# *Child Development*

## A THEMATIC APPROACH

**Houghton Mifflin Company**   Boston   Toronto

GENEVA, ILLINOIS   PALO ALTO   PRINCETON, NEW JERSEY

# Child Development

## A THEMATIC APPROACH

## Second Edition

**Danuta Bukatko**
COLLEGE OF THE HOLY CROSS

**Marvin W. Daehler**
UNIVERSITY OF MASSACHUSETTS, AMHERST

*To Don and Nicholas*

D. B.

*To June, and to Curtis, Joshua, and Renée*

M. W. D.

Sponsoring Editor: Rebecca J. Dudley
Senior Associate Editor: Jane Knetzger
Project Editor: Danielle Carbonneau
Production/Design Coordinator: Caroline Ryan Morgan
Senior Manufacturing Coordinator: Priscilla Bailey

Interior design by Ron Kosciak
Cover design by Harold Burch, Harold Burch Design, NYC
Cover photograph by William Whitehurst, NYC
Anatomical illustrations, charts, and graphs by Networkgraphics

Printed in the U.S.A
Library of Congress Catalog Card Number: 94-76492
ISBN: 0-395-69752-2

23456789-DW-98 97 96 95

# Brief Contents

# Contents

# Preface

As we undertook the revision of this text, we retained the same general vision we had when we wrote the first edition. That is, we wanted students to consider an exciting and complex topic: the factors that influence and shape an individual in his or her most formative years. Yet we also recognized a common dilemma shared by instructors: How do we capture the remarkable breadth and depth of the child's psychological development in the mere thirteen (or fewer) weeks that the course is scheduled? Our question was and still is, How do we help students to sift through the enormous number of developmental "facts" so that they carry away the central knowledge of our field? Furthermore, how do we give students a meaningful sense of the "whole" child, given the specialized study of so many different "parts" of the individual that are characteristic of our field?

To meet these special challenges, our goal has been to provide for the undergraduate student a comprehensive, topically organized, up-to-date picture of child development from conception through adolescence. We emphasize the classic and contemporary research and theory at the core of developmental psychology. As with the first edition, we continue to draw on the growing body of cross-cultural research that helps to elucidate certain fundamental questions about development; in fact, as we approached the revision, we paid special attention to adding cross-cultural and multicultural topics throughout the book. Moreover, in keeping with our belief that research in child development tells an integrated "story," we have added a new element; at various points in the text, we now point out examples of atypical development that can be understood in the context of normal development.

Most important, however, we explicitly draw the student's attention to the themes that replay themselves throughout the course of development, those fundamental, overarching issues that continually resurface and that provide coherence among seemingly disparate research findings. We highlight six basic themes in our discussion of child development:

- What roles do nature and nurture play in development?
- How does the sociocultural context influence development?
- How does the child play an active role in development?
- Is development continuous or discontinuous?
- How prominent are individual differences in development?
- How do the various domains of development interact?

Those familiar with our first edition will notice that we have introduced a new theme, the prominence of individual differences. We decided to include this theme because individual differences are such a common and typical outcome of the multiple processes that contribute to development. Individual differences need to be understood and celebrated as part of the goal of each child's maturing. In introducing this new theme, we elected to incorporate a previous theme, sensitive periods in development, within a broadened interpretation of the debate over whether development is best conceptualized as continuous or discontinuous. The merging of these two themes seemed desirable because a major implication of sensitive periods is that discontinuities can be introduced in development when, for example, certain experiences are unavailable.

By drawing out these themes, we hope to give the reader a means of discovering the "big picture," a way of making sense of the myriad facts that compose the child development literature and a way of understanding the child as a complex, yet integrated being. Moreover, we believe these themes will serve as a tool to stimulate critical thinking among students about the nature of development and how it is best conceptualized. They encourage the student to think about the *process* of development, or *why* development proceeds as it does. We believe that when students engage in this sort of reflection, they also begin to appreciate the ramifications of research and theory for applied issues such as parenting practices, education, and social policy regarding children, which are ultimately concerns for us all.

## Organization and Coverage

We have made several changes in the organization of the book. First, because of the growing literature on cognitive development, we have added an additional chapter on this topic. Chapter 8 is now devoted to a discussion of Piaget's theory of cognition and the contemporary research that his work has stimulated. Chapter 9 provides expanded coverage of the information-processing perspective on cognition. Second, we have integrated the material on social cognition with the topic of moral development in the form of a new chapter (Chapter 12) called "Self and Values." We believe this new organization better reflects the interconnections between the child's growing social awareness and self-regulation skills and his or her developing sense of values.

We begin the text with two chapters that set the stage for the balance of the book. Chapter 1 considers the historical roots of developmental psychology and the research methodologies the field typically employs. We include a discussion of newer research approaches such as meta-analysis and have updated several of the examples used to illustrate research tactics. Chapter 2 introduces the six developmental themes—including the new theme of individual differences—followed by major theories of development. We also discuss how various theorists have taken explicit or implicit positions on the six themes. At the request of several reviewers, we have reduced the emphasis on Freudian theory as the influence of his theoretical formulations continues to wane.

The next three chapters deal primarily with the biological underpinnings and physical changes that characterize child development. Chapter 3 explains the mechanisms of heredity that contribute to human development and evaluates the role of genetics in the expression of many human traits and behaviors. Much of this material has been rewritten so that students who have had little past exposure to these concepts will find it comprehensible. Recent conceptualizations of gene-environment interactions and new material on genetic disorders such as fragile-X syndrome have been added. Chapter 4 sketches the major features of prenatal development and focuses on how environmental factors such as teratogens can modify the genetic blueprint for physical and behavioral development. Updated information on prenatal diagnostic procedures, alternative birth settings, fetal alcohol syndrome, and prenatal exposure to caffeine, cocaine, and AIDS has been incorporated. Greater attention is also given to the consequences of low birthweight in the middle and later school years. Chapter 5 outlines the major features of physical and motor skill development and includes a special section on brain growth and differentiation. We have increased our coverage of motor development in the preschool and middle school years and have added a section on adolescent sexual behavior.

The next group of chapters focuses on the development of the child's various mental capacities. Chapter 6 reviews both the literature on children's learning and the development of perception, including the most recent findings on early intermodal perception as well as perceptual development in older children. Cross-cultural studies and the role of parents in guiding learning are discussed more fully than in the first edition. Chapter 7 describes language development, highlighting the contemporary research on infant language and the social context of language acquisition and considers several different roles, in addition to communication, that language plays in development. Our revision pays greater attention to word learning biases and provides an updated treatment of the linguistic perspective. As mentioned above, Chapter 8 features Piaget's approach to cognitive development as well as recent research spurred by his theory. Perspective-taking skills, formerly treated in the social cognition chapter, are now discussed here. Also new to the text are discussions of infants' understanding of object properties, children's appreciation for natural domains, and research on theory of mind. Chapter 9 continues the discussion of cognitive development from the information-processing perspective. The topic of attention is now treated entirely within this chapter (and no longer in Chapter 6). In addition, we have extended our discussion of early recognition memory and provide more information on children's problem-solving skills. Chapter 10 provides students with a picture of traditional models of intelligence (shortened from the first edition) along with more recent views, such as Sternberg's triarchic theory and Gardner's theory of multiple intelligences. A section on exceptional intelligence has been added in keeping with our goal of incorporating issues of atypical development.

The child's growing social and emotional achievements constitute the focus of the next group of chapters. In light of the enormous interest in children's emotions, we devote all of Chapter 11 to this topic. The second edition provides a more extended examination of emotional development in adolescence and the concept of temperament, as well as recent developments in the attachment literature. Chapter 12 covers two other rapidly expanding areas of interest: social cognition and the bridge it provides to our understanding of moral development. The concept of values has been used to emphasize the broader framework within which research on moral development now takes place. A section on ethnic identity has also been added as an element of the child's growing sense of self. Chapter 13 covers the most recent ideas about gender development, including substantial treatment of gender schema theory. In keeping with new theoretical developments in this field, mention of the relational approach to understanding gender has been added.

In the final portion of the text, we consider the most important external forces that shape the path of child development—the family, the peer group, and the schools and media. Chapter 14 adopts a family systems approach to emphasize how various family members continually influence one another. Specific topics include fatherhood, maternal employment and day care, and divorce. A separate chapter entirely dedicated to the influence of peers, Chapter 15, covers the burgeoning research on this topic. Chapter 16 considers the special influence of schools on child development, along with another powerful aspect of contemporary culture—television. The chapter makes special note of how computers can influence the child's growing skills and abilities.

## *Special Features*

We have incorporated several features in this text to achieve the goals we initially set for this project:

**Key Themes in Development**    Within each chapter, some or all of the six developmental themes listed above serve to organize and provide coherence for the material. As already noted, we see these themes as pedagogical tools designed to help students discern the importance and interrelatedness of various facts, and as vehicles for instructors to encourage critical analysis among students. The themes are highlighted for students in several ways. First, the themes most immediately relevant to a chapter are listed at its start. Throughout the body of the chapter, marginal indicators point to the discussion of a relevant theme. Finally, each chapter closes with a brief synopsis of how the key themes are illustrated in the chapter. Students may, of course, find other themes and additional instances of the six we explore; in fact, we encourage them to do so. Our point is to set in motion in the reader a search for integration and coherence in the vast material that constitutes the scientific study of child development.

**Chronology Charts**    From our own experience as teachers who have adopted a topical approach to child development, we know that students often get so immersed in the theories and research on a given topic that they lose a sense of the child's achievements over time. Consequently, within most chapters, we include one or more Chronology charts, which summarize the child's specific developmental attainments at various ages. One of the points we emphasize in this text, of course, is that there are individual differences in rates, and sometimes in paths, of development. We therefore caution students that these tables are meant only to give a picture of the overall trajectory of development, a loose outline of the sequence of attainments we expect to see in most children. Nonetheless, we believe that these rough guidelines will give students a sense of the patterns and typical timing of important events in the life of the child and that they will serve as another organizing device for the material related to each domain of development.

**Controversies: Thinking It Over**    Important questions about development often have no clear-cut answers. In fact, decisions must frequently be made about children and their families in the face of conflicting research findings or theoretical beliefs. Should children serve as eyewitnesses in courts of law? Should children be academically tracked in school? A special feature found in each chapter considers questions like these to help students critically assess the opposing positions that experts take and to appreciate some of the applied implications of developmental research and theory. These controversies can serve as the foundation for debate and extended discussion in the classroom. In the second edition, we have rewritten the Controversies so that about half of the topics are new. Moreover, we have framed the Controversies in a more open-ended way, concluding with questions designed to stimulate critical thinking among students. To emphasize the critical thinking objectives we had in mind, we have added the subtitle "Thinking It Over."

**Study Aids**     The chapter outlines, chapter summaries, and marginal and end-of-text glossaries all serve to underscore important themes, terms, and concepts. We hope that students will actively utilize these aids to reinforce what they have read in the chapter body. In addition, we employ several strategies to make the material in this text more accessible to students: opening vignettes to capture the reader's interest (about half of these are new), the liberal use of examples throughout the text, and an extensive program of illustrations accompanied by instructive captions.

The result, we hope, is a text that captures for the reader all the excitement and wonder we ourselves feel when we watch a child growing up.

## Ancillaries

The Test Bank and Study Guide that accompany this text were prepared by Carolyn Greco-Vigorito of St. John's University, Staten Island, and Michael Vigorito of Seton Hall University, South Orange, NJ. In addition, we have revised the Instructor's Resource Manual based on the first edition prepared by Carolyn and Michael. A shared set of learning objectives unifies all three supplements.

**Test Bank**     The Test Bank has been expanded to include 2300 multiple-choice items. Each question is accompanied by a key that provides the learning objective number, text page on which the answer can be found, type of question (Fact/Concept or Application), and correct answer. Since we are committed to the idea that students should be encouraged to engage in critical thinking about child development, we have added a series of essay questions for each chapter and a concluding set of essay questions that might constitute part of a cumulative final examination in the course.

**Computerized Test Bank**     All test items are available on disk in IBM or Macintosh formats. Instructors may integrate their own test items with those on disk.

**Instructor's Resource Manual**     The Instructor's Resource Manual contains a complete set of chapter lecture outlines and learning objectives. The manual also contains specific teaching aids such as lecture topics, classroom exercises, demonstrations, and handouts. Thirty new topics for lecture or classroom discussion have been added to the manual.

**Study Guide**     The Study Guide contains the same set of learning objectives that appear in the Instructor's Resource Manual and the Test Bank. In addition, each chapter of the Study Guide includes a key terms review section and a self-quiz consisting of 30 multiple-choice questions. An answer key tells the student not only which response is correct but why each of the other choices is incorrect.

**Transparencies**     A set of transparencies, most in full color, also accompanies the text.

# Acknowledgments

Even a revision of a text could not come to completion without the assistance of numerous colleagues, friends, and others who have provided their professional opinions, time, and inspiration. Our first thanks go once again to our students at Holy Cross and the University of Massachusetts, who enroll in our classes in child development and show us so visibly how they appreciate what they learn. It is the students who continue to serve as the primary inspiration to work on this book.

We also appreciate very much the assistance of reviewers whose questions, comments, and helpful criticisms of the first edition provided the impetus for the changes we made here. We believe we have a better book as a result of their responses. For their many generous contributions in reviewing the first edition or the manuscript for the second, we thank the following individuals:

Kay Alderman
  *University of Akron*
Linda Baker
  *University of Maryland-Baltimore County*
Thomas M. Batsis
  *Loyola Marymount University*
Brian J. Bigelow
  *Laurentian University*
Kathryn N. Black
  *Purdue University-West Lafayette*
Cathryn L. Booth
  *University of Washington*
Phina Bright
  *Nassau Community College*
Eliot J. Butter
  *University of Dayton*
Ralph E. Calhoun
  *University of Central Arkansas*
Rita M. Curl
  *Minot State University*
Nancy Dudley
  *University of Calgary*
Clarie Etaugh
  *Bradley University*
Colleen Gift
  *Highland Community College*
Susan Hegland
  *Iowa State University of Science and Technology*
Janis E. Jacobs
  *University of Nebraska-Lincoln*
Kenneth D. Kallio
  *State University of New York-Geneseo*
Ronald Katsuyama
  *University of Dayton*

Cindy Kennedy
  *Sinclair Community College*
Joel King
  *University of Maine-Farmington*
Sue Kirkpatrick
  *University of Alabama-Huntsville*
Emily J. Krohn
  *Southern Illinois University-Edwardsville*
Frank Laycock
  *Oberlin College*
Malinda Jo Muzi
  *Community College of Philadelphia*
Cherie G. O'Boyle
  *California State University-San Marcos*
Shelley Parlow
  *Carleton University*
Roger D. Phillips
  *Lehigh University*
Rosemary A. Rosser
  *University of Arizona*
Robert F. Rycek
  *University of Nebraska-Kearney*
Shirley S. Shaw
  *Iowa State University of Science and Technology*
Robert S. Siegler
  *Carnegie Mellon University*
Harold W. Stevenson
  *University of Michigan-Ann Arbor*
James K. Uphoff
  *Wright State University*
Charlotte E. Wood
  *Yukon, Oklahoma*
Christopher Ziegler
  *Kennesaw State College*

We also appreciate the contributions of D. Bruce Carter at Syracuse University who provided much of the groundwork for Chapter 12 in the first edition.

In addition, we are extremely grateful to colleagues at our respective institutions for reading and commenting on various chapters or just plain sharing ideas that helped us clarify what we were doing. At Holy Cross, Ogretta McNeil was especially influential in sensitizing us to multicultural issues in development. A special thanks is also due to the staff of Dinand Library at Holy Cross for their gracious assistance in locating reference works and other source materials. At the University of Massachusetts, Daniel Anderson, Carole Beale, Richard Bogartz, Rachel Clifton, Gary Marcus, Nancy Myers, and Philippe Rochat have provided a wealth of information and stimulating ideas in formal seminars and informal hallway conversations.

Once again, the editorial staff at Houghton Mifflin has demonstrated just how professional, talented, dedicated, and knowledgeable they are. Mike DeRocco, our sponsoring editor, continued to show his unwavering enthusiasm for this project and his commitment to making the book successful. We were delighted that Jane Knetzger was able to continue as the developmental editor on the book. As with the first edition, she showed remarkably sharp insights into how we could operationalize our pedagogical goals as we made our way through the revision. Her talents are enormous! Finally, Danielle Carbonneau, our production editor, oversaw the many details involved in producing the revision, and for her conscientious work, we are grateful.

Most of all, though, we would like to thank our families for their continued patience and support as we progressed through this revision. To Don, thanks for once again appreciating the importance of this project, and to Nicky, thanks for understanding why "Mommy can't play now." Nicky continued to be an important source of inspiration, since his own growth has offered numerous, vivid examples of the themes and issues that stand out in child development. Special thanks to June, who continued to accept the demands that such a project entails, and also thanks to Curtis, Joshua, and Renée, who have now become part of the audience for whom this book is intended. We have been eager to make it a valued resource for them and all others who are interested in learning about children and their development.

Danuta Bukatko

Marvin W. Daehler

# Child Development

## A THEMATIC APPROACH

# 1

# *Studying Child Development*

*"When five months old," the noted evolutionary theorist Charles Darwin wrote of his infant son in 1840,*

> *associated ideas arising independently of any instruction became fixed in his mind; thus as soon as his hat and cloak were put on, he was very cross if he was not immediately taken out of doors. When exactly seven months old, he made the great step of associating his nurse with her name, so that if I called it out he would look round for her. . . . when a few days under nine months, he associated his own name with his image in the looking-glass, and when called by name would turn toward the glass even when at some distance from it. When a few days over nine months, he learnt spontaneously that a hand or other object causing a shadow to fall on the wall in front of him was to be looked for behind. (Darwin, 1877, p. 290)*

*In just such informal records of their own offspring, Darwin and other nineteenth-century European scientists were taking the first steps toward the systematic observation of the child that would burgeon in the next century into a flourishing multidisciplinary field. The only surprise is that human development became a focus of serious study comparatively late in the history of Western science, for few fields offer a subject—the developing human being—that undergoes such dramatic transformations over time.*

**Development**, as we will use the term, means all the physical and psychological changes a human being undergoes in a lifetime, from the moment of conception until death. The study of human development is, above all, the study of change. And at no other time of life does change take place at such a rapid pace as in childhood and adolescence. From the very moment of birth, changes in body and behaviors are swift and impressive. Even in a few short months, the newborn who looks so helpless (we will see that the true state of affairs is otherwise) comes to control his own body, to locomote, and to master simple tasks such as self-feeding. In the years that follow, the child learns to understand and speak a language, displays more and more complex thinking abilities, shows a distinct personality, and develops a social network along with the skills necessary to interact with other people. The range and complexity of every young person's achievements in the first two decades of life can only be called extraordinary.

One of the goals of this book is to give you an overview of the most significant changes in behavior and thinking processes that occur in this time span. Accordingly, much of the material you will encounter in the pages that follow will *describe* the growing child's accomplishments in many domains of development. We will begin by observing the formation of basic physical and mental capabilities in children; we will then examine the social and emotional skills children develop as they reach out to form relationships with their family members, peers, and others.

Our second important goal is to help you appreciate just why children develop in the specific ways that they do. That is, we will also try to *explain* development, at least as far as research has led us to understand the causes of varying developmental outcomes in children. How do the genetic blueprints inherited from parents shape the growing child? What is the role of the environment—the people, objects, and events the child interacts with or experiences? How does the society or culture in which the child lives influence development? Does the child play a passive or active role in this process? Do the

**development**  Physical and psychological changes in the individual over a lifetime.

3

changes that take place occur gradually or suddenly? Do all children follow the same developmental pathways at the same ages, and if not, what factors explain individual differences in development? And how do the many facets of development influence one another? As you might imagine, the answers to these questions are neither simple nor always obvious.

**Developmental psychologists** are scientists who study changes in human behaviors and mental activities as they occur over a lifetime. Developmental psychologists rely on the general principles of scientific research to collect information about growth and change in children. This approach has its limitations—researchers have not necessarily studied every important aspect of child development, and sometimes research findings do not point to clear, unambiguous answers about the nature of development. Indeed, researchers often disagree on the conclusions they draw from a given set of data. Nonetheless, scientific fact finding has the advantage of being verifiable and is also more objective and systematic than personal interpretations of children's behavior. As you read the research accounts in the coming pages, the controversies as well as the unequivocal conclusions, we hope you will use them to sharpen your own skills of critical analysis.

Research conducted around the world, especially in the last three decades, has yielded many important insights about the process of human development. Needless to say, a substantial number of these discoveries have practical implications for our interactions with children. For example, newborn nurseries for premature infants now contain rocking chairs so that parents and nurses can rock and stimulate babies previously confined to isolettes. Bilingual education programs capitalize on the ease with which young children master the complexities of language. Many day-care centers teach prosocial behaviors to young children. Throughout this book, we will emphasize both the importance of rigorous research and the practical applications of the knowledge gathered by scientists.

During the first part of this century many psychologists established the norms of development, the ages at which most children are able to accomplish developmental tasts such as walking.

## The Scientific Study of the Child in Western Society

Developmental psychology as a field has grown at an astonishing rate since Darwin recorded his observations of his baby boy. Each year hundreds of books and articles about children's growth are published for professionals interested in specific theoretical issues and for parents or teachers who wish to bring a more informed perspective to the challenging enterprises of child rearing and education. Scientists and laypersons, however, have not always had such a focused and conscious desire to understand the process of child development. In fact, Western societal attitudes toward children have shifted considerably over the last several centuries, a phenomenon that has paved the way for the contemporary emphasis on children as the subjects of scientific study.

**developmental psychology**
Systematic and scientific study of changes in human behaviors and mental activities over time.

### Historical Perspectives on the Nature of Childhood

Contemporary society views childhood as a separate, distinct, and unique period in the span of human life: during this special time children are to be protected, nurtured, loved, and for the most part kept free of adult responsibilities and obligations. Child labor laws try to ensure that children are not abused in the work world, and the institution of public education signals our society's willingness to devote significant resources to their academic training. But childhood was not always viewed in this way. As we look back through time, we see that prevailing beliefs about human nature and the social order shape attitudes about the nature of childhood and hence the treatment and rearing of children (Borstelmann, 1983).

**Children in Medieval and Renaissance Times**    From the Middle Ages through premodern times, European society's attitudes toward children were strikingly different from our contemporary society's. Though their basic needs to be fed and clothed were tended to, children were not coddled or protected in the same way that infants in our society are. As soon as they were physically able, usually at age seven or so, children were incorporated into the adult world of work; they harvested grain, learned craft skills, and otherwise contributed to the local economy. In medieval times, Western European children did not have special clothes, toys, or games. Once they were old enough to shed swaddling clothes, they wore adult fashions and pursued adult pastimes such as archery, chess, and even gambling (Ariès, 1962).

In certain respects, however, premodern European society regarded children as vulnerable, fragile, and unable to assume the full responsibilities of adulthood. Medical writings alluded to the special illnesses of young children,

In premodern Europe, children often dressed like adults and participated in many adult activities. At the same time, though, children were seen as fragile and in need of protection.

and laws prohibited marriages of children under age twelve (Kroll, 1977). Religious movements of this era proclaimed the innocence of children and urged that they be educated. Children's souls, as well as adults', must be saved, said clerics, and they held that parents were morally responsible for their children's spiritual well-being. Parents recognized that children were also a financial responsibility, and helped them to set up their own households as they approached adulthood and marriage (Pollock, 1983; Shahar, 1990). Thus, even though medieval children were incorporated quickly into the adult world, they were recognized both as different from adults and as possessing special needs.

A noticeable shift in attitudes toward children occurred in Europe during the sixteenth century. In 1545, English physician and lawyer Thomas Phayre published the first book on pediatrics. In addition, the advent of the printing press during this century made possible the wide distribution of other manuals on the care of infants and children. The first grammar schools were established and educated upper-class boys in economics and politics. Upper-class girls attended convent schools or received private instruction intended to cultivate modesty and obedience as well as other skills thought to be useful in their future roles as wives and mothers (Shahar, 1990).

Probably one of the most significant social changes occurred as a result of the transition from agrarian to trade-based economies in the sixteenth and seventeenth centuries, and the subsequent growth of industrialization in the eighteenth century. As people relocated from farms to towns and as the production of goods shifted outside the home, the primary role of the family in Western society changed from economic survival to the nurturing of children (Hareven, 1985). Closeness and emotional attachment increasingly became the hallmarks of parent-child relations.

**The Age of Enlightenment** The impact of these sweeping social changes was consolidated by the writings of several key thinkers who shaped the popular understanding of childhood. In the seventeenth and eighteenth centuries, two philosophers proposed important but distinctly different ideas about the nature and education of children. In his famous treatise, *An Essay Concerning Human Understanding,* published in 1690, the British philosopher John Locke (1632–1704) described his views on the acquisition of human knowledge. Virtually no information is inborn, according to Locke. The newborn's mind is a *tabula rasa,* literally a "blank slate," upon which perceptual experiences are imprinted. Locke's philosophy of **empiricism**, the idea that environmental experiences shape the individual, foreshadowed the modern-day psychological school called behaviorism. Locke believed that the use of rewards and punishments, imitation, and the associations that the child formed between stimuli are key elements in the formation of the mind.

In a second work, *Some Thoughts Concerning Education* (1693), Locke expounded further on his philosophy of training children:

> The great mistake I have observed in people's breeding their children . . . is that the mind has not been made obedient to discipline and pliant to reason when it was most tender, most easy to be bowed. . . . He that is not used to submit his will to the reason of others when he is young, will scarce hearken to submit to his own reason when he is of an age to make use of it.

> . . . If the mind be curbed and humbled too much in children, if their spirits be abased and broken by too strict a hand over them, they will lose all vigour and industry and are in a worse state than the former.

**empiricism** Theory that environmental experiences shape the individual; more specifically, that all knowledge is derived from sensory experiences.

These statements convey Locke's belief that early experiences and proper training are important, but that child rearing and education should proceed through the use of reason rather than harsh discipline. In his view, parents must find a balance between being overly indulgent and overly restrictive as they manage their child's behavior. As we will see, many of these same themes resound in contemporary research on good parenting and represent a contrast to the strict discipline characteristic of Western society before the eighteenth century.

The second influential philosopher of the Enlightenment was Jean Jacques Rousseau (1712–1778), a French thinker who embraced the ideal of the child as a "noble savage." According to Rousseau, children are born with a propensity to act on impulses but not necessarily with the aim of wrongdoing. They require the gentle guidance of adult authority to bring their natural instincts and tendencies in line with the social order. In *Émile* (1762), Rousseau set forth these beliefs about child rearing:

> Never command him to do anything whatever, not the least thing in the world. Never allow him even to imagine that you assume to have any authority over him. Let him know merely that he is weak and that you are strong; that by virtue of his condition and your own he is necessarily at your mercy.

> . . . Do not give your scholar any sort of verbal lesson, for he is to be taught only by experience. Inflict on him no species of punishment, for he does not know what it is to be in fault.

Rousseau emphasized the dynamic relationship between the curious and energetic child and the demands of his or her social environment, as represented by adults. A major aspect of the process of development, Rousseau believed, is the resolution of conflicts between the individual tendencies of the child and the needs of the larger society; adults should not have to stifle the child's natural development and spirit through domination. Contemporary theories that acknowledge the active role of the child in the process of development have distinct roots in Rousseau's writings.

Rousseau also advanced some radical ideas about education. Children, he held, should not be forced to learn by rote the vast amounts of information that adults perceive as important. Instead, teachers should capitalize on the natural curiosity of children and allow them to discover on their own the myriad facts and phenomena that make up the world. Rousseau's ideas on the nature of education would be incorporated in the twentieth-century writings of Jean Piaget, a prominent theorist who observed and described the cognitive development of children.

Both Locke and Rousseau emphasized the notion of the child as a *developing,* as opposed to a static, being. Both challenged the supposition that children are merely passive subjects of adult authority, and both advanced the idea that children should be treated with reason and respect. Having been elevated by the efforts of these worthy thinkers to an object of intellectual interest, the child was now ready to become the subject of scientific study.

## The Origins of Developmental Psychology

By the mid- to late 1800s, scholars in the natural sciences, especially biology, saw in the study of children an opportunity to support their emerging theories about the origins of human beings and their behaviors. Charles Darwin, for example, hypothesized that the similarities between the behaviors of humans and those of other species were the result of common evolutionary ancestors. Similarly, Wilhelm Preyer, another biologist, was initially interested in the physiology of embryological development but soon extended his investigations to behavioral development after birth.

Although these early attempts to study childhood scientifically were not explicitly conducted for the purpose of understanding child behavior and were often methodologically flawed, they paved the way for the systematic psychological study of the child that emerged by the end of that century. In the United States and Europe, key researchers who participated in the birth of psychology as an academic discipline began to show an interest in studying children specifically and applied the general methods of scientific observation to this end. By the beginning of the twentieth century, developmental psychology was established as a legitimate area of psychological inquiry.

### The Baby Biographers: Charles Darwin and Wilhelm Preyer

The excerpt at the beginning of the chapter from Charles Darwin's 1840 notes marks one of the first records of the close scrutiny of a child for the purpose of scientific understanding. Eager to uncover important clues about the origins of the human species, Darwin undertook to record in great detail his infant son's behaviors during the first three years of life. Darwin documented the presence of early reflexes, such as sucking, as well as the emergence of voluntary motor movements, language, and emotions such as fear, anger, and affection. When he saw similarities, he linked the behaviors of the young child to other species, as when, for example, he concluded that the infant's comprehension of simple words was not unlike the ability of "lower animals" to understand words spoken by humans (Darwin, 1877).

In 1882, the German biologist Wilhelm Preyer published *The Mind of the Child,* a work that described in great detail the development of his son Axel during his first three years of life. Preyer wrote meticulously of his son's sensory development, motor accomplishments, language production, and memory, even noting indications of an emerging concept of self. Although Preyer followed in the footsteps of several previous "baby biographers," including Darwin, he was the first to insist that observations of children be conducted systematically and scientifically. Accordingly, Preyer advocated that observations be taken unobtrusively and recorded immediately, that they be repeated several times each day, and that whenever possible the recordings of more than one observer be compared.

One major problem with the observations conducted by Darwin, Preyer, and other baby biographers was the subjective nature of the interpretations they made about children's observable behaviors. How do we know, for example, that a given facial expression made by an infant actually signifies "sympathy," a notation Darwin made in his records about his son? The very fact that he was recording his own child's behavior introduces still another dimension of observer bias; parents typically are not the most objective observers of their own child's behavior. Moreover, the baby biographers did not always make their observations at regular intervals: sometimes entries were made in their "diaries" on a daily basis; other times weeks would go by before an entry was made. Nonetheless, by advocating the application of scientific techniques to the study of children, the baby biographers, and Preyer in particular, set in motion the beginnings of the child development movement in the United States.

**G. Stanley Hall: The Founder of Modern Child Psychology** The psychologist perhaps most responsible for launching the new discipline of child study in the United States was G. Stanley Hall, who, in 1878, became the first American to obtain a Ph.D. in psychology. Hall is also known for founding the first psychological journal in the United States in 1887 and, in 1891, the first journal of developmental psychology, *Pedagogical Seminary* (now called the *Journal of Genetic Psychology*). In addition, he founded and served as the first president of the American Psychological Association.

As the first American to study in Europe with the pioneer psychologist Wilhelm Wundt, G. Stanley Hall returned to the United States in 1880 with an interest in studying the "content of children's minds." Adopting the questionnaire method he had learned about in Germany, he had teachers ask about two hundred kindergarten-aged children questions such as, "Have you ever seen a cow?" or "What are bricks made of?" The percent of children who gave particular answers was tabulated, and comparisons were made between the responses of boys and girls, city children and country children, and children of different ethnic backgrounds (Hall, 1891). For the first time, researchers were collecting data in order to compare groups of children, in contrast to previous approaches that had emphasized the detailed examination of individual children.

G. Stanley Hall's greatest contributions to the field lay not so much in the specific ideas he put forth about the nature of development, but rather in his role as "an importer and translator of ideas" (Cairns, 1983). By transplanting the questionnaire method from Europe to the United States, Hall introduced a new method by which researchers interested in children could approach their

G. Stanley Hall is considered to be the founder of modern child psychology.

studies. As president of Clark University, he was also instrumental in bringing another preeminent psychologist to the United States in 1909 to deliver a series of lectures—Sigmund Freud. The ideas of psychoanalysis—specifically, that early childhood experiences could profoundly influence adult thinking and behavior and that development itself might be a stagelike process—were to find a new and receptive audience in America.

**Alfred Binet and the Study of Individual Differences**    The French psychologist Alfred Binet is known primarily as the developer of the first formal assessment scale of intelligence. Binet was a pioneer in the study of **individual differences**, those unique characteristics that distinguish one person from others in the larger group. Although the trend in the United States at that time was to study the psychological characteristics or behaviors that groups of people shared, Binet's work underscored the importance of identifying varying patterns of abilities.

Binet's original interest lay in the general features of children's thinking, including memory and reasoning about numbers. His studies of children's thinking were to provide the basis for more formal tests of children's mental abilities. In response to a request from the Ministry of Public Instruction in Paris for a tool to screen for students with learning problems, Binet and another colleague, Théodore Simon, developed a series of tasks for the systematic measurement of motor skills, vocabulary, problem solving, and a wide range of other higher-order thought processes (Binet & Simon, 1905). This instrument could identify patterns in mental capabilities that were unique to each child.

The idea of mental testing caught on very quickly in the United States, especially among clinicians, school psychologists, and other professionals who were concerned with the practical side of dealing with children. For the first time, it was legitimate, even important, to consider variation in mental abilities from person to person.

**James Mark Baldwin: Developmental Theorist**    Much early developmental psychology emphasized the construction of methodologies for studying children and collecting data about their behavior. James Mark Baldwin, one of the most important American developmental theorists of the early twentieth century, however, made his contributions on another front.

One of Baldwin's most important propositions was that development is a dynamic and hierarchical process involving more than just the accumulation of bits and pieces of knowledge or behavior. As he stated, "Every genetic change ushers in a real advance, a progression on the part of nature to a higher mode of reality" (Baldwin, 1930, p. 86). Moreover, development encompasses two critical processes: habit, or simple repetition of behaviors, and accommodation, the adaptation of organisms to new environments, a process that brings with it a new level of knowledge and awareness (Baldwin, 1895). Baldwin applied these ideas to the domain of cognitive development by suggesting that mental advances occur in a stagelike sequence. The earliest thought is prelogical but gives way to logical, and eventually hyperlogical, or formal, reasoning.

Baldwin is also recognized for his unique ideas about social development and the formation of personality. Instead of characterizing the child as a passive recipient of the behaviors and beliefs endorsed by the larger society, he described the child's emerging self as a product of continual reciprocal interactions between the child and others. Children imitate those around them, and in turn others are affected by the child's behaviors. The proposition that devel-

**individual differences** Unique characteristics that distinguish a person from other members of a larger group.

opment results from a mutual dynamic between child and others took a long time to catch on among psychologists, but this idea, so popular today—and one of the themes of development we are emphasizing throughout this text—is actually almost a century old (Cairns & Ornstein, 1979).

By the start of the 1900s, the foundations of developmental psychology were well laid out. The handful of psychologists of that era who were specifically interested in development, however, was still obliged to invent their own methodologies and devise their own theories, sometimes apart from mainstream psychology (Cairns & Ornstein, 1979). During the early part of this century, several prominent theorists began to publish their ideas about the nature of development. Sigmund Freud detailed the stages in the emergence of personality in his psychoanalytic theory of development. John B. Watson elaborated on how the principles of learning theory could be applied to the development of emotions, such as fear, in children. Jean Piaget began to formulate what would become the most comprehensive theory of cognitive development to date in developmental psychology. Important ideas proposed by each of these theorists will be treated in more detail in the next chapter. Considering how few empirical data had been gathered about children up to that point, however, the theoretical writings of our predecessors were amazingly insightful.

## Developmental Psychology in the Twentieth Century

From the beginning of the century to the mid-1940s, psychologists interested in development concentrated their efforts on gathering descriptive information about children. At what ages do most children achieve the milestones of motor development, such as sitting, crawling, and walking? When do children develop emotions such as fear and anger? What are children's beliefs about punishment, friendship, and morality? It was during this era of intensive fact gathering that many *norms* of development—that is, the ages at which most children are able to accomplish a given developmental task—were established. For example, Arnold Gesell established the norms of motor development for the first five years of life, guidelines that are still useful to psychologists, pediatricians, and other professionals who work with children in diagnosing developmental problems or delays (Gesell & Thompson, 1934; 1938).

The first half of the twentieth century also saw the founding of many major institutes or research centers that attracted bright young scholars who dedicated their lives to the scientific study of children. A further sign of the professionalization of the discipline was the formation of the Society for Research in Child Development in 1933 for scientists who wished to share their growing knowledge of child behavior and development.

Scholars now approach child development from an assortment of disciplines, including anthropology, sociology, education, medicine, biology, and several subareas of psychology (for example, neuropsychology, comparative psychology, and clinical psychology), as well as the specialized area of developmental psychology. Each discipline has its own biases, as defined by the questions each asks about development and the methodological approaches it employs to answer those questions. Nonetheless, our pooled knowledge now gives us a better understanding of development than we might expect from a field that officially began only a century ago.

### Is Childhood Disappearing from Contemporary Society?

We have seen how our understanding of the nature of childhood has been modified as a function of historical and social changes within our society. We have also seen how childhood slowly has come to be viewed as a unique and special time in life worthy of study and special attention. Childhood as an *idea* now occupies a privileged place in contemporary society. Our modern culture, some would even say, prolongs the actual experience of childhood into what bygone eras regarded as adult years. Indeed, by midcentury American society allowed many older teenagers and young adults to remain socially defined as children by virtue of remaining full-time students, relying on their parents for financial and emotional support, and delaying the start of their own families, households, and independent lives. Other observers, however, warn that many signs in post-1950s contemporary culture point to the erosion of this relatively new distinction between childhood and adulthood.

Some of the more visible evidence for this "adulteration" of a protected childhood comes from a merging of adults' and children's clothing styles, games, and tastes in food. Children frequently wear miniature versions of adult jeans, athletic shoes, designer clothing, make-up, and accessories. On the other hand, video games and fast-food restaurants, once thought of as appealing primarily to children, attract numerous adults. Many of the activities and customs that distinguished adults from children in previous decades are now commonly shared by both age groups (Postman, 1982).

More alarming, however, is the suggestion that children now experience many of the problems once exclusively found among adults. Alcoholism, drug abuse, sexual promiscuity, and violent crime increasingly occur among adolescents and even younger children. One factor that may contribute to these problems may be the access children have to the media—television programs, newspapers, and magazines that make available to children portrayals of violence and sexuality that were once taboo (Postman, 1982). In addition, in an era when many parents divorce, children are often forced to provide their parents with emotional support, a reversal of traditional parent-child roles (Winn, 1983).

Contemporary society, this same argument holds, often pushes children to achieve more at earlier ages—as in the example of the young athlete in serious training or the child musician who practices many hours before and after school. Children also experience pressures for academic achievement at earlier and earlier ages. Some parents enroll their two- and three-year-olds in highly structured preschool programs in the hopes that they will read at earlier ages, show increases in their IQ scores, and achieve more once they enter elementary and secondary school (Elkind, 1981b; 1984; Howe, 1990). Children, say the social critics, no longer have time to just be children, to engage in fantasy play, and to live free of the responsibilities and pressures experienced by adults.

Is childhood disappearing? Do we still hold children in a special place in society and protect them from the harsher realities of life? Or do children enter the world of adulthood too soon? What are the costs of their doing so—to the children themselves and to society at large? Should our society take a serious look at this issue? What steps can we take to preserve "childhood" as a special time in the span of human life?  ■

# Research Methods in Developmental Psychology

Like their colleagues in all the sciences, researchers in child development seek to gather data that are objective, measurable, and capable of being replicated in controlled studies by other researchers. Their studies, in other words, are based on the **scientific method**. Frequently, they initiate research to evaluate the predictions of a specific theory (for example, is cognitive development stagelike, as Piaget suggests?). Alternatively, they may formulate a research question to determine an application of theory to a real-world situation (for example, can IQ scores be boosted by early intervention programs for preschoolers?). Regardless of the motivation, the general principles of good science are as important to research in child development as they are to any other research arena. Although many of the methods that child development researchers use are the very same techniques that psychologists routinely employ in other specialized areas, some methodological approaches are particularly useful in studying changes in behavior or mental processes that occur over time.

## The Role of Theories

An essential ingredient of the scientific process is the construction of a **theory**—a set of ideas or propositions that helps to organize or explain observable phenomena. Children display a vast assortment of intellectual, linguistic, social, and physical behaviors, capabilities that also show changes with time. By describing children's accomplishments in a systematic, integrated way, theories *organize* or make sense of the enormous amount of information researchers have gleaned.

Theories of development also help *explain* our observations. Is your neighbor's little boy shy because he inherited this trait, or did his social experiences encourage him to become this way? Did your niece's mathematical skills develop from her experience with her home computer, or does she just have a natural flair for numbers? Psychologists are interested in understanding the factors that contribute to the emergence of behavioral skills and capacities, and their theories are ways of articulating ideas about what causes various behaviors to develop in individual children.

A good theory goes beyond description and explanation, however. It leads to *predictions* about behavior, predictions that are clear and easily tested. If shyness is the result of the child's social experiences, for example, then the withdrawn four-year-old should profit from a training program that teaches social skills. If, on the other hand, shyness is a stable, unchangeable personality trait, then even extensive training in sociability might have very little impact.

Theories usually lead to *hypotheses* about the causes of or influences on behavior, which the researcher then systematically tests. The scientific method

**scientific method**   Use of objective, measurable, and repeatable techniques to gather information.

**theory**   Set of ideas or propositions that helps organize or explain observable phenomena.

dictates that theories must be revised or elaborated as new observations confirm or refute them. The process of scientific fact finding involves a constant cycle of theorizing, empirical testing of the resulting hypotheses, and revision (or even outright rejection) of theories as the new data come in. Later, in Chapter 2, we will examine the major theories of child development and their impact on the field. Here, we consider the methods useful in evaluating theories.

## Measuring Attributes and Behaviors

All researchers are interested in identifying relationships among **variables**, those factors in a given situation that have no fixed or constant value. In child development studies, the variables are individual attributes, experiences, or behaviors that differ from one time to the next or from one person to another. Ultimately, researchers are interested in determining the causal relationships among variables—that is, they wish to identify those variables directly responsible for the occurrence of other variables. Does watching television cause children to behave aggressively? Do withdrawn children have academic problems once they enroll in school? Does the way a parent interacts with a toddler raise or lower the child's later intelligence? In posing each of these questions, researchers are hypothesizing that some attribute or experience of the child is causally related to another attribute or behavior.

The first problem the researcher faces is that of **operationally defining**, or specifying in measurable terms, the variables under study. Take the case of aggression. This term can be defined as parental ratings of children's physical hostility, the child's own reports of his or her level of violent behavior, or the number of hits and kicks recorded by an observer of the child's behavior. The key point is that variables must be defined in terms of precise measurement procedures that other researchers can use if they wish to repeat the study.

The measurement of variables must also be valid and reliable. **Validity** refers to how well an assessment procedure actually measures the variable under study. Parental reports of physical violence, for example, or even the child's own self-reports may not be the best indicators of aggression. Parents may not want a researcher to know about their child's misbehavior, or they may not have complete knowledge of how their child behaves outside the home. Children's own reports may not be very accurate because they may wish to present themselves to adults in a certain way. If a trained observer records the number of hits or kicks the child displays during a school day, on the other hand, the resulting measurement of aggression is likely to be valid.

**Reliability** is the degree to which the same results will be obtained consistently if the measure is administered repeatedly or if several observers are viewing the same behavior episodes. In the first case, suppose a child takes an intelligence test one time, then two weeks later takes the test again. If the test has high *test-retest reliability,* she should obtain similar scores on the two testing occasions. In the second case, two or more observers viewing a child's behavior should agree about what they are seeing (for example, did that child smile in the presence of a stranger?); if they do agree, the test has high *inter-rater reliability*. Both types of reliability are calculated mathematically and are usually reported by researchers in their published reports of experiments; both are very important factors in good scientific research. Measurements of behavior that fluctuate dramatically from one observation time to another or from one observer to another are virtually useless as data.

**variable**   Factor having no fixed or constant value in a given situation.

**operational definition**   Specification of variables in terms of measurable properties.

**validity**   Degree to which an assessment procedure actually measures the variable under consideration.

**reliability**   Degree to which a measure will yield the same results if administered repeatedly.

## Collecting Data

Researchers in developmental psychology employ a range of strategies to gather information about children. Each approach offers advantages and disadvantages, and the choice of research tactic will often depend on the nature of the investigator's questions. If we are interested in exploring children's spontaneous tendencies to behave aggressively as they play (for example, do boys play more aggressively than girls?), we would probably find a *naturalistic approach* most appropriate. If we want to examine how children understand aggression, its antecedents, and its consequences, then we might adopt another strategy, such as a *structured interview* or a *questionnaire*. Sometimes researchers combine data collection methods within a study or series of studies. There is no one right way to study children. Researchers must consider their overall goals and their available resources as they make decisions about how to construct a research study.

**Naturalistic Observation**    Researchers have no better way to see how children really behave than to observe them in natural settings—in their homes, schools, playgrounds, and other places that are part of their everyday lives. After all, the ultimate goal of developmental psychology is to describe

In naturalistic observations, researchers observe and record children's behaviors in real-life settings, such as playgrounds, schools, or homes.

and explain changes in behavior that actually exist. **Naturalistic observations** do not involve the manipulation of variables; researchers simply observe and record behaviors of interest from the natural series of events that unfolds in a real-world setting.

A study by Theodore Wachs and his colleagues (Wachs et al., 1993), for example, used naturalistic observations to assess the relationship between specific caregiver behaviors and the competence of toddlers as they matured from eighteen to thirty months of age. The study was conducted in Egypt. Twice a month, researchers observed children and their caregivers in their homes for a period of thirty minutes, noting such behaviors as how frequently caregivers vocalized to the children and the amount of physical contact between caregiver and child. Several observations were made of toddler behavior, as well, including ratings of the child's alertness, the number of vocalizations made by the child, and the amount of time the child spent actively playing with objects. The results showed that, as in Western families, the more vocal stimulation the caregiver provided, the more alert, vocal, and actively involved with the environment was the child.

The methodology of this study had many positive features. First, Wachs and his co-researchers operationally defined the variables of interest by clearly specifying which behaviors should be recorded. For example, the amount of physical contact given by the caregiver to the child was defined as "the number of times during the observation the child is picked up, held, or carried by an adult or older child" (p. 602). Second, these researchers were aware that caregivers and children might react to the presence of a stranger by behaving in untypical or "unnatural" ways. To reduce such **subject reactivity**, a preliminary observation was conducted when the children were seventeen months of age in order to get the family acclimatized to the presence of observers in the home. Finally, to minimize the effects of **observer bias**—the possibility that the researcher would interpret ongoing events to be consistent with his or her prior hypotheses—two independent observers (one of whom was unfamiliar with the purposes of the study) coded caregiver and child behaviors to ensure reliability of the findings.

An important advantage of naturalistic observations is that researchers can see the events and behaviors that precede the target behaviors they are recording; they can also note the consequences of those same target behaviors. In this way they may be able to discern important relationships in sequences of events. Moreover, naturalistic observations give researchers important insights into which variables are important to study in the first place, insights that may not be derived solely by observing children in the laboratory. Often the trends or phenomena identified in such preliminary studies become the focus of more intensive, controlled laboratory experiments. And, as we mentioned earlier, naturalistic observations have the distinct advantage of examining real-life behaviors as opposed to behaviors that may emerge only in response to some contrived or artificial laboratory manipulation.

Some cautions, however, are in order about this method. First, a wide range of variables may be influencing the behaviors under observation, and it is not always clear which ones have the most impact. What causes young children to be alert, vocal, and involved with their environment? Is it the responsiveness of the caregiver? Or does some other factor, like the child's general health status, play a larger role? Cause-and-effect relationships, furthermore, cannot be deduced. Do vocal caregivers cause toddlers to be alert, or do alert toddlers elicit verbalizations from their caregivers? Answering questions like these requires the systematic manipulation of variables, a tactic that is part of other research approaches.

**naturalistic observation**   Study in which observations of naturally occurring behavior are made in real-life settings.

**subject reactivity**   Tendency of subjects who know they are under observation to alter natural behavior.

**observer bias**   Tendency of researchers to interpret ongoing events as consistent with their research hypotheses.

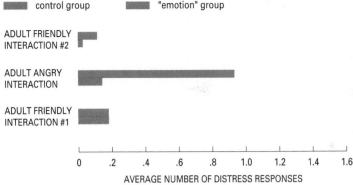

Source: Adapted from Cummings, Iannotti, & Zahn-Waxler, 1985.

**FIGURE 1.1**

**A Structured Observation**

What happens when two-year-old children observe two adults have a friendly interaction, followed by an angry exchange, then by another friendly interaction? The graph shows the average number of distress responses (expressions of anxiety, crying, and so forth) displayed by children who witnessed this sequence of events compared with those of a control group that saw a series of three neutral exchanges. This structured observation showed that exposure to adult anger heightened children's distress.

**Structured Observation**    Researchers cannot always depend on a child to display behaviors of scientific interest to them during observation. Researchers who observe a child in the home, school, or other natural setting may simply not be present when vocalization, sharing, aggression, or other behaviors they wish to study occur. Therefore, developmental psychologists may choose to observe behaviors in a more structured setting, usually the laboratory, where they devise situations to elicit those behaviors of interest to them. **Structured observations** are the record of specific behaviors displayed by the child in a situation constructed by the experimenter. Structured observations, like naturalistic observations, are a way of collecting data by looking at and recording the child's behaviors, but this form of looking takes place under highly controlled conditions.

A study of the effects of adult emotions on the emotions of two-year-olds illustrates how such structured observations are frequently conducted (Cummings, Iannotti, & Zahn-Waxler, 1985). Pairs of children were brought to a laboratory playroom along with their mothers. While the children played, two adults entered the room and engaged first in a friendly, pleasant interaction, then in an angry exchange, and finally in a friendly, conciliatory manner. The emotional reactions of children (particularly bodily or facial expressions of anxiety and vocalizations like crying) during the different phases of the experimental session were recorded by several trained observers. In addition, a control group of children witnessed the adults in a series of three neutral communications. The results (shown in Figure 1.1) indicated that exposure to the adults' angry exchanges generated significant distress among two-year-olds compared with their reactions in the presence of the friendly exchanges.

Although these researchers could have attempted to conduct their study of reactions to adult emotions through naturalistic observation in children's homes or preschools, they might have had to wait a long time for the appropriate interactions to take place spontaneously. Furthermore, adults in natural settings display emotions with varying degrees of intensity, making it difficult for the experimenters to ensure that all of their subjects witnessed exactly the same emotional states. By doing a structured observation, the experimenters could control the precise nature of the adult emotional displays that children saw. The adult actors were carefully trained so that all children witnessed exactly the same emotional scenes in the same order.

**structured observation**    Study in which behaviors are recorded as they occur within a situation constructed by the experimenter, usually in the laboratory.

A liability of structured observations, especially if they are conducted in the laboratory, is that children may not react in the same ways in the research room as they do in "real life." Being in a strange environment with unfamiliar experimenters or other participants in the study may make children behave in ways that are not typical. For example, children may show heightened distress to adult anger when they are in an unfamiliar environment. One solution to this problem is to confirm the results of laboratory studies by conducting similar studies in children's natural environments.

Structured observations can focus on a variety of types of behaviors. Like many structured observations, the study by Cummings and colleagues focused on children's overt actions—in this case, their facial displays and physical activities. Researchers often record other behaviors, such as the number of errors children make in a problem-solving task, the kinds of memory strategies they display, or the amount of time it takes children to learn a specified task. When structured observations are conducted in the laboratory, it is also possible for researchers to obtain *physiological measures,* the shifts in heart rate, brain wave activity, or respiration rate that can indicate the child's reaction to changes in stimuli. This technique is especially useful in examining the behavior of infants, because the range of overt responses usually displayed by very young children is more limited than that of older children.

**The Interview and the Questionnaire**    Sometimes the best way to glean information about what children know or how they behave is not simply to observe them but to *ask* them directly. Researchers have found that talking with children about their conceptions of friendships, gender roles, problem-solving skills—in fact, almost anything in the child's world—has yielded a wealth of material for analysis.

Many investigators use the technique of **structured interviews**, studies in which each participating child is asked the same sequence of questions. For example, the goal of a recent study conducted by Mary Levitt and her colleagues (Levitt, Guacci-Franco, & Levitt, 1993) was to explore the sources of social support for seven-, ten-, and fourteen-year-old children from different ethnic backgrounds. Over three hundred African-American, Anglo-American, and Hispanic-American children were interviewed individually about the people most important in their lives. Each child was questioned by an interviewer of the same cultural background as the child to maximize the child's comfort with the session and the accuracy of his or her responses. Examples of the standard questions employed in this study include "Are there people who make you feel better when something bothers you or you are not sure about something?" and "Are there people you talk to about things that are really important to you?" The results showed that for all children, regardless of ethnic background, the family was an important source of social support. Moreover, members of the extended family (e.g., grandparents, aunts, or uncles) played an increasing role during middle childhood, while peers assumed a significant support role during adolescence.

Another "asking" technique that researchers use with children is to obtain written responses to a standard set of items in a **questionnaire**. Because questionnaires can be administered to large numbers of children at the same time, researchers can use this method to obtain a large set of data very quickly. Questionnaires can also be scored quickly, particularly if the items ask subjects to pick from a set of multiple-choice items or to rate items on a numerical scale. Children, however, may have difficulty understanding the items and may not be able to answer accurately without guidance from an adult. Un-

**structured interview**  Standardized set of questions administered orally to subjects.

**questionnaire**  Set of standardized questions administered to subjects in written form.

der those conditions, oral interviews with individual children may provide more reliable and valid information about how children think and feel.

Researchers who use interviews and questionnaires to collect data from children must be careful, though. Sometimes young respondents, like their adult counterparts, will try to present themselves in the most favorable light or answer questions as they think the researcher expects them to. In the study of children's sources of social support, for example, subjects may say they talk with their parents when they have problems because they know this is the expected response. To prompt subjects to answer as honestly as possible, researchers try not to react positively or negatively as the subject responds and also try to explain the importance of answering truthfully before the start of the interview or questionnaire.

Another way of collecting data by interview is the **clinical method**, a flexible, open-ended technique in which the investigator may modify the questions in reaction to the child's response. A notable early example was Jean Piaget's use of the clinical method to explore age-related changes in children's thinking capabilities. Consider the following segment, in which Piaget (1929) questions a six-year-old boy about the sun:

PIAGET:  How did the sun begin?
CHILD:  It was when life began.

PIAGET:  Has there always been a sun?
CHILD:  No.

PIAGET:  How did it begin?
CHILD:  Because it knew that life had begun.

PIAGET:  What is it made of?
CHILD:  Of fire . . .

PIAGET:  Where did the fire come from?
CHILD:  From the sky.

PIAGET:  How was the fire made in the sky?
CHILD:  It was lighted with a match. (p. 258)

Note how Piaget follows the child's line of thinking with each question he asks. The format of the interview changes with an older boy, age nine years:

PIAGET:  How did the sun start?
CHILD:  With heat.

PIAGET:  What heat?
CHILD:  From the fire.

PIAGET:  Where is the fire?
CHILD:  In heaven.

PIAGET:  How did it start?
CHILD:  God lit it with wood and coal.

PIAGET:  Where did he get the wood and coal?
CHILD:  He made it. (p. 265)

Piaget gained some enormous insights into the thinking processes of children by using the probing, interactive questions typical of the clinical method. Having the flexibility to follow the child's train of thought rather than sticking to a rigid protocol of predetermined questions allows the researcher to gather fresh insights. The weakness of this approach, however, lies precisely in this flexibility. Because the questions asked of different subjects are likely to vary,

**clinical method**  Flexible, open-ended interview method in which questions are modified in reaction to the child's responses.

systematic comparisons of their answers are difficult to make. Moreover, the researcher may be tied to a theoretical orientation that biases the formulation of questions and the interpretation of answers. Nonetheless, the clinical method can be a valuable research tool, particularly in exploring the way children think and reason.

**The Meta-analytic Study**    Sometimes researchers do not actually collect empirical data themselves but instead make a statistical analysis of a body of previously published research on a specific topic that allows them to draw some general conclusions. Instead of looking or asking, they "crunch" data— that is, they combine the results of numerous studies to assess whether the central variable common to all has an important effect. This technique, called **meta-analysis**, is particularly useful when the results of studies in the same area are inconsistent or in conflict with one another.

A good example of meta-analysis is a study conducted by Janet Hyde and her colleagues to assess the existence of sex differences in children's mathematical skills (Hyde, Fennema, & Lamon, 1990). Many researchers have concluded that boys perform better than girls on tests of mathematical skill, particularly after the age of twelve or thirteen (Halpern, 1986; Maccoby & Jacklin, 1974). Such observations have spawned numerous debates about the origins of this sex difference. Is mathematical skill biologically given or is it learned through experiences in the environment? The answer to this question has important educational implications for male and female students. Hyde and her colleagues collected one hundred studies conducted from 1967 through 1987 that examined the question of sex differences in mathematics performance. (This body of studies represented the participation of over 3 million subjects!) For each study, a statistical measure representing *effect size* was computed, a mathematical way of expressing the size of the difference in male and female scores. Hyde and her colleagues (1990) found that the average difference between males and females across all studies was small, leading these researchers to conclude that sex differences in mathematical ability are not large enough to be of great scientific significance.

Conducting a meta-analysis requires the careful transcription of hundreds of statistical figures, a powerful computer, and a good deal of computational skill. Because the researcher taking this approach did not design the original studies, she or he cannot always be sure that the central variables have been defined in identical ways across studies. Moreover, studies that do not present their data in the form necessary for analysis might have to be eliminated from the pool; potentially valuable information might thus be lost. Despite these difficulties, the meta-analytic approach allows researchers to draw conclusions based on a large corpus of research, not just individual studies, and thereby to profit from an accumulated body of knowledge. This technique has recently become increasingly popular in developmental research and has provoked the reevaluation of more than one traditional notion about children. Table 1.1 summarizes the advantages and disadvantages of these four general types of data collection.

## Research Designs

Besides formulating their hypotheses, identifying the variables, and choosing a method of gathering information about children, investigators must select the research design they will use as part of their study. The *research design* is

**meta-analysis**   Statistical examination of a body of research studies to assess the effect of the common central variable.

| Approach | Description | Advantages | Disadvantages |
|---|---|---|---|
| **Naturalistic Observations** | Observations of behaviors as they occur in children's real-life environments. | Can note antecedents and consequences of behaviors; see real-life behaviors. | Possibility of subject reactivity and observer bias; less control over variables; cause-and-effect relationships difficult to establish. |
| **Structured Observations** | Observations of behaviors in situations constructed by the experimenter. | More control over conditions that elicit behaviors. | Children may not react as they would in real life. |
| **Interviews and Questionnaires** | Asking children (or parents) about what they know or how they behave. | Quick way to assess children's knowledge or reports of their behaviors. | Children may not always respond truthfully or accurately; systematic comparisons of responses may be difficult; theoretical orientation of researcher may bias questions and interpretations of answers. |
| **Meta-analytic Studies** | Statistical analysis of other researchers' findings to look for the size of a variable's effects. | Pools a large body of research findings to sort out conflicting findings; no subjects are observed. | Requires careful mathematical computation; variables may not have been defined identically across all studies. |

**TABLE 1.1**

**Advantages and Disadvantages of Information-gathering Approaches**

the overall conceptual approach that defines whether the variables will be manipulated, how many children will be studied, and the precise sequence of events as the study proceeds. Research designs may be fairly complex, and an investigator might choose more than one design for each part of a large study. Generally, however, researchers select from one of three study types: the correlational, the experimental, and the single-case design.

**The Correlational Design**     Studies in which the researcher looks for systematic relationships between variables use the correlational design and are called **correlational studies**. Instead of manipulating the variables, in this design the investigator obtains measures of two or more characteristics of the subjects and sees if changes in one variable are accompanied by changes in the other. Some variables show a **positive correlation**—that is, as the values of one variable change, scores on the other variable change in the same direction. For example, if a positive correlation existed between children's television viewing and their aggression, as the number of hours of TV viewing increased, the number of aggressive acts committed would increase, as well. A **negative correlation** indicates that as scores on one variable change, scores on the other variable change in the opposite direction. Thus, using our example, a negative relationship would exist if aggression decreased as TV viewing increased.

The statistic used to describe the strength of a relationship between two variables is called the **correlation coefficient**, or *r*. Correlation coefficients may range from +1.00 (perfectly positively correlated) to –1.00 (perfectly negatively correlated). As the correlation coefficient approaches 0.00 (which signifies no relationship), the relationship between the two variables becomes

**correlational study**   Study assessing whether changes in one variable are accompanied by systematic changes in another variable.

**positive correlation**   Relationship in which changes in one variable are accompanied by systematic changes in another variable in the same direction.

**negative correlation**   Relationship in which changes in one variable are accompanied by systematic changes in another variable in the opposite direction.

**correlation coefficient (r)**   Statistical measure, ranging from +1.00 to −1.00, that summarizes the strength and direction of the relationship between two variables; does not provide information about causation.

weaker. A rule of thumb is that correlations of .70 or higher usually signify strong relationships, whereas those below .20 represent weak relationships. In most cases, values falling in between indicate a moderate relationship between two variables.

We can use a portion of a study conducted by Sheryl Olson and her colleagues (Olson, Bates, & Kaskie, 1992) to illustrate the key features of correlational research. The objective of these investigators was to see if the style of mother-infant interaction at six, thirteen, and twenty-four months of age was related to children's cognitive ability at age six and eight years. One finding of this study was a correlation of $r = .49$ between the mothers' score on a verbal interaction scale when children were twenty-four months of age and children's scores on the Peabody Picture Vocabulary Test (PPVT) at six years of age. (The PPVT assesses the number of words children understand and is often used as a measure of cognitive ability.) The correlation coefficient indicates that the more frequently and clearly mothers spoke to their two-year-olds, the more words these children understood four years later. In contrast, mothers' scores on a scale of affection correlated $r = .18$ with children's PPVT scores at age six, suggesting no relationship between affection and cognitive ability.

Because researchers do not actively manipulate the variables in correlational studies, they must be cautious about making statements about cause and effect when strong relationships are found. In the above study, for example, do verbal mothers produce children who understand more words, or do verbally skilled children elicit greater talking from their mothers throughout the early childhood years? Still another possibility is that some third factor influences both mother and child's verbal behavior. Perhaps the child's general "sociability," or orientation to and interest in people in the environment, influences both child and mother's verbal behavior. (Olson and her colleagues were actually able to rule out the "sociability" explanation based on other measures obtained in their study.)

Despite these limitations on interpretation, correlational studies are often a useful first step in exploring which variables might be causally related to each other. In addition, in many instances experimenters are unable to manipulate the variables that are the suspected causes of certain behavior. In the study of mother-child interactions, for example, it would be difficult, even unethical, to ask some mothers to speak frequently with their children over a period of time and some mothers to limit verbalizations to their children. In such cases, correlational studies represent the only approach available to understanding the influences on child development.

**The Experimental Design**    The **experimental design** involves the manipulation of one or more **independent variables** (the variables that are manipulated or controlled by the investigator, often because they are the suspected cause of a behavior) to observe the effects on the **dependent variable** (the suspected outcome). One of the major goals of this type of study is to control for as many as possible of the factors that can influence the outcome, aside from the independent variables. Experimental studies are frequently conducted in laboratory situations, where it is possible to ensure that all subjects are exposed to the same environmental conditions and the same task instructions. In addition, **random assignment** of subjects to different treatment groups (in which usually one group is a *control group* that receives no treatment) helps to avoid any systematic variation aside from that precipitated by the independent variables. As a consequence, one distinct advantage of the ex-

**experimental design**  Research method in which one or more independent variables are manipulated to determine the effect on other, dependent, variables.

**independent variable**  Variable manipulated by the experimenter; the suspected cause.

**dependent variable**  Behavior that is measured; suspected effect of an experimental manipulation.

**random assignment**  Use of principles of chance to assign subjects to treatment and control groups; avoids systematic bias.

perimental study design is that cause-and-effect relationships among variables can be identified.

To illustrate the experimental design, consider the following question: are different sweet substances—sucrose, fructose, glucose, and lactose—equally effective in reducing crying in newborn infants? Elliott Blass and Barbara Smith (1992) investigated this question in an experimental study involving one- to three-day-old infants. During the prestimulation phase, each infant rested in a bassinet for five minutes. In the next five-minute phase, each infant received one of five solutions in its mouth—sucrose, fructose, glucose, lactose, or water. The assignment of a particular solution to each infant was randomly determined. Finally, infants were observed for an additional five minutes, the poststimulation phase. During all the observation phases, the amount of infant crying was recorded. Thus, the independent variable was the type of solution infants received and the dependent variable was the percent of time infants cried.

In this experiment, many other factors that could affect infant crying were controlled. For example, the nursery temperature was held at seventy-five degrees, all infants had their diapers changed right before the experimental session began, and all infants were tested in a bassinet. When other variables are controlled, the researcher can be more confident that the independent variable is causing changes in the dependent variable.

Figure 1.2 shows the percentage of time infants spent crying in each phase of the experiment. The graph shows that fructose and sucrose produced the greatest decreases in crying, while lactose and glucose were less effective in soothing infants. Can other hypotheses account for these findings? Because babies were randomly assigned to experimental conditions, it is not likely that the happiest babies were in the fructose and sucrose groups. And because all infants experienced the same experimental procedures except for the type of solution, it is difficult to argue for other explanations of these data.

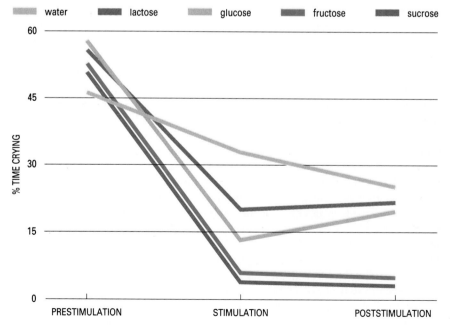

Source: Blass & Smith, 1992.

**FIGURE 1.2**

**An Experimental Study**

In this example of an experimental design, newborn infants were observed for five minutes as they lay in a bassinet (prestimulation) and then received one of four sweet solutions or water for five minutes (stimulation). Finally, they were observed for another five minutes (poststimulation). The percentage of time crying was recorded in each phase. The graph shows that sucrose and fructose resulted in a substantial decrease in crying compared to the other solutions in the stimulation and poststimulation phases of the experiment.

The experimental approach has been the traditional design choice for many developmental psychologists because of the "clean" answers it provides about the causes of developmental phenomena. Yet it has also been criticized for providing a narrow portrait of child development. Development in the real world is likely to be caused by many variables; few changes are likely to be the result of a single or even a few independent variables. In that sense, experimental studies typically do not capture the complexities of age-related changes. Moreover, we have already mentioned that children may not react normally when they are brought into the laboratory setting, where most experiments are conducted. Children may "clam up" because they are shy about being in unfamiliar surroundings with strangers and mechanical equipment. Or they may rush through the experimental task just to get it over with.

In recognition of these problems, many researchers have tried to achieve a more homelike feeling in their laboratories, with comfortable couches, chairs, tables, and rugs instead of sterile, bare-walled rooms filled with equipment. Another tactic has been to conduct **field experiments**, in which the experimental manipulations are actually carried out in a natural setting, such as the child's home or school. In one classic field experiment, Lynette Friedrich and Aletha Stein (1973) randomly assigned children attending their preschools to one of three experimental conditions to see if the type of television program they watched over a period of time affected their behavior during free play. For four weeks, one-half hour each day during a portion of their preschool program, children viewed one of the following: (1) aggressive cartoons ("Batman" and "Superman"), (2) prosocial shows ("Mr. Rogers' Neighborhood"), or (3) neutral films. The results showed that children exposed to aggressive shows declined in obedience to rules and their ability to tolerate delays. In addition, children who were above average in aggression at the start of the study showed more aggression during free play than children who had previously viewed the neutral shows. Finally, children who watched prosocial programs were more likely to stick with tasks they had begun and were more likely to obey rules than children who viewed neutral films. As with laboratory experiments, this study identified a causal effect of television programs on children's social behaviors. Because the only known variation in children's experiences was systematically introduced by the researchers in their manipulation of the independent variable (the type of television show the children watched), changes in behavior could be attributed to type of show. Additionally, the natural setting of this field experiment minimized the problems associated with bringing children into the artificial surroundings of a laboratory.

In some instances, it is not possible for the researcher to randomly assign subjects to treatment groups because of logistical or ethical difficulties. In these cases, the researcher may take advantage of the natural separation of subjects into different groups. **Quasi-experiments** are studies in which researchers investigate the effects of independent variables that they do not manipulate themselves but that occur as a result of children's natural experiences. Suppose, for example, that a researcher wanted to explore the effects of day-care centers of varying quality on children's social competence. It would be unethical to assign children randomly to high- and low-quality centers. Yet in everyday life, children do attend centers that differ in the overall quality of experience they provide. Deborah Vandell and her colleagues (Vandell, Henderson, & Wilson, 1988) observed the free play of four-year-old children who attended good- and poor-quality day-care centers. Good-quality centers were defined as those with better-trained teachers, better adult-child ratios, smaller classes, and more materials than poor-quality centers. When children from the

**field experiment** Experiment conducted in a "natural" real-world setting such as the child's home or school.

**quasi-experiment** Study in which the assignment of subjects to experimental groups is determined by their natural experiences.

two types of centers were compared on a range of social behaviors, Vandell and her colleagues noted that children from the better centers were rated as more socially competent, happier, and capable of more friendly interactions with their peers than children from the poorer centers.

Because the researchers did not randomly assign subjects to each group, we must be careful in how we interpret the results of this and other quasi-experimental studies. The children who attended poor- and good-quality centers may have consistently differed in ways that better account for their differences in social behavior than simply the nature of the day-care center they attended. Families with children in poor-quality centers may have had more limited financial resources and may have been under more stress than those who sent their children to better centers. Aspects of the home climate, rather than qualities of the day-care experience, may in fact have caused differences in children's social behavior and general emotional disposition. At the same time, however, quasi-experimental studies do offer researchers a way of addressing important questions about the complex influences on child development, questions that often have powerful real-world implications.

**The Single-Case Design**     Some notable discoveries about developmental processes have come from the in-depth examination of a single child or just a few children. At times, psychologists make an intensive description of an individual child, much as the baby biographers did. Freud and Piaget both relied heavily on such **case studies** of individuals to formulate their broad theories of personality and cognitive development, respectively. In other instances, researchers introduce experimental treatments to one or a few children and note any changes in their behavior over time. In these **single-case designs**, the purpose of the study is frequently to evaluate a clinical treatment for a problem behavior or an educational program designed to increase or decrease specific activities in the child.

Suppose, for example, we wish to evaluate the effectiveness of a treatment for stuttering in children. One team of researchers selected four boys, aged ten to eleven years, who had difficulties with stuttering (Gagnon & Ladouceur, 1992). Their first step was to record the percentage of stuttered syllables spoken by each boy during the *baseline* period, prior to the start of the treatment. Next, the treatment was begun. During two one-hour sessions per week, each boy received instruction on how to recognize stuttering and how to regulate breathing during stuttering. Special speaking exercises and parent information sessions were also introduced. Finally, the subjects' speech was assessed at one month and six months, following the end of treatment. Figure 1.3 shows the decline in percentage of stuttered syllables for the children from baseline through follow-up periods. Was the treatment effective? The fact that all four of the subjects showed similar declines in stuttering and the fact that stuttering remained low during follow-up several months later suggest that it was.

Single-case designs do not require large groups of children or the random assignment of subjects to groups. Each subject essentially serves as his or her own control by experiencing all conditions in the experiment over a period of time. As with any study involving only one or a few individuals, however, researchers may be limited in their ability to generalize to a larger group of children. Perhaps the child or children they selected for the study were particularly responsive to the treatment, a treatment that might not work as well for other children. In addition, the researcher must be aware of any other circumstances concurrent with the treatment that might have actually produced the behavior changes. For example, did the children in the stuttering study ma-

**case study**   In-depth description of psychological characteristics and behaviors of an individual.

**single-case design**   Study that follows only one or a few children over a period of time.

ture neurologically and did that maturation cause the reduction in speech problems? The fact that the treatment started at different times for each of the four children and was immediately followed by a decrease in stuttering suggests that the treatment and not some other factor caused the changes.

In Table 1.2, we present an overview of the strengths and weaknesses of single-case studies and other research designs we have briefly examined here.

## Strategies for Assessing Developmental Change

The developmental researcher faces a problem unique to this field: how to record the changes in behavior that occur over time. The investigator has two

**FIGURE 1.3**

**A Single-Case Design**

In this example of a single-case design, four boys with stuttering problems were observed during a baseline period. Next, a program to treat their speech problems was begun. The graph shows that the percentage of stuttered syllables declined dramatically following the onset of treatment and remained low during the follow-up period. Because four children showed similar patterns of behavior change, and because the behavior change was maintained long after the treatment was ended, the researchers concluded that their treatment was effective.

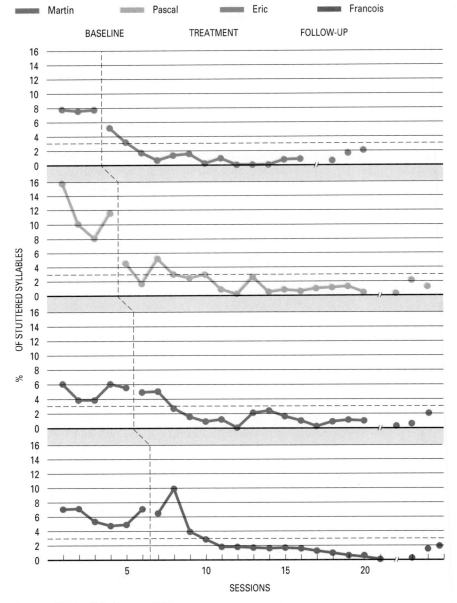

Source: Gagnon & Ladouceur, 1992.

| Design | Description | Strengths | Weaknesses |
|---|---|---|---|
| Correlational Design | Researcher sees if changes in one variable are accompanied by systematic changes in another variable. | Useful when conditions do not permit the manipulation of variables. | Cannot determine cause-and-effect relationships. |
| Experimental Design | Researcher manipulates one or more independent variables to observe the effects on the dependent variable(s). | Can isolate cause-and-effect relationships. | May not yield information about real-life behaviors. |
| Field Experiment | Experiment conducted in real-life, naturalistic settings. | Can isolate cause-and-effect relationships; behaviors are observed in natural settings. | Less control over treatment conditions. |
| Quasi-Experiment | Assignment of subjects to groups is determined by their natural experiences. | Takes advantage of natural separation of children into groups. | Factors other than independent variables may be causing results. |
| Single-Case Design | In-depth observation of one or a few children over a period of time. | Does not require large pool of subjects. | Ability to generalize to the larger population may be limited. |

**TABLE 1.2**

**Strengths and Weaknesses of Research Designs**

choices—to observe individual children repeatedly over time or to select children of different ages to participate in one study at a given time. Each approach has its strengths and limitations, and both have contributed substantially to our understanding of child development.

**The Longitudinal Study**   **Longitudinal studies** are studies in which the same sample of subjects is assessed repeatedly at various points in time, usually over a span of years. This approach has the longest historical tradition in developmental psychology. The early baby biographies were, in essence, longitudinal observations, and several major longitudinal projects initiated in the early part of the 1900s continued for decades. One of the most famous is Lewis Terman's study of intellectually gifted children, begun in 1921 (Terman, 1925; Terman & Oden, 1959).

Terman identified 952 children aged two to fourteen years who had scored 140 or above on a standardized test of intelligence. He was interested in answering several questions about these exceptionally bright children. Would they become extraordinarily successful later in life? Did they possess any specific cluster of common personality traits? Did they adapt well socially? The sample was followed until most subjects reached sixty years of age, and a wealth of information was collected over this long span of time. One finding was that many individuals in this sample had highly successful careers in science, academics, business, and other professions. In addition, contrary to many popular stereotypes, high intelligence was associated with greater physical and mental health and adaptive social functioning later in life.

Longitudinal research is costly and requires a substantial research effort. Subjects followed over a period of years often move or become unavailable for

**longitudinal study** Research in which the same subjects are repeatedly tested over a period of time, usually years.

Longitudinal studies assess the same subjects over a span of years. This strategy for assessing developmental change allows researchers to identify the stability of many human characteristics.

other reasons; just keeping track of them requires constant and careful record keeping. In addition, one might raise questions about the characteristics of the people who remain in the study: perhaps they are less mobile, or perhaps those who agree to participate in a thirty-year study have unique qualities that can affect the interpretation of the project's results (for example, they may be less energetic or they may be more curious about themselves and more introspective). Another difficulty lies in the fact that subjects who are tested repeatedly often get better at the tests, not because of any changes in their abilities, but because the tests become more familiar over time. Subjects who take a test of spatial skill again and again may improve because of practice with the test and not because of any developmental change in their abilities. If the researcher attempts to avert this outcome by designing a different version of the same test, the problem then becomes whether the two tests are similar enough!

One of the biggest methodological drawbacks of longitudinal research is the possibility of an **age-history confound**. Suppose a researcher began a twenty-year longitudinal study in 1970 and found that individuals' gender-role beliefs became less stereotyped as the years progressed. That is, subjects were less likely to believe that females are dependent, passive, and emotional and that males are independent, aggressive, and logical. Are these shifts in attitude associated with development? Or did some historical factor, such as the "women's movement" bring about the changes in beliefs? Because subjects age as historical events occur, it is often difficult to decide which factor affects the results of a longitudinal study.

Despite all these difficulties, the longitudinal approach has distinct advantages not offered by any other research tactic; in fact, certain research questions in child development can *only* be answered longitudinally. If a researcher is interested in identifying the *stability* of human characteristics—that is, how likely it is that early attributes will be maintained later in development—the longitudinal approach is the method of choice. Only by observing the same person over time can we answer such questions as, Do passive infants become shy adults? or, Do early experiences with peers affect the child's ability to form friendships in adolescence? For researchers interested in understanding the process of development and the factors that precede and follow specific developmental phenomena, particularly with respect to individual differences, the longitudinal strategy remains a powerful one.

**The Cross-Sectional Study** Possibly the most widely used strategy for studying developmental differences is the cross-sectional study, in which children of varying ages are examined at the same point in time. Cross-sectional studies take less time to complete and are usually more economical than longitudinal studies.

A good example of cross-sectional research is the investigation of children's memory development conducted by Peter Ornstein and his colleagues (Ornstein, Naus, & Liberty, 1975). The specific goal was to see if age-based changes occur in children's tendency to rehearse (or repeat) a series of words they are asked to remember. Furthermore, the researchers were interested in whether any tendencies to rehearse were accompanied by actual increases in the numbers of words that children remembered. Ornstein and his associates began by asking third-, sixth-, and eighth-graders to study a list of eighteen words and then recall them in any order they wished (a *free recall* procedure). Half of the subjects in each age group were also instructed to rehearse out loud as each word was presented during the study period. The number of times the children repeated the words as well as the number of different words in the rehearsal set (the block of items they actually verbalized each time they

**FIGURE 1.4**

**A Cross-Sectional Study**

Age differences in behaviors can be assessed relatively quickly with the cross-sectional approach. In one such study, Ornstein, Naus, and Liberty found that older children recalled more words than younger children (a), older children rehearsed more frequently than younger children (b), and older children included more items in the set they rehearsed than younger children (c).

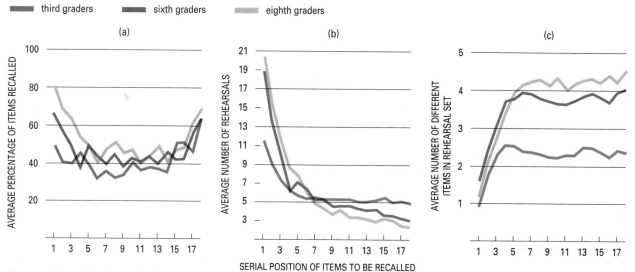

Source: Adapted from Ornstein, Naus, & Liberty, 1975.

rehearsed) were noted. The three panels in Figure 1.4 show the results. First, third-graders had lower levels of recall than the two older age groups, especially for words that had appeared early in the list. Second, third-graders tended to rehearse individual items with less frequency than did older children, again primarily for items at the beginning of the list. Lastly, third-graders included fewer different items in their rehearsal sets; instead of saying over and over several different words from the list to be remembered, they tended to repeat only one or two of the same words. Ornstein and his colleagues (1975) concluded that younger children's poorer levels of recall memory were linked to their use of less effective strategies for remembering.

Using the cross-sectional approach allowed the researchers to make a rapid assessment of changes in memory without waiting for children to grow three or five years older. They were, however, unable to draw conclusions about individual children and about how characteristics observable at one age might be related to characteristics at another age. Did some of the third-graders spontaneously rehearse, even if most of their age mates did not? If so, would these children have the best memories three or five years later? The cross-sectional approach does not provide answers to these kinds of questions. Most cross-sectional studies involve pooling the scores of individual subjects in such a way that the average performance of an entire group of children of a specified age is reported; the average scores of two or more groups of children are then compared. The result is that information about individuals is not the focus of data analysis in this type of study.

Another difficulty with cross-sectional designs is that cohort effects may interfere with our ability to draw clear conclusions. **Cohort effects** are all the characteristics shared by children growing up in a specific social and historical context. For example, many of today's five-year-olds have had extensive peer experience through their enrollment in day-care and other preschool programs, whereas many fifteen-year-olds probably have not. A researcher comparing the two groups might mistakenly conclude that younger children are more sociable than older children, but the differential exposure to age mates early in life—that is, the cohort effect—may be responsible for the findings rather than changes in sociability with age. Cross-sectional studies are a quick means of providing descriptions of age changes in all sorts of behaviors. Where they sometimes fall short is in helping us to understand the processes underlying those age-related changes.

**The Sequential Study**    One way to combine the advantages of both the longitudinal and cross-sectional approaches is the **sequential study**, in which groups of children of different ages are followed repeatedly but for only a few years. For example, a research group wanted to study age changes in patterns of television viewing of the educational program "Sesame Street" (Pinon, Huston, & Wright, 1989). Two groups of children—a group of three- to five-year-olds and a group of five- to seven-year-olds—were followed for a period of two years. During specified weeks within this two-year period, families kept diaries of the children's television viewing. At the same time, the researchers wanted to examine the relationship between a number of family characteristics, such as parental education and maternal employment, and children's tendency to watch "Sesame Street."

Figure 1.5 shows that children's viewing of "Sesame Street" peaked at about age three and a half or four and then declined. These researchers also found that age-related events in the children's lives were associated with the declines after age four. For example, as children entered preschools or kindergartens,

**cohort effect**    Characteristics shared by individuals growing up in a given sociohistorical context that can influence developmental outcomes.

**sequential study**    Study that examines groups of children of different ages over a period of time; usually shorter than a longitudinal study.

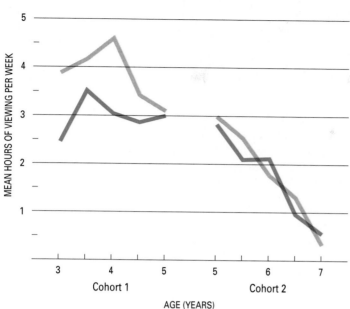

spring start time     fall start time

MEAN HOURS OF VIEWING PER WEEK

3     4     5     5     6     7

Cohort 1          Cohort 2

AGE (YEARS)

Source: Adapted from Pinon, Huston & Wright, 1989.

**FIGURE 1.5**

**A Sequential Study**

Age differences in behavior patterns over time can be assessed by sequential studies. In one such study, television viewing of "Sesame Street" by two age groups, a group of three-year-olds and a group of five-year-olds, was recorded over a period of two years. (Some of the subjects began the study in the spring, others started in the fall.) As the graph shows, children's interest in this show peaked around age four, then declined over the next several years. The sequential approach combines the advantages of the longitudinal and cross-sectional approaches.

they tended to watch less television. Similarly, as mothers returned to work and sent their children to child care, children's viewing decreased. The benefit of the sequential design was that it allowed information about a four-year age span to be obtained in two years. Information about the stability of television viewing for individual children was available, just as it would have been in a longitudinal study. At the same time, the researchers halved the amount of time it took to find out about children's viewing tendencies from ages three through seven. Although most developmental researchers still prefer to conduct cross-sectional studies because of their expediency, the sequential study provides a convenient way of reaping the advantages of both cross-sectional and longitudinal approaches to studying developmental change. Table 1.3 summarizes the relative benefits of each of the research strategies for assessing developmental change.

## Cross-Cultural Studies of Development

Some of the most fundamental questions about the nature of development concern the universality of the various features of psychological growth. Do all children learn language the same way, regardless of the specific language they acquire? Does children's thinking develop in a universal sequence? Are certain emotions common to all children regardless of attitudes about the appropriateness of crying, smiling, or feeling angry in the larger social group in which they live?

If psychological development does display universal features, this circumstance has far-reaching implications. It could imply, for a start, that a child's behavior is largely shaped by biological factors and, more specifically, by the genes that govern the unfolding of some human behaviors. Variations in aspects of psychological development across cultures, on the other hand, imply that the differences in the child's experiences weigh heavily in bringing

| Approach | Description | Advantages | Disadvantages |
|----------|-------------|------------|---------------|
| **Longitudinal Study** | Repeated testing of the same group of children over an extended period of time. | Can examine the stability of characteristics. | Requires a significant investment of time and resources; problems with subject attrition; can have age-history confound. |
| **Cross-Sectional Study** | Comparison of children of different ages at the same point in time. | Requires less time; less costly than longitudinal study. | Cannot study individual patterns of development or the stability of traits; subject to cohort effects. |
| **Sequential Study** | Observation of children of two or more different ages over a shorter period of time than in longitudinal studies. | Combines the advantages of both longitudinal and cross-sectional approaches; can obtain information about stability of traits in a short period of time. | Has same problems as longitudinal studies but to a lesser degree. |

**TABLE 1.3**

**Strategies for Assessing Developmental Change**

about those behaviors. **Cross-cultural studies**, which compare children from different cultural groups on one or more behaviors or pattern of abilities, can be extremely useful in answering questions such as these.

Take, for example, a reported finding about infants' linguistic behaviors. Among young infants in the United States, it has been found that females vocalize more than males under age one year (Lewis, 1969; Lewis & Freedle, 1973). Particularly because this sex difference appears so early in life, it might be tempting to conclude that females are biologically predisposed toward strong verbal skills. Yet a study of Greek infants has demonstrated that male infants show greater vocal responsiveness to their mothers than females do (Roe, Drivas, Karagellis, & Roe, 1985). This one finding alone casts doubt on a biological explanation of sex differences in vocalization.

Cross-cultural studies can present unique challenges to the researcher. If children from two cultural backgrounds are being compared, the researcher must make sure that the tasks are well understood and have equivalent forms despite differences in language or the kinds of activities children are used to doing. For example, children in some cultures may never have seen a photograph or a two-dimensional drawing. Asking these children to categorize objects in pictorial form may place them at an unfair disadvantage if they are to be compared with children who have extensive experience with two-dimensional representations. Moreover, if the researcher is an outsider to the cultural group being observed, he or she may provoke atypical reactions from the individuals under study. Parent-child interactions, peer play, and many other behaviors may not occur as they would in the natural course of events because of the presence of an outside observer. Cross-cultural researchers must thus pay special attention to the possibility of subject reactivity. These problems aside, cross-cultural studies can provide important insights into almost all aspects of child development. For this reason, we will draw on available cross-cultural work as we discuss each aspect of the growth of children.

**cross-cultural study** Study comparing subjects in different cultural contexts.

## Ethical Issues in Developmental Research

All psychologists are bound by professional ethics to treat the subjects under study humanely and fairly. In general, researchers try to minimize the risk of any physical or emotional harm that might occur to subjects from participation in research and to maximize the benefits that will accrue from the findings of their work. The American Psychological Association has drawn up the following specific guidelines for the use of human subjects: First, subjects must give **informed consent** before participating in a research project; that is, they must be told the purposes of the study and informed of any potential risks to their well-being, and then they must formally agree to participate. Second, subjects have the right to decline to participate or to stop participation, even in the middle of the experiment. Third, if subjects cannot be told the true purpose of the experiment (sometimes knowing the experimenter's objective will influence how subjects behave), they must be **debriefed** at the conclusion of the study. When subjects are debriefed, they are told the true objective of the study and the reasons for any deception on the part of the experimenter. Finally, data collected from subjects must be kept confidential. To ensure that experimenters comply with these guidelines, most research institutions have review boards that evaluate any potential risks to subjects and the researchers' compliance with ethical practice.

The same ethical guidelines apply to using children as subjects in research, but frequently the implementation of these guidelines becomes a difficult matter. Who provides informed consent in the case of an infant or young toddler, for example? (The parents do.) Is it proper to deceive children about the purposes of a study if they cannot understand the debriefing? (In general, it is a good idea to avoid any kind of deception with children, such as telling them you are interested in how quickly they learn a game when you are really interested in whether they will be altruistic with their play partner.) Are some subjects of study taboo, such as asking children about their concepts of death, suicide, or other frightening topics that might affect them emotionally? (Such studies, if conducted, must be planned very carefully and conducted only by trained professionals.) What about cases in which treatments are suspected to have beneficial outcomes for children? Can the control group properly have the treatment withheld? For example, if we suspect that children's participation in an early-intervention preschool program will have real benefits for them, should children in the control group be kept out of it? (One solution to

Are children from different cultures similar or different in their behaviors? Cross-cultural studies allow psychologists to see if there are universalities (and therefore perhaps biological factors) in development.

**informed consent** Subject's formal acknowledgment that he or she understands the purposes, procedures, and risks of a study and agrees to participate in it.

**debriefing** Providing research participants with a statement of the true goals of a study after initially deceiving them about its purposes.

- The investigator may not use any procedures that could impose physical or psychological harm on the child. In addition, the investigator should use the least stressful research operation whenever possible. If the investigator is in doubt about the possible harmful effects of the research, he or she should consult with others. If the child will be unavoidably exposed to stress in research that might provide some diagnostic or therapeutic benefits to the child, then the study should be reviewed by an institutional review board.

- The investigator should inform the child of all features of the research that might affect his or her willingness to participate and should answer all questions in a way that the child can comprehend. The child has the right to discontinue participation at any time.

- Informed consent should be obtained in writing from the child's parents or from other adults who have responsibility for the child. The adult has the right to know all features of the research that might affect the child's willingness to participate and can refuse consent.

- If the research necessitates concealment or deception about the nature of the study, the investigator should make sure that the child understands the reasons for the deception after the study is concluded.

- All information about participants in research must be kept confidential.

- If, during the research, the investigator learns of information concerning a jeopardy to the child's well-being, the investigator must discuss the information with the parents or guardians and experts to arrange for assistance to the child.

- The investigator should clarify any misconceptions that may have arisen on the part of the child during the study.

Source: Adapted from the ethical standards set by the Society for Research in Child Development, 1990.

**TABLE 1.4**

**Ethical Guidelines in Conducting Research with Children**

this thorny problem is to offer the control group the beneficial treatment as soon as possible after the conclusion of the study, although this is not always a satisfactory compromise. The control group still has to wait for a beneficial treatment or intervention.)

Many researchers assume that children's vulnerability to risk as they participate in psychological experiments decreases as they grow older. Because infants and young children have more limited cognitive skills and emotional coping strategies, they are viewed as less able to protect themselves and their rights during participation in research. This assumption certainly has some logical basis. Some types of research, however, may actually pose a greater threat to older children. As Ross Thompson (1990) has pointed out, older children are developing a self-concept and a more elaborate understanding of the ways in which others evaluate them. Older children may thus be more susceptible to psychological harm than younger children when the researcher compares their performance with that of others or when they think teachers or parents might learn about their performance. In addition, older children may be more sensitive to research results that reflect negatively on their family or sociocultural group. These situations require awareness on the part of the researcher about the subtle ways in which children can be adversely affected by the research enterprise.

Table 1.4 sets forth the ethical guidelines on using children as subjects in research established by the Society for Research in Child Development. Probably the overriding guiding principle is that children should not be subjected to any physical or mental harm and should be treated with all possible respect. In fact, because children are frequently unable to voice their concerns and have less power than adults do, developmental researchers must be especially sensitive to their comfort and well-being.

# *Summary*

*Developmental psychology* has two main goals: to describe changes in behavior and mental processes that occur over time and to explain the reasons that development occurs in the way it does.

## The Scientific Study of the Child in Western Society

Attitudes toward children have changed in Western society over the centuries. During medieval times, children were quickly incorporated into the adult world although their vulnerability was also recognized. Philosophers such as Locke and Rousseau contributed to a growing interest in the nature of childhood during the seventeenth and eighteenth centuries. The systematic study of children began with the baby biographers of the nineteenth century, who made extensive observations of individual children. At the beginning of the twentieth century, G. Stanley Hall introduced the questionnaire method for studying large groups of children and Alfred Binet led the movement to study individual differences in children's behavior and abilities. Theorists like James Mark Baldwin formulated hypotheses about the nature of the child. Much of the early empirical work in developmental psychology focused on establishing norms of behavior. Today, research in developmental psychology is guided by a rich array of theoretical, empirical, and applied questions.

## Research Methods in Developmental Psychology

Researchers can choose from a number of specific techniques for gathering data about children. *Naturalistic observations* involve the systematic recording of behaviors as they occur in children's everyday environments. *Structured observations,* usually conducted in the laboratory, allow the experimenter more control over the situations that accompany children's behaviors. Researchers can employ *interviews* or *questionnaires* if they are interested in children's own reports of what they know or how they behave. Finally, *meta-analytic studies* permit investigators to analyze the results of a large body of published research in order to draw general conclusions about behavior.

Three basic research designs are employed in psychological research. In the *correlational design,* investigators see if changes in one variable are accompanied by systematic changes in another variable. However, correlations between variables do not prove cause-and-effect relationships. In the *experimental design,* the researcher manipulates one or more independent variables to see if they have an effect on the dependent variable. In the *single-case design,* the researcher intensively studies one or a few individuals over a period of time. Each of these designs offers advantages and disadvantages, with the researcher's choice dictated by the specific questions to be answered as well as the types of resources available.

There are three strategies for assessing developmental change. *Longitudinal studies* test the same subjects repeatedly over an extended period of time. *Cross-sectional studies* examine subjects of different ages at the same time. *Sequential studies* examine children of two or more ages over a period of time, usually shorter than that used in longitudinal studies. *Cross-cultural studies* have a special place in developmental psychology because they often address questions of the universality of human behaviors.

One last important consideration for the researcher is the ethical dimension of conducting studies with children. Children, like all human subjects, must be treated with fairness and dignity and must be protected from harm.

# 2

# Themes and Theories

*Right from the start Robert was a handful. A restless infant who slept poorly and cried frequently, he grew into an extremely active toddler who threw frequent temper tantrums. After his mother died in a car accident, leaving his father as a single parent to rear him, Robert's behavior became an even greater problem. By the time he entered kindergarten, he displayed serious difficulties in participating in group activities and minding teachers. Robert's father had always refused to use physical punishment to discipline his son but now found himself faced with a painful question: had he, in the words of an old saying, "spared the rod and spoiled the child"?*

When we think seriously about how children mature and the best ways to foster their development, common sense seems like the logical place to start. The caregivers responsible for your upbringing were most likely unacquainted with the theories of John Locke, Jean Jacques Rousseau, or other philosophers. Instead, they probably relied on their own experience and the advice of relatives and friends to make decisions about how to encourage your development. Even if you have not been actively involved in child rearing, you also have preconceptions based on your childhood—perhaps further influenced by personal observations, study, or work with children—about "what's best" for them. These kinds of experiences make up the common sense and parenting wisdom by which generations of caregivers have reared children, and they are frequently shared across cultures. In fact, Robert's father might have been more likely to begin spanking his son had he known that the Ovambo of southwest Africa say, "A cranky child has not been spanked," and that Japanese parents were advised at one time to "bring up your beloved child with a stick."

Yet at times common sense not only fails to provide answers but may promote unexpected and possibly even undesirable outcomes. For example, is physical punishment of children a good thing? Caregivers in many societies believe spanking, hitting, and even whipping the child for unacceptable behaviors such as aggression are the best ways to prevent those behaviors. But is this the most desirable response to the child-rearing dilemma Robert's father faces? Perhaps not. Researchers, for example, have found that parents who typically resort to physical punishment often have children who initiate more aggressive acts toward others than children of parents who rely on alternative methods of disciplining inappropriate conduct (Bandura & Walters, 1959; Olweus, 1980). Thus, under some circumstances, physical punishment may encourage, rather than discourage, aggressive actions. In Robert's case, an attentional deficit or some other disorder might underlie his hyperactive behavior, and spanking might be ineffective in helping him to control that behavior. As scientific knowledge of child development has evolved, we can step back from blind acceptance of the untested wisdom and practices of previous generations and validate their effectiveness using the systematic procedures and methods described in Chapter 1.

This is precisely the point at which *theory* enters the picture. As one researcher has stated, "The basic aim of science is theory" (Kerlinger, 1964). Reread this sentence, because it makes a claim you may find surprising. Why are theories so vital to science? For many students, theories seem far less important and interesting than the many intriguing "facts" that surround children and their development. The answer, however, to why theories are so important lies in what they are designed to do. Theories are essential for helping to organize information and to guide further research. An equally important aim of theory is to *explain* behavior.

Theories are established to provide reliable explanations for our observations, a goal that is important in every scientific discipline, not just child development. Being able to explain behavior is not only gratifying, it is essential for translating ideas into applications—creating meaningful programs and ways to assist parents, teachers, and others who work to enhance and promote the development of children. Thus, for example, when a theory proposes that adults are an important source of imitative learning and that parents who display aggressive behavior provide a model for responding to a frustrating situation, we can begin to understand why common proverbs such as "spare the rod and spoil the child" sometimes need to be reevaluated.

In this chapter our discussion focuses on several broad theories and perspectives that have influenced explanations of children's behavior and promoted developmental research. No one theory is sufficient to provide a full explanation of all behavior. Some strive to make sense of intellectual and cognitive development; others focus on social, emotional, and personality development. Theories also vary in the extent to which they present formalized, testable ideas. Thus, some are more useful than others in providing explanations for behavior that can be rigorously evaluated. And they often disagree in their answers to the fundamental questions of development. In fact, before we examine specific theories, let us consider the cluster of basic questions that all theories of development must address.

## Six Major Themes in Developmental Psychology

As you read about each of the many domains of child development—language acquisition, peer relationships, motor skills, recognition of self-worth, and others—you will find that certain questions about the causes and nature of development surface again and again. We call these questions the *themes in development*. In our discussions of language, cognitive, emotional, social, and other aspects of development, you will notice that different theories attempt to address these questions in diverse ways. Good theories, grounded in careful research, help us to think about and understand these major themes.

### What Roles Do Nature and Nurture Play in Development?

All of us have heard the expression "He inherited a good set of genes," or "She had a great upbringing" to explain some trait or behavior. These explanations offer two very different answers to a basic question of child development, one that has fueled a controversy among theorists since before the days of Locke and Rousseau and that continues to rage even today. Dubbed the **nature-nurture debate**, the dispute centers on whether the child's development is the result of genetic endowment or environmental influences.

Do children typically crawl at nine months and walk at twelve months of age because they have learned to do so or because of some inborn unfolding pro-

**nature-nurture debate** Ongoing theoretical controversy over whether development is the result of the child's genetic endowment or the kinds of experiences he or she has had.

gram? Do they readily acquire language because their environment demands it or because they are genetically predisposed to do so? Are boys more aggressive than girls because of cultural conditioning or biological factors? Is the child's level of intellectual functioning an inherited trait or the result of environmental stimulation (or lack thereof)? In each of these areas researchers want to do more than describe the course of the child's achievements; they also want to identify the factors influencing those achievements. In some of these areas, such as the development of intelligence and the emergence of gender roles, the debate over nature versus nurture has become particularly heated.

Why all the sound and fury about such a question? One reason is that the answer has major implications for children's developmental outcomes. If, for example, tested theories suggest that intelligence is guided largely by heredity, then providing children with rich learning experiences may have minimal impact on their eventual levels of intellectual skill. If, on the other hand, research and theory more convincingly show that intellectual development is shaped by environmental events, it becomes vitally important to provide children with the kinds of experiences that will optimize their intellectual growth. Such theories can also have an impact on public policy by affecting how funds are allocated to social and educational programs.

Psychologists now recognize that both nature and nurture play a role in all aspects of behavior, that these two forces together help to mold what the child becomes. Thus, the controversy has shifted from a concern with identifying *which* of these two factors is critical in any given situation. Instead, the question is *how,* specifically, each contributes to development. The problem for researchers is to determine the manner by which heredity and environment *interact* to fashion the behaviors we see in children, and eventually in adults. Theories have taken very different positions on this question.

## How Does the Sociocultural Context Influence Development?

Development does not take place only within the microcosm of the family. Children grow up within a larger social group that has unique customs, values, and beliefs about the proper way of rearing children and the ultimate goals of guiding their development. Think back to your family and the cultural standards and values that determined how you were treated. Were you allowed to be assertive and to speak your mind? Or were you expected to be compliant to adults and never challenge them? Were you encouraged to fend for yourself, or were caregivers, relatives, and even cultural institutions such as the school, church, or a government agency expected to assist with your needs throughout childhood, adolescence, perhaps even into your early adult years? On an even broader scale, how was your development affected by your family's economic status and educational attainments? By your gender and ethnic identity?

The values and resources of the society in which a child lives have major impacts on progress in physical, social, emotional, and cognitive development. These sociocultural factors affect everything from the kinds of child-rearing practices parents engage in to the level of health care and education children receive; they affect children's physical well-being, social standing, sense of self-esteem, "personality," and emotional expressiveness as well. As you explore the various domains of development, you will see that many developmental outcomes seemingly the result of inborn dispositions or the immediate environment are, in fact, heavily influenced by the sociocultural context. And, as with the nature-nurture debate, the precise impact of sociocultural context on various areas of development has generated much heated discussion among theorists.

## How Does the Child Play an Active Role in Development?

When children learn to speak, do they passively record the language they hear in their environment and reproduce it as if they were playing back a tape recording? Or are they more actively engaged in acquiring the sounds, grammar, and meanings of words and putting them together in new ways? Do children compose male and female gender roles simply by imitating the behaviors of men and women around them? Or do they somehow construct mental interpretations of male and female activities that in turn drive their own behavior? Do parents set the emotional tone for interactions with their young infants? Or do infants take the initiative in determining whether playing or bathing will be stressful or happy events? In other words, do infants and children somehow regulate and determine their own development?

Most researchers today believe that children do take an active role in their own growth and development. That active role may be evident at two different levels. The first commences with the various attributes and qualities that children possess or display, such as their curiosity and eagerness for engaging in the physical and social world surrounding them. For example, by virtue of being a boy or girl, being placid or active, being helpful or refusing to cooperate, and by eventually taking an interest in such things as dinosaurs, music, or sports, children elicit reactions from others. Thus, children are not simply passive recipients of surrounding influences, blank slates on which the environment writes; their own capacities and efforts to engage, to get "mixed up" with, their physical and social world often modify the kinds of things that happen to them. This can affect their development in profound ways.

Children grow up in various cultures and social settings that stress unique customs, values, and beliefs. In the United States and many other countries, young children often can be found in classrooms like the one shown here. In other cultures, this kind of formal educational setting may not exist or may take a very different form. Researchers must take into consideration these and many other kinds of sociocultural differences to fully understand development.

A second, perhaps more fundamental, way in which children may contribute to their own development is by actively constructing and organizing ways of thinking, feeling, communicating, and so forth, that assist them in making sense of their world. These psychological processes and conceptualizations may be assembled by children to help them respond to and understand the rich array of physical and social events that comprise their experience. As you will soon see, this view of how children directly influence their own development is theoretically controversial.

## Is Development Continuous or Discontinuous?

Does the way in which children think at age seven or eight change radically after reaching adolescence? Does the two-year-old child enter a "terrible twos" phase in personality development, marked by a refusal to cooperate and frequent shouts of "no!" not found at other ages? What is the best way to explain the differences so immediately apparent when we compare the behaviors and abilities of the one-year-old, four-year-old, nine-year-old, and sixteen-year-old?

Everyone agrees that children's behaviors and abilities change and sometimes in dramatic ways, but there is much less agreement on how best to explain these changes. On one hand, development can be viewed as a *continuous* process in which new attainments in thinking, language, and social behavior are characterized by gradual, steady, small *quantitative* advances. For example, substantial progress in reasoning or problem solving might result from the ability to remember more and more pieces of information. Or as neural coordination and muscle strength gradually improve, the infant may advance from crawling to walking—a progression in behavior that, by anyone's account, has substantial consequences for both child and caregiver. Thus, even though at two given points in time the child may look very different in the ability to think or locomote, it may be continuous, quantitative improvements in the speed, efficiency, or strength with which mental or physical processes are carried out—rather than a dramatic reorganization of some underlying capacity—that underlies these changes.

Alternatively, some theories explain development in terms of the child's progress through a series of **stages**, or periods when innovative developmental accomplishments abruptly surface, presumably because some fundamental reorganization in the thought or capacities underlying behavior has taken place. In this view, development undergoes a rapid transition as one stage ends and a new one begins, followed by a relatively stable period during which the behavior and abilities of the child change very little (see Figure 2.1). *Qualitative* differences in how children perceive, think, feel, or behave mark these periods in their lives. From this perspective, children establish distinctive ways of thinking, for instance, during the early school years and move to another level of thinking in adolescence. Or a child may indeed pass through a unique phase of personality development in toddlerhood dubbed the "terrible twos."

A related issue concerns the importance of certain types of experience at particular points in a child's growth. For example, if an infant does not develop a secure, positive emotional relationship with her caregiver in the first year of life, will her ability to establish positive relationships with others suffer? If a child has not been exposed to a second language by the beginning of adolescence, will he ever be able to achieve native fluency and pronunciation in the new language? Some theories propose that there are **sensitive** or *critical*

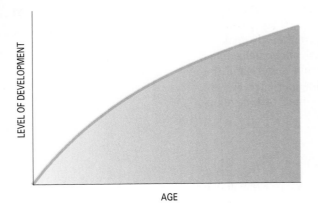
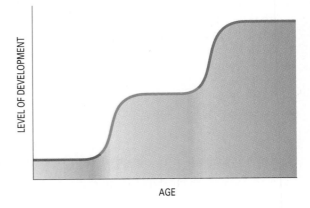

**FIGURE 2.1**

### Development as a Continuous Versus a Discontinuous Process

Children display many changes in their abilities and behaviors throughout development. Theorists, however, disagree on how best to describe these changes. According to some, the best way to explain development is in terms of gradual changes in the structures and processes underlying growth. For others, however, development is believed to undergo a series of stagelike transformations during which underlying processes and structures exhibit rapid reorganization followed by a period of relative stability.

**stage** Developmental period during which the organization of thought and behavior is qualitatively different from that of an earlier or later period.

**sensitive period** Brief period during which specific kinds of experiences have significant positive or negative consequences for development and behavior. Also called *critical period*.

*periods* when the child is highly vulnerable or responsive to particular kinds of environmental events. In other cases, the *lack* of some experience during a sensitive time can lead to behavioral difficulties. For example, some experts believe that the failure to form a strong emotional bond with a caregiver in infancy is linked to serious emotional problems later in childhood. Thus, experience with specific events during a sensitive period could be the basis for new achievements or serious disruptions in development. Such events could help to explain discontinuities in behavior along with which experiences are necessary to ensure that development proceeds in a typical fashion.

Evidence supporting or negating theories about continuity, discontinuity, and sensitive periods in human development is difficult to obtain. For instance, few, if any, aspects of human growth appear to mimic the obvious transformations found in the life cycle of an insect as it changes from egg to larva, to pupa, and finally to adult, periods in which a stable physical organization is followed by rapid reorganization and emergence of a new period in the life cycle. Yet over a period of months and years children do become quite different. Whether these changes are best understood in terms of quantitative or qualitative factors and the degree to which they are dependent upon highly specific experiences are points of frequent disagreement among theories of development.

## How Prominent Are Individual Differences in Development?

Psychologists are very much interested in understanding the changes common to all children as they grow from infant to adult. Thus, we often refer to the "average" or "typical" child as if every baby, six-year-old, or adolescent should be capable of engaging in some specific level of physical, mental, or social activity. But does every child proceed along the same path in their development?

Parents of two or more children frequently comment how different and unique each of them is. One child may have learned to speak before she was a year of age, another not until eighteen months. One may have shown an interest in music, another in athletics. Perhaps one child repeatedly challenged the parents' authority, another adapted to their demands and requests cheerfully.

Biological and experiential differences undoubtedly contribute to wide variations in behavior and competency displayed by children, even those born to and reared by the same set of parents. Although human growth must go forward within certain constraints, development may proceed along many paths and at quite different rates from one individual to another. Theories differ as to how and to what extent the diversity that is found in children's development can be explained by general or individual principles of development.

## How Do the Various Domains of Development Interact?

Many times the child's development in one domain will have a direct bearing on her attainments in other domains. Consider just one example—how a child's physical growth might influence her social and emotional development. A child who has become taller than her peers may experience very different interactions with adults and peers than a child who is small for her age. The taller child might be given more responsibilities by a teacher or be asked more frequently by peers to lead the group. These opportunities may instill a sense of worth and offer occasions for practicing social skills that are less frequently available to the smaller child. As these social skills are exercised and become more refined and advanced, the taller child may receive still more opportunities that promote social, and even cognitive development.

Few theories have considered the interaction among domains of development in depth; nevertheless, this is a vital dimension of the complicated dynamics of development. Our ultimate aim is to understand the child as a whole individual, not just as someone who undergoes physical, perceptual, emotional, cognitive, and social development. To do so, we must keep in mind that no single component of development unfolds in isolation from the rest.

Where do you stand on each of these themes? Do you think development is primarily influenced by nature or nurture? How greatly do you believe a society's trends, values, and resources affect an individual's development? To what extent are you convinced that children actively determine their own futures?

Development takes place on many fronts. Abilities displayed in one domain often interact with abilities in other domains. For example, good physical skills and motor coordination can be a source of positive self esteem, which in turn may foster effective communication and social interactions with others.

Would you describe changes throughout infancy and childhood in terms of continuous or discontinuous processes? How would you explain the diversity you observe in children's development? How do you see advances or difficulties in one domain affecting the child's development in other domains?

These are not easy questions. And, as we take a closer look at specific theoretical approaches, you shall see that they often propose conflicting answers.

## Learning Theory Approaches

Learning theorists study how principles of learning cause the individual to change and develop. **Learning**, the relatively permanent change in behavior as a result of experience, undoubtedly contributes to why the infant smiles as her mother approaches, the three-year-old says a polite "thank-you" in response to his grandmother's present, the five-year-old displays newfound skill in tying her shoes, and the adolescent expresses a clear preference about the most fashionable item of clothing to wear.

In the extreme, some learning theorists believe, as John B. Watson did, that learning mechanisms can be exploited to create virtually any type of person:

> Give me a dozen healthy infants, well-formed, and my own specified world to bring them up in and I'll guarantee to take any one at random and train him to become any type of specialist I might select—doctor, lawyer, artist, merchant-chief, and yes, even beggar-man and thief, regardless of his talents, penchants, tendencies, abilities, vocations, and race of his ancestors. (Watson, 1930, p. 104)

Although present-day supporters of learning seldom take such a radical position on the modifiability of human potential, they are in agreement that basic principles of learning can have a powerful influence on development (Bijou, 1989; Gewirtz & Peláez-Nogueras, 1992; Schlinger, 1992).

### Behavior Analysis

**Behavior analysis** is a theoretical account of development that relies on several basic principles of learning, particularly *classical* and *operant* conditioning, to explain developmental changes in behavior. Behavior analysis sprang from the radical learning position introduced by John B. Watson and was extended in more recent years by B. F. Skinner (1953, 1974) and others.

Nearly a century ago, the Russian physiologist Ivan Pavlov observed that dogs would often begin to salivate to the sound of a bell or some other arbitrary stimulus. Pavlov already knew that food innately triggered the release of saliva. But here was evidence that previously neutral stimuli could also come to have this effect. Pavlov recognized the powerful implications of this observation; responses considered to be reflexive, such as salivation, could, in fact, occur in situations other than those that innately elicited them. This type of learning is called **classical conditioning**. In classical conditioning a neutral stimulus begins to elicit a response after being repeatedly paired with another stimulus that already elicits that response. We learn certain behaviors and emotions as a result of classical conditioning. For example, children and adults may become anxious upon entering a dental office because of its association with previous painful treatments performed by the dentist.

To understand a second basic principle of learning, consider two babies who smile as their caregivers approach. With one baby, the caregiver stops, says

**learning** Relatively permanent change in behavior as a result of such experiences as exploration, observation, and practice.

**behavior analysis** Learning theory perspective that explains the development of behavior by the principles of classical and operant conditioning.

**classical conditioning** Type of learning in which a neutral stimulus repeatedly paired with another stimulus that elicits a reflexive response eventually begins to elicit the reflexlike response by itself.

**operant conditioning** Type of learning in which patterns of behavior that are learned and the frequency with which they are performed depend on whether the behaviors produce rewarding or desired outcomes. Also called *instrumental conditioning*.

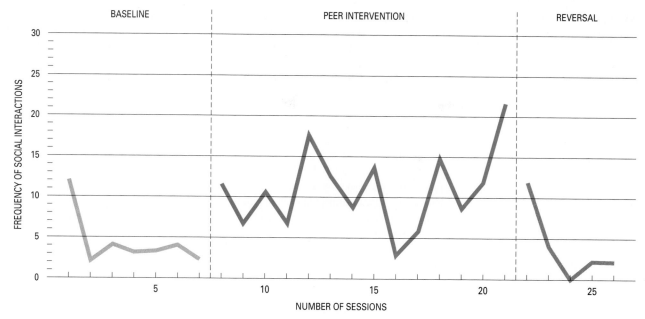

BASELINE | PEER INTERVENTION | REVERSAL

FREQUENCY OF SOCIAL INTERACTIONS

NUMBER OF SESSIONS

Source: Goldstein, Kaczmarek, Pennington, & Shafer, 1992.

**FIGURE 2.2**

**Modifying a Child's Activity Through Behavioral Analysis**

When typical and severely disabled children are integrated into the same school setting, they often do not interact with each other, perhaps because disabled children are not very responsive to their peers. Goldstein et al. (1992) trained normal preschoolers to engage in social communicative activities such as commenting on and acknowledging the behavior of a severely disabled child. During the baseline period, when preschoolers (who had not yet been trained) seldom directed communicative actions toward the disabled child, that child rarely initiated social interactions such as positive gestures toward or eye contact with peers. However, during the intervention period (when peers initiated communicative activities), the severely disabled child began to display more social behaviors. During the reversal period, when peers discontinued their communicative efforts, the disabled child's social responsiveness again declined.

"Hi, baby!" and briefly rocks the cradle. With the other baby, the caregiver walks on past, preoccupied. Or consider two fifth graders, one who receives an enthusiastic response from teacher and peers on her book report, the other whose report is acknowledged with only a polite thank-you from the teacher. Which baby is more likely to repeat his smile when the caregiver nears again? Which fifth grader is more likely to work hard on her next book report? If you reasoned in both cases that the first is more likely than the second because the behavior was followed by a stimulus event (attention or approval) that often increases the frequency of a behavior, you know something about the principle of operant conditioning. **Operant conditioning** (also called *instrumental conditioning*) refers to the process by which the frequency of performance of various behaviors changes depending on whether the behaviors are followed by rewarding or desired outcomes. Behavior analysts have used this principle to account for the emergence of such straightforward behaviors as the one-year-old's waving good-bye to far more sophisticated ventures associated with memory, language, social interaction, and complex problem solving.

Operant and classical conditioning have been shown to have enormous potential for changing behavior. *Behavior modification,* sometimes called *applied behavior analysis,* is concerned with the systematic application of operant conditioning to affect human activity. In one example, Howard Goldstein and his colleagues (Goldstein et al., 1992) investigated whether children with severe behavioral disabilities would display more social interactions such as making positive gestures toward or eye contact with their normal peers if those peers had been taught to initiate communicative strategies such as commenting on and acknowledging the behavior of the severely disabled child. The answer was clearly yes. When the communicative strategies were implemented by peers, the children with disabilities began to display more social behaviors in return, but when the peers stopped such efforts, the social behaviors declined (see Figure 2.2).

Operant and classical conditioning have become powerful means by which teachers, therapists, and caregivers bring about changes in behavior ranging from the elimination of temper tantrums or thumb sucking to encouraging healthy diets and safe driving habits. Even some of its detractors have suggested that behavior analysis may have done more to benefit human welfare than any other psychological theory (Hebb, 1980). For this reason alone, classical and operant conditioning have appealed to many in their efforts to understand development. Yet behavior analysis has drawn extensive criticism. Its critics, including some learning theorists, remain unconvinced that behavior can be understood without taking into account the child's feelings and reasons for engaging in that behavior. In other words, mental, emotional, and motivational factors also play a prominent role in how a child interprets and responds to stimulation. Among various learning perspectives, social learning theory attempts to incorporate these factors into its explanation of complex behavior and development.

## Social Learning Theory

**Social learning theory** emphasizes the importance of learning through observation and imitation of the behaviors displayed by others. Social learning theorists start with the assumption that whether an adult will be friendly, outgoing, confident, and honest rather than shy and perhaps hostile and untrustworthy largely depends on the child-rearing practices parents and caregivers use to socialize him as a child. Although operant and classical conditioning play a substantial role in these child-rearing practices, social learning theorists emphasize **observational learning**, the acquisition of behaviors from simply listening to and watching other people, as a particularly important means of learning new behaviors. The two-year-old who stands before a mirror pretending to shave in imitation of his father is displaying observational learning. Similarly, you may have witnessed the embarrassment of a parent whose three-year-old has expressed a profanity, probably acquired by the same process.

According to Albert Bandura, psychology's most well-known spokesperson for social learning, a society could never effectively convey complex language, social and moral customs, or other achievements to its younger members if each behavior had to be learned solely through operant and classical conditioning. Bandura (1965) notes that significant learning occurs, often completely without error, by the act of watching and imitating another person, a *model*. For example, girls in one part of Guatemala learn to weave simply by watching an expert, an approach to learning new skills common to the fields, homes, and shops of communities all over the world. Social learning theorists propose that many kinds of complex social activities, including the acquisition of gender roles, aggression, prosocial responses (such as willingness to assist others), resistance to temptation, and other facets of moral development are learned primarily through observing others (Bandura & Walters, 1963).

In accounting for the acquisition of complex behaviors, Bandura has increasingly made reference to cognitive processes within his theory, now known as *social cognitive theory*. Bandura (1989) has identified four sets of cognitive processes he believes to be especially important in observational learning. Attentional processes determine what information will be acquired from models and memory processes convert these observations into stored mental representations. Production processes then transform these mental representations into matching behaviors, and motivational processes define which be-

**social learning theory** Theoretical approach emphasizing the importance of learning through observation and imitation of behaviors modeled by others.

**observational learning** Learning that takes place by simply observing another person's behavior.

haviors are likely to be performed. As each of these processes advance over time, observational and other forms of learning become increasingly refined and proficient, and the child becomes more effective in regulating her own behavior as development progresses (Grusec, 1992).

## Learning Theory and Themes in Development

As our discussions of behavior analysis and social cognitive theory suggest, learning theorists do not all share the same views about the prime determinants of development. What stance do behavior analysts and social cognitive theorists take on the six major developmental themes we introduced at the beginning of this chapter?

• *Roles of Nature and Nurture* Behavior analysts believe that although biological and genetic factors may limit the kinds of responses that can be performed and help to define the events that are likely to be reinforcing or punishing, it is the environment that controls behavior. For behaviorists, each child's activity reflects an accumulated history of events associated with reinforcement or punishment, accidentally or intentionally delivered by the environment. In social cognitive theory, biological and other internal factors along with the environment are believed to play a mutual, interactive role in contributing to development (Bandura, 1989).

• *Sociocultural Influence* Behaviorists believe that although societies differ in the behaviors viewed as desirable or unacceptable, the mechanisms of learning are universal for individuals in all cultures. Rewards and punishments provided by the immediate environment are the key to understanding development, although the circumstances under which reward and punishment occur may differ from one culture to the next. Social learning theorists have given the role of the sociocultural context more emphasis by pointing out, for

Children often notice the behavior of others and frequently imitate their activities. Observational learning serves as an important mechanism for acquiring many socially desirable customs and behaviors.

example, that advances in communication technology such as televisio
expanded the opportunity for children and adults in many societies to a
many novel skills and patterns of behavior through observational learnir

• *The Child's Active Role* In keeping with their strong emphasis on er
mental stimulation, behaviorists believe that the child plays a passive r
development. Skinner claimed that "a person does not act upon the worl
world acts upon him" (1971, p. 211). According to Skinner, psycholc
should abolish references to unobservable mental or cognitive const
such as motives, goals, needs, or thoughts in their explanations of behe
Bandura's social cognitive theory moves far beyond behavior analysis by
bracing mental and motivational constructs and processes for interpretin;
understanding others as well as the self. Social cognitive theory therefore ⌄n-
fers a much more active status on the child than does behavior analysis.
Whereas behavior analysts see children adjusting and reacting to their environment, social cognitive theorists see them encoding and processing observations, selecting whether and when to perform modeled behaviors on the
basis of cognitive skills and motivational factors.

• *Development as Continuous/Discontinuous* Both behavior analysts and social learning theorists consider development to be continuous rather than
stagelike, with relatively smooth transitions and without dramatic qualitative
changes. Any departure from this pattern would stem from abrupt shifts in environmental circumstances such as might take place when the child enters
school or the adolescent enters the work environment.

• *Individual Differences* The general principles of classical and operant conditioning and observational learning apply to all individuals. Individual differences arise primarily from the unique kinds of experiences each person receives, for example, the specific models he is exposed to or the particular
behaviors that are rewarded by others in the environment.

• *Interaction Among Domains* Finally, whereas behavior analysts explain development in all domains in terms of the basic principles of learning, social
cognitive theorists stress that learning is linked to the child's physical, cognitive, and social development. Thus, this latter perspective acknowledges the
interaction among different domains of development by recognizing that what
the child learns is a consequence of what he or she feels, believes, and thinks.

## Cognitive-Developmental Approaches

In **cognitive-developmental theory**, behavior reflects the emergence of various psychological *structures,* organized units or patterns of thinking, that influence how the child interprets experience. Cognitive-developmental theories
tend to share the fundamental assumption that normal children display common mental, emotional, and social capabilities despite widely varying experiences (Horowitz, 1987a). Most three- and four-year-olds around the world, for
example, believe that a gallon of water, poured from one container to another
of a different shape, changes in amount or quantity, an error that is rarely
made once children reach seven or eight years of age. Cognitive-developmental theorists explain this profound change in reasoning in terms of children acquiring new ways of understanding their world.

The most extensive and well-known cognitive-developmental theory was put
forward by Jean Piaget. His vigorous defense of physical and mental *action* as

**cognitive-developmental
theory** Theoretical orientation,
most frequently identified with
Piaget, that explains development
in terms of the active construction
of psychological structures concerned with the interpretation of
experience. These structures are
assumed to be established at
roughly similar ages by all children
to form a series of qualitatively distinct stages in development.

the basis for cognitive development and his belief that intellectual capacities undergo *qualitative* reorganization at different stages of development have had a monumental impact, not only on developmental psychologists, but on educators and other professionals working with children as well. More than a decade after his death in 1980, Piagetian insights continue to be disseminated through the writings of his many students and collaborators (Beilin, 1989; 1992). The few pages that we devote here to Piaget's theory will touch upon only his core ideas and concepts. His keen observations and theoretical contributions, however, will be discussed in chapters that follow.

## Piaget's Theory

Piaget's vision of human intellectual development was based on two overriding assumptions about intelligence: (1) it is a kind of biological adaptation, and (2) it becomes organized in various ways as the individual interacts with the external world (Piaget, 1971). Thus, for Piaget, thinking exhibits two kinds of inborn qualities. The first is **adaptation**, a tendency to adjust or become more attuned to the conditions imposed by the environment. The second is **organization**, a tendency for intellectual structures and processes to become more systematic and coherent. Just as arms, eyes, lungs, heart, and other physical structures organize and take shape to carry out biological functions, so too, mental structures become organized in ever more powerful ways to support more complex thought. These changes, however, depend upon the opportunity to look and touch, to manipulate and play with objects, to sort and order materials. From these and other everyday physical and social experiences, the child encounters unexpected and puzzling outcomes that require reorganizations in thought.

**Schemes**    The basic mental structure in Piaget's theory is a **scheme**, a coordinated and systematic pattern of actions or way of reasoning. A scheme is a kind of template for acting or thinking applied to similar classes of objects or situations. The infant who sucks at her mother's breast, at her favorite pacifier, and at her thumb is exercising a scheme of sucking. The toddler who stacks blocks, pots and pans, and then shoe boxes is exercising a scheme of stacking. The six-year-old who realizes that his eight matchbox cars can be stored in an equal number of boxes regardless of how they are scattered about the floor is also exercising a scheme, this time concerned with number. Each of these is a kind of intelligence, a way of knowing and structuring reality.

The infant's schemes are patterns of action applied to objects—sucking, grasping, shaking, and so forth. The older child's schemes will likely involve mental processes and be far more complex as he or she reasons about number, spatial relations, and by adolescence, the universe. At all levels of development, individuals apply schemes as a means of interacting with the environment. For Piaget, earlier schemes set the stage for constructing new and more complex schemes. From simple reflexes like grasping and sucking emerge schemes for holding or hugging or hitting. And from these actions children construct new schemes—for classifying objects, for relating to family and friends, and so forth.

**Assimilation and Accommodation**    Piaget believed that schemes change through two complementary processes. The first, **assimilation**, refers to the process of interpreting an experience in terms of current ways of understanding things. The second, **accommodation**, refers to the modifications in

**adaptation**    In Piagetian theory, inborn tendency to adjust or become more attuned to conditions imposed by the environment; takes place through assimilation and accommodation.

**organization**    In Piagetian theory, the inborn tendency for structures and processes to become more systematic and coherent.

**scheme**    In Piagetian theory, the mental structure underlying a coordinated and systematic pattern of behaviors or thinking applied across similar objects or situations.

**assimilation**    In Piagetian theory, a component of adaptation; process of interpreting an experience in terms of current ways (schemes) of understanding things.

**accommodation**    In Piagetian theory, a component of adaptation; process of modification in thinking (schemes) that takes place when old ways of understanding something no longer fit.

Jean Piaget's keen observations and insights concerning the behavior of children laid the groundwork for his theory of cognitive development. Piaget's ideas about how children's thinking develops have influenced psychologists, educators, and many others in their attempts to understand children.

**equilibration** In Piagetian theory, an innate self-regulatory process that begins with the discovery of a discrepancy between the child's cognitive structures or schemes and results, through accommodation and assimilation, in more organized and powerful schemes for effectively thinking about and adapting to the environment.

behavior and thinking that take place when the old ways of understanding something, the old schemes, no longer fit.

To illustrate these two processes, Piaget used the biological analogy of ingesting and digesting food. For the child to take in nutrients for physical growth, she must first ingest food. The way the child chews it, how enzymes react to it, and the speed and manner in which the muscles of the stomach contract to move food along the digestive tract are examples of accommodating to the particular form or type of food that has been eaten. Once food has been broken down into easily digestible components, the body can assimilate the nutrients using the physical structures available.

Consider another example—the toddler who has begun to walk. He freely moves about the floor of his home but when approaching the steps leading to either the bedroom upstairs or to the basement below, he pauses, says "Stairs," and turns away. He does the same when coming across sets of stairs while visiting his grandmother's or neighbor's house. He recognizes, in other words, perhaps after repeatedly hearing his mother and father say, "Stop! You'll fall down!" that steps are forbidden and *assimilates* instances of staircases in other situations within this scheme or knowledge of "things that can cause me to fall."

One day at the beginning of winter when the temperature has dropped below freezing, he and his father go for a walk outdoors. Following some distance behind, his father suddenly shouts, "Stop! You'll fall down!" The toddler appears puzzled, looking around as if searching for something and at the same time utters, "Stairs." His father, sensing his son's confusion, points to the ice that has formed on the sidewalk on which he is standing and adds, "There aren't any stairs here, but you can fall down on ice, too." Through this new encounter, the child comes to *accommodate* his understanding of "things that cause me to fall" to include not just stairs, but also ice and, eventually, perhaps a slippery rug or toys left lying about on the floor. So too, when the baby first begins to drink from a cup instead of feeding from his mother's breast, he must accommodate to this new experience, shape his lips and mouth in new ways to take in the milk. In a similar manner, the child's intellectual capacities become reshaped and reorganized as she attempts to adjust—that is, accommodate—to new experiences.

For Piaget, assimilation and accommodation are complementary aspects of all psychological activity, processes engaged in a constant tug of war with experience. We attempt to assimilate experience within our current schemes or level of intellectual knowledge. At the same time, however, we are continually pressured to change our understanding, to accommodate, since we are regularly confronted with new experiences that fail to fit our schemes. Just as the toddler needs to recognize the many circumstances that may contribute to his falling down, so too, he and other children throughout their development need to establish increasingly mature schemes for thinking about their world.

Fortunately, adaptation in the form of newer and more complex schemes is the result of this never-ending dynamic. The outcome of increased adaptation is a greater *equilibrium* or balance, a more effective fitting together of the many pieces of knowledge that make up the child's understanding. The process by which assimilation and accommodation bring about more organized and powerful schemes for thinking is called **equilibration**. Each new experience can cause imbalance, which can only be corrected by modification in the child's schemes. In trying to make sense of his or her world, the child develops more adaptive ways of thinking. At some periods in development, schemes

| Stage | Emerging Cognitive Structure (Schemes) | Typical Achievements and Behaviors |
|---|---|---|
| **Sensorimotor (birth until 1½–2 years)** | Sensory and motor actions, initially reflexes, quickly differentiate by means of accommodation and coordinate to form adaptive ways of acting upon the environment. | Infants suck, grasp, look, reach, and so forth, responses that become organized into complex activities such as hand-eye coordination and are applied to the environment to solve problems such as reaching for and manipulating objects. Practical knowledge of space and the consequences of physical actions is acquired. Object permanence and rudimentary symbols, although still closely tied to sensorimotor events, emerge. |
| **Preoperational (1½–7 years)** | Symbols stand for or represent objects and events, but communication and thought remain relatively inflexible, heavily influenced by physical appearance and the child's own perspective. | Children begin to acquire language and mental imagery, to understand drawings and to display pretend play. They may have difficulty understanding that another person sees, feels, or thinks differently from themselves. Thinking appears unidimensional, focused on a single perceptual aspect. Reasoning about categories, relations, space, time, and causality is inconsistent. |
| **Concrete Operational (7–11 years)** | Cognitive operations permit logical reasoning about objects, events, and relationships. Thought, however, remains limited to concrete objects and events. | Children are no longer fooled by appearance. They recognize that some things do not affect quantity and other characteristics of objects and can reason effectively about classes of objects and their relationships. |
| **Formal Operational (11 years and above)** | Operations can be performed upon operations. Thought becomes abstract, and all possible outcomes can be considered. | Adolescents are able not only to imagine, but to reason about hypothetical outcomes. Abstract issues (for example, religion, morality, alternative lifestyles) can be considered and systematically evaluated. Adolescents are able to think about their own thinking. |

**TABLE 2.1**

**Piaget's Stages of Cognitive Development**

may undergo substantial reorganization. These more effective levels of knowledge are the basis for distinguishing one stage of development from another.

**The Piagetian Stages**     Piaget is probably most widely known for his description of stages of cognitive development. He proposed that development proceeds through four stages: *sensorimotor, preoperational, concrete,* and *formal.* These stages are briefly identified in Table 2.1. Each higher stage is defined by the appearance of a qualitatively different level of thinking, an increasingly sophisticated form of knowledge through which the child achieves greater intellectual balance for responding to the environment. However, each new stage does not suddenly appear full-blown; it arises from the integration and incorporation of earlier ways of thinking.

Piaget's wide range of observations, his frequently surprising findings about what infants and children can and cannot do, and his challenging theoretical explanations and assumptions have sparked a wealth of research on cognitive, social, and moral development. Many researchers agree with his findings but disagree with his interpretations of them. For example, Piaget vigorously embraced the notion of children as active participants in their own development, a viewpoint that has been widely adopted by others. However, the central concept of qualitative differences in thinking between children and adults—and particularly of stagelike transformations—has been far less favorably received (Brainerd, 1978; Carey, 1985; Spelke, 1991). Researchers also suggest that Piaget incorrectly estimated the ages at which certain kinds of thinking are displayed and have proposed that infants and children can use symbols or can reason logically far earlier than he theorized (for example, Flavell, Miller, & Miller, 1993; Gelman & Gallistel, 1978; Mandler, 1992). We will consider Piaget's position and the many pieces of evidence in support of, and challenging, his theory more fully in Chapter 8.

## Piaget's Theory and Themes in Development

How does Piaget's theory address the six major themes of development?

• *Roles of Nature and Nurture* Piaget theorized that a number of biologically based factors contribute to cognitive development. Among them is maturation, the gradual unfolding over time of genetic programs for development. Another factor is the child's inherent tendency to act, physically or mentally, upon the environment. As a result of those actions, schemes become modified and changed. Still another factor is equilibration, the self-regulatory process of achieving a more adaptive balance in physically responding to and mentally understanding objects, events, and the relationships among them. Nevertheless, for Piaget development is clearly the product of these factors interacting with experience. Piaget emphasized the interaction between nature and nurture in his cognitive-developmental theory.

• *Sociocultural Influence* For Piaget, children develop in much the same way in all cultures around the world, in part because of the common physical world to which all humans must adapt, and in part because of the common threads that exist within their social environments. Social experience in the form of cultural or educational opportunities, however, could affect the speed and ultimate level of progress in cognitive development.

• *The Child's Active Role* In Piaget's theory, knowledge is far more than simply a mirror or copy of the physical or social world. Instead, knowledge is *constructed*—that is, created and formed by the continuous revision and reorganization of intellectual structures in conjunction with experience. Piaget's constructivist model depicts a mind actively engaged in knowing and understanding its environment. Thinking is active. That activity leads to increasingly more effective ways of thinking. Children, then, are highly active participants in determining what they learn and how they understand reality.

• *Development as Continuous/Discontinuous* Although recognizing continuous changes, Piaget's theory focuses on describing and understanding the ways schemes undergo reorganization and change to form distinctive stages in development. In his later writings and conversations, Piaget began to downplay the importance of stages (Piaget, 1971; Vuyk, 1981). He felt that an overemphasis on stages led to too much concern with describing periods of intellectual stability or equilibrium when, in fact, cognition is always undergoing development. Cognitive development, he eventually concluded, is more like a spiral in which change constantly occurs, although sometimes at faster rates than at others (Beilin, 1989).

• *Individual Differences* Piaget placed very little emphasis on individual differences in development. His goal was to identify the principles that applied to cognitive and other aspects of development in *all* children. Individual differences, where they arise, could stem from variations in biological and/or experiential factors, but were not a primary focus of his theory.

• *Interaction Among Domains* Piaget's cognitive-developmental theory has implications for many other domains of development. For example, his ideas about cognitive development have been used to explain developmental changes in communication, moral thinking, and aspects of *social cognition,* how children understand the thoughts, intentions, feelings, and views of others. Nevertheless, Piaget has been criticized for paying relatively little attention to emotional factors and how social and emotional domains influence cognitive development.

## Information-Processing Approaches

Computer information processing as a metaphor for human thinking has generated so many models and theories that it is difficult to single out any one approach as a prototype. However, many contemporary research programs in developmental psychology are based on assumptions associated with this perspective. One common thread underlying **information-processing** points of view is the notion that humans, like computers, have a *limited capacity* for operating with information. As development proceeds, changes in intellectual structures and more efficient skills, including the implementation of sophisticated strategies, help older children to process information more fully and effectively.

Why have information-processing ideas become so popular in psychology? One reason is disenchantment with learning, Piagetian, and other perspectives for explaining behavior. For instance, although learning theories attempt to identify which kinds of human behaviors are acquired and performed, they have offered fewer insights into what kind of mind we possess to be able to do those things. Piaget's cognitive-developmental theory addresses this latter issue, but his explanations have been difficult to translate into ideas about how the mind actually functions. Contributing to the surge in interest in information processing has been the popularity of the computer as an alternative, albeit limited, model of symbol manipulation.

Humans operate with symbols (information). So do computers. To carry out these manipulations, computers have physical structures (hardware) that follow nonphysical, conceptual programs (software) to function. What analogues to the computer's physical structures and programs might exist in the human mind? The human mind can be said to possess cognitive structures—for example, a short- and long-term memory and an executive system—and processes, for example, strategies, rules, and plans that influence attention, decision making, remembering, and so forth. What sets an information-processing theory apart from most of the other theories is its detailed effort to explain exactly *how* the child comes to identify the letters of the alphabet,

**information processing** Theoretical approach that views humans, much like computers, as having a limited ability to process information.

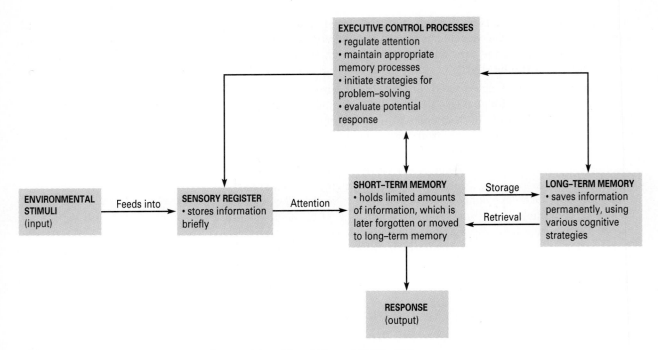

**FIGURE 2.3**

**A Schematic Model of Human Information Processing**

This highly simplified model includes several cognitive structures and processes many information-processing theorists believe to be important in cognitive development. As the arrows indicate, information often flows in several directions between various structures. The goal of information-processing models is to identify those structures and processes at work when a child responds to his or her environment.

Source: Adapted from Atkinson & Shiffrin, 1968.

remember the tables of multiplication, recall the main ideas of a story, give a classmate directions to his home, decide whether it is safe to cross the street, or recognize that a friend has become angry—abilities that are influenced by sensing, perceiving, representing, storing, retrieving, and manipulating a set of information.

A highly simplified information-processing model is shown in Figure 2.3. This model identifies several mental structures through which information may flow as it is registered, manipulated, and stored. In addition, the model suggests ways in which cognitive processes operate on this information. Executive control processes, for instance, may regulate attention; initiate strategies, hypotheses, and plans for solving problems; and evaluate potential response output.

Information-processing models often rely on measures such as time to complete a task, kinds of responses, or errors in performing a task to evaluate what is involved in reasoning, problem solving, or some other activity. Consider the six-year-old who successfully completes a few simple addition problems. The question, from an information-processing perspective, might be, How did she do this task? She may have had lots of practice with this activity, having learned the answer to each particular problem by rote over many weeks and months of exposure. Or she might carry out some kind of strategy that permits her to consistently arrive at the correct answer. For example, she could start with the first number of the addition problem, and then add one unit the number of times indicated by the second number. Thus, for the problem 3 + 5, she may begin at 3 and add 1 to it the necessary five times to arrive at the correct answer.

How could we tell whether she was engaging in the first procedure, primarily retrieving information from long-term rote memory, or the second, utilizing a rule for determining the answer? One clue could come from the length of time it takes to solve various addition problems. If she is using the first technique, she can be expected to solve each problem given to her in about the same length of time. If she uses the second technique, however, she will likely take much longer to answer those problems when the second number is very large and requires more addition.

As this example illustrates, information-processing theorists often attempt to describe the rules and procedures that the child follows in completing a task as a convenient way to summarize how knowledge and thinking develop. For example, in preparing for a quiz on the capitals of European countries, a twelve-year-old might elect to rehearse the name of each city and country over and over, visualize the city's name on a geographic map of Europe, or link it in some other way as a capital to a particular country. These strategies are processing activities that could facilitate remembering the necessary material, and information-processing perspectives would attempt to pinpoint which is actually being used. Advances in memory, concept formation, and problem-solving tasks are often theorized to result from changes in the kinds of rules, strategies, or procedures children employ. Moreover, this perspective has been extended to account for development in many other domains including language acquisition, social skills, even personality development. We will consider information-processing perspectives more fully in a number of the chapters that follow.

## Information-Processing Approaches and Themes in Development

Because of the wide variety of information-processing models theorized to account for changes in cognitive development, we can draw only broad conclusions concerning their positions on the various themes in development.

• *Roles of Nature and Nurture* In contrast to most other theories, information-processing models have had little to say about the nature versus nurture debate. Some basic capacities to perceive and process information are assumed to be present at or before birth, and the system may be attuned to respond in certain ways—for example, to language and other kinds of information. The environment has an obvious impact on development since it provides input for processing by the mind. The implicit assumption in most models is that basic cognitive structures and processes interact with experience to produce changes in the system.

• *Sociocultural Influence* As in the case of learning theory, the sociocultural context of development has largely been ignored by information-processing theorists. This is probably because researchers have typically focused on identifying how the mind operates on specific problems rather than on how the mind is affected by the kinds of problems a culture presents to it.

• *The Child's Active Role* The limitations of the computer as a metaphor for human information processing are most evident when we consider the child's active contributions to development. Whereas computers are generally perceived as passive machines that must be programmed, few information-processing theorists accept this view of the mind. While we do, of course, react to the environment, we also initiate and construct strategies and procedures that assist in processing information more effectively. From this perspective, children take an increasingly active role in controlling their own learning and development.

• *Development as Continuous/Discontinuous* In most information-processing models, cognitive development is theorized to undergo quantitative rather than qualitative changes. For example, children remember increasingly greater numbers of items both in short-term and long-term memory and interpret information and apply various strategies more efficiently and effectively with development. Similarly, the acquisition of new strategies for storing and retrieving information, new rules for problem solving, and new ways of thinking about and processing information are interpreted as shifts in ability that come about because of relatively small, continuous improvements in the capacity to process information. Some information-processing theories, however, include qualitative changes as well.

• *Individual Differences* Most information-processing theories pay little heed to individual differences in development. However, the potential for explaining such differences in terms of variations in rules, strategies, and other procedures for processing information is considerable.

• *Interaction Among Domains* A notable limitation of many information-processing models is their failure to consider emotional, motivational, and other domains of behavior. How social factors such as instructions, modeling, and the cultural context of learning lead to developmental changes in processing information is also rarely spelled out (Klahr, 1989). However, there are an increasing number of information-processing approaches formulated to explain other domains of development. For example, some researchers now interpret the establishment of peer relationships in terms of changes in information-processing capacities. Thus, this type of model has begun to provide fruitful ways of documenting and explaining age-related differences in language, social, and personality development as well as in cognitive development.

## *Psychosocial Approaches*

The theoretical models we have examined so far have been concerned with learning and cognitive development for the most part. With *psychosocial* models, theories which stress societal and cultural influences on development, we shift to a substantially greater focus on emotional growth and personality. At one time Sigmund Freud's theory of personality was extremely influential in explaining emotional and personality development. However, many generations of researchers have reinterpreted and expanded on Freud's ideas. Among these researchers is Erik Erikson, who, along with Freud, theorized that personality development progresses through stages. During each stage the child must resolve conflicts between needs or feelings and external obstacles. The satisfactory resolution of these conflicts leads to a healthy personality and a productive lifestyle. Because of his significant influence on Erikson's thinking, however, we begin by briefly summarizing important features of Freud's developmental theory.

**psychosexual theory of development** Freud's theory that many aspects of an individual's personality originate in an early and broad form of childhood sexuality. The focus of gratification of this sexuality, however, changes from one region of the body to another throughout various stages of development.

### Freud's Psychosexual Theory of Development

Freud proposed in his **psychosexual theory of development** that many aspects of the individual's personality originate in an early and broad form of childhood sexuality. The fuel powering human behavior, according to Freud, was a set of biological instincts that make demands on the mind. The psychological tension induced by these instincts, called *libido* or *libidinal energy,* gradually builds and requires eventual discharge. Under many circumstances this energy is reduced as rapidly as possible. Sometimes, however, tensions such as those associated with hunger or pain in infants cannot be discharged immediately. From these delays, mental structures and behavioral responses eventually become organized to achieve more satisfactory ways of reducing tension. These acts might include such behaviors as calling out to the caregiver as a signal to be fed or eventually learning to feed oneself, responses that reduce libidinal urges by effective, rational, and socially acceptable means.

The locus of tension and the optimal way to reduce needs change with age. Freud identified five stages of psychosexual development, periods during which libidinal energy is usually associated with a specific area of the body. These stages were called the **oral stage**, the **anal stage**, the **phallic stage**, and, after a period of **latency** during middle childhood, the **genital stage**. Table 2.2 summarizes major characteristics of these stages.

Freud believed that the individual's progression through these stages was greatly influenced by maturation. From this perspective, personality developed through periods in which libidinal energy could be satisfactorily reduced by activities associated with a dominant region of the body. However, the environment also played a critical role in this normal progression. Lack of opportunity to have needs sufficiently met or to express them adequately during a critical period was predicted to have negative consequences for the ways in which the child related to others and for feelings of self-worth. The infant whose sucking needs were not gratified, for example, became *fixated,* that is, preoccupied with actions associated with the mouth for the rest of his life.

Freud's theory of psychosexual development has been criticized extensively by later schools of psychology, and by anthropologists and others who argue that his views are culture bound. In particular, it was early noted that the sources of conflict that affect social and personality development differ among societies, especially where family composition and locus of authority depart from the pattern of strong parental influence found in traditional Western societies of his time (Malinowski, 1927). The major theory to address these criticisms has been offered by Erik Erikson.

## Erikson's Psychosocial Theory

Despite the fact that he never received a formal degree after high school, his contributions to psychology earned Erik Erikson prestigious clinical and academic positions as well as the admiration of many. In his classic work *Childhood and Society* (1950), Erikson built upon Freud's developmental theory to chart eight stages of development, as summarized in Table 2.3. The first five stages match Freud's psychosexual model in their time of appearance. The last three describe additional stages of personality development during adulthood.

In his description of these eight stages, Erikson modified Freudian theory in two significant ways. First, he moved away from an accent on biological and sexual sources of tension to an emphasis on the psychological needs to be successfully negotiated at each stage of development. During the first stage (comparable to Freud's oral stage), for example, Erikson theorized that *incorporation* or taking in was the primary mode for acting adaptively toward the world. In Erikson's view, this mode of activity extended beyond the mouth and

**oral stage**  In Freudian theory, the first psychosexual stage, between birth and about one year of age, during which libidinal energy is focused on the mouth.

**anal stage**  In Freudian theory, the second psychosexual stage, between about one and three years of age, during which libidinal energy is focused on control of defecation.

**phallic stage**  In Freudian theory, the third psychosexual stage, between about three and five years of age, when libidinal energy is focused on the genitals and resolution of unconscious conflict with the parent of the same sex leads to establishment of the superego.

**latency**  In Freudian theory, a period from about six to eleven years of age, when libidinal energy is suppressed and energies are focused on intellectual, athletic, and social achievements appropriate to the adult years.

**genital stage**  In Freudian theory, the final psychosexual stage, beginning with adolescence, in which sexual energy is directed to peers of the opposite sex.

| Stage | Focus | Consequences for Personality |
|-------|-------|------------------------------|
| **Oral (birth to 12 months)** | Libidinal energy centered on the mouth. Gratification through sucking, chewing, eating, and biting. | Inadequate opportunity to suck may lead to fixations in the form of thumb sucking or other oral activity such as preoccupation with food, eating, or other forms of taking things in (for example, wealth or power). Also possibility of "biting" (sarcastic) personality. |
| **Anal (1–3 years)** | Libidinal energy centered on the anal region. Gratification through controlling and expelling fecal waste through the anal sphincters. | If toilet-training demands are too lax, fixations may occur in the form of being messy, disorderly, wasteful, or excessively demonstrative. Strict toilet training may result in possessive, retentive (frugal and stingy) personality and excessive concern with cleanliness and orderliness. |
| **Phallic (3–5 years)** | Libidinal energy centered on genitals. Gratification possible through masturbation but more likely through expressions of desire for opposite-sex parent. | Beginning rivalry with members of the same sex. Fixations appear as inordinate ties to opposite-sex parent or difficulty in achieving appropriate relationships with members of same and opposite sex. |
| **Latency (5 years to adolescence)** | Libidinal energy is submerged (latent) and not exhibited through any specific body region. | Because libidinal energy is submerged, there are relatively few important long-term consequences. Much of the energy is channeled into emotionally safe areas, such as intellectual, athletic, and social achievements. |
| **Genital (adolescence and beyond)** | Libidinal energy centered on mature forms of genital stimulation. Gratification directed toward reproductive functions. | Complete independence from parents becomes possible. A balance between love and work marks normal psychosexual development. |

**TABLE 2.2**

**Freud's Five Psychosexual Stages of Development**

psychosocial theory of development   Erikson's theory that personality development proceeds through eight stages during which adaptive modes of functioning are established to meet the variety of demands framed by society.

included other senses such as looking and hearing, and motor systems such as reaching and grasping, systems designed to expand the infant's ways for absorbing and responding to reality. Each subsequent stage identified another important mode for adapting to the environment.

Erikson's second major modification to Freud's theory was to assign society an even more critical role in shaping and forming reality for the child. Communities create their own demands and set their own criteria for socializing the child. In one society an infant may be permitted to breast-feed whenever hungry over a period of several years, whereas infants in another society may be nursed or bottle-fed on a meticulously arranged schedule and weaned within the first year of life. In another example, the timing and severity of toilet training as well as the means by which it is initiated by caregivers may differ vastly from one society to another. Cultures differ in the requirements imposed on the child, yet each child must adapt to his own culture's regulations. Thus, Erikson's **psychosocial theory of development** highlights the child's composite need to initiate adaptive modes of functioning while meeting the variety of demands framed by the society in which she lives.

As in Freudian stages, maturation plays an important role in the movement from one to another of the eight Eriksonian stages. Similarly, Erikson theo-

| Stage | Adaptive Mode | Significant Events and Outcomes |
|---|---|---|
| **Basic Trust Versus Mistrust (birth to 1 year)** | Incorporation—to take in (and give in return) | Babies must find consistency, predictability, and reliability in their caregivers' behaviors. Out of these experiences babies learn to trust the world and themselves or to gain a sense of hope. |
| **Autonomy Versus Shame and Doubt (1–3 years)** | Control—to hold on and to let go | The child begins to explore, to make messes, to say "no!", to make choices. From these opportunities the child comes to understand what is socially acceptable or unacceptable without losing the feeling of being able to manage or the sense of will. |
| **Initiative Versus Guilt (3–6 years)** | Intrusion—to go after | The child begins to make plans, set goals, and persist in both physical and social exchanges. Even though frustration is inevitable, the child's goal is to remain enthusiastic and bold and to gain a sense of purpose. |
| **Industry Versus Inferiority (6 years to puberty)** | Construction—to build things and relationships | The child acquires and extends skills to the wider culture, performs "work," in the sense of education or support of the family. Failure and feelings of inadequacy occur, but the child must be able to feel competent and achieve a sense of skill. |
| **Identity Versus Identity Confusion (puberty to adulthood)** | Integration—to be oneself (or not to be oneself) | The adolescent attempts to bring together experiences to discover his or her identity and place in society. This trying out of many roles should lead to an answer for the question, Who am I? or a sense of fidelity to self. |
| **Intimacy Versus Isolation (young adulthood)** | Solidarity—to lose and find oneself in another | The young adult who has achieved a sense of identity is no longer self-absorbed and can now share himself or herself with another. Inability to do so contributes to feelings of isolation and self-absorption and the absence of a sense of love. |
| **Generativity Versus Stagnation (middle adulthood)** | Productivity—to make and to take care of | The adult not only produces things and ideas through work, but also creates and cares for the next generation. Lack of productive endeavors leads to boredom, stagnation, and the absence of a sense of caring. |
| **Integrity Versus Despair (old age)** | Acceptance—to be (by having been) and to face not being | The older adult reviews his or her life and reevaluates its worth. Acceptance of that life, even though all goals have not been achieved, and of death, contributes to a sense of wisdom. |

**TABLE 2.3**

**Erikson's Eight Stages of Psychosocial Development**

rized that the individual confronts a specific crisis as new demands are imposed by society in each stage. The resolution of each crisis may or may not be successful, but triumphs at earlier stages lay the groundwork for the negotiation of later stages. Moreover, each society has evolved ways of helping individuals meet their needs. Caregiving practices, educational programs, social organizations, occupational training, and moral and ethical support are examples of cultural systems established to foster healthy, productive psychosocial development.

Perhaps the common theme underlying the various features of Erikson's theory is the search for **identity**, or the acceptance of both self and one's society. At each stage this search is manifested in a specific way. The need to develop a feeling of trust for a caregiver, to acquire a sense of autonomy, to initiate exchanges with the world, and to learn and become competent in school

**identity** In Eriksonian psychosocial theory, the acceptance of both self and society, a concept that must be achieved at every stage but is especially important during adolescence.

and other settings are examples of how the infant and child discovers who and what he is and will become. During adolescence the individual confronts the issue of identity directly. But the answer to "Who am I?" is elaborated and made clearer as the individual progresses through each psychosocial stage.

In summary, Erikson redirected Freud's somewhat pessimistic views of personality development away from the need to restrain and control desires toward a consideration of the practices society uses to encourage and promote healthy social and personality development. Erikson, however, painted development with a broad brush, and consequently his theory is frequently criticized for its vagueness. Still, just as Piaget's insights highlighted meaningful issues in cognitive development, so too, Erikson—regardless of the precision of his specific formulations—had a flair for targeting crucial issues in social and personality development.

## Psychosocial Theory and Themes in Development

Our discussion of Erikson's theory has already focused on a number of themes in development, but let's consider them once more.

Erik Erikson outlined eight stages of personality development. His psychosocial theory emphasized that at each stage, individuals must successfully adapt to new forms of demands placed upon them by society. He also stressed that cultures frequently differ in how they help individuals to negotiate these demands.

• *Roles of Nature and Nurture* A biological contribution to behavior, extended from Freud's theory, is evident in Erikson's theory as well. Yet psychosocial theory must be considered interactionist, given the momentous role that the presence and absence of appropriate socializing experiences play in resolving conflicts that arise at every stage.

• *Sociocultural Influence* The broader sociocultural context in which caregivers encourage children to master, explore, and engage in their physical and social environment, especially during the early years of life, plays a critical role in Erikson's theory of development. For Erikson, the sociocultural context is a key factor in understanding an individual's personality and social relationships.

• *The Child's Active Role* In Erikson's theory, the emphasis on establishing an identity for self within society suggests an active role for the child in development. Each stage, in fact, identifies a particular task or way of effectively adapting that is to be achieved in order to sustain a healthy personality.

• *Development as Continuous/Discontinuous* In Erikson's eight stages in personality development, the successful negotiation of earlier stages lays the groundwork for continued psychological growth. The individual unable to work through a crisis at one time, however, may still effectively resolve it at a later stage. From this perspective, Erikson's theory does not view each stage as a critical period, but rather as a major time in which to negotiate important individual and social needs.

• *Individual Differences* The psychosocial stages are common to every individual in every culture. However, the success with which each is accomplished can vary dramatically from one individual to another and from one society to another. Although not specifically focused on individual differences in development, Erikson's theory offers many insights into how and why these might come about.

• *Interaction Among Domains* Although not spelled out in detail, Erikson links social, emotional, and cognitive development together in the individual's efforts to achieve identity. For example, a sense of trust emerges from taking in through the senses as well as the motor system; a sense of industry reflects intellectual competence as well as the ability to interact effectively with others; and discovering one's identity requires the integration of all of one's psychological skills and competencies.

# Contextual Approaches

Psychologists have long recognized not only that children live in vastly different circumstances but that each child experiences a number of overlapping contexts. First is the environment of the immediate family, which is subject to enormous variation: some children grow up in households with a single parent, others with two parents, and still others with grandparents and other relatives; children in foster care, on the other hand, may be shuffled from one family to another. Number of siblings, economic resources, space and privacy, independence, and emotional atmosphere are among the vast assortment of factors that vary in the immediate surroundings of children.

Differences in the contexts of development extend far beyond a child's immediate family, however. Physical surroundings, access to schools, job opportunities, technological innovations, natural disasters, political systems, war, and the cultural dictates of the community form and influence the way in which children are reared. Some of these circumstances will be more supportive of social and cognitive development than others. Beyond the physical and sociocultural contexts in which each child lives is still another—the innate and species-specific predispositions with which individual children come equipped to learn and develop.

In other words, the context of development extends far beyond family or even society. Developmental theories usually focus on immediate experience, defined narrowly in terms of contemporary circumstances and recent events, and how it affects development. Yet culture, the historical legacy of earlier generations of a given social group as well as the evolutionary pressures that have shaped humans to exist in their natural environment, is also a major factor affecting growth. Put another way, the transformation from infant to child to adult takes place via a complex system of multidirectional levels of influence (Gottlieb, 1991). Contextual models, sometimes called *systems* views, are concerned with the effects of this broad range of biological, physical, and sociocultural settings on development. Let us first examine contextual theories that address the sociocultural contributions to a child's development.

## Ecological Systems Theory

The most extensive model of a contextual approach to development is the ecological systems theory proposed by Urie Bronfenbrenner (1986, 1989). Ecological theories stress the need to understand development in terms of the everyday environment in which children are reared, a need fervently advocated by Bronfenbrenner, who argues that "much of contemporary developmental psychology is the science of the strange behavior of children in strange situations with strange adults for the briefest possible periods of time" (Bronfenbrenner, 1977, p. 513). Development, he believes, must be studied not only in the home, but also in the schools, neighborhoods, and communities where it takes place. His **ecological systems theory** emphasizes the immense range

**ecological systems theory**
Bronfenbrenner's theory that development is the joint outcome of individual and experiential events. Experience consists not only of immediate surroundings but also of the larger social and cultural systems that affect an individual's life.

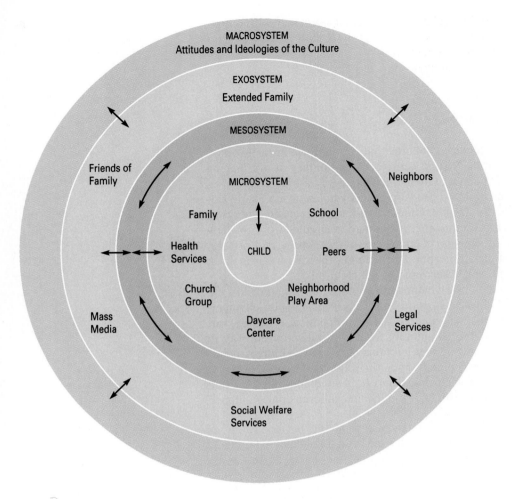

**FIGURE 2.4**

**Bronfenbrenner's Ecological Model**

Source: Adapted from Garabino, 1982.

At the core of Bronfenbrenner's ecological model is the child's biological and psychological make-up, based on individual genetic and developmental history. This make-up continues to be affected and modified by the child's immediate physical and social environment *(microsystem)* as well as interactions among the systems within this environment *(mesosystem)*. Other broader social, political, and economic conditions *(exosystem)* influence the structure and availability of microsystems and the manner in which they affect the child. Finally, social, political, and economic conditions are themselves influenced by the general beliefs and attitudes *(macrosystem)* shared by members of a society.

of situations and contexts individual children encounter and their consequences for development.

One of Bronfenbrenner's major theoretical contributions is his broadened and comprehensive portrait of the environment—the ecological forces and systems that exist at several different, but interrelated, levels. These levels can be conceptualized as a series of concentric rings, as shown in Figure 2.4. At the center is the child's biological and psychological makeup, not only inherited and biologically based factors, but also cognitive capacities and socioemotional and motivational propensities (for example, temperament and personality) for responding to and acting upon the environment. These characteristics and traits have evolved to make humans unique from other organisms, and they are also potential sources of individual differences among children.

Systems with the most immediate and direct impact upon an individual are part of the next ring, the **microsystem**. These include the home and members of the household; social and educational settings (including classmates, teachers, and classroom resources); neighborhoods (including physical layout, friends, and acquaintances); and the workplace. The microsystem comprises the personal qualities of others, the physical and material properties of everyday settings, and the "activities, roles, and interpersonal relations experienced by the developing person" (Bronfenbrenner, 1989, p. 227).

The **mesosystem**, the next ring, is concerned with the interrelationships among the various settings within the microsystem. For example, expectations and events within the family, such as access to books and learning to read, or an emphasis on acquiring basic academic and socialization skills, may have a critical impact on the child's opportunities and experiences in school. When the households of divorced parents are in different neighborhoods, regular and frequent moves back and forth between the two homes have an effect not only on family relationships but also on the range and kinds of friendships with peers that the child can establish.

Social, economic, political, religious, and other settings in which the child takes no immediate part but that directly bear upon those who interact with the child can also influence development. These wider contexts make up the **exosystem**. In technological societies, for example, the child is seldom a member of either parent's work environment. Nevertheless, the parent who encounters a difficult problem at work may bring frustrations home and express them through angry exchanges with members of the family. A neighborhood playground taken over by drug pushers could very well end afternoon softball games with friends. Skirmishes between rival villages or countries may bring poverty if the family breadwinner is killed in fighting. Thus, contexts removed from the child's immediate environment can still have a powerful impact on development.

The broadest context, embracing all others, is the **macrosystem**. The macrosystem includes the major historical events (for example, famines or wars) and the spiritual and religious values, legal and political practices, ceremonies and customs shared by a cultural group. Natural disasters and wars can have a devastating impact on conventional microsystems such as schools and neighborhoods as well as on individual families. Cultural beliefs about child rearing, the role of schools and family in education, the importance of maintaining kinship affiliations, tolerance for different lifestyles, and the ethical and moral conventions of a society affect the child both directly and indirectly through guidelines for acceptable and desirable behavior. The macrosystem represents the accumulated insights of previous generations of caregivers, an evolving wisdom that continues to be transformed by succeeding generations. This historical context, too, has far-reaching consequences for each individual's psychological development.

Bronfenbrenner's ecological systems theory underscores the many levels of a child's surroundings that directly and indirectly interact with the individual to influence development. Specific settings within the microsystem have direct consequences for behavior but are often affected in turn by larger settings and contexts. Researchers frequently use labels to stand for these larger units (for

**microsystem** In Bronfenbrenner's ecological systems theory, the immediate environment provided in such settings as the home, school, workplace, and neighborhood.

**mesosystem** In Bronfenbrenner's ecological systems theory, the environment provided by the interrelationships among the various settings of the microsystem.

**exosystem** In Bronfenbrenner's ecological systems theory, environmental settings that indirectly affect the child by influencing the various microsystems forming the child's immediate environment.

**macrosystem** In Bronfenbrenner's ecological systems theory, major historical events and the broad values, practices, and customs promoted by a culture.

Lev Vygotsky's sociohistorical theory emphasizes the influence that wide variations in cultural experiences may have on development. For example children in some communities have numerous opportunities to learn how snakes are influenced by the sounds of a musical instrument and how to handle them safely. Would you feel comfortable with one in your lap? Might the child pictured here have difficulty understanding your discomfort? By becoming aware of the many different contexts in which development takes place, we can begin to appreciate how they influence attitudes, beliefs, and values.

example, socioeconomic class, ethnic group, or region such as rural and urban). But such labels, Bronfenbrenner argues, fail to give sufficient weight to the belief systems, resources, lifestyles, and cultural values that critically influence and regulate development. To simply state that ethnic differences exist, for example, does not identify the reverberating elements of the broader cultural belief systems that have an impact on development, nor does it acknowledge the interactive, multidimensional nature of the various levels of these systems.

## Vygotsky's Sociohistorical Theory

What is culture? It is, of course, those parts of one's surroundings that have been made and continue to be produced by humans—physical artifacts such as tools and buildings—but also language and the practices, values, and beliefs accumulated over many generations. A culture, in other words, is a *historical,* human-generated facet of the environment that has enormous influence on the way that children are reared. Lev Vygotsky's **sociohistorical theory** emphasizes the unique contextual blend of cultural (historical) and social processes that form the foundation of every child's development.

The range and variety of cultural practices is immense. Some communities emphasize skill in weaving; others, fishing and hunting; still others, athletic prowess. Some encourage allegiance and respect for kin such as grandparents or other elders; others do not. Some view peacemaking efforts superior to war; others do not. A central tenet of Vygotsky's sociohistorical theory is that as children become exposed to and participate in their culture, they begin to internalize and adopt, often with the guidance of a skilled partner such as a caregiver or teacher, more mature and effective ways of thinking about and solving problems with respect to their circumstances.

**sociohistorical theory** Vygotsky's theory of development emphasizing the historical (cultural) and social processes that are part of the context of development for every child.

Infants, of course, are not born with the tools and ways of thinking that are part of a community's history. These, however, can be transferred to children by those who are skilled or knowledgeable in their use. Thus, social interactions involving observations of how others communicate and approach problems using the culture's artifacts are an indispensable part of every child's experience and, therefore, of every child's development (Wertsch, 1989; Wertsch & Tulviste, 1992). For example, in sitting down with and reading to the child, the caregiver is communicating the importance of this activity; eventually the child may come to also value it in her own behavior and as part of her own culture. Vygotsky believed that language is an especially important cultural tool in this dialogue because it too is internalized by the child to affect thinking and problem solving. We will have more opportunity to discuss Vygotsky's ideas in later chapters. As you will see, his views have become especially important in considering the larger context in which development takes place.

## Transactional Theory

Transactional theory begins with and builds upon ecological and sociohistorical views to emphasize the seamless alloy that encompasses development as the child is affected by and, in turn, actively influences, his or her environs (Sameroff, 1987). Development is viewed as dynamic, a never-ending process involving continuing, reciprocal exchanges: people and settings transform the child, who in turn changes the people and setting surrounding him, which then reshape the child again in an endless, unbroken progression. In **transactional theory**, development consists of progressive movement and mutual construction of both environment and individual—an ongoing process with no final goal or outcome to indicate that either development or the context in which it takes place is complete.

A major feature of transactional theory is the child's active influence; the environment is never separable from or independent of the child. Consider the baby born with low birth weight. Such an infant often displays a sharp, shrill cry and has difficulty nursing. Because of these factors and his fragile appearance, a mother who might otherwise feel confident may become anxious and uncertain about her caregiving abilities. Her apprehensions may translate into inconsistent behaviors to which the baby in turn responds with irregular patterns of feeding and sleeping. These difficulties further reduce the mother's confidence in her abilities and enjoyment of her baby, leading to fewer social interactions and less positive stimulation for her baby. As a consequence, achievements in other areas of development, such as language acquisition, may be delayed. What factors, precisely, caused the delay? To answer this question, we might point to the mother's avoidance of her child, but this explanation falls far short of representing the many complex factors that contributed to the mother's behaviors (Sameroff, 1987).

The teenage years offer many good examples of transactional events. The adolescent caught shoplifting at the urging of a friend may set into motion a change in his parents' perceptions of him that further elevates conflict between them. The girl unable to resist her boyfriend's urges to engage in sexual activity may set in motion a course of events that dramatically alters her role from that of student with many friends and freedoms to that of mother with many responsibilities and little time to herself. The contexts for her own development have changed dramatically. Can we reasonably single out one critical

**transactional theory** Theoretical perspective in psychology that highlights the reciprocal relationship between child and environment, emphasizing that development is a seamless alloy formed by the child's being affected by and, in turn, actively influencing the environment.

factor to explain her current situation? Perhaps in some sense, but many factors, both immediate and historical, have formed an intricate and complex web of events leading to this outcome.

The importance of transactional models becomes especially apparent when psychologists apply interventions that attempt to modify the course of development. The mother who has avoided her premature infant because of a widening gulf of anxious reactions brought about by disappointments and unhappy exchanges will need more than simply to be told to start talking to her child to encourage his language development. She may need to gain a greater understanding of the typical problems faced by prematures, receive support and reinforcement for her efforts to initiate confident caregiving skills, and acquire richer insights into how development is affected by experiences, only some of which she can control.

## Ethological Theory

Development is influenced by yet one more broad context. That context is the biological history and constraints that have been a part of human evolution. In the nineteenth century, Darwin and other biologists concluded that adaptive traits—those that improved the likelihood of survival and thus a greater number of offspring for further reproduction—were more likely to be found in succeeding generations of a species. He hypothesized that through *evolution,* the descent of living species from earlier species of animals, humans inherited biological traits and capacities that improved the likelihood of their survival. **Ethology** is the discipline specifically concerned with understanding how adaptive behaviors evolved and what functions they still serve for the continuation of the species.

Ethological theory surfaced in the 1930s when European zoologists such as Konrad Lorenz (1963/1966) and Niko Tinbergen (1951) investigated aggressive actions and the courtship and mating rituals of such animals as the mallard duck and stickleback fish. Their observations led to explanations that took into account the *mutual* interchange between the inherited, biological bases of behavior and the environment in which that behavior was exhibited (Hinde, 1989). Consider, for example, the kinds of questions that Robert Hinde (1965), another well-known ethologist, wanted to answer. How is hormone production in female canaries influenced by temperature and length of daylight? How does this hormone production interact with responsivity to male courtship displays and the initiation of nest building? Questions such as these, concerned with behaviors that arise from the interaction between biological and environmental factors, are typical in research on animals in their natural habitats and are also relevant to the complex behaviors of human beings.

Ethologists have frequently studied caregiver-offspring behaviors designed to provide support and protection, behavioral exchanges between adversaries competing for territory or potential mates, and courtship and other rituals leading to the production of offspring. These social interactions are among the most powerful and important for the survival of any species, including humans. Ethological studies propose answers to questions such as the following: Why do babies cry or smile? Why might the ten-year-old fight or be friendly? Ethologists point out the adaptive value such activities have for the individual in the specific environment in which he or she is growing up.

Konrad Lorenz, an ethologist, is being followed by young geese who have imprinted to him. Imprinting in young animals typically occurs to other members of the same species who, under normal circumstances, are present shortly after hatching or the birth of an animal. One question posed by ethologists is whether human infants also show some form of imprinting.

**ethology** Theoretical orientation and discipline concerned with the evolutionary origins of behavior and its adaptive and survival value in animals, including humans.

Ethological theory proposes that human infants, as well as the offspring of other species of animals, begin life with a set of innate, *species-specific* behaviors common to all members. In human babies, these include reflexes such as sucking and grasping and may also include more complex activities such as babbling, smiling, and orienting to interesting sensory events—behaviors exhibited by normal infants around the world. These species-specific behaviors help infants meet their needs either directly, as in the case of sucking as a means of ingesting food, or indirectly, as in the case of smiling, a behavior that attracts caregivers and encourages them to provide support.

Besides innate behaviors, the young of many species are predisposed to certain kinds of learning that are not easily reversed and promote their continued survival, learning that may occur only during limited sensitive periods in development. One of the best-known examples is found in various species of birds, including geese. Usually within a very short time after hatching, the gosling begins to follow and to prefer being near a particular stimulus. Normally, that stimulus will be another goose, its mother. In acquiring this behavior, the gosling not only learns about its species more generally, but also increases the likelihood of being fed and protected. This form of learning that takes place during a brief interval early in life and that is difficult to modify once established is known as **imprinting**.

Do other animals show imprinting? Mammals such as horses and sheep do. What about human infants? John Bowlby's (1969) theory of attachment suggests that they do, at least to some degree. Bowlby noted that the crying, babbling, and smiling behaviors of young infants signal needs and elicit supportive and protective responses from adults. These behaviors, along with following and talking in older infants, become organized and integrated with the social and emotional reactions of caregivers to form the basis for *attachment,* a mutual system of physical, social, and emotional stimulation and support between caregiver and young. We will discuss attachment more fully in Chapter 11, but ethological principles are evident in a related controversial issue that we introduce here, the issue of bonding of caregiver to infant.

## CONTROVERSY: THINKING IT OVER

### *How Important Is Bonding?*

Does it matter whether infants and their caregivers are together during the first few hours and days after birth? It does for some species of animals, but what about for humans? In 1976 Marshall Klaus and John Kennell reported that the events occurring in the first days following the delivery of a baby are extremely important for establishing a long-term positive relationship between caregiver and infant. One group of mothers experienced the typical sequence of events observed in most hospitals in the United States at that time, a brief glance or two at the baby after delivery and then regularly scheduled twenty- to thirty-minute visits for feeding every three to four hours during the day. A second group of mothers was encouraged to cuddle and engage in skin-to-skin contact with their babies for an hour immediately after birth and to interact with them several additional hours each day during the hospital stay. Observations of these two groups of mothers while in the hospital, a month later, and even after one and two years, revealed that mothers

**imprinting** Form of learning, difficult to reverse, during a sensitive period in development in which an organism tends to stay near a particular stimulus.

permitted the extra interactions cuddled, looked at, soothed, and nurtured their babies more than mothers given the usual hospital routine. Furthermore, infants who were cuddled immediately after birth were reported to perform better on various tests of physical and mental development (Klaus & Kennell, 1976, 1982).

Klaus and Kennell concluded that shortly after giving birth, human mothers enter a sensitive period during which they can establish a strong emotional bond to their infants. This bond may come about because hormones present during the birth process lead the mother to be especially receptive to forming an early attachment. Alternatively, the intense emotional and anxiety-ridden experiences accompanying the delivery process are suddenly replaced and reinterpreted as positive feelings as the mother has the opportunity to focus on her responsive baby. Whatever the reason for this finding, it had an immense impact upon hospital practices throughout the nation, leading many doctors and experts in child care to encourage early and frequent interactions between mothers, and even fathers, and their newborns.

But is this early experience critical? Diane Eyer (1993) has recently claimed that it is not. There is time, she said, not just during the first few days after birth, but throughout the first year of life and even beyond, to develop a close and loving relationship with a baby or young child and to initiate the kind of caregiving and support that will establish a healthy relationship for both parent and child. Others have also challenged the findings reported by Klaus and Kennell, unable to replicate differences in interactions for mothers who do and do not have the opportunity to establish an early bond (Chess & Thomas, 1986; Goldberg, 1983; Svejda, Campos, & Emde, 1980). Furthermore, when cultures that encourage mothers, for example, to have early contact with their babies, or fathers to be involved with the birth process, are compared with cultures that do not promote these activities, few differences emerge in the extent to which nurturance or affection for infants is expressed (Lozoff, 1983).

Have the substantial efforts of doctors and hospitals to augment parent-infant contact shortly after birth been helpful to parenting? Or have these ventures yielded relatively few benefits and fostered needless anxiety for those who have not had this opportunity? Could the enormous investment in early and frequent contact between caregiver and baby help to produce other positive outcomes that researchers have yet to clearly document? What might such benefits be? What are the ethical implications of carrying out research that might help to answer these questions?

The importance of bonding continues to be disputed. Regardless of their position, everyone agrees that parents *should* have the opportunity to participate in the birth and caregiving process to whatever extent is possible and comfortable for them. But should greater efforts be made to ensure that all parents establish a constructive relationship with their offspring as soon after birth as possible? Or do other routes exist for instituting positive and supportive relationships so that mothers and fathers do not feel that their newborns will be permanently harmed by the lack of opportunity to bond?  ■

## Contextual Approaches and Themes in Development

Contextual models are generally in agreement on many of the themes in development, and where differences exist, they are most often found in ethological theories.

- *The Roles of Nature and Nurture* For most contextual theories, nurture is emphasized. Except for ethological theories, the biological contributions to development receive little attention. For ethologists, however, behaviors are closely linked to nature because they have helped, or continue to help, humans survive. Thus, the biological context is every bit as important as other contexts for development. Yet even in ethological theories, the interaction between nature and nurture is considered paramount.

- *Sociocultural Influence* Perhaps more than any other theoretical orientation, contextual theories are concerned with the ways that broad sociocultural patterns affect development. Contextual theories attempt to find evidence for how the larger social systems and settings in which children are reared affect their behavior and shape their minds.

- *The Child's Active Role* Contextual models, even those having an ethological focus, tend to view the child as actively engaged with the environment. In calling for their caregivers, exploring, playing, solving problems, and seeking out playmates, infants and children elicit reactions from the adults and peers around them. Contextual models emphasize that characteristics of the child trigger and alter environmental events and these changes further impact development. Both individual and environment change in highly interdependent ways, and their relationship is *bidirectional,* each influencing the other (Bell, 1968).

- *Development as Continuous/Discontinuous* Contextual models place little emphasis on major qualitative changes in development. Instead, such models describe the continuous ebb and flow of interactions that transpire throughout development to produce incremental change. Most contextual theorists emphasize how the child's unique circumstances promote gradual advances in thought and behavior. However, ethologists often emphasize that particular periods in development are critical for establishing certain competencies. For example, infancy is considered a crucial time for forming emotional ties with caregivers.

- *Individual Differences* Aside from ethological theories, contextual perspectives focus less on highlighting universal experiences that promote development and more on the unique configuration of circumstances that foster cognitive, linguistic, social, and personality development. Given the immense number of factors potentially affecting the child, individual differences are often an important aspect to be explained by such theories.

- *Interaction Among Domains* Not surprisingly, most contextual models are typically concerned with the entire fabric of human growth and claim substantial interactions among cognitive, linguistic, social, and other domains. Ethological theorists especially focus on the interrelationship between biological and other aspects of development.

## Which Theme and Which Theory?

All theories of development, of course, are ultimately concerned with the simple question, What develops? As you have seen amply demonstrated in this chapter, the answers differ. For learning theorists, what develops is a set of responses. For Piaget, it is a set of cognitive structures. For information-processing enthusiasts, it is mental structures and strategies for responding. For psychosocial theorists, it is identity. For most contextual theorists, it is a pattern of mutually supportive individual and cultural relationships. For ethologists, it is adaptive behaviors.

Theories give us models for observing and interpreting behavior. They have had an enormous influence on the way we view children and their development, as the chapters to follow will demonstrate. Why so many different theories? The reason is that each brings an important perspective to understanding development. Some remind us of the importance of emotions, others of cognitive structures. Some keep us honest about the role of our biological nature; others perform the same service for the culture in which we are born and reared. Various theories enrich and broaden our understanding of develop-

**TABLE 2.4**

**The Main Developmental Theories and Where They Stand on the Six Themes in Development**
(Continued on next page.)

| Theme | Learning Theories | Piagetian Theory | Information-Processing Models | Psychosocial Theory | Contextual Theories | |
|---|---|---|---|---|---|---|
| | | | | | Sociocultural | Ethological |
| **What roles do nature and nurture play in development?** | Environment is more important than heredity. | Maturation sets limits on how rapidly development proceeds, but experience is necessary for the formation of cognitive structures. Interaction between nature and nurture. | Of relatively minor concern. Structures and processes presumably have an inherent basis, but experience is likely to be important for their effective operation. | Erikson stressed an interactional position that emphasizes the socialization demands of the society in which a child is reared along with a biological contribution borrowed from Freud's theory. | A major emphasis is the environmental factors that interact with biological structures. | Behavior is biologically based, but the environment elicits and influences these biologically based patterns. |
| **How does the sociocultural context influence development?** | Sociocultural factors are likely to determine which behaviors are reinforced, punished, or available from models, but this level of context is not stressed since the principles of learning are considered to be universal. | Piaget believed the cognitive structures underlying thought are universal. Sociocultural context might affect the rapidity or final level of thinking, but sociocultural differences are not stressed. | Of relatively minor concern. However, the rules, strategies, and procedures acquired to perform tasks may differ from one culture to another. | Erikson incorporated sociocultural context as a major component of his theory. | A critically important determinant of behavior. Culture contains the historical knowledge that has permitted former and current members of the group to interact successfully with the environment. | Not emphasized. Ethological principles of development are presumed to apply in all cultures. |
| **How does the child play an active role in development?** | The child is not active in behavior analysis, but more actively engages the environment to determine what is learned in social cognitive theory. | Knowledge is based on underlying cognitive structures constructed by the child. | The child determines what information is processed and the rules, strategies, and procedures initiated to perform tasks. | The child is actively in search of an identity. | The child plays a central role in determining what kind of environment is established, how it changes and how it further affects behavior. The influences of the child and the environment are bidirectional. | The child is biologically equipped to interact with the environment and actively contributes to developmental outcomes. |

ment. We will frequently draw on their contributions for interpreting the many behaviors of children. We hope you will, too.

At the beginning of this chapter, we asked you to note your position on each of six major themes of development. As we have introduced developmental theories, we have also discussed their positions on these themes. Table 2.4 summarizes these positions for the major theories introduced in this chapter. As you read further in this book, you may find yourself revising your own stand on the six themes. We trace their presence throughout the remainder of this book with marginal cues placed beside important research and discussion that bear on each theme. We also open each chapter with a list of the most relevant themes discussed in it and we conclude each chapter by summarizing how the themes have applied to the developmental domain under discussion.

**TABLE 2.4** (Continued)

**The Main Developmental Theories and Where They Stand on the Six Themes in Development**

| Theme | Learning Theories | Piagetian Theory | Information-Processing Models | Psychosocial Theory | Contextual Theories | |
| --- | --- | --- | --- | --- | --- | --- |
| | | | | | Sociocultural | Ethological |
| Is development continuous or discontinuous? | Continuous. Development is cumulative, consisting of the acquisition of a greater and greater number of learned responses. | Stagelike. Four qualitatively different stages emerge, each involving a reorganization of cognitive structures that permits more effective adaptation to the demands of the world. | Usually continuous. Development consists of the acquisition of more effective structures and processes for performing tasks. | Stagelike, although the individual may return to earlier stages to work through unresolved conflicts. | Continuous. Development involves transactions between the individual and the environment. | Continuous, although there are certain times when particular issues must be resolved. |
| How prominent are individual differences in development? | Individual differences are not emphasized; the laws of learning are universal. However, variations in experience can be a major source of individual differences. | Individual differences are not a primary focus of Piaget's theory. | Little emphasis is placed on individual differences; however, variations in structures, strategies, and other processes could help to explain individual differences in behavior. | Psychosocial stages are universal, however, individuals may proceed through and resolve each need in quite different ways. | Stresses the unique configuration of events that contribute to individual differences in explaining behavior. | Not emphasized. |
| How do the various domains of development interact? | Learning proceeds on many different fronts and is highly situational. | In Piaget's theory, stagelike advances in cognition not only have implications for thinking and problem solving, but also for moral and social development since many achievements in these domains depend on cognitive skills. | Development is usually considered to be domain specific. However, recent efforts have been made to understand social and emotional relationships in terms of information-processing models. | Failure to progress through psychosocial stages may disrupt progress in many different domains besides personality development. | Because of the strong mutual interdependence between individual and environment, all aspects of development are closely interrelated. | Social and psychological aspects of development are intimately linked to biological aspects, and all domains of development are linked together by their common contribution to adaptation. |

# *Summary*

**Six Major Themes in Developmental Psychology**  Theories provide models for understanding the complex phenomenon of human development. At the beginning of this chapter we formulated six recurring investigative questions that developmental theories must answer:

- What roles do nature and nurture play in development?
- How does the sociocultural context influence development?
- How does the child play an active role in development?
- Is development continuous or discontinuous?
- How prominent are individual differences in development?
- How do the various domains of development interact?

The various theories examined in this chapter differ in their answers to these questions and their emphasis in addressing the various themes.

**Learning Theory Approaches**  *Learning theories,* especially *behavior analysis,* emphasize the critical role of the environment and *operant* and *classical conditioning* for bringing about behavioral change. Even complex behaviors are the product of basic principles of learning. *Social learning theories,* particularly *social cognitive theory* as outlined by Bandura, add *observational learning* as an important mechanism by which behavior is continuously modified and changed.

**Cognitive-Developmental Approaches**  Piaget's *cognitive-developmental theory* focuses on the child's construction of schemes or patterns of thought as development progresses through a series of qualitatively different stages. By *assimilation* and *accommodation* a child's *schemes,* or intellectual structures, actively adapt to the demands of the environment and become more organized, rational, and logical. Cognitive structures not only determine the way the child interprets and understands the world but also influence social and moral development.

**Information-Processing Approaches**  *Information-processing models* use the computer as a metaphor to describe the cognitive structures and processes available to children in their efforts to comprehend, reason about, and respond to information. Various perceptual, memory, and other structures as well as attentional, storage, retrieval, and other processes are posited to explain behavior.

**Psychosocial Approaches**  *Psychosocial theory* focuses on personality development. Freud's *psychosexual theory of development,* the predecessor of Erikson's psychosocial theory, posits that development proceeds maturationally through several stages in which specific body systems become especially effective in reducing libidinal energy. Failure to negotiate these stages successfully results in personality disturbances. Erikson's *psychosocial theory of development* emphasizes the sociocultural context in which behavioral needs are met. Development proceeds through a series of crises involving an individual's identity. Individuals who manage to resolve these crises become people who can successfully contribute to society.

**Contextual Approaches**    *Contextual models* view human development from a broader framework. *Ecological systems theory* looks beyond the immediate context of an individual interacting with family, peers, and friends to the broader sociocultural contexts of his or her society. Vygotsky's *sociohistorical theory* views culture as the historical legacy of a community and emphasizes that development results from social interactions in which this heritage is transferred to and becomes part of an individual's way of thinking. *Transactional theories* view the child as actively modifying and affecting the environment so that development is a process that is unending for both. *Ethological theory* pays special attention to the biological heritage each individual brings into the world. This heritage includes a history of species-specific behaviors that have been found to be adaptive throughout evolution.

# 3

# Genetics and Heredity

*"He was shy," Jeremy's mother said. "He's always been shy, ever since he was a baby. I remember those first weeks at the day-care center, how Jeremy clung to me, clutched my hand, even grabbed my leg whenever I started to walk toward a group of children. The teacher said he would get over this timid behavior. But when I came to observe, Jeremy would be off to the side watching what everyone else was doing; he was hardly ever in the center of a group. Every time I saw him like that, it reminded me of myself in grade school. The other kids talked with each other and shared things so easily and always seemed so popular. I guess Jeremy just takes after me. No matter how I tried to encourage him, he hung back from the rest of the group just like I did."*

*She paused. "Cindy was so different. She was usually the center of attention and never bashful about walking up to a stranger. Her schoolteachers often commented about Cindy's enthusiasm in class. She'd usually be one of the first to raise her hand, answer a question, or volunteer to lead the group in some kind of activity. She has all her father's outgoing personality and charm. It comes so naturally to both of them!"*

Parents often describe their children in ways like this, but what precisely are the mechanisms by which we "take after" our parents? Can aspects of personality such as being shy or outgoing be inherited? Though we may readily acknowledge the contribution of nature to eye color, gender, height, and many other physical traits, heredity's role in whether we are complacent or quick tempered, prone to alcoholism, likely to suffer depression, and in other social, emotional, and intellectual traits continues to be questioned. Yet, as Sandra Scarr, a leading researcher in behavioral genetics, has stated, "Parents of two or more children know perfectly well that their children are different for reasons that have nothing to do with their training regimens" (1987, p. 227).

In Chapter 2, we noted how researchers have debated the contributions of nature and nurture in many domains of development. That debate continues today. In fact, in recent years some researchers have become so sympathetic to biologically based explanations of development that Robert Plomin, another leading behavioral geneticist, cautions, "As the pendulum swings from environmentalism, it is important that the pendulum be caught midswing before its momentum carries it to biological determinism" (1989, p. 110).

In this chapter we consider hereditary contributions to development. Major advances in our understanding of the basic biological units of inheritance and their effects on behavior have led to a greater appreciation of the reciprocal, interactive relationship between nature and nurture. A rich variety of physical and social experiences simply does not replace biological determinants of development or vice versa. Instead, experiences mold, modify, and enhance biological predispositions, and conversely, our genetic endowment influences, perhaps even actively promotes, selection and preference for certain kinds of environments. Our goal is to understand just how such complex interactions evolve.

We begin with a brief overview of the principles of heredity. The blueprint for human development is replicated in nearly every cell of our body. This blueprint includes genetic instructions to help distinguish humans from all other species of plants and animals. Regardless of the language we speak, the work we do, the color of our skin, or how friendly we are, we share a genetic underpinning that makes us unambiguously human. But this biological inheritance also contributes to our uniqueness as individuals. All of us, with the exception of identical twins, begin with a set of genetic instructions that, when combined with various experiences, ensures that each of us is and continues to be unique, different from everyone else, though we belong to the same species. Imagine the monotony of a world populated by a single kind of man and a single kind of woman. Biologists emphasize that genetic diversity is important for another reason: it helps ensure the survival of our species.

In this chapter we also examine several examples of hereditary anomalies and diseases that pose problems for development. As researchers have come to learn more about the ways in which genetic abnormalities arise, they have begun to design environments that sometimes help minimize the negative impact of these disorders. We consider, too, how genetic counseling assists parents in deciding whether to have children.

Most psychological development, of course, cannot be linked to simple genetic instructions. Intelligence, temperament, and personality along with several kinds of mental disorders are the outcome of complex interactions between genetic and environmental events. In the final section of this chapter, we consider research involving identical and fraternal twins, siblings, adopted children, and other family relationships for the purpose of unraveling the complex tapestry that genetic and environmental factors weave for cognitive, social-emotional, and personality development. Historically, researchers have often attempted to identify *how much* nature and nurture, respectively, contribute to development. But understanding how these factors *interact* to account for behavior will ultimately yield more insights concerning the process of human development (Wachs, 1983).

## *Principles of Hereditary Transmission*

Whether we have freckles, blonde hair, or display a certain type of personality can be influenced by genetic factors but none of these characteristics is bestowed on us at conception any more directly than our height, which is finally realized only at our maturity. We must make a distinction between what is supplied as our genetic make-up and the kind of individual we eventually become. That difference serves as the basis for distinguishing between **genotype**, a person's constant, inherited genetic endowment, and **phenotype**, an individual's observable, measurable features, characteristics, and behaviors. A given phenotype is the product of complex interactions involving the genotype and the many events that are a part of an individual's *experience*.

Modern theories of the genotype can be traced to a series of experiments reported in 1866 by Gregor Mendel, an Austrian monk. From his observations of the characteristics of generations of peas, Mendel theorized hereditary char-

▶ Roles of nature and nurture

**genotype**  Total genetic endowment inherited by an individual.

**phenotype**  Observable and measurable characteristics and traits of an individual; a product of the interaction of the genotype with the environment.

The biological heritage passed on from mother to daughter is one source of similarities in the four generations of women shown here. Psychologists are interested in determining how this biological heritage interacts with experience to affect physical appearance, intellectual development, personality, and other traits and behaviors.

acteristics are determined by *pairs* of particles called factors (later termed **genes**, the specialized sequences of molecules that form the genotype). He further proposed that the information carried by the individual members of a pair of genes is not always identical. Since differences between the two genes in a pair may exist, the information carried by one gene could dominate or mask the information carried by the other gene. Or the information might interact so that the phenotype would reflect the combined influence of both genes.

Mendel also outlined the basic principle by which genes are transferred from one generation to another. He concluded that offspring randomly receive one member of every gene pair from the mother and one from the father. The parents' **gametes**, or sex cells (egg and sperm), carry only one of the pair of genes. Thus, when egg and sperm combine during fertilization, a pair of genes, one from each parent, is reestablished in the newly created offspring. That individual, in turn, may transmit either member of the pair to subsequent offspring. In this way, a given genotype can be inherited from one generation to the next.

About the same time that Mendel's research was published, biologists discovered **chromosomes**, long threadlike structures in the nucleus of nearly every cell in the body. In the early 1900s, several researchers independently hypothesized that genes were located on chromosomes. Yet another major breakthrough occurred in 1953 when James Watson and Francis Crick deciphered the structure of chromosomes, and in so doing, proposed a powerfully elegant way by which genes were duplicated during cell division. By 1956, researchers documented the existence of forty-six chromosomes in normal human body cells. Research being conducted in the present decade and likely to continue throughout the next is attempting to map the entire **human genome**,

**gene**   Large segment of nucleotides within a chromosome that codes for the production of proteins and enzymes. These proteins and enzymes underlie traits and characteristics inherited from one generation to the next.

**gametes**   Sperm cells in males, egg cells in females, normally containing only twenty-three chromosomes.

**chromosomes**   Threadlike structures of DNA, located in the nucleus of cells, that form a collection of genes. A human body cell normally contains forty-six chromosomes.

**human genome**   Entire inventory of nucleotide base pairs comprising the genes and chromosomes of humans.

the set of genes and sequence of complex molecules that make up the genetic information contained in all forty-six chromosomes.

## The Building Blocks of Heredity

How could hereditary factors play a part in Jeremy's shyness and Cindy's friendliness, or in another child's remarkable mathematical ability or mental retardation? To understand the genotype and its effects on appearance, behavior, personality, or intellectual ability, genetic mechanisms must be discussed at many different levels.

To begin with, every living organism is composed of cells—and in the case of mature humans, trillions of cells. As Figure 3.1 indicates, within the nucleus of nearly all of these cells are the chromosomes that carry genetic information critical to the functioning of that cell. Genes, regions within the strands of chromosomes, determine the production of enzymes and specific proteins in the cell. The genes are, in turn, made up of various arrangements of four different chemical building blocks called **nucleotides** that contain one of four nitrogen-based molecules (*adenine, thymine, cytosine,* or *guanine*). The nucleotides link together in one of only two kinds of pairings to form the rungs or steps of a remarkably long, spiral, ladderlike staircase called **DNA** or **deoxyribonucleic acid** (see Figure 3.2). An average of about a thousand nucleotide pairs make up each gene, although some have substantially more pairings (National Research Council, 1988). Genes differ from each other in the number and sequence of nucleotide pairings and in their location on the chemical spiral staircases, or chains of DNA that we call the chromosomes.

Just as Mendel had theorized, hereditary attributes are influenced by *pairs* of genes, one inherited from the mother and one from the father. Since each member of the pair of genes comprises a segment of a different chromosome, chromosomes, too, come in pairs. The two chromosomes in each pair that code for the same kinds of genetic events are called *homologous* (similar). Human beings have twenty-three homologous pairs or a total of forty-six chromosomes. Figure 3.3 shows a **karyotype** or photomicrograph of these twenty-three pairs. They are numbered from 1 to 22 in the case of the **autosomes**, those pairs of homologous chromosomes that are distinguished from the remaining two chromosomes which genetically determine sex. The two members of the twenty-third set in females, called **X chromosomes**, are relatively large and similar in size and shape. But the two members of this pair for males are quite different. The normal male has one X chromosome and one much smaller **Y chromosome**, a chain of DNA believed to carry far less genetic information. Nevertheless, the Y chromosome has a major function in promoting the development of the male *gonads* (testes) and, consequently, in determining whether an individual will be identified as male or female.

## Cell Division and Chromosome Duplication

Each child begins life as a single cell created when a sperm cell from the father unites with an ovum (egg) from the mother to form a **zygote**, or fertilized egg cell. The developmental processes started by this union are more fully described in Chapter 4. Remarkably, however, nearly every one of the millions of different cells in the newborn, whether specialized for bone or skin, heart or

**nucleotide** Repeating basic building block of DNA consisting of nitrogen-based molecules of adenine, thymine, cytosine, and guanine.

**deoxyribonucleic acid (DNA)** Long, spiral staircase-like sequence of molecules created by nucleotides identified with the blueprint for genetic inheritance.

**karyotype** Pictorial representation of an individual's chromosomes.

**autosomes** Twenty-two pairs of homologous chromosomes. The two members of each pair are similar in size, shape, and genetic function. The two sex chromosomes are excluded from this class.

**X chromosome** Larger of the two sex chromosomes associated with genetic determination of sex. Normally females have two X chromosomes; males, only one.

**Y chromosome** Smaller of the two sex chromosomes associated with genetic determination of sex. Normally males have one Y chromosome; females, none.

**zygote** Fertilized egg cell.

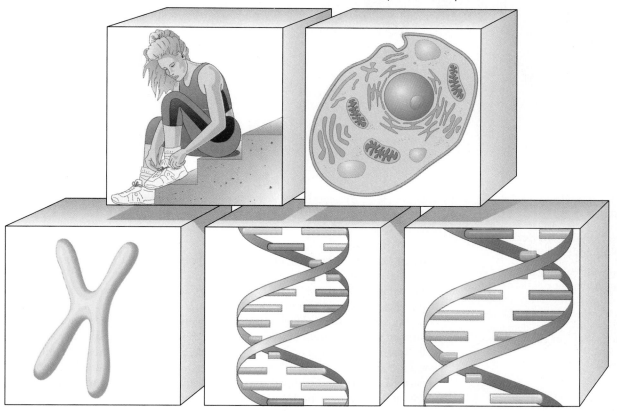

1. The **human body** has about 10 trillion cells. Proteins determine the structure and function of each cell.

2. Most **cells** contain a nucleus. Located within the nucleus are 46 chromosomes which carry the instructions that permit the cell to manufacture various proteins and enzymes.

3. A **chromosome** is a long thin strand of DNA organized as a coiled double helix. A full set of 46 chromosomes contains about 100,000 genes.

4. A **gene** is made up of thousands of nucleotide pairs. Each gene typically has enough information to specify the production of a particular protein.

5. **Nucleotides**, composed of four different kinds of chemical building blocks, are the smallest genetic unit and are paired in specific combinations. A project is now under way to map and sequence the estimated 3 billion pairs of nucleotides that make up the total complement of genes and chromosomes.

**FIGURE 3.1**

**The Building Blocks of Heredity**

Source: Adapted from Isensee, 1986.

Hereditary contributions to development can be observed at many different levels. In this figure you can see five major levels. Nearly every cell in the human body carries the genetic blueprint for development in the chromosomes. Specific regions on each chromosome, the genes, regulate protein and enzyme production and can be further examined in terms of the nucleotides, chemical molecules that are the building blocks for the genes. Each of these different levels of the individual's biological make-up can offer insights into the mechanisms by which the genotype affects the phenotype, the observable expression of traits and behaviors.

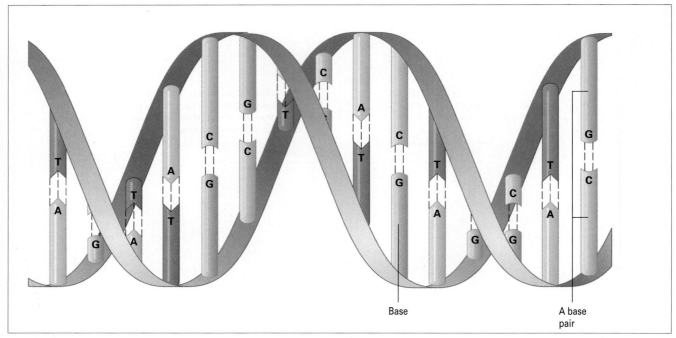

Base

A base pair

**FIGURE 3.2**

Source: Adapted from Alberts et al., 1983.

**The Building Blocks of the DNA Ladder**

The basic building blocks of the human genome consist of four different nucleotides. Each of the four nucleotides—adenine (A), thymine (T), cytosine (C), and guanine (G)—binds with only one other.

**mitosis**   Process of cell division taking place in most cells of the human body that results in a full complement of forty-six chromosomes in each cell; reproduces identical genetic material in succeeding generations of cells.

**meiosis**   Process of cell division that takes place to form the gametes; normally results in twenty-three chromosomes in each human egg and sperm cell rather than the full complement of forty-six chromosomes.

brain, or in some other way, contains the same genetic blueprint established in the initial zygote.

How does this extraordinary duplication of DNA, from one cell to another or from one generation to the next, take place? The division process for most cells is called **mitosis.** During mitosis, genetic material in the nucleus is reproduced so that a full complement of DNA becomes available to each new cell. Before cell division occurs, the chemical bonds linking the nucleotides together to form the rungs of the DNA ladder weaken. Each pair of nucleotides separates as if being unzipped from one another. While this process is taking place, additional nucleotides are being manufactured in the cell to become attached to the separated nucleotides. Because each type of nucleotide can combine with only one other, the newly formed DNA rungs are rebuilt exactly as their original sequence. The two newly constructed DNA strands eventually separate completely so that one becomes a member of each of the two new daughter cells, as depicted in Figure 3.4.

The process of cell division associated with the gametes is called **meiosis.** Meiosis, which results in twenty-three chromosomes in the egg and sperm cells, actually involves *two* successive generations of cell divisions. In the first stage, each of the forty-six chromosomes replicates. However, before the identical replicas split apart, the cell divides and each daughter cell receives only twenty-three chromosomes, one from each of the twenty-three pairs, as pictured in Figure 3.3. In the second stage, the replicas split apart and the two cells divide once more, each again receiving one member of each pair of chromosomes. Thus, from these two successive generations, four cells are produced, each with twenty-three chromosomes. Figure 3.5 illustrates the process of meiosis for sperm cells.

Random segregation of the twenty-three homologous chromosome pairs in the first stage of meiosis yields over 8 million possible combinations of ga-

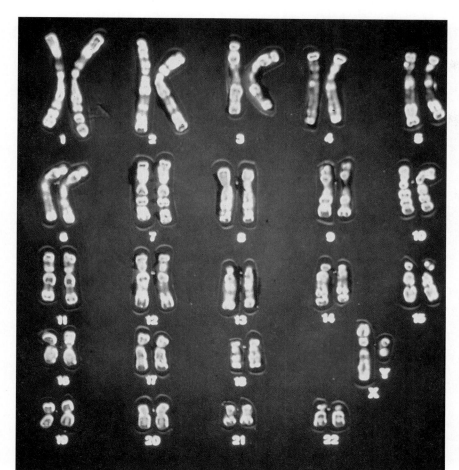

**FIGURE 3.3**

**Chromosomes for the Normal Human Male**

This karyotype depicts the twenty-two homologous pairs of autosomes and the two sex chromosomes for the normal human male. In females the twenty-third pair of chromosomes consists of an XX instead of an XY pair.

metes with one or more different sets of chromosomes. Along with an equivalent number of possible unique arrangements from a mate, mother and father have the potential for producing about 64 trillion offspring differing by one or more chromosomes. But the potential for genetic variability is actually far greater because of the phenomenon known as **crossing over**, a key part of the first stage of meiosis. Before homologous chromosome pairs separate in the first cell division, they mysteriously align, and segments of DNA transfer, or cross over, from one member to the other member of the pair, as shown in Figure 3.6. As a result of the genetic variability ensured by crossing over, it is virtually impossible for someone to have the same genetic make-up as someone else, even another sibling, unless the two are identical twins.

▶ Individual differences

## Gene Expression

▶ Roles of nature and nurture

We have briefly described key structures of inheritance: nucleotides, genes, and chromosomes, and how these structures are replicated in cells of the body, including gametes. But how does the genotype affect the phenotype—how does the underlying genetic blueprint promote the appearance of blue eyes,

**crossing over** Process during the first stage of meiosis when genetic material is exchanged between autosomes.

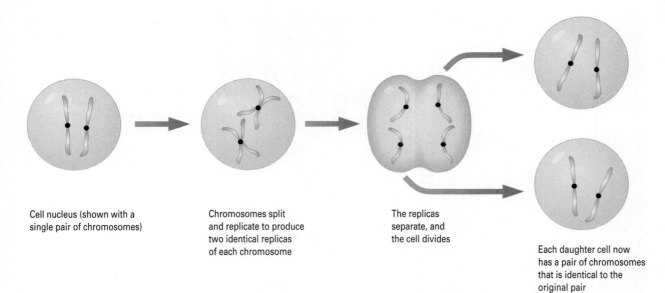

Cell nucleus (shown with a single pair of chromosomes)

Chromosomes split and replicate to produce two identical replicas of each chromosome

The replicas separate, and the cell divides

Each daughter cell now has a pair of chromosomes that is identical to the original pair

**FIGURE 3.4**

**The Process of Mitosis**

The process of mitotic cell division generates nearly all the cells of the body except the gametes. During mitosis, each chromosome replicates to form two chromosomes with identical genetic blueprints. As the cell divides, one member of each identical pair becomes a member of each of the daughter cells. In this manner complete genetic endowment is replicated in nearly every cell of the body.

Cell with 46 chromosomes (only one pair of homologous chromosomes is shown here). Each member of the pair has begun to replicate similar to mitotic cell division.

First meiotic cell division begins but does not proceed as in mitosis. Instead of the replicated chromosome splitting apart, one member of each homologous pair becomes a part of the first-generation daughter cell.

The second meiotic division proceeds after the first is completed; now the replicated chromosome acquired in the first-generation daughter cell splits apart.

Each of the four gametes produced by the two-step process now has acquired one member of the pair of homologous chromosomes.

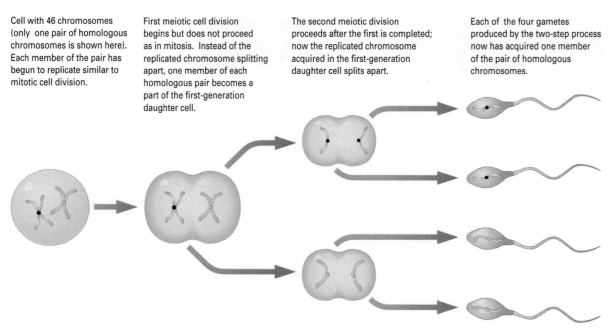

**FIGURE 3.5**

**The Process of Meiosis for Sperm Cells**

As meiosis begins (a), DNA replicates as in mitotic cell division. However, before the replicated arms split apart, one member of each pair of homologous chromosomes moves to become part of each first-generation daughter cell (b). Once the first generation of daughter cells is established, DNA replicas then split as part of the second meiotic division (c). Thus, one replica of one member of the pair of homologous chromosomes is contributed to each second-generation daughter cell (d). From these two successive divisions, four cells, each with 23 chromosomes, is produced.

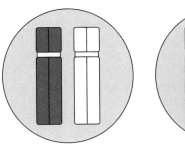  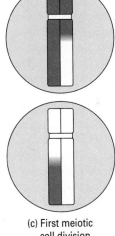

(a) Alignment of
homologous
chromosomes,
each a pair
of sister
chromatids

(b) Crossover

(c) First meiotic
cell division

Source: Adapted from Knowles, 1985.

**FIGURE 3.6**

**Crossing Over: The Exchange of Genetic Material Between Chromosomes**

In the process known as crossing over, genetic material is exchanged between homologous pairs of chromosomes during the first stage of meiotic cell division. (a) Initially, autosomes that have begun DNA replication align with each other. (b) Genetic material between homologous chromosomes is exchanged. (c) One member of each homologous pair of chromosomes randomly segregates or relocates to two different regions of the parent cell, and the first generation of cell division in meiosis takes place.

baldness, and dark skin, or such complex behaviors as shyness, schizophrenia, and intelligent problem solving? The answer begins with the fact that any single gene often can be found in one of several alternate forms. Each of these alternate forms is called an **allele.** The different alleles of a gene, then, are the hereditary foundation for such individual differences as, for example, whether hair will be curly or straight, or eyes will be blue or brown or hazel.

As already pointed out, each of us typically inherits pairs of genes that code for an event, one member from our mother and the other from our father. These genes may be identical—that is, have the same allelic form—or they may differ. When both have the same allelic form, a person's genotype is said to be **homozygous** for whatever characteristic that gene affects. For example, three alleles exist for the gene that governs blood type: A, B, and O. When both inherited versions have the same form—that is, both are A, both B, or both O—a person has a homozygous genotype for blood type. But if an individual inherited two different alleles of the gene for blood type, let's say A and B, that person's genotype is **heterozygous;** he or she has Type AB blood.

The consequences of a homozygous genotype are usually straightforward: the child's phenotype will be influenced by whatever characteristics are specified by that particular allelic form. But the effects of a heterozygous genotype depend on how the alleles influence each other. When a child's phenotype shows the effects of only one of the two alleles, the gene whose characteristics are observed in the phenotype is considered **dominant;** the gene whose influence is not evident in the phenotype is considered **recessive.** For example, a person who inherits both an A and O allele for blood type will still be classified as having Type A; the allele for Type A is dominant; the allele for Type O, recessive.

*Cystic fibrosis,* a leading cause of childhood death among children in North America, provides another example of a dominant-recessive relationship be-

**allele** Alternate form of a specific gene; provides a genetic basis for many individual differences.

**homozygous** Genotype in which two alleles of a gene are identical, thus having the same effects on a trait.

**heterozygous** Genotype in which two alleles of a gene are different. The effects on a trait will depend on how the two alleles interact.

**dominant allele** Allele whose characteristics are reflected in the phenotype even when part of a heterozygous genotype. Its genetic characteristics tend to mask the characteristics of other alleles.

**recessive allele** Allele whose characteristics do not tend to be expressed when part of a heterozygous genotype. Its genetic characteristics tend to be masked by other alleles.

tween alleles of a gene. The vast majority of North Americans inherit a gene pair that does not include the allele for cystic fibrosis; they have a homozygous genotype that contributes to a normal phenotype. About one in twenty-five people of Caucasian ancestry, however, has a heterozygous genotype in which one gene is normal, but the other carries the genetic information that leads to cystic fibrosis. The normal gene is *dominant.* Thus, someone who is heterozygous for this condition can lead an ordinary, productive life. But should two individuals, each with a heterozygous genotype, have children, some of the children can be expected to inherit two normal genes, some both a normal and an abnormal gene, and some two abnormal genes for cystic fibrosis (see Figure 3.7). In the latter homozygous condition, the two recessive abnormal alleles are no longer masked by a normal gene and these children (about one in every 2,500 Caucasians) will suffer from cystic fibrosis. Medical researchers today are actively investigating the potential for *gene therapy,* the replacement of the gene that codes for cystic fibrosis by a normal gene, to reduce and even eliminate the devastating consequences of this inherited disorder (Collins, 1992).

For other genes, the child's phenotype will reflect the influence of both alleles, either in some blended form intermediate to the pattern expressed when the genes are homozygous or in some unblended form in which elements or characteristics of both genes are evident. An individual's mature height, for example, is probably influenced by a blend of alleles inherited for several different pairs of genes that have a bearing on height (Mange & Mange, 1990). When the characteristics of both alleles are observed in some unblended form, the alleles exhibit **codominance.** For example, a child with Type AB blood has inherited a gene for Type A blood from one parent and another gene for Type B blood from the other parent.

A number of traits and characteristics of individuals are affected by single genes exhibiting dominant-recessive patterns between genes (see Table 3.1). But we must be cautious when drawing inferences about these dominant-recessive relationships, even for the characteristics listed in Table 3.1. Many traits are **polygenic**—that is, determined by more than one and possibly many genes. Eye color, for example, although recognized to be largely governed by the dominant-recessive relationship between alleles of a single gene, is influenced by other genes as well. A further complication is that determining whether two alleles exhibit a dominant-recessive pattern, some intermediate blend, or a codominant relationship depends on the yardstick of measurement we use (Mange & Mange, 1990). We will see this chameleonlike quality of gene relationships later when we discuss sickle cell anemia, a condition that affects a high proportion of individuals in some African and African-American populations. Depending on whether sickle cell anemia is examined at the level of its implications for medical care, certain behavioral limitations, or biochemical analysis of the blood, it can be considered to have a recessive, a blended, or a codominant expression, respectively.

▶ Roles of nature and nurture

**codominance** Condition in which individual, unblended characteristics of two alleles are reflected in the phenotype.

**polygenic** Phenotypic characteristic influenced by two or more genes.

## Gene Functioning and Regulation of Development

How do genes influence the development of a phenotype? Although exceptions exist, genetic information is typically conveyed from the DNA in the cell's nucleus to the organic and inorganic substances in the cell outside the nucleus. This process is performed by *ribonucleic acid,* or *RNA,* a molecule somewhat similar to DNA. RNA copies segments of the nucleotide sequences making up genes. The message carried by the RNA initiates a series of biochemical

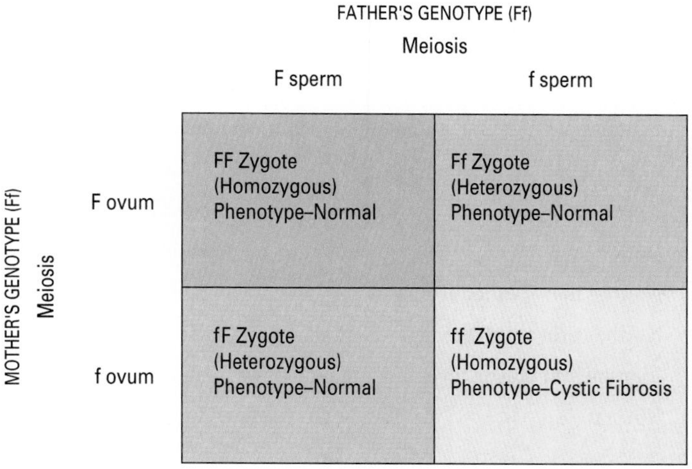

FATHER'S GENOTYPE (Ff)

Meiosis

|  | F sperm | f sperm |
|---|---|---|
| F ovum | FF Zygote (Homozygous) Phenotype–Normal | Ff Zygote (Heterozygous) Phenotype–Normal |
| f ovum | fF Zygote (Heterozygous) Phenotype–Normal | ff Zygote (Homozygous) Phenotype–Cystic Fibrosis |

MOTHER'S GENOTYPE (Ff)
Meiosis

**FIGURE 3.7**

**The Pattern of Inheritance for Cystic Fibrosis**

The inheritance of cystic fibrosis is one of many traits and diseases that is influenced by a single pair of genes. In this figure, F symbolizes a normal allele and f symbolizes the allele for cystic fibrosis. When parents with a heterozygous geno-type for this disease have children, their offspring may inherit a ho-mozygous genotype with normal al-leles (FF), a heterozygous genotype with one normal and one abnormal allele (Ff), or a homozy-gous genotype with two abnormal alleles (ff). Because the normal al-lele dominates, children with a het-erozygous genotype will not exhibit cystic fibrosis. When both alleles carry genetic information for the disease, however, cystic fi-brosis will occur.

processes that eventually produce complex enzymes or proteins to give the cell its unique ability to function. Enzymes act as catalysts, promoting additional bio-chemical reactions whose presence and timing are fundamental to the develop-ment and operation of all organs and systems of the human body. Thus, our ap-pearance and our behavior are, in part, the end result of an extensive chain of biochemical processes started by the instructions carried in the genotype.

The information conveyed by different alleles of a gene may cause one or more biochemical events in the chain to be modified, sometimes in substantial ways. Such a modification occurs, for example, in phenylketonuria, or PKU, a genetic condition in which *phenylalanine*, an amino acid in milk and high-protein foods such as meat, is unable to be metabolized as it is by most individ-uals. As a result, phenylalanine and other metabolic products accumulate in the blood, and the nervous system becomes deprived of needed nutrients. The eventual consequences are often convulsions, severe mental retardation, hyperactivity, and other behavioral problems. Remember, however, that a phe-notype is the product of the interaction between genotype and environment. In the case of PKU, environmental intervention in the form of reducing phenyl-alanine in the diet can help prevent severe mental retardation. Here, then, is an excellent example illustrating that genes do not have all the information built into them to cause particular developmental outcomes; external factors inter-act with the genotype to yield a specific phenotype.

Many mysteries remain concerning how genes influence development. For example, humans are believed to have about 100,000 **structural genes**, genes that code for the production of different kinds of enzymes and other proteins governing the physiological functions of a cell. Yet structural genes account for only about 3 percent of the 100 million nucleotide pairs estimated to be in the human genome (National Research Council, 1988). Some of the remaining DNA consists of another type of gene, called **regulator genes**, that start and stop the functioning of structural genes. Many structural genes do not operate continuously throughout development. They turn on and off (Plomin, 1987). Regulator genes appear to be responsive to environmental signals, factors within and outside the cell itself, to determine when structural genes become activated. Such genes would help explain how cells become differentiated—for example, how a nerve cell, liver cell, or muscle cell is formed despite their

**structural gene** Gene responsi-ble for the production of enzymes and other protein molecules. Hu-mans are estimated to have about 100,000 structural genes, some of which have been located on partic-ular chromosomes.

**regulator gene** Gene that switches other genes on and off.

**TABLE 3.1**

**Alleles of Genes That Display a Dominant and Recessive Pattern of Phenotypic Expression**

| Dominant Traits | Recessive Traits |
|---|---|
| Brown eyes | Gray, green, blue, hazel eyes |
| Curly hair | Straight hair |
| Normal hair | Baldness |
| Dark hair | Light or blond hair |
| Nonred hair (blond, brunette) | Red hair |
| Normal skin coloring | Albinism (lack of pigment) |
| Immunity to poison ivy | Susceptibility to poison ivy |
| Normal skin | Xeroderma pigmentosum (heavy freckling and skin cancers) |
| Thick lips | Thin lips |
| Roman nose | Straight nose |
| Earlobe free | Earlobe attached |
| Cheek dimples | No dimples |
| Extra, fused, or short digits | Normal digits |
| Second toe longer than big toe | Big toe longer than second toe |
| Double-jointedness | Normal joints |
| Normal color vision | Red-green color blindness |
| Farsightedness | Normal vision |
| Normal vision | Congenital eye cataracts |
| Retinoblastoma (cancer of the eye) | Normal eye development |
| Normal hearing | Congenital deafness |
| Type A blood | Type O blood |
| Type B blood | Type O blood |
| Rh-positive blood | Rh-negative blood |
| Normal blood clotting | Hemophilia |
| Normal metabolism | Phenylketonuria |
| Normal blood cells | Sickle cell anemia |
| Familial hypercholesterolemia (error of fat metabolism) | Normal cholesterol level at birth |
| Wilms tumor (cancer of the kidney) | Normal kidney |
| Huntington's chorea | Normal brain and body maturation |
| Normal respiratory and gastrointestinal functioning | Cystic fibrosis |
| Normal neural and physical development | Tay-Sachs disease |

identical genetic make-up. Vast networks of structural, regulator, and probably other kinds of genes interact, both with themselves and with their environment, to affect development.

Complex human activities are typically affected by many genes, but how they influence the wide range of behaviors of interest to psychologists remains largely unknown. Nonetheless, we can identify the consequences of several specific gene mutations as well as chromosomal disturbances having serious repercussions for development. We examine some of these gene and chromosomal abnormalities now to further illustrate the contribution of the genotype to human development.

## *Gene and Chromosomal Abnormalities*

▶ Individual differences

Changes in the structure of genes, or **mutations**, introduce genetic diversity among individuals. Mutations occur relatively often. Nearly half of all human conceptions have been estimated to have some kind of genetic or chromosomal error (Plomin, DeFries, & McClearn, 1990). Most of these are lost through spontaneous abortion very early after conception. A small number will have little impact, but others can have enduring, often negative, consequences on an individual's development. Even if the mutation does not have an immediate effect, it may be inherited from one generation to the next, a major way different alleles of a gene are established in populations of individuals. Still other disorders can be linked to disturbances involving the larger structural units of inheritance, the chromosomes.

About one in twenty individuals below the age of twenty-five have a disorder that can be linked to genetic factors (Baird et al., 1988). Between three and four thousand different disorders associated with specific genes, some inherited and others occurring as mutations, have been identified in humans (National Research Council, 1988; DeLisi, 1988). Many more inherited gene disorders will likely be discovered in the near future as the human genome is mapped more completely.

### Gene Disorders

▶ Individual differences

An estimated 100,000 infants are born each year in the United States alone with some kind of disorder caused by a single dominant or recessive gene. For about 20,000 of these babies the problem is serious (Knowles, 1985). Table 3.2 lists a few of the more important gene disorders that are currently known. In most cases, the effects of inherited disorders are evident at birth (*congenital*), but the consequences of some are not observed until childhood or even late adulthood. We will discuss several dominant and recessive disorders to illustrate their effects on development and the interventions and treatments they entail.

**mutation** Sudden change in molecular structure of a gene; may occur spontaneously or be caused by an environmental event such as radiation. Some mutations are lethal, but others are not and may be passed on from one generation to the next in the form of alleles of a gene.

**Huntington's Disease: Dilemma for Genetic Counseling** About twenty-five thousand Americans have **Huntington's disease.** Many more are at risk for developing it as they enter their adult years. Since Huntington's disease is caused by a dominant gene, each child of an affected parent has a 50 percent chance of acquiring it. The disease continues to be transmitted from one generation to the next because its onset is usually delayed until an

**Huntington's disease** Dominant genetic disorder characterized by involuntary movements of the limbs, mental deterioration, and premature death. Symptoms appear between thirty and fifty years of age and death within twenty years of onset of these symptoms.

| Disorder | Estimated Frequency (live births in U.S.) | Phenotype, Prognosis, and Prenatal Detection |
|---|---|---|
| *Autosomal Dominant Disorders* | | |
| Familial Alzheimer's Disease | Unknown. | Premature onset of loss of cognitive and social functioning often characteristic of senility. Gene located on chromosome 21. Prenatal detection possible. |
| Huntington's Disease | 1 in 18,000. | See text. Gene located on chromosome 4. |
| Marfan Syndrome | 1 in 20,000. | Tall, lean, long limbed, with gaunt face (some believe Abraham Lincoln had syndrome). Frequent eye problems. Cardiac failure in young adulthood common. Suicide second most common cause of death. Associated with increased paternal age. |
| Neurofibromatosis (von Recklinghausen's disease) | 1 in 2,500–3,300. | Symptoms range from a few pale brown spots on skin to severe tumors affecting peripheral nervous system and visibly distorting appearance. Minimal intellectual deficits in about 40% of cases. Gene for major form located on chromosome 17. Gene for other form located on chromosome 22. Prenatal detection possible. |
| *Autosomal Recessive Disorders* | | |
| Albinism | 1 in 10,000–20,000. Several forms; frequency differs among various populations. Most common form occurs in about 1 in 15,000 African Americans; 1 in 40,000 Caucasians; but much more frequently among some Native American tribes (1 in 200 among Hopi and Navajo, 1 in 132 among San Blas Indians of Panama). | Affected individuals lack pigment *melanin*. Extreme sensitivity to sunlight and visual problems. Prenatal detection possible. |
| Congenital Hypothyroidism | 1 in 3,000 of European origin. | Dwarfism, severe mental deficiency. Treatment with thyroid hormones successful but must be continued throughout life. Many countries currently screen newborns for disease. |
| Cystic Fibrosis | Most common genetic disease in Caucasian populations in U.S., especially those of Northern European descent, affecting about 1 in 2,500. One in 25 Americans is carrier. Less common among African-American and Asian-American populations. | Respiratory tract becomes clogged with mucus; lungs likely to become infected. Gene located on chromosome 7. Death often in young adulthood, but individuals may have children. Prognosis for females poorer than for males. Therapy helps delay effects. Prenatal detection possible. Some countries regularly screen newborns for disease. |

**TABLE 3.2**

**Some Inherited Gene Disorders**

| Disorder | Estimated Frequency (live births in U.S.) | Phenotype, Prognosis, and Prenatal Detection |
|---|---|---|
| Galactosemia | 1 in 60,000 | Mental retardation, cataracts, cirrhosis of the liver caused by accumulation of galactose in body tissues because of absence of enzyme to convert this sugar into glucose. Those heterozygous for this condition have half the normal enzyme activity, but this is enough for normal development. Galactose-free diet only treatment. Prenatal detection possible. Some countries currently screen newborns for defect. |
| Phenylketonuria | 1 in 12,000. Somewhat higher rate of incidence in Caucasian and Asian than in African-American populations. | See text. Prenatal detection possible. |
| Sickle Cell Anemia | 1 in 600 African Americans. Also frequently found in malaria-prone regions of world. | See text. Prenatal detection possible. |
| Tay-Sachs Disease | 1 in 3,000 Ashkenazic Jews. Very rare in other populations. 1 in 30 Ashkenazic Jews are carriers; in other populations 1 in 300 are carriers. | Signs of mental retardation, blindness, deafness, and paralysis begin 1 to 6 months after birth. Death normally occurs by 3 or 4 years of age. Prenatal detection possible. |
| Thalassemia (Cooley's anemia) | 1 in 800–2,500 in populations of Greek and Italian descent. Much less frequent in other populations. | Severe anemia beginning within 2 to 3 months of birth, stunted growth, increased susceptibility to infections. Death usually occurs in 20s or 30s. Prenatal detection possible. |

*Sex-linked Disorders*

| Disorder | Estimated Frequency (live births in U.S.) | Phenotype, Prognosis, and Prenatal Detection |
|---|---|---|
| Color Blindness (red-green) | About 1 in 100 males of Caucasian descent see no red or green. About 1 in 15 males of Caucasian descent experience some decrease in sensitivity to red or green colors. | Those who are completely red-green color blind lack either green-sensitive or red-sensitive pigment for distinguishing these colors and see them as yellow. Those who show lesser sensitivity to red or green perceive reds as reddish browns, bright greens as tan, and olive greens as brown. |
| Duchenne Muscular Dystrophy | 1 in 7,000 males. Most common of many different forms of muscular dystrophy. Several forms, including Duchenne, are X linked. | Progressive muscle weakness and muscle fiber loss. Mental retardation in about ⅓ of cases. Few ever live long enough to reproduce. Responsible gene located on short arm of X chromosome; appears to be massive in number of nucleotide pairs. Prenatal detection possible. |
| Hemophilia | 1 in 10,000 Caucasian male births for the most common form. | Failure of blood to clot. Several different forms; not all are sex linked. Queen Victoria of England carrier for the most common form. Potential for bleeding to death, but administration of clot-inducing drugs and blood transfusions reduces hazard. At risk for exposure to blood-transmitted diseases such as AIDS. Prenatal detection possible. |
| Lesch-Nylan Disease | 1 in 15,000. In more than ⅓ of affected males, cause is new mutations. | Recurrent vomiting, cerebral palsy, and mental retardation; self-mutilation, including gnawing of fingers, lips, or mouth. Death at relatively early age. Prenatal detection possible. |

Sources: Based on Beaudet et al., 1989; Headings, 1988; Knowles, 1985; National Genetics Foundation, 1987; Plomin, DeFries, & McClearn, 1990; Stanbury et al., 1989.

**TABLE 3.2** (continued)

**Some Inherited Gene Disorders**

individual is thirty-five to forty years of age. By this time, before its symptoms begin to appear, a carrier may have children. The symptoms, which often appear slowly but relentlessly increase in severity over a period of fifteen to twenty years, usually include personality changes, depression, a gradual loss of motor control and memory, and other mental impairments caused by massive cell death in the brain.

Recent progress in molecular genetics now permits testing of individuals to determine whether they have inherited Huntington's disease. Unfortunately, however, it cannot be cured or treated at the present time. Thus, the decision to carry out such screening presents an enormous conflict for those who have a family history of the disease; the test results can provide a potentially devastating glimpse into their future. *Genetic counselors*, professionals who advise parents about whether their children may or may not inherit a genetic defect, are also confronted with the ethical dilemma of whether to encourage prospective parents to have the test since its results are important for determining if offspring are at risk (Grady, 1987). Screening can be conducted prenatally to determine whether the fetus has inherited Huntington's disease as well.

### Sickle Cell Anemia: A Problem for Genetic Classification

**Sickle cell anemia** is a genetic disorder whose incidence is extremely high in many regions of West Africa and around the Mediterranean basin. It is also found in about one of every six hundred African Americans and in high numbers of Greek Americans and others whose ancestors came from areas where malaria commonly occurs. The defect, inherited as a recessive gene on chromosome 11, introduces a change in a single amino acid in hemoglobin, the molecule permitting the red blood cells to carry oxygen. As a result, red blood cells become crescent shaped rather than round. These sickle-shaped cells are ineffective in transporting oxygen; they also survive for a much shorter duration than normal red blood cells, and the bone marrow has difficulty replacing them. The consequence is often anemia, jaundice, low resistance to infection, and severe pain and damage to various organs when the distorted cells block small blood vessels.

More than 2 million, or about one in every ten, African Americans are carriers of the sickle cell gene. These individuals, who possess a heterozygous genotype, have the **sickle cell trait.** They manufacture a relatively small proportion of cells with abnormal hemoglobin. Few of these individuals show symptoms of sickle cell anemia; most live normal lives. But insufficient oxygen, which may occur in high altitude regions, when flying in unpressurized airplane cabins, or after strenuous exercise, can trigger sickling of red blood cells in those who have the trait. Nevertheless, carriers of the sickle cell gene are more resistant to malaria than are individuals who have normal hemoglobin. This adaptive feature probably accounts for the high incidence and persistence of the trait in populations where malaria is present.

Sickle cell anemia provides a good illustration of the arbitrary nature of classifying phenotypic relationships among alleles (Mange & Mange, 1990). From a medical or clinical perspective, the sickle cell gene is recessive; an individual is likely to suffer anemia or need hospitalization only when the genotype is homozygous and both alleles code for the production of the abnormal red blood cells. From a broader perspective, however, the sickle cell gene reflects an intermediate phenotypic pattern; individuals with a heterozygous genotype have *some* sickled cells, although far fewer than those suffering sickle cell anemia. Thus, individuals with the sickle cell trait *may* endure symptoms of sickle cell

**sickle cell anemia**   Genetic blood disorder common in regions of Africa and other areas of the world where malaria is found and among descendants of these regions. Abnormal blood cells are unable to carry adequate amounts of oxygen.

**sickle cell trait**   Symptoms shown by those possessing a heterozygous genotype for sickle cell anemia.

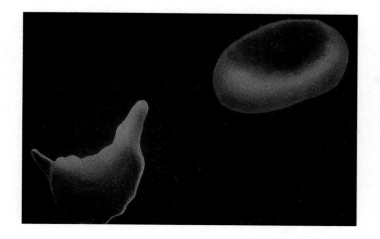

Individuals who suffer from sickle cell anemia, a genetically inherited disorder, have a large proportion of crescent-shaped red blood cells like the one shown on the left. A normal red blood cell is round and doughnut-shaped. Sickle-shaped cells are ineffective in transporting oxygen and may cause damage to various organs and pain by blocking small blood vessels.

anemia if they engage in activities that expose them to oxygen deprivation. From the perspective of biochemists, however, who analyze chains of amino acids, normal and abnormal alleles are really codominant; both kinds of chains are present in heterozygotes. Thus, as pointed out earlier in our discussion of phenotypic expression, the label used to describe the relationship between two alleles really depends on the level of the phenotype we are observing.

### Phenylketonuria: Environmentally Modifiable Genetic Disorder

▶ Roles of nature and nurture

Phenylketonuria (PKU), a recessive metabolic disorder affecting about one in every eleven thousand newborns, is caused by the mutation of a gene on chromosome 12. As indicated earlier, it provides a good illustration of how genes can interact with the environment to foster a particular phenotype or capacity. Treatment to reduce the effects of this debilitating genetic disorder consists of changing the child's environment—in this case, diet.

An infant with PKU is normal at birth. However, retardation begins within six months and becomes severe by four years of age if the condition is untreated. Fortunately, screening performed shortly after birth (required in nearly all areas of the United States and many other countries) can detect elevated levels of phenylalanine. An infant identified as having PKU can then be placed on a diet low in phenylalanine to prevent its more serious effects. Experts agree the diet must be started relatively early, within the first few months after birth, and continued at least through adolescence to ensure nearly normal mental development (Azen et al., 1991).

Even though the more serious consequences of this genetic disorder can be prevented, however, a completely normal prognosis for these children remains problematic (Scriver & Clow, 1988). The diet is difficult to maintain; it requires a careful balance between excessive phenylalanine to prevent neural damage and sufficient nutrients to permit reasonably normal growth. Blood tests may be needed as often as twice a month to keep metabolite concentrations within an acceptable range, a regimen for which child, parents, and testing centers may be ill prepared. Even under optimal conditions, children with PKU may show some growth and intellectual deficiencies, particularly in the area of planning and problem solving (Diamond, 1993; Welsh et al., 1990), and are somewhat more likely to display unusual mannerisms, hyperactivity, and reduced social responsivity (Smith, et al., 1988). The bland and unappetizing diet can be a source of conflict between child and caregiver as well, creating management problems within households attempting to lead relatively normal lives (Scriver & Clow, 1988).

Even those who successfully reach adulthood may not escape further consequences of their inherited disorder. Children born to mothers with PKU often suffer congenital heart defects and mental retardation (Lowitzer, 1987). Elevated levels of phenylalanine in the mother's blood appear to cause serious damage to fetal development. If a mother returns to a low phenylalanine diet before or early in her pregnancy, the risks can be reduced substantially (Platt et al., 1992). Thus, although dietary modifications are helpful, it remains unclear whether this intervention completely eliminates the negative consequences of PKU.

**Sex-linked Disorders**     Relatively few genes are known to exist on the Y chromosome, but the X chromosome carries many. This imbalance has substantial implications for a number of disorders said to be sex linked because the gene associated with them is carried on the X chromosome. Hemophilia, red-green color blindness, and Duchenne muscular dystrophy (see Table 3.2) have nothing to do with differentiation of sex but are sex linked because they are fostered by genes on the X chromosome. As a consequence, these disorders are found much more frequently in males than in females.

As with genes for autosomes, those that are sex linked often have a dominant-recessive relationship. Thus, females, who inherit two genes for sex-linked traits, one on each of the X chromosomes, are much less likely to display the deleterious effects associated with an abnormal recessive gene than are males, who, if they inherit the damaging allele, have no second, normal gene to mask its effects. Hemophilia, a condition in which blood does not clot normally, is a good example since it is nearly always associated with a defective gene on the X chromosome. Because the allele for hemophilia is recessive, daughters who inherit it typically do not exhibit hemophilia; the condition is averted by an ordinary gene on the second X chromosome that promotes normal blood clotting. A female can, however, serve as a carrier. If she possesses a heterozygous genotype for hemophilia, the X chromosome with the abnormal gene has a fifty-fifty chance of being transmitted to either her son or daughter. When the abnormal gene is inherited by a son, he will exhibit hemophilia because the Y chromosome does not contain genetic information to counter the allele's effects. If the abnormal gene is inherited by a daughter, she will be a carrier who may then transmit the allele to her sons and daughters, as has occurred in several interrelated royal families of Europe.

## Chromosome Disorders

Mutations in specific genes are only one of several sources of variation in the human genome. Occasionally whole sections of a chromosome are deleted or duplicated, or an extra chromosome is transmitted to daughter cells during cell division. When this happens, the consequences for normal development are often devastating. Human embryonic growth virtually never proceeds when a complete pair of autosomes is missing or when an extra pair of autosomes is inherited. **Trisomy**, the inheritance of an extra chromosome, also typically results in the loss of the zygote or miscarriage in early pregnancy (Boué, Boué, & Gropp, 1985). However, several specific trisomic patterns may be found in surviving human newborns. One of these, trisomy 21, or Down syndrome, occurs relatively frequently and has a substantial impact on the child, caregivers, and others in the family and community.

**Trisomy 21 (Down syndrome)**    Trisomy 21, one of the most common genetic causes of mental retardation, occurs in about one of every six hundred live births (Beaudet et al., 1989). Physically observable features associated with trisomy 21 include an epicanthal fold to give an almond shape to the eye; flattened facial features; poor muscle tone; short stature; and short, broad hands, including an unusual crease of the palm. Infants with Down syndrome may have congenital heart defects, cataracts or other visual impairments, and deficiencies in the immune system so that susceptibility to infection and leukemia is increased. Intellectual development appears to be markedly slowed and Down syndrome children appear to be less responsive to stimulation generally than are other children (Ganiban, Wagner, & Cicchetti, 1990; Hodapp & Zigler, 1990).

Approximately 95 percent of babies born with Down syndrome have an extra twenty-first chromosome. The majority of these errors originate in egg cells, but some stem from errors of meiosis during the production of sperm cells (Stewart, Hassold, & Kunit, 1988). About 4 percent of infants with Down syndrome have part of chromosome 21, perhaps as little as its bottom third, shifted to another chromosome (National Genetics Foundation, 1987; Patterson, 1987). Another 1 percent of Down syndrome children display a *mosaic* genotype, that is, have chromosomal deviations in only a portion of their body cells. The severity of Down syndrome in these individuals seems to be related to the proportion of cells exhibiting trisomy.

The probability of giving birth to an infant with Down syndrome increases with the age of the mother (see Figure 3.8). Although mothers over age thirty-five give birth to only about 16 percent of all babies, they bear over half the infants with Down syndrome. The age of the father shows only a small, if any, relationship to the occurrence of Down syndrome (Epstein, 1989). To explain these findings, experts have often proposed an "older egg" hypothesis. According to this view, the mother's egg cells, which have begun the first steps in meiosis even before her own birth, undergo change with aging, either because of the simple passage of time or because of increased exposure to potentially hazardous biological and environmental conditions. Older egg cells, those released from the ovaries later in the childbearing years, become more susceptible to chromosomal errors while undergoing the final steps of meiosis when ovulation occurs.

Recent research, however, has failed to confirm that errors occur more often in the ova of older than of younger mothers (Stewart et al., 1988). Some researchers have proposed a "relaxed selection" hypothesis to account for the increased frequency of Down syndrome in older mothers. According to this view, older mothers are less likely than younger mothers to spontaneously abort a zygote with trisomy 21. Though plausible, this explanation can also be challenged. For example, Down syndrome caused by the relocation of a part of

This child has trisomy 21, or Down syndrome. Although trisomy 21 is the leading cause of mental retardation in the United States, when given the opportunity to learn, many children with this chromosomal anomaly can acquire some skills in reading and writing.

**trisomy**    Condition in which an extra chromosome is present.

**FIGURE 3.8**

**Relationship Between Maternal Age and the Incidence of Down Syndrome**

The incidence of Down syndrome increases dramatically as a function of the age of the mother. One in every 1,500 babies born to mothers aged twenty-one has Down syndrome. For forty-nine-year-old mothers, the incidence is much higher: 1 in every 10 babies has Down syndrome. Two explanations, the "older egg" and the "relaxed selection" hypothesis, have been offered to account for these findings.

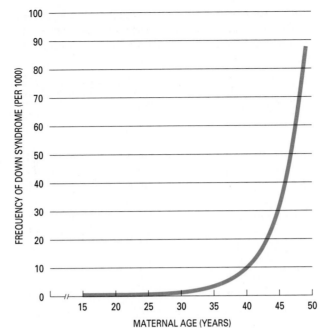

Source: Epstein, 1989.

▶ Roles of nature and nurture

the twenty-first chromosome to another chromosome is not associated with maternal age. Why is a pregnancy more likely to end in younger women when there is an extra chromosome, but not when chromosomal errors occur (Stewart et al., 1988)?

Because of better medical and physical care, more than half of all infants born with Down syndrome now live over thirty years and a quarter beyond fifty years (Patterson, 1987). Furthermore, although in the past the learning abilities of children with Down syndrome were considered to be quite low, many *can* learn and show considerable proficiency in reading and writing. But we still have much to learn about Down syndrome. For example, individuals with trisomy 21 who survive beyond age thirty-five frequently develop the same kinds of abnormal brain cells and show some of the same behavioral symptoms as adults who acquire Alzheimer's disease (Thase, 1988). Alzheimer's disease is characterized by memory and speech disturbances, personality changes, and increasing loss of intellectual functioning, typically in individuals between fifty and seventy-five years of age, although the symptoms may begin much earlier. At least one form of Alzheimer's disease is thought to be inherited, and not surprisingly, the responsible gene appears to be located on chromosome 21.

**Structural Aberrations of Chromosomes**    Other changes in chromosomes, including deletions, duplications, and relocations of *parts* of DNA also occur. As with trisomy, the consequences in most cases are so severe that the pregnancy ends soon after conception. But again this is not always the case. For example, deletion of a small segment of the fifth chromosome is responsible for *cri du chat*, or *cat-cry syndrome*, in which infants exhibit a cry similar to a cat's (and thus its name), severe mental retardation, microcephaly (very small head size), and short stature, as well as other congenital anomalies. Mental retardation and severe physical deformations often accompany structural aberrations observed in other chromosomes as well.

**Sex Chromosome Abnormalities**     As we have already noted, males normally have an X and a Y chromosome, and females have two X chromosomes for the twenty-third pair. But variations in the number of sex chromosomes can be found in humans. For example, an individual may inherit only a single X (XO), an extra chromosome (XXX, XXY, XYY), or even pairs of extra chromosomes (for example, XXXX, XXYY, XXXY). Several of these variations are described in more detail in Table 3.3. Children with sex chromosome anomalies display a wide range of phenotypic expressions; however, large proportions of these individuals lead normal lives.

When an extra chromosome was first identified, a few researchers contended that it was closely linked to an assortment of abnormal and socially unacceptable behaviors. For example, in the 1960s several published reports claimed the XYY pattern existed surprisingly often in hard-to-manage retarded men and highly aggressive inmates in penal institutions and was the basis for their antisocial behaviors. Despite a number of methodological problems with this research, the belief that XYY males are more aggressive than other males was widely disseminated by the media. The extra Y chromosome was even used in courts of law to argue for leniency for criminals who inherited this chromosomal pattern. Today we know that the extra Y chromosome is linked to above-average height and sometimes lowered intelligence. This physical and intellectual combination may account for the slightly elevated percentage of XYY men in prison compared with normal XY males. The crimes these men commit, however, are no more violent than those of other men (Witkin et al., 1976).

The wide variation in phenotypes associated with sex chromosome anomalies, even among those bearing the same karyotype, may be due to experiential factors. Bruce Bender and his colleagues at the University of Colorado School of Medicine studied forty-six children with sex chromosome abnormalities such as those described in Table 3.3 (Bender, Linden, & Robinson, 1987). These children, born between 1964 and 1974, were identified by screening forty thousand consecutive births in the Denver area. Those with sex chromosome abnormalities were more likely to have neuromotor, psychosocial, and language impairments and school problems compared with their siblings who had normal sex chromosome complements. But this was true for school and psychosocial problems only if children were growing up in a family where they experienced severe stress such as exposure to drug abuse or severe illness, lack of effective parenting by caregivers, or poverty. In the absence of such problems, children with sex chromosome abnormalities showed no greater evidence of school or psychosocial problems than their siblings, although they did continue to show more neuromotor and language impairment. What these findings seem to imply is that children with sex chromosome abnormalities may be more vulnerable to disruptions in their caregiving environment than children with a normal complement of sex chromosomes.

▶ Roles of nature and nurture

**Fragile X Syndrome**     Genetic researchers have recently identified a structural anomaly that consists of a pinched or constricted site near the end of the long arm of the X chromosome. This anomaly, termed **fragile X syndrome**,

fragile X syndrome   Disorder associated with a pinched region of the X chromosome; a leading genetic cause of mental retardation in males.

| Disorder | Estimated Frequency (live births in U.S.) | Phenotype and Prognosis |
|---|---|---|
| XO (Turner syndrome) | 1 in 1,200–2,500 females (90% are spontaneously aborted) | *Characteristics.* Short stature, usually normal psychomotor development, but limited development of secondary sexual characteristics. Failure to menstruate and sterility due to underdeveloped ovaries. Webbed, short neck. Near-average range of intelligence but serious deficiencies in spatial ability and directional sense. *Prognosis.* Increased stature and sexual development, including menstruation, but not fertility, can be induced through administration of estrogen and other hormones. In vitro fertilization permits carrying of child when adult. |
| XXX (Triple-X syndrome or "superfemale") | 1 in 500–1,200 females | *Characteristics.* Not generally distinguishable. Some evidence of delay in speech and language development, lack of coordination, poor academic performance and immature behavior. Sexual development usually normal. *Prognosis.* Many are essentially normal, but greater proportion have language, cognitive, and social-emotional problems. |
| XXY (Klinefelter syndrome) | 1 in 500–1,000 males (increased risk among older mothers) | *Characteristics.* Tend to be tall, beardless, with feminine body contour, high-pitched voice. Some evidence for poor auditory short-term memory and difficulty with reading. Testes underdeveloped, individuals sterile. *Prognosis.* Many with normal IQ, but about 20% may have occasional mild to moderate retardation. |
| XYY ("supermale") | 1 in 700–1,000 males | *Characteristics.* Above-average height, near-average range of intelligence. *Prognosis.* Most lead normal lives and have normal offspring. Higher proportion than normal incarcerated, but crimes no more violent than those of XY men. |

Sources: Based on Bender, Linden, & Robinson, 1987; Gorlin, 1977; Knowles, 1985; Linden et al., 1988; Plomin, DeFries, & McClearn, 1990; National Genetics Foundation, 1987.

**TABLE 3.3**

**Examples of Observed Sex Chromosome Abnormalities**

affects about one in every thousand infants and can be inherited from one generation to the next. It is caused by a single gene on the X chromosome (Nussbaum & Ledbetter, 1986). We include it in our discussion of chromosomal errors, however, because its diagnosis can be made on the basis of a physical change in the chromosomal structure (see Figure 3.9).

Fragile X syndrome has attracted widespread attention primarily because of its link to mental retardation. In fact, fragile X and Down syndrome are the most frequent known genetic causes of mental retardation in the United States (Hagerman, 1992). Males with fragile X syndrome commonly have a long narrow face, large or prominent ears, and large testes. Cardiac defects and relaxed ligaments (permitting, for example, hyperextension of finger joints) are also frequent components of the disorder. Behavioral attributes include poor eye contact and limited responsiveness to many forms of external stimulation as well as hand flapping, hand biting, and other unusual mannerisms such as mimicry. Females who possess a heterozygous genotype often show some reduction in intelligence and, to a much lesser extent, some of the physical char-

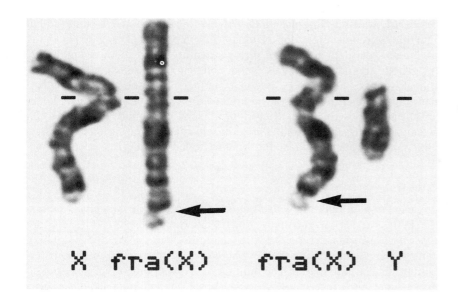

X  fra(X)     fra(X)  Y

**FIGURE 3.9**

**Chromosome Illustrating Fragile X Syndrome**

Fragile X syndrome is one of the most frequent known genetic causes of mental retardation. This photomicrograph illustrates the pinched or constricted portion of the X chromosome in an affected male and one of the pair of X chromosomes in a heterozygous female.

acteristics of the disorder. Most of these women are normal, although, as with other sex-linked gene disorders, they are carriers for the syndrome. In fact, the size of the abnormal segment of the chromosome, along with the severity of the disorder, appear to increase as it is passed from a grandfather, where the mutation first occurred (but who may show no evidence of the disorder), to daughter (who may be minimally affected), to grandson who now displays the disorder full-blown (Coplan, 1993).

▶ Individual differences

## *Genetic Counseling*

Advances in detecting gene and chromosomal defects as well as in understanding the biochemical and metabolic consequences of various inherited disorders have led to a rapidly expanding medical and guidance specialty called **genetic counseling.** Obtaining family histories revealing the occurrence of various diseases among ancestors and relatives is usually the first step. If warranted, parental **genetic screening** may be carried out. From the results of various tests, genetic counselors can provide prospective parents with estimates of the likelihood of bearing a child with a specific disorder. For example, screening can be completed for Tay-Sachs disease in Ashkenazic Jews, sickle cell trait among descendants of regions where malaria is prevalent, thalassemia for individuals of Mediterranean ancestry, and other disorders for which the family history indicates that one or both parents might be carriers. For many conditions, genetic counselors are able to go beyond providing estimates. Through a variety of prenatal tests, they can determine if a particular fetus has a chromosomal abnormality or one of many other kinds of genetic defects.

Prospective parents may wish to consult genetic counselors for a variety of reasons. The National Genetics Foundation indicates that genetic counseling

**genetic counseling** Medical and counseling specialty concerned with determining and communicating the likelihood that prospective parents will give birth to a baby with a genetic disorder.

**genetic screening** Systematic search for certain genotypes using a variety of tests to detect individuals at risk for developing genetic anomalies, bearing offspring with potential chromosome or gene defects, or having genetic susceptibility to environmental agents.

is particularly warranted when a history of disorders is found in a family and in certain other circumstances, for example, when a pattern of previous birth defects, mental retardation, unusual physical features, and medical conditions with a genetic component, such as cancer and heart disease, are found to exist (National Genetics Foundation, 1987). Assurance about the absence of a particular genetic concern is always the preferred message from a genetic counselor, but if the possibility of a hereditary disorder is found, counselors can help couples understand the likelihood of and reasons for various outcomes and the options available in deciding whether to have children.

### Prenatal Screening

If couples at risk for children with a genetic disease elect to conceive, prenatal tests may be carried out for many genetic disorders. These tests, including *amniocentesis, chorionic villus sampling*, and others, are discussed in detail in Chapter 4. They can provide answers about whether specific conditions are present or absent in the fetus. The number of disorders for which prenatal diagnosis is possible is increasing at a remarkable rate and today stands at over two hundred.

Technical advances in genetic screening have provided many benefits to couples. Parents are often reassured that their child will not develop some potential condition. But advances in genetic testing have also led to a number of questions. For example, should screening be mandatory when procedures are available and treatments exist to help alleviate or minimize the impact of some condition? If screening procedures become more widespread, should added counseling resources be provided to deal with the potentially devastating psychological effects of discovering that one is a carrier for a genetic disease? Who would have access to the results of such tests? For example, should insurance companies be allowed to obtain such information? Should such tests be carried out solely to determine the sex of the baby? These are just a few of the many legal and ethical issues that have surfaced in this rapidly advancing field.

---

### CONTROVERSY: THINKING IT OVER

#### *When Is a Parent a Parent?*

Recent advances in the field of genetics and reproductive technology have revolutionized human conception and childbearing along with our traditional notions about definitions of parenthood. Couples at risk for bearing children with a genetic disease or those among the one in six estimated to be unable to have children now can explore many options, in addition to adoption, in their efforts to become parents. Each new alternative brings hope to many couples but raises a tangle of ethical and legal issues as well.

If a male carries a genetic disorder or is infertile, couples may elect *artificial insemination by donor.* In this procedure, a donor, usually anonymous and often selected because of his similarity in physical and other characteristics to a prospective father, contributes sperm that are then artificially provided to the mother when ovulation occurs. Some six thousand to ten thousand children are thought to be conceived by this means every year in the United States (Curie-Cohen, Luttrell, & Shapiro, 1979).

There is little information about how donors are chosen and screened or how they subsequently feel about being the possible biological father to an unknown number of children. Donors in rural areas have voiced concerns that their known children might inadvertently marry and bear offspring with unknown half-siblings (Baran & Pannor, 1989). In addition, whereas adopted children are often informed that they have been adopted, children born via artificial insemination are seldom aware that their legal and biological fathers are not the same person. Even if they are told, however, these children would typically be unable to obtain further information since the approximately thirty sperm banks currently operating in the United States rarely make their records public (Baran & Pannor, 1989).

If a female is the carrier of a genetic disease or is infertile, options include *surrogate motherhood* and *in vitro fertilization*. Surrogate motherhood has sometimes been termed the "renting" of another woman's womb, but this concept is a bit misleading in many cases since the surrogate mother often donates an egg for prenatal development as well as her womb. The surrogate is thus the biological mother as well as bearer of the child who has been conceived by artificial insemination using the prospective father's sperm (Holbrook, 1990). For in vitro fertilization, eggs are removed from a woman's ovaries, fertilized in a laboratory dish with the prospective father's sperm, then transferred to another woman's uterus. In this situation, biological and social mother may be one and the same except during the gestational period when a surrogate mother's womb is used. Alternatively, a woman who cannot conceive normally might undergo in vitro fertilization and carry her own or another woman's fertilized egg during her pregnancy.

Legal, medical, and social controversy swirl around both surrogate motherhood and in vitro fertilization (Kermani, 1992; Knoppers & LeBris, 1991; Macklin & Delaney, 1991; Shore, 1992). Legal debates center on who is the rightful father or mother. In one highly publicized case in the United States involving Baby M, a woman was impregnated by artificial insemination by a man whose wife was afflicted by multiple sclerosis. According to a contract, the surrogate mother was to receive $10,000 for carrying the child. At birth, she would then surrender the child to the couple for adoption. After delivery, however, she refused to relinquish custody of the child. Who should be the legal parent? In the Baby M case, the court ruled against the surrogate mother. In another recent case in California, the court ruled that a baby conceived from a woman's egg and her husband's sperm via in vitro fertilization and carried to term by another woman should be reared by the genetic couple rather than the surrogate mother. Yet the debate surrounding these and similar cases continues as judicial systems try to resolve who is the legal parent: the genetic, the gestational, or the caregiving or social mother.

Other controversies surround the costly medical procedures and complicated ethical and social issues associated with in vitro fertilization and surrogate motherhood. For example, perhaps as many as two hundred clinics in the United States and many more in other countries, often operating as commercial businesses, provide in vitro fertilization services. But perhaps less than 20 percent of their attempts result in live births. Should medical insurance pay the high costs associated with these attempts (Holbrook, 1990)? Will these

In vitro fertilization is one of several new reproductive technologies that has emerged to assist men and women in their attempts to have healthy offspring. In this method, an egg cell is surgically removed from the woman's ovary to permit it to be fertilized by a sperm cell. After cell division begins to take place, the zygote is inserted in the woman's uterus where it can implant and continue to grow. This procedure can be used to bring about pregnancy when one of the partners has a fertility problem. Prior to its insertion in the uterus, individual cells also can be tested to determine whether the zygote carries a hereditary defect.

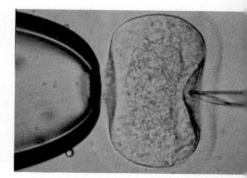

new technologies lead to increased pressures to use genetic engineering to ensure only healthy offspring?

The desire to have their own children is a powerful motive for most couples. New advances in reproductive technology will help many to reach that goal, yet they cause dilemmas that many nations have not fully resolved. ∎

## Developmental and Behavioral Genetics

As our previous discussion indicates, chromosomal errors and particular genes can have drastic, often devastating, effects on physical, intellectual, and social development. Yet the similarities observed among relatives—the quick tempers of two brothers; the wry sense of humor in a mother and daughter; the musical talent of a grandfather and his grandchildren; and for Jeremy's mother, her son's shy, reserved personality, so reminiscent of her own childhood—are not likely to have been influenced by a single, isolated gene. Might these attributes and behaviors reflect a hereditary contribution involving *many* genes? Or are these phenotypic resemblances the result of experiences shared by kin?

▶ Roles of nature and nurture

Many attributes and behaviors are undoubtedly influenced by polygenic relationships. **Behavior geneticists** are researchers concerned with learning to what extent the diversity of traits, abilities, and behaviors exhibited by individuals is influenced by combinations of genes versus experience. This focus on assessing the hereditary and experiential basis of individual differences distinguishes behavior geneticists from ethologists, who are interested in understanding the adaptive value of activities such as attachment and aggression that have biologically evolved and are universally shared by members of the same species.

▶ Individual differences

### The Methods of Behavioral Geneticists

Working with animals such as the fruit fly or mouse, behavior geneticists often use *selective breeding* experiments to learn whether certain phenotypic expressions can be increased or decreased in offspring. In this procedure, members of a species that display a specific attribute are bred to each other, usually over many generations. If the attribute is inherited, subsequent generations of offspring can be expected to display it more and more frequently or strongly. For example, after thirty generations of selective breeding in which mice displaying a high level of activity were bred only to each other as were mice showing only a low level of activity, researchers were able to observe no overlap in terms of the amount of activity displayed by the two groups of mice (DeFries, Gervais, & Thomas, 1978). Those bred for high activity, compared to those bred for low, were thirty times more active. Whereas the high-activity mice would run the equivalent of a football field during two three-minute test periods, the low-activity mice would not even run the equivalent of a first down (Plomin, 1986).

**behavior genetics** Study of how characteristics and behaviors of individuals such as intelligence and personality are influenced by the interaction between genotype and experience.

Selective breeding in mice, rats, chickens, and other species of animals has revealed genetic contributions to many different attributes, including aggressiveness, emotionality, maze learning, and sex drive (Plomin, DeFries, & Mc-Clearn, 1990). But selective breeding, of course, cannot be used to study hu-

**identical twins** Two individuals who originate from a single zygote (one egg fertilized by one sperm), which early in cell division separates to form two separate cell masses. Such twins have an identical genetic makeup. Also called *monozygotic twins*.

man behavior. Instead, behavior geneticists gain information about hereditary and environmental influences on humans by examining resemblances among family members. These studies investigate similarities among *identical* and *fraternal* twins, siblings, and other members of families who are genetically different from one another to varying degrees.

**Identical**, or **monozygotic**, **twins** come from the same zygote: a single egg fertilized by a single sperm. A cell division takes place early in development that creates two separate embryos from this zygote, and the twins are genetically identical. **Fraternal**, or **dizygotic**, **twins** come from two different zygotes, each created from a separate egg and separate sperm. Although sharing the womb at the same time, fraternal twins are no more genetically similar than siblings born at different times, each averaging about half their genes in common.

If identical twins resemble each other more than fraternal twins in some way such as intelligence or shyness, one *potential* explanation for this similarity is their common genotype. The degree of resemblance is usually estimated from one of two statistical measures: concordance rate or correlation coefficient. The **concordance rate** is the percentage of pairs of twins in which both members have a specific attribute when one of the twins is identified as having that attribute. It is used when measuring attributes that are either present or absent, such as schizophrenia or depression. Should both members of every twin pair have a particular trait, the concordance rate would be 100 percent. If only one member of every pair of twins has some particular trait, the concordance rate would be 0 percent.

When attributes vary on a continuous scale so that they can be measured in terms of amount or degree, resemblances are estimated from a *correlation coefficient.* This statistic helps to determine whether variables such as intelligence or shyness, which are measured in some quantifiable way from lower to higher, are more similar for identical than for fraternal twins or more similar among siblings than among unrelated children. A positive correlation exists when both members of a pair of twins typically score at similar levels on an intelligence test. A negative correlation is found when one member of the pair of twins tends to score high, but the other low. Uncorrelated attributes show no relationship to one another. In this case, one twin may score high, but this information does not help us to anticipate how high the other member of the pair is likely to score.

Identical twins may resemble one another more than fraternal twins because identical twins share the same genotype. However, another explanation for any greater resemblance may be that identical twins share more similar experiences. Although some behavior geneticists do not feel the similarity of twins' experiences represents a major problem in twin research (Plomin, De-Fries, & McClearn, 1990), one way to reduce its effects is to study biologically related family members who have been adopted or reared apart from one another in very different environments. If an attribute is greatly influenced by genetic factors, children should still resemble their biological siblings, parents, or other family members more than their adoptive relatives. On the other hand, if the environment is the primary determinant of an attribute, separated children might be expected to resemble their adoptive parents or other adopted siblings more closely than their biological parents or siblings.

Adoption studies pose many challenges for evaluating hereditary and environmental influences because children are often placed in homes similar to those of their biological parents. As a consequence, the contributions of family

These identical twins have already anticipated a question that they probably are asked often. Because their genetic makeup is the same, identical or monozygotic twins typically look very much alike and display very similar traits and behaviors. The study of such twins provides important information about the contributions of heredity and environment to development.

**fraternal twins**   Siblings sharing the same womb at the same time but who originate from two different eggs fertilized by two different sperm cells. Also called *dizygotic twins.*

**concordance rate**   Percentage of pairs of twins in which both members have a specific trait identified in one of the twins.

environment and heredity to an attribute become extremely difficult to tease apart. In addition, information on the biological family may not be readily available in the case of adoption. Because of these kinds of difficulties, major family resemblance projects investigating genotype-environment interactions often combine family, twin, and adoption methods. The Colorado Adoption Project, for example, has been conducting longitudinal research on resemblances between (1) parents and their natural children, (2) adoptive parents and their adopted children, and (3) parents and their biological children who have been adopted into other homes (Loehlin, Horn, & Willerman, 1990). The Minnesota Study of Twins Reared Apart has assessed a variety of psychological and physiological characteristics exhibited by identical and fraternal twins reared together or twins reared apart and having virtually no contact with each other prior to adulthood (Bouchard et al., 1990). These and other longitudinal studies have provided us with valuable information on the genetic and experiential contributions to family resemblance.

▶ Roles of nature and nurture

## Conceptualizing the Interaction Between Genotype and Environment

Historically, the roles of genotype and environment in fostering behavior and its development have often been described in one of two uncompromising forms: behavior is completely determined by the genes, or behavior is completely determined by the environment. Neither of these extreme positions, of course, is advocated today. Instead, researchers often propose an interaction between the two. But what is the nature of this interaction?

### Genotype-Environment Interaction and the Range of Reaction

How a genotype influences development may depend to a great extent on the environment. Similarly, how an environment affects behavior often depends on the genotype. These conditional relationships mark complex *interactions* between genotype and environment; the influence of one upon the other is not constant. Consider the repercussions of inheriting the single-gene condition phenylketonuria (PKU), discussed earlier in the chapter. For persons bearing this genotype, normal intellectual development depends on an environment, in this case a diet, in which protein, more specifically, phenylalanine, is minimized. In contrast, intellectual development for someone without PKU will be largely unaffected, or may possibly even be improved, by the presence of substantial protein in the diet.

▶ Individual differences

Can this same concept of interaction between a single-gene condition and the environment be extended to polygenic factors and experience? It certainly seems possible. For example, some children appear to succeed under rearing conditions to which many other children are highly vulnerable. Large numbers of children are members of families who encounter severe forms of stress; they may live in poverty, a parent may commit crimes or be mentally ill, or the family may be dysfunctional for other reasons. Nevertheless, some of these children display enormous resilience in adapting to such stresses. They will demonstrate extraordinary personal and intellectual achievements, and be socially far above the norm for children reared in such contexts (Garmezy, 1985; Rutter, 1987; Werner & Smith, 1982). An uncommon array of family, community, and other experiential factors, as yet not fully understood, may promote these competencies (Rhodes & Brown, 1991). But some of these suc-

▶ The child's active role

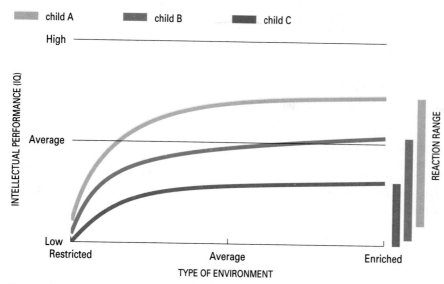

Source: Gottesman, 1963 and Turkheimer & Gottesman, 1991.

FIGURE 3.10

**The Concept of Range of Reaction for Intellectual Performance**

As the product of the interaction between genotype and the environment, the phenotype for any attribute shows a typical range of reaction. For example, the intelligence score of every child, even one who is born with a genotype that will likely lead to mental retardation, will be higher when the environment is optimal for intellectual development. The range of reaction may be greater for some children than for others. For example, all children may show significant intellectual retardation in a severely restricted environment. Although all children will benefit from an enriched environment, the extent to which these benefits are evident in the phenotype will depend on the genotype.

cessful children may also have inherited a combination of genetic qualities that empower them to rise above the environmental circumstances so debilitating to many other children.

The interactive relationship between genotype and environment is emphasized by the concept of **range of reaction**, the notion that, depending on environmental conditions, a phenotype is expressed within broad limits established by the genotype (Platt & Sanislow, 1988). This concept is illustrated in Figure 3.10 for intellectual performance. Think about children with Down syndrome (represented by Child C in Figure 3.10) who are intellectually limited by their genotype. Moving such children from unstimulating institutional settings and engaging them in supportive learning activities helps many to achieve much higher levels of cognitive functioning than is possible when they remain in institutions (Feuerstein, Rand, & Rynders, 1988). However, we *currently* do not know of any environment that will promote in the child born with Down syndrome a level of intelligence routinely exhibited by many children with a normal complement of chromosomes. The performance of children with other genotypes that permit them to reach average or even high intellectual levels (as represented by Child B and A) can be enormously affected too, depending on whether they are reared in stimulating or deprived conditions.

We need to be cautious, however, in thinking about the concept of range of reaction for it reflects only what we presently know about the ways genotype and environment interact (Turkheimer & Gottesman, 1991). For example, at one point, we might have suggested that the potential range of cognitive abilities of children with PKU are like those characterized by Child C. But through a change in their diet, the range of reaction begins to look more like that depicted for Child B or even A. New knowledge and advances in our understanding, particularly of the complex, multidirectional influences that we call environment, may drastically modify the range that is often associated with a genotype in the expression of specific kinds of behaviors (Platt & Sanislow, 1988).

**range of reaction** Range of phenotypic differences possible as a result of different environments interacting with a specific genotype. Also called *norm of reaction.*

▶ Individual differences

**Canalization**    The principle of **canalization**, or a kind of "channeling" of development, suggests yet another way of thinking about genotype-environment relationships. This principle helps to shed light on the emergence of behaviors common to all members of a species as well as on the development of individual differences. As originally proposed by the geneticist Conrad Waddington (1971), a highly canalized attribute is one primarily influenced by the genotype; experiential factors can have an impact on the course of development but only under extreme conditions. Imagine an emerging capacity as a flowing stream or river seeking its course over terrain in which channels of varying depth have been cut. The terrain helps to steer the flow in one of several directions. However, channels are so deeply cut by the genotype for some phenotypes that only extreme environmental pressures can change their course.

In this regard, many aspects of early motor behavior emerge on a fairly regular basis during infancy, and presumably the genotype has carved a relatively deep course for them. However, the emergence of various early motor skills is not completely protected from disturbances in experience (see Chapter 5). Other aspects of early development, including the onset of babbling and such important components of social responsivity as smiling at interesting events, may also be highly canalized.

Recently, Gilbert Gottlieb (1991) has overturned these ideas about canalization, proposing that the channeling of development may come about not only through the genotype, but from early experiential influences as well. Thus, exposure to certain types of critical stimulation may steer development just as can hereditary information. As an example, Gottlieb cites research on mallard ducklings which, if prevented from hearing their own vocalizations and only exposed to a chicken call early in development, later show preferences for the chicken call rather than for sounds produced by members of their own species.

Some attributes and behaviors may be highly canalized early in development but become less so with increasing age. Robert McCall (1981) suggests this is true for intellectual development. Early mental abilities, he believes, are primarily organized by the genotype, and only relatively extreme conditions are likely to change their initial expression. With development, however, intellectual abilities become less heavily influenced by the genotype. From his perspective, the landscape characterizing the interactive relationship between genotype and environment does not remain constant but, in fact, changes throughout development.

▶ Roles of nature and nurture

## Conceptualizing the Correlation Between Genotype and Environment

Although behavioral geneticists attempt to determine what portion of various traits such as activity level, sociability, or intelligence derives from the genes and what portion comes from the environment, the task is laden with problems. Not only do genotype and environment interact, they also are linked or *correlated* with each other in several complex ways (Plomin, DeFries, & Loehlin, 1977; Scarr, 1992; Scarr & McCartney, 1983).

**canalization**  Concept that the development of some attributes is governed primarily by the genotype and that only extreme environmental conditions will alter the phenotypic pattern for these attributes.

**Passive Links**    One correlation between genotype and experience arises from the tendency for parents to establish a child-rearing environment in harmony with their own interests and preferences. Assume, for example, that sociability has some genetic basis. Sociable parents may transmit this orientation to their children either through their genes, through the social environment created in their home, or through an intertwining of both mechanisms.

This kind of correlation between genotype and environment is labeled as *passive* since it has been created for the child by the parents. Jeremy and Cindy might have been influenced by this passive correlation. Jeremy's mother stayed home with him during his first three years of life. Thus, while Jeremy was young, his mother, who was shy, had the opportunity to structure her household and interactions in ways that met her needs, and Jeremy had considerable opportunity to experience the kind of environment his mother preferred. But soon after Cindy was born, her mother returned to work. Cindy spent much more of her infancy and toddler years with a day-care provider who was much more outgoing and sociable. Because for these two siblings both genotype and early environment may have been different, we cannot easily separate their contributions to later social development.

In most families the correlation between the genetic and environmental components of child rearing is likely to be positive—that is, the environment will contain features that support and complement the child's genetic potential. But a negative correlation between genotype and environment is also possible, as when a highly active child is adopted into a sedentary family or when parents elect to provide a rearing environment that departs from their own experience and genetic propensities. A parent who feels that he or she was too shy during childhood and, as a consequence, missed out on many social activities may actively initiate play groups and other activities designed to promote sociability in a child.

**Evocative Links**    Another type of correlation between the genotype and the environment, termed *evocative* or *reactive*, occurs when elements in the environment, particularly other people, support or encourage individual differences that may have a genetic component. An active preschooler is likely to prompt teachers to make sure enough large-muscle toys are available to dissipate some of that energy. A sociable child is more likely to attract the attention of peers than a shy or passive child. Jeremy's preference for standing on the sidelines resulted in a tendency for other children in the preschool to ignore him; Cindy's gregariousness helped to ensure that she was often called on by others in her group. A ten-year-old's propensity for reading may encourage a teacher to offer additional academic exercises for learning. Thus, attributes that may have a biological basis are likely to evoke certain patterns of social interaction involving others, providing an environment complementary to the child's genetic proclivity.

**Active, Niche-picking Links**    In yet another type of correlation between genotype and environment, termed *active*, the child may eagerly seek out and be attracted to experiences more compatible with his or her genotype. Bright children may prefer to exercise their intellect and to play with peers who are also bright. The athletic child may find little pleasure in practicing the piano but spend countless hours skateboarding and playing basketball. Jeremy preferred to play by himself, Cindy to play with others. Any genetic basis for these traits and activities may, in turn, influence the kind of environment a child attempts to create and experience. Sandra Scarr and Kathleen McCartney (1983) describe this kind of linkage as **niche picking** to emphasize that

Niche picking, the tendency of a child to seek out and become attracted to activities that are compatible with her genotype, may be an important aspect of the interaction between nature and nurture. This child, intently focused on her sculpture project, may work hard to display early artistic talents, and as a result, gain continued recognition and much satisfaction from this activity.

▶ The child's active role

niche picking   Tendency to actively select an environment compatible with a genotype.

children and adults selectively construct and engage environments responsive to their genetic orientations.

Scarr and McCartney (1983; Scarr, 1992) believe that the impact of passive, evocative, and active correlations between genotype and environment change with development. Although infants may actively attend to some parts of their environment more than others, their experiences are often determined for them by their caregivers. Thus, initial correlations between genotype and environment are likely to be established by passive factors. As children gain greater independence and control of their environment, however, others around them may begin to notice and support their individual differences and niche picking becomes an increasingly greater factor as children choose their own interests and activities.

This analysis allows us to make another important prediction: under some circumstances, children within the same family will become less similar to each other as they grow older and move away from the common environment provided by their parents. In other words, siblings will select niches more fitting to their individual genotypes than the one their family may have first presented them. When Sandra Scarr and Richard Weinberg (1977) studied adopted children, they obtained support for this prediction. During early and middle childhood, adopted but biologically unrelated children showed similarities in intelligence, personality, and other traits. These resemblances may have come about from adoption procedures that tended to encourage the placement of children in homes somewhat like the child's biological home and from the family environment children shared when adopted into the same home. As adopted siblings neared the end of adolescence, however, they no longer exhibited similarities in intelligence, personality, or other traits. Scarr and Weinberg concluded the passive influence of the common environment established by the adoptive parents had been supplanted by active niche picking. Older siblings more and more effectively exposed themselves to environments that matched their own individual genotypes.

The notion of niche picking may provide us with an even more startling prediction. When identical twins are reared apart, they might in some ways, with increasing age, actually come to resemble each other as much as identical twins reared together! This greater correspondence could come about as others react to their similar behaviors and as opportunities arise for the twins to make more choices. In the Minnesota Study of Twins Reared Apart pairs of identical twins, separated as infants and having no interactions with one another until well into adulthood, revealed remarkable similarities, not only in gait, posture, gestures, and habits such as straightening glasses, but also storytelling skill, spontaneous giggling, phobic tendencies, hobbies and interests—resemblances rarely observed among fraternal twins reared apart and usually not considered to have a strong genetic basis (Bouchard, 1984; Bouchard et al., 1990; Lykken et al., 1992). Furthermore, identical twins reared apart showed as high a correlation on many intellectual tasks and personality variables as those reared together. These results suggest that niche picking could be a powerful means by which behaviors initiated by the genotype are maintained.

▶ Roles of nature and nurture

## Hereditary and Environmental Influences on Behavior

We have little reason to doubt that multiple genes, perhaps often with subtle effects, can influence intellectual and personality development, mental illness, and many other aspects of human behavior. As always, however, sifting through the genetic and environmental contributions to complex human traits and behaviors is an extremely difficult task. Research findings involving studies of family resemblances, adopted children, and identical and fraternal twins reared together and apart can be interpreted in many ways and those interpretations can sometimes have powerful implications for intervention and social policy (Baumrind, 1993; Jackson, 1993; Scarr, 1992; 1993). Should families or communities, for example, expend resources for educational and mental health efforts if there is a substantial biological basis for behavior? Or is this kind of question, concerned with *how much* heredity contributes to variations in the human phenotype, misguided in failing to recognize that educational and social opportunities are essential even where genetic contributions are considerable? Both genetic and experiential factors affect human traits and behaviors, and the more we can learn about *how* they do so, the more we will understand children and the most effective ways to enhance their development.

**Intelligence**    In Chapter 10 we discuss the limitations of using the intelligence quotient (IQ) as the primary symbol of intellectual ability. Unfortunately, most studies have relied on IQ to determine the contributions of genotype and environment to intelligence, and many of these studies suffer from methodological problems as well. Nevertheless, the findings of these studies overwhelmingly indicate that *both* environmental and genetic factors make important contributions to intelligence (Scarr, 1992).

Table 3.4 presents a summary of correlations on IQ test scores between pairs of late adolescents and adults who share different genetic relationships with one another. The contribution of environmental factors is revealed by findings, for example, that individuals who were reared together tend to show somewhat higher correlations for intelligence scores than those with the same genetic relationship who were reared apart. Nevertheless, a substantial role

**TABLE 3.4**

**IQ and Degrees of Relatedness: Similarities of Genetically Related and Unrelated Persons Who Live Together and Apart**

| Relationship | Correlation | Number of Pairs |
|---|---|---|
| **Genetically identical:** | | |
| Identical twins together | .86 | 1,300 |
| Identical twins apart | .76 | 137 |
| Same person tested twice | .87 | 456 |
| **Genetically related by half of the genes:** | | |
| Fraternal twins together | .55 | 8,600 |
| Biological sisters and brothers | .47 | 35,000 |
| Parents and children together | .40 | 4,400 |
| Parents and children apart | .31 | 345 |
| **Genetically unrelated:** | | |
| Adopted children together | .00 | 200 |
| Unrelated persons apart | .00 | 15,000 |

Source: Adapted from Plomin and DeFries (1980).
Note: Based on data from Scarr and Weinberg (1978) and Teasdale and Owen (1985) on older adolescents who are comparable in age to other samples in this table. Younger adopted children resemble each other to a greater degree, with correlations around .24, according to samples of 800 pairs.

for the genotype in intelligence is also evident. There is a pattern of increases in the correlation for IQs as similarity in genotype increases.

Scarr and McCartney's (1983; Scarr, 1992) analysis of developmental changes in patterns of genetic and environmental correlations helps make sense of several additional findings from research on family relatedness and intelligence. For example, IQ scores for younger adopted children reared together are positively correlated (about .24) rather than unrelated as Table 3.4 indicates for older individuals. Moreover, intelligence has been found to be highly correlated for *both* identical and fraternal twins during infancy and early childhood and with increasing age the correlations become even greater for identical twins, yet tend to decline to the level reported in Table 3.4 for fraternal twins (Fischbein, 1981; Wilson, 1978; 1983; 1986). These kinds of findings suggest a greater influence of passive factors (the similar rearing environment created by the parents) on intelligence early in childhood and more opportunity for niche picking later in development.

▶ The child's active role

Identical twins, however, do not always become more similar when they grow older. A recent meta-analysis of twin studies reveals that as twins who have been reared together become older, fraternal, and to some extent identical, twins become more dissimilar on many aspects of intelligence tests. In other words, even identical twins often grow apart as they become older (McCartney, Harris, & Bernieri, 1990) perhaps because they actively attempt to establish a *unique* niche in the family and community, efforts that may also be encouraged by parents of the twins (Schachter, 1982).

How significant is heredity for intellectual development? Assessments of **heritability**, the proportion of variability in the phenotype that can be accounted for by genetic influences, are typically estimated to be about 50 percent for intelligence (Plomin & Rende, 1991). In other words, about half of the variability in intelligence appears to be attributable to genetic factors and the remainder to environmental factors, at least among white American and European middle-class populations, the groups studied most thoroughly. However, a classic investigation carried out by Marie Skodak and Harold Skeels (1949) illustrates the substantial impact environmental influences can have even if intellectual development is highly influenced by hereditary factors. One hundred children born to retarded mothers, most of whom were from low socioeconomic backgrounds, were adopted before six months of age into homes that were economically and educationally well above average. These children displayed above average intelligence throughout their childhood and adolescent years and substantially higher IQs than their biological parents, an outcome reflecting the contribution of environmental factors. Despite their high levels, however, the children's IQs still were substantially correlated with those of their biological mothers, indicating a hereditary contribution to these scores as well.

More recent adoption studies have obtained similar findings (Dumaret, 1985; Horn, Loehlin, & Willerman, 1979; Scarr & Weinberg, 1983). IQ can undergo impressive boosts in some kinds of environments; nevertheless measures of intelligence for adopted children continue to be highly correlated with their biological parents, indicating a genetic contribution (Loehlin, Willerman, & Horn, 1988; Turkheimer, 1991). Moreover, other studies have revealed that certain cognitive abilities such as memory for where an object has been hidden, categorization, and word comprehension, in addition to overall IQ, are significantly influenced by hereditary as well as environmental factors in young children (Emde et al., 1992).

**heritability** Proportion of variability in the phenotype that is estimated to be accounted for by genetic influences.

**Temperament and Personality**    Many personality traits also reflect genetic influences, although their heritability may be less than for intelligence (Loehlin, Willerman, & Horn, 1988). Perhaps the most extensive research on this topic has been concerned with **temperament**, an early appearing constellation of personality traits theorized to have some genetic basis (Buss & Plomin, 1984; Rothbart & Derryberry, 1981; Thomas & Chess, 1977). Arnold Buss and Robert Plomin have identified three broad qualities frequently describing the temperaments of infants and very young children. One of these is *sociability,* the tendency to be shy or inhibited and somewhat fearful of new experiences versus outgoing and uninhibited, qualities that are likely precursors to introversion and extroversion in older children and adults. Another trait is *emotionality,* how easily an individual becomes distressed, upset, or angry, and how intensely these emotions are expressed. The third trait is *activity,* as evidenced by the tempo and vigor with which behaviors are performed.

Selective breeding studies with various species of animals indicate that sociability, emotionality, and activity level have a hereditary component; family resemblance and adoption studies in humans lead to the same conclusion. For example, identical twins consistently show higher correlations for sociability (typically between .40 and .60 on various measures) than fraternal twins (typically between .10 and .30) (Emde et al., 1992; Matheny, 1989; Plomin, 1987; Robinson et al., 1992). Inherited differences in physiological reactivity may underlie these variations in social responsiveness (Kagan, Snidman, & Arcus, 1992). Young children like Jeremy who remain aloof from strangers, including peers, and who are reluctant to begin to play with novel toys, display increased heart rate and muscle tension in unfamiliar situations compared with children like Cindy, who are more outgoing and spontaneous. However, adoption studies also suggest that the personality of parents can play some role in influencing sociability; for example, the shyness of adopted infants has been found to be somewhat related to the shyness of their adoptive parents (Plomin & DeFries, 1985).

Studies comparing infant twins on emotionality and activity also consistently reveal higher correlations for identical than for fraternal twins (Plomin, 1987). As with research on sociability, these studies have used various procedures to evaluate emotionality and activity: experimenter ratings and observations of infants as well as parent interviews and questionnaire ratings. Consistent racial and ethnic differences have been reported as well and have been attributed to genetic differences in temperament. When Daniel Freedman (1979) compared Caucasian and Chinese-American newborns, he found Caucasian babies were more irritable and harder to comfort than Chinese-American infants. As older infants, Chinese-American babies also tended to be more wary when confronted with novel or uncertain situations (Kagan, Kearsley, & Zelazo, 1978).

Does the environment play a significant role in temperament and personality differences? Parents of siblings sometimes think not and often comment on how different their children are, emphasizing how compliant, responsive, and cheerful one child might be and how stubborn, independent, and active another is. Furthermore, studies comparing the personalities of unrelated children in the same household report that the correlations are fairly low and often approach zero, especially in later childhood and adolescence (Plomin & Daniels, 1987).

Does this mean that such traits are really not influenced by the environment and only by heredity? Probably not, since family environments may promote

▶ Individual differences

temperament    Stable, early appearing constellation of individual personality attributes believed to have a hereditary basis; includes sociability, emotionality, and activity level.

▶ The child's active role

*differences* among individual children as well as similarities. Such differences are evident, for example, in the dissimilar ways caregivers often interact with boys and girls (see Chapter 13). But variations in personality also seem to be related to whether a child is first born or later born, tall or short, and other factors that are part of their position in the family and their physical and psychological make-up. Parents and other family members, even the broader community, may encourage different roles for individual children. Of course, children may also actively seek ways to be different, to "stand out" from their siblings and others (Schachter et al., 1976). In other words, environmental factors exist within families that both promote and discourage similarities in temperament and personality.

**Mental Illness**    Investigators are currently conducting intensive research on whether some forms of *manic depression*, a disorder characterized by rapid and large mood swings between feverish activity and withdrawn, depressed behaviors, is influenced by a single gene (Barinaga, 1989). However, some subtypes also may have a polygenic component. Family studies reveal children of a manic-depressive parent are at substantially greater risk for displaying the illness than children without such a parent. Research on twins and adoptees provides further evidence that genotype, not just the environment, plays a role in the transmission of manic depression. The concordance rate for identical twins for manic depression is far higher than for fraternal twins and nontwin siblings (Rosenthal, 1970). The data on adopted children reveal manic depression is about three times greater for adopted children whose biological parents have the illness than for adopted children whose biological parents do not have the illness (Knowles, 1985).

A form of psychopathology that has received even greater attention from researchers is *schizophrenia*, a disorder that includes disturbances in thoughts and emotions such as delusions and hallucinations. As the biological relationship to someone diagnosed as having schizophrenia increases, an individual's risk for the same diagnosis rises. In general, when one twin has schizophrenia, the other twin is about three times more likely to display schizophrenia if identical than if fraternal. Adoption studies provide further confirmation for a role of the genotype (Gottesman & Shields, 1982). Schizophrenia is far more prevalent among adopted children who are the biological offspring of a schizophrenic parent than of a nonschizophrenic parent. Although researchers continue to look for the contributions of a single gene, many feel a polygenic model, which claims schizophrenia is influenced by many genes, provides a better explanation for these findings.

An important point to remember about various forms of mental illness—and about all the other traits we are studying—is that none are 100 percent concordant even in identical twins, despite the similarity of their genetic make-up. Environmental factors are significant for the emergence of psychopathology as well as other forms of behavior. Whether children come to display mental illness is greatly influenced by the number and intensity of environmental stresses such as parental disharmony, poverty, and other dysfunctional living arrangements (Rutter, 1979).

**Other Characteristics**    A variety of other characteristics, including empathy, alcoholism, reading disabilities, inclinations to commit crimes, sexual orientation, susceptibility to various illnesses such as heart disease and cancer, even a propensity to watch television, have been identified as having a genetic linkage (DiLalla & Gottesman, 1991; Mange & Mange, 1990; Plomin,

TABLE 3.5

**The Genetic Basis of Selected Diseases: Twin Data**

Evidence for the genetic basis of diseases and other traits is often supported from comparisons involving the concordance rates observed in identical and fraternal twins. The numbers in parentheses indicate the number of pairs of twins studied.

| Trait | Concordance in Identical Twins | | Concordance in Fraternal Twins | |
|---|---|---|---|---|
| Schizophrenia | 34% | (203) | 12% | (222) |
| Tuberculosis | 37% | (135) | 15% | (513) |
| Manic-depressive psychosis | 67% | (15) | 5% | (40) |
| Hypertension | 25% | (80) | 7% | (212) |
| Mental deficiency | 67% | (18) | 0% | (49) |
| Rheumatic fever | 20% | (148) | 6% | (428) |
| Rheumatoid arthritis | 34% | (47) | 7% | (141) |
| Bronchial asthma | 47% | (64) | 24% | (192) |
| Epilepsy | 37% | (27) | 10% | (100) |
| Diabetes mellitus | 47% | (76) | 10% | (238) |
| Smoking habits (females only) | 83% | (53) | 50% | (18) |
| Cancer (at same site) | 7% | (207) | 3% | (767) |
| Cancer (at any site) | 16% | (207) | 13% | (212) |
| Death from acute infection | 8% | (127) | 9% | (454) |

Source: Adapted from Hartl, 1977.

Corley, DeFries, & Fulker, 1990; Vandenberg, Singer, & Pauls, 1986; Zahn-Waxler, Robinson, & Emde, 1991). For example, concordance rates for identical and fraternal twins for a variety of diseases are indicated in Table 3.5. The number of twins from whom data have been collected is sometimes small (shown in parentheses in Table 3.5) and it is not always possible to determine to what extent heredity and environment are responsible for the typically higher concordance rates in identical twins. But these data are helpful in making one final point. Remember, the genotype codes for proteins and enzymes that, in the context of a cellular environment, influence patterns of neural, hormonal, and brain activity. These, in turn, sustain the development of traits and behaviors in individuals. Identifying a genetic component in this multifaceted array of systems and settings provides knowledge about only one of many levels of influence. Understanding how the genotype along with the environment creates that influence remains a critical goal for unlocking the complex theme of nature and nurture in development.

## THEMES IN DEVELOPMENT

### GENETICS AND HEREDITY

▶ **What roles do nature and nurture play in development?**

As we have seen in this chapter, the phenotype, the observable behaviors and characteristics of an individual, is the product of a complex interaction between the genotype and the environment. Environment includes biological contexts, such as the foods we eat, but more frequently we consider nature and nurture within a framework of trying to understand how experiences provided by caregivers and others affect behavior and development. The relationship between genotype and environment is made more complicated by passive, reactive, and niche-picking correlations. As a consequence, experiential factors become tightly interwoven with the genotype to produce the range and variety of behaviors and characteristics displayed by an individual. Both are necessary; each is indispensable.

▶ **How does the child play an active role in the effects of heredity on development?**

Researchers have begun to recognize the child's active efforts to seek out environments that support and maintain behavioral orientations and preferences that are influenced by hereditary factors. As the child achieves greater control over the environment, he or she has increasing opportunities to find a niche. In other words, behaviors, activities, and skills displayed by the child are not only a consequence of imposed social and physical experiences, but also reflect the selective efforts of the child to discover environments that are interesting, challenging, and supportive. Inherited and environmentally imposed influences may be met with eager support or active resistance to determine each child's unique life history.

▶ **How prominent are individual differences in development?**

Individual differences are pervasive in intellectual, temperamental, and a host of other cognitive, social, and emotional aspects of development. Hereditary and environmental factors are the basis for these differences. A small number of variations in genes differentiate humans from other species of animals and alleles of genes contribute to the wide range of physical, cognitive, emotional, and social adaptations displayed by individuals. These individual differences are not solely produced by genes, but also by a rich medley of physical, social, and cultural contexts in which each individual matures. A distinctive combination of genes and experiences promotes the abundant diversity that can be observed in human abilities and behavior.

## *Summary*

**Principles of Hereditary Transmission**    The structures and principles of heredity must be examined at several different levels including: (1) the individual, (2) the cells making up the body of that individual, (3) the chromosomes located within the nucleus of those cells, (4) the genes comprising segments of each chromosome, and (5) the nucleotide pairs that form the biochemical building blocks for the genes. A central unit of hereditary information is the *gene*. Genes are segments of the twenty-three pairs of chromosomes that are made up of *deoxyribonucleic acid*, or *DNA*.

Variants of pairs of genes, or *alleles*, interact with each other in *dominant-recessive* and other relationships to establish different patterns of inheritance for particular traits or characteristics. *Mitosis* is the process of cell division by which the chromosomes are duplicated in body cells. The *gametes*, or sex cells, are formed by *meiosis*, a process of cell division by which one member of each pair of chromosomes is randomly selected for each sperm or egg cell. This random process, combined with *crossing over*, ensures that every individual, with the exception of identical twins, has a unique hereditary blueprint.

Hereditary contributions to development begin at conception, when the twenty-three chromosomes in a sperm cell are added to the twenty-three chromosomes in the egg. Males and females differ in the composition of the twenty-third pair of chromosomes. For females, both members of the pair are X chromosomes. For males, one is an X and the other a Y chromosome. Gene disorders associated with this twenty-third pair of chromosomes are said to be *sex linked*.

**Gene and Chromosomal Abnormalities and Genetic Counseling**
A number of inherited abnormalities associated with chromosomes and alleles can lead to severe disruptions in physical and behavioral development. *Genetic counseling* provides prospective parents with information on the likelihood of having children affected by birth defects. Environmental influences in the form of treatment and remediation programs can counter the consequences of some of these genetic disorders.

**Behavioral and Developmental Genetics**   A *genotype* constitutes hereditary information and interacts with the environment in which development proceeds to determine the *phenotype*, that is, measurable characteristics, traits, or behaviors. The genotype may establish a range of possible outcomes for development. But the relative contribution of a particular genotype to a phenotype cannot be readily determined and may differ from one individual to the next as a function of environmental conditions. Understanding the genotype-environment interaction is made even more difficult by correlations between them. These include passive events, such as the creation of specific environments for offspring by caregivers with similar genotypes; reactive events such as siblings, peers, and others responding to genetic inclinations in accommodative ways; and active *niche picking* by children attempting to locate and create environments supportive of their individual genetic propensities.

Identifying to what degree and how genotype and environment contribute to development remains a major goal of *behavior genetics*. Most human attributes, whether simple physical traits or complex capacities, are *polygenic;* they are influenced by several genes. Behavior geneticists conduct studies of family members, including identical and fraternal twins, siblings, and adopted children, to demonstrate that both the genotype and the environment make important contributions to intelligence, temperament, personality characteristics, mental illness, and many other aspects of human behavior.

# 4

# The Prenatal Period and Birth

▶ **What roles do nature and nurture play in prenatal development and birth?**

▶ **How does the sociocultural context influence prenatal development and birth?**

▶ **Is development before and after birth continuous or discontinuous?**

▶ **How prominent are individual differences in prenatal development and the newborn?**

*It was a tough meeting. Her boss had not been enthusiastic about the new marketing plans. Carmen knew her ideas were a gamble too. Back in the tranquility of her office, Carmen's thoughts drifted to a more carefree time as a child in her small village in the Caribbean.*

*Then she felt it, the first unmistakable twitching, the fluttery motion of a tiny elbow or foot.*

*Shortly after the baby's conception, she had guessed that she was pregnant. Although she and her husband were thrilled when her hunch was confirmed, the first four months of pregnancy had been difficult. Morning sickness, Carmen's hectic schedule, and her mother's serious illness had left little time to enjoy or appreciate the remarkable time leading up to this first stirring. She had seen the ultrasound image just a few weeks earlier. But it was this distinctive movement within her womb that made it real. She was going to have a baby. Yet concern lurked at the edges of Carmen's exhilaration. She savored a glass of wine with dinner each evening; had she drunk too much? She had stopped smoking as soon as she had learned the news; had it been soon enough? And what about the pressures of this job?*

Nearly every woman likely experiences both pride and apprehension when she learns that she is going to have a baby. Whatever feelings they may have, women are affected by a multitude of social and cultural assumptions and ideas about pregnancy. Although societies differ enormously in their specific beliefs, anthropologists report expectant women around the world are urged to avoid certain activities and to carry out various rituals for the sake of their fetuses. In Western societies, admonitions about pregnancy exist as well; obstetricians may advise a pregnant woman to stop smoking, avoid alcohol, and let someone else clean the cat litter. Did Carmen, then, have good reason to be concerned about her baby?

Fortunately, some of the mysteries connected with this momentous time are beginning to be unraveled. The discussion of prenatal development starts with a brief description of the amazing sequence of events taking place between conception and birth. At no other time does growth proceed so rapidly or do so many physical changes occur in a matter of weeks, days, and even hours. Some cultures, such as the Chinese, tacitly recognize the dramatic events by crediting an infant with a year of life at birth. As we will soon learn, in the typical nine months of confinement to the womb, the fetus has indeed undergone an epic adventure.

Despite the concealed and highly protected setting in which first growth takes place, we are also beginning to fathom the way that drugs, diseases, and other external factors affect prenatal development. After summarizing our understanding of such influences, we briefly consider the birth process and take a first quick inspection of the newborn's states and features.

# The Stages of Prenatal Development

▶ Development as continuous/discontinuous

Three major overlapping periods serve to differentiate the life of the young human organism. **Prenatal development** proceeds from the moment of conception to the beginning of labor; all but the first few days are spent within the confines of the womb. The **perinatal period** begins about the seventh month of pregnancy and continues until twenty-eight days after birth. This period is associated with the impending birth, the social and physical setting for delivery, and the baby's first adjustments to her new world. Among the events included in the perinatal period are the medical and obstetrical practices associated with delivery and the preparations and care provided by parents and others to assist in the transition from the womb to life outside. **Postnatal development** begins after birth. The child's environment now includes the broader physical and social world afforded by caregivers and others responsible for his continued growth.

Prenatal development is divided into three stages. These are the **germinal period**, also known as the **period of the zygote** (from fertilization to the first ten to fourteen days after conception), the **embryonic period** (from about two to eight weeks after conception), and the **fetal period** (from about eight weeks after conception to birth). Movement, cell division, and implantation of the fertilized egg in the uterine wall characterize the germinal period. The formation of structures such as the nervous, circulatory, and respiratory systems and organs mark the embryonic period. In the fetal period, the body grows rapidly, and the organs and systems are refined in preparation for functioning outside the womb. This complex series of events begins the moment sperm and egg fuse.

**prenatal development** Period in development from conception to the onset of labor.

**perinatal period** Period beginning about the seventh month of pregnancy and continuing until about four weeks after birth.

**postnatal development** Period in development following birth.

**germinal period** Period lasting about ten to fourteen days following conception before the fertilized egg becomes implanted into the uterine wall. Also called *period of the zygote.*

**period of the zygote** *See* germinal period

**embryonic period** Period of prenatal development during which major biological organs and systems are formed. Begins at about the tenth to fourteenth day after conception when implantation occurs, and ends at about the eighth week after conception, with the onset of bone formation.

**fetal period** Period of prenatal development marked by relatively rapid growth of organs and preparation of body systems for functioning in postnatal environment. Begins about the eighth week after conception and ends at birth.

## Fertilization

Even before her own birth, the human female has formed approximately 5 million primitive egg cells in her ovaries. Their numbers, however, decline with development; by puberty perhaps only thirty thousand remain. Of this abundant supply, about four hundred will mature and be released for potential fertilization during the childbearing years (Samuels & Samuels, 1986). In contrast, male sperm production begins only at puberty when an incredible 100 million sperm (about a thousand per second) may be formed daily.

The opportunity for human conception begins at about the fourteenth day after the start of the menstrual period. At this time a capsulelike *follicle* housing a primitive egg cell in one of the ovaries begins to mature. As it matures, the follicle moves, eventually ruptures, and discharges its valuable contents from the ovary. The expelled egg cell, or *ovum,* is carried into and begins its journey through the Fallopian tube. This organ serves as a conduit as the egg moves toward the uterus at the leisurely rate of about one-sixteenth inch per

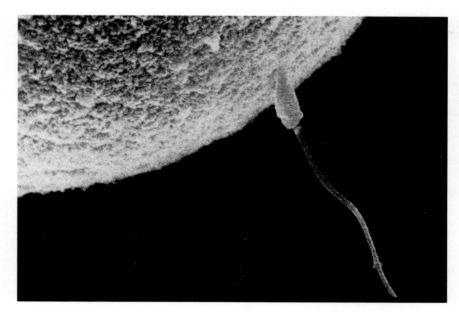

Human development begins with the penetration of the egg by a single sperm, as shown here (egg and sperm are magnified greatly). Although the egg is the body's largest cell and the sperm its smallest, each contributes 23 chromosomes to form the hereditary basis for the development of a new living entity.

hour and provides a receptive environment for fertilization if sperm are present (Abel, 1989). The unfertilized ovum, however, can survive for only about twenty-four hours.

Sperm reach the Fallopian tube by maneuvering from the vagina through the cervix and the uterus. Sperm can migrate several inches an hour with the assistance of their tail-like appendages. Fewer than one hundred may negotiate the six- or more hour trip into the Fallopian tube, but these typically survive about forty-eight hours and sometimes even longer.

If an ovum is present, sperm may become attracted to it (Roberts, 1991). The egg cell prepares for fertilization in the presence of sperm. Cells initially surrounding the ovum loosen their protective grip, permitting the egg to be penetrated by a sperm cell (Nilsson, 1990). As soon as one sperm cell passes through the egg's protective linings, enzymes rapidly transform the ovum's outer membrane to prevent others from penetrating. Genetic material from both cells soon mixes to establish a normal complement of forty-six chromosomes. The egg, the body's largest cell, barely visible to the naked eye, weighs about 100,000 times more than the sperm, the body's smallest cell. Despite the enormous difference in their sizes, both contribute an equal amount of genetic material to form a new entity.

## The Germinal Period

The fertilized egg cell, called a *zygote*, continues to migrate down the Fallopian tube (see Figure 4.1). Within twenty-four to thirty hours after conception the zygote divides into two cells, the first of a series of mitotic divisions called *cleavages*. At roughly twelve-hour intervals these cells divide again to form four, then eight, then sixteen cells. During the cleavages the zygote remains about the same size; thus, individual cells become smaller and smaller.

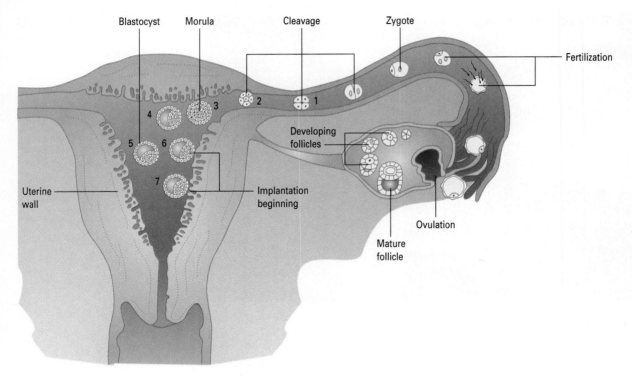

**FIGURE 4.1**

**Fertilization and the Germinal Period**

Source: Adapted from Moore, 1988.

During the early development of the human embryo, an egg cell is released from a maturing follicle within the ovary and fertilization takes place in the Fallopian tube, transforming the egg cell or ovum into a zygote. Cleavage and multiplication of cells proceed as the zygote migrates toward the uterus. Differentiation of the zygote begins within the uterus, becoming a solid 16-cell sphere known as the morula, then a differentiated set of cells known as the blastocyst, which prepares for implantation in the uterine wall. Once implanted, it taps a vital source of nutriments to sustain further development. (The numbers indicate days following fertilization.)

After three days, about the time the migrating zygote is ready to enter the uterus, it has become a solid sphere of sixteen cells called a *morula*. These cells are alike in their capacity to generate a separate identical organism; all contain and have access to the master genetic blueprint. By the fourth day after conception, however, cells begin to segregate in order to carry out specific functions. One group constructs a spherical outer cellular layer that eventually forms various membranes that provide nutritive support for the embryo (Moore, 1989). A second, inner group of cells organizes to form a mass that will develop into the embryo. This differentiated group of cells is now called a *blastocyst*.

About the sixth day after conception, the blastocyst begins the process of attaching to the uterine wall to tap a critical new supply of nutriments. By about the tenth to fourteenth day after conception the implantation process is completed. In preparing for this event, the blastocyst began secreting hormones and other substances to inhibit menstruation, or the shedding of the uterine lining, and to keep the woman's immune system from rejecting the foreign object. One hormone eventually becomes detectable in the woman's urine as a marker in a common pregnancy test.

## The Embryonic Period

The embryonic period, beginning with implantation of the blastocyst in the uterine wall and continuing until about the eighth week after conception, is marked by the rapid differentiation of embryonic cells to form most of the organs and systems within the body. Differentiation is achieved by the migration and production of specialized cells having distinctive functions.

### Formation of Body Organs and Systems

The first step in the formation of various body organs and systems involves the migration of unspecialized embryonic cells to establish a three-layered embryo (Abel, 1989). The three layers serve as the foundation for all tissues and organs in the body. The *endoderm,* or inner layer, will give rise to many of the linings of internal organs such as lungs, the gastrointestinal tract, liver, pancreas, bladder, and some glands. The *mesoderm,* or middle layer, will eventually develop into skeleton and muscles, the urogenital system, the lymph and cardiovascular systems, and other connective tissues. The *ectoderm,* or outer layer, will form skin, hair, and nails, but its earliest derivatives will be the central nervous system and nerves.

How, by simply migrating to a layered configuration, do undifferentiated cells come to establish highly distinctive sets of organs and systems? The immediate environment appears to play a major role. Although at first unspecialized, a cell's potential or fate becomes constrained by its association with neighboring tissues. In other words, cells are induced by their surroundings to take on certain forms and functions. For example, if cells from the ectodermal layer are removed and placed in a culture so that they grow in isolation from other cell layers, they form epidermal, or skinlike, tissues. If placed with a layer of mesodermal cells, however, a nervous system will emerge. The mechanisms inducing such differentiation remain unknown, but biochemical substances are likely to be involved in the influence of the immediate environment on cellular growth (Abel, 1989).

▶ Roles of nature and nurture

Because the embryonic period is the major time for development of organs and systems, many possibilities exist for disruption. We will see some examples later as we discuss the influence of environmental factors on the embryo. Under normal conditions, however, the sequence of primary changes in prenatal development during the embryonic and fetal periods proceeds in a fairly regular pattern. Some of the changes are summarized in the Chronology on page 122.

### Early Brain and Nervous System Development

About the fifteenth day after conception, a small group of cells at one end of the ectoderm begins growing rapidly. The growth creates a reference point for the cephalo (head) and the caudal (tail) end of the embryo and helps to distinguish left from right side. The cells induce the development of the *neural tube,* which in turn initiates the formation of the spinal cord, nerves, and eventually the brain.

Rapid changes in the region of the neural tube begin about the fourth week. At first, the neural tube is open at both ends. The tube begins closing in the brain region and a few days later in the caudal region. Failure to knit shut at either end can have drastic consequences for development. In *anencephaly,* a condition that results when the cephalic region of the neural tube does not close, the cerebral hemispheres do not develop and most of the cortex is missing at birth. Newborns with such a condition survive only a short time. *Spina bifida* is a condition that arises when the caudal region of the neural tube fails to close. The resulting cleft in the vertebral column permits spinal nerves to grow outside the protective vertebrae. In more serious cases the infant may be paralyzed and lack sensation in the legs. Surgery often must be performed after birth to keep the condition from getting worse, but lost capacities cannot be restored, and malformations in brain development and impaired intellectual development often accompany spina bifida (Abel, 1989; Wills, 1993). The frequency of both neural tube defects, now about six in every ten thousand births, has declined sharply over the last twenty years in the United States, especially for anencephaly. A better understanding of nutritional needs early in pregnancy, particularly of folic acid and other components of the vitamin B complex, appears to be one important explanation for the change (Yen et al., 1992).

The second month after conception is marked by continued rapid development of the head and brain. Nerve cells show an explosive increase in number, with as many as 100,000 neurons generated every minute (Nilsson, 1990). Neurons also undergo extensive migration once the neural tube closes and soon begin to make contact with one another. The head greatly enlarges, relative to the rest of the embryo, to account for about half of total body length. Nevertheless, the embryo is still tiny: it is less than one-and-a-half inches long and weighs only about half an ounce. However, nearly all organs are established by this time and the embryo is recognizably human.

One of the most striking milestones is reached in about the fifth week after conception, when the nervous system begins to function. Now irregular and faint brain wave activity can be recorded. Soon, if the head or upper body is touched, the embryo exhibits reflex movements. In a few more weeks muscles may also flex, but it will still be some time before the woman is able to feel any movement.

## The Fetal Period

The transition signaling the change from embryo to fetus is the emergence of bone tissue in about the eighth week after conception. Organ differentiation continues, particularly in the reproductive system and the brain, but the fetal period is dedicated primarily to growth in size and the addition of finishing touches to assist various organs and systems to function. One positive consequence is that the fetus becomes much less susceptible to potentially damaging environmental factors.

During the third month after conception, the fetus increases to about three-and-a-half inches in length and about one-and-a-half ounces in weight. Its movements become more pronounced. At nine weeks, the fetus opens and closes its lips, wrinkles its forehead, raises and lowers its eyebrows, and turns its head. By the end of twelve weeks the behaviors have become more coordinated; the fetus can, for example, display sucking and the basic motions of breathing and swallowing. Its fingers will bend if the arm is touched, and the thumb can be opposed to fingers, an indication that peripheral muscles and nerves are functioning in increasingly sophisticated ways (Samuels & Samuels, 1986).

**The Second Trimester**   By the end of the third month, the fetus has completed the first of three trimesters of prenatal development. In the second trimester, the human body grows more rapidly than at any other time. By the end of the fourth month, the fetus is about eight to ten inches long, although it still weighs only about six ounces. During the sixth month, the fetus rapidly starts to gain weight, growing to about one-and-a-half pounds while reaching a length of about fourteen inches.

By the middle of the second trimester, fetal movements such as those felt by Carmen, commonly identified as *quickening*, are unmistakable to the woman. Activities such as stretching and squirming are exhibited as well. Near the end of this trimester, brain wave patterns begin to look like those observed in the newborn. Should birth occur at this time, there is a small chance of survival if specialized medical facilities are available. Although a baby born at this stage can breathe regularly for a number of hours, the surfaces of air sacs in the lungs tend to stick together, interfering with the transfer of oxygen and carbon dioxide, unless production of a substance that prevents the problem has begun.

**The Third Trimester**   The final months of prenatal development add finishing touches to the astonishing progression. The cerebral hemispheres, the parts of the brain most responsible for complex mental processes, grow rapidly, folding and developing fissures to give them a wrinkled appearance. Myelin, which helps insulate and speed the transmission of neuronal impulses, begins to form and surround some nerve fibers. Brain wave patterns indicating different stages of sleep and wakefulness can also be observed. The sense organs are developed sufficiently to enable the fetus to respond to smell and taste as well as to auditory, visual, and tactile stimulation; learning also appears to be possible. The fetus continues to gain weight rapidly (nearly half a pound per week), although growth slows in the weeks just preceding birth. Control of body temperature and rhythmic respiratory activity remain problematic if birth occurs at the beginning of the third trimester. Nevertheless, **viability**, or the ability of the fetus to survive outside the womb, shows dramatic improvement over the course of these three months.

Birth of a Caucasian baby can be expected about 269 to 274 days after conception; there is evidence that the gestation time may be a few days shorter for Japanese and black babies (Mittendorf et al., 1990). Within the medical profession the common reference for prenatal development is **gestational age**, which is based on the date of onset of the woman's last menstrual period before conception. This method of calculating age makes the embryo or fetus fourteen days older than when age is calculated from the date of conception. But regardless of the method used to determine age, the events that began at conception and continued throughout prenatal development equip the fetus to adapt to perinatal and postnatal events.

▶ Individual differences

viability   Ability of the baby to survive outside the mother's womb.

gestational age   Age of fetus derived from onset of mother's last menstrual period.

### 3 WEEKS*

Precursors to vertebrae begin to organize.
Blood vessels form and connect to precursor of umbilical cord.
Blood vessels and tubes establish primitive, one-chambered heart that starts to beat by 21st day.
Major segments of brain begin to differentiate.
Embryo grows to about 2 millimeters in length (about 1/10 inch).

### 4 WEEKS

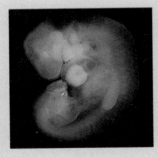

Disc-shaped embryo forms more cylindrical appearance as it folds on cephalo and caudal ends and on right and left side.
Thickening stripe of tissue develops on either side of trunk to begin chest and stomach muscle production. Swelling occurs near upper end of stripe to form arm buds by about day 26. Two days later similar swellings begin at caudal end of stripe to form early buds for lower limbs.
Rudimentary liver, gall bladder, stomach, intestines, pancreas, thyroid, and lungs created.
Nerves begin to form.
Embryo grows to about 6 millimeters (about 1/4 inch) and appears to have tail-like cartilage curving under rump.

### 5 WEEKS

Basic mouth and esophagus develop.
Elbow, wrist regions, and paddle-shaped plate with ridges for future fingers take shape.
Heart differentiates into upper and lower regions.
Embryo grows rapidly, about 1 millimeter a day (.04 inches), but is still less than 1/2 inch in length.

### 6–7 WEEKS

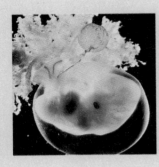

Upper lip, jaws, teeth, eyelids, nostrils, tip of nose, and tongue are formed as head size becomes dominant.
Embryo possesses short, webbed fingers, and foot plate has also begun to differentiate.
Heart divides into four chambers.
Many muscles differentiate and take final shape.
Neurons form rapidly.
Tail-like cartilage regresses.
Embryo begins to show reflexive responses to touch, first around facial region.

### 8–12 WEEKS

Fetus appears to have widely separated eyes and ears set lower in head than they eventually will be.

Eyelids fuse shut about 9th week.

Fingernails, toenails, and hair follicles form.

Fetus begins to show differentiation of external reproductive organs (if male about 9th week, if female, several weeks later).

Bones start to grow.

Startle and sucking responses first appear. Fetus displays hiccups and flexes arms and legs.

## 13–16 WEEKS

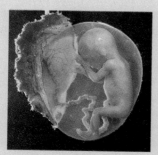

Fingerprints and footprints established.

Spinal cord begins to form.

If female, large numbers of primitive egg cells created.

Other reflexes, including swallowing and sucking, emerge.

Eyelids have closed.

Fetus sprouts soft downlike hair at end of this period.

## 17–20 WEEKS

Fetus becomes covered by cheeselike, fatty material secreted by oil glands that probably protects the skin constantly bathed in amniotic fluid.

Eyebrows and hair visible.

Fetal heartbeat can be heard through woman's abdomen.

Fetus displays stable pattern of sleep and wakefulness and often assumes a favorite position.

## 21–25 WEEKS

Skin appears wrinkled and has a pink to reddish cast caused by blood in capillaries, which are highly visible through translucent skin.

Eyes fully formed and may be opened and closed.

Fetus can see and hear and produce crying sounds if born prematurely.

## 26–29 WEEKS

Fat deposits accumulate beneath surface of skin to give fetus a much less wrinkled appearance.

Downy hair may disappear or may remain and be present at birth.

Hair may begin to grow on head.

Lungs are sufficiently developed to permit breathing of air should birth occur.

Nerve cell formation completed, and brain begins to take on wrinkled and fissured appearance.

## 30–38 WEEKS

Fat continues to accumulate, giving full-term newborn chubby appearance and helping to insulate baby from varying temperatures once born.

Fetus adds about half its total weight.

Skin color turns from red to pink to white or bluish pink for all babies, regardless of racial make-up.

*From conception.

This chart describes the sequence of prenatal development based on the findings of research. There are individual differences in the exact ages at which embryos and fetuses display the various developmental achievements outlined here.

## Prenatal Diagnosis

We saw in Chapter 3 how the new field of genetic counseling assists couples at risk for children with a genetic disease. Prenatal diagnostic procedures now available can detect several hundred types of hereditary and environmentally induced defects. For example, one test carried out in the second trimester on the woman's blood (alpha fetoprotein test) may provide evidence of neural tube defects and other problems. Fetoscopy, the insertion of a fiber optic light to see the fetus or assist in withdrawal of fetal blood, can be used to detect several other anomalies. Among the best-known procedures for prenatal diagnosis are amniocentesis, chorionic villus sampling, and ultrasonography.

**Amniocentesis**     In **amniocentesis** a small amount of amniotic fluid is withdrawn through a syringe inserted in the woman's abdominal wall (see Figure 4.2). Cells collected from the fetus are tested for biochemical composition and chromosomal make-up. Amniocentesis is usually performed during the fourteenth to sixteenth week after conception; tests on the cells often require several additional weeks for completion. The effectiveness of the procedure at earlier times (when the fetus is eleven to fourteen weeks old) is still being explored (Hanson et al., 1992).

Amniocentesis and other fetal tests are typically performed only when there is an increased risk of impaired development. Women older than thirty-five, who have had frequent miscarriages, or who have other children or relatives with genetic defects are good candidates for the test. The risks from the procedure are small, but infection and an increased likelihood of spontaneous abortion exist.

**Chorionic Villus Sampling**     In **chorionic villus sampling** a biopsy or small sample of hairlike projections (*villi*) is taken from the chorion, the outer wall of the membrane in which the embryo develops. The relatively new test permits chromosomal and biochemical analyses as early as the fifth week of prenatal development, although the procedure is usually performed between eight and twelve weeks after conception. Information gained much earlier in pregnancy can considerably reduce uncertainty and anxiety about the possibility of defects (Caccia et al., 1991). The procedure is somewhat more difficult to perform than amniocentesis and is associated with a slightly greater risk of miscarriage and limb malformations (Burton, Schulz, & Burd, 1992).

**amniocentesis**   Method of sampling the fluid surrounding the developing fetus by insertion of a needle; usually performed in the fourteenth to sixteenth week after conception. Used to diagnose fetal genetic and developmental disorders.

**chorionic villus sampling**   Method of sampling fetal chorionic cells; usually performed in eighth or twelfth week of pregnancy. Used to diagnose embryonic genetic and developmental disorders.

**ultrasonography**   Method of using sound wave reflections to provide a representation of the developing fetus. Used to estimate gestational age and to detect fetal physical abnormalities.

**Ultrasonography**     **Ultrasonography**, commonly called *ultrasound,* is now routine in many parts of the world to help determine whether fetal growth is proceeding normally. Sound waves reflecting at different rates from tissues of varying density are represented on video monitors and even printed to form a picture of the baby. The picture can reveal such problems as microcephaly (small head size), cardiac malformations, cleft lip and palate, and neural tube and other physical defects. Studies reveal that the procedure is safe, and it is widely used to verify the age of the fetus as well as to assist lifesaving operations on the fetus within the womb.

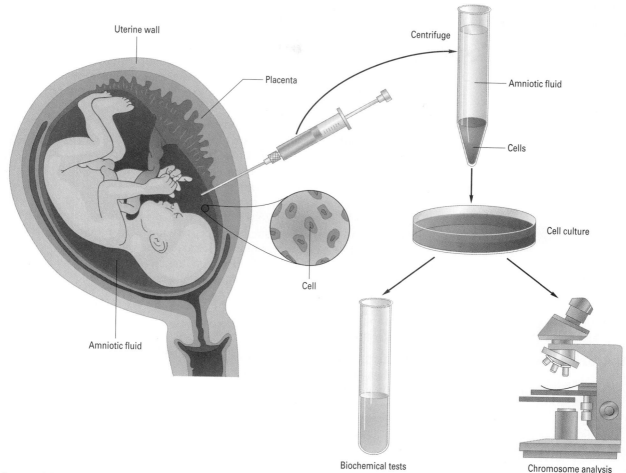

Source: Adapted from Knowles, 1985.

## *Environmental Factors Influencing Prenatal Development*

The union of ovum and sperm, the migration of the zygote to the uterus, the differentiation of organs and systems within the embryo, and the growth of the fetus are among the most intricate and complex phenomena in the universe. We have already seen how individual cells form an environmental context that can have dramatic consequences for tissue development. But what about other environmental factors? What kinds of support do the embryo and fetus receive in their liquid, somewhat buoyant, surroundings and how well protected are they from intrusions?

### Support Within the Womb

The embryo and fetus are sustained by a number of major structures, including the placenta, the umbilical cord, and the amniotic sac. The **placenta**, formed by cells from both the blastocyst and the uterine lining, produces

**FIGURE 4.2  The Process of Amniocentesis**  In this prenatal screening procedure, a needle is inserted into the amniotic fluid surrounding the fetus. A small amount of fluid is withdrawn, and cells shed by the fetus are separated from the fluid by centrifuge. The cells are cultured and submitted to various biochemical and other tests to determine whether chromosomal, genetic, or other developmental defects exist.

**placenta**  Support organ formed by cells from both blastocyst and uterine lining; serves as exchange site for oxygen, nutrients, and waste products.

essential hormones for the fetus. Just as important, it serves as the exchange site where oxygen and nutrients are absorbed from the woman's circulatory system and carbon dioxide and waste products are excreted from the embryo's circulatory system. The transfer takes place via a network of intermingling blood-rich capillaries originating in the woman's and the fetus's circulatory systems. Blood cells are too large to cross the membranes separating the two systems, but smaller molecules of oxygen, carbon dioxide, nutrients, and hormones can traverse the barrier. So too can some chemicals, drugs, and diseases that interfere with fetal development.

The **umbilical cord** is the conduit for blood of the fetus to and from the placenta via two arteries and a vein embedded in a gelatin-like substance about the consistency of a firm rubber hose. The pressure from the circulating blood helps prevent the cord from kinking or knotting.

The fetus lives in the womb surrounded by the fluid-filled **amniotic sac**. Amniotic fluid helps to stabilize temperature, insulates the fetus from bumps and shocks, and contains substances necessary for lung and other aspects of development. The fluid is constantly recirculated and renewed as the fetus ingests nutrients and urinates. Cells from fetal membranes are part of amniotic fluid and can be examined by amniocentesis, the prenatal screening procedure described earlier.

## Teratogens

▶ Roles of nature and nurture

Most fetuses that negotiate the average thirty-eight-week period from conception to birth emerge as healthy vigorous newborns. For example, 95 to 97 percent of infants born in the United States show no evidence of disruptions in their development. Yet, as we saw in Chapter 3, genetic factors can modify normal progress. So too can environmental factors. The study of birth defects and behavioral problems that arise from environmental influences during the prenatal period is called *teratology*. Environmental agents causing such disruptions are known as **teratogens**.

That external agents could upset the course of prenatal development in humans first gained support in 1941 when McAllister Gregg, an ophthalmologist, argued that rubella, commonly called German measles, caused visual anomalies in the fetus. During this same decade many infants born to women exposed to the atomic bomb were reported to have birth defects—a finding that, along with studies involving animals, implicated radiation as a teratogen (Warkany & Schraffenberger, 1947). Yet the full import of these early observations was not understood until researchers documented that women who had taken a presumably harmless drug called *thalidomide* frequently bore infants with arm and leg malformations (McBride, 1961).

**umbilical cord**   Conduit of blood vessels through which oxygen, nutrients, and waste products are transported between placenta and embryo.

**amniotic sac**   Fluid-filled, transparent protective membrane surrounding the fetus.

**teratogen**   Any environmental agent that can cause deviations in prenatal development. Consequences may range from death to behavioral problems.

The thalidomide tragedy made absolutely clear that human embryos could be seriously harmed by an environmental agent without adverse effects to the woman or to others of various ages (Wilson, 1977). In order to accept that environmental agents might disrupt prenatal development, specialists had to give up a fundamental misconception about the relationship between a woman and her fetus. Many experts claimed that a placental barrier filtered out virtually all harmful agents, providing the embryo with a highly insulated, sheltered world. But we now recognize that the embryo may be susceptible to virtually any substance if exposure to that substance is sufficiently concentrated (Samuels & Samuels, 1986).

**Principles of Teratology**    A number of broad generalizations have emerged from extensive research on teratogens since the 1960s (Abel, 1989; Vorhees, 1986; Wilson, 1977). These principles help to order the sometimes bewildering array of adverse consequences that specific drugs, diseases, and other agents have been found to have on development.

- *The Principle of Susceptibility: Individuals within species as well as species themselves show major differences in susceptibility to different teratogens* One example was thalidomide. Extremely large doses of the drug were known to cause abnormal fetal development in rats (Cohen, 1966), but the doses given to pregnant women in Europe and Canada, where thalidomide was administered to reduce morning sickness and anxiety, were considerably smaller. For reasons unknown, human and other primate embryos are far more sensitive than embryos of other species to small doses of thalidomide. More than seven thousand babies were born with limb defects and intellectual retardation before the species difference was recognized. The genotype of an individual woman and her fetus may also affect susceptibility to a teratogen: some fetuses were exposed to thalidomide between the third and eighth week after conception, the interval during which it usually causes anomalies, yet at birth these babies showed no ill effects from the drug (Kajii, Kida, & Takahashi, 1973).

▶ Individual differences

- *The Principle of Critical or Sensitive Periods: The extent to which a teratogen will affect the fetus depends on the stage of development during which exposure occurs* Many human organs and systems are most sensitive to toxic agents during the third to eighth week after conception, when they are still being formed. Figure 4.3 illustrates the periods during which specific organs of the body show the greatest susceptibility to teratogens. It also shows that many body systems are vulnerable to teratogens throughout much of prenatal development. In fact, the brain continues to undergo substantial neural differentiation, migration, and growth during the second and third trimesters of pregnancy and even the weeks and months after birth. As a consequence, exposure to teratogens throughout much of prenatal development may have significant behavioral consequences.

The effect of teratogens on the zygote is not well known. Some researchers believe that many agents typically have no effect in this earliest stage, but others suggest that a common outcome is loss of the zygote. A large proportion of pregnancies terminate before the woman is aware that she is pregnant. Whether many spontaneous abortions are a consequence of teratogenic factors, however, is not known.

- *The Principle of Access: The accessibility of a given teratogen to a fetus or embryo influences the extent of its damage* Many factors determine when and to what extent an embryo or fetus is exposed to a teratogen. Cultural and social practices may prevent or encourage a pregnant woman to use drugs, to be inoculated for certain diseases, or to frequent locations that expose her to chemicals and other toxins. For example, use of cocaine may be socially approved in one segment of a culture, avoided in another. Even when the woman is exposed to the teratogen, it must still gain access to the uterine environment. The way the woman has been exposed to the agent, how she metabolizes it, and how the agent is transported to the womb influence whether a teratogen reaches a sufficient threshold to have some effect.

▶ Sociocultural influence

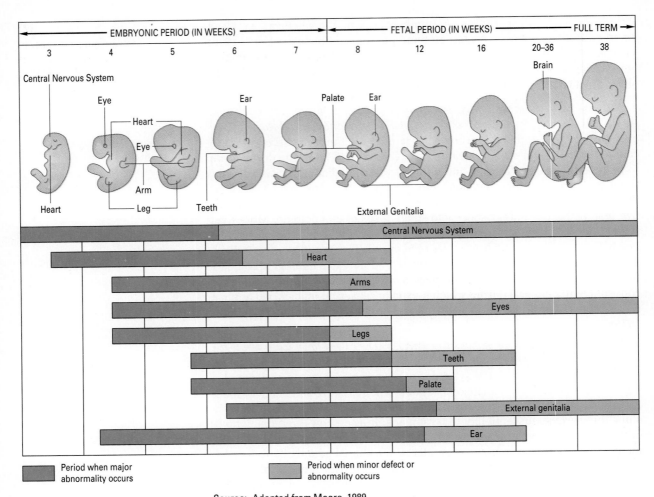

**FIGURE 4.3**

**Sensitive Periods in Prenatal Development**

During prenatal development, organs and systems undergo periods in which they are more or less sensitive to teratogenic influences—environmental agents that can cause deviations in development. The potential for major structural defects (dark-colored sections) is usually greatest during the embryonic period, when many organs are being formed. However, many regions of the body, including the central nervous system, continue to have some susceptibility to teratogens (light-colored sections) during the fetal period.

Source: Adapted from Moore, 1989.

- *The Principle of Dose-Response Relationships: The extent of exposure or dosage level of a given teratogen influences the extent of its damage* The severity of teratogenic effects is often related to level of dosage. The more a woman smokes, for example, the greater is the likelihood that her baby will be of low birth weight and be born prematurely. The concentration of a toxic agent reaching the fetus, however, cannot always be determined based on the woman's exposure to it. The severity of an illness a woman experiences, for example, does not always predict the effect of a disease on the fetus. The woman's physical condition also determines how much of a teratogen reaches the fetus.

- *The Principle of Teratogenic Response: Teratogens do not show uniformly the same effects on prenatal development* Teratogens may cause death or disrupt development of specific organs and systems. They may also have behavioral consequences, impairing sensorimotor, cognitive, social, and emotional development. As previously stated principles reveal, species and individual differences, as well as time, duration, and intensity of exposure play a role in determining what effect a specific teratogen will have on prenatal development. Rubella, for example, may cause visual, auditory, cardiac, or nervous system anomalies, depending on the week of pregnancy in which the woman acquires the disease. Alcohol can cause congenital defects during the embryonic period but may interfere with prenatal weight gain and contribute to postnatal behavioral problems during the second and third trimesters of pregnancy (Abel, 1989). One other important implication of this principle is that very different teratogenic agents can produce a similar pattern of defects. Thus, efforts to pinpoint why a baby was born with a given anomaly are not always successful.

• *The Principle of Interference with Specific Mechanisms: Teratogens affect prenatal development by interfering with biochemical processes that contribute to the differentiation, migration, or other basic functions of cells* This principle helps winnow folk beliefs from scientific explanations of fetal anomalies. Looking at a frightening visual stimulus, for example, has no direct consequence for the fetus. On the other hand, a teratogen such as alcohol may affect development because it interferes with normal fetal metabolism, including neural cell growth and migration. The changes may in turn have physical, behavioral, and other consequences for the developing fetus.

• *The Principle of Developmental Delay and "Sleeper Effects": Some teratogens may cause temporary delays in development with no long-term negative consequences, but others will cause developmental problems only late in development* Although some teratogenic effects may be observed at birth and are permanent and irreversible, other effects may be nullified, especially when a supportive caregiving environment is established. However, the effect of teratogens on development is probably substantially underestimated because many produce "sleeper effects"—those that go unnoticed at birth but seed problems that become apparent in childhood and even later. One of the most highly publicized examples of a sleeper effect involves women who were treated with diethylstilbestrol (DES), a hormone administered from the 1940s through the 1960s to prevent miscarriages. When the children of the women became adults, women showed a high rate of genital tract cancers and men displayed a high incidence of abnormalities of the testes.

## Drugs as Teratogens

Now that we have considered general principles involving teratogens, we can examine the effects that specific kinds of environmental agents have on the embryo or fetus. Among them are a number of substances expectant women may use, either as medicine or as mood-altering devices. Some frequently become part of the intrauterine world as well.

**Alcohol**    Because alcohol readily crosses the placenta, its concentration in the fetus is likely to be similar to that in the woman (Abel, 1981). Simply stated, this means that every time a pregnant woman takes a drink, she may be giving her fetus a drink of proportionate size. Nevertheless, alcohol consumption by pregnant women continues to be acceptable in many cultures. From 9 to 11 percent of pregnant American women are considered heavy or problem drinkers (Abel, 1982). The proportion may be substantially greater in some Western European nations (such as France and Italy) and other countries (U.S. Department of Health, Education, and Welfare, 1978). The definition of *heavy drinking* varies but usually refers to consumption of two or more drinks a day (two 12-ounce glasses of beer, two 2 1/2-ounce glasses of wine, or two 5/8-ounce glasses of distilled spirits) or ten to fourteen drinks during one

▶ Sociocultural influence

week. About 300,000 infants born each year in the United States are thought to have been exposed to this amount of alcohol on a regular basis.

Widespread recognition of the potential dangers of alcohol emerged in the early 1970s when a constellation of deficits, including prenatal and postnatal growth retardation, microcephaly and other abnormal facial features, and mental retardation and behavioral problems such as hyperactivity and poor motor coordination, were observed in babies born of alcoholic women (Jones & Smith, 1973). The estimate is that nearly two in every one thousand pregnant women (about one in forty alcoholic pregnant women) deliver a baby displaying **fetal alcohol syndrome (FAS)** (Abel & Sokol, 1987). It is the most frequent cause of mental retardation in many countries.

Women who drink heavily throughout their pregnancy are far more likely to have children diagnosed with FAS than women who drink moderately or infrequently or who discontinue heavy drinking early in pregnancy (Autti-Rämö et al., 1992; Weiner & Morse, 1988). Heavy drinkers are also more likely than moderate or light drinkers to give birth to infants with *fetal alcohol effects (FAE)*. Manifestations of FAE include less severe forms of mental and growth retardation and more subtle behavioral problems, including hyperactivity, learning and language disabilities, shortened attention span, sleep disturbances, and poor socialization and communications skills that extend into early childhood and continue into adulthood (Autti-Rämö et al., 1992; Streissguth et al., 1989; Streissguth et al., 1991).

How does alcohol produce such effects? One way is by directly modifying cell functioning, including cell differentiation, migration, and growth. Examination of infants with fetal alcohol syndrome who died shortly after birth reveals evidence of structural changes in the brain caused by delays and errors in the ways neurons migrate to form the cortex, or outer layer, of the brain (Clarren et al., 1978). The metabolism of alcohol also requires substantial amounts of oxygen. If oxygen is expended to metabolize alcohol, less oxygen may be available to the fetus for the growth and functioning of neural and other cells (Abel, 1982).

Binge drinking, even on an infrequent basis, may be especially hazardous, because it exposes the fetus to highly concentrated alcohol levels (Chasnoff, 1986). But what about the effects of moderate amounts of alcohol, perhaps even as little as a single drink a day, such as that enjoyed by Carmen? Some researchers have reported that even this small amount is associated with an increase in the number of spontaneous abortions and with reduced alertness, less vigorous body activity, more tremors, and less rapid learning in newborns as compared with babies of women who did not drink (Mills et al., 1984; Streissguth, Barr, & Martin, 1983). The findings are controversial and often disputed. Nevertheless, the American Academy of Pediatrics (1993) has recommended complete abstinence during pregnancy, because no "safe dose" for alcohol has been established.

**Cigarette Smoking**   In the early 1980s nearly one-third of expectant women in the United States smoked (Merritt, 1981). More recently, tobacco use by expectant women has declined to less than 20 percent in the United States. Its use appears to be greatest among Caucasian women, especially those who have not graduated from high school, somewhat less among African-Americans, and lowest among Asian- and Hispanic-American expectant women (Centers for Disease Control, 1992; Fichtner et al., 1990).

Researchers agree that smoking does not cause major congenital defects, but nicotine, or some other of the more than two thousand pharmacological

▶ Individual differences

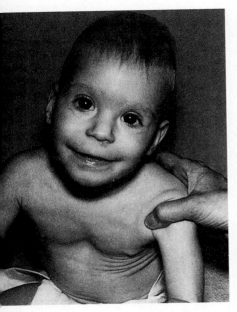

This baby, born to an alcoholic mother, displays the characteristics of fetal alcohol syndrome. These characteristics include microcephaly (small head size), eyes widely set apart, thin, flat upper lip, delayed physical growth, and mental retardation.

▶ Sociocultural differences

**fetal alcohol syndrome (FAS)**
Cluster of fetal abnormalities stemming from mother's consumption of alcohol; includes growth retardation, defects in facial features, and intellectual retardation.

agents found in cigarette smoke (U.S. Public Health Service, 1979), can have serious consequences for fetal and infant mortality, birth weight, and possibly postnatal development (Weinberger & Weiss, 1988; Zuckerman, 1988). The most consistent finding from studies of babies born to smokers, compared with those born to nonsmokers, is their smaller size. The more a woman smokes during pregnancy, the lower her baby's average weight is at birth, even when equated for length of gestation (because babies of women who smoke are also likely to be born a few days early). Babies of women who use tobacco weigh an average of two hundred grams (about seven ounces) less than other babies.

A second consistent finding is an increase in spontaneous abortions, still-births, and neonatal deaths in pregnant women who smoke (Kleinman et al., 1988). For example, in one study involving more than fifty-one thousand births, light smoking (less than one pack a day) was found to increase the risk of fetal death by 20 percent, and heavy smoking (more than one pack a day) by 35 percent (Meyer & Tonascia, 1977). As with alcohol consumption, a reduction in oxygen may account for the effects. Smoking increases carbon monoxide in the blood of both woman and fetus, displacing oxygen in the red blood cells. Nicotine also reduces blood flow to the placenta. These events could explain why a fetus's heart rate goes up when a woman smokes, a reaction that may be designed to maintain adequate oxygen (Samuels & Samuels, 1986). Perhaps for the same reason babies of women who use tobacco tend to have larger placentas and more frequent placental abnormalities compared with babies of the same weight born to nonsmoking women (Meyer & Tonascia, 1977; Weinberger & Weiss, 1988).

The behavioral and long-term consequences of smoking for the newborn are less well understood. Studies have reported that infants born to smokers display poorer learning (Martin et al., 1977) and reduced visual alertness (Landesman-Dwyer, Keller, & Streissguth, 1978), but infant tests of development have not uncovered a consistent pattern of deficits (Eskenazi, 1984). At older ages children of women in Great Britain who smoked during pregnancy have been observed to lag several months behind children of nonsmokers on general ability, reading, and mathematics tests (Butler & Goldstein, 1973), but the finding is confounded by the possiblity of postnatal differences in exposure to smoke, among many other factors. Researchers have noted that women who smoked during and after pregnancy report a greater number of behavioral problems in their four- to eleven-year-olds, although additional factors again could account for the differences (Weitzman, Gortmaker, & Sobol, 1992). In another study of nine- to eleven-year-olds, children of smokers did not differ on a variety of academic, social, and other measures compared with children of nonsmokers (Lefkowitz, 1981). Although the long-term behavioral consequences remain controversial, Carmen's decision to stop smoking makes sense in light of the uncertainty about increased risks for development associated with tobacco use during pregnancy.

**Prescription and Over-the-Counter Drugs**    Legal drugs in addition to alcohol and tobacco can be hazardous for fetal development. Some are known teratogens (see Table 4.1), but knowledge of the effects of many remains perilously limited. Aspirin, for example, has been demonstrated to impair behavioral competence in the offspring of lower animals. One well-controlled study found that aspirin may also be associated with lower IQ in early childhood (Streissguth et al., 1984).

▶ Individual differences

| Drug | Description and Known or Suspected Effects |
|---|---|
| **Alcohol** | See text. |
| **Amniopterin** | Anticancer agent. Facial defects and a number of other congenital malformations as well as mental retardation. |
| **Amphetamines** | Stimulants for the central nervous system, some types frequently used for weight control. Readily cross placental barrier. Fetal intrauterine growth retardation often reported but may be a result of accompanying malnutrition or multiple-drug use (Rodgers & Lee, 1988). |
| **Antibiotics (streptomycin) (tetracycline)** | Streptomycin associated with hearing loss. Tetracycline associated with staining of baby's teeth if exposure occurs during second or third trimester. |
| **Aspirin** | Possibility of increased bleeding in both mother and infant. See text for other complications that can arise. |
| **Barbiturates (pentobarbital) (phenobarbital) (secobarbital)** | Sedatives and anxiety reducers. Considerable evidence of neurobiological and behavioral complications in rats. Readily cross human placenta; concentrations in fetus may be greater than in woman. Newborns may show withdrawal symptoms (Brown & Fishman, 1984). No consistent evidence of long-term effects in humans. |
| **Benzodiazepines (chlordiazepoxide) (diazepam)** | Tranquilizers. Not shown to have teratogenic effects (Rogers & Lee, 1988). Newborns may display withdrawal symptoms (Eskenazi, 1984). |
| **Caffeine** | See text. |
| **Hydantoins** | Treatment for epilepsy. Produce *fetal hydantoin syndrome*, including heart defects, cleft lip or palate, decreased head size, and mental retardation. Controversy continues over whether effects are entirely caused by drug or by conditions associated with the mother, including her epilepsy (Eskenazi, 1984). |
| **Lithium** | Treatment for manic depression. Crosses placenta freely. Known to be teratogenic in pre-mammalian animals. Strong suggestive evidence of increased cardiovascular defects in human infants. Behavioral effects unknown. Administration at time of delivery markedly reduces infant responsivity (Kerns & Davis, 1986). |
| **Sex Hormones (androgens) (estrogens) (progestins)** | Contained in birth control pills, fertility drugs, and other drugs to prevent miscarriages. Continued use of birth control pills during pregnancy associated with heart and circulatory disorders. Behavioral and personality implications suspected. |
| **Thalidomide** | Reduce morning sickness and anxiety. Deformities of the limbs, depending on time of exposure, often accompanied by mental retardation (Gouin-Decarie, 1969). |
| **Tobacco** | See text. |
| **Tricyclics (imipramine) (desimipramine)** | Antidepressants. Some tricyclics cross the placenta. Studies with rats reveal developmental and behavioral disturbances. Studies with humans reveal no consistent findings (Kerns & Davis, 1986). |
| **Vitamins** | Large amounts of vitamin A known to cause major birth defects. Excess amounts of other vitamins may also cause prenatal malformations. |

Note: This listing is not meant to be exhaustive, and other drugs may have teratogenic effects. No drug should be taken during pregnancy without consultation with a qualified physician.

**TABLE 4.1**

**Prescription and Other Frequently Used Drugs and Their Effects on Prenatal**

Caffeine too has been implicated in birth defects in animals, although studies have failed to reveal any consistent link in humans. A typical cup of coffee contains about one hundred milligrams of caffeine. Heavy coffee consumers (more than three cups a day) do tend to have babies of lower birth weight than those who drink less or no coffee (Narod, de Sanjosé, & Victora, 1991). Caffeine also may have behavioral consequences for the fetus. Lawrence Devoe and his colleagues (1993), using ultrasound, recorded biweekly two-hour observations of fetal activity during the final ten weeks of pregnancy from ten heavy caffeine consumers (>500 milligrams, or five cups, daily) and ten low caffeine consumers (<200 milligrams, or two cups, daily). As can be seen in Figure 4.4, the length of time during which fetuses exhibited arousal (defined by irregular heart rate and breathing activity, frequent body movements, and rapid eye movements) was substantially greater in the high caffeine than in the low caffeine groups. The long-term implications of the differences are unknown. Of course, the more highly aroused infants may have consumed more energy, a factor that could contribute to their lower birth weight.

Perhaps an even greater concern is the number of prescription and over-the-counter drugs consumed during pregnancy. The majority of expectant women use at least one medication, and the average found in most studies is more than three (Buitendijk & Bracken, 1991). Little is known about the effects of many products and even less about any interactive consequences when multiple drugs are used. Thus, expectant women are often advised to take *no* drugs during pregnancy, including over-the-counter remedies, or to take them only under the close supervision of their physician. Cautions printed on the labels of cough syrups, pain relievers, antacids, vitamins, and other readily available health aids are there for good reasons.

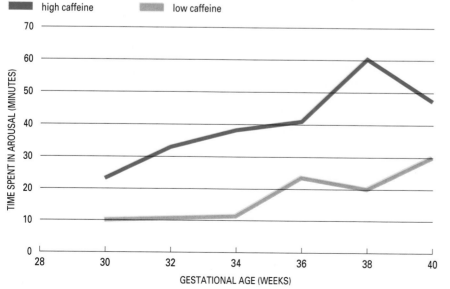

**FIGURE 4.4**

**Caffeine Consumption and Fetal Activity**

Fetuses of women who were heavy caffeine consumers (>500 milligrams, or five cups, daily) showed greater amounts of time (per 2-hour period) in an aroused state, as defined by irregular heart rate and breathing activity, frequent body movements, and rapid eye movements, than fetuses of women who were light caffeine consumers (<200 milligrams, or two cups, daily).

Source: Adapted from Devoe et al., 1993.

**Illegal Drugs**    The effects of illegal drugs such as marijuana, heroin, and cocaine on prenatal development are even more difficult to untangle than the effects of prescription and over-the-counter medications. Drug users are rarely certain of the concentrations or the contents of the drugs they consume. Wide variation in frequency of use, the possiblity of interactions from exposure to multiple drugs, poor nutritional status, inadequate or no prenatal care, and potential psychological and physiological differences before or after taking such drugs compound the problem of isolating their teratogenic effects. The lifestyle of many illegal-drug users is described as essentially chaotic (Chasnoff, 1992). Yet the need to understand the effect of illegal drugs on development has never been greater. About 11 percent of expectant women in the United States are estimated to be drug abusers; some 375,000 infants are born to them each year (National Association for Perinatal Addiction Research and Education, 1988). Others estimate the numbers to be much higher (Gomby & Shiono, 1991).

Researchers have long known from animal experiments that the psychoactive ingredients associated with marijuana cross the placenta and are stored in the amniotic fluid (Harbison & Mantilla-Plata, 1972). The ingredients may even be transferred postnatally through the mother's milk (Dalterio & Bartke, 1979). But the small number of studies attempting to determine the effects of marijuana on either the fetus or postnatal development reveal few consistent findings (Zuckerman & Bresnahan, 1991). As with tobacco use, fetal weight and size appear to be reduced. Length of gestation may also be shorter for heavy marijuana users, a finding consistent with giving marijuana to speed labor, a practice carried out at one time in Europe.

The acoustics of the cries of newborns exposed to marijuana, for example, are higher pitched and more variable, than of those not so exposed (Lester & Dreher, 1989). The differences may be important because they often indicate neurophysiological disturbances in infants exposed to other risks. Visual problems and lower scores on memory and verbal tasks in early childhood also are associated with prenatal exposure to marijuana (Fried, 1986; Fried & Watkinson, 1990), but other differences in the backgrounds of these children may account for the findings. Thus, researchers are as yet unable to determine to what extent marijuana acts as a teratogen.

The effects of other illegal drugs such as heroin and morphine on the infant came to the attention of the public as early as the late 1800s, when doctors reported withdrawal symptoms in newborns whose mothers used these substances (Zagon & McLaughlin, 1984). By the early 1900s heroin and morphine were known to be transmitted through the placenta as well as through the mother's milk. Today, an estimated ten thousand infants born every year in the United States are exposed to heroin or another pharmacologically similar product called *methadone* (Hans, 1989). Often given under regulated conditions as a heroin substitute, methadone appears to have effects on fetal development that are just as serious as heroin's.

Although congenital defects have not been positively linked to heroin and methadone, stillbirths and infant deaths are more frequent and lower birth weight is common. Moreover, 60 to 90 percent of infants born to heroin- and methadone-addicted women undergo withdrawal symptoms such as diarrhea, sweating, distinctive cry characteristics, and irritability. Babies appear overstimulated and are not easily consoled (Zuckerman & Bresnahan, 1991). The signs of distress typically last about ten days for heroin and several weeks for

▶ Individual differences

methadone, but considerably longer under some circumstances. Sleep disturbances, delayed sensorimotor development, and visual and auditory problems are common, perhaps stemming in part from withdrawal experiences or from poor nutrition, other drug exposure, limited care provided by caregivers, or additional factors that often complicate the early lives of these infants. Such problems continue to be reported in older infants and children, although the difficulties may, of course, arise from the disruptive postnatal environment in which many of them grow up. Methadone programs that provide high-quality prenatal care, emphasize adequate nutrition, and furnish other kinds of support to the addict can reduce, and perhaps eliminate, many of the effects (Rodgers & Lee, 1988).

Whereas the frequency of abuse of most illegal drugs stayed level or declined from the mid-1970s to the mid-1980s, cocaine use in the United States tripled and quadrupled among several age groups, including young adults, during these decades (Atkins, 1988). Its use in other countries also appears to have increased. Cocaine in its many forms, including the especially potent and addictive form called *crack*, readily crosses into the placenta. Once it reaches the fetus, it stays longer than in adults, because the immature organs of the fetus have difficulty breaking the substance down. It can continue to influence the baby after birth through the mother's milk. The estimate is that more than 150,000 infants whose mothers abused cocaine during pregnancy are born each year in the United States (Gomby & Shiono, 1991). In some major metropolitan areas nearly one-third of newborns show evidence of exposure to cocaine (Ostrea et al., 1992).

Early reports cited serious repercussions of cocaine exposure for the fetus and infant. Some, such as premature birth, low birth weight, and small head size, have been widely confirmed. Others, such as seizures and strokes, respiratory difficulties, and kidney and genital malformations have also been reported in a troubling proportion of offspring (Chasnoff, 1992). Behaviorally, cocaine-exposed newborns are sometimes described as being easily overstimulated, displaying abnormal motor responses, and having difficulty moving from states of sleep to alertness and back again. However, these patterns of behavior are not observed in most infants or in every study (Woods et al., 1993; Zuckerman & Bresnahan, 1991). When older, such children may show delays in language acquisition, attentional problems, and inability to regulate their own behavior; however, the difficulties appear to be far less widespread than early, often sensationalized, reports suggested (Chasnoff, 1992; Zuckerman & Frank, 1992).

▸ Individual differences

The extent to which later developmental adversity can be attributed to prenatal cocaine exposure, and its oft-accompanied lower birth weight, or to postnatal factors remains difficult to sort out. As Ira Chasnoff (1992) and others point out, the prognosis for children exposed to cocaine in utero improves markedly when interventions are undertaken to reduce or eliminate other risk factors. This drug, along with so many others we have discussed, seems to create potential, but not always inevitable, obstacles to development, and much can be done to improve the outlook for many children.

Because prenatal development is so closely tied to the intrauterine environment, much less research has been conducted on the father's exposure to drugs or other teratogens and their effects on the embryo. However, research with lower animals and some studies with humans suggest that the sperm of men who consume alcohol, cocaine, and other drugs may carry toxic substances that can disrupt normal prenatal development (Yazigi, Odom, & Polakoski, 1991). Still, the woman is regularly assigned far greater responsibility for prenatal events, as the following controversy reveals.

---

## CONTROVERSY: THINKING IT OVER

### Should a Drug-abusing Expectant Woman Be Charged with Child Abuse?

In 1991 perhaps as many as one hundred American women in twenty-three states were arrested on various charges, including child abuse and neglect, delivery of drugs to a minor, and assault with a deadly weapon for allegedly harming their fetus through exposure to potentially harmful drugs (Shoop, 1992). Consider, for example, the circumstances surrounding the prosecution of Jennifer Johnson. Both a son, born in 1987, and a daughter, born in 1989, tested positive for exposure to cocaine. In 1991 Johnson was convicted in Florida of delivering drugs to her children at birth via the umbilical cord. Although that conviction has since been overturned by the Florida Supreme Court, the issues surrounding this and similar cases remain unresolved.

What are an expectant woman's moral and legal responsibilities to the fetus? If sufficient research evidence accumulates to show that a drug is potentially dangerous, should members of a concerned society make every effort, including, if necessary, the threat of criminal charges, to help deter its use and to ensure that every newborn begins life as healthy as possible? Some say yes. Several U.S. states have implemented laws that take such a stance, permitting a newborn to be removed from a parent on the grounds of child abuse or neglect as a result of drug exposure. After all, anyone found to provide such illegal substances to a child would certainly expect to face criminal charges. Is the situation really that much different in the case of a pregnant woman and her fetus?

Others believe the situation is much different and further argue that such efforts are counterproductive. Drug laws, they claim, have proved ineffective in helping large numbers of abusers gain control of their behavior; a woman who undoubtedly began abusing drugs well before her pregnancy would be unlikely to gain control at this point in her life, especially because of the severe shortage of treatment programs to help in dealing with the addiction and limited support services to assist with other aspects of pregnancy. Out of fear of being prosecuted, such legislation, then, would only drive prospective mothers away from the care and treatment needed both for themselves and their fetuses.

The ethical and legal controversies certainly extend well beyond these arguments. For example, should laws designed to protect and benefit children be generalized to the fetus as well? Or is the relationship between a woman and her fetus qualitatively different, one that requires other important considerations, including the right of privacy? Moreover, does enough evidence exist to convincingly demonstrate that a particular drug causes problems for the newborn? Or are poor nutrition and a host of other social and economic-related factors that often accompany drug use, and over which the woman may have little control, the primary culprits in poor fetal development in most cases? If laws concerned with fetal protection are established, should they also be applied to

▶ Development as continuous/discontinuous

situations involving legal drugs such as alcohol and tobacco, which are also believed to have serious potential consequences for development of the fetus?

These are difficult issues to resolve. Is recourse to the judicial system a desirable and effective means of helping the newborn? Or might such laws constitute a smokescreen that obscures and diverts resources from newborns' needs? The costs of drug abuse, not only to the individuals involved but to society as a whole, are considerable. Should litigation be one means of reducing those costs?  ∎

## Diseases as Teratogens

Two to eight percent of babies born to American women are exposed to one or more infectious or parasitic diseases or other forms of illness during pregnancy (Saltzman & Jordan, 1988). Fortunately, most babies are unaffected by these exposures. But some diseases have physical and behavioral consequences for some babies (see Table 4.2). The effects may occur even when the woman is completely unaware of illness.

**Rubella**    Before widespread vaccination the last major outbreak of rubella (German measles) in the United States in 1964 caused congenital defects in an estimated twenty thousand infants (Andiman & Horstmann, 1984). Fewer than twenty cases of congenital problems associated with the disease were reported in this country by the early 1980s (Orenstein et al., 1984). Unfortunately, however, rubella continues to be a major cause of fetal malformations and death worldwide, because vaccination programs are limited in many Third World countries.

▶ Sociocultural influence

The most common problems associated with rubella include growth retardation, cataracts, hearing impairment, heart defects, and mental retardation. Virtually every organ, however, may be affected, depending on when the disease is contracted during prenatal development (Andiman & Horstmann, 1984). Up to 50 percent of infants born to women with rubella during the first month of pregnancy will have congenital abnormalities, but the figure declines to 22 percent, 6 percent, and less than 1 percent during the second, third, and fourth months, respectively (Saltzman & Jordan, 1988).

**Toxoplasmosis**    Toxoplasmosis is caused by a parasite found in many mammals and birds. Twenty to 40 percent of adults in various regions of the United States and Great Britain have been exposed to it (Feldman, 1982; Peckham & Logan, 1993); however, toxoplasmosis is found more frequently in tropical regions. An unusual aspect of the parasite is that part of its life cycle can only be completed in cats. Humans contract the disease by touching cat feces containing the parasite or by eating raw or partially cooked meat, especially pork and lamb, that has been infected by exposure to cat feces. Children and adults are frequently unaware of their exposure, because the infection may have no symptoms or cause only a minor fever or rash.

About 3 percent of women contracting the disease during pregnancy will have an infected baby (MacLeod & Lee, 1988). Infections early in pregnancy when, fortunately, risk of transmission to the fetus is lowest, can have devastating consequences, including growth retardation, jaundice, accumulation of fluid in the brain, and visual and central nervous system damage. Some infants exposed to the disease lack any symptoms at or shortly after birth and only later in

## Sexually Transmitted Diseases

| | |
|---|---|
| **Acquired Immune Deficiency Syndrome (AIDS)** | See text. |
| **Chlamydia** | Nearly always transmitted to infant during delivery via infected birth canal. Estimated 100,000 (of 155,000 exposed in the United States) become infected. Often causes eye infection in infant and some increased risk of pneumonia. Other adverse effects suspected (McGregor & French, 1991). |
| **Gonorrhea** | If acquired prenatally, may cause premature birth. Most frequently contracted during delivery through infected birth canal and may then attack eyes. In the United States and many other countries, silver nitrate eye drops are administered to all newborns to prevent blindness. |
| **Hepatitis B** | Associated with premature birth, low birth weight, increased neonatal death, and liver disorders (Pass, 1987). Most frequently contracted during delivery through birth canal or postnatally. |
| **Herpes Simplex** | Of its two forms, only one is transmitted primarily through sexual activity. Both forms, however, can be transmitted to the fetus, causing severe damage to the central nervous system (Pass, 1987). Most infections occur during delivery through birth canal containing active herpes lesions. Even when treated, the majority of infants will die or suffer central nervous system damage (Nahmias, Keyserling, & Kernick, 1983). If known to carry the virus, women may need to be tested frequently during pregnancy to determine if the disease is in its active, contagious state because symptoms may not be present even when active. If the disease is active, casarean delivery is used to avoid infecting the baby. |
| **Syphilis** | Damage to fetus does not begin until about 18 weeks after conception. May then cause death, mental retardation, and other congenital defects. Infected newborns may not show signs of disease until early childhood. |

## Other Diseases and Maternal Conditions

| | |
|---|---|
| **Cholera** | Increased risk of stillbirth. |
| **Cytomegalovirus** | See text. |
| **Diabetes** | Risk of congenital malformations and death to fetus two to three times higher than for babies born to nondiabetic women (Coustan & Felig, 1988). Excessive size at birth also common. Effects are likely to be a consequence of metabolic disturbances rather than of insulin. Rapid advances in care have helped reduce risks substantially for diabetic women. |
| **Hypertension (chronic)** | Probability of miscarriage or infant death increased. |
| **Influenza** | Some forms linked to increased heart and central nervous system abnormalities as well as spontaneous abortions. |
| **Mumps** | Increased risk of spontaneous abortion and stillbirth. |

**TABLE 4.2**

**Diseases and Other Conditions That May Affect Prenatal Development**

development may mental retardation, neuromuscular abnormalities, impaired vision, and other eye problems become apparent (MacLeod & Lee, 1988).

Because some drugs can reduce the risk of the disease, widespread screening of pregnant women for exposure to toxoplasmosis has sometimes been proposed. Attempting to avoid infection during pregnancy, however, is the most cost-effective method of preventing congenital toxoplasmosis. Meat should be fully cooked and hands frequently washed following meat prepara-

| | |
|---|---|
| **Pregnancy-induced Hypertension** | 5%–10% of expectant women experience significant increase in blood pressure, often accompanied by *edema* (swelling of face and extremities as a result of water retention), rapid weight gain, and protein in urine during later months of pregnancy. Condition is also known as *pre-eclampsia* (or *eclampsia*, if severe) and *toxemia*. Under severe conditions, woman may suffer seizures and coma. The fetus is at increased risk for death, brain damage, and lower birth weight. Adequate protein consumption helps minimize problems. Drugs used to treat high blood pressure may be just as hazardous to fetus as the condition itself. |
| **Rh Incompatibility** | Blood containing a certain protein is Rh positive, Rh negative if it lacks that protein. Hereditary factors determine which type the individual possesses. If fetus's blood is Rh positive, it can cause formation of antibodies in blood of woman who is Rh negative. These antibodies can cross placental barrier to destroy red blood cells of fetus. May result in miscarriage or stillbirth, jaundice, anemia, heart defects, and mental retardation. Likelihood of birth defects increases with succeeding pregnancies because antibodies are usually not present until after birth of first Rh-positive child. A vaccine (Rhogam) can be administered to the mother within 3 days after childbirth, miscarriage, or abortion to prevent antibody formation. |
| **Rubella** | See text. |
| **Smallpox** | Increased risk of spontaneous abortion and stillbirth. |
| **Toxoplasmosis** | See text. |
| **Varicellazoster (chicken pox)** | Skin and muscle defects, intrauterine growth retardation, limb reduction. |

**TABLE 4.2** (continued)

**Diseases and Other Conditions That May Affect Prenatal Development**

tion. Cat litter must be disposed of carefully. Because the parasite can survive in cat feces for a year under some conditions, even work in gardens frequented by cats can be hazardous.

**Cytomegalovirus**    Cytomegalovirus (CMV), which causes swelling of the salivary glands and mononucleosis-like symptoms in adults, is the single most frequent infection found in newborns today. It affects one to two of every one hundred babies, and as many as 20 percent of the infected infants can be expected to sustain some congenital damage (Saltzman & Jordan, 1988). CMV and other members of the herpes virus family share the property of latency; after contacting the disease, an individual may show no symptoms for many years, only to have it recur at any time. No effective treatment exists. CMV is most frequently reported in Asia and Africa and among lower socioeconomic groups, yet 40 to 60 percent of middle- and high-income groups in Europe and the United States have it (Tookey, Ades, & Peckham, 1992; Wentworth & Alexander, 1971). Transmission occurs sexually, through blood transfusions, and by other body fluids. CMV is particularly common in day-care centers, where it can be passed easily from child to child or between child and adult through physical contact.

> ▶ Sociocultural influence

Babies are most frequently exposed to CMV during birth or early thereafter if the disease is active in the mother at these times. But infection can occur within the womb. For infants who acquire the disease prenatally, growth retardation, jaundice, skin disorders, and small head size are common consequences. About one-third of infants showing these characteristics at birth will die in early infancy, and a large percentage of those who survive will be mentally retarded. About half of infants sustaining congenital damage from CMV show no symptoms at birth, but many will subsequently display progressive loss of hearing caused by damage to the auditory nerve or other more subtle defects, including minimal brain dysfunction, visual or dental abnormalities, or motor and neural problems (Andiman & Horstmann, 1984; Pass, 1987; Saltzman & Jordan, 1988).

**Sexually Transmitted and Other Diseases**   Several diseases identified as teratogenic are primarily transmitted sexually, or the infection and its symptoms are usually concentrated in the genitourinary tract (see Table 4.2). Syphilis and certain strains of herpes simplex, for example, are virtually always contracted from infected sexual partners. On the other hand, some, such as acquired immune deficiency syndrome (AIDS) and hepatitis B, can be acquired through exposure to infected blood as well.

Sexually transmitted disease (STDs) can interfere with reproduction in a number of ways. They may compromise the woman's health (AIDS, gonorrhea, hepatitis B, herpes simplex, syphilis), scar or disturb reproductive organs so conception and normal pregnancy cannot proceed (chlamydia, gonorrhea), directly infect the fetus (AIDS, herpes simplex, syphilis), and interfere with healthy postnatal development (AIDS, hepatitis B, herpes simplex, syphilis) (Lee, 1988). In recent years their frequency has risen rapidly in populations around the world. None, however, has had so dramatic an effect as AIDS. AIDS already is, or will soon be, one of the top five leading causes of death among children and adolescents today (Novello et al., 1989). In New York state, for example, AIDS is the first and second most frequent cause of death among one- to four-year-old Hispanic and African American children, respectively (Chu et al., 1991).

Of the estimated ten- to twenty thousand living children infected with human immunodeficiency virus type 1 (HIV) in the United States, most were infected prenatally or during birth (Van Dyke, 1993). As many as one-third of expectant women with HIV infection, the precursor to AIDS, can be expected to deliver an infected infant (Indacochea & Scott, 1992). The more advanced the disease in the mother, the greater the risk to her newborn is. The prognosis for all infected infants is poor. Many will show delayed growth and motor and mental retardation. Even if the HIV infection has not developed into full-blown AIDS, visual, motor, cognitive, social, and communicative skills are all likely to be impaired (Aylward et al., 1992; Levenson et al., 1992).

## Environmental Hazards as Teratogens

Radiation was one of the earliest confirmed teratogens, and it is known to cause genetic mutation as well. Radiation's teratogenic effects include spontaneous abortion, small head size, and other defects associated with the skeleton, genitals, and sensory organs. Even low doses of radiation have been linked to increased risks of cancer and neural damage; pregnant women are urged to avoid unnecessary x-rays and other circumstances in which radiation exposure may be increased.

Chemicals and other elements in the environment pose another significant source of potential risks. Known teratogens include lead, mercury, and cadmium, as well as many elements found in paints, dyes and coloring agents, solvents, oven cleaners, pesticides, herbicides, food additives, artificial sweeteners, and cosmetic products. Careless handling and disposal of such elements

TABLE 4.3

**Occupational Hazards for
Women of Childbearing Age**

| Occupation | Hazardous Substances |
| --- | --- |
| Cleaning Personnel | Soaps, detergents, solvents |
| Electronic Assemblers | Lead, tin, antimony, trichloroethylene, methyl chloride, resins |
| Hair Dressers and Cosmetologists | Hair-spray resins, aerosol propellants, solvents, dyes |
| Health Personnel | Anesthetic gases, x-rays, laboratory chemicals |
| Painters | Lead, titanium, toluene |
| Photographic Processors | Caustics, bromides, iodides, silver nitrate |
| Plastic Workers | Formaldehyde, vinyl chloride |
| Printing Personnel | Ink mists, methanol, carbon tetrachloride, lead, solvents, trichloroethylene |
| Textile and Garment Workers | Formaldehyde, dyes, asbestos, solvents, flame retardants |
| Transportation Personnel | Carbon monoxide, lead |

Source: Adapted from Samuels & Bennett, 1983.

and their excessive production and use—they pervade the foods we eat and the air we breathe—is one problem. But in addition, many women of childbearing age are exposed to hazardous substances in the workplace (see Table 4.3). Even concerns about exposure to video terminals have been voiced, but no evidence now exists to indicate that they are harmful to the fetus (Bentur & Koren, 1991).

With increasing awareness of the negative effect on prenatal development of certain chemicals and other environmental elements have come new and complex social and legal issues pertaining to women in the workplace. Some companies have barred women in their childbearing years from jobs involving hazardous substances as a way of reducing risk. But others have seen the restrictions as ways of preventing women from obtaining good jobs. Furthermore, some elements such as lead may also affect fertility and increase chromosomal aberrations in men (Bentur & Koren, 1991). Thus, both men and women need to be vigilant about environmental hazards in the workplace that could affect offspring they may have.

## Women's Conditions and Prenatal Development

In addition to teratogens, a number of health conditions are associated with increased risk during pregnancy. Several of these (diabetes, pregnancy-induced and chronic hypertension, Rh incompatibility) and their consequences for the fetus are summarized in Table 4.2. Additional factors influencing the prenatal environment include the age of the woman, her nutritional status, and her emotional state.

Teenage mothers give birth to approximately 500,000 babies in the United States each year. Many of them will be unmarried teens who have received little or even no prenatal care, factors that increase the risk for delivering less healthy babies.

▶ Sociocultural influence

**Age**     The number of older mothers is on the rise in the United States as women postpone pregnancy until careers are established or for other reasons. Is pregnancy in older women more risky? As we saw in Chapter 3, the likelihood of having a child with Down syndrome increases markedly during the later childbearing years. Some studies also report increased prematurity and mortality as well as greater difficulty during labor, especially for older women having their first child. However, the findings likely stem from increased health-related problems that generally accompany aging. Healthy women older than thirty-five have no more complications during pregnancy than younger women (Grimes & Gross, 1981; Stein, 1983).

Teenagers, on the other hand, are at considerable risk for delivering less healthy babies (McAnarney, 1987). Lack of adequate prenatal care may be one primary reason. Pregnant teenagers in the United States, particularly those who are very young and unmarried, are much less likely than other women to seek medical services. In any given year one in twenty teenagers is likely to bear a child. Nearly 60 percent of the approximately 500,000 births to teenagers each year will be to unmarried teens (Children's Defense Fund, 1988).

**Nutrition**     What foods are needed for the health of the woman and her fetus? The seemingly obvious but important answer is a well-balanced diet.

Physical and neural growth of the fetus can be severely impaired when a woman fails to maintain a balanced diet or to gain sufficient weight, typically about twenty-five to thirty-five pounds during pregnancy. Because it is a time when neurons and brain growth are proceeding rapidly, extreme malnutrition during prenatal development can be especially detrimental. During World War II, famines occurred in parts of Holland and in Leningrad in the Soviet Union. The incidence of spontaneous abortions, stillbirths, abnormalities of the nervous system, and deaths at or shortly after birth increased markedly in these locations. When the malnutrition occurred during the first few months of pregnancy, death, premature birth, and nervous system defects were especially frequent. When famine occurred later in prenatal development, retardation in fetal growth and low birth weights were more likely (Antonov, 1947).

▶ Sociocultural influence

Diets must be sufficient, not only in terms of amount of food but also in terms of adequate protein, vitamins, and other nutrients. Deficiencies in specific elements such as zinc or iron may result in particular neural or other deficits. Nevertheless, unless deficiencies are so severe that malformations and deficits in neuron formation cannot be overcome, many intellectual problems linked to prenatal undernutrition may be reversed when adequate nourishment and stimulation are provided following birth. In other words, the negative cognitive and social prognosis for malnourished newborns can in many cases be reversed if they are fortunate enough to enter an enriched postnatal environment (Zeskind & Ramey, 1981).

**Stress**    Cultural beliefs about potentially harmful consequences of frightening or stressful events on fetal development are pervasive, and many societies encourage a calm atmosphere for pregnant women (Samuels & Samuels, 1986). In recent studies in which researchers have carefully measured the existence of family conflict, the frequency of positive and negative life events, and the availability of physical and social support for the pregnant woman, the results show that stressful conditions before and during pregnancy result in a pattern of greater complications during pregnancy and birth. For the woman these include preeclampsia or premature labor. For the infant low birth weight, poor respiration, and other problems may result (Nuckolls, Cassel, & Kaplan, 1972). Research with animals indicates that when the female is under stress, blood flow is diverted from the womb and hormones that can interfere with normal growth are released. Stress also may indirectly affect prenatal development by leading a woman to increase smoking, consume more alcohol, or engage in other activities that are known to have teratogenic effects on the fetus (McAnarney & Stevens-Simon, 1990).

▶ Sociocultural influence

Prior medical condition, age, personality, and the social support a pregnant woman receives from family and friends are important factors, however, that lessen the consequences of stress during pregnancy. Among women who experience a variety of life changes before and during pregnancy, those with strong social and personal support have far fewer complications than women without such resources. For example, Jane Norbeck and Virginia Tilden (1983) found that high stress during the year before pregnancy correlates with complications for the infant (low birth weight, respiratory difficulties, and so forth) but only when a woman had few tangible sources of support (to borrow money, to get a ride somewhere, or to get help if she got sick). How well a family functions during stressful times may be a more important predictor of complications during and after pregnancy than how many stressful events are actually experienced (Smilkstein et al., 1984). Other research has found that

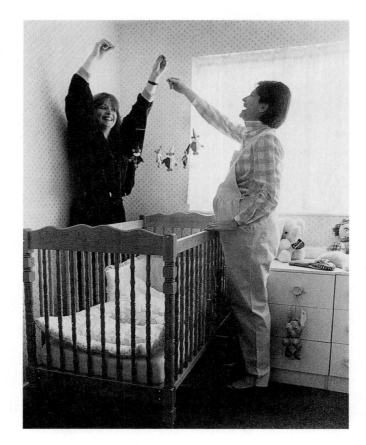

women who receive as little as twenty minutes of psychosocial support addressing concerns and offering encouragement during regular prenatal visits have babies who weigh more than the babies of women who do not receive this support (Rothberg & Lits, 1991).

At the beginning of this chapter we introduced Carmen, who was under considerable pressure at work and worried about the illness of her mother. Although concerned about the consequences of the stresses, Carmen had a supportive husband and other family members with whom to share her apprehensions. She, like others, cannot completely eliminate stress in her life; pregnant women must juggle work, family, and other obligations. To the extent that Carmen establishes opportunities to relax and the people with whom she is comfortable help to manage her stress by providing emotional and social support, she can minimize potentially negative outcomes. Efforts couples initiate to reduce stress or respond to it in adaptive ways can be effective preventive medicine both during pregnancy and after (Samuels & Samuels, 1986).

## A Final Note on Environment and Prenatal Development

After examining the range of teratogens and other factors affecting prenatal development, we may be surprised that babies manage to be born healthy at all. But they are—every day. We should wonder rather at the rich complexity of prenatal development and appreciate more deeply that it proceeds normally so much of the time. Ninety to 95 percent of babies born in the United States, for example, are healthy infants well prepared to adapt to their new environment. Knowledge of teratogens allows prospective parents as well as others in the community to maximize the chances that all infants are equipped to enter the world with as many resources as possible.

## Birth and the Perinatal Environment

When a woman goes into labor, the wet, warm, and supportive world of the uterus undergoes a rapid transformation, and the fetus must adjust to an earth-shaking series of events. During a normal birth the fetus is subjected to increasingly stronger pressure. Uterine contractions, occurring at first only briefly, and about every ten to fifteen minutes apart, begin to take place at shorter intervals and become more powerful, forcing the fetus to enter the narrow birth canal. Pressure, as great as thirty pounds of force, will probably cause the head to become somewhat elongated and misshapen (Trevathen, 1987). At times the fetus may experience brief disruptions in its supply of oxygen as the flow of blood in the umbilical cord is temporarily obstructed. And then the infant emerges head first into a strange new world—drier, possibly colder, and often much brighter and noisier than his previous home. Within minutes the child must begin to take in oxygen. The baby must also soon learn to coordinate sucking, swallowing, and breathing to obtain sufficient nutrients.

Passage from the womb to the outside world initiates momentous physical and other changes for a newborn. The new world introduces others who actively relate to the baby. If the child is wanted, she will be cuddled and talked to, fussed over, and rocked by one, maybe two, perhaps many people. If she is unwanted, she may rarely experience such events. The newborn, in other words, enters a social environment that can be supportive and responsive or barren and uninviting and any number of levels in between. Needs such as nutrition, formerly met by the placenta and various structures in the womb, now depend on social interaction for their gratification. Mothers, fathers, grandparents, siblings, and others become the major environmental resource for physical and psychological growth.

### Childbirth Practices

▶ Sociocultural influence

Societies vary enormously in the techniques and rituals that accompany the transition from fetus to newborn. One fundamental difference is how pregnancy and birth are viewed, either as natural and healthy or as an illness requiring medical care and attention (Newton, 1955). The !Kung, a hunting-and-gathering people living in the Kalahari Desert of Africa, build no huts or facilities for the delivery of babies, because they regard birth as part of the natural order of events requiring no special intervention (Shostak, 1981). In contrast, pregnancy and childbirth in the United States and many other countries during this century have been regarded more as an illness to be managed by professionally trained medical personnel (Dye, 1986). In 1900 fewer than 5 percent of babies were born in hospitals in the United States (Wertz & Wertz, 1977). However, the advent of antiseptic practices, anesthesia and other

Societies differ enormously in their approach to the birth of a baby. Here a midwife from Mauritania, with her own baby swaddled on her back, assists in tying the newborn's umbilical cord.

painkilling drugs, new delivery techniques, and greater knowledge of the anatomy and physiology of gestation led to innovations that transformed childbirth from a natural process to a medical and surgical event. Today, about 99 percent of all babies in the United States are born in hospital maternity wards (National Center for Health Statistics, 1988).

**Medication During Childbirth**    Nearly all births within Western societies are accompanied by some form of medication (Brackbill, 1979). Anesthesia blocks the transmission of pain, analgesics lessen feelings of discomfort, and sedatives relax the woman. All these drugs readily pass through the placenta and enter the fetus's circulatory system. Critics of the routine use of drugs point out that babies whose mothers receive high doses of drugs during labor are reported to be less attentive and responsive to caregivers, more irritable, and to gain weight more slowly than babies exposed to small amounts or no drugs at all (Brackbill, 1979; Brazelton, Nugent, & Lester, 1987). Moreover, some behavioral differences may persist well beyond infancy. Heavy use of drugs during labor has been associated, for example, with an increased incidence of learning disorders among school-aged children (Brackbill, McManus, & Woodward, 1985).

Findings of differences between babies born to medicated and nonmedicated women are not consistent, however, and some experts believe that the negative effects of exposure to drugs at birth have been markedly overstated and occur only when used excessively (Kraemer et al., 1985). As a consequence, women need not experience unreasonable pain or feel guilty if drugs are administered.

**Prepared Childbirth**    Concerns about the effects of drugs used during labor, along with reports of unmedicated but seemingly pain-free delivery by women in other cultures, have led professionals and expectant parents to consider how women can best prepare for the birth of a baby. After observing one woman who reported a pain-free delivery, Grantley Dick-Read, a medical prac-

▶ Sociocultural influence

titioner in Great Britain, concluded that difficult childbirth was fostered largely by the tension and anxiety in which Western civilization cloaked the event. Dick-Read (1959) proposed that women be taught methods of physical relaxation, given information about the process of childbirth, and encouraged to cultivate a cooperative relationship with their doctors to foster a more natural childbirth experience. Others, including Fernand Lamaze (1970), adopted similar ideas, adding procedures to divert thoughts from pain and encouraging breathing activities to support the labor process.

Lamaze and other childbirth education programs (including the National Childbirth Trust in the United Kingdom) have become popular resources for prospective mothers in recent years. Women who attend such classes and adhere to their recommendations generally require lower amounts of drugs during delivery than women who have not participated in prepared childbirth. Women who attend childbirth classes may experience no less pain, but relaxation techniques and an additional element often required in these programs—the assistance of a coach or trainer, usually the father—seem to help counter the pain.

Human birth differs from the birth of other species of mammals in typically requiring some form of assistance (Rosenberg, 1992; Trevathen, 1988). In many cultures the help is provided by friends and relatives or by midwives. Even in the United States childbirth was a social event attended by friends and neighbors until the eighteenth century (Wertz & Wertz, 1977). With the relocation of childbirth to hospitals, however, women were often isolated from family and friends during labor, and a more private and impersonal procedure emerged. However, studies carried out in Guatemala, and more recently in the United States, have shown that a supportive companion during delivery is helpful to women (Kennell et al., 1991; Klaus & Kennell, 1982). In the Guatemala studies first-time mothers were assigned a *doula*, an experienced companion who stayed with the woman and provided support, encouragement, and information about what was happening during labor. Women given these personal attendants spent far less time in labor, required drugs or forceps less frequently, and delivered babies who showed less fetal distress and difficulty in breathing than women who had no doula and received only routine nursing care.

Greater flexibility in position of delivery is another way to provide assistance to women during childbirth. For example, hanging from a bar or standing, squatting, or sitting in special chairs are offered increasingly as options to the traditional recumbent position, especially in European birthing facilities. The alternatives, designed to draw upon any benefits that may accrue from gravity, seem to reduce stress for the baby during delivery, although they may impose slightly increased risk from greater blood loss for the woman (Staff, 1990). Other efforts to make the birth process more gentle, by reducing illumination and noise or delivering the baby under water, have also been proposed (Daniels, 1989; LeBoyer, 1975), although the advantages of these practices for either women or infants have not been fully documented.

**Alternate Birth Settings**    The perception of hospital settings as impersonal and regimented, coupled with a desire to make delivery more relaxing and natural, has led to other revolutionary changes in childbirth practices. Hospitals in the United States began to allow fathers into the delivery room in the early 1970s. Birthing centers within hospitals have become less institutional and more homelike. Home delivery and freestanding birthing centers

▶ Sociocultural influence

(FSBCs) have become further options. For example, nearly 5 percent of babies born in Oregon in the early 1980s were delivered at home or in FSBCs. The alternatives have become popular because women feel more relaxed surrounded by family or friends in a familiar setting, they wish to divorce the experience of pregnancy from the concept of illness, and they feel greater control over what happens to both them and their babies (Eakins, 1984).

Alternative birthing environments do raise the issue of safety, however. Virtually all of the more than 160 FSBCs operating in the United States require women at risk for complications to use traditional medical facilities and have arrangements with nearby hospitals if emergencies arise (Mathews & Sadak, 1991). But for home deliveries, back-up services are often less available, especially when home deliveries take place for economic reasons. The safety of planned home births with licensed midwives in attendance matches that for hospital births (Mathews & Sadak, 1991), but the mortality rate increases nearly twentyfold when home deliveries are unintended. Prenatal planning and screening, along with adequate training of birth attendants, are among the most important factors in making home births relatively safe (Clarke & Bennets, 1982).

## Labor and Delivery

Labor is a complicated interactive process involving three elements: the fetus, the woman, and the placenta. What causes labor to begin? The answer remains largely unknown, although the pituitary gland of the fetus could play a significant role (Trevathen, 1987). Labor is traditionally divided into three stages. The first begins with mild but increasingly severe and frequent contractions that alter the shape of the cervix, preparing it for the fetus's descent. Near the end of the first stage, which lasts an average of eleven hours for first-borns and about seven hours for later-borns, dilation of the cervix proceeds rapidly to allow passage through the birth canal. The second stage consists of the continued descent and birth of the fetus. This stage usually requires a little less than an hour in first-borns and about twenty minutes in later-borns. In the third stage, lasting about fifteen minutes, the placenta is expelled. All times are, however, averages; enormous variations exist from one woman to another.

**Cesarean Birth**    A cesarean birth is the delivery of a baby through a surgical incision in the woman's abdomen and uterus. Cesarean births are recommended when labor fails to progress normally, when the baby's head is very large, or when birth is *breech* (foot or rump first) rather than head first. Concerns about stress on the fetus during birth that might lead to increased risk of brain damage, about vaginal infections that might be transmitted to the baby, and about expensive malpractice suits (should things go awry during vaginal

▶ Sociocultural influence

delivery) have led to a substantial increase in the frequency of cesarean sections in the past twenty years. Today, about 23 percent of deliveries in the United States are cesarean rather than vaginal, a rate that is substantially higher than virtually all other countries; only Brazil and Puerto Rico report higher rates (Centers for Disease Control, 1993).

Women who undergo cesarean section face an increased risk of infection and a longer hospital stay than women who give birth vaginally. Moreover, cesarean babies are likely to be exposed to greater maternal medication. Other concerns center on the different experiences both mother and infant receive under such circumstances. For example, when cesarean babies are delivered before labor begins, they do not have a misshapen head and appear perfectly healthy, but they have substantially lower levels of two stress hormones, adrenaline and noradrenaline, which are known to facilitate respiration by helping to keep the lungs open and clear. The hormones also enhance cell metabolism, circulation of the blood to the brain, and activity level, factors that help the infant make the transition to the new environment and to become responsive to caregivers. Thus, cesarean babies generally tend to have more trouble breathing, are less active, sleep more, and cry less than other babies (Trevathen, 1987).

**Birth Trauma**    The increase in the frequency of cesarean sections in the United States has come about partly because of concerns about birth trauma, or injuries sustained at birth. A potentially serious consequence is *anoxia*, or deprivation of oxygen. Anoxia can result from damage to or lengthy compression of the umbilical cord or head during birth. It may also result from failure of the baby to begin regular breathing after birth. If oxygen deprivation lasts more than a few minutes, the baby can suffer severe damage to the central nervous system.

Fortunately, brief periods of anoxia have few long-lasting effects. Furthermore, an adequate postnatal caregiving environment can be extremely important in helping to counter potentially negative outcomes for infants experiencing periods of anoxia (Sameroff & Chandler, 1975). Concerns about anoxia and other birth traumas, however, have led to the rapidly expanded use of **fetal monitoring devices** during labor. Most of these devices record fetal heartbeat to determine whether the fetus is undergoing stress during delivery. However, some experts question whether the devices are more beneficial than the ordinary stethoscope for making medical decisions in all but high-risk pregnancies (Shy et al., 1990).

## Low Birth Weight

▶ Individual differences

As infant and childhood diseases have come under greater control in recent decades, prevention and treatment of low-birth-weight infants (less than two thousand five hundred grams, or five-and-a-half pounds) has gained increased attention. Study after study has confirmed that as birth weight increases to normal levels, mortality rate rapidly declines (see Figure 4.5). The United States has a higher proportion of infants born with low birth weight than many other developed countries, a major reason that this country's infant mortality rate is also higher (see Figure 4.6). Among the explanations for this poor ranking is a relatively large number of births to teenagers and the lack of prenatal care for some members of the population.

▶ Sociocultural influence

Babies with low birth weight fall into two groups: those born *preterm* (less than thirty-five weeks' conceptual age) whose development has generally proceeded normally but has been cut short by early delivery, and those born near their expected arrival date and who are *small for gestational age* (*SGA*). Thus, low-birth-weight infants comprise a heterogeneous group, perhaps needing separate types of medical treatment and intervention and facing differing developmental outcomes. Congenital anomalies are somewhat more frequent in SGA infants, for example, whereas respiratory distress is more likely among infants who are born preterm (Starfield et al., 1982).

In general, infants born with low birth weight face many obstacles. Cerebral palsy, seizure disorders, and other neurological problems are more frequent

**Fetal monitoring device**    Medical device used to monitor fetal heartbeat during delivery.

## FIGURE 4.5

### Birth Weight and Infant Mortality

Mortality rate is much greater in infants of very low (<1,500 grams) and low birth weight (<2,500 grams) compared with infants of normal birth weight. Advances in the treatment of these infants can help to lower the mortality rate, but an even more effective way to reduce infant mortality may be to provide medical, educational, and social assistance to avoid the causes of low birth weight in infants in the first place.

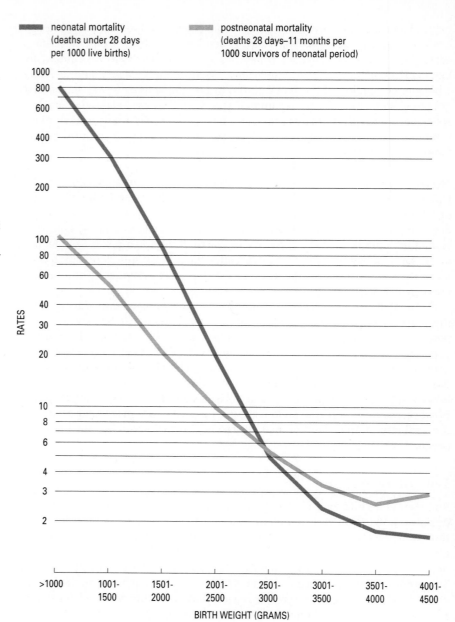

Source: Adapted from Shapiro et al., 1980.

than in babies of normal birth weight. The risk is especially great for infants of very or extremely low birth weight (less than one thousand grams, or about two-and-a-quarter pounds). Respiratory difficulties, hyperactivity, greater frequency of illness, and disruption of parental caregiving and family functioning are common problems for the infants (Blackman, 1991).

Despite their immediate difficulties, low-birth-weight children who manage to survive often do surprisingly well. An analysis of data from more than eighty different studies conducted in North America, Europe, Australia, and New Zealand concluded that only small differences in intellectual and developmental capabilities exist for low-birth-weight compared with normal-weight children (Aylward et al., 1989). Nevertheless, a higher proportion of low- than full-birth-weight children, especially those with extremely low birth weights, display visuomotor deficits, learning disabilities, and behavior problems as children. The problems are likely to result in poorer school achievement and to more frequently require special education intervention (Halsey, Collin, & Anderson, 1993; Marlowe, Roberts, & Cook, 1993; Ross, Lipper & Auld, 1991). Such children also tend to display fewer social skills and experience more peer rejection (Hoy et al., 1992; Landry et al., 1990).

Although greater percentages of low-birth-weight infants suffer disabling conditions, supportive caregiving and intervention designed to assist caregivers and their low-birth-weight children can substantially reduce the extent to which they exhibit deficits (Achenbach et al., 1990; Parker et al., 1992; Ramey et al., 1992). For example, as can be seen in Figure 4.7, Jeanne Brooks-Gunn and her colleagues (1993) found that these children were able to maintain higher levels of performance on cognitive tests when they and their families participated in educational day-care programs, regular home visits, and frequent parent group meetings than when these resources were not available.

**Caring for Low-Birth-Weight Babies** Attempts to reduce complications associated with low birth weight have proceeded on two fronts. Improved medical care has permitted more low-birth-weight, especially extremely low-birth-weight, infants to survive and develop normally. Better regulation of temperature, more careful use of drugs, sensitive monitoring of biochemical functions, and other advances in neonatal intensive care units (NICUs) in the United States (called *special care baby units* in the United Kingdom) have

▶ Roles of nature and nurture

▶ Sociocultural influence

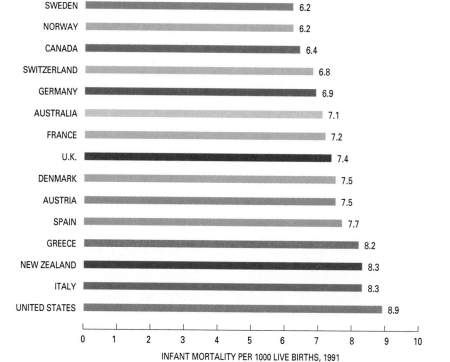

**FIGURE 4.6**

**Infant Mortality in Selected Developed Countries**

The infant mortality rate (deaths before one year of age per thousand live births) is a measure that provides an indication of the overall health of a nation. A number of countries have a lower infant mortality rate than the United States.

| Country | Infant Mortality per 1000 Live Births, 1991 |
|---|---|
| SWEDEN | 6.2 |
| NORWAY | 6.2 |
| CANADA | 6.4 |
| SWITZERLAND | 6.8 |
| GERMANY | 6.9 |
| AUSTRALIA | 7.1 |
| FRANCE | 7.2 |
| U.K. | 7.4 |
| DENMARK | 7.5 |
| AUSTRIA | 7.5 |
| SPAIN | 7.7 |
| GREECE | 8.2 |
| NEW ZEALAND | 8.3 |
| ITALY | 8.3 |
| UNITED STATES | 8.9 |

INFANT MORTALITY PER 1000 LIVE BIRTHS, 1991

Source: United Nations Statistical Office (1993).

This infant, although born prematurely, has the opportunity to explore a rich array of brightly colored toys in his new environment. He also receives frequent handling by caregivers. However, questions remain about how much and what kinds of stimulation are optimal for the development of children born with low birth weight.

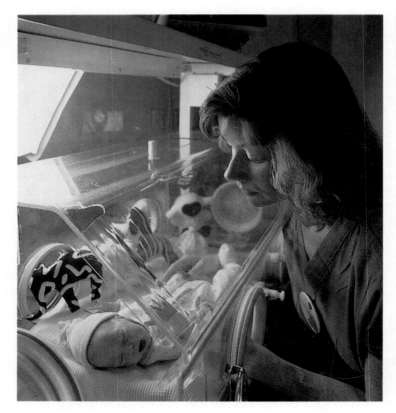

▶ Roles of nature and nurture

proved remarkably effective in reducing mortality rate (Ehrenhaft, Wagner, & Herdman, 1989).

A second major assault on the problem of low birth weight is directed at preventing or at least minimizing its occurrence. Researchers have catalogued a long list of demographic, medical, and behavioral factors associated with low birth weight. Providing adequate prenatal care, meeting nutritional needs, and initiating early and frequent education about the effects of smoking, drugs, and other risk factors both before and during pregnancy can reduce the enormous medical, social, and psychological costs associated with low birth weight.

For an infant born with low birth weight the first major task is to maintain physiological stability. Another critical task is to achieve regular cycles or patterns of activity involving sleep and wakefulness—patterns that infants of normal birth weight routinely display within a few weeks of birth but that infants of low birth weight often take much longer to achieve (Barnard, 1987; Horowitz, 1987b; Gunzenhauser, 1987). They have trouble falling asleep, awakening, maintaining alertness, and settling into regular and efficient feeding schedules (Barnard, 1987).

Are low-birth-weight infants too fragile to receive any stimulation beyond that necessarily imposed by medical treatment? At one time parents were either excluded completely from intensive care units or were cautioned to handle premature babies as little as possible. However, as evidence emerged demonstrating the importance of stimulation for social and intellectual development in full-birth-weight infants, concerns that low-birth-weight infants might

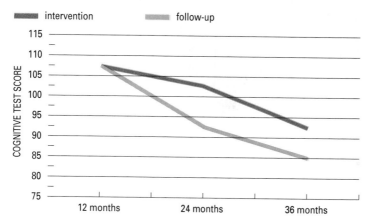

Source: Brooks-Gunn, Klebanov, Liaw, & Spiker, 1993.

**FIGURE 4.7**

**Low-Birth-Weight Children's Cognitive Development as a Function of Intervention**

In a large-scale study investigating the effects of providing home visits and educational child care for low-birth-weight infants and their families, Brooks-Gunn and her colleagues (1993) found that performance on measures of intellectual development was substantially better for those who received the intervention than for those who did not. Although some decline in scores occurred even for the group receiving intervention, it was far less than for those who did not receive the intervention. Both groups performed similarly at the youngest age (12 months), perhaps because tests measuring cognitive skills often are not very sensitive to differences at that age.

not receive adequate stimulation began to surface (Ramey, Bryant, & Suarez, 1987; Thoman, 1993).

Giving low-birth-weight babies appropriate stimulation, many professionals agree, is highly desirable, but what kind should it be? Should caregivers offer compensatory environments, attempting to duplicate what the baby would have gained if still in the womb? Compensatory stimulation, for example, has consisted of the use of oscillating devices or waterbeds to simulate movements the fetus experiences prenatally, muffled recordings of a human voice, a heartbeat, or other sounds to match those usually heard in the womb, and opportunities for nonnutritive sucking, an activity in which the fetus occasionally engages (Korner, 1987; Thoman, 1993). Or, by reasoning that preterm babies must respond to gravity, organize respiratory and digestive functions, and process stimulation much as full-term infants do, should caregiving be enriching, that is, approximate the visual and auditory stimulation, handling, and social contact that a typical newborn might receive (Scafidi et al., 1990; Thoman, 1993)?

Benefits from both types of stimulation have been reported: more rapid weight gain, shorter hospital stays, fewer medical and eating problems, more regular patterns of breathing and heart rate, improvements in sensorimotor development, more regular and longer periods in quiet states, and more appropriate and effective transitions from one state to another (Gorski, 1991; Korner, 1987; Thoman, 1993). However, other studies have failed to find advantages of such stimulation, and even in those that have, not all low-birth-weight babies benefit and there is little evidence that those who do benefit maintain the gains.

Perhaps discrepancies in the findings should not be surprising; treatments have differed greatly and have been of limited breadth or duration. Moreover, children in both treatment and control groups may be exposed to social and rearing conditions upon leaving the hospital that can have a far more powerful influence on later development (Korner, 1987). In addition, an appropriate kind of stimulation for one premature baby at one point in his development may be ineffective, even overstimulating, at another moment. From this perspective the goal of caring for low-birth-weight infants, as for every infant, should be to fit the individual baby's needs with an environment that complements those needs (Gorski, 1991). As Evelyn Thoman recently concluded, "Exploring procedures for providing optimal individualized care is the

▶ Individual differences

emerging notion which will have a major impact on future directions in premature care and research" (1993, p. 15).

Another essential part of successful intervention, both during hospitalization and after the baby goes home, entails the support and encouragement of parents in their efforts to care for low-birth-weight infants. Furnishing parents with opportunities to engage in suitable caregiving in the hospital situation, instructing them to recognize the specific needs of their infant and what behaviors to expect, and providing emotional support from hospital staff, other parents, and service agencies are types of assistance that can have a powerful effect on the development of low-birth-weight children and others with special needs (Korner, 1987). Even simple parent training, such as permitting the mother to observe the administration of a standard infant test or providing her with weekly reports on the infant's activities, has been found to increase the mother's sensitivity to and involvement with her infant and to foster her baby's development (Szajnberg et al., 1987; Widmayer & Field, 1981; Worobey & Belsky, 1982). Such activities may help because they clarify how each low-birth-weight infant attempts to cope with and adapt to the new environment.

## *The Newborn*

Even parents of a healthy infant may be in for a surprise when they see their baby for the first time. Unless delivered by cesarean section, the baby is likely to have a flattened nose and a large distorted head, produced when the bones of the skull override one another during passage through the narrow birth canal. The skin of all babies, regardless of racial background, is a pale pinkish color and often is covered by an oily cheeselike substance (the vernix caseosa) that protects against infection. Sex organs are swollen by high levels of sex hormones.

If the parents are startled, though, just imagine what kind of adjustment the baby must make. An infant's most immediate need after emerging from the birth canal is to breathe. Pressure on the chest during delivery probably helps to clear the baby's fluid-filled lungs, but the shock of cool air, perhaps accompanied by jiggling, a slap, or some other less-than-gentle activity by a birth attendant, makes the first breath more like a gasp, quickly followed by a reflexive cry. The umbilical cord can continue to pulse for several minutes after birth, and in most societies the cord is not cut until after it ceases to do so (Trevathen, 1987). In the United States, however, the cord is usually cut immediately, a practice under criticism, because the placenta continues to provide an oxygen-rich source of blood for a short time after delivery (Desmond, Rudolph, & Phitaksphraiwan, 1963).

▶ Sociocultural influence

The second major task the baby must accomplish upon entering the world is to regulate body temperature. Babies lose body heat about four times more rapidly than adults, because of their lower fat reserve and relatively large body surface (Bruck, 1962). As a consequence, newborns are often quickly separated from their mothers and placed under heaters. They can, however, effectively maintain their temperature when held by their mothers (Hill & Shronk, 1979).

### Assessing Newborns

Newborns typically weigh five-and-a-half to ten pounds and measure eighteen to twenty-two inches in length. Many medical measures for evaluating their

| Vital Sign | Ratings | | |
|---|---|---|---|
| | 0 | 1 | 2 |
| Heart rate | Absent | Slow (below 100) | Over 100 |
| Respiratory effort | Absent | Slow, irregular | Good, crying |
| Muscle tone | Flaccid | Some flexion of extremities | Active motion |
| Reflex responsivity | No response | Grimace | Vigorous cry |
| Color | Blue, pale | Body pink, extremities blue | Completely pink |

Source: From Apgar, 1953.

**TABLE 4.4**

**The Apgar Scoring System**

The Apgar Scale is given at and shortly after birth to diagnose the physical condition of a newborn. The ratings for each vital sign are added for a total score ranging from 0 to 10. An infant who scores less than 4 is considered at risk.

health have become available in recent years, but one routinely administered is the *Apgar Scale* (Apgar, 1953). Assessed normally at one and five minutes after birth, the Apgar measures five vital signs: heart rate, respiratory effort, muscle tone, reflex responsivity, and color. Each vital sign is assigned a score of 0, 1, or 2 based on the criteria described in Table 4.4. In the United States 90 percent of infants receive a total score of 7 or better; those who score less than 4 are considered at risk.

A more extensive measure developed by T. Berry Brazelton (1973), the *Neonatal Behavioral Assessment Scale* (*NBAS*), evaluates the baby's behavior on a variety of dimensions such as ability to interact with the tester, responsiveness to objects in the environment, reflex motor capacities, and ability to control behavioral state. Typical questions include, Does the baby watch while the examiner moves her head back and forth and side to side and calls out the baby's name in a high-pitched voice? Does the baby cuddle or resist being held? Does the baby remove a cloth placed over his face, grasp a forefinger placed in his hand, attempt to hold his head upright while in a sitting position, and become quiet within a reasonable time after being fussy?

Newborn performance on the NBAS has been used to assess neurological condition and can indicate whether certain prenatal or perinatal conditions, as well as intervention programs, have had an effect (Korner, 1987; Tronick, 1987). An NBAS score can also predict later developmental outcomes. Babies who score poorly on the scale continue to be somewhat less responsive to caregivers in the first few months after birth (Vaughn et al., 1980). In general, however, the predictive validity of the NBAS (along with other infant tests) for long-term development is only modest at best (Brazelton, Nugent, & Lester, 1987). Nevertheless, parents who observe while examiners give the NBAS or who are trained to give it themselves seem to become more responsive to and effective in interactions with their infants (Worobey, 1985).

## Newborn Sleep States

Babies sleep. They sleep a lot. But newborns and young infants display a wide variety of states: regular and irregular sleep, drowsiness, alert inactivity, alert activity, and crying. Crying or distress usually begins with whimpering but swiftly shifts to full-scale cries, often accompanied by thrashing of arms and legs. During alert activity the infant also exhibits vigorous, diffuse motor

▶ Individual differences

▶ Sociocultural influence

**FIGURE 4.8**

**Developmental Changes in Sleep Requirements**

The young infant not only sleeps more than children or adults but also spends a substantially greater proportion of that time in rapid-eye-movement (REM) sleep. Newborns fall asleep and wake up in the REM state. By about age two or three, however, children begin sleep in the non-REM (NREM) state, the pattern also observed for older individuals. Moreover, very young infants may alternate between REM and NREM sleep every fifteen to twenty minutes, changes that occur much less frequently in older individuals.

activity, but such exertions are not accompanied by signs of distress. During alert inactivity the baby is relatively quiet, at least in terms of motor activity, but actively engages in visual scanning of the environment. In this state the baby appears most responsive to sensory stimulation and may be learning a great deal.

Although individual differences are great, newborns average sixteen to seventeen hours of sleep a day. The duration of sleep and wake cycles is extremely short, and babies are easily disrupted by external stimulation. As the weeks pass, babies gradually sleep less but for longer periods; by about three to five weeks of age a pattern begins to emerge in which the longest sleep periods take place at night (Thompson, 1982). But naps during the day continue to be a regular occurrence through the preschool years. In fact, in some cultures such naps are never eliminated.

The development of sleep patterns differs substantially across various cultures. In the United States parents are often eager to have their infants adopt a routine that matches their own. A significant milestone is reached when the baby of three or four months finally sleeps through the night. In some cultures, such as the Kipsigi of rural Kenya, however, infants are permitted more flexible sleep patterns and they will not sleep through the night until much older (Super & Harkness, 1982).

Like adults, infants display two distinct sleep states. During active or *REM* (rapid-eye-movement) sleep, eye movements and muscle jerks are frequent, and breathing and heart rate are irregular. During quiet sleep (*NREM*) eye and muscle movements are few, and physiological activity is more regular. The proportion of time spent in the two states, however, shifts dramatically during the first year of life (see Figure 4.8). In fact, the large amount of sleep required by infants is largely a result of their greater need for REM sleep.

Active or REM sleep has been linked to dreaming, but it is not clear that young infants dream. Even if they do, why do they spend so much time in REM sleep? REM sleep is believed to be important for normal brain activity (Roffwarg, Muzio, & Dement, 1966). *Autostimulation theory* proposes that REM sleep provides powerful stimulation to the central nervous system, which

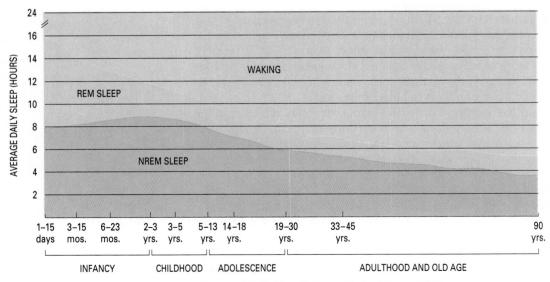

Source: Adapted from Roffwarg, Muzio, & Dement, 1966.

in adults is interpreted as sensory and motor activity associated with dreaming. According to this theory, stimulation during REM sleep compensates for the relatively brief number of hours each day the infant is awake. Infants kept awake for relatively lengthy periods of time show reduced amounts of REM sleep, and premature infants, whose wakeful periods are even more limited, show more REM sleep than full-term babies (Boismer, 1977; Roffwarg, Muzio, & Dement, 1966). If autostimulation theory is correct, it is a further demonstration of how important stimulation is for development, even at those times when considerable sleep is essential as well.

## THEMES IN DEVELOPMENT

## THE PRENATAL PERIOD AND BIRTH

▶ **What roles do nature and nurture play in prenatal development and birth?**

Prenatal development is the product of complex interactions involving genetic instructions inherited from parents (see Chapter 3) and the expectant woman's physical and emotional conditions: exposure to drugs, diseases, hazardous chemicals, stressful living conditions, and adequate diet, and the use of medication before and during pregnancy and during labor. We have seen, for example, that differentiation of organs and systems in the embryo typically obeys principles established by biochemical and physiological processes. Yet these processes do not operate in a vacuum. Teratogens and various intrauterine conditions can radically alter the normal path. Thus, events in the life of the woman may change the immediate environment within her womb, with drastic consequences for the fetus. The reactions, attitudes, and availability of the newborn's caregivers and the stimulation they provide are other major sources of potential influence on the baby's development.

▶ **How does the sociocultural context influence prenatal development and birth?**

The immediate internal environment of the fetus and the interactions of caregivers for the newborn can be influenced dramatically by the larger social, economic, and cultural settings in which pregnancy and birth take place. The woman's actions during pregnancy are often modified or regulated by a network of expectations, advice, and resources provided by the culture in which she lives. An expectant woman in one community, for example, may have access to medical and other kinds of care that provide a more healthy environment for the fetus than a woman in another community. Industry or governing units may legislate controls on chemical pollution in one country, ignore them in another. Scientific and technological advances in prenatal testing, birthing practices, and newborn care may be available in one region of the world but not another; even when available, however, not all parents may have the economic resources or desire to use them. Support provided by societies to deal with these problems can be a major factor in the infant's successful development.

▶ **Is development before and after birth continuous or discontinuous?**

When the zygote attaches to the uterine wall and taps a new source of nourishment, its course of development changes dramatically. Once the various organs and systems are formed and become less susceptible to environmental disruptions, the fetus achieves a vastly different status. The process of birth itself is a major transition. Such dramatic changes fit with discontinuous or stagelike descriptions of development. So too do the marked shifts in vulnerability to teratogens observed during prenatal development. Underlying the progressions, however, are biochemical and physiological processes governing cell proliferation, differentiation, and the emergence and functioning of biological systems that can be seen as continuous. Many dramatic changes are essentially the product of modest quantitative modifications in the multifaceted complex environment that promotes development.

▶ **How prominent are individual differences in prenatal development and the newborn?**

Newborns everywhere undergo many common gestational experiences to reach this point in their development; however, individual differences already have begun to surface. Many differences arise because, contrary to once widely held beliefs, the fetus is not immune to the influences of the larger world. Because of exposure to teratogens and other maternal conditions, babies will differ in their physical and behavioral qualities and their ability to cope with and adapt to their new environment. As a result, some infants may require extensive medical and social care. Greater knowledge of and sensitivity to those differences by caregivers, whether exhibited by a newborn with special needs such as one with low birth weight or by an infant who falls within the typical range of assessments for newborns, can help to ensure success for the continued development of every child.

## Summary

**The Stages of Prenatal Development**     Prenatal development is the period that extends from conception to birth. During this time a newly fertilized ovum is transformed from a single-celled zygote into the complex active organism that is the newborn. During the *germinal period*, about the first ten to fourteen days after conception, the zygote migrates from the Fallopian tube to the uterus, becomes multicelled, and implants in the uterine wall to gain access to a new source of nutrients directly from the woman.

The *embryonic period* begins after implantation and continues until about the eighth week after conception. This period is marked by development of the *placenta* and other supportive structures within the uterine environment and by the differentiation of cells into tissues that form the major organs and systems of the embryo. Many vital organs, including the brain, begin forming at this time. The embryo is susceptible to a variety of *teratogens*, environmental agents that can disrupt development and interfere with later behavior.

The *fetal period*, beginning in about the eighth week after conception and lasting until birth, is marked by continued growth and refinement of organs and systems. Neurons continue to form and migrate during this period. Brain activity, sensory reactions, and movement are more easily detected, and by the beginning of the third trimester of pregnancy the fetus may be able to survive should birth occur prematurely.

**Environmental Factors Influencing Prenatal Development**   Many drugs, diseases, chemicals, and other agents can cross the placental barrier and induce fetal death, produce congenital malformations, and contribute to other negative outcomes in development. The effects of exposure to a specific teratogen depend on many factors, such as the genetic susceptibility of the woman and her fetus, stage of fetal development, and means of access and level of exposure of the teratogen to the fetus. Teratogens can have different consequences, ranging from transient delays to irreversible defects to outcomes apparent only much later in development. Conditions of the woman, including how much stress she experiences, the availability of social and emotional support, and her nutritional and health status, can also influence fetal development.

**Birth and the Perinatal Environment**   The practices and procedures surrounding the birth and initial care of a baby are part of the *perinatal period* of development. Cultures differ enormously in their methods of managing childbirth. Differences include where the baby is born, who is present at birth, and how much and what kinds of medication are made available to the woman during labor. Concerns about isolated and restrictive regimens, as well as an overreliance on medication in traditional hospital settings, have led to a variety of more natural methods of preparing for and delivering children in many Western societies.

As infant and childhood diseases have come under increasing control, researchers have directed their attention to the prevention and treatment of low-birth-weight infants. Despite the immediate obstacles facing both preterm and small-for-gestational-age babies, many become normal children and adults. Compensatory and enrichment programs increase early weight gains and other aspects of early development and have come to increasingly recognize the individual needs of low-birth-weight infants.

**The Newborn**   The brief but climactic beginnings taking place prenatally and perinatally set the stage for the long course of *postnatal development*. Newborns have the immediate task of responding to their new environment. Tests such as the Apgar and Neonatal Behavioral Assessment scales provide some indication of the baby's physiological state and ability to interact with caregivers and respond to stimulation. Newborns and infants display a number of sleeping and waking states, and a relatively large proportion of their sleep time is engaged in REM sleep, a state that may provide them with stimulation even when asleep.

# 5

# Physical Growth and Motor Skills

## Key Themes in This Chapter

▶ What roles do nature and nurture play in physical growth and motor skill development?

▶ How does the sociocultural context influence physical growth and motor skill development?

▶ How does the child play an active role in the process of physical growth and motor skill development?

▶ Are physical growth and motor skill development continuous or discontinuous?

▶ How prominent are individual differences in physical growth and motor skill development?

▶ How do physical growth and motor skill development interact with other domains of development?

*She had not been able to sleep very well the previous night. Maybe that was why she felt so tired. Or maybe it was the grueling tennis match in which she was now engaged. She was only fourteen, but this match was for the state high school championship. Erin had faced similar situations before. Just three months earlier, her teammates had looked to her to score the final points to win the league basketball title. She had not let them down. Now she was on the spot again, in a completely different sport.*

*"Competitive from the day she was born," her mother always said of Erin, but there was much in Erin's family life to encourage her athletic abilities. Her father had been a university basketball player, and her brothers were constantly playing basketball in the front yard; she joined them whenever they'd let her. From the age of eight she attended sports camp faithfully, spending two months each summer engaged in swimming, field hockey, soccer, tennis, any sport in which she could participate. By the age of ten Erin was good—very good—at most sports, although she was one of the shortest girls in her class. After she turned twelve, however, Erin began to grow rapidly and now was taller than many of her classmates, including some of the boys.*

*Erin played a tough match, but she lost. She was disappointed but not devastated. She knew she had played well. Erin's athletic proficiency contributed to a core of self-esteem solid enough to survive temporary setbacks. Erin would draw on her reserve of confidence often in the course of the many tumultuous physical, social/emotional, and cognitive transformations that comprised her adolescent years.*

Physical growth and advances in motor skills are among the most readily apparent indicators of development throughout infancy, childhood, and early adulthood. The changes are accompanied by less obvious, but no less revolutionary, neurological changes in the brain. What is more, physical growth, brain growth, and the development of motor skills significantly influence, and in turn are affected by, social, emotional, and cognitive dimensions of development. Consider how newfound motor skills can, for example, dramatically stimulate cognition. The infant who begins to reach for and grasp objects acquires fresh and powerful means of both gaining information about her world and influencing it. Equally, the child just beginning to crawl—simply by being forced to pay attention to various surfaces or the location of objects to investigate—learns a tremendous amount about her environment.

The reactions of others to the child's changing physical appearance and accomplishments can elicit and encourage new activities or stifle and interfere with them. The child just beginning to crawl may confront new barriers—the side of a playpen, a gate, or a loud "no" from the caregiver. The toddler who insists on dressing himself but still lacks the fine motor skills for buttoning and unbuttoning may become easily frustrated, overtaxing his mother's patience as she tries to get him to day care and herself to work on time. His need for increasing autonomy and his efforts to master new motor skills are two facets of the same developmental impulse, but his mother may have other agendas to consider in fostering them.

A young adolescent such as Erin, satisfied with the changes her body has undergone, may feel confident not only about learning new physical activities but in initiating new social relationships as well. Conversely, the child who fails to display certain skills or who lacks attributes valued in a society—who is shorter, less coordinated, or otherwise physically distinctive—may receive strikingly different treatment than the child who is tall, strong, or athletic.

How do body, brain, and motor skills develop? Are they determined only by genetic factors or do parenting, cultural, or other environmental events influence their course? How important are such elements as appearance, early maturity, and physical prowess? Are the many physical differences that can be readily observed among children important or not? The answers can be found by examining the distinctive ways in which the child's body, brain, and motor skills develop. Another important consideration is the effect that physical growth and the acquisition of motor skills have upon progress in other domains and how these other factors influence physical development in turn. We begin with a description of physical growth.

## Body Growth and Development

The mysterious ability of a living organism to grow is a phenomenon that never loses its capacity to amaze. For parent and child alike the ever-higher pencil marks on the bathroom wall are eloquent testimony to the passage of time. A long-absent aunt who cries, "My, how you've grown!" may summon a grin from the wary seven-year-old or a blush from the self-conscious thirteen-year-old, but she is confirming for them the social importance of this sign of increasing physical maturity.

We tend to use the words *grow* and *develop* interchangeably in describing the physical transformations of childhood, but they do not refer to the same processes. Strictly speaking, *growth* is the increase in size of the body or its organs. *Development* refers not only to changes in size but also to the orderly patterns, such as growth spurts, and the more complicated levels of functioning associated with physical and other changes.

### Norms of Growth

By recording information about the size and weight of large numbers of children from various populations, we can determine whether a particular child's

Variation in height is just one of the many ways that children of the same age differ in their physical development. These individual differences are most pronounced as children approach the adolescent years. Although the same age, perhaps the ability of these children to play the clarinet is as varied as their heights and the clothes they wear.

individual growth falls within the range expected for her chronological age and ethnic background. These **norms**, quantitative measures that provide typical values and variations in height and weight for children, have also become an essential reference for attempting to answer questions about how biological and experiential factors influence growth.

Length and Height     The most rapid increase in body length, as we saw in Chapter 4, occurs during the fourth month of prenatal development when the fetus grows about 1.5 millimeters a day (Sinclair, 1985). Babies continue to grow rapidly, albeit at a somewhat slower rate, during the remaining prenatal weeks and also postnatally, especially during their first six months. In fact, if growth rate during the first six months after birth were sustained, the average ten-year-old would be about one hundred feet tall (McCall, 1979). Moreover, some researchers believe sudden growth spurts of one-quarter to one-half inch may occasionally occur literally overnight in infants and toddlers (Lampl, Veldhuis, & Johnson, 1992). One rule of thumb is that girls reach approximately half their adult height at about one and one-half years of age, boys at about two years of age (Krogman, 1972).

Throughout infancy and childhood boys and girls grow at similar rates, although individual children of course may differ enormously. At about ten or eleven years of age, however, many girls begin an adolescent growth spurt, a period when growth occurs at nearly double the rate of childhood. Because the growth spurt usually does not start in boys until about two years later, girls may tower over their male peers for a brief period in early adolescence. Figure 5.1 depicts the pattern of growth for children during their first eighteen years. Derived from measurements obtained in a cross-sectional sample of boys and girls in England in 1965, the pattern is typical of many populations of children.

▶ Individual differences

Weight     In contrast with height, the maximum rate of increase in weight occurs shortly after birth, as shown in Figure 5.1. In the first few days after delivery newborns typically lose excess body fluids and shed 5 to 10 percent of their birth weight. But then infants usually make rapid weight gains, normally doubling their birth weight in about five months and tripling it by the end of the first year (Pinyerd, 1992). If the gains for the first six months were

**norms**  Measure of average values and variations in some aspect of development such as physical size and motor skill development in relation to age.

FIGURE 5.1

## Growth Curves for Height and Weight in Boys and Girls

Babies shoot up faster than teenagers and gain weight just as rapidly, as this chart of average individual growth in height and weight for British boys and girls in 1965 shows. Note how boys and girls are similar in height and weight until adolescence, when girls typically show an adolescent growth spurt about two years before boys. The later growth spurt found in boys, however, is usually more intense, and they often overtake girls in height and weight.

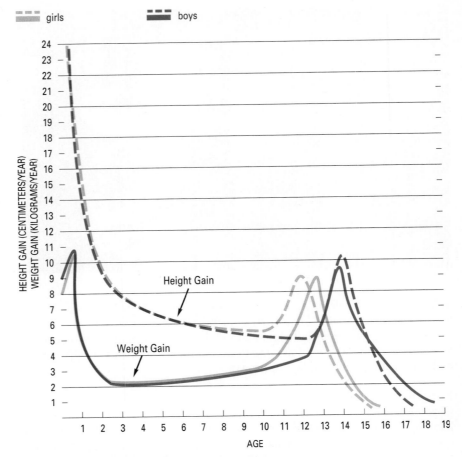

Source: Adapted from Tanner, Whitehouse, & Takaishi, 1966.

sustained, the average ten-year-old would weigh in at about 240,000 tons (McCall, 1979). Weight gains are smallest during childhood between the ages of two and three and gradually increase until just before adolescence. During the adolescent growth spurt, however, a girl can expect to put on thirty-five pounds, a boy forty-five pounds.

## Patterns in Body Growth

The development of individual systems within the body often proceeds at rates different from that of the body as a whole. The most dramatic example probably is head size. Two months after conception the head constitutes nearly 50 percent of total body length. By birth, however, head size represents only about 25 percent, and by adulthood it accounts for 12 to 13 percent of total body length, as Figure 5.2 shows.

Other organs, including the muscles and the respiratory and digestive systems, follow the pattern of overall general weight change: substantial gains during the first two years; a slower, more stable increase throughout childhood; and a rapid increase during adolescence. The central nervous system

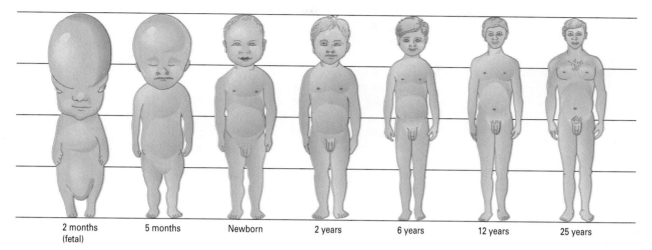

| 2 months (fetal) | 5 months | Newborn | 2 years | 6 years | 12 years | 25 years |

Source: Adapted from Robbins et al., 1928.

**FIGURE 5.2**

**Changes in Body Proportions During Prenatal and Postnatal Growth**

The size of the human head in proportion to the rest of the body shows striking changes over the course of prenatal to adult development. Two months after conception, the head comprises about half of the entire length of the body. By adulthood, the head makes up only about 12 to 13 percent of total body length. The head's tendency to grow more rapidly than regions of the body near the "tail" demonstrates the pattern of cephalocaudal development.

along with the head shows an early and extremely rapid increase in weight. By five or six years of age 90 percent of the adult level for brain and head size has been reached. The reproductive system, not surprisingly, follows a strikingly different pattern; only during adolescence do organs associated with reproduction begin to mature and rapidly approach their adult size.

The patterns mirror the functional importance of various systems of the body at specific points in development. The brain's relatively early maturity makes possible neural involvement in many aspects of early behavior acquisition and development. Similarly, the increase in the weight of the reproductive organs during adolescence is an important component in the emergence of adult sexual maturity.

**Directionality of Growth**   The varying growth trends we observe in many parts of the body follow two common patterns of development. **Cephalocaudal development**—cephalocaudal combines the Greek words for *head* and *tail*—describes the tendency for systems and parts of the body near the head to grow more rapidly than those more distant from the head. In Chapter 4 we noted that the neural tube closes earlier at the end near the head than at the lower end of the spinal column and that upper limbs differentiate earlier than lower limbs, as predicted by the cephalocaudal principle. The pattern is also evident in the more rapid rate of development of the head compared with the rest of the body. **Proximodistal development** refers to the finding that regions near the middle of the body also tend to differentiate more rapidly than regions near the periphery. A good example is the ability of infants to control body parts nearer their trunk, such as their upper arms and legs, much sooner than areas more distant, such as their fingers and toes.

**cephalocaudal development**
Pattern that organs, systems, and motor movements near the head tend to develop earlier than those near the feet.

**proximodistal development**
Pattern that organs and systems of the body near the middle tend to develop earlier than those near the periphery.

Not all physical changes conform to the cephalocaudal or proximodistal principles of development. During the adolescent growth spurt, for example, some parts of the body undergo rapid growth in a pattern almost the reverse of the proximodistal principle. We are all familiar with the teenager who seems to be all hands and feet. Hands and feet are in fact usually the first body parts to show a dramatic change during this period; they are followed by arms and legs and, last of all, the trunk (Tanner, 1978). An adolescent, in other words, is likely to outgrow his shoes first, then his trousers, and finally his jacket.

▶ Individual differences

**Individual and Group Differences**    Children show substantial deviations from the norm in their rates of physical growth and development. Individual variations in size are already noticeable at birth. For example, boys already tend to be slightly longer and heavier than girls at this time (Copper et al., 1993). Individual differences in growth continue throughout infancy and childhood, often becoming especially evident during the adolescent years, when children are likely to show enormous variation in the timing, speed, and duration of the adolescent growth spurt. In the United States the onset of rapid adolescent growth typically occurs between the ages of ten and fourteen for girls and twelve and sixteen for boys (Sinclair, 1985). A girl who once towered over her childhood friends may suddenly find at age thirteen that she is looking up to them—temporarily, at least. A boy whose athletic skills were unremarkable may find himself the starting center for the junior high basketball team if he undergoes an early adolescent growth spurt.

▶ Sociocultural influence

Variability in growth occurs among ethnic and cultural groups as well. For example, American infants of African heritage tend to weigh slightly less than American infants of European heritage at birth, even when social class, gestational age, and other factors known to affect birth weight are equated (Goldenberg et al., 1991). Ethnic and cultural variability are further exhibited throughout childhood as Figure 5.3, illustrating the average height of eight-year-old girls from thirty-seven cultures, reveals.

▶ Role of nature and nurture

## Determinants of Body Growth and Development

Developmental psychologists try to understand the roles of nature and nurture in human physical growth just as in other aspects of development. On the one hand, the contributions of nature, or heredity, are often suggested by correlations in size among biologically related family and cultural members, in the onset and pattern of other physical changes, and by research indicating significant biological factors in physical development. On the other hand, nurture, or environment—including diet, disease, and social and emotional circumstances—has a bearing on physical growth as well. But just how do biology and environment affect physical development?

**Genetic Factors**    A person's height is likely to be closely related to that of her mother and father. A late-maturing adolescent often shares late maturity with other family members (Rallison, 1986). What is true for the family in miniature is also true for larger human populations that are genetically related. The Lese of Zaire, for example, are much taller as a group than their nearby

▶ Individual differences

neighbors the Efe, the pygmies of the Ituri rain forest. Even body proportions differ among ethnic groups; leg and arm lengths are relatively greater in individuals of African descent than in other racial groups, when length of the torso is the same (Sinclair, 1985). Such similarities and differences implicate genetic

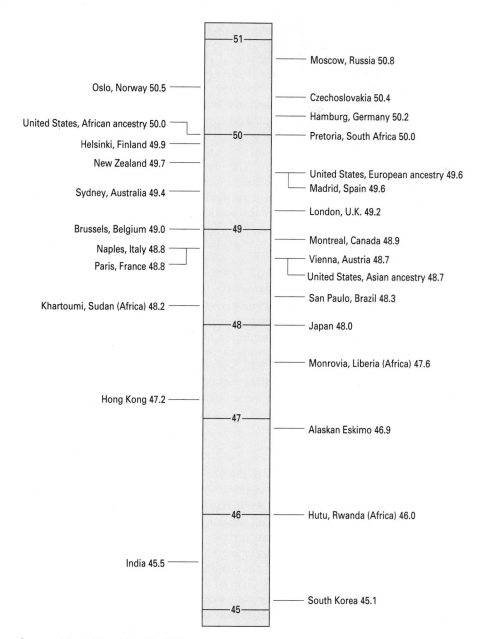

Oslo, Norway 50.5

Moscow, Russia 50.8

United States, African ancestry 50.0

Czechoslovakia 50.4

Hamburg, Germany 50.2

Helsinki, Finland 49.9

Pretoria, South Africa 50.0

New Zealand 49.7

United States, European ancestry 49.6

Madrid, Spain 49.6

Sydney, Australia 49.4

London, U.K. 49.2

Brussels, Belgium 49.0

Montreal, Canada 48.9

Naples, Italy 48.8

Vienna, Austria 48.7

Paris, France 48.8

United States, Asian ancestry 48.7

Khartoumi, Sudan (Africa) 48.2

San Paulo, Brazil 48.3

Japan 48.0

Monrovia, Liberia (Africa) 47.6

Hong Kong 47.2

Alaskan Eskimo 46.9

Hutu, Rwanda (Africa) 46.0

India 45.5

South Korea 45.1

Source: Adapted from Meredith, 1978.

**FIGURE 5.3**

**Ethnic and Cultural Differences in Growth**

Ethnic and cultural differences in growth are strikingly apparent in this graph of the average height of eight-year-old girls from selected regions of the world. Girls in northern and eastern Europe are nearly a half foot taller, on average, than girls in India at this age; similar results are found for boys. These variations may reflect both hereditary and environmental conditions.

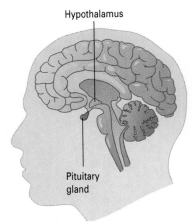

Hypothalamus

Pituitary gland

**FIGURE 5.4**

**Two Important Organs of the Brain That Affect Growth and Physical Development**

The hypothalamus and the pituitary gland, located near each other at the base of the brain, are two organs believed to play a central role in the regulation of growth. The hypothalamus may be the locus for a growth center that compares actual height with a genetically determined template for height. Hormones released by the hypothalamus stimulate the release of other hormones by the pituitary gland that promote growth.

▶ Individual differences

factors in physical development. But genes do not control growth *directly.* Genes regulate physical development by means of neural and hormonal activity in different organs and body systems. The neural and hormonal factors make up the biological mechanisms that carry out genetic instructions.

**Neural Control**   Many researchers believe that the brain includes a growth center, a genetically established program or template that monitors and compares expected and actual rates and levels of growth for the individual (Sinclair, 1985). The claim has been supported by observations of **catch-up growth**, an increase in growth rate that often occurs if some environmental factor interferes with normal increases in height during infancy or childhood. Illness or malnutrition, for example, may disrupt physical growth, but if the duration and severity are limited and do not occur at a critical time, the child's rate of growth often accelerates once she recovers. The acceleration continues until height "catches up" to the level expected, had no disruption occurred.

The presence of a growth center is also suggested by the converse finding—**lagging-down growth** (Prader, 1978). Some rare congenital and hormonal disorders produce unusually rapid growth; if the disorder is corrected, growth halts or slows until actual and projected height match the pattern of growth established before the disruption. Where might this neural control center for growth be located? Researchers have theorized that the orchestrator of genetic instructions for growth is the *hypothalamus,* a small region near the base of the brain (see Figure 5.4). Special cells in the hypothalamus may maintain the records for comparing actual with genetically programmed growth and may direct other cells in the hypothalamus to produce hormones that directly affect growth.

**Hormonal Influences**   One key mechanism for converting genetic instructions into physical development is provided by hormones, the secretions of substances from various glands of the body. Hormones travel in the bloodstream to influence cells in other regions of the body. A dozen or more hormones affect growth, often by regulating the manufacture of still other hormones that directly stimulate cell division (Tanner, 1978).

As the suspected site of the growth center, the hypothalamus plays an important role in coordinating the formation and release of many growth-related hormones. For example, chemical stimulation from cells in the hypothalamus triggers or inhibits production of several hormones in the nearby *pituitary gland* (see Figure 5.4), including one known as *human growth hormone* (*HGH*). Infants with insufficient HGH may be nearly normal in size at birth, but their growth slows dramatically over the ensuing months and years; they typically reach an adult height of only about four or four and a half feet. HGH, however, only indirectly promotes growth in bone and other cells. It affects growth by furthering the production of *somatomedins*, specialized hormones produced by many other cells in the body that directly regulate cell division for growth (Underwood, 1991).

The hypothalamus and pituitary gland interact to stimulate the production of other hormones important for physical changes, including those that occur during puberty. However, variations in amounts of many hormones, so long as they fall within a reasonable range, do not account for individual differences in height. Tall and short people may manufacture ample supplies of HGH and somatomedins; individual differences seem to depend on the sensitivity of cells to the hormones (Tanner, 1978). For example, the pygmy Efe produce normal quantities of HGH but seem unable to use it to produce one kind of somatomedin important for typical growth (Merimee, Zapf, & Froesch, 1981).

**Nutrition and Health**    For a large proportion of the world's children such environmental factors as adequate nutrition and exposure to diseases may be the primary determinants of whether physical growth proceeds normally or even at all. We pointed out some consequences of malnutrition for fetal development in Chapter 4, and as the phenomenon of catch-up growth indicates, illness and poor nutrition can affect postnatal growth as well. Data collected during much of the first half of the twentieth century from one city in Germany revealed that the average height of children at various ages increased gradually over the years, a trend reported in most Western societies. However, during World Wars I and II, when food was far more limited in that city, the pattern of gradual increments in average height leveled off and even showed a decline in some years for some age groups (Howe & Schiller, 1952).

Dietary supplements designed to raise nutrition to an adequate level have a positive influence on children's physical growth and development, suggests a recent study conducted by the Harvard School of Public Health in Bogotá, Colombia. All family members in a group in which infants were at risk for malnutrition were given additional food to enrich their diets. The supplements were begun when the woman was in her third trimester of pregnancy and were continued for all family members until the target child reached three years of age. At the end of the period children who received the supplement were on average more than an inch taller and nearly one and a half pounds heavier than children in families who did not receive the supplement. Although the differences were not enormous, the targeted children continued to be larger at age six as well, three years after the supplements were discontinued (Super, Herrara, & Mora, 1990).

Severe protein-energy malnutrition can have a devastating effect on growth. Infants with *marasmus* fail to grow because they lack sufficient calories. Consequences include eventual loss in weight; wrinkly, aged skin; an abdomen that is often shrunken; and a hollow appearance to the body. Another prevalent form of protein-energy malnutrition is *kwashiorkor*, or failure to develop, either because the diet contains an inadequate balance of protein or includes potentially harmful agents such as toxins (Hendrickse, 1991; Jellife & Jellife, 1992). Kwashiorkor typically appears in a child aged one to three years who has been weaned, usually because of a newborn, and whose subsequent sources of protein are inadequate or contaminated.

The symptoms of kwashiorkor—lethargic behavior and an apathetic look, wrinkled skin, a distended stomach, and a thin, wispy, reddish orange cast to the hair—have been depicted in all their horror by the world media repeatedly. Kwashiorkor leads to deterioration of the brain, and although some of the damage can be quickly reversed when adequate nutrition is reinstated early (Gunston et al., 1992), long-term cognitive deficits and poorer school-related performance as a result of impaired attention and memory may continue (Galler et al., 1990). Some deficits may be an indirect result of the malnutrition—the outcome of lessened motivation or curiosity and inability to respond to or effectively engage the environment (Pollitt et al., 1993; Ricciuti, 1993). Deficiencies in other specific nutritional elements—for example, vitamins A, B complexes, D, and K, as well as iron and calcium—are also linked to growth disorders affecting hundreds of thousands of children in various regions of the world (Hansen, 1990).

▶ The child's active role

**catch-up growth**    Increase in growth rate after some factor such as illness or poor nutrition has disrupted the expected, normal growth rate.

**lagging-down growth**    Condition in which, after periods of rapid acceleration because of congenital or hormonal disorders, growth is slowed so that subsequent increases in height conform to those normally expected for the individual.

The smaller of the two children shown here may be suffering from kwashiorkor as suggested by the somewhat distended, bloated appearance of the child's stomach. Kwashiorkor can be found in communities where the diet of the young child fails to include sufficient protein or where toxins may be present in the limited food that is available.

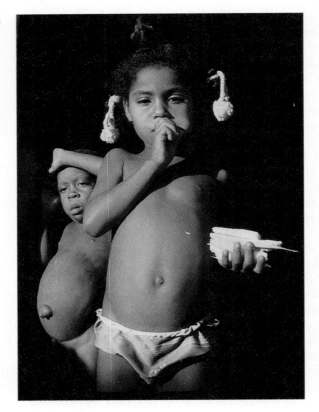

▶ Interaction among domains

**Social-Emotional Factors**   How important are social-emotional factors in physical growth? Early studies of institutionalized children (Ribble, 1943; Spitz, 1946b) painted vivid images of massive disruption in physical growth, even death, if a warm consistent caregiver was unavailable to the infant. Although alternative explanations may exist for these early observations, lack of social and emotional support do appear to be a contributing factor in many cases of **failure to thrive**, a label applied to any child below the third percentile in weight or height compared with other children of the same age.

When no specific genetic, biological, or medical basis (including poor nutrition) can be identified for growth retardation, it is labeled *nonorganic failure to thrive syndrome.* Infants and young children with the syndrome tend to be more passive and apathetic and display less facial expressivity than other infants and children (Abramson, 1991). Although the syndrome may stem partly from characteristics of the infant or child—for example, difficulty in temperament or nursing or unresponsiveness to the caregiver—nonorganic failure to thrive may originate or be further aggravated by emotional deprivations, psychological traumas, or some other aspect of inadequate caregiving, including abuse and neglect (English, 1978; Rallison, 1986). For example, mothers of these infants are often reported to display less pleasure, positive affect, and support in their communications and interfere or act more arbitrarily while engaging in activities with their infants than other mothers (Drotar et al., 1990; Liggon et al., 1992; Skuse, 1985). Clearly, the importance of the environment for physical development extends beyond making adequate nutrition available.

Growth retardation can be reduced by social and educational programs concerned with promoting development. In the study carried out on infants at risk in Colombia, researchers included twice-weekly home visits to stimulate learning and development until the target child was three years of age. The home visitor provided advice and support to the parents to improve caregiver-child interactions but offered no specific instructions on nutrition or other health-related topics. The intervention alone eventually resulted in gains in height and weight by the time the children were six years old. Even greater growth benefits occurred when food supplements were combined with the home visits. Fewer than 20 percent of the children who received both types of intervention were considered growth retarded, as compared with more than half the children in the control group (Super, Herrara, & Mora, 1990). The findings demonstrate that programs designed to improve emotional and social support within the family, along with adequate nutrition, can have a substantial effect on physical growth.

**Secular Trends**     Knowledge of nutrition and medical treatment of disease has changed dramatically in many societies in recent generations. When a pattern of change in the environment occurs over generations as a result of such factors, it is called a **secular trend.** As any young woman who has ever tried on her grandmother's wedding dress knows, children today not only grow faster but are taller than previous generations in most regions of the world. In many European countries slight increases in average height occurred from 1825 to 1875. Substantially greater increases occurred from the late 1800s to the middle of this century, and a slower increase or even stability in size has been found since the 1960s. Between 1880 and 1950 the average height of Western European and American children increased by nearly four inches. Similar findings have been reported for other cultures, although for different generations. For example, the most substantial changes in height in Japan took place between 1950 and 1970 (Tanner, 1978).

▶ Sociocultural influence

What accounts for the dramatic increases in physical growth? Generational differences undoubtedly stem from improved nutrition, medical care, and the abolition of child labor. Similar factors may account for the greater height and more rapid maturation, within a single generation, of children from professional, highly educated, and urban families compared with children from poorer families and those in rural populations (Tanner, 1978). Medical and economic changes have brought significant improvements to the physical growth and development of children around the world. And perhaps, as the recent data from Colombia suggest, a better understanding of the ways to support and encourage child development and family relationships, that is, greater knowledge of the social, emotional, and psychological needs of children, may provide yet another round of improved physical growth in future generations of children.

## The Social-Emotional Consequences of Body Growth

▶ Interaction among domains

We have seen in the previous section a few of the ways in which social and emotional contexts can affect growth. But how important is physical size in

**secular trend**   Consistent pattern of change over generations.

the way others respond to people and for the development of their sense of worth?

▶ Individual differences

**Height**  Many societies share a mystique about tallness, the notion that height directly correlates with such traits as competence and leadership. Some individuals have argued that height has a dramatic bearing upon the work people do, their success, the social lives they lead, their attractiveness to others, and their self-esteem and sense of worth (Gillis, 1982). Research has shown that the height of a child does affect impressions of her ability. Mothers of young children of the same age, for example, perceive taller boys as more competent (able to get along better with others, less likely to cry when frustrated, and so forth) and treat smaller boys as younger and in a more overprotective manner (Eisenberg et al., 1984; Rotnem, 1986). The same is true of children judged to possess relatively mature facial features (Zebrowitz, Kendall-Tackett, & Fafel, 1991). Moreover, boys believe it is important to be tall and muscular (Cobb, 1954); those substantially shorter than the average height for their age report extensive teasing from their peers, greater dissatisfaction with their skills, especially in athletic endeavors, and increasing unhappiness as they approach adolescence (Finch, 1978).

Surprisingly, lower self-esteem among children of short stature is not consistently reported (Rieser, 1992). Nevertheless, older boys especially often yearn to be tall and athletic in appearance. Until recently, little could be done to alter the course of a child's rate of growth or eventual height. Today, however, human growth hormone can be produced synthetically. For those children whose lack of growth stems from insufficient HGH, the breakthrough represents an enormously positive step in promoting growth. However, increasing numbers of children who are genetically short or whose delay in growth is a normal part of their pattern of maturation are also being given HGH in an effort to speed or increase their height.

Should such treatments, motivated by perceptions and expectations about the benefits of being tall rather than by a medical condition, be encouraged? Neither the effectiveness nor the potential for negative side effects of such supplemental hormones is fully understood. Attempting to alter normal physical development to conform to a cultural stereotype is a drastic action that raises many ethical issues. The argument that such treatment forestalls negative social and emotional consequences is often countered with the charge that the stereotype, not the child, is what needs to be modified.

▶ Sociocultural influence

**Obesity**  Common criteria for obesity include weight 20 percent in excess of the weight considered ideal for a person's height, age, and sex or other measures of body fat (such as skin-fold thickness) above the eightieth percentile for the child's reference group (Dietz, 1983; Epstein & Wing, 1987). Being overweight has strong social-emotional consequences in all cultures. American society tends to view obesity negatively, although in earlier eras it carried the positive connotations of substance and prosperity and still does in many developing countries (Sobal & Stunkard, 1989). For example, adolescent females in some societies are encouraged to increase their body fat in preparation for marriage (Brown & Konner, 1987). However, in industrialized societies excess body fat is rarely viewed positively by people of any age (Feldman, Feldman, & Goodman, 1988). When children as young as six describe drawings or photographs of people who are chubby or thin, they are likely to label obese figures as "lazy," "cheater," or "liar," although the children seldom apply such terms to their overweight friends (Kirkpatrick & Sanders, 1978; Lawson, 1980). Moreover, overweight ten- and eleven-year-olds experience more negative interactions involving peers than other children do (Baum & Foreham, 1984).

Disease and medical conditions rarely cause obesity (Dietz, 1983). Genetic factors may predispose some children to obesity, however. Adopted children show a closer relationship to the weight of their biological parents than their adoptive parents', and identical twins, whether reared together or apart, show similar levels of weight (Stunkard et al., 1990). Overweight parents often have obese children, although this relationship may reflect either hereditary or environmental influences, because parents serve as models for their children's eating and exercise habits (Epstein, Wing, & Valoski, 1985).

▶ Roles of nature and nurture

Does this mean that a fat baby stays fat? Not always, although about 20 percent of overweight babies continue to be obese as children (Woolston, 1987). A heavy infant is about twice as likely as an infant of normal weight to be obese later in life, and the longer a child continues to be overweight, the more likely it is that he will remain obese as an adult (Epstein, Wing, & Valoski, 1985). Heavier infants and young children appear to form greater numbers of fat cells than their counterparts of average weight (Hirsch, 1975). As a consequence, overweight children may have difficulty escaping a pattern of obesity laid down by these cells early in development. The problem of weight control may be made more complicated by the tendency of obese children to be more sensitive to external food-related cues and less responsive to internal hunger cues than their normal-weight peers (Ballard et al., 1980; Costanzo & Woody, 1979).

Health surveys and other studies conducted in the United States reveal a substantial increase in obesity in African American, European American, and Native American children in recent decades (Byers, 1992; Gortmaker et al., 1987). What are the reasons for this secular trend? Researchers have advanced various hypotheses. For example, compared with a generation ago, children spend greater amounts of time in more sedentary activities such as watching television (Gortmaker et al., 1987). More limited physical activity has been accompanied by dietary shifts from fresh fruits and vegetables to calorie-laden snack and convenience foods. Whatever the reason, this is an instance in which the cultural context, while attaching a negative label to a physical condition on one hand, may actively promote it on the other. Perhaps for these reasons weight reduction programs have had limited success with children; effective treatment procedures may need to approach the problem from many different fronts (Spence, 1986).

▶ Sociocultural influence

## The Brain and Nervous System

Now that we have a sense of body growth and development, we can begin to examine other important physiological and physical changes that accompany increasing maturity. In particular, we focus on changes in the brain and nervous system as well as motor skill development. Information about the central nervous system, for example, can help to unravel many complexities, not only in the growth of motor skills but in cognitive, social, and other domains as well.

## The Developing Brain

Even before birth, brain growth is rapid, as Figure 5.5 shows. The weight of the brain swiftly increases, from about 4 percent of adult weight at five months after conception to about 25 percent at birth and about 80 percent of adult weight by four years of age (Spreen et al., 1984). Much of that growth takes place in the *cerebral cortex*, the region of the brain most closely identified with mental processing and complex human behavior.

Compared with other regions of the brain, the cerebral cortex is relatively late in its development. The *brain stem* and *midbrain*, involved in basic reflexes and sensory processing, as well as such essential biological functions as digestion, elimination, and respiration, are fairly well established at birth. Within the cerebral cortex, regions associated with motor and sensory funcu-

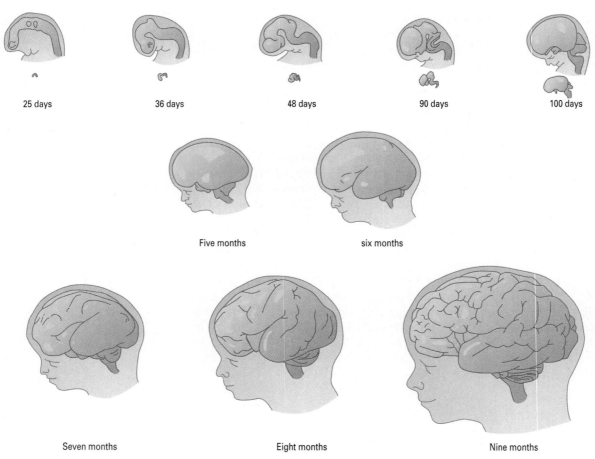

| 25 days | 36 days | 48 days | 90 days | 100 days |

| Five months | six months |

| Seven months | Eight months | Nine months |

**FIGURE 5.5**

**The Developing Human Brain**

Source: Adapted from Cowan, 1979.

During prenatal development the human brain shows dramatic increases in size, and the cerebral cortex takes on a convoluted pattern to increase surface area. During the last trimester of prenatal development the shape of the brain takes on an adultlike appearance, and by birth most of the neurons have been formed. The brain's weight increases most dramatically from about the fifth prenatal month until the infant is about two and a half years of age. The drawings have been made to a common scale; however, the first five have been enlarged to a common size to show details.

tions tend to be among the first to mature. Even within these areas a cephalo-caudal and proximodistal pattern of growth is evident: neural development allied with control of the head and upper body progresses more quickly than neural development associated with the lower trunk or legs.

With development, **neurons**, cells that carry electrochemical messages as neural impulses, *proliferate*—that is, increase in number. Neurons also *migrate*—move to various regions of the brain—and *differentiate*—increase in size, complexity, and functioning. One notable aspect of differentiation is the increased number and kinds of *synapses,* the space-filled junctures associated with the branches of the neuron that permit it to communicate with other neurons. Parts of many neurons also become surrounded by **myelin**, a sheath of fatty material that serves to insulate and speed neural impulses by about tenfold. An estimated ten times more **glial cells** (from the Greek word for *glue*) than neurons also form within the brain (Blinkov & Glezer, 1968). Glial cells provide the material from which myelin develops, facilitate the transfer of nutrients to neurons, and establish a scaffolding for neuron migration (Tanner, 1978).

**Neuron Proliferation**  The production of new nerve cells is known as *neuron proliferation.* Neuron production in humans begins near the end of the first month of prenatal development, shortly after the *neural tube* closes, and much of it, at least in the cerebral cortex, is completed before birth (Casaer, 1993; Parmelee & Sigman, 1983). Thus, at a very early age a finite but very large number—certainly well over 100 billion—of young neurons are formed (Shatz, 1992).

▶ Development as continuous/discontinuous

**Neuron Migration**  Shortly after their formation neurons move from the neural tube, where they were produced, to other locations within the brain. How do neurons know where to migrate and when to stop migrating? Both neurochemical and mechanical information probably play a role. Young neurons attach to and maneuver along the surface of fibers of glial cells radiating to the region of their destination, detaching at programmed locations. Both the production and migration of large numbers of neurons in the cortex occur in waves, especially during the seventh and eleventh weeks of gestational age (Spreen et al., 1984). Neurons may migrate a great distance, passing through levels of older neurons that already have reached their final destination. The consequence can be an *inside-out pattern* of development in which layers of nerve cells nearer the outer surface are younger than layers deeper in the cortex (Rakic, 1981). Some teratogens, including mercury and alcohol, are known to interfere with the onset and path of neuron migration (Abel, 1989). In fact, developmental defects ranging from mental retardation to behavioral disorders, including some forms of schizophrenia and dyslexia, have been linked to interference in the migratory patterns of nerve cells (Nowakowski, 1987).

▶ Development as continuous/discontinuous

▶ Roles of nature and nurture

**neuron**  Nerve cell within central nervous system electrochemically designed to transmit messages between cells.

**myelin**  Sheath of fatty cells that insulates and speeds neural impulses by about tenfold.

**glial cells**  Brain cells that provide the material from which myelin is created, nourish neurons, and provide a scaffolding for neuron migration.

**Neuron Differentiation**  Whereas neuron proliferation and migration for the most part take place prenatally, neuron differentiation—the process of enlarging, forming connections with other neurons, and beginning to function—flourishes postnatally and perhaps continues even into adulthood. These changes, along with the growth of glial cells and other supportive tissues, including myelin, contribute to the substantial increase in the size of the brain postnatally.

▶ Roles of nature and nurture

Some aspects of neuron differentiation proceed without external stimulation. Experience, however, plays a major role in the selection, maintenance, and strengthening of connections among many neurons (Shatz, 1992). Work investigating the effects of vision on brain development in cats illustrates the complex relationship (Hubel & Wiesel, 1979). By the time a kitten's eyes open, neurons in the visual receptor areas of the cerebral cortex have already established some connections and may respond, for example, to sensory information from either eye or to visual patterns with a broad range of characteristics. But the neurons become far more selective and tuned to specific kinds of sensory information as the kitten experiences specific forms of visual stimulation. Some neurons may, for example, begin to respond to information arising from one or the other eye only and to transitions in dark-light patterns in the visual field that are vertical or horizontal or at some other spatial orientation.

Without stimulation and the opportunity to function neurons are unlikely to establish or maintain many connections with other neurons; their synaptic density is substantially reduced (Huttenlocher, 1990). Formation of the myelin sheath can also be disrupted, and neurons may even die (Kalil, 1989). In fact, one theory holds that massive cell death occurs during normal development in some regions of the brain, although perhaps not in the cerebral cortex (Huttenlocher, 1990). In birds, for example, 40 to 75 percent of all neurons are estimated to die within a few days of completing cell migration (Spreen et al., 1984). Here again we see the complex interaction between biological and environmental events in development. The typical infant is genetically equipped with the capacity to generate many synaptic connections, perhaps in far more neurons than a person will ever need (Kalil, 1989). That surplus provides the opportunity for a rich variety of experiences to affect development, and should damage or destruction occur to some neurons early in life, other nerve cells can replace them.

## Plasticity in Brain Development

Because of the unspecialized nature of young neurons, the brain possesses **plasticity**, or the ability within limits for alternate regions of the cerebral cortex to take on specialized sensory, linguistic, and other information-processing requirements (Kolb, 1989). Infants or children who suffer damage to regions of the cerebral cortex that process speech, for example, are often able to recover, because neurons in other parts of the cortex take on this function. On the other hand, the prognosis for recovery of language in adults after an accident or stroke is often much poorer, because the remaining neurons in various regions of the brain have already become dedicated to processing certain kinds of experiences (Lenneberg, 1967).

William Greenough and his colleagues have proposed that neurons in human and other mammalian brains exhibit two different kinds of plasticity (Greenough, Black, & Wallace, 1987). Some neurons are sensitive to *experience-expectant information.* As a result of a long evolutionary process, these neurons begin to grow and differentiate rapidly about the time they can be expected to receive the kinds of stimulation important to their functioning. In many mammals, for example, parts of the visual cortex involved in depth or pattern perception develop quite rapidly shortly before and after the eyes open or, in the case of people, shortly before and after birth. Research with lower animals indicates that visual deprivation during these periods—being reared in the dark or without patterned light, for example—results in the permanent

▶ Development as continuous/discontinuous

**plasticity** Capacity of immature systems, including regions of the brain and the individual neurons within those regions, to take on different functions as a result of experience.

loss of some kinds of depth and pattern vision, losses that do not occur when equivalent lengths of deprivation occur at other periods (Movshon & Van Sluyters, 1981).

Other neurons are sensitive to *experience-dependent information.* Many kinds of events cannot be expected to occur at predicted times during development. Each person learns different and unique things, even into old age. The distinctive perceptual features forming the image of a neighbor or the attributes defining the concept of democracy are unique representations recorded within an individual's neural system. This type of learning, also assumed to be linked in some way to neuron differentiation, can occur at any time in development. Here, then, is a form of plasticity that extends beyond sensitive periods of development and implicates neural differentiation as a critical aspect of brain functioning throughout a person's lifetime.

## Brain Lateralization

One of the brain's most obvious physical characteristics is that it can be divided into two mirrorlike structures, a *left* and *right hemisphere.* By and large, in humans sensory information and motor responses on the left side of the body are processed by the right hemisphere; sensory information and motor responses on the right side of the body are processed by the left hemisphere. In addition, in most adults the left hemisphere is especially involved in language functioning, whereas the right hemisphere is usually involved in processing spatial, emotional, or other nonverbal information (Michel, 1988; Saxby & Bryden, 1985). But these differences are by no means absolute. For example, speech is primarily controlled by the left hemisphere in about 95 percent of right-handed adults but only in about 70 percent of left-handed adults (Kinsbourne & Hiscock, 1983). Furthermore, in all individuals the right hemisphere can comprehend and initiate speech, although it may be more limited in its capacity to do so.

A major developmental question is whether hemispheric specialization exists at birth or whether the brain shows progressive **lateralization**, the process of one hemisphere's dominating the other in terms of a particular function. Based on research on left-hemisphere damage in children, Eric Lenneberg (1967) proposed that at least until age two both hemispheres are capable of carrying out language functions equally well and that lateralization increases only gradually until adolescence. In other words, throughout childhood one hemisphere may process language nearly as well as the other.

Other researchers suggest lateralization begins much earlier (Kinsbourne & Hiscock, 1983), perhaps as a consequence of exposure to fetal testosterone (Geschwind & Galaburda, 1987; McManus & Bryden, 1991). For example, most infants lie with the head oriented to the right rather than to the left, an orientation that later predicts hand preference (Michel, 1988), and even before three months of age most babies more actively use and hold objects longer in the right than in the left hand (Hawn & Harris, 1983). They also turn more frequently to stimulation coming from the right than the left side (Siqueland & Lipsitt, 1966). Futhermore, infants are able to better identify changes in speech sounds heard in their right ear and to detect changes in the timbre of musical notes better in their left ear (Best, Hoffman, & Glanville, 1982). However, the evidence of early hemispheric differences does not preclude the possibility that at later ages either hemisphere is capable of taking over the other's functions if necessary.

▶ Individual differences

**lateralization** Process by which one hemisphere of the brain dominates the other. In most individuals the left hemisphere is more involved in language processing, whereas the right is more involved in processing spatial and emotional information.

# Motor Skill Development

With development cartilage is transformed to bone, and bones elongate and increase in number to become scaffolding to support the body in new physical orientations. As the central nervous system matures, neural commands begin to coordinate thickened and enlarged muscles, permitting more powerful and refined motor activities. Cephalocaudal and proximodistal principles are evident in the emergence of many motor skills. The principles are augmented by two other complementary patterns: *differentiation*, the enrichment of global and relatively diffuse actions with more refined and skilled ones, and *integration*, the increasingly coordinated actions of muscles and sensory systems. Throughout infancy and childhood motor skills become more efficient, coordinated, and deliberate or automatic as the task requires. At the end of this period many skills become highly specialized talents: youngsters such as Erin are already athletes; others her age are concert musicians.

Motor skill development was a prominent focus of study early in the history of developmental psychology but received little attention from researchers during the 1950s and 1960s. More recently, enormous interest in this topic has reemerged. If, as Piaget suggested, sensorimotor activity serves as the prototype and first stage in the construction of knowledge, the acquisition, coordination, and integration of basic motor skills can provide important insights into early cognitive and perceptual development as well (Benson, 1988; Bushnell & Boudreau, 1993).

▶ Interaction among domains

## The First Actions: Reflexes

At first glance newborns seem helpless and incompetent. Babies eat, sleep, and cry; their diapers always seem to need changing. Yet a more careful look reveals that infants enter their new world with surprisingly adept sensory abilities, along with **reflexes**, the involuntary reactions to touch, light, sound, and

Among the reflexes that babies display is the swimming reflex. When young infants are placed in water, breathing is suspended and they engage in swim-like movements with their arms and legs.

**reflex**  Involuntary movement in response to touch, light, sound, and other forms of stimulation; controlled by subcortical neural mechanisms.

other kinds of stimulation, some exhibited even prenatally. Reflexes are among the building blocks that soon give rise to voluntary movements and the attainment of developmental milestones or significant achievements in motor skills.

Along with breathing and swallowing, *primitive reflexes* such as rooting and sucking (see Table 5.1) provide nourishment for survival of the infant. At least among humans' evolutionary ancestors others, such as the Moro and palmar reflexes, helped protect newborns from danger. *Postural reflexes*, such as stepping, swimming, and body righting (surprisingly similar to later voluntary movements) appear to be designed to maintain a specific orientation to the environment. If some primitive or postural reflexes are absent, are too strong or too weak, are of unequal strength when normally elicited from either side of the body, or continue to be exhibited beyond certain ages, a pediatrician may

| Name of Reflex | Testing Procedure | Response | Developmental Course | Significance |
|---|---|---|---|---|
| *Primitive Reflexes* | | | | |
| **Palmar or Hand Grasp** | Place finger in hand. | Hand grasps object. | Birth to about 4 months. | Absence may signal neurological defects; persistence could interfere with voluntary grasping. |
| **Rooting** | Stroke corner of mouth lightly. | Head and tongue move toward stimulus. | Birth to about 5 months. | Mouth is brought to stimulus to permit sucking. |
| **Sucking** | Place finger in mouth or on lips. | Sucking begins. | Birth to about 6 months. | Ensures intake of potential nutrients. |
| **Moro** | (1) Sit child up, allow head to drop about 20 degrees backward, or (2) make a loud noise, or (3) lower baby rapidly. | Baby extends arms outward, hands open; then brings hands to midline, hands clenched, spine straightened. | Birth to about 5–7 months. | Absence may signal neurological defects; persistence could interfere with acquisition of sitting. |
| **Plantar or Foot Grasp** | Place pressure on ball of foot. | Toes curl as if grasping. | Birth to about 9 months. | Absence may signal spinal cord defect. |
| **Babinski** | Stroke bottom of foot. | Toes fan and then curl. | Birth to about 1 year. | Absence may signal neurological defects. |
| **Asymmetric Tonic Neck Reflex** | Place baby on back, arms and legs extended, and rotate head 90 degrees. | Arm on face side extends, arm on back side of head flexes. | About 1 month to 4 months. | Absence may signal neurological defects; persistence could prevent rolling over, coordination. |

**TABLE 5.1**

**Typical Reflexes Observed in Newborns and Infants**

| Name of Reflex | Testing Procedure | Response | Developmental Course | Significance |
|---|---|---|---|---|
| **Postural Reflexes** | | | | |
| **Stepping** | Hold baby under arms, upright, leaning forward. | Makes walklike stepping movements. | Birth to about 3 months. | Absence may signal neurological defects. |
| **Labyrinthine** | (1) Place baby on back. | Extends arms and legs. | Birth to about 4 months. | Absence may signal neurological defects. |
| | (2) Place baby on stomach. | Flexes arms and legs. | | |
| **Swimming** | Place baby in water. | Holds breath involuntarily; arms and legs move as if trying to swim. | Birth to about 4 to 6 months. | Absence may signal neurological defects. |
| **Placing** | Hold baby under arms, upright, top of foot touching bottom edge of table. | Lifts foot and places on top of table. | Birth through 12 months. | Absence may signal neurological defects. |
| **Landau Reaction** | Place baby on stomach, hold under chest. | Lifts head, eventually other parts of body, above chest. | Head at 2 months, other parts of body later. | Absence may signal neurological defects; inadequate muscle tone for motor development. |
| **Body Righting** | Rotate hips or shoulder. | Rotates remainder of body. | 4 months to more than 12 months. | Absence may signal neurological defects; difficulty in gaining postural control and walking. |

Many of the reflexes displayed by the newborn can also be elicited during the later weeks of fetal development (Gundy, 1987). Considerable variability exists among infants in the way in which many reflexes are displayed and ages at which they can be elicited (Touwen, 1974). The presence or absence of any single reflex provides only one among many indicators of healthy or atypical development.

**TABLE 5.1** (continued)

**Typical Reflexes Observed in Newborns and Infants**

begin to suspect neurological impairment and developmental difficulties for the baby.

## Sudden Infant Death Syndrome

To survive in the postnatal environment the infant must synchronize rooting and sucking with swallowing and breathing. In fact, the inability to coordinate these reflexes often makes nursing difficult for premature infants (Rosenblith & Sims-Knight, 1985). But organizing and controlling breathing can be a problem for a small number of older infants as well. The abrupt unexplained death of a baby or toddler who stops breathing during sleep is known as **sudden infant death syndrome (SIDS)**. The deaths are particularly alarming, because they occur with no identifiable warnings.

**sudden infant death syndrome (SIDS)** Sudden, unexplained death of infant or toddler as a result of failure to continue breathing during sleep.

SIDS, sometimes known as *crib death*, is estimated to occur in about two of every thousand live births in the United States. Much higher rates exist in some other countries, including New Zealand and Australia (Orenstein, 1992). The frequency of SIDS peaks two or three months after birth, and SIDS rarely befalls infants younger than three weeks or older than one year. Thus, the highest incidence occurs at a time when basic automatic respiratory reflexes governed by the brainstem begin to be supplemented by the voluntary cortex-regulated breathing essential for vocalization and the emergence of speech. Perhaps during this formative period voluntary and involuntary breathing are not sufficiently orchestrated to provide a fail-safe system that ensures breathing continues during sleep (Burns & Lipsitt, 1991).

Although no specific cause has been identified, SIDS is associated with a bewildering number of factors: the colder months of the year, bottle feeding, economically depressed neighborhoods, having a cold, being a male, later born, or a member of a multiple birth, low birth weight, and maternal cigarette smoking or drug dependency (Goyco & Beckerman, 1990). An additional related factor may be placing babies in a prone (on their stomach) sleeping position especially on a soft mattress, pillow, or other material. Although the prone position is often recommended in the United States, the American Academy of Pediatrics (1992) recently has advised pediatricians to suggest that otherwise healthy infants be put to sleep on their side or back to avoid rebreathing exhaled air which may become trapped in soft bedding material. James McKenna and his colleagues (McKenna et al., 1990) have suggested yet another aspect of sleeping arrangements may be a factor in SIDS—infants and toddlers in separate rooms rather than in bed with their mothers. In co-sleeping arrangements mothers and infants synchronize sleep, breathing, and arousal patterns. McKenna and his colleagues suggest that the synchrony could help arouse infants from *apnea*, irregular patterns or temporary cessations in breathing.

Historically and in many cultures yet today, co-sleeping for mothers and infants is the norm. For example, Mayan mothers seem to view putting very young children in a separate room at night as almost the equivalent of child neglect. However, American mothers typically justify such a practice, especially after the baby is a few months old, as a way to encourage self-reliance and independence (Morrelli et al., 1992). Decisions about sleeping arrangements are deeply ingrained in cultural beliefs concerning the values of closeness and interdependence or of privacy and self-reliance. But whether the recent tendency in some cultures to favor separate sleeping arrangements for mother and infant has a bearing on SIDS remains to be proved.

## Motor Milestones

In addition to reflexes, babies exhibit **rhythmical stereotypies**, repeated sequences of motions performed with no apparent goal (Thelen, 1979). Rubbing one foot against the other, rocking back and forth, bouncing up and down, swaying side to side, striking or banging objects, mouthing and tonguing activities, and shaking and nodding the head are just a few of the activities produced as movements to exercise bones, joints, and muscles. In older children and adults the recurrent display of such behaviors is generally considered evidence of abnormal development, but in infants the actions are common. Although probably not entirely governed by deliberate directed efforts,

**rhythmical stereotypies** Repeated sequences of movements such as leg kicking and hand waving or banging that seem to have no apparent goal.

▶ The child's active role

Once a baby can stand, he will often cruise or move about by stepping side to side while holding onto objects or other people. It is one of the many milestones infants achieve in their diligent attempts to gain independent locomotion.

stereotypes, along with some early reflexes, may eventually be recruited and progressively integrated into organized voluntary motor skills and activities (Thelen, Kelso, & Fogel, 1987).

During their first year infants also begin to display directed voluntary actions as they gradually gain neuromotor control of their head, arms, and legs. Some of these—grasping, crawling, and walking, for example—are motor milestones: once mastered, new worlds are open to the infant. Moreover, they cause caregivers to respond to the infant in different ways—childproofing the home to prevent accidents, encouraging greater independence, expecting more mature behavior. Most achievements in infant movement illustrate progress in (1) *postural control*, the ability to maintain an upright orientation to the environment; (2) *locomotion*, the ability to maneuver through space; and (3) *manual control*, the ability to manipulate objects (Keogh & Sugden, 1985).

**Postural Control**    Keeping the head upright and stable at about two to three months of age represents one of the first milestones in infant motor development. As the Chronology on page 185 indicates, this achievement is followed by mastery of other significant postural skills, such as maintaining an upright sitting position, moving to a standing position, and standing alone without assistance. The milestones, built on various postural reflexes among other things, often reflect a cephalocaudal progression. Head control, for example, precedes control of the trunk, and command of the legs is the last to develop. The integration of postural skills is also important. For example, being able to keep head upright while sitting, or standing on a stable surface is one thing; being able to do this when motion is added from being carried about or during self-movement requires integration of far more information to retain motor control (Keogh & Sugden, 1985).

**Locomotion**    Achievements in standing, crawling, sitting, and walking are also summarized in the Chronology on page 185. One early milestone in locomotion is the ability to roll over. Then comes success at initiating forward motion, a skill marked by considerable variation. Some infants use their arms to pull and their legs to push, others use only arms or legs, and still others scoot forward while sitting. *Crawling*, locomotion with stomach touching the floor, may soon give way to *creeping*, locomotion on hands and knees. Then again it may not, and the varieties of forward motion invented by babies often generate lively and entertaining discussions among caregivers.

Once babies are able to pull themselves upright, they often *cruise*—that is, move by holding on to furniture or other objects while stepping sideways. Forward walking while holding on to someone's hand typically follows. By about twelve months of age half of American babies walk alone, a skill that continues to be refined throughout infancy and early childhood. Mary Shirley (1931), for example, placed olive oil or powder on the soles of babies' feet to record how they walked across a length of paper. When they first began to walk, toddlers did so with feet widely separated, and their toes were pointed outward, yielding a waddle, which likely helped to maintain balance. Beginning walkers also take short steps, gradually increasing their length during the next few months; then they increase the rate at which they take those steps to establish a pace that is more automatic and natural (Bril & Brenière, 1992).

Prewalking and walking skills likely depend on the growth of higher brain centers, but even before independent walking many of the components of this skill are evident. For example, babies six months of age, placed on a treadmill and held so they do not have to support their full weight, display alternating stepping similar to that involved in walking (Thelen & Ulrich, 1991). Even six-week-olds, if lying on their backs, produce surprisingly coordinated leg movements (Thelen, Skala, & Kelso, 1987).

**Manual Control** At birth and in the first few weeks that follow babies typically keep their hands closed in fistlike fashion. By about four months of age infants awkwardly pick up an object by grasping it with the palm of the hand. Over the next few months they display a shift from using the inner palm to using opposing thumb and finger tips (see Figure 5.6), a progression that culminates in a *neat pincer grasp* at about nine months of age (Connolly & Elliott, 1972). This development in turn sets the stage for the elegant manual control required to hold, inspect, and manipulate different objects. As a consequence, the baby not only learns about objects but also begins to learn about her ability to control them (Karniol, 1989).

▶ The child's active role

Before grasping can take place the infant must also make progress in reaching. Newborns display *prereaching*, an attempt to initiate contact with objects that catch their attention, but their efforts are neither accurate nor coordinated with grasping (Bushnell, 1984). Movements do show speeding up and slowing down and changes in direction nonetheless similar to those involved in later more accurate reaches (Hofsten & Rönnqvist, 1993). Directed reaching, which

Sophisticated eye-hand coordination and the ability to simultaneously perform different functions with each hand are two important accomplishments that assist the curious toddler in gaining increasingly effective manual control of her environment.

## FIGURE 5.6

### Changes in Grasping Techniques

Changes in grasping progress along several dimensions. With development the infant becomes increasingly capable of rotating the thumb so that it closes opposite the index finger rather than to the side. Additionally, at first objects are clutched near the inner palm. As finger and thumb dexterity increase, grasping takes place nearer the thumb region and the tips of the fingers, culminating in the neat pincer grasp.

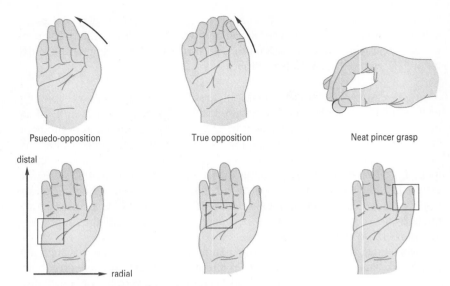

Psuedo-opposition          True opposition          Neat pincer grasp

Source: Adapted from Connolly & Elliott, 1972.

infants tackle in vastly differing ways, begins at about three months of age (Thelen et al., 1993). By about five to six months infants display mature, *ballistic* reaches, rapidly and accurately retrieving an object in the visual field. Although the ability to see their own hand is not necessary in these reaches, babies eventually do appear to make use of such visual cues to help them retrieve an object (Ashmead et al. 1993; Clifton et al., 1993).

Another important component of motor skill is increased coordination between the two hands. Infants often attempt to grasp objects with both hands, but once babies gain greater postural control, such as being able to sit by themselves, one-handed reaches become far more frequent (Rochat, 1992). Coordination also involves complementary hand orientations, such as holding a toy dump truck in one hand while using the other hand to fill it with sand. This *functional asymmetry* emerges at about five to six months of age but becomes especially refined as the child enters the second year and begins to display self-help and advanced motor tasks requiring sophisticated use of both arms and hands.

## Motor Skills in Preschool and Later-Childhood Years

Many fundamental motor skills that the child acquires in the first two years of life continue to be modified and refined in the preschool and elementary school years. Among them are more effective body and eye-hand or eye-foot *coordination*, evident in greater sophistication in the ability to hop and skip or perhaps to kick, dribble, and catch a ball; better *balance*, noted in the ability to walk greater distances on a beam or stand on one foot for a longer period of time; increased *speed*, shown in the ability to run short distances more rapidly; improved *agility*, revealed, for example, in improved capacity to shift directions quickly while running; and greater *power*, shown by the ability to jump higher or longer distances or to throw a ball farther and faster than previously. The Chronology on pages 185–6 summarizes major accomplishments in early childhood for some of these abilities.

| CHRONOLOGY | Motor Skill Development |
|---|---|
| 2 MONTHS | Holds head steady when held upright.<br>Lifts head up. |
| 3 MONTHS | Holds head steady while being carried.<br>Rolls over. |
| 4 MONTHS | Grasps cube. |
| 6 MONTHS | Sits without support.<br>Stands holding on to something. |
| 7 MONTHS | Rolls: back to stomach.<br>Begins to attempt to crawl and/or creep.<br>Displays true thumb opposition in holding cube. |
| 8 MONTHS | Achieves sitting position without help.<br>Pulls to standing. |
| 9 MONTHS | Walks holding furniture (cruises).<br>Demonstrates fine prehension (neat pincer grasp).<br>Bangs two objects held in hands. |
| 10 MONTHS | Walks with help.<br>Plays pat-a-cake. |
| 11 MONTHS | Stands alone. |
| 12 MONTHS | Walks alone.<br>Turns pages of book.<br>Drinks from cup. |
| 14 MONTHS | Builds tower using two cubes.<br>Scribbles. |
| 15 MONTHS | Walks sideways and backward.<br>Attempts to use spoon and fork. |
| 17 MONTHS | Walks up steps. |
| 20 MONTHS | Kicks ball forward.<br>Throws ball overhand. |

| 2–3 YEARS | Jumps up several inches using both feet. |
| | Begins to show true run rather than hurried walk. |
| | Balances on one foot for one second. |
| | Throws ball, but feet remain stationary. |
| | Extends arms outstretched to catch a ball. |
| | Draws primarily in the form of scribbles. |
| | Eats with a spoon. |

| 3–4 YEARS | Walks upstairs, alternating feet. |
| | Able to produce standing long jump of about a foot. |
| | Flexes elbows to catch a ball and trap it against chest. |
| | Hops. |
| | Cuts paper with scissors. |
| | Uses lines to form boundaries of objects in drawing pictures. |
| | Brushes teeth without help. |
| | Puts on T-shirt. |
| | Buttons and unbuttons articles of clothing. |

| 4–5 YEARS | Walks downstairs, alternating feet. |
| | Gallops and skips by leading with one foot. |
| | Transfers weight forward to throw ball. |
| | Attempts to catch a ball with hands. |
| | Eats with a fork. |
| | Dresses without help. |

| 5–6 YEARS | Walks on a balance beam. |
| | Jumps about one foot vertically, broad jumps about three feet. |
| | Displays adultlike skill in throwing and catching. |

| 6–7 YEARS | Ties shoes. |
| | Writes some numbers and words. |

Source: Bayley, 1993; Cratty, 1986; Frankenburg et al., 1992; Gallahue, 1989; Newborg, Stock, & Wnek, 1984; Roberton, 1984; Winner, 1986.

This chart describes the sequence of motor skill development based on the findings of research and indicates the age at which approximately half of the infants or children tested in the United States begin to demonstrate the skill. Children often show individual differences in the exact ages at which they display the various developmental achievements outlined here.

In general, activities that permit the exercise of large muscles are of considerable interest to toddlers and preschoolers. The activities include pulling and pushing things, stacking and nesting large objects, and eventually riding toys such as kiddie cars and tricycles. As preschoolers begin to organize their interests and display more investment in energetic games and athletic activities by jumping, hopping, running, balancing, and catching or throwing a ball, feats that emphasize speed, strength, and efficiency of performance become frequent ingredients of their everyday schedule. When young children initially attempt to execute these skills, they often fail to prepare or follow through on their actions; the speed or force needed to complete them in a mature way is absent. Before finally demonstrating mastery of a skill, children may have difficulty synchronizing all the complex movements.

Some motor exercises also foster greater competence in self-help skills (such as dressing and grooming), assembling items (such as stacking and puzzle construction), and eventually skills involving sophisticated dexterity such as writing and drawing. For example, older preschoolers begin to supplement their large-muscle and athletic exercises with coloring and drawing, cutting and sculpting, and other activities that demand small-muscle coordination, a longer attention span, and more sophisticated planning and organization.

Improvements in motor skills during the middle childhood years usually arise from producing faster, more complex movements in a more coordinated fashion and in a wider variety of contexts and circumstances (Keogh & Sugden, 1985). Movements become more efficient and effective as well as better controlled in relation to the force needed to complete them. Any parent who has tried to avoid a three-year-old's fastball fired at pointblank range will have a healthy appreciation for developmental changes in performing such actions with reasonable force. With the exception of balance, boys tend to slightly outperform girls on many motor tasks (Gallahue, 1989) by the time they enter elementary school. Differences between boys and girls, may become especially large, however, for some activities as they enter the adolescent years, as Figure 5.7 indicates for running speed and the distance a youngster can throw a ball.

▶ Development as continuous/discontinuous

While athletic skills improve dramatically during the school years, so too does fine motor coordination. This is perhaps no more apparent than in progress in drawing and writing. At six or seven, children may be limited to printing relatively large uppercase letters of the alphabet, which can be done with motions involving the entire arm. Yet in a few years this will be supplanted by cursive writing of normal size, which demands more sophisticated wrist and finger movements. In addition, new interest in model construction or needlework, mastering the complex finger sequencing to play musical instruments, and drawing more detailed and more faithful representations of objects are further evidence that motor skills are undergoing significant developmental advancement.

As children grow older, the range of differences in individual abilities often increases (Clark, 1988). The effect may, of course, stem from practice, because some children focus on developing particular skills relevant to their social and cultural milieu. The acquisition of expertise or specialized motor skills in sports, dance, crafts, hobbies, playing musical instruments, and in some cultures trade or work-related endeavors permits older children to engage their environment with increasing competence, become more effective members of their society, and gain greater social status among peers and adults.

▶ Individual differences

## Determinants of Motor Development

To what extent do the emergence, refinement, and integration of motor skills depend on genetic or maturational factors? Or are the dramatic changes a consequence of practice, cultural, or other experiential factors? Many pioneers in developmental psychology advocated a strong maturational theory to account for the orderly acquisition of motor skills. But the empirical findings often raised enough questions to suggest that changes in motor skills, as in other

▶ Roles of nature and nurture

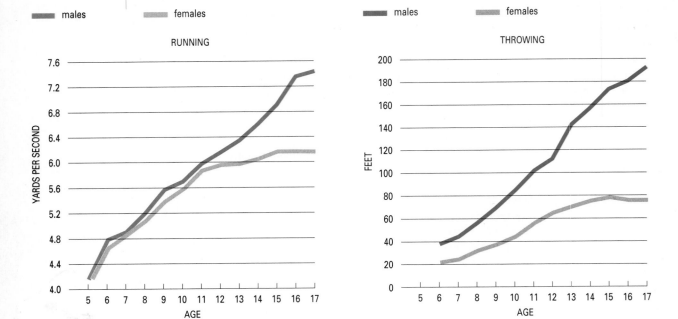

**FIGURE 5.7**

**Running Speed and Throwing Distance for Boys and Girls at Different Ages**

Boys tend to outperform girls on many motor skill tasks during the elementary school years as indicated by these data on speed of running and distance throwing a ball, summarized from a number of studies carried out since 1960. The differences between boys and girls often increase substantially as children enter the adolescent years.

Source: Gallahue, 1989, adapted from Haubenstricker & Seefeldt, 1986.

domains of development, are better understood as the unique confluence of biological and experiential factors.

**Biological Contributions**    The tendency for motor skills to develop predictably and in progressively differentiated and integrated ways provides one of the strongest arguments in support of a genetic or maturational basis for their development. Although individual differences exist, even intellectually and physically disabled babies routinely attain major milestones in an order similar to the average childs'. For example, blind children acquire many abilities at ages remarkably similar to when sighted infants acquire those abilities; only actions involving visuomotor coordination and independent locomotion are delayed in blind children (Adelson & Fraiberg, 1974). Children with Down syndrome also evidence the usual order of achievements, although they need more time, particularly when health complications such as heart disease are present (Zausmer & Shea, 1984). Other studies reveal greater concordance in sitting up and walking for identical than for fraternal twins and great similarity in gross motor activities such as running, jumping, and throwing in children who are closely related biologically (Malina, 1980). Perhaps, then, infants and children are *genetically preadapted* to righting and balancing reflexes, bone and muscle growth, and a maturing central nervous system designed to interact effectively over time with the physical and social environment (Kopp, 1979).

**Experiential Contributions**    Could experiential variables also play a role in motor development? With respect to the acquisition of expert motor skill, the answer is most certainly yes, but it may be true even for attaining fundamental developmental milestones. Lack of opportunity to engage in physical activity does seriously interfere with reaching developmental milestones, as research conducted in the 1940s and 1950s on children reared in institutions revealed. For example, in an orphanage in Teheran, Iran, Wayne Dennis (1960) found that babies who spent most of their first year lying in cribs and receiving few other forms of stimulation typically did not walk before age three or four. Observations of blind children also reveal that reaching for objects, crawling, and walking are substantially delayed. Yet when special programs encourage blind infants to acquire self-initiated movement, they do so at ages more comparable to their sighted peers' (Fraiberg, 1977).

In the Navajo culture babies are often swaddled for most of the day. Wayne Dennis' research with Hopi infants who received the same kind of experience suggests that this baby, despite the lack of opportunity to practice sitting up, crawling, and standing alone, will begin to walk about the same time as an infant who has not been swaddled.

Before these observations were made, a number of investigators conducted studies in the 1930s with sets of twins to test the role of experience in motor skill development. Typically, one twin received extensive training in such skills as handling blocks, climbing stairs, or roller skating; the other twin did not (Gesell & Thompson, 1934; Hilgard, 1932; McGraw, 1935). However, when given a chance to acquire the skills, the untrained twin often rapidly achieved the same level of accomplishment as the trained twin. Additionally, Wayne and Marsena Dennis found that specific training or practice yielded few benefits in learning to walk (Dennis & Dennis, 1940). Dennis noted that some Hopi Indian mothers practiced the tribal tradition of tightly swaddling their babies in a cradleboard. The mother strapped the board to her back for all but about an hour a day during her waking hours for the first six to twelve months of her child's life; the babies had little opportunity to practice sitting up, crawling, and walking. Other Hopi mothers adopted the practice of rearing infants without swaddling. Dennis found that swaddling had little bearing on when infants initiated walking, an observation reconfirmed in a more recent study of the effects of Hopi rearing customs (Harriman & Lukosius, 1982).

What can we conclude from these investigations? Only that specific training or practice seldom enhances the acquisition of a skill. The normal range of daily activities in which infants and children are engaged or, in the case of infants reared on cradleboards, the experience gained in strengthening their postural orientation, appear sufficient to promote normal locomotor development (Rosenblith & Sims-Knight, 1985). But consider another more recent finding. Philip Zelazo and his colleagues (Zelazo, 1983) asked whether infants from one to seven weeks of age, given a few minutes of daily practice in the placing and stepping reflexes, retained the reflexes and began walking earlier than infants who received no special training or whose legs were passively moved back and forth. Zelazo found that they did retain the reflexes and began walking earlier. He concluded that experiences that prevent the loss of certain reflexes provide a foundation for early walking. Thus, his research suggests that activities that maintain or encourage various components of complex motor skills can influence their development.

Esther Thelen (1983; Thelen & Ulrich, 1991) has applied a far broader perspective to such findings. She has argued that all complex motor skills, such as the onset of walking require the assembling and reassembling of multiple processes involving, among other things, motivation, elements of the nervous system that regulate posture and balance, increased bone and muscle strength, and changes in body proportions. The assemblages are constrained by the *biodynamics* of the human body, such as the physical and mechanical characteristics of limbs and body segments, muscles, and neural control mechanisms. However, when people attain the right configuration of underlying components, they display a new level of skill. Neither biological nor experiential factors alone are responsible for the opportunity to display this new level of skill. Instead, motor development is a dynamic system; its multiple components become "tuned," some perhaps through maturation, others by experience, into more effective action (Lockman & Thelen, 1993).

▶ Sociocultural influence

## Cross-Cultural Differences

Given the emphasis on viewing motor skills as a complex system, it should not be too surprising that racial, ethnic, and cultural differences in motor development are reported (Werner, 1972). At birth and continuing throughout their first year African babies typically outperform infants of other ethnic and racial backgrounds on a variety of motor skills (Lester & Brazelton, 1982; Werner, 1972). American children of African heritage have also been found to run faster, throw farther, and to have greater skill in balancing than American children of other ethnic and racial backgrounds (Bonds, 1969; Huntsinger, 1969). Yet the factors contributing to these differences are not easy to disentangle. Consider, for example, the work Charles Super (1976) conducted in a fairly prosperous community in rural Africa. He spent three years testing all sixty-four children born from 1972 to 1975 in a high-altitude region of Kenya. His monthly tests revealed that the babies were able to sit, stand, and walk an average of a month earlier than babies in the United States.

Parents in the African community made extensive efforts to teach the skills to their children. For example, they provided special props to encourage the infant to sit or held the baby's hands in a sequence of structured activities involving walking. In fact, their language contained distinctive words to denote the specialized training. The training also has been observed in more than a dozen other regions of East Africa. The more likely caregivers were to promote specific motor skills, the earlier their children tended to display them. For example, 93 percent of one group of caregivers said they taught their babies to crawl, and babies in this group began crawling at about five and a half months of age. In contrast, only 13 percent of the caregivers in a nearby cultural group expressed support for teaching their infants to crawl, and these babies did not crawl until they were about eight months of age. Caregivers in some of the cultures also believed it was important to teach babies to walk, and as already described, carried out exercises to encourage them to do so. Their infants continued to exhibit the stepping reflex until walking began, a finding that confirms Zelazo's hypothesis about the contribution of training in attaining this developmental milestone.

Although genetic, biological, nutritional, and other factors could contribute to the cultural differences, one finding strongly implicates child-rearing efforts. Super found that advanced motor development in this part of Kenya was limited to sitting, standing, and walking, skills considered important to the cultures. Other milestones not taught or valued, such as head control or the ability to roll over, were acquired later than when American infants attain them. A similar finding has been reported in Jamaica. Some mothers perform special stretching and massaging exercises to encourage their infants to sit and walk alone (Hopkins & Westra, 1990). Mothers who performed these exercises and expected their children to sit and walk early had children who reached the specific milestones sooner than other children. Still, we cannot be certain whether training focused on particular skills or more general experiences are responsible for cultural differences. Children in East Africa, for example, spend more time in an upright position, seated on a caregiver's lap or riding on her back, than children in the United States (Super, 1976). The activities may strengthen trunk and leg muscles to aid the earlier appearance of sitting, standing, and

Different cultures may implement a variety of practices to foster the development of motor skills and physical coordination. Here Mexican girls are encouraged to acquire the graceful movements of a folkdance by practicing with bottles on their heads.

walking. At the present time we do not know whether the ethnic differences reported earlier for American children reflect biological or experiential factors. However, based upon the complex dynamic systems that contribute to motor development, we can anticipate that both genetic and learning opportunities may play a role.

Now consider the children of the Ache of Eastern Paraguay, who are significantly delayed in acquiring a host of motor skills. For example, walking is reported not to begin until twenty-one to twenty-three months of age (Kaplan & Dove, 1987). This small band of people, engaged in hunting and gathering, do not encourage the acquisition of motor skills in infants. When families migrate to the forests, the women closely supervise their children younger than three years of age, preventing them from venturing more than a yard or so into the uncleared vegetation and spending 80 to 100 percent of their time in physical contact with them (Kaplan & Dove, 1987). For the Ache, keeping infants in close reach may be crucial for their continued survival. One consequence is less opportunity for infants to practice motor skills. Because the Ache have been relatively isolated and the total population at times quite small, genetic factors cannot be ruled out as contributing to the delay, but cultural concerns and efforts to either promote or discourage the acquisition of motor skills appear to have a significant effect on delays in their development.

## Physical Maturity

Having learned about some substantial advances in physical size and brain and motor skill development taking place during infancy and childhood, we can now begin to examine the many changes that accompany the transition to physical maturity. The growth spurt of early adolescence is only one of numerous indicators that signal approaching physical maturity. Attending the growth spurt are important changes in the body that reflect sexual maturity as well. We briefly consider some of the progressions marking the passage from late childhood to early adulthood and a few of the psychological issues that a young person may confront during this time.

## Defining *Maturity*

The large variation in rate and final level of growth among individuals and for various parts of the body compel the use of criteria other than size to determine physical maturity. One reliable indicator of physical growth and its culmination is provided by **skeletal maturity**, that is, the extent to which *ossification,* the chemical transformation of cartilage into bony tissue, has taken place.

The change of cartilage into bone begins prenatally about the eighth week after conception when cartilage in the ribs and in the center of the long bones of the arms and legs is transformed into bone. The process continues into late adolescence or early adulthood, when bones in the wrist and ankle are finally completely formed. Degree of ossification is determined by x-rays of the size, shape, and position of bones, particularly those in the hand and forearm. Although skeletal maturity has become the standard for determining physical growth, other highly visible markers of maturity appear just before and during the adolescent years. These important markers for young teenagers and their parents comprise a series of transformations associated with **puberty**, that developmental milestone when a young person gains the ability to reproduce.

During puberty the *primary sexual organs*—testes and penis in males; vagina, uterus, and ovaries in females—enlarge and become capable of functioning. *Secondary sexual characteristics* that distinguish men from women, such as facial hair or breasts, also mature. Puberty is accompanied by other changes that catapult adolescents from a childlike to an adultlike appearance. Boys take on a more muscular and angular appearance as their shoulders widen and the fat tissue of childhood is replaced with muscle. Girls' hips broaden, a change especially adaptive to bearing children. Girls also tend to retain a higher proportion of fat to muscle tissue and assume a more rounded appearance overall than boys.

Like the growth spurt, the timing of each of the many events associated with puberty varies enormously from one young person to another. Within each individual, moreover, the various signs of puberty emerge at different times (Brooks-Gunn & Reiter, 1990). As a rule, however, this cluster of characteristics tends to appear somewhat earlier in girls than in boys. Figure 5.8 identifies several events associated with sexual maturity and the average age at which those events take place for boys and girls.

Typically, enlargement of the testes in boys begins at about eleven and a half years of age, pubic hair starts to appear about six months afterward, and growth of the penis, deepening of the voice, and rapid increase in height begin six months after that. The first spontaneous ejaculation of semen normally occurs about a year after the penis begins to enlarge. Further markers, such as the growth of facial and body hair, appear even later. In some boys, however, the indicators of increased sexual maturity make their appearance at much younger or older chronological ages. The growth of the testes, for example, may begin as early as nine and a half years of age and be nearly complete by

▶ Development as continuous/discontinuous

▶ Individual differences

**skeletal maturity**  Extent to which cartilage has ossified to form bone; provides the most accurate estimate of how much additional growth will take place in the individual.

**puberty**  Developmental period during which a sequence of physical changes takes place that transforms the individual from immaturity to one capable of reproduction.

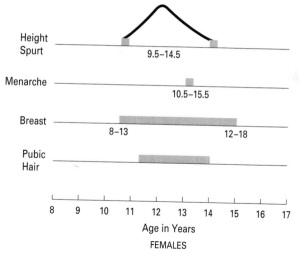

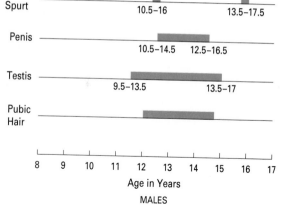

Source: Adapted from Marshall & Tanner, 1970.

FEMALES / MALES

FIGURE 5.8

**Normal Range of Ages in the Development of Sexual Characteristics in Males and Females**

The various changes accompanying puberty for males and females have a typical age of onset and cessation, but the specific times vary within individuals as well as between individuals. The peaking lines connecting onset and cessation of the timeline for height spurt reflect changes in the rate of increase in height over the duration of the growth spurt. The numbers under the time lines mark the earlier and later ages when these transitions take place for many children. Note especially the age differences for girls and boys.

▶ Roles of nature and nurture

age thirteen and a half for some boys, when such growth is just beginning for other boys.

The onset of various signs of approaching sexual maturity in girls is every bit as variable as that for boys. Breast development and rapid growth increase typically begin in the tenth year, the appearance of pubic hair in the eleventh year, and underarm hair about the thirteenth year. **Menarche**, the first menstrual period, often occurs before the thirteenth birthday and after peak height increments—but, as with all other indicators of puberty, its age of first appearance varies considerably from one girl to the next. Menarche is usually considered the indicator of sexual maturity in females, although it is not synonymous with actual reproductive ability. *Ovulation,* the release of an egg cell during menstruation, may not occur for another twelve to eighteen months after menarche.

What triggers these remarkable changes? As was true with the growth spurt, the brain—including the hypothalamus and pituitary gland—and various hormones appear to be centrally involved. In girls the hypothalamus may monitor metabolic cues associated with body size or the ratio of fat to muscle, because weight appears to be a good predictor of onset of menarche and because extremely high levels of exercise and poor nutrition can delay its occurrence (Frisch, 1983; Moffitt et al., 1992). Pituitary secretions stimulate the *adrenal glands,* located just above the kidneys, to increase the manufacture of a hormone that plays an important role in the growth spurt and the emergence of underarm and pubic hair in girls. Still other *gonadotropic* (gonad-seeking) hormones released by the pituitary gland stimulate the production of estrogen and progesterone by the ovaries and regulate the menstrual cycle. Estrogen promotes the development of the breasts, uterus, and vagina as well as the broadening of the pelvis.

Gonadotropic hormones also contribute to the production of sperm and elevate the production of testosterone by the testes in boys. For boys testosterone promotes further growth in height, an increase in size of the penis and testes, and the appearance of secondary sexual characteristics such as pubic and facial hair.

**menarche** First occurrence of menstruation.

## Early Versus Late Maturity

Today, adult height in most industrialized societies is typically reached by about age seventeen; a century ago, final height was often not achieved until about age twenty-three (Rallison, 1986). Changes in the age of menarche reveal a similar trend to increasingly earlier and earlier occurrences over recent generations (see Figure 5.9). The secular changes stem from improved socioeconomic conditions, including more adequate nutrition, but differences in development among individuals continue to be evident during the adolescent years. Do these individual, often transitory, differences during adolescence affect socioemotional development? The answer appears to be yes, but let's first consider how young people feel about the changes accompanying puberty.

▶ Interaction among domains

Most teenagers express concerns about their changing appearance. Their worries may stem from increasingly sophisticated cognitive skills as well as from the physical events themselves. Research investigating how young people view puberty has focused on girls and their reactions to menarche, which may occur suddenly and unexpectedly (Greif & Ulman, 1982). Girls who are relatively unprepared for menarche, either because of lack of information or because of its early onset, perceive the event more negatively than other girls, whose reactions are often a mixture of positive and negative feelings (Koff, Rierdan, & Sheingold, 1982; Ruble & Brooks-Gunn, 1982).

Today, because of both earlier and more complete education, girls' reactions to menarche appear to be less negative than in previous generations, at least in developed countries (Brooks-Gunn, 1984). Greater communication within the family correlates with a more positive attitude (Brooks-Gunn & Ruble, 1980), but girls are reluctant initially to talk about their first menstruation with friends (Brooks-Gunn et al., 1986). Parents may also display considerable uneasiness or embarrassment about discussing such events, especially fathers, who rarely participate in providing information about it (Paikoff &

**FIGURE 5.9**

**Secular Trends in the Age of Menarche**

There is evidence for a secular trend in the decrease in age for the onset of menarche from 1845 through 1960. Although most of the data were obtained by questioning adolescents and young adults, some, especially from earlier generations, depended on the memory of older individuals.

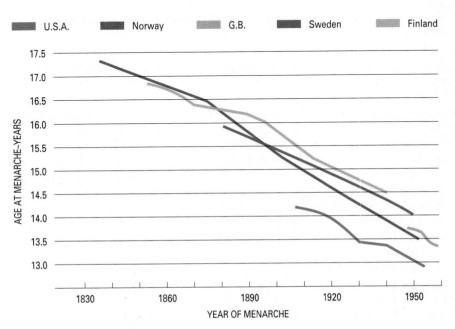

Source: Adapted from Tanner, 1962.

Brooks-Gunn, 1991). Moreover, conflict, particularly between mother and daughter, tends to increase at this time, a factor that could contribute to ambivalent emotional reactions to this new sign of maturity (Holmbeck & Hill, 1991; Steinberg, 1988).

Limited research conducted with boys suggests that they are often uninformed, other than through reading, about their first spontaneous nocturnal emission of sperm. Perhaps for this reason their feelings about the event are mixed and they seldom talk about it with others (Gaddis & Brooks-Gunn, 1985). Yet in American culture, and probably in most, early maturity is positive in many respects for boys (Alsaker, 1992; Peterson, 1988). Compared with early maturers, late-maturing boys report more negative feelings about themselves, feel more rejected, express stronger dependency and affiliative needs, and are more rebellious toward their parents (Mussen & Jones, 1957). Although late maturers want to be well liked and accepted, their efforts to obtain social approval often translate into attention-getting, compensatory, and childish behaviors disruptive to success with peers and adults (Mussen & Jones, 1958). The differences continue to be observed even into adulthood (Jones, 1965).

What are girls' reactions to early and late maturity? Here the picture is somewhat different (Alsaker, 1991; Greif & Ulman, 1982; Simmons, Blyth, & McKinney, 1983). Early maturity may enhance status and prestige for girls just as for boys, but it can also be embarrassing, decrease their popularity, at least among age mates, and lead to greater social pressure and expectations from older friends, parents, and other adults to conform to more mature behavior patterns (Brooks-Gunn, 1989). The findings of one study of Swedish girls beginning when they were ten years of age reveal some social consequences of early maturity (Magnusson, Stattin, & Allen, 1986). Girls reaching menarche early were more likely than late-maturing girls to engage in a variety of norm-breaking activities—staying out late, cheating on exams, pilfering, or using alcohol. This was especially true for the girls who matured first—they preferred older and more mature friends who may have inspired their greater independence from socially approved conventions of behavior. Indeed, among those maturing early but reporting no older friends, the frequency of norm-breaking activities was about the same as for girls who matured later (see Figure 5.10). As they grew older, early maturers with and without older friends began to look more alike in their frequency of many norm-breaking activities, and later maturers began to engage in such activities as use of alcohol as often as early maturers. Still, a few unacceptable behaviors, such as the use of drugs, remained higher throughout adolescence among early-maturing than among late-maturing girls.

How young adolescents feel about pubertal changes and evaluate their own status in relation to their peers may help to explain the findings on early and late maturity. Consider the cultural ideals of beauty and maturity that exist in most Western societies. Slenderness and long legs are considered desirable traits in women. Although initially taller than their peers during the growth spurt, early-maturing girls have less opportunity to grow tall and often end up somewhat shorter, heavier, and more robust than their later-maturing peers (Faust, 1983). The physical outcomes deviate from the ideal portrayed in the media; not surprisingly, early-maturing girls are therefore less satisfied with their weight and appearance than late-maturing girls. On the other hand, early-maturing boys more quickly assume the rugged muscular physique stereotypically portrayed in American society as ideal for men and are more pleased by their weight and appearance than late-maturing boys (Peterson, 1988).

▶ The child's active role

▶ Sociocultural influence

## FIGURE 5.10

**Norm-breaking and Menarcheal Age for Girls With and Without Older Friends**

Among adolescent girls norm-breaking activities, age of menarche, and availability of older friends have been found to correlate. Although early maturers tended to engage in more norm-breaking activities than late maturers, their behavior was markedly influenced by the availability of older friends. In contrast, the presence of older friends had little influence on norm-breaking activities for those girls who matured at later ages.

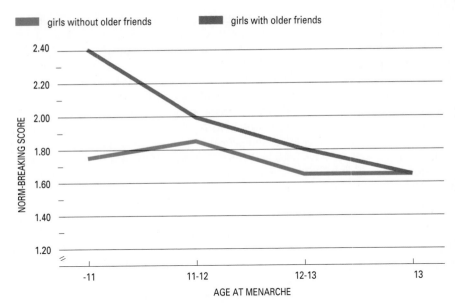

girls without older friends          girls with older friends

Source: Adapted from Magnusson, Stattin, & Allen, 1986.

Girls who mature early and boys who mature late are also out of step with most of their classmates. Young people usually prefer friends who share interests, and interests change with increasing maturity. Late-maturing boys may find that their peers move on to other pursuits, making it more difficult to maintain positive relationships with their friends. Early-maturing girls may redirect friendships to older peers. But this desire can be a problem, because it may contribute to increased behavior and school problems and greater personal unhappiness caused by pressures to conform to older peers (Magnusson, Stattin, & Allen, 1986; Simmons et al., 1987). In other words, biological, immediate social, and broader cultural factors combine to help define the consequences of early and late maturity.

## Dieting and Eating Disorders

In the United States many youth, especially women, indicate that they are unhappy with their weight. In fact, more than 40 percent of high school women report that they are dieting (Centers for Disease Control, 1991). Similar percentages occur in Australia and probably in many other Western countries (Paxton et al., 1991). Concern about weight seems especially prevalent in Caucasian and Hispanic youth, less so for African American young women.

A substantial number of teenagers, especially girls, many who are not obese, go to great and even life-threatening lengths to reduce their weight. *Anorexia nervosa* and *bulimia nervosa* are two self-initiated forms of such extreme weight control. Anorexia nervosa is a kind of self-imposed starvation most frequently found in Caucasian, middle- to upper-income young women (Harris, 1991). Anorexics appear to be obsessed with the avoidance of appearing too heavy and as a consequence become dangerously thin. As weight loss becomes severe, muscle tissue degenerates, bone marrow changes, menstrual periods are disrupted, and cardiac stress and arrhythmia can occur. Bulimia

▶ The child's active role

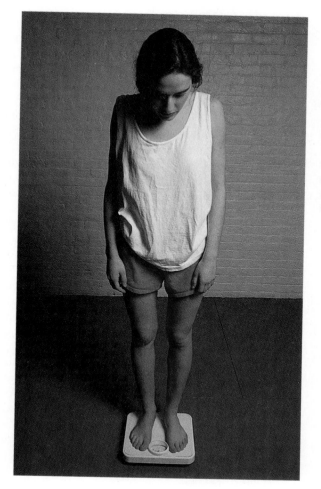

Concerns about weight become especially common among girls during the adolescent years. Cultural ideals associated with physical size and attractiveness may foster unrealistic efforts to control weight and contribute to anorexia nervosa, a kind of self-imposed form of limiting weight gain that can have serious health consequences.

nervosa is an eating disorder in which the individual engages in recurrent bouts of binge eating, consuming enormous quantities of food, alternating with self-induced vomiting. Although sharing with anorexics an intense concern about weight, bulimics often fall within a normal weight range for their age and height.

A substantial increase in these disorders has been reported since the 1970s, and their frequency may be greater in certain groups, such as athletes and dancers, who are especially concerned about their weight or physical appearance (Phelps & Bajorek, 1991; Taub & Blinde, 1992). Eating disorders could begin as part of the larger spectrum of anxieties adolescents and young adults experience about physical changes during puberty (Lask & Bryant-Waugh, 1991). Cultural ideals of physical attractiveness, insecurities about family and friends, the hormonal or physiological changes that may be occurring, and concerns about puberty may interact. Thus, sociocultural, psychological, and biological factors may be contributing factors, but the treatments most effective for dealing with such disorders have not been determined. Nevertheless, individuals experiencing eating disorders should be strongly encouraged to seek professional help.

▶ Sociocultural influence

▶ Interaction among domains

## Adolescent Sexual Behavior

Few changes accompanying puberty are as contentious in many families as the increased sexuality that attends physical maturity. Anthropological research indicates that the majority of cultures are likely to permit or tolerate some sexual activity during the teen years. But Western societies have generally been more restrictive in the expression of sexuality (Schlegel & Barry, 1991). Nevertheless, increasing numbers of teenagers in the United States are engaging in sexual relations and at younger ages (see Figure 5.11). Similar levels are often reported in other Western nations (Newcomer & Baldwin, 1992).

What are the factors that seem to play a role in whether a teenager will engage in sexual intercourse? Teenagers who perceive their parents as permissive about discipline and rules are more likely than other teenagers to initiate sexual relationships. But those who see their parents as most strict in these matters are more sexually active than teenagers who view their parents as moderately restrictive (Miller et al., 1986). Sexually active older siblings, absence of the father in the home, difficulty in school, early dating activity, friends engaged in such behavior, absence of religious practices and beliefs, and participation in other risk-taking behaviors all correlate with early sexual behavior (Santelli & Beilenson, 1992).

Aside from the moral and ethical issues adolescent sexual behavior raises, there are other important health and social consequences. Among the most frequent concerns are sexually transmitted diseases, teenage pregnancy, and the tendency of teenage parents to drop out of school (White & De Blassie, 1992). Moreover, compared with twenty-five years ago, when they do become pregnant, a far lower proportion of teenagers in the United States now marries (Glazer, 1993). This trend, along with increased sexual activity and inconsistent contraceptive use, translated into pregnancy for approximately 20 percent of unmarried American women of European heritage aged eighteen years or

**FIGURE 5.11**

**Number of Women in the United States Reporting First Intercourse at Ages Younger Than 18, 1958–1984**

Since the 1950s an increasing proportion of teenagers is reporting first intercourse at younger ages, as this figure for women indicates. The rates may be higher for men.

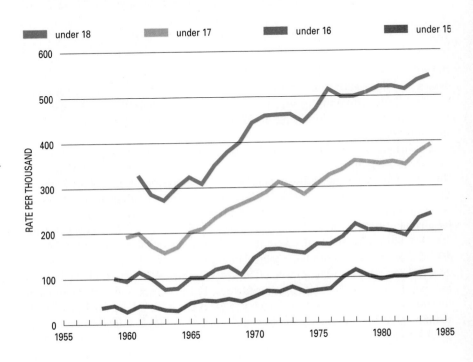

younger and 40 percent of African heritage during the 1980s (Furstenberg, Brooks-Gunn, & Chase-Lansdale, 1989). Nearly half the pregnancies terminate before the birth of a baby, but well over 300,000 babies are born every year to single teenaged women in the United States. Only about half of these women will finish high school. Moreover, their children will often have difficulty when they begin school (Lawrence, 1983). The long-term negative consequences of becoming a single parent at so young an age are just some of the reasons adolescent sexual behavior is of so much concern, not just to the families of teenagers but to the professionals who work with them as well.

## CONTROVERSY: THINKING IT OVER

### *Should Sex Education Be Part of the School Curriculum?*

Because of the risks associated with sexual activity, such as pregnancy and contracting AIDS or other sexually transmitted diseases, many working with elementary, junior high, and high school students in the United States and other countries have argued that young people need to be better educated about their sexuality. Nearly everyone agrees that instruction about sex should begin in the home at a young age, taught by parents. But beyond that consensus is much less accord about sex education.

Parents generally wish to see instruction about sexuality provided in the school; polls conducted on the issue seem to reveal a preference for such instruction. For example, it is not unusual to find that about 80 percent of adults in the United States believe that sex education is appropriate, and when given the opportunity, only a small proportion of parents ask to have their children excused from sex education classes (Fine, 1988). In fact, sex education is either required or recommended in nearly all states today and in many other countries where formal education is offered (Cole et al., 1993).

So what then is this controversy about sex education all about? The answer of course is what the curriculum should be. From the perspective of some the emphasis should be on encouraging young people to abstain from engaging in sexual relationships until they are married or, at the least, until they are mature enough to effectively handle the complex interpersonal relationships and consequences. To promote anything other than abstinence sends a mixed message that communicates a double standard: "Avoid sexual relationships, but in case you can't, here is what you should know."

From the perspective of others, however, sex education in the school should not be presented within the context of moral or prescriptive lessons but instead should clearly provide information and access to resources that will help young people be comfortable with their emerging sexuality. Perhaps a somewhat tempered perspective is that while young people should be encouraged to postpone sexual involvement, many teenagers, even older children, are already taking part in sexual activity, are unlikely to change their behavior, and therefore need to learn to engage in it responsibly and safely.

Tests of the effectiveness of various sex education curricula have often yielded mixed results (Glazer, 1993; Stout & Rivara, 1989). While their knowledge of sexuality typically increases, young people do not consistently report that they are involved in less sexual activity or engage in it more responsibly or safely, nor has the incidence of teenage pregnancy always been found to decline. On the other hand, little evidence exists to indicate that sex education programs increase sexual activity, another fear that is occasionally expressed.

Why might these efforts have had limited effect? Is it that such programs need to be offered at earlier ages, because many young people do not participate in sex education classes until they are already sexually active (Santelli & Beilenson, 1992)? Or is it that the curricula typically provided on this topic have been uninteresting and ineffective, presenting extensive information about the biology of reproduction but little about the social skills needed to respond to the many pressures exerted among young people to engage in sexual relationships (Howard & McCabe, 1990; Miller et al., 1990)? Would the outcome be different if the programs were more comprehensive, supplemented by multifaceted efforts of parents, youth and religious leaders, other community resources, and the mass media (Shamai & Coambs, 1992)? Have the programs stressing abstinence, which for the most part have only recently gained widespread adoption, not been in schools long enough to prove themselves (Olsen et al., 1991)? Or are these latter programs too biased and narrow in their focus, often emphasizing fear instead of knowledge, extolling a simplistic solution to a complex problem that can have life-and-death consequences for young people today?  ■

## THEMES IN DEVELOPMENT

### PHYSICAL GROWTH AND MOTOR SKILLS

▶ **What roles do nature and nurture play in physical growth and motor skill development?**

Physical growth, brain development, and the acquisition of motor skills are the product of complex systems influenced by both biology and experience. Biological processes, both genetic and hormonal, augment growth, the proliferation and migration of neurons, and events associated with the development of motor skills. At the same time the transformation from relatively immature infant to increasingly competent child and adolescent is affected by experience and the many different forms of influence provided by caregivers. Important stimulation ranges from providing adequate emotional, social, and nutritional support for physical growth to practice and training in encouraging the acquisition of motor skills and talents.

▶ **How does the sociocultural context influence physical growth and motor skill development?**

Physical growth and motor skill development are embedded within and often determined by the settings, resources, and beliefs promoted by the society in which children live. For example, the extent to which a culture encourages specific skills, from the acquisition of motor milestones to skilled athletic ability, or values a particular physical attribute, such as being slender, affects the efforts of children to display these qualities. Furthermore, knowledge of nutrition, views about physical appearance, and the availability of leisure time, as well as educational practices, have established secular trends for many aspects of development, including growth in height, onset of menarche, and the prevalence of obesity.

▶ **How does the child play an active role in the process of physical growth and motor skills development?**

Babies seem to be intrinsically motivated to exercise rudimentary motor skills, as displays of rhythmic stereotypies suggest. Furthermore, once a child attains locomotion or other skills, she provokes new reactions from caregivers that may include being denied access to cupboards and light sockets or prevented from pouncing on the usually patient family dog. New physical competencies may also be exercised to improve their speed, accuracy, and efficiency. From these efforts can emerge expertise that fuels further progress in athletic, artistic, and other endeavors. Rapid growth or early maturity may affect not only the child's interests but also the expectations and reactions of others. Excessive concerns about weight, for example, and the emergence of sexual maturity may influence the kinds of interactions in which the child or adolescent engages both within and outside the home—interactions that can have dramatic consequences for future development.

▶ **Are physical growth and motor skill development continuous or discontinuous?**

Physical growth, brain development, and the acquisition of motor skills show spurts at certain times in development. The patterns often give rise to conceptions of stagelike development. But even dramatic changes in behavior such as those that occur with the attainment of motor milestones in infancy or during pubertal changes of adolescence are grounded in processes undergoing continuous transformations. Small incremental changes in the relative strength of muscles or production of hormones, for example, may initiate substantive dynamic reorganizations in complex systems of behavior. Physical and skill changes observed in children may bring about dramatic reactions from others and may result in perceptions of stagelike growth and motor skill development.

▶ **How prominent are individual differences in physical growth and motor skill development?**

Individual differences are a hallmark of physical growth and motor skill development. The variation may arise from biological or experiential factors that can limit or augment development. The differences can significantly influence the child and the reactions of others, as early or late maturity or precocious or delayed skill acquisition demonstrate. Individual differences are pervasive and readily apparent and an important aspect of behavior to be appreciated as well as explained.

▶ **How do physical growth and motor skill development interact with other domains of development?**

A child's physical size and weight, as well as improvements in the execution and coordination of motor skills, have dramatic influences on the responses and expectations of caregivers, peers, and others and in turn on how the child feels about his body and abilities. For example, once she is capable of walking, the child has a greater ability to initiate independence, which may lead her parents to grant more freedoms and at the same time demand more responsibilities. Similarly, the young adolescent's status with peers is often influenced by signs of his physically maturing body and other aspects of physical stature, coordination, and skill. These qualities are evaluated by others and influence the child's evaluation of self.

## *Summary*

**Body Growth and Development**    *Norms* obtained on physical growth reveal a common pattern of rapid changes in height and weight in the months before and after birth, much slower but regular increases in size beginning at about two years of age, and a final growth spurt before or during early adolescence. Growth is also marked by considerable variation among individuals and cultural groups and for specific systems of the body. *Cephalocaudal* and *proximodistal* principles apply to many patterns of physical growth.

Biological factors help regulate growth. Cells in the hypothalamus may determine whether growth is proceeding according to genetic instructions. Many *hormones* interact in complex ways to influence growth as well. Nutrition, disease, and even social-emotional experiences further affect physical development. Improved nutrition and prevention of disease have yielded secular increases in final height over the last several centuries in many regions of the world. Yet malnutrition and inadequate, neglectful, or abusive caregiving can result in severe stunting of growth. Insufficient rates of growth and obesity have significant consequences for the child's social interactions with others and appear to be major concerns for children and their families.

**The Brain and Nervous System**    Brain growth proceeds rapidly during fetal and early postnatal development. Much of neuron proliferation and migration to various locations in the brain occurs before birth; however, differentiation of neurons continues throughout development. Differentiation may proceed at critical or sensitive times for experience-expectant information but occurs throughout development for experience-dependent information. *Glial cell* formation, *myelination*, and the operation and organization of nervous system networks also begin prenatally and continue to develop after birth. Infants display behaviors suggestive of hemispheric specialization, or *lateralization*, at birth, but both hemispheres may have equal potential for higher-order processing of information.

**The Development of Motor Skills**    Infants display *reflexes* and spend considerable time producing stereotypies that may serve as building blocks in the neuromotor programs underlying complex voluntary behavior. Postural, locomotor, and manual control undergo regular patterns of differentiation and integration. Throughout infancy and childhood, motor skills become more efficient and quick. Failure to integrate higher-order voluntary and lower-order brain reflex mechanisms controlling breathing is hypothesized as one cause of *sudden infant death syndrome* (*SIDS*).

Genetic preadaptation may assist in initiating the emergence of milestone motor skills, but research indicates that experience is equally important for their acquisition. Many processes influenced by both biological and environmental factors contribute to individual and cross-cultural differences in the appearance of early motor skills and later skill acquisition.

**Physical Maturity**    Maturity is most effectively defined not by size but by ossification of bone material. Many signs of approaching sexual maturity, including the adolescent growth spurt, begin earlier in girls than boys. Boys in Western societies seem to benefit from early maturity, but the effects for girls are less clear. The different consequences may stem from the reactions and pressures of peers and perceived cultural values about body size and shape. Eating disorders and new patterns of sexual behavior appear to be major concerns for adolescents and their families.

# 6

# *Learning and Perception*

▶ **What roles do nature and nurture play in learning and perceptual development?**

▶ **How does the sociocultural context influence learning and perceptual development?**

▶ **How does the child play an active role in learning and perceptual development?**

▶ **How prominent are individual differences in learning and perceptual development?**

▶ **How do learning and perceptual development interact with development in other domains?**

*"I saw little Liana stick out her tongue! Honest, I was making faces, stickin' out my tongue at her. She really did, she did the same thing to me!" shouted six-year-old Miguel as he raced over to his father. His grandmother, overhearing Miguel's excited outburst in the kitchen, could not help but smile. She thought about her son, Liana and Miguel's father, born three decades before. The new doctor on the reservation had said that babies could neither see nor hear at first. But a few hours with her newborn had led Greyeagle to doubt that claim.*

*Liana's father also started to wonder about his daughter's abilities. Was this what the nurses had meant when they declared that Liana, the newest member of their tribe, would learn from the moment she was born? She was only two days old; could Liana already have learned how to imitate her brother? Then it hit him. Although quite proud of Miguel, he would much rather he teach Liana something about the customs of their village!*

Few questions have attracted more attention from developmental researchers than what a newborn can learn or hear or see or feel. Only twenty-five or thirty years ago obstetricians and pediatricians, even some psychologists, might have answered, "Very little and perhaps nothing at all" (Haith, 1990). But a different answer has emerged recently. Newborns can imitate tongue protrusions and learn other responses. They can also see. If newborns can see their surroundings, can they also hear—for example, a mother's lullaby? Can they identify the subtle smells of their mother's body, feel the prick of a nurse's pin or the pain of circumcision? How do opportunities to learn and gain information change with age? Do the changes depend on the opportunity to experience certain sights, noises, odors, or other events? Might a child reared in the angular world of city skyscrapers, for example, see and learn about things far differently than a child growing up in a tropical rain forest?

These are precisely the kinds of questions psychologists have often asked. Why? Because the answers provide information about the many things infants and children can perceive and learn about people, objects, and events. Perception and learning are fundamental processes by which children come to understand and respond to their world. Perception, the interpretation of sensory information from visual, auditory, and other sensory receptors, is the vehicle by which all information about the world is gleaned. Learning, a means of acquiring new skills and behaviors from experience, is an extremely important form of adaptation. Through learning children avoid dangers, achieve satisfactions, and become contributing members of the family, community, and culture in which they live. What perceptual and learning abilities do infants have? How do early abilities develop? Let's begin with learning in infants and children and then consider their sensory and perceptual development.

## *Learning in Infancy and Childhood*

Learning includes mechanisms that permit adaptation to the environment. The wide variety of learning infants and children display helps them to increase their likelihood of survival, respond to the demands of their physical and social environments, and achieve goals and solve problems. Children learn, for example, that a stove can be hot, that hitting a sibling will make their parents angry. From watching other children present a class project, they learn how to make theirs as interesting or better for classmates. How early do these important capacities appear in infants and young children?

▶ Roles of nature and nurture

### Basic Learning Processes in Infancy

Basic forms of learning appear quite early in babies. Evidence of this comes from experiments involving *classical* and *operant conditioning* and from studies of imitation and habituation.

**unconditioned stimulus (UCS)** A stimulus that, without prior training, elicits a reflexlike response (unconditioned response).

**unconditioned response (UCR)** The response that is automatically elicited by the unconditioned stimulus (UCS).

**conditioned stimulus (CS)** A neutral stimulus that begins to elicit a response similar to the unconditioned stimulus (UCS) with which it has been paired.

**conditioned response (CR)** A learned response that is exhibited to a previously neutral stimulus (CS) as a result of pairing the CS with an unconditioned stimulus (UCS).

**positive reinforcement** Occurrence of a stimulus that strengthens a response when it follows that response. Also known as a reward.

**negative reinforcement** Withdrawal of an aversive stimulus that, upon its removal, serves to strengthen a preceding response.

**Classical Conditioning**      As we saw in Chapter 2, in *classical conditioning* a neutral stimulus, as a result of being paired with an event that triggers an inborn response, comes to elicit a response similar to the one triggered by the event. Consider, for example, a nipple placed in a newborn's mouth; it tends to elicit sucking. The nipple is an **unconditioned stimulus** (**UCS**); the sucking response it elicits is an **unconditioned response** (**UCR**). After a series of trials in which a neutral stimulus—say, a distinctive odor—is paired with the nipple (the UCS), the odor may also begin to elicit sucking even when the nipple is not present. The odor has become a **conditioned stimulus** (**CS**), and the sucking response it initiates, a **conditioned response** (**CR**). Table 6.1 summarizes the sequence of steps in classical conditioning for this and other typical examples.

Classical conditioning can be shown in infants within hours after birth. Elliot Blass and his colleagues (Blass, Ganchrow, & Steiner, 1984) demonstrated this by pairing a tactile stimulus, stroking of the newborn's forehead (CS), with the delivery of a sugar solution to the mouth (UCS) that elicited sucking (UCR). Newborns learned to orient and initiate sucking (CR) with stroking of the forehead (CS) alone. But other types of classical conditioning are difficult for infants to learn. For example, researchers have not been successful at conditioning infants younger than three or four weeks of age with responses to aversive stimuli such as foot withdrawal at loud noises or a painful prick. Perhaps the youngest infants lack the motor and neural abilities to escape noxious events; they must depend upon caregivers for protection until they acquire simple locomotor skills for avoiding aversive stimuli (Rovee-Collier, 1987).

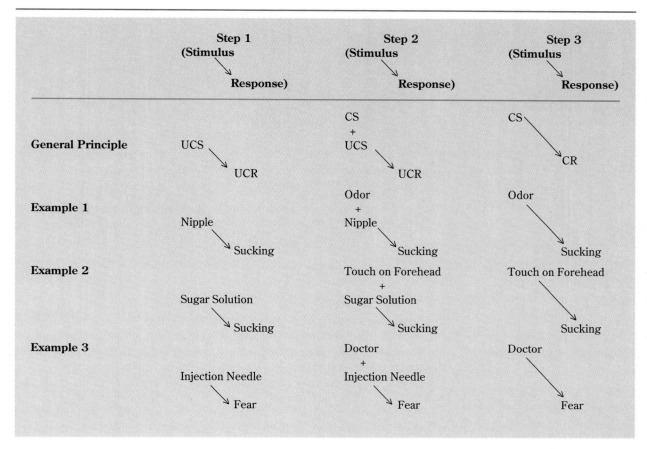

|  | Step 1 (Stimulus → Response) | Step 2 (Stimulus → Response) | Step 3 (Stimulus → Response) |
|---|---|---|---|
| **General Principle** | UCS → UCR | CS + UCS → UCR | CS → CR |
| **Example 1** | Nipple → Sucking | Odor + Nipple → Sucking | Odor → Sucking |
| **Example 2** | Sugar Solution → Sucking | Touch on Forehead + Sugar Solution → Sucking | Touch on Forehead → Sucking |
| **Example 3** | Injection Needle → Fear | Doctor + Injection Needle → Fear | Doctor → Fear |

However, other important associations, particularly those surrounding feeding activity, may be acquired through classical conditioning shortly after birth.

**Operant Conditioning**     In *operant* (or *instrumental*) *conditioning* the frequency of spontaneous, sometimes novel, behaviors changes as a result of positive and negative consequences. Put another way, behaviors tend to increase when followed by rewards (**positive reinforcement**) or the removal of aversive events (**negative reinforcement**) and to decrease when followed by the loss of rewards (**negative punishment**) or an aversive outcome (**punishment**). Figure 6.1 summarizes these relationships and provides examples of positive and negative reinforcement and different forms of punishment.

Operant conditioning can also be exhibited by infants in the first few hours and days after birth. For example, newborns increase or decrease pressure during sucking in response to the availability of milk, a positive reinforcer (Sameroff, 1972). And as with classical conditioning, operant conditioning seems to work best with behaviors significant to infants, such as searching for (head turning, mouthing) and obtaining food (sucking). Even premature infants weighing only two or three pounds show evidence of learning through conditioning; in a two-week period they come to more quickly touch and maintain longer contact with a toy bear that exhibits a breathing pattern similar to

**TABLE 6.1**

**Examples of Classical Conditioning**

Classical conditioning is learning in which a neutral cue (conditioned stimulus), through its association with a cue (unconditioned stimulus) that naturally elicits a reflex-like response (unconditioned response), comes to elicit the same response (conditioned response).

**negative punishment**     The withdrawal or loss of a desired stimulus or reward that, upon its removal, weakens or decreases the frequency of a behavior.

**punishment**     Aversive stimulus, or the removal of a pleasant stimulus, that decreases the frequency of a response when it is the outcome of that response.

**FIGURE 6.1**

**Positive Reinforcement, Negative Reinforcement, and Punishment**

TYPE OF STIMULUS

|  | Pleasant | Unpleasant |
|---|---|---|
| **Delivered** (ACTION OF STIMULUS) | Positive reinforcement (increases behavior through administration of a desired stimulus) Example: Infant says "cookie" → Mother gives praise → Infant says "cookie" again | Punishment (decreases behavior through administration of an adversive stimulus) Example: Toddler throws toys → Father yells, "Stop it" → Toddler stops throwing toys |
| **Withdrawn** | Negative punishment (decreases behavior through the removal of a desired stimulus) Example: Teenager out past curfew → Parent grounds teenager → Teenager meets curfew next week | Negative reinforcement (increases behavior by removing an aversive stimulus) Example: Child cleans messy room → Parent stops "nagging" → Child keeps room clean |

▶ Interaction among domains

their own rate of respiration than to a bear that shows no respiratory activity (Thoman & Ingersoll, 1993). Full-term babies only a few weeks of age can acquire complex chains of behavior such as making two head turns in one direction and two in the other through operant conditioning (Papousek, 1967).

Sensory stimuli seem to be especially powerful reinforcers for infants. Babies will work hard, modifying the frequency or rate of vocalizing, smiling, and other behaviors under their control to see and hear things or to continue receiving other stimulation (Lipsitt, 1982). The sensory stimulation, of course, typically occurs in the presence of parents, grandparents, neighbors, and siblings who, as a major source of reinforcers, encourage the baby to become responsive to them.

**Imitation**   What about the ability to imitate? Andrew Meltzoff and M. Keith Moore (1983, 1992) and other researchers argue that babies are able to imitate a variety of responses, including tongue protrusion, mouth opening, and possibly even facial expressions portraying such emotions as happiness, sadness, and surprise (Field et al., 1982). Although some investigators have been unable to replicate their results, many others, including the authors of one study involving infants from Nepal (see Figure 6.2), report surprising success in observing imitation by neonates (Reissland, 1988).

Even more controversial is what the imitative behaviors mean. Piaget (1962), for example, claimed infants younger than eight to twelve months could imitate someone else's behavior but only when able to see themselves making these responses. Because babies cannot view their own faces, imitative facial gestures would be impossible, according to Piaget, until after about one year of age when new symbolic capacities emerge. From this perspective, then, facial gestures are stereotyped rigid responses that are triggered by and tethered, so to speak, to limited forms of stimulation. In other words, infants can respond to just a few kinds of stimuli, and this behavior is innate, a kind of reflexive motor activity and not really a form of imitation (Anisfeld, 1991; Jacobson, 1979; Over, 1987).

▶ Roles of nature and nurture

Meltzoff and Moore (1989, 1992) counter that infants imitate a variety of responses, express their imitations in many ways, and have a tendency to exhibit

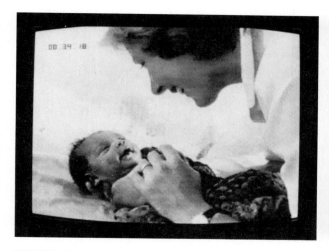 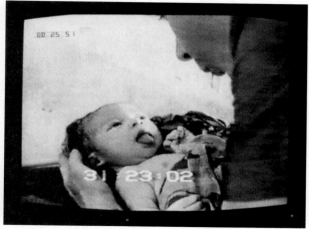

**FIGURE 6.2**

**Facial Imitation in Newborns**

Within an hour after their birth, babies in Nepal showed different responses when an experimenter used pursed versus widened lip movements. On the left, the baby broadens his lips in response to widened lips by the model. On the right, the baby exposes his tongue in response to pursed lips by the model. The findings support the highly controversial position that even newborns are capable of imitating facial gestures.

their imitations only to other people and not to inanimate objects—all of which works against the view that such behaviors are simply a fixed pattern of reflexive actions. They propose instead that infants imitate in order to continue interacting with others. Thus, imitation has an important social-communicative function, and these behaviors mark the earliest games in which babies engage to learn more about others in their new surroundings. By their second six months of age babies display even more frequent and precise imitations, matching a wide range of exhibited behaviors (Kaye & Marcus, 1981).

According to Piaget and others (McCall, Parke, & Kavanaugh, 1977), at about eighteen to twenty-four months of age children exhibit **deferred imitation**, the ability to imitate well after some activity has been demonstrated. Piaget believed deferred imitation, along with pretend play and the emergence of language, marked an important transition from one stage of thinking to the next, providing one of the first major sources of evidence for symbolic capacities. Here too researchers have challenged Piaget's position and claim that deferred imitation can be observed at much earlier ages. For example, nine-month-olds copy simple actions, such as knocking over a particular block or pushing a button, equally well both immediately and twenty-four hours after seeing the action (Meltzoff, 1988). Moreover, toddlers as young as fourteen months who see a peer pulling, pushing, poking, and inserting toys at the laboratory or at a day-care center will reproduce the behaviors in their own home as much as two days later when given the same toys (Hanna & Meltzoff, 1993).

The capacity for deferred imitation appears to exist much sooner than previously assumed. In fact, the results accord well with research on memory showing that infants younger than one year can recognize stimuli hours and days later. The findings are also important from a social learning perspective, providing clear and compelling evidence that infants, as well as older children, can learn many new behaviors by observing others.

▶ Interactions among domains

**deferred imitation** Ability to imitate a model's behavior hours, days, and even weeks after observation.

**Habituation**    The gradual decline in the intensity, frequency, or duration of a response to the repetitious occurrence of a stimulus is known as **habituation**. Even newborns display habituation. For example, they may show less arousal as they are repeatedly patted on the arm or hear the same bell ring and ring. Habituation is thus a simple adaptive form of learning—learning to ignore things that offer little new information and in a sense have become boring. Unlike other kinds of learning, however, habituation does not usually lead to new behaviors.

Once babies have habituated to an event, they often display a renewed response to a change in the stimulus. For example, if touched on the leg instead of the arm or exposed to a sound other than the ringing of a bell, they may become aroused once again. The return of a response is an example of **recovery from habituation** (sometimes called **dishabituation**) and suggests that the baby perceives the new stimulus as different from the old one.

▶ Individual differences

Low-birth-weight, brain-damaged, and younger babies tend to habituate less rapidly than older more mature infants (Krafchuk, Tronick, & Clifton, 1983; Rovee-Collier, 1987). In fact, as we shall see in Chapter 10, in infants rapid habituation and recovery from habituation to new stimuli is associated with greater intelligence and cognitive capacities in later childhood. Thus, although it is a simple form of learning, habituation may nonetheless be an important process in intellectual development.

## Learning Throughout Childhood

How do older children learn the many complex behaviors that they are able to display? One answer has been that caregivers or "instructors" reinforce actions of the child that are more and more like the behavior that the child is expected to acquire. Consider the six-year-old learning to write the letters of the alphabet. At first, of course, neither the size nor shape may be skillfully reproduced, but the teacher may express considerable satisfaction with these early efforts. With practice and as the child's ability improves, however, the teacher may expect a far more legible symbol before granting praise to the student.

▶ The child's active role

Although the process may extend to many situations in the home or at school in which children are expected to learn, it is difficult to imagine that the systematic implementation of reinforcers and punishment is the key to mastering many vital tasks of childhood. What seems to be missing from this explanation of how children learn is their active role in observing and interpreting events occurring in their culture. For example, at about age two, children readily imitate actions performed on objects. When that happens, it seems to promote continued play with the objects by both the model who begins the action and the observer who imitates the action so that there is an escalation of social and imitative games between children (Eckerman & Stein, 1990). Mothers also report that two-year-olds increasingly imitate responsible behaviors such as chores and self-care (pretending to cook, brushing teeth) rather than affective or attention-getting actions such as laughing and sighing or shouting and pounding (Kuczynski, Zahn-Waxler, & Radke-Yarrow, 1987). Thus, observational learning, along with the parents' direct application of reinforcers and punishments, no doubt plays a powerful role in the socialization of young children.

**habituation**    Gradual decline in intensity, frequency, or duration of a response over repeated or lengthy occurrence of the same stimulus.

**recovery from habituation**    Reinstatement of the intensity, frequency, or duration of a response to a stimulus that has changed. Also called *dishabituation*.

**dishabituation**    *See* recovery from habituation

**The Cultural Context of Learning**    The sophisticated conventions required for interacting with others; the physical and intellectual skills, techniques, and procedures demanded in play and work; and the rapidly expanding knowledge of the world evident throughout childhood depend on learning (Paris & Cross, 1983). Knowing how to address a revered elder, care for a flock of sheep, read and solve complex mathematics problems, and navigate from one location to another within the city, over mountainous countryside, or between widely dispersed islands are skills acquired through learning. Much of what children learn is culturally prescribed: the games to be played, the chores to be performed, the relationships to be respected, and the activities to be valued.

As we saw in Chapter 2, social learning theorists have considered observational learning one important way that children acquire many complex social and cognitive skills (Bandura, 1977b). Individuals often learn behaviors important to the community by observing the activity of others who in turn provide watchful guidance. Lev Vygotsky made such *social activity* the cornerstone of his theory of development. A child's knowledge is cultivated by formal and informal exchanges with caregivers, peers, and tutors who convey the information a culture has to offer (Vygotsky, 1978). Consider, for example, how a sensitive caregiver arranges tasks and materials to help a child solve a problem. The caregiver defines the difficulty of the task by dispensing useful background information, demonstrating appropriate actions, guiding and directing behavior, and allowing the child to take control whenever possible. The teacher or caregiver may sometimes lead and oversee and at other times stand back and let the student demonstrate his skill.

▶ Sociocultural influences

With the assistance of an expert, children can often contribute to the completion of tasks that they would otherwise be unable to perform. This skilled potter provides a scaffolding for her unskilled student, molding his hands and guiding his efforts to produce a product in which both can take pride.

**Scaffolding**    The concept of **scaffolding** is a way of thinking about the social relationship involved in learning from another person (Wood, Bruner, & Ross, 1976). A scaffold is a temporary structure that gives support necessary to accomplish a task. An effective caregiver or teacher provides such a structure in problem-solving situations, perhaps by defining the activity to be accomplished, by demonstrating supporting skills and techniques in which the learner is still deficient, and by motivating the beginner to complete the task. The collaboration advances the knowledge and abilities of the apprentice, as illustrated by the following study of a toddler learning to label objects. Anat Ninio and Jerome Bruner (1978) visited the child in his home every two weeks from his eighth month until he was two years old. One commonly shared activity that they observed was reading from a picture book, with the boy's mother providing the scaffold for the child to learn more about his language.

> The mother's (often quite unconscious) approach is exquisitely tuned. When the child responds to her "Look!" by looking, she follows immediately with a query. When the child responds to the query with a gesture or a smile, she supplies a label. But as soon as the child shows the ability to vocalize in a way that might indicate a label, she raises the ante. She withholds the label and repeats the query until the child vocalizes, and then she gives the label if the child does not have it fully or correctly.
>
> Later, when the child has learned to respond with shorter vocalizations that correspond to words, she no longer accepts an indifferent vocalization. When the child begins producing a recognizable, constant label for an object, she holds out for it. Finally, the child produces appropriate words at the appropriate place in the dialogue. Even then the mother remains tuned to the developing pattern, helping her child recognize labels and make them increasingly accurate. For example, she develops two ways of asking, "What's that?" One, with a falling intonation, inquires about those words for which she believes her child already knows the label; the other, with a rising intonation, marks words that are new. (Bruner, 1981, pp. 49–50)

Scaffolding involves a teaching/learning relationship that uses the expert or tutor who intervenes as required and gradually withdraws as assistance becomes unnecessary. Patricia Greenfield (1984) observed this phenomenon among girls learning to weave in Zinacantan, Mexico. Beginners, in the presence of at least one expert weaver (usually the mother), started by weaving small items and performed only the simpler parts of the task. The more experienced the learner, the less likely the teacher was to intervene to complete the more technically difficult steps. Novices were more likely to receive direct commands from the teachers, whereas experienced weavers were more likely to receive statements or comments. Both verbal and nonverbal assistance declined as the girls became increasingly proficient weavers, although the expert continued to be a role model for both specific techniques and more general principles of weaving. Remarkably, the scaffolding provided by the tutor yielded a woven product from beginners indistinguishable from those completed by expert weavers.

▶ Sociocultural influence

These examples illustrate what Vygotsky (1978) called the **zone of proximal development**, that is, the span or disparity between what children are able to do without the assistance of others and what they are often able to accomplish by having someone more expert assist them at key points. Vygotsky claimed that the most effective assistance from the expert is that just slightly beyond or ahead of the child's current capacities.

As the phenomenon of scaffolding and the zone of proximal development suggest, a role model who is sensitive to the learner's level of knowledge contributes greatly to the effective transmission of skills. The effect can be demon-

**scaffolding**    Temporary aid provided by one person to encourage, support, and assist a lesser-skilled person in carrying out a task or completing a problem. The model provides knowledge and skills that are learned and gradually transferred to the learner.

**zone of proximal development**    Range of various kinds of support and assistance provided by an expert (usually an adult) who helps children to carry out activities they currently cannot complete but will later be able to accomplish independently.

strated in tasks as diverse as the three-year-old's learning to distinguish the colors and shapes of pictures (Diaz, Neal, & Vachio, 1991) to fifth-graders learning how to carry out long division in mathematics assignments (Pratt et al., 1992). Of course, some tutors may be better at these activities than others. James Wertsch and his colleagues report an example of how teachers sometimes differ from parents in their approach to assistance (Wertsch, Minick, & Arns, 1984). Five- and six-year-olds from rural Brazil were asked to construct a replica of a toy barnyard. Either a mother or a teacher assisted in completing the task. Mothers were far more directive with their children than were teachers, pointing to specific pieces in the model or identifying them by explicit verbal references. Such an interaction provides opportunities for the problem solver different from one in which the child is expected to take more initiative. A child who is given direct instruction may be learning less about planning and organizing his approach to the problem, an essential part of many social and cognitive tasks (Clausen, 1991).

Despite the differences, parents can be remarkably effective as role models and teachers. They have the opportunity to engage in frequent one-on-one interactions with their children, to monitor closely and assess progress in all domains of development, and to gain substantial knowledge of their children's abilities. They also have great personal and emotional investment in the development of their offspring. Still, substantial differences among parents as effective role models exist. And the differences can have important consequences. For example, among intervention programs in the United States designed for communities in which preschoolers are at substantial risk of being unprepared for formal schooling, successful programs appear to be those that train parents to be useful role models and teachers in interactions with their children (Garber, 1988). In addition, effective teachers of older children, even in large formal classroom settings, appear to provide supportive scaffolds to promote their students' learning (Brown & Reeve, 1987).

▶ Individual differences

Recently, Barbara Rogoff and her colleagues (1993) have suggested that the extent to which children and adults take an active role in learning skills, values, and knowledge of their community differ across cultures. In general, in all communities adults provide a scaffolding for children to begin engaging in mature activities, a process they label *guided participation*. However, children take on a greater burden of responsibility for managing their attention, desire, and interest in mature activities in communities in which they are routinely in the company of adults. The guidance provided by caregivers in this context is likely to be in the form of supporting children's observations and efforts rather than in the form of instruction. In contrast, when much of a child's day is spent separate and apart from adults, the child will need more directed lessons and training to acquire mature skills. In this context, the caregivers assume comparatively greater responsibility in helping children to observe and understand the world.

▶ Sociocultural influences

Rogoff and her colleagues (1993) found that in communities in India and Guatemala, where young children could watch and enter into adult social and work activities, caregivers were likely to assist and support their children in carrying out the more mature responsibilities, such as learning to dress themselves or play with a new toy. On the other hand, in middle-income communities in Turkey and the United States, where children were more likely to be segregated (and parents could not be as consistently attentive and supportive), caregivers were likely to promote play and conversation or provide lessons or learning opportunities in interacting with children to teach them new skills. These interactions, in other words, looked more like the kind typically found for older children in formal school settings. Thus, although all caregivers provided guidance for more mature behavior in each community, its specific form differed, a confirmation of the diversity of ways in which learning may be encouraged in various cultural contexts.

We have described how infants and children learn in several different ways. We have also considered the important role that habituation, classical and operant conditioning, and observational learning typically play in determining what is learned as well as how learning proceeds. Although these basic learning mechanisms are essential for acquiring new patterns of behavior and enriching each individual's skills and competencies, researchers have come to recognize that development involves much more. To understand development, psychologists also must consider sensory and perceptual capacities as well as how infants and children represent and think about the information that becomes available to them. In later chapters we will examine the development of cognitive and information processing skills more closely, but let's turn now to a consideration of sensory and perceptual development.

## Sensory and Perceptual Capacities

Can she see me? Can she hear me? This is what many wonder when they hold an infant, even as they seem to be answering their own questions with a resounding yes by vocalizing, making funny facial expressions, touching, caressing, and rocking the baby. Still, the uncertainty remains: do infants register the information and if so, how do they interpret it?

More than a century ago William James (1890) theorized that for the newborn the world must consist of a "big blooming buzzing confusion." This view was built on the notion that the infant has to learn the pattern of features associated with a particular perceptual stimulus. Only by repeated experiences associated with distinct sensation could the infant come to appreciate the human face, for example, or a particular set of sounds as an organized, perceptually important event.

▶ Roles of nature and nurture

Is this theory valid today? Some researchers think not. James and Eleanor Gibson and many of their students have offered a strikingly different view of the early perceptual capacities of infants (Pick, 1992). For them, babies come into the world responsive to important structural aspects of the stimuli to which they are exposed. They already have organized perceptual systems that permit them to adaptively respond to sensory stimulation. Of course, experience affords ever greater opportunity to determine which properties of sensory events are stable and important and which can be ignored.

To delineate the different positions psychologists often distinguish between **sensation**, the registration of a basic unit of information such as a visual feature or aspect of sound by a sensory receptor or the brain, and **perception**, the process of organizing and interpreting sensations. Perception occurs when the infant recognizes his mother's face on sight or interprets a sequence of sounds as a familiar lullaby. Sensations are the building blocks; perception is the order and meaning imposed on those basic elements.

**sensation** Basic information in the external world processed by the sensory receptors.

**perception** Process of organizing and interpreting sensory information.

Today, most developmental psychologists think that the sensory world of the neonate is less chaotic and more organized than James suggested. As we consider evidence supporting this view, we can make two broad observations about research on sensory and perceptual development. First, vision has been studied far more thoroughly than any other sensory domain. To some extent

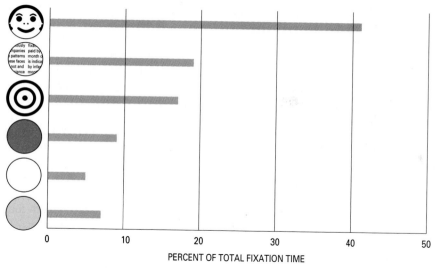

**PERCENT OF TOTAL FIXATION TIME**

0   10   20   30   40   50

Source: Adapted from Fantz, 1961.

**FIGURE 6.3**

**Preferential Looking**

When Robert Fantz showed infants two to three months of age the different visual stimuli shown here, he found that babies preferred to look at those that illustrated some pattern (for example, a facelike figure, newsprint, or a bull's eye) more than those that consisted of a single solid color. The finding, using the preferential looking procedure, was an important early demonstration that infants have the capacity to discriminate different visual stimuli. Note that the greatest preference was exhibited for the facelike stimulus.

this bias reflects the widespread belief that sight provides the major source of information for humans. Visual development, however, has also been easier to study than hearing, smell, and other senses. Second, in recent years the knowledge of sensory and perceptual development in newborns and young infants has expanded far more rapidly than the knowledge of these developments in older infants and children (Aslin & Smith, 1988). The disparity reflects the efforts of researchers to uncover the earliest appearance of sensory and perceptual capacities and the finding that many major changes in these domains occur in the first few months after birth.

## Studying Infant Sensory and Perceptual Capacities

How can we possibly know what babies see or hear or smell when they are unable to tell us about it in words? Researchers have devised ingenious techniques, some quite simple, to help answer this question. Most techniques are based on measures of **attention**—that is, alertness or arousal focused on a specific aspect of the environment. For example, when infants display attentional differences, such as looking longer at some things than others, they may be communicating that they can perceive differences among them. A closer look at several types of studies illustrates this point.

**Preferential Behaviors**    In 1958 Robert Fantz placed babies on their backs in an enclosed criblike chamber. Through a peephole he and his colleagues observed how long the babies gazed at different visual stimuli inserted in the top of the brightly illuminated chamber. Observers were able to determine where the infant was looking, because the reflection of the stimulus could be seen on the *cornea*, the outer surface of the baby's eyes, as she looked at it. Using this method, Fantz (1961) found that infants attended to some things longer than others. For example, babies one to six months old looked at disks decorated with bull's eyes, stripes, newsprint, or facelike figures far longer than solid-colored circles (see Figure 6.3).

**attention**   State of alertness or arousal that allows the individual to focus on a selected aspect of the environment.

The simple methodology encouraged many researchers to study the visual capacities of infants by observing their *preferential looking*, their tendency to look at some things more than others. The procedure has some limitations, however. What can we conclude, for example, when the infant looks at both members of a pair of stimuli for the same amount of time? Is the infant unable to discriminate the two, or does he prefer to look at one just as much as the other? Nor can we be certain that when the baby gazes at a stimulus he is processing its features.

Despite the limitations, babies often show preferences in what they attend to, and this simple procedure has proved to be enormously useful in assessing their visual capacities. In fact, by using special photographic techniques involving infrared lights and appropriate film, researchers can pinpoint specific regions and aspects of a figure at which the baby looks and how she visually inspects a stimulus. Such procedures have revealed, for example, to which features of a human face infants are most likely to attend, as shown in Figure 6.4.

**Habituation**     In another technique that capitalizes on the infant's tendency to prefer looking at some things more than others, babies are shown the same stimulus for relatively lengthy periods or in a series of trials. *Habituation* of attention, the simple form of learning described earlier, is the typical outcome. A change in the stimulus, however, may elicit *recovery from habituation*, or if the habituated stimulus is paired with one that is dissimilar, the infant may show a preference for the new one, both indicators that the child has perceived a difference.

By measuring habituation and recovery from habituation Alan Slater and his colleagues (1991) claim that newborns distinguish a change in both orientation and size of an angle. In a series of trials three- to five-day-olds were shown a simple stimulus such as that depicted in Figure 6.5. As expected, their attention to it dropped markedly; the newborns displayed habituation. Then some infants were shown that stimulus paired with one rotated to a different orientation or with lines in the same orientation but forming a different angle. When

## FIGURE 6.4

### Visual Scanning

Using specialized techniques, researchers can often pinpoint the specific features in a visual stimulus at which infants are looking. Here the typical patterns of scanning these facelike stimuli by a one- and two-month-old have been recorded. Note how the younger infant's gaze tends to be directed to the outer or external regions of the facial stimulus—that is, hair and chin. The older infant's gaze is more frequently directed to inner features such as the eyes and mouth.

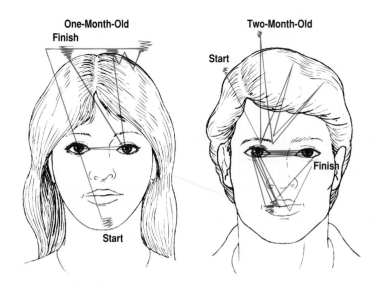

Source: Adapted from Salapatek, 1975.

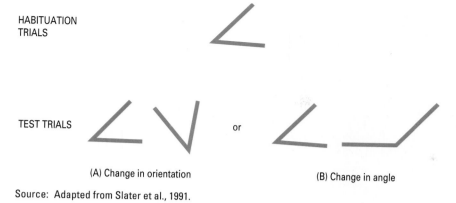

HABITUATION
TRIALS

TEST TRIALS

or

(A) Change in orientation

(B) Change in angle

Source: Adapted from Slater et al., 1991.

**FIGURE 6.5**

**Discriminating Orientation and Angle**

Using a habituation procedure, Slater and colleagues (1991) concluded that even newborns could discriminate both the size of an angle and its orientation. In one study an angle similar to the top one shown here was presented to babies in a series of trials until their attention to the stimulus greatly declined. Babies were then shown the same figure paired with another that had either been rotated (A) or with its contours rearranged to form a complementary angle (B). Newborns preferred attending to the stimulus rotated to a new orientation, and in other experiments newborns could also recognize a change in the angle of the stimulus. Researchers have found that habituation procedures provide considerable information about many sensory and perceptual capacities of infants.

the orientation changed, newborns showed a marked preference for attending to the novel stimulus. In subsequent experiments the babies appeared to distinguish angular changes as well. The results suggest that even newborns are able to detect specific features such as the orientation and angle of a simple array.

Habituation and recovery from habituation are processes that reveal abilities in other sensory domains. Infants, for example, often turn their heads away from unpleasant odors. Yet just as adults frequently report that they no longer notice a lingering unpleasant smell, infants also habituate to repeated presentations of the same odor. However, a baby who starts turning his head away again when a slightly different odor is presented demonstrates that he can distinguish the old and new smells.

**Operant Conditioning**    More complex forms of learning such as operant conditioning can be used to further test an infant's ability to discriminate sensory cues. To receive milk and other tangible rewards, including interesting visual and auditory patterns, for example, babies will learn to suck faster or slower, to turn their heads, to look, and to perform other behaviors that indicate discrimination of sensory stimuli.

Operant conditioning procedures figure prominently in research on auditory perception. One procedure popularized by Peter Eimas and his colleagues (1971), called *high-amplitude sucking*, has proved especially informative. Babies are given a special nipple designed to record their rate of sucking. A baby who sucks energetically or at a rapid rate may be rewarded by hearing some pleasant sound—for example, the consonant-vowel pairing *pa*. After the infant hears *pa* repeatedly, the rate of sucking typically declines as he habituates to the stimulus. What will the baby do when a different sound such as *ba* is introduced? Infants as young as one month of age begin to suck at a high rate again in order to keep hearing *ba;* they can discriminate the new consonant-vowel pair from *pa*. In other words, one-month-olds are already able to distinguish some important sounds that occur in language.

In addition to these behavioral methods—preferential looking, habituation, and operant conditioning—procedures using physiological responses such as heart rate or the neurological activity of the brain and even of individual neurons can be recorded to clarify the sensory and perceptual abilities of infants. Fortunately, the results of the various methods have often complemented each other in providing information about infant sensory and perceptual capacities.

The newborn must perform a variety of visuomotor responses including focusing his eyes on the features of his mother's face if he is to make sense of this new source of information. Visuomotor skills undergo rapid improvement during the first few months of life, one factor that permits a baby to soon recognize his caregiver's face.

## Vision

▶ The child's active role

Because newborns have limited motor skills, we are often tempted to assume that their sensory systems—their eyes, ears, nose, mouth, and skin—must be passive receptors awaiting stimulation. But Eleanor J. Gibson and James J. Gibson convincingly argue that perceiving is an active "process of *obtaining* information about the world (J. J. Gibson, 1966). We don't simply see, we look" (E. J. Gibson, 1988, p. 5). The Gibsons's emphasis on the active nature of the visual system applies to all sensory domains at every developmental level; even neonates mobilize sensory receptors to respond to stimulation flowing from their bustling environment.

**Visuomotor Skills**    The eye includes a lens designed to refract, or bend, light. As a result, visual images are focused onto the *retina*, that part of the back of the eye housing the sensory receptors for light. The lens of the human eye is variable; small involuntary muscles change its shape so that images of objects viewed at different distances are brought into focus, a process called **visual accommodation**. When the lens works effectively, the eye sees things clearly.

Newborns display limited visual accommodation, but the process improves rapidly to nearly adultlike levels by about three months of age (Aslin, 1987a). Poorer accommodative ability, along with the relatively small size of the eye, tends to cause images to be projected behind rather than on the retina (Banks, 1980). In addition, the *pupillary reflex*, which controls the amount of light entering the eye, tends to be sluggish during the first few months after birth, further reducing the ability to focus (Aslin, 1987a). As a result, infants are unable to detect small details of stimuli. However, they discriminate best those patterns and objects about eight to twenty inches away, the typical distance of a caregiver's face when holding or feeding the baby.

**visual accommodation**  Visuomotor process by which small involuntary muscles change the shape of the lens of the eye so that images of objects seen at different distances are brought into focus on the retina.

Eye movements are another essential part of looking. **Saccades**, rapid shifts or movements of the eye to inspect an object or to look at something in the periphery of the visual field, are produced within hours of birth (Lewis, Maurer, & Kay, 1978). At first, the saccades are initiated sluggishly and cover only small distances; neonates must launch a sequence of them to "catch up" to a peripheral target (Aslin, 1987a). They typically become more accurate, however, during the first three to four months. Yet the age at which saccades become fully adultlike remains uncertain (Bronson, 1990; Hainline et al., 1984).

Humans exhibit another pattern of eye movements, **smooth visual pursuit**, which consists of maintaining fixation on a slowly moving target almost as if the eyes were locked onto it. Newborns display only brief periods of smooth pursuit (Kremenitzer et al., 1979), and its execution continues to improve through eight months of age (Shupert & Fuchs, 1988). Nevertheless, infants readily turn their eyes and head to follow a moving object and prefer looking at a moving object to looking at a static visual array (Nelson & Horowitz, 1987).

In looking toward an object both eyes normally move together in the same direction. Sometimes, however, the eyes must rotate in opposite directions, turning toward each other as, for example, a person tries to see a fly that has landed on her nose. This response, called **vergence**, occurs when fixations shift between far and near objects; otherwise, a person would see double images. Vergence occurs irregularly in infants younger than two months (Aslin, 1987b). For example, young babies' eyes may fail to rotate far enough toward each other to converge on a visual target. By three months of age, however, the baby exhibits the ability more regularly. The development of some mechanisms for perceiving depth depend on this coordination, and if vergence is not readily demonstrated during the first few years of life, children may begin to suffer a permanent loss in depth perception (Banks, Aslin, & Letson, 1975).

### Acuity and Color Perception

How well are young infants able to see despite their immature visuomotor skills? The question concerns **visual acuity**, the ability to discriminate *contours*—that is, transitions in dark-light shading that signal borders and edges of elements in a visual array. One common test of visual acuity used with children and adults, the *Snellen test*, is based on identifying letters or other symbols on a chart twenty feet away.

Babies, of course, cannot name letters, so other procedures are used to test their visual acuity. Several methods have been devised, but one that provides a reasonably good measure relies on preferential looking. As an array of, say, black and white stripes appears more frequently (the stripes become narrower), the pattern becomes more difficult to see, and the stimulus eventually appears to be gray. Infants unable to detect the stripes quickly lose interest, preferring instead to attend to a pattern that they can still detect. By pairing stimuli with different frequencies of stripes and observing preferential looking, researchers can gauge the visual acuity of infants.

Two key findings emerge from the many investigations of visual acuity in infants. First, even newborns detect contours, although their acuity is much poorer than that of children or adults. In fact, acuity under some conditions is estimated to improve more than forty-five-fold from birth to adulthood. Although some studies suggest far better acuity in very young infants, babies are certainly not able to see fine features of stimuli. Second, acuity improves rapidly during the first six months after birth. The improvement owes to im-

**saccade** Rapid eye movement to inspect an object or to view a stimulus in the periphery of the visual field.

**smooth visual pursuit** Consistent, unbroken tracking by the eyes that serves to maintain focus on a moving visual target.

**vergence** Ability of the eyes to rotate in opposite directions to fixate objects at different distances; improves rapidly during first few months after birth.

**visual acuity** Ability to make fine discriminations among elements in a visual array by detecting contours, transitions in light patterns that signal borders and edges.

proved visuomotor skills, development of the neural pathways for vision, and changes in the shape and physical characteristics of the eye, including a dramatic increase in the number of visual receptors in the retina (Banks & Dannemiller, 1987).

Can babies also see colors? Once again the answer is yes and at very young ages. The retina contains two major types of receptor cells: *rods*, sensitive only to the intensity of light (functioning already at birth), and *cones*, sensitive to the different wavelengths of light. The cones contribute to color perception. Although infants may not see the full range of hues available to adults, color vision can be found by two or three months after birth and may be possible even earlier (Adams, Maurer, & Cashin, 1990). In fact, by four months of age, babies prefer looking at red and blue to green or yellow, a preference also evident in adults (Teller & Bornstein, 1987). Thus, color preferences may not be simply learned but may instead reflect certain biological contributions.

In summary, basic visuomotor skills and sensory capacities are available to infants. Babies can look at and see a richly patterned and probably colorful array of events. Their vision is not as keen as it soon will become, but newborns and infants are certainly not blind. In their first few months vision is limited to the more glaring and distinctive features, but these seem more than adequate for perception—that is, for interpreting and giving meaning to the visual environment that is an integral part of their new sensory world.

▶ Roles of nature and nurture

**Perception of Pattern and Form**    Few questions fascinate psychologists more than when and how infants recognize patterns and other configurations of visual arrays. Some have proposed that babies are born with the ability to perceive wholes and units. Others have argued the more traditional view, that this capacity is acquired only through extensive visual experience; infants become aware of or construct perceptions of integrated, holistic, and meaningful visual figures through repeated opportunities to process contours, angles, shading, and other primary sensory features.

As we have already learned, neonates do discriminate basic and relatively simple elements of stimuli, such as their contour, angles, and motion (Bronson, 1974; Haith, 1980; Karmel & Maisel, 1975). At two to three months of age things change. Now infants inspect and analyze the components more systematically, scanning a greater variety of features in a complex stimulus. A good example of the developmental change is exhibited by the **externality effect**—infants younger than about two months typically focus on a few of the outer contours of a complex stimulus and explore the internal features less systematically. Older infants tend to scan the internal features of a complex stimulus as well (Maurer, 1983; Salapatek, 1975).

▶ The child's active role

We saw an illustration of the externality effect in the discussion of preferential looking. Babies younger than two months tend to fixate on external contours of the face such as hair or the chin line; older infants much more frequently inspect internal features such as eyes or the mouth. The developmental difference is found when babies view other stimuli, such as two geometric figures, one inside the other. Very young infants can attend to the smaller internal figure when it shows movement or when its brightness is increased, but their attention is usually affected by the presence of an outer contour (Bushnell, Gerry, & Burt, 1983; Ganon & Swartz, 1980). On the other hand, older infants seem to carry out a much more deliberate, organized visual search, exploring and looking at the entire pattern or array.

**externality effect**    Tendency for infants younger than two months of age to focus on the external features of a complex stimulus and to explore the internal features less systematically.

Other experiments provide further evidence that babies perceive entire forms and patterns at least within a few months of birth. For example, when two-month-olds are habituated to a rectangle, they show recovery of habituation to a square but not if the rectangle is simply rotated (Schwartz & Day, 1979). In other words, they recognize that the figure has changed and can ignore its orientation. One especially convincing illustration of form perception involves subjective, or gradient-free, contours. Look at the Kanizsa figure shown in Figure 6.6. What should be apparent is a highly visible white triangle standing above three black disklike figures at each of its corners. But closer inspection should reveal that the brain subjectively assumes the triangular form; no contour is present to mark its edges. Infants, perhaps as young as one or two months and certainly by three to four months, perceive the subjective figures too, a powerful demonstration that perception of a triangular array, not of isolated features, is taking place (Ghim, 1990; Treiber & Wilcox, 1980). Numerous findings confirm that attention to the configuration of a pattern begins soon after birth and continues to improve throughout infancy (Dodwell, Humphrey, & Muir, 1987).

Some perceptual patterns are especially significant to the infant. Recall the findings shown in Figure 6.3, that babies prefer looking at facelike stimuli to some other kinds of visual patterns. Do even newborns recognize faces, perhaps the specific faces of their caregivers? Based on the discussion so far, it should not be surprising that by about two months of age infants do assign great importance to the face, attending to it more than other equally complex arrays. But an even earlier, perhaps innate, preference also makes evolutionary sense, because faces are a vital source of information for social and emotional relationships. Some researchers claim that newborns display such a preference, at least for moving configurations that approximate a face—two eyelike representations above a mouthlike representation—to other arrangements of the same components (Johnson et al., 1991). Mark Johnson (1992)

▶ Interaction among domains

▶ Roles of nature and nurture

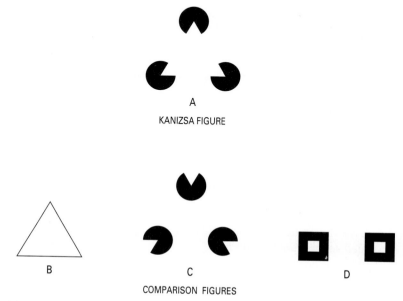

A

KANIZSA FIGURE

B

C

COMPARISON FIGURES

D

Source: Adapted from Treiber & Wilcox, 1980.

**FIGURE 6.6**

**Infants' Subjective Perception of Form**

Infants as well as adults perceive the subjective triangular figure appearing in the Kanizsa figure (a) even though no contour is present to define it. After becoming habituated to the Kanizsa figure, babies are shown other figures, including a standard triangle formed by visible contours (B), the indented circular figures rotated to abolish the subjective triangle (C), or a completely different array of stimuli (D). Infants show the least recovery from habituation to the normal triangle (B), suggesting that they perceived the triangular shape produced by the Kanizsa figure.

suggests that the inborn preference arises from a fairly primitive visual system that functions in newborns. By about two months of age the capacity is supplanted by a more sophisticated system that effectively explores and discriminates faces from other equally complex stimuli. The primitive system helps to ensure that the infant begins to attend to an important perceptual array—the face—as other visual capacities more fully develop.

When does a baby discriminate her mother's face from that of another person's? Perhaps within days after birth (Bushnell, Sai, & Mullen, 1989). However, the ability may be based on recognition of a specific feature rather than a full appreciation of her mother's appearance. Nevertheless, within three months of age babies recognize photographs of their mothers and prefer pictures of her to those of someone else (Barrera & Maurer, 1981b). The conclusion is that infants are attracted to and identify significant aspects of the human face early in their development and make rapid strides in perceiving and recognizing this important social stimulus.

▶ The child's active role

**Perception of Objects**    The visual environment is made up of objects as well as surfaces that must be distinguished from each other. How does a baby perceive a rattle as separate from the table on which it lies? The family dog as distinct from the floor on which he sits? James J. Gibson (1979) argued that the dynamic flow of visual information created by movement of objects or of a person's eyes, head, or body, called **kinetic cues**, provides infants with abundant information for distinguishing objects.

A series of experiments carried out by Philip Kellman, Elizabeth Spelke, and their colleagues supports James Gibson's position in regard to infants as young as three months of age (Kellman & Spelke, 1983; Kellman, Spelke, & Short, 1986; Spelke, Hofsten, & Kestenbaum, 1989). Babies viewed a rod, the midsection of which was occluded by a rectangular block; only the ends of the rod were visible (see Figure 6.7). What do infants perceive in these circumstances? A single complete rod partially hidden by the block? Or two short rods with the space between them covered by the block? To find out, the babies were habituated to the rod and block. As Figure 6.7 shows, in some conditions the rod and block moved in different ways during habituation. The results revealed that infants interpret the occluded rod as complete, not broken, so long as its two ends appear to be moving together and independent of the block during habituation trials, even when the two visible ends of the rod are of quite different shapes. But if neither the rod nor block moves, rod and block shift together in the same direction, or only the occluding block moves during habituation trials, infants do not "fill in" the unseen portion of the rod; they seem to treat the stimulus as two short rods separated by an intervening space.

▶ Roles of nature and nurture

Is perception of a coherent object innate? Might even newborns interpret the rod as complete in such situations? One study suggests that the answer is no (Slater et al., 1990). Under movement conditions in which older infants treat the separated segments as novel, newborns treat the complete rod as novel. Newborns do not seem to fill in or make perceptual inferences about the occluded segment of the stimulus.

**kinetic cue**  Perceptual information provided by movement of eyes, head, body, or of objects in the environment; important source of information for depth perception, even for infants.

The importance of kinetic cues, motion in general, for early infant perceptual development is demonstrated in yet another phenomenon known as *biological motion*. Bennett Bertenthal and his colleagues (1985) programmed lights to move as if they were attached to the head and major joints of a person walking. In other conditions the pattern of lights was inverted or an equivalent

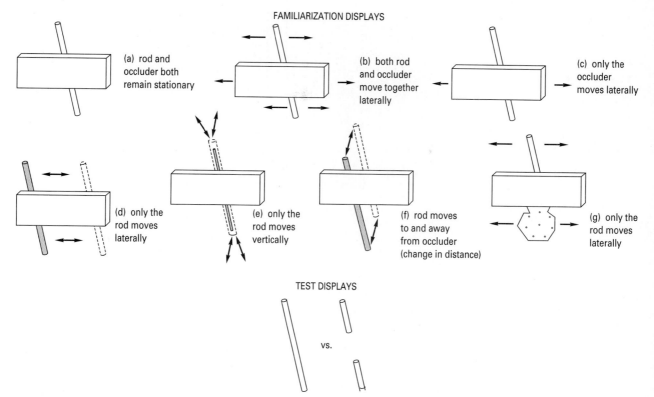

FAMILIARIZATION DISPLAYS

(a) rod and occluder both remain stationary

(b) both rod and occluder move together laterally

(c) only the occluder moves laterally

(d) only the rod moves laterally

(e) only the rod moves vertically

(f) rod moves to and away from occluder (change in distance)

(g) only the rod moves laterally

TEST DISPLAYS

vs.

Source: Adapted from Spelke, 1985.

Under some conditions four-month-olds respond as if they perceive an occluded rod as a single complete figure. Infants are habituated to one of the seven familiarization displays shown here and then are presented with the test displays. After viewing conditions A, B, and C, infants respond to the complete rod in the test display as novel, indicating they perceived the rod in A, B, and C to be broken. When shown conditions D, E, F, or G, however, infants appear to perceive the rod as a connected whole, showing less attention to the complete rod than to the broken rod in the test display. The results indicate the ability of young infants to infer unity and coherence for objects. Recent research suggests newborns do not make these perceptual inferences.

**FIGURE 6.7**

**Inference of Unity and Coherence**

amount of motion was shown, but the lights were scrambled so that the motion did not simulate the appearance of a person walking. After habituating to one of these displays, three-month-olds could perceive the change when either of the other displays was shown. By five months of age, however, infants exhibited greater reactions after habituating to the display depicting humanlike movement, which suggests that the "walker" had taken on special meaning for infants this young (Proffitt & Bertenthal, 1990).

**Depth Perception**    In addition to seeing objects to the left and right and above and below, people note the depth or distance of objects. Yet visual images are received on the retina in two dimensions. When and how do people acquire the ability to perceive depth? One source of information is *binocular* vision. Sensory information differs slightly for each eye. The ability to fuse the two distinct images to perceive a single object is called **stereopsis**, a capacity

**stereopsis** Ability to perceive a single image of an object even though perceptual input is binocular and differs slightly for each eye; significant source of cues for depth perception.

**FIGURE 6.8**

**The Visual Cliff**

In the visual cliff, used to test depth perception, a baby is placed on the plank at the center and a caregiver attempts to coax the child to cross to either side. Infants are much less likely to crawl on the glass support when the textured surface appears far below than when it is immediately beneath the glass.

that improves markedly during the first four months after birth. Stereopsis provides clues to depth as effectively for six-month-olds as for adults (Fox et al., 1980; Held, Birch, & Gwiazda, 1980).

Still other sources of information about depth and distance are available to infants. A classic series of studies involving the **visual cliff** suggests that kinetic cues are among them. The visual cliff consists of a large sheet of glass bisected by a relatively narrow plank. A patterned surface is placed immediately under the glass on one side, but much farther below the glass on the other side (see Figure 6.8). Richard Walk (1968) found that an infant placed on the plank and old enough to crawl can usually be coaxed to cross the shallow side but is much less likely to crawl over the deep side. In one study Walk put a patch on one eye of each young subject to eliminate binocular cues to depth. Infants were still far more reluctant to crawl over the deep side, perhaps because the kinetic cues provided by their own head and body movements signaled depth.

The shallow and deep sides of the visual cliff can even be identified by babies too young to crawl. Placed face down on the glass surface, two- to three-month-olds respond differently to the two sides of the cliff; they become quieter, less fussy, and show a greater decrease in heart rate on the deep side than on the shallow side (Campos, Langer, & Krowitz, 1970). Such reactions suggest that infants have not yet associated anxiety or fear with depth and find the visual information provided by the deep side more interesting than the shallow side. In fact, kinetic cues may already influence attention at birth, be-

**visual cliff** Experimental apparatus used to test depth perception in which the surface on one side of a glass-covered table is made to appear far below the surface on the other side.

NEWBORN     Shows minimal accommodation; limited, sluggish saccades; incomplete vergence.
Detects contours, but acuity and contrast sensitivity remain relatively poor.
Prefers attending to highly visible contours, angles, features in motion, and three-dimensional over two-dimensional stimuli.
Exhibits externality effect.

1–3 MONTHS     Shows accommodation; near normal adultlike vergence.
Smooth visual pursuit emerges, as does color vision.
Discriminates cues to depth.
Responds to rapidly expanding visual images.
Explores internal as well as external features of stimuli.
Recognizes shape of simple figures and more detailed patterns and objects.
Prefers attending to increasingly complex patterns, including those with facelike organization.

4–8 MONTHS     Exhibits stereopsis.
Saccadic eye movements become larger, more rapid, and accurate.
Shows adultlike smooth visual pursuit.
Acuity and contrast sensitivity approach normal.
Displays fear of depth on visual cliff.
Discriminates many pictorial (two-dimensional) cues to depth.
Distinguishes symmetrical from asymmetrical patterns.
Processes "subjective" contours.
Perceives occluded objects as wholes.
Becomes responsive to "biological motion."

This chart describes the sequence of visual development in infancy based on the findings of research. Children often show individual differences in the exact ages at which they display the various developmental achievements outlined here.

cause newborns prefer looking at three-dimensional objects to looking at two-dimensional figures (Slater, Rose, & Morison, 1984).

Sudden expansion or contraction of an image provides yet another kind of kinetic cue to an object's location. Infants older than three weeks produce avoidance-like behaviors such as blinking and backward head movements in reaction to rapidly expanding shadows that suggest an impending collision. However, they do not respond this way to rapidly shrinking shadows, if the expansion suggests that the object will miss, or if it appears to include an opening such as a doorway (Ball & Tronick, 1971; Carroll & Gibson, 1981; Náñez, 1988). Younger infants fail to exhibit these different reactions, either because they have not learned what the visual cues might mean or they are too immature to respond to them.

▶ Roles of nature and nurture

Finally, other cues, collectively described as *pictorial* because they can be perceived in photos or two-dimensional arrays, signal depth. Pictorial cues include relative size (near objects appear larger), shadows, interposition of surfaces (one surface hides another), and linear perspective (lines converging toward a horizon). Infants begin to use many of the cues to identify nearer configurations by about five to seven months of age (Granrud et al., 1984; Yonas & Owsley, 1987). Thus, infants respond very early in development to an abundant array of cues signaling depth and those necessary for perceiving space and objects as three-dimensional.

In summary, when does the infant begin to perceive patterns, objects, and depth? The answer is at least within the first two to four months (Ghim & Eimas, 1988). Newborns are attracted to and detect features of their visual environment. Their capacity to process larger, more organized, and meaningful patterns emerges soon thereafter, as visuomotor and sensory processes mature and are modified by experience. The development of visual abilities in infancy is summarized in the Chronology on page 225. Based on their early ability to construct and recognize coherent, integrated perceptual arrays, researchers conclude that the infant's visual world is far less of a "blooming buzzing confusion" than William James suspected.

## Audition

Just as medical opinion once held that newborns are blind, so too it asserted that newborns are deaf (Spears & Hohle, 1967). However, the fetus appears to be listening well before birth; sound not only affects brain wave patterns and heart rate of babies during their last few weeks in utero (Aslin, 1987b) but also fetal activity as revealed by ultrasound scans during exposure to sound (Kisilevsky & Muir, 1991).

Perhaps the most persuasive evidence that fetuses hear comes from several studies indicating that newborns prefer to listen to the sounds they heard before birth. Anthony DeCasper and Melanie Spence (1986) asked expectant women to read aloud a passage from Dr. Seuss's *The Cat in the Hat*. Women read the passage twice a day during the last six weeks of pregnancy; their fetuses were exposed to the story for a total of about three and a half hours before they were born. Two or three days after birth the babies listened to either the same passage or a new story while outfitted with a special pacifier that recorded rate of sucking. Depending on rate of sucking, the recording of the story would turn on or off.

▶ Roles of nature and nurture

When newborns could hear *The Cat in the Hat*, they modified their rate of sucking to listen to it but not to the new story. The results indicate that some kind of learning about the Dr. Seuss story took place prenatally. In fact, research suggests that a woman's voice is transmitted more loudly to her fetus in the fluid-filled prenatal environment than when broadcast through the air (Richards et al., 1992). The precise nature of what the fetus hears remains a mystery. However, prenatal voice familiarity may help to explain why newborns also prefer to listen to their mother's voice to that of a stranger (DeCasper & Fifer, 1980).

**Hearing**    There is little research on exactly how well babies hear in the first few months after birth. Six-month-olds, however, detect high-frequency sounds nearly as well as preschoolers, who in turn are able to hear such sounds better than adults (Schneider et al., 1986). Furthermore, by six months of age babies are able to distinguish two different high-frequency sounds much as adults do (Olsho, 1984). On the other hand, the ability to hear low-frequency sounds greatly improves during the first two years and probably until about ten years of age (Trehub et al., 1988; Yoneshige & Elliott, 1981). Thus, in contrast to visual sensitivity, which becomes nearly adultlike by six to eight months, some aspects of auditory sensitivity take a lengthy period to develop.

Can infants determine the direction and distance from which a sound is coming? Shortly after birth babies display **sound localization**, the ability to locate a sound in space, by turning their head or eyes in the direction of the sound. This early ability, which may be reflexive, declines during the first two months and then reemerges at about four months of age in the form of a more deliberate search for sound (Field et al., 1980). The ability to locate the precise position from which a sound originates markedly improves throughout infancy and into early childhood (Ashmead, Clifton, & Perris, 1987; Morrongiello, 1988; Morrongiello, Fenwick, & Chance, 1990). By six to eight months of age infants also already begin to appreciate the distance from which a sound emanates. At this age babies in the dark are less likely to attempt to retrieve an object producing a sound beyond their reach than one located within their reach (Clifton, Perris, & Bullinger, 1991).

**Perception of Sound Patterns**   Are babies able to perceive patterns in sound? Can they distinguish music from noise? Might they even have a preference for some kinds of music? Two- and three-month-olds do recognize changes in intervals between brief bursts of sound (Demany, McKenzie, & Vurpillot, 1977). Six-month-olds can distinguish more complex rhythms, such as a change from three groups of three bursts of noise (a three-three-three pattern) to either two groups (a five-four pattern) or one group (a nine-element pattern). By one year of age babies also distinguish the numbers of elements in a group (for example, a four-one-four versus three-three-three pattern) (Morrongiello, 1984).

At eight months of age babies recognize changes in short six-note melodies, including a transposition in key and the shift of a single note in a sequence to either a higher or lower frequency (Trehub, Bull, & Thorpe, 1984; Trehub, Thorpe, & Morrongiello, 1985). Babies are indeed sensitive to rhythmic and melodic contour (Trehub, 1987). In fact, four-and-a-half- to six-month-olds can boast of some budding capacities as music critics. Carol Krumhansl and Peter Jusczyk (1990) chose short passages of Mozart minuets and introduced brief pauses at locations judged by adults to be either natural or awkward places for a musical phrase to end. Babies preferred looking at a loudspeaker that played only natural versions to those that played unnatural versions of the Mozart selections. The ability to detect satisfying musical phrasings may be important not only for appreciating music but also for the phrasing and sound rhythms that commonly underlie speech.

**Speech**   Research on infants' basic hearing abilities has often been conducted to answer one question: how soon do babies perceive human speech? The ability to interpret speech sounds as meaningful elements of language probably begins in the second six months of life. That developmental story is discussed in Chapter 7. Do even younger infants discriminate speech sounds, and if so, how are they able to do this?

The smallest unit of sound that affects the meaning of a word, called a **phoneme**, consist of bursts of acoustic energy produced at several different frequencies. Phonemes are surprisingly complicated stimuli, and a difference of less than one-fiftieth of a second in the onset or transition of a frequency of sound is enough for adults to discriminate the distinctive phonemes /p/,/b/,

▶ Interaction among domains

**sound localization** Ability to determine a sound's point of origin.

**phoneme** Smallest unit of sound that changes the meanings of words.

| | |
|---|---|
| NEWBORN | Recognizes auditory events that were repeatedly produced by the woman when fetus was still in utero.<br>Discriminates mother's and stranger's voice.<br>Localizes sound reflexively. |
| 1–3 MONTHS | Recognizes simple auditory patterns.<br>Discriminates many, if not all, basic sounds used in language.<br>Makes deliberate efforts to locate sound, an ability that continues to improve throughout early childhood. |
| 4–8 MONTHS | Detects and discriminates high-frequency tones nearly as well as, sometimes better than, children or adults; ability to detect low-frequency tones continues to improve throughout childhood.<br>Recognizes melodic rhythms, transposition in key, note changes, phrasing in music.<br>Begins to lose some phoneme discriminations if not heard in native language. |

This chart describes the sequence of auditory development in infancy based on the findings of research. Children often show individual differences in the exact ages at which they display the various developmental achievements outlined here.

and /t/ in the sounds *pa, ba*, and *ta*. (Linguists use slashes to identify the phonemes of a language.) Are infants able to hear the differences? Indeed they are. In fact, by six months of age and often much earlier, babies probably distinguish every sound of importance in any of the hundreds of languages spoken around the world (Werker, 1989).

▶ Roles of nature and nurture

How are infants able to detect the subtle differences? Two answers with very different implications for language development have been proposed. One possibility is that babies are born with a "speech module," an innate capacity to detect and process the subtle and complicated sounds that make up human language (Fodor, 1983). The complexity of language acquisition, according to this view, requires such a specialized ability, because the cognitive skills of infants and young children are so limited. Another view is that phoneme discrimination hinges on general auditory capacities, capacities not limited to processing speech sounds or even necessarily unique to humans but capacities that infants are able to exploit quite early in development.

What evidence exists for either of these positions? Two research findings lend support to the view that speech perception involves special language-oriented mechanisms. The first comes from the extremely complex relationship between the acoustic properties of phonemes and their perception. For example, the /b/ phonemes of the words *beak* and *book* are quite different acoustically, although people treat the sounds as equivalent. Researchers argue that the absence of a simple set of rules for perceiving the phoneme /b/ in the two words makes the presence of a special mechanism for speech perception highly likely (Kuhl, 1987).

A second finding is based on **categorical perception**, the classification as the same of sounds that differ on some continuous physical dimension, except when on opposite sides of a critical juncture. For example, the English consonants /b/ and /p/ in the sounds *ba* and *pa* differ only in *voice onset time (VOT)*, the period in which the vocal chords begin to vibrate relative to the release of air by the vocal apparatus. Small changes in VOT are not heard as more or less like *ba* or *pa*. Instead, English speakers only hear *ba* as long as VOT continues to fall on one side of the categorical boundary and only *pa* when it falls on the other side. But if the difference in VOT crosses a critical point, the phoneme boundary, the two sounds are readily distinguishable. Infants as young as one month already demonstrate categorical perception for many different speech sounds (Aslin, 1987b; Kuhl, 1987).

However, researchers remain uncertain whether people are born with a special sensory mode for speech, because categorical perception can be found with sounds other than those found in speech. Monkeys, even chinchillas, also distinguish speech sounds categorically (Kuhl & Miller, 1978; Kuhl & Padden, 1983), a finding that argues against a specialized innate ability to process phonemes in humans.

Regardless of what accounts for phoneme perception, developmental psychologists fully concur that infants display many abilities important to acquiring language but also lose some competencies when the sounds are not a part of their auditory environment. For instance, younger infants appear to be more sensitive than older infants to phonemes found in languages other than their own. In one study six- to eight-month-olds reared in an English-speaking environment could readily discriminate among phonemes used in Hindi, whereas eleven- to thirteen-month-olds had more difficulty with this task (Werker & Lalonde, 1988). Adults could regain the lost discriminations only with considerable practice (Werker, 1989). Other research carried out in the United States and Sweden confirms that the language an infant hears affects his perception of phonemes by six months of age (Kuhl et al., 1992). Researchers selected two different vowel sounds, one that occurred only in English, the other only in Swedish. Six-month-olds were more likely to ignore variations in the vowel sound they heard in their own language than the vowel foreign to their language experience.

▶ Sociocultural influence

As with vision, psychologists have often been surprised at the many competencies displayed by infants with respect to sound. The Chronology on page 228 summarizes some of the early developmental abilities displayed in this domain.

## Smell, Taste, and the Cutaneous Senses

Developmental researchers have given far less attention to smell, taste, and the *cutaneous senses*—the receptor systems of the skin responsible for perceiving touch, pressure, pain, and temperature—than to vision or hearing. These senses do function shortly after birth and furnish crucial adaptive and survival cues for the baby. Smell, for example, may be critical for determining what is edible and may also be involved in early attachment to the caregiver.

**Smell**   Facial expressions, changes in rate of respiration, and approach-avoidance activities involving head turning are just a few of the responses indicating that newborns detect odors. But studying infants' olfactory capacities is difficult, because no simple system exists for classifying odors and because

**categorical perception** Inability to distinguish between sounds that vary on some basic physical dimension except when those sounds lie at opposite sides of a critical juncture point on that dimension.

the intensity of the odors at the receptor level is extremely difficult to control. The typical procedure consists of a series of trials in which a researcher holds a stimulus-saturated cotton swab just beneath the baby's nose for a few seconds. Do babies turn up their noses at the unpleasant smell of rotten eggs? Can they detect the food-related smells of fish, butter, banana, or vanilla? They most certainly do (Engen, Lipsitt, & Kaye, 1963; Rieser, Yonas, & Wikner, 1976; Steiner, 1979). Moreover, newborns become increasingly sensitive to these and other odors during the first few days of life (Lipsitt, Engen, & Kaye, 1963; Self, Horowitz, & Paden, 1972).

Parent-infant recognition occurs by smell among many species of animals. Can human infants identify their caregivers this way as well? Aidan MacFarlane (1975) offered two breast pads to newborns, one worn by the infant's mother and the other unused. Two- to four-day-olds oriented toward both pads about the same amount of time, but by five days of age infants turned their heads longer in the direction of the pad the mother had used. By six days of age infants also preferred a pad obtained from their own mother to one from an unfamiliar mother.

What cues are babies detecting, a mother's milk or odors from her body? Perhaps both. A series of experiments conducted by Richard Porter and his colleagues (Cernoch & Porter, 1985; Makin & Porter, 1989; Porter et al., 1992) has revealed that two-week-olds are generally attracted to a breast pad worn by a nursing mother, regardless of whether the mother is familiar. However, nursing (but not bottle-fed) two-week-olds also recognize the unique odor of their mother's body, orienting more to a breast or underarm pad worn by their own mother than to one worn by someone else. The findings suggest that after the close and frequent contact involved in nursing, neonates become familiar with and able to discriminate their caregivers from others on the basis of odor.

▶ Roles of nature and nurture

To test the familiarity hypothesis, René Balogh and Richard Porter (1986) taped a substance releasing either a cherry or ginger fragrance inside the bassinets of twenty-four newborns. The substance remained for about twenty-three hours, and babies were tested with the odors within forty-eight hours of birth. Girls, but not boys, demonstrated a clear preference for the familiar stimulus, results consistent with the hypothesis that early exposure to an odor can lead to its preference. Sex differences in this and other studies with infants indicate that girls are more sensitive to odors than boys, a finding also reported in tests of olfactory capacities of children and adults (Doty et al., 1984; Makin & Porter, 1989).

One additional finding of interest is that within the first few days of birth and after brief contact, mothers can identify their infants on the basis of odor. Fathers, grandmothers, and aunts also can recognize newborn kin by their smell alone. In other words, humans may inherit some family olfactory signature to which they are sensitive or are able to learn quickly (Porter, Balogh, & Makin, 1988).

**Taste**    Receptors for the basic tastes of sweet, sour, salty, and bitter, located mostly on the tongue and nearby regions of the mouth, develop well before birth; the fetus may already taste as it swallows amniotic fluid. Facial expressions and rate of sucking reveal that newborns can certainly discriminate among tastes (see Figure 6.9). Sweet stimuli, for example, elicit a relaxed facial expression resembling a smile; sour stimuli, lip pursing or a puckered expression; bitter stimuli, mouth openings as if expressing disgust (Steiner, 1979).

▶ Roles of nature and nurture

Innate preferences for some tastes may help infants to meet nutritional needs and protect them from harmful or dangerous substances (Crook, 1987). The preferences can, however, be modified by experience. For example, babies fed

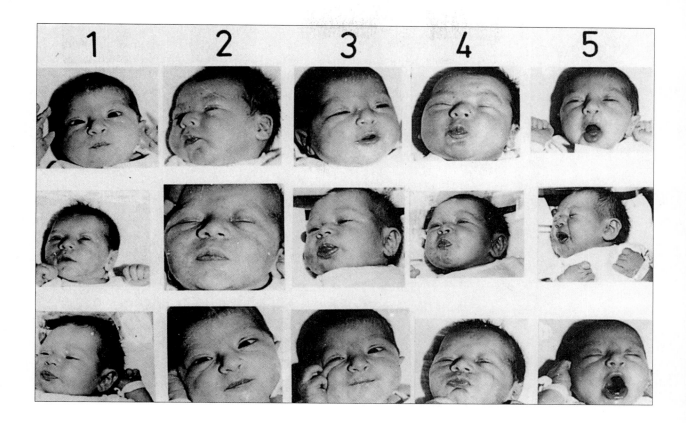

sweeter fluids in the first few months after birth ingest more sweet water at six months of age than babies not given this experience (Beauchamp & Moran, 1982). The desire for salt in a specific food may also be established early in infancy (Beauchamp & Cowart, 1990; Harris & Booth, 1985; Sullivan & Birch, 1990). Although learning appears to be important for the emergence of odor and taste preferences, we should also note that until they reach about two years of age, children will put just about anything into their mouths. Thus, among the most important things they must learn is what *not* to eat (Rozin, 1990).

**Touch, Pressure, Pain, and Temperature**    Skin contains more than one hundred types of receptors sensitive to touch, pressure, pain, and temperature (Reisman, 1987). As we saw in Chapter 4, even the fetus responds to touch. In the newborn stimulation can also elicit a variety of reflexes (see Chapter 5), and pin pricks and other painful events initiate crying. The skin's receptors undergo further development after birth, and during the first month babies become increasingly sensitive to painful events (Humphrey, 1964; McGraw, 1941). Although work on pain sensitivity is limited because of ethical concerns, circumcision and other medical procedures involving newborns have come under increasing scrutiny, because these operations are performed without anesthesia. Babies recover from such surgery rapidly, however, feeding and responding to caregivers normally after only a few minutes (Marshall et al., 1982). They also typically fall asleep after surgery, which may assist in their recovery from stress within a few hours (Gunnar et al., 1985).

A difficult problem for newborns, particularly premature infants, is regulation of body temperature (Moffat & Hackel, 1985). Cooling awakens babies, makes them more restless, and increases their oxygen consumption, re-

**FIGURE 6.9**

**Discriminating Tastes**

Babies produce different facial expressions depending on what they taste. The first column shows the resting face of three different newborns. Column 2 shows the same babies after they received distilled water—their expressions show very little change. The babies' facial expressions after sweet stimulation are more likely to be positive and relaxed, resembling a smile or licking of the upper lip as shown in column 3. However, their mouths become more pursed after sour stimulation (column 4) and more arch-shaped after bitter stimulation (column 5).

sponses that may facilitate heat production. Because newborns are unable to sweat or pant, exposure to high temperatures produces reddening skin, less activity, and more sleep, events that decrease heat production and assist heat loss (Harpin, Chellappah, & Rutter, 1983). When warm, babies also assume a sunbathing position, extending their extremities, perhaps a good clue for caregivers trying to decide whether a baby is too warm (Reisman, 1987).

Finally, just as caregivers can recognize their babies by odor shortly after birth, so too can they recognize them by touch. Recent research indicates that after only a couple of hours of contact, mothers can identify their babies on the basis of stroking only the back of their hand (Kaitz et al., 1992). This ability, perhaps adaptive in encouraging caregivers to be responsive to their offspring, is another illustration of the sensory communication that can take place between infant and caregiver to facilitate their social interaction.

▶ Interaction among domains

## CONTROVERSY: THINKING IT OVER

### *Can the Fetus Benefit from a "Sensory Curriculum"?*

Many caregivers are eager for children to have experiences that promote their development. For example, despite lack of evidence supporting long-term beneficial effects, some parents faithfully initiate exercises involving words spelled on flashcards to foster the early appearance of reading skills in their toddlers. With the finding that the fetus also has sensory capacities, a new kind of "curriculum" has entered the caregiving marketplace. This one involves patterned sounds—complex auditory or vibroacoustic events (such as heart- or drumbeat sounds), sometimes even words, numbers, and letters, steadily relayed to the fetus by a belt worn by the expectant woman or by some similar means. But such technological gadgetry is really only one aspect of this philosophy—other people may repeatedly play certain kinds of music in their home or engage in other repetitious practices during pregnancy in an effort to stimulate the unborn's sensory receptors and nervous system.

Researchers have demonstrated that during the third trimester the fetus becomes responsive to vibroacoustic stimulation (see Figure 6.10). Thus, the possibility of promoting prenatal learning and development certainly exists. Could certain kinds of fetal sensory curricula then be beneficial? Might such experiences give newborns a head start in knowing which sensory events are important or in stimulating their thought processes? Would familiarity with sensory stimulation also help to relax and comfort the infant in the months following birth? Why not begin sensory education as early as possible?

One concern is that the efforts are not only unproductive but even potentially harmful. For example, low-frequency sounds emanating from outside the womb are somewhat amplified for the fetus (Richards et al., 1992). Could some become so intense as to actually damage delicate sensory organs just beginning to function? Expectant women exposed to noisy workplaces or a rock concert sometimes report considerable activity in their fetus. Is this a positive response? Or a sign that the fetus is attempting to get away from the stimulation? Is the expenditure of so much energy beneficial to exercising muscles and joints? Or is such excitation potentially stressful? Would the newborn benefit from a prenatal sensory curriculum? Or is stimulation from the pregnant woman's normal speech and physical activities sufficient for optimal develop-

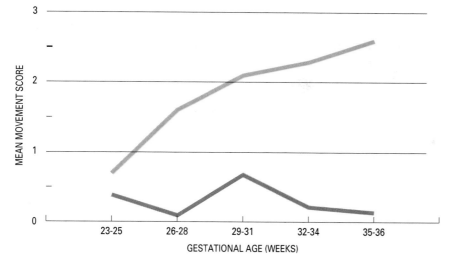

Source: Adapted from Kisilevsky, Muir, & Low, 1992.

**FIGURE 6.10**

**Vibroacoustic Stimulation and Movement by the Fetus**

Ultrasound scans reveal that by about twenty-six weeks (gestational age) the fetus is likely to begin movements when a buzzing vibrating stimulus is placed on the woman's abdomen near the fetus's head (experimental trials). When the stimulus is presented in a similar position a short distance from the woman's abdomen (control trials), the fetus seldom moves. Although it is not certain whether the fetus is processing both sound and vibration, the results confirm that early in prenatal development the fetus is responsive to sensory information. Should the fetus be provided with a "sensory curriculum" to help promote the new capacities? or could such stimulation pose a danger to the fetus?

ment? Remember that overstimulation of premature infants is a major concern for their well being. Should it be a concern for fetuses as well? ■

## Intermodal Perception

When sensory information is coordinated in order to perceive or make inferences about some aspect of an object, we are demonstrating **intermodal perception**. The toddler who hears his mother's voice calling from another room expects to see her when he enters that room. The sight of a cup provides information about how to shape the mouth to drink from it. If we recognize that the cup holds milk, we also expect it to taste a certain way and that we cannot pick the milk up with our fingers as we can pieces of popcorn. Sometimes, of course, we can be fooled. A luscious-looking dessert may taste like cardboard. A good ventriloquist really does make it appear that the dummy is talking.

When does intermodal perception develop? The question has been debated for decades. In fact, the research on infant tongue protrusion discussed earlier suggests intermodal perception exists early in infancy. If newborns imitate tongue protrusions, they must somehow understand that the sight of another's actions can be mimicked by their own mouth movements. Thus, some researchers argue that intermodal perception must be innate (Meltzoff & Moore, 1992).

A kind of intermodal perception may indeed exist at birth, according to the Gibsons (E. J. Gibson, 1982; J. J. Gibson, 1979). To them, perception is initially *amodal*, that is, undifferentiated; a newborn is unable to distinguish which sense is being stimulated. For example, if an object is visible and makes a noise, the baby perceives only something interesting and orients, to whatever extent possible, all receptors to it. Thus, intermodal perception does not depend on learning to coordinate the various senses (Spelke, 1987). Instead, with experience infants and children begin to recognize which sense is being stimulated, part of a process the Gibsons call **perceptual differentiation**.

▶ Roles of nature and nurture

**intermodal perception** The coordination of sensory information to perceive or make inferences about the characteristics of an object.

**perceptual differentiation** Process postulated by Eleanor and James Gibson in which experience contributes to the ability to make increasingly finer perceptual discriminations and to distinguish stimulation arising from each sensory modality.

This toddler very likely feels the soft, cold texture of snow while at the same time sees its white, fluffy qualities. Both visual and tactual cues will change if she holds onto it long enough and she may soon add another sensory input, taste, if she hasn't done so already. Stimulation often takes place through several sensory modalities.

The Gibsons's position is a controversial one. Another explanation of intermodal perception emphasizes the initial separateness of the senses; only after repeated experiences, this argument runs, are babies able to coordinate sensory information. Thus, intermodal perception involves, for example, learning that when objects are shaken, some rattle and make noise and others do not, an object that feels soft can also look soft, and a square peg does not fit into a hole that appears to be round. According to this viewpoint, intermodal perception is the outcome of *enrichment*, the association of sensations from two or more modalities, or from a more Piagetian perspective, the outcome of *constructing* schemes involving multisensory experiences (Spelke, 1987). Note that learning is important in each of these views. The point of contention is whether intermodal perception comes about by breaking complex undifferentiated stimulation into its specific constituents or by combining unique sensory experiences through association.

**Sight and Sound**    To determine whether infants link visual and auditory events Elizabeth Spelke (1976) developed a simple procedure in which four-month-olds could look at either of two films shown side by side. At the same time infants could hear a soundtrack coming from a speaker located between the two viewing screens. The soundtrack matched events in one of the two films, for example, an unfamiliar woman engaged in a game of peek-a-boo or someone playing percussion instruments. Would infants pay more attention to the film synchronized with the soundtrack? Spelke found this to be the case, at least when the percussion sounds could be heard.

Four-month-olds can match not only auditory and visual tempo and rhythm but other auditory-visual cues as well (Bahrick, 1992; Lewkowicz, 1992). In one study babies were shown two films, one depicting wet sponges being squeezed, the other two blocks being clapped together (Bahrick, 1983). When babies heard a squishing sound, they attended more to the film showing the sponges; when they heard a banging sound, they attended more to the film of the rigid blocks. Five-month-olds could even link sounds such as an auto coming and going with concordant visual progressions of approaching and retreating movement (Walker-Andrews & Lennon, 1985). Intermodal perception in infants extends to social relationships as well. For example, three-and-a-half-month-olds are likely to look at the parent, seated to one side, whose voice is coming from a speaker centered in front of the baby (Spelke & Owsley, 1979). By six months babies who hear a strange male or female voice also look longer at a face of the same sex than the face of the opposite sex, although three-month-olds do not show this ability (Francis & McCroy, 1983).

Intermodal cues can influence perception in some perhaps unexpected ways. Speech perception, for example, may be greatly affected by what a person sees. Harry McGurk and John MacDonald (1976) played videotapes of an adult uttering simple syllables such as *ba ba*. Sometimes, however, the video picture was synchronized with another sound, such as *ga ga*. Three-year-olds, older children, and adults often reported hearing something quite different—for example, *da da* or another utterance. By five months of age babies also seemed to recognize auditory-visual correspondence, preferring to attend to facial expressions articulating sounds that match to facial expressions that do not match what they are hearing (Kuhl & Meltzoff, 1988).

**Sight and Touch**    By six months of age infants who explore an object with their hands alone can recognize it by sight alone (Pineau & Streri, 1990; Rose,

Gottfried, & Bridger, 1981; Ruff & Kohler, 1978). But several experiments suggest that coordination of visual and tactile information exists much earlier when the mouth is used to explore objects. In one study one-month-olds were allowed to mouth either a smooth or nubby sphere, neither of which they could see. When permitted to view the objects, they preferred to look at the one they had not mouthed (Meltzoff & Borton, 1979). In another experiment one-month-olds also recognized objects they mouthed but—perhaps because of a difference in the procedure—preferred looking at the familiar object to looking at the unfamiliar one (Gibson & Walker, 1984). Babies can even be surprised by a discrepancy between vision and touch. Emily Bushnell (1981) showed infants a solid object within a box. Its location was distorted by mirrors, so that when babies reached for it they touched another object differing in size, shape, and texture. Infants younger than nine months of age failed to investigate the novel object actively or search for the one they could see, but older infants did both.

Research has not yet yielded a simple verdict on whether intermodal perception is present at birth or is only gradually acquired. Both positions may contain some truth (Spelke, 1987). Coordination among looking, listening, and touching can be found in infants only a few weeks of age, possibly younger, a serious challenge to the view that these abilities are learned or constructed only after much experience. Yet there is substantial evidence that intermodal perception also changes with experience. Much of the knowledge and skill that underly intermodal perception can only be gained through opportunities to look at, listen to, and smell, taste, and touch the surrounding world.

▶ Roles of nature and nurture

The discussion of sensory and perceptual capacities shows that very young infants can boast of surprisingly sophisticated competencies undergoing rapid improvement and refinement. Babies come equipped to gain access to a rich variety of sensory stimulation and quickly come to make sense of it. Their perceptual development reveals an order and purpose beautifully adapted to the goal of responding to and learning from experience. We must conclude that babies, as well as older children, are highly competent information processors, able to explore and learn through vision, hearing, touch, smell, and taste. Furthermore, they interpret and organize information in many ways that appear to be similar to the older child's, and adult's. This does not mean, of course, that infants perceive and interpret their surroundings in exactly the same way as older children and adults. It does mean that they are equipped with sensory and perceptual tools that allow them to become responsive to family, community, and culture in an astonishingly short amount of time.

## *Perceptual Development Throughout Childhood*

Richard Aslin and Linda Smith (1988) have noted a predicament facing anyone interested in learning about perceptual development after infancy. As research has increasingly found sophisticated abilities in newborns and infants, the importance of studying perceptual development at older ages has seemingly faded. Perception also becomes more difficult to investigate without considering at the same time the child's developing linguistic and cognitive skills. Nevertheless, several important features of perceptual development are evident throughout childhood. For example, as you grew older, did you find more

▶ Interaction among domains

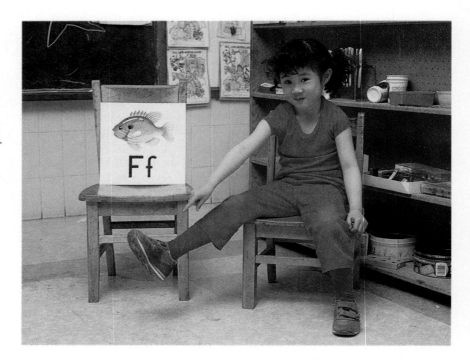

In learning to read, children must begin paying attention to consistencies and variations in letters and text, aspects of their visual environment that they may have largely ignored before. Attention to similarities and differences extend to the auditory domain as well. This young student points to another object which begins with the same sound as _fish,_ her _foot._

quickly which pictures were exactly alike among the six on the page? And did it become easier to spot the answer when "Sesame Street" asked, "Which of these things is not like the others?" As you progressed from a preschooler to a sophisticated schoolchild, you solved these problems better and faster. Children's perceptual skills become better focused, organized, and more confined to the meaningful and important features of the environment—in other words, perception becomes increasingly efficient with development. Eleanor Gibson (1969, 1982, 1988) has outlined one major view of perceptual learning to account for such findings.

## Perceptual Learning

Eleanor Gibson's theory of perceptual learning emphasizes three changes with age: increasing specificity in perception, improved attention, and more economical and efficient acquisition of perceptual information. Much of the infant's first year is spent in learning the sensory properties of objects, the spatial layout of his world, and the perceptual repercussions of his actions. But perceptual learning continues. For example, children acquire new kinds of visual discriminations when they learn to read. They must begin to pay attention to consistencies and variations in letters and text, aspects of their visual environment that they may have largely ignored before.

▶ The child's active role

Eleanor Gibson and her colleagues (E. J. Gibson et al., 1962) created different sets of letterlike figures such as those shown in Figure 6.11. One member of each set was designated a standard, but each set included variations of that standard. A straight line, for example, might be redrawn as a curved line, the standard rotated or reversed, a break introduced in a continuous line, or its perspective changed by tipping or elongating some aspect of the figure. Children four through eight years of age were shown a stack of each set of figures and asked to pick out only those identical to the standard.

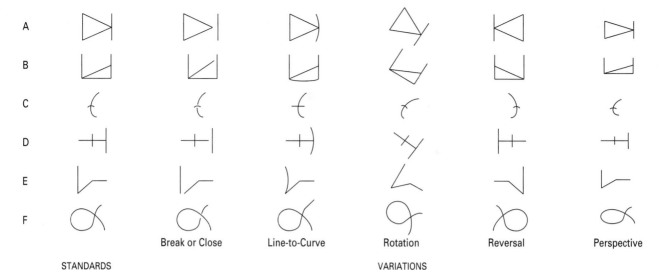

| | | Break or Close | Line-to-Curve | Rotation | Reversal | Perspective |
|---|---|---|---|---|---|---|

STANDARDS                                              VARIATIONS

Source: Adapted from Pick, 1965.

**FIGURE 6.11**

**Sensitivity to Perceptual Differences**

Column 1 of this figure gives different letterlike forms used as standards in a sorting task. Columns 2 through 6 display various transformations of each standard. Four- to eight-year-olds, shown a stack of the figures and asked to select only those identical to the standard, commit relatively few errors on variations that involve a break in the figure, presumably because the distinction is important for identifying many objects as well as alphabetic symbols. With increasing age errors involving rotation, reversal, and line/curve variations decrease substantially because, according to Eleanor Gibson, children who are beginning to learn to read must pay attention to these features of the stimuli. Errors involving perspective remain high at all ages, perhaps because the transformation is not important for identifying either objects or letters of the alphabet.

Children made many more errors for some kinds of variations in the stimuli than for others. For example, children of all ages seldom confused the standard with versions that contained breaks, perhaps because these features are important for identifying common objects in the environment as well as letters of the alphabet. On the other hand, older children did substantially better than younger children in discriminating rotations and reversals and line/curve transformations, presumably because children learning to read must begin to distinguish such variations. Finally, children of all ages found it difficult to discriminate changes in perspective from the standard, a variation that can and should normally be ignored for identifying both physical objects as well as letters of the alphabet.

Eleanor Gibson believes the age-related improvements in performance on this activity do not come about by reinforcing children to make the discriminations. In fact, when asked to classify the letterlike forms in a series of trials, children showed steady improvement in sorting without any feedback about how accurate they were. Gibson argues that through repeated exposure to and inspection of letters of the alphabet children are afforded the opportunity to recognize certain critical features distinguishing such figures. Opportunities to experience the regularities and differences among similar stimuli, not the systematic reinforcements of parents or teachers, enable children to distinguish them. Perceptual learning, then, is not only indispensable for infants learning to distinguish objects but also throughout development for learning to read and accomplish many other technical skills that demand subtle and sophisticated perceptual discriminations.

## Part-Whole Perception

As we have already learned, within a matter of weeks after birth babies can see patterns, forms, and objects—the wholes, so to speak, not just their isolated features, and we cannot rule out the possibility that they do so even earlier. The perception of preschoolers appears to be frequently influenced by wholes;

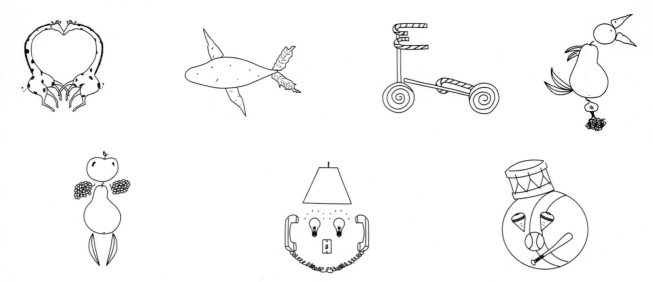

**FIGURE 6.12**

Source: Adapted from Elkind, Koegler, & Go, 1964.

**Part-Whole Perception**

Stimuli were created by Elkind and his colleagues to test whether young children can perceive both the parts and the whole. Younger children reported only seeing the parts. When the wholes are made simpler than those shown here, however, even three-year-olds can see both the parts and the whole. Difficulty in reporting both may stem from conceptual and verbal constraints rather than from perceptual limitations.

▶ Interaction among domains

they occasionally have difficulty making precise and systematic judgments about the similarity of objects based upon a single feature or attribute (Smith, 1989). Whereas older children are more likely to classify stimuli on one or a few dimensions (for example, size, shape, color, or some other specific dimension), preschoolers seem to approach such tasks from a more global perspective, grouping things on the basis of their overall similarity. For example, preschoolers might put a red rubber ball with a slightly smaller ball of pink yarn, because their overall appearances are similar, whereas older children might lump the red rubber ball with a white foam ball of exactly the same size, using the size dimension as the criterion for defining similarity. Whether they see the parts or features rather than the whole is probably greatly influenced by how complex and distinctive both levels are.

A related question is whether children are able to see both the wholes and parts. Consider the stimuli shown in Figure 6.12, a set of figures with identifiable pieces arranged to form meaningful wholes. David Elkind and his colleagues asked children from ages four to nine to describe what they saw (Elkind, Koegler, & Go, 1964). Younger children generally reported only the parts. Only eight- and nine-year-olds were likely to mention both wholes and parts, leading the researchers to conclude that younger children have difficulty perceiving both features. But more recent studies have revealed that when the parts and the wholes are relatively simple stimuli or the parts are arranged in configurations that can influence each other, children as young as three process both levels (Prather & Bacon, 1986; Stiles, Delis, & Tada, 1991).

In summary, developmental trends in childhood concerning the perception of parts and wholes must be interpreted cautiously. On simple perceptual tasks preschoolers can perform as older children do, and if older children or adults are given limited time or a difficult task, their perception is also likely to take on a less complicated quality, such as reporting only the whole (Smith & Kemler-Nelson, 1984). The findings suggest that cognitive rather than percep-

Does the environment influence perceptual development? Some have argued that a child who grows up in a culture where linear perspective is uncommon, as is the case in many parts of Africa and island regions in the Pacific Ocean, will perceive things differently than a child who grows up in a "carpentered" environment—one filled with straight lines, right angles, and many opportunities to see distances based on orderly linear cues.

tual factors may be primarily affecting performance on many perceptual tasks (Smith & Evans, 1989).

## Experience and Perceptual Development

How do experience and inborn sensory capacities interact to determine perception? Throughout the history of psychology this has been an important question, and it continues to be so as medical and technical advances provide opportunities to compensate for some kinds of sensory disabilities. For example, blind children can perceive the existence of distant objects, presumably from changes in auditory cues they receive while moving about (Ashmead, Hill, & Talor, 1989). As a consequence, blind infants are being fitted with sonic devices to help them hear echoes to signal the direction, distance, and other qualities of objects. The effects of these efforts are still to be demonstrated, but we can be sure of one thing from research on sensory deprivation: experience is extremely important for maintaining many perceptual capacities.

▶ Roles of nature and nurture

Evidence of the importance of experience in preserving perceptual capacities comes from many sources. When infant monkeys are reared with light but no contours or patterns are visible, their ability to discriminate objects is gradually and permanently lost (Riesen, 1965). The same appears true in humans as studies of infants born with cataracts have demonstrated (Walk, 1981). Research with kittens indicates the ability to perceive contours of different orientations requires exposure to a variety of horizontal, vertical, and oblique patterns of stimulation (Blakemore & Mitchell, 1973). Moreover, if a person's eyes do not function together during the first months and years of life, her binocular vision may be permanently affected (Aslin & Dumais, 1980). Thus, there are sensitive periods early in perceptual development during which visual stimulation must occur to prevent the loss of perceptual capacities.

▶ Individual differences

Experiential factors may also help to explain cross-cultural differences in perception. Environments around the world differ in their degree of "carpen-

▶ Sociocultural influence

teredness" (Segall, Campbell, & Herskovits, 1966). In most urban, technically advanced societies, houses are constructed on rectilinear principles, which involve perpendicular and right-angle dimensions. Even the layout of roads and other artifacts of the environment often follow these principles. In other environments, such as in Oceanic and many African cultures, walls and roofs may be curved and straight lines and angular intersections may be few.

In one study field workers administered several optical illusions to samples of children and adults in locations in Africa, the Philippines, and the United States (Segall, Campbell, & Herskovits, 1966). The two horizontal lines in the Müller-Lyer illusion (see Figure 6.13) are actually the same length, as are the horizontal and vertical segments of the horizontal-vertical illusion. The researchers theorized that individuals living in a carpentered environment, who often see rectangular intersecting contours, would have greater difficulty seeing the lines as equal in the Müller-Lyer illusion than people living in noncarpentered environments. They based this prediction on the fact that inward-pointing finlike perspectives often accompany edges that are seen as nearer, and outward-pointing finlike perspectives are frequently associated with edges seen as farther away. Thus, in the case of the Müller-Lyer illusion an individual perceives greater depth when the fins point outward and judges the line to be longer. They also predicted that because the vertical line in the horizontal-vertical illusion might signal depth, that is, a line receding in space, the illusion of the vertical line as longer should be greater among people living in open plains or deserts, who regularly experience such cues to distance, than among people residing in heavily wooded tropical forests. In fact, their results conformed to the predictions.

Other research has challenged the carpentered-world hypothesis. Nevertheless, children and adults in cultures with minimal formal education, little experience with pictures, or artworks that incorporate few depth cues are unlikely to perceive pictures or photos in three dimensions (Pick, 1987). Thus, the ways in which children and adults interpret their sensory environment can be greatly affected by cultural opportunities, a finding that fits well with the conclusion that perception is influenced by experience.

**FIGURE 6.13**

**Cross-Cultural Differences in Perception**

Is one of the two horizontal lines in the Müller-Lyer illusion longer than the other? What about the vertical and horizontal lines in the horizontal-vertical illusion? Children and adults who live in "carpentered" environments are more susceptible to these illusions than people who live in forested regions where cues to distance are less prevalent.

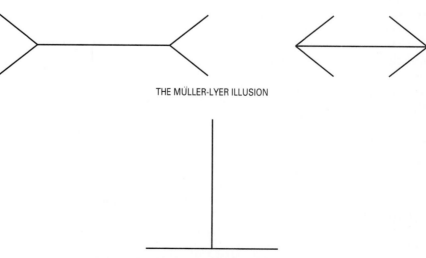

THE MÜLLER-LYER ILLUSION

THE HORIZONTAL-VERTICAL ILLUSION

## THEMES IN DEVELOPMENT

### LEARNING AND PERCEPTION

▶ **What roles do nature and nurture play in learning and perceptual development?**

When we review the enormous advances in learning and perceptual development made by infants and children, we can only be impressed by the remarkably adaptive resources immediately available to them for gaining knowledge of their environment. The basic mechanisms of learning—habituation, classical and operant conditioning, perhaps even imitation—are found ready to influence development at or shortly after birth. Although a newborn's sense organs and brain undergo many changes, they are sufficiently developed to provide rudimentary capacities to see, hear, feel, taste, and smell. Thus, babies are biologically ready to begin to perceive the world, and their behavior is readily influenced by the familiar and the novel that enter into their experience. We have also seen, however, that sensory and perceptual capacities improve substantially as a result of further maturation and experiential fine-tuning. Through such mechanisms the environment has an early and powerful role in determining which capacities are acquired and maintained.

▶ **How does the sociocultural context influence learning and perceptual development?**

Occasions provided by the culture—the behaviors that are reinforced and punished and the opportunity to observe others engaged in work, play, and social interactions—have substantial effects on what a child learns. Although formal instruction and education may be provided to assist learning in some societies, in all cultures the actions of caregivers and role models provide plentiful opportunities for children to gain knowledge of what is socially accepted and expected. Specific cultural demands, such as discriminating the printed word, and culturally related physical layouts, such as carpentered environments, may have considerable bearing on perceptual development.

▶ **How does the child play an active role in learning and perceptual development?**

While mechanisms of learning typically do not emphasize an active role for the child, what the child has learned certainly contributes to the kinds of interactions to which he will be exposed and to opportunities for further learning. In this sense the knowledge and skills that the child possesses actively contribute to further social interactions, learning, and development. With respect to perceptual development, Eleanor Gibson's theory highlights the important role that the activity of the child, including visuomotor and other sensorimotor mechanisms, plays in perception and its development. Children construct perceptions of whole multisensory arrays at an early age, and their perceptual learning increasingly reflects deliberate and organized exploration of the environment.

▶ **How prominent are individual differences in learning and perceptual development?**

All normal children are equipped with the basic capacities to learn and perceive. But those capacities in fact provide the basis for extraordinary individual differences to emerge as each child experiences various caregiving role models, educational practices, cultural conventions, and other phenomena unique to her circumstances. What is learned establishes the knowledge base upon which a rich variety of accomplishments and skills is displayed. Accompanying these may also be different ways of using the senses and perceiving the environment so that people's views of the world are different as well.

▶ **How do learning and perceptual development interact with development in other domains?**

Learning plays a substantial role in almost every aspect of development. The child learns social skills, acceptable ways to express thoughts and feelings, techniques for academic and occupational success, and numerous other behaviors. The child who learns about the alphabet, about having to sit quietly in the classroom, about when and when not to speak to an elder, or about behaviors effective in hunting, shepherding, domestic, or other activities can be expected, depending on his culture, to achieve social status, prestige, and other resources that will benefit his development in many other domains. Furthermore, gains in perception are substantially influenced by physiological and neural advances. Rapidly improving intellectual and motor skills introduce demands for making new perceptual discriminations such as reading, that, once mastered, lead to further cognitive, social, and other progress.

## *Summary*

**Learning in Infancy and Childhood**    Learning includes mechanisms that permit adaptation to the environment. Infants are capable of *classical* and *operant conditioning, habituation* and *recovery from habituation*, and possibly *imitation* as well. Thus, babies are equipped to adapt to their environment and to learn from it. Observational learning plays a major role in socialization as well as in acquisition of knowledge. Caregivers and tutors often provide a *scaffold* to assist learning, permitting children to make progress in the acquisition of a wide range of skills in a social context. For Vygotsky, social interactions taking place in the *zone of proximal development* provide maximum opportunities for children to acquire the knowledge and skills important to society.

**Sensory and Perceptual Capacities**    Although it was once assumed that newborns' sensory receptors did not yet function, today we know that every sense is operative at birth and in some cases even before birth. The conclusion has emerged from studies revealing preferential behaviors for certain kinds of stimuli, habituation to familiar stimuli and recovery to new ones, and learning to discriminate among various objects and events.

Newborns both look for and see visual events. Within a few months of birth the lens of the baby's eye readily accommodates to the varying distances of objects to permit seeing them in focus. Newborns also display *saccadic* eye movements, which in a matter of weeks become more rapid and accurate in the exploration and search for stimuli in the visual field. Ability to perform *smooth visual pursuit* is limited but improves during the first eight months as well. *Vergence*, the capacity to focus both eyes on an object, reaches a mature level even sooner.

*Visual acuity* is limited, but newborns can detect contour, and their ability to see edges and transitions in surfaces under varying intensities of light is nearly adultlike by six months of age. Color vision and *stereopsis* emerge within the first few months of life and in fact may be present even earlier. Other cues to depth, such as *kinetic cues* based on self-induced movement or movement in the environment, are available to young infants. Sensitivity to many two-dimensional cues in pictures begins to be evident at about five to seven months of age, at least among children in the United States.

Newborns do not examine patterns of stimuli systematically and are often attracted to larger external features showing high contrast or movement. By two to three months of age infants perceive more detailed patterns and begin to prefer looking at such things as the human face, although they may display a bias to attend to the human face even earlier. Kinetic cues are important for the detection of the unity and coherence of objects and signal movement arising from another person.

Ability to detect sounds and their location appears at birth, although the ability undergoes substantial improvement during the first few months. In fact, auditory sensitivities continue to improve throughout childhood. Auditory pattern perception is present by about three months of age, and infants prefer patterns that conform to acceptable phrasing in musical passages. Moreover, infants are able to discriminate most, if not all, sounds used in different languages, a capacity that becomes limited by the end of the first year as a result of exposure to only a subset of sounds in the language(s) the baby hears. The phenomenon, along with *categorical perception* of speech sounds, has given rise to theoretical debates about whether speech perception is performed by special acoustic mechanisms or by more general auditory capacities.

Newborns can discriminate basic tastes and pleasant and unpleasant smells. They agree with adults' judgments of the pleasantness of odors and quickly recognize the smell of their caregiver. Babies also respond to tactile stimuli and demonstrate intermodal perception. The latter capacity has raised numerous questions about whether the senses are differentiated at birth and how knowledge of the multiple sensory cues of objects is acquired through experience.

**Perception in Childhood**     Investigations of perceptual development in children have been infrequent. Research based on Eleanor Gibson's theory of perceptual learning has revealed that perception becomes more focused, organized, and confined to the meaningful and important features of the environment. Perception becomes increasingly efficient as children have opportunities to learn about the constant and critical features of their sensory environment. Children perceive both the parts and wholes of stimuli. Opportunity early in development to observe patterns, depth, and sounds important in language helps to maintain perceptual abilities. Perceptual learning may contribute to differences among children from various cultures in their perception of their environment.

# 7

# Language

## Key Themes in This Chapter

▶ **What roles do nature and nurture play in language development?**

▶ **How does the sociocultural context influence language development?**

▶ **How does the child play an active role in the process of language development?**

▶ **Is language development continuous or discontinuous?**

▶ **How prominent are individual differences in language development?**

▶ **How does language development interact with development in other domains?**

*It is hard to believe just how quickly and easily infants and children master the range of complex verbal and nonverbal skills that make up human communication. Consider the sophisticated efforts of an infant named Carlotta, after less than a year of life, to gain an adult's attention:*

> *At [10 months, 18 days], we observed the first instance in which Carlotta extends her arm forward to show an object to the adult. She is playing with a toy already in her hand; suddenly, she looks toward the observer and extends her arm forward holding the toy. In the next 2–3 weeks, this behavior increases and stabilizes until we observe Carlotta looking around for objects not already in her grasp, and immediately presenting them while awaiting adult response. (Bates, Camaioni, & Volterra, 1975, p. 216)*

*Carlotta's gesture, as documented by the researchers, seems to be sending the nonverbal message, "Here, look at this!"*

*A few months later, as Carlotta sits outside the kitchen, she looks at her mother, says, "Ha," and looks toward the kitchen. After her mother carries her in, Carlotta points to the sink. Her mother gives her a drink of water. On two separate occasions this infant has been able to make her communications perfectly clear to observers.*

Now consider a statement made by a five-year-old boy: "Daddy, look how your pants are sulking!" (Chukovsky, 1963). By age five, most children have moved from Carlotta's effective but rudimentary mix of verbal and nonverbal messages to the complex achievements reflected in this sentence. They have mastered the bewildering variety of sounds in their native language to produce recognizable words, and they understand the meanings of words reasonably well. Although this boy may not yet possess the vocabulary to describe falling pants accurately, he can still state the words in correct order so that his meaning is clear. And if he spares his father embarrassment by whispering his message so that other people cannot hear, the child has shown himself to be aware of the interactive and sociocultural rules of communication.

By the age of five, in fact, most children have become highly proficient listeners and speakers, a marvel indeed given the plethora of sounds, vocabulary words, grammatical rules, and social conventions that go into producing mature adult-sounding speech. You are not likely to have a vivid memory of the way in which you learned to speak—most of us have little specific recall of this extremely complex yet somehow entirely natural process—but if you have ever tried to learn a foreign language, you probably have some sense of how remarkable children's mastery of communication is. How do infants and children manage such a seemingly overwhelming task?

In this chapter we will first examine the major milestones in the acquisition of communication and language skills from infancy through childhood: what is the sequence of events as the child comes to comprehend and produce language? Next, we will look at the most important theories of language development. What factors account for the observable commonalities in how children acquire language? Of all the themes of development, none has been more central to theories of language development than the nature-versus-nurture debate—the extent to which either biological predispositions or environmental influences dictate the child's developing linguistic competence. Finally, we will briefly examine the functions of language, particularly as they interact with children's growing cognitive skills and ability to regulate their own behavior.

## *The Course of Language Acquisition*

A baby's contact with language is—initially, at least—noticeably one sided. Although she may gurgle or coo, most of her experience is as a listener. Among her first tasks is to learn to identify the myriad sounds that make up her native language. That is, she must distinguish specific sounds in the stream of spoken language, note the regularities in how they are combined, recognize which combinations constitute words, and eventually—when she makes the transition from listener to speaker—form the consonant-vowel combinations that are the building blocks of words and sentences. The fundamental sound units and the rules for combining them in a given language make up that language's **phonology**. If you have studied a foreign language, you will recognize that some sounds appear only in certain languages, such as the prolonged nasal *n* sound in Spanish or the French vowel that is spoken as if *e* and *u* are combined. Furthermore, each language has its own rules for combining sounds. In English, for example, the *sr* combination does not occur, whereas *sl* and *st* appear frequently. Even at this basic level of phonology, the child has to absorb an enormous amount of information about those sounds and combinations of sounds that are acceptable in her native language.

Another basic language skill the child must master is linking the combinations of sounds he hears to the objects, people, events, or relationships they label. **Semantics** is the meaning of words or combinations of words. *Cookie* is an arbitrary grouping of sounds, but it is used by speakers of English to refer to a specific class of objects. The child thus attaches words to conceptual groups, learning when it is appropriate to use them and when it is not (for example, *cookie* does not refer to all objects or edible goods found in the bakery). The child also learns that some words describe actions *(eat)*, whereas others describe relationships (*under* or *over*) or modify objects (*chocolate* cookie). Mapping combinations of sounds to their referents (that is, the things to which words refer) is a major task in the acquisition of language.

As the child begins to combine words, she learns the principles of **syntax**, or the grammatical rules that dictate how words can be combined. The order in which words are spoken conveys meaning—"Eat kitty" and "Kitty eat" do not mean the same thing, even in the simplified language of the young child. A

**phonology**  Fundamental sound units and combinations of units in a given language.

**semantics**  Meanings of words or combinations of words.

**syntax**  Grammatical rules that dictate how words can be combined.

word's position in a sentence can signify whether it is an agent or the object of an action, for example. The rules of syntax vary widely from one language to another, but within a given language they operate with consistency and regularity. One of the most remarkable features of language acquisition is the child's ability to detect the regularity of syntax and use it to create meaningful utterances of his own without much direct instruction.

The process of acquiring language also includes learning **pragmatics**, the rules for using language effectively and appropriately according to social conventions. The effective use of language includes a host of nonverbal behaviors, rules of etiquette, and even changing the content of speech according to the identity of the listener and the context of the communication. How do you ask someone for a favor? Not, the child soon learns, by saying, "Hey, you—get me that ball!" If someone does not hear what she said, the child also learns that adding a gesture can sometimes complete the communication. And the way to speak to an adult who has some authority will probably include more polite forms and fewer terms of familiarity than when speaking to a peer. As they are acquiring language, then, children are also absorbing the equally important sociocultural dimension of pragmatics.

Clearly, language is a multifaceted skill with many overlapping dimensions, from understanding and uttering sounds to appreciating the sometimes subtle rules of social communication. Despite the complexities, by the time they are four or five years old most children speak much as adults do. Their progress in mastering vocabulary, syntax, and pragmatics continues during the school years and thereafter, but the essential elements of the language system are acquired in an impressively brief period.

## From Sound to Meaning: Phonological and Other Prelinguistic Skills

What does it take to learn a language? The infant's first step consists both of attending to the sounds of speech as a special type of auditory stimulation and also of deciphering phonology, the units of sound that occur in a given language. Thus, during much of the infant's first year the emphasis is on phonological development, both in receiving messages from others and in being able to produce them on his own.

**Early Responses to Human Speech** Right from birth the human infant has a special sensitivity to the sounds made by other human beings. Newborns show a distinct preference for human voices to other sounds and like to hear their own mother's voice more than a stranger's (DeCasper & Fifer, 1980; Gibson & Spelke, 1983). Of most significance, however, is that infants respond in specific ways to small acoustic variations in human speech that distinguish one word or part of a word from another.

As Chapter 6 explained, the basic building blocks of spoken language are called *phonemes*—the smallest units of sound that change the meanings of words. In the words *pat* and *bat*, for example, the phonemes */p/* and */b/* make a big difference in the meaning of the word. Recall from Chapter 6 that infants as young as one month can discriminate different phonemes and that they do so categorically, ignoring small acoustic variations in a sound unless the sound pattern crosses a phonemic boundary (Aslin, Pisoni, & Jusczyk, 1983; Kuhl, 1987). At two months of age, infants add to their repertoire the ability to discriminate vowels (Marean, Werner, & Kuhl, 1992). As Chapter 6 also pointed

**pragmatics** Rules for using language effectively within a social context.

out, younger infants are actually more sensitive than older infants to differences in phonemes that occur across languages.

Infants are also able to detect broader differences in speech sounds, such as a foreign language being spoken. For example, researchers reported that four-day-old French infants could distinguish their native language from Russian. After they displayed habituation of their sucking response in the presence of one language, the infants showed dishabituation in the presence of the new language. They also preferred their native language. These infants, however, could not detect the difference between two unfamiliar languages (Mehler et al., 1988).

Later in the first year, at nine months of age, infants are especially attentive to familiar patterns of sounds that occur in their native language. Peter Jusczyk and his colleagues found that Dutch and American infants preferred listening to unfamiliar words in their own respective languages to listening to words in an unfamiliar language (Jusczyk et al., 1993). It seems, then, that as infants approach the end of their first year, they zero in on the distinctive features and patterns of speech that appear in the language they hear most often.

Spoken language also varies in its **prosody**—the patterns of intonation, stress, and rhythm that communicate meaning. One example of a prosodic feature is the pattern of intonation that distinguishes questions from declarative statements. When you raise your voice at the end of a question, you are signaling a different communicative intent than when you let your voice fall at the end of a declarative sentence. Researchers have found that infants prefer the prosodic features associated with the high-pitched, exaggerated, musical speech, often called "baby talk," that mothers typically speak to their young children. Figure 7.1 illustrates some of the acoustical properties of mothers' speech to infants. In one study, Anne Fernald (1985) trained four-month-olds to turn their heads to activate a loudspeaker positioned on either side of them. Infants were more likely to make this response if their "reward" was a female stranger's voice speaking as she would to a baby than if she used normal adult speech. In a subsequent study, researchers found that it was the high pitch of the "baby talk" that infants preferred, not the loudness or rhythm of that speech (Fernald & Kuhl, 1987). In light of these preferences, it seems fitting that mothers from cultures as diverse as France, Italy, Germany, Britain, Japan, China, and the Xhosa tribe of southern Africa have been found to raise their pitch when they speak to their young infants (Fernald, 1991; Papousek, 1992).

In summary, infants show an amazing ability to respond to some important elements of human speech, abilities that prepare them for the even more sophisticated language achievements to come. Because these competencies appear so early in life, they suggest that human language has biological underpinnings. At the same time, the role of the environment in language acquisition is clear. The baby's ability to distinguish his native language from others, his preference for that language, and his increasing difficulty in making phoneme discriminations in nonnative languages demonstrate that the specific language the child hears exerts a steady influence on his linguistic skills, even in the first year of life.

▶ Roles of nature and nurture

**Cooing and Babbling: Prelinguistic Speech**   Well before the child utters her first word, she produces sounds that increasingly resemble the language spoken in her environment. At birth, the infant's vocal capabilities are limited to crying and a few other brief sounds such as grunts, sighs, or clicks.

**prosody**   Patterns of intonation, stress, and rhythm that communicate meaning in speech.

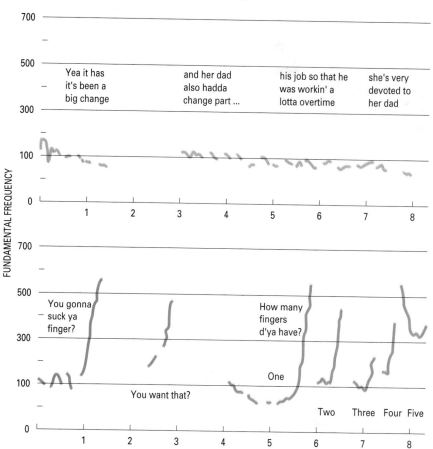

**FIGURE 7.1**

**The Acoustical Properties of Maternal Speech to Infants**

These two samples of maternal speech show the special acoustical qualities that make speech to infants (bottom) distinct from speech to adults (top). The Y-axis represents fundamental frequency, a measure of auditory pitch. Note the frequent use of modulation of pitch and the predominant presence of high pitch in maternal speech to infants. Babies seem to be especially responsive to the qualities of this type of speech.

Source: Adapted from Fernald, 1985.

Between six and eight weeks a new type of vocalization—**cooing**—emerges. These brief vowel-like utterances are sometimes accompanied by consonants, usually those produced in the back of the mouth, such as /g/ or /k/. Infants coo when they are in a comfortable state or when a parent has made some attempt to communicate, either with speech or coos of his own. In the weeks that follow, the infant's vocalizations become longer and begin to include consonants formed at the front of the mouth, as in /m/ or /b/.

The next significant accomplishment is the emergence of **babbling**, the production of consonant-vowel combinations such as *da* or *ba*. Most children begin to babble at about three to six months and refine their skills in the succeeding months. To many listeners, the infant's babbling sounds like active experimentation with the production of different sounds. In the succeeding weeks, the infant will repeat syllables, such as *bababa* or *dadada*. The repetition of the same consonant-vowel pair is called **reduplicated babbling**. At nine or ten months the child's babbling includes more numerous and complex consonant-vowel combinations, as well as variations in intonation. In fact, a

**cooing** Vowel-like utterances that characterize the infant's first attempts to vocalize.

**babbling** Consonant-vowel utterances that characterize the infant's first attempts to vocalize.

**reduplicated babbling** Repetition of simple consonant-vowel combinations in the early stages of language development.

casual listener might think that the child is actually speaking, although he is not yet producing real words.

The changes in children's productive capabilities are linked to physiological changes in their vocal apparatus and central nervous system that occur during the first year. In the months after birth, the infant's larynx descends farther into the neck, the oral cavity grows, and she can place her tongue in different positions in her mouth (not just forward and back as at birth). At the same time, the cortex of the brain replaces the brainstem in controlling many of the child's behaviors. In general, early reflexlike vocalizations, such as cries, fade as more controlled voluntary utterances, such as coos and babbles, enter the child's repertoire (Stark, 1986).

Are these early prelinguistic utterances influenced by the language infants hear around them? Some language researchers believe that babbling is predominantly under the control of biological maturation and is little influenced by the native language (Lenneberg, 1967). According to this view, infants from different cultures should evidence the same patterns and sounds of babbling, with only random variations among individuals. Other researchers believe that the language the infant hears influences the nature of his vocalizations, even those that precede intelligible words. Recent studies have shown distinct differences in babbling among infants from varying cultures. One group of researchers conducted a *spectral analysis* of the vowel sounds made by ten-month-olds in Paris, London, Algiers, and Hong Kong. The procedure involved translating the acoustic properties of speech into a visual representation of the intensity, onset, and pattern of vocalization. Infants from different countries varied in the average frequencies of the sounds they produced; the differences paralleled those of adult speakers from the same country (Boysson-Bardies et al., 1989). Thus, the child's linguistic environment has a distinct effect on his own speech before he can speak true words.

Another way to assess the role of experience in the development of babbling is to compare the preverbal utterances and other language-related behaviors of deaf children with those of hearing children. If exposure to spoken language is a critical element in the development of babbling, deaf children should show patterns of linguistic production different than those of hearing children. For many years psychologists thought that there were strong resemblances between the vocal babbling of deaf and hearing infants (Appleton, Clifton, & Goldberg, 1975; Fry, 1966). Moreover, a recent study of two deaf infants exposed to sign language showed that they made repetitive, rhythmic hand gestures akin to babbling at ten months of age (Petitto & Marentette, 1991). Such findings support a maturational explanation of babbling. However, another study of nine deaf infants showed that none of the children had uttered reduplicated babbling by ten months of age, whereas all twenty-one of the hearing subjects produced well-formed syllables by that age (Oller & Eilers, 1988). Evidently, exposure to spoken language plays a significant role, at least in the production of speech sounds.

That most infants, regardless of their culture, begin to coo and babble at similar ages suggests that biological factors direct the onset of these behaviors. Nature thus plays a distinct role in the emergence of the child's utterances. But even at this early stage of language development, the form of the child's vocalizations is influenced by the language spoken around her. And, as the case of spoken speech among deaf infants suggests, the biological blueprint of language emergence can be altered when children are not able to process spoken language.

**Gesture as a Communication Tool**    Late in the first year, before or as they speak their first words, many children begin to use such gestures as pointing, showing, or giving as a means of communicating with other people (Bates, Camaioni, & Volterra, 1975). As we saw at the beginning of the chapter, Carlotta, the infant Elizabeth Bates and her colleagues observed, was able to display several kinds of nonverbal communication. When Carlotta held up her toy, she was using a **protodeclarative communication** that, much like a declarative sentence, called the adult's attention to the object. When she pointed to the kitchen sink, Carlotta used a **protoimperative communication** intended to get the adult to do something (Bates, 1979). Often (as when Carlotta wanted her drink of water), children's gestures are accompanied by direct eye contact with the communication's recipient. They may also repeat their communications if the message is not understood. This constellation of behaviors and the context in which they occur suggest that children use gestures as a purposeful means to an end (Scoville, 1983).

Similarly, Linda Acredolo and Susan Goodwyn (1988) found that when a child is between eleven and twenty-four months of age, he uses gestures not just to show or request but also to symbolize objects or events. The child may signify a flower, for example, by making a sniffing gesture or the desire to go outside with a knob-turning motion. A significant number of children's gestures recreate the function of objects, rather than their form or shape. For example, subjects in their study would put their fist to one ear to signify a telephone or wave their hands to signify a butterfly.

Acredolo and Goodwyn believe there is a strong relationship between the development of gestures and verbal abilities because both appear at approximately the same time in development, with gestures usually preceding words by a few weeks (Acredolo & Goodwyn, 1988; Goodwin & Acredolo, 1993). Recognizing that one thing can symbolize another represents a major cognitive advance, one that is essential for the use of both gestures and spoken language. Gestures drop out of the child's repertoire by the middle of the second year, however, because they are less useful when the "listener" is out of view and they are usually correctly understood by a limited number of adults. Parents also probably tend to encourage the child's verbalizations more than they do the use of gestures (Acredolo & Goodwyn, 1990a).

## Content: The Acquisition of Semantics

Few moments in life rival the excitement parents feel when they hear their children say their first words, typically at about one year of age. "Cookie," "Mama," and "Dada" are joyfully entered into the baby book alongside other momentous events, such as the infant's first steps. Certainly, the uttering of first words is a major accomplishment, marking the visible entry of the child into the world of spoken shared communication. The child's comprehension and production of words also signal a new focus in the mastery of language—semantic development. Although he continues to refine his understanding of phonology, the major task confronting him now is unraveling the meanings of words.

**The One-Word Stage**    From about twelve to twenty months of age, most children speak only one word at a time. Children's first words are most frequently **nominals**, labels for objects, people, or events, although action words (*give*), modifiers (*dirty*), and personal-social words (*please*) also occur (Nelson,

**protodeclarative communication**    Use of a gesture to call attention to an object or event.

**protoimperative communication**    Use of a gesture to issue a command or request.

**nominals**    Words that label objects, people, or events; the first type of words most children produce.

Beginning about one year of age, many young children begin to use gestures to cummunicate, a sign that they are putting into practice the various facets of language.

1973). Children's early words usually refer to people or objects important in their lives, such as parents and other relatives, pets, or familiar objects. Children are also more likely to acquire labels for dynamic objects (*clock, car, ball*) or those they can use (*cup, cookie*) than for items that are stationary (*wall, window*). Figure 7.2 shows how the proportion of word types changes in the vocabularies of children in the one-word stage.

Children acquire their first ten words slowly; the typical child adds about one to three words to her repertoire each month (Barrett, 1989). From about age eighteen months onward, however, many children show a virtual explosion in the acquisition of new words. This remarkable period in language development is called the **vocabulary spurt** (Barrett, 1985; Bloom, 1973). In one recent longitudinal study of vocabulary growth in one- to two-year-olds, some learned to say as many as twenty new words, mostly nouns, in every week of the vocabulary spurt (Goldfield & Reznick, 1990). Figure 7.3 shows the rapid rate of vocabulary growth for three children in the middle of their spurt. Within the same two-month period children also typically show a spurt in the number of words they understand (Reznick & Goldfield, 1992). In addition to learning new labels for objects and actions, children begin to use words to express internal states (*yay!*) and to direct the actions of others (*go*) (Nelson, 1973).

Many of the child's first words are bound to a specific context: that is, the child uses the word to label objects in limited situations. Lois Bloom (1973) observed that one nine-month-old used the word *car* only when she was looking out the living room window at cars moving on the street. She did not say "car" to parked cars, pictures of cars, or cars she was sitting in. This type of error, when the child applies a label to a narrower class of objects than the term signifies, is called an **underextension**. Over time, the child begins to use single words more flexibly in a wider variety of contexts (Barrett, 1986).

Another type of error, called **overextension**, occurs when children apply a label to a broader category than the term signifies. For example, a toddler may

**vocabulary spurt**  Period of rapid word acquisition that typically occurs early in language development.

**underextension**  Application of a label to a narrower class of objects than the term signifies.

**overextension**  Tendency to apply a label to a broader category than the term actually signifies.

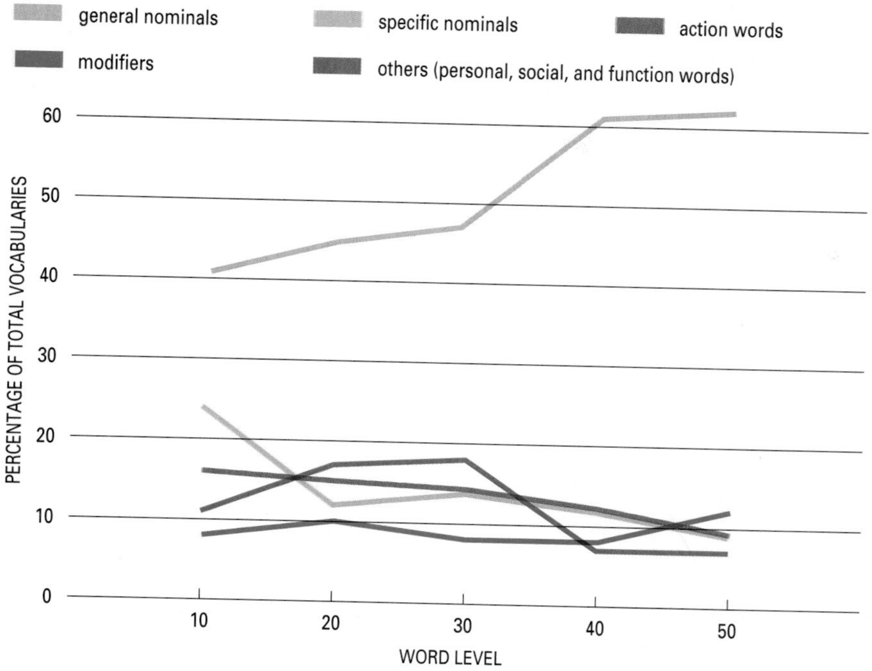

general nominals    specific nominals    action words
modifiers    others (personal, social, and function words)

Source: Adapted from Nelson, 1973.

**FIGURE 7.2**

**Changes in the Proportion of Word Types in Children's Vocabularies**

As children's vocabularies grow from only a few words to fifty words (the horizontal axis on this graph), the proportion of general nominals (*cat, dog*) increases dramatically. The proportion of other types of words children learn—such as specific nominals (*Mommy*), action words (*go*), modifiers (*pretty*), and personal-social words (*please*)—remains fairly stable or even declines slightly as their vocabulary increases.

call a horse or cow "doggie." The child often applies the same word to objects that look alike perceptually (Clark, 1973). At other times, the child may misuse a word when objects share functions, such as calling a rolling quarter a "ball" (Bowerman, 1978). As with underextensions, the child's use of overextensions declines after the second year.

**Comprehension Versus Production**    If you have ever tried to learn a new language, you undoubtedly found that it was easier to understand what another speaker was saying than to produce a sentence in the new language yourself. An important point to remember about children's early language is that the child's **receptive language**, what he comprehends, far exceeds his **productive language**, his ability to say and use the words. In one study, for example, parents reported an average of 5.7 words produced by their ten-month-olds but a comprehension average about three times greater, 17.9 words (Bates, Bretherton, & Snyder, 1988).

That young children understand so much of what is said to them means they have acquired some important information about language before they actually speak. They know that people, objects, and events have names. They know that specific patterns of sounds represent objects and events in their environment. Most important, they begin to appreciate the usefulness of language as a means of expressing ideas, needs, and feelings.

**Individual Differences in Language Development**    Although children show many common trends in the way they acquire language, they also show significant individual differences in rates and types of language production. You may have heard a family member or friend report that her child said

**receptive language**  Ability to comprehend spoken speech.

**productive language**  Meaningful language spoken or otherwise produced by the individual.

## FIGURE 7.3

### The Vocabulary Spurt in Three Young Children

Many children show a vocabulary spurt, a sharp rise in the number of new words they learn, as they approach two years of age. However, children may begin their spurts at different ages, as the graph clearly shows. Child A showed an early spurt, beginning at fifteen months. Child B's spurt began at the more typical age of eighteen months. Child C showed a late spurt at twenty-one months.

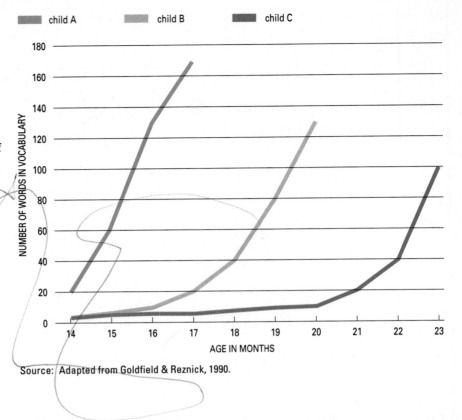

Source: Adapted from Goldfield & Reznick, 1990.

▶ Individual differences

virtually nothing for two or three years and then began speaking in complete sentences. Although such dramatic variations in language milestones are not frequent, children sometimes show unique patterns in their linguistic accomplishments, patterns that still lead to the attainment of normal language by later childhood.

One example of wide individual variation is the age at which children say their first word. Some children produce their first distinguishable word as early as nine months, whereas others may not do so until sixteen months (Barrett, 1989). Similarly, some children show good pronunciation, whereas others have difficulty making certain sounds, consistently substituting *t* for *k*, or *b* for *v*, for example (Smith, 1988). In addition, not all children display the vocabulary spurt (Acredolo & Goodwyn, 1990b), or they may start their spurts at different ages, as indicated in Figure 7.3.

Children may also differ in the content of their one-word speech. Most one-year-olds tend to use nominals predominantly, displaying what Katherine Nelson (1973) termed a **referential style**. Other children show a different pattern. Rather than naming objects, these children frequently use words that have social functions, such as *hello* or *please*, thus displaying an **expressive style**. Expressive children use words to direct the behavior of other people or to comment on them. Referential children tend to have larger vocabularies and show more rapid advances in language development, at least in the early stages (Bates, Bretherton, & Snyder, 1988; Nelson, 1973).

How do we explain these individual differences in the rates and styles with which children acquire language? There are several hypotheses. Perhaps individual differences result from differences in the neurological structures that control language or from inborn differences in temperament. For example, ex-

**referential style** Type of early language production in which the child uses mostly nominals.

**expressive style** Type of early language production in which children use many social words.

pressive children may be more sociable by nature. Another possibility is that parents influence the rate and form of children's vocabulary development. Some parents, for example, may spend a great deal of time encouraging their infants to speak, and they may focus especially on labeling objects. Others may be more relaxed about letting the infant proceed at his own pace. Researchers have confirmed that the overall amount of speech parents produce when their infants are sixteen months is related to the acceleration of vocabulary growth in infants (Huttenlocher et al., 1991). In another study, the amount of time parents spent reading stories to their twenty-four-month-olds predicted the child's language ability up to two years later (Crain-Thoreson & Dale, 1992).

▶ Roles of nature and nurture

**Deriving the Meanings of Words** The number of new words the child learns grows rapidly from the age of eighteen months through the preschool years. According to one estimate, children learn more than fourteen thousand new words by the time they enter school (Carey, 1978). There are several hypotheses about how children learn the meanings of words.

One suggestion is that certain elements in early parent-child interactions provide children with clues to the meanings of words. For example, parents of infants tend to label many objects, often in the context of joint book reading or the child's manifest interest in a particular object or person in her surroundings (Ninio & Bruner, 1978). A typical scenario goes like this: The infant turns his head, points, and maybe even coos as the family dog enters the room. The mother also turns and looks, saying, "Doggie." Such interactions, in which the parent follows the child's attention and labels the target of his interest, are common between nine and eighteen months of age. Researchers have noted that these are precisely the conditions under which infants seem to remember the words that name objects. For example, one researcher found that children's vocabulary development is strongly related to the tendency of parents to label objects at which the child points (Masur, 1982). In other studies researchers report that when an adult supplies a label *after* rather than *before* the child has looked at an object, the child comprehends the label better (Dunham, Dunham, & Curwin, 1993; Tomasello, 1988, 1992). Thus, children seem to learn words best when they already have the object in mind.

▶ The child's active role

As the child begins to speak, parents continue to supply her with information about word meaning, often in the form of corrections when she makes a mistake. "That's not a glass; that's a cup," or "Your soup is not hot; it's cool" are examples of parental verbalizations that not only point out the child's error but provide the correct words. Children profit from these forms of *linguistic contrast* to learn new terms and labels (Au & Laframboise, 1990).

Some researchers also believe that the child acquires word meanings by a process called **fast-mapping**, in which the context in which the child hears words spoken provides the key to their meaning. Often the child's initial comprehension of a word is an incomplete guess, but a fuller understanding of its meaning follows from successive encounters with it in other contexts (Carey, 1978). Suppose the child hears his mother say, "This room looks *messy*!" in the midst of the youngster's toy-strewn bedroom. He might surmise that the word *messy* refers to some characteristic of the room that has to do with the toys being out of the toybox. Another time, he might hear his father say, "You look *messy*," as the child climbs out of the sandbox. Noticing his dirty T-shirt and sneakers and drawing on his previous interpretation of the word, he concludes that *messy* refers to a state of disarray. Children are often able to derive the meanings of words quickly, even when the exposure is brief, if the context in which new words are heard is meaningful (Rice & Woodsmall, 1988).

**fast-mapping** Deriving meanings of words from the context in which they are spoken.

▶ Roles of nature and nurture

Still other researchers believe that young children have certain biases in word learning. Consider the child who hears a new word such as *eggbeater*. What does that word mean? Logically, it could refer to a host of objects or perhaps an action instead of an object. Testing the numerous hypotheses could take an inordinate amount of time. Several researchers argue that children are biased to form more restricted hypotheses about the meanings of words; if they were not, children would not learn language so rapidly and with so few errors. *Constraints* on word learning, presumed by many theorists to be innate, give young children an edge in figuring out the meanings of words from the vast array of possibilities.

One hypothesized bias in word learning is called the *principle of contrast*. According to Eve Clark (1987, 1988, 1992), children assume that two different words will have two different meanings. For example, suppose a child already knows the word *dog* and hears a new word, *horse*. She will assume the new word has a contrasting meaning and search for features in the newly labeled four-legged creature that distinguish it from a dog. A related idea, called the **mutual exclusivity bias**, is that young children tend to assume that new words label unfamiliar objects (Markman, 1987, 1990). Researchers have been able to demonstrate experimentally that children tend to treat new words as labels for new objects rather than as synonyms for words they already know. For example, Ellen Markman and Gwyn Wachtel (1988) showed three-year-olds pairs of objects; in each set one object was familiar and the other was not (for example, a banana and a pair of tongs). When children were told, "Show me the *x*" where *x* was a nonsense syllable, they tended to select the unfamiliar objects. The mutual exclusivity bias emerges at about age three and continues to play a role in the way in which older children and adults attach meaning to new words (Merriman & Bowman, 1989).

Other biases in word learning include the child's assumption that a new word labels an entire object, rather than a part or feature of the object, and that the same new word can be extended to include other objects that are taxonomically similar. Consider a study conducted by Ellen Markman and Jean Hutchinson (1984). Four- and five-year-olds looked at a picture as the experimenter labeled it with a nonsense syllable. For example, a cow was called a *dax*. Then two other pictures were presented, in this case a pig and milk. When asked, "Can you find another dax?," most children pointed to the pig, not the milk. In contrast, when children heard no label for the cow and were simply instructed to "find another one," they tended to associate the cow with milk.

Not all researchers agree that constraints on word learning are critical in the earliest stages of language acquisition. For example, Katherine Nelson (1988, 1991) has pointed out that most studies like those described previously have involved preschoolers who already have a good deal of experience with language. Thus, it is difficult to argue for innately given constraints on word learning; perhaps word learning biases arise from experiences with language. Moreover, she suggests, early word learning is better understood in the context of the child's growing representations of events that are important in his life and the social interactions he experiences. Nonetheless, the idea that children are predisposed to learn certain aspects of language continues to be popular, not only in explaining semantic development but the emergence of syntax as well.

## Form: The Acquisition of Syntax

At about the time of the child's second birthday, another significant achievement in language production appears—the child becomes able to produce

**mutual exclusivity bias** Tendency for children to assume that unfamiliar words label new objects.

There may be constraints on how children learn new words. Children will assume, for example, that a new word such as "eggbeater" labels an unfamiliar object.

more than one word at a time to express ideas, needs, and desires. At first, two-word utterances, such as "Doggie go" and "More juice," prevail, but the child soon combines greater numbers of words in forms that loosely resemble the grammatical structure of her native language. In combining words, the child is displaying an awareness of the different syntactic categories into which words fall. "Doggie go" illustrates the child's understanding of nouns and verbs as distinct classes of words. Moreover, when children combine words, they are stating more than just labels for familiar items; they are expressing relationships among objects and events in the world. All this represents no small feat for a two-year-old.

### Early Grammars: The Two-Word Stage

At first, children's two-word utterances consist of combinations of nouns, verbs, and adjectives, without the conjunctions, prepositions, and other modifiers that give speech its familiar flow. Because speech at this stage usually contains only the elements essential to getting the message across, it is often described as **telegraphic speech**.

In his systematic observations of the language of three children, Martin Braine (1976) noted that speech at this stage contained a unique syntactic structure, which he dubbed **pivot grammar**. The speech of the children he observed contained noticeable regularities: one word often functioned in a fixed position while other words filled in the empty slot. For example, one child in this study said, "More car, more cookie, more juice, more read." In this string of utterances *more* functions as a *pivot word*, an anchor for a variety of *open words*. The child's grammar could consist of [pivot word + open word] as in the example, or [open word + pivot word], as in "Boots off, pants off, water off." Table 7.1 contains several other examples of a two-year-old's early word combinations.

Other linguists have described other regularities in children's grammars that reflect the incorporation of semantic knowledge with the use of syntax. For example, Table 7.2 summarizes the regularities of child speech in the

**telegraphic speech** Early two-word speech that contains few modifiers, prepositions, or other connective words.

**pivot grammar** Early two-word grammar in which one word is repeated and a series of other words fills the second slot.

**TABLE 7.1**

**One Child's Pivot Grammar**

This table shows several examples of one two-year-old's two-word speech. Frequently, one word—the pivot word—is repeated while several other words—open words—fill the other slot. The pivot word can occupy either the first or second position in the child's utterances.

| | | | |
|---|---|---|---|
| no bed | boot off | more car | airplane all gone |
| no down | light off | more cereal | Calico all gone |
| no fix | pants off | more cookie | Calico all done |
| no home | shirt off | more fish | all done milk |
| no mama | shoe off | more high | all done now |
| no more | water off | more hot | all gone juice |
| no pee | off bib | more juice | all gone outside |
| no plug | | more read | all gone pacifier |
| no water | | more sing | salt all shut |
| no wet | | more toast | |
| | | more walk | |
| | | outside more | |

Source: Adapted from Braine, 1976.

two-word stage that one researcher found in ten different cultures (Brown, 1973). In children's verbalizations, agents consistently precede actions, as in "Mommy come" or "Daddy sit." At the same time, inanimate objects are usually not named as agents. The child rarely says, "Wall go." To avoid making this utterance she must know the meaning of *wall* and that walls do not move. The child's semantic knowledge is thus related to the production of highly ordered two-word utterances.

Many experts currently believe that no one syntactic system defines the structure of early language for all children (Maratsos, 1983; Tager-Flusberg, 1985). Some children may speak with nouns, verbs, adjectives, and sometimes adverbs in the pivot grammar described by Braine, whereas others pepper their speech with pronouns and other words such as *I, it,* and *here* (Bloom, Lightbown, & Hood, 1975). Most researchers agree, however, that individual children frequently use consistent word orders and that their understanding of at least a small set of semantic relationships is related to that word order. Moreover, numerous detailed observations of children's language indicate that they never construct "wild grammars"; some utterances, such as "Big he" or "Hot it," are simply never heard (Bloom, 1990). Such observations have distinct implications for explanations of syntactic development.

▶ Individual differences

**Later Syntactic Development**   At age two and a half, children's speech often exceeds two words in length and includes many more of the modifiers and connective words that enrich the quality of speech. Adjectives, pronouns, and prepositions are added to the child's repertoire (Valian, 1986). Between the ages of two and five, the child's speech also includes increasingly sophisticated grammatical structures. **Inflections**—endings to words (such as *-s, -ed,* and *-ing*) that signal plurals or verb tense—become incorporated in routine utterances, as do more articles and conjunctions. Also, the child comes to use negatives, questions, and passives correctly.

In her examination of language acquisition in four children, Lois Bloom (1991) found a predictable sequence in the use of negatives. Initially, children

**inflection**   Alteration to a word, such as tense or plural form, that indicates its syntactical function.

| Semantic Relation | Examples |
|---|---|
| agent + action | Mommy come; Adam write |
| action + object | eat cookie; wash hand |
| agent + object | Mommy sock; Eve lunch |
| action + location | sit chair; go park |
| entity + location | lady home; baby highchair |
| possessor + possession | my teddy; Daddy chair |
| entity + attribute | block yellow; box shiny |
| demonstrative + entity | dat book; dis doggie |

Source: Adapted from Brown, 1973.

**TABLE 7.2**

**Examples of Semantic Relations in Child Syntax**

Children's word orders often reflect knowledge of semantic relationships, such as the idea that agents precede actions or that actions are followed by locations. Roger Brown believes that the semantic relations shown in this table are incorporated in the syntactic constructions of children in many different cultures.

use the negative to express the nonexistence of objects, as in "no pocket," said as the child searches for a pocket in her mother's skirt. In the second stage, children use the negative as they reject objects or events. For example, one of Bloom's subjects said "no sock" as she pulled her sock off her foot. Finally, negatives are used to express denial, as when the child states "No dirty" in response to her mother's comment about her dirty sock. Young children form negatives not just by putting the negative marker at the beginning of an utterance but also by embedding it deep within a statement, as in "My sweetie's no gone" (de Villiers & de Villiers, 1979).

Questions, too, are formed in a fairly consistent developmental sequence, although not all children display the pattern we are about to describe (Maratsos, 1983). Children's earliest questions do not contain inverted word order but consist instead of an affirmative sentence or a declarative preceded by a *wh*-word (*who, what, why, when, where*), with a rising intonation at the end of the statement ("Mommy is tired?"). Subsequently, children form questions by inverting word order for affirmative questions, such as "Where will you go?" but not negative ones ("Why you can't do it?"). Finally, by age four, children form questions for both positive and negative instances as adults do (Klima & Bellugi, 1966).

One of the more difficult linguistic constructions for children to understand is the passive voice, as in "The car was hit by the truck." Children typically begin to comprehend the meaning of a passive construction by the later preschool years, but they may not use this grammatical form spontaneously and correctly until several years later. Generally, children understand passive constructions that convey some action, such as "The boy was kissed by the girl," before they understand those without action, such as "John was liked by Mary" (Maratsos et al., 1979). This finding suggests that action is a salient feature, not only as children learn their first words but also as they acquire the rules of syntax.

One interesting phenomenon of the preschool and early school years is the child's tendency to use **overregularizations**, the application of grammatical rules to words that require exceptions to those rules. From time to time, young children use words such as *goed* or *runned* to express past tense, for example, even if they previously used the correct forms, *went* and *ran*. Although

**overregularization** Inappropriate application of syntactic rules to words and grammatical forms that show exceptions.

they are mistakes, the constructions indicate the child is learning the general rules for forming past tense, plurals, and other grammatical forms (Marcus et al., 1992).

What are the common patterns in children's acquisition of the complexities of syntax? We have seen that children comprehend negatives, questions, and passives well before they can correctly produce them. In addition, children's own uses of these sophisticated grammatical forms begin as imperfect versions that gradually approach the more adult versions. Thus, the child's progression to mature speech shows a distinct orderliness. Accounting for the consistencies in children's acquisition of syntax remains a major challenge for psychologists concerned with language development.

## Context: The Acquisition of Pragmatics

▶ Sociocultural influence

Just as important as semantic and syntactic rules are cultural requirements or customs pertaining to the proper use of speech in a social context. Is the child speaking with an elder or a peer? Is the context formal or informal? How does the speaker express politeness? Each situation suggests some unique characteristics of speech, a tone of voice, a formal or more casual syntactic structure, and the choice of specific words. In the context of playing with a best friend, a "Gimme that" might be perfectly appropriate; when speaking with the first-grade teacher, saying, "Could I please have that toy?" will probably produce a more favorable reaction. These examples demonstrate the child's grasp of pragmatics.

**Acquiring Social Conventions in Speech**     When do children first understand that different situations call for different forms of speech? When Jean Gleason and Rivka Perlmann (1985) asked two- to five-year-olds and their parents to play "store," they observed that at age three some children modified their speech depending on the role they were playing. For example, one three-and-a-half-year-old boy who was the "customer" pointed to a fake milk bottle and said, "I want . . . I would like milk." His revision showed an understanding that an element of politeness is required of a customer. Preschoolers also have some limited understanding that different listeners are typically spoken to in different ways. In a study in which four- and five-year-olds were asked to speak to dolls portraying adults, peers, or younger children, they used more imperatives with dolls representing children and fewer with dolls that were adults and peers (James, 1978).

The child's facility with social forms of politeness increases with age. Researchers in one study instructed two- to six-year-olds to *ask* or *tell* another person to give them a puzzle piece. Older children were rated by adults as being more polite than the younger children, particularly when they were asking for the puzzle piece. Usually, older children included such words as *please* in their requests of another person (Bock & Hornsby, 1981).

▶ Roles of nature and nurture

Parents undoubtedly play a significant role in at least some aspects of the acquisition of pragmatics, especially because they deliberately train their children to speak politely. Esther Greif and Jean Gleason (1980) observed the reactions of parents and children after children had received a gift from a laboratory assistant. If the child did not say "thank you" spontaneously (and most of the preschoolers in the sample did not), the parent typically prompted the child with "What do you say?" or "Say thank you." Parents also serve as models for politeness routines; most parents in the study greeted the laboratory assistant upon entry and said goodbye when the assistant departed.

Incorporating social conventions into language often involves learning subtle nuances in behaviors, the correct words, vocal intonations, gestures, or facial expressions that accompany speech in different contexts. Children may get direct instruction on the use of forms of politeness, but it is not yet clear exactly how they acquire the other behaviors that accompany socially skilled communication.

### Referential Communication

A group of experiments that has been especially useful in providing information on children's awareness of themselves and others as effective communicators centers on **referential communication**, situations that require the child either to talk about a topic specified by the experimenter or to evaluate the effectiveness of a message describing some sequence of events. Researchers note whether the child's message is sufficient to communicate his intent or, alternatively, whether the child is able to detect ambiguous or uninformative components in the messages he hears.

A classic experiment in referential communication was conducted by Robert Krauss and Sam Glucksberg (1969), who asked four- and five-year-olds to describe a series of unfamiliar geometric forms to another child who could not see them (see Figure 7.4). The speaker had to provide the listener with enough information to duplicate an array the speaker was constructing. The results showed that children at this age often rely on personal descriptions of the stimuli ("It looks like Daddy's shirt"), messages that are not particularly helpful to the listener. Thus, young children's ability to understand the requirements of the listener and to adjust their speech to meet those needs is limited when they are describing unfamiliar items.

Initially, children's poor performance in referential communication tasks conducted under highly controlled laboratory conditions was attributed to their cognitive *egocentrism*—that is, their inability to understand the perspectives of other individuals. Observations of children's natural interactions with one another suggest, however, that well before they enter school children appreciate the requirements of the listener and can modify their speech in accordance with those requirements.

In a study of the communication skills of preschool-aged children, Marilyn Shatz and Rochel Gelman (1973) asked four-year-olds to describe a toy to either an adult or a two-year-old listener. When the children spoke to a younger child, they shortened their utterances, used simple constructions, repeated utterances, and employed more attention-getting devices than when they spoke to an adult. Other researchers have also observed that even two-year-olds use techniques to make sure their message gets across during the normal interactions that occur in a nursery school. Children point, seek eye contact with listeners, and use verbal attention getters such as "hey" to ensure that listeners hear what they have to say (Wellman & Lempers, 1977).

Older children—for example, those in the first or second grade—show the ability to detect problems in the messages of others and can even suggest revisions. The ability to evaluate the adequacy of a communication is called **comprehension monitoring**. Carole Beal (1987) asked children to trace a route on a road map according to a set of instructions that was read to them. Most children were able to identify uninformative instructions as such and to suggest revisions that would make the message clearer.

**referential communication**
Communication in situations that require the speaker to describe an object to a listener or to evaluate the effectiveness of a message.

**comprehension monitoring**
Ability to evaluate the adequacy of a communication.

Observations of children's interactions with each other suggest that even preschoolers appreciate the requirements of the listener and can modify their speech in accordance with those requirements.

▶ Interaction among domains

The mature use of language involves the ability to understand the demands of the situation, to be sensitive to the needs of the listener, and to employ subtle nuances in speech compatible with the situation. The child's failure to acquire the social skills that are a part of effective communication can have broad consequences in the qualities of relationships she establishes with parents, teachers, and peers, among others.

## Abstraction: The Acquisition of Metalinguistic Awareness

During the period of most rapid language learning—from about eighteen months through age five—children may not have a full understanding of what it means for a sentence to be grammatical or how to gauge their linguistic competencies, even when their speech is syntactically correct and effective in delivering a communication. The ability to reflect abstractly on the properties of language and to conceptualize the self as a more or less proficient user of this communication tool is called **metalinguistic awareness**. By most accounts, the child does not begin to think about language in this way until at least the early school years, although some early indicators that this ability is emerging are evident before that.

**Reflecting on Properties of Language**    One of the first studies to explore children's ideas of the function of grammar was conducted by Lila Gleitman and her colleagues (Gleitman, Gleitman, & Shipley, 1972). The investigators had mothers read grammatically correct and incorrect passages to their two-, five-, and eight-year-old children. After each sentence, an experimenter said "good" at the end of an acceptable passage, such as "Bring me the ball," or "silly" at the end of an unacceptable one, such as "Box the open." When the children were given the opportunity to judge sentences themselves, even the youngest children were generally able to discriminate between correct and in-

**metalinguistic awareness**  Ability to reflect on language as a communication tool and on the self as a user of language.

Source: Adapted from Krauss & Glucksberg, 1969.

**FIGURE 7.4**

**An Experiment in Referential Communication**

In Krauss and Glucksberg's (1969) study of referential communication, four- and five-year-old children had to describe a series of unfamiliar geometric forms (represented here as blocks) to other children who could not see them. In this illustration, for example, the speaker on the left must explain to the listener on the right which forms to place on the stacking peg. The results showed that children this age are generally ineffective in transmitting this type of information. Research in more naturalistic settings, however, demonstrates that preschoolers can engage in effective referential communication.

correct versions. They were not able, however, to correct improper constructions or to explain the nature of the syntactic problem until age five.

Not until the age of six or seven do most children appreciate that words are different from the concepts to which they are linked. Four-year-olds frequently believe that *train* is a long word, for example, because its referent is long (Berthoud-Papandropoulou, 1978). Similarly, preschoolers believe that the labels for objects can be changed—that is, a *dog* can arbitrarily be called a *cat*, and that the animal will shift from barking to meowing (Osherson & Markman, 1975). Some changes in metalinguistic understanding are undoubtedly linked to advances in cognition, particularly the development of more flexible and abstract thought.

▸ Interaction among domains

**Humor and Metaphor**   One visible way in which children demonstrate their metalinguistic awareness is through language play—creating funny words, telling jokes or riddles, or using words in a figurative sense. The way in which children comprehend and produce humorous verbalizations undergoes clear developmental changes from the preschool to later school years. Children who are three to five years old frequently experiment with the sounds of words, altering phonemes to create humorous facsimiles (for example, *watermelon* becomes *fatermelon*) (McGhee, 1979). By the early school years, the basis of children's humor expands to include riddles or jokes based on semantic ambiguities, as in the following:

QUESTION: How can hunters in the woods find their lost dogs?
ANSWER: By putting their ears to a tree and listening to the bark.

Still later—as every parent who has ever had to listen to a seemingly endless string of riddles and jokes from a school-aged child can testify—children begin to understand and be fascinated by jokes and riddles that require them to discern syntactic ambiguities (Hirsch-Pasek, Gleitman, & Gleitman, 1978), as in:

| | |
|---|---|
| NEWBORN | Prefers human voices.<br>Discriminates among phonemes.<br>Discriminates own language from other languages.<br>Cries. |
| 1–4 MONTHS | Discriminates among vowels.<br>Is sensitive to prosodic features of speech.<br>Coos. |
| 6–12 MONTHS | Babbles.<br>Prefers unfamiliar words in own language to other languages.<br>Produces gestures to communicate and symbolize objects. |
| 12–18 MONTHS | Produces single-word utterances.<br>Comprehends fifty-plus words. |
| 18–24 MONTHS | Displays vocabulary spurt.<br>Begins to use two-word utterances. |
| 2 1/2–5 YEARS | Produces multiword utterances.<br>Uses inflections, negatives, questions, and passive voice.<br>Shows growth in vocabulary and use of syntax.<br>Displays overregularizations.<br>Appreciates humor and metaphor.<br>Shows growth in referential communication skills and other aspects of pragmatics. |
| 6+ YEARS | Shows metalinguistic awareness. |

This chart describes the sequence of language development based on the findings of research. Children often show individual differences in the exact ages at which they display the various developmental achievements outlined here.

QUESTION: Where would you go to see a man-eating shark?
ANSWER: A seafood restaurant.

Thus, children's appreciation of humor mirrors their increasingly sophisticated knowledge of the various features of language, beginning with its fundamental sounds and culminating with the complexities of syntactic and semantic rules. It appears that each change in the orientation of children's humor comes after they have conquered a particular facet of language.

Similarly, children's understanding of **metaphor**, figurative language in which a term that typically describes one object or event is applied to another context (for example, calling a shadow a "piece of the night," or skywriting a

**metaphor**  Figurative language in which a term is transferred from the object it customarily designates to describe a comparable object or event.

"scar in the sky"), undergoes developmental change. Even preschoolers show a rudimentary comprehension of figurative language, especially when it refers to perceptual similarities between two objects. A four-year-old understands expressions such as "A string is like a snake," for example (Winner, 1979). In later childhood and adolescence, children understand and even prefer metaphors grounded in conceptual relationships, such as "The volcano is a very angry man" (Silberstein et al., 1982).

The development of metalinguistic skills necessarily follows the acquisition of phonological, semantic, and syntactic knowledge. After all, to be able to reflect on and even play with the properties of language demands that a person first possess a basic understanding of those properties. In addition, metalinguistic skill is probably tied to advances in thinking skills in general. Just how children move from concrete to abstract thinking and come to reflect on their thought processes are topics to which we will return in the next chapter when we discuss the development of cognition.

## The Sequence of Language Acquisition: An Overview

The Chronology on page 264 provides a summary of the child's progression in attaining language. Three points about the sequence are especially noteworthy. First, language development proceeds in an orderly fashion. Although individuals may vary in the ages at which language milestones are attained or in the precise form of their achievements, children do not acquire language in a haphazard fashion. Second, the child learns language rapidly and with seemingly little effort. With the exception of those with some serious physical or psychological problem, all children learn to speak within only a few years, despite the diverse range of skills required. Third, children produce *generative* language. That is, they do not merely duplicate what others say but create novel and unique expressions of their own. How can we account for these remarkable achievements? Although we have already alluded to some possibilities in decribing language development, it is time to more closely examine several major theoretical positions.

## Explaining Language Acquisition

Psychologists, linguists, and others intrigued by the question of language development have proposed a number of theories to account for the sequence of acquisition. The theories range from biological and linguistic accounts that underscore the importance of innate language predispositions to theories that emphasize the children's experiences in the environment. This section examines five major perspectives on the development of language.

### The Biological Perspective

The human brain contains several areas associated with the understanding and production of language. As we saw in Chapter 5, the right and left hemispheres of the brain have specialized functions, a phenomenon called *lateralization*. The primary regions that control language processing in most people are found in the left hemisphere. A major question arising from knowledge of the brain's involvement in language is the extent to which the milestones of

## FIGURE 7.5

**The Two Portions of the Left Cortex of the Brain Responsible for Language Processing**

Broca's area governs the production of speech, and Wernicke's area is responsible for the comprehension of speech. Damage to the former produces expressive aphasia, whereas damage to the latter leads to receptive aphasia.

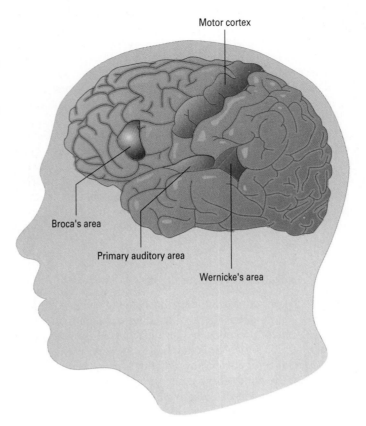

Motor cortex

Broca's area

Primary auditory area

Wernicke's area

▶ Interaction among domains

**Broca's area** Portion of the cerebral cortex that controls expressive language.

**expressive aphasia** Loss of the ability to speak fluently.

**Wernicke's area** Portion of the cerebral cortex that controls language comprehension.

**receptive aphasia** Loss of the ability to comprehend speech.

language acquisition are controlled by physiological maturation of brain structures and, more specific, by lateralization.

**The Brain and Language**    Studies of adults who have suffered brain damage because of stroke, traumatic injury, or illness have pinpointed two specific regions in the left hemisphere that play a vital role in the ability to use language. The first is **Broca's area**, located in the left frontal region near the motor cortex (see Figure 7.5). Patients who have damage in this region evidence **expressive aphasia**, or the inability to speak fluently, although their comprehension abilities remain intact. The second region, **Wernicke's area**, is in the temporal region of the left hemisphere, close to the areas of the brain responsible for auditory processing. Damage to Wernicke's area results in **receptive aphasia**, in which speech seems fluent, at least on the surface, but contains nonsense or incomprehensible words; the ability to understand the speech of others is also impaired.

An important finding is that both children and adults with lesions, or injuries, to the left side of the brain show language impairments more frequently than those whose damage occurs in the right side of the brain (Witelson, 1987). Children, however, are more likely than adults to recover language functions (Annett, 1973; Basser, 1962). Eric Lenneberg (1967) contended that before the age of two, children's brains are not yet lateralized, and each side thus has equal potential for controlling language; damage to one area may be overcome because another part of the brain will take those functions over. Lenneberg believed that lateralization proceeds slowly through childhood until adultlike characteristics emerge at puberty. Chief among the characteristics of maturity is a loss of *plasticity*, the ability of the brain to recover from damage.

Newer evidence suggests, however, that children already show lateralization of the hemispheres in the first few months of life and do not become more lateralized with age (Best, Hoffman, & Glanville, 1982; Molfese & Molfese, 1979, 1980, 1985). For example, Dennis and Victoria Molfese (1980) found greater brain wave activity in reaction to speech stimuli in the left hemisphere than in the right hemisphere in infants aged one week to ten months. Thus, greater plasticity of the human brain during childhood may be independent of the phenomenon of lateralization (Witelson, 1987).

Lenneberg (1967) also argued that several other features of language acquisition suggest a strong biological component. Like motor milestones, language milestones are attained in a predictable sequence, regardless of the environment in which the child grows up (except for a few rare cases of extreme environmental deprivation). In addition, all languages share such features as phonology, semantics, and syntax, elements that Lenneberg and others believed were derived from the biologically determined capabilities of human beings. Indeed, children do seem to be driven to learn language, even in the absence of linguistic stimulation. One group of researchers found a group of congenitally deaf children who were not taught sign language and failed to learn oral communication (Feldman, Goldin-Meadow, & Gleitman, 1978). Even so, the children developed a unique gestural system of communication that followed the same sequence as that of hearing children, that is, a one-symbol stage followed by a two-symbol stage, and so forth.

▶ Roles of nature and nurture

**Critical Periods and Language Learning**    In order to speak and comprehend normally, Lenneberg (1967) claimed children must acquire all language basics by adolescence, when physiological changes in the brain make language learning more difficult. He thus proposed a *critical period* for the acquisition of language. A few rare case studies of children who have been isolated from social contact for protracted periods support his position. One girl, Genie, had minimal human contact from the age of twenty months until thirteen years because of isolation imposed by her parents. She did not speak at all. After she was found and received extensive therapy, Genie made some progress in learning words but never learned to speak normally, showing special difficulty in completely mastering the rules of syntax (Curtiss, 1977). Other evidence comes from studies of deaf people who learned American Sign Language (ASL) at different times in life. Elissa Newport (1990) found that subjects who learned ASL after the age of twelve showed consistent errors in the use of grammar, whereas subjects who were exposed to ASL from birth displayed a normal course in the development of the language.

Another implication of Lenneberg's hypothesis is that children will also find it difficult to learn a second language if they begin during or after adolescence. In fact, Lenneberg claims that few of those who learn a second language after adolescence will sound like native speakers. Here, too, there is evidence to support his ideas. Jacqueline Johnson and Elissa Newport (1989) assessed the ability of Chinese and Korean immigrants who learned English as a second language to judge the grammatical correctness of more than two hundred English sentences. Some subjects started to learn English as early as age

▶ Development as continuous/discontinuous

Studies of second language learners indicate that younger children may have an advantage over older children and adults in attaining proficiency.

three, others not until age seventeen or later. As Figure 7.6 shows, the older they were before learning English, the poorer their scores on the grammar test were. Other analyses showed that factors such as length of experience with English, amount of formal instruction in English, or identification with American culture could not account for the findings. Newport (1990) concludes that "in language . . . the child, and not the adult, appears to be especially privileged as a learner" (p. 12).

### FIGURE 7.6

**Second Language Learning as a Function of Age**

Johnson and Newport (1989) administered a test of English grammar to Chinese and Korean immigrants who had learned English as a second language at different ages. The graph shows that the older the subjects were when they learned English, the poorer their test scores were. The data provide support for the critical-period hypothesis of language learning.

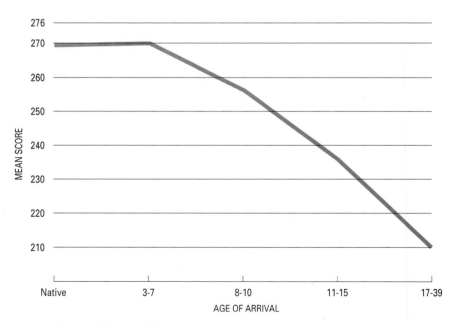

Source: Johnson & Newport, 1989.

Critics point to problems in interpreting some of the research cited in support of the critical-period hypothesis. Genie, for example, may have suffered serious cognitive, physiological, and emotional deficits because of her prolonged isolation from other humans, deficits that could well account for her lack of mature language. Deaf people who learn ASL later in life still learn a good deal about the syntactic system and are able to communicate. And many individuals who learn a second language in adulthood acquire the phonology, vocabulary, and syntax of that language with nativelike proficiency (Snow, 1987b). In fact, in the early stages of acquisition adults typically learn a second language more rapidly than children (McLaughlin, 1984). Nonetheless, children may have a distinct advantage over adults in language learning, making early childhood an ideal time to acquire a second language.

To summarize, the common sequence in the emergence of language abilities is the strongest evidence of a biological explanation for language development. An explanation based solely on biology, however, cannot account for all aspects of language development. Languages vary enormously in the way they express relations and concepts. Let us take one example: how specificity versus generality is expressed. In English, we say "I want *the* car" or "I want *a* car" to represent the two ideas. In some African languages, however, different intonation patterns rather than different words convey the distinction (Maratsos, 1989). Clearly, biology alone cannot explain the vast differences in the way languages express ideas or that children do in fact end up speaking different languages, depending on their culture. It is obvious that a place must be found for the role of nurture, or experience.

▶ Roles of nature and nurture

▶ Sociocultural influence

## The Learning Perspective

One of the earliest attempts to explain language acquisition came from learning theorists. B. F. Skinner (1957) and other behaviorists regarded language as a behavior like any other, the appearance and development of which could be accounted for by the basic principles of learning. Reinforcement and imitation were the mechanisms that explained the child's acquisition of phonology, semantics, syntax, and pragmatic rules.

▶ Roles of nature and nurture

Learning theorists believe that productive language is initially shaped through the selective reinforcement of the child's earliest vocalizations. At first, utterances that even remotely resemble the child's native language are rewarded by caregivers with smiles, hugs, or an enthusiastic "Good!" whereas other random sounds are ignored or discouraged. Gradually, parents and others expect the child's verbalizations to conform more closely to the phonological and syntactic structure of their language before they will reward her. Later in infancy, the verbalization "Baba" may not receive the reinforcements it once did when the child signals for her bottle; only a more accurate pronunciation will do.

Imitation also plays a significant role, according to the learning theorists. As parents and other more experienced users of language label objects for the child and speak in syntactically correct sentences, they provide models of competent and mature language use for young language learners. Children do, after all, learn the phonology, syntax, and conversational rules of the culture into which they are born; they must be influenced by the linguistic models in their environment.

Do parents differentially reinforce grammatically correct and incorrect sentences with any consistency? Some evidence suggests that parents tend to respond to the truth value of children's utterances rather than their grammatical

Imitation plays an important role in language acquisition; children learn the sounds, words, grammatical constructions, and gestures that accompany spoken language by observing those around them.

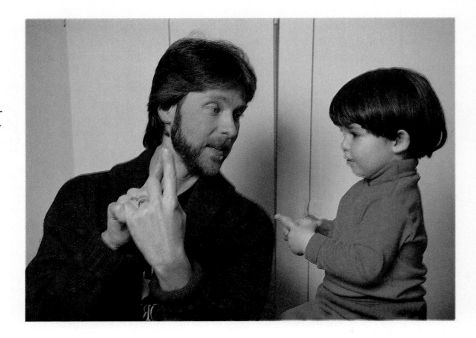

correctness. Thus, a grammatically flawed statement, such as "I no like spinach," might be followed by "Yes, I know" from the parent, whereas a perfectly constructed "I'm sleeping" would probably be met with "No, you're not" (Brown & Hanlon, 1970).

Parents, however, do sometimes provide indirect feedback about the correctness of child speech. Mothers (the parent whose verbalizations to children have been studied most) often follow the child's grammatically incorrect utterances with **recasts**, repetitions of the child's verbalization with some elaboration: when the child says, "Ball fall," her mother might reply, "Yes, the ball fell." Recasts provide children with cues that their verbalization needs improvement and a model for how to improve. Children often imitate the parent's recasts (Farrar, 1992). On the other hand, parents frequently follow the child's grammatically correct utterances with extensions of the topic rather than expansion of the child's syntactic form. Extensions of the topic suggest to the child that his message was understood and therefore correctly expressed (Penner, 1987). Other researchers have noted that parents are more likely to ask for clarification after a poorly formed sentence than a well-formed one (Bohannon & Stanowicz, 1988; Demetras, Post, & Snow, 1986). Thus, although parents do not always directly reinforce the grammatical correctness of child speech, they do provide subtle feedback regarding the child's use of syntactic rules.

While learning theory may help us to understand some facets of language acquisition, the theory does have some significant limitations. One is its inability to account for the occurrence of *overregularizations*, as when the preschooler uses a word such as *goed* or *runned*. The child is not likely to encounter models for these grammatical mistakes in her language environment. It is also unlikely that parents encourage children to generate these erroneous constructions. The phenomenon of overregularization suggests instead that children actively abstract the general rules for forming tenses, plurals, and

**recast**   Repetition of a child's utterance along with some new elements.

other grammatical forms from the language they hear spoken around them and then overuse the rules.

Another important limitation of the learning perspective is the assumption that the child plays a passive role in acquiring language. We have already seen that even in the earliest stages of learning language, children actively experiment with the production of sounds regardless of the reactions of caregivers. They point to objects that their parents subsequently label for them and create two- or three-word utterances that others have never spoken to them. Indeed, the fact that so much of language acquisition is "child driven" lies behind the emergence of alternative theories of language development.

▶ The child's active role

## The Linguistic Perspective

Noam Chomsky (1980, 1986) and other linguists emphasize the structures that all languages share, those syntactic regularities that are quickly identified by the young language learner in the course of everyday exposure to speech— as when the child learning English notices that nouns representing agents precede verbs and nouns representing the objects of actions follow verbs. According to Chomsky, children possess an innate system of language learning, called *universal grammar*, that predisposes them to notice the general linguistic properties of any language. As children are exposed to a specific language, a process called *parameter-setting* takes place. That is, "switches" for the grammatical rules that distinguish English from Japanese or Arabic from French are set. After abstracting the general rules of language, children apply them to form their own novel and creative utterances. Language learning, say most linguists, is distinct from other forms of learning; there are constraints on what the child will be predisposed to learn, and language learning is governed by distinct principles, separate from those that guide cognition and other domains. Furthermore, many linguists believe that language is a uniquely human enterprise, not part of the behavioral repertoire of other species.

▶ The child's active role

▶ Roles of nature and nurture

Research evidence supports many of the tenets held by linguists about how language is acquired. Children learn syntactic rules for forming plurals, past tense, and other grammatical forms rapidly in their first five years and can even apply them to words they have never heard before. In a famous experiment, Jean Berko (1958) demonstrated this phenomenon by presenting children with several nonsense words such as *wug*. Children were able to state correctly that the plural form of *wug* was *wugs*, although they had never heard made-up words such as these. Moreover, linguistic theories fare better than learning theories in explaining the occurrence of overregularizations; these can be seen as the product of a language learner who has done too good a job, implementing rules even in cases where there are exceptions.

What kinds of cues does spoken language provide to children for deducing the rules of syntax? Some clues may come from the phonology or sounds of language. Is the word *record* a noun or a verb, for example? The answer depends on which syllable is stressed; if the first, the word is a noun, if the second, it is a verb. Children may pick up cues from stress, the number of syllables in a word, or other tips from the sounds of language to help them classify words as nouns, verbs, or other grammatical categories (Kelly, 1992).

Other cues about syntax may come from the meanings of words. According to the **semantic bootstrapping hypothesis**, for example, when children

**semantic bootstrapping hypothesis** The idea that children derive information about syntax from the meanings of words.

learn that a certain animal is called a *dog,* they also notice that it is a thing (or noun) and later in development, that it is an agent (subject) or recipient (object) of action (Pinker, 1984, 1987). The tendency to make such assumptions is hypothesized to be innate.

Linguistic approaches help to explain just how children can master the complex, abstract rules that characterize all languages, given what some have called the "impoverished input" provided by the environment (Lightfoot, 1982). That is, the stream of speech most children hear is fraught with incomplete or ungrammatical utterances. Nor do children learn language from explicit teaching of the rules of grammar or lists of vocabulary words. However, critics point out that linguistic approaches may reflect more the biases of adult theoreticians who attempt to describe the logical necessities of language achievements than the actual processes used by children. In addition, it is not clear that language abilities are limited to the human species, as many linguists claim. In the past several decades, there have been several attempts to train members of the ape family to use language, all with some apparent success (Gardner & Gardner, 1971; Premack, 1971; Rumbaugh, Gill, & von Glaserfield, 1973). However, many early studies were criticized on methodological grounds (Terrace et al., 1979). Nevertheless, in one recent well-controlled study, an ape named Kanzi was raised from infancy with exposure to human speech similar to that provided to a young girl named Alia. When Kanzi was eight years old and Alia was two, they were tested on their ability to comprehend an assortment of novel sentences, such as "Take the potato outdoors." On many of the sentences, ape and child performed equally well (Savage-Rumbaugh et al., 1993). Therefore, language may have an evolutionary heritage in species that predate humans. Whatever its shortcomings, though the linguistic approach has helped to capture some of the complexities of language development overlooked by other theoretical perspectives.

## The Cognitive Perspective

▶ Interaction among domains

Language follows from the path set by advances in the child's thinking processes, according to the cognitive perspective on language. Theorists vary, however, in the precise way they link cognition with language.

In Piaget's framework, children must have certain knowledge about the concept to which a given label applies before they can use names for objects, events, or people. In particular, infants must have grasped fully the notion of *object permanence,* the fact that an object continues to exist even when it is no longer in view. In addition, Piaget believed that during most of their first two years, children do not yet use symbolic schemes; hence, their language abilities are quite limited before this age. Once the **semiotic function**, or the cognitive ability to symbolize, emerges, however, language becomes possible. According to Piaget, changes in underlying cognitive structures that precede language explain why children's first words usually name objects, rather than other semantic categories, and also account for the rapid expansion of vocabulary at the age of eighteen months.

**semiotic function**  Ability to symbolize objects.

Other theorists argue that children's language attainments reflect different emerging cognitive skills. For example, it may be no accident that children's first words tend to be nouns such as *dog* and not *animal* or *collie.* Learning to organize objects at this intermediate level seems to be easier for young children than using either broader or more specific categories (Mervis, 1984; Mervis & Crisafi, 1982; Rosch et al., 1976), and the child's language reflects this cognitive preference. Growth in memory, the ability to analyze and dissect complex stimuli, as well as the ability to classify objects in the first place, are other candidates for cognitive precursors of language (Bates, Thal, & Marchman, 1991).

Do cognitive achievements precede linguistic milestones, as Piaget and others suggest? In studies in which researchers have explored the relationship between attainment of object permanence and language, the correlations have been only moderate or weak (Corrigan, 1979). On the other hand, Elizabeth Bates and her colleagues found that skills such as imitation, tool use, and the complex manipulation of objects do predict language attainments (Bates et al., 1979). Alison Gopnik and Andrew Meltzoff (1986) have identified still other cognitive skills that seem to crop up just before certain language accomplishments. For example, children who can find a hidden object after it has been moved from one location to another begin within a few weeks to use words such as *gone* to signify disappearance. Similarly, they begin to use words representing success and failure (for example, *there* and *uh-oh*) after learning to solve a complex means-ends task, such as using a stick to obtain an object. Gopnik and Meltzoff (1987, 1992) also noted that children who are able to sort groups of toys into two distinct categories, such as dolls and cars or boxes and balls, have more words in their vocabulary. According to these researchers, children develop linguistic labels consistent with cognitive problems that interest them at a given stage of development.

Does cognitive development lay the groundwork for language, or does language development follow a unique and independent path, as the linguists maintain? The answer is not yet clear. If anything, perhaps the two domains develop independently but concurrently and overlap at certain points in development, especially at the early stages of language learning (Rice, 1989).

## The Social Interaction Perspective

Many researchers of child language hold as a central tenet that language is a social activity, one that arises from the desire to communicate with others and that is nurtured in social interactive contexts. While acknowledging the biological and innate predispositions of the young human organism to learn language, proponents of this position emphasize the role that experiences with more mature, expert speakers play in fostering linguistic skill. Children need support and feedback as they make their first attempts at communication. They also need models of appropriate speech, models whose speech does not exceed children's processing abilities. Many qualities of parental speech directed at children are well suited to the child's emerging receptive and productive skills. That is, parental speech often operates within the child's *zone of proximal development* to provide the *scaffolding* for language development, concepts outlined in Chapter 6 in relation to the child's general learning process.

▶ Interaction among domains

▶ Roles of nature and nurture

Parents have a unique way of talking to their young children. Most parents present a scaled-down version of spoken language as they interact with their young offspring, a version that contains simple, well-formed sentences and is

When caregivers talk to infants and young children, they employ simple sentences, exaggerate their intonation, and speak with a high pitch. Infants are especially responsive to these qualities of "motherese."

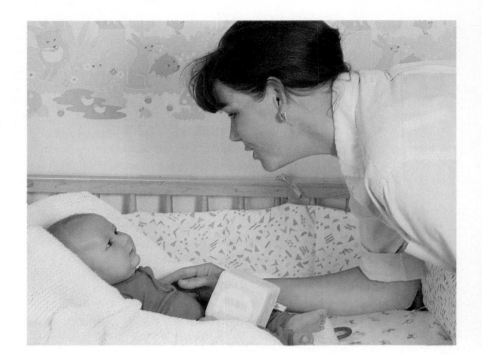

punctuated by exaggerated intonation, high pitch, and clear pauses between segments of speech (Newport, 1977). Caregivers describe concrete events taking place in the present and often refer to objects with diminutives such as *kitty* or *doggie*. **Motherese**, as this form of communication is called, also includes repetitions of what the child has said as well as many questions. Questions, in particular, serve to facilitate the occurrence of **turn taking**, the alternating vocalization by parent and child. Some questions are also used as **turnabouts**, elements of conversation that explicitly request a response from the child, as in "You like that, don't you?" or "What did you say?" Finally, as noted earlier in this chapter, *recasts* are an especially important component of motherese because they highlight for the child the discrepancies between the child's simple utterance and a more advanced form (Nelson, 1989).

Consider the following exchange between one seven-month-old, Ann, and her mother, observed by Catherine Snow (1977):

| MOTHER | ANN |
|---|---|
| *Ghhhhh ghhhhh ghhhhh ghhhhh* | |
| *Grrrrr grrrrr grrrrr grrrrr* | |
| | (protest cry) |
| Oh, you don't feel like it, do you? | |
| | *aaaaa aaaaa aaaaa* |
| No, I wasn't making that noise. | |
| I wasn't going *aaaaa aaaaa*. | |
| | *aaaaa aaaaa* |
| Yes, that's right. | |

**motherese**   Simple, repetitive, high-pitched speech of caregivers to young children; includes many questions.

**turn taking**   Alternating vocalization by parent and child.

**turnabout**   Element of conversation that requests a response from the child.

Notable in the exchange is the mother's pattern of waiting for her child's vocalization to end before she begins her response, an example of turn taking. If the child had spoken actual words, a real conversation would have taken place. The mother also repeated the child's vowel-like sound but embedded it in more elaborate speech. By the time the infant reaches eighteen months, the mother's tendency to expand or explain her utterances becomes even more pronounced, as in the following brief episode (Snow, 1977):

| MOTHER | ANN |
|---|---|
| | (blowing noises) |
| That's a bit rude. | |
| | Mouth. |
| Mouth, that's right. | |
| | Face. |
| Face, yes, mouth is in your face. What else have you got in your face? | |
| | Face. (closing eyes) |
| You're making a face, aren't you? | |

According to Snow (1984), two general principles operate during caregiver-child interactions. First, parents generally interpret their infants' behaviors as attempts to communicate, even when that interpretation may not seem warranted to an objective observer. Second, children actively seek relationships among objects, events, and people in their world and the vocal behaviors of their caregiver. The result of these two tendencies is that parents are motivated to converse with their children and children have a mechanism for learning language.

▶ The child's active role

Motherese may serve a number of functions in the child's growing competence with language. First, this form of speech may assist the child's acquisition of word meaning. Mothers tend to say the names for objects more loudly than other words in their speech to infants, and often they place the object label in the last position in their sentence, as in "Do you see the *rattle?*" (Messer, 1981). Mothers also tend to highlight new words by raising their pitch as they say them (Fernald & Mazzie, 1991). Second, the intonations of motherese may facilitate the child's acquisition of syntax. One recent study demonstrated that seven- to ten-month-olds oriented more frequently to motherese that contained pauses at clausal boundaries than to motherese that was interrupted within clauses. Infants did not show differential preferences in response to regular adult speech (Kemler Nelson et al., 1989). Another study showed that at nine months, infants show a similar sensitivity to even smaller grammatical units, the phrases within a sentence (Jusczyk et al., 1992). The prosodic features of motherese may thus assist the infant in identifying syntactically relevant elements of language. Finally, exposure to motherese may provide lessons in conversational turn taking, one aspect of pragmatics that governs speech in interactions with others.

Are there any other effects of interactions with caregivers on child language development? Researchers have observed that the more mothers talk with their children, the more words their children acquire (Huttenlocher et al., 1991; Olson, Bayles, & Bates, 1986; Tomasello & Todd, 1983). It is not just how much mothers talk to their children that makes a difference, however; *how* they talk also matters. When mothers use many directives to control their children's behaviors and are generally intrusive, language development is slowed. When mothers (or teachers) use questions and conversational turn taking to elicit language from children or follow the children's vocalization with a response, language development proceeds more rapidly (Hoff-Ginsberg, 1986; McDonald & Pien, 1982; Nelson, 1973; Valdez-Menchaca & Whitehurst, 1992). By engaging their young children in conversations, mothers are increasing children's attention to the properties of language and are at the same time providing them with a rich set of information about those characteristics (Hoff-Ginsberg, 1990). One context in which mothers' speech tends to be particularly lavish is during book reading. Erika Hoff-Ginsberg (1991) found that when mothers and two-year-olds were reading books, mothers showed the greatest diversity in the vocabulary they used, the greatest complexity of syntax, and the highest rate of replies to their children as compared with other contexts, such as meal time or toy play. As a result of such findings, many child development experts encourage parents to read to their young children.

As important as motherese may seem, however, it is not a universal phenomenon. Although features of motherese have been observed in many different languages (Gleason & Weintraub, 1978), mothers in some cultures adopt a distinctly different style in talking with their infants. Consider the following two examples of maternal speech, one an American and the other Japanese, as observed by Anne Fernald and Hiromi Morikawa (1993):

▶ Sociocultural influence

AMERICAN MOTHER: That's a car. See the car? You like it? It's got nice wheels.
JAPANESE MOTHER: Here! It's a vroom vroom. I give it to you. Now you give it to me. Give me. Yes! Thank you.

While American mothers tend to name objects and focus on the exchange of information, Japanese mothers rarely name objects, using them instead to engage their infants in social routines. Perhaps it is not surprising, then, that American infants use substantially more nouns in their speech at nineteen months of age. Similarly, other researchers have noted that Japanese mothers ask fewer questions but use more nonsense sounds and songs than American mothers (Bornstein et al., 1992; Toda, Fogel, & Kawai, 1990). Thus, mothers may have different agendas as they speak with their children, and their style of speech may subtly shape the child's utterances.

Another example of variation in the use of motherese can be found in the Kaluli society of Papua New Guinea. In this culture, talking with others is a highly valued social skill, yet few adult verbalizations are directed to infants. Infants may be called by their names, but until they pass their first year, little else is said to them. When mothers do begin to talk to their babies, their speech contains few of the elements of motherese. Turn taking, repetitions, and elaborations are absent; usually, mothers simply make a directive statement that requires no response from the child. Nevertheless, Kaluli children eventually become proficient users of their language (Schieffelin & Ochs, 1983). Joint linguistic interactions between caregiver and child may thus not be absolutely essential to the emergence of language.

Linguistic exchanges with other interaction partners—fathers, siblings, peers, and others—may uniquely influence the child's eventual level of linguistic skill. For example, when fifteen-month-olds "converse" with their fathers, they experience more communication breakdowns than when they talk with their mothers. Fathers more often request clarification, change the topic, or do not acknowledge the child's utterance after they fail to understand what she says (Tomasello, Conti-Ramsden, & Ewert, 1990). Thus, in communicating with fathers children are challenged to make adjustments in order to maintain the interaction. Children are normally exposed to a rich and varied range of linguistic stimuli from different communication partners; many theorists believe that this fact ensures that children will learn the details of linguistic structures that may not be present in the verbalizations of a single conversation partner, such as the mother (Gleitman, Newport, & Gleitman, 1984; Wexler, 1982).

In summary, each of the five theoretical positions makes an important contribution to the understanding of language development. Specialized biological structures are responsible for human language processing, and biology evidently also sets the child's early predispositions to be responsive to the unique features of language. The child's cognitive growth assists in the acquisition process. Part of the child's task, one that he does well, is to filter out the regularities that occur in spoken language so that he can use the general rules to create his own utterances. At the same time caregivers provide models of correct speech, deliver indirect feedback as to the correctness of the child's utterances, and by using motherese provide linguistic data compatible with the child's level of language skill. Given the complexities involved in language development, it is no wonder that explanations of the phenomenon are multifaceted.

## CONTROVERSY: THINKING IT OVER

### *What Is the Source of Children's Reading Difficulties?*

Once children enter school, they are expected to master yet another type of language-based skill—reading. Children must map the visual information given by letters to specific sounds and from these patterns discern words and their meanings. For some children, this complex process flows smoothly and relatively effortlessly. But for a sizable minority of children, perhaps as much as 25 percent of children in school, learning to read is a slow and difficult process (Stedman & Kaestle, 1987). When a child's reading level is significantly below expectations based on his intelligence, he is often diagnosed as *dyslexic*.

What is the underlying cause of dyslexia? Early hypotheses focused on possible visual perception problems, presumably neurologically based, that cause children to perceive letters in reverse, to identify *d* as *b* or *p* as *q*. Although there is some evidence of perceptual deficits (Lovegrove, 1991), more recently, two other broad views of reading difficulties have become more prominent.

One position states that poor readers have general cognitive deficits. For example, poor readers may take a global approach to identifying words rather than focusing on the features or details that define a word (Frith, 1985). One researcher found that poor readers did as well as good readers in identifying letters at the beginnings of words; their performance dropped, however, when they were asked to identify letters in the middle or end positions of words (Venezky, 1976). Children with reading problems may also have general difficulties in learning rules, especially rules that are irregular or contain exceptions (Manis et al., 1987).

The second broad view on reading impairment states that poor readers have problems linked specifically to linguistic processing abilities rather than general cognitive processes (Stanovich, 1988, 1992). Children who have difficulty with reading have problems in associating the sounds that go with each letter or combination of letters (Shankweiler & Liberman, 1990). There is ample evidence that poor readers have difficulties when they must decide whether two words rhyme, when they are asked to read pseudowords such as *mog* or *lun*, and when they are asked to partition a word into phonemes (Siegel, 1993a). Furthermore, phonological problems seem to have a small relationship to the broader cognitive skills measured by intelligence tests, so the impairment may be distinctly linguistic (Siegel, 1993b).

Why might it be important to isolate the causes of reading problems in children? What are the implications of each view of reading difficulties—perceptual, cognitive, linguistic—for helping children to improve their reading? Are the three major views necessarily mutually exclusive, or could there be multiple causes of reading problems? Finally, how do the theoretical debates on the causes of reading disability mirror controversies about the nature of language development in general?  ■

## *The Functions of Language*

Aside from its obvious usefulness as a social communication tool, what functions does language serve? Does the human propensity to learn and employ language affect other aspects of functioning—specifically, mental processes, the regulation of behavior, and socialization? At the very least, language enriches the human experience by providing a useful vehicle for enhancing cognition and behavior; it also exerts powerful influences on other areas of human activity. Here we will examine briefly some broad effects of language on the domains of cognition, behavior, and socialization.

▶ Interaction among domains

### How Language Influences Cognition

The relationship between language and cognition has been a controversial subject for many years, especially with respect to the issue of which activity precedes the other. Some psychologists and anthropologists have argued that language shapes thinking, whereas others contend that cognition paves the way for language. Most now acknowledge that the link between language and cognition is bidirectional and that each domain influences the other. We have already pointed out some ways cognition might influence language. How might language have a powerful influence on the child's cognitive attainments?

**Language, Memory, and Classification**    If you ask a child to perform a cognitive task, such as remembering a list of words or grouping a set of similar objects, you will notice that he will often spontaneously use language to aid his performance. The best examples of this behavior come from research findings on developmental changes in children's memory. There are distinct differences in the way preschool and school-aged children approach the task of remembering. Older children are far more likely to employ deliberate strategies for remembering than are younger children, strategies that typically involve the use of verbal skills. In one study, John Flavell and his colleagues (Flavell,

Beach, & Chinsky, 1966) asked kindergarten, second-, and fifth-graders to watch as the experimenter pointed to three pictures in an array of seven. The children's job was to point to the same three pictures either immediately or after a delay of fifteen seconds. During the delay, the experimenters noticed that most children in the oldest group made spontaneous lip movements, suggesting that they were verbally repeating the items to be recalled. Moreover, the superior performance of the oldest group on the memory test was attributed to their spontaneous repetition of the names of the items. The use of verbal labels seemed to bridge the gap between the time the items were first seen and the time they were to be recalled.

Language can also influence how children categorize related groups of objects. Stan Kuczaj and his colleagues showed children twelve unfamiliar objects that could be grouped in three sets (Kuczaj, Borys, & Jones, 1989). Children who were taught the names of one category member from each group were more successful in sorting the objects than children who were not given labels. Language provides children with cues that classes of stimuli differ from each other and can thus influence how children form conceptual groups. If some four-legged animals are called *dogs* and others are called *cats*, the different linguistic labels will highlight for the child that there are differences in the features of these two groups.

**Bilingualism and Cognition**    One of the more interesting ways in which the influence of language on thought has been studied has been to compare, on a variety of tasks, the performance of bilingual children equally fluent in two languages with monolinguals fluent in only one. Bilingual children have been characterized as more analytic and flexible in their approach to different types of thought problems. Sandra Ben-Zeev (1977) compared monolingual children with children who spoke both Hebrew and English and found that bilinguals performed better on a symbol substitution task. The task required that subjects substitute certain words in a series of sentences for others, such as *spaghetti* for *I* in the sentence "I am cold." Bilingual children also perform better than monolinguals on nonverbal problems, such as the Raven Progressive Matrices (see Figure 7.7) (Hakuta & Diaz, 1985). Finally, bilingual children have been found to display greater metalinguistic awareness than monolingual children, even those who might be chronologically older. Given sentences such as "Why is the cat barking so loudly?" bilingual children were more likely than monolingual children to ignore conflicting semantic information and state that the sentences were grammatically correct (Bialystok, 1986).

One hypothesis to explain their superior performance is that bilingual children are forced to think more abstractly and analytically because they have

**FIGURE 7.7**

**Cognitive Achievements of Bilingual and Monolingual Children**

Bilingual children outperform monolinguals on nonverbal tests such as the Raven Progressive Matrices, which requires children to select the segment that correctly fits into the larger pattern. Bilingual children generally seem to be more analytical than monolinguals in their approach to various problem-solving tasks.

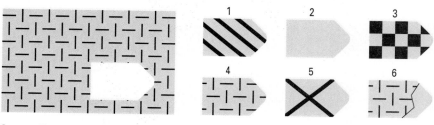

Source: From Raven, 1962.

had experience with analyzing the structure and detail of not just one language but two. A second possibility is that they are generally more verbally oriented in their thinking and have a greater tendency to produce verbalizations that enhance their performance even in nonverbal tasks. Last, they may have an increased objective awareness of language and hence, more control over cognitive processing in general (Bialystok, 1991; Diaz & Klingler, 1991). Whatever the mechanism, these studies demonstrate that speaking a second language affects cognitive processes.

## How Language Influences Self-regulation

▶ Interaction among domains

Language takes on special significance in its increasing role in regulating behavior as the child develops, according to two prominent Soviet psychologists, Lev Vygotsky and Alexander Luria. Vygotsky (1962) believed that the child's initial utterances serve an interpersonal function, signaling others about her affective state. In the preschool years, however, speech takes on a different function. Specifically, the child's **private speech**, or overt, audible "speech-for-self," comes to guide her observable activities. If you have ever observed a toddler coloring and simultaneously saying something like, "Now, I'll use the blue crayon. I'll make the sky blue," you have seen an example of private speech. Eventually, speech-for-self becomes interiorized; **inner speech** dictates the direction of the child's thoughts.

▶ Development as continuous/discontinuous

Luria (1961) expanded these ideas by proposing three stages in the verbal regulation of behavior (see Table 7.3). In the first stage, encompassing the ages of about eighteen months to three years, the verbalizations of others can prompt motor activity, but they rarely inhibit behavior. In an experiment in which children were to squeeze a rubber ball according to the commands of an adult, they would start pressing after the command "Go!" but did not stop when given negative commands such as "Don't squeeze." In the second stage, lasting from about three to five years of age, children's external

**TABLE 7.3**

**Luria's Stages of the Verbal Regulation of Behavior**

| Age | Characteristics | Example |
|---|---|---|
| **18 Months–3 Years** | Verbalizations of others initiate child's motor behavior but do not inhibit it. | Child squeezes ball when adult says, "Go," but does not stop squeezing when adult says, "Don't press." |
| **3–5 Years** | Adult's or child's own speech initiates and inhibits behavior but only if physical qualities of speech match task requirements. | If child says, "Go, go," child squeezes ball twice; if child says, "I shall press twice," child will only squeeze once. |
| **5+ Years** | Content of child's internalized speech controls thoughts and actions. | Child says, "I shall press twice" and squeezes rubber ball two times. |

**private speech**   Child's vocalized speech to himself that directs behavior

**inner speech**   Interiorized form of private speech

Young children often use private speech when they are engaged in new or challenging tasks. This overt "speech-for-self" guides children's behaviors and is eventually interiorized.

speech (either from others or vocalized overtly by the children) can increasingly initiate and inhibit behavior but only if the physical qualities of the speech match the requirements of the task. If children said, "Go, go," they squeezed the rubber ball twice; if they said, "I shall press twice," however, they squeezed the ball only once. Finally, at about age five, children's speech becomes internalized to control thoughts and actions. In addition, the content of speech, and not just its superficial qualities, becomes effective in regulating behavior.

Attempts to find empirical support for the ideas of Vygotsky and Luria have met with mixed success. One problem has been the failure to observe much overt speech-for-self among preschoolers, although that may be a function of the particular settings and tasks psychologists have used (Fuson, 1979). On the other hand, in one study, when children younger than four and a half were given negative commands in a loud voice—such as "Don't touch your toes!"—they were more likely to perform the prohibited act than when the instruction was issued softly. That is, the loudness of the command was more powerful in initiating a behavior than the content was in stopping it. In contrast, older children attended more to the content of the message than its physical qualities (Saltz, Campbell, & Skotko, 1983). Moreover, Laura Berk (1986) noted that when first-graders were solving math problems in school, they engaged in high levels of externalized private speech to guide their problem solving. Third-graders also showed evidence of private speech but a more internalized form, through mutterings and lip movements as they attempted to solve math problems. Thus, children do use private speech in some contexts, and they progress from overt private speech to a more interiorized form.

How important is private speech in directing behavior? You may have noticed that you tend to talk to yourself when you are under stress or when you have a lot to do. Research has confirmed that children, like adults, use private speech when they find tasks difficult or when they make errors, and that when they use task-relevant private speech, their performance on a variety of tasks improves (Berk, 1992). In addition, a longitudinal study has demonstrated that as children progress from overt to more internal private speech, they also show fewer distracting body movements and greater sustained attention in school (Bivens & Berk, 1990). Such studies suggest that language becomes an increasingly powerful regulator of children's behavior as they develop.

## How Language Influences Cultural Socialization

▶ Sociocultural influence

Still another way in which language can have a broad influence on development is by helping children to discern the social roles, relationships, and values of their culture. Many languages have specific grammatical forms that are used to convey gender, age, or social power. In acquiring language, children are sensitized to the specific ways their own culture creates social order. For example, in Japanese, the word particle *zo* signifies affective intensity and a male speaker and the particle *wa*, hesitancy and a female speaker. Children learning Japanese are therefore likely to associate hesitancy with females and forcefulness with males (Ochs, 1990). In many other languages, specific words have formal and informal versions, with the formal used when speaking with individuals who have more authority or power and the informal with individuals of equal status or who are related. Again, such linguistic distinctions highlight important social relationships within the cultural group.

A good example of how language can influence socialization comes from traditional Samoan culture, in which community and group accomplishments are emphasized over the attainments of individuals. In Samoan speech, few verbalizations include praise or blame for individuals. Most statements concern the success or failure of the group and emphasize the life of the community. When Samoan children are exposed to verbalizations of this type, they are being socialized into the collective orientation of their culture (Ochs, 1990).

Researchers are just beginning to explore the ways in which the words and social conventions within a specific language are related to cultural values and beliefs. However, it is apparent that through language children are learning far more than simply how to communicate; they are also learning about the broader belief systems of their society.

---

## THEMES IN DEVELOPMENT

---

### LANGUAGE

▶ **What roles do nature and nurture play in language development?**

There are several indicators that nature sets early human dispositions to develop language: the infant's sensitivity to phonemes and prosody, the child's tendency to progress through language milestones in a predictable sequence, and the devotion to language functions of certain portions of the brain are just some examples. Nurture, in the form of the child's experiences with more mature language users, interfaces with these biological tendencies to lead him to acquire the phonology, semantics, and syntax of a particular language and to learn the social conventions that accompany spoken language in his culture.

▶ **How does the sociocultural context influence language development?**

Cultures vary in the extent to which caregivers use motherese with their growing children, a factor that may influence the rate of language acquisition. The specific elements of phonology, semantics, syntax, and pragmatics also vary widely across languages. Often, the content and structure of a specific language provide cues to the culture's social order and values.

▶ **How does the child play an active role in the process of language development?**

Even in the earliest stages of language acquisition, children often influence which objects or people caregivers will label when they look at or point to specific items. Although children do benefit by merely listening to language use in the environment, they also actively use context and other word-learning biases to derive the meanings of words. In addition, their rapid acquisition of the rules of syntax and their production of overregularizations suggest that children abstract the regularities in language to generate their own verbalizations.

▶ **Is language development continuous or discontinuous?**

Descriptions of early language production often seem stagelike because children appear to spend distinct periods of time in a babbling stage, one-word stage, and so on. However, recent studies suggest that there are more continuities than previously thought between different stages in language acquisition. For example, the sounds in infant babbling are related to the language the child will eventually speak. Luria posits that there are stages in the verbal regulation of behavior. However, rather than disappearing at a particular age, private speech often resurfaces, even among older children and adults, when tasks become difficult or stressful.

▶ **How prominent are individual differences in language development?**

Children frequently show striking differences in the rate at which they achieve language milestones. They may differ, for example, in the age at which they say their first words or when, even if, they show a vocabulary spurt. Some may develop a referential style of speech, whereas others may speak expressively. Nonetheless, there is a pronounced regularity in the sequence of language attainments by children, regardless of the culture in which they grow up.

▶ **How does language development interact with development in other domains?**

In early childhood, the ability to produce spoken language parallels the physiological maturation of the vocal apparatus and the central nervous system. The emergence of language also coincides with the onset of certain cognitive skills, such as conceptual understanding. Language is nurtured largely within the context of social interactions with caregivers. Thus, physical, cognitive, and social factors affect the process of language acquisition. By the same token, language has a clear effect on other domains. Children's use of language enhances their ability to remember, form concepts, and as studies of bilinguals suggest, may even promote analytic thinking and mental flexibility. In addition, children's ability to be successful communicators can have important repercussions for social relationships with parents, peers, and others.

## *Summary*

**The Course of Language Acquisition**   Acquiring language is a developmental task with four main components: phonology, semantics, syntax, and pragmatics. In the early stages of acquisition, children focus on *phonology;* they learn to segment and produce the basic sounds of language and show a predisposition to respond to language as a unique auditory stimulus. During the first year, they vocalize by *cooing* and *babbling* but also communicate and symbolize objects by producing gestures.

By one year, most children are speaking in one-word utterances, usually *nominals*, or nouns. A general characteristic of *semantic* development, the learning of word meanings, is that children comprehend far more language than they are able to produce. Children learn the meanings of words through fast-mapping, parental labeling of objects that children point to, linguistic contrast, and their tendency to have biases in learning labels for objects. Their growing conceptual knowledge is also thought to be part of learning word meanings. Although there are specific ages at which most children achieve language milestones, children also show individual differences in patterns of acquisition.

Once children begin combining two or more words, they show evidence of *syntactic* awareness, the grammatical rules that state how words are combined. Although it is difficult to describe their grammar, children use *inflections* and other systematic relationships between words to convey meaning. Later in childhood, children learn to form negatives, questions, and use the passive voice. Two other later developments are the acquisition of *pragmatics*, the social conventions regarding effective communication, and *metalinguistic awareness*, the ability to reflect abstractly on language as a communication tool and the self as a language user.

**Explaining Language Acquisition**   Theories of language development have centered primarily on the nature-nurture debate. Those leaning toward a biological explanation have pointed to the regularities in language attainments across cultures and the brain structures specifically devoted to language processing. A major question stemming from the biological position is whether a critical period exists for the acquisition of language. Learning theorists have emphasized the role of shaping, reinforcement, and imitation in language acquisition. Linguistic theorists emphasize the child's abstraction of general grammatical principles from the stream of speech. Cognitive theorists point out that certain advances in thinking, such as classification skills, precede language attainments. Finally, social interaction theorists highlight the characteristics of caregiver-child speech that facilitate development, such as the use of *recasts, turn taking*, and simple clear verbalizations.

**The Functions of Language**     Language serves numerous functions in the child's life in addition to simple communication. It can influence specific cognitive processes, such as memory or classification. It can serve to direct the child's behavior in the form of *private speech* and, later, *inner speech*, particularly when tasks are new or difficult. Last, it can play a role in the socialization of the child by introducing him directly to specific values and expectations of the child's native culture.

## Key Themes in This Chapter

▶ **What roles do nature and nurture play in cognitive development?**

▶ **How does the sociocultural context influence cognitive development?**

▶ **How does the child play an active role in the process of cognitive development?**

▶ **Is cognitive development continuous or discontinuous?**

▶ **How prominent are individual differences in cognitive development?**

▶ **How does cognitive development interact with development in other domains?**

*Observing his sixteen-month-old daughter Lucienne, the developmental psychologist Jean Piaget recounts what happened when he placed an intriguing watch chain inside an empty matchbox:*

> *I put the chain back into the box and reduce the opening to 3 mm. It is understood that Lucienne is not aware of the functioning of the opening and closing of the match box and has not seen me prepare for this experiment. She only possesses two preceding schemas: turning the box over in order to empty it of its contents, and sliding her fingers into the slit to make the chain come out. It is of course this last procedure that she tries first: she puts her finger inside and gropes to reach the chain, but fails completely. A pause follows during which Lucienne manifests a very curious reaction. . . . She looks at the slit with great attention; then, several times in succession, she opens and shuts her mouth, at first lightly, then wider and wider! [Then] . . . Lucienne unhesitatingly puts her finger in the slit, and instead of trying as before to reach the chain, she pulls so as to enlarge the opening. She succeeds and grabs the chain. (Piaget, 1952b, pp. 337–338)*

What Piaget witnessed in this episode is a very clear demonstration of a young child in the process of *thinking*. Lucienne solved a simple problem by paying attention to the dilemma before her, relying on her memory for information about how to extract objects, and opening and closing her mouth to display what needed to be done with the matchbox. Although Lucienne's problem-solving behavior is a far cry from the more sophisticated thought of, say, the adolescent, who can solve complex logical problems or remember vast amounts of new information, she is displaying some impressive cognitive skills for a child not far past her first birthday.

One of the most active research areas of child development focuses on **cognition**—those thought processes and mental activities including attention, memory, concept formation, and problem solving evident from early infancy onward. Do young children remember as well as older children? Does the way in which children form concepts change? Do older children solve problems the same way that younger children do? These are the types of questions that psychologists interested in cognitive development ask.

Virtually every aspect of a child's development, in fact, has some connection to emerging cognitive capabilities. We have already seen in Chapter 7 that a

**cognition** Processes involved in thinking and mental activity, such as attention, memory, and problem solving.

child's use of language is linked to her growing conceptual development. Once she understands concepts such as "animal" or "flower," she can apply the labels to members of these classes. Similarly, the child's growing knowledge of effective social interaction can influence the quality of her relations with peers. In the domain of emotional development, the infant's fear of separation from the caregiver follows from the realization that people continue to exist even when they are no longer within sight—another cognitive advance. These are just a few of the numerous examples of how changes in thinking influence and interact with other areas of the child's development.

We begin our discussion of cognitive development by considering Piaget's theory, one of the most important theoretical positions that has framed research on children's thought. In addition to summarizing his major ideas and evaluating his contributions to our understanding of cognitive development, in this chapter we also discuss several topics explored by contemporary researchers who have been influenced or provoked by Piaget's writings. These topics include the development of children's understanding of physical objects, their ability to classify objects, and their understanding of concepts such as number and space. We also examine what children understand about psychological states, their own and those of others.

## Piaget's Theory of Cognitive Development

▶ The child's active role

As we saw in Chapter 2, Piaget believed that children are actively involved in the construction of knowledge, incorporating new information into already existing knowledge structures, or *schemes*, through *assimilation*. As a result, schemes are modified or expanded through the process of *accommodation*. The outcome is greater *equilibrium* or balance among the pieces of knowledge that make up the child's understanding. An important implication of this proposition is that what a child can understand or mentally grasp at any given point in time is heavily influenced by what the child already knows or understands. At the same time, the child's schemes are constantly being transformed, as equilibrium is continually disrupted by the never-ending flow of information from the world around him.

▶ Development as continuous/discontinuous

As a stage theorist, Piaget maintained that thought becomes qualitatively reorganized at several points in development. Thus, even though early schemes lay the foundation for later knowledge structures, schemes in one stage bear little resemblance to those in other stages. The child's progression through the *sensorimotor, preoperational, concrete operational*, and *formal operational* stages reflects major transitions in thought in which early action-based schemes evolve into symbolic, then logical, and finally abstract mental structures. In Piaget's theory, the child who is at a given stage will display certain characteristic features of thought, no matter what the specific content of that thought, be it numbers, classes of objects, or spatial arrangements.

### Stages of Development

Piaget maintained that all children progress through the stages of cognitive development in an invariable sequence in which no stage is skipped. In addition, each stage contains a period of formation and a period of attainment. When the child begins a new stage, his schemes are somewhat unstable and loosely organized. By the end of the stage, his schemes are well formed and well organized. Even though Piaget provided age norms for the acquisition of each stage, he believed that, because cognitive development is the result of maturational factors working in concert with environmental experiences, some children might reach a stage more quickly or more slowly, depending on the opportunities for learning their environment provided. Ultimately, though, there is a universal regularity in the evolution of thought, according to Piaget.

**The Sensorimotor Stage (Birth to Two Years)**     The most striking characteristic of human thinking during the **sensorimotor stage** is its solid basis in action. Each time the child reaches for an object, sucks on a nipple, or crawls along the floor, she is obtaining varied feedback about her body and its relationship to the environment that becomes part of her internal schemes. At first, the infant's movements are reflexive, not deliberate or planned. As the child passes through each of the six substages of the sensorimotor period, her actions become progressively more goal directed and aimed at solving problems. Moreover, she is able to distinguish self from environment and learns about the properties of objects and how they are related to one another. Table 8.1 summarizes the major features of each substage of the sensorimotor period.

A significant accomplishment of the sensorimotor stage is the infant's progression toward **means-ends behavior**, the deliberate use of an action to accomplish some goal. During the early substages of sensorimotor development, the infant often initiates actions accidentally rather than purposefully. When Piaget's daughter Lucienne was three months old, she was observed to shake her bassinet

> by moving her legs violently (bending and unbending them, etc.), which makes the cloth dolls swing from the hood. Lucienne looks at them, smiling, and recommences at once. (Piaget, 1952b, pp. 157–158)

Lucienne repeated her kicking to make the dolls shake in what Piaget calls a **circular reaction**, the repetition of a motor act because of the pleasure it brings. Her first kick, however, was totally accidental. Several months afterward, when Lucienne was eight months old, Piaget placed a new doll over the hood of her bassinet. This time her behavior reveals a greater degree of intentionality:

▶ The child's active role

> She looks at it for a long time, touches it, then feels it by touching its feet, clothes, head, etc. She then ventures to grasp it, which makes the hood sway. She then pulls the doll while watching the effects of this movement. (Piaget, 1952b, p. 256)

Throughout the first two years, the child increasingly uses actions as a means of obtaining some end or goal. She experiments with new means toward reaching the same goal and uses familiar behaviors to attain new goals.

A second aspect of sensorimotor development is the child's gradual separation of self from the external environment. Initially, the child derives pleasure from actions that center on her own body. At three months of age, Lucienne "strikes her quilt with her right hand; she scratches it while carefully watching what she is doing, then lets it go, grasps it again, etc." (Piaget, 1952b, p. 92). The circular reaction, in this case, was repeated because of the satisfying sensations it brought to Lucienne's hand. A few months later, in the episode of the swinging dolls, Lucienne's kicking in the bassinet produced a gratifying result in the external environment. In general, the child becomes less centered on the self and more oriented to the external world.

**sensorimotor stage**   In Piagetian theory, the first stage of cognitive development—from birth to approximately two years of age—in which thought is based primarily on action.

**means-ends behavior**   Deliberate behavior employed to attain a goal.

**circular reaction**   In Piagetian theory, repetition of some action or behavior because of the pleasure it brings.

| Substage | Major Features | Object Concept |
|---|---|---|
| Reflexive Activity (0–1 month) | Formation and modification of early schemes based on reflexes such as sucking, looking, and grasping | No attempt to locate objects that have disappeared |
| Primary Circular Reactions (1–4 months) | Repetition of behaviors that produce interesting results centered on own body | No attempt to locate objects that have disappeared |
| Secondary Circular Reactions (4–8 months) | Repetition of behaviors that produce interesting results in the external world | Search for objects that have dropped from view or are partially hidden |
| Coordination of Secondary Schemes (8–12 months) | Combination of actions in order to achieve a goal | Search for completely hidden objects |
| Tertiary Circular Reactions (12–18 months) | Experimentation with different actions to achieve the same goal or observe the outcomes | Ability to follow visible displacements of an object |
| Invention of New Means Through Mental Combinations (18–24 months) | Thinking through of potential solutions to problems and imitation of absent models | Ability to follow invisible displacements of an object |

**TABLE 8.1**

**The Six Substages of Piaget's Sensorimotor Stage**

A third important accomplishment of this stage is the attainment of the **object concept**, or *object permanence*. Infants who possess the object concept realize that objects continue to exist even though they are not within immediate sight or within reach to be acted upon. Up to three months of age, the saying "out of sight, out of mind" characterizes the child's understanding of objects. At about four months of age, she will lift a cloth from a partially covered object or show some reaction, such as surprise or puzzlement, when an object disappears. At about eight months of age, she will search for an object that has completely disappeared—for example, when it has been covered entirely by a cloth. In the last two phases of the attainment of the object concept, she will be able to follow visible and then invisible displacements of the object. In the first instance, the twelve-month-old will follow and find a toy that has been moved from under one cloth to another, as long as the movement is done while she is watching. In the second instance, the eighteen-month-old can find an object moved from location A to location B, even if the displacement from A to B is done while she is not looking.

The completion of the sensorimotor stage and the beginning of the next stage is signaled by the child's display of *deferred imitation*, the ability to imitate a model who is no longer present. At age sixteen months, Piaget's daughter Jacqueline was playing with a boy who suddenly had a dramatic temper tantrum. The next day, the normally well-behaved Jacqueline mimicked the little boy's behaviors with remarkable accuracy. To do so, she must have had the ability to represent the boy's overt behaviors in internal form and to draw on

**object concept** Realization that objects exist even when they are not within view. Also called object permanence.

A significant attainment in infancy is the child's understanding of object permanence. Children under about 3 to 4 months of age act as if a hidden or obstructed object no longer exists.

that representation hours later. This ability to represent events and objects internally marks the beginning of a major transition in thought.

**The Preoperational Stage (About Two to Seven Years)**    The key feature of the young child's thought in the **preoperational stage** is the *semiotic function,* the child's ability to use a symbol, object, or word to stand for something. He can play with a cardboard tube as if it were a car or draw a picture of the balloons from his third birthday party. The semiotic function is a powerful cognitive ability because it permits the child to think about past and future events and to employ language. In fact, Piaget asserted that language would not be possible without this significant characteristic of thought; the child must possess the general cognitive ability to let one thing stand for another before words can be used to represent objects, events, and relationships. The semiotic function is also a prerequisite for imitation, imagery, fantasy play, and drawing, all of which the preschool child begins to manifest.

Despite this tremendous advance in thinking, preoperational thought has distinct limitations. One is that children in this stage are said to be **egocentric**, a term that describes the child's inability to separate his own perspective from that of others. Put into words, his guiding principle might be, "You see what I see, you think what I think." An example is the three-year-old who thinks he is hiding from an older sibling or parent by crouching behind a chair. Even though his legs and feet might be sticking out for all present to see, the youngster believes he is well concealed because he himself is unable to see anyone. According to Piaget, the preschooler's egocentrism has ramifications for both his social communicative behavior and his perceptual skills. As we saw in Chapter 7, Piagetian theory predicts poor referential communication skills in children under age seven years and, as we will see later in this chapter, the inability to appreciate the perspectives of others in perceptual tasks.

▶ Interaction among domains

**preoperational stage**   In Piagetian theory, the second stage of development—approximately from two to seven years of age—in which thought is now symbolic in form.

**egocentrism**   Preoperational child's inability to separate his or her own perspective from that of others.

The second limitation of preoperational thought lies in the child's inability to solve problems flexibly and logically. The major tasks that Piaget used to assess the status of the child's cognitive development are called the **conservation tasks**. These "thinking problems" generally require the child to observe some transformation in physical quantities that are initially equivalent and to reason about the impact of the transformation. Figure 8.1 shows several conservation tasks.

Suppose we use the conservation of liquid quantity task to illustrate how the preoperational child thinks. The four- or five-year-old will usually quickly agree that two equal-size glasses of water (A and B) have the same amount of liquid. If the liquid from A is poured into the tall cylinder C, however, the child will state that C now has more than B. According to Piaget, this error is the result of several limitations in preoperational thinking. One is **centration**—that is, focusing on one aspect of the problem, in this case the height of the cylinder—to the exclusion of all other information, such as its narrower width, that could help produce a correct solution. A second cognitive trait at work here is lack of **reversibility**. The preoperational child cannot mentally reverse the action of pouring from C to A; if he could, he would realize that the two containers still contain the same amount of liquid as they did at the start of the problem. Third, the preoperational child tends to **focus on states** rather than on the events that occur between states. It is as if he has stored two static photographs of containers A and B, and then B and C, rather than a video of the sequence of events. He fails to realize the connection between the two components of the conservation problem and, as a result, fails the conservation task.

### The Concrete Operational Stage (About Seven to Eleven Years)

Children enter the **concrete operational stage** when they begin to be able to solve the conservation tasks correctly. At first, the six- or seven-year-old may solve only a few of the simpler problems, such as conservation of length, number, or liquid quantity. Later, she will succeed on tasks that involve area or volume. Piaget called this extension of the same cognitive structures to solve increasingly difficult problems within a given stage *horizontal décalage*.

The reason for this shift is that the child is now capable of performing **operations**, mental actions such as reversibility that allow him to reason about the events that have transpired. He can pour the liquid back from C to A "in his head" or think about the narrow width of the tall cylinder as compensating for its height. In other words, the child now thinks logically, although the physical components of the problem must still be present (if not externally in the world, then as images in the mind). The child's thought is also less egocentric, allowing him to understand that other individuals' perceptions, beliefs, and feelings might be different from his own. The concrete operational child is becoming a true "thinker," as long as there are specific objects or events that his logic can be applied to.

### The Formal Operational Stage (About Eleven Years and Beyond)

By the time the child reaches adolescence, she will most likely have moved to the final stage in Piaget's theory, the **formal operational stage**. Thinking in this stage is both logical and abstract. Problems like "Bill is shorter than Sam, but taller than Jim. Who is tallest?" can now be solved without seeing the individuals or conjuring up concrete images of them. The adolescent can also reason **hypothetically**; that is, she can generate potential solutions to

**conservation tasks** Problems that require the child to make judgments about the equivalence of two displays; used to assess stage of cognitive development.

**centration** In Piagetian theory, tendency of the child to focus on only one aspect of a problem.

**reversibility** In Piagetian theory, the ability to mentally reverse or negate an action or transformation.

**focus on states** Preoperational child's tendency to treat two or more connected events as unrelated.

**concrete operational stage** In Piagetian theory, the third stage of development—approximately from seven to eleven years of age—in which thought is logical when stimuli are physically present.

**operation** In Piagetian theory, mental action such as reversibility.

**formal operational stage** In Piagetian theory, the last stage of development—approximately from eleven to fifteen years of age—in which thought is abstract and hypothetical.

**hypothetical reasoning** Ability to systematically generate and evaluate potential solutions to a problem.

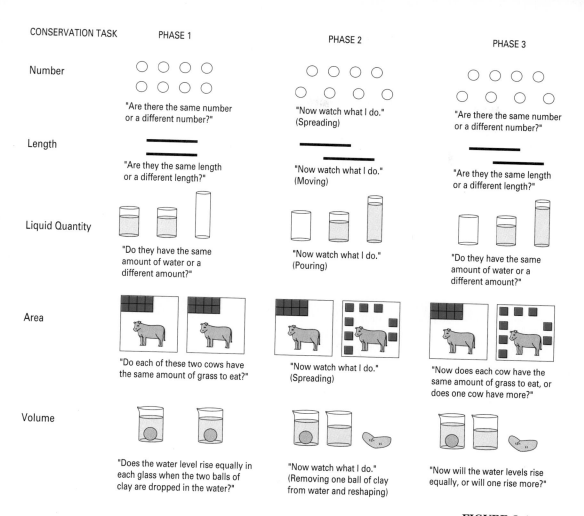

**CONSERVATION TASK**

| | PHASE 1 | PHASE 2 | PHASE 3 |
|---|---|---|---|
| Number | "Are there the same number or a different number?" | "Now watch what I do." (Spreading) | "Are there the same number or a different number?" |
| Length | "Are they the same length or a different length?" | "Now watch what I do." (Moving) | "Are they the same length or a different length?" |
| Liquid Quantity | "Do they have the same amount of water or a different amount?" | "Now watch what I do." (Pouring) | "Do they have the same amount of water or a different amount?" |
| Area | "Do each of these two cows have the same amount of grass to eat?" | "Now watch what I do." (Spreading) | "Now does each cow have the same amount of grass to eat, or does one cow have more?" |
| Volume | "Does the water level rise equally in each glass when the two balls of clay are dropped in the water?" | "Now watch what I do." (Removing one ball of clay from water and reshaping) | "Now will the water levels rise equally, or will one rise more?" |

**FIGURE 8.1**

**Examples of Conservation Tasks**

In the first phase of all conservation tasks, the child agrees that two stimulus arrays are equivalent. In the second phase, one of the stimuli is physically altered but remains equivalent to the other. In the third phase, the child is questioned about the equivalence of the arrays. The child who conserves will respond that the arrays remain the same.

problems in a thoroughly systematic fashion, much as a scientist approaches an experiment.

Piaget's pendulum problem allows us to examine the thinking of the formal operational adolescent. In this task, the subject is shown an object hanging from a string and is asked to determine the factor that influences the frequency of oscillation, the rate at which the pendulum swings. The length of the string, the weight of the object, the force of the push on the object, and the height from which the object is released can all be varied. How do children in earlier Piagetian stages approach this problem? Children in the preoperational and concrete operational stages typically try various manipulations in a haphazard fashion. They might compare the effect of a long string attached to a heavy weight and a short string tied to a light weight. Or they vary the weight of the object and force of the push, but leave out length of the string. In contrast, formal operational children are both systematic and complete in testing the potential influences on oscillation. For example, while keeping weight constant, they observe the effects of varying length, push, and height. While keeping length the same, they investigate the effects of varying weight, push, and height, and so forth. Most adolescents, Piaget observed, could correctly determine that the length of the string was the critical factor in how fast the pendulum swings (Inhelder & Piaget, 1958).

In the social realm, achieving abstract thought means that the adolescent can think about the nature of society and his own future role in it. Idealism is not uncommon at this developmental stage because he understands more fully concepts such as justice, love, and liberty and thinks about possibilities, not just realities. In some ways, the adolescent may be more of a "dreamer" or utopian than the adult because he has not yet had to confront the practical facts of living and working in the world (Inhelder & Piaget, 1958).

The contemplative nature of adolescent thought may manifest itself in two other ways, according to David Elkind (1976, 1981a). First, adolescents may believe that others scrutinize and evaluate them as much as they think about themselves. This belief, called the **imaginary audience**, may cause a young girl to avoid going out because she just got braces on her teeth ("Everybody will see me!") or may make a teenage boy avoid answering a question in class because he is certain all his classmates will think he is "dumb." Second, adolescents may show signs of a **personal fable**, the belief that they are unique, that no one can fully understand them, and even that they are invulnerable. A teenage boy prohibited from going to a late-night rock concert by his parents might say, "You just don't understand how important this is to me!"

The development of formal operational thought represents the culmination of the reorganizations in thought that have taken place throughout each stage in childhood. By adolescence thought has become logical, flexible, and abstract, and its internal guiding structures are now highly organized.

## Implications for Education

Piaget's theory carries some clear implications for teaching children. The first is that the individual child's current stage of development must be carefully taken into account as teachers plan lessons. For example, if a seven-year-old is in the stage of concrete operations, she should be given problems involving actual physical objects to observe or manipulate rather than abstract word problems or diagrams (Flavell, 1963). Similarly, a four-year-old preoperational child might have difficulty with tasks requiring the use of logic; a more fruitful strategy might be to foster the imagination and creativity that result from the recently acquired semiotic function. By encouraging drawing, pretend play, and vocal expression, teachers can capitalize on the preschooler's cognitive strengths.

A second, related implication is that what the child knows already will determine what new information he is able to absorb. Because his current cognitive structures limit what he will be able to assimilate, it is important for the teacher to be aware of the child's current state of knowledge. In addition, cognitive advances are most optimally made when new material is only slightly different from what the child already knows (Ginsberg & Opper, 1988). Thus, the teacher's task is to plan lessons that are tailored to the needs of the individual child rather than the class as a whole and to be flexible in devising instructional materials that stretch the child one step beyond what he already knows.

**imaginary audience** An individual's belief that others are examining and evaluating him.

**personal fable** The belief that one is unique and perhaps even invulnerable.

According to Piaget, the ideal way to educate children is to actively involve them in the discovery of scientific or mathematical principles.

One of Piaget's most important statements about cognitive development is that it is the result of the *active engagement of the child.* Early sensorimotor schemes and later mental operations are all founded first on the child's physical activity and later on mental actions. Thus education, too, must be structured in such a way that it will promote the child's active participation. Instead of emphasizing rote learning, teachers following a Piagetian model provide children with experiments allowing them to discover scientific principles on their own. Children do not memorize numerical relationships, such as the multiplication tables, but discover them by manipulating sets of objects under the close guidance of the teacher. According to Piagetian thinking, active learning of this sort promotes deeper and more enduring understanding.

▶ The child's active role

Educational programs based on a Piagetian model have varied in their instructional goals—some have emphasized the teaching of specific skills such as conservation, and others have focused on more general principles, such as fostering children's active participation in the educational process (Crain, 1992). Many of these programs have been specifically targeted for preschool-aged children, probably for good reasons. One difficulty in implementing Piagetian-based education in higher grades is that individualized instruction is not always possible when there are twenty or more students in a classroom; in preschool classrooms, which tend to have fewer students, individualized instruction is more feasible. Nevertheless, many teachers have found inspiration in the rich theoretical framework Jean Piaget devised for thinking about how and what to teach children.

## Evaluating Piaget's Theory

That Piaget's theory has stimulated so much research in developmental psychology is not surprising, given its wide-ranging scope. In sheer numbers of empirical studies generated by the writings of one person, Jean Piaget has no rival in developmental psychology. Like all good theories, Piaget's has spawned a host of debates about the fundamental nature of cognitive change.

These debates are a tribute to the power of his ideas and his contribution to the scientific process.

Contemporary evaluations of Piaget's theory have raised several key points. First, did Piaget provide an accurate portrayal of the ages at which different cognitive skills are acquired? Second, does cognitive development proceed in a stagelike fashion? Third, could there be alternative explanations for the behaviors Piaget observed in children of different ages?

**What Are the Ages of Acquisition?** One major criticism of Piaget's theory is that he underestimated the abilities of infants and young children. Many researchers have found that when cognitive tasks are simplified or restructured or when children are observed in more naturalistic settings, they display cognitive skills at much earlier ages than Piaget believed possible.

Take the object concept, for example. Piaget maintained that the first real notions about the permanence of objects do not occur until about eight or nine months of age, when infants will search for objects that are completely covered. Renée Baillargeon (1987a), however, was able to demonstrate that infants as young as four months old have a rudimentary understanding of the continuing existence of objects. Figure 8.2 shows the phases of this experiment. At first, the infants observed a screen that rotated 180 degrees over repeated trials. As you might expect, they showed habituation of visual fixation to this display after it was repeated for several trials. Next, a box was placed behind the screen so that as the screen rotated, it occluded the box. In the *possible event* condition, the screen stopped moving at the point where it hit the box. In the *impossible event* condition, the box was surreptitiously removed and the screen passed through the space the box would have occupied. In two control conditions, the screen either moved or stopped, as in the two experimental conditions, but no box was present. Infants looked significantly longer

**FIGURE 8.2**

**Do Infants Have an Object Concept?**

In Baillargeon's experiment, infants were habituated to a screen rotating 180 degrees (A). Next, infants in the *impossible event* condition saw the screen seeming to pass through the location of a box (B, on left), while infants in the *possible event* condition saw the screen stopping at the location of the box (C, on left). Infants in the *impossible event* condition looked significantly longer at this event, suggesting that they were puzzled by what they saw and therefore had an object concept. The control conditions (shown at right) were included to make sure that infants were not responding to the arc of the screen's movement.

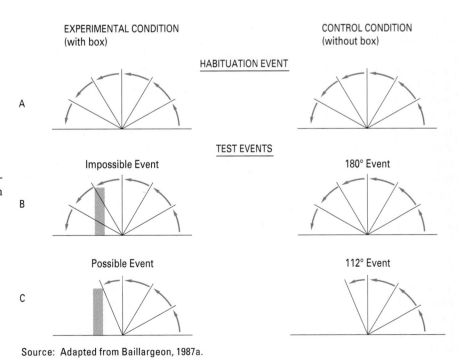

EXPERIMENTAL CONDITION (with box)

CONTROL CONDITION (without box)

HABITUATION EVENT

A

TEST EVENTS

Impossible Event

B

Possible Event

C

180° Event

112° Event

Source: Adapted from Baillargeon, 1987a.

at the impossible event than the possible event, apparently noticing that the screen was moving through the space that should have been occupied by the box. Looking did not differ in the two control conditions, indicating that the type of movement did not determine the infants' looking. Thus, infants seemed to be aware that the box in the impossible event condition should have had an effect on the movement of the screen, even though they could not see it. This awareness, argues Baillargeon, is an indicator of the object concept.

Similarly, Rochel Gelman (1969) noted that conservation of number could be demonstrated in five-year-old children who, in Piaget's view, are still in the preoperational stage of development and lack the logical thought structures to perform this task correctly. Gelman first determined that all the subjects in her sample were unable to conserve numbers. Then she provided training on the "oddity problem." On each trial, children saw three stimuli and were directed to indicate which one was different from the other two. On some trials, the "odd" stimulus differed in number from the other two; on others, the "odd" stimulus was different in length. After the training period, the children were tested on the conservation of length and number. The majority performed correctly even when they were tested several weeks after the training period. In fact, in later work, Gelman has shown that under some circumstances, even three- and four-year-olds are able to conserve number after training (Gelman, 1972).

Part of the difficulty in assessing when children are capable of various types of thought may have to do with how they are asked questions. Even adults may fail a conservation of weight task if they are asked "When do you weigh more, when you are running or walking?" as opposed to "When do you weigh more, when you are running or walking, or do you weigh the same?" (Winer, Craig, & Weinbaum, 1992). Likewise, young children may be fully capable of logical, operational thought, but may be misled by the way the interviewer asks them questions. They may simply "give in" to one of the two options presented by the experimenter when the first type of question is asked.

Piaget himself was not as concerned with the specific ages at which children acquired cognitive skills as he was with the sequence of development. For others, however, the fact that many cognitive attainments occur earlier than he suggested is problematic. As researchers sought explanations for the presence of cognitive skills at earlier ages, they raised other questions about the nature of cognitive development.

**Is Cognitive Development Stagelike?**    If cognitive development proceeds in stages, there should be common features in how children think within a stage and distinctive differences in how they think across stages. One problem with Piagetian theory is that it posits more consistency in performance within a given stage than is actually found in the behavior of children. In one study, Ina Uzgiris (1968) tested children who should have been in the stage of concrete operations on conservation of quantity, weight, and volume. The same tasks were tested with different materials, such as plasticine balls, metal cubes, and plastic wires. Many children were able to conserve when one material was used (say, plasticine balls) but not when another was employed (say, metal cubes). If conservation is indeed tied to the presence of logical thought structures, it should not matter which materials are used to conduct the conservation tests.

Other researchers have noted that the correlations among various abilities predicted to co-occur within the stage of concrete operations are much lower

▶ Development as
continuous/discontinuous

than would be expected if development were truly stagelike (Gelman & Baillargeon, 1983). Piaget maintained, for example, that before children could conserve number they had to understand the principle of *class inclusion*, the idea that some groups of objects are subsets within a larger set. "Dogs" are a subset of "animals," just as "five" is a set contained within "six." Yet children can conserve number by the age of six or seven and still not fully understand the concept of class inclusion (Brainerd, 1978a).

Because of these findings many contemporary researchers now believe that development shows more continuity than Piaget suggested. What seems to vary among children of different ages, say the critics, is not their cognitive skills but the degree to which the same basic skills are displayed in a wide variety of more and more complex situations (for example, Brainerd, 1978b). Another position retains an emphasis on stagelike development but suggests that when new levels of thinking are reached, they are less broadly and generally applied than Piaget initially proposed. Cognitive development, these theorists say, proceeds as outlined by Piaget, but in some domains—say number or spatial relationships—growth is more rapid than in other domains (for example, Fischer, 1980). We will consider these perspectives more fully in our discussion of neo-Piagetian approaches to cognitive development.

**Are There Alternative Explanations for Development?**    Many studies have confirmed Piaget's general claims about the patterns of behavior children display at different ages. Without special training, for example, most children under age six or seven years fail conservation tasks, whereas older children perform them successfully. Adolescents are indeed capable of solving problems more systematically and abstractly than their younger counterparts. Yet many psychologists disagree with Piaget about the precise mechanisms that account for such patterns in the development of thinking processes.

The basic challenge to Piaget's theory centers on whether cognitive development is best understood in terms of emerging symbolic, logical, and hypothetical thought structures or whether some other explanation is more tenable. A case in point is the successful training of conservation by Rochel Gelman (1969) as previously described. Gelman suggests that young children normally fail conservation tasks because they fail to attend to the correct portions of the problem, not because they lack mental operations like reversibility. If children's attention is directed to the salient cues, Gelman and others argue, they will be successful in conserving. Younger children may also be less skilled at remembering than older children, forgetting elements of problems that are essential to reaching the correct solution. Thus, cognitive development may result from a change in how information is gathered, manipulated, and stored rather than from the alteration of cognitive structures themselves.

▶ Roles of nature and nurture

▶ Individual differences

▶ Sociocultural influence

Another central Piagetian tenet is that maturation, in conjunction with experience, is responsible for the unfolding of more sophisticated thought structures. The heavy emphasis Piaget places on maturation implies that the sequence of development is universal. Yet not all children reach the stage of formal operations, and some do not even attain the highest levels of concrete operations. Many American adults, in fact, fail to display formal operational thought (Neimark, 1979). Moreover, members of many non-Western cultures do not display formal operational thinking, especially when they have little experience with formal schooling (Dasen, 1972; Rogoff, 1981).

At the same time, specific kinds of cultural experiences may accelerate the emergence of conservation and formal operational thought. Douglass Price-

Williams and his colleagues examined two groups of rural Mexican children six to nine years old on standard conservation problems (Price-Williams, Gordon, & Ramirez, 1969). Half of the children came from pottery-making families, the other half from families who practiced other trades. Children who had experience in manipulating clay for pottery making were far more likely to conserve than the other children. Studies such as these imply that the child's experiences in the sociocultural context may shape the nature of thought to a greater degree than Piaget acknowledged. They also challenge the notion that Western scientific thinking represents the highest form of thought and the endpoint of development (Greenfield, 1976). The ability to solve problems like a miniature scientist may be highly valued in our own culture, but less so in cultures in which other skills such as hunting, farming, or even social facility are more essential to successful living.

Despite these criticisms, several important strands of Piaget's work run through contemporary ideas about cognitive development. First and foremost is the idea that children are active participants in their own growth: few researchers believe that children merely absorb information like sponges. Moreover, many modern accounts of cognition assume that what the individual knows at a given time determines the knowledge he or she can acquire, a distinctly Piagetian idea. Finally, Piaget opened the doors to the exploration of important topics in cognitive development. How do infants understand the properties of objects? How do children classify objects that have potential relationships to one another? What do children understand about the properties of numbers? What do children understand about different mental states, their own and those of others? These questions, suggested by Piaget's pioneering work, are being actively explored by contemporary developmental psychologists.

## Concept Development

When and how does the child begin to understand that horses, dogs, and cats all belong to a common category called "animals"? When does she realize that numbers like "2" or "4" represent specific quantities, no matter what objects are being counted? And how does she mentally organize her spatial environment, such as the layout of her house or the path from home to school? In each case, we are concerned with the ways in which the child organizes a set of information about the world, using some general or abstract principle as the basis for that organization. In other words, we are describing the child's use of **concepts**.

As one psychologist put it, "Concepts and categories serve as the building blocks for human thought and behavior" (Medin, 1989). Concepts allow us to group isolated pieces of information on the basis of common themes or properties. The result is greater efficiency in cognitive processing. Suppose someone tells you, "A quarf is an animal." Without even seeing one, you already know many of the quarf's properties—it breathes, eats, locomotes, and so on. As we have already seen, concepts also underlie one of our most powerful human capabilities—language. And as we shall see in the next chapter, concepts are at the heart of strategies that improve still other cognitive activities, such as memory. Thus, understanding how concepts develop is an important concern of developmental psychologists.

**concept**  Definition of a set of information on the basis of some general or abstract principle.

## Properties of Objects

The most fundamental early concepts, of course, have to do with the objects infants and young children encounter. What exactly do they understand about the properties of objects, for example, the fact of their continual existence or how one object might cause another to launch forward or zigzag across the room?

**The Object Concept**    We have already discussed how Piaget believed that significant accomplishments like the object concept emerge late in the first year of life, and do not become fully elaborated until the second year. We have also seen that experiments like those of Renée Baillargeon suggest that by three to four months of age, infants understand far more about the properties of physical objects, like the object concept, than Piaget surmised (Baillargeon, 1987a; Baillargeon & DeVos, 1991).

According to Baillargeon, infants this young not only understand that objects exist when out of sight, but also that their size continues to be preserved as well (Baillargeon, 1987b). In a series of experiments involving the rotation of a screen similar to that shown in Figure 8.2, the rectangular box was either upright (as shown in Figure 8.2) or lying flat. Three- and four-month-olds seemed to understand that the screen could not rotate as far when the box was in the upright position as when lying down. Moreover, if the object was something that could be squeezed, like a ball of gauze they had previously played with, they were not surprised by the continued rotation of the screen in front of it. They did show surprise when the screen seemed to rotate past the position of a hard and rigid box. Apparently, young infants have already begun to develop ideas about properties of objects such as their height and rigidity.

A series of studies by Adele Diamond and her colleagues further demonstrates the extent of young infants' knowledge about objects. A common error when the child is about seven to nine months of age is the $A\bar{B}$ (or "A, not B") error. Piaget noted that if an object was hidden in one location, A, found by the infant, and then in full view of the infant, moved to location B, the child would mistakenly but persistently search for the object in location A. Piaget hypothesized that the infant's incomplete knowledge of the object concept leads to this error, in large part because the sensorimotor scheme for searching in location A still controls the child's thought. Diamond, however, proposes that other factors account for the $A\bar{B}$ error.

Diamond noticed, when watching infants make the $A\bar{B}$ error, that even though some infants would mistakenly *reach* for A, they would actually *look* at B, the correct location of the hidden toy (see Figure 8.3) (Diamond, 1985). They behaved as if they knew the correct location of the toy but could not stop themselves from reaching to A. In other studies, adult monkeys, who normally perform successfully on the $A\bar{B}$ task, make mistakes identical to seven- to nine-month-old human infants when given brain lesions in very specific areas of their frontal cortex. These are the brain areas that control the inhibition of responses (Diamond & Goldman-Rakic, 1989). Diamond (1991) proposes that infants have the object concept well before age seven months but that, due to the physical immaturity of this special cortical area, they cannot suppress their tendency to reach for location A. Lending support to this hypothesis is recent data showing that infants who are successful in the $A\bar{B}$ task display more powerful brain electrical activity from the same frontal region of the cortex (Bell & Fox, 1992). Thus, the behaviors originally observed by Piaget in the $A\bar{B}$ task

▶ Interaction among domains

may be due to infants' inability to inhibit reaching, not the lack of object concept.

**Physical Causality** Imagine the following scene: a red brick moves halfway across a screen, hits a green brick, and the green brick moves across the rest of the screen. Most adults would conclude that the red brick *caused* the green brick to glide across the screen. They would not reach that conclusion, however, if they saw the bricks did not touch each other, or if there was a pause between the time the two bricks made contact and the time the green brick started to move (Michotte, 1963).

In a series of experiments, Alan Leslie showed that infants as young as six months of age show similar reactions (1982, 1984; Leslie & Keeble, 1987). In one condition, infants observed one object collide with and propel another object forward for a series of trials. After they showed habituation to this scene, they viewed the reverse situation in which the second object hit and launched the first. Infants showed dishabituation, that is, they treated the two event sequences (depicted in Figure 8.4) as if they were different. In a control condition, infants were habituated to the same events, but the second object moved only after a delay. Now, though, when the event was reversed, little dishabituation was observed. These experiments showed that infants noticed something unique about causal events. Other research has demonstrated that for infants to react to physical causality, the same objects must be used repeatedly during habituation trials. Reactions to physical causality diminish when the objects themselves change from trial to trial (Oakes & Cohen, 1990; Cohen & Oakes, 1993). Thus, it seems that the infant's conceptual understanding of physical causality appears early in life and develops as a result of repeated experiences with specific objects.

**FIGURE 8.3**

**Alternative Explanations for the AB Error**

In the first photograph, a toy has been hidden first in the right well (location A), then in the well on the left (location B) as the infant looks on. The next three photographs show that even though the infant reaches for location A, he looks persistently at location B, suggesting he has the object concept when there are visible displacements of the object. Diamond (1991) believes that infants reach for the incorrect location because of failure to inhibit motor responses.

**FIGURE 8.4**

**A Demonstration of Infant Discrimination of Physical Causality**

In Leslie's experiments, six-month-old infants viewed stimulus sequences that occurred under different conditions. The top row shows a red brick moving and touching a green brick, after which the green brick moves. Infants habituated to this sequence showed dishabituation when the reverse sequence (depicted in the bottom row) was shown. In another condition, the red brick moved and touched the green brick, but the green brick moved only after a delay. Infants habituated to this latter sequence did not show as much dishabituation to the reversal.

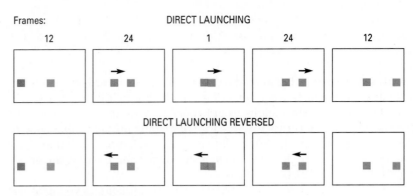

Source: Leslie & Keeble, 1987.

Findings such as these stand in sharp contrast to Piaget's ideas about the development of concepts of causality. Piaget (1930, 1974) believed that up until the early school years, ages seven or eight years, children lack an awareness of physical causality. Furthermore, once they are verbal and can discuss causality, they make two kinds of errors: **animism**, attributing lifelike properties to inanimate objects (for example, boats do not sink because they are clever), or **artificialism**, believing that naturally occurring events are caused by people (for example, clouds move because people move). In Piaget's view, children are slow to shed their animistic and artificial beliefs; the latter may persist until age ten years or so (Piaget, 1929).

Of course, the infant studies described above do not suggest a full-blown appreciation of the concept of causality; they simply imply that before age one year, infants notice something unique about contiguous event sequences where one object seems to "cause" another to do something. How do slightly older children—preschoolers—understand concepts of causality? Apparently, again, better than Piaget thought they did.

Susan Gelman and Kathleen Kremer (1991) attempted to replicate some of Piaget's studies by asking preschoolers, "Do you think people made (or make) __?" where the blank was filled in by an object such as the sun, moon, dogs, flowers, dolls, and shoes. Few of the children showed evidence of artificialism; most recognized that objects such as dolls are made by humans, but that the sun and moon are not. Moreover, these young children often cited natural causes for the behaviors of living things (for example, birds fly because they have bones) and human causes for the artificial objects (for example, cars go uphill because people make them). Why the discrepancy with Piaget's observations? Gelman and Kremer (1991) postulate that direct questions, such as the ones they used, were more likely to tap children's underlying knowledge of causality than the free-ranging interview questions employed by Piaget.

## Classification

Aside from learning about the properties of single objects, as in the object concept, children also quickly learn about relationships that can exist among sets of objects. Sometimes objects resemble each other perceptually and seem to "go together" because they are the same color or shape. Other times, the relationships among objects can be more complex; the perceptual similarities may not be as obvious and moreover, some sets can be embedded within others.

**animism**  The attribution of lifelike qualities to inanimate objects.

**artificialism**  The belief that naturally-occurring events are caused by people.

Cocker spaniels and Great Danes, two different-looking dogs, can be classified together in the group "dogs" and both breeds fit into a larger category of "animals." As with many other cognitive skills, Piaget believed that before the age of seven years, children's ability to classify objects, particularly in the manner of the latter example, was limited. Ask a young child who sees six brown beads and three white beads, all of which are wooden, "Do I have more brown beads or wooden beads?" Chances are the four- or five-year-old will respond, "More brown beads." According to Piaget, preoperational children lack the logical thought structures to permit understanding that some classes can be subsets of others (Piaget, 1952a).

Piaget was right in claiming that classification skills undergo changes with development, but the research that followed his has revealed a far more complex portrait of this cognitive skill. As mentioned above, objects can be classified on the basis of a number of relations. They can be grouped together because they look alike (triangles go with other triangles, circles with circles), a *perceptually based grouping.* Objects can also be grouped together because they often function together or complement one another (spoon goes with cereal), a *thematic relation.* Finally, objects can be grouped together because they belong to a common higher-order group, as in pear-apple (both fruits), or horse-dog (examples of animals). *Taxonomic groupings,* as these classes are called, require children to cluster objects that may not always look alike or function similarly into a grouping based on some abstract principle. Even within taxonomic groupings, children might display several different types of understanding. To understand that pear-apple go together may be very different than understanding that a McIntosh is an apple, which is a fruit.

**Early Classification**     One of the earliest signs of classification skills in young children occurs toward the end of the first year, when they begin to group perceptually similar objects together. Susan Sugarman (1982, 1983) carefully watched the behaviors of one- to three-year-old children as they played with successive sets of stimuli that could be grouped into two classes, such as plates and square blocks, or dolls and boats. Even the youngest subjects displayed a spontaneous tendency to group similar objects together by pointing consecutively to items that were alike. At age two, children went one step further and began to move objects resembling each other into two distinct groups—that is, plates with plates and blocks with blocks. Thus, the tendency to group objects together on the basis of shared perceptual characteristics emerges early in development.

Between ages one and three years, children experience a rapid growth in classification skills. Infants as young as fourteen months successively touch objects that appear in common contexts, such as "kitchen things" and "bathroom things" (Mandler, Fivush, & Reznick, 1987). Two-year-olds will match items on the basis of both thematic and taxonomic relations, putting a baby bottle with a baby or a shoe with a boot. Younger children, though, are more likely to group items taxonomically when items show perceptual similarities. For example, linking a shoe with a boot is easier for the two-year-old than linking a shoe with a shirt (Fenson, Vella, & Kennedy, 1989).

It is not until children are age seven years or so that they spontaneously use the different kinds of relationships possible within taxonomic classes. In one recent study, for example, four- and seven-year-old children were asked to say "the first word you think of" as they were given different stimulus words. The stimulus list included words like shirt, pants, socks, dog, cat, guinea pig, and so on. Whereas seven-year-olds typically said words like "animal" or "collie" when they heard the word "dog," four-year-olds were more apt to say "cat," or even more commonly a word like "bark" (Lucariello, Kyratzis, & Nelson, 1992). That is, only school-aged children showed a tendency to use the vertical relations within a taxonomic category, while preschoolers employed horizontal or thematic relations. Thus, as they grow older, children become capable of using a wider range of relations to classify objects, their exclusive reliance on shared perceptual features lessens, and they display spontaneous hierarchical knowledge of categories.

**Basic-level Categories**　　Eleanor Rosch and her colleagues have proposed another way of framing our understanding of the way concepts develop in children (Rosch et al., 1976). These researchers believe that some groupings of objects can be described as *basic level;* that is, objects go together when they look alike and can be used in similar ways, and when we can think of "average" members of the class. "Chair" is an example of a basic-level concept because virtually all chairs have seats, legs, and backs; all are used for sitting; and we can think of such a thing as a "typical" chair. In contrast, other concepts are *superordinate level.* Members of superordinate-level groups, such as "furniture," do not necessarily share many perceptual attributes, and they are broader and more general than basic-level concepts. Rosch and her colleagues believe that because basic-level groups carry more information, especially perceptual information, than superordinate-level groups, they are easier for children to process. Figure 8.5 gives another example of a basic-level and a superordinate-level grouping.

　　Rosch and her colleagues found that children under the age of five years readily put together four pictures of different shoes or four pictures of different cars; that is, they could sort according to basic-level groupings (Rosch et al., 1976). In fact, a recent study shows that the ability to sort basic-level stimuli is evident as early as eighteen months of age (Gopnik & Meltzoff, 1992). Children in Rosch's study could not, however, proficiently sort on the basis of superordinate category by putting a shoe, shirt, sock, and pants together until they reached the age of eight or nine years. These results, like those described above, reaffirm that children's classification skills undergo significant development in the years from three to nine.

▶ Roles of nature and nurture

**Natural Domains**　　Some concepts or categories of objects are easier to acquire than others, several developmental psychologists have said recently. Just as children seem to be biologically "programmed" to learn language rapidly and easily (see Chapter 7), so too do they seem to learn about certain conceptual domains quickly and effortlessly. In other words, some objects and events in the environment offer "privileged relationships" for the child to learn about (Gallistel et al., 1991). Among these so-called **natural domains** is knowledge about biological entities.

　　Children show a dramatically early ability to classify animate versus inanimate objects. For example, a twenty-four-month-old child will show obvious surprise when a chair seems to move forward on its own (Golinkoff et al., 1984). Three-year-olds know that living things can feel emotions, but inanimate objects cannot; they say a person can feel sad, but a doll or a rock cannot (Gelman, Spelke, & Meck, 1983). Even subtle distinctions between animate

**natural domains**　Concepts or categories that children acquire especially rapidly and effortlessly.

and inanimate objects are made. Shown a mechanical monkey, young children in Susan Carey's (1985) studies said the monkey physically resembles a person, but cannot eat or sleep like a human being.

Similarly, preschool children view the qualities of biological offspring, such as the color of a flower, as derived from a parent—a biological source. In contrast, they recognize the qualities of nonbiological artifacts, such as the color of a can, as mechanically derived. Thus, preschoolers already form a distinction between reproduction involving biological kinds and production involving the manufacture of inanimate objects (Springer & Keil, 1991). Preschoolers also begin to recognize that other processes, such as growth, illness, healing, and death, are unique to biological organisms (Backscheider, Shatz, & Gelman, 1993; Rosengren et al., 1991; Siegal, 1988).

Part of the usefulness of concepts, of course, is that they permit us to make assumptions about other category members, as in our example of the "quarf" above. That is, we go beyond the information given, perhaps even beyond the similarity of perceptual features of objects, to make conceptually based judgments or inductions about them. According to Susan Carey (1985) and Frank Keil (1989), children's inductions are largely guided by "theories" they construct about the nature of specific concepts. For the domain of biological entities, Carey found that children's theories become revised with development to allow more and more accurate judgments. For example, a four-year-old, told that humans have "omenta," will say that only other animals that are very similar to humans also have "omenta." Their theories about biology center around what they know about humans. In contrast, an older child would state that

**FIGURE 8.5**

**Basic- and Superordinate-level Categories**

The left panel gives an example of objects that are considered a basic-level grouping. These stimuli share perceptual features and an "average" member of the class can be thought of. The right panel gives an example of a superordinate-level grouping. Members of such classes do not necessarily share many perceptual features and it is more difficult to think of an "average" class member. Basic-level categories are easier for young children to employ than superordinate-level groupings.

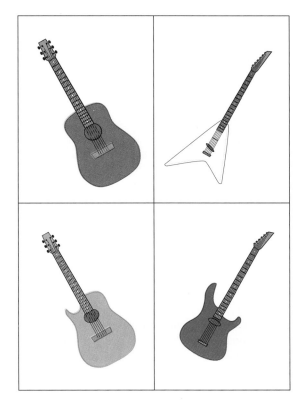

even animals physically dissimilar from humans have "omenta." Their theories of biology extend beyond resemblances to human beings to the broader properties that characterize living things. According to Carey, then, concept development in the biological domain is actually the development of a systematic and coherent *theory* of biology.

▶ Sociocultural influence

**Culture and Classification**     Just why do classification skills develop precisely as they do? Does the process involve theory development as Carey and others maintain? Even though children show earlier achievements in classification than Piaget supposed, was he right in suggesting that increasingly logical thought structures are responsible for growth in these skills? Are some concepts indeed innately easier to learn than others? Implied in all of these questions is the notion that at least some facets of concept development will be similar among children across different cultures. However, research also suggests that the sociocultural context in which an individual grows up cannot be ignored. For example, one variable—the experience of formal schooling—may be key to understanding some aspects of concept formation. Consider again the development of taxonomic classification among older children.

One group of researchers found that residents of rural Mexico without much formal schooling tended to group objects on the basis of their functional relations. "Chicken" and "egg" were frequently classified together because "the chicken lays eggs." On the other hand, subjects with more education relied on taxonomic classification, grouping "chicken" with "horse" because "they are animals" (Sharp, Cole, & Lave, 1979). It may be that taxonomic classification strategies are taught explicitly in schools or that education fosters the development of more abstract thought, a basic requirement for taxonomic grouping.

Other cultural differences may also be important in concept development, specifically, by influencing the types of theories children and adults construct about groupings of objects and events. Sheila Walker (1992) studied understanding of biological kinds among rural, urban poor, and highly educated adults in western Nigeria, where familiarity with supernatural beliefs is more widespread than in the United States. Subjects were asked questions about the identity of animals that underwent transformations in religious ritualistic contexts and in nonritualistic contexts. Adults from all backgrounds were more likely to accept a change in the biological identity of an organism—say a cat changing to a dog—in the ritualistic context than in the nonritualistic context. This finding sheds further light on the view that classifications are theory-based by pointing out the substantial role that cultural contexts—in this case, a context where the supernatural is familiar—can play in those theories. Any full explanation of the development of classification skills will have to take into account the experiences of children within their specific sociocultural context.

## Numerical Concepts

Children as young as two years of age frequently use number terms, either to count toys, snacks, or other items or in playful ways, such as shouting, "One, two, three, jump!" as they bounce off their beds (Saxe, Guberman, & Gearhart, 1987). But do young children really understand the full significance of numbers as a tool for establishing quantitative relationships? Or are they merely repeating a series of words they have heard someone else say without fully appreciating the conceptual underpinnings of those words?

Piaget's (1952a) position was that children under the age of seven years or so—before they enter the concrete operational stage—do not have a full grasp

By the age of four years, many children show the ability to count and appreciate at least some of the principles of numerical relationships.

of the meaning of numbers. One indication is the failure of preoperational children to succeed in the conservation of number task. In this problem, you will recall, children see two equal rows of objects—say, red and white poker chips—as shown in Figure 8.1. Initially, the rows are aligned identically, and most children will agree that they have equal numbers of chips. But when the chips in one row are spread out, the majority of children state that this row now has more chips even though no chips have been added or subtracted.

Preoperational children, Piaget maintained, fail to comprehend the **one-to-one correspondence** that still exists among items in the two rows; that is, each element in a row can be mapped onto an element in the second row with none left over. Moreover, he believed that young children have not yet attained an understanding of two important aspects of number. The first is **cardinality**, or the total number of elements in a class—as in *six* red poker chips. The second is **ordinality**, the order in which an item appears in the set, as in the *second* poker chip. According to Piaget, the child must grasp both these concepts in order to judge two sets of items equivalent.

Many contemporary researchers believe that Piaget underestimated preschool children's understanding of number concepts. For example, two-year-olds will correctly point to a picture with three items, and not a picture with one item, when asked, "Can you show me the three fish?" (Wynn, 1992). By age four years, many children say number words in sequence and, in so doing, appreciate at least some basic principles of numerical relationships. Rochel Gelman and her associates have argued that even young children have knowledge of certain important fundamental principles of counting (Gelman & Gallistel, 1978; Gelman & Meck, 1983). Among these principles are (1) using the

**one-to-one correspondence** Understanding that two sets are equivalent in number if each element in one set can be mapped onto a unique element in the second set with none left over.

**cardinality** Principle that the last number in a set of counted numbers refers to the number of items in that set.

**ordinality** Principle that a number refers to an item's order within a set, as in the third finisher in a race.

same sequence of counting words when counting different sets; (2) employing only one counting word per object; (3) using the last counting word in the set to represent the total number; (4) understanding that any set of objects can be counted; and (5) appreciating that objects can be counted in any order.

Recent studies suggest that when young children count, their words are not empty of numerical meaning. In one experiment, three- and four-year-olds saw six dolls and five rings and were asked, "There are six dolls. Is there a ring for every doll?" Most of the four-year-olds used number words to answer questions about one-to-one correspondence. For example, many said, "No, because there are six dolls and five rings" (Becker, 1989). Similarly, many preschoolers spontaneously resort to counting when they encounter the following type of problem. Six dolls are arranged in a row. Two dolls are given two teddy bears each. If the rest of the dolls get two teddy bears each, the children are asked, how many teddy bears are needed? (Becker, 1993). In addition, children aged four years are able to compare quantities, answering correctly such questions as "Which is bigger, five or two?" (Siegler & Robinson, 1982). Thus, their understanding of number terms includes relations such as "larger" and "smaller." One interesting pattern, though, is that young children have more difficulty in making such comparisons when the numbers themselves are large (ten versus fourteen) or when the difference between two numbers is small (eight versus nine). The same is true when children have to add, subtract, and perform other calculations with numbers (Levine, Jordan, & Huttenlocher, 1992).

Once children enter school, of course, they are expected to master the formal properties of numbers through mathematics. Lauren Resnick (1986) believes that before children learn the systematic rules for addition, subtraction, algebra, and the like, they develop intuitive concepts about how numbers can be manipulated. How would Pitt, one of her seven-year-old subjects, add 152 and 149?

> I would have the two 100's, which equals 200. Then I would have 50 and the 40, which equals 90. So I have 290. Then plus the 9 from 49, and the 2 from the 52 equals 11. And then I add the 90 plus the 11 . . . equals 102. 102? 101. So I put the 200 and the 101, which equals 301. (p. 164)

All this came from a young boy who had mastered only first-grade arithmetic! Resnick suggests that the additive properties of numbers are relatively easy for children to understand, whereas relations, such as ratios, and transformations, such as algebraic expressions, are more difficult. Therefore it is not surprising that many children experience difficulties with mathematics beyond the early elementary school years. One way to ameliorate the difficulty might be to frame more complex mathematical operations in terms of simple additive properties, at least when they are first being learned.

Thus, young children understand a good deal about numbers and their usefulness in describing relations among objects. In the course of their cognitive development, children become more adept at dealing with larger quantities and manipulate numbers in more sophisticated ways, such as addition, subtraction, and other mathematical operations. Many of their intuitive understandings about the properties of numbers can help them as they learn the more formal aspects of quantitative relations.

## Spatial Relationships

From early infancy onward, children organize the objects in their world in still another way—according to relationships in space. Where does the toddler find his shoes or an enticing snack? Usually, the infant and young child have developed a mental picture of their homes and other familiar physical spaces to guide their search for missing objects or to reach a desired location. For the older child, spatial understanding extends to finding her way to school, grandparents' homes, or other more remote locations. As he did for many other areas of cognitive development, Piaget set forth some of the first hypotheses about the child's concepts of space, ideas that have been modified or enriched by later researchers.

During infancy, Piaget (1954) stated, the child's knowledge of space is based on her sensorimotor activities within that space. The child, for example, searches for objects by using *egocentric* frames of reference. That is, if a ball disappears under a couch or chair, the infant represents its location in relation to her own body ("to the left of my arm") rather than in relation to some other external object ("to the left of the door"). Only with the advent of symbolic ability at the end of the sensorimotor stage are children able to use frames of reference external to the self.

Many researchers have confirmed that children, in the absence of environmental cues, indeed rely on the positions of their own bodies in space to locate objects. For example, experimenters in one study hid an object under one of two covers situated to the left and right of their nine-month-old subjects. The infants readily learned to locate the item in one of the two positions, either to the right or to the left, depending on which training condition they were in. After the training trials, the children were shifted to the opposite side of the table, a 180-degree change in position. Now infants were unable to locate the hidden objects, a finding that suggests they were relying on the position of the object relative to their own bodies in order to find it (Bremner & Bryant, 1977). In an interesting modification, however, the investigator made the covers of the two hiding locations of distinctively different colors. Under these conditions, infants were able to locate the hidden toy even when they were moved to a different position around the table (Bremner, 1978). Thus, infants are *not* egocentric when other information is available to assist in finding objects.

After infancy, children quite literally reach out into the world for cues denoting spatial relationships. The ability to use **landmarks** denoting the physical locations of objects helps preschool-aged children find objects in larger spatial environments. Linda Acredolo and her colleagues demonstrated this skill in an experiment in which three- through eight-year-olds were taken on a walk through an unfamiliar building in one of two conditions (Acredolo, Pick, & Olsen, 1975). In the first condition, the hallway through which the experimenter led each subject contained two chairs. In the second, there were no chairs. The subjects saw the experimenter drop a set of keys during the walk with each child, and in the "landmark" condition this event occurred near one of the chairs. Later, when children were asked to retrieve the keys, performance was best in the "landmark" condition for the preschoolers; older children did well regardless of the experimental condition. Thus, prominent landmarks help younger children to encode specific locations within their spatial environment.

Alexander Siegel and his associates believe that knowledge about large-scale spaces proceeds from landmark knowledge to route mapping (Siegel, Kirasic, & Kail, 1978). **Route mapping** consists of knowledge about sequential directional changes that must take place as one negotiates a path through space, such as, "Take a left at the store, then a right at the traffic light." Children rely on this form of spatial representation during their early school years.

**landmark** Distinctive location or cue that the child uses to negotiate or represent a spatial environment.

**route mapping** Child's use of sequential directional changes to negotiate or represent a spatial environment.

▶ Roles of nature and nurture

▶ Interaction among domains

**configurational knowledge**
Child's use of landmarks and routes in integrated, holistic ways to represent physical space.

**perspective taking** Ability to take the role of another person and understand what that person is thinking, feeling, or knows, often with the purpose of solving some problem in communicating or interacting with that individual.

At age ten years or so, children display even more sophisticated spatial understanding, called **configurational knowledge**, which is the ability to represent landmarks and routes as integrated, holistic entities. They can draw reasonably accurate maps of their neighborhood or the spatial layout of their school (Anooshian & Young, 1981; Curtis, Siegel, & Furlong, 1981).

Developmental improvements in spatial knowledge are associated with the child's increasing familiarity with a given physical space. In the study conducted by Siegel and his associates, when kindergartners were walked through a model town several times, they were able to produce maps of the town as accurate as those of fifth-graders. Their ability to produce a mature spatial layout, one that required configurational representation, was enhanced simply by having experience with that physical space (Siegel, Kirasic, & Kail, 1978). Instructions to "look back" as the child is traversing a path can help, too. Twelve-year-olds (but not six-year-olds) who took a walk on an unfamiliar university campus were better able to find their way back to their starting point if they were periodically reminded to "turn around and look where we came from" (Cornell, Heth, & Rowat, 1992).

In summary, young children initially locate objects in space by using simple cues, especially the position of objects relative to their own bodies. Gradually, their spatial representations include more discrete elements, especially cues that are external to the self such as landmarks, and their representations become better integrated. Why does spatial knowledge develop in this way? A likely explanation is that the child's growing attentional and memory skills contribute to the ability to process, retain, and integrate more numerous physical cues.

## *Understanding Psychological States*

Our knowledge extends beyond understanding of physical objects, classes, number, and space. It also includes an awareness of our mind and how it and the minds of others work. How do children understand and judge the motives, feelings, needs, interests, capacities, and thoughts of playmates, siblings, parents, and others? And how and when do children come to understand and reflect on the psychological states of the self? This type of cognition, thinking about the self and its relationship to the social world, is called *social cognition*. In comparison to the world of physical objects and events, thinking about the social world presents unique challenges to the developing child. People may act unpredictably; their feelings and moods, and even their appearances, may shift. Just how children piece together their understanding of social experiences has been the focus of several lines of research.

### Perspective Taking: Taking the Role of Others

**Perspective taking** is the ability to put oneself in another person's place, to consider that person's thoughts, feelings, or knowledge in order to interact with him more effectively. We have already seen one aspect of perspective taking in Chapter 7, which examined developmental differences in communicating with another person. To successfully explain something to another person, the child must have knowledge of the other's background and abilities. By "putting oneself in another's shoes," a child can also more effectively assist or support that person. When and how does this ability develop in young children?

**What Do Others See? Visual Perspective Taking**    One basic element of perspective taking is understanding what others see. For example, does the child realize that his sister, standing across the room, cannot see the brightly colored pictures in the book he is eagerly examining? In 1956, Jean Piaget and Barbel Inhelder published a classic experiment illustrating children's limited knowledge of the visual perspective of others. Children seated in front of three different papier-mâché mountains (see Figure 8.6) were asked to indicate what a doll would see in viewing the array from various locations. Four- to six-year-olds showed considerable *egocentrism* in their responses; they typically indicated that the doll's view would be identical to their own. By six to nine years of age, children began to realize the doll's perspective would be different, although they still had difficulty figuring out what the doll would actually see. Nine- and ten-year-olds were able to determine the doll's perspective accurately. More recent research has shown that the difficulty of the doll and mountain task may have led Piaget and Inhelder to underestimate children's role-taking competence. When simpler visual arrays or familiar everyday scenes are used, or when the method of interviewing children is simplified, three- and four-year-olds can answer some of these kinds of questions reasonably well (Borke, 1975; Newcombe & Huttenlocher, 1992).

John Flavell and his colleagues have identified two levels of visual perspective-taking skill in children (Flavell, 1978; Lempers, Flavell, & Flavell, 1977).

**FIGURE 8.6**

**Visual Perspective Taking**

How well can children adopt another person's visual perspective? Piaget asked this question by seating a child at a table (in location 1) containing three "mountains" of different size and color, then asking the child how the scene would look to a doll (or another person) seated at other locations (locations 2 and 3) around the table. Piaget found that preschoolers often chose a view similar to their own. More recent research indicates that preschoolers can be more successful with this task when familiar and easily distinguishable scenes are used.

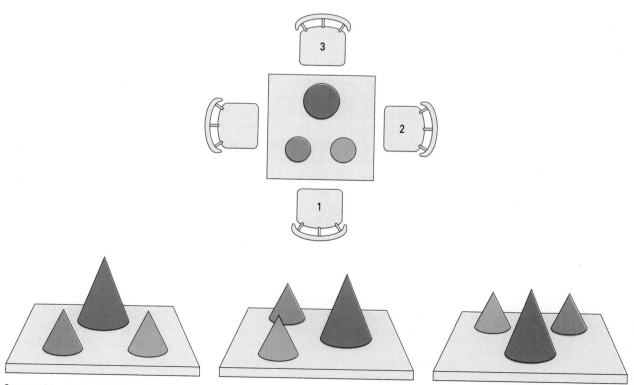

Source: Adapted from Phillips, 1975.

At the first level, from late infancy until about three years, children realize that their own and another's view are not identical. Thirty-month-olds, for example, acknowledge that an object they can see, but screened from another person, will be visible only to themselves. Toddlers may even adjust pictures or objects to help others see them more easily (Flavell, Shipstead, & Croft, 1978). Thus, very young children recognize a different visual perspective for others.

A second, more advanced level of visual perspective taking appears in three- and four-year-olds and continues to be refined for several years thereafter. Now children begin to succeed in determining the *specific* limitations of another's view. Four-year-olds, for example, can say whether an object seen by another will look right side up (Masangkay et al., 1974). They also realize that a view of one portion of an animal may not provide enough cues to allow someone else to determine what the animal is *doing* but, until age six, believe others will have little difficulty *identifying* the animal even if only a few ambiguous details are visible (Taylor, 1988). Throughout the early school years children become increasingly proficient at determining how the relationships among specific features of a complex array will change when viewed from several perspectives (Rosser, 1983). These advances reflect cognitive gains both in differentiating oneself from another and in knowledge of space and spatial relationships (Shantz, 1983).

**What Do Others Think? Conceptual Perspective Taking**     To interact effectively with others, children must learn that friends, family members, and classmates not only see things in other ways than their own, but also have different kinds of knowledge about things. What evidence exists for developmental differences in children's conceptualizations of the thoughts and cognitions of others? Several lines of research have provided answers to this question.

One simple illustration comes from research on *privileged information*. The typical procedure in these experiments is to provide facts to the child that are unavailable to another and then to observe whether the child is aware of the discrepancy. In one study, two- to six-year-olds watched a film of a boy seated at a table (Mossler, Marvin, & Greenberg, 1976). The accompanying sound track described how much the boy wanted to have a cookie. Children then viewed the film again, this time with their mothers. For the second showing, however, the sound track was turned off. Asked if their mothers knew the boy wanted a cookie, children two to four years of age had difficulty realizing their mothers would not know. But children between four and six years of age recognized that their mother did not have this information. By this age, then, children begin making a distinction between what they and others know.

In another line of research, John Flavell studied children's emerging ability to understand the *recursive* nature of thought (Flavell, Miller, & Miller, 1993; Flavell et al., 1968; Miller, Kessel, & Flavell, 1970). Recursive events refer to those that can take place repeatedly, perhaps indefinitely, over a series of steps. Thought is considered to be recursive because we can reflect on the possibility that others are thinking about what we are thinking, and so on, through many levels of "you're thinking that I'm thinking. . . ." Figure 8.7 illustrates an example of a one-loop recursion ("The boy is thinking that the girl is thinking of her father") and a two-loop recursion ("The boy is thinking that the girl is thinking of the father thinking of the mother").

Throughout the elementary school years, children's responses hint at an increasing understanding of the recursive nature of thought. Flavell found, how-

ONE-LOOP RECURSION        TWO-LOOP RECURSION

Source: Adapted from Miller, Kessel, & Flavell, 1970.

**FIGURE 8.7**

**How Recursive Thinking Develops**

Children often have difficulty with complex levels of recursive thinking. In this one-loop example, they must understand that "the boy is thinking that the girl is thinking of father" and in the two-loop example, that "the boy is thinking that the girl is thinking of the father thinking of the mother." Recursive thought continues to improve into adolescence, an indication that advanced levels of perspective taking probably require abstract and hypothetical reasoning available only to individuals capable of formal operational thought.

ever, that many children have difficulty understanding the sophisticated level of reasoning required in this process. For example, only about half the children at eleven years of age grasped a one-loop recursion, and about a third of eleven-year-olds understood two-loop recursions. This knowledge improves well into adolescence and may depend upon the more abstract and hypothetical reasoning associated with formal operational thought (Shantz, 1983).

In still another approach, Robert Selman has proposed a model of perspective taking that emphasizes an orderly sequence of development in which role-taking undergoes qualitative shifts from one age to the next (Selman, 1976, 1980; Selman & Byrne, 1974). To formulate this model Selman used children's responses to social dilemmas describing two individuals in conflict. Here is an example:

> Holly is an eight-year-old girl who likes to climb trees. She is the best tree climber in the neighborhood. One day while climbing down from a tall tree she falls off the bottom branch but does not hurt herself. Her father sees her fall. He is upset and asks her to promise not to climb trees any more. Holly promises.
>
> Later that day, Holly and her friends meet Sean. Sean's kitten is caught up in a tree and cannot get down. Something has to be done right away or the kitten may fall. Holly is the only one who climbs trees well enough to reach the kitten and get it down, but she remembers her promise to her father. (Selman & Byrne, 1974, p. 805)

▶ Development as continuous/discontinuous

| Level | Features | Typical Responses to the Story of Holly |
|---|---|---|
| **0** *Egocentric Role Taking* (about 3–6 years) | The child has little understanding of another's point of view; the child's perspective extends to everyone else. | If child concludes Holly will rescue the kitten, other characters in the story, including the father, are assumed to approve of the action. "She will save the kitten because she doesn't want the kitten to die"; if her father finds out he will be "Happy, he likes kittens" (p. 305). If the punitive consequences of breaking a promise to the father are brought to the child's attention, he may decide Holly would not save the kitten after all; the child fails to grasp the discrepancy in his conflicting responses. |
| **1** *Subjective or Differentiated Perspective* (about 6–8 years) | The child realizes that others may have another perspective but thinks all will agree if everyone has the same information and has difficulty anticipating disagreements and resolving any conflicts that remain. | The child who says Holly should climb the tree realizes her father might get angry, but only if she fails to tell him about the good reason for climbing the tree. She thinks that as long as both Holly and her father have the same information, they will arrive at similar evaluations of the situation. "If he didn't know why she climbed the tree, he would be angry. But if Holly tells him why she did it, he would realize she has a good reason" (p. 304). |
| **2** *Self-reflective Role Taking* (about 8–10 years) | In addition to realizing that others may have different perspectives, the child also becomes aware that they can appreciate his perspective. Thus, the child understands that two perspectives may differ even though the same information is available to both of them. One consequence is that the child can begin to anticipate the reactions of others to his behaviors. He still, however, cannot consider his own and others' perspectives simultaneously. | The child might respond to Holly's dilemma by saying her father will understand Holly's feelings and will not punish her. By making such a claim, the child recognizes that Holly and her father can have different perspectives. "The father may think breaking a promise is worse, but he'd understand that Holly thinks saving the kitten's life is more important" (p. 305). Although the child realizes Holly's father will be unhappy, he is still unable to consider how that conflicting perspective might need to be resolved in a way that is fair for both Holly and her father. |
| **3** *Mutual Role Taking* (about 10–12 years) | The child begins to appreciate the recursive and embedded nature of thinking about others. Both self and others can be viewed mutually and simultaneously. | Now the child is able to consider the views of both Holly and her father at the same time. He describes Holly's and her father's positions from the vantage point of a neutral person. |
| **4** *Societal and In-depth Role Taking* (about 12–15 years) | Social conventions are seen as a means of attempting to resolve the dilemma. Different values are respected, but if the dispute remains unresolved, the values of the larger social or cultural group or "generalized other" become the arbiter. | The child explaining Holly's rationale for retrieving the kitten might make reference to society's beliefs concerning humaneness to animals or assisting neighbors in times of difficulty. Alternatively, if the child says that Holly elected not to climb the tree, she might refer to the importance of honoring and respecting adult authority and demands. |

Source: Based on Selman, 1976.

**TABLE 8.2**

**Selman's Stages of Social Perspective Taking**

Holly has promised her father that she will not climb trees any more. But she is the only person able to climb a tree to get a kitten that is caught in it. This table summarizes the perspectives that children at different ages take in attempting to resolve this kind of conflict.

After listening to this story, children were asked the following kinds of questions: Does Holly know how Sean feels about the kitten? How will Holly's father feel if he finds out she climbed the tree? What does Holly think her father will do if he finds out that she climbed the tree?

Based on children's responses to these dilemmas, Selman distinguished five levels or stages of role-taking ability (see Table 8.2). Children approximately three to six years of age are either unable to recognize that others have a different perspective or, if able to do so, have little desire to maintain the distinction between their own and the other's perspective. On the other hand, children from six to eight years of age begin to recognize that people with different information or other responsibilities may have dissimilar thoughts and feelings about a situation. Children this age, however, continue to have difficulty anticipating viewpoints that conflict with their own. Around eight to ten years of age, children realize that others are able to think about the child's perspective. Thus, they are becoming aware of one-loop recursions in thought, anticipating how others will think about their actions. Still, the perspectives of self and others are not considered simultaneously or from a neutral, third-party position. This capacity emerges at the next stage, sometime between ten and twelve years of age. Now children can step outside the situation to consider several points of view at the same time. Finally, adolescents consider the views of the larger society and bring them to bear upon the dilemma. The teenager can take the group perspective and recognizes that conflicts and problems need to be resolved in ways that satisfy the society at large.

Research provides some support for Selman's developmental model. For example, when researchers tested forty-one first- to sixth-grade boys two and five years later, all children showed increases in their level of responding over the period (see Figure 8.8) (Gurucharri & Selman, 1982). Only eight boys failed to advance at least one full level in five years, and only one child showed a decline in responding at any time during testing. Other research shows that children progressively advance to higher levels without skipping previous ones (Selman, 1980; Selman & Byrne, 1974), furnishing additional evidence for the claim that perspective taking undergoes invariant stagelike advances during childhood.

What factors play a significant role in explaining the development of perspective taking? Research shows that performance on Piagetian conservation tasks is associated with the development of perspective-taking skill. Children unable to think at a concrete operational level typically fall at the lowest level in Selman's model (Keating & Clark, 1980; Krebs & Gilmore, 1982). We are uncertain, however, whether reversibility or other aspects of concrete and formal operational thought account for advances in perspective-taking skills (Shantz, 1983). Furthermore, we cannot rule out possible contributions from other factors (Higgins & Parsons, 1983). Why not? Because numerous changes take place in children's environments that can affect their role-taking activities. As a child develops, her roles expand to include pupil as well as daughter, athlete, musician, playmate, leader, or follower among her peers. These expanding opportunities to participate in social interactions with others are likely to foster developmental changes in perspective-taking ability.

▶ Interaction among domains

## The Child's Theory of Mind

Children's understanding of their social world extends beyond perspective-taking skills. Emerging as part of their competencies is an expanding and in-

## FIGURE 8.8

### Improvements in Perspective Taking

Children in first grade who were evaluated on their social perspective-taking ability showed substantially higher levels of performance over a five-year period between testing at time 1 and time 3, as the results shown here indicate. Each line in the graph shows the performance of an individual child. Similar changes were observed for children in the second through sixth grades. In fact, only one child showed a measurable decline in performance over testing intervals. Failure to find many regressions and other evidence to indicate that children do not skip levels provide support for Selman's claim that perspective taking progresses through qualitatively different stages of development.

▶ Interaction among domains

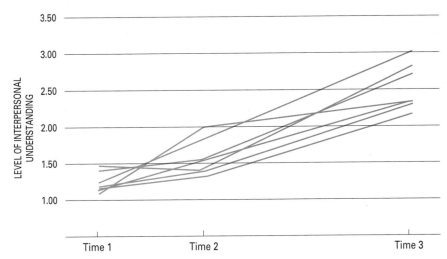

Source: Adapted from Gurucharri & Selman, 1982.

realism   The inability to distinguish between mental and physical entities.

creasingly coherent appreciation of the kinds of mental qualities that contribute to the behavior of self and others. Did the playmate who broke a favorite toy *intend* to do the damage? Might Dad feel *angry* when he sees the broken pieces of his new coffee mug? Would a close friend *believe* that Mom will not let them go to the park alone? Many of our social behaviors are guided by the judgments and inferences we make about the desires, feeling states, beliefs, and thoughts of other people (Astington, Harris, & Olson, 1988; Wellman, 1990). In fact, it would be rare to *not* be concerned with the mental states of others in the normal course of interactions with them.

When do children become aware of the concept of mental states, their own and those of others? How are these ideas acquired and how do they change with development? Once again, Piaget has provided much of the impetus for research on this topic. His position was quite clear. As Piaget put it, "The child knows nothing about the nature of thought . . ." (Piaget, 1929, p. 37). Dubbing this characteristic of children **realism**, Piaget maintained that children are not capable of distinguishing between mental and physical entities until the school years. To the child under the age of eight, dreams and mental images are as real as any event in waking, conscious life. To the same child, thinking is a behavior produced by the body, usually, the mouth or the head; physical and mental acts are one and the same.

Despite Piaget's strong claims, developmental researchers have uncovered considerable evidence to the contrary. By age three, children readily distinguish between mental and physical entities, and after that age, show further developments in their understanding of their own mental states and those of others (Flavell, 1993). Children apparently have a well-articulated "theory of mind" by the time they are ready to enter school.

In one experiment, for example, three-year-olds were told stories such as the following: "Judy doesn't have a kitty, but right now she is thinking about a kitty." Could they see or touch the kitty? Could the kitty be seen by someone else or touched at some time in the future? Children had no problem in identifying this as a mental event, one in which the kitty could not be seen or touched. In contrast, when they heard other stories, as in "Judy had a kitty," they correctly stated that these real events could be seen and touched (Wellman & Estes, 1986). Other research indicates that by twenty-eight months of age, children realize when others are engaged in pretend or "make-believe" activity (Harris et al., 1991; Harris & Kavanaugh, 1993).

Young children also understand the meaning of specific mental states. Three-year-olds understand the concepts of "desire" and "pretend," although they still have difficulty with the concept of "belief" (Lillard & Flavell, 1992). The typical "false belief" task, used to assess children's understanding of "belief," proceeds as follows. Children are shown a doll named Maxi who puts some chocolate in a cupboard and leaves the scene. Maxi's mother moves the chocolate to a new location. When Maxi returns, children are asked, "Where will he look for the chocolate?" Most three-year-olds say in the new location. Four-year-olds, though, recognize that Maxi holds a "false belief" and will look for the chocolate in the cupboard (Wimmer & Perner, 1983). Similarly, three-year-olds have some difficulty understanding that their own past beliefs may not be the same as their current beliefs; four-year-olds no longer have this difficulty (Gopnik & Slaughter, 1991; Wellman, 1990).

Why do younger children have difficulty with the "false belief" task? Perhaps they fail to understand that beliefs, which are mental states, need not match external reality. But quickly over the next year, that realization becomes part of the child's cognitive repertoire. In fact, this may be a very significant cognitive transition for all children (Flavell, 1988). Children from several cultures including China, Japan, and the preliterate Baka society of Cameroon show similar developmental changes in their understanding of "beliefs" (Avis & Harris, 1991; Flavell et al., 1983; Gardner et al., 1988). A provocative possibility, if there is indeed a universal pattern in the emergence of the "theory of mind," is that this concept may have distinct biological roots.

▶ Roles of nature and nurture

## CONTROVERSY: THINKING IT OVER

### Is Childhood Autism the Failure to Develop a Theory of Mind?

Childhood autism is a puzzling disorder affecting about one or two of every one thousand children born. The disorder, more common among boys than girls, is characterized by the child's preference to be alone, poor eye contact and general lack of social skills, oftentimes the absence of meaningful language, and a preference for sameness and for elaborate routines. Some autistic children show unusual skills, such as being able to recite lengthy passages from memory, put together complex jigsaw puzzles, or create intricate drawings. Often, these children will show a fascination with spinning objects or repeating the speech patterns of someone else. The hallmark trait, though, is the lack of contact these children have with the social world, starting at an early age. Kanner's (1943) description of one autistic boy captures the syndrome well: "He seems almost to draw into his shell and live within himself" (p. 218).

Since Leo Kanner first identified this psychopathology, numerous causes of autism have been proposed, ranging from deprived early emotional relationships with parents to defective neurological wiring in the brain. An intriguing suggestion recently put forth by a team of researchers is that autistic children,

Researchers have found that between two and three years of age, children understand the meaning of certain mental states, such as "pretend."

for biological reasons, lack the ability to think about mental states. That is, they lack a "theory of mind" that most children begin to develop during the preschool years. Consider how autistic children behave in one standard task testing the child's theory of mind. As in the "false belief" task described above, children are told a story about Sally and Anne, represented by puppets, who are playing together. Sally puts a marble in a basket and leaves the room. Anne moves the marble to a box. Sally returns. Where will Sally look for her marble? Normal children, at age four, typically state that Sally will look in the basket, realizing that Sally does not have the same information that they have. In contrast, most nine-year-old autistic children tested with this problem still think Sally would look in the box (Baron-Cohen, Tager-Flusberg, & Cohen, 1993; Frith, 1993). These results indicate that the autistic children could not conceptualize the mental state of another individual. Autistic children, the argument proceeds, have severe deficits in communication and social interaction precisely because they cannot appreciate what the contents of another person's mind might be.

But this may not be the whole story, according to other researchers. True, autistic children may have a cognitive deficit, but this deficit is different from a failure to develop a theory of mind. Claire Hughes and James Russell (1993) included autistic children in a task involving three boxes, each with a transparent window. A candy was placed in one of the boxes while the child and an "opponent" in the game closed their eyes. Then, the child, who could see through the box's window though his opponent could not, was asked to tell the opponent which box contained the candy. He was also told that by misleading the opponent, he could obtain the candy for himself. Autistic children persistently "gave away the secret," telling the opponent exactly where the candy was, even if this meant the opponent got to keep the candy for twenty trials. This finding, of course, is exactly what would be predicted according to those

**4–9 MONTHS**   Develops object concept.
Notices events containing physical causality.
Relies primarily on own body, but also simple landmark cues to locate objects in space.

**12–18 MONTHS**   Classifies objects according to physical similarities.

**18–30 MONTHS**   Classifies according to thematic and simple taxonomic relations.
Understands the meaning of simple number terms.
Realizes others can have different visual perspectives.
Distinguishes between animate and inanimate objects.
Begins to understand "pretend" and "make-believe."

**3–4 YEARS**   Understands basic principles of counting.
Uses landmarks to negotiate spatial environments.
Is aware of specific limitations in visual perspectives of others.
Begins to consider privileged information.
Develops a "theory of mind."

**7–9 YEARS**   Classifies according to superordinate relations.
Displays intuitive concepts about numbers.
Uses route mapping to represent spatial environments.

**10 YEARS**   Shows configurational knowledge in spatial relations.
Can consider own and the perspective of others simultaneously.

This chart describes the sequence of cognitive development based on the findings of research. Children often show individual differences in the exact ages at which they display the various developmental achievements outlined here.

who claim autistic children lack a "theory of mind." In another condition, though, there was no opponent in the game; if the child told the experimenter which box contained the candy, the candy simply went into a pile. Only if the child pointed to the wrong box did the child get the candy. Autistic children still persisted in pointing to the box that contained the candy—even when there was not another "mind" or person to try to understand. Thus, Hughes and Russell concluded that the essential problem for autistic children is their inability to disengage attention from the target object.

What *are* the primary differences between autistic and normal children? Is there a way to tease apart whether it is the absence of a theory of mind or a deficit in controlling attention? Given these two hypotheses, what are the implications for treatment? Finally, are there still other cognitive mechanisms that might explain these observations of autistic children? For example, some researchers have proposed that problems in retrieving information from memory (Boucher, 1981) or problems in processing social meaning (Rutter, 1983) are responsible. Are these hypotheses also plausible? ■

# Neo-Piagetian Approaches

We have seen throughout this chapter how Piaget's theory and observations of children have sparked a wealth of research on cognitive development. The major achievements described in this chapter are outlined in the Chronology on page 319. We have noted that some of Piaget's ideas, such as the active participation of the child in the construction of her own knowledge, have been widely and enthusiastically embraced. Other central tenets of his theory have met with more skepticism. For example, just how broad and general are the features of a child's thinking within a given stage of development? Or does cognitive development proceed in a more "modular" fashion, proceeding rapidly in some domains and more slowly in others? Put another way, does cognitive development proceed in a *domain-general* or *domain-specific* way?

Several researchers have modified and expanded Piaget's theory to address some of these criticisms. Because their ideas build on those initially proposed by Piaget, these psychologists are often called neo-Piagetians. Like Piaget, neo-Piagetians believe that children show distinct—even stagelike—advances in general thinking skills, probably because of maturation. They also agree that what the child knows at a given time heavily influences what he will be able to learn and think about. Neo-Piagetians, though, are much more willing than Piaget to acknowledge the role that specific experiences have in shaping the child's knowledge in a given area (Flavell, 1992).

## Fischer's Skill Theory

▶ Development as
continuous/discontinuous

▶ Roles of nature and nurture

▶ Individual differences

Kurt Fischer, like Piaget, proposes that the emergence of general, broad thinking skills contribute to cognitive development (1980; Fischer & Pipp, 1984; Fischer & Farrar, 1988). These are organized into four stages or "tiers"—reflex, sensorimotor, representational, and abstract. Unlike Piaget, though, Fischer adds that within the same individual, skills may develop more rapidly in some domains—say numerical understanding or classifying familiar objects—than others, depending on the child's experiences. The child who is given ample access to art materials but not to math problems, for example, may show greater skill in the first area than the second.

In Fischer's theory, skills are similar to Piaget's schemes: mental structures that stem from action. In contrast to schemes, however, which are highly generalized structures, skills are more specific to particular objects and tasks. If the environment supports a variety of skills, development in all skills will proceed relatively evenly. Fischer suggests, however, that uniform access to skill development is unlikely. At any one time in development, most children show different levels of skill depending on the domain, be it numerical reasoning, spatial understanding, classification of objects, and so forth. Specific skills used in limited contexts eventually become more powerful and are used in more generalized contexts (Fischer & Bidell, 1991). By emphasizing the emergence of separate skills that are heavily dependent on the specific experiences available to the child, Fischer offers a picture of development that is more continuous and gradual than proposed by Piaget.

## Case's Theory

Robbie Case (1985, 1992) has also built on many Piagetian ideas. Case proposes four stages of development similar to those outlined by Piaget. Case's theory differs most notably from Piaget's, however, in terms of its explanation of transitions from one stage to the next. Case proposes that infants begin life with certain innate, but limited, capacities and attentional resources. Through both maturation and sensorimotor practice, the infant's actions gradually become more efficient and automatic, eventually permitting a child to think about as well as to act upon these objects and entities, and still later to integrate information about their dimensions, features, and qualities to solve problems.

▶ Development as continuous/discontinuous
▶ Roles of nature and nurture

Beyond infancy, the increasing efficiency of cognitive *operations*, processes such as identifying stimuli and recognizing relationships among them, paves the way for greater memory capacity. If a substantial amount of mental effort is expended on identifying or recognizing stimuli, fewer resources are available for storage and retention of information. Conversely, as children become more proficient at identifying letters, colors, and other features of stimuli, they will have more resources available for remembering. A simple experiment illustrates how these principles work. Three- and six-year-olds were asked to perform two tasks—repeat a list of words one at a time as fast as possible and then recall those same lists of words. Children who were quick to repeat the words had better memory scores than children who were slower at repetition (Case, Kurland, & Goldberg, 1982). As operational efficiency increased with development, more cognitive resources were available for remembering.

According to Case, increases in the ability of children to process information quickly are tied to maturational changes in the nervous system as well as to practice with various cognitive activities. One important physiological change that occurs through adolescence is the *myelinization* of areas of the cortex that control alertness and higher-order thinking processes (Yakovlev & Lecours, 1967). Because myelinization is responsible for speeding neural transmissions, it is plausible that this process is related to the increasing speed of cognitive processing. Practice also helps. The more times the child identifies numbers, words, or other stimuli, the more facile she will become in this activity. As a result of practice and experience, children develop *central conceptual structures* that guide their performance in specific domains, such as numerical or spatial reasoning. As you will see in Chapter 9, many of the ideas proposed by Case draw from another theoretical school of cognitive development—the information-processing perspective.

▶ Interaction among domains

▶ Roles of nature and nurture

---

## THEMES IN DEVELOPMENT

### COGNITION: PIAGETIAN PERSPECTIVES

▶ **What roles do nature and nurture play in cognitive development?**

A central tenet of Piaget's theory is that maturation, in conjunction with experience, is responsible for the child's cognitive growth. Neo-Piagetian theorists echo the same theme. Thus, the interaction between nature and nurture is central in these theories. When we examine the child's concept development, we may find that certain natural domains offer the child "privileged relationships" to learn about. The role of nature is implicated here. At the same time, studies of concept formation in different cultures suggest that experiences, like formal schooling, also play a role in determining whether children will display specific kinds of classification skills.

▶ **How does the sociocultural context influence cognitive development?**

Piaget's theory emphasizes the universal cognitive attainments of all children, regardless of their cultural background. However, research has shown that the sociocultural context cannot be ignored. For example, not all children in all cultures attain formal operational thought. We have also seen that children with formal schooling employ taxonomic classification more frequently than unschooled children and that theories about biological kinds may be influenced by cultural beliefs.

▶ **How does the child play an active role in the process of cognitive development?**

A central assumption in Piaget's theory of cognitive development is that the child actively organizes cognitive schemes and knowledge to more effectively adapt to the demands of the environment. In fact, this idea, a cornerstone of Piaget's work, is widely accepted by developmental psychologists of different theoretical persuasions.

▶ **Is cognitive development continuous or discontinuous?**

The extent to which cognitive advances are stage-determined is an issue that remains to be resolved. Piaget, of course, stressed stagelike attainments in thinking. Others who have empirically reevaluated his work make claims for more continuous changes in cognition in their focus on the underlying basic processes that contribute to development. This latter view will be more fully elaborated in the next chapter.

▶ **How prominent are individual differences in cognitive development?**

Piaget emphasized the common features of thought displayed by all children. His explicit goal was to explain the general characteristics of cognition as children moved from the sensorimotor through formal operational stages of development. Although Piaget acknowledged that some children might reach a given stage earlier or later than others, his main concern was not with individual differences among children. Others, including the neo-Piagetians, argue that children may show greater or lesser abilities within particular domains, depending on the specific experiences they are exposed to. Thus, there may be substantial individual differences in cognitive development among children of similar ages.

▶ **How does cognitive development interact with development in other domains?**

The child's emergent cognitive skills interface with almost every other aspect of development. For example, a child's decreasing cognitive egocentrism will affect his ability to make judgments in perspective-taking tasks, which have important social ramifications. By the same token, development in other domains can influence cognitive growth. For example, cognition may be affected by maturation of the central nervous system, which is hypothesized to contribute to the development of the speed and efficiency of cognitive processing. The child's thinking is thus both the product of, as well as a contributor to, development in many other domains.

## *Summary*

**Piaget's Theory of Cognitive Development**     One of the most comprehensive theories of cognitive development was proposed by Jean Piaget. Piaget championed the active role of the child in the construction of knowledge and the transformation of cognitive schemes as a result of maturation combined with experience. Piaget believed that development proceeded from *sensorimotor*, through *preoperational, concrete operational*, and *formal operational* stages. The child's thought in each stage has unique characteristics, beginning with the action-based schemes of the sensorimotor stage and progressing to the symbolic, then logical, and finally abstract thought of succeeding stages. Challenges to Piaget's theory have focused on whether his description of the ages of acquisition of cognitive skills is accurate, whether development is indeed stagelike, and whether there are alternative explanations for the behaviors he observed among children.

**Concept Development**     An important area of cognitive development is the emergence of concepts. Infants have a good grasp of the *object concept* and preliminary notions of the concept of physical causality. One-year-olds begin to group items together on the basis of perceptual similarities, and slightly older children rely on thematic and taxonomic relations. By age seven, children are able to employ more complex hierarchical relations as they sort objects. Similarly, children show an awareness of the concept of numbers before starting school, and later develop an intuitive understanding of mathematical operations such as addition. The development of spatial concepts begins with the child's use of *landmarks* and proceeds to *route mapping* and *configurational knowledge*. Spatial knowledge is related to the child's ability to select useful landmarks and familiarity with a given physical space.

**Understanding Psychological States**     Children begin to show *perspective taking* during the preschool years, and this ability improves in successive years. Selman offers an alternative to Piaget in describing the development of perspective-taking skills. A related achievement is the child's acquisition of a "theory of mind," an understanding of the difference between mental and physical states as well as what is meant by mental concepts such as "belief" and "desire." This understanding is fairly well formed before children start school.

**Neo-Piagetian Approaches**     Fischer and Case have expanded and modified Piaget's original ideas to include the possibility that achievements within specific domains are an integral part of cognitive development. Fischer emphasizes the development of skills in specific domains, while Case describes the impact of greater cognitive efficiency on thinking as a whole.

# 9

## Cognition:

### The Information-Processing Approach

▶ **What roles do nature and nurture play in cognitive development?**

▶ **How does the sociocultural context influence cognitive development?**

▶ **How does the child play an active role in the process of cognitive development?**

▶ **Is cognitive development continuous or discontinuous?**

▶ **How prominent are individual differences in cognitive development?**

▶ **How does cognitive development interact with development in other domains?**

*"Tomorrow's science test is going to be really tough," Nate lamented to his friend on the way home from school. "I should have paid more attention in class and kept up with my reading assignments. Now I have to study so much material!" Normally a good student, Nate had been preoccupied with the success of his baseball team. Now there was a price to be paid as he prepared for the next day's test. Nate knew one "trick" for remembering the colors of the spectrum— just think "ROY G. BIV" for red, orange, yellow, green, blue, indigo, and violet. And to remember about wavelengths, he could visualize the long red rays stretching out from the sun like a person's hair and the short violet ones forming the stubble of the sun's beard. But there was so much more to remember. Maybe he could just repeat the main ideas over and over to himself. One thing he knew for sure—next time he would not save all of his studying for the night before the test.*

Nate, as it turns out, had a pretty good understanding of his mental capabilities. He knew that paying attention in class was helpful and that certain techniques like rehearsal, mental imagery, and other "tricks" could help him remember information. He also knew that there were limits to what he could accomplish in the few hours he had to prepare for his exam. In fact, many aspects of Nate's own thinking—attention, memory, even the fact that he could evaluate his thought capabilities—have been topics of great interest for developmental psychologists. As Nate rightly surmised, attention *is* important in the attainment of knowledge, and although there *are* limits to one's memory capabilities, there are also techniques that can be used to improve memory performance.

In this chapter, we continue our examination of cognitive development, this time from an important alternative to the Piagetian approach, the information-processing perspective. First, we will summarize the major features of this theoretical model. Next we will survey several topics that have been studied extensively from the viewpoint of information-processing theory including attention, memory, and problem solving. Finally, we close this chapter with a consideration of how the child's sociocultural environment affects cognitive development, paying close attention to the special role that parents and teachers might play in this process.

# The Information-Processing Approach

As we saw in Chapter 2, information-processing theorists believe that human cognition is best understood as the management of information through a system with limited space or resources. In the information-processing approach, mental processing is usually broken down into several components or levels of activity. For example, memory processes are often partitioned into *encoding, storage,* and *retrieval* phases. Moreover, information is assumed to move forward through the system in time and each stage of processing is of some duration (Massaro & Cowan, 1993; Palmer & Kimchi, 1986).

Many traditional information-processing models are called **multistore models** because they posit several mental structures through which information flows sequentially, much as data pass through a computer. Most multistore models distinguish between psychological structures and control processes. Psychological *structures,* as we saw in Chapter 2, are analogous to the "hardware" of a computer and typically include (1) a *sensory store,* which holds new information in essentially raw form, like an echo or an enduring visual image, for very brief periods of time; (2) *memory stores* (often separated into *working memory* and *long-term memory*), which retain information for seconds, minutes, or even years; (3) a *central processor* that oversees and coordinates the components in the system; and (4) a *response system* that allows the individual to produce an answer to a problem or question. The *control processes* are mental activities that move information from one structure to another, much like "software" functions for the computer.

Suppose someone asks you to repeat a list of words: shoe, car, truck, hat, coat, bus. If you have paid attention to all of the words and have "input" them like a well-functioning computer into your cognitive system, the first stage of processing would take place in the **sensory store**. Information is held here for a fraction of a second in a form very close to the audible sounds in which you experienced it. Next, the words may move to the memory stores. The first is **working memory** (often also called *short-term store*), which holds information for no more than a couple of minutes. If you were to repeat the words over and over to yourself in an attempt to rehearse them, you would be employing a control process to retain information in working memory. You might also use **long-term memory**, the repository of more enduring information, and notice that the items belong to two categories, clothing and vehicles. The central processor, which functions like an executive decision maker, oversees this communication among the structures of the information-processing system. Finally, when you are asked to say the words aloud, your response system functions to help you reproduce the sounds you heard moments earlier.

Other theorists in this field have advanced a **limited-resource model** of the cognitive system that emphasizes a finite amount of available cognitive energy that can be deployed in numerous ways, but only with certain tradeoffs. Unlike multistore models, limited-resource models put their emphasis on the allocation of energy for various cognitive activities rather than on the mental structures themselves. The basic assumption is that the pool of resources available for processing, retaining, and reporting information is finite (Bjorklund & Harnishfeger, 1990). In one such model, introduced in Chapter 8, Robbie Case proposes an inverse relationship between the amount of space available for operating on information and that available for storage (Case, 1985; Case, Kurland, & Goldberg, 1982). *Operations,* as we have seen, include processes such as identifying the stimuli and recognizing relationships among

**multistore model** Information-processing model that describes a sequence of mental structures through which information flows.

**sensory store** Memory store that holds information for very brief periods of time in a form that closely resembles the initial input.

**working memory** Short-term memory store in which mental operations such as rehearsal and categorization take place.

**long-term memory** Memory that holds information for extended periods of time.

**limited-resource model** Information-processing model that emphasizes the allocation of finite energy within the cognitive system.

them; *storage* refers to the retention of information for use at a later time. If a substantial amount of mental effort is expended on operations, less space is available for storage or retention.

Similarly, Robert Kail (1986, 1991a, 1991b) proposes that a central component of cognitive development is an increase in processing speed with age. As children grow older, they can mentally rotate images, name objects, or add numbers more rapidly. More resources then become available for other cognitive tasks.

In the simple memory experiment we just examined, the effort used to identify the words and notice the categorical relationships among them will determine the space left over for storing those words. If we are proficient or very fast at recognizing words and their relationships, storage space will be available. If these tasks cost us substantial effort, however, our resources will be taxed and little will be left for the task of remembering.

How do these two general information-processing frameworks, the multi-store model and the limited-resource model, account for cognitive development? Multistore models allow for two possibilities. Changes in cognition can stem from either an increase in the size of the structures—the "hardware"—or from increasing proficiency in employing the "software" or control processes. For example, the capacity of the mental structure working memory may increase with age, or as children grow older, they may increase their tendency to rehearse items to keep information in working memory or even push it into long-term memory. Limited-resource models suggest that what changes during development is processing efficiency. As children become more proficient in manipulating information, more internal space is freed up for storage.

## The Development of Attention

Have you ever noticed that sometimes a seven- or eight-year-old can spend hours absorbed in a single activity, like doing a jigsaw puzzle or playing Nintendo, whereas a toddler seems to bound from activity to activity? Most of us have a sense that older children are better able to "pay attention" to a given task than younger children. Parents read brief stories to their two-year-olds but expect their adolescent offspring to read long passages from novels. Preschool teachers present their charges with only occasional brief structured tasks, like painting or coloring; high school teachers expect their students to follow their lessons for a half hour or more at a time. Clearly, children's attentional processes undergo recognizable changes with development.

**Attention** has been conceptualized as a state of alertness or arousal that allows the individual to focus on a selected aspect of the environment, often in preparation for learning or problem solving (Kahneman, 1973). Attention represents the first step in cognitive processing and, as such, is a critical phase. Unless information enters the system in the first place, there will be few opportunities to develop memory, concepts, or other cognitive skills. Children with a poor capacity to attend will have difficulties in learning, the ramifications of which can be enormous, especially as they enter school. Research evidence corroborates that children who have greater attention spans and persistence in tasks at ages four to five years have higher intelligence scores and school achievement by the time they get to second grade (Palisin, 1986).

**attention** State of alertness or arousal that allows the individual to focus on a selected aspect of the environment.

▶ Interaction among domains

▶ The child's active role

attentional inertia   Continued
sustained attention after an initial
period of focused attention.

## Focusing Attention

One of the most obvious developmental trends that takes place is the dramatic increase in the child's ability to *focus* attention on some activity or set of stimuli. Holly Ruff and Katharine Lawson (1990) observed one-, two-, and three-and-a-half-year-old children while they played with an array of six toys. There was a steady linear increase with age in the amount of sustained attention directed to individual toys. On average, one-year-olds showed focused attention for 3.33 seconds, two-year-olds for 5.36 seconds, and three-and-a-half-year-olds for 8.17 seconds. The attention span continues to increase throughout the early school years and adolescence, and shows a particularly marked improvement around age ten years (Milich, 1984; Yendovitskaya, 1971).

Why does focused attention increase with age? It may be that maturation of the central nervous system is partly responsible. The reticular activating system, the portion of the lower brain stem that regulates levels of arousal, is not fully mature until adolescence. Another factor may be the increasing complexity of the child's interests. Young children seem to be intrigued by the physical properties of objects, but since these are often not too complex, simply looking at or touching objects leads quickly to habituation. On the other hand, older children are more concerned with creative and varied ways of playing with objects (Ruff & Lawson, 1990). As the child actively generates more possible uses for stimuli, her attention becomes more captivated by them. Thus, the child's overall cognitive development and her active engagement with stimuli feed back to influence attention.

One other aspect of sustained attention has been revealed in studies examining how children watch television. Daniel Anderson and his colleagues have noted that when children watch programs like "Sesame Street," the longer they look at the screen, the longer they keep looking (Anderson, Choi, & Lorch, 1987). If preschool children attended to the TV program for fifteen seconds, it was highly unlikely that they would be distracted by other environmental events. This greater likelihood of continued looking after longer initial looks is called **attentional inertia**. Research has yet to reveal how attentional inertia might change with age. However, it may serve a valuable function in cognitive growth by maintaining the flow of information passing through the system.

## Deploying Attention

A second developmental change that takes place in attentional processes is that older children become more able to control their attention in a systematic manner—that is, they *deploy* their attention effectively—as, for example, when they are comparing two complex stimuli. The work of Eliane Vurpillot (1968; Vurpillot & Ball, 1979) illustrates these developmental changes in how children attend to their environment. Children were shown a picture of two houses, each having six windows, and were asked to judge whether the houses were identical (see Figure 9.1). As they inspected the houses, their eye movements were filmed by a camera. Preschoolers scanned the windows less thoroughly and systematically than older children. For example, when the houses were identical, four- and five-year-olds looked at only about half of the windows before making a decision, but older children looked at nearly all of them. When the windows differed, older children were more likely than younger children to stop scanning as soon as they detected a discrepancy. Fi-

Source: Adapted from Vurpillot, 1968.

**FIGURE 9.1**

**Comparing Houses**

Children were asked to explore houses to make judgments about whether they were the same or different while a camera photographed their eye movements. Preschoolers explored the windows less thoroughly, efficiently, and systematically than older children.

nally, older children were more likely to look back and forth at windows in the same locations of the two houses; younger children displayed more haphazard fixations, looking at a window in one house, then a different window in the other house.

In another experiment, Patricia Miller and Yvette Harris (1988) found that children not only become more systematic, but they also use more *efficient* attentional strategies as they grow older. Preschoolers were asked to determine whether two rows of six drawings of toys were the same or different. To accomplish this task, they had to open doors that covered the pictures. Three-year-olds tended to be systematic, but not very efficient; they opened one entire row first, then opened the next row. In contrast, the four-year-olds adopted a systematic *and* more efficient strategy for comparing; they opened each vertically aligned pair from one end of the array to the next. Perhaps as a consequence, the older subjects were more accurate in their judgments about whether the rows were identical or not.

## Selective Attention

Still another aspect of attention that changes with development is the ability to be *selective*. Older children are much more likely than younger children to ignore information that is irrelevant or that distracts from some central activity or problem (Lane & Pearson, 1982). An experiment conducted by George Strutt and his colleagues illustrates this effect (Strutt, Anderson, & Well, 1975).

Children of ages six, nine, and twelve years participated in a *speeded classification task*. They were given decks of cards that varied on one or more stimulus dimensions: form (circle or square), orientation of a line (horizontal or vertical), and location of a star (above or below the center). The objective was to sort the cards on the basis of one predetermined dimension as quickly as they could. But what happened when an irrelevant dimension was added to the cards in the deck? This manipulation interfered with the ability of six-year-olds to sort the cards but had little effect on the performance of older children. What about the effect of adding a second irrelevant dimension? Again, the six-year-olds were the most dramatically affected by the addition of distracting information.

The ability to attend to some parts of an event or activity to the exclusion of others signals the child's increasing skill at controlling his own cognitive processing. Contributing to this change may be the child's growing understanding that his attentional capacity is limited and that cognitive tasks are best accomplished with focused attention. In other words, the child shows gains in **metacognition**, the knowledge and awareness of his own cognitive processes. Some evidence of that knowledge appears during the preschool years. In one study, three- and four-year-olds were asked if they would rather listen to pairs of stories simultaneously or one at a time. The three-year-olds were willing to listen to two tape recorders at once, but the four-year-olds preferred to listen to one at a time (Pillow, 1988). Thus, the development of attention involves an awareness of attention as a limited resource, coupled with more focused, systematic, and selective allocation of that resource.

## Problems with Attention: Attention Deficit Hyperactivity Disorder

▶ Individual differences

Between 5 and 10 percent of children in the United States, usually boys, show a pattern of impulsivity, high levels of motor activity, and attention problems called *attention deficit hyperactivity disorder* or ADHD (American Psychiatric Association, 1987; Ross & Ross, 1982). These children often have academic difficulties in school, may develop problems in their social relationships, and are frequently treated with stimulant medications such as Ritalin that serve to "slow them down." The disorder is puzzling, since its cause is unclear and an unambiguous diagnosis is often difficult to obtain. At the same time, for parents, teachers, and the children themselves, the consequences of the disorder—poor school achievement, behavior management problems, and low self-esteem among them—can be serious.

▶ Interaction among domains

As the diagnostic label implies, a major assumption about the nature of ADHD is that these children have some type of deficit in attention. But what precisely is the nature of that deficit? One hypothesis is that ADHD children are highly distractable; they have difficulty in being selective when they are confronted with numerous stimuli that compete for their attention. A recent experiment comparing ADHD boys with normal boys as they watched television demonstrates this effect (Landau, Lorch, & Milich, 1992). Each boy in the study watched four segments of a show called "3-2-1 Contact" for fourteen minutes, half the time with several distracting toys in the room and half the time without them. All subjects were told that they would have to answer some questions about the televised segments at the end of the viewing period. Figure 9.2 shows that when distracting toys were present, ADHD boys paid about half as much attention to the shows as the normal boys. However, the two groups of boys did not differ in their attention in the absence of distracting

**metacognition** Awareness and knowledge of cognitive processes.

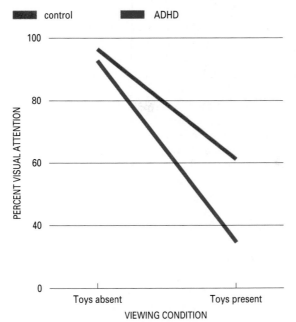

control     ADHD

Source: Landau, Lorch, & Milich, 1992.

**FIGURE 9.2**

**Attention in ADHD Boys**

Boys diagnosed with ADHD do not differ much from normal boys in their attention to television when there are no distracting items in the room. However, in the presence of distracting toys, ADHD boys show a noticeable drop in the percent of time they watch a television show. These findings suggest that children with ADHD have difficulty with selective attention.

toys. These results suggest that ADHD children do not have a pervasive problem in sustaining attention; rather, they have difficulty in filtering out extraneous stimulation.

The underlying causes of attention problems in ADHD children, presumed to be neurological in clear-cut cases, are still not well understood. Moreover, the precise nature of the attention deficit continues to be debated. Some researchers have maintained that the ability to focus or sustain attention long enough to complete a task is impaired (Douglas, 1983). Others say that the ability to deploy attention, to control where attention will be directed, is adversely affected (Pearson & Lane, 1990). Still others, noting that ADHD children display appropriate levels of attention in some situations but not others, suggest that attention deficits are not the primary difficulty at all. Rather, more global problems in controlling many types of behavior, including those related to motor actions as well as attention, are at the core of this disorder (Sergeant, 1988). Clearly, a better understanding of ADHD is needed to sharpen its clinical diagnosis and to develop treatment strategies for these children.

## *The Development of Memory*

Few cognitive skills are as basic as the ability to store information encountered at a given time for potential retrieval seconds, minutes, days, or even years later. It is hard to imagine how any other cognitive activity, such as problem solving or concept formation, could take place without the ability to draw on previously experienced information. How could we classify dogs, horses, and giraffes into the category "animals" unless we remember the common shared features of each? How could we solve a problem like Piaget's pendulum task, described in Chapter 8, without remembering the results of each of our mini-experiments with the length of the string, weight of the object, and so on? In one way or another, memory is a crucial element in most of our thinking.

Memory, however, is far from a simple or unitary construct. One distinction, for example, is drawn between episodic and semantic memory. **Episodic memory** is defined as memory for events that have occurred at a specific time and place in the past ("What did you do on your first day of school?"). **Semantic memory**, on the other hand, consists of general concepts or facts that are stored without reference to a specific previous event ("How many inches are there in a foot?"). We can make another distinction, between recognition and recall memory. Tasks that measure **recognition memory** require subjects to indicate if a picture, word, or other stimulus has been encountered before ("Have you seen this picture on previous trials of this experiment?"). All that is usually required of the subject is a "yes" or "no" answer or some other simple response that signals an item has been encountered before. In **recall memory** tasks, subjects must reproduce previously presented stimuli ("Tell me the twelve words you heard me say a few minutes ago."). The fact that memory can be conceptualized in such different ways has complicated the task of describing developmental processes. Nevertheless, two decades of research on this multifaceted area of cognition have begun to suggest some clear and predictable trends in the development of memory.

## Recognition Memory

How early can we demonstrate the presence of memory? How long do those memories last? How much information can be retained through recognition memory? Two techniques useful in documenting young infants' perceptual abilities and discussed in Chapter 6, *habituation* and *operant conditioning*, have also been fruitful in yielding answers to these questions about infants' and young children's abilities to recognize previously experienced stimuli.

Much of the earliest research on infant recognition memory has been conducted by Joseph Fagan, who used the habituation procedure. First, a visual stimulus such as a photograph of a human face or geometric figure (some examples are shown in Figure 9.3) is presented to the infant for a predetermined period of time. On a subsequent trial, the same stimulus is paired with a completely new item, and the time the infant spends looking at each is recorded. In this *paired-comparison procedure*, infants typically look longer at the novel stimulus than at the familiar one, suggesting that they remember the familiar item.

Using this basic approach, Fagan (1974) has demonstrated that five- to six-month-olds familiarized with black-and-white photos of human faces for only a few minutes retain information about them for surprisingly long periods of time. When the recognition test occurred three hours or up to fourteen days after the initial familiarization, infants showed consistently longer visual fixations to the novel stimulus. This is an impressive level of performance for infants only a few months old.

Carolyn Rovee-Collier and her colleagues have used a different technique relying on operant conditioning to demonstrate infants' early memory capabilities (Rovee-Collier & Hayne, 1987; Rovee-Collier & Shyi, 1992). As shown in Figure 9.4, infants lie in a crib with a ribbon running between their ankle and an overhead mobile. Within a few minutes, infants recognize the contingency between their foot kicks and the movement of the mobile—their rate of kick-

**episodic memory** Memory for events that took place at a specific time and place.

**semantic memory** Memory for general concepts or facts.

**recognition memory** Ability to identify whether a stimulus has been previously encountered.

**recall memory** Ability to reproduce stimuli that have previously been encountered.

Source: Adapted from Fagan, 1974.

**FIGURE 9.3**

**Infant Recognition Memory**

Fagan tested infant recognition memory by using visual stimuli in a paired-comparison procedure. For each row, one of the stimuli was presented repeatedly until habituation occurred. Then one of the other stimuli in the row was paired with the familiar stimulus to see if infants preferred the novel item. Infants only a few months old looked longer at novel items up to fourteen days after the initial familiarization.

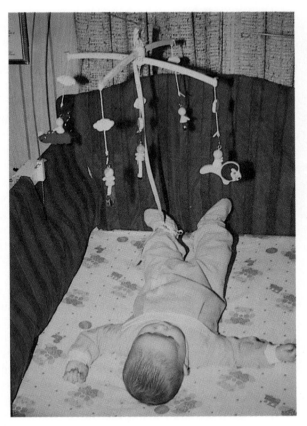

Source: Rovee-Collier & Hayne, 1987.

**FIGURE 9.4**

**Using Operant Conditioning to Study Early Memory**

Infants in Rovee-Collier's studies had a ribbon attached between their foot and an interesting mobile overhead. Infants quickly learned that kicking made the mobile move. When the mobile was removed and then reintroduced after a delay interval, infants showed that they "remembered" it by vigorously kicking again.

ing increases dramatically. Suppose, however, that the mobile is removed from the crib for two weeks. When the mobile is reintroduced, do infants remember that this is the object that can be moved with a foot kick? The answer is yes: three-month-olds vigorously kicked when the familiar mobile was replaced over the crib, but did not kick as much when a brand-new mobile was put in the same position (Enright et al., 1983).

These early memories are easily disrupted, however, by changes in the context of the task. Suppose an infant learns the original contingency between a foot kick and the movement of the mobile when she is in a playpen lined with a yellow cloth with green squares. Twenty-four hours later, the mobile is reintroduced, but the cloth liner is now blue with red stripes. Now infants do not show a memory for the previous day's events; they do not kick nearly as much as they did at the end of training the previous day (Rovee-Collier et al., 1992). Thus, infants six months of age and under encode very detailed and specific information about an event, even when that information is not central or the focus of attention.

At just how young an age do infants display recognition memory? And precisely how long do early infant memories last? Two recent studies address these questions. One experiment shows that even newborns can retain information for at least a twenty-four-hour period (Swain, Zelazo, & Clifton, 1993). On the first day of the study, newborns heard a tape of a word, either "beagle" or "tinder," which was repeated during the experimental session while an observer recorded the number of head turns the infant made toward the sound. As you would expect with the habituation procedure, the number of head turns declined over the session. One day later, one group of infants heard the same word again, while a second experimental group heard a new word. Infants in the first group made fewer head turns toward the stimulus word and more head turns away from it compared with infants in the second group. Evidently, they remembered some very specific properties of the auditory stimulus for a duration of many hours.

The second study is perhaps even more dramatic in demonstrating the long duration of early memories. A number of children had participated in a study of infant auditory localization when they were six months of age. The experimental task had required them to reach in the dark for a shaking rattle. Now, almost two years later, these same children revisited the laboratory and experienced the same experimental conditions without any instructions or description of the task. In comparison to the control group, children who had prior experience with the experiment during their infancy were much more likely to reach out in the dark for the shaking rattle (Perris, Myers, & Clifton, 1990). Evidently, an event that was experienced only briefly at six months of age was accessible in memory two years later!

Not only does recognition memory appear early in life, but the levels of recognition accuracy among older infants and preschool-aged children are impressive. Marvin Daehler and Danuta Bukatko (1977) showed one-and-a-half- to three-and-a-half-year-old children forty pictures of common objects. The stimuli reappeared paired with novel pictures after up to fifty intervening stimuli. Nevertheless, children of all ages showed consistently greater visual attention to the new pictures, indicating good memory for the large number of pictures they had previously seen. With somewhat older, more verbal children, researchers have found that three- to five-year-olds recognized more than three-fourths of the hundred pictures they had viewed as many as twenty-eight days earlier (Brown & Scott, 1971).

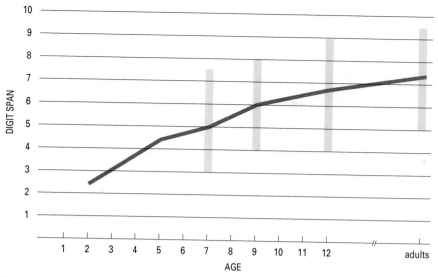

Source: Adapted from Dempster, 1981.

**FIGURE 9.5**

**Developmental Changes in Memory Span**

In the memory span task, subjects are asked to repeat a string of digits after an interval of a few seconds. The points on the curve represent the average number of digits subjects are able to recall. The bars represent the ranges of typical performance at each age. Memory span increases throughout childhood and approaches the adult level between ages ten and twelve years.

In summary, the ability to recognize previously viewed stimuli appears to be rudimentary, present right from birth. Recognition memory is enduring and, at least among slightly older children, encompasses the retention of a good deal of information. The ability to distinguish the familiar from the novel probably has a biological basis because it appears so early in human infants and is evident in other species as well. Considering how important memory is to other cognitive activities, it is not surprising that this early form of retention should be so robust and appear so early in the developmental process.

▶ Roles of nature and nurture

## Developmental Changes in Recall

Suppose someone asks you to repeat a string of digits, such as a phone number. Like most adults, you should be able to repeat between seven and nine digits with relatively little difficulty as long as no more than approximately thirty seconds elapse after you first hear the digits. Tasks like these measure **memory span**, the number of stimulus items that can be *recalled* after a brief interval. Children under the age of ten years remember fewer items than do adults. As Figure 9.5 shows, two-year-olds typically remember only about two items, four-year-olds about three or four, and seven-year-olds about five items (Dempster, 1981).

Do these changes in memory span occur because the storage capacity of memory increases? That is, does the "hardware" of the information-processing system hold increasingly greater amounts of information as the child grows? The findings of numerous memory experiments suggest that this is not necessarily the case. Instead, children's ability to employ **memory strategies**, activities to enhance the encoding and retrieval of information, increases with age. Children seven years and older are more likely than younger children to rehearse items or reorganize them into more meaningful, and hence more memorable, units. For instance, noting that the numbers 1, 3, 5, and 7 form the sequence of odd numbers makes the list easier to recall. So does simply repeating them over and over. Alternatively, we have already seen in Chapter 8

**memory span** Number of stimulus items that can be recalled after a brief interval of time.

**memory strategy** Mental activity, such as rehearsal, that enhances memory performance.

**FIGURE 9.6**

**Developmental Differences in Free Recall**

This graph shows the probability that a word will be recalled by third-, sixth-, and eighth-graders in a free-recall task. Few developmental differences appear in memory for the last few items in the list, but older children show elevated levels of recall for the first few items. This pattern suggests that older children are more likely to produce memory strategies such as rehearsal to remember the early items.

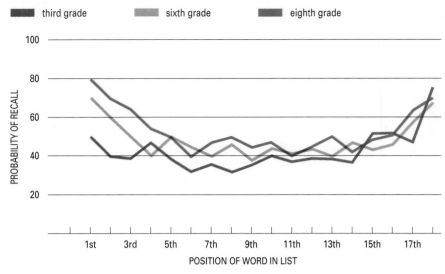

Source: Adapted from Ornstein, Naus, & Liberty, 1975.

that Robbie Case and his colleagues have proposed that increases in memory span can be understood as a result of the increasing operational efficiency children display as they mature (Case, Kurland, & Goldberg, 1982). As operational efficiency increases, more cognitive resources are available for storage.

The memory span task is usually believed to tap working memory, or short-term memory, because the interval between presentation of the stimuli and the memory test is relatively brief. Other recall studies have examined the ability of children to remember lists of words, sentences, or other items for longer than a few seconds. Nearly all of these experiments demonstrate that older children remember more information than younger children do.

In *free-recall* tasks, children are given a list of words or objects that they are to repeat, after a specified delay period, in any order they wish. As Figure 9.6 shows, few developmental differences in recall are usually noted for items later in the list. Children of all ages recall these well, at least by the time they are of elementary school age. Older children, however, show a clear advantage for recalling items that had appeared in the early or middle positions (Ornstein & Naus, 1978; Ornstein, Naus, & Liberty, 1975). The fact that older children show good memory for early items is called the **primacy effect**, whereas elevated memory for later items is called the **recency effect**.

How can we account for age-related differences in patterns of recall? The recency effect is viewed as the extraction of information from more immediate memory, a task that is usually not too demanding for children aged four years and older. However, as we saw with memory span, as children grow older they tend to display more memory strategies. Developmental differences in the primacy effect can be explained as the result of the tendency of older children, those aged seven years or greater, to engage in deliberate strategies to improve recall. They repeat items aloud, make up sentences connecting the items, or think of mental images that connect the items. In fact, much of the research on memory development has centered on detailing the types of strategies that children of different ages display. We now turn to these investigations.

**primacy effect**   Tendency for subjects to display good recall for early items in a list.

**recency effect**   Tendency for subjects to show good recall for the last few items in a list.

**Memory Strategies**    How do you make sure that you remember your grocery list or where you hung your coat in a restaurant coatroom? Or, as in the case of Nate, the under-prepared student described at the beginning of the chapter, how do you make sure you remember important facts and concepts for a test in school? Ordinarily, you must perform some activity to make sure that the stimuli are correctly and enduringly encoded in the first place. As a mature rememberer, you often capitalize on cues that may later "trigger" retrieval. Thus, you might say the words in your grocery list over and over to yourself ("milk, eggs, bread; milk, eggs, bread") or note the characteristics of the location of an object ("I hung my coat next to the bright red one"). In general, as children grow older, they become more likely to employ self-generated strategies for both encoding and retrieval and to take advantage of external information that can potentially aid recall.

▶ The child's active role

We have already identified one useful memory tactic—**rehearsal**—simply repeating, either aloud or silently, items to be remembered. The fact that young children are unlikely to engage spontaneously in rehearsal is well documented. In a study mentioned in Chapter 7, investigators asked kindergartners, and second- and fifth-graders to observe as an experimenter pointed to three specific pictures in an array of seven (Flavell, Beach, & Chinsky, 1966). When children were asked to point to the same sequence after a fifteen-second delay, fifth-graders showed significantly greater accuracy than the other two age groups. More importantly, during the delay period the researchers recorded any signs that children might have been rehearsing the items to be remembered, such as moving their lips or vocalizing to themselves. They found that 85 percent of the fifth-graders engaged in spontaneous rehearsal, whereas only 10 percent of the kindergartners did. Moreover, children who rehearsed showed the best recall. In other words, there was a direct link between the child's production of this strategy and memory performance.

Not only does the tendency to rehearse increase with age, the nature of the **rehearsal set** (the items actually repeated by the subject during the delay period) changes, too. Peter Ornstein and his coresearchers asked third-, sixth-, and eighth-graders to remember a list of eighteen unrelated words (Ornstein, Naus, & Liberty, 1975). In one condition of the experiment, subjects were instructed to rehearse out loud whatever list items went through their minds as each additional stimulus word was presented. Table 9.1 shows the rehearsal sets for a third- and an eighth-grade subject. In general, third-graders tended to repeat only the current item and perhaps one immediately preceding word, whereas eighth-graders constructed a more cumulative rehearsal set. Thus, older children tend to engage in active, purposive behaviors designed to ensure that they remember as many stimulus items as possible.

Older children also engage in another important memory strategy called **organization**, the tendency to reorder items to fit some category or higher-order scheme. If the items to be recalled can be grouped conceptually, older children do so, and the amount they recall increases accordingly. For example, if the stimulus list contains *animals, furniture, vehicles,* and *clothing,* ten- and eleven-year-olds spontaneously cluster conceptually related items together as they recall them, whereas five- and six-year-olds do not (Moely et al., 1969). Furthermore, giving children explicit instructions to group the words or objects they are to remember into categories significantly enhances recall (Bjorkland, Ornstein, & Haig, 1977; Black & Rollins, 1982). Even if young children do not cluster stimulus lists categorically on their own and are not shown how to do so, they are often still able to profit from organizational structure. For example,

**rehearsal**    Memory strategy that involves repetition of items to be remembered.

**rehearsal set**    Items actually repeated by subjects as they engage in rehearsal.

**organization**    Memory strategy in which subjects reorder items to be remembered on the basis of category or some other higher-order relationships.

| | Rehearsal Sets | |
| --- | --- | --- |
| **Word Presented** | **Eighth-Grade Subject** | **Third-Grade Subject** |
| **Yard** . . . . . . . . . . | Yard, yard, yard | Yard, yard, yard, yard, yard |
| **Cat** . . . . . . . . . . . | Cat, yard, yard, cat | Cat, cat, cat, cat, yard |
| **Man** . . . . . . . . . . | Man, cat, yard, man, yard, cat | Man, man, man, man, man |
| **Desk** . . . . . . . . . . | Desk, man, yard, cat, man, desk, cat, yard | Desk, desk, desk, desk |

Source: Adapted from Ornstein, Naus, & Liberty, 1975.

**TABLE 9.1**

**Rehearsal Sets of a Third- and an Eighth-Grader**

As children grow older, they are more likely to employ a rehearsal set that includes more items from the list to be remembered. In this example, with one exception, the third-grader repeats only the word that has just been presented by the experimenter. In contrast, the eighth-grader incorporates previous items from the stimulus list into the rehearsal set.

Marion Perlmutter and Nancy Myers (1979) presented two- to four-year-old children with objects from related categories (animals, transportation, utensils) or unrelated categories (bell, clock, drum, flag, horse, leaf, pen, star, truck). Children from both age groups remembered significantly more objects from the related list. The fact that older, school-aged children tend to order items spontaneously within some meaningful framework means that they have a powerful tool in the service of memory.

Still another helpful memory technique is the use of **elaboration**, thinking of a sentence or image that links together items to be remembered. If you have to remember the list "cat, shoe, piano," you might construct the sentence, "The cat wearing shoes played the piano," or think of a visual image portraying this scene. Elaboration is one of the latest memory strategies to appear; usually children do not spontaneously use images or elaborative verbalizations until adolescence or later (Pressley & Levin, 1977).

One last facet of the strategic behavior of older children is their tendency to use **retrieval cues**, aids that help them to extract information already stored in memory. One of the best illustrations of this phenomenon comes from a study conducted by Akira Kobasigawa (1974). Children ranging in age from six through eleven years were shown twenty-four pictures of objects that belonged to eight categories. For each stimulus item, a cue card was provided that served to categorize it. For example, pictures of a monkey, camel, and bear were accompanied by a picture of a zoo with three cages; a seesaw, slide, and swing were presented with a picture of a park. There were three experimental conditions: (1) a control condition, in which children were given standard free-recall instructions; (2) a cue condition, in which at the time of recall, children were told they could consult the cue cards if they wanted to; and (3) a directive-cue condition, in which children were specifically asked to name the items that went with each cue card. Figure 9.7 shows the results. In the directive-cue condition, few developmental differences in recall emerged—children of all ages performed at high levels compared with the control condition. When left to their own devices in the cue condition, however, only the older children chose to use the cue cards as retrieval aids. As a result, their memory was clearly superior to that of the younger subjects in the same condition.

Throughout this discussion, the recurring theme has been the tendency of children over seven years of age to initiate some activity that will improve their recall. It is important to note that when younger, nonstrategic children are in-

**elaboration** Memory strategy in which subjects link items to be remembered in the form of an image or sentence.

**retrieval cue** Aid or cue to extract information that has already been stored in memory.

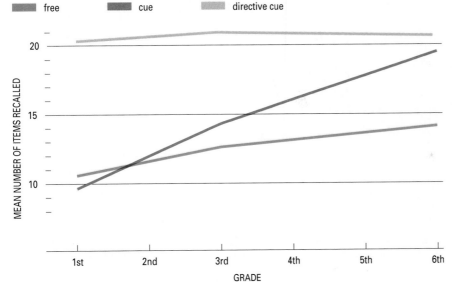

free     cue     directive cue

MEAN NUMBER OF ITEMS RECALLED

20

15

10

1st    2nd    3rd    4th    5th    6th

GRADE

Source: Adapted from Kobasigawa, 1974.

**FIGURE 9.7**

**Developmental Differences in the Use of Retrieval Cues**

These data from Kobasigawa's experiment show that children directed to use retrieval cues performed extremely well on a memory test regardless of age. When they were given the option of using retrieval cues, however, only the oldest children chose to use the cues and therefore recalled the greatest number of items. The free-recall condition shows the typical levels of performance when no cues were available to assist memory.

structed to employ strategies such as rehearsal, organization, or the use of retrieval cues, their recall markedly improves (Bjorkland, Ornstein, & Haig, 1977; Keeney, Cannizzo, & Flavell, 1967; Moely et al., 1969; Ornstein & Naus, 1978). The only exception appears to be when children are first learning a strategy; there seems to be a transition time such that when younger children first employ a memory strategy, their recall does not improve substantially (Miller, Woody-Ramsey, & Aloise, 1991). Overall, however, younger children simply do not generate memory strategies on their own, a phenomenon termed **production deficiency** (Flavell, 1970).

At the same time, preschool-aged children are not completely deficient in the use of strategies. For example, when preschoolers are instructed to "remember" a set of objects, they are more likely to name and look at them than children who are instructed to "play with" the objects (Baker-Ward, Ornstein, & Holden, 1984). Thus, strategy use does not suddenly appear among seven-year-olds. There is a developmental progression that leads to a greater degree and more varied forms of strategy use.

▶ Development as continuous/discontinuous

**Sources of Memory Strategies** How can we explain children's tendency to become more strategic and planful with age? There are several possibilities. One is that children are taught memory strategies directly or indirectly by parents and teachers. Barbara Moely and her colleagues (Moely et al., 1989) noted that 83 percent of the elementary school teachers they interviewed said that they encouraged their pupils to employ repetition to learn vocabulary words, science concepts, and other material. However, when these researchers directly observed classroom activities in grades kindergarten through six, they found relatively little teacher instruction about strategies. Teachers conveyed the greatest amount of direct information on how to improve thinking in grades two and three (Moely et al., 1992).

Do parents play a role? Hilary Ratner (1984) found a positive relationship between three-year-olds' memory performance and the frequency with which

▶ Roles of nature and nurture

**production deficiency** Failure of children under age seven years to spontaneously generate memory strategies.

When teachers present lessons in an organized, integrated manner, children may discover strategies for improving their memories.

their mothers asked them questions about past events. Such memory demands may help children to learn about encoding and retrieval processes that aid memory.

Direct instruction in using memory strategies may not be as important as the exposure children have to environments that provide information in an organized, structured way (Ornstein, Baker-Ward, & Naus, 1988). For example, teachers usually present lessons in a cohesive, integrated manner. Pupils who have this repeated experience may discover on their own memory strategies that can be applied to other situations. Support for this idea comes from a recent study in which third-graders were given the chance to spontaneously sort a group of highly related pictures. They were given no explicit instructions on how to sort the stimuli. Later, when they had a group of items that were only loosely associated, they grouped them categorically and showed high levels of recall for those items. Indirect experience of this type was actually more effective in producing improved memory than explicitly telling children how to sort the groups of stimuli (Best, 1993). Thus, children may deduce techniques for improving memory from experiences with manipulating information.

Another explanation for the emergence of strategies is that children become more conscious of their own thinking capabilities with age and realize the need to produce strategies. **Metamemory**, an aspect of metacognition, refers to the understanding and ability to reflect on memory as a process. It includes the ability to assess one's own memory characteristics and limitations, the demands made by different memory tasks, and the strategies likely to benefit memory (Flavell & Wellman, 1977; Guttentag, 1987). It also includes the ability to monitor the contents of one's own memory and to make decisions about how to allocate cognitive resources ("Have I memorized everything thoroughly? Do I still need to study some items?") (Kail, 1990). Advances in each of these aspects of metamemory may be responsible for improvements in memory as children get older. For example, unlike older children, younger children often manifest unrealistic ideas about the extent of their memories. When John Flavell and his colleagues asked nursery school through fourth-grade children to predict the number of pictures they could recall in a set of

**metamemory** Understanding of memory as a cognitive process.

ten, many of the youngest subjects stated that they could remember them all (Flavell, Friedrichs, & Hoyt, 1970). In fact, they could actually recall only three or four. In contrast, older children were much more accurate in estimating their memory span. Similarly, older children have a better understanding that shorter lists are easier to remember than longer ones and that events from the distant past are more difficult to remember than more recent events (Lyon & Flavell, 1993; Kreutzer, Leonard, & Flavell, 1975; Wellman, 1977). Thus, children's general knowledge about the characteristics of memory increases with age.

Finally, it may be that the child's general knowledge about the world must develop. For example, for a child to use the strategy of organization, she must appreciate the conceptual categories that objects can belong to. Before she can categorically cluster *couch, chair,* and *table* in a list of words to be recalled, she must understand that they all belong to the category *furniture.* In other words, the child's production of memory strategies arises, in part, from her expanding general knowledge base.

**Memory and the Growth of General Knowledge**     Do younger children ever remember more than older children or adults? In a unique experiment, Michelene Chi (1978) found that in certain situations they do. Adults along with children averaging ten years of age were asked to remember lists of ten digits presented by the experimenter. Typically, the adults' performance surpassed the children's. However, when the memory task consisted of reproducing chess positions previously seen for only ten seconds on a chessboard, children significantly outperformed their adult counterparts. How did they accomplish this remarkable feat? Chi (1978) explains that the children who participated were experts in the game of chess, whereas the adults (who were college educated) had only casual knowledge of the game. These children's greater knowledge probably enabled them to see familiar patterns of chess pieces that they could efficiently encode, whereas adults were probably seeing random arrangements of rooks, knights, and pawns. Thus, *domain-specific knowledge*, information about a specific content area, can be influential in the individual's ability to remember.

Memory researchers now recognize that the knowledge the child has already acquired can influence subsequent memory. Thus, many psychologists have begun to explore the nature and development of *semantic memory*, knowledge about the meanings of words, concepts, and other general knowledge. An important question here is, How is knowledge stored internally? One popular hypothesis is that information about the world is stored in the form of **networks**, groups of associations in which closely related items are represented in close proximity. Thus, for example, the concepts "sunset," "sunrise," and "clouds" are stored in close proximity to one another, while "apples" or "ambulance" are more distant.

David Bjorkland (1987) suggests that if a network representation of semantic memory is accurate, then what changes with development is the number of items stored in semantic memory, the number of features or links associated with each item, and the strength of the relationships among items. As children become more familiar with new and different objects and concepts, more and stronger links are established with other concepts and relations among items are more easily activated. Thus, Bjorkland maintains that as children mature, they become more able to retrieve information automatically. Memory development, according to Bjorkland, is more than just the emergence of effortful

**network**  Model of semantic memory that consists of associations among closely related items.

By the time they reach three or four
years of age, many children display
organized general knowledge of
familiar routines, such as eating
dinner.

strategy use—it is the greater use of *effortless* processing. This, in turn, leaves
more space available for storage. These ideas are consistent with the limited-
resources concept of cognition.

The effect of a growing knowledge base on memory has been described in
one other way—in terms of scripts. **Scripts** are the organized schemes of
knowledge individuals possess about commonly encountered events. For
example, by the time they are three or four years old, most children have a
general schematic representation for the events that occur at dinner time—
cooking the food, setting the table, sitting down to eat—as well as for other
routine events such as going to school or attending a birthday party (Fivush,
1984; Nelson & Gruendel, 1981). When they are asked to remember stories
based on such familiar scripts, children typically recall script-based activities
like "eating dinner" better than other details less related to scripts (McCartney
& Nelson, 1981). Similarly, when they witness a logically ordered event that
resembles past real-life activities or scripts, like making "fundough," they remember more details about the event than when the event consists of arbitrary
segments, such as different activities in sand play (Fivush, Kuebli, & Clubb,
1992). This tendency to remember familiar sequences of events that are linked
through temporal order is evident in children as young as eleven months of
age (Bauer & Mandler, 1992). Thus, scripts serve as general frameworks

**script**   Organized scheme or
framework for commonly experienced events.

within which specific memories can be stored and may be one of the earliest building blocks for memory.

Two of the great challenges facing those interested in cognitive development are finding the most useful way of describing semantic memory and accounting for developmental changes in the representations and relationships among the items it contains. Moreover, research will undoubtedly continue to illuminate how general knowledge plays an important role in the child's ability to recall information for specific objects and events.

## Memory Development: An Overview

We have seen that one form of memory, recognition memory, is evident in the very youngest infants and contains detailed, specific information for long durations. In recall memory tasks, there are clear developmental improvements. What is it, then, that develops during memory development? First, effective and deliberate strategies, such as rehearsal and organization, that serve to strengthen or impose meaning on stimuli to be recalled. Second, knowledge in the broader sense—knowledge about one's own cognitive processes, general information about objects and their relations, and knowledge about common sequences of events. In the multistore model of information processing, memory development means the development of control processes that move information to long-term storage and facilitate the communication among stores. In the limited-resource model, strategy use and greater access to semantic memory promote operational efficiency, leaving more room for storage.

## CONTROVERSY: THINKING IT OVER

### *Should Children Provide Eyewitness Testimony?*

The research on children's memory, particularly recognition memory, suggests that their ability to remember events from the past is very impressive. But as children are increasingly called upon to testify in courts after they have witnessed or been victims of abuse, neglect, or other crimes, their capability to render an accurate account of past events has been questioned by some. At the heart of the matter is whether children's memories of past events are susceptible to suggestive or leading questions by attorneys, clinicians, or other interrogators (Ceci & Bruck, 1993). Can they be misled by certain kinds of information or questions? Are they able to report events accurately in the highly charged setting that often accompanies this kind of testimony?

Some researchers report that children, especially preschoolers, are likely to misreport a past event under certain conditions. Stephen Ceci and his colleagues tested children ages three through twelve years on their ability to remember the details of a story (Ceci, Ross, & Toglia, 1987). A day later, children in one of the experimental conditions were asked leading questions that distorted the original information, such as "Do you remember the story about Loren, who had a headache because she ate her cereal too fast?" In the original story, Loren had a stomach ache from eating her eggs too fast. Compared with children who did not hear misleading questions, children who heard bi-

ased questions made more errors on a subsequent test in which they were required to select pictures that depicted the original story—they chose the pictures showing a girl eating cereal and having a headache. This tendency to err
was especially pronounced in children ages four and under.

On the other hand, other researchers believe that younger children are no
more suggestible than older children or adults. In one study, children witnessed a live staged event of an argument between two adults. The researchers found no age differences in susceptibility to misinformation (Marin
et al., 1979). Although college students in this study were able to recall more of
the details of the event two weeks later, children aged five, eight, and twelve
years were no more likely to "fall for" misleading information than young
adults.

Several factors may influence just how suggestible children are. One is the
perceived power of the person doing the questioning. For example, in Ceci's
study described above, misinformation provided by an adult had more of an
impact on distorting memory than misinformation provided by another child.
Secondly, when children are asked questions repeatedly, particularly "yes-no"
questions, they are likely to change their answers or speculate inappropriately
(Poole & White, 1991; Poole & White, 1993). Preschoolers, especially, may
perceive the repeated question as a signal that their first answer was incorrect.
Finally, children may be particularly vulnerable in the emotionally charged atmosphere of the courtroom, especially when they are the victims of abuse or
assault and are in the presence of the person they are accusing (Goodman et
al., 1991; Goodman et al., 1992).

Should children be called upon to give eyewitness testimony? If so, what is
the best way for professionals in the criminal justice system to encourage
children to give reliable eyewitness accounts? What kinds of ethical issues are
involved in conducting research on this topic? Finally, how do we protect children as well as the rights of defendants in such confrontational settings?  ■

## *The Development of Problem-solving Skills*

One of the most powerful and uniquely human cognitive skills is the ability to
solve problems. Whether you are completing an analogy, computing an arithmetic solution, or testing a scientific hypothesis, problem solving typically involves several steps or phases. Oftentimes, you start with planning the steps to
the solution of the problem, considering both the information you have at the
start and the final goal. Clearly, you must attend to the portions of the problem
that are relevant to its solution. You will probably select from a number of
strategies to help you achieve your goal (for example, count on your fingers or
use a calculator). In many cases, you must rely on your understanding of what
different symbols in the problem (for example, "+" or "=") represent. Frequently, you must draw on a body of information from memory and examine
relationships among several pieces of that information. Once you have the solution, you will often apply this new knowledge to similar contexts. Given the
number of steps involved and the complex, intertwined relationships among
them, you can see why problem solving is considered to be an example of what
is called "higher-order thinking."

What are the earliest instances of problem-solving activity in humans? In the
beginning of Chapter 8, we saw a good example of problem solving in the

young toddler when Lucienne Piaget opened the matchbox. Recent evidence suggests that even younger infants are capable of solving problems, combining several subgoals in order to reach an interesting toy. In an experiment conducted by Peter Willatts and Karen Rosie (1989), twelve-month-old infants saw a barrier in front of a cloth, on which was placed a string attached to a toy (Figure 9.8). To get the toy, infants had to remove the barrier, pull the cloth, and then pull the string. In a control condition, the toy was not attached to the string. Infants in the first group tended to remove the barrier without playing with it, quickly pulled the cloth, and grasped the string in order to reach the toy. Their behavior suggested that reaching the attractive toy was of utmost interest. In contrast, infants in the control group played with the barrier, were slower to reach for the cloth, and frequently did not grasp the string, probably because they recognized that the barrier, cloth, and string could not help in bringing the toy closer. Willatts and Rosie (1989) concluded that infants are capable of putting together several subgoals with the deliberate intent of reaching a goal.

Problem-solving skills become more elaborate and complex as children pass through the preschool and school years. A major question has been

**FIGURE 9.8**

**Simple Problem Solving by Infants**

This one-year-old knocks down the barrier and pulls the cloth to obtain the string to which an attractive toy is attached. Such behavior suggests that young infants can deliberately put together several subgoals in order to reach a goal.

whether the child's increasing proficiency in solving complex and abstract problems results from an abrupt, qualitative shift in the ability to think logically, or whether improvements in problem solving occur because of gradual gains in memory, attention, and other component cognitive skills. As we saw in Chapter 8, Piaget believed in abrupt qualitative shifts; he felt that the cognitive structures that permit completely logical and abstract thought do not evolve until adolescence when children reach the stage of formal operations. In contrast, many information-processing theorists have emphasized the continuous growth and refinement of component skills involved in problem solving. According to them, children of all ages possess the fundamental ability to manipulate information in a logical fashion but may forget some of those elements during the process of problem solution or not attend to them sufficiently in the first place. With age, however, improvements in children's attention, memory, or other cognitive skills result in corresponding improvements in problem solving. Let us take a closer look at the components of problem solving that are considered essential in information-processing views of cognitive development.

## Components of Problem Solving

Just think about the typical day of the average school-aged child and you will undoubtedly discern many problem-solving situations the child encounters: a set of arithmetic problems to complete on a worksheet at school, a computer maze or jigsaw puzzle to solve for fun, or several bus routes to choose from in order to get to an after-school job. There are several "executive" cognitive skills that more mature and efficient problem solvers deploy, much like the central processor directs the various functions of a computer. For instance, can I add these numbers in my head or should I get a calculator? What is the best strategy to use—should the puzzle be started with the edge pieces or the entire top left corner? Will learning how to do a simple computer maze provide any clues about how to do a more complex one? As researchers have explored children's problem solving, they have discovered a number of developmental changes in important components that characterize higher-order thinking.

**Representation**     One of the most basic capacities required for problem solving, most information-processing theorists agree, is the ability to use symbols—images, words, numbers, pictures, maps, or other configurations that represent real objects in the world. As we noted in Chapter 8, Piaget argued that children were not able to think with symbols, that is, to use representations, until near the end of the sensorimotor stage of development at about eighteen months of age. Others, however, have challenged this position and argue that representational capacities are evident much earlier in infancy. Jean Mandler (1988) has pointed out a number of early abilities displayed by infants that support this thesis. For example, we noted in Chapter 7 that infants begin to use gestures to stand for objects or events prior to age one year. Similarly, Baillargeon's experiments on object concept in infancy, described in Chapter 8, suggest that infants must hold some internal representation of objects in order to show surprise when they apparently disappear.

Although infants may have basic representational capacities, there is substantial evidence that they become far more sophisticated in recognizing that external symbols of real objects in the world can be used to further their problem-solving efforts. For example, Judy DeLoache (1987) asked two- and three-year-olds to search for a small toy hidden in a scale model of a room. Next, the

An important skill that emerges about
age three is the understanding that a
symbol or model may *represent* a
real-life event.

children were brought into a life-size room that corresponded to the scale model they had just seen. Could they find the real-life toy that corresponded to the smaller replica in the previous segment of the experiment? If they saw a small Snoopy toy under a miniature couch, would they look for a large Snoopy under the couch in the life-size room? The three-year-olds could find the hidden object on over 70 percent of the trials. But the two-year-olds could do so on only 20 percent of the trials. Later, when both age groups were asked to locate the toy back in the scale model, they did so with few errors. Thus, the search failures of two-year-olds in the life-size room were not due to memory problems. DeLoache concluded that two-year-olds have difficulty in understanding that a scale model *represents* a life-size room. By age three, however, children understand that a symbol or model can "stand for" a real-life event.

Another way to understand the role of representations in children's problem solving is to observe their use of maps. Children show developmental gains here, as well. In one study, kindergartners through sixth-graders were shown a map of their classroom and were asked to place stickers denoting their seat, the location of the teacher, the location of the experimenter, and so forth. Even kindergartners were successful with this task, showing a basic understanding that maps represent a given physical space and that there is a correspondence between the physical location and the space on a map. But performance declined for all children, especially the younger groups, when the map was rotated 180 degrees relative to the actual classroom scene. Only the fifth- and sixth-graders showed evidence of beginning to understand correspondences when map and classroom did not match in alignment (Liben & Downs, 1993). Thus, after children attain a general understanding that symbols on maps represent real-life locations, they must still refine their understanding to include the precise geometric relationships depicted on maps, even when the map and the actual location are not aligned with each other.

**Planning**     One of the hallmarks of a mature problem solver is the ability to plan an approach to obtaining a goal. Planning, of course, depends on representational capacities since symbols may be employed or manipulated as part of the plan. Moreover, planning has at least two aspects: first, deciding on the

▶ The child's active role

**FIGURE 9.9**

**The Tower of Hanoi**

In the Tower of Hanoi problem, the child must move three cans stacked on one peg to the third peg, duplicating the array shown in the foreground. Only one can may be moved at a time, and a smaller can may not be placed on a larger one. This problem gives researchers the opportunity to study developmental changes in children's planning activities as they solve problems.

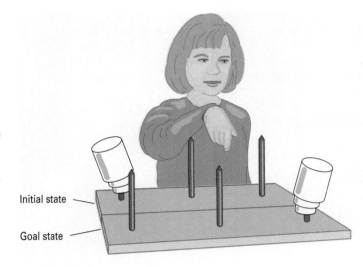

Initial state

Goal state

steps one needs to take ahead of time, and second, knowing when to be flexible and perhaps modify or discard advance plans if the situation calls for it (Baker-Sennett, Matusov, & Rogoff, 1993).

David Klahr's classic research using the Tower of Hanoi problem, illustrated in Figure 9.9, shows that there are clear developmental differences in planning (Klahr, 1978; Klahr & Robinson, 1981). In this problem, one of three pegs has three cans of different sizes stacked on it. The goal is to move the cans to the third peg so they end up in the same order as they were on the first peg. Two rules apply: only one can may be moved at a time, and a smaller can cannot be placed on a larger one.

Klahr found that six-year-olds were better planners than three-year-olds in two respects. They were more likely to pursue long-term goals, and they could keep more subgoals in mind as they attempted to solve the problem. For example, three-year-olds single-mindedly moved the cans to the final peg without thinking of the intermediate steps that might be necessary; their plan encompassed only the short-term goal to get the cans to the final peg. They could only think of one or two steps in attaining the goal and broke the rules of the game. In contrast, six-year-olds used five or six steps in solving the problem, looking ahead a step or more as they planned their moves and anticipating potential traps or obstacles to their placement of the cans.

With development children also show changes in the flexibility of their planning. This phenomenon is illustrated by another study in which children were asked to plan a route through a maze (Gardner & Rogoff, 1990). When the task involved no time pressure, seven- to ten-year-olds planned the entire route through the maze before they drew in the path. However, when the experimenter told children to work as fast as they could, these older children used a more efficient approach under the circumstances—they planned less. Younger children, aged four to seven years, were less likely to adapt their planning strategies to the particular demands of the task.

**Strategy Choice**   When a child encounters a problem, say an addition problem, he will most likely choose from among several strategies. Robert Siegler has closely examined children's strategies as they solve simple addi-

▶ The child's active role

tion problems and has found that children often have more than one approach they rely on (Siegler & Shrager, 1984; Siegler & Jenkins, 1989; Siegler & Crowley, 1991). Most children, he noted, first turned to one strategy, but also usually had a back-up strategy or two. Having multiple strategies affords the child useful flexibility as he encounters new situations and gains new knowledge (Siegler, 1989).

Suppose the child's assignment is to add the numbers 3 and 1. Several strategies are possible. The child can represent each number on his fingers and then count to the total. Alternatively, he can represent the larger number on his fingers and then count off the smaller number. Or he can simply retrieve the information from memory. Siegler found that if the problem was simple, children drew on memory for the answer since that approach is the fastest (Siegler & Shrager, 1984). If the problem was more difficult, however, children used other strategies that ensured greater accuracy, such as counting on their fingers.

With development, as children have more successes with solving problems and become more confident about their approach, they are more likely to use memory as opposed to finger-counting to solve addition problems. They also learn new strategies, often when they fail to solve a problem and need to search for alternative solutions. But children can learn from their successes, too. Siegler and Jenkins (1989) noticed that children often came up with new strategies on problems they had solved correctly earlier in the experiment.

However, children do not merely substitute one strategy for another as they become more mature problem solvers. Rather, they incorporate new blends of strategies as new ones are learned and older ones are discarded. Children are constantly selecting from a pool of multiple strategies, depending on whether the task demands that they be fast or accurate, and depending on what they remember about the success of that strategy in the past (Siegler, 1989).

**Transferring Skills**    One final essential element in higher-order thinking is the ability to use what you have learned in one situation and apply it to other similar problems. How well do children extend their existing problem-solving skills to new circumstances? This has been a long-standing question in psychology, particularly among researchers who have studied the role of *generalization* in learning. It has also been a question of paramount importance to educators, who assume that children will find some application in their everyday lives for what they have learned in the classroom.

The ability to transfer knowledge requires children to have learned the original problem well, to note the resemblance between the old and new problems, and to apply the appropriate activities to the new problem. This process is called **analogical transfer** in that the child must notice the one-to-one correspondence that exists between the elements of one problem and another, and then must apply the familiar skills to the novel context.

An experiment by Ann Brown and her coresearchers illustrates how this process can occur (Brown, Kane, & Echols, 1986). In this study, three- to five-year-old children were read a story in which a magical genie had to move his jewels from one bottle across a high wall to another bottle. Several items were available to help the genie: glue, paper clips, sheets of paper, and so on. The experimenter and each child enacted the solution, rolling up the paper into a tube and using it to transport the jewels from one bottle to the other. The children were then presented with a different problem having the same general solution (a rabbit who needs to get his Easter eggs across a river can roll paper

**analogical transfer**    Ability to employ the solution to one problem in other similar problems.

into a tube to transport them). Whether the children were able to transfer the solution to a new problem depended on whether they recalled the goal structure of the previous problem. If they remembered the major actor, his goal, and the solution to his problem, even three-year-olds could solve the new problem. In fact, based on children's performance on a variety of problem-solving tasks employed by Ann Brown and other researchers (Baillargeon & DeVos, 1991; Brown, 1990), Usha Goswami (1992) has concluded that certainly toddlers, and possibly even infants, demonstrate analogical transfer.

Brown hypothesizes that for transfer of problem solving to take place, the child must represent the problem in general mental terms, that is, to abstract out the goal, problem, and solution dissociated from the specific fact that it was a genie who had to transfer jewels. Children can be encouraged to discern such common goal structures in consecutive problems. Zhe Chen and Marvin Daehler (1989) found that when six-year-olds were explicitly prompted to formulate an answer to the question of how problems were alike, they then performed significantly better on a transfer problem than control subjects who did not receive this training. Thus, parents and teachers may play a crucial role in facilitating the transfer of learning by pointing out commonalities across the solutions to several problems.

▶ Roles of nature and nurture

## Formal Reasoning

Many of us associate problem solving with the types of formal reasoning tasks that we have encountered in science or mathematics classes in school or on the occasional aptitude tests given in different grades. Among the typical formal reasoning tasks studied by developmental psychologists are *analogies* (for example, "boat:rudder" as "bicycle:handlebars"), *class inclusion* problems (for example, "If there are six roses and three daisies, are there more flowers or more roses?") and *transitive inference* problems (for example, "If Sue is taller than Becky, and Becky is taller than Allison, who is taller, Sue or Allison?"). These tasks share the common requirement that the child consider relations among objects in order to draw a logical conclusion, and as such, allow us to understand more about the child's awareness of logical relationships.

**Analogies**    A common type of formal reasoning task is the analogy, where the individual is required to detect a similarity between one set of relations and another. That is, if A:B, then C:?. Intuitively, we might judge this type of problem to be difficult for children; but evidence suggests, to the contrary, that three- and four-year-olds can solve analogies if they understand the underlying relations among the stimulus items. For example, Usha Goswami and Ann Brown (1989) showed three-, four-, and six-year-olds pictures laid out in a series depicting analogical relations. One set showed playdough, cut playdough, and an apple. Children were to supply the next item in the series, choosing from a pool of pictures that included a cut apple. A surprising number of children were successful in this task, probably because of their sufficient experiences with objects that have been cut.

An alternative framework for understanding analogical reasoning is provided by Robert Sternberg and his associates (Sternberg & Nigro, 1980; Sternberg & Rifkin, 1979). Sternberg believes that analogical reasoning can be partitioned into a number of component processes. One is *encoding*, inputting the relevant features of the related objects. Another is *mapping*, comparing the features of A and C in the analogy. *Inference* refers to noting the relationship between A and B. Sternberg's research reveals that eight-, ten-, and twelve-year-olds all showed evidence of using these and other components in solving analogies. The major developmental difference was that older subjects were much faster in carrying out these component processes.

**Class Inclusion**    In one of Piaget's classic tasks, the class inclusion problem, children are asked questions like, "If there are seven horses and three cows, are there more horses or animals?" (Inhelder & Piaget, 1964). Preoperational, and sometimes even concrete operational children, often mistakenly say, "There are more horses." Piaget attributed young children's errors on this problem to their failure to understand that one class of objects, in this case horses, can simultaneously also be a part of another class, like animals. In other words, Piaget said, there are fundamental differences in the logical reasoning abilities of younger versus older children.

However, there are alternative explanations for children's difficulties with class inclusion problems. For example, when children's attention is drawn to the part-whole relations within the problem, they answer correctly more frequently. In one study, five- and six-year-olds were shown pictures of frogs labeled as mother, father, and four babies. In some instances, children were asked, "Who would have more pets, someone who owned the baby frogs or someone who owned the family?" In this case, the word "family" draws the child's attention to the qualities of the group far more than when the question is phrased, "Who would have more pets, someone who owned the baby frogs or someone who owned the frogs?" The latter is the form of the standard class inclusion question. Children who were asked questions of the first type were more likely to answer correctly than when they were asked the standard class inclusion question (Markman & Siebert, 1976). Thus, the logic demanded by class inclusion tasks may be available to preschool children, although their reasoning may be easily disrupted by difficulties in processing the specific content or wording of the problem (Markman, 1989).

**Transitive Inferences**    If stick A is longer than stick B, and B is longer than stick C, then what is the relationship between A and C? To solve this problem, the child must perform a *transitive inference*; that is, she must decide on the relationship between two objects based on their relationships to other objects. All the information necessary to solve the problem is available; the child must simply put it together correctly. Piaget (1970) observed that preoperational children have difficulty with problems like these, and suggested that they do not have the logical thought structures to make the required inferences.

However, other researchers have noted that children as young as four years of age show the ability to make transitive inferences when the problem is modified slightly. For example, Peter Bryant and Tom Trabasso (1971) asked preschoolers to learn the relationships among a series of sticks of different sizes, although the children could not see the actual length of the sticks. Thus, they learned that A is greater than B, B is greater than C, C is greater than D, and D is greater than E. The critical part of this experiment was that Bryant and Trabasso made sure their subjects thoroughly learned the initial premise information. Next, children were asked to compare the lengths of B and D, even though they had not directly learned about the relationship between these two specific sticks. Approximately 78 percent of the four-year-olds correctly stated that B is greater than D. Why were these young children so successful? Bryant and Trabasso maintained that young children are capable of making transitive inferences when their memory for each component of the problem is insured. When they fail the task, it is not so much because they are illogical, but because they have forgotten the initial premises.

Still another explanation has been proposed for young children's failures on transitive inference problems. Charles Brainerd and Valerie Reyna (1990, 1992, 1993) suggest that children's failures on transitive inference problems are less the result of a failure of memory than of their use of a different approach to problem solution. According to these researchers, children use the "gist" of the premise information rather than the precise and accurate details that are provided by a verbatim memory. Thus, they might encode that "things are getting smaller to the right" as they receive information about the relationships among sticks. Sometimes, though, other irrelevant "gists" interfere or the child's "gist" does not include the full amount of information necessary to solve the problem logically. Under such circumstances, children (and, occasionally, adults as well) will make errors.

Research on children's formal reasoning thus demonstrates that while preschoolers demonstrate certain basic logical abilities, they improve as their attention, memory, speed of processing, and general knowledge grow. Perhaps the key to children's improvement, though, lies in still another aspect of cognitive development. Some researchers maintain that adolescents are indeed better formal reasoners than younger children because they begin to understand more about the nature and requirements of logical reasoning. That is, they can *think* about what is necessary for thinking. For example, around the age of ten years, children begin to appreciate the concept of *logical necessity*. In one study, researchers presented fourth- and seventh-graders, as well as college students, with premises and conclusions, some of which did not describe truthful relations (Moshman & Franks, 1986). One set was "If dogs are bigger than elephants and elephants are bigger than mice, then dogs are bigger than mice." Could subjects recognize that the conclusion, "Dogs are bigger than mice," was logically necessary even though the premise information was not true? Not until about ten or twelve years of age, according to the findings. Fourth-graders unflinchingly attended to the truth value of the premise information; they could not grasp the concept of logical necessity of a problem's solution as the seventh-graders and adults could. Thus, noticeable improvements in the ability to engage in formal reasoning seem to be strongly related to this growth in understanding about the nature of logic (Byrnes & Overton, 1988; Goswami, 1991; Moshman, 1990).

## The Development of Problem Solving: An Overview

What can we conclude from the growing body of research on children's problem-solving skills? First, young children are far more competent in formal reasoning and other kinds of problem-solving tasks than Piaget surmised. We do not have to wait until adolescence to observe logical reasoning in children since under the right circumstances, preschoolers can solve analogies, class inclusion problems, and transitive inferences. Second, children do improve in their ability to solve formal reasoning and other types of problems, but their improvements seem to be less tied to abrupt shifts in cognitive abilities than smooth, continuous increments in several component cognitive processes. With age, children's broader knowledge base, improved memory, more efficient processing, and greater attention to the relevant pieces of the problem all contribute to better performance. Children also become more adept at using representations, planning, experimenting with different strategies, and transferring solutions as they attempt to solve various kinds of problems. In other words, not only do children show improvements in the component cognitive skills required for problem solving, but they also become more adept at directing and managing their own cognitive activity.

To summarize, we have chronicled numerous developmental changes in children's attention, memory, and problem solving in this chapter. The most notable accomplishments are outlined in the Chronology on page 354. As you can see, the changes involve the ability to input information, to manipulate and store it, and to direct the flow of information through the system. Whether the information-processing approach will continue to dominate the field of cognitive development as it does now remains to be seen. Undoubtedly, though, this model has been extremely useful in uncovering some of the mysteries of the child's mind.

# The Context of Cognitive Development

As we saw in Chapters 2 and 6, Lev Vygotsky (1978), the prominent Soviet psychologist, wrote that the child's cognitive growth must be understood in the context of the culture in which he lives. Vygotsky believed that adults cultivate in children the particular skills and abilities valued by their cultural group and that the regulation and guidance of the child's behavior by others is gradually replaced by internalized self-regulation. As adults engage in interactions with children, they provide the *scaffolding*, or framework, for the child's subsequent attainments, especially when those experiences are just one step ahead of what the child already knows within the *zone of proximal development*. In this section, we explore the ways in which children's cognitive skills vary across different cultures and look at the microcosm of adult-child interactions as a way of understanding the development of cognition.

▶ Sociocultural influence

## Cross-Cultural Differences in Cognition

Both Piaget and the information-processing theorists assume that cognitive processes function in similar ways across cultures, that there are universal qualities to the nature of thinking. But researchers who have studied memory, classification, and other cognitive skills among children from diverse cultures have shown that although children's thinking from culture to culture may show common features, there are notable differences as well.

Take, for example, the typical free-recall task described earlier in this chapter. Michael Cole and his colleagues examined how children and adults from the Kpelle tribe of Liberia remembered two kinds of lists—words that were potentially categorizable and unrelated words (Cole et al., 1971). We already know that American children remember more words as they grow older and tend to categorize them into conceptual groups with age. The Kpelle, however, exhibited few developmental differences in recall—all age groups performed poorly. Moreover, Kpelle subjects showed almost no evidence of clustering similar items together in their recall. The only exception was that subjects who had some experience in school tended to cluster and recall more words than their nonliterate counterparts.

| | |
|---|---|
| NEWBORN | Shows recognition memory for simple stimuli. |
| 1 YEAR | Performs simple problem solving by combining subgoals. |
| 2 YEARS | Has memory span of about two items.<br>Uses naming and looking as simple memory strategies. |
| 3 YEARS | Shows recognition memory for fifty-plus items.<br>Has memory span of about three items.<br>Knows scripts for familiar routines.<br>Understands that scale models represent real objects.<br>Shows analogical transfer following training.<br>Can solve simple analogies. |
| 4–6 YEARS | Uses systematic and efficient attention strategies.<br>Has memory span of about four to five items.<br>Can think of several steps in planning solutions to problems.<br>Can solve class inclusion problems.<br>Can solve transitive inference problems. |
| 7–8 YEARS | Produces rehearsal as a memory strategy.<br>Has memory span of about five to six items.<br>Shows flexibility in planning solutions to problems. |
| 9–10 YEARS | Shows improvement in focused and selective attention.<br>Produces accurate estimates of memory span.<br>Produces organizational strategies for memory.<br>Can use symbols on maps that are not aligned with the physical space they represent.<br>Appreciates the concept of logical necessity. |
| 11 YEARS | Produces elaboration strategies for memory.<br>Uses retrieval strategies for memory. |
| 13 YEARS | Uses cumulative rehearsal sets. |

This chart describes the sequence of cognitive development based on the findings of research. Children often show individual differences in the exact ages at which they display the various developmental achievements outlined here.

Similar findings come from studies of other cognitive skills. In Chapter 8, we saw that children and adults living in the rural Yucatán region of Mexico tended to classify objects together on the basis of functional similarities rather than taxonomically. For example, they would group a food item with a utensil rather than putting food items and utensils into two separate groups. Once again, formally educated children and adults behaved differently from their

The cognitive activities emphasized within various cultures can influence the modes of thinking that children develop. For example, researchers have observed that cross-cultural differences in children's memory and classification skills parallel their cultural experiences.

less educated peers—they were more likely to group items taxonomically, just as older American children are (Sharp, Cole, & Lave, 1979). Similarly, a recent study showed that formal schooling is more closely tied to children's advances in making transitive inferences than is their chronological age (Artman & Cahan, 1993).

An important variable, then, is children's experience with formal instruction in school. Barbara Rogoff (1981) suggests that schooling may influence the development of cognitive skills in four ways: (1) by emphasizing the importance of searching for general rules; (2) by teachers' use of verbal instruction, which invites abstract thought; (3) by teaching specific skills such as memorizing and classifying; and (4) by leading to literacy, the ability to read and write, which, in turn, enhances specific cognitive skills.

But children from other cultures, even when they have little or no schooling, do not always do more poorly than educated American children. Barbara Rogoff and Kathryn Waddell (1982) compared Mayan children living in rural Guatemala with American children on a memory test that required the reconstruction of an organized spatial scene. Both groups of children were shown a scene containing mountains, buildings, a road, a lake, and trees. Children watched as the experimenter placed twenty objects in the scene and removed them. They were then asked to place the objects in the same locations. The children from these two cultural groups showed no differences in performance on this task. When memory for meaningful, spatially organized information was being tapped, children of both cultures performed equally well. On the other hand, Mayan children performed poorly on memory tasks they had little experience with, such as learning lists of unrelated words.

Studies such as this suggest that it is important to consider the activities that are valued and common within a culture in trying to explain the emergence of cognitive skills. Some cultures may provide children with more experience in grouping objects together on the basis of function, for example. In other cultures, in which many children attend school, other modes of classification may be directly taught. Some cultures value literacy, whereas others value trade skills, such as weaving or making pottery. Thus, children ultimately show different cognitive attainments depending on the skills and abilities that are promoted in the context in which they grow up.

Although the cognitive end products may differ, however, the process through which children learn to think in culturally specific ways may be universal. Many developmental psychologists now agree with Vygotsky that at least one critical process is the way adults convey particular cognitive skills as they engage in cognitive activities and problem-solving tasks with children (Rogoff, 1989).

## The Role of Parents and Teachers

▶ Roles of nature and nurture

Just how are the cognitive skills and activities valued in a given sociocultural context transmitted to children? One mechanism could well be imitation—children learn by watching how parents, older siblings, and other skilled thinkers approach various cognitive tasks (Azmitia & Perlmutter, 1989). Another is the instruction provided by parents and teachers within the zone of proximal development. Two recent lines of research illustrate how this process takes place with two rather different skills: planning the solution to a problem and reading.

In the first research program, Barbara Radziszewska and Barbara Rogoff (1988) examined how nine- and ten-year-old children learned to plan errands. One group of children worked with their parents to organize a shopping trip through an imaginary town, while a second group of children worked with a peer to plan the expedition. Children who worked with adults were exposed to more sophisticated planning strategies; they explored a map of the town more frequently, planned longer sequences of activities, and verbalized more of their plans. Instead of using a step-by-step strategy ("Let's go from this store to the next closest store") as the peer pairs did, children working with adults formulated an integrated sequence of actions ("Let's mark all the stores we have to go to in blue and see what is the best way between them"). In the second part of the experiment, all the children were observed as they planned a new errand in the same town, this time by themselves. Children who had initially worked with their parents employed more efficient planning strategies than children who had worked with peers.

Why does collaboration with adults work so well? In a follow-up study, Radziszewska and Rogoff (1991) observed that when children work with adults, they participated in more discussion of the best planning strategy—more "thinking out loud"—than when children worked with peers who had expertise in planning. When working with adults, children are generally more actively involved in the cognitive task, while they tend to be more passive observers when their tutor is another child.

A second set of studies was an exploration of how teachers might foster the emergence of reading comprehension strategies in junior high school students (Brown et al., 1991; Palincsar & Brown, 1984, 1986). The students received instruction in four reading skills: summarizing, clarifying, self-directed questioning, and predicting. Using an instructional method called *reciprocal teaching*, students and teachers took turns in generating these activities. For one paragraph, the teacher summarized the theme, isolated material that

Children who participate in planning activities with adults later show more sophisticated planning strategies than children who work solely with peers. The instruction provided by parents and teachers often provides the scaffolding for learning advanced cognitive skills.

needed to be clarified, anticipated questions, and predicted what would happen next. For the next paragraph, the students engaged in these four activities. Table 9.2 gives an example of the teacher-student exchanges that typically occur with this method.

The results of training were impressive. Whereas during the pretests students averaged 20 percent correct in answering ten questions from reading a paragraph of material, after twenty sessions of reciprocal teaching, they averaged 80 percent correct on similar tests. Six months later, students trained in this method moved up from the twentieth percentile in reading ability in their school to the fifty-sixth percentile. The key to the success of reciprocal teaching was the interaction between teacher and students. Teachers modeled the appropriate use of each of the four comprehension skills and adjusted their instructions according to the needs of the individual students.

Both sets of studies described here show that parents and teachers can and do provide children with direct instruction about how to succeed in different cognitive tasks. But several ingredients are necessary for the child to fully grasp that skill and be able to use it on her own in other contexts. First, both adult and child must be motivated—the adult to find occasions to push the child forward and the child to engage in the activity in the first place. Second, the adult must be facile at modifying the skill in question so that it suits the needs of the child. Lastly, the adult must be adept at assessing the child's current level of competence and judging the level of difficulty the child is able to master. That is, the adult must be able to locate and work within the zone of proximal development (Belmont, 1989). The result is a constantly modulated interaction leading to the child's cognitive development.

**Reciprocal Teaching**

| | |
|---|---|
| *Student 1:* | (*Question*) My question is, what does the aquanaut need when he goes under water? |
| *Student 2:* | A watch. |
| *Student 3:* | Flippers. |
| *Student 4:* | A belt. |
| *Student 1:* | Those are all good answers. |
| *Teacher:* | (*Question*) Nice job! I have a question too. Why does the aquanaut wear a belt? What is so special about it? |
| *Student 3:* | It's a heavy belt and keeps him from floating up to the top again. |
| *Teacher:* | Good for you. |
| *Student 1:* | (*Summary*) For my summary now: This paragraph was about what aquanauts need to take when they go under the water. |
| *Student 5:* | (*Summary*) And also about why they need those things. |
| *Student 3:* | (*Clarify*) I think we need to clarify gear. |
| *Student 6:* | That's the special things they need. |
| *Teacher:* | Another word for gear in this story might be equipment, the equipment that makes it easier for the aquanauts to do their job. |
| *Student 1:* | I don't think I have a prediction to make. |
| *Teacher:* | (*Prediction*) Well, in the story they tell us that there are "many strange and wonderful creatures" that the aquanauts see as they do their work. My prediction is that they'll describe some of these creatures. What are some of the strange creatures you already know about that live in the ocean? |
| *Student 6:* | Octopuses. |
| *Student 3:* | Whales? |
| *Student 5:* | Sharks! |

Source: Palincsar & Brown, 1986.

**TABLE 9.2**

**An Example of Reciprocal Teaching**

This conversation illustrates the types of exchanges that typify reciprocal teaching. The teacher and students model question-asking, summarizing, clarifying, and predicting. Students who participated in this program showed significant gains in their reading comprehension.

## THEMES IN DEVELOPMENT

### COGNITION: THE INFORMATION-PROCESSING APPROACH

▶ **What roles do nature and nurture play in cognitive development?**

Some of the changes in cognition documented by information-processing theorists have links to underlying alterations in the structure of the brain. For example, changes in attention, and perhaps the speed of information processing, may be associated with maturation of parts of the central nervous system. These connections between cognition and biology point to the role of nature. On the other hand, the child's exposure to specific experiences that nurture the emergence of cognitive skills is also important. As an example, the child's exposure to formal schooling shapes just how he will perform on a memory task or initiate plans in a problem-solving task. Similarly, parents and teachers serve as important models for how to approach cognitive tasks such as planning or reading.

### ▶ How does the sociocultural context influence cognitive development?

The culture in which the child grows up plays a vital role in cognitive development, according to Vygotsky. His claims have been supported by cross-cultural studies that demonstrate differences in cognitive skills, such as organizing information and memory, depending on where the child grows up. Cognitive skills may be transmitted directly by parents, teachers, or other experts in the environment. They may also be transmitted more indirectly through the types of problems and tasks children are confronted with. An especially important variable seems to be whether a given culture provides children with the experience of formal schooling.

### ▶ How does the child play an active role in the process of cognitive development?

Many of the child's cognitive achievements reflect active, not passive, processing. From the child's increasing control of her attention to the deployment of memory strategies, from the use of planning in problem solving to the selection of strategies in problems, the portrait of the child that emerges from studies of cognition is of an engaged, dynamic processor of information.

### ▶ Is cognitive development continuous or discontinuous?

Most information-processing researchers reject the notion that there are qualitative stagelike changes in cognition with development. Their studies have confirmed that many cognitive achievements in the childhood years, such as improvement in formal reasoning, are related to small, successive increments in component cognitive skills, such as attention and memory.

### ▶ How prominent are individual differences in cognitive development?

Information-processing theorists have focused on documenting general changes in cognition with age, and until recently, have been relatively unconcerned with individual differences. Nonetheless, the general features of information-processing skill may vary from child to child. A case in point is ADHD, where there seem to be significant disruptions in attention skills. Individual differences may also be observed in the extent and effectiveness with which strategies are implemented in memory and problem solving although these have not yet been systematically examined.

### ▶ How does cognitive development interact with development in other domains?

There are many examples of how cognition is influenced by development in other domains. For example, cognition may be affected by maturation of the central nervous system, which is hypothesized to contribute to the development of focused attention and the speed of information processing. Cognition can also be influenced by the child's emotional state, as illustrated by research on eyewitness testimony. According to Vygotsky, social interactions with parents, teachers, and others form the basis for cognitive development within a given cultural context. At the same time, cognitive development affects how the child functions in other arenas, such as language, emotion, and social interactions.

## *Summary*

**The Information-processing Approach**    Information-processing theories emphasize the flow of information through the cognitive system. *Multistore models* include such structures as the sensory store, working memory, and long-term memory, along with control processes such as rehearsal. *Limited-resource models* describe tradeoffs made between energy used to operate on stimuli and the room left over for storage.

**The Development of Attention**    There are several important developmental changes in attention. These include the child's increasing ability to focus attention for longer durations, to control attention systematically and efficiently, and to select certain aspects of the environment to attend to while ignoring others. These changes appear to be tied to maturation of the central nervous system and to advances in other aspects of cognition, such as the ability to think about the potential uses of objects and *metacognition*. A developmental disorder thought to be linked to problems in attention is *attention deficit hyperactivity disorder*.

**The Development of Memory**    Although even infants display good *recognition memory*, the ability to *recall* previously seen stimuli increases with age. Improvements in memory result in part from the tendency of older children to spontaneously produce strategies that enhance memory. Among these are *rehearsal, organization, elaboration*, and *retrieval strategies*. Children develop these strategies as their *metamemory*, or awareness of memory, develops. They may also learn strategies indirectly from experiences with structured, organized information. The growth of general knowledge in the form of *semantic memory* and *scripts* is also related to improvements in memory.

**The Development of Problem-solving Skills**    Even though infants show the ability to solve simple problems, significant advances in problem solving continue through adolescence. Children show advances in several components of problem solving, including the ability to use representations, to plan, to choose strategies, and to transfer skills from one problem to another. Even though preschoolers show basic logical reasoning capabilities, children's ability to engage in formal reasoning improves with age as attention, memory, and general knowledge improve. Another important developmental change is the ability to appreciate the principle of logical necessity.

**The Context of Cognitive Development**     The culture in which the child lives is an important influence on cognitive development. According to Vygotsky, adults play a critical role in the transmission of skills, particularly as they teach children within the zone of proximal development. The availability of formal schooling is another key variable. In describing and explaining cognitive development, we must take into consideration the valued and frequently used skills within a given cultural context.

# 10

# Intelligence

*Son Van Nguyen stared intently at the questions he couldn't answer while the other students in the test room kept on busily marking their score sheets. Son was embarrassed to be stuck, and especially embarrassed about the nature of the questions he was having trouble with. After only nine months in America, this ten-year-old was proud of the English he had learned, and he was at the top of his class in math. Now he was in serious trouble on portions of a test some of his slower American classmates seemed to be sailing through.*

*At lunchtime he compared notes with Manuela Gomez, whom he considered an "expert" on American life because her family had lived in the States a good four years longer than his family had. "What does* inscription *mean?"*

*"Oh, that's easy. It's words you write or carve on something, like a tombstone."*

*Son was impressed but suspicious. "How did you know that?"*

*"It's the same in Spanish, inscripción."*

*She was acting so superior he almost didn't want to confess his ignorance. Just as he feared, when he asked her another question about the test, she hooted with laughter. "Are you ever dumb! Don't you know anything? Everybody knows Christopher Columbus discovered America. We all knew that back in Chihuahua before we even moved here."*

*Son's worst fears about himself had just been confirmed. Although the teachers never mentioned the word, he knew, like all the other children did, that he had just taken an intelligence test. And at that moment the truth seemed only too plain to Son: compared with his classmates, he was not intelligent.*

Psychologists who have tested large numbers of children and adults on intelligence tests have found noticeable differences in individual performance, like those that presumably occurred between Son and many of his classmates. What do these differences mean? In contrast to cognitive psychologists, who are interested in identifying *common processes* in children and adults' thinking, some researchers focus on identifying and explaining *individual differences* in mental capabilities. Researchers look for these differences in subjects' responses on tests of word meanings, general knowledge, and visual-spatial performance and describe the results as a measure of intelligence.

What is intelligence? To the layperson, that term usually includes the ability to reason logically, speak fluently, solve problems, learn efficiently, and display an interest in the world at large (Siegler & Richards, 1982; Sternberg et al., 1981). Most of us probably have a sense that the ability to profit from

| 6-Month-Olds | 2-Year-Olds | 10-Year-Olds | Adults |
|---|---|---|---|
| Recognition of people and objects | Verbal ability | Verbal ability | Reasoning |
| Motor coordination | Learning ability | Learning ability; problem solving; reasoning (all three tied) | Verbal ability |
| Alertness | Awareness of people and environment | | Problem solving |
| Awareness of environment | Motor coordination | | Learning ability |
| Verbalization | Curiosity | Creativity | Creativity |

Source: Adapted from Siegler & Richards, 1982.

**TABLE 10.1**

**Popular Notions of Age-Specific Intelligence**

This table shows the five most important traits that characterize intelligence at different ages according to one survey of college students. The students identified perceptual and motor abilities as most important for infants. They saw problem solving and reasoning as abilities that become increasingly important later in development.

experience and adapt to the environment are also part of intelligent human functioning. We might even postulate that intelligent behavior is defined by different kinds of skills at different ages, as did the college-aged subjects in one study of popular notions of intelligence (see Table 10.1). Yet despite the average person's ability to give what sounds like a reasonable description of intelligent behavior, in the field of psychology the formal definition of intelligence has proven surprisingly elusive. Even though the concept has been the object of research and theorizing for over a century, no one definition has been commonly agreed upon, and no one measurement tool assesses intelligence to everyone's satisfaction.

Despite the lack of consensus on how to define and measure it, we now have many tests designed to measure intelligence in children as well as adults. These tests are routinely used in schools as well as in medical, mental health, and employment settings to make decisions about educational strategies, therapeutic interventions, or job placements. Given this widespread use of intelligence tests, it is vital that we closely examine the concept of intelligence and how it is measured.

Our objective in this chapter is to present both historical and contemporary ideas about intelligence—what it is, how we measure it, and the factors that influence it—while keeping in mind that many of the long-standing controversies about this topic are still unresolved. For the most part, the type of intelligence we will be describing is academic intelligence, which includes the kinds of perceptual, verbal, spatial, and reasoning skills traditionally associated with successful performance in school. We will see, however, that because psychologists have taken a renewed interest in intelligence in recent years, newer definitions incorporate broader skills such as social adaptability or artistic talent.

## What Is Intelligence?

Among the many attempts to define intelligence, the most pressing issue has been and continues to be whether intelligence is a unitary phenomenon or whether it consists of various separate skills and abilities. In the first view, an intelligent person has a global ability to reason and acquire knowledge that manifests itself in all sorts of ways, such as memorizing a long poem or solving a maze. Intelligence by this definition is a general characteristic that shows up in multiple and varied observable behaviors and activities of any one person. In the second view, an intelligent person may possess specific talents in some areas but not others and so, for instance, may be able to compose a sonata but not solve a simple mathematical problem. The various component skills of intelligence are seen as essentially independent, and each individual may have areas of strength and weakness.

The second major issue has been the best way to conceptualize intelligence. Should it be defined in terms of the *products* individuals generate, such as test scores? Or should it be defined in terms of the *processes* people use to solve problems? The earliest theories about intelligence came from the *psychometric tradition*, which emphasized the quantification of individual differences in test scores to establish a rank order of capabilities among the subjects tested. More recently, psychologists have put forth alternative ideas about the nature of intelligence based on theories about the processes people employ to acquire knowledge.

## Psychometric Approaches

The notion that human beings might differ from each other in certain skills originated in the late nineteenth century with the work of Sir Francis Galton. Galton (1883) believed that people differ in their ability to discriminate among varying physical stimuli, such as auditory tones of different pitch, and in their speed of reaction to sensory stimuli. Such differences, according to Galton, were largely innate. Expanding on these ideas, James McKean Cattell (1890) devised a series of psychophysical tests that assessed a person's ability to sense physical stimuli or perform different motor actions. It was Cattell who coined the term *mental test*. Based on subsequent empirical studies, the idea that intelligence is functionally equivalent to psychophysical skill was temporarily shelved, but the idea of testing individuals to compare their levels of performance was not.

▶ Individual differences

The first formal intelligence test was created in 1905 by Alfred Binet and Théodore Simon. Commissioned by the minister of public instruction in Paris to devise an instrument that would identify children who could not profit from the regular curriculum in the public schools because of lower mental ability, Binet and Simon (1905) designed a test that assessed children's ability to reason verbally, solve simple problems, and think logically. With the Binet-Simon test, the mental testing movement was born, and psychometrics became firmly entrenched as a model for understanding intelligence.

**Psychometric models** of intelligence are based on the testing of large groups of individuals to quantify differences in abilities. The basic assumption is that some people will perform better than others and that those who perform below some average or normative level are less intelligent, whereas those who perform above that level are more intelligent. Thus, if a large group of ten-year-olds scores an average of 20 out of 40 points on a test, and one ten-year-old youngster scores 35, she is considered more intelligent than other children her age. Within the general psychometric framework, however, theorists have taken contrasting positions on the exact nature of intelligence.

**Spearman's Two-Factor Theory.** Charles Spearman (1904) believed that intelligence consisted of two parts: *g*, a general intelligence factor that he

**psychometric model** Theoretical perspective that quantifies individual differences in test scores to establish a rank order of abilities.

equated with "mental energy," and $s$'s, or specific knowledge and abilities such as verbal reasoning or spatial problem solving that were evident only in specific tasks. According to Spearman, $g$ is involved in any task requiring cognitive activity and accounts for commonalities in levels of performance that people typically demonstrate in various kinds of intellectual tasks. Thus, the influence of $g$ might enable a person to obtain a high score on a verbal test as well as on a test of visual-spatial skill.

Spearman (1923, 1927) claimed to find high correlations among tests of various mental abilities, concluding they were caused by the presence of the single factor $g$. Not all statisticians agreed with Spearman that the data on relatedness of test scores fit his conceptual model. The idea that intelligence was a unitary phenomenon, however, took hold in some theoretical camps.

**Thurstone's Primary Mental Abilities**     In contrast to Spearman, Louis Thurstone (1938) believed that intelligence is comprised of several distinct fundamental capabilities that are completely independent of one another. After analyzing the intelligence test scores of many college students, Thurstone concluded that there was little evidence for $g$. Instead, he proposed that the following seven mental abilities are components of intelligence: *visual comprehension*, as measured by vocabulary and reading comprehension tests; *word fluency*, the ability to generate a number of words (for example, those beginning with "b") in a short period of time; *number facility*, the ability to solve arithmetic problems; *spatial visualization*, the mental manipulation of geometric forms or symbols; *memory*, the ability to recall lists of words, sentences, or pictures; *reasoning*, the ability to solve analogies or other problems involving formal relations; and *perceptual speed*, the ability to recognize symbols rapidly.

Subsequent studies found that the correlations among Thurstone's seven skill areas were higher than he initially thought, but Thurstone continued to maintain that any underlying general skill is secondary in importance to the separate skill areas themselves (Thurstone, 1947). In this new conception of intelligence, individuals possess areas of strength and weakness rather than the global entity of intelligence.

**Guilford's Structure-of-Intellect Approach**     J. P. Guilford (1967, 1985) extended Thurstone's ideas about discrete mental abilities in a model that proposes 150 factors in intelligence. These factors are generated by three elements: *operations, contents*, and *products*. According to Guilford, there are five operations, mental processes like memory or divergent production (the ability to produce several different answers to a question). There are also five contents, or modalities to which intelligence can be applied. For example, some tasks require visual processing, while others are auditory in nature. Finally, there are six products which an individual may master; these include units, classes, or relations involving a series of objects. Operations, contents, and products can be combined in a multiplicative fashion to create a $5 \times 5 \times 6$ matrix, resulting in 150 different aspects of intelligence (shown in Figure 10.1).

By giving individuals tests designed to assess specific combinations of contents, operations, and products, Guilford (1985) claimed to find empirical evidence for a substantial number of the factors represented by the small cubes in Figure 10.1. Not all researchers agree, however, that human intellectual abilities can be broken down into all these separate categories.

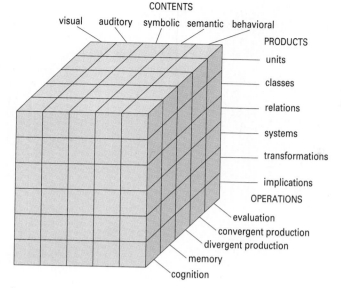

Source: Adapted from Guilford, 1985.

**FIGURE 10.1**

**The Intelligence Cube**

Guilford's model of intelligence consists of 150 factors, the products of 5 types of content × 6 products × 5 operations. Each factor (the small cubes) represents a unique feature of intelligence as a whole, represented by the larger cube.

**Fluid and Crystallized Intelligence**   According to Raymond Cattell and John Horn, a distinction can be made between two types of intelligence, each with a unique developmental course (Cattell, 1971; Horn, 1968; Horn & Cattell, 1967). **Fluid intelligence** consists of biologically based mental abilities that are relatively free of cultural influence, such as the ability to remember a list of words or to group abstract figures together. **Crystallized intelligence** consists of skills that are acquired as a result of living in a specific culture, such as knowledge of vocabulary, reading comprehension, or general information about the world. Because it is thought to be tied to physiological maturation, fluid intelligence is believed to increase until adolescence, when it levels off and then declines in later adulthood. On the other hand, crystallized intelligence is hypothesized to increase over much of the life span because individuals are continually acquiring knowledge as they live in their cultural group.

Horn and Cattell's (1967) early studies substantiated the idea that fluid intelligence increases until subjects are in their twenties and then declines. They also found that older adults obtained higher scores on tests of crystallized intelligence than younger adults did. Other researchers have failed to replicate these findings, however, and have pointed out the problems of cross-sectional studies, in which cohort effects could account for apparent declines in intelligence (Schaie, 1974).

Suppose, for example, we examine a group of ten- and forty-year-old subjects on a test of visual-spatial skill and find that the ten-year-olds outperform the forty-year-olds. Can we definitively conclude that fluid intelligence declines? The answer is no. In contrast to the forty-year-olds, the group of ten-year-olds has grown up in an age of technological advances, in which many children have substantial experience with video games and other forms of electronic media that might influence their ability to perform on the test of visual-spatial skill. More generally, longitudinal studies are also problematic because a group of forty-year-olds that has been followed for the past thirty years may not share

▶ Roles of nature and nurture

▶ Sociocultural influence

▶ Sociocultural influence

**fluid intelligence**  Biologically based mental abilities that are relatively uninfluenced by cultural experiences.

**crystallized intelligence**  Mental skills derived from cultural experience.

According to Cattell and Horn, crystallized intelligence consists of skills that are acquired as the result of living in a specific culture.

many educational, cultural, or historical experiences with a group of ten-year-olds who are moving into adulthood today. In other words, the generalizability of the findings from one cohort to another may be limited. When researchers have combined the longitudinal and cross-sectional designs to address some of these methodological problems, they find that decreases in intelligence test scores, if they occur, happen after the age of sixty years or so (Schaie, 1983; Schaie & Hertzog, 1986).

In summary, psychometric models of intelligence have been valuable in demonstrating individual differences in performance on questions about general information, vocabulary, nonverbal reasoning, and on a variety of other mental tasks. Moreover, although psychometric models have not definitively resolved the debate about whether intelligence is a unitary trait or a cluster of separate abilities, the patterns of correlations among tests for different skills suggest the presence of some underlying general factor as well as several specific skills (Kail & Pellegrino, 1985). Some researchers, however, have challenged the idea that asking people questions about knowledge they have *already* acquired is a good indicator of intelligence. Many have chosen an alternative path to understanding intelligence—studying the processes by which people learn and acquire information.

## Information-processing Approaches

Newer theoretical ideas about intelligence are directly derived from the information-processing model of cognition discussed in Chapter 9. The analysis of each step involved in the chain of cognitive processes, from encoding to retrieval, has generated definitions of intelligence based on concepts such as speed of processing, growing knowledge base, or metacognitive skill. Rather than identifying the structures of mental ability, as the psychometricians did, information-processing theorists have focused on describing the mental processes necessary to accomplish different types of tasks. In this section, we will briefly consider three formulations of intelligence that are based on the general principles of information-processing theory.

**Intelligence as Speed of Processing**   Individuals vary in the speed with which they conduct certain cognitive activities. For example, studies with infants show that some babies habituate more quickly than others to visual stimuli and show a more pronounced reaction when a novel stimulus appears. Michael Lewis and Jeanne Brooks-Gunn (1981) showed a group of three-month-old infants a picture of twenty straight colored lines repeated over six trials. On the seventh trial, twenty curved colored lines appeared. Some infants in this study were more likely than others to habituate quickly to the repeated straight lines and to show rapid recovery of attention to the novel stimulus. Data from this and other studies suggest that individual differences in visual attention exist from early childhood and reflect variations in the speed of processing visual information (Bornstein & Benasich, 1986; Colombo et al., 1991).

▶ Individual differences

People also vary in the time it takes them to react in simple psychophysical tasks, an idea that goes back to the work of Galton and Cattell. Consider, for example, a typical *choice reaction-time* task. A subject sits in front of an apparatus that contains eight lights, her finger resting on a "home" button. As soon as one of the eight lights comes on, the subject is required to move her finger to a button below that light to turn it off. People show notable differences in the speed with which they carry out this task. Several researchers have proposed that such individual differences in speed of processing information might be related to intelligence, particularly *g*, the general intelligence originally described by Spearman (Jensen, 1982; Jensen & Munroe, 1979; Vernon, 1983).

Is there evidence that speed of information processing is a component of intelligence? As we will soon see, infants who are rapid habituators perform more effectively than infants who habituate less rapidly on a variety of intelligence and other cognitive tasks when they are several years older. Similarly, researchers have observed at least moderate relationships between reaction-time measures and scores on standardized tests of intelligence among adults (Jensen, 1982; Vernon, 1983). At the same time, individuals may differ in the speed of their processing because of variations in motivation and attention to the task rather than differences in intellectual ability (Marr & Sternberg, 1987). Some subjects in the choice reaction-time task may become distracted by the equipment in the experimental room or may become anxious, and hence slower, in their attempts to do their best. Because reaction times are measured in fractions of a second, they are particularly vulnerable to these types of disruptions.

In addition, different cultures and ethnic groups place varying emphases on the value of speed in mental processes. In our own Western culture, we place high priority on getting things done quickly, but the same may not be true for cultures in which time is not a major part of daily routines. If a person does not have a heightened consciousness of time and speed, he might not choose to perform mental tasks rapidly, even when he has the capability to do so (Marr & Sternberg, 1987). Thus, we must be cautious about interpreting the results of choice reaction-time and other tasks that assess speed of processing as an element of intelligence.

▶ Sociocultural influence

**Sternberg's Triarchic Theory of Intelligence**   Robert Sternberg (1985) has recently proposed a broad new theory of intelligence based on the principles of information processing. The **triarchic theory** of intelligence

**triarchic theory**   Theory developed by Robert Sternberg that intelligence consists of three major components: (1) the ability to adapt to the environment; (2) the ability to employ fundamental information-processing skills; and (3) the ability to deal with novelty and automatize processing.

▶ Sociocultural influence

▶ The child's active role

(see Figure 10.2) is derived from three major subtheories that describe mental functioning in a far more encompassing framework than theories we have described thus far, incorporating what cognitive psychologists have learned in the past two decades about how people think.

The first of these subtheories, called the *contextual subtheory*, asserts that intelligence must be considered as an adaptation to the unique environment in which the individual lives. This means, for example, that we would not administer an intelligence test designed for children in the United States to children from a completely different culture, such as that of the Australian aborigines. In Sternberg's words, intelligence consists of "purposive adaptation to, and selection and shaping of, real-world environments relevant to one's life" (1985, p. 45). Intelligent persons are thus able to meet the specific demands placed on them by their environment, by learning to hunt if that skill is required by their culture, or by perfecting reading or mathematical skills in societies in which formal education is stressed. By the same token, intelligent persons will change their environment to utilize their unique skills and abilities most effectively. For instance, changing jobs or moving to a different locale may demonstrate intelligent adaptive behavior, according to Sternberg.

The *componential subtheory* focuses on the internal mental processes involved in intelligent functioning, including the ability to encode, combine, and compare stimuli—those basic aspects of information processing described in Chapter 9. Other components of intelligence are higher-order mental processes, such as relating new information to what is already known. Finally, the ability to plan, monitor, and evaluate one's performance—the metacognitive activities we described in Chapter 9—is also part of intelligent functioning. Thus, Sternberg stresses *how* individuals acquire knowledge rather than *what* they know as indicators of intelligence.

The *two-facet subtheory* describes the intelligent person in terms of: (1) her ability to deal with novelty, and (2) her tendency to automatize cognitive processes. Devising a creative solution to an unfamiliar problem or figuring out how to get around in a foreign country are examples of coping successfully with novelty. Automatization takes place when the individual has learned initially unfamiliar routines so well that executing them requires little conscious

**FIGURE 10.2**

**The Triarchic Theory of Intelligence**

According to Sternberg, intelligence has three major facets, or "subtheories," all based on the individual's ability to process information.

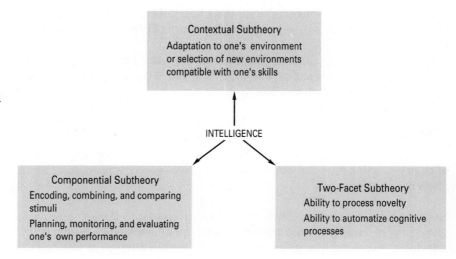

An important aspect of Sternberg's triarchic theory of intelligence is the individual's ability to adapt to the demands of the environment. In our culture, for example, there is a heavy demand for verbal skills and literacy.

effort. Learning to read is a good example of this process. The beginning reader concentrates on the sounds symbolized by groups of letters and is very aware of the process of decoding a string of letters. The advanced reader scans groups of words effortlessly and may not even be aware of her mental activities while in the act of reading.

The triarchic theory captures the enormous breadth and complexity of what it means to be intelligent. Sternberg believes that it is futile to try to encapsulate this human quality with one measure or number because such a number would mask the extremely different patterns of abilities that individuals show. One child might have exceptional componential skills but behave maladaptively in his environment. Another might be highly creative in encountering novel problems but show poor componential skills. Thus, it is problematic—if not impossible—to devise a test of intelligence that could be applied to groups of individuals.

**Gardner's Theory of Multiple Intelligences**    Howard Gardner defines intelligence as "an ability (or skill) to solve problems or to fashion products which are valued within one or more cultural settings" (1986, p. 74). Gardner (1983) also noted, though, that people often show marked individual differences in their ability to process specific kinds of information. Accordingly he identified the following seven distinct intelligences:

▶ Individual differences

*Linguistic:*   A sensitivity to the meaning and order of words, as well as the functions of language;
*Musical:*   A sensitivity to pitch, tone, and timbre, as well as musical patterns;
*Logico-mathematical:*   The ability to handle chains of reasoning, numerical relations, and hierarchical relations;
*Spatial:*   The capacity to perceive the world accurately and to transform and recreate perceptions;

*Bodily-kinesthetic:*  The ability to use one's body or to work with objects in highly differentiated and skillful ways;

*Intrapersonal:*  The capacity to understand one's own feelings and use them to guide behavior;

*Interpersonal:*  The ability to notice and make distinctions among the moods, temperaments, motivations, and intentions of others.

Gardner finds support for the existence of these discrete areas of intelligence on several fronts. For each skill, he says, it is possible to find people who excel or show genius, such as Mozart, T. S. Eliot, or Einstein. It is also possible, in many instances, to show a loss of or deficit in a specific ability through damage to particular areas of the brain. Lesions to the parts of the left cortex specifically dedicated to language function, for example, produce a loss of linguistic intelligence. Yet the other intelligences usually remain intact. Finally, it is possible to identify a core of information-processing operations uniquely relevant to each of the areas. For musical intelligence, one core process is sensitivity to pitch. For bodily-kinesthetic intelligence, it is the ability to imitate the movement made by another person.

How do each of the intelligences develop? Gardner believes that propensities or talents in certain areas may be inborn but that the child's experiences are also of paramount importance. Some children, for example, may show a unique ability to remember melodies, but all children would profit from exposure to musical sequences. Moreover, Gardner reminds us that it is important to remember the cultural values the child is exposed to. In our culture, linguistic and logico-mathematical skills are highly valued and are emphasized as measures of school success. Among the Puluwat islanders of the South Pacific, the navigational skills required for successful sailing are of paramount importance, and hence spatial intelligence receives great recognition in that culture.

Although no formal test is yet available to assess individuals on the various intelligences, Gardner's theory has refueled the debate over intelligence as a unitary construct or a set of distinct skills. The theory of multiple intelligences clearly falls into the latter category.

▶ Interaction among domains

▶ Roles of nature and nurture

▶ Sociocultural influence

One of the distinct abilities identified by Howard Gardner in his theory of multiple intelligences is musical intelligence, a sensitivity to pitch, tone, timbre, and musical patterns.

What is intelligence? The psychometric and information-processing views emphasize reasoning and problem-solving skills as key components of intelligence. Newer approaches have broadened our understanding of intelligence to include adaptability to one's environment, social skill, and even control of one's body and self-understanding. In addition, psychometric models help to identify patterns of individual differences in performance, and information-processing models have begun to identify and describe the precise mental activities involved in intelligent behavior. Yet few theories explicitly describe the *development* of intelligence. Most models of intelligence are derived from data gathered from young adults and provide few suggestions about the way intelligence changes from early childhood through adulthood.

## *Measuring Intelligence*

Over the years, we have come to use the term *IQ* as a synonym for *intelligence*. In fact, the abbreviation *IQ* means "intelligence quotient" and refers only to the score a person obtains on the standardized intelligence tests now widely used in Western societies. The results of these tests have become so closely associated with intelligence as an attribute of human functioning that we have virtually ceased to make a distinction between them. Yet as we saw in our opening scene about Son, the IQ score may or may not be a good indicator of intelligent functioning.

Standardized tests of intelligence are based on many shared assumptions about how this characteristic is distributed among individuals. IQ scores are assumed to be normally distributed in the population, as shown in Figure 10.3, with the majority falling in the middle of the distribution and fewer at the up-

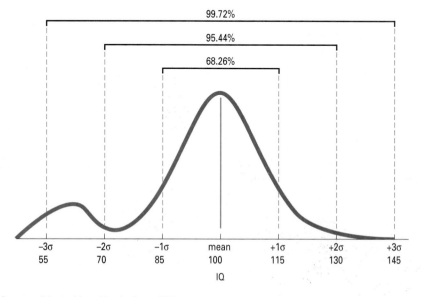

Source: Adapted from Vandenberg, 1971.

**FIGURE 10.3**

**How Intelligence Is Distributed in the General Population**

Intelligence scores are assumed to be normally distributed in the population, with a mean score of 100. Most people's scores fall within 15 points (or one standard deviation) above or below the mean, and almost the entire population falls within three standard deviation units of the mean. In actuality, a slightly greater number of individuals than we would theoretically expect fall at the lower end of the distribution, probably because of genetic, prenatal, or early postnatal risks that can affect intelligence.

per and lower extremes. The average or *mean* IQ score on most tests is 100. Usually a statistical measure of the average variability of scores around the mean, or *standard deviation*, is also calculated. The standard deviation gives a picture of how clustered or spread out the scores are around the mean. On many tests, the standard deviation has a value of 15, which means that most individuals differ from the mean score of 100 by 15 points or less.

The normal distribution of scores can also be partitioned into "standard deviation units." As Figure 10.3 shows, the majority of IQ scores (about 68 percent) fall within one standard deviation on either side of the mean, and almost all scores in the population (about 99 percent) fall within three standard deviations above or below the mean. In actuality, the percent of scores below the mean is slightly greater than the theoretical normal distribution would predict. This fact is probably the result of genetic, prenatal, or early postnatal factors that can put young infants at risk for lower intellectual development (Vandenberg & Vogler, 1985; Zigler, 1967).

## Standardized Tests of Intelligence

Educators, clinicians, and others who must assess and diagnose children have a number of standardized tests to choose from. **Psychometricians**, psychologists who specialize in the construction and interpretation of tests, typically administer a new test to a large sample of subjects during the test construction phase, both to assess the test's reliability and validity (see Chapter 1) and to establish the norms of performance against which other individuals will be compared. Some intelligence tests are designed to be administered to individual children; others can be given to large groups.

**Infant Intelligence Tests**     Most tests of infant intelligence are based on norms for behaviors that are expected to occur in the first year or two of life. Because most of the infant's accomplishments are in the domains of motor, language, and socioemotional development, these areas appear most frequently on the various tests. Almost without exception, the tests are administered individually to infants.

Perhaps the most widely used infant test is the *Bayley Scales of Infant Development*, designed by Nancy Bayley (1936, 1969, 1993) to predict later childhood competence. The test consists of two scales: the Mental Scale assesses the young child's sensory and perceptual skills, memory, learning, acquisition of the object concept, and linguistic skill. The Motor Scale measures the child's ability to control and coordinate the body, from large motor skills to finer manipulation of the hands and fingers. Table 10.2 shows some sample items from each scale. Designed for infants from one through forty-two months of age, the test yields a *developmental index* for both the mental and the motor scale. That is, the infant's scores are compared to the scores for the standardization sample (the large sample of normal infants whose performance was assessed at the time the test was developed) and are expressed in terms of how much they deviate from the average scores of that sample. The Bayley scales also contain a Behavior Rating Scale to assess the infant's interests, emotions, and general level of activity as compared with the standardization sample.

One of the most recently developed measures of infant intelligence is the *Fagan Test of Infant Intelligence*, designed for infants between six and twelve months old and based on infants' recognition memory capabilities. During the test, the child sits on the parent's lap and views a picture for a predetermined

**psychometrician** Psychologist who specializes in the construction and interpretation of standardized tests.

| Age | Mental Scale | Motor Scale |
|---|---|---|
| 2 months | Turns head to sound<br>Plays with rattle<br>Reacts to disappearance of face | Holds head erect and steady for 15 seconds<br>Turns from side to back<br>Sits with support |
| 6 months | Lifts cup by handle<br>Looks for fallen spoon<br>Looks at pictures in book | Sits alone for 30 seconds<br>Turns from back to stomach<br>Grasps foot with hands |
| 12 months | Builds tower of 2 cubes<br>Turns pages of book | Walks with help<br>Throws ball<br>Grasps pencil in middle |
| 17–19 months | Imitates crayon stroke<br>Identifies objects in photograph | Stands alone on right foot<br>Walks up stairs with help |
| 23–25 months | Matches pictures<br>Uses pronoun(s)<br>Imitates a 2-word sentence | Laces 3 beads<br>Jumps distance of 4 inches<br>Walks on tiptoe for 4 steps |
| 38–42 months | Names 4 colors<br>Uses past tense<br>Identifies gender | Copies circle<br>Hops twice on 1 foot<br>Walks down stairs, alternating feet |

Source: Bayley, 1993.

**TABLE 10.2**

**Sample Items from the Bayley Scales of Infant Development**

period of time. The familiar picture is then presented alongside a novel one and the infant's looking time to the novel stimulus is recorded. As you saw in Chapter 9, infants show their "memory" for the familiar stimulus by looking longer at the new item. Several of these "novelty problems" are presented in succession. The test is designed to screen for children at risk for intellectual deficits based on the premise that their response to novelty is depressed. In one study, scores that infants obtained on the Fagan Test of Infant Intelligence correlated +.49 with their scores on several standard tests of intelligence at age three years. Furthermore, it was found over a series of studies that if infants directed less than 53 percent of their visual fixations to the novel stimuli, they were especially likely to fall into the category of "intellectually delayed" (Fagan & Montie, 1988).

**Individual IQ Tests for Older Children**    The two most widely used individually administered intelligence tests for school-aged children are the Stanford-Binet Intelligence Scale and the Wechsler Intelligence Scale for Children-Revised (or WISC-R). Both are based on the psychometric model and measure similar mental skills.

The *Stanford-Binet Intelligence Scale*, adapted from the original Binet scales by Lewis Terman of Stanford University, was most recently revised in 1986 (Terman, 1916; Terman & Merrill, 1937; Terman & Merrill, 1973; Thorndike, Hagen, & Sattler, 1986). When Binet originally designed the test, he chose mental tasks the average child at each age could perform. He also assumed that if children of a specific age—say, eight years—performed like their older counterparts—say, ten years—they had a higher *mental age*. By the same token, if an eight-year-old passed only the items the average six-year-old could answer, he had a lower mental age. Thus, intelligence was the extent to which children resembled their age mates in performance.

Terman translated, modified, and standardized the Binet scales for use in the United States. He also borrowed from William Stern, a German psychologist, an equation for expressing the results of the test. The child's **intelligence quotient**, or **IQ**, was computed as follows:

$$\text{mental age}/\text{chronological age} \times 100$$

Thus, a ten-year-old who obtained a mental age score of 12 would have an IQ of 120. The Stanford-Binet Intelligence Scale came rapidly into use among educators and clinicians eager to find a useful diagnostic tool for children.

The Stanford-Binet test assesses four broad areas of mental functioning: verbal reasoning, abstract/visual reasoning, quantitative reasoning, and short-term memory. The test is scaled for use with individuals from two years of age through adulthood. During the administration of the test, children are given tasks according to year level. Once they fail all or most of the tasks for two consecutive year levels, the test session is terminated. In the newest edition of the Stanford-Binet, the concept of mental age has been replaced by a **deviation IQ**. The child's score in each of the four test areas is compared with the performance of similar-aged children in the standardization sample, and an IQ score is obtained for each. An overall IQ score can also be computed. Thus, this test permits psychologists not only to assess the child's overall abilities but also to isolate specific areas of strength and weakness.

The *Wechsler Intelligence Scale for Children*, the major alternative to the Stanford-Binet, is scaled for use with children aged six through sixteen years. The original version was constructed in 1949 by David Wechsler. The revised version, called the WISC-R, contains three scales: (1) the Verbal Scale, which includes items assessing vocabulary, arithmetic skills, digit span performance, and knowledge of general information; (2) the Performance Scale, which includes tests of visual spatial skill, puzzle assembly, and arranging pictures to form a story; and (3) a Full Scale IQ, which represents a composite of the two (Wechsler, 1974). Figure 10.4 shows some items resembling those from each scale of the WISC-R. Thus, like the Stanford-Binet, this test allows the examiner to assess patterns of strength and weakness in the child's mental abilities. In addition, like the Stanford-Binet, the child's score on the WISC-R is computed on the basis of the deviation IQ.

A relatively new intelligence test for two- through twelve-year-olds is the *Kaufman Assessment Battery for Children* or *K-ABC* (Kaufman & Kaufman, 1983). This test is based on the assumption that intelligence is related to the quality of mental processing; the focus is on how children produce correct solutions to problems rather than on the content of their knowledge. The test includes three scales: (1) the Sequential Processing Scale, which assesses the ability to solve problems in a step-by-step fashion; (2) the Simultaneous Processing Scale, which tests the ability to solve problems through integration and organization of many pieces of information; and (3) the Mental Processing Composite, a combination of the first two scales. The K-ABC also includes an Achievement Scale to assess knowledge the child has acquired in the home and school. Figure 10.5 illustrates some of the items found on the K-ABC.

Most of the items on the K-ABC were specifically designed to be neutral in content so that processing differences among children could be validly assessed. That is, the intent was to minimize the influence of the child's previous learning history on performance. In addition, the emphasis in test administra-

**intelligence quotient (IQ)** Numerical score received on an intelligence test.

**deviation IQ** IQ score computed by comparing the child's performance with that of a standardization sample.

VERBAL SCALE

General Information
1. How many nickels make a dime?
2. Who wrote *Tom Sawyer?*

General Comprehension
1. What is the advantage of keeping money in a bank?
2. Why is copper often used in electrical wires?

Arithmetic
1. Sam had three pieces of candy and Joe gave him four more. How many pieces of candy did Sam have all together?
2. If two buttons cost fifteen cents, what will be the cost of a dozen buttons?

Similarities
1. In what way are a saw and a hammer alike?
2. In what way are an hour and a week alike?

Vocabulary
This test consists simply of asking, "What is a _____?" or "What does _____ mean?" The words cover a wide range of difficulty.

PERFORMANCE SCALE

Picture Arrangement

I want you to arrange these pictures in the right order so they tell a story that makes sense. Work as quickly as you can. Tell me when you have finished.

Object Assembly

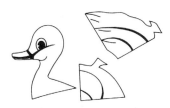

Put this one together as quickly as you can.

## FIGURE 10.4

**Sample Items from the Wechsler Intelligence Scale for Children—Revised**

The WISC-R contains two scales: the Verbal Scale and the Performance Scale. Shown here are examples that resemble items from the several subtests that contribute to each scale.

## SEQUENTIAL PROCESSING

| | | |
|---|---|---|
| HAND MOVEMENTS: | Watch my hand. Now, you try it. |  |
| NUMBER RECALL: | Say these numbers just as I do. | 5 – 4 – 8 – 1 – 10 |
| WORD ORDER: | Cat–hand–shoe–ball. Now touch the pictures that I named. | |

## SIMULTANEOUS PROCESSING

| | | |
|---|---|---|
| GESTALT CLOSURE: | What is this? | |
| TRIANGLES: | (Child is given three triangles). Now try to make one like this. |  |
| SPATIAL MEMORY: | See these pictures? | 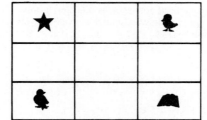 |
| | Point to where you saw the pictures. | 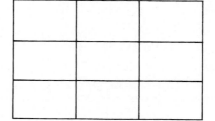 |

Source: Kaufman & Kaufman, 1983.

tion is on obtaining the child's best performance. Whereas administration of the Stanford-Binet and the WISC-R requires strict adherence to test protocol, examiners giving the K-ABC are encouraged to use alternate wording, gestures, or even languages other than English to make sure the child understands what is expected. Thus, in terms of its content and its mode of administration, the K-ABC represents a departure from many traditional tests of intelligence.

**Group Tests of Intelligence**     Not all intelligence tests are administered to individual children. Many of us remember the experience of having our normal school routine altered so the class could take a special test, one that we were told would assess our special talents and abilities. Group tests are obviously less time consuming and more efficient to administer and score than are individual tests. Because the child must work relatively independently on the group test, however, she may be at a disadvantage if she has poor reading skills or language difficulties. Moreover, individual tests often provide the examiner with clinical insights apart from the responses to the test items themselves; a school psychologist, for example, might note during the test session that a child is overly anxious or has a poor attention span. Such insights are lost in group testing situations. Despite these drawbacks, however, group tests have been shown to be as reliable and valid as individual tests (Lennon, 1985). Some examples of group tests include the *Otis-Lennon School Ability Test*, the *Differential Aptitude Tests*, and the *Test of Cognitive Skills*.

**Piagetian Tests of Intelligence**     Piaget's theory, which we described in Chapters 2 and 8, also represents an approach to understanding intelligence. Piaget's description of cognitive development as an adaptive process and his delineation of the child's progression from simple, sensorimotor-based mental activities to rational, abstract thought clearly portray the growth of the child's intellectual functioning. In that sense, it is one of the few conceptualizations of intelligence that is distinctly developmental. Piaget emphasized process and structure—that is, how children come to know what they do and how internal representations of their knowledge change—rather than the specific contents of children's minds. Some researchers have attempted to devise a standardized test that taps those Piagetian notions of intelligence.

One Piagetian test is called the *Concept Assessment Kit* (Goldschmid & Bentler, 1968). In this test, the child must solve a number of conservation problems that assess her ability to think in a concrete operational way. Among the tasks in the test are conservation of number, mass, and liquid. The child's responses to each conservation problem are noted, as well as any rationale or justification she provides for the answer, and her scores are compared with those of a normative sample. This test is appropriate for children aged four through seven years, when the transition from preoperational to concrete operational thought is typically made. Scores on the Concept Assessment Kit are moderately correlated with scores on more traditional measures of IQ (Goldschmid, 1967).

**Intelligence Tests: An Overview**     In summary, the most widely used intelligence tests are based on the idea that levels of performance on academic types of tasks reveal something about an individual's general mental abilities. They often assume that intelligent persons will have acquired a specific body of knowledge that many other members of our Western industrialized culture have also learned. Newer tests like the *Fagan Test of Infant Intelligence*, the *Kaufman*

**FIGURE 10.5 (facing page)**

**Sample Items from the Kaufman Assessment Battery for Children**

The K-ABC contains a Sequential and a Simultaneous Processing Scale. One of the goals of this test is to assess intelligence apart from the specific content children may already have learned.

*Assessment Battery,* and the Piagetian *Concept Assessment Kit* assess intelligence from alternative perspectives that emphasize differences in mental processing activities such as recognition memory capacity or the ability to think logically. So far, however, no test captures the breadth of human intelligent functioning as it displays itself in adaptive behavior overall or in specific dimensions such as social competence, artistic talent, or other nonacademic skills.

## Stability and Prediction

Intelligence tests were first developed with the goal of predicting children's future functioning. Binet, you recall, was asked to design a tool that would anticipate children's achievement in school. Those who followed with other theories and assessment tools for measuring intelligence likewise assumed, either explicitly or implicitly, that scores on the tests would forecast the individual's successes or failures in some areas of life. Moreover, many (although not all) psychologists assumed that "intelligence" was a quality people carried with them over the whole span of their lives. They believed, in other words, that IQ scores would show continuity and stability.

### The Stability of IQ

If intelligence is a reasonably invariant characteristic, then a child tested repeatedly at various ages should obtain approximately the same IQ scores. In one major longitudinal research project, the Berkeley Growth Study, a group of children was given intelligence tests every year from infancy through adulthood. The correlations between the scores obtained during the early school years and scores at ages seventeen and eighteen years were generally high; the correlation between IQ scores at ages seven and eighteen years, for example, was .80 (Jones & Bayley, 1941; Pinneau, 1961). Even though the results point to a great deal of stability, however, about half of the sample showed differences of 10 points or more when IQ in the early school years was compared with IQ in adolescence.

In another extensive project, the Fels Longitudinal Study, the stability of intelligence was assessed from the preschool years to early adulthood. Although correlations for scores were high when the ages were adjacent, they were much lower as the years between testing increased; the correlation between IQ score at ages three and four years was .83, but dropped to .46 between ages three and twelve years. Furthermore, as in the Berkeley data, individual children frequently showed dramatic changes in scores—sometimes as much as 40 points—between the ages of two and seventeen years (McCall, Appelbaum, & Hogarty, 1973; Sontag, Baker, & Nelson, 1958). Taken together, the results of these two major longitudinal studies suggest that, for many children, IQ scores are often remarkably stable, especially if the two test times are close together, but that large fluctuations in individual scores are also possible.

▶ **Roles of nature and nurture**

Why do the scores of some children shift so dramatically? The presence or absence of family stress can be one factor. Children in the Berkeley study who showed significant declines in IQ often also experienced a dramatic alteration in life experience, such as loss of a parent or a serious illness (Honzik, Macfarlane, & Allen, 1948). Similarly, a recent longitudinal study showed that there is a relationship between IQ scores and the number of environmental risk factors a child is exposed to (Sameroff et al., 1993). As children matured from ages four to thirteen years, those with lower IQ scores also experienced the greater number of risks, factors such as unemployment of a parent, physical illness of a family member, or absence of the father from the household. The child's per-

Longitudinal studies have demonstrated that parents who encourage intellectual achievement have children who show noticeable gains in IQ.

sonality attributes or parental interaction styles can also play a role. In the Fels study, children who showed gains in IQ were described as independent, competitive in academics, and self-initiating. In addition, the parents of these children encouraged intellectual achievement and used a discipline style that emphasized moderation and explanation. In contrast, children whose IQ scores decreased with age had parents who were overly restrictive or permissive in discipline style (McCall, Appelbaum, & Hogarty, 1973). This body of studies suggests that IQ scores are vulnerable to environmental influences that can affect the child's performance on a test at a given point in time or, more broadly, his motivation to achieve in the intellectual domain.

**The Stability of Infant Intelligence**     The correlations between scores on infant intelligence tests and IQ scores in later childhood have been particularly low, at least according to research conducted before the start of this decade (Kopp & McCall, 1980; McCall, Hogarty, & Hurlburt, 1972). In one review of studies measuring IQ at age one year and again at ages three through six years, it was found that the average correlation was only .14 (Fagan & Singer, 1983). In another, Nancy Bayley (1949) reported essentially no relationships between scores obtained in the first four years of life and young adulthood. Only when children reached age five years were correlations of .60 seen with adult scores (see Figure 10.6).

Several hypotheses have been advanced to explain why infant IQ scores do not correlate well with scores later in childhood. One possibility, of course, is that there is no such thing as a general intelligence factor (or *g*) or that if it exists, it is not a stable trait. Another possibility is that intelligence in infancy differs qualitatively from intelligence in later years, implying that intellectual development is discontinuous. One problem in drawing any conclusions is that the types of skills measured by infant intelligence tests are very different from those measured by tests such as the Stanford-Binet and WISC-R. Recall, for example, some of the items from the *Bayley Scales of Infant Development*, many of which center on the child's sensory and motor accomplishments: the ability to

▶ Development as continuous/discontinuous

## FIGURE 10.6

### Is Intelligence Stable Over Time?

The graph shows the correlations between IQ scores obtained in infancy and childhood and IQ scores at age eighteen years. Note that IQ scores obtained before age four years are poor predictors of subsequent IQ.

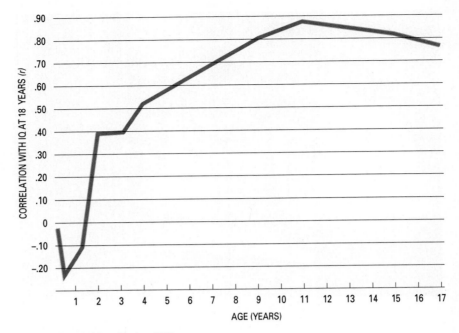

Source: Adapted from Bayley, 1949.

roll over, reach, or jump on one foot. We have little reason to believe that the infant's skill in these areas should be related to the verbal, memory, and problem-solving skills measured by traditional IQ tests for older children.

On the other hand, recent tests that assess the infant's response to familiar and novel stimulus items hold more promise in identifying those features of mental functioning that might remain constant over a span of years. Recall that the *Fagan Test of Infant Intelligence*, based on the infant's tendency to respond to novelty, correlates well with IQ scores three years later. Several other researchers have reported strong relationships between both recognition memory and speed of habituation during infancy and IQ at ages one through eight years (Bornstein & Sigman, 1986; McCall & Carriger, 1993). Infant recognition memory is also strongly related to language proficiency and performance on other cognitive tests in later childhood (Rose, Feldman, & Wallace, 1992; Thompson, Fagan, & Fulker, 1991). When the characteristics of visual attention are used as measures, mental development seems to be more continuous than developmental psychologists previously thought. Moreover, these data suggest that the ability to discern the familiar from novel may represent a fundamental cognitive skill that plays a role in other higher-order mental processes.

▶ Interaction among domains

**The Predictive Utility of IQ Tests**     What do IQ tests predict? IQ tests do a good job of telling us which children will be successful in school and which will have difficulties. Most studies have found that the correlations between intelligence tests and measures of educational achievement average about .50, with the correlations slightly higher for elementary school children than for high school or college students (Brody & Brody, 1976; Jensen, 1980). In addition, the correlations are strongest with academic subjects emphasizing verbal skills. In one study, the correlation between IQ and reading comprehension was .73, but only .48 in geometry (Bond, 1940). One reason that IQ scores are so successful at predicting school achievement is that many of the skills required in intelligence tests overlap with the skills essential to educational success. Verbal fluency, the ability to solve arithmetic problems, and rote memory, some of the abilities measured by IQ tests, are part of most children's school routines. Thus, IQ tests predict best exactly what they were originally designed by Binet to foretell.

Do IQ tests predict any other developmental outcomes besides school success? IQ scores are related to job status during adulthood. In his longitudinal study of children with IQs of 140 or higher, Lewis Terman (Terman, 1925; Terman & Oden, 1959) found that many of these exceptionally bright individuals eventually became scientists, executives, and college faculty members. As usual, however, we must be cautious about how we interpret correlational data. If, as we saw earlier, IQ scores are strongly related to educational achievement, it may be that occupational success is the result of education and not a direct result of IQ. In fact, researchers who have applied advanced statistical techniques to unravel the directions of influence among IQ, education, and occupation have demonstrated that IQ influences educational attainment and has little additional direct influence on occupation (Fulker & Eysenck, 1979; Jencks, 1972).

Aside from these relationships, however, IQ scores have typically not been found to be related to other measures of success in life. IQ scores do not necessarily predict the amount of money an individual earns, physical or mental health, or general life satisfaction (Lewis, M., 1983; McClelland, 1973). A likely explanation is that IQ tests measure only a restricted set of skills that do not provide a full picture of intelligence as the ability to adapt to the environment.

Because IQ tests predict a limited number of developmental outcomes, many psychologists advocate their use only for educational purposes—to identify gifted children or to provide students who have lower intellectual capabilities with special educational services. Even here, some experts caution that making major educational decisions based solely on IQ test scores can be dangerous. For example, the child may obtain a low score on a given test because of poor motivation, unfamiliarity with the English language, or vastly different cultural experiences. Moreover, when the child is labeled an "underachiever" or a "slow learner" on the basis of an IQ score, teachers and parents may have lower expectations of that child, a phenomenon that can further lower her achievement. Finally, IQ test scores usually do not have direct implications for specific remedial education practices or instructional techniques (Boehm, 1985). Thus, many recommend that psychologists who employ IQ tests also rely on other measures of the child's abilities, such as classroom observations or teacher reports, and that examiners be familiar with the cultural backgrounds of the children they assess (Weinberg, 1989).

## Exceptional Intelligence

Less than 3 percent of the population falls outside the typical range of intelligence, that is, beyond two standard deviation units of the mean for IQ scores. A child who obtains an IQ score greater than 130 is generally regarded as gifted, whereas a child who obtains a score below 70 is often classified as mentally retarded.

**Giftedness**    The U.S. Office of Education has defined giftedness as a capability or potential ability in any of the following areas: (1) intellectual ability, (2) academic aptitude, (3) creativity, (4) leadership, and (5) visual or performing arts (Marland, 1972). Gifted children are identified as having exceptional general intellectual skill and may have unique special talents, as well, such as unusual musical ability or facility with mathematics.

Probably the most extensive study of the gifted was conducted by Lewis Terman beginning in 1921 (Terman, 1954; Terman & Oden, 1959). Over a thousand children with IQ scores of 140 or greater were studied longitudinally from early adolescence into their adult years. What were these children like? Contrary to popular stereotypes, they were not frail, sickly, antisocial "bookish" types. They tended to be taller than average, physically healthy, and often assumed positions of leadership among their peers. By the time they were young adults, about 70 percent of those in the sample completed college (a very high proportion for that generation), and many obtained advanced degrees. The majority entered professional occupations where they became very productive as adults, authoring books, plays, and scientific articles, for example. Unfortunately, however, because the children in Terman's sample were nominated by their teachers, gifted children who were more quiet or who did not fit a teacher's conception of a "good student" were probably overlooked. Thus, while the findings of Terman's large-scale study show that gifted children generally enjoyed many successes in life, the results must be viewed with caution.

▶ Roles of nature and nurture

Does giftedness simply reveal itself naturally during the childhood years? Not according to other researchers examining the underpinnings of exceptional talent. In one study, two children who were expert chess players and one who was an accomplished musician were found to spend many hours practicing their skills under the tutelage of special teachers (Feldman, 1979). In another, world-class musicians, mathematicians, and athletes reported that their childhood years were marked by strong encouragement of their early natural abilities. Parents, coaches, and teachers were important sources of motivation, and typically, these talented individuals spent years in intensive training of their skills (Bloom, 1982).

Drawing upon his triarchic theory of intelligence, Robert Sternberg has extended our understanding of giftedness beyond the psychometric criterion of high IQ score. According to Sternberg (1981, 1986), gifted children show several unique information-processing skills. First, when solving problems, they tend to spend much of their time in planning—selecting and organizing strategies and information, for example—and less time with encoding the details stated in the problem. That is, their approach tends to be more "global" than "local," reflecting greater metacognitive skills. Second, Sternberg hypothesizes that gifted children are better able to deal with novelty and to automatize their information processing. Given novel, unusual insight problems, for example, gifted children are better able to recognize useful strategies for solutions compared with children of average ability (Sternberg, 1986).

Finally, gifted children are apparently more efficient and speedier in processing stimuli that match their particular talents. Veronica Dark and Camilla Benbow (1993) asked extremely gifted seventh- and eighth-graders to judge, as quickly as they could, whether two stimuli were the same or different. When the stimuli were digits, the response patterns of students who were the most gifted in mathematics showed faster access to numerical representations than other children. The response patterns of students who were the most gifted in verbal skills showed faster access to verbal representations when the stimuli were words. Based on their analysis of many studies of giftedness, Dark and Benbow (1993) concluded that the difference between gifted and other children is not qualitative; rather it is simply a matter of degree, in this case, the degree to which basic cognitive skills are used quickly and efficiently.

**Mental Retardation**     According to the American Association on Mental Retardation, mental retardation is defined as subaverage intelligence combined with limitations in two or more adaptive behaviors that are first evident during the childhood years (Luckasson et al., 1992). Adaptive behavior refers to a range of social skills typically required to function in the everyday world, such as self-care skills, the ability to get to school or home on one's own, or eventually, the capacity to find a job and handle personal finances. This broad definition is framed by four assumptions outlined in Table 10.3. Levels of retardation are sometimes identified, ranging from mild to profound. While the mildly retarded child can usually be expected to profit from school instruction and to eventually live independently as an adult, a profoundly retarded child will require special assistance with almost every aspect of daily functioning throughout life.

As we saw in Chapters 3 and 4, some cases of mental impairment are linked to genetic factors, as in the case of Down syndrome or PKU, or to experiences in the prenatal or perinatal environment that interfere with brain and central nervous system development and functioning, such as exposure to rubella or oxygen deprivation during birth. When there is a clear biological cause, the retardation is called *organic*. Generally, the most severe forms of retardation fall into this category. In other cases, the retardation has no obvious organic roots, but rather is suspected to result from an impoverished, unstimulating environment, the inheritance of the potential for a low range of intelligence, or a combination of both. About 70 to 75 percent of cases of mental retardation fall into this category called nonorganic or *familial retardation* (Zigler & Hodapp, 1986). Usually, the level of retardation for children in this second class is mild or moderate.

Are children with mental retardation qualitatively different from children with at least average intelligence, or do their mental capacities differ only in degree? Psychologists who have studied the cognitive processing of children with familial retardation have noted that they show deficits on a number of fronts. First, they have difficulty in focusing attention on the task at hand, becoming easily distracted. Second, they show notable deficits in working memory and an impoverished general knowledge base. One reason may be that they rarely produce the strategies for remembering typically displayed by children of average or above-average intelligence, strategies like rehearsal and or-

▶ Roles of nature and nurture

**TABLE 10.3**

**Assumptions in Defining Mental Retardation**

Recent efforts to identify mental retardation have focused increasingly on the specific adaptive limitations that children sometimes display as the accompanying assumptions illustrate.

### Four Essential Assumptions in Defining Mental Retardation

1. Valid assessment respects cultural and linguistic diversity along with communication and behavioral differences;

2. Limitations in adaptive skills are found within community settings appropriate for similar-age peers and identify the individual's precise needs for support;

3. Specific adaptive limitations often co-exist with competencies and personal strengths in other areas; and

4. With continuing effective supports, individuals with mental retardation generally improve in ability to function.

Source: Adapted from Luckasson, R., Coulter, D., Polloway, E., Reiss, S., Schalock, R., Snell, M., Spitalnik, D., and Stark, J., *Mental Retardation: Definition, Classification, and Systems of Supports, 9th edition*. Washington, DC: American Association on Mental Retardation.

ganization described in Chapter 9. Thus, their ability to retain information in both short- and long-term memory is hampered. Finally, children who have nonorganic retardation oftentimes fail to transfer knowledge from one learning situation to another. If the child was trained, for example, to repeat a string of digits to improve recall, he would fail to employ that strategy when given a new, but similar task like recalling a set of letters (Campione, Brown, & Ferrara, 1982). All of these findings suggest that mentally retarded children develop just like children of average intelligence, just slower. On the other hand, say some experts, we do not know if children with organic retardation have the same structure of intelligence as others. Their developmental progression in attaining cognitive skills may be unique (Zigler & Hodapp, 1986).

Negative stereotypes are often associated with the label "mental retardation," and over the years there has been much debate about what term best capsulizes intellectual impairment. Specialists have offered various alternative labels, such as "slow learners," "exceptional children," or "special needs children," but these terms are not necessarily widely accepted. Other controversies concern the effective care and education of children with mental retardation. The trend in recent years has been to "deinstitutionalize" all but the most profoundly retarded. Likewise, the placement of children in special education schools and classrooms has given way to the practice of *mainstreaming* retarded children within normal classrooms, where they are encouraged to participate in and benefit from as many regular classroom activities as their abilities permit.

## *Factors That Influence Intelligence*

▶ Roles of nature and nurture

In Chapter 3 we saw that genetics can influence intelligence. Chromosomal abnormalities and single-gene effects such as the fragile X syndrome, Down syndrome, and PKU can have profound effects on the child's intellectual growth. The higher correlations among IQ scores of identical twins reared apart compared with fraternal twins or nontwin siblings reared in the same environment and the strong correlations between IQs of adopted children and their biological parents also suggest a role for heredity.

Yet even if we agree that genetic differences contribute, perhaps even substantially, to the child's intellectual competence, it would be a mistake to conclude that IQ scores are not influenced by environmental experiences (Angoff, 1988; Scarr, 1981). Take, for example, two traits very strongly influenced by heredity—physical height and the presence of the trait for PKU. In each instance, the presence of the genotype bears a great resemblance to the phenotype. Yet it is also true that environmental factors can influence the eventual outcome for the child. Recall the secular trends in physical height discussed in Chapter 5, and remember also from Chapter 3 that dietary modifications for infants born with PKU can result in essentially normal mental development. In each case, a highly canalized human characteristic is modified by the environment. The ever-present role of the environment is an important factor to keep in mind as we discuss the roots of intelligence.

What factors are especially important in shaping the child's intellectual attainments? We begin by examining group differences in IQ scores, findings that have provided much of the backdrop for the nature-nurture debate. Next we examine those elements of the child's home experience that might be crucial to mental growth as well as the role of the sociocultural environment in shaping specific mental skills. Finally, we consider the impact of early-intervention programs on the intellectual attainment of children from culturally different backgrounds. In each case we will see that there are many conditions, even given the contributions of heredity, under which intelligence is not fixed but modified by the timing, extent, and range of environmental experiences.

## Group Differences in IQ Scores

Children from different socioeconomic and ethnic backgrounds do not perform equally well on traditional IQ tests. One well-established finding is that African American children in the United States typically score 15 points lower than Caucasian children on tests such as the Stanford-Binet and the WISC-R (Jensen, 1980; Loehlin, Lindzey, & Spuhler, 1975). Another finding is that children from lower socioeconomic classes obtain lower IQ scores than those from middle and upper classes (Deutsch, Katz, & Jensen, 1968; Lesser, Fifer, & Clark, 1965). Of the many hypotheses put forward about the sources of these differences, some have rekindled the nature-nurture debate and others focus on the validity of IQ tests for minority and lower-class children.

**Racial Differences in IQ and Nature vs. Nurture**    In 1969, Arthur Jensen published a paper suggesting that racial differences in IQ scores could, in large part, be accounted for by heredity. According to Jensen, there is a high degree of *heritability* in IQ; that is, about 80 percent of the variation in IQ scores in the population could be explained by genetic variation. Because racial and ethnic subgroups within the population tend not to marry outside their groups, he argued that African American–Caucasian differences in IQ scores had a strong genetic component.

▶ Roles of nature and nurture

Jensen's propositions created a storm of controversy. One of the most immediate criticisms was that *within-group* estimates of heritability could not be used to explain *between-group* differences in performance. Even if the heritability of IQ were .80 for both Caucasian and African American populations (actually the heritability estimates for IQ had been derived solely from samples of Caucasian children and their families), other factors, such as differences in the environmental experiences of each group, could still not be ruled out in explaining racial differences in IQ scores (Loehlin, Lindzey, & Spuhler, 1975). For example, a 15-point difference in IQ could still arise if most Caucasian children grew up in enriched environments and most African American children experienced environments that did not promote optimal intellectual development.

Sandra Scarr and Richard Weinberg's (1976, 1978, 1983) **cross-fostering study**, in which children were raised in environments markedly different from that of their biological families, demonstrated just how this effect might take place. In their transracial adoption study, Scarr and Weinberg selected 101 Caucasian middle-class families who had adopted African American children, most of whom were under one year of age at the time of adoption. Many of these families also had biological children of their own. The adoptive families were highly educated, were above average in occupational status and income, and had high IQ scores. The biological families of the adopted children had lower educational levels and lower-status occupations.

Scarr and Weinberg found that the average IQ of the African American adopted children during childhood was 106, higher than the average score of both African Americans and the general population. The researchers argued

**cross-fostering study**    Research study in which children are reared in environments that differ from those of their biological parents.

that because the adopted children were raised in environments in which they were exposed to Caucasian culture and the verbal and cognitive skills customarily assessed in IQ tests, they performed better than African American children with similar genetic backgrounds who did not have that experience. At the same time, however, the IQs of the adopted children were more strongly correlated with the educational levels of their biological parents ($r = 0.36$) than with the IQs of their adoptive parents ($r = 0.19$). Thus, the role of heredity cannot be ruled out. Figure 10.7 illustrates a similar pattern of findings obtained in the Adolescent Adoption Study, which examined relationships between IQ scores of natural and adoptive parents and their adopted children who were between sixteen and twenty-two years of age (Scarr & Weinberg, 1983).

Many researchers reject a genetic explanation of racial differences in IQ as too simplistic. We have seen in Chapter 3 that heredity and environment interact in complex ways to produce varied developmental outcomes; neither, by itself, is sufficient to explain most human behaviors. Furthermore, in the United States race is a variable confounded by the other variables of social class, educational achievement, educational opportunities, and income. All these factors can contribute to the types of learning experiences young children undergo. Parents with greater financial resources can provide the books, toys, and other materials that stimulate intellectual growth. Moreover, families with economic stability are likely to experience less stress than economically unstable families, a factor that can be related to intellectual performance, as we saw earlier in this chapter. Rather than settling the nature-nurture question, racial differences in IQ have served to highlight the complexity of interactions among variables associated with intelligence.

▶ Sociocultural influence

**Test Bias**    Another hypothesis to account for group differences in IQ scores is based on the notion of **test bias**. According to this view, the content of traditional tests is not familiar to children from some social or cultural backgrounds. In other words, traditional psychometric tests are not *culturally fair*. Recall the dilemma faced by Son Van Nguyen at the beginning of this chapter and the erroneous conclusion he drew about his own intelligence based on his failure to define "inscription" and to answer the question "Who discovered America?" Unfortunately his test score may reflect the same conclusion. Children who have not encountered such specific information in their own cultural experience will fail those items and score lower on many intelligence tests.

What happens when tests that are more culturally fair are administered to children from varied sociocultural backgrounds? The research findings are mixed. In Chapter 7, you were introduced to the *Raven Progressive Matrices*, a nonverbal test of reasoning ability that is assumed to contain minimal cultural bias. Caucasian children still score significantly higher on this test than African American children do (Jensen, 1980). Yet when another culturally fair test, the *Kaufman Assessment Battery*, was administered to children of different cultural backgrounds, the difference in test scores between Caucasian and African American children was smaller than when tests such as the WISC-R are given (Kaufman, Kamphaus, & Kaufman, 1985).

Finally, there are questions about whether minority children have the same experiences with, and attitudes toward, taking tests as majority children do. Some of the skills required to perform well on standardized tests include understanding directions, considering all response alternatives before selecting one, and attending to one item at a time (Oakland, 1982). Minority children

**test bias**   Idea that the content of traditional standardized tests does not adequately measure the competencies of children from diverse cultural backgrounds.

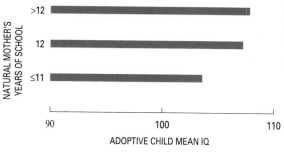

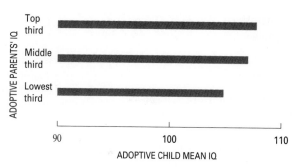

Source: Adapted from Scarr & Weinberg, 1983.

**FIGURE 10.7**

**The Influence of Heredity and Environment on IQ**

In the Adolescent Adoption Study, the IQ scores of adopted teenagers and young adults who had spent most of their childhoods with their adoptive families were compared with their natural mothers' educational level (an estimate of IQ) and with their adoptive parents' IQ scores. The left graph shows that children whose mothers had more years of school had higher IQ scores, indicating a role for heredity. The right graph shows that children who had higher IQ scores tended to have adoptive parents who also had higher scores, suggesting a role for the environment.

▸ Roles of nature and nurture

may not have this basic "savvy" about how to take tests. Since most tests do not permit examiners to be flexible in how the test is administered, they may underestimate minority children's skills (Miller-Jones, 1989). Moreover, minority children may score lower simply because they do not see the point of performing well or have not acquired the same drive to achieve in academic settings that is part of the majority culture (Gruen, Ottinger, & Zigler, 1970; Zigler & Butterfield, 1968).

Not all researchers are convinced that test bias and motivational factors play a large part in explaining the lower IQ scores of certain groups of children (Jensen, 1980). Even for the skeptics, however, these ideas have highlighted the importance of trying to structure test situations so that *all* children are given the opportunity to display their best performance.

## Experiences in the Child's Home

The generally lower performance of children from minority groups and lower socioeconomic classes on IQ tests has prompted many researchers to take a closer look at how interactions in the home as well as the values of the larger culture might affect intellectual development. Not surprisingly, some elements in caregiver-child interactions are related to higher scores on IQ tests.

**The HOME Inventory**   In 1970, an ambitious project got under way in Little Rock, Arkansas. Initiated by Bettye Caldwell and her associates (Caldwell & Bradley, 1978), the goal of the project was to identify characteristics of the young child's environment that might be related to later competence, including intellectual achievement. A sample of infants and their parents was recruited for a longitudinal study that would last eleven years.

The *Home Observation for Measurement of the Environment (HOME)* inventory was designed to measure a number of characteristics of the child's home surroundings, including the quality of caregiver-child interactions, the availability of objects and activities that might stimulate the child, and the types of experiences family members provide to nurture the child's development (see Table 10.4 for the subscales and some sample items). Researchers collected data for the inventory through interviews and direct observations in the children's homes and gave children in the sample standard intelligence and school achievement tests. The results identified several key features of the home environment as related to subsequent IQ (Bradley, 1989).

**TABLE 10.4**

**Subscales of the Home Observation for Measurement of the Environment (HOME)**

The HOME Inventory assesses several features of the home environment. Subscales (1), (4), and (5) were found to be significantly correlated with the child's later IQ and language competence.

**(1) Emotional and Verbal Responsivity of Mother**
*Sample item:* Mother caresses or kisses child at least once during visit.

**(2) Avoidance of Restriction and Punishment**
*Sample item:* Mother does not interfere with child's actions or restrict child's movements more than three times during visit

**(3) Organization of Physical and Temporal Environment**
*Sample item:* Child's play environment appears safe and free of hazards.

**(4) Provision of Appropriate Play Materials**
*Sample item:* Mother provides toys or interesting activities for child during interview.

**(5) Maternal Involvement with Child**
*Sample item:* Mother tends to keep child within visual range and to look at the child often.

**(6) Opportunities for Variety in Daily Stimulation**
*Sample item:* Child eats at least one meal per day with mother and father.

Source: Adapted from Elardo & Bradley, 1981.

First, significant correlations were found among several measures of the home environment taken at twelve months and children's IQ scores at ages three and four-and-a-half years. Particularly important were scales that measured parental emotional and verbal responsivity to the child, the availability of appropriate play materials, and parental involvement with their children (Bradley & Caldwell, 1976; Elardo, Bradley, & Caldwell, 1975). The correlations among these factors and the child's later IQ ranged from .39 to .56. Second, HOME scores at age two years were significantly related to language competencies at age three years (Elardo, Bradley, & Caldwell, 1977). The same three scales on the HOME inventory were especially related to the child's linguistic competence. The most recent follow-up of these children showed that parental involvement and provision of toys at age two years were significantly related to school achievement at age eleven years (Bradley, 1989).

▶ Interaction among domains

This series of studies shows that important processes occur between children and their parents early in life that can have long-lasting implications for future intellectual achievement. For one thing, children who have responsive parents may develop a sense of control over their environments, and their resulting general socioemotional health may facilitate intellectual growth. In addition, the opportunity to play with toys may provide contexts for children to learn problem-solving skills from their parents as well as the chance to develop knowledge from direct manipulation of the play materials. Language development is also enhanced because verbal interactions with parents during play and at other times teach children the properties of spoken speech (Bradley & Caldwell, 1984).

**Parenting Practices**    Several other parental variables are related to children's subsequent IQ scores. Kevin Marjoribanks (1972) interviewed almost two hundred parents about their intellectual expectations for their eleven-year-old boys, their emphasis on the use of language, and their desire to promote independence and activity in their children. The boys were also given several mental tests. The results showed that parents who "pressed" for achievement, independence, and linguistic skill and, in general, valued intellectual accomplishment had sons with higher scores, particularly on verbal tests. One caution is in order in interpreting these data, however, as well as the results of the HOME studies. As with any correlational research that uncovers relationships, we do not necessarily know the direction of influence. In the case of the Marjoribanks (1972) study, for example, it could be that bright, intelligent boys elicited higher expectations from their parents rather than the other way around. Similarly, in the HOME studies, intelligent infants may have engendered more parental responsiveness and involvement simply because of their greater exploration of the environment or advanced verbal skills.

Some of these difficulties are addressed in a study by Luis Laosa (1982), who used sophisticated statistical techniques to extract information about the directions of influence in correlational relationships. In order to see how certain parental characteristics and behaviors might directly influence children's intellectual development at age three years, Laosa studied fifty families through interviews, observations of mother-child interactions, and standardized tests of children's intellectual levels. From this rich set of data, a number of strong causal relationships emerged.

Several aspects of parenting practices predicted children's IQ scores. Among them were how much time family members spent reading to the child as well as the extent to which mothers used physical demonstration, or modeling, as a teaching strategy with their children. Another extremely important factor was the mothers' socioeducational values. This variable was expressed through the mothers' educational and occupational status, as well as the amount of reading they did with their children. It is significant that reading to children and modeling problem-solving tasks proved to be substantial influences. Reading and the verbal exchanges that accompany it provide an excellent context for the development of verbal skills, which are a primary component of intelligence tests. Furthermore, three-year-old children are cognitively capable of profiting from modeling as a teaching style, whereas more complex forms of teaching may be beyond the preschooler's cognitive reach.

Of course, many questions remain about the specific ways in which the child's home environment influences intellectual attainment. For example, are there teaching strategies, aside from modeling, that may be more effective in promoting intellectual advances in older children? Are there other important parental behaviors that have not yet been identified? And—in keeping with the position that parent-child effects are often reciprocal—what is the child's role in the parent-child interactions that foster intellectual development? One of the principal aims of current research is to identify more of the specific family characteristics that lead to intellectual advances across the span of childhood.

## The Child's Sociocultural Environment

Children from different cultural backgrounds often display unique patterns of intellectual abilities. For example, the Inuit people of the Arctic region show exceptional visual-spatial skills compared with those of United States residents (Berry, 1966; Vernon, 1966). How does the larger culture within which the child lives influence her level or pattern of mental abilities?

▶ Sociocultural influence

The role of culture in intellectual development might be examined in terms of activities and behaviors essential for adaptation and survival. The Inuits de-

The child's sociocultural background can influence specific patterns of intellectual skills. For example, among the Inuits, superior visual-spatial skills may be tied to that culture's emphasis on hunting and gathering in large, expansive terrains.

pend on hunting and gathering in their native terrain, activities that require the ability to perceive small changes in large, expansive fields of vision; in this context, the prominence of their visual-spatial skills is understandable. Similarly, as we saw in Chapter 8, Mexican children with extensive experience in making clay pottery were more advanced in a Piagetian measure of intelligence—the conservation of quantity task—compared with children without experience in pottery making (Price-Williams, Gordon, & Ramirez, 1969). Intensive practice in specialized skills that are an integral part of one's cultural experience can heighten "intelligence" in those domains.

Another way to understand the role of culture is in terms of parental beliefs about children that affect their interaction styles. When Shirley Brice Heath (1983) examined the communication patterns of middle- and lower-class parents as they interacted with their children, she found some striking differences. Middle-class parents tended to ask their children frequent questions and expected children to be able to provide explanations. They tended to give their children lots of reasons for events and behaviors even when their children were only one month of age. Lower-class parents, in contrast, delivered frequent commands without providing a rationale and expected children to show what they knew rather than to tell what they knew. Moreover, children in these families were discouraged from asking questions, which were viewed as a sign of disrespect. Although this study focused on social class differences more than cultural differences, we can see how a culture's views about the proper place of children and the behaviors appropriate for parents and their offspring may translate into specific interaction styles that influence intellectual styles.

One additional way in which the culture into which the child is born can influence patterns of intellectual activity is the degree to which that culture emphasizes formal schooling. Cross-cultural studies have shown that children with formal education are more likely to use mnemonic strategies to learn lists of words and to classify objects according to a consistent rule (Sharp, Cole, & Lave, 1979; Wagner, 1978). Although memory and classification performance, the dependent measures in these studies, are not explicit indices of intelligence, they are cognitive skills frequently embedded in psychometric tests. Moreover, if intelligence is assumed to be reflected in IQ scores, children may learn specific skills in school that enable them to do well on intelligence tests (Ceci, 1991). Performing on a time-limited test, understanding and following directions, and being able to consider a number of response alternatives are all general test-taking skills that children are likely to absorb in school. Furthermore, the answers to specific questions found on intelligence tests, such as "Who discovered America?" or "What is the distance from New York to Los Angeles?" are usually learned in school.

## CONTROVERSY: THINKING IT OVER

### Can Early Intervention Programs Boost IQ?

During the 1960s, the idea of compensatory education became popular in the United States. Researchers wanted to see if the poor performance of children from lower socioeconomic classes on IQ and achievement tests could be improved if they received the kinds of cognitive stimulation presumably present in the lives of middle-class children. If compensatory education programs worked, the idea that IQ is malleable or modifiable by experience would receive strong support, and a genetic explanation of class and race differences in IQ would be less tenable.

The first federally funded program for compensatory education was Project Head Start, begun in the 1960s as a preschool enrichment program for "underprivileged children." The program includes nutritional and medical assistance as well as a structured educational program designed to provide cognitive stimulation. The first evaluations of Head Start were disappointing. In 1969, the Westinghouse Learning Corporation/Ohio University report compared the intellectual development of about four thousand children from similar backgrounds, half of whom had participated in the first Head Start programs around the country and half of whom did not participate in Head Start. There were essentially no differences in the intellectual performance of the two groups; both remained below the norms for their age groups. This evaluation, however, has been criticized on a number of grounds, including that the evaluation was done prematurely, just barely after the program got off the ground.

More recent evaluations of Head Start have yielded more optimistic results. The Head Start Evaluation, Synthesis, and Utilization Project was an attempt to summarize all research on the impact of Head Start (McKey et al., 1985). This review concluded that Head Start produced significant effects on the intellectual performance of program participants, at least for the short term. Head Start children performed well in the first year or two after they started elementary school, showing average gains of 10 points in IQ score, but the effects of the program faded in subsequent years.

Project Head Start is a federally funded program designed to provide nutritional and medical assistance, as well as to strengthen the school readiness skills of children growing up in poverty. Children who attend Head Start show gains in some measures of educational achievement and social competence, and at least short-term increases in IQ scores.

Another important early intervention project begun in 1972, the Carolina Abecedarian Project, was aimed at preventing the lower intellectual functioning of children at risk (Ramey & Campbell, 1981; Ramey, Lee, & Burchinal, 1989). A sample of 121 poor, pregnant women with low educational achievement and low IQ scores (an average of 84) was selected. Once the infants were born, roughly half were assigned to the experimental group and half to the control group. Infants in the experimental group received medical care, nutritional supplements, and a structured program of day care that emphasized the development of cognitive, language, social, and motor skills. In addition, the researchers provided a toy-lending library and a home visiting program as well as parent support groups. This was a comprehensive, multifaceted program intended to alter as much as possible the developmental outcomes for this high-risk sample. During the first year, there were few differences between infants in the experimental and control groups on their Bayley scores. From age eighteen months onward, however, the IQs of the experimental group consistently exceeded those of the control group. Yet some researchers remain pessimistic about the significance of these findings. For example, Herman Spitz (1986) pointed out that by age five years, the differences between the experimental and control groups diminished to an average of only seven points. Therefore, say the critics, the effects of this intensive intervention were only transitory.

Is Head Start "America's most successful educational experiment" as some have claimed (Zigler & Muenchow, 1992)? Or are early intervention programs examples of social experiments that failed? Why might the initial gains of Head Start and Abecedarian children have "washed out" in successive years? Are IQ scores the best indicators of the impact of Head Start and other early intervention programs? One collaborative study of the effects of eleven early intervention programs showed that children who had participated were less likely to be assigned to special education classes, less likely to be "held back" in grade, and were more likely to cite their school achievements as a source of pride than nonparticipants (Lazar & Darlington, 1982). Edward Zigler, a key figure in the formulation of Project Head Start, and his colleagues have also suggested that Head Start children show gains in social competence (Zigler & Berman, 1983; Zigler & Trickett, 1978). Are these outcomes just as important as gains in IQ scores?

---

## THEMES IN DEVELOPMENT

## INTELLIGENCE

▶ **What roles do nature and nurture play in the development of intelligence?**

The nature-nurture debate becomes an especially charged and thorny issue in the matter of intelligence. Few psychologists would dispute that heredity plays a role in the child's intellectual development. For example, early individual differences in the speed of infant habituation and recognition memory may signal differences in some aspects of later intellectual functioning. In addition, genetic effects such as Down syndrome and the high correlations between IQ scores of identical twins reared apart suggest a role for "nature." Yet research also shows that the child's early experiences within the home together with the intellectual skills that are touted by the larger culture modulate how his genetic blueprint comes to fruition.

▶ **How does the sociocultural context influence the development of intelligence?**

Culture broadly influences the kinds of skills that its members value and nurture and that are believed to constitute "intelligence." Is speed of executing tasks important? Are good visual-spatial or verbal skills essential in successful adaptation to the environment? A culture's demands and expectations frame the way in which intelligent behavior will be defined in the first place. From the narrower perspective of performance on standardized IQ tests, children who have experiences consistent with the knowledge tapped by test items will perform well, while those whose backgrounds are different will be at a disadvantage. Other sociocultural factors often associated with social class, such as parental emphasis on intellectual achievement or the amount of emotional stress within the family system, can also impinge on IQ test performance.

▶ **How does the child play an active role in the development of intelligence?**

Traditional psychometric theories have rarely assumed that the child plays an active role in affecting her own intelligence. However, the information-processing perspective has focused on executive control skills, the child's ability to monitor his own cognitive processes, and other cognitive activities as significant contributors to intellectual development. Moreover, Piaget's theory, which can be viewed as a general theory of intelligence, emphasizes the child's active construction of knowledge.

▶ **Is the development of intelligence continuous or discontinuous?**

Some would argue that intelligence does not really develop at all—that it is a stable, relatively unchanging, inborn human characteristic. Information-processing theorists, in contrast, see intelligence as largely the by-product of normal continuous developmental processes wherein the child learns more complex relations about stimuli in the world and becomes capable of more sophisticated cognitive processing with age. Piaget views intellectual development as stagelike, and formal tests based on his theory assess which stage of thinking best characterizes the child.

▶ **How prominent are individual differences in the development of intelligence?**

From the psychometric perspective, the concept of intelligence is rooted in the assumption that there are individual differences in performance on certain mental tasks. Other theories, particularly Gardner's theory of multiple intelligences, stress the patterns of strength and weakness a given individual may show across a spectrum of domains. Studies of how the environment influences intelligence also suggest that an individual's score on an IQ test can be a function of the specific parenting practices she has experienced or other elements of the childhood environment.

▶ **How does the development of intelligence interact with development in other domains?**

Children who obtain high scores on intelligence tests are more likely to be successful in school and, as adults, to hold high-status jobs and be productive in them. Thus, to some extent, IQ scores can predict certain aspects of success in life. According to more recent theoretical perspectives, the child's experiences in various domains can also influence intelligence. For example, in Gardner's theory of multiple intelligences, bodily-kinesthetic intelligence can be fostered through athletic experiences and interpersonal intelligence can grow through extensive social experience.

## *Summary*

**What Is Intelligence?**  Definitions of intelligence vary in two major ways: (1) whether intelligence is seen as a global characteristic or a set of separate abilities, and (2) whether the emphasis is on the products or processes of intelligent behavior. The *psychometric model* emphasizes individual differences in test scores, whereas information-processing models underscore the mental activities that individuals engage in as they solve problems.

**Measuring Intelligence**  Intelligence is usually expressed in terms of the *intelligence quotient (IQ)*, the individual's score derived from an intelligence test. Most intelligence tests, administered both individually and to groups, are based on the psychometric model and assess a range of verbal, visual-spatial, and problem-solving skills. Common intelligence tests for infants are the *Bayley Scales of Infant Mental and Motor Development* and the *Fagan Test of Infant Intelligence*. School-aged children are most frequently tested with either the

*Stanford-Binet Intelligence Scale* or the *Wechsler Intelligence Scale for Children-Revised (WISC-R)*. More recently, tests based on alternative conceptions of intelligence have grown in popularity.

For many children the scores obtained on IQ tests are stable over time, especially after the age of five years, although individual children can show dramatic fluctuations. Studies of infant attention and memory suggest that there may be some continuities in mental abilities. IQ scores generally predict academic success but are not necessarily related to other measures of life satisfaction. While most children fall within the normal range of IQ scores, some score at the upper and lower boundaries of exceptionality.

**Factors That Influence Intelligence**   Intelligence is the result of the complex interaction between heredity and environment. Racial and social class differences in IQ scores illustrate the difficulty of drawing simple conclusions about the sources of intelligence. One problem is that estimates of the heritability of IQ do not necessarily explain between-group differences in scores. *Test bias* can be a factor in the performance of children from some social or cultural backgrounds on tests designed for the cultural mainstream. The child's experiences in the home and the skills valued by the larger culture can have an impact on the child's level and pattern of intellectual performance.

# 11

# Emotion

▶ **What roles do nature and nurture play in emotional development?**

▶ **How does the sociocultural context influence emotional development?**

▶ **How does the child play an active role in the process of emotional development?**

▶ **Is emotional development continuous or discontinuous?**

▶ **How prominent are individual differences in emotional development?**

▶ **How does emotional development interact with development in other domains?**

*Among the Gusii tribe of Kenya, a typical interaction between mother and child takes place: The Gusii mother maintains a bland, neutral expression, constantly avoiding her infant's gaze, especially when the child becomes excited or agitated. When the infant begins to show strong signs of emotion by crying, laughing, or thrashing her arms and legs, the mother physically restrains her. The mother also nods her head and makes repetitive noises to maintain a calm emotional state in her infant. Although mother and child rarely engage in face-to-face play, when they do the mother makes a deliberate attempt to minimize strong emotional content.*

*Contrast this scene with one in our own culture: The mother raises her eyebrows and opens her mouth, making an "Oohh" sound suggesting surprise. Her baby eyes her with fascination, chortles, then smiles. The mother reacts with an expressive "Yeesss!" and claps her hands. The baby lets out a squeal of delight.*

The very different nature of these two interactions raises some fundamental questions about the nature of human emotions and the forces that guide emotional development. Are our emotions innately determined, the result of a biological "prewiring"? Or are our displays and conceptions of emotions derived from learning the rules and conventions of our culture? On the surface, the two mother and child scenes might suggest that nurture, not nature, is the determining factor. The Gusii culture places great importance on suppressing intense emotions, probably to maintain harmony in the small tribal living units characteristic of that group. In the United States, in contrast, intensity of emotional expression is consistent with the energetic approach to life that Americans value (Dixon et al., 1981). These differing cultural norms are reflected in the parenting styles of each culture and the behaviors eventually displayed by children. At the same time, however, as we will see in this chapter, recent research with young infants suggests that emotions possess biological underpinnings as well.

The exchange between the American mother and her infant suggests another related question about emotional development: to what extent do children play an active role in the emergence of the full range of their emotions? Do children passively record and mimic the emotional expressions of others at the same time as they are learning the contexts in which to display them? Do emotions appear when some internal biological clock marks the appropriate developmental moment for them to appear, again suggesting a passive role for the child? Or is there something special about the context of social interactions in which the dynamic between *both* partners, caregiver and child, produces the emotional capabilities and dispositions we eventually observe in the adolescent and young adult?

In this chapter we will see how children's expression and understanding of emotions change with age. Many of their accomplishments are tied to advances in cognition that permit them to think about complex feeling states in themselves as well as in others. Finally, even though emotions are the personal expression of the individual's moods or feeling states, they also function as a mode of communicating with others. Given the social dimension of emotions, we can investigate the role they play in the child's relationships with others, specifically in the special "attachments" that emerge between child and caregivers. What is the psychological significance of these emotional bonds and how do they influence the child's later development?

## *What Are Emotions?*

Although many of us have an intuitive understanding of what an emotion is, the formal psychological definition of this term proves to be surprisingly elusive. Many theorists agree, however, that **emotions** are a complex set of behaviors produced in response to some external or internal event, or *elicitor,* and that they include several components. First, emotions have a *physiological* component, involving changes in autonomic nervous system activities such as respiration and heart rate. Fear or anxiety, for example, may be accompanied by more rapid breathing, increased heart rate and blood pressure, and perspiration. Second, emotions include an *expressive* component, usually a facial display that signals the emotion. Smiles, grimaces, cries, and laughter overtly express a person's emotional state. Third, emotions have an *experiential* component, the subjective feeling or cognitive judgment of having an emotion (Izard, Kagan, & Zajonc, 1984). Just how a person interprets and evaluates an emotional state depends on his level of cognitive development and the experiences he has had. For a child to state, "I feel happy," he must recognize the internal cues and external contexts associated with "happiness," which are derived from experience. In addition, he must have a relatively mature concept of the self as a feeling, responding being, a sign of cognitive maturity.

▶ Interaction among domains

### Measuring Emotions

Given the complex nature of emotions, how to measure them becomes an important issue for researchers because all three dimensions—physiological, expressive, and cognitive—must be taken into consideration. One approach is to record changes in physiological functions such as heart rate (acceleration or deceleration), heart rate variability (the individual's basic heart rate pattern), or EEG patterns showing brain activity as affective stimuli are presented (Fox & Davidson, 1986). Another strategy is to conduct fine-grained analyses of the child's facial expressions or vocalizations. Tiny movements of the muscles in the brow, eye, and mouth regions produce the facial configurations associated with joy, sadness, anger, and other emotions (Izard & Dougherty, 1982). Similarly, the frequency, loudness, duration, and sound patterns of the child's vocalizations indicate emotion (Papoušek, Papoušek, & Koester, 1986). Finally, the child's interpretations of her own and others' emotions can be assessed

**emotions** Complex behaviors involving physiological, expressive, and experiential components produced in response to some external or internal event.

through the use of self-report measures (for example, "Tell me how often you felt cheerful in the last week") and tasks requiring the child to label, match, or produce emotional expressions ("Tell me how the person in this picture feels" or "Show me the person who feels sad").

Although each methodological approach has helped to illuminate aspects of the child's emotional life, researchers must be cautious when they interpret their data. When physiological changes such as decelerated heart rate occur as the infant watches a lively segment of "Sesame Street," is he experiencing happiness, interest, or fear? The emotion that corresponds to a specific reaction of the nervous system is not always clear. Likewise, an overt emotional expression such as crying might represent a number of possible internal emotional states, such as sadness, joy, or fear. Self-reports of the child's emotional states present their own difficulties. As we saw in Chapter 1, children may answer researchers' questions in the way they think they *should* rather than on the basis of how they really feel. Others may be reluctant to discuss their inner feelings at all. Despite these methodological difficulties, researchers have learned a good deal about emotional development in the last two decades.

## The Functions of Emotions

What role do emotions play in the psychological development of the child? On one level, they serve to organize and regulate the child's own behavior. If a child is learning to ride a two-wheel bicycle and succeeds in tottering down the sidewalk without keeling over, she undoubtedly will feel elated and probably more motivated to practice this new skill for a few more minutes or even hours. If, on the other hand, she falls repeatedly or even injures herself, she may feel angry and discouraged and quit riding for a few days. Thus, the child's emotional states regulate what she will decide to do (Campos et al., 1983).

Emotions also have important links to cognition. Children often smile, show surprise, or even display fear as they engage in cognitive activities. For example, the infant who perceives depth as he is perched over the rail of his crib will express wariness. A ten-month-old who observes an object disappear behind a screen acts surprised; she has the concept of object permanence and understands the object still exists but is perplexed over its whereabouts. The school-aged child beams proudly at the mastery of an intellectual challenge such as completing a difficult puzzle or school assignment. In each case, the child's cognitive activity leads to the display of an emotion. In fact, researchers often use these emotional responses to assess children's mental skills.

▶ Interaction among domains

Not only do many cognitive processes produce emotional expressions, the child's emotional state can also influence cognitive processes, such as level of attention or ability to learn. In one experiment, children were instructed to think of an event that made them feel either happy or sad. Children who were induced in this way to feel a positive affective state learned a shape discrimination problem significantly faster than those induced to feel a negative emotion (Masters, Barden, & Ford, 1979).

Of special importance is the fact that emotions serve to initiate, maintain, or terminate interactions with others. The baby's cry or smile almost invariably prompts contact with the caregiver. A toddler's frustration and anger over an unshared toy may lead him to abandon a playmate temporarily. In fact, a social dialogue completely devoid of emotional content is unusual. "Moods," more enduring emotional states, may help us to understand the child's personality attributes, such as the tendency to be shy, dependent, or aggressive. Personality traits, too, can influence the frequency and form of the child's social contacts. Thus, understanding emotional development can increase our appreciation of a broad range of children's accomplishments in other domains.

## *Theories of Emotional Development*

Are human emotions biologically based, preprogrammed responses to specific environmental stimuli, or are they the products of the myriad learning experiences that accumulate over the course of infancy and childhood? The familiar nature-nurture debate has an historically rich tradition when we turn to the varying ways in which the emergence of human emotions has been explained.

### The Foundations of Modern Theory: Darwin and Watson

▶ Roles of nature and nurture

The biological underpinnings of emotion were emphasized by Charles Darwin, the nineteenth-century scientist most known for his theory of evolution. According to Darwin (1872, 1877), emotions and their expressions in humans and animals have endured because they serve a survival function by preparing the organism for action and signaling to others the action to be taken. On encountering a predator, for example, some apes will express fear with a bared-teeth grimace before fleeing. Other members of the troop read this expression and take similar action. In this way, emotions play a role in the survival of both organisms and species.

As we saw in Chapter 1, in his investigation of human emotions Darwin made extensive observations of his own children, keeping a diary of their emotional expressions and states. He identified seven basic emotions, each with its own accompanying facial expression: anger, fear, affection, pleasure, amusement, discomfort, and jealousy. He argued that humans from many different cultures show similar expressions for the basic emotions and that human expressions were similar to those of other primates. Darwin concluded that emotions and their expression are innate and biologically determined.

With the emergence of behaviorism in the first part of the twentieth century, this prevailing view shifted. Emotions, like most other responses in the child's repertoire, were now seen as products of the child's learning experiences. John Watson, in his book *Behaviorism* (1930), stated that three emotional reactions—fear, rage, and love—are innate, but are emitted to only a limited range of stimuli. Loud noises, for example, automatically result in the display of fear in very young infants. Through learning, however, these primitive emotions develop into the more complex array of affective responses that children and adults produce to various stimuli.

To illustrate his theory, in his famous case study of little Albert, Watson demonstrated that fear of a specific object could be learned through the process of classical conditioning. Albert, an eleven-month-old infant, initially showed no fear responses to a white rat, although loud sounds did elicit a marked reaction from him. Watson systematically paired the sound of a steel bar being struck by a hammer, producing a startle or fear reaction, with every attempt Albert made to touch the white rat. Eventually the sight of the rat

There are many cross-cultural commonalities in the expression of certain emotions. Such commonalities suggest biological underpinnings to emotional displays.

alone made Albert begin to whimper and cry, a reaction Watson called a **conditioned emotional response**. Moreover, Albert showed a generalization of the fear response to other objects that were similar in appearance, such as a rabbit and a piece of fluffy cotton. Although researchers today would raise ethical questions about conducting such an experiment because of the potential psychological harm to the child, this early study does point out how basic learning processes can account for the display of emotions to initially neutral stimuli.

## Contemporary Perspectives on Emotional Development

Modern-day theorists are more likely than either Darwin or Watson to acknowledge the interaction of biological and environmental factors in explaining the complexity and range of the child's emotional behaviors and experiences. Nevertheless, some investigators continue to stress the biological foundations of emotions, whereas others believe that the child's socialization history and the cognitions underlying emotions play a more significant role.

▶ Roles of nature and nurture

### Biologically Based Explanations
The main champions of a strong biological view of emotions today are Paul Ekman and Carroll Izard. Ekman (1972, 1973) conducted numerous studies of how people in various cultures understand emotions and concluded that there are universal facial expressions for certain basic emotions that are interpreted in similar ways across cul-

**conditioned emotional response** Emergence of an emotional reaction to an originally neutral stimulus through classical conditioning.

tures. Ekman showed photographs of six faces depicting happiness, sadness, anger, fear, surprise, and disgust to subjects in the United States, Japan, Chile, Brazil, and Argentina. As they looked at each photograph, subjects were asked to identify the emotion displayed. Ekman (1972) found a high degree of agreement across cultures as to which emotions were being depicted.

Similarly, Izard believes that because certain emotional expressions are displayed by very young infants, they are necessarily innate and have distinct adaptive value (Izard, 1978; Izard & Malatesta, 1987). When the newborn infant tastes a bitter substance such as quinine, for example, she will pull up her upper lip, wrinkle her nose, and squint her eyes, indicating that she has detected the unpleasant stimulus. No learning is necessary to produce this reaction of disgust. The caregiver observing this type of signal might respond by removing a potentially harmful substance from the baby's mouth, thereby ensuring her well-being. The experience of emotion, Izard states, is the automatic product of the internal sensory feedback the individual elicits from making the facial expression; wrinkling the face produces the feeling of disgust. Izard also maintains that once an emotion is activated, it motivates the individual in turn to act. The experience of disgust, in other words, may lead the baby to spit out the distasteful substance.

Both Ekman and Izard acknowledge that learning may play a role in emotional development, especially as children learn to control and regulate their emotions. They maintain, however, that the role of biological factors is paramount and that emotions originate in the genetic blueprints with which the child begins life.

**A Cognitive-Socialization Explanation**     Michael Lewis and Linda Michalson (1983) have provided an alternative account of the emotional life of the child, one that emphasizes both the cognitive activities involved in emotional experiences and the role of socialization. According to these theorists, an environmental event does not produce directly an emotional expression. Instead, the child relies on cognitive processes to assess the event, how it compares with past events, and the social rules surrounding the event. Suppose, for example, the child encounters a barking dog. Whether he cries with fear or smiles at the noisy animal depends on the child's past experiences with dogs (has he ever been bitten?) and on what parents and others have instructed him to believe about animals ("Barking dogs will bite—stay away!" or "Some dogs get excited when they want to play—it's okay"). Cognitive processes thus act as **mediators**, or mental events that bridge the gap between environmental stimuli and the response the individual ultimately expresses. According to Lewis and Michalson, this conceptualization accounts for individual differences in emotional reactions when the same event produces different responses from two people.

According to Lewis and Michalson, socialization plays an important role in shaping the time and the manner in which emotions are displayed. Children in our culture learn that it is appropriate to feel happy at birthday parties and sad when a friend's grandmother dies and that a smiling and sad face should be made at these events, respectively. Socialization also guides the way in which emotions are managed. Young children in many cultures, for example, learn to inhibit expressions of fear and anger. Finally, socialization directs the way in which children label and interpret emotions. When the young child cries due to a physical injury and the parent says, "That hurts, doesn't it?" the interpretation provides pain as the reason for the tears. When crying is the response to a

▶ Interaction among domains

▶ Individual differences

**mediator**  Cognitive process that bridges the gap between an environmental event and the individual's eventual response to it.

tower of toy blocks falling over, the parent may provide a different interpretation for the child, such as "That's frustrating." These kinds of communications serve as an important vehicle for children to learn how to interpret their own emotional states.

# *Expressing, Recognizing, and Understanding Emotions*

Researchers focus on emotional development from various angles. First, they examine whether children change in the way they *express* their own emotions. Do infants exhibit the full range of emotions that we see in adults or does a developmental progression occur in the types of emotions that children display? Second, do children change in their skill in *recognizing* emotions in others, in reading the facial expressions, vocalizations, and other body movements that carry messages about positive or negative affect? Last, are children likely to change in how they *understand* emotions, such as the events that precipitate and follow an emotional display or the complexities of masking emotions?

## Early Emotional Development

Much of the groundwork for emotional development occurs during the first year or so of life. Parents and young infants rely less on language to communicate with each other than on nonverbal signals that frequently are laden with emotional overtones. Just what behaviors are infants capable of showing and "reading"? The answer to this question bears directly on the roles of nature and nurture in emotional development.

### Emotional Expression in Infancy
Even newborn infants are capable of producing the facial expressions associated with several emotions, including interest, distress, disgust, joy, sadness, and surprise (Field, Woodson et al., 1982; Izard, 1978). In studies of infants' affective displays, observers who are asked to label emotions depicted in slides and videotapes of infant faces have identified each of these discrete emotions reliably. By four months of age, the infant has added anger to her repertoire; by seven months, expressions of fear appear (Izard et al., 1980). The fact that these discrete facial expressions appear so early in infancy, before much learning could have taken place, provides strong support for the idea that emotional expressions are to some extent biologically determined. Moreover, because these emotions appear to be genetically determined, they are often called **basic** (or *primary*) **emotions**.

Besides displaying a wide range of expressive signals, infants show a high rate of change in their facial displays, sometimes spontaneously and sometimes in response to the expressions of others. Carol Malatesta and Jeannette Haviland (1982), for example, found that as three-month-olds engaged in face-to-face play with their mothers, they changed their expression about once every seven seconds. As you might expect, the facial displays of infants often produce a reaction from the caregiver—delight at the infant's smile and concern at an expression of distress, for example. In fact, Malatesta and Haviland (1982) noted that mothers responded to infant expressions 25 percent of the time, often by matching expressions. Thus, caregivers' responses to infants'

▶ Roles of nature and nurture

**basic emotion**   Emotion such as joy, sadness, or surprise that appears early in infancy and seems to have a biological foundation. Also called *primary emotion.*

signals lead to interactions that play a crucial role in their developing relationship.

Although even the earliest displays of basic emotions usually are recognized readily by adults, their form and the conditions that elicit them may change over the first few months. The development of two important emotional expressions in infancy—smiling and crying—demonstrates these changes.

**Smiling**    One of the most captivating and irresistible infant behaviors is the smile. In the newborn this behavior occurs primarily during the state of REM sleep, when dreaming is thought to occur, in bursts of several smiles in succession (Emde & Koenig, 1969). The mouth stretches sideways and up, producing a simple version of the eagerly anticipated expression. Although many hypotheses attempt to explain why very young infants produce this facial gesture (including the popular but mistaken notion that "gas" is responsible), the most consistent finding is that neonates smile when they experience a shift in physiological arousal state, as when they fall asleep or become drowsy (Wolff, 1987).

At approximately two weeks of age, the form of the smile changes. The corners of the lips retract even farther, the cheek muscles contract, and the skin around the eyes wrinkles. Now the infant smiles during states of wakefulness, sometimes in response to familiar voices and sounds, sweet tastes, and pleasant food odors (Fogel, 1982; Steiner, 1979). By three months of age, smiles increase in frequency and occur in the presence of visual stimuli, most notably the sight of the baby's primary caregiver, usually the mother (Adamson & Bakeman, 1985; Fogel, 1982). Because this "social smile" plays a substantial role in initiating and maintaining interactions between the infant and significant adults in her life, it is considered an important milestone in infant development.

At about four months of age, infants begin to laugh as well as smile, initially at the presence of tactile or auditory stimuli such as tickling or interesting verbalizations, and later at amusing visual events such as the game of peek-a-boo (Sroufe & Waters, 1976). Thus, what began as a spontaneous, reflexlike behavior that occurs during certain physiological states becomes a voluntary, controlled response that serves an important social-communicative function.

Several aspects of smiling and laughter are important to note. First, the developmental course of these positive emotional expressions is related to the child's increasing cognitive maturity. With age, the child smiles and laughs to increasingly complex stimuli, stimuli that are incongruent with his past experiences, or that suggest events that he remembers from the past. One-year-olds laugh at stimuli such as their mother walking like a penguin or sucking on a baby bottle; they also laugh in anticipation of being kissed on the stomach (Sroufe & Wunsch, 1972). In each situation, children rely on their memory of familiar events to perceive novelty or incongruity. Second, children become increasingly active in producing on their own the stimuli that generate smiling and laughter. After age two years, for example, children will laugh more when they cover an observer's face with a cloth than when the observer covers her own face (Sroufe & Wunsch, 1972). Finally, the shift from smiling as a reflexlike behavior to a controlled, voluntary response parallels the increasing maturation of the cerebral cortex, which is responsible for higher-order mental processes and deliberate, goal-directed behaviors.

▶ The child's active role

▶ Interaction among domains

▶ The child's active role

▶ Interaction among domains

**Crying**     Crying is another common way in which infants express emotion. Newborn babies cry for a variety of reasons, but primarily because they are hungry, cold, wet, in pain, or disturbed from their sleep. The nature of the baby's distress is often reflected in the type of cry she emits. In an extensive study of eighteen infants observed in their homes, Peter Wolff (1969) identified three patterns of crying. The first is the *basic* (or hungry) *cry*, a rhythmical sequence consisting of a vocalization, pause, intake of air, and pause. The second is the *angry cry*, in which extra air is forced through the vocal cords during the vocalization segment of the basic cry. Finally, in the *pain cry*, the infant produces a long vocalization followed by an even longer silence as he holds his breath and then gasps.

Like smiling, crying is a response that promotes contact between the infant and the caregiver. Mothers usually react to their young infant's cries promptly, especially an angry or pain cry, and when they do, infants actually cry less in succeeding weeks and months (Bell & Ainsworth, 1972; Wolff, 1969). The first order of business is usually to make sure that the infant's physical needs are met. Other effective techniques for soothing the crying infant include providing a pacifier, swaddling with a blanket, and tapping some part of the body—that is, providing some form of rhythmic or continuous stimulation (Brackbill, 1975). Picking up the baby and holding her on the caregiver's shoulder also is soothing, probably because this act provides the infant with a broad range of stimulation that distracts her from crying (Korner, 1972).

By the time the infant is one or two months of age, the causes of crying are no longer purely physiological. Infants will cry when the caregiver leaves the room or when a favorite toy is removed. At about this time, a new type of cry emerges—the *fussy* or *irregular cry*, which varies in intensity, is less rhythmical, and seems to function as a demand for particular objects or actions. At eight months of age, the infant will pause in crying to see if the mother or other adults are receiving the message (Bruner, 1983). As the infant gains more voluntary control over his vocalizations, cry patterns become even more varied and controlled and are displayed in a wider range of situations to signal an assortment of different messages. Individual differences in the crying patterns of some infants also might be useful in diagnosing developmental abnormalities. Malnourished infants, for example, display more variability in the pitch of their cries, whereas children who have suffered oxygen deprivation have shorter cries of high pitch (Michelsson, Sirvio, & Wasz-Hockert, 1977; Zeskind, 1981). Variations in individual patterns of crying may affect caregiver-infant relationships. In particular, the infant's *shrill* or *aversive cry*, typical of the preterm baby, may interfere with the normal interactions that pave the way for healthy parent-child relationships (Zeskind & Lester, 1981).

▶ Individual differences

▶ The child's active role

**Recognizing and Imitating Others' Expressions**     Besides producing expressions themselves, infants are capable of discriminating and responding to emotional displays in others. Several remarkable studies conducted by Tiffany Field and her colleagues suggest that three-day-old infants are capable of imitating the facial expressions for happiness, surprise, and sadness when they are modeled by an adult (Field, Woodson et al., 1982, 1983). Infants widened their eyes and opened their mouths on "surprise" trials, drew back their lips on "happiness" trials, and tightened their mouths and furrowed their brows on "sadness" trials. Based on the faces the babies made, observers correctly guessed which expressions the babies had seen at levels significantly

According to some research, three-day-old infants are capable of imitating expressions for happiness (top), sadness (middle), and surprise (bottom) when they are modeled by an adult.

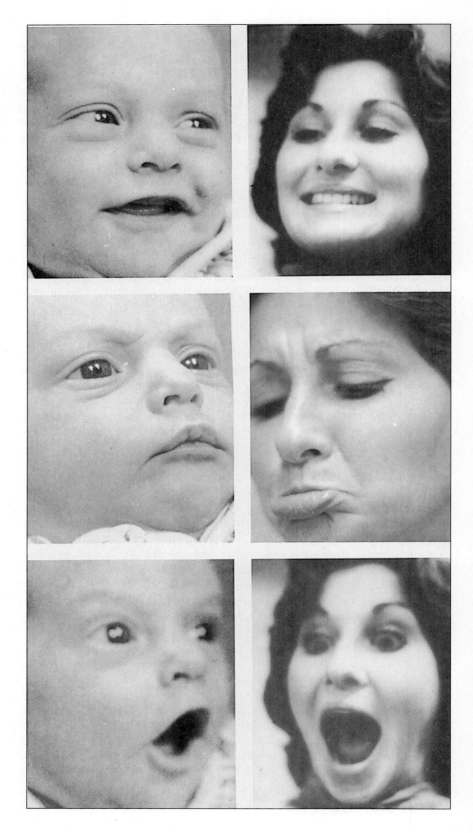

**Showing Preferences for Adult Facial Expressions**

When three-month-olds were shown a neutral face (far left) paired with one of the other photos of a smile, they consistently preferred to look at the smile and looked longer at the more intense smiles.

above chance. Although some researchers offer alternative explanations for these findings (see Chapter 6), many believe that infants have an early sensitivity to emotional expressions in others.

Other researchers use the *habituation paradigm* to examine the infant's ability to recognize facial expressions in photographs. Typically, a stimulus representing one emotional expression is presented repeatedly while the amount of the infant's visual fixation is monitored. After looking time decreases to a certain predetermined level, a stimulus containing a new expression is presented. If the infant's looking time increases, there is good reason to believe that she has detected the change in expression. Researchers have also examined whether infants show preferences for some expressions over others.

The use of these experimental procedures has shown that three- and four-month-olds are able to distinguish among several expressions, particularly happiness versus anger, surprise, and sadness and that they prefer to see joy over anger (Barrera & Maurer, 1981a; LaBarbera et al., 1976; Young-Browne, Rosenfeld, & Horowitz, 1977). They can even identify variations in a single expression. Three-month-olds in one experiment consistently preferred looking at photographs of a woman exhibiting a smile over a neutral expression (see Figure 11.1) and looked longer at increasingly intense versions of the smile (Kuchuk, Vibbert, & Bornstein, 1986).

**Social Referencing** Do infants derive meaning from the facial expressions they observe in others, or do they simply respond to changes in isolated facial features that contribute to these expressions (for example, the upward curve of the mouth in the smile)? Because some researchers report, as noted in Chapter 6, that infants under the age of two or three months do not scan systematically the entire human face, it seems unlikely that they are responding to any expression as a totality. In fact, it is not until the latter half of the first year that infants show evidence they understand the meaning of facial expressions.

At this age, a phenomenon called **social referencing** indicates an infant's ability to interpret facial expressions. If infants are placed in an unfamiliar situation or encounter a strange object and are uncertain how to respond, they often will look to their caregiver for cues. The facial expression displayed by the caregiver typically will influence the infant's own emotional response and subsequent actions. For example, in one study, twelve-month-olds were placed on the shallow side of the visual cliff apparatus, which, as we saw in Chapter 6, can be used to assess the perception of depth. They were coaxed to move toward the place on the cliff where the surface apparently drops off. At this point, half of the subjects' mothers posed a happy expression and the other half ex-

**social referencing** Looking to another individual for emotional cues in interpreting a strange or ambiguous event.

hibited fear. Of the infants whose mothers smiled, 74 percent crossed the deep side of the cliff. In contrast, *none* of the infants whose mothers showed fear crossed the deep side. Moreover, these babies tended to produce fearful expressions on their own faces (Sorce et al., 1985). Thus, not only did infants "read" the expression they saw on their mother's face, they also correctly interpreted its message.

▶ The child's active role

Social referencing provides a good example of the child's active involvement in the process of emotional development. When he encounters a puzzling or ambiguous event, he actively seeks information from the environment about how to react. He then uses the emotional expression of others to derive meaning from that event and decide on a course of action (Tronick, 1989).

**Emotions as Regulators of Social Interactions**     Observations of infants' ability to express and identify emotions in the context of interactions with others have suggested to developmental psychologists that emotions serve an important function in regulating and modulating early social exchanges. This dynamic process begins at about two or three months of age, when, as in the second scene that opened this chapter, the infant looks into the adult's eyes and shows a "social smile" or a cry, to which the adult responds. The adult vocalization or facial expression, in turn, often precipitates another emotional response from the infant. Such episodes of reciprocal, mutually engaging cycles of caregiver-child behaviors are called **interactive synchrony**. During the first year, interactive synchrony characterizes about 30 percent of face-to-face interactions between infants and caregivers (Tronick & Cohn, 1989).

At about three months, primary caregivers typically assume the major responsibility for guiding interactions, producing repetitions of exaggerated faces and vocalizations to which the infant pays rapt attention (Stern, 1974). Infants, without doubt, notice and react to their mothers' displays. When moth-

Beginning about two to three months of age, infants and their caregivers begin to show *interactive synchrony,* cycles of reciprocal coordinated face-to-face interactions.

**interactive synchrony**     Reciprocal, mutually engaging cycles of caregiver-child behaviors.

ers do not return a smile but show a still face or a neutral pose, infants respond with a quizzical or sober look, avert their gaze, and touch themselves or some nearby object (Toda & Fogel, 1993; Tronick et al., 1978). When mothers show a positive expression, the infant follows suit. If mothers look depressed, infants react by averting their gaze and sometimes crying (Cohn & Tronick, 1983). By about six to nine months of age, infants more clearly take the initiative; the infant's displays of positive affect now more often precede the mother's (Cohn & Tronick, 1987). Thus, throughout early infancy, the child becomes an increasingly active partner in an emotionally toned interactive "duet" with the caregiver.

▶ The child's active role

But what about the other 70 percent of the time, when infant-caregiver interactions are *asynchronous* or uncoordinated with each other? Edward Tronick and his colleagues believe that these episodes, which constitute the majority of infant-caregiver relations, also play an important part in normal emotional development. A common occurrence after a sequence in which infant and caregiver are not coordinated is the infant's attempt to repair the "interactive error." When the mother looks sad, for example, the infant's subsequent gaze aversion or crying encourages the mother to modify her own behavior, and frequently she does (Cohn & Tronick, 1983). Thus, episodes of asynchrony provide infants with the opportunity to learn about the rules of interaction, and in cases in which they are able to repair an interaction, give them a sense of mastery or control over their environment (Tronick & Cohn, 1989).

Affective exchanges between infant and caregiver lay the groundwork for social behavior and emotional dispositions at later ages. For example, researchers find that infants of clinically depressed mothers express a good deal of negative affect in face-to-face interactions, probably in response to the disengagement of the mothers (Cohn et al., 1986). These infants tend to express more sadness and anger, and their negative affect extends to other adults, even those who are not depressed (Field et al., 1988; Pickens & Field, 1993). Moreover, the dominance of specific emotions during early mother-child interactions culminates in a general mood or background emotional state that pervades the child's own behaviors (Tronick, Ricks, & Cohn, 1982). The child then brings this general affective tone to new situations—for example, an anxious child is likely to interpret a new event as fearful, whereas a happy child might react with curiosity. Finally, the nature of the affective exchanges between mother and child influences the strength of the emotional bond—or *attachment*—between them. Infants who engage in attempts to elicit responses from mothers by smiling, vocalizing, or crying at six months of age are more likely to have healthy attachments at the age of one year than children who withdraw from such interactions (Tronick, Ricks, & Cohn, 1982). As we will see later in this chapter, healthy attachments, in turn, have been found to be related to many other positive developmental outcomes in social and cognitive functioning. Hence, the tone of these early interactions is a crucial facet of child development.

## Later Emotional Development

Beyond infancy, the child's emerging linguistic capabilities and cognitive growth result in still more changes in emotions. She expresses new and more complex emotions, such as guilt, shame, and pride, or more varied forms of joy and fear, earlier basic emotions. With the advent of language, she can communicate feelings by verbalizing instead of just furrowing her brow and crying or making some other facial display. She also gains a more comprehensive understanding of emotions, their antecedents and their consequences, both in herself and in others.

▶ Interaction among domains

**Expressing Complex Emotions**    By their second year, many children begin to show emotions that reflect a more complex understanding of social relationships. Shame, guilt, and envy, for example, each require the child to understand the perspective of another person—that they might be disappointed in the child, might be hurt, or might feel affection for a third party. Such emotions also require a consciousness about the self and one's relations to others, a facet of cognitive development (Campos et al., 1983; Lewis, 1989). Emotions like envy and guilt are accordingly known as **complex emotions**.

Mothers report seeing the first signs of guilt and shame at about eighteen months of age (Emde, 1980; Izard & Malatesta, 1987). This is the same age at which children begin to make reparations for damage they have caused to others, such as hugging a peer hit a few moments earlier or showing remorse for coloring on the couch (Zahn-Waxler & Radke-Yarrow, 1982). At age two years, children also show visible signs of jealousy. The child might wedge himself between mother and father as they are hugging, or hit a sibling that a parent just kissed (Cummings, Zahn-Waxler, & Radke-Yarrow, 1981). You might recall from Chapter 7 that this is the same age at which children begin to evidence early referential communication skills, which also require an awareness of the perspectives of others. As the child understands more about the social world and the relationships and feelings of others, her own feeling states become increasingly sophisticated as well.

At the same time that more complex emotions emerge, the child also begins expressing the basic emotions in more varied and controlled ways. During the preschool years, for example, children show an increase in the tendency to smile by raising their upper lip and exposing the upper teeth, a form of smile that is considered the most sociable. By age four years, children begin to reserve this smile almost exclusively for same-sex peers (Cheyne, 1976).

Another emotion, fear, also undergoes developmental changes, particularly in the types of stimuli that elicit it. Whereas early expressions of fear are made in response to loud noises or strange people, later in childhood fear occurs as a response to more complex events, such as the possibility of failing in school or being rejected by peers (Morris & Kratchowill, 1983; Rutter & Garmezy, 1983). Thus, as the child's cognitive skills and social awareness grow, he expresses more complex emotions or more elaborate and controlled forms of the basic emotions.

▶ Interaction among domains

**Understanding Emotions**    Children begin to use language to describe feeling states between eighteen and thirty-six months of age, shortly after they begin to talk. Inge Bretherton and Marjorie Beeghly (1982) asked mothers of twenty-eight-month-olds to keep a diary of their children's verbalizations that referred to psychological states. Table 11.1 shows the percentage of children who used words for various emotions to describe either themselves or others. Besides being able to apply a wide range of terms to express both positive and negative feelings, these children also were able to discuss the conditions that led to a specific emotion and the actions that followed as a consequence. Several children, for example, made statements similar to "Grandma mad. I wrote on wall," suggesting an understanding of the reasons for another's emotion. Another type of utterance made by several children—"I cry. Lady pick me up

**complex emotion**    Emotion such as guilt and envy that appears later in childhood and requires more complex cognitive and social skills.

| Emotion Terms | Percentage of Children Using Word for Self or Others |
|---|---|
| **Positive** | |
| Good (moral) | 93 |
| Love | 87 |
| Like | 80 |
| Funny | 77 |
| Have fun | 67 |
| Happy | 60 |
| (Feel) good | 47 |
| To be all right | 37 |
| Have a good time | 30 |
| Proud | 27 |
| (Feel) better | 27 |
| Surprised | 13 |
| **Negative** | |
| Bad (moral) | 87 |
| Scared | 73 |
| Mad | 73 |
| Sad | 57 |
| Scary | 40 |
| Yucky | 33 |
| Messy | 30 |
| Angry | 17 |
| (Feel) bad | 10 |

Source: Adapted from Bretherton & Beeghly, 1982.

**TABLE 11.1**

**The Emotion Vocabulary of 28-month-olds**

Mothers of thirty 28-month-old children collected data on their children's verbalizations that referred to psychological states. This table shows the percentage of children who used emotion terms to describe themselves or others. The majority of children used at least some emotion terms.

and hold me"—signifies an understanding that emotions may be related to subsequent actions.

From the age of three to four years and onward, children become more proficient in verbally describing the causes and consequences of emotions (Barden et al., 1980). Children tend to agree that certain events, such as receiving a compliment, lead to happy emotions, whereas others, such as being shoved, lead to negative feelings. Furthermore, they are able to suggest ways of ameliorating another's negative emotions, such as hugging a crying sibling or sharing toys to placate an angered playmate (Fabes et al., 1988). Knowledge about emotions can have ramifications for the child's social development. For example, children who have substantial knowledge about the emotions that usually accompany given situations, such as fear during a nightmare, are better liked by their peers (Denham et al., 1990). The reason may be that children who have greater knowledge about emotions are more likely to respond appropriately to the emotional expressions of their age-mates.

▶ Interaction among domains

By the time they enter school, children possess an even more sophisticated understanding of emotions. They appreciate the phenomenon that emotions fade with time (Harris, 1983). They also begin to understand that changes in thoughts may lead to changes in feelings—that thinking happier thoughts, for example, might make a sad mood go away (Weiner & Handel, 1985). As children approach adolescence, they comprehend the possibility of experiencing two contrasting emotions at the same time, like feeling happy to get a bike as a gift but disappointed that it is not a ten-speed (Harter & Buddin, 1987).

One of the skills that appears later in childhood is the ability to mask or "fake" an emotional state. By this time, children understand behaviors prescribed by cultural rules (for example, you are supposed to look happy when you are given a gift even if you don't like it) or behaviors necessary to obtain certain goals (you should smile even if you don't feel well if you want your mother to allow you to go to a friend's party). Paul Harris and his associates (Harris et al., 1986) examined this skill in using emotional **display rules**, the cultural guidelines about when and how to express emotions, by asking six- and ten-year-old children to listen to stories in which the central character felt either a positive or negative emotion but had to hide it. Here is one such story:

> Diana has just had a haircut. The hairdresser cut off too much hair and she looks really silly. At school Diana's friends laugh at her and tell her that she looks like a hedgehog. Diana tries to pretend that she doesn't mind.

After hearing the story, children were to describe verbally the facial expression of the protagonist along with how this person *really* felt. Even six-year-olds could state that the emotion displayed would not match the emotion felt, although ten-year-olds provided a fuller explanation. These results suggest that by the middle school years children have developed a broad understanding of the social norms and expectations that surround the display of feelings.

As they approach adolescence, children's concepts of emotions center increasingly on internal psychological states. That is, whereas younger children identify their own emotional states based on the situations they are in ("I'm happy when it's my birthday"), preadolescents and adolescents refer more frequently to their mental states ("I'm happy when I feel good inside") (Harris, Olthof, & Meerum Terwogt, 1981). In explaining why emotions fade with time, younger children refer to the fact that situations change—sadness over a lost dog gives way to happiness when the family adopts another dog. At age ten years, their explanations center around notions of forgetting or not thinking about one's previous emotional state (Harris et al., 1985). Preadolescents also have better insights into the feelings and motives of others than do younger children. Fifth-graders in one study, for example, accurately identified the emotions felt by an adult based on the content of a conversation the adult was having with a third party. They were also able to elaborate on the reasons that person felt the way he did (Rothenberg, 1970).

In summary, emotional development in older children is affiliated closely with advances in cognition that allow them to think in more abstract and complex terms. In addition, it is apparent that the way in which children express and understand emotions can be a major component in their success with social relationships. We will see in Chapter 15 that children who are popular with their peers know how to deliver positively toned messages to their playmates. Similarly, the emergence of guilt and shame is related to moral development and altruism, two other important facets of social development.

**Emotions During Adolescence**   By many popular accounts, adolescence is a unique phase in emotional development. Many laypeople, as well as professionals, believe that adolescence is a time of "storm and stress," of emotional turmoil and extreme moodiness. Does research substantiate this belief? Although the evidence is somewhat mixed, several recent studies suggest that

**display rules**   Cultural guidelines about when, how, and to what degree to display emotions.

adolescents do experience more negative emotions than children of other ages, and in fact, may be at risk for psychological problems such as depression (Larson & Lampman-Petraitis, 1989; Petersen & Hamburg, 1986; Rutter, 1991).

In one recent study, for example, fifth- through ninth-graders wore electronic pagers for one week as they went through their normal daily routines. At random times over the week, the researchers "beeped" the subjects, signaling that they should rate their mood just before the signal. In addition, the children and their parents filled out questionnaires assessing the number of positive and negative life events they experienced in the past six months. Figure 11.2 shows the results. Ninth-graders reported more negative affect than the fifth-graders; moreover, for these young adolescents, negative emotions were associated with a greater number of negative life events, such as changing schools, breaking up with a boyfriend or girlfriend, or getting along poorly with parents (Larson & Ham, 1993).

For some adolescents, negative emotional states become more extreme and manifest themselves as depression, a psychological disorder characterized by depressed mood for enduring periods of time, eating and sleeping problems, low self-esteem, loss of energy, and other symptoms. According to recent estimates, roughly 35 percent of adolescents experience depressed mood, and about 7 percent meet the criteria for clinical depression, with girls experiencing higher rates of depression than boys (Petersen et al., 1993). Why are adolescents especially vulnerable? Several explanations are possible. Changes in self-image may accompany the many biological changes in the body associated with puberty. Cognitive growth may mean the adolescent thinks more about the self and her future. A switch from elementary to secondary school may mean adjustments in peer group relationships. Family relationships also

▸ Interaction among domains

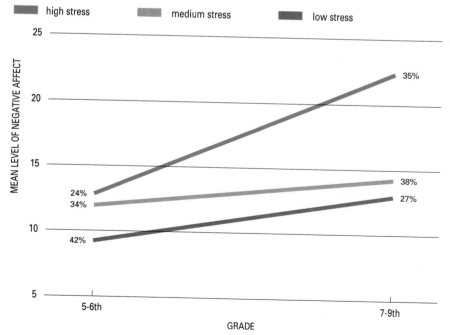

**FIGURE 11.2**

**Frequency of Negative Affect Among Adolescents**

To assess the types of emotions experienced by older children and adolescents, researchers "beeped" subjects during their daily routines and asked them to report how they felt. The mean percent of negative affect is shown along the y-axis. The percentages indicated within the graph show the proportion of students in each grade reporting low, medium, or high stress. Ninth-graders reported more negative affect than fifth-graders and those who reported more stress in their lives were especially likely to experience negative emotions.

may change; parents may have reached a stage in their relationship where they consider divorce, for example (Petersen et al., 1993; Rutter, 1991). Clearly, understanding and preventing depression in adolescents requires a consideration of several domains of development.

## Variations in Emotional Development

So far, our account of emotional development has emphasized commonalities across children in the expression and interpretation of emotions. Despite the generalities we have observed, especially in the emotional behaviors of infants, however, there are noteworthy variations in emotional development among individuals and cultural groups. Some of these variations suggest an important role for socialization in emotional development, while others suggest that biological factors play a role.

**Sex Differences in Emotions**    According to the familiar stereotype, females are more emotionally expressive and more sensitive to the emotional states of others than are males. Do boys and girls actually differ in any facet of emotional development? Several recent studies suggest that the answer is yes. During the first six months of infancy, girls tend to show more positive emotions, including interest and joy, than boys (Matias & Cohn, 1993). In another study with older children, when seven- and twelve-year-olds played a game with a peer, girls were more likely than boys to show a positive or negative emotion when the peer made a comment such as "she looks friendly" or "she doesn't look nice" (Casey, 1993). Later in adolescence, girls smile more than boys both on their own initiative and in response to the smile of another (Hall & Halberstadt, 1986). Girls also begin to show more anxieties than boys during the school years—fears about tests, family issues, health, and other concerns (Orton, 1982; Scarr et al., 1981). Finally, some researchers report that girls are better than boys at decoding the emotional expressions of others (Hall, 1978, 1984).

Observations of parents' behaviors suggest that many of these sex differences may be taught or modeled directly. For example, mothers and fathers spend more time trying to get their infant daughters to smile than they do their infant sons (Moss, 1974). Mothers of preschoolers also mention feeling states more often when they talk with their daughters than with their sons (Dunn, Bretherton, & Munn, 1987). When a group of researchers recorded the facial expressions of mothers as they played with their two-year-old children, they found that mothers were significantly more expressive with girls than with boys. Girls were exposed to a greater range of emotions and received more social smiles (Malatesta et al., 1989). In general, parents encourage girls to maintain close emotional relationships and to show affection, whereas they instruct boys to control their emotions (Block, 1973). Thus, while biological explanations of sex differences cannot be ruled out completely, many of the emotional behaviors we see in males and females appear to be influenced by their learning histories.

▶ Roles of nature and nurture

▶ Sociocultural influence

**Cross-Cultural Differences in Emotions**    The tendency of children to express and detect emotions varies as a function of the culture in which they are raised. American children, for example, tend to smile more in response to the smile of a stranger than do Israeli children (Alexander & Babad, 1981). On the other side of the emotional spectrum, Chinese children are better able to identify fearful and sad situations than are American children (Borke, 1973). These differences may reflect the child's incorporation of particular cultural beliefs about emotions.

A study of crying among the Kipsigis of Kenya provides a good example of how parenting practices reflect cultural values and shape the child's emotional responses. In the Kipsigis culture, crying is regarded as a positive behavior among infants, but as a negative behavior among older children, particularly as they approach their passage to adulthood. To discourage crying in her growing children, the Kipsigi mother does not hurry to pick up or hug her crying child. Instead, she waits for the child to approach her. And rather than focusing on the child's behavior and the reasons for it, she encourages the child to talk about other things and to return to the activities in which he had been engaged (Harkness & Super, 1985). We saw at the beginning of this chapter how, in a similar fashion, Gusii mothers prepare their children for a style of emotionally neutral interactions with others. Thus, the cultural norms governing emotions, mediated through parental behaviors, serve to elaborate and refine the child's earliest emotional tendencies.

**Temperament**    Emotions are not just transitory states of feeling and expression; often, we discern a child's more enduring emotional mood and describe her personality as "cheerful" or "hostile," "easy-going" or "irritable." Many researchers find that infants and children vary in **temperament,** a style of behavioral functioning that encompasses the intensity of expression of moods, distractibility, adaptability, and persistence. Individual differences among infants in these qualities often remain relatively stable over time, even through middle childhood (Pedlow et al., 1993).

▶ Individual differences

Stella Chess and Alexander Thomas (1982, 1990, 1991) have offered one conceptualization of temperament, identifying three basic patterns that many children display:

- The *"easy"* child generally has positive moods, regular body functions, a low to moderate energy level in responses, and a positive approach to new situations. This child establishes regular feeding and sleeping schedules right from early infancy and adapts quickly to new routines, people, and places.
- The *"difficult"* child is often in a negative mood, has irregular body functions, shows high-intensity reactions, withdraws from new stimuli, and is slow to adapt to new situations. The difficult child sleeps and eats on an unpredictable schedule, cries a good deal (and loudly), and has trouble with new routines.
- The *"slow-to-warm-up"* child is somewhat negative in mood, has a low level of activity and intensity of reaction, and withdraws from new stimuli. However, with repeated exposure to new experiences, these children begin to show interest and involvement.

Chess and Thomas (1991) note that children with different temperaments will evoke different patterns of reactions from their parents, teachers, and peers. "Easy" children usually elicit the most positive reactions from others, while children from the other two temperament categories typically draw more negative reactions. Later in life, children with "easy" temperaments may adjust more readily to important transitions, such as the start of school or making new friends. An important dimension of development, say Chess and Thomas, is the "goodness of fit" between the child's temperament and the

▶ The child's active role

**temperament**    Stable, early appearing constellation of individual personality attributes believed to have a hereditary basis; includes sociability, emotionality, and activity level.

demands placed on him by his environment, specifically parents, teachers, peers, and others.

In another set of studies, Jerome Kagan and his colleagues (Kagan et al., 1984; Kagan, Reznick, & Snidman, 1988) have noted that some infants have a tendency to show wariness and fearfulness when they encounter unfamiliar people, objects, or events, while others react with interest, spontaneity, and sociability. Both the first group, called *inhibited*, and the second, called *uninhibited*, tend to show their distinctive styles from infancy through middle childhood. Moreover, studies comparing identical and fraternal twins on these dimensions of temperament suggest that the tendency to be inhibited or uninhibited has a genetic component (Emde et al., 1992; Robinson et al., 1992). Other researchers have defined temperament similarly in terms of the tendency toward expressivity in manifesting basic emotions such as fear or pleasure (Goldsmith & Campos, 1982, 1990) or more generally, in terms of excitability and the ability to regulate the self and one's level of arousal (Rothbart, 1986).

▶ Roles of nature and nurture

Does early temperament predict any of the child's characteristics later in life? It appears so, according to the results of several recent studies. For example, the extent to which an infant tends to show negative emotions at three months of age predicts that child's poorer cognitive abilities at age four years even when factors such as the mother's responsiveness are ruled out as influences on the child (Lewis, 1993). In the domain of social relationships, preschool boys who exhibit a style of expressing negative affect tend to have poorer social skills and lower status among their peers (Eisenberg et al., 1993). Similarly, infants who tend to express anger and frustration score higher on measures of aggression at age six to seven years than children who expressed less anger as infants (Rothbart, Ahadi, & Hershey, 1994). It seems that the relatively stable emotional style a particular child displays may have far-reaching impact.

▶ Interaction among domains

## *Attachment: Emotional Relationships with Others*

One of the most widely discussed and actively researched aspects of emotional and social development is **attachment**, the strong emotional bond that emerges between infant and caregivers. Attachment is not the same as dependency, which refers to the child's reliance on others to meet her basic needs. The child may become more independent with age while still remaining attached to certain people in her life. Attachment should also be distinguished from *bonding,* which we saw in Chapter 2 refers to the caregiver's emotional tie to the infant. The concept of attachment occupies a prominent place in developmental psychology because of its link with successful cognitive, social, and emotional development throughout childhood.

How does attachment emerge between infant and caregiver? In what ways is this emotional bond expressed? What roles do the caregiver and infant play in its formation? What is the significance of attachment in the later development of the child? Do we observe the same patterns of attachment among children across cultures? In this portion of the chapter we will describe the course of attachment in infancy and early childhood and explore the answers to these questions.

**attachment** Strong emotional bond that emerges between infant and caregiver.

# The Origins of Attachment: Theoretical Perspectives

What forces govern the emergence of attachment? Psychological explanations have varied over the last several decades according to the dominant theoretical orientation. Learning theorists emphasize the importance of the feeding situation, ethologists identify biological predispositions, and cognitive theorists focus on the child's advances in thinking. Let us examine each of these perspectives in turn.

**Learning Theory**     Learning theorists believe that certain basic drives, such as hunger, are satisfied by *primary reinforcers*, rewards that gratify biological needs. In the case of the young infant, an important primary reinforcer is food. Other rewards, called **secondary reinforcers**, acquire their reinforcing qualities because of their association with primary reinforcers. Because they are connected repeatedly with the reduction of the hunger drive, mothers acquire secondary reinforcing properties. Eventually the mother's presence in contexts outside feeding is rewarding to the infant.

Is the activity of feeding related to the emergence of infant-mother attachments, as learning theorists predict? Evidently not, according to a series of classic experiments conducted by Harry Harlow and his associates (Harlow & Zimmerman, 1959). These investigators separated infant monkeys from their mothers and provided them instead with extended contact with two surrogate mothers, one a figure made of wire mesh and the other a figure covered with terry cloth. The wire surrogate was equipped for feeding half the monkeys; the terry-cloth surrogate fed the other half. The infant monkeys lived with both their surrogates for at least 165 days, during which time several observations were made of the monkeys' behaviors. One measure was the number of hours per day spent with each surrogate. As Figure 11.3 shows, infant monkeys preferred the cloth "mother" regardless of which surrogate was providing nour-

Harlow's experiments showed that infant monkeys reared with surrogate mothers preferred the cloth mother even when the wire mother provided nourishment. Here, the infant monkey is actually nursing from the wire mother, but still maintains contact with the cloth mother.

**secondary reinforcer**     Object or person that attains rewarding value because of its association with a primary reinforcer.

**FIGURE 11.3**

**Forming Attachments: The "Cloth Mother" and "Wire Mother" Experiment**

Harlow's research showed that infant monkeys spent more time with a cloth surrogate mother than a wire surrogate mother, regardless of which one fed them. This graph shows how much time infant monkeys spent with each surrogate as a function of feeding condition.

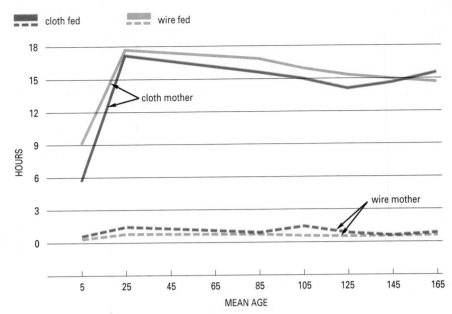

Source: Adapted from Harlow & Zimmerman, 1959.

ishment. In a subsequent test of attachment, when a frightening stimulus such as a mechanical spider was introduced into the monkeys' cage, the monkeys chose the cloth mother to run and cling to, even if they had been fed by the wire mother.

Harlow's findings challenged the view that attachments are based on the mother's acquisition of secondary-drive characteristics. The fact that the infant monkeys did not seek out the surrogate that fed them under either normal or stressful conditions led Harlow to conclude that "contact comfort," the security provided by a physically soothing object, played a greater role in attachments than the simple act of feeding.

**The Ethological View**    Proponents of the ethological position state that attachments occur as the result of the infant's innate tendency to signal the caregiver and the caregiver's corresponding predisposition to react to these signals. As a result, the infant and caregiver are brought together, a bond is forged between them, and the survival of the infant is ensured. In other words, attachment is an adaptive, biologically programmed response system that is activated early in the infant's development and that follows many of the principles of *imprinting* described in Chapter 2.

▶ Roles of nature and nurture

The principal spokesperson for this perspective, John Bowlby (1958, 1969), initially was concerned with the detrimental effects of institutionalization on infants and young children. Scientists in the late 1940s had reported that children who spent extended periods of time in hospitals and orphanages during their early years often showed serious developmental problems, including profound withdrawal from social interactions, intellectual impairments, and in some cases, physical delays (Skodak & Skeels, 1949; Spitz, 1946a). Bowlby proposed that the cause lay in the lack of a close emotional bond between child and primary caregiver.

Bowlby maintained that attachments develop in a fixed sequence, beginning with the infant's emission of **signaling behaviors**, such as crying and smiling. In the first two months, most infants emit these signals indiscriminately, but by six months of age, smiles and cries become increasingly restricted to the presence of the caregiver, usually the mother. From six to twelve months of age, clearer signs of the infant's strong attachment to the caregiver develop. At that point, most infants become visibly upset at the mother's departure, a phenomenon called **separation protest**, and will also show signs of greeting her upon her return. Once they are able to move about, infants will ensure their nearness to their mother by approaching and clinging to her. About the same time, they also display **stranger anxiety**, a wariness and fear at the approach of someone unfamiliar. The final phase of attachment occurs at about three years of age, when the relationship between mother and child becomes more of a partnership and the child comes to appreciate the mother's feelings, motives, and goals. The regularity with which infants show this sequence of behaviors, says Bowlby, suggests its biological basis.

According to Bowlby, infants become attached to those who respond consistently and appropriately to their signaling behaviors. Thus, Bowlby saw the maladaptive development of institutionalized infants as a consequence of the absence of the dynamic, contingent interaction between child and caregiver. Although the basic physical needs of children were met in institutional settings, it was often at the convenience of the caregiver's schedule rather than in response to the child's behaviors. Today, some researchers have moved away from the idea that infants' signals and caregivers' responses to them are innately "wired in." Nonetheless, Bowlby's general scheme about the origins and course of attachment has framed numerous investigations of the development of attachment.

**Cognitive-Developmental Theory**    Followers of Piaget assert that the development of attachment depends on the child's prior acquisition of certain cognitive capabilities, specifically the concept of *object permanence*. Before he can show stranger or separation anxiety, the infant must have an understanding of the continuing existence of objects and people. To be able to show stranger anxiety, for example, the child must have some internalized representation of the caregiver against which to compare the stranger's face. Similarly, separation protest depends on the infant's realization that the caregiver continues to exist, in a location apart from him.

▶ Interaction among domains

Is there evidence to suggest that recognition of object permanence either precedes or accompanies stranger and separation anxiety? Research has shown that object permanence and strong indications of attachment are present in eight-month-olds almost simultaneously (Schaffer & Emerson, 1964). Moreover, infants who are in the more advanced stages of the development of object concept display stronger, more forceful protests when their mother departs (Lester et al., 1974). Evidently, advances in thinking do play at least some role in the development of attachments.

## The Developmental Course of Attachment

For the most part, research has confirmed the sequence of behaviors outlined by Bowlby in the emergence of attachment. Infants can discriminate their mother's face from that of a stranger at two days of age and their mother's voice and smell a few days after that (DeCasper & Fifer, 1980; Field et al.,

**signaling behavior**    In ethological theory, a behavior such as crying or smiling that brings the caregiver physically close to the infant.

**separation protest**    Distress shown by the infant when the caregiver leaves the immediate environment.

**stranger anxiety**    Fear or distress shown by an infant at the approach of an unfamiliar person.

▶ Interaction among domains

**FIGURE 11.4**

**The Changing Pattern of Infant Attachments**

During the first year, indiscriminate attachments decline and attachment to the mother increases beginning at about seven or eight months of age. The line labeled *specific attachment* refers to infant attachment behaviors directed to specific individuals, such as fathers, grandparents, and other caregivers, but also includes the mother. Specific attachments also increase toward the latter half of the first year.

1984; MacFarlane, 1975). However, they emit their signals to anyone who is available. By about seven months of age, these indiscriminate behaviors give way to attachments to specific people, most notably the mother or primary caregiver. Stranger anxiety becomes full blown, and separation anxiety is usually manifested as well. In the months that follow, children show evidence of multiple attachments to fathers, substitute caregivers, and grandparents (Schaffer & Emerson, 1964). Figure 11.4 displays these developmental trends.

At age two years most children continue to show strong attachments, but by age three years some of the manifestations of this bond begin to change. Separation distress diminishes for most children, probably because of advances in cognition. For example, children begin to appreciate the fact that even though the caregiver may depart for several hours, she always returns (Marvin, 1977). Four-year-olds have even less need to maintain close physical proximity to the caregiver. As they develop insights into the perspectives of others and as their communication skills improve, they can understand better the reasons for temporary separations and can express their emotions in ways other than crying or clinging. The sequence of changes in emotional development and attachment is summarized in the Chronology on the next page.

**Measuring Attachment**    The **Strange Situation**, developed by Mary Ainsworth and her associates, is a standardized task that is employed frequently to measure the quality of the child's emotional ties to her mother (Ainsworth et al., 1978). Table 11.2 shows the eight episodes that comprise this measure, which is administered in a laboratory setting.

On the basis of her extensive observations of the patterns of behaviors shown by infants, Ainsworth (Ainsworth et al., 1978) distinguished three patterns of attachment, *secure attachment* and two categories of *insecure attachment:*

• *Secure attachment* Children in this group showed many clear signs of attachment by displaying stranger anxiety, separation anxiety, and greeting the

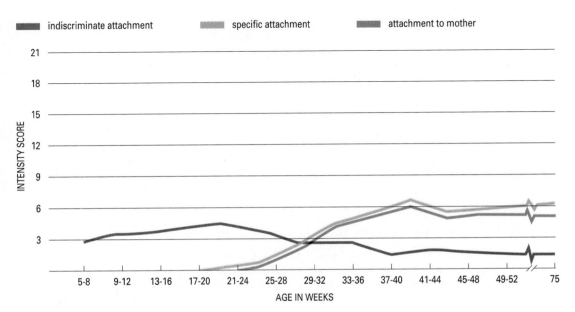

Source: Adapted from Schaffer & Emerson, 1964.

## CHRONOLOGY    Emotional Development

| NEWBORN | Discriminates mother's face, voice, and smell from others.<br>Expresses interest, distress, disgust, joy, and sadness.<br>Imitates facial expressions for happiness, surprise, and sadness.<br>Smiles during REM sleep.<br>Cries when has physical needs. |
|---|---|
| 1 MONTH | Displays "fussy cry." |
| 3 MONTHS | Smiles at caregiver.<br>Distinguishes among anger, surprise, and sadness.<br>Participates in interactive synchrony. |
| 4 MONTHS | Expresses anger.<br>Laughs in response to tactile and auditory stimuli. |
| 7 MONTHS | Expresses fear.<br>Shows specific attachments, stranger anxiety, and separation anxiety. |
| 12 MONTHS | Begins to display social referencing. |
| 18–24 MONTHS | Displays guilt, shame, and envy.<br>Uses words to describe feeling states. |
| 3–4 YEARS | Smiles more to same-sex peers.<br>Describes the causes and consequences of emotions.<br>Shows decline in separation distress and other attachment behaviors typical of infancy. |
| 6–7 YEARS | Understands that emotions fade with time and that thoughts can control emotions. |
| 10–12 YEARS | Understands the possibility of feeling two emotions at once.<br>Can mask or "fake" emotions.<br>Has concepts of emotions based on internal feeling states. |

This chart describes the sequence of emotional development based on the findings of research. Children often show individual differences in the exact ages at which they display the various developmental achievements outlined here.

mother enthusiastically upon her return. They also used the mother as a *secure base for exploration*, exploring their new surroundings but looking or moving back to their mother as if to "check in" with her. They obviously felt comfortable in the presence of their mother and distressed and apprehensive in her absence.

• *Avoidant attachment* Infants in this category were not as enthusiastic in greeting the mother when she returned to the laboratory room. In fact, they

**Strange Situation** Standardized test that assesses the quality of infant-caregiver attachment.

| Number of Episode | Persons Present | Duration | Brief Description of Action |
|---|---|---|---|
| 1 | Mother, baby, and observer | 30 seconds | Observer introduces mother and baby to experimental room, then leaves. |
| 2 | Mother and baby | 3 minutes | Mother is nonparticipant while baby explores; if necessary, play is stimulated after 2 minutes |
| 3 | Stranger, mother, and baby | 3 minutes | Stranger enters. Minute 1: stranger silent. Minute 2: stranger converses with mother. Minute 3: stranger approaches baby. After 3 minutes mother leaves unobtrusively. |
| 4 | Stranger and baby | 3 minutes or less[a] | First separation episode. Stranger's behavior is geared to that of baby. |
| 5 | Mother and baby | 3 minutes or more[b] | First reunion episode. Mother greets and comforts baby, then tries to settle him again in play. Mother then leaves, saying bye-bye. |
| 6 | Baby alone | 3 minutes or less[a] | Second separation episode. |
| 7 | Stranger and baby | 3 minutes or less[a] | Continuation of second separation. Stranger enters and gears her behavior to that of baby. |
| 8 | Mother and baby | 3 minutes | Second reunion episode. Mother enters, greets baby, then picks him up. Meanwhile stranger leaves unobtrusively. |

[a]Episode is curtailed if the baby is unduly distressed.
[b]Episode is prolonged if more time is required for the baby to become reinvolved in play.

Source: Campos et al., 1983.

**TABLE 11.2**

**The Episodes of the Strange Situation**

tended to avoid or ignore her, playing in isolation even when she was present in the room.

• *Ambivalent attachment* Tension characterized the behaviors these children showed toward their mothers. Although they displayed noticeable proximity-seeking behaviors when the mother was in the room, sometimes clinging excessively to her, they also showed angry, rejecting behavior, even hitting or pushing her away. Some children in this category were extremely passive, showing limited exploratory play, except for bouts of crying that were used as signals to be picked up and held.

In Ainsworth's original study, 63 percent of the infants were categorized as securely attached, 29 percent were avoidantly attached, and 8 percent were ambivalently attached. In our society, the behaviors of the securely attached group are generally seen as the healthiest, most desirable pattern against which other patterns are compared.

A newer way of measuring attachment is the *Q-sort*. In this method, mother and infant are observed for a specified period of time, after which the observer sorts through a series of cards containing descriptions of the mother-infant relationship. Several piles are created from "least characteristic" to "most characteristic" of the child. The child's attachment score is based on the extent to which these ratings correlate with the characteristics of a securely attached child defined by a panel of experts on childhood attachment (Waters & Deane, 1985).

**The Antedecents of Secure Attachment** How do secure, high-quality attachments develop? Research by Mary Ainsworth and her colleagues suggests that the mother's style of interacting with her infant and her responsivity to the baby's signals may be key factors. In addition, the ability of the caregiver and infant to achieve moments of interactive synchrony may also be important.

▶ Roles of nature and nurture

Ainsworth and her associates visited the homes of twenty-six infants and their mothers for about four hours every three weeks during the entire first year of the infants' lives (Ainsworth, Bell, & Stayton, 1971, 1972, 1974). When they were about a year old, infants were brought to the laboratory to be tested in the Strange Situation and were classified according to the quality of attachment to their mother. An attempt then was made to find relationships between the attachment classification and specific maternal behaviors observed earlier. The results of this study indicated that mothers of securely attached infants were *sensitive* to the child's signals, noticing his cues and interpreting them correctly. These mothers were *accepting* of their role as caregiver. They displayed *cooperation;* mothers of securely attached infants would wait until the child finished her activity or was in a good mood before imposing a request. Gentle persuasion was used rather than assertive control. Mothers in this group were also *accessible*, providing quick responses to the child's signals, particularly crying. They were not distracted by their own thoughts and activities. In contrast, mothers of the insecurely attached group were often rigid, unresponsive, and demanding in their parenting style and did not feel positively about their role as caregiver.

Other researchers have found that mothers of securely attached infants have higher self-esteem, feel more competent, and see themselves as more accepted by their own parents and peers than do mothers of insecurely attached infants (Tronick, Ricks, & Cohn, 1982). Mothers of securely attached children have also been found to be more affectionate, more positive, and less intrusive in their vocalizations compared with mothers of insecurely attached infants (Bates, Maslin, & Frankel, 1985; Isabella, 1993; Izard et al., 1991; Roggman, Langlois, & Hubbs-Tait, 1987). Yet recent research has also raised the possibility that characteristics of parental caregiving are less important for predicting the quality of attachment than originally thought (Rosen & Rothbaum, 1993). Although parental factors are predictors, just how influential they are remains unclear.

Interactive synchrony may also be important in the emergence of attachments. One group of researchers observed the interactions of mothers and their infants at one, three, and nine months of age, recording each instance in which the infants' and mothers' behaviors co-occurred and produced a mutually satisfying outcome. For example, if the infant gazed at the mother, the mother verbalized, or if the infant fussed and cried, the mother soothed him. The infants' attachments were then assessed at one year of age. According to the results, securely attached infants had experienced a greater number of synchronous interactions in the prior months (Isabella, Belsky, & von Eye,

1989). Therefore, in accounting for the emergence of secure attachment, it is important to consider maternal behavior *as it is related to the child's behavior*.

**Attachments to Fathers**    Because mothers traditionally have fulfilled the role of primary caregiver, most of the emphasis in this chapter, and in the field of child psychology, has been on the emotional bond that develops between child and mother. With large numbers of women participating in the labor force, however, and challenges to the assumption that females have the exclusive role in child care, many caregiving responsibilities have been assumed by others either within or outside the family. Moreover, researchers in developmental psychology have begun to recognize the glaring absence of information on how another important family member—the father—interacts with his children. The result has been a growing literature on father-child interaction.

In general, fathers spend far less time interacting with and caring for their children than mothers do. Estimates on just how much time vary, ranging from an average of fifteen to twenty minutes per day to about three hours a day, compared with an average of eight or nine hours each day for the mother (Kotelchuk, 1975; Lewis & Weinraub, 1974). Nevertheless, many infants clearly do form attachments to their fathers. In the Strange Situation, these infants show signs of separation anxiety when their father leaves the room and greet him upon his return. They also use him as a secure base for exploration (Kotelchuk, 1976). Mothers may still be preferred in certain circumstances, as in the presence of a stranger or when children seek to be comforted (Cohen & Campos, 1974). When fathers spend time in face-to-face interactions with their infants and display sensitivity and playfulness, however, their infants show clear signs of attachment to them (Chibucos & Kail, 1981; Cox et al., 1992).

Infants show clear signs of attachment to fathers, especially when fathers spend time in rewarding, mutually engaging interactions with them.

Given the opportunity, fathers can become partners in strong, secure attachments.

**Temperament and Attachment**   Caregivers are not solely responsible for the emergence of attachment. Because the formation of attachments takes place in the context of interactions between caregiver and infant, it seems reasonable to postulate that the infant's own style as a communication partner might be influential in the growth of an affectional bond.

▶ The child's active role

Several researchers have reported a link between infant characteristics such as irritability and proneness to distress and subsequent attachment behaviors in the Strange Situation (Bates, Maslin, & Frankel, 1985; Goldsmith & Alansky, 1987; Miyake, Chen, & Campos, 1985). For example, one recent study found that two-day-old infants' proneness to distress when a pacifier was removed from the mouth was related to insecure attachment at fourteen months of age (Calkins & Fox, 1992). Researchers must be cautious, however, before they conclude that temperament *produces* these outcomes; parental behaviors may influence *both* temperament and attachment in the infant. Even if children have biologically based temperaments, these might be modified by specific parenting practices very early in development. A young infant who is hard to arouse, for example, might elicit vigorous stimulation from the caregivers. In response, that child may become much more active, even irritable. Thus, her original temperament has been modified and parents may develop an entirely new mode of interaction in conjunction with the infant's altered style (Sroufe, 1985).

▶ Individual differences

▶ Roles of nature and nurture

What can we conclude, then, about the causes of attachment? The characteristics of both caregiver and infant play a role, as does the synchrony between the behaviors they emit toward each other. Healthy emotional relationships are the result of dynamic, constantly evolving forms of human interaction where both partners—caregiver and child—play a role.

**The Modifiability of Attachments**   How stable are attachments, once they are formed? The attachment classification given to an infant at age twelve months typically remains the same when measured at eighteen months (Waters, 1978). Using a measure of attachment specifically developed for testing older children and based on behavior during a reunion with the mother, Mary Main and Jude Cassidy (1988) found that classifications made at six years of age could be predicted from classifications that had been made at twelve months of age for 84 percent of the sample. Thus, attachment patterns established during the course of the first year are maintained for relatively long periods of time.

▶ Development as continuous/discontinuous

Attachment patterns do not always remain stable, however. Stresses or changes in the family's circumstances can affect the quality of attachment. In a large-scale study conducted in Minneapolis, Brian Vaughn and his colleagues examined attachment classifications of infants at twelve months and again at eighteen months of age (Vaughn et al., 1979). The majority of these infants' families were living at or below the poverty level. Most of the mothers were single parents, and many of the families experienced a significant change such as a shift in residence or the addition or loss of an adult in the living group during the six months between observations. In this study, 20 percent of the infants who had been securely attached at twelve months of age were insecurely attached at eighteen months. Furthermore, shifts from secure to insecure attachments were associated with maternal reports of a greater number of stressful events in their lives, such as loss of employment, financial problems, or illness. As another study showed, however, when new mothers from low socioeconomic backgrounds are provided with a volunteer coach who provides social support and information about child rearing, secure attachments among infants are more likely to result (Jacobson & Frye, 1991).

**Attachment and Later Development**    The importance of attachment has been underscored by research findings showing that secure attachments are related to positive developmental outcomes in both social and cognitive spheres when children become older. Leah Matas and her associates assessed the quality of attachments of forty-eight infants when they were eighteen months of age (Matas, Arend, & Sroufe, 1978). Six months later, these same children were observed for the quality of their play and their problem-solving style. Children who had earlier been categorized as securely attached were more enthusiastic and compliant with their mothers' suggestions in the problem-solving tasks and showed more positive affect and persistence than their insecurely attached counterparts. They also engaged in more symbolic play and displayed less crying and whining.

▶ Interaction among domains

These same securely attached children were found to be more socially competent with their peers at age three and a half years, showing more leadership, greater sympathy, and less withdrawal from social interactions (Waters, Wippman, & Sroufe, 1979). They also evidenced stronger signs of "ego-resiliency" at age five years, meaning they responded to problems in a flexible, persistent, and resourceful manner (Arend, Gove, & Sroufe, 1979). In contrast, insecurely attached infants, particularly those who show avoidant patterns, do not fare so well in the preschool years, according to another study (Erickson, Sroufe, & Egeland, 1985). Children with this attachment classification were found to display many maladaptive and undesirable behaviors, such as high dependency, noncompliance, and poor social skills in peer interactions. They also were described by teachers as hostile, impulsive, and withdrawn.

The effects of early attachments may carry over well into adolescence and the adult years, perhaps because children construct *internal working models* of relationships that influence their future emotional ties to family, friends, and romantic partners (Bowlby, 1973; Main, Kaplan, & Cassidy, 1985). Adolescents who evidence secure attachments to their parents, in the sense of expressing affection for and trust in their parents, generally have high self-esteem and a strong sense of personal identity, and display social competence (Rice, 1990). They also engage in more constructive problem solving when discussing controversial topics, such as dating and household rules, with their parents (Kobak et al., 1993). Furthermore, the quality of an individual's attachment during childhood may influence her parenting style as an adult. Margaret Ricks (1985) studied the intergenerational effects of attachment by assessing the self-esteem and childhood recollections of twenty-eight middle-class mothers. Mothers of securely attached infants had higher self-esteem scores and more positive recollections of their own childhood relationships with parents and peers. Evidently, then, there are strong links between the quality of early parent-child interactions and developmental outcomes throughout childhood, and even adulthood.

## Three Special Cases: Prematurity, Adoption, and Abuse

In some contexts, the ideal pattern of caregiver-child interaction may be disrupted—as, for example, when mother and infant are physically separated during the early days of their partnership because of the infant's premature birth or when the child is placed for adoption and nonbiological parents assume the caregiving role. Other children are the victims of physical abuse or neglect. Is there any evidence that attachments suffer in such cases? A consideration of these issues will illuminate further the ways in which early caregiver-child relationships are related to subsequent child development.

Prematurity    The preterm infant looks and behaves differently from the infant with the benefit of a full thirty-eight weeks in utero. The premature infant, in all likelihood, will be very small and fragile looking, less alert and responsive to stimulation, and more difficult to comfort. Cries, but not smiles, are very frequent (Goldberg, 1979). In addition, mothers and their premature infants usually are separated physically, sometimes for several weeks, while the baby receives the medical care necessary to ensure his well-being and even survival. If attachments were based largely on mutually rewarding infant-caregiver interactions, we might expect premature infants to develop insecure attachments with their mothers.

In the hospital nursery, mothers of premature infants do, indeed, behave in a markedly different manner than mothers of full-term infants. Mothers of premature babies touch, hold, and smile at their babies less often than do mothers of full-term infants (DiVitto & Goldberg, 1979). As their babies get older, however, mothers of premature infants actually become more active than mothers of full-term babies in stimulating them: they initiate and maintain more interactions, even to the point of being excessive. These behaviors may stem from the mother's desire to alter the premature's unresponsive pattern or to stimulate the child in an effort to spur slowed development. As Figure 11.5 shows, infants often react to these maternal behaviors by averting their gaze, as if to shut out the added stimulation (Field, 1977, 1982).

Given the difference in maternal styles with prematures, is there a corresponding impact on the attachments of these infants? In a comparison of twenty full-term and twenty premature infants at eleven months of age, Ann Frodi and Ross Thompson (1985) observed no significant differences in the

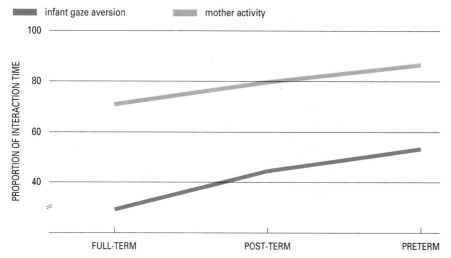

**FIGURE 11.5**

**Maternal Interactions with Premature Babies**

After an initial period of inactivity following the birth of their child, mothers of premature infants become more active in their exchanges with their infants compared with mothers of full- and post-term infants. At the same time, premature babies display more gaze aversion, as if they are seeking to terminate their mothers' overstimulation.

Source: Adapted from Field, 1982.

patterns of attachments. Most of the children in both groups were observed to be securely attached. By one year of age, many premature infants "rebound" from the negative effects of early birth, especially if they encounter a responsive, supportive environment. Mothers may also adapt their styles in later months to conform more closely with the rhythms and needs of the child. Thus, the early developmental risk posed by prematurity does not lead automatically to enduring problems in mother-child relations or other developmental patterns.

**Adoption** By the time they reach middle childhood and adolescence, adopted children show a noticeably higher incidence of psychological and academic problems compared with children who are not adopted (Brodzinsky et al., 1984). Because most adoptions involve the separation of the infant from the biological mother at an early age, the disruption of the attachment process might play a role.

One of the few investigations of this issue showed that separation of the infant from the biological parents at six to seven months of age produces socioemotional difficulties even ten years later, particularly in the child's ability to form relationships with others (Yarrow et al., 1973). Separation at an earlier age, however, may have less of an impact. When Leslie Singer and her colleagues assessed the attachments of adoptive and nonadoptive infants between thirteen and eighteen months of age, they found no difference in the classifications of attachments between these two groups (Singer et al., 1985). Most of the infants fell into the securely attached category. In this group, most of the adoptive placements had occurred at fairly early ages, the majority by three months of age. At this age children have not yet developed the concept of object permanence, and the early manifestations of attachment, such as stranger anxiety and separation anxiety, have not occurred. As in the case of premature infants, events that interfere with the establishment of stable relationships in the first part of infancy do not necessarily forecast poor attachment. These studies of adoption also suggest that disrupting stable relationships with caregivers later in infancy can be more harmful and that the first few months of life may represent a sensitive period for emotional development.

▶ Development as continuous/discontinuous

**Abuse** Physically or psychologically abused children are at risk for an assortment of cognitive and socioemotional difficulties. Because the trauma that accompanies within-family violence can be enduring, especially with repeated episodes of abuse, it should not be surprising that attachments between abused children and their parents take on an aberrant character.

Infants and toddlers who have been maltreated by their caregivers are likely to fall into a recently identified category of insecure attachment called **disorganized/disoriented attachment**, in which children show fear of their caregiver, confused facial expressions, and an assortment of avoidant and ambivalent attachment behaviors (Main & Solomon, 1986). Approximately 80 percent of maltreated infants fit this attachment profile (Carlson et al., 1989). Like other attachment categories, the disorganized/disoriented pattern may predict later developmental outcomes. For example, in one recent study, 71 percent of preschoolers who showed high levels of hostile behavior toward peers had been categorized as having disorganized attachments during their infancy (Lyons-Ruth, Alpern, & Repacholi, 1993). In another study, researchers found that when children with disorganized/disoriented attachments were six years

**disorganized/disoriented attachment** Infant-caregiver relations characterized by the infant's fear of the caregiver, confused facial expressions, and a combination of avoidant and ambivalent attachment behaviors.

old, they tended to be depressed, disorganized in behavior, and even self-destructive in response to questions about their parents or family life (Main, Kaplan, & Cassidy, 1985).

Why do these maladaptive attachments form? Abusive parents tend to react negatively to many of their child's social signals, even positive ones. When Ann Frodi and Michael Lamb (1980) observed the reactions of abusive and nonabusive mothers to videotapes of smiling and crying infants, abusive mothers were more aroused physiologically by both cries and smiles than were nonabusive mothers and were less willing to interact with an infant, even a smiling one, than nonabusive mothers. These findings suggest, at the very least, that the abused infant has an unwilling and psychologically distant interaction partner.

In addition, abused children experience fear, an emotion that leads them to seek comfort from the caregiver but also makes them wary of further abuse. Thus, the tendency to seek proximity to the caregiver is counterbalanced by the tendency to avoid that same person. The resulting behaviors, such as freezing and appearing dazed, are characteristic of children in the disorganized/disoriented attachment category.

Taken together, studies of premature and adopted children reveal that secure attachment relationships can develop in circumstances that are less than optimal during the early part of infancy. At the same time, however, when interactions between caregivers and infants deviate too much from the ideal, either in terms of their partnership's time of onset or in the emotional tone of interactions, the consequences for the child can be serious and enduring.

## Cross-Cultural Variations in Patterns of Attachment

In recent years, the Strange Situation has been used to assess the nature of attachments of infants in Japan, Israel, and several countries in Western Europe. In one of the first uses of the Strange Situation outside the United States, Karin and Klaus Grossmann and their associates observed German infants and mothers during the infants' first year of life (Grossmann et al., 1985). As in the Ainsworth studies, these researchers noted a relationship between maternal sensitivity and infant attachment; securely attached infants had mothers who responded to them in a warm, responsive manner. They noted, however, some interesting variations as well. First, most infants (49 percent) were not classified as securely attached but instead were scored as avoidantly attached. Second, although mothers varied in the sensitivity of responding when infants were two months of age, they did not vary by the time the infants were ten months old—most mothers had *low* sensitivity ratings by this time.

Grossmann and her colleagues interpreted their findings in the context of the different attitudes toward child rearing held by parents in Germany and the United States. The emphasis in German culture is on fostering independence in one's offspring, encouraging the development of an obedient child who does not make demands on the parents. Responding to the infant's every cry is considered inappropriate because it is seen as "spoiling" the child. Thus, German mothers' tendency to pick up their children less frequently and for shorter periods of time and to display less affection reflects the goals of socialization in that culture.

Studies of children in Israel portray a similar theme. Many Israeli infants are raised in the group setting of the kibbutz. While parents go to work, children are cared for by the *metapelet*, or caregiver, beginning some time between six and twelve weeks of age and continuing after the first year. Children visit with

▶ Sociocultural influence

Many Israeli children are raised in the group setting of Kibbutz. Children visit with their parents in the evening and at other times during the day, but most of their time is spent with the nonparental caregiver and peers.

their parents in the early evening and often during other parts of the day, but most of their time is spent with the nonparental caregiver and peers. Do such arrangements interfere with the formation of attachments to mothers? Early studies suggested that such was not the case; infants raised on the kibbutz displayed clear signs of protest at separation from their mothers. At the same time they also displayed signs of attachment to the metapelet (Fox, 1977). A more recent study, however, showed that the experience of being raised on the kibbutz was related to the more frequent display of ambivalent attachments compared with American children and Israeli children raised in cities (Sagi et al., 1985). How are we to interpret these latter findings?

One possibility, of course, is that being raised in a group setting results in greater insecurity. In the child care setting of the kibbutz, it may not always be possible for the metapelet to respond to each infant's signals promptly and predictably. It would be consistent with attachment theory, then, to predict the insecure patterns that have been found. There is, however, another feasible explanation. Children in the kibbutz have relatively few experiences with strangers compared with American children, who often visit shopping malls, playgrounds, and other locations filled with unfamiliar people. It may be, then, that kibbutz infants are as securely attached to their parents as any other children but are simply tense and anxious in the unfamiliar context of the Strange Situation.

Some researchers have suggested that the Strange Situation is not the optimal measure of the child's emotional feelings toward the caregiver (Lamb et al., 1985). Instead of assessing the qualities of children's affective bonds, it may be gauging instead the influence of other social and cultural experiences. This idea is supported by studies that show that specific experiences in infancy may dampen the child's protests to the mother's departure. A child who has had frequent experiences with the mother leaving and subsequently returning, for example, may show little or no separation protest even though he is securely attached (Kagan, 1976).

The cross-cultural studies reviewed in this section underscore the point that variations in children's experiences and in cultural expectations for their behavior may influence responses to elements of the Strange Situation and may not reflect the actual intensity of emotional bonds between caregiver and child. As we begin to evaluate the impact of nonmaternal child care on children in our own society, we should be cautious about the measures we use to draw our conclusions.

## CONTROVERSY: THINKING IT OVER

### *Does Day Care Affect Attachment?*

One of the most troublesome and difficult decisions many parents face concerns alternative child care arrangements when both mother and father work. As Table 11.3 shows, about 60 percent of mothers with preschool-aged children work, and over 50 percent of women with infants under one year of age are employed (U.S. Bureau of the Census, 1992). In fact, this latter group represents the fastest-growing category of women in the labor force. A substantial number of children are therefore receiving nonparental care, many beginning very early in their lives. Does this form of early experience influence the formation of attachments?

Part of the problem is that many variables are operating when the child receives nonparental care. Is it the mother's absence or the quality of substitute care that produces any observable effects on child behavior? These two factors are difficult to unravel from each other. Does the age at which alternative care began make a difference? It may, but researchers have not always considered this variable when conducting their studies. Does it matter whether the child

| | Percent of Women in the Labor Force | | |
|---|---|---|---|
| **Age of Child** | **1975** | **1985** | **1991** |
| With children under 18 | 44.9 | 60.8 | 66.8 |
| Under 6, total | 36.7 | 53.4 | 59.9 |
| Under 3 | 32.7 | 50.5 | 56.8 |
| 1 year or under | 30.8 | 49.4 | 55.8 |
| 2 years | 37.1 | 54.0 | 60.5 |
| 3 to 5 years | 42.2 | 58.4 | 64.7 |
| 6 to 13 years | 51.8 | 68.2 | 72.8 |
| 14 to 17 years | 53.5 | 67.0 | 75.7 |

**TABLE 11.3**

**Labor Force Participation Rates of Women with Children Under Age 18**

This table shows the percentage of women with children under age eighteen who are employed outside the home (the table shows only the data for women whose husbands are present in the home). The participation rates for this group of women have grown rapidly since 1975, especially for those with children age one year and under.

Source: Adapted from U.S. Bureau of the Census, 1992.

receives full-time or part-time care? Perhaps—but again, it has been difficult to control this factor in research studies because of the tremendous variation in caregiving schedules. In addition, the kinds of alternative care children receive vary a great deal, ranging from a single caregiver coming to the home, to out-of-home family day care in which another parent may provide care for several children, to center-based care. Given these complexities, it is understandable that simple and direct answers to parents' questions have not been forthcoming.

When Alison Clarke-Stewart and Greta Fein (1983) reviewed a large number of studies on day care and attachment, they concluded that children in day care may behave differently from home-reared children but only in some components of the Strange Situation. Day-care children do not react differently from home-reared children to the mother's departure; they both protest or ignore her to the same degree. Day-care children, however, tend to spend less time in close proximity to their mothers, both in the presence and in the absence of a stranger. In addition, although the majority of studies show no difference, a sizable minority find more avoidant responses in day-care children than home-reared children when they are reunited with their mothers.

Jay Belsky and Michael Rovine (1988), for example, reported that infants who received more than twenty hours per week of nonmaternal care when they were under one year of age were more likely to be classified as insecurely attached and showed more avoidance of the mother at reunion compared with infants who received less nonmaternal care. Boys seemed to be the most vulnerable. Belsky and Rovine pointed out that 50 percent of the infants receiving nonmaternal care did form secure attachments. Positive relationships were related to several child and mother characteristics: the child was more likely to be an "easy" baby, the mother was more sensitive and empathic, and the mother expressed more satisfaction with her marriage. Also, secure attachments with mothers were more prevalent when the nonmaternal caregiver was the father. Overall, however, Belsky and Rovine conclude that "extensive nonmaternal (and nonpaternal) care in the first year is a risk factor in the development of insecure infant-parent attachment relationships" (p. 165).

Does this mean that day care predisposes children toward impaired attachments? The answer is no, according to Clarke-Stewart and Fein (1983). The behaviors observed in day-care children are subject to a number of other interpretations. It is possible that day-care children are showing a precocious move toward independence which most parents view as a desirable goal of socialization. They also may be used to interacting with unfamiliar people and to the comings and goings of their mother, and their behavior may simply reflect these socialization experiences, not insecure attachment.

Belsky and Braungart (1991) examined some of these hypotheses in a subsequent study of the specific behaviors of infants receiving either more or less than twenty hours per week of alternative care. Did the infants with extended day-care experience show greater independence and less stress when reunited with their mothers in the Strange Situation compared with infants who had less nonparental care? The answer is no, according to the follow-up study: infants with extended day-care experience whimpered and fussed more and played less with objects compared with infants with less day-care experience.

As you can see, this controversy is far from resolved. Why might the infants with more day-care experience be showing greater distress? Do the results of the Belsky and Braungart (1991) study necessarily mean that parents should refrain from sending their infants to day care for too many hours per week? Given the economic factors that necessitate that both parents work, what can society do to ease their burden in seeking alternative caregiving arrangements? Drawing on the research on good "mothering" and good "fathering," what would be the qualities of good day-care centers?

---

## THEMES IN DEVELOPMENT

---

### EMOTION

▶ **What roles do nature and nurture play in emotional development?**

As we have stressed throughout this chapter, both nature and nurture contribute to the child's emotional development. Biology assumes a larger role in the child's early emotional capacities, as in the infant's ability to express and detect basic emotions such as joy and sadness. However, socialization and cognitive development become more prominent as explanations of later emotional expression and understanding, particularly for complex emotions such as guilt and envy. Ethologists and child temperament researchers also maintain that nature guides the formation of attachments between children and caregivers, but other researchers suggest that qualities of parenting style are equally important.

▶ **How does the sociocultural context influence emotional development?**

Different cultures place varying emphases on emotionality itself and on the specific emotions considered appropriate to display. For example, among the Kipsigis, crying is actively discouraged almost as soon as children complete their infancy. A culture's beliefs and values also can influence the child's responses in the Strange Situation. For example, German children often are classified as avoidantly attached, but their behavior simply may reflect parental stress on independence.

▶ **How does the child play an active role in the process of emotional development?**

The child is hardly docile in the construction of her emotional repertoire. There are numerous examples of how the child plays an active role in emotional development, including the phenomenon of social referencing, the infant's role in producing interactive synchrony with the caregiver, and the role of the child's temperament in the formation of attachments.

▶ **Is emotional development continuous or discontinuous?**

Attachment patterns established during the first year of life are maintained for relatively long periods of time and forecast many desirable developmental outcomes. Thus, many researchers believe infancy is a sensitive period for the formation of attachments. Studies of adopted children, in particular, suggest that better socioemotional outcomes result when infants are placed with their adoptive parents prior to the age of six months.

> ▶ **How prominent are individual differences in emotional development?**

Individual differences are especially evident in the enduring emotional moods infants and children display. Children, for example, may be "easy," "difficult," or "slow to warm up" in temperament, or may display inhibited or uninhibited styles. These relatively stable individual differences may affect how parents and others react to the child, and in turn, influence other developmental outcomes such as attachment.

> ▶ **How does emotional development interact with development in other domains?**

Emotions are closely intertwined with both cognition and social behavior. On the one hand, cognitive achievements, such as the attainment of object permanence or the ability to interpret social and personal experiences, lay the groundwork for advances in attachment and emotional expression. Similarly, children often learn about emotions through social experiences, such as interactions with their caregivers. On the other side of the equation, successful emotional development in the form of attachment is associated with positive social and cognitive achievements later in childhood. Children who are skilled at understanding and expressing emotions also have better relations with their peers.

## *Summary*

**What Are Emotions?**   *Emotions* are complex responses to internal or external events that include physiological, expressive, and experiential components. They are measured in a variety of ways, ranging from physiological measures and observer judgments of facial expressions to self-reports about moods and feelings. Emotions serve to organize and motivate the child's behavior, influence cognitive processes, and regulate social interactions. Thus they play a comprehensive role in the child's development.

**Theories of Emotional Development**   Some theorists, like Izard, propose that certain *basic emotions* such as joy and disgust are innate and that their expression has adaptive value. Environmental stimuli directly produce emotional responses that result in the experience of emotion. Cognitive-socialization theorists, like Lewis, emphasize the role of experience in transmitting to the child the appropriate times and ways of expressing emotions. Thus, individuals may express different emotions in response to the same stimulus.

Research with infants reveals that many emotional expressions are made from birth. Among these are joy, sadness, surprise, and disgust. However, the form of emotional expressions, such as smiling and crying, changes over the first year, as do the circumstances in which emotions are displayed. Advances in cognition are, in part, responsible, as is the maturation of portions of the brain that direct voluntary behaviors. Young infants also identify the emotional expressions of others and in many instances will imitate them. By the latter half of the first year, infants will use the emotional expressions of others to guide their behaviors, a phenomenon called *social referencing*. Infants' emotional expressions, in conjunction with those of caregivers, often co-occur in a synchronous manner, called *interactive synchrony*, laying the foundations for the formation of attachments.

Older children display more *complex emotions* such as guilt and envy, as well as more controlled use of basic emotions. Preschoolers understand many of the situations that give rise to specific emotions and the consequences of displaying them. School-aged children appreciate that they can control emotions with their own thoughts and that sometimes two emotions can be experienced simultaneously. The ability to disguise emotions appears later in childhood, as does an understanding of the nature of emotions based on internal feeling states. Many of these changes are related to cognitive development. Sex differences and cultural variations in the display of emotions also suggest a role for socialization.

**Attachment: Emotional Relationships with Others**    The strong affectional bond between child and caregiver is known as *attachment*. Learning theorists explain attachment as the product of the mother's association with feeding and other activities the infant finds pleasurable. Ethologists say that attachment is an innate, adaptive phenomenon that promotes proximity between infant and caregiver and thus ensures the infant's survival. Cognitive-developmental theorists link attachment to the infant's cognitive advances, specifically the emergence of object permanence.

*Stranger anxiety* and *separation anxiety*, two of the most pronounced indicators of attachment, typically emerge at about seven or eight months of age. Three basic patterns of attachment—*secure, avoidant,* and *ambivalent*—have been identified on the basis of the *Strange Situation* task. Secure attachments, in particular, are related to the most favorable developmental outcomes for the child. Several variables predict the formation of secure attachments, including the sensitivity and responsiveness of the caregiver, the temperament of the child, and the synchrony in their interactional behaviors. Studies of prematures, adoptees, and abused children indicate that attachments can be formed under less than optimal circumstances, but that extreme deviations in caregiver-child interactional patterns can have serious negative consequences for the child. For example, many abused children show *disorganized/disoriented attachments*. Cultural variations in attachment patterns suggest that what seem to be insecure attachments may be caused by factors other than inadequate caregiver-child interactions.

# 12

## Self and Values

## Key Themes in This Chapter

▶ **What roles do nature and nurture play in the development of the self and of values?**

▶ **How does the sociocultural context influence the development of the self and of values?**

▶ **How does the child play an active role in the development of the self and of values?**

▶ **Is the development of the self and of values continuous or discontinuous?**

▶ **How prominent are individual differences in the development of the self and of values?**

▶ **How does the development of the self and of values interact with development in other domains?**

*Michael had just finished his math assignment when he heard the door slam and the loud angry voice. "Kids today!" his grandfather fumed to no one in particular. "A couple of 'em almost ran me down on the sidewalk. Didn't bother to apologize. One even yelled, 'Get out of my way!' as she chased after her friends. Kids don't respect anybody—not even themselves, wearing those funny clothes, dying their hair every color you can think of, poking holes in their ears, even their noses! I suppose if I had stopped 'em, they'd have taken a swing at me or even worse. . . ." His voice trailed to a mutter.*

*Michael had heard such tirades before, had been told repeatedly how the world has changed, how young people today do not know right from wrong, are just plain troublemakers. Michael also worried about reports on the news—the first-grader who punched his teacher, the large number of sixth-graders who felt cheating was okay, the junior high students suspended for bringing knives and guns to school.*

*Does his grandfather have a point? Just what values do young people have today?*

To instill in children a sense of satisfaction with who they are and to recognize the standards of conduct considered acceptable and ethical within their community are among the most important goals of society. We expect children and adults to take pride in their accomplishments, to learn to judge right from wrong, and to inhibit actions that harm family, friends, or neighbors. Broadly speaking, survival as a member of a social community depends on the ability to foster behaviors, such as helping, cooperation, and sharing, that benefit others. Children display an awareness of self and the consequences of their conduct, both good and bad, early on, but these undergo noticeable changes with development. One goal of this chapter is to describe age-related changes in the development of self, moral behavior, and values.

Michael's grandfather believes that in his neighborhood a positive sense of self and of courtesy and concern for others has declined. Although it is not possible to address here whether such a change has taken place, the concerns voiced by Michael's grandfather are not new. Philosophers, theologians, and scientists have argued for years over the basic goodness or evil of human nature and the role of children's experiences in channeling whatever inborn tendencies they may have in either direction. In this sense the nature-nurture debate remains embedded in contemporary discussions of the roots of self, moral behavior, and values. A second goal of this chapter is to examine research that sheds light on how self, moral behavior, and values are promoted by society. Let's begin by considering the child's emerging understanding of self.

## *The Concept of Self*

"I know how."
"Look! See what I did!"
"I'm smart."
"I'm stronger than you!"
"I'm really good at this!"

These statements express in no uncertain terms what children believe they can do, what they think they are like, how they feel about their abilities. The statements reveal the child's awareness of self. How does this understanding of **self**—as someone who is an independent unique person, able to reflect on her own beliefs and characteristics—develop?

To answer this question researchers have found it useful to adopt a distinction first offered by William James (1892) more than a century ago. For James, there were two components of self, the "me," or *objective self,* and the "I," or *subjective self.* The "I," or subjective component, consists of several key realizations about the self: (1) I can be an agent of change and can control events in my life (sense of autonomy); (2) my experiences are unique and accessible to no one else in exactly the same way (sense of individuality); (3) my past, present, and future are continuous (sense of stability); and (4) I can reflect upon— that is, think about—my self (sense of reflection, or self-consciousness). All contribute to the sense of the subjective "I."

James's objective, or the "me" aspect of self, often is called *self-concept.* An individual's self-concept includes an understanding of his physical qualities, possessions and status, skills, and psychological characteristics, including personality, beliefs, and value systems.

### Self as Object

Self as object, the **self-concept**, consists of that unique set of traits and characteristics that identify an individual as observed by that individual, not by someone else. The awareness starts with the person's basic capacity to identify her own face and body.

**Self-recognition**    When can young children, responding to their reflection or picture, declare, "That's me!"? When do they know what they look like? To answer these questions, researchers have found the household mirror a helpful tool. A toddler younger than fifteen to eighteen months shows little evidence of recognizing himself in a mirror. How do we know that? If a spot of rouge, for example, is placed surreptitiously on a child's nose, a toddler of about eighteen months of age who looks in the mirror is likely to touch or rub

**self**    Realization of being an independent, unique, stable, and self-reflective entity; the beliefs, knowledge, feelings, and characteristics that the individual ascribes to his or her own personhood.

**self-concept**    Perceptions, conceptions, and values one holds about oneself.

her nose, which indicates that she has formed a concept of what her face ordinarily does or does not look like (Amsterdam, 1972; Bertenthal & Fischer, 1978; Lewis & Brooks-Gunn, 1979). In just a few more months she will also say, "That's me," when asked, "Who's that?" as she stares at a picture or mirror image of herself.

The consequences of becoming aware of his physical appearance can be enormous for a toddler. For one thing, it may be linked to the appearance of self-conscious emotions such as embarrassment, shame, and pride that emerge at about this age, as we saw in the discussion of emotional development in Chapter 11 (Lewis, 1990; Lewis et al., 1989). For another, self-recognition seems to develop hand in hand with a growing awareness of others as distinct individuals. For example, a toddler who displays self-recognition on the mirror task also is likely to attend to a partner of a similar age and to encourage that child to play with matching toys, which indicates increased interest in sharing and enjoyment of the other child's activities (Asendorpf & Baudonnière, 1993). Thus, at a very young age children have begun to unwrap a major piece of the total package of their self-concept, the first of many steps in the development of their identity.

▶ Interaction among domains

**Self-definition**     A self-concept is made up of much more than appearance. If asked to answer the question "Who are you?" a preschooler might say, "I'm a boy. I'm strong. I know the letters of the alphabet. I like pizza. I live with my mother and father. I go to nursery school." Thus during the preschool years, knowledge of self extends beyond physical features to include activities the child likes and is good at, his possessions, and his relationships to others. In defining themselves, a common theme for children at this age is to establish a **categorical self**, that is, to classify themselves in terms of membership in certain groups based on their sex, age, skills, what they own, where they live, and who their friends are.

Are preschoolers also aware of having psychological and social attributes? As we pointed out in Chapter 8, rapidly accumulating evidence indicates that preschoolers know quite a bit about their own mental activities. The findings suggest that preschoolers possess knowledge of themselves that goes beyond appearance and actions. Thus, responses such as "I have a friend" or "I'm a happy person" are among their self-descriptions. Preschoolers consistently select self-statements that reflect moods, feelings, achievements, and other psychological and social orientations. Self as object, as *me,* even for a young child, includes a sense of a psychological and social being (Damon & Hart, 1988; Eder, 1990).

▶ Interaction among domains

When children reach about seven years of age, a new element enters their self-descriptions. Whereas younger children describe themselves in terms of typical categorical activities ("I run fast"), older children begin to make relational statements. For example, in response to the question "Who are you?" a fifth grader might say, "I can run faster than anyone else in my class," "I'm not as pretty as my older sister," or "Other children in my class are better than I am at math." The emphasis shifts from a kind of itemization of skills, actions, or social and psychological qualities to a comparison of their qualities with others' (Livesley & Bromley, 1973; Ruble, 1983; Secord & Peevers, 1974). Resemblance to others in terms of appearance, skills, abilities, and social and psychological traits is an important factor in defining self during these years.

As children become older, self is viewed in terms of more abstract qualities and becomes increasingly differentiated (Harter & Monsour, 1992; Secord & Peevers, 1974). The emphasis further shifts to how these attributes spur inter-

**categorical self** Conceptual process starting in the early preschool years in which the child begins to classify him- or herself according to easily observable categories (sex, age, physical capacities, skills, and so forth) that can be used to distinguish people.

## FIGURE 12.1

### Concerns About Opposing Attributes

From early to middle adolescence students increasingly report opposite or conflicting descriptions of self that depend on whether their evaluation is framed within the perspective of classroom, friends, close relationships, or parents. Concerns about these opposite or conflicting views increase at the same time. However, both the number of opposite attributes assigned to self and concerns about their effect on defining self begin to decline in later adolescence, as young people establish a more integrated identity and recognize that contradictions may be normal and of some value.

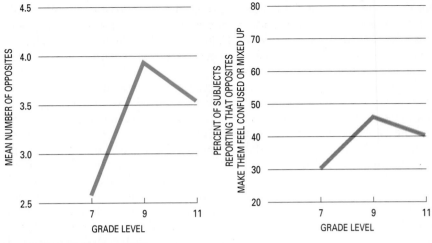

Source: Harter & Monsour, 1992

▸ Sociocultural influences

actions with others and affect social relationships. The changes are evident in such responses from young adolescents as "I play sports . . . because all the kids like athletes" and "I'm an honest person . . . people trust me because of it" (Damon & Hart, 1988).

By early adolescence self can be viewed from multiple, even opposing, perspectives. Susan Harter (1986) asked whether someone can have both positive and negative qualities. Can a person be both "smart" and "dumb" or "nice" and "nasty"? She found a substantial increase in the belief in this possibility between the seventh and ninth grades. The number of opposites, and concerns about them—feeling confused or bothered by qualities of self that reverse when interacting with parents, with friends or in a romantic relationship, or as a member of the classroom—becomes greatest during middle adolescence as Figure 12.1 indicates (Harter & Monsour, 1992). But these concerns lessen as adolescents become older and establish a more integrated and coherent picture of self that interprets contradictions as normal and even as having some value, depending on the situation. In addition, views of self in older adolescents become organized into principled ideas and comprehensive plans that include a more extended future and larger goals. For example, whether a boy is handsome or not is less important than taking pride in his self. Perceiving the self as helpful is important, because it makes the world a better place in which to live.

How universal is this developmental process? Can cultural, religious, and social class differences influence the development of self-concepts? William Damon and Daniel Hart (1988) believe that a sequence other than that outlined here for middle-income children in the United States is possible, even likely, in communities that encourage other levels of autonomy and independence. In some societies, for example, possessions or membership in the family or a social group may be far more important in determining perceptions of self than individual qualities, abilities, and achievements (Levine & White, 1986).

To illustrate their point, Damon and Hart (1988) studied children living in a fishing village in Puerto Rico. The residents were relatively poor and had few educational and social services available to them. Children typically attended school for no more than three or four years, and jobs often depended on a network of family and social relationships. Compared with middle-income youngsters from mainland regions of the United States, the Puerto Rican children voiced far more apprehension about whether their *behavior* was good or bad than whether they were competent or talented. A twelve-year-old might say it is important to be nice and respect people because misbehavior would mean that "everybody will hit and hate me or not help me." The Puerto Rican children consistently expressed greater concern than their mainland counterparts about whether others approved of their actions than about their relative competence with respect to some skill or capacity.

In cultures in which individual superiority is rewarded less than contributions to the collective community—for example, the Samoan culture—researchers may find that evaluations of self in terms of individual competencies are not seen as desirable. Many factors could contribute to these differences. The lives of children vary across cultures and communities in terms of styles of parenting, formal education, social structure, and the expectations of parents, peers, and community leaders. For example, in many Asian cultures, greater compliance to parental expectations, an emphasis on common academic tasks in school settings (Stevenson et al., 1986), and a high regard for modesty in interactions with others may contribute to a far different concept of the self than found in many western nations. All these factors may affect the self-concepts children develop.

**Social Comparison**    During the early and middle school years, as we already have indicated, children begin to reference others in describing themselves. Whether Jim feels he is nice or can run fast, or Ellen believes she is smart or throws a ball well, depends on how Jim or Ellen stacks up against age mates and friends. How important is this process, called **social comparison**—the tendency of people to use others as mirrors to evaluate their own abilities, interests, and values? The answer appears to be that it becomes increasingly important as children move through the elementary school years. For example, when five-, seven-, and nine-year-olds were told that they did better than or not as well as peers in a ball-throwing contest in which they could not actually determine their success, nine-year-olds based predictions of their future performance on the feedback they received: those told that they were successful predicted they would continue to show superior ability; those told that they were less successful expected to continue to perform more poorly than children who received no feedback. Five- and seven-year-olds, however, were unaffected by the information; they predicted that they would do equally well, regardless of how they compared with others (Ruble et al., 1980).

Children, of course, observe things happening to others even in the preschool years. Two pieces of candy of unequal size given to two four-year-olds can easily initiate conflict. At this age, however, observing others seems to be an especially important way of learning how to respond or of gaining new skills for mastering a task (Butler, 1989; Ruble, 1983). The motivation of younger children for attending to others often seems to be to find out how to do something (Veroff, 1969). To illustrate this point Diane Ruble (1987) recorded how frequently children in kindergarten, first, second, and fourth grades looked at other students or made comparative comments to them as they worked independently in the classroom. The comparisons were classified as showing an interest in achievement ("What page are you on?") or nonachievement (looking

THE CONCEPT OF SELF

▶ The child's active role

**social comparison**  Process in which individuals define themselves in relation to the skills, attributes, and qualities of others; believed to become especially important in contributing to self-concept during the middle childhood years.

A child's conception of self is often influenced by how others evaluate his activities and abilities. Athletic skill, for example, may be publicly recognized through the awarding of trophies. Moreover, at this age the child's definition of self is likely to include a comparison with others in terms of how well he is able to perform such activities.

at another child but not her work). The latter activity provides more information about how to behave than about how to compete. Ruble found that comparisons involving achievement increased substantially between kindergarten and first grade and continued at high levels among older children. Non-achievement comparisons, on the other hand, declined from kindergarten through fourth grade; older children seemed to engage in social comparisons as a way of determining how well they were doing, whereas younger children seemed to be checking on what they should be doing.

In fact, young children frequently are unrealistic about their skills; they claim that they will do far better than they actually can (Butler, 1990). By attending to the attributes and qualities of others, children may gain a more realistic means of predicting how well they will do. For example, Ruble (1987) found that children in kindergarten and first grade who more frequently made social comparisons involving achievement tended to have greater knowledge of their relative standing in the classroom.

As children approach the adolescent years and grow more competent in a task, they become less likely to look to others to evaluate how well they are doing and instead begin to use their own measures of performance on that task to judge success (Ruble & Flett, 1988). Here we may be seeing the dawning of a shift from social comparison to a more self-reliant and principled standard for evaluating self. This basis for a self-concept, rooted in internalized norms of mastery and competence, fits the criteria that mature individuals use to evaluate their identity and often is observed in later adolescence and early adulthood.

In summary, the development of self as object reveals a fascinating progression, beginning with the toddler's recognition of his separateness from others in terms of physical appearance and features. Among preschoolers, self is usually organized around category membership, but children this young also have some understanding of psychological capacities. The self-concepts of older children increasingly reflect a consideration of others and involve active comparison. The process eventually gives way during the adolescent years to more formalized autonomous standards for judging self, especially in areas in which the young person feels competent. Of course, social and cultural conditions may have an enormous effect on these progressions.

## Self as Subject

Just as we can ask a child what she knows about her physical features or personal characteristics, so too can we ask whether a child realizes that she influences and controls her surroundings, remains the same person over time, or is a unique individual. Such questions inquire about a child's understanding of her sense of agency or autonomy, individuality, and stability, and her capacity to reflect on these abilities. What do children know about such matters?

**The Sense of Agency**     The belief that a person can determine and influence things probably has its roots in infancy (Lewis & Brooks-Gunn, 1979). Robert White (1959) suggested that babies are born with a desire to master their environment, an ambition he termed **effectance motivation**. The active infant repeatedly stacks blocks, bangs pots, smiles to caregivers, and plays peek-a-boo, activities that often lead to consequences that the infant has learned to anticipate. If she cries, she typically is picked up, rocked, and nursed. The one-year-old who says "Mama" or other new words often may become the center of attention. From the feedback associated with crying or saying new words, infants may learn to expect what will happen and how to make it happen again. As a result, they eventually begin to see themselves as in control, capable of reaching desired goals and having the knowledge and means to do so.

By about two years of age many children begin to protest the attempts of others to help them in an activity such as dressing. Some researchers believe that the protests further reveal an early desire to be an agent or to master an activity (Kagan, 1981; Lutkenhaus, Bullock, & Geppert, 1987). At about this same time children also look to adults after completing a task as if to share

▶ The child's active role

▶ Roles of nature and nurture

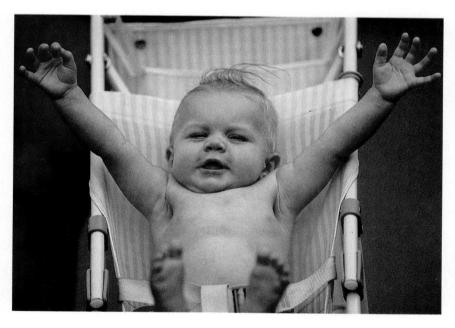

This infant may have already gained a rudimentary sense of agency. His outstretched arms seem to say, "Pick me up!" His behavior illustrates one of the many ways that even babies actively influence the things that happen to them.

**effectance motivation**   Inborn desire theorized by Robert White to be the basis for the infant's and child's efforts to master and gain control of the environment.

their success (Stipek, Recchia, & McClintic, 1992). The finding suggests that the consequences of social feedback, along with the child's observations of his activity, enter into a sense of competence at an early age.

As children mature, they believe that the world becomes increasingly responsive to their actions. For example, if asked, "How did you get to be the way you are?" a preschooler is likely to refer to uncontrollable factors ("I just grew. . . . My body just got bigger"), whereas a ten-year-old mentions her own efforts ("From getting good grades in school from studying"). By age thirteen, children also acknowledge the contributions of others to their sense of agency ("I learned from my parents, I even learned from friends, just listening to 'em and talking to 'em"), and older adolescents incorporate in their reasoning principled personal and moral qualities ("Well, I decided to be kind to people, because I've seen lots of kids hurt other kids' feelings for no reason, and it's not right or fair. . . .") (Damon & Hart, 1988).

How is this enthusiasm for mastery preserved and encouraged? The answer is complex, but as we have already seen, a responsive physical and social environment may be essential. To further illustrate, researchers in one study placed mobiles above the heads of infants for ten minutes a day during a period of fourteen weeks (see Figure 12.2). When babies could make the mobile rotate rapidly by moving their heads on a pressure-sensitive pillow, they quickly learned to do so. But for other babies the mobile rotated independent of the child's activity or simply remained stationary. When these infants subse-

**FIGURE 12.2**

**Learning Not to Learn**

Babies who are given the ability to control the motion of a mobile by moving their head on a special pillow normally learn to master the mobile's movement quite rapidly. However, infants who are initially not enabled to control the mobile but then are given the opportunity to do so have great difficulty learning to make the mobile move. Lack of opportunity to have an effect on the environment may sow the seeds for learned helplessness.

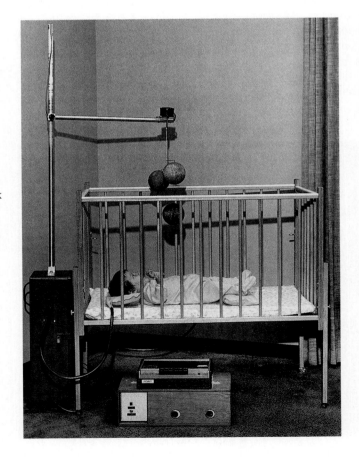

quently were given the opportunity to control the mobile by using the pillow, they did not learn to do so, even after extensive training (Watson, 1971; Watson & Ramey, 1972). The infants seemed to have lost the ability to master the activity by failing to make the connection between their head movements and the motion of the mobile.

Do individual children differ in their sense of self-determination and control? Indeed they do. Some children are convinced that what happens to them depends on their actions, that their choices, decisions, and abilities govern whether outcomes are good or bad, successful or unsuccessful. Asked how to find a friend, such a child might say, "Go up to someone you like and ask them to play with you." Asked how to do well on a test, the child might answer, "Study for it and you'll get smart!" These children are said to have an **internal locus of control** (Rotter, 1966). Carol Dweck and Elaine Elliott (1983) note that such children have a strong **mastery orientation**, a belief that success stems from trying hard; failures, these children believe, are usually conditions to be overcome by working harder or with greater effort. A primary benefit of this orientation is a sense of having the *ability* to do well in a variety of situations.

Other children, in contrast, exhibit an **external locus of control**; they feel that luck, fate, or others have an inordinate influence on what happens to them (Rotter, 1966). Asked why he cannot catch a ball, such a child might say, "The others throw it too fast." Asked why he got a poor grade, this child might say, "The teacher doesn't like me." Such children often express little confidence in their ability and feel powerless to influence the future. They perceive themselves as not having the *ability* to achieve, perhaps because their efforts have not led to regular success. In place of a sense of mastery, the child has a sense of **learned helplessness**, the feeling of having little ability and therefore no reason to initiate efforts at doing well (Dweck & Elliott, 1983).

Differing beliefs about competency have been shown to have a powerful bearing on academic achievement, participation in athletics and physical activities, popularity, and self-esteem (Nowicki & Strickland, 1973). The child who thinks passing to the next grade depends on whether a teacher likes her, rather than on how hard she works, may have little reason to strive for success. Those with an internal locus of control, and who recognize choices in pursuing a goal, perform better in school and on standardized tests of achievement than children with an external locus of control or who are not aware of various ways of doing well (Chapman, Skinner, & Baltes, 1990; Findley & Cooper, 1983).

Children who display learned helplessness are caught in a vicious cycle of self-fulfilling events, anticipating failure and rationalizing that they have little control over what happens, even if they have displayed competence in similar situations before (Dweck & Elliott, 1983). They are especially likely to expect failure on tasks found difficult in the past and may avoid such tasks when given further opportunity to work on them (Dweck, 1991). Deborah Phillips (1984) reports that nearly 20 percent of fifth-graders with high ability limit their goals and persistence in school activities. In the academic realm this pattern is found more frequently among girls than boys, perhaps because girls are more likely than boys to view their failures in terms of such uncontrollable factors as lack of ability (Crandall, 1969; Dweck, Goetz, & Strauss, 1980; Dweck & Repucci, 1973; Stipek & Hoffman, 1980). The pattern can even be observed among children as young as five or six years of age (Heyman, Dweck, & Cain, 1992).

▶ Individual differences

**internal locus of control** Individual's sense that his or her own efforts and activities influence success and failure and the events that happen to him or her. Contrast with *external locus of control*.

**mastery orientation** Belief that achievements are based on one's own efforts rather than luck or other factors beyond one's control.

**external locus of control** Individual's sense that outside factors such as luck, fate, and other people primarily influence success and failure and the events that happen to him or her. Contrast with *internal locus of control*.

**learned helplessness** Belief that one has little control over situations, perhaps because of lack of ability or inconsistent outcomes.

However, children this young interpret failures on a task as not being "good" in a more global, moral sense rather than in terms of intellectual ability.

Children who gain little mastery over their environment or who are offered conflicting and inconsistent reactions—as, for example, by abusive parents—seem most likely to display learned helplessness. Competent adults grow up in families in which they are encouraged to take on appropriate responsibilities as children, invited to participate in family discussion, encouraged to be independent, and in which parents are available to provide clear and consistent discipline (Block, 1971). Parental warmth and support during problem-solving efforts, especially by the father, seem to have positive benefits for a child's perception of competence as well (Wagner & Phillips, 1992).

Teachers also may play a major role in fostering a sense of mastery or helplessness, at least with respect to academic achievement (Dweck et al., 1978). When children already do well, teachers can promote a mastery orientation by rewarding stable inner qualities, such as the sense of ability, as they encourage children's efforts. When children do poorly, however, the teacher's criticisms should focus on nonintellectual and temporary factors that may have reduced the student's performance rather than on the child's intrinsic ability, thereby encouraging effort when the next opportunity arises. The guidelines stem from the assumption that for those who perceive themselves as helpless, a sense of agency will be established only when their beliefs about the causes of their failures are changed (Dweck, 1975). Children must be convinced that their failures are not from lack of ability but from insufficient effort or some other factor that can be modified easily.

To illustrate this point Dweck identified twelve children who displayed learned helplessness on math tasks and asked them to complete a series of difficult math problems that they were unable to solve. The children then participated in twenty-five training sessions. Six children were given problems on which they could consistently succeed and received tokens to emphasize their success, a procedure introduced to build self-confidence. The other six children were assigned to *attribution retraining,* a procedure designed to change their beliefs about the cause of their failures. During each session these children received a small number of "failures" and were explicitly told that they needed to work harder; lack of success thus was directly tied to their effort rather than their inability.

When the two groups of children attempted the initial set of problems again, those in the attribution retraining group showed a clear improvement in performance; the other children did not. The children whose training emphasized success continued to view themselves as unable to do well on mathematics problems, but children receiving attribution retraining persisted longer and were more likely to credit any remaining failures to lack of effort. Thus, the attribution retraining led them to recognize that they had the means to change outcomes, an important element in encouraging them to be agents in charge of their behavior. Attribution retraining has now become an important method that parents and teachers use in attempting to replace self-limiting styles and attitudes with positive and fulfilling approaches to success, a means of converting learned helplessness into a greater sense of mastery and agency (Dweck, 1986).

**The Sense of Individuality**     How does a child know that she cannot become someone else? In other words, what do children understand about individuality and uniqueness? In one recent study young people were asked,

"What makes you different from everybody else in the world?" Preschoolers usually answered with their name ("Cause there is only one person with my name"), their possessions, or specific features of their bodies. Eight- to ten-year-olds added comparative statements involving abilities, activities, and personality ("Well, I think I'm friendlier than most kids I know"). Young adolescents were more likely to list unique psychological and other traits ("The way I act . . . One thing else, I worry a lot . . . Yeah, I worry too much and a lot of things that a lot of kids don't care about"). Older adolescents adopted even stronger views involving unique personal feelings and orientations ("Nobody else sees things or feels the same way about things as I do") (Damon & Hart, 1988).

The answer that emerges from this research is that the child gains his sense of individuality early and first links it to observable physical characteristics and features. As children grow, they begin to compare themselves with others, especially their private feelings and thoughts, and these qualities become the central criteria for the child's claim to uniqueness.

### The Sense of Stability

Is an individual essentially the same person today that she was a year ago or will be a year from now? As with her sense of individuality, the child's understanding of her continuity begins quite early, but the explanation for this stability changes with development. Asked, "If you change from year to year, how do you know it's still always you?" preschoolers cite personal name ("My name, and then I would know if it was me if someone called me"), physical features, possessions, or other categorical qualities as proof. An eight- to ten-year-old is likely to refer to stable personal or internal qualities ("I know it's me because I still know the things I knew five years ago"). Young adolescents link the sense of continuity to others ("I'll still have my family. . . . They always know I'm me and not someone else"). An older adolescent is likely to state his certainty more abstractly ("Well, nothing about me always stays the same, but I am always kind of like I was a while ago") (Damon & Hart, 1988).

Here, just as for their individuality, children's sense of a stable self gradually expands from physical, highly observable attributes to include both inner psychological and broader contextual elements. Moreover, as children mature, they judge inner psychological qualities as increasingly important in decisions about their stability of self (Aboud & Skerry, 1983).

### The Sense of Reflection

When does the ability to reflect upon or contemplate the self emerge? Robert Selman (1980) suggests that the capacity does not begin until early adolescence. The advent of reflection, along with new ways of thinking abstractly, helps to explain the preoccupations of young teenagers with appearance and worth—that is, their growing *self-consciousness* about who they are. In fact, David Elkind (1981a) has proposed that young adolescents exhibit a kind of egocentrism, an excessive preoccupation with themselves as the object of their thought. They go overboard in assuming that others are just as concerned as they about their looks, feelings, and thoughts. For them there is an *imaginary audience,* a sense of continually being on stage and being observed by others.

Another consequence of the capacity to reflect upon the self is a greater appreciation of how the mind contributes to experience. A fourteen-year-old may say, "I can fool myself into thinking I don't miss my lost puppy." An older adolescent, however, often realizes that she cannot always completely control her

▶ Interactions among domains

The ability to reflect upon or contemplate one's own looks, feelings, and ideas may not emerge until the adolescent years. At this time we occasionally begin to observe a young person as if "lost" in thought. Sometimes those reflections exhibit a form of egocentrism or excessive preoccupation with one's own feelings and ideas.

feelings and that her behavior may be affected, even if she is unaware of those feelings. Thus, the sense of reflection forms the basis for eventually distinguishing between conscious and unconscious psychological processes (Damon & Hart, 1988).

## Self-esteem: Evaluating Self

We turn now to another component of self, **self-esteem**, or self-worth, the positive feelings of merit and the extent to which the child believes his attributes and actions are good, desired, and valued. This component of self appears to be related to social affiliations, success in school, and overall mental health. For example, later life satisfaction and happiness have been linked to high self-esteem (Bachman, 1970; Crandall, 1973); depression, anxiety, and poor adjustment in school and social relationships have been linked to low self-esteem (Damon, 1983).

**Defining Self-esteem**   How should we describe a child's self-esteem if she takes pride in how smart she is, concludes that she is not very good at sports (but sports are unimportant anyway), and is unsure whether she is pretty enough to become a movie star? Work by Susan Harter (1987) and others (Eccles et al., 1993b) has revealed that children often give different evaluations of self when asked about academic competence, athletic skill, social acceptance, or physical appearance. Still, by about eight years of age children can make global assessments to answer such questions as, "Do you like yourself?" and "Are you happy the way you are?" The responses children make to these broad inquiries, however, are not a simple summation of all the different evaluations they make in regard to their specific attributes and abilities. How then does the child arrive at a global sense of worth?

William James (1892) theorized that self-esteem depends on the success a person feels in areas in which that person wants to be successful. Others emphasize that self-esteem originates in how a person thinks others see him; the

**self-esteem**   One's feelings of worth; extent to which one senses one's attributes and actions are good, desired, and valued.

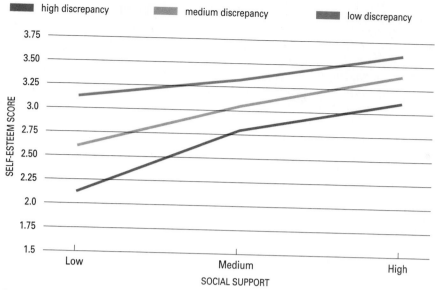

high discrepancy    medium discrepancy    low discrepancy

SELF-ESTEEM SCORE

3.75
3.50
3.25
3.0
2.75
2.50
2.25
2.0
1.75
1.5

Low        Medium        High

SOCIAL SUPPORT

Source: Adapted from Harter, 1987.

**FIGURE 12.3**

**How Self-esteem Develops**

Self-esteem reflects the combined influence of social support and the discrepancy between the child's perceived and desired competence in some ability or attribute. Harter divided elementary school children into three groups based on these two measures. Those with highest self-esteem reported high social support and a low discrepancy between perceived and desired competence. Those with lowest self-esteem reported low social support and a high discrepancy between perceived and desired competence. The findings suggest that parents, teachers, and others concerned with increasing self-esteem need to consider both the kind of social encouragement and positive regard they provide and children's own feelings about what they believe is important.

*generalized other*—the combined evaluations of parents, peers, and teachers influential in a person's life—helps to determine his sense of worth (Cooley, 1902; Mead, 1934).

To determine whether both the importance of being successful in a highly regarded domain and the perceived evaluations of others affect self-esteem, Harter (1987) obtained ratings of how children viewed themselves in scholastic competence, athletic competence, social acceptance, physical appearance, and behavioral conduct and in terms of global success. Harter further asked children how critical it was for them to do well in each of these domains. Harter reasoned that greater discrepancies between perceived competence and the importance of a domain, especially those highly valued, would be linked to lower self-esteem. Children additionally rated how others (parents, peers) viewed them, felt they were important, liked them, and so on.

For children in the third to eighth grades, the more a rating of importance in an area outstripped a child's perception of her competence, the lower the child's sense of her overall worth was. In fact, children with low self-esteem seemed to have trouble disregarding the significance of areas in which they were not skilled (Harter, 1985). In contrast, children with high self-esteem minimized the value of those domains in which they were not especially competent and gained considerable satisfaction from areas in which they were relatively successful. But Harter found that the perceived social support of others also correlated with the child's sense of self-worth. As Figure 12.3 shows, elementary school children with low discrepancy *and* high social support scores showed superior levels of self-worth. Children with high discrepancy and low social support, however, displayed the lowest levels of self-esteem. Thus, both factors contributed to overall sense of worth. The results suggest that efforts to improve self-esteem in children require both a supportive social milieu and the formation and acceptance of realistic personal goals.

Are some domains more important than others for a child's overall sense of worth? The answer appears to be yes. Boys and girls of elementary and middle

▶ Sociocultural influences

▶ Interactions among domains

▶ Individual differences

▶ Sociocultural influences

**identity (personal)** Broad, coherent, internalized view of who a person is, what a person wants to be, believes, and values that emerges during adolescence.

school age who were dissatisfied with and keenly concerned about their physical appearance tended to have especially low self-esteem. Although discrepancies were also important in other domains, they correlated less highly with judgments of overall self-worth. Harter (1987) speculates that in American culture the relationship stems from the enormous emphasis in movies, television, and teen magazines on appearance as the key to success and acceptance. As children become older, discrepancy scores on social acceptance take on increasingly greater significance, whereas discrepancy scores on athletic competence show a decline in importance (Harter, 1987). Other research indicates that positive judgments by peers about social acceptance and academic ability near the beginning of the school year correlate with improved self-worth at the end of the year (Cole, 1991).

**Developmental Changes in Self-esteem**    In general, the self-esteem of children in early elementary school is high. Yet as they approach adolescence, self-esteem for a substantial portion, especially girls, declines (Block & Robins, 1993; Simmons & Blyth, 1987; Wigfield et al., 1991). The change accompanies major transitions, such as the onset of puberty, entry to junior high school, and substantial realignments in friendship patterns. Often the decline accompanies a lowering of perceived competence in academic subjects such as math. However, if girls retain a warm strong orientation toward others, they are more likely to maintain high self-esteem throughout these transitions. Perhaps the association should not be surprising, given that warm responsive parenting is linked to high self-esteem in young people in the first place (Bishop & Ingersoll, 1989). And, as the earlier review of a sense of agency suggested, coping strategies that lead young people to attribute success to their competence and mastery is certainly another critical element in maintaining high self-esteem (Brooks, 1992).

Relatively little cross-cultural research on self-esteem has been reported although several studies comparing children from the United States and Taiwan have revealed a consistent pattern; Chinese children report lower self-esteem than their counterparts in the United States (Chiu, 1992–93; Stigler, Smith, & Mao, 1985; Turner & Mo, 1984). The reasons for this difference may stem from cultural practices in Taiwan that emphasize humility rather than pride in one's accomplishments or qualities and provide less opportunity to receive social or public displays of success in academic and other settings. Also, Taiwanese family rearing patterns emphasize obedience rather than individual achievement. Furthermore, although children in Taiwan often do excel academically, other ways of gaining high self-esteem may be less available to them.

### Identity

The burgeoning sense of self, along with the capacity to reflect on individual qualities, serves as the nucleus for the construction of an **identity**, a broad, coherent, internalized view of who a person is, what a person wants to be, believes, and values. A sense of identity solidifies and gives meaning to such fundamental questions about self as, Who am I? Why do I exist? And what am I to become? Knowledge of self is woven from the many roles a person plays in society. A healthy identity, Erik Erikson pointed out (see Chapter 2), is fabricated during adolescence and young adulthood but builds on earlier progress in accepting and trusting others, in being encouraged to explore interests and desires, and in acquiring feelings of competence and skill. By establishing a fully integrated identity, the adolescent creates a healthy personality for the transition to mature adulthood.

**The Adolescent Identity Crisis**     The period of adolescence has sometimes been viewed as filled with stress and uncertainty about self, riddled with sudden and frequent mood shifts, a time dubbed the **identity crisis**. Does such a crisis really take place? Erikson (1963) pointed out that in establishing an identity, adolescents enter into a period of intense reflection on and dissatisfaction with who they are and what they are like. During these years thoughts and behavior often are devoted to exploring alternatives before commitment to a course of action with respect to social relationships, vocation, and lifestyle (Marcia, 1980).

As they approach the teen years, adolescents often engage in new ways of behaving and thinking that involve greater autonomy, independence, and expressions of intimacy with others. For example, teenagers increasingly view their actions and conduct as personal, their own business, so to speak (Smetana, 1988), and come to believe strongly that such things as family chores, eating habits, curfews, and personal appearance are up to them, not their parents. Needless to say, this view can introduce conflict within the family, especially for parents who may wish to maintain control.

Other research suggests, however, that conflict for many adolescents is far less frequent and traumatic than the idea of a crisis would suggest (Hill, 1987; Powers, Hauser, & Kilner, 1989). From this perspective the vast majority of adolescents are sociable, well-adjusted individuals on their way to adopting the mores and values of their culture and effectively coping with the pressures and demands placed on them by their society (Offer, 1987). A key element in the successful negotiation of these years appears to be a supportive family, educational, and social milieu that resonates with the needs and interests of adolescents (Eccles et al., 1993a). For example, as children progress from elementary to junior high school, they find greater emphasis on control and discipline, less positive personal support from teachers, and more competitiveness and public evaluation of their work. The changes, however, conflict with adolescents' need for fewer intellectual pressures and more opportunity to take charge in exploring and resolving uncertainties about their identity (Eccles et al., 1993a). From bargaining over their choices of friends and activities to use of the telephone or the family car, adolescents also test new ways of communicating with and relating to parents and others in authority (Powers, Hauser, & Kilner, 1989). Thus, parents, teachers, and others have an important role in providing reassurance and support while permitting teenagers to weigh their ideas in less evaluative contexts. Being able to establish a point of view seems to promote a strong sense of personal identity (Grotevant & Cooper, 1986; Hauser et al., 1987).

Is there an identity crisis during adolescence? Perhaps not for the vast majority of teenagers. Yet 10 to 20 percent of adolescents do experience serious mental health problems, and many of them receive little attention from professionals. One especially significant problem is suicide. As many as five thousand young people aged fifteen to twenty-four commit suicide annually in the United States; the number of attempted suicides is estimated to be one hundred times greater (Berman, 1987). Whether there is an identity crisis or not, many adolescents need to confront and resolve serious mental health problems.

**identity crisis**     Period, usually during adolescence, characterized by considerable uncertainty about the self and the role the individual is to fulfill in society.

▶ Sociocultural differences

**Ethnic Identity**    Among the factors affecting a young person's identity is ethnic and racial background. **Ethnic identity** refers to the sense of belonging to a specific cultural group as opposed to simply adopting its social practices, known more generally as *acculturation* (Phinney, 1990). Research conducted in the United States suggests that preschool and younger children, even when members of a racial minority group, display a bias for choosing dolls or pictures depicting white individuals when asked who they are most like, who they want most to be like, or who they prefer (Spencer & Markstrom-Adams, 1990). But the bias may stem from conceptual and methodological problems as well as sociocultural stereotypes that make it difficult to interpret how young children understand such questions.

As they become more capable of reflecting on and exploring their heritage, older children and adolescents do grapple with their racial and ethnic identity. Because the majority culture often views minority groups in a stereotypical and negative light, the majority culture might assume that identifying with a minority ethnic or racial group could set the stage for personal conflict and confusion. Yet little evidence exists for this scenario; in fact, self-esteem among minority children can be as strong as self-esteem among others, especially when minority children have come to understand and value their ethnicity (Phinney, 1989; Spencer & Markstrom-Adams, 1990). Valuing ethnicity seems to be fostered by warm parents who are sensitive to ethnic issues (Phinney & Rosenthal, 1992). Moreover, young people may evidence a high level of ethnic identity whether the minority group enjoys relatively elevated or low status in the majority culture (Rosenthal & Feldman, 1992). However, our understanding of ethnic identity and its development remains quite limited, even though about 30 percent of youth in the United States alone are members of minority groups (Wetzel, 1987).

## *Self-regulation and Self-control*

Impulsive and easily upset, infants and young children have difficulty behaving in a patient or deliberate manner. Eventually, however, parents and others demand that children control their behavior. A three-year-old may be expected to stay away from the fireplace, to use the toilet, to say thank you, to share and put away toys. Older children and teenagers are asked to assume ever greater responsibility for their actions and to conform to socially accepted rules and standards. But this transition, from being dependent to becoming responsible and self-reliant, may be a long and difficult one. A mother may have great difficulty persuading her daughter, eager to show her tricycle-riding prowess, that it is a playmate's turn. And countless parents have wrestled with how best to convince their offspring that completing their homework is an important way of becoming better prepared for the future.

**Self-regulation** refers to the capacity of a person to monitor and direct his own activities to achieve certain goals or meet the demands imposed by others. **Self-control**, a related concept, signifies the ability to comply with expectations of caregivers or other adults, especially in their absence. Self-control is especially important for achieving ethical or moral behavior. However, let's first consider the development of self-regulation and self-control, apart from their broader ethical and moral implications.

**ethnic identity**    The sense of belonging to a particular cultural group.

**self-regulation**    Process by which children are expected to control their own behaviors in accordance with the standards and desires of their caregivers and community, especially in the absence of other adults.

**self-control**    Ability to comply with sociocultural prescriptions concerning ethical or moral behavior.

## Developmental Changes

For infants and young children regulation of behavior might best be labeled *co-regulation* (Kopp, 1987); the children and their caregivers jointly manage behavior. Throughout a child's development, but especially during the earlier years, adults continue to play an important part in overseeing a child's activity (Maccoby, 1984a). Efforts to limit behaviors begin in many families when babies are about eight or nine months old, when their newly acquired motor skills increase their risk of injury; in some households restraining devices such as playpens and gates appear. For their safety infants about one year of age may be warned to avoid dangerous or unhealthy objects and situations ("Don't touch the knife"; "Don't play with the cat litter"; "Hold on to my hand"). Efforts to preserve possessions ("Don't play with the VCR") and to not harm others ("Don't pinch") are also common admonishments at about this time (Gralinski & Kopp, 1993).

As toddlers approach eighteen months of age, adults often initiate broader efforts to control children's behaviors. These efforts emphasize following such family routines as putting away toys, self-care, and being more independent (e.g., walking rather than being carried) (Gralinski & Kopp, 1993). Designed to help organize the child's activities, requests include touching and other nonverbal attempts to get the toddler's attention, as well as pointing out things to be done and how to do them. By the time children reach twenty-four to thirty months of age, parental demands may decline in frequency as children become familiar with requests and respond to them more routinely (Kopp, 1987).

Children's self-initiated attempts to obey appear during the second year. A thirteen-month-old, for example, may look at, perhaps even approach and touch, an electrical outlet while saying, "No, no!" During the second and third year self-restraint improves rapidly. For example, in a **delay-of-gratification** task, in which the child is asked to wait some period of time before performing an activity or attaining some highly desired outcome (such as playing with an attractive toy or eating a piece of candy), eighteen-month-olds have great difficulty complying. Between two and three years of age children become increasingly more effective at delaying their behavior (Vaughn, Kopp, & Krakow, 1984). Thus, although the development of self-control first begins with attempts by others to govern the young child's actions, the efforts are relinquished and transferred gradually; the warnings and guidance of others become less direct, perhaps even less necessary, and the child takes on more responsibility for regulating his behavior. How does this shift come about?

Toddlers are often asked to begin to regulate behaviors and activities so that they are displayed in socially acceptable ways. One such activity that most toddlers are expected to master is control of body functions.

▶ The child's active role

## The Influence of Language and Attention

As we saw in Chapter 7, Lev Vygotsky (1962) and his students, particularly Alexander Luria (1961, 1969), theorized that language plays a pivotal role in the regulation of behavior. Consider what David, a preschooler, says while playing alone with Tinkertoys, as recorded by an observer:

> The wheels go here, the wheels go here. Oh we need to start it all over again. We need to close it up. See, it closes up. We're starting all over again. Do you know why we wanted to do that? Because I needed it to go a different way. Isn't it going to be pretty clever, don't you think? But we have to cover up the motor just like a real car. (Kohlberg, Yaeger, & Hjertholm, 1968, p. 695)

▶ Interaction among domains

**delay of gratification**  Capacity to wait for some period of time before performing a tempting activity or attaining some highly desired outcome; a measure of individuals' ability to regulate their own behavior.

According to Vygotsky, David's *private speech* is a form of self-regulation (Wertsch, 1985). Intended for no one else, the conversation appears to keep David on track by organizing and praising his efforts to construct a toy car. Before about three years of age, Vygotsky maintained, only the speech of others exerts any kind of control. As we noted in Chapter 7, over the next several years the child becomes better able to initiate, maintain, or inhibit behavior, first through speech spoken aloud, as in David's case, and then as expressed silently, in the mind (Mischel & Mischel, 1977).

As we also pointed out in Chapter 7, observations of the speech habits of preschoolers engaged in various activities do not always support Vygotsky's view that verbalization contributes to more competent performance (Kopp, 1987). One reason may be that expressions intended for self-regulation are most likely to occur in circumstances especially challenging to the child (Frauenglass & Diaz, 1985). Thus, a child who talks to herself might be expected to do less well on a task than a child who proceeds silently; after all, the silent child may no longer need verbalizations to assist him in problem solving.

Donald Meichenbaum and Joseph Goodman (1971) have carried the relationship between verbalization and self-regulation one step further by training children to use language to control their behavior. In one study they asked impulsive seven- to nine-year-olds to observe an adult engaged in a pencil-and-paper motor task. The adult verbalized the task requirements, ways of directing and guiding responses, and positive feelings about performance, uttering comments such as "I have to go slowly. . . . Draw the line down, good. Good, I'm doing fine so far." Simply having children observe this activity was not enough to help their performance. Successful training required a series of steps that mirrored Vygotsky's developmental model of self-regulation. Children had to perform the task first while being instructed by an adult, then while instructing themselves out loud, and finally by instructing themselves silently. Through this kind of training the verbal communications provided by the adult and eventually adopted by children helped children meet the demands for self-reliant, systematic, and deliberate behavior.

Meichenbaum (1977) suggests that verbalizations help regulate behavior, because they direct attention to key dimensions and features of a task, assist in establishing and organizing ways to engage in activities, and preserve important task-related information in memory. The importance of attentional factors in self-control becomes apparent when we examine the kinds of verbal expressions most effective in delay-of-gratification tasks. For example, the child directed not to eat a marshmallow who says "The marshmallow is yummy"— words that focus attention *on* the forbidden treat—or who talks about sad things such as falling and hurting himself—ideas that provide little diversion—shows less delay than someone who sings a pleasant but distracting nursery rhyme such as "Three Blind Mice" (see Figure 12.4) (Mischel, Ebbesen, & Zeiss, 1972). A fidgety third-grader eager for recess might be better advised to direct her attention to reading a book of her choice than staring at the classroom clock.

Again, a developmental shift can be found in who assumes responsibility for regulating attention. At first, caregivers are more likely to initiate attempts to focus or distract the child. To illustrate this point George Holden (1983) observed mothers and their two-and-a-half-year-olds as they completed grocery shopping, an activity that can rapidly test the limits of most caregivers, because grocery displays are enticing. Holden found mothers were frequently forced to respond to their children's requests in this setting and used a variety

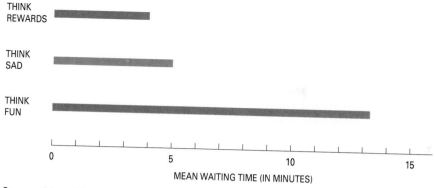

THINK
REWARDS

THINK
SAD

THINK
FUN

0       5       10       15

MEAN WAITING TIME (IN MINUTES)

Source: Adapted from Mischel, Ebbesen, & Zeiss, 1972.

**FIGURE 12.4**

**Delay of Gratification and Attention to the Desired Goal Object**

Preschoolers find it far easier to delay gratification if they are asked to think and talk about things that are fun than if asked to think and talk about either sad things or about the reward that they can eventually receive. Encouraging young children to consider fun things effectively distracts their attention from other highly desired goal objects.

of tactics to do so: reasoning, not responding, physically or verbally intervening, acknowledging children's desires, and attempting to distract children. Mothers who tried to anticipate conflicts, either by diverting children's attention in advance or by engaging them in an interesting conversation, were most effective in preventing conflict while grocery shopping. Sensitive and consistent mothers who learned to use strategies to direct, maintain, and redirect their children's attention appeared to be most effective in regulating their behavior (Holden & West, 1989; Kopp, 1987).

During later preschool and early school years children acquire their own attentional strategies as a means of preserving goals and supporting long-term ambitions. For example, in a delay-of-gratification task preschoolers often prefer to place in front of themselves a tempting reward rather than a picture of it or some other irrelevant item. In doing so they unnecessarily increase their exposure to the forbidden object, look at it more, and have greater difficulty delaying their response to it. By age five, children are less likely to create such self-defeating arrangements; they prefer to wait with the tempting reward covered rather than uncovered (Mischel & Mischel, 1983). Some will even shield their eyes, play games with their hands and feet, or try to go to sleep to help manage the delay (Cournoyer & Trudel, 1991; Mischel, Shoda, & Rodriguez, 1989).

▶ The child's active role

Older children show greater metacognitive understanding of helpful attentional and other tactics for regulating their activities (Mischel & Mischel, 1983). An eleven-year-old, for example, offered the following recommendation about distracting the self: "You can take your mind off of it and think of Christmas or something like that. But the point is—think about something else." By this age, then, children begin to reflect on ways they can most effectively control their behavior.

▶ Interaction among domains

## Individual Differences

Even ten years later children better able to initiate delay-of-gratification strategies as preschoolers stand apart from children less able to delay gratification as preschoolers. Adolescents who had greater self-regulatory capacities as preschoolers are described by their parents as more academically and socially competent and better able to handle frustration and temptation. They also are reported to be more attentive, deliberate, and intelligent. In addition, they seem better able to tolerate stress and cope with social and personal problems, even

▶ Individual differences

when their intellectual performance is similar to those less able to delay gratification (Mischel, Shoda, & Rodriguez, 1989; Shoda, Mischel, & Peake, 1990).

Jeanne Block and Jack Block (1980) have identified yet another component of self-regulation—flexible and adaptive behavior in appropriate settings—that shows evidence of stable individual differences. Shouting, running, and responding impulsively, for example, may be unacceptable within the classroom but highly appropriate during recess. Some children display elasticity and are able to modify their behavior easily as the situation demands throughout childhood; others consistently show far less flexibility.

What accounts for these individual differences? Genetic and constitutional factors may contribute, but researchers generally agree that socialization practices also play a significant role. Caregivers who encourage and use self-regulation provide opportunities for children to acquire skills, attitudes, and habits that promote persistence and effort and reduce frustration, yielding both social and academic benefits (Mischel, Shoda, & Rodriguez, 1989). Parents also need to strike a proper balance in dispensing appropriate control and encouraging self-regulation. Overcontrolling adults tend to have grown up in families that emphasize considerable structure, order, and tradition in their values (Block, 1971). Adults with relatively little control, on the other hand, tend to have grown up in families in which little emphasis was placed on achievement and responsible behavior and in which each parent had different caregiving values.

Self-regulation, in summary, begins as a joint venture between child and caregiver, but as children mature, most parents gradually relinquish and transfer the supervisory role to their offspring. By verbally directing children's activities and attention, caregivers provide role models and specific techniques that children can adopt. Individual differences in these abilities emerge by the preschool years and are consistently maintained throughout adolescence. Some of the transitions in that ability, along with other major aspects of development of self, are summarized in the Chronology on page 459.

▶ Roles of nature and nurture

## *Moral Development*

Psychologists began to study *moral development,* the process by which an individual comes to understand what society accepts as right and wrong, during the early years of the twentieth century. After all, few aspects of development have more far-reaching implications for human understanding than the values society holds about acceptable behaviors and relationships. On a more practical level, with the emergence of handbooks for parents on the "how-to's" of rearing a child, experts attempted to identify those disciplinary techniques that would produce a child of good moral character. Educators too were interested in finding ways in which the school curriculum could foster high standards and conduct in students. The issues remain of concern today.

Psychological theories vary in the aspects of moral development that they emphasize. Theories arising from Freud's view of personality focus on *affective* dimensions of moral development. According to this perspective, the emotional relationships children have with their parents influence the degree to which they incorporate parental standards of conduct. Social learning theories emphasize the child's acquisition of moral *behaviors,* such as the tendency to behave acceptably and to resist temptation. Cognitive-developmental theories center on moral *reasoning,* or how the child thinks about moral problems and

## CHRONOLOGY — Understanding Self and Self-regulation

| | |
|---|---|
| 8–9 MONTHS | Parent initiates attempts to regulate infant's behavior. |
| 12–15 MONTHS | Parent's efforts to control behavior emphasize toddler's safety, preservation of property, and avoidance of harm to others. <br> Toddler shows first signs of self-regulation. |
| 15–18 MONTHS | Recognizes self in mirror and photos. <br> Parent's increased efforts at co-regulation emphasize family routines, self-care, and increased independence. |
| 18–30 MONTHS | Begins to be capable of delaying gratification. |
| 2 1/2–6 YEARS | Defines self by categorical judgments. <br> Recognizes agency for physical and cognitive achievements. <br> Exercises overt self-regulation using language. <br> Recognizes increasingly effective ways to delay gratification. |
| 6–9 YEARS | Defines self by social comparisons. <br> Displays global self-esteem. <br> Recognizes agency for social achievements. <br> Exercises self-regulation through internalized language. |
| 10–13 YEARS | Defines self in terms of social roles. <br> Begins to use autonomous criteria for evaluating self. <br> Recognizes contradictory views of self. <br> Shows metacognitive understanding of self-regulation. |
| 13+ YEARS | Defines self in terms of principled values. <br> Begins to accept and resolve contradictory views of self. <br> Begins to address issues of identity. <br> Recognizes self within the broader society. |

This chart describes the sequence in the development of understanding the self and self-regulation based on the findings of research. Children often show individual differences in the exact ages at which they display the various developmental achievements outlined here.

judges right and wrong. Each perspective makes a unique contribution to the understanding of the development of values.

## Freud's Theory

Sigmund Freud's theory of moral development ([1925]1961) emphasized the *internalization* of moral standards as a by-product of the child's progression through the stages of psychosexual development. Specifically, Freud believed that the acquisition of a moral sense is achieved near the end of the *phallic stage,* by about the age of five or six, when the *Oedipal complex* is resolved in

▶ Development as continuous/discontinuous

boys. According to Freud, the boy experiences intense emotional conflict when sexual attraction to his mother cannot be fulfilled and hostile feelings toward his father (his competitor for his mother's affections) cannot be acted upon. The boy's primary fear is that he will be punished by castration and that he will lose his parents' love.

The Oedipal conflict becomes resolved, Freud concluded, when the young boy suppresses his instinctual urges and allies himself with his powerful same-sex parent—his father. Through this process of *identification* the child acquires his father's moral values and standards. Another outcome is the formation of the **superego**, the component of the child's personality that functions both as a **conscience** (by identifying what not to do) and **ego ideal** (by identifying appropriate and desirable behaviors). The child's suppressed aggressive tendencies are turned inward so that his moral transgressions are followed by guilt feelings and the desire for self-punishment. The child generally tries to avoid feelings of guilt by acting in accordance with the internalized notions of his parents' wishes.

Among the controversial aspects of Freud's theory is its prediction that girls will develop a weaker moral sense than boys. In the counterpart of the Oedipal complex, dubbed the *Electra complex* for girls, the daughter experiences a strong attachment to her father. The resolution of this conflict does not involve nearly the same emotional intensity for girls as it does for boys. Girls, for example, cannot fear castration. As a result, the girl's identification with her mother occurs with less force, and the superego or conscience, according to Freud, is not as strong.

Attempts to validate the various claims made by Freud have not met with much success. Little evidence exists to show that the child's identification with the same-sex parent or fear of losing parental love leads to internalization of moral standards (Hoffman, 1970, 1971). Moreover, many have reacted strongly to the notion that moral development is inferior or incomplete in girls. For example, Carol Gilligan (1982) maintains that Freud's theory is a male's view of male development that fails to explore the unique dimensions of the female experience as they pertain to morality. Furthermore, contemporary research shows that children begin to develop concepts of morality well before the age at which Freud hypothesized that the superego emerges (Emde et al., 1991; Lamb, 1991). In fact, the early internalization of rules seems to arise in the child's second year of life as the ability to recognize anger or displeasure in the emotional reactions and communications of caregivers increases (Kochanska, 1993). Despite these criticisms, Freud's emphasis on moral development as the internalization of society's standards, the central role parents play in the process, and the import of the child's emotions for moral development are ideas that have endured.

## Social Learning Theory

▶ Roles of nature and nurture

▶ Development as continuous/discontinuous

According to social learning theory, the rewards and punishments dispensed by parents and others in response to the child's behaviors shape their conduct, as do the actions and verbalizations that children see parents and others use (Aronfreed, 1976; Bandura, 1977b). In this sense, moral values are learned like any other behavior. Social learning theorists see morality as a process of incremental growth in appropriate actions and increasing conformity with the rules of society. In addition, this school emphasizes the child's overt observable behaviors rather than his moral reasoning and moral judgment. Although they speak of the child's internalization of moral standards, social learning theorists

Among the issues sparking controversy in development is how a child learns which behaviors are acceptable and unacceptable. Research on moral development and values has examined the roles of cognition and affect in an effort to fully understand the socialization of culturally permissable behavior. The effort to instill rules and regulations typically begins in the family, but other agencies, such as the school, play a significant role in this process as well.

generally are not concerned with how the child thinks about moral problems. Throughout this process children play a somewhat passive role, absorbing the moral prescriptives of the parents and their culture more broadly.

How convincingly does the social learning model explain moral development? Laboratory studies investigating one form of moral behavior, the child's ability to resist temptation—for example, learning not to play with a forbidden toy—suggest that the child's reinforcement history is indeed a factor. Children quickly learn not to touch an attractive toy, if an adult mildly reprimands them for initiating activities with it. In other words, they respond to the punishments doled out by the adult.

Several factors influence children's tendency to transgress when left alone in the room with the forbidden toy after they have been punished. First, as social learning theory predicts, the timing of the punishment during the initial training plays a role. When the punishment is administered as the child reaches for the forbidden toy but before she actually touches it, instead of after the child has picked up the toy, the child is less likely to violate the adult's commands during the "temptation period," when the adult is no longer present. Learning theory predicts that punishments will be most effective if they closely follow the undesired behavior—in this case, when first reaching for the forbidden toy. Second, the provision of a verbal explanation of why the toys are prohibited also has an effect. When children are told, for example, that the attractive toys might break if they are handled, children are much less likely to violate the adult's prohibition. According to social learning theorists, verbalizations facilitate the internalization of morally acceptable and unacceptable behaviors (Aronfreed, 1969, 1976).

Parents and others serving as models can also influence whether a child commits a transgression. Children who observe a role model committing a prohibited act, such as touching a forbidden toy, are more likely to perform the act themselves, whereas children observing a role model who resists temptation commit fewer transgressions (Rosenkoetter, 1973). However, it seems that role models are more powerful in *disinhibiting* than in inhibiting behavior that violates a rule or expectation; children are more likely to follow a role model's deviant behaviors than his compliant ones (Hoffman, 1970).

▶ The active role of the child

**superego** In Freudian theory, a mental structure that monitors socially acceptable and unacceptable behavior.

**conscience** In Freudian theory, the part of the superego that defines unacceptable behaviors and actions, usually as also defined by the parents.

**ego ideal** In Freudian theory, the part of the superego that defines the positive standards for which an individual strives. This component is acquired via parental rewarding of desired behaviors.

▶ Interaction among domains

▶ The active role of the child

▶ Interaction among domains

▶ Development as
continuous/discontinuous

Many aspects of moral development can be explained by social learning theory. The results of experiments demonstrating that reinforcements influence the child's tendency to transgress and that role models influence the child's compliance with prohibitions are but a few examples of compatible findings. Some experts contend, however, that social learning theorists do not adequately consider the child's thinking and reasoning about moral issues. Elliot Turiel (1983), for example, underscores the importance of children's judgments about and interpretations of the punishments administered by adults. In his view the early punishment in the forbidden-toy experiments is effective because of extremely clear communication about what behaviors are acceptable and unacceptable—the toy should not be touched. In contrast, when punishment is delivered late, the child may become confused, thinking that the behavior is acceptable in those first few moments of holding the toy before the adult expresses her displeasure. Thus, the child's inability to sort out conflicting messages, rather than the late timing of reinforcement, may lead to persistence of the "deviant" behavior.

Newer versions of social learning theory assign a larger role for cognitive processes in the emergence of moral values. In Albert Bandura's social cognitive theory (1986), children develop internalized standards of conduct, cognitive representations that they derive by observing role models and by processing the explanations of moral behavior delivered by parents and others. Children attempt to behave in ways consistent with those representations. A thorough consideration of the child's reasoning processes, however, has traditionally been absent from learning theories. As we will see in the next section, it has been left to other theorists, such as Jean Piaget and Lawrence Kohlberg, to describe changes in the child's ability to reason about moral questions.

## Cognitive-Developmental Theories

Cognitive-developmental explanations of moral development highlight the ways in which children reason about moral problems. Should a person ever steal, even if the transgression would help another person? Are there any circumstances under which lying is acceptable? The child's ability to think through the answers to such questions depends on his ability to reason and to consider the perspectives, needs, and feelings of others. In other words, moral development is intimately connected with advances in general thinking abilities.

The two most prominent cognitive-developmental theorists concerned with moral development have been Jean Piaget and Lawrence Kohlberg. Both have suggested stage theories in which children's reasoning about moral issues is qualitatively different depending on their level of development. Each theory presumes that children pass through the stages in an unvarying sequence, without skipping any stages. Both also assume that earlier forms of thought lay the foundation for more mature reasoning abilities. An implication of both theories is that children across different cultures will show notable similarities in the way they advance in their moral reasoning.

**Piaget's Theory**    As was the case in his work on cognitive development, Piaget ([1932] 1965) derived his ideas about moral development from systematic and extensive observations of children, in this case in two contexts—as they played a formal game with a shared set of rules and as they encountered moral dilemmas created to assess thinking about ethical problems. Piaget began by exploring children's understanding of rules as an essential ingredient in constructions of morality. He observed and interviewed children playing marbles, a popular children's game. Children were asked several questions about this game: What are the rules? Can new rules be invented? Where do rules come from? Have they always been the same?

Piaget concluded that children's developing appreciation for the rules of the game of marbles occurred in several stages. Preschoolers, he stated, are not guided by rules. They engage in the activity for the pure pleasure it provides, and their play is largely solitary. Thus, young children may hide marbles or throw them randomly, ignoring the formal rules of the game. By about age six, children become aware of rules and begin to regard them as sacred and inviolable. They believe that rules, handed down by adults, must be respected and always existed in the same form; people have played marbles in exactly the same way over the years. By about ten years of age children understand rules to be the result of cooperation and mutual consent among all the participants of the game. Thus, rules may be modified to suit the needs of the situation if all the players agree.

▶ Development as continuous/discontinuous

The second method Piaget used to study moral development consisted of noting responses of children to moral dilemmas, stories in which a central character committed a transgression; the intentions of that character and the consequences of his act varied. What follows is a pair of such stories:

A. A little boy who is called John is in his room. He is called to dinner. He goes into the dining room. But behind the door there was a chair, and on the chair there was a tray with fifteen cups on it. John couldn't have known that there was all this behind the door. He goes in, the door knocks against the tray, bang go the fifteen cups, and they all get broken!

B. Once there was a little boy whose name was Henry. One day when his mother was out he tried to get some jam out of the cupboard. He climbed up onto a chair and stretched out his arm. But the jam was too high up and he couldn't reach it and have any. But while he was trying to get it he knocked over a cup. The cup fell down and broke. (Piaget, [1932] 1965, p. 122)

Which boy is naughtier? Younger children typically choose John, the child who broke more cups. According to Piaget, children younger than about ten are in the stage of moral development called **moral realism**, or *heteronomy*. They judge the rightness or wrongness of an act by the objective visible consequences—in this case, how many cups were broken. They do not consider the boys' intentions to behave well or improperly.

**moral realism**   In Piaget's theory of moral development, the first stage of moral reasoning, in which moral judgments are made on the basis of the consequences of an act. Also called *heteronomy*.

In the stage of moral realism, rules are viewed as unbreakable; if the rules are violated, the child sees punishment as the inevitable consequence. The belief in **immanent justice** is reflected in such statements as "That's God punishing me," when the child accidentally falls off a bike after lying to her mother, for example. Although the fall is unrelated to the child's transgression, she believes the causal link exists. Children in this stage also believe in **expiatory punishment**, the notion that a punishment need not be related to the wrongful act, if it is severe enough to teach a lesson. Thus, stealing a friend's toy can be punished by any means, not necessarily by returning the toy or making reparations, so long as the retribution is harsh.

**immanent justice**   Young child's belief that punishment will inevitably follow a transgression.

**expiatory punishment**   Young child's belief that punishment need not be related to a transgression as long as the punishment is severe enough.

From a limited ability to reason about moral issues children progress to **moral relativism**, or *autonomy*. Now the transgressor's motives are taken into account. Henry is named as the naughtier boy; he intended to misbehave, although he broke only one cup. The child no longer believes every

**moral relativism**   In Piaget's theory of moral development, the second stage of moral reasoning, in which moral judgments are made on the basis of the actor's intentions. Also called *autonomy*.

▶ Interaction among domains

violation will be punished but that punishments should relate to the misde-
meanor so that the individual appreciates the consequences of his act. Piaget calls this concept **punishment by reciprocity**.

What precipitates the shift from moral realism to moral relativism? Piaget
points to changes in the child's cognitive capabilities, especially decreasing
egocentrism (see Chapter 8), as one important element. To understand a person's intentions, for example, the child must be able to appreciate the point of
view of another person as distinct from her own. Another important factor is
the opportunity to interact with peers. Peer interactions force the child to
consider the thoughts and feelings of others and eventually lead to an understanding of their intentions and motives. Parents can further encourage the
transition from realism to relativism, notes Piaget, by encouraging mutual respect and understanding, by pointing out the consequences of the child's actions for others and articulating their needs and feelings as parents.

**Evaluating Piaget**     How well does Piaget's theory stand up? Research has
confirmed that reasoning about moral problems shifts as children grow older.
Children from many different cultures, social classes, and of varying intellectual abilities show an increasing consideration of intentions in judging the actions of another person; beliefs in immanent justice, expiatory punishment,
and obedience to authority decline with age (Hoffman, 1970; Lickona, 1976).
Piaget's assertion that cognitive growth underlies changes in moral reasoning
has also received support. As children reach the stage of concrete operations,
become less egocentric, and demonstrate improved ability to take the perspective of another, they rely less on adult authority and are more likely to base
their moral responses on the principle of reciprocity (Lee, 1971).

As for Piaget's contention that peer interaction promotes advances in moral
thought, the evidence is mixed. Children reared on the Israeli kibbutz, or collective farm, where they have extensive experience with peers right from early
infancy, display levels of moral reasoning similar to those of peers who grew
up in nuclear family settings (Kugelmass & Breznitz, 1967). At the same time,
other researchers have noted a positive relationship between sophistication of
moral thought and opportunities to interact with peers in clubs, activities, and
other settings (Harris, Mussen, & Rutherford, 1976; Keasey, 1971; Kruger,
1992).

Although many general aspects of Piaget's theory have been confirmed,
some particulars have been challenged. For one thing, Piaget maintains that a
child at a given stage should display all the characteristics associated with
moral reasoning at that level, that is, his thought should show internal consistency. But children who believe in immanent justice sometimes fail to respond
to moral dilemmas only on the basis of objective consequences or adult authority (Lickona, 1976). Young children also can be sensitive to the intentions
behind a given act. One set of researchers asked kindergarten, second-grade,
and fifth-grade children to listen to stories about a girl who was being aggressive with another. In the "hostile" condition the aggressive act was intended to
make the victim feel bad. In the "prosocial" condition the aggressive act protected someone else (for example, "Betty grabs the ball from Andrea so no one
gets hit by it"). Even the youngest children indicated that aggression in the
hostile condition was worse than in the prosocial condition, demonstrating
their awareness of the intentions behind the aggressor's behavior (Rule, Nesdale, & McAra, 1974). Furthermore, even children as young as seven seem to
realize that whether another person has authority does not depend simply on

**punishment by reciprocity**   Belief that punishment should be related to the transgression.

being an adult but instead on the social position that gives an adult, or even a peer, the status to make demands on another (Laupa, 1991).

Piaget's theory has made important contributions to the understanding of moral development by emphasizing a previously little-considered dimension—the child's cognitive skill. It is clear from Piaget's work that the child's conceptualization of what is moral becomes more elaborate and complex with age and that any attempt to understand moral development must include an explanation of the child's thought as well as behavior. Subsequent theorists, Kohlberg in particular, have found Piaget's writings a useful springboard for their own theoretical formulations.

**Kohlberg's Theory**   As did Piaget, Lawrence Kohlberg (1969, 1976) has proposed a stage theory of moral development in which progress through each stage proceeds in a universal order and regression to earlier modes of thinking is rare. Kohlberg based his theory on children's responses to a set of dilemmas that put obedience to authority or the law in direct conflict with helping a person in need. One of the most famous of these dilemmas is this story of a man's attempt to help his dying wife:

▶ Development as continuous/discontinuous

> In Europe, a woman was near death from cancer. One drug might save her, a form of radium that a druggist in the same town had recently discovered. The druggist was charging $2,000, ten times what the drug cost him to make. The sick woman's husband, Heinz, went to everyone he knew to borrow the money, but could only get together about half of what it cost. He told the druggist that his wife was dying and asked him to sell it cheaper or let him pay later. But the druggist said, "No." The husband got desperate and broke into the man's store to steal the drug for his wife. Should the husband have done that? Why? (Colby et al., 1983, p. 77)

Using an analysis of the reasoning of boys, who ranged in age from ten to sixteen, who responded to nine of these dilemmas, Kohlberg initially identified three general levels of moral orientation, each with two substages, to explain the varying responses of his subjects (see Table 12.1). At the first level, called the **preconventional level**, the child's behavior is motivated by external pressures—avoidance of punishment, attainment of rewards, and preservation of his own self-interests. Norms of behavior are not yet derived from internalized principles, and the child's needs and desires are primary.

At the next level, the **conventional level**, conforming to the norms of the majority and maintaining the social order have become central to the child's reasoning. He now considers the point of view of others, along with their intentions and motives. The child also feels a sense of responsibility to make contributions to society and to uphold the laws and institutions that serve its members by keeping the system going.

Finally, at the **postconventional level**, the individual has developed a fuller understanding of the basis for laws and rules. They are now seen as the result of a social contract that all individuals must uphold because of shared responsibilities and duties. The individual recognizes the relative and sometimes arbitrary nature of rules, which may vary from group to group. Certain principles and values, however, such as justice and human dignity, must be preserved at all costs.

Kohlberg emphasized that changes in the child's perspective-taking ability are the basis for shifts in moral reasoning. The focus of the younger child is on the self and personal needs, but children increasingly appreciate the perspectives of others by the end of the preconventional level and throughout the con-

**preconventional level**   In Kohlberg's theory, the first level of moral reasoning, in which morality is motivated by the avoidance of punishments and attainment of rewards.

**conventional level**   In Kohlberg's theory, the second level of moral reasoning, in which the child conforms to the norms of the majority and wishes to preserve the social order.

**postconventional level**   In Kohlberg's theory, the third level of moral reasoning, in which laws are seen as the result of a social contract and individual principles of conscience may emerge.

| Stage | Motivation | Typical Moral Reasoning |
|---|---|---|
| | **Preconventional Level** | |
| 1 **Punishment and obedience orientation** | The primary motive for action is the avoidance of punishment: | *Pro:* If you let your wife die, you will get in trouble. You'll be blamed for not spending the money to save her and there'll be an investigation of you and the druggist for your wife's death. |
| | | *Con:* You shouldn't steal the drug because you'll be caught and sent to jail if you do. If you do get away, your conscience would bother you thinking how the police would catch up to you any minute. (Kohlberg, 1984, p. 52) |
| 2 **Naive instrumental hedonism** | Actions are motivated by the desire for rewards: | *Pro:* If you do happen to get caught you could give the drug back and you wouldn't get much of a sentence. It wouldn't bother you much to serve a little jail term, if you have your wife when you get out. |
| | | *Con:* He may not get much of a jail term if he steals the drug, but his wife will probably die before he gets out, so it wouldn't do him much good. If his wife dies, he shouldn't blame himself; it isn't his fault she has cancer. (Kohlberg, 1984, p. 52) |
| | **Conventional Level** | |
| 3 **Good boy morality** | The child strives to avoid the disapproval of others (as distinct from avoidance of punishment): | *Pro:* No one will think you're bad if you steal the drug but your family will think you're an inhuman husband if you don't. If you let your wife die, you'll never be able to look anyone in the face again. |
| | | *Con:* It isn't just the druggist who will think you're a criminal, everyone else will, too. After you steal it, you'll feel bad thinking how you've brought dishonor on your family and yourself; you won't be able to face anyone again. (Kohlberg, 1984, p. 52) |

**TABLE 12.1**

**Kohlberg's Six Substages of Moral Development**

ventional level. By the postconventional level children consider the self and others within the context of the larger society. According to Kohlberg, changes in perspective-taking ability are promoted by providing opportunities for children to discuss others' points of view. Exposure to higher levels of moral reasoning displayed by older peers and adults, which can precipitate cognitive advances in children, also is critical.

▶ Development as continuous/discontinuous

**Evaluating Kohlberg**   Numerous investigations of Kohlberg's theory have confirmed stagelike transitions in moral reasoning. For example, Anne Colby and her colleagues (1983) followed Kohlberg's original sample of adolescent boys during a twenty-year period and noted that their responses to moral dilemmas fit within the developmental stages delineated by Kohlberg (see Figure 12.5). With few exceptions, subjects progressed upward through the stages, although as adults most individuals still reasoned at the conventional level. In fact, so few subjects responded at the highest stage of the postconventional level that Kohlberg (1984; Kohlberg, Levine, & Hewer, 1983) came to question whether the last stage (stage 6) was justified. Moral development also was found to correlate positively with IQ and educational level, con-

| Stage | Motivation | Typical Moral Reasoning |
|---|---|---|
| **Conventional Level (cont.)** | | |
| **4 Authority-maintaining morality** | An act is always wrong if it violates a rule or does harm to others: | *Pro:* You should steal it. If you did nothing you'd be letting your wife die, it's your responsibility if she dies. You have to take it with the idea of paying the druggist.<br><br>*Con:* It is a natural thing for Heinz to want to save his wife but it's always wrong to steal. He still knows he's stealing and taking a valuable drug from the man who made it. (Kohlberg, 1984, p. 50) |
| **Postconventional Level** | | |
| **5 Morality of contract and democracy** | The individual is concerned with self-respect and maintaining the respect of others. Laws must be obeyed, because they represent a social contract, but they may sometimes conflict with moral values: | *Pro:* The law wasn't set up for these circumstances. Taking the drug in this situation isn't really right, but it's justified to do it.<br><br>*Con:* You can't completely blame someone for stealing, but extreme circumstances don't really justify taking the law in your own hands. You can't have everyone stealing when they get desperate. The end may be good, but the ends don't justify the means. (Kohlberg, 1984, p. 50) |
| **6 Morality of individual principles of conscience** | Individuals are concerned with upholding their personal principles and may sometimes feel it necessary to deviate from rules when the rules conflict with moral principles: | *Pro:* This is a situation which forces him to choose between stealing and letting his wife die. In a situation where the choice must be made, it is morally right to steal. He has to act in terms of the principle of preserving and respecting life.<br><br>*Con:* Heinz is faced with the decision of whether to consider other people who need the drug just as badly as his wife. Heinz ought to act not according to his particular feelings toward his wife, but considering the value of all the lives involved. (Kohlberg, 1984, p. 51) |

**TABLE 12.1**

**Kohlberg's Six Substages of Moral Development** (continued)

sistent with Kohlberg's emphasis on the cognitive basis of moral judgment. More recently, Lawrence Walker (1989) has confirmed that six- through fifteen-year-old children tested during a two-year period showed significant gains in moral reasoning and that few children skipped stages or regressed to earlier forms of reasoning.

Cross-cultural studies in countries as diverse as India, Turkey, Japan, Nigeria, and Finland also have found that children show development of moral reasoning, from preconventional to conventional levels, without skipping stages and without regressing to previous stages. Postconventional reasoning, observed infrequently, is reported more commonly in urban cultures and is virtually absent in tribal and village folk societies (Snarey, 1985).

▶ Sociocultural influences

As with Piaget's theory, however, researchers have been unable to confirm some specific propositions in Kohlberg's outline of moral development. Is perspective-taking skill important in spurring advances in moral reasoning? Researchers report no relationship between the two variables about as often as they report a significant one (Kurdek, 1978). Do individuals within a stage respond consistently to different moral dilemmas, as Kohlberg maintains they

## FIGURE 12.5

### The Development of Moral Reasoning

In a longitudinal follow-up study of Kohlberg's original sample, Colby and her colleagues confirmed that subjects showed consistent upward advances in moral reasoning with age. The graph shows the extent to which subjects gave responses characteristic of each of Kohlberg's six stages from age ten through adulthood. With development, responses associated with the preconventional level (stages 1 and 2) declined, while responses associated with the conventional level (stages 3 and 4) increased. Few young adults moved to the postconventional level of moral reasoning.

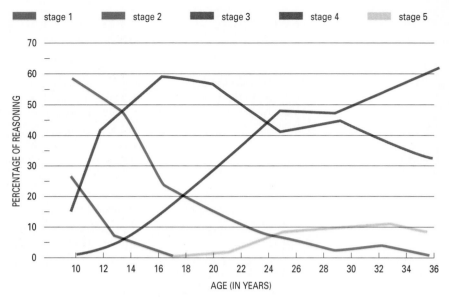

Source: Adapted from Colby et al., 1983.

▶ Sociocultural influences

should? In one study of seventy-five college students who responded to five moral dilemmas, not one person received the same stage score for all stories (Fishkin, Keniston, & MacKinnon, 1973). Thus, while individuals may exhibit a particular stage, they also display considerable variation in their reasoning about moral issues. Finally, investigators have reported that when they do not continue their education, some adults tend to remain at one stage of moral reasoning or a small percentage move down instead of up through the stages (Rest, 1983).

One last criticism of Kohlberg's theory is that it fails to capture the many modes of moral reasoning evident in individuals and different cultural groups. In responding to moral dilemmas, people growing up on the Israeli kibbutz often address the importance of the principle of happiness for everyone (Snarey, 1985). Asian cultures too emphasize the idea of the collective good and harmonious social order. The desirable way to resolve disputes is by reconciling people who are in conflict, not relying on laws to control their behavior. Thus, families often preserve harmony by holding conferences to settle disputes between individuals. Kohlberg's moral dilemmas, which require a choice between rules and the needs of individuals, do not permit the expression of this cultural principle (Dien, 1982). Likewise, Indian cultures emphasize the value of all life, not just human life; thus, a most serious transgression, as expressed by orthodox Hindu children and adults, is eating beef, chicken, or fish (Shweder, Mahapatra, & Miller, 1987). Such a concept does not appear in Kohlberg's outline of moral development. Buddhist beliefs about limits to self and to the value of intervention in preventing suffering are also difficult to reconcile within Kohlberg's framework (Huebner & Garrod, 1991). Thus, the movement of the individual toward the fullest understanding of the principle of justice, at least as conceptualized by Kohlberg, may be a singularly Western phenomenon.

One criticism of Kohlberg's theory of moral development is that it fails to encompass the values found in other cultures. For example, judgments of postconventional reasoning are infrequent even in western societies and are rarely found in many other societies. Until researchers have a greater understanding of cultural values, such as those being conveyed by this father to his son, our understanding of the development of moral reasoning will remain incomplete.

## CONTROVERSY: THINKING IT OVER

### *Are There Sex Differences in Moral Development?*

In one of his studies Kohlberg reported that most males function at the higher stage, whereas most females reason at the lower stage, within the conventional level of moral reasoning (Kohlberg & Kramer, 1969). The report provoked a strong reaction from some members of the psychological community and led Carol Gilligan to propose that moral development takes a different, not inferior, course in females (1982, 1988; Gilligan & Antonucci, 1988). Gilligan states that because of their tendency to be concerned with relationships, caregiving, and intimacy, females tend to develop a **morality of care and responsibility** in contrast to the **morality of justice** described by Kohlberg. The morality of care and responsibility is concerned with self-sacrifice and relationships with others rather than with the tension between rules and the needs and rights of the individual.

An eleven-year-old girl's response to the story of Heinz and his wife illustrates the ethic of care that Gilligan holds to be typical of females:

> If he stole the drug, he might save his wife then, but if he did, he might have to go to jail, and then his wife might get sicker again, and he couldn't get more of the drug,

**morality of care and responsibility** Tendency to make moral judgments on the basis of concern for others.

**morality of justice** Tendency to make moral judgments on the basis of reason and abstract principles of equity.

and it might not be good. So, they should really just talk it out and find some other way to make the money. (Gilligan, 1982, p. 28)

Although this response might receive a low score in Kohlberg's system because of its seemingly wavering noncommittal nature, Gilligan believes it reflects a mature understanding of the crisis a relationship might undergo when a law is broken.

Are there sex differences in moral development? Are there sex differences in cultures in which an emphasis on care and responsibility seem to be more highly valued? Could such differences challenge Kohlberg's fundamental position of stages in moral development? Of the large number of investigations based on Kohlberg's tasks, only a few report substantial differences between males and females in level of moral reasoning (Walker, 1984). In fact, males and females often use both the morality of justice and the morality of care in responding to moral dilemmas (Kahn, 1992; Smetana, Killen, & Turiel, 1991; Walker, deVries, & Trevethan, 1987).

Could a major benefit of Gilligan's work be that it expands our understanding of what constitutes moral values? Could Kohlberg's emphasis on justice, Gilligan's emphasis on care, and other viewpoints—focused, for example, on virtue, altruism, and so forth—provide an even more complete picture of moral development, not only in males and females but in different cultural groups as well (Brabeck, 1983)?  ■

**Morality as Domain-specific Knowledge**   As we have seen, definitions of morality can vary enormously, and which aspects of behavior are judged acceptable or unacceptable often are enbedded within the broad fabric of social knowledge and values. Elliot Turiel (1983; Turiel, Hildebrandt, & Wainryb, 1991) draws a distinction in social-cognitive development between the domains of moral and societal values. The *moral domain* consists of rules that regulate a person's own or another's rights or welfare; examples are the concepts of justice and responsibility toward others. The *societal domain* is knowledge of the social world. Within this domain **social conventions** are the rules that regulate social interactions, such as how to dress appropriately for a given occasion and what degree of formality to use in speaking to someone. In contrast to moral knowledge, social conventions can vary dramatically from culture to culture.

▶ Sociocultural influences

Turiel hypothesizes that the moral and societal domains develop along separate paths and that most theories of moral development have confused the two. Children begin distinguishing moral and social-conventional rules by the age of three (Smetana & Braeges, 1990). To illustrate, preschoolers will respond differently depending on whether the transgressions of their playmates violate a social or a moral rule. When a child violates a moral rule—for example, by intentionally inflicting harm or taking another's possessions—other children typically react by physically intervening or making statements about the pain experienced by the victim. On the other hand, when children observe another person violating a social convention—such as eating while standing instead of sitting—they either do not react or simply comment on the rules surrounding proper social behavior (Nucci & Turiel, 1978). In addition, when questioned about social-conventional transgressions, most children say such an act would be acceptable if no rule existed about it in school, whereas moral transgressions are wrong, are more serious, and should receive greater punishment,

**social conventions** Behavioral rules that regulate social interactions, such as dress codes and degrees of formality in speech.

even if the school has no rule pertaining to them (Smetana, Schlagman, & Adams, 1993).

How do children come to appreciate the distinction between moral and social conventions? Perhaps through the greater emotional affect associated with moral transgressions than with social infractions. When a child observes a peer hitting someone or is a victim of retaliation himself, the abuse may arouse a high degree of emotion in him. For example, when first- and third-graders are asked to rate how they would feel if they were hit without provocation or if their toys were stolen by another child, they are more likely to indicate a negative emotion than when they line up outside the wrong classroom. Furthermore, children frequently justify intervening in a moral transgression by referring to their own or the victim's emotional state (Arsenio & Ford, 1985). Events that share emotional reactivity may cluster in the child's memory, whereas social violations form their own cluster.

▶ Interaction among domains

**Evaluating Cognitive-Developmental Theories** Domain-specific approaches, such as Elliot Turiel's, place less emphasis on qualitative transitions in moral thinking and focus instead on how the child's experiences lead to cognitive constructions of moral and social values. In contrast, Piaget and Kohlberg believe that age-related changes in how children reason about moral problems proceed in a stagelike manner. Older children are more likely than younger children to consider the intentions, feelings, and needs of others and to rely on abstract moral principles, such as the concept of justice, as they make moral judgments. The changes in moral reasoning parallel more general changes in cognitive abilities (Stewart & Pascual-Leone, 1992).

▶ Development as continuous/discontinuous

Cognitive-developmental approaches fill a void left by Freudian and social learning theories by acknowledging that how the child thinks about moral situations and social conflict is every bit as important as how she feels or behaves. However, the approaches also have shortcomings. A most important concern is whether moral reasoning is related to moral behavior. Scores on reasoning tests do not always correlate with tendencies to avoid cheating, to help others, or to abide by rules (Blasi, 1980; Kurtines & Greif, 1974; Richards et al., 1992). The highest relationships are found between moral reasoning and specific negative social behaviors, such as aggression and delinquency. Adolescent boys who display high levels of antisocial behavior tend to score low on moral reasoning tests (Bear, 1989; Blasi, 1980). Another limitation of cognitive-developmental theories is that current formulations do not capture the full range of moral principles individuals use in making ethical judgments. Thus, contemporary researchers continue to explore moral reasoning across different cultures and between the sexes (Gilligan, Lyons, & Hanmer, 1989).

Although they highlight different facets of moral progress, Freudian, social learning, and cognitive-developmental theories (summarized in Table 12.2) all portray the child as moving from a self-orientation to an other-orientation. They also share the view of a child motivated initially by external events, such as rewards and punishments or the need to affiliate with the parents. With development the standards of morality become internalized. Ultimately, however, a complete theory of moral development should describe the ways in which the affective, cognitive, and behavioral dimensions are related to one another. Perhaps research on more positive aspects of moral development can shed additional light on these complex interrelationships.

| Theory | Emphasis | Path of Development | Process of Moral Development |
|---|---|---|---|
| **Freudian** | Affective dimensions | Stagelike | Resolution of Oedipal/Electra conflict followed by identification with same-sex parent |
| **Social Learning** | Moral behavior | Continuous | Reinforcement and modeling of standards of behavior followed by internalization of those standards |
| **Cognitive-Developmental** | | | |
| **Piaget** | Moral reasoning | Stagelike | Growth in cognitive and perspective-taking skills that lead to more abstract, other-oriented principles of morality |
| **Kohlberg** | Moral reasoning | Stagelike | |
| **Turiel** | Moral reasoning | Continuous | Growth in knowledge of moral rules as distinct from social conventions |

**TABLE 12.2**

**The Major Theories of Moral Development**

▶ Interaction among domains

prosocial behavior   Positive social action performed to benefit others.

altruism   Behavior carried out to help another without expectation of reward.

empathy   Vicarious response to the feelings of others.

# Prosocial Behavior and Values

A young child consoles a friend in distress, helps her pick up the pieces of a broken toy, or shares a snack. These **prosocial behaviors**, social actions performed to benefit others, have come under increasing investigation in recent years as another way of understanding the development of values and moral behavior in children. Among prosocial behaviors is **altruism**, behavior carried out to help others without expectation of rewards for the self. In contrast to research that focuses on justice and rights, prosocial and altruistic responses have a less obligatory, legalistic quality about them (Kahn, 1992). Acts of kindness or assistance are often discretionary but highly valued in many communities. Grade school children who tend to help others have better social skills (Eisenberg & Mussen, 1989), are more popular with peers (Gottman, Gonso, & Rasmussen, 1975; McGuire & Weisz, 1982), and are more self-confident, self-assured, and better adjusted (Mussen et al., 1970) than those who do not. Thus, altruism is associated with many desirable outcomes, particularly in children's social relationships. Given this fact, it seems important to understand what influences the emergence of these qualities.

## The Development of Prosocial Behaviors and Altruism

Several contemporary theorists believe that before a child can behave altruistically, he must feel **empathy**, a vicarious emotional response to the feelings of others that includes sympathetic concern for the person in need of assistance (Batson & Oleson, 1991). Even infants show signs of sensitivity to the distress of others. Two- and three-day-olds cry when other infants cry, but they may not cry in response to other, equally loud noises (Simner, 1971). In addition to crying, ten- to fourteen-month-olds may whimper or silently attend to expressions of distress from another person. Often they respond by soothing themselves, by sucking their thumb or seeking a parent for comfort (Radke-Yarrow & Zahn-Waxler, 1984). Perhaps because children at this age do not distinguish the boundaries between self and another individual clearly, consoling the self is a form of coping with another's distress.

Between one and two years of age new behaviors emerge—touching or patting the victim as if to provide solace, seeking assistance for the person in distress, even giving her something to provide comfort, such as a cookie, blanket, or teddy bear. The victim's emotional state also might be labeled with expressions such as "Cry," "Oh-oh!" or "Hurting" (Radke-Yarrow & Zahn-Waxler, 1984). As we saw in Chapter 11, children show sensitivity to the emotional states and needs of others well before they achieve a sophisticated level of cognitive functioning. Accompanying that sensitivity are actions that have an unmistakably altruistic character, a quality that some believe to have a genetic basis.

Preschool children display more varied and complex responses to the needs of others. In a classic study of sympathy, Lois Murphy (1937) observed that children show a host of reactions to a peer's distress in a nursery school setting. Among them are comforting and helping the victim, asking questions of the troubled child, punishing the agent of the child's distress, protecting the victim, and asking an adult for help. When asked why they share with or help someone else, nursery school children often state they simply want to or refer to the needs of the other person (Eisenberg-Berg & Neal, 1979).

Although many researchers report that helping and sharing increase with age, others note that older children actually help or share less (Radke-Yarrow, Zahn-Waxler, & Chapman, 1983). This lack of consensus about how altruism develops in the years from six to sixteen may stem in part from the wide range of research approaches, from naturalistic to staged laboratory experiments. In addition, the child's self-interests and the expectations of others, along with genuine altruism, may enter into decisions about whether to assist a person in need or engage in other prosocial activity.

A popular belief is that girls are more nurturing, caring, and empathic than boys and because of these qualities are thus more altruistic. Is there any evidence that this is so? On the whole, children display few sex differences in the amount of helping and sharing (Radke-Yarrow, Zahn-Waxler, & Chapman, 1983). For example, when actually in the presence of a crying baby, girls are no more likely to assist than boys (Zahn-Waxler, Friedman, & Cummings, 1983). But there are sex differences in how prosocial behaviors are expressed. For one thing, girls who hear a recording of an infant crying express more verbal sympathy than boys do. The tendency for girls to be more expressive about prosocial activities is consistent with at least some research indicating that girls are more frequently rewarded by parents for helping than are boys (Fagot, 1978a). Girls may be trying to simply live up to societal expectations for females. Yet despite cultural stereotypes and differential patterns of parental reinforcement, evidence for sex differences in altruism are not strong.

**The Relationship Between Empathy and Helping**   Martin Hoffman (1975, 1976, 1982) postulates that a child behaves prosocially—for example, attempts to alleviate distress in others—as a way to relieve her own empathic distress. Thus, if a boy sees that a friend who has just fallen down on the playground is crying, he feels uncomfortable. He knows how painful a skinned knee feels and shares his friend's anguish. To feel better himself the boy rushes to his playmate and helps him to the school nurse's office. There are other alternatives—the boy could look away or cover his ears so he does not

▸ Roles of nature and nurture

▸ Sociocultural influences

hear his friend's cries, but these responses could result in feelings of guilt. Thus, in Hoffman's scheme, empathic distress prompts prosocial behavior.

How strong is the connection between empathy and prosocial behavior? Because of difficulties associated with measuring empathic distress, especially when children are asked to report their feelings, a consistent link between empathy and assisting others has not always been shown. However, empathy also can be assessed by using nonverbal measures, such as facial expressions (e.g., sadness) or behavioral gestures that connote empathy or lack of it (e.g., looking away from the distressed person). When such measures are used, empathy is found to relate to helping and sharing, and as children grow older, the relationship grows distinctly stronger (Eisenberg, 1986; Eisenberg & Miller, 1987; Underwood & Moore, 1982). The young child may show signs of empathic distress yet not know what form, if any, the assistance should take (Hoffman, 1975, 1976). If a playmate is crying as the result of a fall, should she be helped to stand up or left alone? Should the child say something comforting or reassuring or simply keep silent? As children mature, they have more opportunities to learn about the range of prosocial behaviors that they can express. Their understanding of the distinction between self and other also matures and with it the realization that the other person's distress can be relieved by taking some action. The stronger relationship between empathy and prosocial behavior in later childhood probably reflects these elements.

Do children help others only in order to reduce their own empathic distress? The answer seems to be no. When Randy Lennon and Nancy Eisenberg (1987) observed preschoolers in semistructured play, virtually every time a child shared a toy with another, both she and the recipient displayed positive emotions before and after the sharing. Such findings are not explained easily by the concept of empathic distress and indicate that empathy needs to be more broadly construed as a response to both positive and negative emotions. Moreover, C. Daniel Batson (1990) has argued that care and concern for others is truly altruistic, that is, often expressed independent of personal needs as a result of empathy for others.

▶ Sociocultural influence

**Prosocial Reasoning: Cross-Cultural Investigations**    One framework within which to assess the development of prosocial reasoning has been formulated by Nancy Eisenberg (1986). In each of her prosocial dilemmas the needs of one person are in conflict with those of another individual or group. The following story is an example:

> One day a girl (boy) named Mary (Eric) was going to a friend's birthday party. On her (his) way she (he) saw a girl (boy) who had fallen down and hurt her (his) leg. The girl asked Mary to go to her house and get her parents so the parents could come and take her to the doctor. But if Mary did run and get the child's parents, she would be late for the birthday party and miss the ice cream, cake, and all the games. What should Mary do? Why? (Eisenberg, 1986, p. 135)

**hedonistic reasoning**    Form of prosocial reasoning in which children say they will help in order to obtain material rewards.

**needs-oriented reasoning**  Form of prosocial reasoning in which children express a concern for the physical or psychological needs of others.

**approval and interpersonal orientation**    Form of prosocial reasoning in which children's reasons for assisting someone in need are based on the social approval or disapproval of others.

Many preschool and some young school-aged children in the United States use **hedonistic reasoning**, saying they would help in order to gain affection or material rewards such as candy or cake. **Needs-oriented reasoning** prevails in the years up to age seven or eight, when children express a concern for the physical or psychological needs of others ("He needs help" or "She's hurt"). An **approval and interpersonal orientation** is prevalent in the middle childhood years as the child's responses increasingly take into consideration the reactions of others. For example, a nine- or ten-year-old might

| Level | Age | Characteristics |
|-------|-----|-----------------|
| **Hedonistic reasoning** | Preschoolers and young elementary school children | Preoccupation with gain for the self as a result of being or not being altruistic |
| **Needs-oriented reasoning** | Preschoolers and elementary school children | Concern for the physical and psychological needs of others although they may conflict with own |
| **Approval and interpersonal orientation** | Elementary and high school students | Reliance on stereotypes of good and bad and seeking approval from others for helping or not helping |
| **Empathic and/or transitional reasoning** | Older elementary and high school students | Concern for feelings of others and use of norms for prosocial behavior |
| **Internalized reasoning** | High school students | Maintenance of self-respect for living up to internalized values and beliefs; belief in rights of all individuals and importance of fulfilling societal obligations |

Source: Adapted from Eisenberg, 1986.

**TABLE 12.3**

**Levels of Prosocial Reasoning**

Nancy Eisenberg has outlined the accompanying progression in prosocial reasoning. Children move from a concern with the self to a concern for others and show more internal abstract bases for helping as they grow older.

comment that Mary should help because then "the other girl would like Mary." During the later elementary years and into high school more **empathic reasoning** emerges ("I'm trying to put myself in her shoes"), and in older adolescents **internalized reasoning** focuses on the importance of such emotions as happiness and pride to match internalized abstract principles of behavior concerned with fulfilling societal obligations, avoiding guilt and maintaining self-respect.

Table 12.3 outlines the stages of prosocial reasoning. As with other views of moral development, there is a progression from concern for external consequences to a more internalized, principled foundation in reasoning, although hedonistic responses may show some increase during the adolescent years, especially in boys (Eisenberg et al., 1991). The judgments also relate to behavior; children who reason hedonistically tend to help other children less frequently, whereas children of a similar age who reason empathically are more likely to donate toys, stickers, or other valuable objects to others (Eisenberg & Shell, 1986; Eisenberg-Berg & Hand, 1979).

When asked to reason about prosocial dilemmas, children in other Western industrialized societies display similar patterns of development. German, Italian, and Polish children, for example, show the same progression from hedonistic to needs-oriented reasoning as children in the United States (Boehnke et al., 1989; Eisenberg et al., 1985). In other cultures, however, there are variations in the sequence. For example, elementary school children reared on the Israeli kibbutz reflect a more mature level of prosocial reasoning, voicing concern about the humaneness of the central character and the importance of internalized norms ("She has a duty to help others") (Eisenberg, Hertz-Lazarowitz, & Fuchs, 1990). A somewhat different picture is provided by children from the Maisin tribe, a coastal village society of Papua New Guinea. Here children maintain a needs orientation well into adolescence and even adulthood (Tietjen, 1986). These patterns of prosocial reasoning mirror the values emphasized by each culture (Eisenberg, 1986). On the Israeli kibbutz the goal of con-

▶ Development as continuous/discontinuous

**empathic reasoning** Form of prosocial reasoning in which children attempt to put themselves in another's place and understand that person's feelings.

**internalized reasoning** Form of prosocial reasoning in which internalized beliefs and principles are followed to fulfill societal obligations and maintain self-respect.

Some children grow up in cultures in which they contribute to the needs of the community, by helping with harvesting, for example. Children raised in group-oriented societies tend to behave more prosocially than children reared in settings that emphasize individualism.

tributing to the good of the entire community is stressed, whereas among the Maisin, children are taught explicitly to be aware of and respond to the needs of particular other individuals, as opposed to the larger social group.

If cross-cultural differences are found in reasoning about prosocial matters, might children also show differences in the tendency to behave prosocially? Nancy Graves and Theodore Graves (1983) studied the inhabitants of Aitutaki Island, one of the Cook Islands in the South Pacific. A tremendous economic shift, from a subsistence to an industrialized market economy, has taken place on parts of this island and has produced corresponding changes in family structure and the roles of family members. Children living in the unaffected rural villages grow up in extended families in which they make substantial contributions to family and community goals. They participate in most community affairs, are sent by elders to share food and goods with other village members, and bring the family contribution to church each week. In contrast, children growing up in urban, more modernized settings are reared in nuclear families and participate less in both family and community functions.

Graves and Graves (1983) observed that children five and six years of age in the urban communities were less likely to assist others in their homes and surrounding environs than were children in rural settings. The researchers conclude that prosocial behavior is more likely in societies in which the predominant ethic is one of interdependence and group orientation and in which the child participates in cooperative work experiences than it is in cultures that emphasize individualism and self-reliance.

▶ Roles of nature and nurture

**The Role of Socialization** What role do child-rearing techniques play in the emergence of prosocial behavior? As social learning theory would predict, reinforcement can be influential. Both material (for example, money, candy, tokens) and social rewards ("You're a good boy!") increase the likelihood that children will share with or help another, although social rewards and acknowledgments seem to motivate greater care and concern for others (Smith et al., 1979; Grusec, 1991). Opportunities for observational learning are another po-

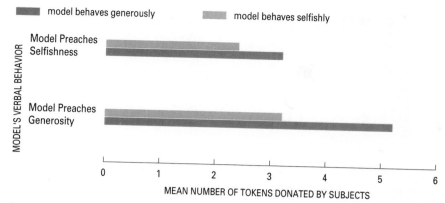

Source: Adapted from Rushton, 1982.

**FIGURE 12.6**

**The Effects of Role Models' Actions and Words**

When children in one laboratory experiment heard a model preach about generosity and then give away half of her winnings to charity, they were far more likely to make a donation themselves than when the model preached about generosity but behaved selfishly. On the other hand, when the model preached about selfishness but behaved generously, children were more likely to donate than when the model spoke and behaved selfishly. The verbal message still had an effect, though. Children in this latter condition were less likely to be altruistic compared with when the model's actions and words were altruistic.

tent factor. When a child sees someone make a donation to a needy person or group, he is likely to be charitable as well (Grusec & Skubiski, 1970).

What role models do appears to be more important than what they say, as an experiment by J. Philippe Rushton (1975) revealed. The experiment had four conditions: half the subjects saw someone who, after participating in a bowling tournament, gave 50 percent of her winnings to a charity; half saw someone who kept all the winnings. In addition, some children then heard the role model they had observed lecture about the importance of being generous; others heard the role model say selfishness is permissible. Thus, one group of children saw a generous role model who also preached about the need to share, another group of children saw a selfish role model who broadcast support for being selfish. Still a third group of children saw a generous role model who proclaimed support for being selfish and a fourth group of children observed a selfish model who trumpeted the need to be generous. As Figure 12.6 shows, the role model's behavior was more powerful than the verbal message she delivered in influencing children's tendency to donate, although the message also increased altruism.

The content of caregivers' verbal communications seems to be especially important. When parents use **induction**, that is, explain why transgressions are wrong, provide a rationale for rules and regulations, and present a reason for prosocial activity, their children are more likely to practice prosocial behaviors (Hoffman, 1975; Zahn-Waxler, Radke-Yarrow, & King, 1979). For example, a parent might say, "Don't pull Sam's hair! That hurts him. You don't like to have your hair pulled, do you?" Such messages emphasize clear communication about standards for behavior, arouse empathic feelings, and stimulate perspective taking (Eisenberg & Mussen, 1989). In contrast, a far less effective means of fostering prosocial behavior involves **power assertion**, forceful commands, physical punishment, or removal of material objects or privileges to influence behavior. For example, the parent might yell, "Stop that! You're not watching TV tonight!" as her son pulls his brother's hair.

Another socialization technique that may be just as effective as induction is emphasizing the child's prosocial characteristics. When told, "I guess you're the kind of person who helps others whenever you can," a child's tendency to behave prosocially is greatly increased (Grusec & Redler, 1980; Mills & Grusec, 1989). Perhaps attributing to the child a sense of concern for others changes her self-concept and she strives to behave in a manner consistent with that image (Grusec, 1982). Parents do not make prosocial attributions about

**induction** Parental control technique that relies on the extensive use of reasoning and explanation as well as the arousal of empathic feelings.

**power assertion** Parental control technique that relies on the use of forceful commands, physical punishment, and removal of material objects or privileges.

Parents who frequently explain why
misbehaviors are unacceptable and
provide a rationale for rules tend to
have children who act more altruistically compared with parents who use
power assertive techniques.

their children often, but it is precisely the rarity of these comments that may
make them so powerful in the eyes of the child (Grusec, 1991).

In summary, prosocial behaviors have their beginnings in the early empathic
responses of the child to the emotional states of others. The child's reasoning
about prosocial conflicts increasingly takes into account the feelings and needs
of others. When adults praise altruistic acts and encourage children to think
about their own prosocial traits, children show an increase in positive moral behaviors. Moreover, parents serve as extremely potent role models of concern
for others. The study of prosocial behavior and altruism has helped to demonstrate how the development of values involves the complex interplay of affect,
cognition, and behavior. The Chronology on page 479 summarizes many of the
aspects of moral and prosocial development described in this chapter.

## Values and Education

Since the mid-1970s many public officials and citizens have expressed renewed interest in providing children with formal education about values. Indeed, training on moral values and sometimes even religious, work, and other
values is often incorporated in school programs, especially those in Asia but in
some Western nations as well (Cummings, 1988). However, in the United
States and other countries values training in public schools usually is limited
to civics. Alarmed by the climbing rates of teenage pregnancy, crime, and
substance abuse, as well as the breakdown of family, religious, and other socializing agencies, some individuals believe that children should be exposed to
values training beginning in the elementary school years if not before.

## CHRONOLOGY — Understanding Moral and Prosocial Development

| | |
|---|---|
| NEWBORN | Reacts to cries of other infants in primitive empathic way. |
| 10–14 MONTHS | Shows various signs of empathy to distress of another but often soothes the self. |
| 1–2 YEARS | Assists another in distress by patting, touching, or offering material objects. |
| 3–6 YEARS | Discriminates moral and social-conventional rules. Judges moral dilemmas according to objective consequences and believes in immanent justice and expiatory punishment. Hedonistic and needs-oriented judgments dominate prosocial decisions. |
| 7–10 YEARS | Reasons according to rewards and punishments expected from authority figures. Approval and concerns about the reactions of others guide judgments about assisting others. |
| 10–16 YEARS | Judges moral dilemmas according to intentions of actor and believes in punishment by reciprocity. Reasons on the basis of rules and laws with a belief in maintaining social order. Empathic reasoning appears in prosocial judgments. |
| 16+ YEARS | Reasons according to internal principles of justice and care. Internalized principles guide prosocial behavior. |

This chart describes the sequence in the development of moral and prosocial behavior and judgments based on the findings of research. Children often show individual differences in the exact ages at which they display the various developmental achievements outlined here.

Several moral education programs have been based on knowledge of the psychological development of children. One type, using Kohlberg's theory, introduces children to moral conflicts and to moral reasoning one stage above the child's own. In one study junior and senior high school students met twice each week to discuss conflicts similar to Kohlberg's moral dilemmas. After listening to a conflict, adolescents were encouraged to supply possible resolutions and to consider the consequences of each solution. The trainer made a deliberate attempt to promote open discussion and alternative points of view. After nine weeks participants showed significant increases in moral reasoning scores, compared with control children who did not participate in the program (Blatt & Kohlberg, 1975).

Still others have argued that educational programs need to go well beyond a concern with reasoning about moral justice in order to strengthen other values such as caring (Noddings, 1992). For example, some programs have used **cooperative learning**, peer groups that work on joint projects, in order to influence prosocial development. In one two-year project conducted in Tel

**cooperative learning** Peer-centered learning experience in which students of different abilities work together in small groups to solve academic problems. Often these groups compete against each other within the classroom.

▶ Interaction among domains

Aviv, children were divided into small groups to work on academic projects in a collaborative fashion, investigating a topic, preparing a report, and presenting the findings to the class (Hertz-Lazarowitz & Sharan, 1984). The hypothesis was that this experience would encourage mutual help and support, the exchange of ideas and resources, and mutual acceptance. Teachers received extensive training in promoting social skills among their students, including actively listening to peers, sharing thoughts and resources, and cooperation. The program was conducted in three elementary schools; when it ended, children were compared with those in traditional schools on a number of academic and social dimensions.

Compared with those in traditional schools, children in the project showed an increase in higher-level thinking skills (for example, evaluation, comparison, and analysis) and creativity, and they also reported a more positive social climate in the classroom. The most important finding from the perspective of moral development, however, was an increase in the frequency of prosocial behaviors displayed by program participants. Children preferred to work with another child in the class and were significantly more altruistic and cooperative than students from the traditional group. Note that specific moral principles were not taught as part of the experimental curriculum. Nevertheless, when exposed to a steady climate of cooperative peer interaction, prosocial behavior developed without explicit instruction.

Surprisingly, developmental researchers have seldom investigated the many potential influences exposure to religious education and other social organizations such as scouting, boys' and girls' clubs, and other community programs may have on the development of values. Yet many parents would probably claim that such activities also can play a vital role in the development of moral, prosocial, and other behaviors considered important by society. For example, in one study of children who were given training in their Jewish or Christian religion, children as young as ten were found to distinguish between moral issues that they consider to be unalterable (stealing, hitting, damaging another's property) and conventional religious practices (such as dress customs, dietary laws, and worship activities) that might change in certain cir-

In one type of moral education program, participants discuss moral conflicts and exchange alternative points of view. After participating in one such program, junior and senior high school students showed significant increases in moral reasoning scores compared with control children who did not have this experience.

cumstances or not apply to other individuals. Thus, they can distinguish moral issues involving justice and human welfare associated with their religion from social conventions that arise from exposure to their particular faith (Nucci & Turiel, 1993). In other words, recognizing what is moral and what is socially determined applies to religious rules as well as to secular relationships.

# THEMES IN DEVELOPMENT

## SELF AND VALUES

▶ **What roles do nature and nurture play in the development of the self and of values?**

Although early, biologically based tendencies for children to display a mastery orientation and empathy may exist, most researchers have described how the child's subsequent cognitions and social experiences shape self and values. For example, feedback from others certainly plays an enormous role in the child's characterization of self and prosocial behavior. Theorists such as Piaget and Kohlberg do suggest that maturation contributes in part to changes in moral reasoning. But even they believe that children's experiences with peers and other socializing agents play a large role in spurring moral reasoning.

▶ **How does the sociocultural context influence the development of the self and values?**

Children's evaluations of themselves are greatly determined by how closely they measure up to autonomy, loyalty, cooperation, perseverance, and other qualities stressed by the culture. Self-esteem is affected by how well children adhere to societies' expectations concerning beauty, athletic skill, hunting prowess, academic ability, and so forth. Moral reasoning and behavior further reflect the values of a culture. When responsibilities to the larger social group are emphasized, children tend to be more caring and display more prosocial reasoning than when the culture emphasizes the role of the individual. In addition, groups place different weights on law-and-justice versus other values, such as harmonious interactions with others. Children's responses to moral dilemmas often reflect their culture's unique beliefs.

▶ **How does the child play an active role in the development of the self and of values?**

Caregivers take on initial responsibility for instituting standards in the behavior of young children. As they gain cognitive and social skills, children initiate efforts to control their own activities and are assumed to internalize the values of the larger society. Children can also begin to recognize that they are competent individuals, capable of influencing and controlling their environment in realistic ways. Their judgments about the appropriateness of moral and prosocial actions are assumed to influence their behavior as well.

▶ **Is the development of the self and of values continuous or discontinuous?**

Although the child's understanding of self undergoes many developmental changes, evidence that these are stagelike remains limited. Even the identity crisis, often considered a hallmark of adolescence, may not be experienced by all youth and reflects a culmination of many earlier, gradual changes. Several influential theories of moral development are stage theories, specifically those of Piaget and Kohlberg. The empirical evidence, however, suggests that reasoning about moral, prosocial, and other values may occur at several levels within the same individual. Although stage theories are popular, domain-specific approaches emphasizing continuous growth are commonplace as well.

▶ **How prominent are individual differences in the development of the self and of values?**

Because the reactions of others play an important role in the development of self, children may differ enormously in how they view themselves and in how they interact with their world. Some may develop confidence and a sense of control, others may express considerable uncertainty and a sense of helplessness. As a result of their socialization experiences and opportunities to interact with peers, children also display considerable differences in their moral and prosocial values.

▶ **How does the development of the self and of values interact with development in other domains?**

Cognitive skills, such as the ability to reason abstractly about the feelings and intentions of others, are involved in the evaluations of self and moral judgments. Emotions such as empathy contribute to prosocial behaviors and altruism. Physical changes and capacities, as well as the social environment, can dramatically affect self-esteem and the emergence of identity. At the same time development of the self and of values has an effect on other domains. For example, high self-esteem and prosocial activity are associated with healthy peer interactions. Development of the self and of values represents an important intersection of affect, cognition, and social experience.

## Summary

**The Concept of Self**   Researchers concerned with the development of *self*—the beliefs, knowledge, and feelings that an individual uses to describe and explain his personal characteristics—make the distinction of self as object and self as subject. Self as object consists of *self-concept,* the perceptions, ideas, and beliefs a person holds to be true of herself. Self as subject consists of how a person initiates, organizes, and interprets experience.

Children's sense of themselves as objects is first evident in their self-recognition at about fifteen to eighteen months of age. During the preschool years they begin defining themselves in terms of a *categorical self,* that is, by referring to various categories that provide membership in one group or another. By the early school years *social comparisons* involving others become important, and by the adolescent years children's effects on others and their relationships to broader sociocultural ideals become a central part of defining themselves.

Among the elements of self as subject are a sense of agency, individuality, stability, and reflection. Infants seem to be born with an intrinsic desire to gain control of their world, but to the extent an environment provides consistent feedback, children acquire an increasing sense of agency. Children with an *in-*

ternal locus of control or a *mastery orientation* believe that they have considerable influence over what happens to them. Children with an *external locus of control* or who experience *learned helplessness* feel that they have little influence over what happens to them.

*Self-esteem* consists of the positive or negative feelings a person has about himself. Preschoolers are able to make this evaluation for specific domains; by the early school years self-esteem takes the form of an overall sense of worth. Self-esteem is affected by feedback from others as well as how successful the child feels he is in areas that are believed to be important. Although self-esteem in adolescents may decline somewhat, many teenagers successfully establish an *identity* with relatively minimal disruption to their lives and those around them.

**Self-regulation and Self-control**    Efforts to control behavior in most societies begin in the second half of the first year of life and continue throughout childhood. At first these efforts are initiated primarily by caregivers, then take the form of co-regulation. Self-initiated attempts to control behavior become more evident as children demonstrate increasing capacities for *delay of gratification* and other forms of compliance, planning, and orderly behavior. Verbal, attentional, and cognitive mechanisms are the means by which behavior comes under self-control.

**Moral Development**    *Moral development* is the child's acquisition of the standards of conduct considered ethical within her culture. Freudian theory focuses on the affective relationship between the child and parents. Social learning theory centers on the emergence of moral behavior. Cognitive-developmental theories emphasize moral reasoning. All the perspectives concur in describing moral development as a movement from self-orientation to other-orientation in which the child *internalizes* external societal standards.

Among the factors contributing to moral development are reinforcements children receive from parents and other agents of socialization. Observational learning is especially potent in the development of moral behaviors. Cognitive-developmental theorists, such as Piaget and Kohlberg, have outlined stages in the development of moral thought. In Piaget's theory children progress from *moral realism* to *moral relativism* as their cognitive capabilities mature. In Kohlberg's outline most children advance through three levels of moral reasoning: the *preconventional, conventional,* and *postconventional levels.* Kohlberg maintains that the child's increasing perspective-taking skills are largely responsible for the shifts. Newer domain-specific approaches describe how children acquire moral knowledge that is distinct from social-conventional knowledge.

**Prosocial Behavior and Values**    Researchers have demonstrated that prosocial and altruistic behaviors occur early in childhood, beginning with the *empathy* of young infants for the distress of others, followed by distinct efforts of preschool children to help others. Children who are empathetic and show high levels of *prosocial reasoning* tend to help others. In addition, children who are rewarded for prosocial behaviors and observe parents and others acting in the same way tend to help others more frequently. Parents who use *induction* as a disciplinary technique and apply prosocial attributions to their children, and children who grow up in cultures in which group values are important, are especially likely to have sons and daughters who express care and concern for others.

# 13

# Gender

▶ **What roles do nature and nurture play in gender development?**

▶ **How does the sociocultural context influence gender development?**

▶ **How does the child play an active role in the process of gender development?**

▶ **Is gender development continuous or discontinuous?**

▶ **How prominent are individual differences in gender development?**

▶ **How does gender development interact with development in other domains?**

*"Nicky," one of the authors said to her five-year-old son, "what do you think should be on the cover of this book? It's about children, you know."*

*"Well," he thought for a moment, "how about a picture of a child?"*

*"A boy or a girl?" asked the mother.*

*"How about one of each?" was the answer. The mother was pleased that her son chose a girl as well as a boy. She had tried hard to teach him to think about gender in nonstereotypical ways—and his willingness to include girls seemed like an indication that her efforts were successful.*

*"What should they be doing?" the mother continued.*

*"Well, how about having the boy play with a computer?" he quickly responded.*

*"And the girl?" she asked.*

*"I think she should have a tea party or something."*

This five-year-old's response is consistent with many **gender stereotypes** that exist in our society, that is, our beliefs and expectations about the characteristics of females and males. Boys, according to these stereotypes, are active, aggressive, independent, and interested in technology and science. Girls, on the other hand, are passive, nonaggressive, and socially oriented. To what extent are such common beliefs actually manifested in the everyday behaviors of children? Are any differences due to the biological makeup of males and females? Does socialization play a large role? And how do children themselves understand the concept of gender? We will address these four central questions in this chapter.

Before we proceed, however, we need to consider terminology. Each of us is classified at birth as either a boy or a girl; that is, we are assigned a *biological sex.* In general, the word "sex" is used when statements or comparisons are being made about males or females as biological entities. Thus, we speak of whether children display "sex differences" in behaviors or traits. The word "gender," on the other hand, refers to *inferences* we make about the qualities of males and females (Deaux, 1993). *Gender,* in other words, is a distinctly psychological concept. Thus, for example, the biological classification of sex—the result of differences in sex chromosomes and the prenatal differentiation of the genitalia—has enormous implications for **gender-role development**, the process by which children acquire the characteristics and behaviors prescribed for males and females in their culture.

Before the mid-1960s, most psychologists regarded the socialization of children into traditional masculine and feminine roles as both a natural and a de-

**gender stereotypes** Expectations or beliefs that individuals within a given culture hold about the behaviors characteristic of males and females.

**gender-role development** The process by which individuals acquire the characteristics and behaviors prescribed by their culture for their sex. Also called *sex-typing.*

sirable outcome of development. Behavioral sex differences were viewed as inevitable and were linked to comparable sex differences among nonhumans (Kohlberg, 1966; Mischel, 1966; Shaw & Darling, 1985). But changes in social values in the mid-1960s, especially those accompanying the women's movement, shifted the ways in which psychologists approached sex differences and gender-role socialization. Many of the questions that interest developmental psychologists today represent both a challenge to traditional assumptions about the nature and origins of gender roles and sex differences and a concerted effort to determine the developmental processes that underlie children's acquisition and enactment of gender roles.

## *Sex Differences: Real or Imagined?*

Throughout the recorded history of Western civilization, females and males have been assumed to differ in temperament, interests, educability, and susceptibility to mental illness, among other characteristics. Many of these beliefs persist unchanged in contemporary gender stereotypes.

### The Stereotypes: What Are They?

Suppose a large group of college students is asked to rate the typical man or woman on a number of psychological attributes. Will they rate certain traits as more typical of males than of females, and vice versa? A study in which 128 college students were asked to do precisely this task revealed that characteristics such as independence, aggression, and self-confidence were associated with masculinity, and emotional expressiveness, kindness, and gentleness were associated with femininity (Ruble, 1983). Table 13.1 lists many additional traits the students ascribed to each sex.

These gender stereotypes are not limited to our own society. Researchers asked children and adults from thirty nations in North and South America, Europe, Africa, and Asia to indicate whether certain traits are associated with men or women more frequently in their culture. The results showed that children from all the countries begin to acquire information about gender stereotypes before the age of five years (the youngest age studied), that this information is consolidated in the early school-age years (six to nine years of age), and that the process of learning gender stereotypes is completed by early adolescence (Williams & Best, 1982).

This same research also showed many cross-cultural similarities in the stereotypes adults attributed to males and females. Perceived masculine personality characteristics generally fell into a category psychologists describe as **instrumental** characteristics, or attributes associated with acting upon the world, such as being assertive, achievement oriented, and independent. Perceived feminine characteristics could be classified as **expressive**, or associated with emotions and interactions with other people.

Despite the many similarities in gender stereotypes across cultures, some differences occurred between nations in the specific characteristics attributed to males and females. For example, Italian adults stereotypically associated "endurance" with women, although most adults in other countries felt that this was a masculine trait. Nigerian adults felt that "affiliation" was neutral,

**instrumental characteristics**
Characteristics associated with acting upon the world; usually considered masculine.

**expressive characteristics**
Characteristics associated with emotions or relationships with people; usually considered feminine.

| Male Characteristics | Female Characteristics |
|---|---|
| Independent | Emotional |
| Aggressive | Grateful |
| Acts as leader | Kind |
| Self-confident | Creative |
| Dominant | Gentle |
| Active | Understanding |
| Ambitious | Aware of others' feelings |
| Outspoken | Enjoys art and music |
| Adventurous | Tactful |
| Competitive | Considerate |
| Likes math and science | Home oriented |
| Takes a stand | Cries easily |
| Makes decisions easily | Devotes self to others |
| Skilled in business | Strong conscience |

Source: Adapted from Ruble, 1983.

**TABLE 13.1**

**Stereotypic Characteristics Attributed to Males and Females**

When college students were asked to rate a typical man or woman on a number of personality traits, strong patterns emerged among traits that were seen as associated with each sex. Male traits generally fall into a cluster called *instrumentality*, female traits into a cluster called *expressiveness*.

whereas adults in other countries said it was a feminine characteristic. Thus, we cannot say that specific characteristics are always attributed to males or to females. We can say, however, that the tendency to stereotype on the basis of sex is found in a variety of cultural settings.

▶ Sociocultural influence

## What Sex Differences Actually Exist?

In light of such durable and pervasive stereotypes about "femaleness" and "maleness," it is logical to ask whether researchers have documented actual differences in the characteristics or behaviors of females and males. Before we address this question, however, let us first consider a number of possible patterns for how such differences can occur.

Figure 13.1 illustrates three possible kinds of sex differences for any hypothetical set of scores, be they verbal skills, visual-spatial ability, or any other measure of an attribute or behavior. In graph A, males and females show no overlap and a wide average difference. In graphs B and C, the two sexes overlap (minimally in graph B and considerably in graph C), but males and females both display a greater range among themselves than in graph A, illustrated by the wider bell-shaped curves. Notice, in fact, that in graph C, some females are more different from other females (and some males from other males) than the two sexes are on average different from one another. The pattern of sex differences illustrated in graph C is far more common than those in graphs A and B. In general, average differences between the sexes are less than the variability in performance within each sex. This is an important point to keep in mind as we examine the empirical evidence.

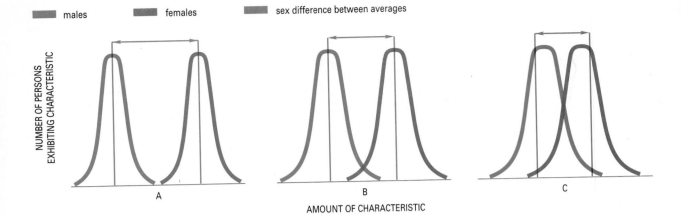

NUMBER OF PERSONS EXHIBITING CHARACTERISTIC

A      B      C

AMOUNT OF CHARACTERISTIC

## FIGURE 13.1

### Possible Patterns of Sex Differences

Differences of any sort, including sex differences, may be of several varieties. The horizontal axis in this series of graphs represents scores on some psychological test that assesses a skill or attribute. In this particular example, females show higher average scores than males. Graph A illustrates a difference in which no overlap exists between the sexes. Graph B illustrates a sex difference in which males and females, on average, differ dramatically, although some males have scores that are higher than the lowest scores of females. Graph C illustrates a sex difference in which considerable overlap exists in the scores of males and females, although the averages of the two groups are still different. Most of the psychological differences between the sexes are of the sort illustrated in graph C.

**Physical Attributes**     Females and males physically differ in a number of ways, including the make-up of their chromosomes, their genitalia, and levels of certain hormones. Females are physically more mature at birth, whereas males show a special physical vulnerability during infancy. Compared with females, males are more likely to be miscarried, die in infancy, or develop hereditary diseases. They are also more likely than females to experience longer and more difficult births (Jacklin, 1989). Later in infancy and childhood, females walk, talk, and reach other developmental milestones earlier than males. By later childhood and adolescence, females reach puberty earlier and males develop greater height, weight, and muscle mass than females (Maccoby & Jacklin, 1974).

**Cognition**     In 1974, Eleanor Maccoby and Carol Jacklin performed an extensive review of the psychological literature on sex differences. They surveyed sixteen hundred studies that examined sex differences in behaviors and tabulated the number of studies that found sex differences favoring girls, the number favoring boys, and the number showing no sex differences. In the area of cognitive skills, Maccoby and Jacklin concluded that girls are more skilled in verbal areas such as reading and vocabulary, whereas boys excel in tasks requiring visual-spatial skills.

More recent meta-analyses of cognitive sex differences, however, indicate no substantial sex differences in verbal skills (Feingold, 1988; Hyde & Linn, 1988). Interestingly, Maccoby and Jacklin's conclusion about verbal skills may have been accurate at the time it was made. Alan Feingold's (1988) meta-analysis of Preliminary Scholastic Aptitude Test (PSAT) scores from over seventy thousand high school juniors who took the test in the years 1960, 1966, 1974, and 1983 indicates that before 1974, girls outperformed boys on the verbal section of this test. Beginning in 1974 (the date of publication of Maccoby and Jacklin's review), however, sex differences in verbal skills disappeared.

In another meta-analysis of over a hundred studies of sex differences in mathematics skills, the investigators concluded that boys and girls showed no overall sex differences in mathematics skills either (Hyde, Fennema, & Lamon, 1990). When the scores of participants of different ages and from specific groups were examined separately, however, sex differences in certain aspects of mathematics performance did emerge. During elementary school, for example, girls showed a slight superiority over boys in the area of computation; in the high school and college years, on the other hand, males did moderately better than females on tests of mathematical problem solving. Among groups selected for either poor performance (such as children from compensatory education programs) or exceptional performance (such as students in gifted and talented programs), males performed better than females in tests of mathematical problem solving. Interestingly, sex differences in mathematics skills seem to be diminishing just as they did in verbal skills: studies published before 1973 are more likely to show a sex difference in this area than studies published after 1973. When differences across all the studies are averaged, males show only a very slight advantage. Figure 13.2 illustrates the overall size of this sex difference.

In fact, the only notable sex difference in cognitive skills currently supported by empirical evidence is visual-spatial skills. Visual-spatial skills involve a number of abilities, all of which require the ability to visualize and transform figures or objects in the mind. Figure 13.3 illustrates three tests of visual-spatial skills—spatial perception, mental rotation, and spatial visualization. As you can see, spatial perception tasks require subjects to ignore distracting information to locate horizontal and vertical. Mental rotation tasks demand that subjects transform two- and three-dimensional figures "in their heads." Spatial visualization tasks require subjects to analyze relationships among different spatial representations.

Marcia Linn and Anne Petersen (1985, 1986) conducted a meta-analysis of thirty-eight studies of visual-spatial skills in boys and girls that had been published between 1974 and 1982. The results indicated no sex differences on spatial visualization tasks. Males do, however, show superior performance on mental rotation, and, to a lesser extent, spatial perception (the tasks depicted in the middle and top portions of Figure 13.3, respectively). Sex differences in mental rotation ability emerge at about age ten years, usually the youngest age at which such tests can be used. Sex differences in spatial perception are noticeably larger after age eighteen years.

**Social Behaviors**    Maccoby and Jacklin (1974) concluded that there are few actual sex differences in the area of social behaviors. Overall, the sex differences observed in social behaviors are most often the type illustrated in

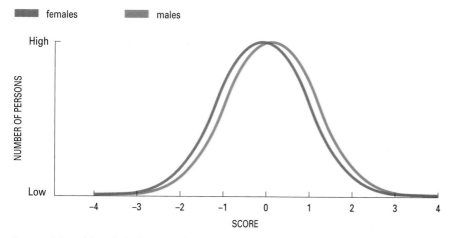

Source:  Adapted from Hyde, Fennema, & Lamon, 1990.

**FIGURE 13.2**

**Sex Differences in Mathematics Skills**

Although sex differences in mathematics skills do exist, these differences are quite small. This graph illustrates the size of the average sex difference. The horizontal axis represents scores converted to a standardized form.

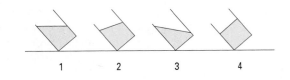

## FIGURE 13.3

### Sex Differences in Visual-Spatial Skills

Tests of visual-spatial skills typically assess spatial perception (top), mental rotation ability (middle), or spatial visualization (bottom). In the top panel, subjects are asked to indicate which bottle has a horizontal water line. In the middle panel, subjects must identify the two responses that depict rotated versions of the standard. In the bottom panel, subjects are asked to identify the simple geometric figure on the top within the more complex figure underneath. Generally, males perform better than females on spatial perception and mental rotation tasks.

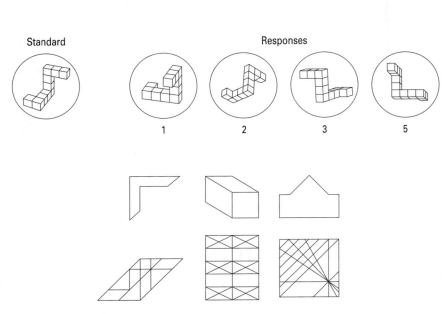

Source: Adapted from Linn & Petersen, 1985.

graph C of Figure 13.1. Although average scores of boys and girls are consistently different in some areas, there is considerable variability in the performance of children within each sex. The single most notable exception to this pattern is aggression.

One of the most consistent findings in the research on sex differences is that, beginning in the preschool years, males are more aggressive than females. They engage in more rough-and-tumble play, display more physical aggression, try to dominate peers, and subsequently display more antisocial behaviors than girls (Block, 1983; Huston, 1985). Meta-analyses substantiate that sex differences in aggression are the greatest among preschoolers, and decrease through the college years (Eagly & Steffen, 1986; Hyde, 1984, 1986). Even though males generally are more aggressive than females, however, the size of the sex difference varies as a function of where the aggression occurs and the type of aggression being measured. The largest sex differences are found in naturalistic settings such as playgrounds and when physical aggression, as opposed to verbal aggression, is measured.

Meta-analyses confirm that sex differences in other social behaviors, when they occur at all, tend to be fairly small. For example, studies show few consistent differences between the sexes in empathic behavior (Eisenberg & Lennon, 1983). Women report that they are more empathetic and cry more than men do, but no sex differences emerge when physiological or unobtrusive measures are used to assess empathy. Some researchers report that girls display more social smiles and gazing than boys do, especially in late adoles-

One of the consistent sex differences in social behavior is the tendency for boys to display more aggression than girls, especially during the preschool years.

cence (Eisenberg & Lennon, 1983; Hall & Halberstadt, 1986). Other evidence suggests that females may be more vulnerable to anxiety and less confident in problem-solving situations than males (Block, 1983). Surveys of middle-class girls also indicate that when they reach adolescence, they report a dramatic decline in self-esteem (American Association of University Women, 1992). These findings must be interpreted with caution, however, since they may reflect the fact that females are more likely than males to report their feelings and emotional states.

One last area in which moderate sex differences have been noted is in the ability to decode the nonverbal expressions of others. Judith Hall's (1984) review of research on this issue shows that female children and adults from widely varying cultures are better than males at identifying the positive versus negative emotions signified by nonverbal cues, particularly as they are transmitted through facial expressions. Moreover, after infancy, females are better than males at recognizing faces.

## Sex Differences: An Overview

In summary, the research literature on actual sex differences in behavior indicates that even though the behavior of people in general shows great variability, males and females are more alike than they are different. Psychologically, male and female children reliably differ on very few dimensions, most notably visual-spatial skills, aggression, and to some extent the ability to decode social messages from nonverbal cues. In fact, many sex differences that we think are "real" actually exist only in the form of gender stereotypes.

If the research indicates greater similarity than differences between males and females, why do stereotypical beliefs persist? One explanation may be that we notice, and therefore retain our beliefs, when boys and girls display behaviors consistent with stereotypes. In contrast, when a girl or boy behaves in a manner inconsistent with a stereotype, we ascribe this pattern to an individual difference. Thus, when Billy fights (a stereotypically masculine activity), we say that "boys will be boys." But when he cooks and helps around the house in

In general research shows that there are fewer actual sex differences in behavior than gender stereotypes lead us to believe. Stereotypes may persist, though, because we attribute behaviors inconsistent with the stereotypes to individual differences among children.

stereotypically feminine tasks, we comment on "how helpful" (not "how feminine") he is compared with other boys his age. Perhaps, too, stereotypes result from the tendency of children (and adults) to form cognitive categories of social groups (Martin, 1991). Upon seeing one similarity between people in a group (for example, in terms of physical characteristics), we may be tempted to conclude that they resemble each other in other ways, too.

## *Theories of Gender-Role Development*

What are the origins of sex differences in behavior? This question was explored by many researchers in the 1960s and 1970s, when it was assumed that actual sex differences were more numerous among children than contemporary research indicates. Biological, social learning, and cognitive theorists all contributed ideas about the origins of male and female characteristics.

Even though contemporary research shows that actual sex differences in behavior are relatively few, they are still differences that must be explained. In other words, children still show some behaviors that are *sex-typed*, or aligned with the definitions of masculinity and femininity in their culture. Most researchers today, however, are less interested in choosing one particular theoretical position to account for gender-role development than they are in identifying the complex interplay of biology, socialization, and the child's understanding that underlies this process.

### Biological Theories

▶ Roles of nature and nurture

Biologically based explanations for sex differences focus largely on the influence of chromosomes, hormones, and the structure of the brain on behavior.

These factors often work in ways that illustrate the complex interactions of biological systems to produce sex-differentiated behaviors.

As we saw in Chapter 3, the presence of an X or Y sex chromosome begins a complex process that leads to sexual differentiation. Between six and twelve weeks after conception, the XY chromosomal configuration leads to the development of testes and the secretion of a class of male hormones called **androgens**, a process that leads to further sexual differentiation. The penis and scrotum develop in response to the metabolism of *testosterone,* an androgen that is actually present in both sexes, but in greater amounts in males (Whalen, 1984). In the absence of an XY configuration and the associated greater amounts of androgens, the female structures develop (Hood et al., 1987). These differences in biological structures form the bases for children to be labeled "boy" or "girl," the categorization of *biological sex.*

**Hormones and Behavior**    Prenatal exposure to hormones, particularly androgens, influences the developing fetus in ways that may have an impact on biology and, perhaps, postnatal behavior. Most important for our discussion, androgens influence the developing organization of the central nervous system and the brain (Gorski, 1980; MacLusky & Naftolin, 1981). Hormone-related sex differences in the central nervous system may, in turn, have important influences on behavior and abilities.

Take the example of aggression. Explanations of sex differences in aggression from a biological perspective have relied on two major sources: experiments in which androgens have been administered systematically to female animals during prenatal development, and human studies that have found correlations between levels of androgens and aggressive behavior. The animal studies show that when androgens are administered to female rats during their prenatal development, they subsequently display increased aggressive behaviors, such as threats and rough-and-tumble play, compared with nor-

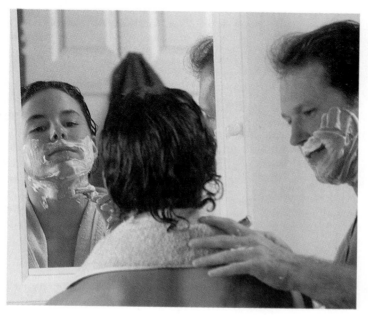

Hormones clearly play a role in the physical maturity of girls and boys. Their role in determining psychological attributes, however, may be more subtle and complex.

**androgen**    Class of male or masculinizing hormones.

mally developing females. These findings have been replicated in rats, monkeys, and a number of other species (Goy, 1970; Parsons, 1980).

Among humans, females may be exposed prenatally to large amounts of androgens either because their adrenocortical glands malfunction and allow excess androgens to circulate (a condition called *adrenogenital syndrome,* or *AGS*), or because their mothers received drugs to prevent miscarriage that also elevated androgen levels. Both groups of females frequently are born with masculinized genitals. Behaviorally, these genetic females are more likely to engage in rough and active physical play than are females not exposed to prenatal androgens (Money & Ehrhardt, 1972). Still another body of research shows that during puberty, when levels of testosterone in males begin to rise, aggressive behavior increases (Hood et al., 1987; Olweus et al., 1980; Susman et al., 1987).

Although this type of evidence implies a causal link between male hormones and aggression, some controversy about the relationship exists (Tieger, 1980). First, while hormones have been shown to precede and presumably influence certain behaviors like aggression, those behaviors may themselves have an impact on hormone levels. That is, levels of hormones, including testosterone, can also change *in response* to changes in the environment (Hood et al., 1987). In stressful situations, for example, testosterone levels in males decrease (Parsons, 1980). Similarly, among nonhuman males, increases in androgen levels frequently follow, rather than precede, an aggressive encounter (Hood et al., 1987). Thus, the link between aggression and levels of androgens is not unidirectional and it is difficult to make causal statements. Moreover, studies of androgenized girls are difficult to interpret because parents were aware of their daughters' masculinized appearance at birth and may have tolerated or even encouraged more "boylike" behaviors. Finally, as we will see later in this chapter, there is ample evidence to show how powerful a factor socialization can be in promoting aggression in boys. Even if biology sets some early predispositions toward aggression in males, the role of social experiences cannot be ruled out.

If hormones do, indeed, affect sex-typed behaviors, their effects are both subtle and complex. In a longitudinal study of the relationship between sex hormones in the blood at birth and later behaviors, investigators found that these substances affect males and females differently (Jacklin, Maccoby, & Doering, 1983; Jacklin et al., 1984; Jacklin, Wilcox, & Maccoby, 1988). One set of outcomes concerned *progesterone,* a hormone present in both males and females, but in greater amounts in females. In males, higher levels of progesterone in infancy are associated with greater physical strength and less timidity at age three years; in girls, however, higher levels of progesterone are linked to lower strength and are unrelated to timidity. Similarly, elevated levels of testosterone in infancy are unrelated to visual-spatial skills at age six years among boys; among girls, greater amounts of testosterone are associated with worse performance on tests of visual-spatial skills at age six years.

The sex-differentiating effects of sex hormones on male and female development are puzzling. It may be that males and females differ in the levels of hormones necessary to produce an effect, such as poor visual-spatial skill. Sex hormones also may be metabolized by males and females in different fashions, resulting in paradoxical, or at least different, effects.

**Brain Lateralization**　　A second way in which biology can influence sex differences in behavior is through the organization and functions of the brain.

A prominent biological explanation for sex differences in visual-spatial skills involves the process known as *lateralization of the brain.* During the course of development, as we saw in Chapter 5, the two halves of the brain become increasingly specialized to handle different types of information, such as speech perception and speech production. According to one version of the lateralization hypothesis, girls' brains mature more quickly and lateralize earlier than boys'. Since verbal skills are thought to develop sooner than visual-spatial skills, and since rapid maturation of the brain is assumed to produce less eventual lateralization, the verbal skills of girls are presumed to be more evenly distributed across the hemispheres. Verbal processing in the right *and* left hemispheres, in turn, interferes with the visual-spatial processing that usually takes place predominantly in the right hemisphere. Because lateralization takes longer in boys, it is hypothesized, their cerebral hemispheres become more specialized than girls'. The net result is that their visual-spatial skills are stronger. Some research evidence confirms that children (regardless of sex) who mature early score better on verbal tasks than on spatial tasks, whereas the reverse pattern holds true for late maturers (Waber, 1976).

Before we accept the lateralization hypothesis, however, we should note that there are also nonbiological explanations of sex differences in visual-spatial skills. One such explanation relies on the contrasting play experiences of boys and girls. According to this formulation, masculine play activities, such as using building blocks, facilitate the development of visual-spatial skills in boys (Block, 1983). Evidence for this explanation was found in a study in which preschool children were given practice in discerning a diamond within a patterned background. The data indicated that although boys were initially superior on visual-spatial problems, their superiority disappeared after the practice sessions (Connor, Schackman, & Serbin, 1978). Thus, it is suggested, sex-typed play activities may account for sex differences in visual-spatial skills.

**Cross-Cultural Patterns of Sex Differences**   The contexts in which gender-role development occurs are many and varied. Children who grow up in urban, suburban, and rural areas in industrialized nations and children who grow up in nonindustrialized societies all acquire the gender roles exhibited in their culture. Cross-cultural studies can shed some light on biological explanations of sex typing. If sex typing results solely from biological influences, then we would expect to see great unanimity in gender roles across periods of history and in different cultures. If, on the other hand, gender roles reflect values that are peculiar to a given era or culture, we would expect to see variability in the characteristics defined as masculine and feminine by different cultures or at different points in time. For example, the meta-analyses showing that verbal superiority of girls has disappeared in the last two decades suggest that these sociocultural forces do play a role.

Margaret Mead's (1967/1949) classic research on sex differences in Melanesian societies illustrates the differences that emerge across cultures. In the 1930s, before the onset of modernizing influences, Mead studied three nonindustrial tribes living in New Guinea: the Arapesh, the Tchambuli, and the Mundugumor. These three tribes exhibited gender roles that differed both from each other and from those seen in our society. Among the Arapesh and Mundugumor tribes, roles were not strongly differentiated by sex, although the two tribes exhibited very different personality characteristics and behavior. Arapesh men and women both adopted what we would identify as a "feminine" role. Both parents cared for children, were emotional, cooperative, and

▶ Sociocultural influence

nonassertive. The Mundugumor men and women, in contrast, adopted "masculine" roles regardless of their biological sex. Men and women alike were extremely aggressive, and the women detested childbearing and child rearing. Mead (1967/1949) described this tribe as devoting "all of their time to quarreling and headhunting" (p. 54). Finally, the roles Tchambuli men and women played in their society, although sex differentiated, reversed our masculine and feminine constructs. Tchambuli men, adopting gender roles our society would deem feminine, were artistic, socially sensitive, and concerned with the feelings of other people. Tchambuli women were assertive and industrious, characteristics our society would consider masculine. Indeed, in this society the women handled business affairs while the men stayed at home, painting and practicing their dance steps.

The patterns of sex typing Mead observed in these three tribes provide evidence that the gender roles seen in our society are neither natural nor universal. Gender roles are prescribed by cultures to fill specific social needs and goals. But, as we can see from the Arapesh and the Mundugumor, sex differentiation in roles does not always occur. Thus, although biological factors in gender-role development cannot be ignored, neither can they account for the diversity of roles that occurs across cultures.

## Social Learning Theory

▶ Roles of nature and nurture

One of the primary mechanisms accounting for sex differences in behavior, social learning theorists maintain, is sex-differentiated treatment of boys and girls. According to this position, boys and girls are reinforced and punished differentially for specific behaviors, which leads them to behave in gender-typed ways. Girls, for example, may be rewarded for playing with dolls and punished for climbing trees, whereas boys may receive just the opposite treatment. Thus, because children are motivated to seek reinforcement and avoid punishment, they will behave in a sex-typed fashion.

According to social learning theory, a powerful vehicle for the transmission of gender roles is imitation. Parents can be especially potent models for sex-typed behaviors.

Children attend both to the consequences of their own behavior and to the consequences others face for their behavior. In fact, imitation, or modeling, may be an even more powerful means by which children learn gender roles. By observing the experiences of other people, children develop expectancies for reinforcement and punishment of their own behavior. These expectancies may influence an individual's behavior as strongly as do the actual experiences of reward or punishment (Bandura, 1969, 1977a). Children have numerous opportunities to observe models behaving in gender-stereotypic ways in the home, in the outside world, and in the media. Each time a child sees that Dad fixes things around the house and Mom does most of the cooking and cleaning, or that most little boys play baseball while little girls play house, she is adding to her storehouse of sex-typed behaviors.

Several factors influence whether children will imitate the sex-typed behaviors of others. Albert Bandura and others have proposed that children's *attention* to models in the first place is influenced by both the sex of the model and the **sex typicality** of the model's behavior—how characteristic it is of the model's own sex (Bandura, 1977a; Perry & Bussey, 1979). According to this hypothesis, boys would, in general, be more likely than girls to attend to the behavior of male models, although they would be less likely to attend to a male model who was exhibiting "feminine" behavior. The prediction that individuals will pay greater attention to same-sex models is based on the notion that observation of same-sex models should provide children with greater information about potential consequences for their own behavior. In addition, Bandura suggests, children *recognize* that certain behaviors are sex-typed, especially as they observe the frequencies with which males and females, as a group, perform certain behaviors. Finally, Bandura (1977a) proposes that *motivational* factors, such as reward seeking and attempts to retain a sense of mastery, will influence behavior in a variety of realms. As children grow older, they rely less on others to regulate their behavior and more on *self-regulation,* based on personal standards of gender-appropriate behavior (Bandura, 1986). Because this more recent formulation of social learning theory incorporates cognitive processes such as attention, it is often called *social cognitive theory.*

▶ Interaction among domains

Several studies have supported the idea that children are more likely to imitate same-sex than other-sex models (Bussey & Bandura, 1984; Bussey & Perry, 1982). Thus, same-sex parents, peers, and characters in the media can be powerful influences on the child. In addition, other studies have found that children are more likely to imitate models who behave in sex-typical ways than models who behave in sex-atypical ways (Perry & Bussey, 1979).

Moreover, self-regulation of sex-typed behavior does seem to increase with development, as a recent study by Kay Bussey and Albert Bandura (1992) shows. Two- to four-year-old children privately rated how they would feel if they played with a series of toys, some of which were masculine (for example, a dump truck), some feminine (for example, a baby doll), and some neutral (for example, a xylophone). As Figure 13.4 shows, younger children expressed relatively neutral self-evaluations about playing with masculine and feminine toys. Older children, in contrast, indicated more positive self-evaluations when imagining they might play with toys geared for their own sex.

Social learning theories offer the best explanation for the roles that parents, peers, and others play in gender-role development. They also provide a credible set of explanations for children's imitation of sex-typical behavior. Traditional social learning explanations, however, appear to be limited by the

**sex typicality** The extent to which a behavior is usually associated with one sex as opposed to the other.

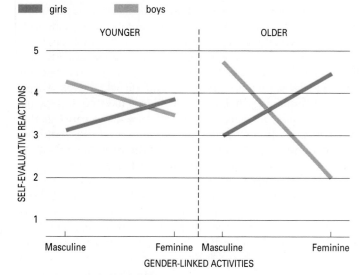

girls    boys

YOUNGER    OLDER

GENDER-LINKED ACTIVITIES

## FIGURE 13.4

**Self-Evaluations During Same-Sex Activities**

Two- and four-year-old children rated how they would feel while they played with masculine, feminine, or neutral toys. As the graph indicates, younger children, especially girls, gave relatively neutral self-evaluations for playing with masculine and feminine toys. In contrast, older children said they would feel better about themselves when they played with same-sex toys.

Source: Bussey & Bandura, 1992.

theoretical emphasis on observable behavior rather than on cognitive processes. The recent inclusion of cognitive and emotional phenomena such as attention, recognition, and motivation may facilitate the ability of this theory to explain nonbehavioral aspects of gender-role development.

### Cognitive-Developmental Theories

Cognitive-developmental theories focus on the ways in which children understand gender roles in general and themselves as males and females in particular. In cognitive-developmental theories, *gender* is emphasized as a conceptual category, a way of classifying people on the basis of their overt appearance or behaviors.

▶ Interaction among domains

▶ Development as continuous/discontinuous

**Kohlberg's Cognitive-Developmental Theory**    Lawrence Kohlberg (1966) proposed that gender roles emerge as a consequence of stagelike developments in cognition. The most basic of these cognitive milestones is acquisition of **gender identity**, the knowledge that self and others are female or male. This concept, which is acquired between ages two and three years, is crucial to later gender-role development because it provides a basic categorizing principle with which children begin to divide the world.

After acquiring gender identity, around their fourth birthday children develop **gender stability**, a sense that gender does not change over time. Children who have acquired gender stability recognize that they were born one sex and will grow up to be a member of that same sex. Despite this knowledge, however, they may not yet be aware of the fact that genitalia determine biological sex. Rather, children assume that external factors (such as clothing or hair length) are the determinants of sex. Thus, a young boy may believe that he was a baby boy and will grow up to be a "daddy" (gender stability), but only if his behavior and physical characteristics (such as hair length) remain masculine.

**gender identity**    Knowledge, usually gained by age three years, that one is male or female.

**gender stability**    Knowledge, usually gained by age four years, that one's gender does not change over time.

Children's lack of awareness of the genital basis of gender indicates their lack of **gender constancy**. This term refers to the child's awareness that changes in external characteristics, behaviors, or desires are not accompanied by a change in biological sex. Thus, a boy may wear a dress and a girl may play with toy soldiers without altering their respective biological sexes. Kohlberg proposes that gender constancy, like other forms of Piagetian cognitive skills (such as conservation skills), is acquired at about age seven years.

For Kohlberg, the acquisition of gender constancy marks the child's mature awareness of the concept of gender differentiation. Moreover, because children value both their own sex and themselves, they are motivated to behave in a gender-typical fashion. From Kohlberg's perspective, cognitive development facilitates *self-socialization* among children. Kohlberg believes that children are internally motivated by their positive self- and same-sex evaluations to behave in a manner consonant with their conceptions of what is sex appropriate. External motivators (such as reinforcements and punishments) are of minimal importance in the process of self-socialization.

▶ The child's active role

Research has confirmed that children progress from attaining gender identity to gender stability and, finally, gender constancy from about two to nine years of age (Fagot, 1985; Slaby & Frey, 1975). This trend appears for children from several cultures including Argentina, Belize, Kenya, Nepal, and American Samoa (DeLisi & Gallagher, 1991; Munroe, Shimmin, & Munroe, 1984). In recent years, the notion that children actively organize social information on the basis of gender has been even further elaborated by other theorists.

**Gender Schema Theory**   Another cognitive-developmental theory is the *gender schema theory* (Bem, 1981; Martin & Halverson, 1981, 1987). Like Kohlberg's theory, gender schema theory adopts Piagetian concepts and stresses the importance of the acquisition of gender identity and children's intrinsic motivations to behave in a gender-typical manner. Unlike Kohlberg, however, gender schema theory does not stress the attainment of gender constancy but rather focuses on the influence of children's active construction of gender knowledge on their behavior (Bem, 1981; Martin & Halverson, 1987; Signorella, 1987).

▶ The child's active role

Carol Martin and Charles Halverson (1981) have proposed that children first acquire gender identity and then, in their attempts to create order in their social worlds, begin to construct two **gender schemas**, or cognitive organizing structures for information relevant to gender. The first one, the *same-sex/opposite-sex schema,* refers to the child's knowledge of one sex or the other. This is a fairly primitive cognitive structure comprised largely of gender stereotypes, such as "boys fix cars" and "girls sew." Children also develop a second, more elaborate, gender schema about behaviors relevant to their own sex. This *own-sex schema* provides a basis for guiding children's behavior. Thus, even though both boys and girls know that girls sew, girls are more likely to be motivated to learn to sew, whereas they may not want to learn how to fix a car. Researchers have confirmed that children explore neutral objects labeled as intended for their sex more than they explore such objects labeled for the other sex. Moreover, up to one week later, children remember more details about the "same-sex" objects than they do about the "other-sex" objects, even when they are offered a reward for remembering details (Bradbard et al., 1986).

**gender constancy**   Knowledge, usually gained around age six or seven years, that one's gender does not change as a result of alterations in appearance, behaviors, or desires.

**gender schema**   Cognitive organizing structure for information relevant to sex typing.

According to Martin and Halverson (1981), children's gender schemas serve as a potent means of organizing information about their social worlds. Gender schemas may also have the effect of distorting information inconsistent with the schema. Thus, when children see a female doctor, for example, they may distort the information to make it consistent with their gender schema, turning the doctor, in their minds, into a nurse (Cordua, McGraw, & Drabman, 1979). Many studies have documented these kinds of distortions in children's memories for stereotype-inconsistent information (Carter & Levy, 1988; Martin & Halverson, 1987).

Cognitive-developmental theories are an effective way of explaining how children's own knowledge contributes to their gender-role development. Concepts such as gender identity and self-socialization have proven to be useful ways to explain gender-role development. In addition, we have seen how children employ their prior conceptions of the sex typicality of models in deciding whether to imitate modeled behavior, a phenomenon predicted by cognitive-developmental theories. In short, how children *think* about gender seems to have far-reaching consequences.

To sum up, each of the preceding theories has some value for explaining the source of sex differences. The biological theories provide a basis for understanding the physiological underpinnings of male and female behavior. Social learning theory provides a mechanism for explaining how children learn discrete aspects of sex-typical behavior. Cognitive-developmental approaches explain how children's concepts of gender become integrated in their minds. Although each theory explains a specific feature of gender-role development better than the other theories do, none of them taken alone is adequate to explain the multifaceted nature of this aspect of development.

## How Children's Knowledge of Gender Develops

How children *think* about gender, it seems, may be of greater significance than actual sex differences in behavior. Anyone who has spent time with children, as a researcher or casual observer, cannot help but note that children pay attention to and organize much of their world around gender as a social category (Martin, 1991). Exactly what do children know about gender at various ages and, further, does this knowledge influence their actual behavior?

### Gender Identity

Theories of gender-role development, especially cognitive theories, are virtually unanimous in contending that children's gender identity plays a vital role in promoting gender-typical behavior. Gender identity is such a basic psychological categorization that, except in rare circumstances, individuals are unlikely to desire a change in their sex, nor is a change likely to be easy. John Money and Anke Ehrhardt (1972) maintain that once a child has attained gender identity, any attempt to change it would have negative outcomes such as depression or severe psychopathology. In clinical studies of children who were born one sex but subsequently relabeled as another (for example, be-

▶ Development as continuous/discontinuous

cause of ambiguous genitalia or surgical accidents), Money and Ehrhardt (1972) conclude that gender reassignment is successful only if it occurs before three or four years of age.

Most children learn to label themselves correctly as female or male between the ages of two and three years (Huston, 1985). Precisely when children develop this distinction can forecast subsequent patterns of behavior. Beverly Fagot and Mary Leinbach (1989) found that some children developed gender identity early (before the age of twenty-eight months), others not until later. Boys and girls who were early identifiers engaged in significantly more gender-typical play, such as play with building toys for boys and doll play for girls, than did late identifiers. At two to three years of age, children able to apply gender labels correctly to others also have greater knowledge of gender stereotypes (Fagot, Leinbach, & O'Boyle, 1992).

▶ Individual differences

How does gender identity develop? Perhaps parents and others provide this information directly by saying things to their young children like, "There's another little boy just like you" or "Be a good girl now, won't you?" Beverly Fagot's research also shows that children who are adept at using gender labels tend to have mothers who engage in sex-typed play with their children and espouse traditional beliefs about gender roles themselves (Fagot, Leinbach, & O'Boyle, 1992). Many researchers contend, however, that the messages about gender roles are so clear and pervasive in our society that even aside from the role that parents may play, children can't help but notice them.

▶ Roles of nature and nurture

## Gender Schemas

Most children can select pictures labeled as "boy" or "girl" at about two to two and a half years of age (Etaugh, Grinnell, & Etaugh, 1989; Leinbach & Fagot, 1986; Thompson, 1975). And as we just saw, they also apply gender labels to themselves and choose toys appropriate for their sex at about the same age. Thus, children show the ability to categorize social information on the basis of gender at an early age. Some children, however, seem to be more likely to use gender as a classification scheme than others.

As we saw earlier in this chapter, gender schemas are cognitive constructions that influence children's behavior and their interpretation of gender-relevant information. Some children tend to be *gender schematic*—that is, they possess a strong gender schema, exhibit more consistent sex typing in their behavior, and process information along gender lines. In contrast, children who are *gender aschematic* possess a weaker gender schema, are less sex typed behaviorally, and focus their attention on aspects of information that are not related to gender.

▶ Individual differences

How do researchers determine whether children are gender schematic or aschematic? A popular technique is to measure the amount of time children take to choose between pairs of toys that are differently (masculine-feminine pairs) or similarly (feminine-feminine pairs) sex typed. Researchers assume that gender-schematic children should choose relatively quickly between masculine-feminine pairs of toys and take relatively longer to choose from masculine-masculine and feminine-feminine toy pairs. Gender-aschematic children, on the other hand, should take comparable amounts of time to choose between all pairs of toys (Carter & Levy, 1988).

Results from a number of studies indicate that gender schemas influence the way in which children process gender-related information. For example, gender-schematic children find it difficult to remember information about pictures of people engaged in sex-atypical activities, such as a boy playing with a

▶ Interaction among domains

doll, whereas they can easily remember information about people engaged in sex-typical activities, such as a girl playing with a tea set (Signorella, 1987). These effects are apparent as early as age twenty-five months, at least among boys (Bauer, 1993). Similarly, children distort stereotype-inconsistent information by actually changing the sex of the person engaged in the sex-atypical behavior. Gender-schematic children who see a picture of a boy playing with a doll are more likely to remember seeing a picture of a girl playing with a doll than a picture of a boy playing with a gender-typical toy (Carter & Levy, 1988).

The development of gender schemas in young children has important implications for gender-role development. Because gender-schematic children often distort information according to their beliefs about gender, they are unlikely to remember events that are inconsistent with those beliefs. Thus, they are less likely to believe that violations of gender-role norms are acceptable because they remember so few instances (if any) of people who behaved in a sex-atypical fashion. Gender-aschematic children, in contrast, are more likely to believe that stereotypes are flexible and that they are permitted to engage in a wider variety of behaviors regardless of the gender association of those activities.

Why do many children become gender schematic? According to Bem (1983), children become gender schematic to the extent that they experience gender as a relevant social category. Thus, for example, when differences between males and females are frequently pointed out to them by parents, teachers, or peers, children themselves will use gender as a way of classifying social information. Furthermore, both peers and adults stress conformity to gender-typical roles, a fact that makes it difficult for most children in our society to become truly gender aschematic (Bem, 1983).

## Gender Stereotypes

Children begin to acquire *gender-role stereotypes* and employ them as guides for their behavior from age two years onward. For example, Spencer Thompson (1975) examined the levels of gender-stereotype knowledge and sex-typed preferences exhibited among a group of twenty-four-, thirty-, and thirty-six-month-old children. Children's sex-typed preferences were assessed by asking them to choose between pairs of photographs of identical objects, one of which was stated to be "for girls" and the other "for boys." Stereotype knowledge was assessed by asking children to sort photos of common sex-typed objects into boxes called things "for boys and men" and "for girls and women."

Children's performance on these tasks indicated significant developmental differences in children's sex-typed preferences and knowledge of stereotypes. Although twenty-four-month-olds did not show consistent sex-typed preferences, thirty-month-old children consistently preferred "same-sex" over "opposite-sex" objects. This tendency was even stronger among the thirty-six-month-old children tested.

Similarly, older children showed more knowledge of gender stereotypes than the younger children, although even the youngest children were surprisingly knowledgeable. Twenty-four-month-olds identified 61 percent of the items consistently with the stereotypes; thirty-month-olds identified 78 percent; and thirty-six-month-olds identified 86 percent. Thus, these data indicate that children have already begun to develop a knowledge of gender stereotypes by the age of two years and that they develop preferences for behaviors and objects associated with their own sex by thirty months of age.

Other research has shown that children as young as two to three years of age begin to associate specific behaviors and future roles with each sex with star-

By two to three years of age, children show a fairly extensive understanding of gender stereotypes, the beliefs and expectations of the characteristics of males and females. Through the early and middle school years, this knowledge becomes even more fully elaborated.

tling consistency. Deanna Kuhn's data indicate that young preschoolers believe that girls are nonaggressive, talk a lot, play with dolls, and will grow up to be a nurse or a teacher. They say, in contrast, that boys are aggressive, play with trucks and cars, and will grow up to be the boss (Kuhn, Nash, & Brucken, 1978).

By age six or seven, children's knowledge of sex-typed activities is essentially "perfect." Lisa Serbin and her colleagues (Serbin, Powlishta, & Gulko, 1993) asked five- through twelve-year-olds to state whether twenty stereotyped objects (for example, hammer, rifle, stove, broom) belonged to male or female categories. As Figure 13.5 indicates, all children, regardless of age, showed extensive knowledge of the stereotypes. The figure also shows that children's knowledge of stereotyped personality traits (for example, gentle, emotional, adventurous, messy) expands through the middle school years. As children grow

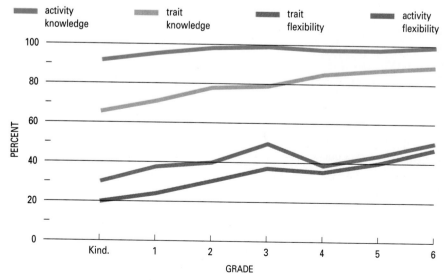

Source: Serbin, Powlishta, & Gulko, 1993.

**FIGURE 13.5**

**Developmental Trends in Gender-Role Knowledge**

When kindergartners through sixth-graders were asked to identify which of twenty stereotyped objects were masculine and which were feminine, all children were at least 90 percent correct (see the line for "activity knowledge"). If they were asked, however, to indicate if objects could be used by both sexes, a developmental increase in flexibility was observed (the line for "activity flexibility"). Knowledge of stereotyped traits and flexibility for those traits both increased over the age span studied.

older, however, their knowledge of stereotypes also becomes more flexible. If researchers employ questions that do not require children to state that a trait or behavior must be "male" or "female," that is, if they allow the child to say "both," older children are more willing to acknowledge that activities and traits can go with both sexes (Serbin, Powlishta, & Gulko, 1993; Signorella, Bigler, & Liben, 1993). Even when children believe that stereotypes can be violated, however, they do not want to associate with people who engage in counterstereotypical behavior (Carter & McCloskey, 1984). Thus, recognition of flexibility of gender stereotypes does not indicate that children find sex-atypical behavior acceptable, but merely that they recognize that exceptions can occur.

The Chronology below summarizes the attainment of gender stereotypes and other aspects of gender-role development described in this chapter. How

## CHRONOLOGY   Sex-Role Development

PRENATAL PERIOD
Sex chromosomes and genitalia develop.
Sex hormones influence brain and physical development.

BIRTH
Infant receives label as boy or girl.

2–3 YEARS
Child labels own gender.
Identifies pictures labeled as "boy" or "girl."
Shows knowledge of gender-role stereotypes.
Prefers same-sex playmates and toys.
If boy, shows more aggression.
If girl, shows better ability to recognize faces.

4–5 YEARS
Attains gender stability.
Shows even stronger preferences for same-sex playmates and toys.
Displays decline in cross-gender behavior.
Enforces gender-role norms in peers.

6–10 YEARS
Attains gender constancy.
Responds increasingly negatively to cross-gender play in peers.
If girl, shows greater ability to decode nonverbal social cues.
If boy, shows better performance in mental rotation tasks.
Shows more knowledge of and flexibility in gender-role stereotypes.

16–18 YEARS
Shows less interest in sex-segregated interactions.
If girl, shows more social smiles and gazing.
If boy, shows better performance in spatial-perception tasks.
Shows greater tolerance for sex-atypical behaviors.
Sex differences in aggression diminish.

This chart describes the sequence of sex-role development based on the findings of research. Children often show individual differences in the exact ages at which they display the various developmental achievements outlined here.

do children acquire gender stereotypes and other knowledge about gender so thoroughly and so early in life? Children may be taught this information by their parents, peers, teachers, or the media, or they may infer that a stereotype or actual sex difference exists by observing systematic patterns of behaviors in the males and females around them (Martin & Halverson, 1987). In fact, the messages sent from the social world are so profound that many psychologists look to the child's socialization experiences as a fundamental way of explaining gender-role development.

# *The Socialization of Gender Roles*

The earliest messages about the social world, of course, come from the child's parents, and in this regard communication about gender roles is no different from any other aspect of social development. From the moment of birth, when parents in our culture ask, "Is it a boy or a girl?" the sex of their child is a very prominent characteristic—one that elicits specific behaviors and reactions from mothers and fathers. As children branch out to social relationships with their peers, gender-role socialization continues in very powerful ways—in the games children play, the relationships they form, and how they react to each other's behaviors. Finally, another significant influence on gender-role development is the child's experiences in schools, in which teachers and the instructional materials they use can confirm (or disconfirm) early gender-role beliefs and behaviors.

▶ Roles of nature and nurture

## The Influence of Parents

Traditionally, developmental psychologists have believed that one of the most important sources of information about gender for children is the behavior of their parents and the environment they create (Katz, 1987). Sometimes the messages are subtle. Parents commonly provide their children with sex-differentiated toys and room furnishings (Rheingold & Cook, 1975). They buy sports equipment, tools, and vehicles for their sons and dolls and doll furniture for their daughters. Boys' rooms typically are decorated in blue, girls' in yellow (Pomerleau et al., 1990). When parents provide boys and girls with differing physical environments, they send messages that boys are indeed different from girls and set sex-related limits on the types of behavior that are acceptable and appropriate.

Other times the messages are more direct. Research has shown that parents treat children differently on the basis of sex in early infancy, beginning at ages younger than those at which actual behavioral sex differences emerge (Fagot & Leinbach, 1987). Adults play more roughly with a male infant, tossing him in the air and tickling him vigorously, than they do with female infants (Huston, 1983). During infancy and childhood, girls are more likely than boys to be protected and sheltered by adults, whereas boys are given greater opportunities to explore their environments than girls are given (Block, 1983; Burns, Mitchell, & Obradovich, 1989). Adult females respond more quickly to crying babies whom they think are little girls, and parents encourage more nurturance in the play of their daughters than in the play of their sons (Condry, Condry, & Pogatshynik, 1978; Huston, 1983).

A revealing series of studies has been conducted to determine whether sex-differentiated treatment of infants results from infant behaviors or from gender stereotypes adults hold. In these "Baby X" studies, adults, who are often parents, are asked to interact with or observe a baby who is labeled as either male or female regardless of the child's actual sex. Information about a baby's sex has proved to be an important determinant of adults' behavior. Adults interpret the motivations of babies differently depending on the sex they believe the child to be. When subjects were asked to interpret why a baby was crying, people who thought the baby was a boy said "he" was angry, whereas those who thought the baby was a girl said "she" was frightened (Condry & Condry, 1976). Similarly, adults interacting with "boy" babies rarely offer them dolls even when these infants expressed an interest in dolls by reaching or grabbing at them (Seavey, Katz, & Zalk, 1975). Clearly the perceived, not the actual, sex of a child influences adults' responses in at least some instances.

**Direct Reinforcement**   Parents take an active role in teaching and encouraging gender-typical behavior in their children, at least according to some research findings. For example, when their children are as young as age three, parents react more negatively when their daughters assert themselves than when their sons do. Fathers, in particular, tend to react positively when their daughters display compliant behavior and reward their sons for assertiveness (Kerig, Cowan, & Cowan, 1993). Similarly, parents give boys more positive evaluations and girls more negative evaluations when children are working on solving different problems (Alessandri & Lewis, 1993). Parents also respond positively to boys who play with blocks and manipulate objects and reinforce girls' play with dolls and requests for help (Fagot & Leinbach, 1987). Fathers appear to be especially concerned about what they perceive as masculinity in their sons, at least during the preschool years (Jacklin, DiPietro, & Maccoby, 1984). Such concern is often expressed in parental interviews as well as in the consistently negative manner in which fathers respond to sex-atypical behavior in their sons.

A recent meta-analysis of 172 studies of parents' differential socialization of girls and boys suggests, however, that we must be cautious about how much weight we give to the role of direct parental reinforcement in accounting for the various facets of gender-role development. In general, the overall impact of parental socialization was judged to be small in most areas of socialization, including achievement expectations, dependency, and aggression. The only socialization area that showed a significant effect was in parental encouragement of sex-typed activities, such as doll play for girls and playing with tools for boys (Lytton & Romney, 1991). It is in these contexts in particular, then, that children may acquire well-defined ideas about maleness and femaleness.

**Parental Attitudes**   Another way in which parents influence gender-role development in their children is more indirect—through their own general beliefs about masculine and feminine roles. Many parents believe that children as young as two years old differ along gender-stereotypic lines (McGuire, 1988). They report, for example, that their own sons like sports, enjoy using tools, and are energetic. On the other hand, parents of girls say their daughters like to be admired, play with dolls, and like clothes. Such beliefs are frequently translated into sex-differentiated treatment in the types of chores boys and girls are assigned to do around the house—boys take out the garbage and mow the lawn; girls do more chores within the house, such as cleaning and cooking (Lackey, 1989).

Parents, but especially fathers, are likely to stress academic and nonacademic achievement more for their sons than for their daughters (Eccles, 1983). In elementary school, parents have higher academic achievement expectations for their daughters than for their sons (Maccoby & Jacklin, 1974). Beginning in adolescence, however, parents expect their sons to perform better in academics than their daughters, especially in areas such as mathematics (Eccles, 1983). Parents may convey such expectations directly (for example, through statements such as, "Girls are never very good at math") or indirectly (for example, through encouraging boys and girls to pursue differing occupational goals). Parents' encouragement of children's play with traditionally sex-typed toys may also have an impact on their academic endeavors. For example, parents may discourage daughters from male-typed play, such as with blocks or construction toys, a pattern that may have the unintended consequence of inhibiting the development of visual-spatial skills in girls.

**Gender in Nontraditional Families** A series of profound changes that have taken place in the traditional American family over the last several decades may have an impact on gender-role development. First, an increasing number of children spend a large part of their lives in families headed by a single parent, usually the mother (Huston, 1983). According to social learning theorists, the absence of significant male models from the home should have an effect on the process of imitation, especially among boys. Second, as we described in Chapter 11, mothers increasingly are employed outside the home while their children are still young. Thus, these women may be providing their children with alternative models for feminine behavior.

Although few studies have addressed the development of gender roles in single-parent families, a large number of studies have been conducted on

▶ Sociocultural influence

Children whose mothers work possess more flexible gender-role concepts compared with children whose mothers do not work outside the home. Girls also show higher levels of achievement motivation when their mothers are employed outside the home.

gender-role development in children from families in which mothers are employed outside the home. In general, maternal employment facilitates the development of flexibility in children's conceptions of gender roles. Children with employed mothers are more likely to believe that both males and females can exhibit a wide variety of behaviors and personality characteristics than children whose mothers are not employed outside the home. The effects on daughters of employed mothers are particularly dramatic. Mothers who work outside the home have daughters who show higher levels of achievement motivation and are more likely to have personality styles that blend male-typed and female-typed traits than are the daughters of mothers who do not work outside the home (Hoffman, 1979; Huston, 1983). The effects of maternal employment on sons are mixed. Boys whose mothers work outside the home are more likely to have flexible views of women's roles than are the sons of nonworking mothers, but sons of both types of mothers have equally masculine personalities and display equally masculine types of behavior (Hoffman, 1979).

Psychologists are also interested in the effects of nontraditional fathers—that is, those who take primary responsibility for child care—on children's gender-role development. Despite the high level of interest in the topic, however, little work to date has been conducted on this group of men because very few fathers adopt even a moderate amount of child-care responsibility. Indeed, studies of labor distribution in households in which both parents work indicate that husbands' child-rearing behavior increases very little when their wives go to work (Nielsen, 1990).

## The Influence of Peers

Another major influence on children's gender-role development is the peer group. Peer groups not only provide children with opportunities for particular kinds of play, but also offer a forum in which children can learn about social behavior and social interactions by watching models and obtaining feedback about their own behaviors. When children begin to interact with their peers, they enter an arena in which adult input is indirect and the opinions and behaviors of age mates become increasingly important. And although peers influence children in a variety of social dimensions, nowhere is their influence more marked than in the area of gender-role socialization (Carter, 1987).

**Early Play Patterns**   The influence of peers on gender-role development can be observed even among very young children. Carol Jacklin and Eleanor Maccoby (1978) observed pairs of unacquainted same-sex and mixed-sex pairs of two-year-olds to determine the influence of peers on toddlers' behavior. Children were dressed in a sex-neutral fashion (in yellow jumpsuits) and allowed to play in a room with their mothers present but nondirective. As Figure 13.6 shows, the behavior of toddlers varied as a function of the sex of their play partner even though the toddlers were unaware of the true sex of the other child. In other words, the *behaviors* of the neutrally dressed children seemed to precipitate different reactions in their play partners. In general, children displayed more social behaviors—both positive overtures and negative acts—when they played with a peer of the same sex. Girls were more likely to be passive when they played with a boy peer than when they played with a girl peer. In addition, girls in girl-girl pairs exhibited greater sharing of toys and were less likely to become upset and cry than when they were in mixed-sex pairs. Finally, boys were less likely to obey a verbal prohibition from a girl than from a

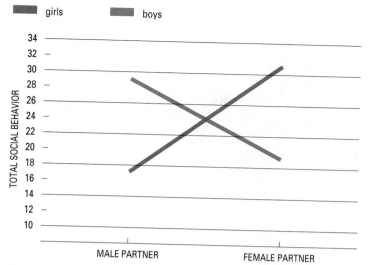

Source: Adapted from Jacklin & Maccoby, 1978.

**FIGURE 13.6**

**Social Behavior as a Function of the Child's Play Partner**

In a study by Jacklin and Maccoby, unacquainted two-year-olds were observed as they interacted with either a same-sex or opposite-sex partner. The amount of social behavior (both positive overtures and negative acts such as aggression) was greater when children played with a peer of the same sex.

boy. Already at this young age, the dynamics of peer interactions were markedly influenced by the sex of the partners.

**Peer Enforcement of Gender Roles**     Peers continue to exert a strong influence on children's adoption of sex-typical behaviors as they begin preschool. A number of studies have shown, for example, that children respond differentially to sex-typical and sex-atypical behavior in their peers. Children may reward behavior they like by complimenting a child or by engaging in mutual play, and they may punish a behavior they do not approve of by name calling. Preschoolers and kindergartners reliably punish boys who engage in sex-atypical behavior, such as playing with dolls, while rewarding them for engaging in sex-typical behavior, such as playing with trucks (Fagot, 1977; Lamb, Easterbrooks, & Holden, 1980; Lamb & Roopnarine, 1979). In contrast, girls are rewarded for engaging in sex-typical behavior, such as playing house, but apparently there are no consequences for them when they engage in sex-atypical behavior (Fagot, 1977). The differential responses of peers toward boys and girls who engage in sex-atypical behavior persist through at least the sixth grade (Carter & McCloskey, 1984).

The pressures exerted by the peer group apparently work. Children are responsive to the positive and negative feedback they receive from their peers. They are likely to continue to engage in a sex-typical behavior in response to reinforcement and to terminate behaviors that are punished by their peers (Lamb, Easterbrooks, & Holden, 1980). Furthermore, feedback from same-sex peers may be especially important. Beverly Fagot (1978a) found that both two-year-old girls and boys were more likely to continue a behavior if a same-sex peer responded positively and to discontinue a behavior if a same-sex peer responded negatively. If the peer was of the other sex, however, the peer's feedback was largely ineffective. Interestingly, data indicate at the same time that among these young children, sex-atypical play is likely to be inhibited even in the presence of a peer of the other sex (Serbin, Connor, Burchardt, & Citron, 1979).

Both boys and girls may engage in cross-gender activities. However, peers react more negatively to cross-gender behavior in boys than in girls.

▶ Individual differences

**Cross-Gender Behavior**   Children who fail to respond to their peers' disapproval of sex-atypical behavior are a fascinating group. These children exhibit **cross-gender behavior**; that is, they adopt, in whole or in part, a variety of characteristics typical of the other sex (Fagot, 1977). Cross-gender boys, for example, exhibit a strong interest in feminine games and activities and play "dress-up" in girls' clothes. Cross-gender boys are likely to become social isolates over time because their male peers refuse to interact with them even when they play in a masculine fashion, and their female peers seem merely to tolerate their presence. Cross-gender girls, in contrast, appear to suffer very little for their sex-atypical behavior. At least in the preschool years, cross-gender girls cross play groups easily, playing with boys at boy games and girls at girl games (Fagot, 1977). Thus, the consequences of cross-gender behavior are much more severe and long lasting for boys than for girls.

The tendency for children to disapprove of cross-gender behavior increases with age. When researchers interviewed kindergartners through sixth-graders to determine how these children would respond to hypothetical cases of cross-gender behavior in their peers, older children reported that they would respond more negatively to cross-gender behavior than did younger children (Carter & McCloskey, 1984). Moreover, children stated that they would respond more negatively to cross-gender behavior in their male than in their female peers. The degree of negativity exhibited by children was particularly surprising. Only one child reported that she would respond positively toward a cross-gender child, and children were virtually unanimous in their opinion that they would not want to play with a cross-gender child. Children's reports of how they would respond ranged from the fairly innocuous "I'd stay away" to reports that they would physically abuse cross-gender children.

Similar results were obtained when researchers asked preadolescents to describe the personal qualities of an actor who played a gender-inappropriate game with children of the opposite sex. If a boy actor played jumprope with a

**cross-gender behavior**   Behavior usually seen in a member of the opposite sex. Term generally is reserved for behavior that is persistently sex atypical.

group of girls, he was viewed as significantly less popular compared with female actors or a male actor playing a masculine game (Lobel et al., 1993). In another study of preadolescents attending summer day camps, researchers found that children who violated gender boundaries by associating with members of the opposite sex were rated as substantially less popular with peers (Sroufe et al., 1993). As we shall see in Chapter 15, popularity with peers is, in turn, associated with other significant developmental outcomes. Children who are unpopular often have low self-esteem, poor academic achievement, and may be prone to aggression. Thus, cross-gender behavior can be stigmatizing and potentially far-reaching in its effects.

**Sex Segregation**    The influence of peers on sex typing in children's behavior is undoubtedly enhanced as a result of the fact that boys and girls tend to interact in separate groups: starting at age three or four, boys play with boys and girls play with girls (Maccoby, 1988, 1990). This phenomenon is called **sex segregation.** In one observation of a hundred children on their preschool playgrounds, four-year-olds spent three times as much time with same-sex partners as with opposite-sex partners. By age six, they spent eleven times more time with peers of the same sex (Maccoby & Jacklin, 1987). This tendency to prefer same-sex peers is maintained at least until early adolescence (Maccoby, 1990). As a result, the range of behaviors open to children and acceptable to their peers is limited by their choice of playmates of the same sex.

Maccoby (1990) believes that children's experiences in same-sex groups foster different styles of social interaction in boys and girls. As boys play in their characteristic rough-and-tumble fashion or in team sports and games, they develop assertive, dominance-seeking styles of interaction. In contrast, girls' groups, which are oriented toward relationships and shared intimacy, promote cooperation and mutual support as well as a tendency to preserve the cohesiveness of the group. According to Maccoby, the same-sex peer group is an extremely powerful socialization environment throughout childhood.

Sex segregation begins to break down as children enter the period of adolescence and begin to think about dating. The pressures of heterosexual interactions, however, may enhance rather than diminish the push toward conformity with sex-role norms (Eccles, 1987; Petersen, 1980). This pattern is particularly obvious among teenage girls, many of whom abandon "tomboyish" behaviors that were acceptable during an earlier period of development (Huston & Alvarez, 1990).

**Adolescent Peer Influences**    Peer acceptance and rejection become increasingly important during adolescence. Although sex-typing pressures remain high, popularity among adolescents in both sexes relies more on positive personality characteristics, such as leadership abilities and politeness, rather than merely the presence of sex-typed behavior (Sigelman, Carr, & Begley, 1986). Thus, the presence of cross-gender personality characteristics or behaviors may not lead to isolation from peers among older adolescents to the extent that it does for younger children (Huston & Alvarez, 1990; Katz and Ksansnak, 1994). Adolescents' greater tolerance for sex-atypical personality characteristics may reflect their increasing cognitive abilities—specifically, their ability to consider multiple dimensions as they make judgments about individuals, including abstract qualities such as their trustworthiness or loyalty. It is also during adolescence that males and females show more attributes

▶ Interaction among domains

▶ Interaction among domains

**sex segregation**  Clustering of individuals into same-sex groups.

characteristic of both sexes as they begin to think about how gender roles affect their life decisions, such as career choice (Eccles, 1987).

### Is It Possible or Desirable to Raise Children in a Nonsexist Fashion?

We are currently witnessing a shift in thinking about gender-role socialization in our society. Experts are questioning the desirability of socializing children into differing roles on the basis of sex alone—that is, they advocate raising children in a *nonsexist* fashion (Bem, 1983; Pogrebin, 1980). Advocates of nonsexist child rearing point out that traditional sex typing encourages children to learn specific skills and roles that may be inconsistent with their interests or abilities. Sex typing, they argue, narrows the field of choices that children can make, forcing them to choose among alternatives that limit the myriad possible behaviors available to human beings.

How might parents raise their children in a nonsexist way? Sandra Bem (1983) suggests, first, that parents provide their children with information about the biological bases of gender at about the time children form their gender identities. Children should be apprised of the fact that genitals—not clothing, appearance, or behavior—determine gender. Second, parents should screen reading materials, television, and movies so that children have opportunities to view both sexes engaged in sex-typical and sex-atypical activities. Finally, Bem suggests that parents provide their children with a "sexism schema." According to Bem, just as we may teach our children to recognize that other families have social values that are different from those held in our family (with regard to religion or politics, for example), we can teach children that other people may hold beliefs about the sexes that are different from our own.

Because gender is strongly emphasized in contemporary culture, however, raising children to be nonsexist may be an arduous, if not impossible, task. Children are exposed to powerful gender-stereotypical messages in their interactions with their peers and teachers as well as from the media. Is it possible for parents to surmount such influential societal forces? Is imparting parental philosophies to the child enough?

If raising children in a nonsexist way can be successful, is it desirable? As we have just seen, many children who behave nontraditionally, especially boys who act in "feminine" ways, suffer significant negative consequences from their peers. What other societal changes must accompany shifts in parental child-rearing tactics so that children can feel comfortable about crossing gender boundaries? In particular, what can be done about the strong pressures peers and other social forces exert, especially on boys, to behave in sex-typed ways?

### The Influence of Teachers and Schools

Teachers, like peers and parents, treat children differentially according to sex, reinforce and punish sex-typed behaviors, and model sex-typical behavior for the children who study with them. Moreover, schools may foster sex typing through the teaching materials and curriculum that children are exposed to. For example, a recent survey of children's readers found that although boys and girls were portrayed with almost equal frequency, girls were more often the characters in stories in need of rescue and boys were rarely shown doing housework or displaying emotions (Purcell & Stewart, 1990).

**Teacher Attitudes and Behaviors**   Teachers, like other adults, often express stereotypical, gender-based views about the capacities of their students. They believe that female students are feminine and male students are masculine, although more experienced teachers are less likely to hold stereotyped beliefs and are more likely to treat students in an egalitarian fashion than are less experienced teachers (Fagot, 1978a; Huston, 1983). When teachers are asked to nominate their best students or those with the most potential, they are more likely to nominate boys than girls. They are especially likely to name boys as most skilled in mathematics. When teachers are asked to think of students who excel in language or social skill, they are more likely to name girls (BenTsvi-Mayer, Hertz-Lazarowitz, & Safir, 1989). These patterns in teacher responses occur despite the fact that actual sex differences in many of these domains are minimal.

In addition, teachers respond differently to students on the basis of student sex as opposed to behavior. Boys, for example, receive more disapproval from teachers than girls do during preschool and elementary school, even when boys and girls are engaged in similar amounts of disruptive behavior (Huston, 1983; Serbin et al., 1973). Teachers' behavior may reflect a belief that boys are more likely than girls to cause trouble in the classroom unless rules are strictly enforced (Huston, 1983). On the other hand, teachers pay more attention to girls when they sit quietly in the front of the classroom, whereas the amount of attention paid to boys is high regardless of where they sit (Serbin et

Research shows that boys and girls have different experiences within the typical classroom. For example, girls receive more attention from teachers when they sit quietly in front of the classroom, whereas boys typically get a high amount of attention regardless of where they sit.

al., 1973). Moreover, within elementary school classrooms, teachers tend to call on boys more often than girls and give them more explicit feedback regarding their answers. When girls answer, they are more likely to receive a simple acceptance from the teacher ("okay") whereas boys tend to receive more praise, constructive criticism, or encouragement to discover the correct answer (Sadker & Sadker, 1994). Thus, boys receive more explicit academic instruction and tend to dominate classroom interactions.

Just as teacher behavior can perpetuate stereotypes, however, it can also change sex-typing patterns among children in classroom settings. Lisa Serbin and her colleagues (Serbin, Connor, & Iler, 1979; Serbin, Tonick, & Sternglanz, 1977) have found that teachers can reduce sex segregation by using reinforcement to facilitate cooperative cross-sex play among preschoolers and kindergartners. For example, when teachers praise children who play in mixed-sex groups by pointing out their cooperative play to the class and complimenting the children, cross-sex play increases.

**Student Attitudes Toward Coursework**    Research indicates that students, teachers, and parents alike view some academic subjects as masculine and others as feminine (Huston, 1983). As we have noted earlier, mathematics is generally seen as a masculine activity and reading is seen as feminine (Eccles, 1983; Eccles et al., 1993; Huston, 1983; Yee & Eccles, 1988). This sex typing is not limited to American schoolchildren. In a study of first- through fifth-grade Taiwanese Chinese, Japanese, and American boys and girls, the investigators found that most children felt that boys were better in mathematics and girls were better at reading (Lummis & Stevenson, 1990). Moreover, boys in these three societies predicted that they would do better in mathematics in high school than girls predicted they would do, although no sex differences were found in children's predictions of their future reading skills.

Students' attitudes toward academic subjects can influence whether they will, in fact, be exposed to these subjects and acquire their specific skills. Jacquelynne Eccles asked fifth- through twelfth-graders to complete questionnaires about their perceptions of their mathematics skills, their attributions for success and failure in mathematics, the value of mathematics for them, and their plans to take mathematics courses in the future (Eccles, 1983; Yee & Eccles, 1988). In addition, she gathered scores on both classroom and standardized mathematics tests. Eccles and her colleagues collected data over a two-year period, allowing them to examine how mathematics attitudes at one point were related to later attitudes and experiences.

Although there were no sex differences in children's classroom or standardized mathematics test scores, girls perceived themselves as less competent at mathematics, were less willing to take mathematics courses in the future, and saw mathematics as less valuable than did boys. Moreover, girls and boys differed in their explanations for success and failure in mathematics. Girls explained success in terms of *external attributions,* such as luck or teacher liking, and failure in terms of *internal attributions,* such as a lack of intelligence or skill. Boys, in contrast, explained failure by external attributions ("the teacher hates me") and success by internal attributions ("I'm smart"). Children's attitudes were predictive of later enrollment in mathematics classes. Girls were more likely to drop out of mathematics courses or to take lower-level mathematics courses than were boys of the same ability levels. Moreover, girls developed higher levels of anxiety about mathematics than boys did. Clearly, children's sex-stereotyped views of courses can have an enormous impact on the direction their studies take.

**Sex Differences in Achievement Expectancies**     A variety of factors may contribute to sex differences in children's interest in academic subjects and their expectancies for academic success. One of these factors may be sex typing in the content of the curriculum. In one study a group of investigators used two computer-based mathematics tutorials differing in sex typing to assess children's skills (Cooper, Hall, & Huff, 1990). The "masculine" tutorial was a typical arcade-type game designed to teach division in a war game format in which guns fired at tanks in response to children's answers to the problems. Tanks exploded when children answered correctly; incorrect responses produced misses. The "feminine" tutorial taught division of fractions using a word-oriented, nonaggressive format. Besides measuring children's liking for the two programs, the investigators collected children's perceptions of stress and their competence on the war game program (no scores were available for the feminine tutorial). Overall, children preferred the tutorial program designed for their own sex and reported feeling less stress when working on the same-sex than the other-sex tutorial. In addition, boys' performance was superior to the performance of girls on the masculine tutorial. (No comparisons of performance were made on the feminine task.) Thus, sex typing of curricular content may affect children's preferences and performance in academic areas.

Another factor that appears to influence children's academic expectancies is the nature of evaluative feedback they receive for their academic work and nonacademic behavior. Carol Dweck and her colleagues have proposed that evaluative criticism is more likely to result in both feelings of incompetence and lowered expectations of success if it is *discriminate*—in this case, directed primarily at academic work—than if it is *indiscriminate*—that is, directed at both academic and social behavior (Dweck et al., 1978). Dweck and her colleagues found that boys received greater indiscriminate criticism from teachers (over two-thirds was for nonacademic behavior), whereas over two-thirds of the criticism girls received concerned their academic efforts. Thus, girls' lower academic expectations may reflect the fact that their academic work is more likely to be criticized. In contrast, since teachers are generally more critical of them, boys may attribute negative feedback to the attitude of teachers rather than to the quality of their intellectual performance.

Girls do, in fact, show greater self-criticism of their academic work than boys do. Karin Frey and Diane Ruble (1987) have studied instances of self- and peer criticism for academic work in classroom settings. Children between the ages of five and ten years were observed at work in academic tasks in their classrooms, and their spontaneous critical and complimentary comments about themselves and their peers were tallied. Several sex differences emerged in the nature of comments children made. Overall, both girls and boys made more self-compliments than self-criticisms, but boys showed a greater number of self-congratulatory statements relative to self-criticisms than girls did (see Figure 13.7). Boys complimented themselves and criticized their peers more than girls did, whereas girls criticized themselves and complimented their peers more than boys did. Girls also were more likely to attribute their failures to a lack of ability ("I'm so stupid") than boys were. Thus, the patterns of girls' self-criticism match the discriminate criticism they hear from their teachers.

**FIGURE 13.7**

**Self-Evaluation in Boys and Girls**

In a study of kindergartners through fourth-graders, Frey and Ruble found that both boys and girls make more self-congratulatory comments than self-critical ones, but girls show a greater proportion of self-critical comments relative to self-congratulatory comments about their classroom performance. The data here are shown as the proportion of self-congratulatory comments minus self-critical comments.

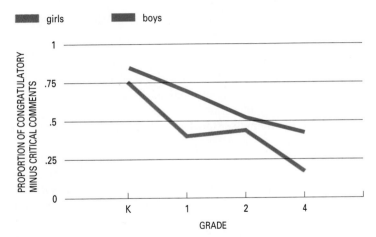

Source: Adapted from Frey & Ruble, 1987.

▶ Sociocultural influence

# Androgyny and the Relational Approach: New Conceptualizations of Gender

Changes in society's conceptions of the desirability of traditional sex typing have been reflected in changes in psychological theories. Although earlier theorists and researchers (Kohlberg, 1966; Mischel, 1966) assumed that sexatypical behavior was undesirable and perhaps indicative of psychopathology, more recent conceptions of gender-role development have taken two new directions. Rather than assuming that traditional masculine and feminine roles are the most desirable, some psychologists have suggested that blending both sets of traits may expand our abilities to respond adaptively to the demands of our environments. Others maintain that male and female development *are* different, but in ways that can be valued and embraced.

## Androgyny

Traditionally, psychologists treated masculinity and femininity as opposite ends of a bipolar dimension: the more masculine one was, the less feminine, by definition, one could be. Sandra Bem (1974, 1975) challenged this view by proposing that masculinity and femininity were not mutually exclusive, as the bipolar formulation would suggest, but rather were separate measurable dimensions of personality. Thus, a person of either sex could be assertive in situations in which that behavior was necessary and nurturant when nurturance was required. From Bem's perspective, **androgyny**, or the coexistence of both masculine and feminine characteristics, allows the individual to be maximally adaptive.

Psychological androgyny should not be confused with the ways in which androgyny is presented in the popular media. From a psychological perspective, people whose physical appearance is ambiguous, neither distinctively male nor distinctively female, are not necessarily androgynous. In Bem's formulation, *androgynous* people are those who exhibit high levels of both masculine and feminine personality characteristics. Persons who are highly masculine

**androgyny**   Gender-role orientation in which a person possesses high levels of personality characteristics associated with both sexes.

|  |  | Masculinity Score | |
|---|---|---|---|
|  |  | High | Low |
| **Femininity Score** | **High** | Androgynous | Feminine |
|  | **Low** | Masculine | Undifferentiated |

**TABLE 13.2**

**Classification of Sex Typing**

In Sandra Bem's (1974, 1975) classification scheme, persons who score high on traits associated with both masculinity and femininity are "androgynous"; those low on both dimensions are classified as "undifferentiated." "Feminine" and "masculine" individuals are those who score high on one sex-typing dimension and low on the other.

and possess fewer feminine characteristics are designated as *masculine,* whereas those who are highly feminine and possess fewer masculine characteristics are designated as *feminine.* Persons who have few masculine and feminine characteristics are classified as *undifferentiated.* Table 13.2 presents this classification scheme.

Psychological health and popularity with peers have been found to be associated with androgyny. For example, androgynous adolescents are better adjusted psychologically than are sex-typed or undifferentiated people (Ziegler, Dusek, & Carter, 1984). Similarly, androgynous adolescents are liked better by their peers and report feeling less lonely than do other groups of adolescents (Avery, 1982; Massad, 1981). Androgynous adolescents also are more likely to have resolved identity crises than are nonandrogynous adolescents (Dusek, 1987). Finally, androgynous girls are more likely to attribute success to internal factors, such as their own efforts or hard work, than to external factors, such as chance or the influences of others (Huston, 1983).

▸ Interaction among domains

How does an individual become androgynous? A variety of theories have been proposed. It has been suggested, for example, that parental characteristics such as nurturance or maternal employment are likely to lead to the development of androgyny. The data on relationships between parental characteristics and androgyny in children are sparse, however. Another possibility involves the child's growing ability to conceptualize the self and social roles in complex, abstract terms. Eccles (1987) has proposed that children cannot become androgynous before adolescence because they are still in the process of acquiring a sex role. During adolescence, however, children's abilities to conceptualize sex roles in a more abstract manner lead them to view sex-role stereotypes as descriptive statements about regularities in behavior rather than as prescriptions for acceptable behavior. Simultaneously, as adolescents strive to define their identities, they may consider factors other than gender as a means of characterizing themselves. Though androgynous role models are likely to foster gender-role transcendence, according to Eccles (1987), it is the convergence of cognitive developmental changes and the emergence of self-definition, rather than external factors such as models, that allow children to transcend traditional roles and emerge as androgynous.

▸ Interaction among domains

## The Relational Approach

Instead of emphasizing the blending of male and female traits, some theorists maintain that the development of females is unique and different from the development of males. For example, in Chapter 12, we saw how Carol Gilligan (1982) defined a "morality of care and responsibility" for females, a distinctive orientation toward relationships that characterized responses of females to moral dilemmas, in contrast to the "morality of justice" that typified male responses. Similarly, Jean Baker Miller (1976) maintains that a central feature of female development, largely ignored by mainstream developmental psychology, is the tendency to seek out and maintain relationships with others. This tendency represents a marked departure from the widely held notion that child development is, in large part, the process of becoming independent, autonomous, and self-reliant. For females, development may mean *more*, not less, connection with others. Further, instead of characterizing these tendencies of females as "dependency," a term that has negative connotations, theorists of the relational school believe they are an important source of gratification and self-fulfillment (Miller, 1991; Surrey, 1991).

This new framework opens up new interpretations of certain important developmental time periods. For example, adolescence has traditionally been seen as a phase where children desire to separate from their parents, to realize their own potentials and strike out on their own. For females, however, breaking away from parents may not be the goal. Instead, the adolescent girl may wish to change the form of her relationships, but still maintain them (Surrey, 1991). The dilemma of reconciling her inclinations toward relationship with her knowledge that the larger society expects her to "break away" may lead to intense conflicts for the adolescent female (Gilligan, Lyons, & Hanmer, 1990). Young girls who were at one time outspoken might become reluctant to speak out about their feelings; they may lose confidence in themselves and their relationships with other females may suffer (Brown & Gilligan, 1992).

Researchers taking the relational approach have begun to assess these theoretical ideas by conducting extensive interviews with girls, exploring the connections between their life circumstances and their feelings. This perspective holds promise in shedding new light on the nature of female development, and represents a signficant departure from more traditional views of gender development.

## THEMES IN DEVELOPMENT

### GENDER

▸ **What roles do nature and nurture play in gender development?**

According to some theorists, biological influences such as hormones and brain lateralization underlie sex differences in aggression and visual-spatial skill, and some experimental evidence is indeed consistent with such hypotheses. However, just as hormones, for example, can influence behavior, so too can behavior influence levels of hormones. According to social learning theorists, the child's socialization experiences with parents and peers and in school contribute substantially to observed sex differences, as does the child's knowledge of gender-role stereotypes. Children learn about gender roles very early in life, well before actual sex differences in most behaviors are observed. Research also shows that parents, peers, and teachers treat boys and girls differently, providing support for the nurture position.

▶ **How does the sociocultural context influence gender development?**

Most cultures hold stereotypical beliefs about gender roles, although the specific characteristics associated with each sex can vary. The particular behaviors exhibited by males and females can also vary according to culture. Such findings demonstrate that although the tendency to stereotype is widespread, the characteristics associated with each sex are not necessarily fixed. Changes within American society, as in the proportion of women who are employed outside the home, underscore the idea that children's gender-role development can be affected by shifting sociocultural trends.

▶ **How does the child play an active role in the process of gender development?**

The child's active role in the construction of gender-based knowledge is emphasized in cognitive-developmental theories of gender development. For example, many children construct gender schemas based on their socialization experiences, schemas that in turn influence how they process gender-related information and how they themselves behave.

▶ **Is gender development continuous or discontinuous?**

Theorists like Kohlberg describe gender development as a stagelike process. Kohlberg hypothesized that children progress through a sequence of attaining gender identity, gender stability, and gender constancy. In contrast, social learning theorists describe the cumulative and incremental effects of reinforcement and modeling on sex-role development. Research evaluating stage theories has confirmed that children pass through the sequence of gender awareness outlined by Kohlberg but has failed to validate the relationship of the entire sequence to gender-role behaviors.

▶ **How prominent are individual differences in gender development?**

Some children acquire gender identity earlier than others; these children tend to behave in more sex-typed ways and have greater knowledge of gender stereotypes than children who acquire gender identity later in life. Later in childhood, some children tend to be gender schematic; that is, they tend to organize their world along sex-divided lines. These children may even distort information to be consistent with their strong gender schemas. Finally, some children exhibit patterns of cross-gender behavior. These tendencies are usually met with negative feedback from peers, especially if the cross-gender child is a boy.

▶ **How does gender development interact with development in other domains?**

Attainments in cognition are thought to be related to many aspects of gender-role development. Bandura describes cognitive processes, such as attention, that influence which models, male or female, children will imitate. Kohlberg suggests that general cognitive advances pave the way for gender knowledge, such as gender constancy. By the same token, the child's state of gender-role development can influence cognitive processing. Gender-schematic children, for example, may show memory distortions consistent with their gender-role beliefs. Moreover, a particular classification of gender role, androgyny, is associated with psychological health and popularity with peers.

# *Summary*

**Sex Differences: Real or Imagined?**   *Gender stereotypes,* beliefs about the typical behaviors and characteristics of females and males, exist in numerous cultures. Often, identified male characteristics are *instrumental,* including traits like independence and assertiveness, whereas identified female characteristics are *expressive,* emphasizing emotionality and sociability. In actual fact, however, male and female characteristics show more similarities than differences.

In terms of quantifiable differences between the sexes, males are physically stronger but more vulnerable in infancy compared with females. Though past research showed that females had superior verbal skills and males excelled in mathematics and visual-spatial skills, recent studies suggest that verbal and mathematical skill differences, for the most part, have disappeared. In social behavior, the most consistent finding is that males are more aggressive than females, particularly during early childhood. In addition, some evidence suggests that females are more skilled than males at decoding nonverbal social-emotional messages, such as the meanings of facial expressions.

**Theories of Gender-Role Development**   Different theories of gender-role development make unique contributions to our understanding of this phenomenon. Biological theories suggest that hormones, such as *androgens,* and brain lateralization help to explain sex differences in aggression and visual-spatial skill. Social learning theories claim that reinforcement and imitation of same-sex models who behave in sex-typical ways explain many sex differences. Cognitive developmental theories stress how the child's growing awareness of and identification with her own sex—in the successive notions of *gender identity, gender stability,* and *gender constancy*—influence sex typing. Alternatively, *gender schemas,* or cognitive constructs, are thought to influence gender-role development.

**How Children's Knowledge of Gender Develops**   Children's knowledge about gender grows rapidly during early childhood. Gender identity is usually formed by age three, an accomplishment that appears to be linked to sex-typed preferences in play activities and knowledge of stereotypes. Some children also tend to rely on gender schemas more than others as they process social information, a tendency that often makes them distort perceptions about sex-atypical behavior. Children become aware of gender stereotypes for many activities and traits during the preschool years, but their ideas become more flexible as they approach adolescence.

**The Socialization of Gender Roles**   From birth onward, parents treat children differently on the basis of biological sex. Boys and girls are provided with sex-differentiated toys, and their parents tend to stress adherence to traditional gender-role norms. Fathers, in particular, appear concerned about their children's sex typing and exert an important influence on the development of sex-typed behavior in children. Parents are particularly upset when sons engage in sex-atypical behavior.

Children are perhaps the most ardent enforcers of gender-role norms. They develop a firm grasp on behaviors that are expected of their sex and enforce compliance with gender-role norms in their peers. Same-sex play and preferences for sex-typical toys and activities become the norm during the preschool and early elementary school years. These patterns of preferences persist at least through adolescence. Children who consistently behave in a cross-gender fashion are likely to become socially isolated from the rest of their peer group.

Schools also exert an important influence on the development of sex typing in children. Teachers treat children differently in the classroom, focusing more of their attention on boys than girls. Boys and girls also acquire differing expectations about their academic skills. These separate expectations can influence the child's choice of academic courses and, ultimately, of occupation.

**Androgyny and the Relational Approach: New Conceptualizations of Gender**    *Androgyny* is a gender-role orientation in which the individual possesses high levels of both feminine and masculine traits. Studies indicate that androgyny is associated with healthy psychological adjustment and may be linked to cognitive growth and the emergence of self-definition. The relational approach attempts to define the elements of female development that may be unique or different from male development. According to these theorists, females are more oriented to seeking and maintaining relationships than are males; this quality has significance for other dimensions of psychological development.

# 14

## The Family

*Seven-year-old Joey looked at his loaded dinner plate and announced, "I'm not hungry. Can I just have dessert?" "No, you may not!" his embarrassed mother replied as she turned toward her houseguest. "I can't think why he gets like this. He's stubborn as a mule." The guest wondered why no one mentioned that Joey, in full view of his mother, had eaten most of a gift box of cookies before dinner.*

*"I don't want this! It stinks! You stink!" Joey pushed away his plate, got up from the table, and ran to the television, which he turned up to full volume.*

*"Turn that down this minute or go to your room!" his mother ordered. Joey ignored her. "He's been like this since his father and I split up," she told her guest in a lowered voice. "Everything's so different now. I feel like I have to be two parents instead of one. He used to be such a good boy. Don't take that cookie!" Joey removed his hand from the cookie box and gave his mother a mournful, pleading look. "All right, but just one!" Joey took two and returned to the TV.*

This episode represents but one brief experience in Joey's life, but the accumulation of experiences such as these within the context of the family can have a distinct effect on the developing child. Families are central to the process of **socialization**, the process by which children acquire the social knowledge, behaviors, and attitudes valued by the larger society. Parents, siblings, and others within the family unit are the people with whom the child usually spends the most time and forms the strongest emotional bonds, and they thus exert the most power in the child's life.

The study of the influence of the family is no simple matter, however. For one thing, the child's experiences within the family can be affected by other factors, such as divorce or parental employment status, factors that can change the nature of interpersonal dynamics within the family. Joey's family experiences both before and after his parents' separation, for example, can have potentially long-lasting effects on his development. Moreover, the direction of influence within families runs along several paths. Just as parents and siblings affect the child's behavior, the child affects the reactions of other family members. Because the family experience includes fluid, constantly changing effects and outcomes for its various members, studying the effect of the family presents a special research challenge to developmental psychologists.

In a sense, virtually every domain of development is deeply influenced by the family environment. Cognition, moral awareness, gender identity, and emotional growth all are nurtured largely within the family. Our goal in this chapter is to focus on the role that specific family members play in the child's social development, with special attention to adaptive and maladaptive patterns of interaction. We will see also how the family itself is a structure in flux, shaped by cultural values and shifting demographic trends such as divorce and maternal employment. The effect of these changes in family structure on

**socialization** Process by which children acquire the social knowledge, skills, and attitudes valued by the larger society.

the individual child's development is a major concern for developmental psychologists.

# Understanding the Family

Historians, sociologists, and anthropologists who study the family as a social unit point to the changes in its structure and functions over the last two centuries. With the industrialization of nineteenth-century America, for example, the extended family, in which secondary relatives such as grandparents, aunts and uncles, or cousins lived in the same household as the primary family, gave way to the nuclear family, consisting solely of parents and their offspring living in a single household. Similarly, as we saw in Chapter 1, the modern notion that families are havens for nurturing the child's growth and development was not always prevalent. As we look back in history, we see that the family has been a changing social structure, and all signs indicate that it will continue to take different shapes in the future as a reflection of larger social, economic, and historical trends.

## The Demographics of the American Family

▶ Sociocultural influence

No one family structure is typical of contemporary American society. The 1950s model of a two-parent family with two children and a nonworking mother has become more myth than reality. For example, as Figure 14.1 shows, only 74 percent of children younger than eighteen years lived with two parents in 1991, compared with 85 percent in 1968. Today, over 25 percent of American children live with only a single parent (U.S. Bureau of the Census, 1992). A climbing divorce rate and the rise in single-parent births have contributed to this trend. Presently, more than 50 percent of all marriages end in divorce (compared with about 15 percent in 1960), and more than 25 percent of all births are to single women (Bumpass, 1990; U.S. Bureau of the Census,

**FIGURE 14.1**

**Demographic Changes in Family Structure**

The number of children living with two parents has declined since 1968, and the number living with a single parent (most frequently the mother) has increased dramatically. About one-fourth of American children live with a single parent. The greater rate of divorce and single-parent births has contributed to this trend.

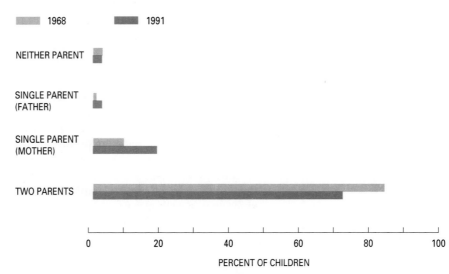

Source: Adapted from U.S. Bureau of the Census, 1978, 1992.

1992). Moreover, because adults now marry at later ages and more couples decide to have fewer children, many children today grow up with older parents and fewer siblings (Rossi, 1987). Finally, as we reported in Chapter 11, over 65 percent of married women with children younger than eighteen years work outside the home, compared with about 45 percent in 1975. In fact, fewer than 15 percent of American families consist of a working father, homemaker mother, and children. All of these changes in family structure have distinct implications for the child's experiences within the family.

## A Systems Approach

Many child development researchers have found it fruitful to focus on family dynamics, the interactions among all members of the group, rather than on the structure of the family per se, as they study the impact of the family. An important influence on contemporary thinking about the family is **systems theory**. The premise is that all members influence each other simultaneously and that the interactions flow in a circular reciprocal manner. In systems theory (see Figure 14.2), the individual child's development is understood as being embedded in the complex network of multidirectional interactions among all family members (Belsky, 1981; Bronfenbrenner, 1979, 1986).

Systems theory assumes that families undergo periods of stability and change. The family tends to adapt in order to maintain a state of *homeostasis,* or equilibrium. Thus, as children attain milestones, such as going to school or entering adolescence, the family system must readjust in order to absorb the

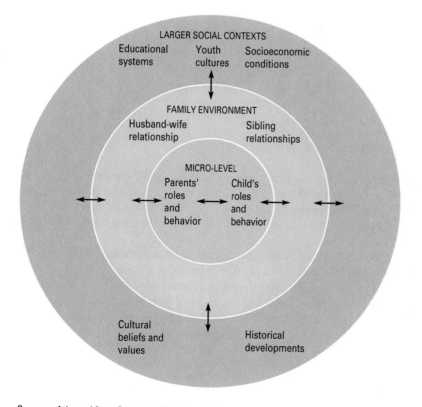

Source: Adapted from Peterson & Rollins, 1987.

**FIGURE 14.2**

**The Systems Model of the Family**

According to systems theorists, reciprocal influences among family members occur at three levels: the individual or microlevel, the family environment, and the larger social context. At the microlevel, parent and child influence each other directly. Within the family, relationships among particular individuals, such as husband and wife, can affect interactions with children. Finally, larger social factors, such as the presence of economic stress, can affect parent-child relations. The individual child's development is thus embedded in this network of multidirectional interactions.

**systems theory**   Model for understanding the family that emphasizes the reciprocal interactions among various members.

▶ The child's active role

child's new routines or demands for independence. At other times families may experience crises, such as financial hardship, moving, or divorce. Here, changing external circumstances oblige the child and all other family members to adapt to the new situation. Systems theory, then, regards families as dynamic, self-regulating social groups (Minuchin, 1988).

Families usually contain several subsystems, such as the relations maintained between spouses, among siblings, and between parent and child. A single family member is usually a member of more than one subsystem at the same time. The child has a relationship with each parent as well as with one or more siblings; mothers and fathers are spouses as well as parents. The quality of each of these separate relationships can have an impact on other relationships. Thus, for example, mothers who feel their marriages are close and confiding tend to be more sensitive and warm with their infants, and fathers who express similar feelings are more positive about their paternal role (Cox et al., 1989). Similarly, when parents have high-quality marital relationships, their relationships with their children are warmer (Miller et al., 1993). Siblings have more positive interactions with each other, too (MacKinnon, 1988). Within the systems model, family members have reciprocal influences on one another, and there are several layers of such interactions.

▶ Sociocultural influence

The family system is itself embedded in larger social networks, including the economic, political, legal, and educational forces that are part of the larger culture. Events in the workplace, school, and other extrafamilial settings can affect individual family members and hence the interactions that occur within the family unit. When one or both parents becomes unemployed, for example, the family experiences stress that often is expressed in increased conflict between parents and children (Flanagan, 1990). In other instances, both parents may work outside the home, which requires children to function independently, cooking their own meals or performing other household tasks. The *social ecology* of child development—that is, the impact of broad sociocultural factors on the child's social, cognitive, and emotional growth—has been given increasing emphasis by developmental psychologists.

## *Parents and Socialization*

In most cultures, the primary agents of the child's socialization are parents. Teachers, peers, and the media—as we will see in the next two chapters—also play a significant role, but perhaps no other individuals in the child's life have the power or influence of parents on future behaviors, attitudes, and personality.

Parents affect the child's socialization in three primary ways. First, they socialize their children through direct training, providing information or reinforcement for the behaviors they find acceptable or desirable. Parents may, for example, encourage their children to share with playmates or instruct them on how to become acquainted with an unfamiliar peer. Second, as they interact with their children, parents serve as important models for the child's attitudes, beliefs, and actions. For example, parents who are warm, engaging, and verbally stimulating tend to have children who are popular in school. Finally, parents manage other aspects of the child's life that in turn can influence their social development. Parents choose the neighborhood in which the family lives; they also may enroll children in sports programs, arrange birthday parties, and invite children's friends to spend the night, all of which influence children's peer networks (Parke et al., 1988).

Of course, parents' major concerns and activities shift as the child develops. Parents of infants focus on caregiving activities and helping the child to learn such skills as self-feeding, dressing, and toileting. By the time their child is two years old, parents begin more deliberate attempts at socialization. Parents of preschoolers help their children to regulate their emotions—to control angry outbursts, for example—and start to instill social skills, such as polite forms of speech and sharing during play with peers. Parents of elementary school children are likely to be concerned with their children's academic achievement. When their children approach adolescence, most parents encourage independent, rational, and value-based decision making as their youngsters prepare to enter their own adult lives.

Parental roles also shift with development. Throughout early childhood, parents closely monitor much of their child's activity. Once the child enters school, parents play less of a supervisory role. They begin to expect their children to be cooperative members of the family by avoiding conflicts and sharing in household tasks. Parents and children begin to negotiate as they make decisions and solve family problems. Finally, during adolescence, parents observe the child's participation in the larger social world, in school and community activities and close personal relationships with peers. While parents are encouraging independence in some domains such as school achievement, they may also be exerting more control in other domains, such as their children's social activities (Maccoby, 1984b; Maccoby & Martin, 1983; McNally, Eisenberg, & Harris, 1991).

As this quick sketch suggests, the child's own development often precipitates shifts in parental roles. As the child's language and cognitive skills mature, parents place greater expectations on her social communication behaviors. As she enters school, parents nurture greater independence. The physical changes associated with puberty often signal to parents that more mature child-adult interactions, such as deferring at times to the child's wishes rather than rigidly restricting his activities, are warranted (Steinberg, 1981). As systems theory suggests, the individual child's development within the family represents an ongoing give-and-take between child and parent, obliging continual readjustment by all members to reinstate family equilibrium.

▶ The child's active role

▶ Interaction among domains

## Styles of Parenting

Even the casual observer of parents interacting with their children in public places such as parks, shopping malls, and supermarkets will notice markedly different styles of parental behavior. Some parents are extremely controlling, using crisp, firm commands void of explanations to restrict their children's behavior. Others seem not to notice as their charges create chaos and pandemonium. Researchers have established that the pattern of interactions a parent adopts is an important variable in influencing the child's later development.

In a landmark series of observational studies, Diana Baumrind (1971, 1973) recorded the interpersonal and behavioral styles of nursery school children as they engaged in normal school activities. She also watched as they worked on a series of standardized problem-solving tasks, such as completing a set of puzzles. In addition, Baumrind gathered information on parenting styles by observing how mothers interacted with their children in both play and structured teaching settings, watching parents and their children in the home, and

Research has shown that parents who expect mature behavior from their children, provide explanations for their requests, and are supportive and warm in their interactions have children who display instrumental competence.

interviewing parents about their child-rearing practices. The children and parents were observed again when children were eight or nine years old. Based on these extensive observations, Baumrind identified several distinct patterns of parenting.

Some parents, Baumrind found, were extremely restrictive and controlling. They valued respect for authority and strict obedience to their commands and relied on coercive techniques, such as threats or physical punishment, rather than reasoning or explanation, to regulate their children's actions. They were also less nurturant toward their children than other parents in the study. Baumrind identified these as **authoritarian parents**. The second parenting style belonged to the group she called **permissive parents**. These parents set few limits and made few demands for mature behavior from their children. Children were permitted to make their own decisions about many routine activities such as TV viewing, bedtime, and mealtime, for example. Permissive parents tended to be either moderately nurturant or cool and uninvolved. The third group of parents was high on both control and nurturance. These **authoritative parents** expected their children to behave in a mature fashion but tended to use rewards more than punishments to achieve their ends. They communicated their expectations clearly and provided explanations to help their children understand the reasons for their requests. They also listened to what their children had to say and encouraged a dialogue with them. Authoritative parents were distinctly supportive and warm in their interactions with their children. Figure 14.3 summarizes the characteristics of these three parental styles as well as a fourth style, *uninvolved* parents, which has been described in later research.

Baumrind found a cluster of behavioral characteristics in children linked with each parental style. The offspring of authoritative parents were friendly with peers, cooperative with adults, independent, energetic, and achievement oriented. They also displayed a high degree of self-control. This set of characteristics often is termed **instrumental competence**. In marked contrast, children of authoritarian and permissive parents did not exhibit the social

**authoritarian parent** Parent who relies on coercive techniques to discipline the child and who displays a low level of nurturance.

**permissive parent** Parent who sets few limits on the child's behavior.

**authoritative parent** Parent who sets limits on a child's behavior by using the technique of induction and who displays a high degree of nurturance.

**instrumental competence** Child's display of independence, self-control, achievement orientation, and cooperation.

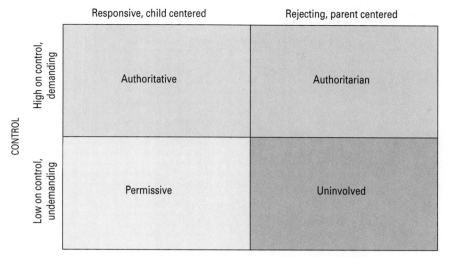

NURTURANCE

**FIGURE 14.3**

**Patterns of Parenting as a Function of Control and Nurturance**

Four parenting styles can be identified in terms of the extent to which parents set limits on the child's behavior (control) and the level of nurturance and responseness they provide.

Source: Adapted from Maccoby & Martin, 1983.

responsibility and independence associated with instrumental competence. Children who had authoritarian parents appeared unhappy, and boys tended to be aggressive, whereas girls were likely to be dependent. Children of permissive parents, on the other hand, were low on self-control and self-reliance.

The effects of parenting style extend to other dimensions of child development and reach into the adolescent years. Authoritarian parenting, especially with its use of coercive techniques for controlling behavior, is associated with less advanced moral reasoning (Hoffman, 1970; Boyes & Allen, 1993), lower self-esteem (Loeb, Horst, & Horton, 1980), and poorer adjustment to starting school (Barth, 1989). Extremely controlling and negative parenting also is associated with higher levels of aggression in children (Maccoby & Martin, 1983), poor peer relations (Putallaz, 1987), and lower school achievement in adolescence (Dornbusch et al., 1987). In contrast, by the time children reach adolescence, those with authoritative parents show more prosocial behaviors, fewer problem behaviors such as substance abuse, greater academic achievement, and higher self-confidence than adolescents whose parents use other parenting styles (Baumrind, 1991; Lamborn et al., 1991).

▶ Interaction among domains

Researchers have also identified a fourth parenting style—the **uninvolved parent** (Maccoby & Martin, 1983). Like some in Baumrind's permissive group, these parents seem uncommitted to their parental role and emotionally detached from their children. Often these parents give greater priority to their own needs and preferences than the child's. These parents may be uninterested in events at the child's school, unfamiliar with his playmates, and have only infrequent conversations with him (Pulkkinen, 1982). Uninvolved parenting is related to children's lower self-esteem (Loeb, Horst, & Horton, 1980), heightened aggression (Hatfield, Ferguson, & Alpert, 1967), and lower control over impulsive behavior (Block, 1971).

The most desirable developmental outcomes are associated with authoritative parenting, which has two key characteristics—setting limits on the child's

**uninvolved parent** Parent who is emotionally detached from the child and focuses on his or her own needs as opposed to the child's.

Middle class parents tend to use commands and self-oriented induction with their adolescent children. The first technique is used when parents want to have an immediate impact and the second when they are concerned with long-term goals.

behavior and responding to the child's needs and actions with warmth and nurturance. These themes echo the discussion of sensitive parenting and attachment presented in Chapter 11. Why does authoritative parenting work so well? There may be several explanations. First, when parents make demands for mature behavior from their children, they make explicit the responsibilities that individuals have toward one another when they live in social groups. When parents set forth clear, consistent guidelines for behavior, they make the child's job of sorting out the social world much easier. Second, when parental demands are accompanied by a reasonable explanation, children are more likely to accept the limitations on their actions. Third, when parents take into account the child's responses and show affection, children are likely to acquire a sense of control over their actions and derive the sense that they have worth. One study confirms, for example, that adolescents who have authoritative parents have a healthy sense of autonomy and self-reliance and feel a sense of control over their lives (Steinberg, Elmen, & Mounts, 1989). Thus, the net outcome of authoritative parenting is a competent child who shows successful psychological adjustment.

## Strategies of Parental Control

Parents set limits on their children's behavior for a variety of reasons, ranging from protecting their safety to controlling socially unacceptable behaviors such as temper tantrums and aggression against others. What specific techniques do parents use to regulate their children's actions? In Chapter 12, we examined two disciplinary techniques, induction and power assertion. *Induction,* which includes the extensive use of reasoning, explanation, and communication of clear standards of behavior, is the method that characterizes authoritative parenting. *Power assertion,* a directive style that includes physical punishment, forceful commands, and the removal of material objects and privileges, is the disciplinary approach of authoritarian parents. Still a third technique is *love withdrawal,* in which a parent reacts to the child's behavior by ignoring her, reacting coldly, or otherwise implying that affection will not be restored until the child obeys.

▶ The child's active role

We have already seen that induction is related to the most desirable child behaviors, whereas power assertion is associated with greater aggression, lower moral reasoning, and other negative outcomes in children. Love withdrawal presents its own problems. Although children are likely to comply with parental requests when love withdrawal is used as a disciplinary strategy, they may also avoid the parent as a consequence (Chapman & Zahn-Waxler, 1981, as cited in Maccoby & Martin, 1983). Because of such potential negative side effects, most child-rearing experts do not recommend the use of this strategy.

**How and When Do Parents Discipline?**    As their children progress from ages one to three, mothers decrease their reliance on physical means of control, such as pulling the child away from a forbidden object (for example, a stove) or forcibly holding his hand, and more frequently use verbal commands, reprimands, and persuasion. These changes in maternal control parallel children's expressions of noncompliance. Initially, children display passive or defiant behaviors, such as whining and temper tantrums, to protest parental control. Older preschoolers attempt to negotiate with parents ("I'll do it later, OK?" or "I have a better idea!"). Some researchers believe that the parental shift to discipline based on reasoning is derived from the child's active bargaining and parents' recognition of the child's growing autonomy (Kuczynski, et al., 1987). It is also interesting to note that even among two-year-olds, compliance on the part of the child is associated with maternal use of persuasion and suggestion, whereas defiance is associated with maternal use of power assertion (Crockenberg & Litman, 1990). Perhaps as their own experience in child rearing grows, parents come to recognize that control techniques based on reasoning often get the best results.

▶ The child's active role

A survey of middle-class mothers and fathers of seventh- and ninth-graders yielded information on parenting strategies with older children (Smith, 1988). Parents were asked to recall any efforts to influence their children in the past year in such areas as choosing subjects in school, the amount of time spent doing homework, choice of peer associates, and several other common situations in which parents and children often disagree. The two most prevalent techniques upon which parents relied were commands—that is, making imperative statements without threats ("Go clean your room, please!")—and self-oriented induction. *Self-oriented induction* consists of parental suggestions about the costs and rewards to the child of his behavior ("Spending more time on your homework will boost your grades"). When parents were concerned with producing an immediate result, as when household chores were to be done or when a curfew was being set, they issued commands. When long-term consequences of the child's actions were involved, as in decisions relating to school, parents opted for self-oriented induction. Thus, at least for this middle-class sample of parents and children living in intact families, many parents usually relied on their legitimate power and on reasoning, rather than on physical coercion or threats, to direct their children's behavior.

How often do parents exercise their authority over children? Obviously, the extent of parental control varies as a function of the age of the child, parental child-rearing philosophy, and the specific behaviors displayed by the child. Observations of family interactions in the home, however, tell us that mothers of preschool children issue commands or disapprove of their behaviors about once every three to four minutes and that these children disobey about 25 percent of the time (Wahler & Dumas, 1989). As children grow older and become more attuned to parental expectations and are more capable of regulating their own behaviors, the need for parental control diminishes or changes.

**Punishment**   In recent decades, the most widely discussed parental control technique has been *punishment,* the administration of an aversive stimulus or withdrawal of rewards to decrease the frequency of undesirable behaviors. Punishment, a form of power assertion, can include spanking, sharp verbal threats, or the loss of such privileges as TV viewing time or playtime with friends. Laboratory studies carried out in the tradition of learning theory show that certain ways of administering punishment are more effective than others.

Ross Parke (1969) studied how several variables influence the effectiveness of punishment in the forbidden-toy experiment originally described in Chapter 12. In the initial phase of the experiment, first- and second-grade boys were presented with pairs of toys, one attractive and one less so. Whenever the child touched the attractive toy, he was punished by the sound of an irritating buzzer. One variable was the timing of the punishment. The punishment for some children occurred before they touched the attractive toy, whereas the punishment for others was delivered after they had already held the toy for a few seconds. Another variable was the degree of punishment—the intensity of the buzzer was either high (96 decibels) or low (65 decibels). A third variable was the amount of "cognitive structure," or explanation, provided for not touching the toy. Some children were simply told not to touch the toy or a buzzer would sound. Others were given an elaborate explanation, that some toys should not be touched because they break or wear out. The prohibition, along with its justification and the consequences of misconduct, was stated clearly. The last variable was the amount of nurturance displayed by the experimenter; the experimenter played with some of the children and gave them lots of approval before the experiment but did nothing extra with others.

Following the initial phase, an observer looked through a one-way mirror while the child was left alone with the prohibited toys. Figure 14.4 summarizes the results. Overall, children who had received the early punishment, the louder buzzer, and greater cognitive structure in the initial phase were less likely to touch the taboo items than children who had experienced late punishment, a less intense punishment, or less cognitive structure. The experimenter's nurturance was less important, although other studies have demonstrated that nurturant adults are more effective at inhibiting children's misbehaviors than are nonnurturant adults (Parke & Walters, 1967). The most powerful factor influencing the children's behavior, in fact, proved to be providing an explanation. As the test period progressed, children in the group given low-cognitive structure began to touch the attractive toys, suggesting that the effects of punishment were wearing off. Children in the group given high-cognitive structure, however, continued to resist touching. Thus, the re-

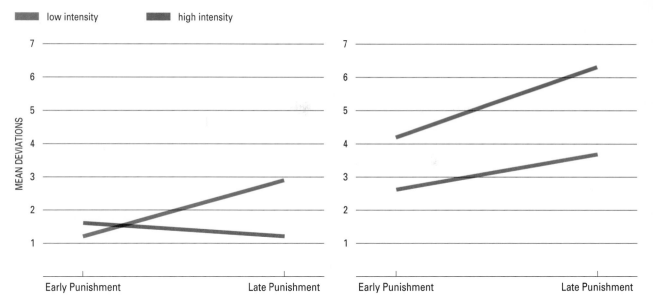

Source: Adapted from Parke, 1969.

sults of this study imply that reasoning, or induction, is a more effective technique than punishment for controlling children's behavior.

The effectiveness of punishment also depends on the consistency with which it is applied. As we saw in the case of Joey and the cookies at the beginning of the chapter, children become particularly disobedient and aggressive when parents prohibit a behavior on one occasion and permit it on another. In one study, parents of delinquent boys displayed more inconsistent disciplinary practices than parents of nondelinquent boys (Gleuck & Gleuck, 1950). Consistency among caregivers (**interagent consistency**), as well as the consistency of one caregiver from one occasion to the next (**intra-agent consistency**), are both important factors in giving children clear, unambiguous messages about acceptable and unacceptable behaviors (Deur & Parke, 1970; Sawin & Parke, 1979).

Although punishment can inhibit a child's misbehavior, many psychologists believe that physical tactics such as spanking or hitting, should not be used at all. In a 1985 survey of three thousand parents, Murray Straus and Richard Gelles found that 90 percent of parents of three- and four-year-olds reported striking their children in the previous year, as did 75 percent of parents of nine- and ten-year-olds. Infants and adolescents were spanked less often (Straus & Gelles, 1986). Thus, in the United States many parents resort to physical punishment, at least on occasion, as a way to control their children's behavior. Most Americans, according to survey data, believe that it is morally correct to hit a child who misbehaves (Straus, Gelles, & Steinmetz, 1980).

Physical punishment does modify the child's behavior in the short run, but its use is also associated with many negative outcomes. The most serious is aggression, especially among boys (Martin, 1975; Rollins & Thomas, 1979; Weiss et al., 1992). For example, Dan Olweus (1980) found that aggression in a sample of adolescent Swedish boys was related to maternal reports of having been hostile and rejecting during their son's childhood. In addition, parents

**FIGURE 14.4**

**Variables That Influence the Effectiveness of Punishment**

In a complex experiment designed to assess the effects of several aspects of punishment on children's subsequent behavior, Parke found that, in general, children deviated less if (1) punishment was administered early, (2) a high-intensity punishment was used (a loud buzzer), and (3) children were provided with cognitive structure or explanation of why they were being punished. As these graphs show, deviations tended to remain low in the high–cognitive structure condition. When cognitive structure was low, however, the effects of intensity and timing were more pronounced.

**interagent consistency** Consistency in application of disciplinary strategies among different caregivers.

**intra-agent consistency** Consistency in a single caregiver's application of discipline from one situation to the next.

who reported using physical punishment, threats, and violent outbursts had more aggressive sons than those who did not use such techniques. Many experts believe that parents who use punishment serve as models of aggression for their children (Parke & Slaby, 1983). Children may learn that hitting, kicking, or pinching are acceptable methods for resolving conflicts. For example, physically abused toddlers are twice as likely as nonabused toddlers to direct physical assaults at peers in their day-care centers (George & Main, 1979). Moreover, especially when children do not receive much attention from their parents, the spotlight placed on them when they are being punished actually may be a positive reinforcement. As a consequence, children maintain the behavior parents were trying to eliminate.

Another undesirable outcome is that children who are punished frequently eventually avoid the punishing agents (Redd, Morris, & Martin, 1975). Parents are likely to be more effective as socializing agents if their children maintain good relations with them than if the children become physically and emotionally removed.

Finally, under some circumstances, an overreliance on physical punishment can set the stage for child abuse. Parental acts of abuse often start out as attempts to discipline the child, and abusive parents rely more on power assertion, including physical punishment, than do nonabusive parents (Oldershaw, Walters, & Hall, 1986; Parke & Collmer, 1975). Among abusive families, a light slap can escalate more quickly into a physical assault on the child than it would in nonabusive families.

**Time-Out**  A reasonable alternative to physical punishment is called **time-out** from reinforcement, a technique derived from the laboratories of behavior analysts. The principle that underlies time-out is simple. When the child transgresses, she is removed from all possible sources of reward, even subtle or accidental ones. That is, she is taken immediately to a quiet, neutral place and remains alone until the undesired behavior ceases or a short period of time, usually two to five minutes, has elapsed. Parents or teachers can set up a "time-out chair" in a remote area of the home or school where no distractions are likely to occur. At the conclusion of the time-out period, the child is permitted to return to routine activities (Varni, 1983).

A study by Robert McMahon and Rex Forehand (1978) illustrates how parents can control inappropriate mealtime behaviors in their preschool-aged children by using time-out. Whenever the child exhibited behaviors such as throwing food, screaming, or leaving the table before the end of the meal, mothers were instructed to follow a particular sequence of responding. First, the mother issued a command to stop the behavior. If the child did not comply, time-out began; the child was taken to another room for two minutes, left alone, and then returned to the table. At the same time, mothers were told to praise their child often for appropriate mealtime behaviors. Figure 14.5 shows the percentage of inappropriate behaviors displayed by a five-year-old boy in the study during baseline (the period before treatment), treatment, and follow-up sessions six weeks later. As the graph shows, the child's problem behaviors decreased markedly within just two treatment sessions.

Time-out has been found effective in reducing or eliminating a variety of troublesome behaviors in children, including temper tantrums, fighting, and self-injurious behaviors (Varni, 1983). Time-out also gives both children and parents the opportunity to "cool down" after all parties have become aroused. Even well-meaning parents may find their emotions rising when the child per-

**time-out**  Disciplinary strategy in which a child is removed from all possible sources of reinforcement, both positive and negative, after committing a transgression.

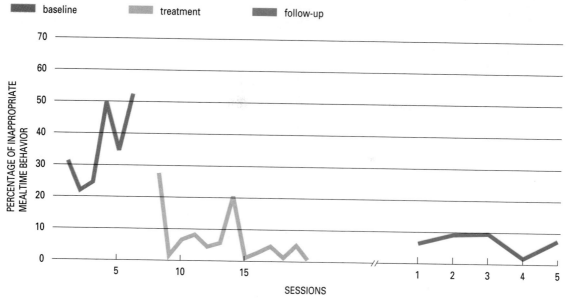

Source: Adapted from McMahon & Forehand, 1978.

sists in misbehaving. By allowing tempers to dissipate, parents who use time-out are more likely to fall back on adaptive strategies when management of the child's behaviors is required. Table 14.1 summarizes some general principles for effective use of time-out.

**The Role of Attributions**     *Attribution theory* suggests that an individual's behavior depends on the inferences he makes about other people's actions—why they behave as they do, what traits they possess, and so on. Theodore Dix and Joan Grusec (1985) hypothesize that the kinds of attributions parents make about their children, particularly the causes of their children's behaviors, will influence the parenting strategies they adopt. If, for example, a parent believes that a three-year-old is throwing a tantrum at the supper table because she wants her dessert immediately, the parent will probably insist that she first eat all her vegetables. If, on the other hand, the parent suspects the child is ill, the parent would probably remove the child from the supper table and nurture and console her.

**FIGURE 14.5**

**Time-Out as a Parental Control Technique**

Time-out can be an effective means of reducing a child's undesirable behaviors. Bill, the five-year-old child whose behavior is diagrammed here, was sent to time-out every time he acted inappropriately at mealtime. His mother also praised him frequently for desirable behaviors. The graph shows that Bill's inappropriate behaviors decreased dramatically compared with the baseline period, and they remained low in frequency during the follow-up phase six weeks later.

- Remove events that reinforce the undesired behavior, such as parental attention.
- Be consistent in applying time-out whenever the undesired behavior occurs.
- Keep the time-out period relatively brief, usually only a few minutes.
- Clearly communicate the conditions leading to time-out.
- Provide the child with an alternative desirable behavior to replace the undesired one.

**TABLE 14.1**

**Elements of the Effective Use of Time-Out**

Source: Sulzer-Azaroff & Mayer, 1977.

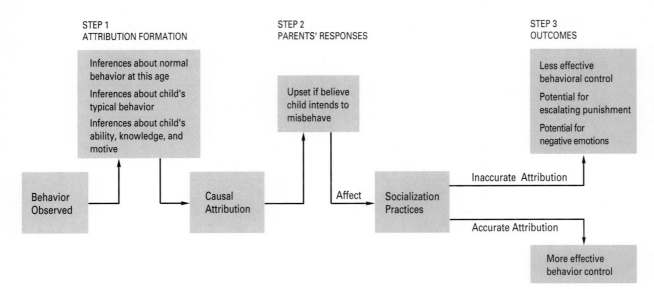

STEP 1
ATTRIBUTION FORMATION

STEP 2
PARENTS' RESPONSES

STEP 3
OUTCOMES

Inferences about normal behavior at this age

Inferences about child's typical behavior

Inferences about child's ability, knowledge, and motive

Upset if believe child intends to misbehave

Less effective behavioral control

Potential for escalating punishment

Potential for negative emotions

Behavior Observed

Causal Attribution

Affect

Socialization Practices

Inaccurate Attribution

Accurate Attribution

More effective behavior control

## FIGURE 14.6

Source: Adapted from Dix & Grusec, 1985.

### The Attribution Model of Socialization

Dix and Grusec hypothesize that parents' judgments about the child's intentionality in misbehaving are critical in determining their response. Parents become more upset if they believe the child intended to transgress and select more forceful control strategies than they do if they believe the transgression was unintentional. If their attributions are correct, they will be effective in controlling behavior. If they make the wrong attribution, however, they will be less effective, may escalate the level of punishment, and may produce negative emotions in themselves and the child.

Figure 14.6 presents a schematic diagram of Dix and Grusec's (1985) attribution model of socialization. The flow of events proceeds as follows. First, the parent observes the child's behavior and judges whether it is typical for the child or normative for her age group. The parent assesses whether the child has the skills, knowledge, and motive to behave intentionally in a certain way. Do most three-year-olds have tantrums to get dessert? Is throwing a tantrum a typical behavior for that child? Parents make a causal attribution about the child's intentions. Next, parents' attributions affect their emotional and behavioral responses to the child. Parents become more upset and act more forcefully if they believe the child intends to misbehave—in this case, screaming for the explicit purpose of obtaining dessert. Finally, if parents have made the correct attribution, they will be effective in controlling the child. But if they are wrong, the child may continue to misbehave, and both parents and child may feel negative emotions rising.

To examine the influence of attributions, Dix and his colleagues asked mothers and fathers of four-, eight-, and twelve-year-olds to react to several vignettes of child misconduct. In one story, for example, the actor fails to obey his mother's request to clean up the living room, an explicit violation of a norm. In another, the central character fails to act altruistically and eats candy, while a boy without money to buy a snack looks on. All characters were represented as the same age and sex as the parent's own child. The results showed that parents of older children (who also heard stories about older children) made more attributions of the child's intentionality than parents of younger children (Dix et al., 1986).

In a second similar study, parents were more upset when they believed a child's transgressions were intentional or controllable. Furthermore, the more upset they were, the more they thought it important to respond forcefully to the child's actions (Dix, Ruble, & Zambarano, 1989). Thus, parents believe there are age differences in children's ability to control their behaviors, and they choose different parenting behaviors as a function of those beliefs.

**Children's Influence on Parenting Strategies**    The attribution model described here suggests that a child's behaviors may set in motion a series of parental judgments about the child's intentions and how the parent should respond. Another perspective on how the child influences the parent's choice of control strategies is provided by Richard Bell (1971; Bell & Harper, 1977). In his **control theory**, Bell suggests that parents and children have upper and lower limits of tolerance for the types of behavior each shows the other. When the behavior of one approaches the other's upper limit, the recipient tries to reduce the excessive behavior with increasing levels of intensity. Thus, for example, a parent whose son is having a temper tantrum might first try to talk to him, then remove him to his room, and finally resort to physical punishment. Likewise, if the child's behavior approaches the parent's lower limits—in the child's shyness or withdrawal at the doctor's office, for example—the parent may try to stimulate the child by coaching her to speak and then promising her a reward if she vocalizes.

Control theory implies that when children's misbehavior pushes parents to their "upper limits," parents will respond with more forceful and firmer control techniques. Furthermore, some children may transgress to this extent more frequently than others. Support for this idea comes from a study of six- to eleven-year-old boys, sixteen normal and sixteen classified as conduct disordered because of their persistent aggression, fire setting, truancy, or temper tantrums. Mothers of conduct-disordered children were observed as they interacted with their own child, another conduct-disordered child, and a normal child. Similarly, mothers of normal children interacted with their own child, another normal child, and a conduct-disordered child. Mothers were unaware of the classification of children who were not their own. The researchers coded the frequency of the mothers' positive and negative behaviors as well as the number of requests they made for a change in the child's behavior. Both groups of mothers made more negative responses and requests to the conduct-disordered children than to the normal children. Thus, it was the type of child, and not the type of mother, that determined the tone of the interaction (Anderson, Lytton, & Romney, 1986). It very well could be that children who evidence a persistent behavioral style of pushing parents to their "upper limits" precipitate a pattern of authoritarian, power-assertive parenting.

## Problems in Parenting

In some instances, such extreme maladaptive styles of interaction develop between parent and child that physical and psychological harm can occur to both. Understanding the dynamics of these families is essential to any attempt at intervention and also provides an even greater understanding of how all families, healthy and dysfunctional, work as systems.

**The Coercive Cycle: Skills Deficits in Parenting**    In some families, maladaptive patterns of interaction escalate to the point at which children become extremely aggressive and antisocial. Gerald Patterson (1976, 1982, 1986) has conducted extensive longitudinal studies of boys who exhibit pathological aggression and concludes that their behavior was learned from routine family interactions in which both parents and children engaged in coercive behavior.

In Patterson's studies, preadolescent boys labeled as highly aggressive by schools, courts, or the families themselves were compared with nonaggressive boys from normal families during a period of several months. Detailed observations were made of family interactions in the home, including the sequences

▶ The child's active role

control theory   Hypothesis about parent-child interactions that suggests that the intensity of one partner's behavior affects the intensity of the other's response.

of behaviors displayed by parents, the target children, and their siblings. Patterson learned that the families of antisocial boys were characterized by high levels of aggressive interaction that rewarded coercive behaviors. When they were younger, the antisocial boys performed minor negative behaviors, such as whining, teasing, or yelling, in response to the aggression of another family member. About 70 percent of these behaviors were reinforced by the acquiescence of the child's interaction partner; in other words, the parent or sibling backed down and the submission negatively reinforced the child's aggression. At other times, parental attention to the child's aggression was positively reinforcing. In addition, although parents were observed to nag, scold, or threaten their children, as Joey's mother in the chapter opening, they seldom followed through on their threats. Such sequences between the target child and other family members occurred as often as hundreds of times each day in the aggressive families. Over time, the target boys' aggression escalated in frequency and progressed to physical assaults.

At this point, many parents attempted to control their sons' aggressive behaviors, but in doing so the parents also became highly aggressive. The coercive chains increased in duration to form long bursts of negative interactions and often resulted in hitting between parent and child. Figure 14.7 illustrates how the **coercive cycle** of reciprocal aggression between parent and child operates. After extended experience in these maladaptive familial exchanges, boys became out of control and acted violently in settings outside the home, such as the school. Aggression in school was related in turn to poor peer relations and academic failure, adding to the chain of negative events in the boys' lives.

▶ Interaction among domains

Can such extreme patterns of aggression be controlled? Patterson and his colleagues have intervened in the maladaptive interactions of aggressive families by training parents in basic child management skills (Patterson et al., 1975). They focused on teaching parents to use discipline more effectively by dispensing more positive reinforcements for prosocial behaviors, using reasoning, disciplining consistently, and setting clear limits on even minor acts of aggression. Children significantly decreased their rates of deviant behavior after only a few weeks, and the results were maintained for as long as twelve months after the initial training period (Patterson & Fleischman, 1979). As an added benefit, parents' perceptions of their children became more positive (Patterson & Reid, 1973).

**Attentional Deficits and Problems in Parenting**     Another model of dysfunctional parenting has been proposed by Robert Wahler and Jean Dumas (1984, 1989). Instead of assuming that parents in dysfunctional families use poor child management strategies, these researchers suggest that troubled families experience stresses from the larger social system that make parents inattentive to the dynamics of child care. For example, a mother who is concerned about marital or financial problems will be hard pressed to attend closely to her child's behavior or to the effects on the child of her own parenting behaviors. In an evaluation of the long-term effect of a skills-based parent training program, Dumas and Wahler (1983) found that the program's success or failure was tied closely to measures of socioeconomic status and social isolation. Parents who were removed from contacts outside the family and who were subject to the greatest financial strain were least likely to succeed with the training program.

▶ Sociocultural influence

**coercive cycle**     Pattern of reciprocal aggression between parent and child.

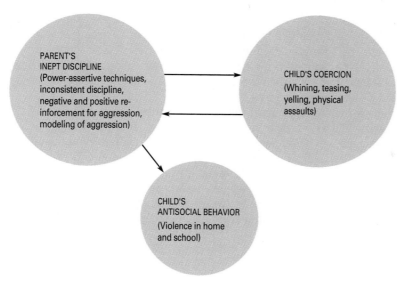

Source: Adapted from Patterson, 1986.

**FIGURE 14.7**

**The Coercive Cycle**

A coercive cycle of behavior often develops between parents and their antisocial boys. Initially, the boy may exhibit mildly negative behaviors that the parent reacts to first by scolding or nagging but eventually by backing down. With these responses, the parent negatively reinforces the child's aggression, acts as an aggressive role model, and is inconsistent. At other times, parental attention positively reinforces the child's aggression. As a consequence, the boy's aggression escalates, further heightening the parent's aggression. The result is a cluster of antisocial behaviors displayed by children at home and school.

According to the attentional deficit model, parents may know about good parenting practices or may learn them readily, but they often do not apply them. Because they are distracted by other family problems, such parents typically overlook the child's positive behaviors or make hasty judgments that their children are misbehaving. Stressed parents also develop a limited repertoire of responses to their children. Instead of experimenting with various child management techniques to determine the most effective one, they fall back on stereotypical, repetitive methods that are often coercive. Parental depression may add to the problem. Several researchers have found that depressed mothers are especially likely to mislabel their child's behavior (Brody & Forehand, 1986; Greist, Wells, & Forehand, 1979).

Wahler and Dumas (1989) believe that any long-term parent intervention program should include the following elements: (1) training parents to modify their habits so they focus on the child's prosocial as well as aversive behaviors; (2) providing parents with coping strategies for external stressors, such as loss of employment or financial hardship; and (3) offering social support networks so that parents can receive assistance with the day-to-day problems of living. In other words, by providing parents with ways to cope with external stress, clinicians and counselors can help them refocus on more positive ways to interact with their children.

**Child Abuse**    About 3 million children were reported abused or neglected in the United States in 1992 (Children's Defense Fund, 1994). In fact, these statistics may represent an underestimate, because many cases of abuse are not reported (Emery, 1989). Aside from the immediate physical and psychological consequences of abuse, children who are the victims of family violence are predisposed to a number of developmental problems. Maltreated infants and toddlers are more likely to be anxiously attached to their mothers than are children who are not maltreated (Egeland & Sroufe, 1981a; Schneider-Rosen et al., 1985). These children are thus vulnerable to the social, emotional, and cognitive impairments associated with insecure attachment. Preschool and

▶ Interaction among domains

school-aged children with a history of abuse score lower on tests of cognitive maturity and manifest low self-esteem and school learning problems (Aber & Allen, 1987; Barahal, Waterman, & Martin, 1981; Eckenrode, Laird, & Doris, 1993; Hoffman-Plotkin & Twentyman, 1984). Emotionally, they may display withdrawal and passivity or, on the other hand, aggressive, oppositional patterns of behavior, patterns that may be linked to their generally poor relationships with peers (Martin & Beezley, 1976; Salzinger et al., 1993). They also frequently display symptoms of clinical depression (Sternberg et al., 1993). Finally, abused and neglected children are at risk for delinquency and violent criminal behavior in adulthood (Widom, 1989) and may be prone to become abusive parents. In one study, women who had been abused as children were followed for a period of three years. Seventy percent were observed to maltreat their children or provide borderline care. Among women who were not abused, only one did not provide adequate care (Egeland, Jacobvitz, & Papatola, 1987).

The causes of abuse are neither simple nor easily ameliorated. Research on the interaction patterns in abusive families suggests that they differ in several respects from those in normal families. Perhaps most significantly, parents in abusive families tend to rely on coercive or negative strategies for modifying their children's behavior, even for routine or mild discipline problems. In general, members of abusive families interact infrequently with each other, but when they do, the tone is negative. In one study, mothers in abusive families displayed 40 percent fewer positive interactions and 67 percent more negative interactions with their children than did nonabusive mothers (Burgess & Conger, 1978). In another study, abusive and nonabusive mothers were observed as they engaged in a sequence of preparing a meal, playing, and cleaning up with their preschool-aged children. Abusive mothers relied heavily on power-assertive techniques, such as threats, humiliation, or physical contact, to alter their children's behavior, whereas nonabusive mothers used predominantly positive strategies, including reasoning, bargaining, or modeling. Abusive mothers issued more than twice as many commands to their children as nonabusive mothers and also were inconsistent in reinforcing their children's compliance. Whereas the nonabusive mothers positively reinforced every instance of their children's obedience to a request, abusive mothers dispensed positive and negative reinforcements with equal frequency (Oldershaw, Walters, & Hall, 1986). As we saw earlier, inconsistent punishment usually leads to the persistence of undesirable behaviors in children.

▶ The child's active role

Certain characteristics of children are also more commonly observed in abusive families. Parents often describe the abused child as irritable, difficult to put to sleep, and prone to excessive crying (Ounsted, Oppenheimer, & Lindsay, 1974). A group at special risk for abuse is premature infants, who tend to have high-pitched, aversive cries and a less attractive appearance (Parke & Collmer, 1975). Abusive parents become especially sensitized to some of the child's objectionable behaviors and show heightened emotional reactivity to the child's cries or noncompliance (Frodi & Lamb, 1980; Wolfe, 1983). Older children in abusive families tend to be more aggressive and less compliant than children of similar ages from control families (Bousha & Twentyman, 1984; Egeland & Sroufe, 1981a; Parke & Collmer, 1975). Thus, both parental and child factors may contribute to a dynamic of physically and psychologically harmful interactions.

Last, abusive families tend to be isolated from the outside world and have fewer sources of social support than nonabusive families. In one study, abusive parents reported that they were less involved with the community than nonabusive parents were; they tended not to join sports teams, go to the library, or take classes (Trickett & Susman, 1988). In another study, some mothers who were at risk for becoming abusive because of their own family history had normal positive relationships with their children. These mothers also had extensive emotional support from other adults, a therapist, or a mate. In contrast, high-risk mothers who subsequently became abusive experienced greater life stress and had fewer sources of psychological support (Egeland, Jacobvitz, & Sroufe, 1988).

How can the spiral of abuse be broken? The guidelines provided by Wahler and Dumas (1989) provide a good start. Specifically, interventions should teach basic parenting skills, provide parents with mechanisms to cope with their emotional tension, and offer social support, such as child-care or counseling services (Belsky, 1993; Wolfe, 1985). Moreover, observers have noted our society's general acceptance of violence as a means of solving problems. This tendency is evident in the widespread endorsement of physical punishment as a technique for disciplining children, as well as in the pervasive displays of violence in the media (Belsky, 1980, 1993; Hart & Brassard, 1987). Altering broader societal attitudes about violence may be an additional and necessary step in breaking the cycle of child abuse.

## Cultural and Social Class Variations in Parenting

Do broader sociocultural beliefs and values play a role in parental socialization practices? If so, do children show specific patterns of behavior as a result of their different cultural experiences? Recent research suggests that the answer to both questions is "yes."

▶ Sociocultural influence

**Cross-National Differences**   Beatrice Whiting and Carolyn Edwards (1988) have provided an extended analysis of variations in parenting by comparing societies as diverse as rural Kenya and Liberia with urban America. Despite vast differences in economic, social, and political conditions, many similar overarching patterns are apparent in the ways parents (specifically, mothers) socialize their children. With infants and toddlers, the universal emphasis is on nurturance—that is, providing routine care along with attention and support. By the time the child reaches age four or five years, most parents shift their focus to control, correcting or reprimanding misbehavior. Finally, when children reach school age, parents become concerned with training their children in the skills and social behavior valued by their cultural group.

At the same time, though, there were notable differences. For example, mothers from rural villages in Kenya and Liberia emphasized training children to do chores responsibly and placed a high premium on obedience. From an early age, children were taught how to care for the family's fields and animals, and they assumed a major role in caring for younger siblings. Children were punished for performing tasks irresponsibly and were rarely praised. Consistent with this orientation to child rearing was the family's dependence on women and children for producing food. Because women in these cultures typically had an enormous workload, they delegated some tasks to children as soon as children were physically capable of managing them; because accidents and injury to infants and the family's resources must be prevented, deviant behaviors were not tolerated in children. Children growing in these communities were highly compliant to mothers' commands and suggestions.

An even more controlling style characterized the Tarong community in the Philippines, where subsistence farming was the mainstay, but responsibilities for producing food were more evenly distributed among the group's members. When the mother did not rely so much on her children to work for the family's survival and when the goals of training were thus less clear, arbitrary commands and even punishing became more common. Children were scolded frequently for being in the way of adults or playing in inappropriate places. By middle childhood, Tarong children showed a marked decline in their tendency to seek attention from or be close to their parents.

These patterns provided striking contrast to the "sociability" that characterized the middle-income American mothers in the sample. Interactions between mothers and children consisted of significant information exchange and warm, friendly dialogues. Mothers emphasized verbalization, educational tasks, and play, and they were liberal in their use of praise and encouragement. Because children in American society normally do not work to ensure the economic survival of the family unit, firm training and punishing were not part of these parents' styles. The emphasis on verbalization and educational activities was consistent with the high value Americans place on social interactions and schooling.

Other researchers, examining parent-child relationships in Asian cultures, have reaffirmed the idea that culture affects parenting styles. Japanese mothers use less physical punishment and more verbal reasoning to control their children than American mothers (Kobayashi-Winata & Power, 1989). Japanese culture emphasizes responsibilities and commitments to others, a socialization goal that is achieved more effectively through reasoning than through power-assertive techniques. Japanese children, in fact, comply with rules at home and in school more than their American counterparts do. Similarly, when Chinese parents are asked to describe their child-rearing practices, they report a greater emphasis on control and achievement in children than do American parents (Lin & Fu, 1990). In Chinese society, character development and educational attainment are highly valued, and parental practices follow directly from these larger societal goals.

As Whiting and Edwards (1988) point out, parents around the world resemble each other in numerous ways because of the universal needs of children as they grow and develop. But it is also true that the specific ecology of each culture, its socialization goals, and the demands it places on the family unit can dramatically shape parenting practices and the course of the individual child's socialization.

**Social Class Differences**     Reliable social class differences exist in parenting practices. Middle-class mothers more frequently use induction, or reasoning, as they discipline their children than do lower-class mothers, who tend to use power-assertive techniques. Middle-class mothers are also liberal in giving their children praise and generally verbalize more than lower-class mothers, who in turn more frequently utter such commands as, "Do it because I say so!" and dispense less positive reinforcement (Hoffman, 1984).

Social class (typically defined by father's occupation) by itself, however, is not a variable that provides neat or meaningful explanations, because it is usually associated with other variables, such as access to health care, nutrition, physical environment, and educational experiences. Moreover, even within low-income families, significant variations in parenting styles can occur. For example, younger low-income mothers and mothers who are less religious tend to use more power-assertive parenting styles than older mothers or those who have strong religious beliefs (Kelley, Power, & Wimbush, 1992). Thus, we must be cautious about making sweeping generalizations about the role of social class in parenting.

Vonnie McLoyd (1990) has provided an extended analysis of the growing literature on families under economic stress that illuminates the effects of social class. Because African American children experience a disproportionate share of the problems of poverty (a rate of 41 percent for African American children at the time of her analysis compared with 13 percent for Caucasian children), she focused on the social and family dynamics that can affect this racial minority. In McLoyd's analysis, economic hardship has a serious negative impact on children's socioemotional development because of the *psychological distress* it causes parents. Parents under stress have a diminished ability to provide nurturant, consistent, involved care for their children. Children growing up with poverty are thus at risk for depression, poor peer relations, lower self-esteem, and conduct disorders. In one study, for example, poor African American and Caucasian mothers were interviewed about their parenting practices. Those who reported being under greater psychological stress found parenting to be more difficult, were less nurturant with their children, and discussed money and personal problems more often with their children than mothers who reported less stress (McLoyd & Wilson, 1989). Similar findings have been reported for Caucasian middle-class families from the midwestern United States during a time of economic downturn. Rand Conger and his colleagues (Conger et al., 1992) found that parents who experienced economic hardship reported greater emotional distress, and this factor in turn was related to less skillful parenting. The disruptions in parenting were related to adjustment problems in the adolescent boys in the sample. These seventh-graders reported more feelings of hostility and depression than those whose families were not experiencing economic hardship.

At the same time, the demands that poverty makes on African American families may be related to unique family structures and socialization goals that are adaptive for their situation and help them to cope. For example, a significant number of African American children grow up in an extended family. About 10 percent of African American children younger than eighteen grow up with a live-in grandparent, three times as many as Caucasian children (Beck & Beck, 1989). Extended family members often bring additional income, child-care assistance, and emotional support and counseling to families under stress, especially when the parent is single (Wilson, 1986). In addition, African American children often are socialized to have a positive orientation to their racial group and to develop interdependence and cooperation, as opposed to independence and competition. These characteristics fit with the needs of a group of children who often find barriers to individual achievement (Harrison et al., 1990). Thus, although economic stress can have a negative effect on family dynamics, it can also foster alternative family structures and socialization goals that help meet the needs of children.

## *Relationships with Mothers, Fathers, and Siblings*

Because women traditionally have been seen as the primary caregivers for children, most studies of parenting practices in the psychological literature

Researchers have noted that fathers are "tuned in" to the signals displayed by their babies, as when a diaper needs to be changed. When they are given the opportunity, fathers respond to children in much the same way that mothers do.

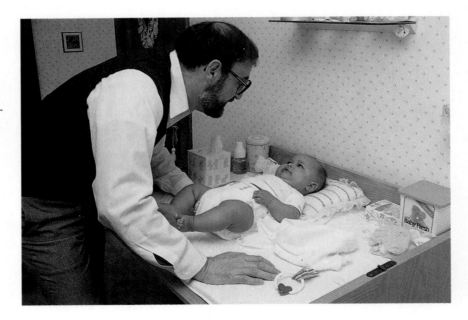

have focused almost exclusively on mothering. A decade's research on fathers, however, as well as even more recent studies of sibling relationships, has provided a much broader understanding of how each distinct relationship within the family influences the individual child's development.

## Mothering Versus Fathering: Are There Differences?

For the most part, mothers still bear most of the responsibility for child rearing in American society, whether they are employed outside the home or not. Research, however, resoundingly reveals that fathers are also significant figures in their children's lives and are clearly competent in their parental role as well.

In this chapter, as well as in Chapter 11, we have underscored maternal sensitivity and responsiveness as key factors in fostering optimal child development. Studies have shown that fathers are just as responsive as mothers to the signals of their infants, and when given the opportunity, they interact with their babies in ways similar to mothers. One team of researchers measured the physiological responsiveness of mothers and fathers as they observed quiet, smiling, or crying babies on a video monitor (Frodi et al., 1978). Mothers and fathers showed similar changes in heart rate, blood pressure, and skin conductance when the babies smiled or cried. In another study of maternal and paternal behaviors directed to infants in the newborn nursery, Ross Parke and Sandra O'Leary (1976) found that fathers were just as likely as mothers to hold, touch, and vocalize to their babies.

After the newborn period, fathers and mothers begin to manifest somewhat different styles of interacting with their infants. When they play face to face with their babies, fathers tend to provide physical and social stimulation in staccato bursts, whereas mothers tend to be more rhythmic and soothing (Yogman et al., 1977). Fathers engage in physical and unpredictable "idiosyncratic" play with their infants—they throw them up in the air, move their limbs, and tickle them—whereas mothers spend more time in caregiving activities or calm games such as "pat-a-cake" (Lamb, 1976; Yogman, 1982). As a consequence, infants prefer fathers when they wish to play and seek out mothers when they desire care and comfort. This dichotomy in parental styles of interaction continues at least until middle childhood (Russell & Russell, 1987).

Despite their responsiveness and competence as parents, most fathers spend less time with their children than mothers do. Using a national sample, Joseph Pleck (1982) found that employed fathers whose children were younger than five spent an average of twenty-six minutes per day in caregiving or other interactions with their children. With children aged six to seventeen that figure dropped to sixteen minutes per day. In general, fathers spend about one-third the time that mothers do in direct contact with their children, even when the mother works outside the home (Ishii-Kuntz & Coltrane, 1992; Lamb et al., 1987). Some exceptions do exist, most notably in nontraditional families in which fathers may even serve as the primary caregiver. Furthermore, the extent of paternal involvement with children increased in the 1970s and 1980s (Juster, 1987). The bulk of the evidence suggests, however, that although fathers are capable and responsive parents, they still have fewer interactions with their children than mothers do, especially in direct caregiving activities.

Why are fathers relatively uninvolved? Some may hold traditional beliefs about which family member should be responsible for child care. Another reason may be that fathers are not confident in their caregiving skills. Because males are typically not exposed to child care through such experiences as babysitting and home economics courses, they may feel insecure about feeding, bathing, or diapering a child (Lamb et al., 1987). Still another obstacle may be the resistance of mothers. Survey data with a national sample showed that only 23 percent of employed mothers and 31 percent of unemployed mothers stated that they wanted more help from their husbands in child care (Pleck, 1982). It may be that women are socialized so strongly to excel in the caregiving role that they are reluctant to relinquish it, even if it places extraordinary demands on their time.

**The Father's Influence on Child Development**   Do fathers have a unique influence, different from that of mothers, on the process of child development? During the 1960s and 1970s psychologists believed that they did, based on studies of the effects of father absence, especially on boys. Boys growing up without fathers were more likely to have problems in academic achievement, gender-role development, and control of aggression (Biller, 1974; Lamb, 1981). An important theoretical construct driving much of the research was *identification*—the idea that boys assimilate the characteristics, attitudes, and behaviors of their fathers as they form an intense emotional bond with them. Presumably, boys without fathers did not have an identity figure or model for appropriate masculine, instrumentally competent behavior and thus suffered deficits in cognitive, social, and emotional domains.

Identification with the father may be less important than other variables, however. Michael Lamb (1987) points out that the effects of father absence may not result from the loss of a masculine identity figure for the son but rather from the loss of a source of emotional and financial support for the entire family. The tension and stress that result may produce maladaptive patterns of parenting, which in turn generate undesirable developmental outcomes for boys. Boys may be particularly vulnerable because they seem to be more generally susceptible than girls to the effects of deviant environments (Rutter, 1986).

A more contemporary view is that fathers make recognizable contributions to family life in general, and child development in particular, but those contributions simply reflect aspects of good parenting. In other words, good fathering resembles good mothering, and the child will thrive by having two parents who fill those roles instead of just one. For example, the father's warmth emerges as a more powerful variable than his masculinity in predicting competence, achievement, and gender-role identity in sons (Radin, 1981; Radin & Sagi, 1982). In fact, the father's warmth is more powerful than the mother's warmth in predicting children's feelings of academic competence (Wagner & Phillips, 1992). When fathers express positive affection toward their first-born children, siblings also seem to act more prosocially toward each other than when fathers do not (Volling & Belsky, 1992).

In addition, there are some noteworthy effects when fathers are more highly involved than the norm in child-care activities, that is, when they assume an equal or almost equal share of the responsibilities for feeding, bathing, and caring for children or when they are the primary caregivers. In one study, fathers and mothers of preschoolers were interviewed about their participation in child-care tasks, and their children were given a number of standardized tests of achievement and psychosocial adjustment. Fathers who were highly involved in caregiving activities had children who believed they controlled the events in their lives, scored higher on tests of cognitive competence, and held fewer stereotyped gender-role beliefs than children whose fathers were less involved. One reason for some of these gains might be that fathers of the better-adjusted children spent more time in providing cognitively stimulating activities for their children, especially their daughters (Radin, 1982). When fathers participate in child care, they are providing an added source of enrichment for both their sons and their daughters.

▶ Sociocultural influence

**Cross-Cultural Studies of Fathering**  As in the United States, fathers in many cultures are becoming increasingly involved in the care of their children, especially during the newborn and infancy periods. In Britain, Sweden, West Germany, and Australia, fathers are beginning to participate more fully as parents (Hwang, 1987; Jackson, 1987; Nickel & Kocher, 1987; Russell, 1987). The Swedish government in particular has established social policies designed to encourage paternal participation. Among the benefits available to fathers are a ten-day paid leave after the birth of the baby, a leave during the child's first year (most of which is compensated), and the option of reducing the workday by as much as two hours until the child is eight years old. About 85 percent of Swedish fathers take advantage of the newborn leave policy (Hwang, 1987).

In contrast, there are some societies in which fathers' participation is comparably low, particularly those with strong cultural beliefs about the proper roles for mothers and fathers. When investigators examined fathers' involvement in child care in a small town north of Rome, they found that few fathers were present at the births of their children, and once their infants were home, they did virtually no physical caregiving. Most of their infant-directed behaviors emanated from a distance; they looked at, talked to, or whistled at their child but were unlikely to pick up the baby to play. As the child grew older, the fathers became even more passive and distant (New & Benigni, 1987).

A closer look at this culture's beliefs about parenting provides some insights into these fathers' lack of involvement. First, both women and men held the strong general belief that only a woman can properly care for a child, that is, respond to physical needs and provide affection and nurturance. The father's role required him to provide financial support for the family. Second, parents held rigid ideas about specific aspects of infant care, with cleanliness and proper nutrition, for example, of great concern. Most parents interviewed in this study believed that only mothers had the specialized skills to care for the child "properly." Finally, the father had few opportunities to be alone with the child, because members of the extended family, usually women, were frequently present. Fathers probably felt reluctant to have their interactions with infants scrutinized by so many experts.

In summary, fathers are capable of engaging in responsive parenting right from their children's infancy, and their children seem to benefit. They may not always be given the opportunity to participate in caregiving, however, because of cultural beliefs about the proper role of fathers or because of their unfamiliarity with child-care routines. As fathers in some societies participate more fully in child care, the lives of both sons and daughters are likely to become markedly enriched.

## Siblings

As do parents, siblings serve as important sources of the child's social attitudes, beliefs, and behaviors. Although they may not wield as much power as parents, siblings certainly do attempt to control each other's behaviors (ask

Only children often achieve more than children with two or more siblings, probably because parents have more time for high quality interactions with an only child.

anyone who is not an only child!) and may be models for both desirable and undesirable actions. An emerging body of research on sibling relationships has provided yet another perspective on how families influence development.

**The Only Child**     One way to assess the impact of siblings on development is to examine children who have none. Are there notable differences between only children and children with one or more sisters or brothers? Popular opinion depicts the only child as spoiled, demanding, self-centered, and dependent (Thompson, 1974). But research evidence suggests the contrary, that only children may enjoy the benefits of having their parents' exclusive attention. Toni Falbo and Denise Polit (1986) summarized the results of 115 studies of only children and concluded that overall only children showed higher achievement and intelligence scores than children with siblings. In addition, only borns ranked higher on measures of character—that is, the tendency toward leadership, personal control, and maturity—than children with siblings. No overall differences emerged between only children and children with siblings on assessments of sociability and personal adjustment.

In explaining these findings, Falbo and Polit (1986) found support for the hypothesis that features of the parent-child relationship account for the advantages only children enjoy in certain domains. Only children were found to have more positive relationships with their parents than children having siblings. This effect probably is the result of parents of one child having more time to spend with their son or daughter and the generally high quality of their interactions (Falbo & Cooper, 1980). Parents and children in one study, for example, exchanged more information in mealtime conversations in one-child families than in families having two or three children (Lewis & Feiring, 1982). First-time parents are also more anxious about their child-rearing techniques and may thus be more vigilant and responsive to their child's behaviors (Falbo & Polit, 1986).

Falbo and Polit's (1986) meta-analysis showed that parent-child relations in one- and two-child families are actually more similar than different. Only when a third child is born does the quality of parent-child relations diminish significantly. Parents of more than two children probably become more relaxed about their child-rearing strategies and also have significantly more demands placed on their time. The result is less responsiveness and fewer deliberate attempts to instruct their children, aspects of parenting related to cognitive achievements.

**Family Size and Birth Order**     Children growing up in contemporary American society have fewer siblings than children in earlier eras. In 1991 the average American family included one or two children (U.S. Bureau of the Census, 1992). Many children thus grow up with only one other sibling. Does the size of the family make any difference in child development?

In general, children from smaller families have higher intelligence test scores, achieve higher levels of education, and display higher self-esteem (Blake, 1989; Wagner, Schubert, & Schubert, 1985). As we have just seen, one reason for these effects may be that parents in larger families have less time to spend with their children and may not provide the kind of cognitive stimulation that children receive in smaller families. Another important factor is financial; parents of more children often experience greater economic stress, which in turn may diminish the quality of their parenting (Rutter & Madge, 1976).

▶ Interaction among domains

▶ Interaction among domains

Regardless of family size, the child's birth order, whether first born or later born, can also be a factor in development. Like only children, first-borns tend to score higher on IQ tests and have higher achievement motivation than other children (Glass, Neulinger, & Brim, 1974; Zajonc, Markus, & Markus, 1979). They also tend to be more obedient and socially responsible (Sutton-Smith & Rosenberg, 1970). All these effects probably stem from the greater attention parents give to their first children. Later-borns seem to have an advantage in the social sphere, however. Youngest siblings tend to have better peer relationships than first-borns and are more confident in social situations (Lahey et al., 1980; Miller & Maruyama, 1976).

**The Impact of a Sibling's Arrival**   The birth of a sibling can have a dramatic effect on the life of a first-born child. Research on the consequences of a second child's arrival generally confirms that "sibling rivalry" is no myth. Judy Dunn and Carol Kendrick (1982) followed the progress of family relationships among forty first-born children who experienced the arrival of a sibling sometime between their first and fourth birthdays. Dunn and Kendrick observed normal home routines during the mother's last month of pregnancy and again when the baby sibling was one, eight, and fourteen months old. They also interviewed the mother at each stage about the elder child's eating and sleeping habits, moods, and other routine behaviors.

For the majority of children, the arrival of a sister or brother was related to marked changes in behavior; they became more demanding, clingy, unhappy, or withdrawn. Accompanying these changes in the child's behavior were significant decreases in maternal attention toward them; mothers engaged in less joint play, cuddling, and verbalization with their first-borns and in general initiated fewer interactions with the older child. At the same time, restrictive and

▶ Interaction among domains

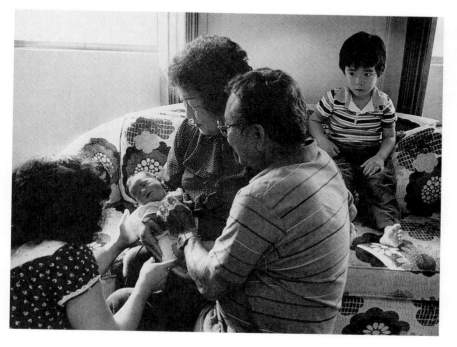

This young boy's reaction to a new sibling is quite typical. Although many children become clingy, withdrawn, or demanding when a new sibling first arrives, these reactions can be diminished if parents prepare the older child for the infant's arrival and involve him in the infant's care.

punitive maternal behaviors increased. Over time, Dunn and Kendrick (1982) noted, two distinct patterns of sibling relationships emerged. Among some sibling pairs, almost all interactions eventually became friendly and positive, whereas for others, a persistent pattern of hostility and aggression became the norm. The first pattern was more likely if mothers had previously prepared the older child for the newborn's arrival by referring to the infant as a person with needs and desires. Engaging the older child in care for the infant also seemed to have positive consequences. In contrast, negative relationships between siblings resulted if the older child experienced a sharp drop in maternal contact. The discrepancy in pre- and postsibling maternal contact made the most difference; children who had less contact with their mother before the sibling's birth were not so profoundly affected by her attention to the new infant.

The arrival of a sibling demands a big adjustment for the older child, especially because another individual begins to compete for the parents' attention and affection. Siblings are highly aware of the differential treatment parents may knowingly or unwittingly bestow on them. The greater the perceived discrepancy is, the greater the sibling conflict will be (Dunn, 1988). But not all aspects of sibling relationships are negative. Dunn and Kendrick (1982) noted that in certain circumstances siblings fill a void in parent-child relationships. When the mother and her older child have difficulties in their interactions, siblings may provide the attention and affection missing from the maternal relationship, thus helping to keep the family system in equilibrium.

**Sibling Interactions Among Older Children**    How do older children interact as siblings? For one thing, children tend to fight more with their siblings than with their friends. When fifth- through eighth-grade students were asked to describe conflicts with their siblings, they reported that they allowed quarrels with siblings to escalate, often to the point at which parents had to intervene, whereas they tried to resolve conflicts with friends. Most of the time, siblings fight about privacy and interpersonal boundaries (Raffaelli, 1989). In addition, interactions between siblings tend to be more negative when the older sibling is a male (MacKinnon, 1989a).

Sibling relationships typically change from middle childhood through adolescence. Duane Buhrmester and Wyndol Furman (1990) administered the Sibling Relationship Questionnaire to third-, sixth-, ninth-, and twelfth-graders, to assess several dimensions of sibling interactions. Older siblings reported being more dominant and nurturant toward their younger siblings, and younger siblings confirmed that they received more often than dispensed dominance and nurturance. These differences between older and younger siblings apparently disappear with the passage of time, however. The older subjects in the sample reported having more egalitarian relationships with their siblings as well as less intense feelings of both warmth and conflict. Initial differences in power and nurturance usually disappeared when the younger sibling was twelve years old, now more competent and in less need of guidance and emotional support.

The quality of sibling interactions can be affected by the style of parenting mothers and fathers choose. In one study, mothers who used nonpunitive control techniques and encouraged curiosity and openness to experience had children who were more prosocial toward each other than mothers who were punitive and restrictive (Brody, Stoneman, & MacKinnon, 1986). Fathers may have an even greater influence on sibling relationships. Fathers who express more positive behavior toward their children by hugging them or praising

Older siblings often serve as powerful models for all sorts of behaviors for younger family members, as this picture of two brothers demonstrates.

them, and who attempt to be fair to each sibling, have children who likewise express more positive behavior and display less conflict toward each other. The relationship of father-child behavior is noticeably stronger than mother-child behavior (Brody, Stoneman, & McCoy, 1992; Brody et al., 1992).

In summary, while the presence of siblings may mean that the child has fewer opportunities to interact with parents, it also provides the context for developing other unique skills. Older siblings have opportunities to become nurturant and assertive, and younger siblings have more models for a range of behaviors than only children. Although many children grow up with siblings, we are just beginning to understand the role they play in child development.

## *Families in Transition*

As we saw at the start of this chapter, the traditional nuclear family has been disappearing slowly from mainstream American society. Single-parent families, dual wage-earner families, and reconstituted families—in which adults who remarry bring their respective children into new families—are becoming more and more prevalent and offer new circumstances to which children must adapt. What are the effects of these emerging family structures on child development? Research shows that child development is not influenced so much by changes in family structure per se but by the ways in which structural changes affect interpersonal relations within the family.

# Maternal Employment

In the last two decades, the percentage of married women with children in the labor force has increased dramatically. The working mother is now the norm. What is the effect of maternal employment on child development?

When psychologists compare children of employed mothers with children of women who remain at home, few differences emerge on measures of cognitive achievement and socioemotional development, at least for middle class subjects (Heyns, 1982; Hoffman, 1984, 1989). If anything, daughters of employed mothers derive some benefit; they are likely to show greater independence, achievement, and higher self-esteem than daughters of nonworking mothers. Apparently, these girls profit from having a successful, competent role model, at least as these qualities are recognized by the larger society. (Women who remain home "work," too, but traditionally have not been afforded recognition or status for that role.) One variable that may make a difference, though, is when mothers return to work. A recent study of more than 1,000 three- and four-year-old children indicated that when their mothers returned to work during their first year, scores on a cognitive test tended to be lower and the number of behavior problems tended to be higher than those of children whose mothers waited until the second year to return to work (Baydar & Brooks-Gunn, 1991).

For children from low-income families, however, maternal employment is related to some clear benefits for children. A recent longitudinal study examined 189 second-grade children, most of whom were born to adolescent mothers and 41 percent of whom lived in households with incomes below the poverty level. For this sample, maternal employment during the child's first three years was associated with greater household income, with a higher quality home environment as assessed by the HOME inventory (see Chapter 10), and with higher math achievement in school among the children as contrasted with the effects when mothers did not work (Vandell & Ramanan, 1992).

In general, the clearest effect of maternal employment involves the sex-role attitudes of both sons and daughters. As we saw in Chapter 13, when mothers work outside the home, their children are less likely than children of at-home mothers to hold stereotypical beliefs about males and females and are more likely to see both sexes as competent (Hoffman, 1984, 1989). When both mother and father work, sons and daughters have the opportunity to see both parents in multiple roles, as powerful, competent wage earners and as nurturant, warm caregivers, a factor that may contribute to more egalitarian beliefs.

Overall, maternal employment is not a simple, "neat" variable when it comes to studying child development. Some mothers work out of sheer economic necessity, while others are more concerned with realizing personal or career goals, for example. As Lois Hoffman (1989) points out, the effect of maternal employment is better understood through its effects on family dynamics, parental attitudes, and the alternative child-care arrangements the family has chosen. It is to these factors that we now turn our attention.

**Maternal Employment and Parent-Child Interaction**     Mothers who work full time outside the home spend less time caring for their children, whether they are infants or high school–aged, than mothers who stay at home (Hill & Stafford, 1980). In terms of direct one-to-one mother-child interaction, however, there are no significant differences between employed and nonemployed mothers (Goldberg, 1977; Richards & Duckett, 1994). Employed mothers often compensate for the time they miss with their child during the work week by allocating more time for them on weekends and evenings (Easter-books & Goldberg, 1985). Thus, working mothers try to establish "quality time" with their children to make up for the hours they are separated from them. The picture for fathers is less clear. Although some studies show that fathers assume more responsibilities for child care when the mother works, others indicate that they do not (Baruch & Barnett, 1981; Pederson et al., 1982; Pleck, 1983).

Does the quality of parent-child interaction differ between mothers who do and do not work? Employed mothers as a group tend to stress independence training (Hoffman, 1989), a characteristic in children that will help the family function more smoothly, given the more limited time mothers and fathers have to perform routine activities. Some researchers also report that employed mothers are more responsive and verbalize more to their children and engage in more social play than mothers who are not employed (Crockenberg & Litman, 1991; Pederson et al., 1982; Schubert, Bradley-Johnson, & Nuttal, 1980).

Overall, what matters more than whether the mother works or not is her attitude toward mothering and work, and why she is working or staying home. In one study of mothers of infants, those women who remained at home contrary to their preference had higher scores on tests of depression and stress than two other groups—mothers who preferred to be home and were not in the labor force and employed mothers who valued their positions in the work world (Hock & DeMeis, 1990). We saw earlier in this chapter that parental stress has been implicated as a factor in less consistent and less nurturant parenting. On the other hand, when maternal employment produces tension, parenting practices also may suffer. Researchers have found that mothers who worked more than forty hours per week, for example, were more anxious and unhappy, and they had less sensitive and less animated interactions with their infants than mothers who worked less than forty hours per week (Owen & Cox, 1988).

**The Effects of Day Care**    It is almost impossible to extract the influence of maternal employment as a variable from the effect of the alternate caregiving arrangements made for the child. The two factors almost invariably occur together.

Child-care arrangements take various forms, from in-home care provided by a relative or paid caregiver to group care in a formal organized center. As Table 14.2 shows, up until age two most children are cared for in another home by a relative or someone else, and only a small percentage of children attend an organized day-care center. This finding raises an interesting issue concerning the effect of day care on development. With rare exceptions, researchers have compared children who have spent varying amounts of time in center-based day care with children who have been reared by their parents at home. We must interpret the findings of this research cautiously, because the more common home-based care of young children whose mothers work—care in another person's home—has yet to be studied extensively.

Chapter 11 discussed the effects of day care on a specific aspect of development—the child's attachment to his mother. Here we consider the broader effects of alternate caregiving on child development. One area in which some (but not all) researchers have noted an effect of day care is in intellectual performance. Day-care children tend to outperform children reared at home by their parents on standardized tests of IQ as well as measures of problem-solving

| Age of Child | Child's Home | | Another Home | | Organized Child-Care Facility | Other[1] |
|---|---|---|---|---|---|---|
| | Relative | Nonrelative | Relative | Nonrelative | | |
| Under 1 year | 22.9 | 8.3 | 15.1 | 23.3 | 14.1 | 16.4 |
| 1 to 2 years | 26.1 | 6.6 | 14.3 | 27.0 | 18.1 | 7.8 |
| 3 to 4 years | 21.6 | 5.1 | 11.7 | 17.2 | 34.3 | 10.0 |

Source: Adapted from U.S. Bureau of the Census, 1990.
[1]Includes mother caring for child at work, child caring for self, and child attending kindergarten or grade school.

**TABLE 14.2**

**Child-Care Arrangements for Children Whose Mothers Work**

This table shows the percentage of children who receive different forms of child care. Most infants, toddlers, and preschoolers whose mothers work receive child care provided by a relative or nonrelative, either in the child's home or the home of the caregiver.

ability, creativity, language development, and arithmetic skills (Clarke-Stewart & Fein, 1983). Day-care programs that stress cognitive activities have a greater effect on IQ scores than those that simply provide caregiving (McCartney et al., 1985). Moreover, the effect of day care on intellectual achievements shows up years later when children are in elementary school. In one study that examined the academic achievements of sixth-graders, the amount of time children had spent in high-quality day-care centers during infancy was positively related to their mathematics grades and their tendency to be enrolled in programs for the gifted (Field, 1991). In another study, conducted in Sweden, children who had started day care before the age of one year performed better in school at age thirteen than those who had started day care later in infancy; children who had no out-of-home care had the lowest levels of school performance (Andersson, 1992).

Day care also produces effects in the realm of social development. Specifically, children with experience in day care are more socially competent. They show greater self-confidence, assertiveness, independence, and behave more prosocially with peers than home-reared comparison groups. In addition to showing more positive behaviors, however, day-care children also more frequently display aggression toward peers and noncompliance with adults, at least according to some, but not all, studies of this behavior (Clarke-Stewart & Fein, 1983). Two factors have been proposed as explanations for day-care children's advanced social behaviors: the extensive peer contacts they have and the prosocial instruction explicitly provided by many caregivers (Hamilton & Gordon, 1978; Rubenstein & Howes, 1979). As for their greater aggressive and noncompliant behavior, Alison Clarke-Stewart (1989) suggests that day-care children are simply more likely to think independently but have not yet mastered the social skills to negotiate for the attainment of their goals.

To summarize, day care has few negative effects on children and may even facilitate cognitive and social development. It is important to remember, however, that most studies of day care have been conducted in high-quality centers, often associated with universities and populated by middle- to upper-class children. But many parents do not have the opportunity or financial resources to send their children to programs of such high caliber. What are the effects of less-than-excellent programs on children? Preliminary research suggests that when children are enrolled in low-quality centers before age one, they have more difficulty with peers and are distractible and less task oriented in kindergarten than children who are enrolled at later ages and those who attend high-quality centers (Howes, 1990). Thus, it is essential for parents to be aware of the elements of high-quality day care.

**Choosing a Day-Care Center**   Both the federal government and many states have set minimum requirements for day-care services that regulate the qualifications of teachers, staff-child ratios, the size and safety of the physical facility, and the provision of nourishing meals. Although the guidelines and laws provide for *minimum* standards, most parents are concerned with providing their child with the best possible care during the hours they are employed. Alison Clarke-Stewart (1982) has drawn on the expanding body of research findings on day care to compile the following suggestions for parents:

- Center-based care is more likely to include educational opportunities for children than home-based care, such as that provided by babysitters and family day care. On the other hand, children are more likely to receive one-to-one supervision and authoritative discipline in home-based care.
- Children are most likely to thrive intellectually and emotionally in programs that offer a balance between structured educational activities and an open, free environment.
- The caregiving environment should provide ample physical space (at least twenty-five square feet per child) and a variety of materials and activities to foster sensorimotor, social, and cognitive development.
- The interaction style of the caregiver is a key aspect of quality care. The caregiver should be actively involved but not restrictive with the children. The caregiver should also be responsive and offer positive encouragement.
- Caregivers who have training in child development and continuing opportunities for education are most likely to provide high-quality care.
- The individual characteristics of the child should be taken into account. Some children will probably do well in a program in which structure and openness are balanced, but others might profit from either more structure or a more flexible and relaxed program.

To date, research shows that day care has few negative effects on young children, and may even facilitate cognitive and social development. Particularly important is the caregiver's warmth and responsiveness.

Other important factors include a high staff-to-child ratio, an overall group size that is not too large, and low staff turnover. Research has shown, for example, that when the staff-child ratio is at least one to three for infants, one to four for toddlers, and one to nine for preschoolers, the quality of caregiving and of children's activities within the center are both good. Likewise, when the overall class size is six or fewer for infants, twelve or fewer for toddlers, and eighteen or fewer for preschoolers, children have better quality experiences than in larger groups (Howes, Phillips, & Whitebook, 1992).

In essence, the qualities of good day care mirror the qualities of good parenting. In other words, parents should seek a warm, responsive environment in which the child is provided, at least some of the time, with opportunities for structured play and prosocial learning.

## The Effect of Divorce

As we pointed out at the start of this chapter, the statistics are dramatic—the divorce rate among couples in the United States has tripled since 1960, and estimates suggest that 40 to 50 percent of children born in the late 1970s and early 1980s will live through the divorce of their parents (Glick & Lin, 1986). Far from being an atypical event, divorce affects a significant proportion of American children. Unfortunately, the effects of divorce on children are rarely

▶ Sociocultural influence

positive; the absence of one parent, the emotional and financial tension, and sometimes continuing conflicts between parents that accompany divorce frequently lead to a range of psychological problems for both boys and girls, at least in the period immediately following the breakup of the family. The ability of children to cope with the stresses of divorce, particularly in the long run, depends on a number of variables. Most important is the way parents manage the transition in family structure.

A major longitudinal study of the effect of divorce on parents and children conducted by E. Mavis Hetherington and her associates illuminated how parental separation affects children and how the nature of parent-child interactions changes (Hetherington, Cox, & Cox, 1982). The researchers compared two groups for a period of two years, a sample of forty-eight preschool-aged middle-class children whose parents divorced, and another group of forty-eight middle-class children matched on several variables, such as age and sex, whose families were intact. In all the divorced families, mothers had custody of their children. During the course of the study, the researchers made several assessments of both parents and children, including parental interviews, observations of parent-child interactions in the laboratory and at home, observations and ratings of children's behavior in the home and at school, and personality tests.

The results of the study indicated that the worst period for most children was the first year after the divorce, when they exhibited many negative characteristics, such as aggression, distractability, and noncompliance. The extent of their undesirable behaviors even surpassed those of children from intact families with a high level of conflict, and it was particularly noticeable in boys. Two years after the divorce, many of the effects on children had diminished, especially for girls. In a six-year follow-up, however, many boys continued to show patterns of aggression and noncompliance, academic difficulties, poor relations with peers, and extremely low self-esteem (Hetherington, 1989).

▶ Interaction among domains

A look at family interaction styles after divorce helps to account for the poor initial adjustment of children. Hetherington and her colleagues noted that soon after they separated from their husbands, mothers tended to adopt a more authoritarian style of parenting (Hetherington, Cox, & Cox, 1982). They gave out numerous commands and prohibitions and displayed little affection or responsiveness to their children. These mothers were undoubtedly having problems coping with their new status as single parents in both emotional and practical terms. At the same time, the fathers withdrew, participating little in the management of their children's behavior. Children, particularly boys, became less compliant, and mothers in turn responded with increased restrictiveness and punitiveness. Caught up in a spiral of frustration, helplessness, and feelings of incompetence, these mothers responded negatively to many of their children's behaviors, even those that were neutral or positive, and despite their harsh threats, followed up on few of the directives they gave. The result was a coercive cycle of parent-child interaction like that described earlier in this chapter and typified by this chapter's opening scene between Joey and his mother.

Other researchers have confirmed that many children show heightened aggression, lower academic achievement, disruptions in peer relationships, and depression after their parents' divorce than they had previously (Camara & Resnick, 1988; Stolberg & Anker, 1984; Wallerstein, Corbin, & Lewis, 1988). Children aged six to eight years seem to have the most difficulty adjusting; they are old enough to recognize the seriousness of the family's situation but do not yet have the coping skills to deal with feelings of sadness and guilt that often accompany the change in family structure (Wallerstein & Kelly, 1980). Older children often have a better understanding of divorce and the notion that conflicts between parents must somehow be resolved (Kurdek, 1989). However, even adolescents often suffer negative psychological consequences after their parents divorce. Adolescent boys, in particular, are more prone to using alcohol or illicit drugs after their parents separate than boys in a control group whose parents remained married (Doherty & Needle, 1991). Sibling interactions also suffer. Carol MacKinnon (1989b) observed elementary school-aged children as they played games with their siblings in the laboratory. Siblings whose parents had been divorced for one year or longer showed more teasing, quarreling, physical attacks, and other negative behaviors toward each other than children from intact families. Given these deleterious consequences and the prevalence of divorce, is there anything that can be done to ease the adjustment of children? Research findings suggest some potentially useful strategies.

**Adjusting to Divorce**    The consequences of divorce are not always so grim for all children. Hetherington (1989) observed that after six years, some of the children in her original study recovered from the family crisis and showed a healthy adaptation to their new family lifestyle, whether their mother remarried or not. These children displayed few behavior problems, high self-esteem, successful academic performance, and positive relations with peers.

What factors were associated with this favorable pattern of adjustment? For one thing, mothers of children in this group had become less authoritarian and more authoritative in their parental style, encouraging independence but also providing a warm, supportive climate for their sons and daughters. If their mother was not available, many of these children had contact with some other caring adult, a relative, teacher, or neighbor. In addition, several children in this category had responsibility for the care of another individual—a younger sibling, an aged grandparent, or someone with a physical or emotional problem. These relationships may have offered children an opportunity to feel needed and provided an alternative source of emotional gratification and support. In contrast, mothers of children with long-lasting adjustment problems continued to manifest coercive styles of interaction. Mothers and sons were especially likely to fall into this pattern. Finally, children are more likely to show successful adjustment to divorce when conflict between divorced parents is low, when the child maintains a relationship with the noncustodial parent, and when the child does not feel "caught" between the two parents (Buchanan, Maccoby, & Dornbusch, 1991; Guidubaldi, Perry, & Cleminshaw, 1984; Kurdek & Berg, 1983; Wallerstein & Kelly, 1980).

Divorce represents a difficult transition for all members of the family. A key variable to understanding its effect is the quality of relationships among all family members—the more conflict and negative emotion associated with the process and the more prolonged the maladaptive patterns of interaction, the worse the outcomes for the child.

## CONTROVERSY: THINKING IT OVER

### What Type of Custody Arrangement Is Best for Children of Divorce?

fter divorce, most children reside with their mother, in large part because of long-standing societal beliefs about the privileged nature of mother-child relationships. Yet, when children live with their mothers after a divorce, they are more likely to experience economic hardship than if they live with their fathers. Studies find that income for divorced women with children declines an average of 30 percent, while the income for fathers declines much less or even increases (Burkhauser et al., 1991; Weitzman, 1985). Children living with their mothers also typically show a dramatic impairment in relationships with their fathers. For example, the National Survey of Children found that more than half of children of divorce did not see their fathers *at all* in the past year (Furstenberg et al., 1983).

Many states now have laws that favor joint custody of children following divorce. In most cases, this means that both parents have equal responsibility for making decisions about the child's medical care and education, that is, they have *joint legal custody*. In other cases, it also means that children reside for substantial periods of time with each parent. This arrangement refers to *joint physical custody*.

Some experts believe that joint custody results in negative outcomes for children because it increases the likelihood that children will be exposed to their parents' hostility and will feel caught in the conflict between their parents (Johnston & Campbell, 1987; Reppucci, 1984; Stahl, 1984; Wallerstein & Kelly, 1980). If joint custody means the child must change residence during the year, relationships with friends and experiences in school may also be disrupted.

Others note no differences in the adjustment of children in joint-custody versus sole-custody families (Kline et al., 1989), while still other evidence suggests that children may adapt better when they are in the custody of the same-sex parent (Camara & Resnick, 1988; Warshak & Santrock, 1983). For example, a recent analysis of data from several hundred high school sophomores whose parents divorced shows that adolescents who lived with their same-sex parent were less likely to drop out of high school than those who lived with their parent of the opposite sex (Zimiles & Lee, 1991).

On what basis should child custody decisions be made—the incomes of the parents, the child's preferred parent, or the same-sex parent—or should the mother usually obtain custody? Does the research on adjusting to divorce have any implications for whether sole- or joint-custody arrangements might be better for the child? Even if joint custody arrangements have been made, can the child's relationships with each parent be truly equal? What types of research should developmental psychologists conduct to obtain clearer answers to this vexing but important issue? ■

**Relationships with Stepparents**    Approximately 75 percent of divorced individuals remarry, the majority within five years after their divorce (Glick, 1984). As a consequence, about 35 percent of children born in the early 1980s will live with a stepparent (Glick, 1989). For children who have just experienced the separation of their parents, the introduction of a new "parent" represents yet another difficult transition.

▶ Interaction among domains

Like divorce, a parent's remarriage often leads to aggression, noncompliance, academic difficulties, and poor peer relations among children (Bray, 1988; Zill, 1988). The child usually has more difficulty adjusting when stepparents have larger numbers of their own children, when children from two previous marriages are assimilated into one family, and when the custodial parent and stepparent have a new biological child of their own (Santrock & Sitterle, 1987; Zill, 1988). Adolescents have more problems adjusting to their new family than younger children, perhaps because their growing autonomy leads them to be more confrontational with parents (Brand, Clingempeel, & Bowen-

Woodward, 1988). In addition, girls in the middle school and adolescent years do not adjust as well as boys to parental remarriage; girls especially withdraw from their stepfathers (Brand, Clingempeel, & Bowen-Woodward, 1988; Vuchinich et al., 1991). Adjustment to a parent's remarriage can take time; in one study, adolescents showed little evidence of adjustment during the twenty-six months that they were studied (Hetherington & Clingempeel, 1992).

Drawing from data collected in a national survey of parent-adolescent relations, Frank Furstenberg (1987) found that stepparents reported reservations about their ability to discipline and provide affection to stepchildren. At the same time, stepchildren confirmed that stepparents were less involved than their biological parents in their care and supervision. Thus, stepparents seem not to fit the profile of authoritative parenting described earlier in this chapter, and the benefits of that parenting style are not realized.

Some difficulties in stepfamilies may stem from the uncertain social roles of stepparents. Should they be as strict as the biological parent, or will the child see too much control as intrusive? Stepparents who are trying to win the affections of their "new" children may be reluctant to use strong discipline. And, as with any new parent and child, stepparents and children need time to build their emotional relationship. Parental remarriage can have either positive or negative consequences for children, depending on how the custodial parent and stepparent manage the transition.

## Families in Transition: An Overview

We have seen that changes in the structure of the American family affect child development to the extent that they influence the interactions among members of the family system. Maternal employment, divorce, and remarriage can alter the emotional tone of parent-child interactions as well as the types of control strategies parents select, and it is the control strategies that can have a profound effect on the intellectual and socioemotional development of the child. Considering how prevalent changes in family structures have become and how many children are affected by them, it is imperative that ways be established to support families undergoing these transitions. Assistance with child care, parent training programs for dysfunctional families, and counseling support for families experiencing stress are some of the programs that can be helpful.

---

## THEMES IN DEVELOPMENT

### THE FAMILY

▶ **How does the sociocultural context influence family processes?**

Many goals that parents have for their children's socialization are governed by attitudes held by the larger society, values and beliefs that change over time. Parents will emphasize cooperation, achievement, and sociability, for example, to the extent that the larger social group values these characteristics. Culture also influences who participates in child care and to what extent; in some cultures, for example, fathers and siblings take part in many routine child-care tasks. Finally, economic and social trends, such as family size, single parenthood, maternal employment, alternative child care, divorce, and remarriage, can alter family structures. The changes in family dynamics introduced by these factors can have far-reaching consequences for child development.

▶ **How does the child play an active role in family processes?**

As integral members of the family system, children can have significant effects on interactions with parents, siblings, and others. The dramatic physical and cognitive changes associated with development oblige parents and siblings to adapt to the rapidly altering capabilities and needs of the child. In general, parents and siblings react to the child's growing independence and competence by displaying less dominance and regulation. In addition, the child's behaviors may influence the parents' choice of discipline style in such a way that aggressive, difficult children elicit more authoritarian parenting and premature children may be at risk for abuse.

▶ **How do family processes interact with other domains of development?**

The child's experiences within the family, particularly the type of parenting style to which the child is exposed, can have broad consequences for development. For example, children who experience authoritarian parenting show less advanced moral reasoning, lower self-esteem, poorer relations with peers, poorer school adjustment, and higher levels of aggression than children who experience authoritative parenting. Similarly, interactions with siblings often provide children with opportunities to develop such social skills as nurturance and assertiveness. Finally, transitions in families can introduce both new opportunities and new stresses in the lives of children that can affect their emotional, social, and cognitive development.

## *Summary*

**Understanding the Family**   Many social scientists conceptualize the family as a *system* in which each relationship influences other relationships. In addition, the family is vulnerable to larger social influences such as cultural values and economic trends. Most psychologists recognize that the key to understanding the child's development lies in family dynamics.

**Parents and Socialization**   Parents serve as the child's primary *socialization* agents by teaching their children directly, serving as powerful models, and controlling other aspects of the child's social life. One important element of parenting is the general style with which parents relate to their children. *Authoritative parenting,* characterized by moderate control and high nurturance, is associated with cooperation, independence, achievement orientation, and healthy peer relations among children. *Authoritarian parents* rely excessively on power-assertive techniques and display less nurturance and affection. Their children frequently are aggressive, have lower levels of moral reasoning, poor self-esteem, poor peer relations, and lower school achievement. *Permissive* and *uninvolved parents* also tend to have children with developmental problems.

Punishment can alter the child's behavior in the short run, particularly if it is accompanied by an explanation and is used consistently. Physical punishment can, however, result in more aggression in children as well as avoidance of the punishing agent. For these reasons, experts recommend induction and *time-out* as techniques. Problems in parenting, such as the *coercive cycle* and child abuse, illustrate how power assertion can lead to escalating levels of violence within the family.

Cross-cultural and social class variations in parenting reflect the pressures exerted by larger social forces. In some rural societies in which children contribute to the family's subsistence, for example, they are expected to care for siblings and strictly obey their parents. Families affected by economic hardship provide another example of how an external factor can place stress on parents and influence their parenting style.

**Relationships with Mothers, Fathers, and Siblings**    Although mothers have traditionally assumed the caregiver role, fathers and siblings also play an important role in the child's socialization. Fathers typically do not spend as much time with their children as mothers but behave similarly when they are given the opportunity. One difference is that fathers tend to engage in more physical interactions with their infants and young children. Sensitive, responsive fathering is associated with many desirable outcomes in children.

Siblings also affect development. The presence of siblings usually means that parents have less time to spend with younger children; this fact may explain the generally higher achievement of only and first-born children. Sibling relations change over the course of development. Preschool-aged siblings have both aggressive and prosocial exchanges, and older siblings are more dominant and nurturant than younger siblings. These differences among siblings diminish as they get older.

**Families in Transition**    In today's society, more families include mothers who work and more families experience divorce. Maternal employment is associated with higher levels of achievement, independence, and self-esteem in girls and less stereotyped gender-role attitudes in both boys and girls. More important than the fact of maternal employment is the mother's interaction style and the quality of substitute care the child receives. Mothers who are satisfied with their life circumstances and who display adaptive parenting techniques have well-adjusted children. Studies of day care generally show that children who attend high-quality day care are more cognitively and socially competent than children reared solely at home by their parents.

Children whose parents divorce evidence socioemotional and academic difficulties, especially boys. Many effects disappear after the first year following the divorce, particularly among girls. Parental separation typically means increased stress on the family, a factor that can lead to ineffective parenting. Successful adjustment to divorce among children is associated with low parental conflict in the period after separation. Children, especially adolescents, also have difficulty adjusting to the remarriage of their parents. These difficulties may stem, in part, from the reluctance of stepparents to exhibit nurturance or control in their interactions with their stepchildren.

# 15

## Peers

▶ **How does the sociocultural context influence peer relations?**

▶ **How does the child play an active role in peer relations?**

▶ **Are developmental changes in peer relations continuous or discontinuous?**

▶ **How prominent are individual differences in peer relations?**

▶ **How do peer relations interact with other domains of development?**

*It was the start of the first day of school. Jan Nakamura, the third-grade teacher, surveyed her new charges as they played in the schoolyard before the bell rang. It was a familiar scene: The boys played a raucous game of kickball, cheering their teammates and urging victory. The girls gathered in small groups, talking with great animation about their summer experiences and their excitement about school. As always, certain children in both groups were the center of activity; they seemed to attract their age mates as a pot of honey draws bees. Other children seemed to fall into the background; few of their peers approached or spoke to them. Already Jan had a sense that third grade would be easier on some of these fresh new faces than others.*

In many ways, Jan's intuitions were correct. She would find, as she learned to match names to faces in this year's class, that many of the playground stars made the transition to a new grade more easily than some of the less popular children. Research evidence suggests that the ability to have successful and rewarding interactions with peers during childhood can be the harbinger of successful later adjustment and that poor peer relations are often associated with a range of developmental problems. Boys and girls who have good peer relationships enjoy school more and are less likely to experience academic difficulties, drop out of school, and commit delinquent or criminal acts in later years than age mates who relate poorly with their peers (Ladd, 1990; Morison & Masten, 1991; Parker & Asher, 1987). Children who are accepted by their peers are also less likely to report feeling lonely, depressed, and socially anxious than children who are rejected (Cassidy & Asher, 1992; Crick & Ladd, 1993; Hymel & Franke, 1985; Vosk et al., 1982). Of course, the quality of peer relations is not the only factor that predicts later developmental outcomes. Nevertheless, experiences with peers play a substantial role in the lives of most children and thus have become an important focus of developmental research.

What do child development theorists say about the role of peers? Social learning theorists believe that peers exert a heavy influence on the child's socialization by means of modeling and reinforcement. Piaget (1965/1932) and Vygotsky (1978) have discussed the ways in which peer contacts alter the child's cognitions, which can, in turn, direct social behavior. Piaget contends that peer interactions prompt—even coerce—the child to consider the viewpoints of others, broadening her social perspective-taking ability and diminishing her egocentrism. The result is a greater capacity for social exchange. Vygotsky maintains that contact with peers, especially those who are more skilled in a given domain, stretches the child's intellectual and social capacities. As a result of experiences with peers, the child internalizes new modes of thinking and social interaction and then produces them independently.

The number of studies examining peer relations in childhood and adolescence has skyrocketed in the last decade, due in part to a recognition of prevalence of peer experiences in children's lives and the undoubted power of peers as socializing agents. Researchers have especially focused on changes in peer relations with age, the dynamics of peer groups, and the factors that are related to social competence with peers. Because we humans are "social" beings, it is not surprising that our childhood experiences in social groups play such a large part in making us what we are.

## Developmental Changes in Peer Relations

Compared with any other human relationship, the special feature of peer relations is their egalitarian nature. In fact, strictly speaking, the term **peer** refers to a companion who is approximately the same age and developmental level. Parent-child interactions are characterized by a distinct dominant-subordinate hierarchy that facilitates the child's socialization as parents use their authority to transmit information about social rules and behaviors. Peers, however, usually function as equals, and it is primarily among equals that children can forge such social skills as compromising, competing, and cooperating. Thus, experiences with peers afford the child unique opportunities to construct social understanding and to develop social skills (Hartup, 1977, 1989; Youniss & Smollar, 1985).

▶ Interaction among domains

Relationships with peers also contribute to the child's developing sense of self. Peers provide the child with direct feedback (verbal and sometimes nonverbal) about how well he is doing in the academic, social, and emotional realms, information that can significantly influence the child's self-esteem. Peers also provide a natural comparison against which the child can gauge his own accomplishments (Furman & Robbins, 1985). "Am I really a good athlete?" "How am I doing as a student?" A child can answer questions like these by comparing his own abilities to those of his peers.

The way in which children relate to their peers undergoes significant developmental changes. At first, peers are simply interesting (or, at times, annoying) companions in play, but eventually they assume a larger and more crucial part in the child's social and emotional life. Children's peer networks start out small. But as children enter day care and school, and as their cognitive, language, and social skills develop, their peer networks expand in size, and their relationships with a subset of those peers grow in intensity.

### Early Peer Exchanges and Play

Infants show distinct reactions to peers even in the first few months of life. The sight of another baby often prompts a three-month-old to become generally aroused and active, a reaction that is very different than the ritualized greeting she usually reserves for her mother (Fogel, 1979) or the rapt and quiet attention she displays to her reflected image (Field, 1979). At six months, diffuse responses to peers give way to more specific signals, such as smiles, squeals, touching, and leaning in their direction (Hay, Nash, & Pedersen, 1983;

**peer** Companion of approximately the same age and developmental level.

Maudry & Nekula, 1939; Vandell, Wilson, & Buchanan, 1980). Older babies crawl toward one another and explore each other's facial features (Vandell & Mueller, 1980). Thus, from early on, infants recognize something special and interesting about strangers who resemble them in size and features. At the same time, most peer interactions during infancy are brief, lasting only a few seconds, and usually do not involve mutual exchanges of behaviors (Eckerman, Whatley, & Kutz, 1975; Vandell & Wilson, 1982).

In the second year, social exchanges with peers become longer and more coordinated. Two children will jointly manipulate toys and other objects, each child taking a turn playing and then offering the object to the playmate. Children also begin to play simple games together, such as hide-and-seek or tag, activities that require taking turns and switching roles (Howes, 1987a, 1987b). Later in toddlerhood, between the ages of two and three years, children engage in peer interactions more frequently. These interactions, instead of revolving around objects such as toys, contain many positive social and affiliative behaviors, such as giving attention, smiling, sharing, and cooperating (Bronson, 1981).

Mildred Parten (1932) found that the peer relations of young children are characterized by three forms of play. In **solitary play**, children play alone with toys, apart from other children and without regard for what they are doing. One child might be stacking rings while another does a puzzle; neither notices or cares about the other's activities. In **parallel play**, children play independently while they are beside or close to other children. Several children might be gathered at a sandbox, one digging with a shovel, another making "pies," and still another dragging a truck through the sand. Even though they are in close proximity, one child's activities do not influence the play of the others. In **cooperative play**, children interact. They share toys, follow one another, and make mutual suggestions about what to do next. Although Parten believed that a stagelike developmental progression took place from solitary to parallel and then cooperative play, more recent

▶ Development as
continuous/discontinuous

In parallel play, children play independently while they are beside or close to other children. Preschoolers may also show patterns of solitary and cooperative play.

**solitary play** Individual play, performed without regard for what others are doing.

**parallel play** Side-by-side independent play that is not interactive.

**cooperative play** Interactive play in which children's actions are reciprocal.

▶ Interaction among domains

research suggests that all three types of play occur among preschoolers (Barnes, 1971; Rubin, Maioni, & Hornung, 1976).

Preschoolers also begin to display **social pretend play** (also called *sociodramatic play*), in which they invoke "make-believe" to change the function of objects, create imaginary situations, and enact pretend roles, often with the cooperation of one or two peers (Rubin, Fein, & Vandenberg, 1983; Smilansky, 1968). Children use sticks and pots as band instruments, ride "magic carpets" together, and play "Mommy and Daddy." Growth in the child's cognitive, perspective-taking, and communication skills helps explain these changes (Hartup, 1983; Howes, 1987a). To conceive of a stick as representing a flute, for example, the child must develop symbolic capabilities that allow him to let one object represent another. For a young girl to play "Mommy," she must relinquish her own perspective and appreciate another person's social role—what "mommies" do and how they speak to children. Finally, for complex and coordinated exchanges of pretend play to occur, as when one child sets the table and prepares the food while the other cries like a baby, children must understand the rules of social dialogue and communication. When we watch three-year-olds engage in pretend play with one another, we are witnessing an intersection of their growing competence in several arenas—social, language, and cognitive skills (Howes, Unger, & Seidner, 1989).

## The School Years and Adolescence

Elementary school–aged children begin to participate more in group activities than in the dyads (or two-person groups) that characterize earlier peer relations. As noted in Chapter 13, they show a clear preference for same-sex peers and, to a lesser extent, children who are racially similar. In fact, as Figure 15.1 shows, the tendency to play with other children of the same sex begins in the preschool years and grows stronger throughout the elementary school years (Maccoby & Jacklin, 1987). It's not that children dislike children of the opposite sex; they simply prefer to play with same-sex peers (Bukowski, Gauze, Hoza, & Newcomb, 1993). Quarrels and physical aggression with peers wane, although older children do use abusive language such as threats and insults when they have conflicts with their peers. Concurrently, prosocial behaviors such as sharing and helping others increase (Hartup, 1983).

A special form of play, called **rough-and-tumble play**, emerges around age two years and becomes more visible during the elementary school years, especially among boys. Children chase each other, pretend to fight, or sneak up and pounce on each other. Rough-and-tumble play differs from aggression in that children do not intend to hurt one another and it often occurs between children who like each other. Smiling and laughing often accompany rough-and-tumble play, and children will often continue to play together after a bout, all signs that these interactions are friendly. In one naturalistic observation of seven-, nine-, and eleven-year-olds, rough-and-tumble play took up about 10 percent of the children's playground time (Humphreys & Smith, 1987). In another study, kindergartners, second-, and fourth-graders were observed on their school playgrounds during recess. For some children—popular children—episodes of rough-and-tumble play were often followed by organized games with rules rather than aggression. A playful chase, for example, often led to a game of tag. In addition, popular children who engaged in rough-and-tumble play had higher scores on a test

**social pretend play** Play that makes use of imaginary and symbolic objects and social roles, often enacted among several children. Also called *sociodramatic play*.

**rough-and-tumble play** Active, physical play that carries no intent of imposing harm on another child.

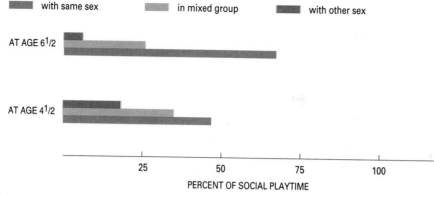

Source: Adapted from Maccoby & Jacklin, 1987.

**FIGURE 15.1**

**Changes in Time Spent with Same-Sex Friends During Early Childhood**

The amount of time children spend with same-sex peers increases dramatically during early childhood, as this study of children's behavior during free play at school shows. At the same time, the proportion of time spent playing with opposite-sex peers decreases noticeably.

of social problem solving. These results suggest that, for some children, rough-and-tumble play provides a context for learning role exchange (for example, "Now you chase *me*") and prosocial behaviors like cooperation. On the other hand, when unpopular children played roughly, they were more likely to end up in a real physical fight. Their rough-and-tumble play escalated into aggression 28 percent of the time and was positively correlated with a measure of general antisocial behavior (Pellegrini, 1988).

What kinds of activities do school-aged children most frequently engage in with their peers? A survey of eighty-one fifth- and sixth-graders in Canada showed that peer activities are diverse (Zarbatany, Hartmann, & Rankin, 1990). Subjects were asked to scan a list of twenty-nine activities and rate how often they participated in each activity with their peers. As Table 15.1 shows, preadolescents spend a lot of time talking with each other, participating in sports, and listening to music or watching television together. These activities are likely to serve a number of functions, including promoting relationships, providing opportunities for learning, and allowing children to validate their own interests and self-worth.

Peer relations during adolescence become more intense on one level and involve larger networks on another level. Adolescents form close, intimate friendships with a subset of their peers, relationships they greatly value. Many children also form **cliques,** groups of five to ten children usually in the same class at school who frequently interact together (Brown, 1989). Clique membership is often supplemented by identification with a **crowd,** a larger group of peers with a specific reputation, such as "jocks" or "brains." Members of crowds do not necessarily spend time together but share a label based on a stereotype. It is interesting that even though youngsters may see themselves as members of particular cliques, their membership in crowds is often identified or labeled by others (Brown, 1989). That is, a girl might not see herself as a "brain" but receive that label from peers who observe her academic achievements and studious behaviors. Membership in cliques and crowds in the middle and later school years reflects the child's growing need for group belonging at a time when he is orienting away from parents and other adults. At the same time, the values encouraged by parents can influence the crowds their adolescent children become affiliated with. If a parent encourages achievement, for example, the child's academic success may place her in the group of "brains" (Brown et al., 1993). The norms of

**clique**   Peer group of five to ten children who frequently interact together.

**crowd**   Large group of peers that is characterized by specific traits or reputation.

**TABLE 15.1**

**Peer Activities in Later Childhood**

Fifth- and sixth-graders were asked to indicate those peer activities they spent the most time engaged in. They rated a series of activities on a scale in which 0 indicated the activity was never conducted and 7 indicated the activity was conducted more than once a day. The results (average ratings) showed that preadolescents participate in a wide range of activities with each other, from conversing to simply watching TV.

| Activity | Time Spent |
|----------|-----------|
| Conversing | 6.76 |
| Hanging out | 6.57 |
| Walking at school | 5.65 |
| Telephone | 5.63 |
| Travel to/from school | 5.57 |
| TV/records | 5.39 |
| Physical games | 5.26 |
| Noncontact sports | 5.17 |
| Academic | 5.15 |
| Acting silly | 5.12 |

Source: Adapted from Zarbatany, Hartmann, & Rankin, 1990.

cliques and crowds can be powerful shapers of behavior; they often provide the adolescent with prescriptions on how to dress, act, and even what ambitions to have for the future.

As adolescents approach young adulthood and feel more secure with their self-identities, they are less interested in cliques and crowds and become oriented once again toward relationships with individuals. Third- through twelfth-graders in one study were asked to list their closest friends in the entire school as well as the people they spent time with (Shrum & Cheek, 1987). Analysis of the patterns of relationships among children showed that there was a sharp decline toward later adolescence in the percentage of students who were members of cliques.

One other significant change in adolescence is that some peer relations begin to include elements of sexuality. Dating becomes one of the major social activities of adolescence, and interest in peers of the opposite sex is generally heightened (Damon, 1983). During this time, adolescents develop new social skills, such as the ability to have mutually engaging conversations with members of the opposite sex, that reinforce this shift toward romantic relationships. Again, interest in members of the opposite sex reflects the adolescent's concerns with entering the adult world. The Chronology on page 569 summarizes these major developmental changes in peer relations.

## Peer Group Dynamics

When we observe preschoolers or elementary school children, we see that they often associate in groups. Peer groups, however, become especially visible and significant during the middle school and early secondary school years (Crockett, Losoff, & Petersen, 1984). Adolescents frequently "hang out" in groups, desire to be members of the most popular groups, and look to the peer group for standards of appearance, conduct, and attitudes. Parents may find

| | |
|---|---|
| 3 MONTHS | Reacts with arousal or attention to presence of a peer. |
| 6–9 MONTHS | Directs smiles, touches, and other signals toward peers. Approaches peers. |
| 2–4 YEARS | Jointly manipulates objects with one or two other peers. Engages in simple turn-taking games with peers. Shares, smiles, and cooperates with peers. Shows bouts of physical aggression with peers. Displays solitary, parallel, cooperative, and social pretend play. |
| 5–9 YEARS | Participates in group activities. Displays less physical aggression and more prosocial behaviors toward peers. Displays rough-and-tumble play. |
| 10–14 YEARS | Forms intimate friendships. Joins cliques. Becomes affiliated with a crowd. Feels greater peer pressure to conform. |
| 15–18 YEARS | Participates less frequently in cliques and crowds. Becomes more interested in peers of the opposite sex. |

This chart describes the sequence of peer relations based on the findings of research. Children often show individual differences in the exact ages at which they display the various developmental achievements outlined here.

that their son or daughter *must have* a certain haircut or *must buy* a particular video game, only to discover that everyone else in the child's circle of friends has the same "look" or library of games. The social dynamics of large groups are often different than the dynamics of two-person groups, or dyads; the power exerted by the group in shaping how the child acts and thinks can be enormous.

## Peer Group Formation

How do peer groups form in the first place? Undoubtedly, they coalesce on the basis of children's shared interests, backgrounds, or activities. Children associate with other members of their classroom, their soccer team, or other members of the school band, for example. Other variables, like socioeconomic status or ethnic and racial group membership, can also be a factor. Youngsters often join with others of similar social class or ethnic/racial background (Clasen & Brown, 1985; Larkin, 1979). As we have seen both in Chapter 13 and

Peer groups form when children participate in cooperative activities that involve some common goal or purpose. Here, fifth graders participate in a camp activity intended to build group solidarity.

in this chapter, gender is another powerful variable; groups, for the most part, tend to be of the same sex throughout childhood and early adolescence.

A particularly enlightening description of how peer groups form and operate can be found in a classic experiment called the Robber's Cave Study, named after the state park in Oklahoma where it took place. Muzafer Sherif and his colleagues invited twenty-two fifth-grade boys who did not know each other to participate in a summer camp program (Sherif et al., 1961). The boys were divided into two groups who lived in separate parts of the state park. Initially, each group participated in its own program of typical camp activities—hiking, crafts, structured games—and was unaware of the existence of the other group. In this initial period of the experiment, each group began to develop a unique identity, and individual members performed distinct roles in relation to this group identity. One group became "tough"; the boys swore, acted roughly, and ridiculed those who were "sissies." Members of the other group were polite and considerate. As group solidarity grew, members decided to name themselves, the former calling themselves the Rattlers and the latter the Eagles.

The experimenters found that when they deliberately structured certain situations to encourage cooperation, group identities could be further strengthened. One day, for example, each group returned to the campsite only to find that the staff had not prepared dinner; only the uncooked ingredients were available. The boys quickly took over, dividing up the tasks so that some cooked, others prepared drinks, and so forth. Some boys assumed a leadership role, directing the suppertime activities, and others followed their directives. It was quite apparent that the boys had a strong sense of identity with the group and that the group had a clear structure. In other words, for both the Rattlers and the Eagles, there was strong intragroup cooperation and identity.

Another change in circumstances made the group identities even more pronounced. The camp counselors arranged for the Rattlers and Eagles to meet and organized a series of competitions for them, including games like baseball and tug-of-war. The effects of losing in these competitions were dramatic. The losing group became very disharmonious and full of conflict. Members accused each other of causing the loss, and some boys who had previously enjoyed status and prestige were demoted in standing if they had contributed to the group's humiliation. After these initial conflicts, however, group identity became stronger than ever. The effects of competition on behavior *between* the groups were even more pronounced. The Rattlers and Eagles verbally antagonized each other and retaliated for a loss in the day's competition by raiding each other's campsites and stealing possessions such as comic books and clothing. Each episode forged intragroup identity but also increased intergroup hostility.

In the last phase of this social experiment, the counselors attempted to lessen the bad feelings between the Rattlers and the Eagles by having them share meals or watch movies together. Instead of promoting harmony between the groups, however, this tactic produced continuing hostilities, punctuated with fights and verbal assaults. In contrast, when the experimenters created situations in which the two groups had to work together to achieve some common goal, antagonisms between them began to crumble. One hot day, for example, when the counselors "discovered" that the water pipeline for the campsites was broken, boys from both the Rattlers and the Eagles began to search together for the broken pipes. On another occasion, the food delivery truck broke down; again, the boys all worked together to restart the engine. The acrimonious behavior between the two groups diminished, and boys from the two groups actually began to form friendships with one another.

Thus, groups form when individuals share activities and have some common goal or purpose. Identity with the group becomes stronger as children have more and more rewarding interactions within them and as the group's goals are accomplished. Groups also quickly develop structures wherein some members assume a more dominant role than others. Group identity becomes especially strong when there is competition with other groups, but an undesirable outcome is that intergroup conflict rises. Barriers between groups break down when they actively work together to achieve some common, overarching goal. Few studies of the formation and function of peer groups match the scope of the Robber's Cave Study, which has revealed many of the intricacies of peer group dynamics, and in doing so, suggests strategies for breaking down animosities between children's peer groups.

## Dominance Hierarchies

The scene: a standard laboratory playroom on a university campus. Six elementary school boys, strangers to one another, are brought together to play for forty-five minutes, five days in a row. Beginning the first day, researchers discover, the boys establish dominance hierarchies, distinct levels of social power in the relationships among group members. Some boys initiate more activity, verbally persuade the other group members to act a certain way, or use aggression to get their way. Others play a more submissive role, giving in to the actions of the dominant boys. Based on the frequencies with which these behaviors are displayed, each boy can be rated as most or least dominant or somewhere in between (Pettit et al., 1990).

▶ Individual differences

As laboratory studies and field experiments like the Robber's Cave Study show, the dominance relations among members of the peer group form quickly and remain stable over a period of months or even longer (Strayer & Strayer, 1976). Especially among younger children, dominance is established through physical power and aggression; the most powerful children are those

▶ The child's active role

who physically coerce or threaten the other members of the group into compliance. The basis of dominance changes, however, as group members get to know one another. When preschoolers are observed over the period of a school year, for example, their aggression is highly correlated with dominance in the beginning of the year but is unrelated to dominance by the end of the year (LaFreniere & Charlesworth, 1983). As children approach adolescence, the basis for dominance shifts from physical power to characteristics such as intelligence, creativity, and interpersonal skill (Pettit et al., 1990; Savin-Williams, 1980).

What function do dominance hierarchies have in the social behavior of children? First, groups can more easily meet their objectives when certain individuals within the group assume a leadership role. Ethologists have long observed that many species of animals, especially primates, have clear lines of power that probably enhance the obtaining of food, protection against natural enemies, and control of reproduction. Among children, dominance hierarchies can serve to get games going on the playground or accomplish school projects that require group efforts. Second, dominance hierarchies make social relationships more predictable for members of the group. Each individual has a specific role, whether as leader or follower, and the behaviors associated with those roles are often clearly defined (Savin-Williams, 1979). Finally, dominance hierarchies are thought to control aggression among members of the group. Usually, once the most dominant members of the group have emerged, few other members resort to aggression. In one naturalistic observation of preschool children's free play, for example, only 20 percent of the interactions among children were classified as counterattacks to aggression (Strayer & Strayer, 1976).

## Peer Pressure and Conformity

One of the most widely accepted beliefs about peer groups is that they control the behavior of children, sometimes more than parents and other adults would like. And in fact, peer pressure *is* a very real phenomenon. When seventh-through twelfth-graders were asked to rate how much pressure they felt from age mates in several domains, they did report pressure and the greatest was to just be involved with peers, that is, spend time with them, go to parties, and otherwise associate with them (Brown, Clasen, & Eicher, 1986; Clasen & Brown, 1985). They also felt pressure to excel and to complete their education. Contrary to popular opinion, however, they reported the least peer pressure to engage in misconduct, such as smoking, drinking, or having sexual relations. Older adolescents, however, felt more pressures toward misconduct than younger adolescents.

How willing are children to conform to these peer pressures? Again, when researchers ask them, children give different answers depending on their age (Berndt, 1979; Brown, Clasen, & Eicher, 1986; Gavin & Furman, 1989). Vulnerability to peer pressure peaks in early adolescence, usually between the sixth and ninth grades (see Figure 15.2), and may lead to conflicts with parents. In fact, adolescents report the greatest number of disagreements with their parents right around the ninth-grade mark. By late adolescence, however, the influence of peers on conformity declines. Thus, the relationship between age and peer conformity is a curvilinear one.

These developmental changes can be explained, in part, by the adjustments that youths must make at different points in adolescence. Most young adolescents are moving from elementary school to a middle school or junior high school, where many students are strangers to each other and new relationships must be established. For many children, this is an anxiety-ridden task; they fear that they "won't know anybody," a phrase many a preadolescent's parent has heard. In addition, adolescents in junior high typically move from one class to another over the course of the day; the peer group does not remain constant as it did in elementary school, and relationships may be more difficult to establish in this context. As they are adjusting to the new school setting, young adolescents also become more independent from their parents and increasingly search for their "selfhood." By conforming to the norms of the peer group and thereby becoming accepted, young adolescents are meeting many of their socioemotional needs, especially the need for affiliation. By virtue of their style of parenting, parents may also be responsible for adolescents' tendencies to seek out the peer group. When parents of young adolescents maintain their power and restrictiveness, limiting their children's opportunities for decision making, their children tend to turn to their peer group for advice (Fuligni & Eccles, 1993).

In contrast, older adolescents are approaching a new phase in their lives, a time when they must seek jobs, further their education, or make other major decisions. These are individual choices of great importance that require less input from peers. The older adolescent has also developed a stronger sense of self and feels less need to rely on the advice or norms of the peer group (Brown, 1989). Thus, the role of the peer group varies with the developmental tasks of different age groups.

Exactly how do peer groups exert their pressure? Most likely by rewarding individuals who conform to the group's norms and reacting negatively to those who resist. Children who conform to the norms of the group get invited to the "right" parties or receive compliments on their attire. Those who don't conform may get "the silent treatment" or, worse yet, become the objects of teasing and ridicule. Few researchers have actually observed the dynamics of peer groups as they try to enforce norms, but subjects in some studies report that negative interactions within peer groups increase during early adolescence and decrease in late adolescence. The same developmental trend shows up when subjects are asked how much they are bothered by these negative inter-

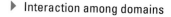 Interaction among domains

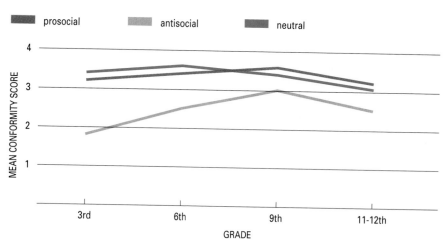

**FIGURE 15.2**

**Developmental Changes in Conformity to Peer Pressure**

Conformity to peer pressure, whether it involves prosocial, antisocial, or neutral behavior, peaks in early adolescence, then declines. The higher numbers in this graph represent greater willingness to conform.

Source: Adapted from Berndt, 1979.

actions; children are increasingly bothered in early adolescence and less bothered toward the end of the adolescent years (Gavin & Furman, 1989).

Finally, how much do the pressures placed by peers conflict with those exerted by parents? As we saw earlier, peers, like parents, expect the growing child to be competent and to achieve in school. In that sense, peers and parents pressure children toward some of the same goals. We also saw, however, that as adolescents approach young adulthood, the pressures to engage in behaviors frowned on by adults increase. Moreover, the results of one study show that when young adolescents strongly value conforming to adult norms (for example, by saying that getting drunk and skipping school are negative), they are less popular with their peers. Conversely, adolescents who place less value on conforming to adult norms are more popular (Allen, Weissberg, & Hawkins, 1989). Thus, adults and peers provide overlapping support in encouraging general competence, but conflicting pressures when it comes to certain behaviors like drinking or smoking that older adolescents are sometimes likely to experiment with.

## Peers as Agents of Socialization

Like parents, teachers, and the media, peers are the child's source of information about the "do's and don'ts" of the social world. Because children have such extensive social relations with their peers, there are few better sources of feedback on acceptable and unacceptable behaviors. Peers socialize their age mates in two main ways—as models and as reinforcers. In their behaviors, peers also reflect the values of the larger society.

### Peers as Models

According to social learning theory, the greater the similarity between a model and an observer, the more likely it is that the observer will imitate the model's behavior (Bandura, 1969). Peers, therefore, are prime candidates for prompting imitation in children. Although peer imitation declines by middle childhood, it occurs quite frequently in the early years. In one study, the number of imitative acts occurring in the free play of preschoolers averaged 14.82 per hour (Abramovitch & Grusec, 1978).

There is ample evidence that a whole host of social behaviors can be transmitted through peer modeling. Display of aggression is a prime example. When children observe a peer acting aggressively with toys, they spontaneously perform similar aggressive acts (Hicks, 1965). On the opposite end of the spectrum, models can promote sharing and other altruistic acts in observer children (Elliott & Vasta, 1970; Hartup & Coates, 1967). Gender-role behaviors, too, can be influenced by peer models. Most children are reluctant to play with toys meant for the opposite sex. Yet if a peer model displays cross-sex play, children's tendency to follow suit increases (Kobasigawa, 1968; Wolf, 1973).

A powerful variable influencing imitation is the model's competence as perceived by the observer child, especially when new skills or behaviors are involved. Children prefer older, friendly models who are similar to themselves in background and interests (Brody & Stoneman, 1981; Hartup & Coates, 1967; Rosekrans, 1967). Especially in the realm of social behaviors, children may im-

▶ Interaction among domains

itate competent peer models over adult models because they see the behaviors selected by peers as more appropriate for themselves.

## Peers as Reinforcers

Peers not only model certain behaviors, they also actively reinforce their friends' behaviors. Peers communicate clear signals about the social behaviors they prefer and those they won't tolerate, messages that may either maintain or inhibit the child's behaviors. Consider the case of sex-typed behaviors. Researchers observed the reactions of peers as preschool-aged children engaged in sex-appropriate or inappropriate play in their nursery schools (Lamb & Roopnarine, 1979). They found that boys who engaged in male-typed activities such as playing ball or chase received more praise and approval (mostly from other boys) than girls did when they attempted these same behaviors. Similarly, peers more frequently reinforced girls than boys who played dolls, kitchen, or assumed female character roles. Peers controlled behavior through punishment, too, although it was reserved largely for cross-sex activities. This study demonstrates how forcefully peers can enforce stereotypical codes of behavior for boys and girls by directly rewarding activities consistent with those codes.

▶ Interaction among domains

In the same way, the frequency of other social behaviors such as aggression can be regulated by peer reactions. In their observations of aggression among preschoolers, Gerald Patterson and his colleagues noted that about three-fourths of the aggressive behaviors that took place were reinforced by victims' compliance or submission (Patterson, Littman, & Bricker, 1967). The consequence was that aggressors maintained their combative styles of interaction. If a peer responded with counteraggression, however, the perpetrator was less likely to repeat the action with that child, choosing either another victim or another behavior. Thus, peers powerfully affect one another by means of their positive and negative reactions.

## Peers as Transmitters of Cultural Values

In a broad sense, the way a culture or society organizes peer experiences for children can serve as a vehicle for conveying its primary values and ideals. For example, some children are raised in *collective* settings in which they experience group care from infancy onward and contact with peers remains extensive through adolescence. Children who grow up in such peer-oriented contexts exhibit some behaviors and traits that distinguish them from children raised in societies that stress individualism and independence.

▶ Sociocultural influence

Urie Bronfenbrenner's (1970) comparative study of peer experiences in the former Soviet Union and several Western nations, including the United States, demonstrates how specific types of peer interactions can shape individual psychological characteristics and beliefs. At the time Bronfenbrenner's observations were conducted, a significant proportion of Soviet children attended preschool institutions. In this setting, group experiences predominated from the beginning. Infants were placed in playpens with five to seven other children, and although caregivers provided a good deal of individual attention, group consciousness was deliberately fostered. Children were encouraged to engage in group games and other forms of collective play and were explicitly taught the value of sharing.

Peers often actively reinforce the child's behaviors, giving clear signals about the behaviors they prefer and value.

At age seven years children entered a formal school program in which the emphasis on group activities continued. Each classroom was divided into "links," rows of students who together were responsible for preparing lessons, conducting projects, and maintaining discipline. Links frequently competed against each other for the teacher's approval, but the success of the link depended on cooperation among its members. Thus, children often helped each other with homework assignments and enforced disciplinary rules so that the link could earn privileges (for example, going to recess first) and positive evaluations from the teacher. Here are some sample observations:

> "What are you fooling around for? You're holding up the whole link," whispers Kolya to his neighbor during the preparation period for the lesson. And during the break he teaches her how to organize better the books and pads in her knapsack.

> "Work more carefully," says Olya to her girl friend. "See, on account of you, our link got behind today. You come to me and we'll work together at home." (Bronfenbrenner, 1970, pp. 63–64)

▶ Interaction among domains

What is the impact of this strong group orientation during childhood? Bronfenbrenner conducted a series of studies examining moral decision making and antisocial behavior in Soviet children. In one study, 150 twelve-year-olds were tested on their readiness to cheat and commit other moral transgressions. In one condition, children were assured that their answers would be kept confidential. In two other conditions, subjects were told that teachers or peers, respectively, would learn their answers. Compared with children from the United States, England, and West Germany, Soviet children were much less willing to behave antisocially, but especially if they thought their peers would know the outcome. American children, in contrast, were *more* likely to transgress if they thought their peers might learn the results (Rodgers, Bronfenbrenner, & Devereux, 1968). What would the Soviet children do if they learned that a peer had committed a transgression? In another study, Bronfenbrenner (1964) learned that most would take personal initiative in correcting their classmate's behavior. In contrast, the Swiss children in his sample responded that they would tell an adult or do nothing.

Similarly, the "other orientation" of children living on the Israeli kibbutzim is apparent in their moral reasoning and prosocial behavior. We saw in Chapter 12 that children growing up in this peer-oriented setting make more advanced prosocial judgments. Kibbutz-reared children also behave more cooperatively than urban Israeli children when they play games that allow either for competition or for cooperation (Shapira & Madsen, 1969). Thus, through their day-to-day experiences with peers, children are directly or indirectly given strong messages about the general values and philosophies of their culture.

## Peer Popularity and Social Competence

Parents, teachers like Jan Nakamura in this chapter's opening scene, and others who have the opportunity to observe children over time usually notice the two extreme ends of the sociability spectrum: some children seem to be at the center of many activities, from school projects to playground games, whereas others are ridiculed or ignored. Frequently, the patterns of peer acceptance that become established in the early school years persist for years afterward, along with the psychological rewards or disappointments that accompany them. Psychologists have uncovered several factors related to peer acceptance and popularity and have applied this knowledge to helping children at the unpopular extreme of the spectrum.

### Measuring Peer Acceptance

Given the relationship between peer acceptance and later development that was described at the start of this chapter, the task of identifying children with problems in this domain is all the more important. Psychologists have relied on teachers or their own observations of children's behaviors to assess the quality of peer relations, but they especially rely in the assessments provided by the child's age mates.

Peer assessments frequently consist of a **sociometric nomination** measure in which children are asked to name a specified number of peers (usually between three and five) who fit a certain criterion. For example, children might be asked to "name three classmates you especially like (or dislike)" or "list three peers you would like to walk home from school with." The number of positive or negative nominations the child receives from other children serves as a measure of his popularity. Alternatively, children are sometimes asked to rate each peer in the class or group on a **sociometric rating scale**, a series of items such as "How much do you like to be with this person at school?" (see Figure 15.3). The target child's average rating by the other children is the index of peer acceptance.

Peer nomination measures, in turn, are used to classify children's *peer status. Popular* children receive many more positive ("like") than negative ("dislike") nominations. *Rejected* children, in contrast, receive few positive but many negative nominations; they are overtly disliked by their peers. *Neglected* children receive low numbers of nominations in either category; although they lack friends, they are not actively disliked (Asher & Dodge, 1986). *Controver-*

**sociometric nomination** Peer assessment measure in which children are asked to name a specified number of peers who fit a certain criterion, such as "peers you would like to walk home with."

**sociometric rating scale** Peer assessment measure in which children rate peers on a number of social dimensions.

## FIGURE 15.3

### A Sociometric Rating Scale

In this peer assessment tool, the child is asked to rate each peer on a series of items, such as "How much do you like to play with this person at school?" The average rating each target child receives from her peers is an index of peer acceptance.

Name _____

EXAMPLES:

HOW MUCH DO YOU LIKE TO PLAY WITH THIS PERSON AT SCHOOL?

| | I don't like to | | | | I like to a lot |
|---|---|---|---|---|---|
| Louise Blue | 1 | 2 | 3 | 4 | 5 |
| Russell Grey | 1 | 2 | 3 | 4 | 5 |
| John Armon | 1 | 2 | 3 | 4 | 5 |
| Andrea Brandt | 1 | 2 | 3 | 4 | 5 |
| Sue Curtis | 1 | 2 | 3 | 4 | 5 |
| Sandra Drexel | 1 | 2 | 3 | 4 | 5 |
| Jeff Ellis | 1 | 2 | 3 | 4 | 5 |
| Bill Fox | 1 | 2 | 3 | 4 | 5 |
| Diane Higgins | 1 | 2 | 3 | 4 | 5 |
| Harry Jones | 1 | 2 | 3 | 4 | 5 |
| Jill Lamb | 1 | 2 | 3 | 4 | 5 |
| Steve Murray | 1 | 2 | 3 | 4 | 5 |
| Jo Anne Norman | 1 | 2 | 3 | 4 | 5 |
| Pam Riley | 1 | 2 | 3 | 4 | 5 |
| Jim Stevens | 1 | 2 | 3 | 4 | 5 |

HOW MUCH DO YOU LIKE TO PLAY WITH

| THIS PERSON AT SCHOOL? | 1 | 2 | 3 | 4 | 5 |
|---|---|---|---|---|---|
| | I don't like to | | | | I like to a lot |

Source: From Asher, 1985.

▶ Individual differences

*sial* children receive high numbers of both positive and negative nominations. They have a high degree of "social impact" because they are active and visible, but they are generally not preferred as social partners (Coie, Dodge, & Coppotelli, 1982). Finally, *average* children do not receive extreme scores on peer nomination measures. Table 15.2 summarizes these categories of peer status.

What exactly is it about unpopular children that makes them so unappealing to their classmates and places them so consistently in an undesirable status? This is a particularly important question if we want to intervene in these children's "at risk" position.

## Characteristics of Popular and Unpopular Children

Peer popularity is related to a number of variables, some of which lie within the child's control and some of which, unfortunately, do not. The child's physical attractiveness, name, and perhaps motor skills fall into the latter category, whereas social skills belong to the former.

**Physical Attractiveness** When asked to rate photographs of unfamiliar children, both preschool and elementary school-aged children believe that children with attractive faces are more friendly, intelligent, and social than unattractive children (Dion & Berscheid, 1974; Langlois & Stephan, 1981). Correlations between children's ratings of peers' attractiveness and sociometric

| | | Positive Peer Nominations | |
| --- | --- | --- | --- |
| | | Many | Few |
| Negative Peer Nominations | Many | Controversial | Rejected |
| | Few | Popular | Neglected |

**TABLE 15.2**

**Classifications of Peer Status**

The number of positive and negative peer nominations received determines whether a child's peer status is classified as controversial, rejected, neglected, or popular. Average children receive less extreme scores on peer nomination measures.

measures of peer acceptance typically range between +0.35 and +0.50, indicating a moderately strong relationship between these two variables (Cavior & Dokecki, 1973; Lerner & Lerner, 1977). Body type makes a difference, too. For example, boys with broad shoulders and large muscles are the most popular, and short, chubby boys are the least popular (Staffieri, 1967). The reasons for these stereotypic beliefs are unknown, but they can lead to self-fulfilling behaviors in children who have been labeled (Hartup, 1983). For example, a child who receives peer attention because of attractiveness may have numerous opportunities to develop the social skills that lead to even greater peer acceptance. Finally, as we saw in Chapter 5, boys who mature early during adolescence and girls who mature later are more likely to be accepted by peers.

▶ Interaction among domains

**Name**    The attractiveness of a child's name, as perceived by peers, is positively correlated with his popularity. When researchers asked several classes of ten- to twelve-year-olds to rate the attractiveness of first names of peers in their group, they found a substantial relationship between these ratings and ratings of peer popularity obtained one month later (McDavid & Harari, 1966). As with the child's physical appearance, the mechanisms underlying this relationship are not well understood, but one possibility is that parents who choose a unique name may have other characteristics that influence the child's social behaviors. They may, for example, be eccentric parents who encourage nonconformist behaviors in their children. Another possibility is that peers are more wary of a child that is "too different," even in name alone, and may be less likely to initiate conversations or invite that child to play. The child with the unusual name may thus have fewer opportunities to develop social skills. Whatever the case, in our society a child with the name "Elmer" might have a bigger task in establishing relationships with peers than a "Michael" or "William."

**Motor Skills**    Another factor related to peer acceptance is the child's proficiency in motor activities. Both boys and girls who are coordinated, strong, and skilled in activities such as throwing a ball are rated as more popular by peers and as more socially competent by their teachers and parents (Hops & Finch, 1985). It may be that the value our society places on athletic prowess is reflected in children's preferences in playmates. Alternatively, motor skill may facilitate the manipulation of objects and game-playing that constitute the majority of children's shared activities. Those who are talented in this arena will naturally have more peer contacts and eventually be better liked.

▶ Interaction among domains

▶ Sociocultural influence

▶ The child's active role

**Social Skills**    One of the most important factors in peer acceptance is the constellation of social behaviors displayed by popular and unpopular children. Researchers who have observed the overt activities of accepted and unaccepted peers have learned that each presents a distinct behavioral profile. In general, popular children engage in prosocial, cooperative, and normative behaviors and show a high degree of social skill. In contrast, rejected and neglected children behave in aggressive, withdrawn, or other socially inappropriate ways for which they receive little social reinforcement (Parkhurst & Asher, 1992).

For example, when Gary Ladd (1983) observed third- and fourth-grade students during recess, he noted several differences in the behavioral styles of popular and rejected children. Popular children spent more time in cooperative play, social conversation, and other positive social interactions with peers than their rejected counterparts. Rejected children, on the other hand, spent more time engaging in antagonistic behaviors such as arguing and playing in a rough-and-tumble fashion, or playing or standing alone at a distance from peers.

According to the results of another study that examined the peer-directed behaviors of first- and third-grade boys, neglected and controversial children display still other clusters of behaviors (Coie & Dodge, 1988). Neglected boys were the least aggressive of any group observed. They tended to engage in isolated activities and had low visibility with peers. Controversial boys were intellectually, athletically, or socially talented and very active, but they were sometimes prone to anger and rule violations. The mixture of their positive and negative social behaviors thus elicited a concomitantly mixed reaction from their classmates. Thus, children may be unpopular with their peers for a number of reasons ranging from social withdrawal to outright aggression.

The social competence of popular children becomes markedly apparent when they are asked to enter a group of unfamiliar children who are already at play. Kenneth Dodge and his colleagues observed as individual kindergarten children entered a room where two other children they did not know were

Children who lack social skills may be rejected or neglected by their peers. In contrast, popular children display prosocial behaviors and display a wide range of social knowledge.

already playing with blocks (Dodge et al., 1983). Popular, rejected, and neglected children used different tactics to gain entry into the group, with popular children generally the most successful. Rejected children tended to disrupt the group's ongoing activity by pushing the blocks off the table or by making intrusive statements, usually about themselves (for example, "I have a baby brother"). In return, their peer hosts responded negatively to them. Neglected children were not disruptive but employed another ineffective strategy. Instead of making some verbal or nonverbal attempt to join the group, these children passively watched as their peers played—and they were ignored. Popular children seemed to know exactly what to do. Rather than bringing attention to themselves or disrupting the group's activities, they made statements about their peers or what they were doing, such as, "That looks like a fun game you are playing." These diplomatic verbalizations paved the way for their smooth integration into the group.

In the second part of this same research project, Dodge and his associates organized play groups for seven- and eight-year-old boys during the summer when school was out of session. None of the boys knew each other at the outset, so that it was possible to observe how they initiated entry into a play group under natural circumstances. Boys who were successful in entering a group that was already playing followed a three-step sequence that consisted of: (1) waiting and watching the group, (2) mimicking the group's activity—for example, playing basketball or singing, and (3) making a group-oriented statement, such as describing what the group was doing. In general, successful children began with low-risk tactics and, as they received positive feedback, moved toward higher-risk strategies. They also kept the focus of attention on the peer group rather than on themselves.

Popular children are particularly effective at maintaining cohesive social interactions with their peers. When Betty Black and Nancy Hazen (1990) observed the social entry behaviors of preschool-aged children, they found that disliked children made significantly more irrelevant comments when they spoke with peers. The following segment illustrates how such a conversation might go:

MARY: "We're being witches here, and I am the mean witch."
SANDY: "My mom is taking me to get shoes today." (p. 387)

In contrast, children who were liked tended to maintain organized, thematically coherent conversations with their peers.

Thus, observations of popular children show that they display a range of social skills that their more unpopular age mates often lack. But does their social skill actually cause their popularity, or do children develop reputations that precipitate subsequent successful or maladaptive patterns of social interaction? A child who is initially rejected because of his appearance, for example, may develop an aggressive style in retaliation. Gary Ladd and his associates examined this question more closely by observing preschool children in the playground during three 6-week intervals in the beginning, middle, and end of the academic year (Ladd, Price, & Hart, 1988). Episodes of cooperative play, arguments, and other positive and negative forms of interaction were recorded. In addition, children's sociometric status was assessed at each of these three points in time. The results showed that children who engaged in more cooperative play at the beginning of the school year made gains in peer acceptance by the end of the school year, whereas children who frequently argued showed a decline in acceptance by the middle of the school year. These results are consistent with the idea that children's behaviors precede their social status.

## The Origins of Social Competence

What factors are responsible for the skilled social behaviors of some children and the seeming social ineptness of others? Researchers draw their answers from a number of perspectives, from the early attachment relationships children form with their caregivers to capabilities in processing the subtle cues that form such an integral part of social interactions.

▶ Interaction among domains

**Attachment Relationships**    As we saw in Chapter 11, infants who are securely attached to their caregivers may be predisposed to have positive peer relations in toddlerhood (Waters, Wippman, & Sroufe, 1979). A plausible hypothesis is that in their relationships with caregivers children have the opportunity to learn and practice a variety of social skills, such as turn taking, compromise, and effective communication. Once honed and refined, these abilities can later be employed with peers and other individuals in the child's life. Attachment also teaches children about emotional ties—how to recognize affection and how to show it. This knowledge about the central ingredients of relationships may assist children as they expand their social worlds (Hay, 1985; Sroufe, 1983). Recent research, however, provides conflicting findings regarding early attachment and later peer relationships. One longitudinal study confirms that five-year-olds who have more positive friendships with peers tended to have secure attachments with their parents during infancy (Youngblade & Belsky, 1992). Another study, in contrast, found no significant relationship between children's attachment classification with mothers at age twelve months and their competence with peers at four years of age (Howes, Matheson, & Hamilton, 1994).

**Parental Influences**    Parents play an influential role in the relationships their children have with peers. Broadly speaking, parents who exhibit an authoritative style (see Chapter 14) such that they are responsive, nurturant, and provide verbal explanations tend to have children who are popular and who display prosocial behaviors with peers. In contrast, children of authoritarian, power-assertive parents are more likely to be classified as rejected (Dekovic & Janssens, 1992; Hart et al., 1992).

Parents serve as important models of social competence for their children; they may also provide explicit instruction on appropriate ways to behave in social situations. In one study, mothers of popular and unpopular preschoolers were observed as they introduced their children to a pair of peers busily playing with blocks. Mothers of unpopular children tended to disrupt the ongoing play and use their authority to incorporate their own child into the group. In many ways, their behaviors resembled those of the unpopular children we discussed earlier. In contrast, mothers of popular children encouraged them to become involved in play without intervening in the activity of the host peers. Moreover, in a subsequent interview, these mothers displayed greater knowledge of how to encourage their children to make friends, resolve conflicts, and display other positive social behaviors (Finnie & Russell, 1988). Others have noted that compared with mothers of less popular children, mothers of popular children are generally less disagreeable and demanding when they play with their children and are more likely to focus on feelings when they talked with both their children and others (Putallaz, 1987).

When parents create opportunities for their children to have experiences with peers, as these mothers are doing, their children may benefit from the ability to practice social skills.

Finally, parents can influence children's social competence on another level—by managing their children's social activities. Parents vary in the extent to which they create opportunities for their children to have experiences with peers, which provide the context for the emergence of social skills. Some parents seek out play groups for their preschoolers, enroll them in nursery school, or periodically get together with friends who have children. When parents deliberately arrange peer contacts for their preschoolers, their children have a greater variety of playmates, a greater number of consistent play partners, display more prosocial behaviors at preschool, and have higher sociometric status (at least among boys) than when parents do not make such efforts (Ladd & Golter, 1988; Ladd & Hart, 1992). Opportunities to interact with peers provide the child with a natural arena to discover those behaviors that generate positive responses from peers and those that do not.

Day Care    When children have more experience with peers because they are enrolled in day care, they show greater social competence than children reared solely at home by their parents. Carollee Howes (1987a) has conducted an extensive longitudinal study of the peer relationships of one- to six-year-old children who were enrolled in child-care programs. Among her findings was the discovery that popular or average-status children had entered child care at earlier ages (about ten to nineteen months on average) than rejected children (about thirty to thirty-three months). Early experience was not the sole important factor, however. Howes found that the stability of the peer group was significant, as well. Toddlers who had spent a year or more with *the same peers*

▶ The child's active role

▶ Interaction among domains

**FIGURE 15.4**

**Social Competence: An Infor-
mation-Processing Model**

Kenneth Dodge has proposed a
five-step model of social competence based on the child's growing
social information-processing
skills. The process begins when
the child is able to correctly encode and then interpret a social
cue. The child next generates a set
of possible responses and evaluates
the potential outcomes of each. Finally, he enacts the behavior he internally selected. The origins of
these five steps lie in the child's biological make-up, his past experiences, and the social cues
surrounding the event. Children
low in social competence may have
difficulties at any step in this
model.

were more socially competent in that they showed more cooperative forms of
play. These children were also rated by teachers as having fewer difficulties
than children who had moved to a different group. Evidently, experiences with
peers do indeed provide an excellent context for mastering social skills, especially if there is sustained contact with familiar age mates.

**Social Cognitive Development**    The studies of peer group entry strategies described here vividly illustrate that the social competence of children
includes an array of intertwined cognitive and behavioral skills. A five-step
information-processing model of social competence recently formulated by
Kenneth Dodge (see Figure 15.4) suggests more precisely how cognitions and
behaviors are related and where problems in social functioning might occur
(Dodge, 1986; Dodge et al., 1986).

According to Dodge, the first step in processing social information is to focus on the correct cues. For example, suppose a boy initiates a conversation
with a peer who is a girl. It is more important for the child to encode the girl's
facial expression ("Is that a smile or a sneer?") than the color of her clothing.
Second, the child must meaningfully interpret the social cues based on his
past experiences. Most children would interpret a scowl on a peer's face as a
sign of hostility and a smile as a mark of friendliness. In the third step of processing, the child generates one or more potential behavioral responses. If he
perceives the peer as hostile, he may contemplate avoiding her or matching
her hostility. If he reads her signals as friendly, he may consider smiling back
or beginning to talk. Fourth, the child learns to evaluate the potential consequences of each possible behavior. Hostility and aggression could lead to
physical harm while avoidance might not and hence might be preferable. Finally, the child enacts the chosen response verbally or physically, monitors
the outcome of his behavior, and if necessary, modifies it, engaging in the five-
step cycle over again. This model, it is apparent, includes a number of steps at
which things can go wrong to disrupt a smooth, mutually rewarding social
interaction.

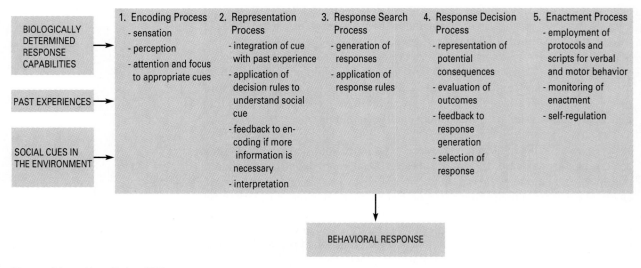

Source: Adapted from Dodge, 1986.

Studies of peer relations suggest that popular children are more skillful than unpopular (and, in particular, rejected) children at several steps in the model. First, they are better able to encode and decipher social information correctly. In one study, elementary school children were asked to label the emotions depicted in sets of pictures. For example, one was a series of faces depicting anger, happiness, sadness, disgust, surprise, and fear. Rejected children were less able to make correct identifications of the emotions represented in these stimuli than were popular children (Monfries & Kafer, 1987).

Second, rejected children often make incorrect attributions about the behaviors of peers. In one experiment, researchers asked children to view videotaped episodes of an actor destroying a second actor's toy with either hostile, prosocial, accidental, or ambiguous intent. Both rejected and neglected children tended to attribute hostile intentions to the actor's actions, even when the acts were accidental or prosocial. Popular children were more often correct in their judgments (Dodge, Murphy, & Buchsbaum, 1984). In fact, rejected children maintain their hostile attributions even when they are told the victim in a story feels happy (Keane & Parrish, 1992). Numerous studies have confirmed that aggressive children, in particular, tend to make more hostile attributions about the intentions of others than nonaggressive children. This finding holds true for children from the middle school years through adolescence and for children from different ethnic backgrounds (Dodge & Somberg, 1987; Graham, Hudley, & Williams, 1992; Slaby & Guerra, 1988). As a result of these mistaken attributions, aggressive children often retaliate with further negative behavior. It is apparent that a correct "reading" of social events is a necessary early step in skilled interpersonal behavior.

Third, rejected children tend to offer inappropriate strategies for solving social problems and have difficulty in devising alternative paths to attain their social goals (Rubin & Krasnor, 1986). Researchers typically assess social problem-solving skills by presenting children with hypothetical social dilemmas and examining their proposed solutions. Researchers in one study asked kindergarten children to react to a series of dilemmas in which, for example, one child takes away another's toy. Unpopular children were much more likely than popular children to recommend an aggressive solution, such as, "Punch him" or "She could beat her up." When asked to suggest ways to initiate new social relationships or maintain old ones, these children were vague or appealed to adult authority (Asher & Renshaw, 1981). Kenneth Rubin and Linda Krasnor observed children's strategies for solving social problems in naturalistic settings and noted that rejected children were rigid in their attempts (Rubin & Krasnor, 1986). If, for example, a rejected child failed to convince another child to give him an object, he simply repeated the same unsuccessful behavior. Popular children often tried a different approach to attaining their goal, indicating a broader and more flexible repertoire of social problem-solving skills.

Popular children thus possess social knowledge that leads to successful interactions with their peers and also behave in ways that manifest this expertise. They know what strategies are needed in order to make friends (for example, ask others their names, invite them to do things) and can describe prosocial behaviors that tend to foster peer relationships (for example, be generous, keep promises) (Wentzel & Erdley, 1993). They also recognize that the achievement of their social goals may require time and work and adjust their behaviors according to the sometimes subtle demands of the situation (Asher, 1983). Rejected children, on the other hand, have a more limited awareness of how to solve social problems, believing particularly in the effectiveness of aggression. Unfortunately, their antagonistic actions frequently lead to a spiral of continuing rejection. As they become disassociated from more socially skilled popular peers, they have fewer opportunities to learn the basics of successful social interaction from them. Moreover, the child who receives consistently negative feedback from peers would probably be hard pressed to be positive, cooperative, and friendly. Neglected children have their own special problems. Rubin and Krasnor (1986) believe that this special category of children does not display social cognitive deficits but rather insecurities and anxieties about the consequences of their social actions. What they need is more self-confidence in their abilities to interact with and be accepted by their peers.

## Training Social Skills

Can children be taught the elements of socially skilled behavior and thereby gain greater acceptance from their peers? Several forms of intervention, usually employed in schools and clinical settings, have produced changes in children's interpersonal strategies.

**Modeling**    One effective training technique is *modeling*—that is, exposing children to live or recorded models displaying desirable behaviors. For example, one research team presented a group of socially withdrawn preschoolers with short videotapes depicting young children engaging in social behaviors accompanied by a narration of their thoughts (Jakibchuk & Smeriglio, 1976). The sound track included the following self-directed statements as the model approached a group of peers: "Those children over there are playing together. . . . I would like to play with them. But I'm afraid. I don't know what to do or say. . . . This is hard. But I'll try. . . . I'm close to them. I did it. Good for me. . . ." Compared with their baseline behaviors, withdrawn children who watched these videotapes for four days increased the number of their social interactions and in turn were the objects of more positive social behaviors from others. The results were dramatic when children who received this treatment were compared with children who received no treatment at all or who saw a nature film (see Figure 15.5). From the perspective of social learning theory, by identifying with the model, observing how the model acted, and noting the positive consequences of the model's behavior, children were able to expand their repertoire of social behaviors, and increase their likelihood of performing these behaviors.

**Reinforcement**    A second type of intervention uses social or material *reinforcement* to shape socially skilled behaviors and increase their frequency, a technique of operant conditioning. Suppose a withdrawn child merely looked at a group of peers playing on the opposite side of the room. The teacher or parent immediately reacts with a "Good!" or a pat on the head. Next the young child might take a few steps in the direction of the group. Again, the teacher promptly delivers a reinforcer. The teacher rewards each successive approximation to the target behavior—in this case, joining the group—until the child has actually entered the group. In general, direct reinforcement of social behaviors is a very effective technique, especially for increasing their frequency (Schneider & Byrne, 1985).

Sometimes the operant approach is combined with other techniques such as modeling. In one investigation, withdrawn nursery school children received

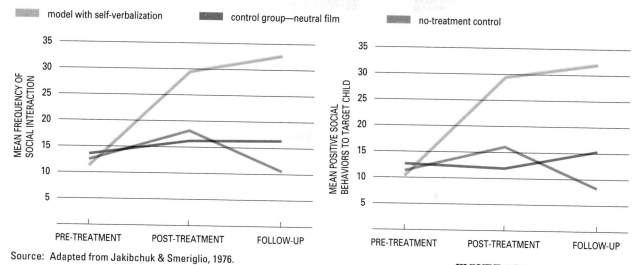

Source: Adapted from Jakibchuk & Smeriglio, 1976.

**FIGURE 15.5**

**Training Social Skills**

In an experiment that evaluated the effects of several treatment strategies with socially withdrawn preschoolers, researchers found that children who observed a model approach a group of peers while verbalizing his thoughts later increased in their number of social interactions compared with the pretreatment (or baseline) period. These children also received more positive social behaviors from others. The graphs show both measures for this treatment group compared with a group that saw a neutral film and with a no-treatment control group. These last two groups were included to make sure that any gains in social behavior were not the result of simple contact with the experimenters or exposure to a film per se.

social reinforcement whenever they interacted with their peers. Those who also saw a model demonstrating social interactions showed the greatest gains in the amount of time they spent with peers (O'Connor, 1972).

Coaching  The most popular training technique has been *coaching,* or direct instruction in displaying an assortment of social behaviors. In this approach, a verbal presentation of the "right" and "wrong" ways to act is frequently accompanied by discussion about why certain techniques work and by opportunities for children to *role-play,* or act out the desirable behaviors. The goal is to expand children's knowledge of socially desirable behaviors and to develop social problem-solving skills. For example, in one social skills training program, elementary school children learn how to join a conversation:

TEACHER: Chances are that if you don't know how to start talking with another person or join in when others are talking, you won't be a part of many conversations. . . . For example, pretend that some of your classmates are talking about a TV show that you happened to see last night and you want to get in on the conversation. . . . What you might do is walk over to the group and, when there is a slight pause in the talking, say something like, "Are you talking about 'Star Trek'? I saw that and really liked it a lot too." At this point you have joined the conversation.
Next, you want to make sure that you participate in what's going on. You should listen and add comments to what is being said. . . . Can you give me different examples of how you can now add to or take part in a conversation or what else you would say?
(Michelson et al., 1983, pp. 116–117)

Karen Bierman (1986) has added still another component to a social skills training program based on coaching—conducting the intervention as a cooperative activity among both popular and unpopular peers. Each target child in her group of preadolescents met with two socially accepted classmates for ten half-hour sessions to produce a film together but also to receive coaching on expressing feelings, asking questions, and displaying leadership. This two-pronged approach led to greater improvements in conversational skills than social skills training alone, possibly because peers could observe firsthand the positive changes occurring in initially unskilled children and could reinforce them immediately.

Children as young as four years of age can profit from training programs that explicitly teach social skills. George Spivack and Myrna Shure (1974) provided preschoolers and kindergarten-aged children with several months of instruction on how to solve social problems. For example, situations like the following were presented: "This girl wants that boy to get his wagon out of the way so she can ride by." Children were asked to generate solutions to the problems and were then asked to evaluate their merits. Children were also taught other skills, such as how to evaluate the emotional expressions of others and how to cope with their own feelings of frustration. At the end of the program, the participants showed significant gains in their ability to solve social problems. Moreover, aggressive children showed fewer disruptive and more prosocial behaviors and withdrawn children became more socially active, even one year after the formal instruction ended.

## CONTROVERSY: THINKING IT OVER

### Can Social Skills Training Programs Change a Child's Peer Status?

Modeling, reinforcement, and coaching have all been effective in treating both aggression and social withdrawal in children (Schneider & Byrne, 1985). Moreover, some studies find that children show gains in their sociometric status following their participation in a social skills training program (Ladd & Asher, 1985). This finding is consistent with the large body of evidence showing that popular children are socially skilled. Shouldn't unpopular children gain status when they acquire similarly adept social behaviors?

Social acceptance does not always follow social skills training, however. For example, in one study, third- through fifth-graders who were low on peer acceptance were given four weeks of training in skills such as greeting others, extending invitations, and carrying on conversations. Even though these children showed greater knowledge and use of social skills than the control groups who didn't receive explicit training, there were no significant changes in their acceptance by peers (La Greca & Santogrossi, 1980). Perhaps unpopular children have reputations that outlast the positive changes in their interpersonal behaviors (Hymel, Wagner & Butler, 1990). Under such circumstances, should children who have learned new social skills be transferred to another school to "start fresh" with a new group of peers, as some have suggested (Perry, Williard, & Perry, 1990)?

Another factor to consider is the types of attributions peers make about the unpopular child. If children see the target child as *responsible* for his own problems, his obesity or social withdrawal, for example, they like him less than when he is viewed as not responsible (Juvonen, 1992). Should social skills training programs therefore be extended to popular children to convince them that their unpopular peers are *not responsible* for their traits? Could there be repercussions for the target children themselves when they hear that they are not responsible for their own behaviors? What is the best way to design social skills training programs so that unpopular children gain in social status? ■

# Children's Friendships

Certain peer relations are special. They are marked by shared thoughts and experiences, trust, intimacy, and joy in the other's company. Children's relationships with friends differ from those with other peers. Friends express more emotion and loyalty toward each other, see each other more frequently, and both cooperate and disagree more than mere acquaintances (Bigelow, Tesson & Lewko, 1992; Hartup & Sancilio, 1986). In fact, when researchers observe the face-to-face interactions of sixth-graders with a friend versus an acquaintance, they note more positive affect, more playfulness, more involvement, and fewer physiological signs of stress in the child-friend pairs (Field et al., 1992). Even though childhood friendships may not endure, their impact on social and emotional development can rival that of the family and may provide a needed buffer when children feel psychological strains.

## Children's Patterns and Conceptions of Friendship

About 80 percent of three- to four-year-old children spend a substantial amount of time with at least one peer who is a "strong associate" or friend. Most preschoolers observed in their nursery school classrooms spend at least 30 percent of their time with one other peer, usually someone of the same sex (Hinde et al., 1985). For the three-year-old, however, the concept of "friend" does not encompass the full range of psychological complexities it does for the older child. At this age, the term is virtually synonymous with "playmate."

Preschoolers' activities with friends usually consist of games, object sharing, and pretend sequences (for example, "You be the baby and I'll be the Mommy"). Conversations between friends often contain a good deal of social comparison, a search for differences as well as similarities. Preschool children are fascinated not so much by the specific nature of things they have in common as they are by the fact that they *have* things in common. Hence the following typical conversation recorded by Jeffrey Parker and John Gottman (1989):

A: "We both have chalk in our hands."
B: "Right!"

Preschool children try to avoid disagreements and negative affect in their interactions with friends, more so than older children do (Gottman & Parkhurst, 1980).

In the middle school years (roughly ages eight through twelve years), children are very concerned with being accepted by their peers and avoiding the insecurity that peer rejection brings; both factors motivate friendship formation. Most friends are of the same age and sex, although relationships with younger and older children occasionally occur as well. Cross-sex friendships are rare, however. Researchers in one study even found their fifth-grade subjects to be openly resistant to the idea that they might have a friend of the opposite sex (Buhrmester & Furman, 1987). By the time children approach

**FIGURE 15.6**

**Changes in Time Spent with Friends over Childhood**

The amount of time that children spend with friends, especially friends of the same sex, increases from childhood to early adolescence. By the eighth grade, children say they spend more time in the company of a same-sex friend than with either parent.

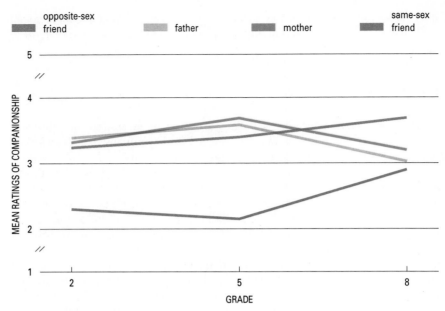

Source: Adapted from Buhrmester & Furman, 1986.

preadolescence, the time they spend with same-sex friends surpasses the time they spend with either parent (see Figure 15.6).

In middle childhood, friendship interactions typically include conflicts as well as cooperation (Hartup et al., 1993), and gossip becomes a predominant format for communication, as the following episode between two girls illustrates:

E: Oh, see, um, you know that tub she gave us for the spider?
M: Yeah.
E: She acts like she owns the whole thing.
M: The whole spider.
E: I know.
(Parker & Gottman, 1989)

Parker and Gottman (1989) believe that gossip allows children to sample the attitudes and beliefs of their age mates without taking the risk of revealing their own views. Because gossip involves the sharing of "privileged" information, it also solidifies the child's membership in the friendship circle.

During this age period, the internal psychological aspects of friendship grow in importance. When sixth-graders are asked, "How do you know that someone is your best friend?" they respond with statements like, "I can talk to her about my problems" or "He'll keep a secret if you tell him." In other words, intimacy and trust as well as loyalty, generosity, and helpfulness become integrated into the child's understanding of friendship (Berndt, 1981). Girls, in particular, speak of the value they place on intimacy in friendship relations. Girls cite the importance of sharing confidences and private feelings with friends far more frequently than boys do and find their same-sex friendships to provide more support than do boys (Buhrmester & Furman, 1987; Furman & Buhrmester, 1992; Jones & Dembo, 1989). This tendency, however, may stem in part from their stereotyped knowledge that female relationships are *supposed* to be close (Bukowski & Kramer, 1986).

Boys' friendships are usually extensive, involving a larger circle of friends and group activities. Girls' friendships, in contrast, tend to be intensive, with smaller networks of friends and a good deal of affective communication and self-disclosure.

Sex differences in concepts of friendship are accompanied by heightened differences in the structure of boys' and girls' friendship networks during the middle school years. Boys' friendships are usually *extensive;* their circle of friends is larger, and play is frequently enacted in groups. For boys, friendship is oriented around shared activities, especially sports (Erwin, 1985). In contrast, girls' friendships tend to be *intensive.* Girls have smaller networks of friends, but they engage in more intensive affective communication and self-disclosure. Girls usually play with only one other girl and may even be reluctant to include a third girl in the relationship. Girls also become more distressed over the breakup of a friendship (Eder & Hallinan, 1978; Maccoby & Jacklin, 1987; Waldrop & Halverson, 1975). It may be that these sex differences in friendship patterns are derived from the games children play. Boys are encouraged to play group games and team sports, like baseball, which involve a number of children and do not promote intimacy and close interaction. Girls' games, such as "house" and "dolls," involve smaller groups and provide an ideal environment for the exchange of thoughts and emotions. Another possibility is that sex differences in friendships are due to larger socialization forces that foster sensitivity to others and affective sharing in girls and autonomy and emotional reservedness in boys (Winstead, 1986).

By adolescence, the importance of intimacy in friendship is firmly solidified. Adolescents say that they value the ability to share thoughts and feelings with friends and expect mutual understanding and self-disclosure in friendships (Bigelow & LaGaipa, 1975; Furman & Bierman, 1984). They share problems, solutions to those problems, and private feelings with friends. These qualities fit the needs of individuals who are struggling to define who they are and who they will become. A sample exchange between two adolescent friends drawn from Parker and Gottman's (1989) research illustrates these themes:

A: I don't know. Gosh, I have no idea what I want to do. And it really doesn't bother me that much that I don't have my future planned. [laughs]
B: [laughs]
A: [laughs] Like it bothers my Dad a lot, but it doesn't bother me.
B: Just tell your dad what I always tell my Dad: "Dad, I *am*."
A: [laughs] Exactly!
B: "And whatever happens tomorrow, I *still* will be!"

Adolescents continue to prefer same-sex friends, although the frequency of boy-girl interactions increases. Adolescents also say that the time they spend with their friends is the most enjoyable part of their day (Csikszentmihalyi & Larson, 1984). Friendship is thus a key element in the social and emotional life of the older child.

## Friendship and Social Cognition

▶ Interaction among domains

▶ Development as continuous/discontinuous

Robert Selman (1981) believes that developmental changes in children's conceptions of friendships are grounded in their social perspective-taking ability—that is, their capacity to understand the viewpoints, thoughts, and feelings of another person (see Chapter 8). Put another way, conceptions of friendship are linked to advances in social cognition. Selman has proposed a five-stage model of the development of friendship concepts that reflects the growing perspective-taking abilities of children:

*Stage 0 (about 3–7 years): Momentary Physicalistic Interaction*   Friendship is defined strictly in terms of physical proximity. A friend is someone who lives nearby or is a playmate.
*Stage 1 (about 4–9 years): One-Way Assistance*   Friends are conceptualized as helpers. The child who helps pick up a spilled lunch, for example, is a friend.
*Stage 2 (about 6–12 years): Fair-Weather Cooperation*   The roles of reciprocity and mutual adjustment in friendship are recognized, but definitions of friendship still center around self-interest rather than mutual concerns. Arguments can terminate the relationship.
*Stage 3 (about 9–15 years): Intimate and Mutually Shared Relationships*   The affective and durable qualities of friendship are recognized. However, friendships can contain an element of possessiveness.
*Stage 4 (12 years–adult): Autonomous and Independent Friendships*   Friendship is seen as an avenue for mutual support and a way in which both partners may derive psychological strength from each other. The importance of relationships with others is now recognized.

In Selman's model, young children's egocentricity limits their conception of friendship to concrete, self-oriented situations. Once they have gained the ability to reflect on the legitimacy of another's perspective—and, later, on how individuals relate to larger social groups—children's notions of friendship expand to include reciprocity and respect for the internal needs and desires of the other.

In addition, say other psychologists, as children gain an increasingly sophisticated understanding of the concept of *reciprocity,* their ideas of friendship are altered. Young children conceptualize reciprocity concretely; they match a peer's helping or sharing, for example, with a similar behavior of their own.

Adolescents view reciprocity in a more abstract way; they see friendships as entailing mutual cooperation and a sharing of identities rather than just sharing objects (Youniss, 1980). Thus, the older child's more elaborate reasoning capabilities are assumed to pave the way for abstract, psychological concepts of friendship.

Research on children's understanding of friendship relies almost exclusively on their ability to verbalize their ideas about what friends do and why they are valuable. Other studies on how children behave with friends, however, show that children's friendships are far more complex than they themselves are able to describe. One clue to that complexity comes from investigations of how children form friendships in the first place.

## How Children Become Friends

How do two previously unacquainted children form a friendship? What behaviors must occur to produce an affiliative bond between these two peers? A time-intensive investigation by John Gottman (1983) provides a fascinating glimpse into the process of friendship formation among children who initially met as strangers. Gottman's method involved tape-recording the conversations of eighteen unfamiliar dyads aged three to nine years as they played in their homes for three sessions. Even in this short time, friendships among some of the pairs began to emerge. In all cases, each member of the pair was within one year of the age of the other. Some were same-sex pairs, others opposite-sex. The behaviors of the child whose home it was (the host child) and the visiting child (the guest) were coded separately; the sequences of behaviors displayed by these children—that is, how one child's behavior influenced the other's—were also analyzed.

Children who "hit it off" in the first play session showed several distinct patterns of interaction. First, they were successful in exchanging information, as in the following conversation one pair had:

A: "Hey, you know what?"
B: "No, what?"
A: "Sometime you can come to my house."

Children who became friends made efforts to establish a common ground by finding activities that could be shared together or by identifying similarities and differences between them.

In addition, any conflicts that occurred as they played were successfully resolved, either by one member of the dyad explaining the reason for the disagreement or by one child complying with the other child's demands, as long as they were not excessive or unreasonable. Alternatively, as activities escalated from simply coloring side by side ("I'm coloring mine green") to one child's issuing a command ("Use blue. That'd be nice"), children who became friends tempered this potential conflict by de-escalating the intensity of play (in this case, going back to side-by-side coloring) or using another element of play that was "safe"—namely, information exchange (for example, "I don't have a blue crayon. Do you?"). In contrast, children who did not become friends often persisted in escalating their play until the amity of the situation disappeared. Children who became friends thus modulated their interactions to preserve a positive atmosphere.

Over time, other social processes also came into play. One influential variable was the clarity of communication, as evidenced by a child giving clear answers to requests for information from the other. The following sequence is an example of a clear communication:

A: "Hand me the truck."
B: "Which truck?"
A: "The red one."

Also significant was the amount of self-disclosure in children's interactions—that is, one child's revelation of feelings in response to a question about them from the other.

Friendship formation, like other aspects of peer interaction, requires a sensitivity to social cues and knowledge of how to manage interactions that have positive and negative moments. And indeed socially skilled children have more friends than socially unskilled children do.

## The Functions of Friendship

By virtue of their special qualities, friendships contribute to the child's development in ways that are different from other, more transient, peer interactions. Friendships involve extended contact between peers and a significant affective investment from each child. Thus they provide a fertile ground for the child's social and emotional development.

▶ Interaction among domains

Because friendships include the sharing of affection and emotional support, especially among older children, they may play a vital role in protecting children from anxiety and stress. For example, boys seem to adjust better to the practical and psychological consequences of divorce when they have friends (Wallerstein & Kelly, 1980). In addition, children who have close and intimate friendships have higher levels of self-esteem, less anxiety and depression, and are more sociable in general compared with those with few close friends (Buhrmester, 1990; Mannarino, 1978). Because many of these studies are correlational, the direction of influence is not always clear. That is, less anxious children may be more capable of forming intimate friendships, or the reverse may be true—friendships may make them less anxious. Nonetheless, it is reasonable to hypothesize that friends provide an important source of social support and feedback about one's competence and self-worth. In fact, as Figure 15.7 shows, even having just one "best friend" can mean less loneliness for the child (Parker & Asher, 1993; Renshaw & Brown, 1993).

Interactions with friends also provide a context for the development of certain social skills such as cooperation, competition, and conflict resolution. In one study, researchers observed teams of four- and five-year-olds playing a game in which cooperation led to both partners winning, whereas competition led to losses for both (Matsumoto et al., 1986). Teachers independently rated the degree of friendship for each pair of children. The results showed that the greater the degree of friendship, the more the children cooperated to win the game. In another longitudinal study of three-year-olds in day care, Carollee Howes (1983) observed that children showed the greatest increases in the complexity of their social interactions—their ability to initiate an interaction or participate in an elaborate exchange, for example—within the context of playing with one or two stable friends. Such gains were not observed when children played with peers who were not friends.

Similarly, because of their investment in friendships, when children have conflicts with friends they frequently seek to negotiate and resolve those conflicts rather than letting the argument escalate or result in the end of the

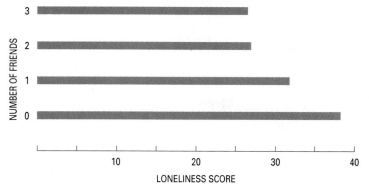

Source: Renshaw & Brown, 1993.

**FIGURE 15.7**

**Friendship as a Buffer Against Loneliness**

Having even one "best friend" can significantly lower children's reports of loneliness. In this study, third- through sixth-graders filled out a questionnaire assessing their feelings of loneliness and social dissatisfaction partway through the school year. A high score indicates greater feelings of loneliness. Children who had a reciprocal relationship with at least one friend had significantly lower loneliness scores than children who had no

friendship. William Hartup and his colleagues, observing four-year-olds in nursery school over a period of several weeks, noted any instances of spontaneous conflict in which one child attempted to influence another but met with resistance (Hartup et al., 1988). They found that when conflicts occurred between friends, children were more likely either to negotiate and bargain or to physically turn away from the situation. When conflicts occurred between nonfriends, children were more likely to stand firm and insist on their original goal.

Finally, the intimacy required in friendships may also promote healthier relations with others later in life. Harry Stack Sullivan (1953) believed that the capacity for intimacy nurtured by same-sex friendships in childhood provides the foundation for intimacy in more mature adult relationships. The failure to acquire this capacity in the formative years of childhood may impair a person's later functioning as a romantic partner, spouse, or parent. Although little research has been conducted to evaluate the validity of this claim, the idea that there is continuity between the capacity for intimacy in childhood and later life continues to have broad appeal.

## THEMES IN DEVELOPMENT

## PEERS

▶ **How does the sociocultural context influence peer relations?**

Cultures vary in the amount of peer experience they structure for children. For example, children in some countries are reared with peers from early childhood. As more children in our society enter day care, they also have more extensive experiences with peers than previous generations. In general, children who spend more time with peers show advances in social development and often show a tendency to prefer cooperation to competition. In most societies, peers pressure their age mates to conform to specific cultural values, such as sex-typed behaviors. Culture can also influence the standards that shape peer acceptance. For example, in our society, athletic capabilities and social skill are highly valued, and as a consequence, children who are proficient in these domains typically enjoy more peer popularity.

▶ **How does the child play an active role in peer relations?**

On one level, many of the physical qualities the child possesses influence the reactions of peers. Attractiveness, body build, motor skill, and rate of maturation all engender different responses from other children. On another level, the child's social skill clearly affects how peers react. Children who can accurately read the emotions of others, gauge the consequences of their own behaviors on others, and know the strategies that facilitate good social discourse are more popular with their peers. Similarly, children who are aggressive and display physical power often rise to the top of peer group dominance hierarchies, but may become unpopular with peers, as evidenced when those peers are asked to name children they like or prefer to associate with.

▶ **Are developmental changes in peers relations continuous or discontinuous?**

According to Parten, the development of play with peers progresses in a stage-like fashion. Similarly, Selman has proposed a stage theory of children's understanding of friendship. However, research now shows that preschoolers often concurrently display several types of play. In addition, young children's interactions with friends suggest more complexity than Selman's social cognitive model hypothesizes.

▶ **How prominent are individual differences in peer relations?**

Children vary in the extent to which they are accepted by their peers. Some children are popular, while others are rejected, neglected, or controversial. A child's popularity may be linked to aspects of physical appearance, name, motor skills, and social skills.

▶ **How do peer relations interact with other domains of development?**

First, healthy relations with peers are associated with a number of successful developmental outcomes in other arenas. Popular children do well in school, have high levels of self-esteem, and suffer fewer emotional difficulties, such as depression, than unpopular children. Second, the ability to interact successfully with peers is related to attainments in several other developmental domains. Children who are reared in a positive emotional environment and who are good at deciphering emotional cues tend to be more socially competent with peers. The formation of early emotional attachments and growth in social knowledge may also play a role. The child's emerging cognitive capabilities—especially perspective-taking skills—make it possible for her to think about the reactions and expectations of others and to anticipate the consequences of her own behaviors. Clear communication skills add to her effectiveness in establishing successful relationships with peers. Successful peer interaction is thus both a product of and a contributor to the child's emotional, cognitive, and social achievements.

## *Summary*

**Developmental Changes in Peer Relations**    Children show a direct interest in their *peers* from infancy, although coordinated social interchanges, such as turn taking, do not emerge until the age of two years or so. Preschool children typically engage in three kinds of play: *solitary play, parallel play,* and *cooperative play.* They also engage in *social pretend play.* Children's relationships with peers display their growing linguistic, cognitive, and social competencies.

During the school years and adolescence, peer groups assume greater importance for children. Children associate in same-sex groups and groups based on other similarities, such as shared interests. *Rough-and-tumble play* is frequently observed. Adolescents form larger groups called *cliques* and *crowds;* toward the end of adolescence, they develop interest in peers of the opposite sex.

**Peer Group Dynamics** Children typically show strong identity with the peer groups they join, feelings that become solidified when the group members work together toward some common goal. At the same time, conflicts between peer groups can occur. One way to break down such intergroup hostilities is to have groups work together on some common goal. Peer groups quickly form organized structures, called *dominance hierarchies,* in which some children become leaders and others, followers. Dominance hierarchies seem to serve a number of adaptive social functions.

Susceptibility to peer pressure heightens during early adolescence but declines as young adulthood approaches. Peers pressure each other to spend time together and, less frequently, to misbehave. Peers enforce their norms by reacting positively to individuals who conform and negatively to those who resist. At times, peer pressures are in direct conflict with pressures from adults.

**Peers as Agents of Socialization** Peers are important agents of socialization who model and reinforce both prosocial and undesirable behaviors for others. Peers can also play a role in transmitting to children the values of the larger social group.

Peer acceptance is measured through such peer assessment devices as *sociometric nominations* or *sociometric rating scales.* The child's peer status is related to his physical attractiveness, name, motor skills, and social skills. In general, popular children engage in prosocial behaviors, know how to enter peer groups, and are effective at maintaining cohesive social interactions.

Social competence may have its roots in the child's earliest attachment relationships, but it is also influenced by parental styles of social interaction. Socially competent children are also better at perceiving and interpreting social cues and have good social problem-solving ability. Modeling, reinforcement, and coaching are some of the techniques that have been used to enhance social skills in children who have social problems such as aggression and withdrawal.

**Children's Friendships** Friendships are an important part of children's peer relations. Preschoolers view friends as peers to play with, but with development they come to value friends for their psychological benefits. Children approaching adolescence increasingly see their friends as providers of intimacy and trust. These changes in children's concepts of friendship parallel changes in social cognition. Children form friendships by keeping social interactions positive in tone, exchanging information, and, at later ages, by clear communication and self-disclosure. Friendships provide a context for developing skills such as cooperation and conflict resolution and may help the child to learn the benefits of intimacy in relationships.

# 16

## School and Television

▶ **How does the sociocultural context influence the child's experiences with school and television?**

▶ **How does the child play an active role in experiences with school and television?**

▶ **How do the child's experiences with school and television interact with development in other domains?**

*"Double click on the icon for your word-processing software," Allison told her classmate Jamie, a new student seated at the computer next to her. "Then call up your file by using the dialog box." She was patiently trying to help Jamie pick up the basics of using the computer. He struggled for a moment to get his timing down as he used the mouse. Then he beamed as he saw the phrases of the essay he had begun yesterday appear on the screen. In a few minutes, he was typing away.*

*"Now save your file," she added as she saw him finish. "And make sure your disk doesn't have that virus that was going around here yesterday—you could lose everything!"*

Such exchanges between twelve-year-olds in a junior high school computer laboratory are more commonplace than ever; the words may sound strange to some adults, but to many children, they have clear and practical meaning. Childhood in the 1990s is an enterprise vastly different from growing up even two decades ago. Would a seventh-grader in the 1970s have had the vaguest idea what Allison and Jamie were talking about?

Computers, television, and videocassette recorders now are an important feature of most schools and many homes. A host of questions has sprung up around these technological marvels as we consider their influence on child development. Can children learn more effectively, both at school and at home, with electronic tools? Will their social development be impaired if they get "hooked" to a computer or television screen? What other aspects of their cognitive or social development might the new technology be affecting? Rapid technological advances have created a new sociocultural climate within which children's growth takes place.

Historically, of course, parents and peers have played the major role in socializing children and helping them build their cognitive skills, and parents and peers carry on this role in contemporary society as well. Schools, too, play a significant part, and we will take a closer look at their effects, pedagogical and social, in this chapter.

## School

In many nations today, children are legally required to attend school; academic accomplishment is the chief point of emphasis. The main aim of education is to provide children with the skills necessary to function as independent, responsible, and contributing members of society. The child's experiences in school can also have a profound effect on other aspects of development, most notably self-concept and psychological well being.

By the time children graduate from high school, they have logged nearly fifteen thousand hours in school. Thus, it is important to understand the nature of that experience and how variations produce specific effects in the child. Several factors in the school experience influence learning and socialization, including the school's physical ecology, the educational philosophies of school personnel, transition points in schooling, and most important, the attitudes and behaviors of teachers.

## What Are the Effects of School on the Developing Child?

As we discussed in Chapter 9, societies vary in the extent to which they stress the experience of formal schooling. Rural agrarian subcultures in some countries, for example, do not have compulsory schooling. Experience in school in turn cultivates such cognitive skills as rote memory, taxonomic classification, and logical reasoning (Rogoff, 1981; Rogoff & Morelli, 1989). One especially powerful outcome of schooling is the development of literacy, the ability to read and write using the symbol system of a culture's language. Literacy is virtually a prerequisite for survival in our own society, and it is linked to other specific cognitive and linguistic attainments, such as the ability to decipher the auditory components of language and to analyze grammatical correctness (Scribner & Cole, 1981).

The ability to read and write will assume even more importance in our society during upcoming decades. As adolescents approach adulthood in the twenty-first century, they will find that more and more jobs will be in the professional and technical sectors, areas that require not only reading and writing skills but also the ability to communicate, reason, and apply mathematical and scientific concepts (Jackson & Hornbeck, 1989). The responsibility for fostering these skills will lie mainly with the schools.

**Academic Achievement**  In some measure, most children attain the basic goals educators and parents have set for academic achievement in school. In 1991, 85 percent of young adults completed high school, although the dropout rates were higher for students from low-income families and racial and ethnic minorities (Rumberger, 1987; U.S. Bureau of the Census, 1992).

How well are children learning in schools? Several major national surveys conducted since 1980 conclude that levels of academic achievement among American students are declining or do not compare well with those of students from other industrialized countries. Here are some representative data:

- American high school students score lower on most standardized tests of achievement than they did in the 1950s (National Commission on Excellence in Education, 1983).
- About 13 percent of seventeen-year-olds in the United States are functionally illiterate—essentially, they cannot read or write—and the rate of illiteracy among minority youth may be as high as 40 percent (National Commission on Excellence in Education, 1983).
- Only 11 percent of all thirteen-year-olds can be categorized as adept readers, meaning they can understand relatively complicated written information (Mullis & Jenkins, 1990).

| | 10-Year-Olds (grades 4/5) | 14-Year-Olds (grades 8/9) |
|---|---|---|
| Australia | 9 | 10 |
| Canada (English-speaking) | 6 | 4 |
| England | 12 | 11 |
| Finland | 3 | 5 |
| Hong Kong | 13 | 16 |
| Hungary | 5 | 1 |
| Italy | 7 | 11 |
| Japan | 1 | 2 |
| Korea | 1 | 7 |
| Netherlands | — | 3 |
| Norway | 10 | 9 |
| Philippines | 15 | 17 |
| Poland | 11 | 7 |
| Singapore | 13 | 14 |
| Sweden | 4 | 6 |
| Thailand | — | 14 |
| U.S.A. | 8 | 14 |

**TABLE 16.1**

**Science Achievement in Seventeen Countries**

This table presents the rank order of countries in science achievement of ten- and fourteen-year-old children. The rank of 1 represents the highest scores on international science tests designed to measure knowledge of basic science concepts. (some of the data indicate tied ranks.)

Source: Adapted from International Association for the Evaluation of Educational Achievement, 1988.

- Only 13 percent of eighth-graders wrote essays that were adequate or better when the task required them to "compare and contrast" (Applebee et al., 1990).
- Students from the United States ranked fourteenth out of seventeen major industrialized countries on a test of science achievement, as shown in Table 16.1 (International Association for the Evaluation of Educational Achievement, 1988).
- Students from the United States ranked twelfth out of fourteen countries in a recent comparison of eight-graders' mathematics capabilities (U.S. Department of Educaton, 1992).

These results are both alarming and perplexing. Have American schools shirked their commitment to academic excellence? Have the characteristics of the student population changed in some way? There are no simple explanations for the national survey data, nor are there quick, obvious ways to remedy the problems. What these results call for plainly, however, is a better understanding of how parents, peers, *and* schools contribute to students' academic attainments.

**Factors Predicting Academic Success**    Before we consider the specific influences of schools, let us first examine the role of several other factors that

▶ Interaction among domains

are associated with academic success. Not surprisingly, parents are of paramount importance. Several recent studies demonstrate that the climate that parents create in the home and the feelings of competence and control they instill in children are related to children's academic performance.

Consider, for example, a model proposed by Wendy Grolnick and her colleagues (Grolnick, Ryan, & Deci, 1991) and illustrated in Figure 16.1. According to these researchers, parental support for their children's autonomy (e.g., encouraging independent decision making) and their involvement with their children (e.g., spending time talking with children about their problems) are related to the strength of children's "inner resources." That is, children develop feelings of competence, autonomy, and control, which, in turn, have an influence on academic performance. To test these ideas, the researchers measured both parental and child qualities that were components of the model, as well as children's academic success. Using sophisticated statistical techniques, they were able to show that, for the most part, they observed the relationships they had predicted. Other researchers have confirmed that authoritative parenting (characterized by warmth and extensive verbal explanation) and the social support provided by parents predict, at least indirectly, exactly how well children do in school during the middle school years and adolescence (DeBaryshe, Patterson, & Capaldi, 1993; Dubow et al., 1991; Steinberg et al., 1992).

Peers make a difference, too. As early as fourth grade, children tend to sort themselves into groups that have different levels of school motivation, and children who are members of a particular group at the start of the school year become even more aligned with the group's motivation level by the end of the school year (Kindermann, 1993). Peers may also enhance or offset the effects of different parenting styles on children's academic achievement. Laurence

## FIGURE 16.1

**A Model of Parental Influences on Children's Academic Achievement**

One model of children's academic achievement suggests that parental involvement and support of children's autonomy predict children's "inner resources." The latter include children's feelings of control, competence, and autonomy. These characteristics of the child, in turn, predict academic achievement. Research has found support for the major elements of this model.

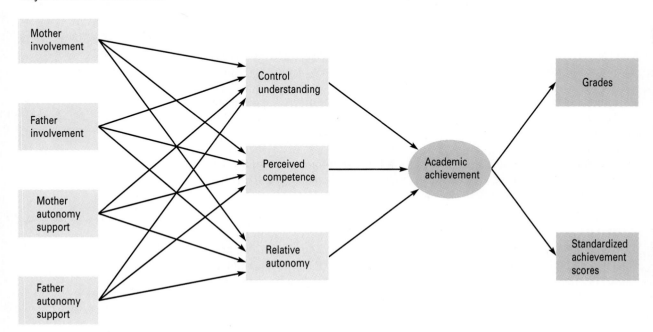

Source: Grolnick, Ryan, & Deci, 1991.

Steinberg and his associates found that among Asian American adolescents, for example, peer support for academic excellence lessened the negative effects of authoritarian parenting on academic achievement. For Caucasian adolescents, peer support for achievement complemented their parents' tendency to be authoritative (Steinberg, Dornbusch, & Brown, 1992).

Finally, still another factor that can affect academic performance of older children is whether they hold jobs before or after school. In general, adolescents who work more than fifteen to twenty hours per week attain poorer grades and show less commitment to school than adolescents who work fewer hours or not at all (Steinberg et al., 1982; Steinberg, Fegley, & Dornbusch, 1993). Taken together, the research described here suggests that children's academic achievement is best understood from the ecological perspective described in Chapter 2.

**Self-esteem**   In addition to building academic skills, children's experience in school can have a major effect on their feelings of competence and self-worth, both in a general sense and in terms of academic self-esteem. School-mates and teachers provide constant feedback to children about how they are doing, from casual comments friends make at recess ("You did great on that poem this morning!") to the formal academic grades determined by the teacher.

▶ Interaction among domains

In general, there is a positive correlation between academic achievement, usually measured by grades, and self-esteem. Students who obtain good grades have more favorable attitudes about themselves (Byrne, 1984). But does high self-esteem lead students to perform better in school, or does academic competence nurture the development of high self-esteem? Most experts agree that both processes are at work. One research team measured the self-concept and mental abilities of children as they began kindergarten and then took successive measures of their reading ability and self-concept during the next two years. The results showed that initial measures of self-esteem were good predictors of reading achievement in second grade (Wattenberg & Clifford, 1964).

By the same token, experimental studies have demonstrated that academically competent children can be made to feel more negative about themselves when they experience failure. In an illustrative experiment, two groups of high-achieving children were given a test of self-esteem and then three academic tests. Children in the experimental group were given a slip of paper after the last test that stated that they had failed. Their scores on a subsequent test of self-esteem declined, but the scores of the control group remained the same (Gibby & Gibby, 1967). Although contemporary researchers might question the ethics of subjecting students to such stress in a psychological experiment, the results clearly point to the power of performance feedback in shaping students' feelings about themselves. A more recent two-year study of sixth- and seventh-graders confirms that students who showed gains in self-esteem started out with a more favorable school climate and higher teacher evaluations of their work habits than those who did not show gains (Hoge, Smit, & Hanson, 1990).

## The Physical Environment of the School

Among the characteristics of schools that play a role in the child's development are school size, class size, and the physical layout of the classroom. Each factor influences the frequency and range of opportunities for students to interact with teachers and peers in the school setting.

**School Size**    Although there is some controversy over the importance of school size, any significant effects found by researchers usually favor students from smaller schools (Rutter, 1983). In a major study of thirteen high schools ranging in size from thirteen to more than two thousand students, researchers noted that students from smaller schools were less alienated, participated more in school activities, felt more competent, and found themselves more challenged (Barker & Gump, 1964). One probable reason is the greater availability of roles for students to fill in smaller schools, particularly leadership roles. Students who have the opportunity to edit the school newspaper or be captain of the band typically receive positive feedback from parents, teachers, and peers for fulfilling these roles. They are also likely to identify strongly with the school and develop a greater sense of personal control and responsibility.

▶ The child's active role

**Class Size**    Class size is another important aspect of school structure. In general, children in small classes show academic advances greater than children in large classes do. Few investigations have actually randomly assigned children to classes of different sizes to explore the effects on achievement, although this procedure would allow us to draw the strongest conclusions about the causal influence of class size. In one study of seventy-six schools across one state, however, precisely this procedure was followed. Kindergarten children and teachers were randomly assigned to one of three conditions: small classes of thirteen to seventeen students, regular classes of twenty-two to twenty-five students, or regular classes with a teacher's aide. By the end of first grade, children in the small classes showed markedly greater improvements in performance on standardized tests of reading and mathematics than children from regular classes, although the presence of an aide did improve scores somewhat. The benefits of small classes were especially pronounced for minority children (Finn & Achilles, 1990).

Why do smaller classes work? For one thing, teachers probably have greater enthusiasm and higher morale when they are not burdened with large numbers of students. Teachers also have more time to spend with individual students, and students are more likely to be attentive and engaged in classroom activities in small classes (Finn & Achilles, 1990).

**The Physical Arrangement of the Classroom**    The way in which a classroom is set up affects both student-teacher and student-student interactions. In the typical traditional classroom, precisely aligned rows of desks face the teacher to enhance communication between the teacher and individual pupils. This arrangement discourages interactions among students, which are viewed as disruptive to the learning process. Also, it provides clear zones that foster greater student-teacher exchange: students seated across the front row and down the center aisle (see Figure 16.2) are most likely to interact with the teacher (Gump, 1978). Even gregarious and actively involved students become less engaged with the teacher when they are seated outside the "action zone" of the traditional classroom (Koneya, 1976).

The best way to encourage the attention and active participation of more students in the class is to place the desks in a circle so that all students have equal access to the teacher. Researchers have noted that when desks are arranged this way, children raise their hands more frequently and make more

This crowded classroom in a public school in the United States does not afford children with the best learning environment. Children in smaller classes show higher scores on standardized achievement tests.

spontaneous comments about the lesson than when desks are positioned in rows and columns (Rosenfield, Lambert, & Black, 1985).

## Philosophies of Education

The traditional model of education emphasizes the role of the teacher as a transmitter of information to students and channels the major interactions in the classroom so that they flow from teacher to student. Students are required to work on problems and assignments individually, their work is evaluated accord-

Source: Adapted from Adams & Biddle, 1970.

**FIGURE 16.2**

**The "Action Zones" of the Traditional Classroom**

Students who sit in the front row and the center aisle of the classroom are likely to have the greatest number of interactions with the teacher. The best way to encourage the participation of more students is to arrange the desks in a circle.

ing to widely shared standards, and a climate of competition is the norm. Teachers assume an authority role, and their goal is to convey primarily academic information, as opposed to personal, emotional, or social knowledge. Alternative models of education, however, deemphasize the teacher as authority, the student as individual learner, and the academic environment as competitive.

**The Open Classroom**     In the **open classroom**, students are encouraged to collaborate, and the teacher's primary role is to structure lessons so that they offer opportunities for intellectual sharing and problem solving. Movable furniture, large open spaces, and activity centers replace the fixed, regular rows of student desks to encourage pupil interaction. The teacher is often considered a joint partner in the learning process, a collaborator in the process of discovery; team teaching is also common. Goals other than the strictly academic are equally valued: fostering the child's creativity, inquisitiveness, and socialization. Rarely are one child's accomplishments compared with those of others; instead, achievement is measured by the degree of progress the individual child shows.

Many ideas behind the open classroom had their origins in the work of John Dewey (1938/1963), an educational philosopher of the early part of this century. Dewey believed two things about education: it should capitalize on the child's natural interests and curiosity, and it should integrate the child into the larger society. Thus, for example, in Dewey's experimental school, arithmetic and science were taught in the context of cooking and carpentry; it was assumed that as children conducted these basic social activities, they would develop a spontaneous interest in more formal academic information.

Likewise, contemporary open classrooms provide children with structured opportunities to "discover" principles of science, mathematics, and other academic subjects. Instead of reading a chapter on photosynthesis, children may have access to a science table where they can manipulate the amount of sunlight and water different plants receive during a period of days to determine those elements necessary for green leaves. Another activity center might be devoted to mathematical problems and so forth. Children are free to explore different areas of the room under the careful guidance of the teacher.

*Open classrooms* like the one shown in this picture contain a number of unique features: large open spaces, movable furniture, and activity centers designed to help children learn by "discovery."

**open classroom**   Nontraditional educational approach that emphasizes peer interaction, free-flowing movement of students around different activity centers in the classroom, and structured opportunities for students to "discover" knowledge.

| Results (percent of studies) | | | | |
|---|---|---|---|---|
| Variable (number of studies) | Open Better | Traditional Better | Mixed Results | No Significant Differences |
| Academic achievement (102) | 14 | 12 | 28 | 46 |
| Self-concept (61) | 25 | 3 | 25 | 47 |
| Attitude toward school (57) | 40 | 4 | 25 | 32 |
| Creativity (33) | 36 | 0 | 30 | 33 |
| Independence and conformity (23) | 78 | 4 | 9 | 9 |
| Curiosity (14) | 43 | 0 | 36 | 21 |
| Anxiety and adjustment (39) | 26 | 13 | 31 | 31 |
| Locus of control (24) | 25 | 4 | 17 | 54 |
| Cooperation (9) | 67 | 0 | 11 | 22 |
| (Overall average) | (39) | (4) | (24) | (33) |

Source: Adapted from Horwitz, 1979.

**TABLE 16.2**

**The Effects of Open Versus Traditional Classrooms**

The results of 102 studies show that although open classrooms have few effects on academic achievement, they are likely to promote creativity, curiosity, independence, and a number of other desirable social characteristics.

Do children in open classrooms display academic and social profiles different from those who learn in traditional classrooms? As Table 16.2 shows, in the realm of academics, more than one hundred studies point to no consistent differences in the average performance of children in one classroom type versus the other (Horwitz, 1979). In the realm of social development, however, children from open classrooms show clear gains. A large body of empirical work shows that open classroom students are generally more cooperative, have a wide variety of interactions with peers in both work and socially related matters, and develop broad networks of relationships with peers (Hallinan, 1976; Horwitz, 1979; Minuchin & Shapiro, 1983). Thus, open classrooms represent an interesting and promising experiment in educational practice.

▶ Interaction among domains

**Peer Learning** Several unique peer-centered learning experiences demonstrate that there are benefits to experimenting with educational models that deemphasize teacher-to-student transmission of information. One such model introduced in Chapter 12 is *cooperative learning,* in which students work in groups rather than individually to solve academic problems or complete assignments.

A prime example is the *Student Teams-Achievement Divisions* (STAD) method developed by Robert Slavin (1990b). Students are assigned to four- or five-person learning teams composed of children with a range of abilities. Each group is deliberately structured to contain both boys and girls and children

▶ Interaction among domains

from a variety of racial or ethnic backgrounds. After the teacher introduces a new topic or set of materials, team members in each group work on related problems, quiz each other, and study together until they decide collectively that they understand the unit. Then each individual is quizzed to assess her knowledge, and the amount of improvement from her previous quiz average is added to the team score. This method ensures that even low-achieving students feel they have made a contribution to the group. Teams with the highest scores, individuals who most exceeded previous performance, and individuals who received perfect scores are recognized in a weekly class newsletter.

Cooperative learning works. Students who participate in STAD classrooms show greater achievement in language arts, social studies, and mathematics than control subjects who learned the same material from more traditional methods. Using specific group rewards—that is, overt public recognition of the teams' accomplishments—has proved to be an especially important factor in producing gains. In addition, the STAD program increases the number of cross-racial friendships, improves self-esteem, and produces more favorable attitudes toward academic achievement (Slavin, 1990b). Like the children in the Robber's Cave Study described in Chapter 15, when these students work in groups toward common objectives, barriers to interpersonal relationships dissolve and commitments to the goals of the group are strengthened.

Another form of peer learning is called **peer collaboration**. Here, pairs of students work jointly on the same problems without competing with other groups. An illustration of how this method works comes from a study by Erin Phelps and William Damon (1989). Fourth-graders worked in pairs on mathematics and spatial reasoning problems, some requiring rote learning and copying and others formal reasoning. The children had to supply the answers to such problems as $2 \times 2 = ?$ (rote learning) or, at other times, solve problems involving ratios and proportions (formal reasoning). After six sessions of peer collaboration, children showed significant gains in per-

One form of peer learning is called *peer collaboration,* where pairs of students work together on science or mathematics problems. Compared with students who receive more traditional methods of instruction, peer collaborators show significant increases in performance in these academic subjects.

**peer collaboration** Peer-centered learning experience in which pairs of students work together on academic problems, usually without competing against other students.

formance on math and spatial problems compared with a control group that did not receive the intervention. This effect occurred for tasks that required formal reasoning but not for those that required rote learning or copying. Another interesting outcome was that the superiority that boys showed over girls on spatial problems at the start of the study was significantly diminished. Peer collaboration thus improves certain forms of learning among elementary school children.

Two major theoretical viewpoints help to explain the positive effects of peer learning. According to both Piaget (1926) and Vygotsky (1978), peer interactions encourage the advancement of cognitive skills. In Piagetian theory, the cognitive conflicts and disequilibrium created in peer exchanges produce reorganizations in the child's thinking. Vygotsky believes that peers facilitate cognitive growth not only because they often operate within similar *zones of proximal development* but also because they display enough differences that one student's advanced knowledge in a given area can provide the *scaffolding* for another student.

Another reason peer learning is effective is that it heightens children's motivation to learn. In team learning, an individual's goals can only be met if the group is successful and group members pressure individual students to display their best efforts. Consistent with the tenets of behavior theory, peer praise or criticism serves to regulate the individual accomplishments of group members (Slavin, 1987b).

▶ Interaction among domains

---

## CONTROVERSY: THINKING IT OVER

### Should Students Be Grouped According to Academic Ability?

Separating children into groups according to ability is standard practice in most North American schools. Sometimes students are simply given colorful group names, such as the Jets and the Falcons. Other times the names are less likely to obscure the true ranking criterion for the groups—some children are the Advanced Readers, others are the Slow Readers. Regardless of the names, most students and their parents realize they are being grouped (or "tracked") according to their academic abilities. One of the longest-running controversies in American education centers on the pros and cons of just this sort of grouping.

The arguments for tracking are numerous. Proponents of this procedure maintain that ability grouping helps teachers adapt their instructional styles to the specific needs of students. Bright students are more likely to be challenged and motivated when they are grouped with other bright students and can advance at a more rapid pace than if they are left in slower classrooms. Slower learners, in turn, are spared the embarrassment of continual failure and have more opportunities to participate when they do not have to compete with bright students. They can learn more when they receive more individual attention from the teacher and when the pace of learning is adjusted to their level of ability. Many educators have found these arguments convincing. As a consequence, grouping students according to academic ability is common in most elementary and secondary schools, whether it is for reading groups within an elementary class or curriculum tracks (for example, college preparatory versus vocational) in the higher grades.

Critics point out, however, that ability grouping can have several damaging consequences. Chief among these are the low expectations and diminished morale that slow learners often develop (Persell, 1977; Rosenbaum, 1980). When students find they are in a lower track, they often feel demoralized and begin to live out the expectations of others. One student's comments during a research interview poignantly illustrate this point:

> I felt good when I was with my [elementary] class, but when they went and separated us—that changed us. That changed our ideas, our thinking, the way we thought about each other, and turned us to enemies toward each other—because they said I was dumb and they were smart. . . . The devil with the whole thing—you lose—something in you—like it goes out of you. (Schafer & Olexa, 1971, pp. 62–63)

There are other problems, too. Because many teachers prefer not to teach students in the lower tracks, some educational researchers maintain that those students actually get poorer-quality instruction (Gamoran, 1989; Oakes, 1985). In addition, students from lower socioeconomic levels and racial and ethnic minorities are more likely to be grouped in lower tracks because they are low achievers (but not necessarily because they are low in ability) (Persell, 1977; Rosenbaum, 1980). Most of the time, once students are placed in a given academic track, it is exceedingly difficult for them to switch to another, especially because the grouping is often presumed to reflect innate ability rather than achievement level. Thus, tracking may serve to perpetuate the degree of access students from various economic and ethnic backgrounds have to educational resources.

In two major overviews of the research on academic ability grouping in elementary and secondary schools, Robert Slavin (1987a, 1990a) concluded that this educational strategy has no overall effect on the academic achievements of students. The only exception is that elementary school children who are grouped across grades according to reading ability (as when higher-level first-graders are grouped with lower-level second-graders) or within grades for mathematics instruction achieve at slightly higher levels. Given the potential negative effects of tracking, Slavin argues that there is no good reason to continue this popular educational practice. On the other hand, Slavin's analysis included studies that relied almost exclusively on standardized tests as measures of achievement, measures that may not capture the benefits of tracking, because they do not necessarily measure what students are actually taught in school (Hallinan, 1990).

Which arguments about academic tracking seem most compelling? What research should psychologists conduct to further evaluate the pros and cons of academic tracking? Are there alternative ways to structure classroom experiences to provide more comprehensive benefits for students than academic ability grouping?  ■

## School Transitions

In addition to the physical ecology of school and philosophies of education, the structuring of the school experience influences development in one other way: the school transitions children are expected to make at specific ages. Most children begin kindergarten at the age of five or six, and the way in which they adjust to this first experience of school frequently determines how much they will like later grades. A second important transition occurs for most children in adolescence, when entering junior or senior high school makes new academic and social demands on them.

**Starting School**     Few times in a child's life are as momentous as the first day of school. Parents typically find this a time of mixed emotions, of eager anticipation of the child's future accomplishments coupled with anxieties about whether school will provide positive and rewarding experiences for their child. Children find they have many major adjustments to handle—accommodating to a teacher and a new physical environment, making new friends, and mastering new academic challenges. The success with which children make the initial transition to school can set the tone for later academic and socioemotional development. Because these early behavior patterns and impressions of school have a way of persisting, we need to identify and understand the factors that make adjustment to school smooth and successful.

To identify the variables connected with a positive transition to school, Gary Ladd and Joseph Price (1987) followed a sample of fifty-eight children as they moved from preschool to kindergarten. Assessing subjects on a number of social measures at three times—before entering kindergarten, at the beginning of the school year, and at the end of the school year—the investigators found that both the social behaviors of the children and the familiarity of the group they entered contributed to healthy school adjustment. Children who as preschoolers displayed high levels of cooperative play and had extensive positive social contacts were well liked by the other kindergartners and were rated as involved with peers by teachers. Children who had been aggressive in preschool tended to be disliked by their kindergarten peers and were rated as hostile by teachers.

▶ Interaction among domains

Peer acceptance was also facilitated by the presence of familiar peers in the kindergarten classroom. It is possible that a nucleus of familiar others provides a secure base from which to develop other social relationships. Moreover, the presence of familiar peers was related to more positive attitudes toward school and fewer anxieties at the start of the school year. In general, factors promoting continuity between the preschool and kindergarten experiences were most beneficial to the child's adjustment, suggesting that parents should consider ways to foster their children's friendships with peers who will be future classmates.

The quality of early peer relationships in school can have even more far-reaching effects on a child's adjustment. Gary Ladd (1990) found that children who had more classroom friends early in the school year had higher levels of social and academic competence, fewer absences from school, fewer visits to the nurse, and less behavioral disruptiveness than those with fewer friendships. These results underscore the fact that the transition to school can be a particularly crucial time in development and that successes in one domain—peer relations—are related to successes in another—competence in school.

▶ Interaction among domains

**A Second Transition: Junior High**     Another important transition occurs later in many children's schooling careers when they move from elementary school to a middle school or junior high school. In our society, this time is usually the visible signal of childhood's end and the beginning of adolescence. Once again, children must adapt to new teachers, peers, and physical environment, but now, rather than staying with the same classmates in the same room for most of the school day, they move from class to class, each usually with its own set of students. Frequently, the difference in student body size is dramatic from elementary school to junior high school. In one study, the mean school size from grade 6 to grade 7 increased from 466 to 1,307, and the mean number of children in each grade went from 59 to 403 (Simmons et al., 1987). It is no wonder that many researchers report a decline in school satisfaction in preadolescence as well as a drop in grades and participation in extracurricular activities (Epstein & McPartland, 1976; Hirsch & Rapkin, 1987; Schulenberg, Asp, & Petersen, 1984; Simmons & Blyth, 1987).

▶ Interaction among domains

Some researchers have also observed a decline in self-esteem at this time, particularly among preadolescent girls, and an increase in physical complaints (Hirsch & Rapkin, 1987; Simmons et al., 1979; Simmons, Rosenberg, & Rosenberg, 1973). Early-maturing sixth-grade girls have been found to have better images of themselves when they attend schools with kindergarten through eighth-grade classes, presumably because they feel less pressured to adopt dating and other activities that become prevalent among seventh- and eighth-graders. On the other hand, those girls entering puberty at more typical ages, and at about the same time that they enter a new school program or undergo other significant transitions, tend to have lower images of themselves and more difficulties in school, possibly because multiple changes in life are difficult to handle (Simmons, Burgeson, & Carleton-Ford, 1987).

For some adolescents, the difficulties encountered in junior high school may set in motion a pattern of academic decline that results in their dropping out of school (Eccles & Midgley, 1988). According to some experts, this is because the junior high school experience does not fit the specific developmental needs of preadolescents. At a time when youngsters are seeking stronger peer associations and a supportive climate for resolving identity issues, they are confronted with an educational environment that is more impersonal than elementary school and fragments peer relationships. In addition, the transition to junior high school frequently happens to coincide with several other life changes, such as the onset of puberty, dating, family disruptions (such as divorce), or new neighborhoods because of a family move. Entry into a new educational setting compounds the stresses with which many preadolescents are already coping (Simmons, Burgeson, & Carleton-Ford, 1987).

What happens when alternatives to the traditional junior high school and high school structures are instituted? In one study, students about to begin high school were assigned to special homerooms in which the teacher played an expanded role in providing academic and personal counseling, contacted parents when students were absent, and encouraged other communication with parents. Thus, the homeroom teachers in this setting provided more social support than usual throughout the entire first year of high school. Students were also assigned to classes so that they took their major academic subjects with many of the same students, a strategy that presumably would enhance peer support and provide a stable environment for students. At the end of the school year, students from this program showed higher levels of academic success and less psychological dysfunction than a control group; after four years, they showed a substantially lower dropout rate from school (21 percent) than the controls (43 percent) (Felner & Adan, 1988; Felner, Ginter, & Primavera, 1982).

We see from these studies that whenever children are confronted with a school transition, whether it be the start of kindergarten or the start of secondary school, they adjust best if they have social and emotional supports adequate to cope with the demands of the new environment. When children are buttressed by strong relationships with peers and teachers, they show higher academic performance, less anxiety, and more favorable attitudes toward school than when they lack these supports.

## Teachers: Key Agents of Influence

No single factor in the school experience plays a more critical role in student achievement and self-esteem than teachers. The expectations teachers have of students, their classroom management strategies, and the climate they create in the classroom are all major elements in student success or failure.

**The Role of Expectations**    A highly publicized study by Robert Rosenthal and Lenore Jacobson (1968) documented how teachers' expectations of students' performance could affect students' actual attainments. The researchers told teachers that certain elementary school children could be expected to show sudden gains in intellectual skills during the course of the school year based on their scores on an IQ test administered at the beginning of the term. In reality, the students they designated as "rapid bloomers" were chosen randomly. When Rosenthal and Jacobson administered the IQ test again at the end of the school year, the targeted children indeed showed significantly greater improvement than other students in the class, an outcome they called the *Pygmalion effect*. The authors explained the findings by suggesting that teachers somehow treated the targeted children differently based on their beliefs about the children's intellectual potential, thereby creating a self-fulfilling prophecy.

The original research conducted by Rosenthal and Jacobson (1968) has been criticized for oversimplifying the variables that contribute to student achievement. Teacher expectations alone cannot explain why some children are more successful than others in school. Subsequent studies, however, have confirmed that high achievers *are* treated differently in the classroom; they are given more opportunities to participate, more time to answer questions, receive more praise for being correct, and receive less criticism than lower achievers (Minuchin & Shapiro, 1983). In other words, the classroom climate is most supportive for those who have already demonstrated success, whereas those who most need the teacher's attention and encouragement may actually get it least.

Most teachers are undoubtedly unaware of the ways in which their expectations influence their own behaviors toward students. Yet the forms of interactions that ensue can have important repercussions for students' academic accomplishments and their feelings of self-worth.

**Classroom Management Strategies**    Students achieve most in school when their teachers maximize the time spent in actual learning. This statement may seem obvious, but the reality is that not all school time is spent in direct instruction. Effective teachers plan their lessons well, monitor the entire classroom continuously, minimize the time spent in disciplining children who misbehave, and keep transitions between activities brief and smooth (Brophy, 1986). They make sure there is little "dead time" in the classroom when students are unoccupied, and they keep the focus on instruction.

Another key ingredient in a teacher's success is his active involvement in the learning process. This means that teachers remain personally involved in every phase of instruction, from the initial presentation of a new lesson to supervising the individual work of students. *Involvement* also refers to the

One of the most important factors in the child's experience in school is the encouragement provided by the teacher. Effective teachers are involved in all phases of instruction, provide clear feedback, and create a positive emotional climate in the classroom.

teacher's enjoyment and knowledge of students. Even when students are working in groups, teachers who guide the discussion or progress of the group will produce higher levels of mastery and feelings of competence than those who leave students completely on their own (Brophy, 1986; Skinner & Belmont, 1993). Effective teachers also provide clear feedback to students on the quality of their performance and on what is expected of them (Rutter, 1983).

Finally, the way in which teachers structure daily classroom activities and deliver feedback can affect students' self-esteem, particularly the conceptions they form about their academic abilities. Generally speaking, when teachers assign similar tasks to all students, students will have more opportunities to make comparisons among themselves, to see how they "stack up" against each other. Those comparisons are harder to draw when, for example, pupils are given choices of several math or reading assignments. When teachers organize tasks according to student ability levels (for example, high- and low-ability reading groups), they are also creating a structure that encourages students to compare themselves. Moreover, when teachers assign grades frequently, make public announcements about grades, and openly emphasize the poor accomplishments of some students, they create situations in which students are likely to conclude that "I'm smarter (or dumber) than you." Children actively process the information, sometimes explicit and sometimes more subtle, that teachers deliver about their abilities. The net result is that some will inevitably see themselves as less competent than others (Rosenholtz & Simpson, 1984).

**The Classroom Climate**    Students achieve less when they are the targets of frequent criticism or ridicule from the teacher. On the other hand, when the classroom provides a warm, friendly environment, student achievement is high (Linney & Seidman, 1989). Teachers who set limits on students' behaviors do make the classroom run more smoothly, but the use of physical punishment is associated with poor attendance and delinquency (Rutter, 1983). In a large-scale investigation of the effectiveness of secondary schools, Michael Rutter and his colleagues found that schools in which students received frequent praise and that provided a pleasant, comfortable environment had children who were more likely to complete school and achieved more than children in other kinds of school environments (Rutter et al., 1979). Positive feedback encourages both acceptable behavior and achievement as well as fostering high student morale (Rutter, 1983). Like the authoritative parents discussed in Chapter 14, teachers who control students but use reasoning and positive emotions are likely to foster the greatest academic and personal gains among their students (Baumrind, 1972).

A particularly important dimension is the extent to which the teacher promotes *autonomy,* or student initiative within the classroom. When children perceive that teachers give them responsibility within the classroom, they have higher self-esteem scores than when teachers are perceived as controlling and directive (Ryan & Grolnick, 1986). The effects of controlling strategies are not necessarily simple, however. In one experiment, some teachers were pressured to improve fourth-grade children's performance in a problem-solving task, and others were simply instructed to facilitate ways in which children learned to solve the problems. Teaching strategies for the next ten minutes were then carefully observed. The results showed that controlling behaviors from teachers produced declines in children's problem-solving performance but only when teachers were pressured. In other words, other factors accompanying control, such as teacher stress and tension, may also affect students' performance (Flink, Boggiano, & Barrett, 1990).

▶ The child's active role

As this entire section shows, teachers play the major role in structuring the child's classroom experiences, those precise forms of interaction that occur in the fifteen thousand hours the child spends in the classroom from kindergarten through high school. The teacher determines which child will be called on to respond to a question, whether that child will be praised or criticized, and which academic tasks she will perform. The teacher also sets the emotional tone in the classroom and establishes how much autonomy children have. All these decisions can have profound effects on children. In some circles, it has become popular to blame teachers for all the failings of the educational system. This is certainly unfair, because the child's school success arises from a myriad of factors: his cognitive capabilities, the attitudes and behaviors of parents, and as we will see, even cultural beliefs about schooling. In many educational systems, teachers also face the pressures of high student-teacher ratios, lack of parental or administrative support for alternative classroom approaches, and the social problems of students who live in poor neighborhoods. At the same time, it is important for teachers to be aware of both the obvious and the subtle ways in which their own behaviors deeply influence the developing child.

## Cultural Differences in School Achievement

The school experience is not the same for children from different racial and ethnic backgrounds. Children who attend school bring with them attitudes about school that are first nurtured within their families, as well as cultural beliefs that may be in synchrony or in conflict with the predominant belief system of the school. Are schools, for example, the vehicle for economic and personal advancement? Cultural and ethnic groups may vary in their re-

▶ Sociocultural influence

sponses to this question. Is verbal, rational expression (which is emphasized in schools) the optimal means of human communication as opposed to emotional or spiritual sharing? Again, cultures may vary in the extent to which they value some skills over others. One of the major challenges facing educators is how to ensure the academic success of children coming from a range of cultural-ethnic backgrounds.

**School Achievement Among Minority Children**    A persistent finding in the research on school achievement is that African American children score significantly lower than Caucasians on many measures of academic performance. For example, the Coleman report, a national study of elementary and secondary school students sponsored by the government in 1966, found that African American children scored significantly below Caucasian children on tests of reading comprehension, verbal skill, mathematical ability, and knowledge of general information (Coleman, Campbell, & Mood, 1966). Later studies showed similar patterns: on measures of achievement in academic subjects and verbal and mathematical aptitude, African American children consistently scored lower than Caucasian children, although the gap has decreased more recently (Jones, 1984). Explanations for these patterns of findings have taken many turns over the years.

In the 1960s, the prevailing explanation for the school difficulties of minority children centered on the *cultural deficit hypothesis,* the notion that some deficiency in the backgrounds of minority children did not prepare them for the academic demands of school. An inescapable fact was that African American children were overrepresented among lower socioeconomic groups. Thus, some researchers hypothesized that these children came from unstimulating, pathological, or stressful homes and, in the absence of early experiences promoting cognitive development, suffered deficits in thinking skills that led to failure in school. As a consequence, the focus of many early-intervention programs was on remediating the cognitive deficits.

Herbert Ginsberg (1972) dispelled many of the popular beliefs of the time by pointing out that rather than being culturally deficient, minority children are culturally different. That is, the behaviors displayed by many African American children help them to adapt to their specific life circumstances. For example, rather than having poor language skills, African American children speaking Black English display rich images and poetic forms when speaking to each other. More recently, other psychologists and educators have come to believe that we must consider the cultural backgrounds of the members of any minority group to understand their school failure or success. According to the **cultural compatibility hypothesis**, school instruction produces greater improvements in learning if it is consistent with the practices of the child's own culture (Tharp, 1989).

**The KEEP Model**    An example of an educational intervention specifically designed to be compatible with the child's cultural background is the Kamehameha Early Education Program (KEEP), developed by Roland Tharp and his collaborators in Hawaii (Tharp et al., 1984). Like many minority children in other parts of the United States, youngsters of native Hawaiian ancestry have been the lowest achieving in the state. In one administration of a standardized test of reading achievement, more than half of native Hawaiian children scored below the fortieth percentile. School achievement deteriorated from the first grade on. Native Hawaiian children were also found to be overrepresented

**cultural compatibility hypothesis**  Theory that school instruction is most effective if it is consistent with the practices of the child's background culture.

among juvenile offenders arrested for serious crimes such as larceny, rape, and homicide.

The KEEP program was instituted as an early-education program in language arts for kindergarten through third-grade children. Several unique features of the program were tied to the practices and beliefs of traditional Hawaiian culture. First, because collaboration and cooperation are highly valued in that society, classrooms were organized into small groups of four to five children working on independent projects under the close supervision of a teacher. Teachers made a deliberate attempt to establish warm, nurturant relationships with their charges through the frequent use of praise and the avoidance of authoritarian methods of control. Second, the program attempted to improve responsiveness to teachers by capitalizing on the tendency of native Hawaiian children to engage their peers in rich and animated verbal interactions. Each day teachers conducted small-group discussions of some academic topic and did not discourage children's interruptions, overlapping speech, and rapid-paced discussions. Third, reading was taught with the aim of developing comprehension as opposed to mechanics, and children were encouraged to relate personal experiences that were triggered by reading a given text.

What were the results of this broad-based intervention? Participants in KEEP scored at approximately the national norms for several tests of reading achievement, whereas control subjects from similar low-income backgrounds continued to place below national averages (Tharp et al., 1984). The KEEP program is an excellent example of how modifying classroom practices to incorporate cultural patterns of language, communication, and social organization can enhance the school performance of children.

**African American Culture and Education**   In keeping with the cultural compatibility hypothesis some have argued that for many African American students, a conflict exists between their background culture and the social and cognitive structure of traditional schools. For example, the spiritualism, expressiveness, and rich oral tradition characteristic of an African American heritage frequently clash with the materialism, emotional control, and emphasis on printed materials characteristic of European Americans and their schools (Boykin, 1986; Heath, 1989; Slaughter-DeFoe et al., 1990).

The experience of racism can compound the problems. African American children may perceive that academic success does not necessarily lead to occupational or economic success, or they may believe that "acting white" is the only way to achieve success. John Ogbu (1974) found that inner-city African American children do poorly on academic tests because they do not take them seriously, do not persevere, and do not see their performance as linked to later success. Ogbu (1986) also maintains that although African American parents value education for their children, they have an inherent lack of trust in the traditional system because of its deep ties to segregation.

A study of achievement patterns of African American and Caucasian children in the first two years of school provides some support for the idea that larger sociocultural forces account for the lower achievement of minority children. Karl Alexander and Doris Entwistle (1988) found that African American and Caucasian first-graders did not differ significantly on a standardized test of verbal and quantitative achievement when they were assessed at the beginning of the school year. But by the end of the year and during the second year, the scores of African American and Caucasian students began to diverge noticeably. The achievements of Caucasian students were significantly related to parental variables, such as parents' expectations of their grades and assessments of their abilities. This relationship did not hold for African American students, however. The authors hypothesize that African American parents may be less attentive to the performance levels of their children or may be less involved in providing academic supports because of external pressures they face, such as economic hardship. Alexander and Entwistle's data, however, are also consistent with another possibility—that parental influences may diminish in the face of other, more powerful factors in influencing the achievement of African American children, such as those identified by Ogbu.

**Achievement Among Asian Children**    Since the mid-1980s, Harold Stevenson and his associates have been conducting comparative research in three countries on the academic abilities of Taiwanese Chinese, Japanese, and American students in an attempt to account for the academic superiority of Asian students, particularly in the areas of mathematics and science. In one of the earlier studies, first- and fifth-grade students from all three countries were tested on a battery of specially designed cognitive tasks that assessed, among other things, spatial relations, perceptual speed, auditory and verbal memory, and vocabulary (Stevenson, Lee, & Stigler, 1986). Tests of reading and mathematics achievement were also administered to these children from middle- to upper-class backgrounds. The results showed that Chinese children scored significantly higher in reading achievement than American children, who in turn performed above the level of Japanese children. American children scored noticeably lower in mathematics than the other two groups did (see Figure 16.3). Ten years later, in a follow-up study, American children declined even further compared to their Chinese and Japanese peers in mathematics achievement (Stevenson, Chen, & Lee, 1993).

The distinctive patterns of achievement could not be explained by superior cognitive skills in any one group. The researchers found no predictive relationships between scores on the various cognitive assessments and scores on achievement tests. In fact, what was striking was the similarity across cultural groups in the children's cognitive profiles by the time they were in the fifth grade (Stevenson et al., 1985).

**FIGURE 16.3**

**Academic Achievement as a Function of Sociocultural Context**

Chinese students score higher than American students on tests of reading achievement. By the first grade, both Chinese and Japanese students show clear superiority to American students in mathematics. (The vertical axis represents standard scores.)

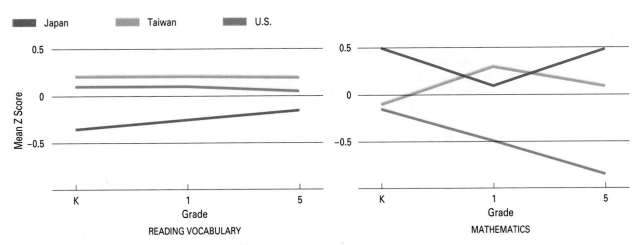

Source: Adapted from Stevenson, Lee, & Stigler, 1986.

What, then, accounts for the differing patterns of achievement in reading and mathematics? Stevenson's research group has found significant differences in children's school routines and the attitudes and beliefs of parents among the three cultures. One important difference occurred in the percentage of classroom time actually spent in academic activities. For fifth-grade students, the figures were 64.5 percent for American children, 91.5 for Chinese children, and 87.4 for Japanese children. Chinese and Japanese children also spent about fifty more days in school during the year than American children did. Furthermore, American children spent more than twice as much time on language arts as on mathematics, whereas Chinese and Japanese children spent equal amounts of time on each. Thus, the American children did not receive nearly as much instruction in mathematics as their Chinese and Japanese counterparts did (Stevenson, Lee, & Stigler, 1986). In addition, Japanese and Chinese teachers were far more likely to spend time in mathematics classes directly teaching the entire class, whereas American children spent more than half their time in mathematics classes working alone (Stigler, Lee, & Stevenson, 1987).

The research group also examined attitudes and behaviors related to homework. American children spent substantially less time doing homework, an average of 46 minutes per day among fifth-graders, according to mothers' estimates, compared to 114 and 57 minutes for Chinese and Japanese children, respectively. American mothers were not dissatisfied with the small amount of homework their children received, nor were Chinese and Japanese mothers dissatisfied with the large amounts their children were assigned (Stevenson, Lee, & Stigler, 1986).

The data highlight the fact that a number of factors other than pure cognitive ability determine the child's level of achievement in school. As we have seen throughout this section, the characteristics of the given school (especially the events that transpire in the classroom), parental attitudes, and larger cultural influences are all related to patterns of academic success or failure. As we also saw at the outset of this chapter, academic performance can have important repercussions for the child's self-esteem and personal adjustment. If we are concerned about the educational attainments of students and their overall psychological development, research on the influence of schools reveals that there are ways to more fully engage children of all ability levels and of diverse sociocultural backgrounds.

## Computers

Perhaps there is no more visible symbol of the technological age than the computer. Just as most adults are now likely to encounter computers in their daily experiences, so too are children, particularly in school. As of 1990, 97 percent of public schools provided computers for instructional purposes, and more than 40 percent of the students in these schools used computers in some way during the school year. The percentage of elementary school children using computers in school is slightly higher than the percentage of high school students (U.S. Bureau of the Census, 1992). In addition, as Figure 16.4 shows, elementary school children commonly interact with drill-and-practice software, which provides direct instruction and exercises, and high school students tend to do their own programming (Becker & Sterling, 1987).

The number of households in which computers are present is also growing. According to some estimates, more than 22 million American households have

▶ Sociocultural influence

**FIGURE 16.4**

**Patterns of School Computer Use Among Children***

Children of all ages use the computer in school, but the kinds of programs they use vary by age. Elementary school children, for the most part, perform drill-and-practice exercises on the computer. Older children learn to write programs and engage in other more sophisticated computer activities. (*As perceived by primary computer-using teacher at each school.)

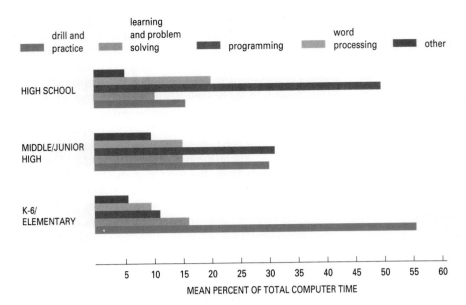

Source: Adapted from Becker and Sterling, 1987.

computers, and that number is likely to increase as the technology becomes more affordable (U.S. Bureau of the Census, 1992). Moreover, computer games are staples in many children's play routines. So ubiquitous are computers in contemporary American society that many now speak of computer literacy as a skill akin to reading.

Quite naturally, parents, educators, and researchers have begun to question the effect computers will have on children's development. Some wonder specifically about effects on academic achievement: can computer-presented instructional materials enhance the child's mastery of academic subjects? Others are concerned with broader aspects of cognitive development: does experience with computers influence the ways in which children tackle problem solving and other cognitive tasks? Still others fear that young computer "hackers" who spend long hours glued to the video screen may be missing other significant experiences, particularly the social interactions crucial to their socioemotional development. The pervasive presence of computers in today's world makes the questions raised by their critics and advocates well worth exploring.

Researchers are just beginning to investigate systematically how children are influenced by contact with computers. The emerging message is clear: there is no such thing as an "effect of computers" per se on child development. What matters, rather, is the way children use them (Salomon & Gardner, 1986).

**Academic Mastery** The first relatively widespread use of computers in education began in the 1960s, when **computer-assisted instruction (CAI)** was touted as a valuable, efficient educational tool. CAI programs serve primarily to supplement classroom instruction, providing highly structured tutorial information along with drill-and-practice exercises in content areas such as mathematics and reading. Several principles are presumed to make CAI programs effective teaching tools. First, the child can work through a lesson at

**computer-assisted instruction (CAI)** Use of computers to provide tutorial information and drill-and-practice routines.

her own pace, reviewing topics if necessary. CAI thus provides an individually paced learning experience in which the content can be tailored to the specific needs of the student. Second, the child receives immediate feedback about the correctness of his responses to questions and exercises and may even receive periodic summaries of performance. These features usually enhance learning and heighten motivation. Finally, CAI programs often employ sound effects and graphics designed to promote the child's attention to, and interest in, the material being presented.

How effective are CAI approaches to instruction? Much early research found that children, and especially "slow learners," obtained higher scores on standardized tests of achievement when traditional classroom instruction was supplemented with CAI (Lieberman, 1985). More recently, meta-analyses of the hundreds of studies evaluating CAI have shown that on average, students with CAI experience improve in achievement test scores and that this effect is moderately strong (Lepper & Gurtner, 1989). CAI is especially effective with elementary school and special-needs children, who seem to profit most from individualized approaches to learning (Kulik, Kulik, & Bangert-Drowns, 1985; Niemiec & Walberg, 1987). Children given CAI experience also have more positive attitudes toward computers and the subject area they are studying (Kulik, Bangert, & Williams, 1983).

Although CAI continues to be popular, newer educational software places less emphasis on rote memorization and more emphasis on providing children with opportunities to use higher-order thinking skills as they master academic subjects. Consider the example of fourth- and fifth-graders who are learning about the laws of physics, such as the principle that once an object is set in motion, an equal force in the opposite direction is necessary to stop it. In a study of how computers can help children learn the laws of motion, one group of children received tutorial material followed by questions and feedback, along the lines of the traditional CAI approach (Rieber, 1990). Another group was given a different type of computer experience, a simulation in which they were allowed to experiment with a free-floating starship, the speed of which they could increase or decrease. As the children interacted with the starship, they could observe the effects of their physical manipulations on its course and "discover" the laws of motion. Still a third group, serving as a control, was given the lesson material with no questions or simulation experiences. Students who participated in the simulations later obtained higher scores on a test of the laws of motion than those in the other two groups. One reason may be that the simulation encouraged students to make a more active mental engagement with the scientific principles underlying the motion of the starship. Software such as the starship simulation allows students to conduct experiments they might not be able to try in the typical elementary school science laboratory and is a prime example of how computer instruction can extend beyond simple drill-and-practice routines to enhance academic learning.

▶ The child's active role

**Cognition**    More than simply vehicles of direct instruction, computers may also be a means of enriching analytic thinking skills and creativity, particularly when children learn to do their own programming. Seymour Papert (1980), a creator of the computer language Logo, believes that programming experiences represent an ideal setting for learning because children can test their own theories and models of physical laws, mathematical relationships, and other forms of knowledge. Under such conditions, claims Papert, children can master abstract concepts and ideas much earlier than they normally would.

▶ The child's active role

Because it is specifically designed for children, the Logo program has been the focus of most studies investigating the influence of programming on children's cognition. Logo is an interactive program that allows children to create graphic displays by instructing a "turtle," a triangular pointer, to move around on the computer screen. To draw a square, the child might write this program:

```
TO SQUARE
FORWARD 100
RIGHT 90
FORWARD 100
RIGHT 90
FORWARD 100
RIGHT 90
FORWARD 100
RIGHT 90
END
```

After using the Logo program, many children begin to have spontaneous insights about how to make their programming more efficient—by, for example, modifying the sequence of commands just given to read:

```
TO SQUARE
REPEAT 4
    FORWARD 100
    RIGHT 90
    END
```

Here the child realizes that the goal can be achieved by "factoring" two commands, an example of more abstract, higher-order thinking.

Papert (1980) maintains that by using Logo to direct the pointer's path, children become familiar with notions of planning and debugging (fixing errors and learning from that process) as well as heuristic strategies for solving problems. **Heuristic strategies** are those mental reflections that focus on accomplishing a goal—as in dividing a problem into smaller parts or connecting it to other successfully solved problems. Furthermore, because computer programming requires the precise articulation of the steps necessary to reach a solution, children should also become aware of the logical and hierarchical nature of problem solving. The result, according to Papert, is a broad and significant change in the child's cognitive processes.

Researchers evaluating these claims have reported conflicting results. Some have found little transfer of skills from programming to other problem-solving tasks. Children with one year of experience with Logo, for example, do not show appreciable superiority in their ability to plan a sequence of events, such as how to schedule a series of classroom tasks efficiently (washing the board, watering the plants, and so forth) compared to children who did not learn to program (Pea, Kurland, & Hawkins, 1985).

Other researchers, however, have reported that children with Logo experience often show significant cognitive gains. For example, Douglas Clements (1986) randomly assigned thirty-six first-graders and thirty-six third-graders to one of three experimental groups: a Logo programming group, in which children had extensive experience in using the language; a CAI group, in which children participated in reading and mathematics tutorials and drills; and a control group, which participated in regular classroom lessons without computers. All children were administered several tests of general cognitive

**heuristic strategies** Methods of problem solving that involve higher-order analyses, such as subdividing the problem into smaller parts or comparing it with previously solved problems.

skill and academic achievement both before and twenty-two weeks after the study period. Although children in the three groups did not differ on measures of reading and mathematics achievement by the end of the study, children in the programming condition scored significantly higher on several measures of cognitive competence. First, the Logo group displayed the highest scores on tests of classification, which required the sorting of geometric shapes and objects as well as class inclusion, and seriation, in which objects had to be ordered from tallest to shortest. Second, this group's members also showed superior ability in monitoring their own cognitive processes—for example, by identifying the parts of a problem they did not understand. Finally, the Logo group received the highest scores on a test of creativity.

Experience with Logo has also been linked to greater spatial cognitive skill, enhanced rule learning, and a reflective cognitive style, in which children solve problems slowly and accurately rather than quickly and with many errors (Clements & Gullo, 1984; Gorman & Bourne, 1983; Mayer & Fay, 1987). In addition, children who have programmed with Logo show greater ability in analyzing the process of problem solving in abstract terms. Thus, they can say what information is necessary to solve a problem and identify problems that have similar structures (Nastasi, Clements, & Battista, 1990). One of the hypothesized reasons for the emergence of these higher-order problem-solving skills is that Logo is often used in group settings in which pairs or small groups of children help each other to solve programming problems. In these contexts, children often disagree on ways to conceptualize a given problem (for example, how to make a house with the turtle) and share several potential solutions. As children attempt to resolve their cognitive conflicts, they are pushed to more advanced modes of thinking (Nastasi, Clements, & Battista, 1990).

The studies show that the computer itself, as well as the interactions with peers it often precipitates, may function within the child's zone of proximal development (Salomon, Globerson, & Guterman, 1989). Children who are capable of learning cognitive skills, such as spatial relations or mathematical concepts, may be pushed to acquire the skills in their interactions with sophisticated software programs or as they work on joint problem-solving tasks with peers. Although some researchers believe that Papert's initial claims about the power of the computer to shape cognition were overstated, others hold that "intelligent" computer programs and experiences with programming languages have vast potential in enhancing children's thinking skills (Khayrallah & Van Den Meiraker, 1987; Salomon, Globerson, & Guterman, 1989).

**Social Development**    Contrary to popular opinion, the interactions a child has with the computer do not necessarily displace other activities of a more social nature, nor is computer use itself necessarily a solitary activity. In one survey of more than five hundred children, those with microcomputers at home resembled nonowners in the frequency with which they visited friends, participated in club meetings, and engaged in sports (Lieberman, 1985). In fact, the computer may actually stimulate the formation of social relationships. Children who play computer games say they visit their friends more often than those who do not, for example (Lieberman, 1985). Furthermore, children who work on computer projects in schools tend to collaborate and share ideas more in these settings than they do in other school activities (Hawkins et al., 1982). In one observation of four-year-olds who had a computer in their child-care center, 63 percent of the time they spent at the computer was in joint participa-

▶ Interaction among domains

When children employ the computer in school, they often have a partner. Computers can promote collaborative learning and provide opportunities for social development.

tion with a peer. In addition, the researchers found that 70 percent of the interactions consisted of active sharing of the computer (Muller & Perlmutter, 1985). Thus, rather than inhibiting social interactions, computer activities may actually promote them, especially when teachers encourage group problem solving as opposed to individual projects (Bergin, Ford, & Hess, 1993). As they work on shared projects or spontaneously exchange ideas at the computer, children have opportunities to develop skills in cooperation and social problem solving.

**Sex Differences**    *Computer.* Ask children ranging from kindergarten age to twelfth grade to rate this word on a scale that is labeled M (for male) at one end and F (for female) at the other. Ask them also to rate how much they like the item. Researchers who have followed this procedure have found that children of all ages place computers toward the "male" side of the rating scale and that boys like computers more than girls do (Wilder, Mackie, & Cooper, 1985). Other researchers have reported that boys are far more likely to enroll in computer camps (by a ratio of three to one) than girls are and that males outnumber females in computer courses in school (Hess & Miura, 1985; Linn, 1985). School computer labs are also far more likely to be populated by male students than female students during free time (Fish, Gross, & Sanders, 1986). If, as we saw before, experiences with computers can affect children's academic, cognitive, and social development, these sex differences have far-reaching implications for both girls and boys.

It is interesting to note that girls do not shy away from all computer activities. For example, although girls do not spend as much time as boys doing programming or playing computer games, they are just about equally disposed to use word-processing programs (Lockheed, 1985). Moreover, when girls do enroll in computer-programming classes, their performance is no different from that of their male classmates (Linn, 1985). Finally, no sex differences in interest in computers are observed when children are kindergarten age (Bergin,

Ford, & Hess, 1993). Why, then, do we see sex differences in the tendency to use computers among older children?

Several explanations are possible. First, teachers and parents may encourage boys to use computers because of their own stereotypic beliefs about appropriate activities for each sex. Parents, especially, may see computer skills as linked to promising careers for their sons and may be more willing to invest in computers, software, and camp programs for them than they would be for their daughters. Second, girls may be less attracted to the aggressive and competitive themes that frequently characterize computer games and educational software, many with titles such as "Submarine Attack" or "Alien Intruder" (Hess & Miura, 1985). Finally, both boys and girls are socialized to link computers with science and mathematics, academic subjects that are frequently perceived as more appropriate for boys (Lockheed, 1985). Unfortunately, the persistence of the stereotypes builds unnecessary barriers for girls to have the experiences with computers that promote abstract, analytical thinking.

In summary, computers add a unique dimension to children's experiences by encouraging them to engage in active and analytical reflection on the nature of problem solving and by promoting exchanges with peers, interactions that may further enhance both cognitive and social development. Early signs are that computers enhance, rather than detract from, the process of development.

# Television

According to most estimates, American children watch a great deal of television. Almost all (98 percent) American homes have at least one television set (U.S. Bureau of the Census, 1992), and as much as one-third of a child's waking life in our society will have been spent watching television (Nielsen Co., 1988). That is more time than children spend in any other activity except sleep (Huston, Watkins, & Kunkel, 1989). Moreover, with the advent of cable television and videocassette recorders (VCR), children have more opportunities than ever to spend time in front of a television screen. In the United States, almost three-quarters of all children have access to a VCR in their homes, and about two-thirds have cable programming (U.S. Bureau of the Census, 1992). Psychologists do not yet have much data on the effect of VCRs and cable television, but after thirty years of research we can say that television plays a recognizable role in the child's cognitive and social development.

▶ Sociocultural influence

## Patterns of Television Viewing Among Children

How much television do American children watch? Babies as young as six months of age attend to television and on average are exposed to more than one hour per day (Hollenbeck & Slaby, 1979). Estimates of viewing times for older children vary from about nine hours per week (Anderson et al., 1986) to about twenty-eight hours per week (Nielsen Co., 1988). Television viewing among children shows large individual differences, however. One research team investigating the viewing habits of three- to five-year-olds found that some children did not watch television at all during a one-week span, whereas others watched as much as seventy-five hours. Moreover, individual patterns of TV viewing were found to remain stable during a period of two years. Thus, the television-viewing habits children acquire in early childhood can be relatively long lasting (Huston et al., 1990).

As Figure 16.5 shows, the time children spend attending to television increases dramatically during the preschool years, especially after age two and a half; peaks between the ages of ten to twelve; and declines during adolescence (Anderson & Levin, 1976; Anderson et al., 1986; Calvert et al., 1982). Boys and girls watch television for equally long periods of time, but children from lower socioeconomic levels tend to be more frequent viewers than children from higher-income backgrounds (Greenberg, 1986).

As they grow older, children also show changes in the types of programs they prefer to watch. Preschoolers prefer to watch nonanimated informative programs specifically designed for children, such as "Sesame Street" or "Mister Rogers' Neighborhood." These programs feature language that children can comprehend easily and characters that are repeated across segments, and they do not require the child to integrate complex elements of a plot or story. Interest in these programs peaks at ages three and a half to four and then declines. From ages three to five, children watch more cartoons; by ages five to seven, they watch comedies and entertainment shows aimed at general audiences. With age, then, children watch shows that make increasing demands on their ability to comprehend plots and themes (Huston et al., 1990). Their choices may also be influenced by their parents; although they tend to watch childrens' programs alone, children often view general audience programs selected by their parents (St. Peters et al., 1991).

## Children's TV Viewing: Active or Passive?

▶ The child's active role

Contrary to popular belief, television viewing is not always a passive process in which a mesmerized child sits gazing at the screen. That their preferences for shows change with age is just one example of the ways in which children actively control their TV viewing. Daniel Anderson and his colleagues have conducted numerous studies further demonstrating that children's selection of television programs is influenced by their ability to comprehend content. Certain formal, or structural, features of television do serve to draw the viewer in, particularly such sound effects as laughter, music, and children's and women's voices. Other features, such as visual cuts, motion, and special sound effects, maintain the child's attention (Alwitt et al., 1980). But the formal features of television programs are not the sole determinants of what children watch.

**FIGURE 16.5**

**Hours of TV Watching as a Function of Children's Age**

The amount of time children spend watching television increases throughout early childhood, peaks at about age ten or twelve years, then declines in adolescence.

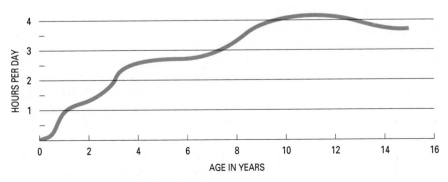

Source: Adapted from Liebert & Sprafkin, 1988.

Television is a powerful influence on child development. According to some estimates, as much as one-third of a child's waking life will have been spent watching television.

Anderson and his coresearchers recorded the visual attention of two- and five-year-olds as they watched a one-hour, specially edited version of "Sesame Street" in a laboratory room (Anderson et al., 1981). The videotape contained a regular program segment along with other portions that were altered to reduce the show's comprehensibility while keeping its formal features constant. In one version the dialogue was presented backward, in another the auditory portion was dubbed in Greek, and so on. The results indicated that children's visual attention was greater during the normal portions than in any of the altered segments. In other words, children actively direct their attention to those portions of the show that they most readily understand; they are not influenced by sound effects or visual cuts alone.

Children do not always have control of the programs they watch. Families frequently view television together, and parents often pick the shows everyone will see. Furthermore, children's program selections are limited by those shows the broadcasters choose to air on a given day and at a given time. Thus, children are frequently exposed to programming that falls outside their range of comprehension (Huston et al., 1990). Nevertheless, much of children's television viewing is guided by their active selection of programming they understand.

## Children's Comprehension of Television Programs

What exactly do young children understand about the various behaviors, roles, and stories that unfold during the programs they watch? Are there developmental changes in children's comprehension of TV programs? Many television shows have complex plots and use subtle cues that require inferences about characters' motives, intentions, and feelings. In addition, most programs contain changes of scene that require watchers to integrate information from several scenes. Research indicates that clear developmental differences exist in children's ability to understand information from television shows, differences that accompany changes in cognitive processing.

Preschoolers can understand short story segments in programs that are specifically targeted for children. When five-year-olds in one study saw four segments from "Sesame Street," each a few minutes long, they were later able to remember the most central elements of each story (Lorch, Bellack, & Augsbach, 1987). When the plots and themes of television shows become more complex, however, young children have difficulties.

More specifically, when they watch programs designed for general audiences, younger children are less likely than older children to remember the *explicit* content of programs; that is, they are less able to recognize the discrete scenes that are essential to understanding the plot. Second- and third-graders in one study remembered only 65 percent of the central content as compared to 90 percent and more for eighth-graders. Even when they do remember explicit information, younger children frequently fail to grasp the *implicit* content communicated by relationships between scenes (Collins et al., 1978). For example, young children may fail to understand a character's motive for aggression if the message is communicated in two scenes separated by several other sequences (Collins, 1983).

▶ Interaction among domains

W. Andrew Collins (1983) believes that children's comprehension of implicit content is tied to their emerging cognitive skills, specifically the ability to integrate two pieces of information separated by time or other events. He further suggests that the children's general knowledge and previous experiences can affect their comprehension of the programs they watch. Suppose, for example, that children are asked to retell the content of a show about a murder and the suspect's eventual capture. Children frequently mention *script-based* knowledge (see Chapter 9), drawing from their general storehouse of information on the events that surround the relationships between police and criminals. Older children are more likely than younger children, however, to describe content that was specific to the program they had watched, such as that some police officers in the show did not wear uniforms (Collins, 1983). As children's general knowledge about the world grows, their comprehension of more detailed specific information in television programs expands as well.

Other research has shown that still another skill—children's growing verbal competency—underlies their ability to understand TV programs. When five-year-olds were given standardized IQ tests and were tested on their memory of the central and incidental events on a thirty-five-minute television program, their scores on the verbal subscales of the IQ test correlated significantly with their ability to comprehend the show's central events (Jacobvitz, Wood, & Albin, 1989).

One other important developmental change occurs in relation to television viewing, and that is in children's ability to recognize that most television programming is fictional. Most five- and six-year-olds do not understand that television characters are actually actors playing roles, and it is not until age eight and older that the majority of children understand this concept. There are some exceptions: even kindergartners realize that cartoons are fantasy, and a few also understand that news shows are real. By second or third grade, children are increasingly able to distinguish between fantasy and reality on television by using contextual cues provided by the programs themselves, such as the genre of the show or whether animation appears. If a child labels a program as a cartoon or an entertainment show, he will see it as pretend; if he labels it as a news or sports show, he concludes that it is real. With age, children are more likely to consider the specific events and actions carried out by characters, rather than simply the type of show, in determining whether a program is about real life or fantasy (Dorr, 1983).

# Television's Influence on Cognitive and Language Development

Most preschoolers these days readily recognize Big Bird and the Cookie Monster as characters from "Sesame Street," the popular educational program specifically designed to teach cognitive skills to preschool children. But they also learn a lot more, according to research on educational television. Evaluations of the effects of such shows as "Sesame Street" demonstrate that television can teach children a range of problem-solving, mathematical, reading, and language skills.

**Cognition**    "Sesame Street" was specifically designed to provide entertaining ways to teach children—especially those who might be underprepared for school—the letters of the alphabet, counting, vocabulary, and similar school-readiness skills. The programs also deliberately include both male and female characters from many racial and ethnic backgrounds. One of the first comprehensive evaluations of the influence of "Sesame Street" was conducted by the Educational Testing Service shortly after the program's inception in 1969 (Ball & Bogatz, 1970). Subjects were preschool children, many from disadvantaged backgrounds, who were tested on an array of cognitive measures both before and after viewing "Sesame Street" at home for a season. Those who watched the show most frequently showed the greatest gains on several skills, including writing their name and knowing letters, numbers, and forms (see Figure 16.6). A second study conducted two years later found that frequent viewers obtained higher scores on a standardized vocabulary test, adapted better to school, and had more positive attitudes toward school and people of other races than nonwatchers did (Bogatz & Ball, 1972). Thus, the show had effects not only on children's cognitive skills but also on their prosocial attitudes.

Despite the apparent successes of "Sesame Street," critics held that the gains made by children who watched the show, although statistically significant, were actually quite small. Rather than closing the gap between underprivileged and advantaged children, they further suggested, the show might actually widen it. Because children in the evaluation studies were given incentives to watch the program, they may have watched it more than they normally

▸ Interaction among domains

**FIGURE 16.6**

**Television and Enhancement of Language Skills**

Preschool children who watch "Sesame Street" show gains in a number of prereading skills, including the ability to recite the alphabet and write their names. The graph shows that children who watched the show the most displayed the greatest gains in performance. (Children in quartile 1 rarely watched the show; those in quartile 2 watched two to three times per week; those in quartile 3 watched four to five times per week; and those in quartile 4 watched more than five times per week.)

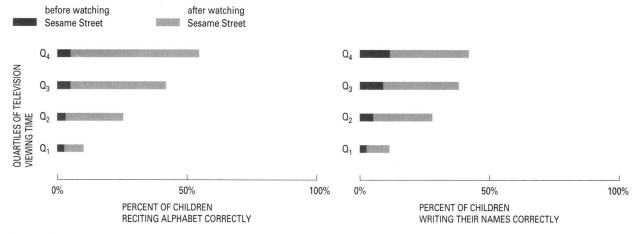

Source: Adapted from Liebert & Sprafkin, 1988.

would have. According to the skeptics, in real life—that is, without the incentives—advantaged children would be more prone to watch the program and thereby benefit from it. Still another problem was that many children in the evaluation study watched "Sesame Street" with an adult present. Did the show itself have an effect, or did the presence of the adult make a difference (Cook et al., 1975)?

A recent study by Mabel Rice and her associates (Rice et al., 1990) helps to rule out some of these criticisms. A large sample of three- and five-year-olds was studied during a two-year period. Diaries of television viewing were collected from the families; children's vocabulary skills were also tested. The results showed that parents viewed children's programs less than one-fourth of the time that children watched them and furthermore that the amount of parental co-viewing did not predict children's later vocabulary. Thus, the show itself, not parental presence, was associated with gains in vocabulary. In addition, the sample included families from a broad range of socioeconomic backgrounds. Contrary to earlier suggestions, the findings indicated no relationship between socioeconomic level and the amount of time children spent watching "Sesame Street."

"Sesame Street" has also been criticized for its short, unrelated segments, a fast-paced format that some developmental psychologists believe may actually impede learning. Jerome and Dorothy Singer (Singer & Singer, 1983) caution that repeated exposure to fast-paced programs may cause children to become overly aroused and inattentive. Children may also come to expect equally high-tempo learning experiences in school and, not finding them, may fail to develop reflective, sustained strategies for learning. Although provocative, these criticisms of "Sesame Street" have not been fully tested through empirical research.

Language    The study by Mabel Rice and her colleagues (1990) mentioned earlier suggests that television can promote children's language development. Many programs targeted for children, such as "Mister Rogers' Neighborhood," include simplified language, repetitions, recasts, and elaboration on the meanings of words. As we saw in Chapter 7, these devices can enhance the child's acquisition of vocabulary and syntax (Rice, 1983). Parents also sometimes use television as a "video picture book" in which events portrayed on the show stimulate verbal exchanges and language learning. When mothers watch television with their preschoolers, they frequently identify objects, repeat new words, ask questions, or relate the content of the show to the child's own experience (Lemish & Rice, 1986). Such verbal interactions are especially likely when parent and child watch age-appropriate shows such as "Sesame Street."

Is there direct evidence that television can function as a vehicle for vocabulary acquisition? Investigators exposed three- and five-year-olds to twenty new words in a fifteen-minute animated television story and found that both age groups showed gains in comprehension after only two viewings. Three-year-olds learned an average of one to two new words, and five-year-olds learned four to five words (Rice & Woodsmall, 1988). These findings are all the more impressive considering the brevity of exposure of the children to new vocabulary items and the limited efforts of the experimenters to highlight or exaggerate the new words.

## Television's Influence on Social Development

Whipping a towel over his shoulders, a seven-year-old jumps off the couch after watching the movie *Superman* on television. A brother and sister brandish toy swords, the brother mimicking the low voice of Shredder in *Teenage Mutant Ninja Turtles*. These common scenes in American households illustrate the power of television to influence children's behavior through direct imitation. Sometimes the messages are more subtle: a male announcer's authoritative voice decrees that a new detergent is twice as effective as other brands or that a sugary cereal is fortified with vitamins. When mostly men's voices are heard in television commercials, the indirect message is that males, more than females, have the knowledge and authority to make such definitive statements. Whether by directly providing models for children to imitate or by indirectly offering messages about social categories, television can promote behaviors as diverse as aggression and sex typing. Psychologists and those who make social policy have been particularly concerned about how television affects the child's social behavior and understanding, for better or for worse.

▶ Interaction among domains

**Aggression**   Any child turning on the television has an extraordinarily good chance of encountering the portrayal of violence. On average, five to six acts of physical aggression per hour occur on prime-time television. The rate is even higher on weekends, when children's programming predominates (Gerbner et al., 1986). For more than two decades, concerned parents and psychologists alike have asked the pressing question: does viewing televised violence produce aggression in children? Hundreds of research studies have examined this issue, and several reports on the topic have been issued by government agencies and professional organizations. The report of the Surgeon General's Scientific Advisory Committee on Television and Social Behavior in 1972, the report of the National Institutes of Mental Health in 1982, and the American Psychological Association in 1985 agree—there is a small but consistent causal relationship between viewing aggression on TV and aggressive behavior in children (Huston, Watkins, & Kunkel, 1989).

These photos, taken from Bandura's classic experiments, illustrate with stark clarity the power of imitation in influencing children's aggression. In the top row, an adult model displays various aggressive actions against a "Bobo doll." The middle and bottom rows depict the sequence of imitative aggression shown by a male and female subject in the experiment. Their behaviors closely mimic the specific actions they had previously seen the adult perform.

Many researchers believe that televised violence provides children with frequent and potent models for aggression, models that—in keeping with the principles of social learning theory—suggest to the child that physical attacks are acceptable in a person's repertoire of behaviors. According to social learning theory, two processes operate: first, children may learn new acts of aggression, and second, aggressive behaviors already in their response repertoire are disinhibited (Bandura, 1969).

In a series of laboratory studies designed by Albert Bandura and his colleagues (Bandura, Ross, & Ross, 1963a, 1963b) to explore the effects of viewing aggression, nursery school children were randomly assigned to one of five experimental conditions. The first group watched from behind a one-way mirror as a model in the next room performed a series of unusual acts of physical and verbal aggression at a plastic, inflated Bobo doll. For example, the model hit the doll with a hammer, kicked it, and said, "Hit the Bobo doll!" and "Kick the Bobo doll!" A second group of children watched a model perform the same actions, but the presentation was on film. A third group watched an adult disguised as a cartoon figure behave like the models in the previous two conditions. A fourth group observed an adult model behaving in a nonaggressive manner, sitting quietly and ignoring the Bobo doll and the toys associated with aggressive behavior. The last group of children saw no model at all.

Figure 16.7 shows the mean number of aggressive responses displayed by children in each condition. Children who had seen an aggressive model performed a large number of imitative aggressive acts, copying even the subtle details of the model's behaviors. In addition, they frequently added their own forms of physical and verbal aggression. Most important, from the standpoint of this discussion, the performance of children in the film-model group was no different from that of subjects who saw the real-life model. Models on film were just as powerful as "live" models in eliciting aggression.

Some researchers have questioned whether the act of punching a Bobo doll should be considered aggressive rather than "playful" behavior and whether the film segment used by Bandura resembles the kinds of scenes depicted in actual television programs (Freedman, 1984). Another criticism is that when the child sees a violent program in the laboratory without the myriad other stimuli that occur under more natural conditions, his attention becomes fo-

**FIGURE 16.7**

**The Effect of Watching Modeled Aggression**

After children saw a live, filmed, or live dressed-up "cartoon" model behave aggressively in the laboratory (bottom three bars), they were much more likely to imitate the model's aggression than were children who had seen no model at all or viewed a model behaving nonaggressively.

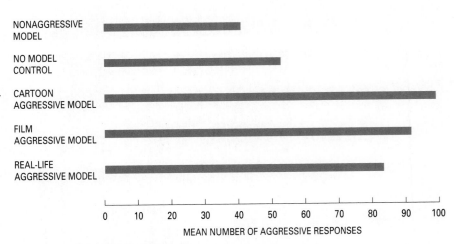

Source: Adapted from Bandura & Walters, 1963.

cused on the experiment's theme. The child may think that the experimenter condones or even expects aggression and therefore behaves more aggressively then he normally would. Finally, laboratory studies of aggression may have limited generalizability to real-life situations. Most studies have not used real TV shows as stimuli, and observations are typically conducted in settings unlike those most children experience in their daily routines.

Field experiments in which children are exposed to actual television programs and are observed in more natural contexts respond to many of these criticisms. You may recall from Chapter 1 that in one such study, Lynette Friedrich and Aletha Stein (1973) found that preschool children who viewed violent cartoons declined on several measures of self-control, including the ability to tolerate delays, obedience to school rules, and task persistence. At the same time, children who saw prosocial programs displayed higher tolerance for delays, more rule obedience, and greater task persistence than control children.

Large-scale correlational studies add to the evidence connecting violence on television with aggression. One study of almost one thousand children showed that aggression and televised violence are actually linked in a reciprocal way (Huesmann, Lagerspetz, & Eron, 1984). The investigators asked each subject's peers to rate how aggressive the child was, and they also noted how much television violence each child watched. After the data were collected during a period of three years, the results showed that the amount of violent TV shows children watched at the start of the study predicted how aggressive they were three years later. In turn, aggression also influenced TV viewing. Children who were aggressive at the start of the study watched more violent shows three years later than they did initially. The results are consistent with a bidirectional model of influence: children become more aggressive after a diet of violent television, and their aggression seems to stimulate even more viewing of violent shows.

Can parents do anything to mitigate the potentially harmful consequences of certain television shows on their children's behavior? One obvious tactic is to limit the amount of time children are permitted to watch violent programs. Another is to watch television with their children and discuss the negative consequences of violence. By suggesting prosocial methods of conflict resolution, parents can help youngsters develop a more critical attitude toward the programs they watch (Dorr, 1986). In a school-based intervention program, 170 children who frequently watched violent programs were divided into an experimental and control group. During a period of six to eight weeks, children in the experimental group participated in regular training sessions in which they were taught that (1) the behaviors of aggressive TV characters are not representative of the way most people act, (2) aggressive scenes on TV are not real but are staged by means of special effects and camera techniques, and (3) the average person uses more positive strategies to resolve interpersonal problems than those shown on violent TV programs. Discussions of these issues followed the presentation of a high-action "superhero" show. During the same time period, control subjects saw nonviolent shows and participated in neutral discussions. By the end of the study, children in the experimental group were significantly less aggressive than the control children, demonstrating that the real-life behaviors of children can be modified by effecting changes in their attitudes about television (Huesmann et al., 1983).

**Prosocial Behavior**     Just as television can encourage negative social behaviors, it can also foster prosocial development. We saw in the field experiment conducted by Friedrich and Stein (1973) that children who watched "Mister Rogers' Neighborhood" for a four-week period increased in their prosocial interpersonal behaviors. Other researchers have also found that programs that contain messages about cooperation, altruism, and sharing promote these behaviors in children.

Consider what happens, for example, when children view two segments from Lassie, one that shows the main character, Jeff, risking his life to save a puppy and one that does not show an example of helping. Children were randomly assigned to one of the two conditions or, alternatively, watched an episode from the "Brady Bunch" series. After children saw one of the shows, they were invited to play a game in which they could earn points to win desirable toys. While the children played, the experimenters played a tape of a dog's barking that became increasingly frantic. Children who saw the prosocial episode of "Lassie" were much more likely to show helping behaviors than children in the other two conditions (Sprafkin, Liebert, & Poulos, 1975).

A meta-analysis of 190 studies of prosocial television indicates that such programs can have powerful effects on children's behavior. In fact, the statistical findings indicated that the effects of prosocial programming are even greater than the effects of antisocial programming on children's behavior (Hearold, 1986). Unfortunately, the power of television to influence children in these positive ways has yet to be used fully.

**Gender Stereotypes**     Television shows such as "The Cosby Show" and "Growing Pains" portray males and females in nontraditional roles in which fathers cook and care for their children and women are employed outside the home. These programs, however, are not standard fare on commercial television. Women appear in only one-third or fewer of the roles in television programs and commercials, and when they do they typically play romantic or family roles. Working women, when they are shown, are likely to be employed in sex-typed positions (for example, as secretaries and nurses); if they occupy positions of authority, they are often cast as villains (Huston & Alvarez, 1990). Consistent with stereotypes of female behavior, girls and women on television act nurturantly, passively, or emotionally. In contrast, males are more frequently the central characters of television shows, and they act forcefully, have more power and authority than women, and display reason rather than emotion (Lovdal, 1989; Signorielli, 1989).

The televised stereotypes of male and female behaviors apparently do affect children. Correlational studies show that the more television children watch, the more they identify with stereotyped roles of their own sex (Frueh & McGhee, 1975; McGhee & Frueh, 1980). Other research shows that the children most likely to be affected by the sexist content of television are middle-class girls of above-average intelligence, the same group of children who otherwise display liberal gender-related attitudes (Morgan, 1982). Longitudinal studies point out that the correlations do not arise simply because sex-typed children watch more television. Michael Morgan's work (1982, 1987) shows that the viewing habits of adolescents during the initial phases of his studies correlated slightly with their gender-role attitudes, but the relationships became stronger six months and one year later, suggesting that beliefs about male and female roles change after a heavy diet of television viewing.

In the same way that television is able to reinforce traditional gender-role standards, it has the power to make these standards less stereotyped. In 1975, a television series called "Freestyle" was developed to counteract children's stereotypical beliefs about sex-typed characteristics and behaviors. Each episode presented stories of people in sex-atypical activities. In one episode, for example, a mother returns to work after teaching the other members of her family how to take care of themselves by performing household chores. The story revolves around the father's recognition that his wife's job increases her self-esteem and the happiness of the family and depicts his gradually increasing pleasure in performing "feminine" household chores. Studies of children who watched this series indicate that they were more accepting of nontraditional roles, activities, and occupations than children who did not watch the series. In addition, changes in children's beliefs persisted for as long as nine months after viewing the series (Johnston, Ettema, & Davidson, 1980).

**Consumer Behavior**    In 1989, American children aged four to twelve spent $6 billion of their own money on candy and other snacks, toys and games, clothing, electronic equipment, and an assortment of other consumer goods (McNeal, 1990). Because of their tremendous spending power, either directly or through their parents, children are the targets of a significant number of television commercials. Of special concern to many child advocates is the proliferation of television shows linked to specific toys (for example, cartoon shows that portray the same characters as toys) and product endorsements for expensive items, such as athletic shoes, by popular sports figures and other celebrities, all of which put pressure on children to spend money.

Children who are heavy television viewers respond to the messages of commercials. For one thing, they frequently request the cereals and other foods they see advertised (Taras et al., 1989). However, children do not always recognize commercials as messages specifically intended to influence their behavior; four- and five-year-olds, for example, believe that "commercials are to help and entertain you." It is usually not until children are eight years of age or older that they understand that commercials are intended to influence viewers' buying habits (Ward, Reale, & Levinson, 1972). Because young children are not able to critically evaluate the information presented to them in commercials, they may pressure their parents to purchase expensive toys and clothes, heavily sugared foods, and other products (Kunkel & Roberts, 1991).

Fortunately, children respond to materials designed to educate them about commercials. When children in one study saw one-minute segments describing the intent of commercials and the fact that they were not always truthful, they were more skeptical about the product claims than children who had not seen these educational messages (Christenson, 1982).

In summary, television holds enormous promise in enhancing children's intellectual and social functioning. In addition to providing a rich source of intellectual stimulation, television can convey potent and influential messages about prosocial behaviors, nonstereotyped gender roles, and responsible consumer behavior. Many critics of television, however, hold that the medium's potential to promote desirable developmental outcomes thus far has gone largely untapped.

## THEMES IN DEVELOPMENT

### SCHOOL AND TELEVISION

▶ **How does the sociocultural context influence the child's experiences with school and television?**

The society in which the child grows up determines whether she will have any exposure to school, computers, or television in the first place. Not all cultures emphasize formal schooling, and not all children have access to television or computers. In terms of school, the child's background culture may either harmonize or conflict with the predominant values of the educational system. In the latter case, children may experience academic failure as well as lower self-esteem. The KEEP model suggests that children's academic performance climbs when educational practices are compatible with the child's cultural background.

▶ **How does the child play an active role in experiences with school and television?**

In their schooling experiences, children show greater academic achievement and higher self-esteem when school structures facilitate their greater participation in the educational process. In addition, educational techniques such as peer collaboration, classroom autonomy, and computer activities in group contexts all seem to foster development by promoting the child's active involvement. In their television viewing, children actively direct their attention to programs they understand, although sometimes they are more passively exposed to programs selected by others.

▶ **How do the child's experiences with school and television interact with development in other domains?**

Children's developmental accomplishments affect their school experience and vice versa. Children who have good peer relations are more likely to adjust well to school in the first place. Once in school, children typically have experiences that can promote their intellectual advancement, peer relations, and self-concept. For example, open classrooms can enhance peer interaction skills, and the academic feedback students receive can influence self-esteem. Peer learning techniques especially foster developmental accomplishments in many domains. Experiences with computers, too, can facilitate cognitive and social development.

As children's cognitive skills grow, so does their ability to comprehend both the explicit and implicit information portrayed on television. At the same time, educational television programs can enhance cognitive growth in such areas as prereading skills. Moreover, television can influence social behavior through the strong messages it portrays about violence, prosocial acts, and gender-role stereotypes.

School    The major influence school exerts on children lies in fostering academic achievement and shaping their self-esteem. Several aspects of the school's physical environment—school size, class size, and the physical arrangement of the classroom—bear on development. Generally, smaller schools and classes, as well as circular seating arrangements, are beneficial to students by promoting their active participation in the educational process. Philosophies of education, which are translated into specific teaching models, also play a role. Some alternative educational practices, such as the *open classroom, peer collaboration,* and *cooperative learning,* have been found to produce especially positive effects on students' social and personal development.

The ways in which children adjust to school transitions, such as the start of school or junior high school, can influence their subsequent attitudes toward and accomplishments in school. The most important element of the school experience, however, is the teacher. Teachers' expectations, classroom management techniques, and the classroom climate all make a difference in students' academic achievement and self-esteem.

Children's school achievement can vary according to their cultural background. The results of the KEEP project demonstrate that children's academic performance climbs when educational tactics incorporate elements of their background culture. Children who go to school in Asian societies show higher levels of achievement than American children, especially in mathematics and science, patterns that are associated with elements of students' classroom experiences.

Computers can influence both cognitive and social development. Children with *computer-assisted instruction (CAI)* experience show modest gains in academic achievement, and children who are exposed to tutoring software or programming show gains in higher-order cognitive skills, such as *heuristic strategies* for problem solving. Computers can enhance social development by stimulating peer exchanges as students attempt to solve problems. Boys are more likely than girls to learn computer skills, which may be the result of gender-role stereotypes among parents, teachers, and the students themselves.

Television    One of childhood's most frequent activities is watching television. Children show increases in the amount of television they view until they reach adolescence, at which point TV viewing declines. Although the formal features of television often guide young children's attention, children also actively attend to the portions of programs they comprehend. As children's cognitive and verbal skills expand, so does their ability to comprehend both the explicit and implicit elements of programs. Television can promote certain prereading skills, such as knowledge of the alphabet and numbers, as well as improve children's vocabulary. Television can also influence social behavior, specifically in the display of aggression, prosocial behavior, gender-role stereotypes, and consumer behavior.

# Glossary

**Accommodation** In Piagetian theory, a component of adaptation; process of modification in thinking (schemes) that takes place when old ways of understanding something no longer fit.

**Adaptation** In Piagetian theory, inborn tendency to adjust or become more attuned to conditions imposed by the environment; takes place through assimilation and accommodation.

**Age-history confound** In longitudinal studies, the co-occurence of historical factors with changes in age; affects the ability to interpret results.

**Allele** Alternate form of a specific gene; provides a genetic basis for many individual differences.

**Altruism** Behavior carried out to help another without expectation of reward.

**Amniocentesis** Method of sampling the fluid surrounding the developing fetus by insertion of a needle; usually performed in the fourteenth to sixteenth week after conception. Used to diagnose fetal genetic and developmental disorders.

**Amniotic sac** Fluid-filled, transparent protective membrane surrounding the fetus.

**Anal stage** In Freudian theory, the second psychosexual stage, between about one and three years of age, during which libidinal energy is focused on control of defecation.

**Analogical transfer** Ability to employ the solution to one problem in other similar problems.

**Androgen** Class of male or masculinizing hormones.

**Androgyny** Gender-role orientation in which a person possesses high levels of personality characteristics associated with both sexes.

**Animism** The attribution of life-like qualities to inanimate objects.

**Approval and interpersonal orientation** Form of prosocial reasoning in which children's reasons for assisting someone in need are based on the social approval or disapproval of others.

**Artificialism** The belief that naturally-occurring events are caused by people.

**Assimilation** In Piagetian theory, a component of adaptation; process of interpreting an experience in terms of current ways (schemes) of understanding things.

**Attachment** Strong emotional bond that emerges between infant and caregiver.

**Attention** State of alertness or arousal that allows the individual to focus on a selected aspect of the environment.

**Attentional inertia** Continued sustained attention after an initial period of focused attention.

**Authoritarian parent** Parent who relies on coercive techniques to discipline the child and who displays a low level of nurturance.

**Authoritative parent** Parent who sets limits on a child's behavior by using the technique of induction and who displays a high degree of nurturance.

**Autosomes** Twenty-two pairs of homologous chromosomes. The two members of each pair are similar in size, shape, and genetic function. The two sex chromosomes are excluded from this class.

**Babbling** Consonant-vowel utterances that characterize the infant's first attempts to vocalize.

**Basic emotion** Emotion such as joy, sadness, or surprise that appears early in infancy and seems to have a biological foundation. Also called *primary emotion*.

**Behavior analysis** Learning theory perspective that explains the development of behavior by the principles of classical and operant conditioning.

**Behavior genetics** Study of how characteristics and behaviors of individuals such as intelligence and personality are influenced by the interaction between genotype and experience.

**Broca's area** Portion of the cerebral cortex that controls expressive language.

**Canalization** Concept that the development of some attributes is governed primarily by the genotype and that only extreme environmental conditions will alter the phenotypic pattern for these attributes.

**Cardinality** Principle that the last number in a set of counted numbers refers to the number of items in that set.

**Case study** In-depth description of psychological characteristics and behaviors of an individual.

**Catch-up growth** Increase in growth rate after some factor such as illness or poor nutrition has disrupted the expected, normal growth rate.

**Categorical perception** Inability to distinguish between sounds that vary on some basic physical dimension except when those sounds lie at opposite sides of a critical juncture point on that dimension.

**Categorical self**  Conceptual process starting in the early preschool years in which the child begins to classify him- or herself according to easily observable categories (sex, age, physical capacities, skills, and so forth) that can be used to distinguish people.

**Centration**  In Piagetian theory, tendency of the child to focus on only one aspect of a problem.

**Cephalocaudal development**  Pattern that organs, systems, and motor movements near the head tend to develop earlier than those near the feet.

**Chorionic villus sampling**  Method of sampling fetal chorionic cells; usually performed in eighth or twelfth week of pregnancy. Used to diagnose embryonic genetic and developmental disorders.

**Chromosomes**  Threadlike structures of DNA, located in the nucleus of cells, that form a collection of genes. A human body cell normally contains forty-six chromosomes.

**Circular reaction**  In Piagetian theory, repetition of some action or behavior because of the pleasure it brings.

**Classical conditioning**  Type of learning in which a neutral stimulus repeatedly paired with another stimulus that elicits a reflexive response eventually begins to elicit the reflexlike response by itself.

**Clinical method**  Flexible, open-ended interview method in which questions are modified in reaction to the child's responses.

**Clique**  Peer group of five to ten children who frequently interact together.

**Codominance**  Condition in which individual, unblended characteristics of two alleles are reflected in the phenotype.

**Coercive cycle**  Pattern of reciprocal aggression between parent and child.

**Cognition**  Processes involved in thinking and mental activity, such as attention, memory, and problem solving.

**Cognitive-developmental theory**  Theoretical orientation, most frequently identified with Piaget, that explains development in terms of the active construction of psychological structures concerned with the interpretation of experience. These structures are assumed to be established at roughly similar ages by all children to form a series of qualitatively distinct stages in development.

**Cohort effect**  Characteristics shared by individuals growing up in a given sociohistorical context that can influence developmental outcomes.

**Complex emotion**  Emotion such as guilt and envy that appears later in childhood and requires more complex cognitive and social skills.

**Comprehension monitoring**  Ability to evaluate the adequacy of a communication.

**Computer-assisted instruction (CAI)**  Use of computers to provide tutorial information and drill-and-practice routines.

**Concept**  Definition of a set of information on the basis of some general or abstract principle.

**Concordance rate**  Percentage of pairs of twins in which both members have a specific trait identified in one of the twins.

**Concrete operational stage**  In Piagetian theory, the third stage of development—approximately from seven to eleven years of age—in which thought is logical when stimuli are physically present.

**Conditioned emotional response**  Emergence of an emotional reaction to an originally neutral stimulus through classical conditioning.

**Conditioned response (CR)**  A learned response that is exhibited to a previously neutral stimulus (CS) as a result of pairing the CS with an unconditioned stimulus (UCS).

**Conditioned stimulus (CS)**  A neutral stimulus that begins to elicit a response similar to the unconditioned stimulus (UCS) with which it has been paired.

**Configurational knowledge**  Child's use of landmarks and routes in integrated, holistic ways to represent physical space.

**Conscience**  In Freudian theory, the part of the superego that defines unacceptable behaviors and actions, usually as also defined by the parents.

**Conservation tasks**  Problems that require the child to make judgments about the equivalence of two displays; used to assess stage of cognitive development.

**Control theory**  Hypothesis about parent-child interactions that suggests that the intensity of one partner's behavior affects the intensity of the other's response.

**Conventional level**  In Kohlberg's theory, the second level of moral reasoning, in which the child conforms to the norms of the majority and wishes to preserve the social order.

**Cooing**  Vowel-like utterances that characterize the infant's first attempts to vocalize.

**Cooperative learning**  Peer-centered learning experience in which students of different abilities work together in small groups to solve academic problems. Often these groups compete against each other within the classroom.

**Cooperative play**  Interactive play in which children's actions are reciprocal.

**Correlation coefficient (r)**  Statistical measure, ranging from $+1.00$ to $-1.00$, that summarizes the strength and direction of the relationship between two variables; does not provide information about causation.

**Correlational study**  Study assessing whether changes in one variable are accompanied by systematic changes in another variable.

**Cross-cultural study**  Study comparing subjects in different cultural contexts.

**Cross-fostering study** Research study in which children are reared in environments that differ from those of their biological parents.

**Cross-gender behavior** Behavior usually seen in a member of the opposite sex. Term generally is reserved for behavior that is persistently sex atypical.

**Crossing over** Process during the first stage of meiosis when genetic material is exchanged between autosomes.

**Crowd** Large group of peers that is characterized by specific traits or reputation.

**Crystallized intelligence** Mental skills derived from cultural experience.

**Cultural compatibility hypothesis** Theory that school instruction is most effective if it is consistent with the practices of the child's background culture.

**Debriefing** Providing research participants with a statement of the true goals of a study after initially deceiving them about its purposes.

**Deferred imitation** Ability to imitate a model's behavior hours, days, and even weeks after observation.

**Delay of gratification** Capacity to wait for some period of time before performing a tempting activity or attaining some highly desired outcome; a measure of individuals' ability to regulate their own behavior.

**Deoxyribonucleic acid (DNA)** Long, spiral staircase-like sequence of molecules created by nucleotides identified with the blueprint for genetic inheritance.

**Dependent variable** Behavior that is measured; suspected effect of an experimental manipulation.

**Development** Physical and psychological changes in the individual over a lifetime.

**Developmental psychology** Systematic and scientific study of changes in human behaviors and mental activities over time.

**Deviation IQ** IQ score computed by comparing the child's performance with that of a standardization sample.

**Dishabituation** *See* recovery from habituation

**Disorganized/disoriented attachment** Infant-caregiver relations characterized by the infant's fear of the caregiver, confused facial expressions, and a combination of avoidant and ambivalent attachment behaviors.

**Display rules** Cultural guidelines about when, how, and to what degree to display emotions.

**Dominant allele** Allele whose characteristics are reflected in the phenotype even when part of a heterozygous genotype. Its genetic characteristics tend to mask the characteristics of other alleles.

**Ecological systems theory** Bronfenbrenner's theory that development is the joint outcome of individual and experiential events. Experience consists not only of immediate surroundings but also of the larger social and cultural systems that affect an individual's life.

**Effectance motivation** Inborn desire theorized by Robert White to be the basis for the infant's and child's efforts to master and gain control of the environment.

**Egocentrism** Preoperational child's inability to separate his or her own perspective from that of others.

**Ego ideal** In Freudian theory, the part of the superego that defines the positive standards for which an individual strives. This component is acquired via parental rewarding of desired behaviors.

**Elaboration** Memory strategy in which subjects link items to be remembered in the form of an image or sentence.

**Embryonic period** Period of prenatal development during which major biological organs and systems are formed. Begins at about the tenth to fourteenth day after conception when implantation occurs, and ends at about the eighth week after conception, with the onset of bone formation.

**Emotions** Complex behaviors involving physiological, expressive, and experiential components produced in response to some external or internal event.

**Empathic reasoning** Form of prosocial reasoning in which children attempt to put themselves in another's place and understand that person's feelings.

**Empathy** Vicarious response to the feelings of others.

**Empiricism** Theory that environmental experiences shape the individual; more specifically, that all knowledge is derived from sensory experiences.

**Episodic memory** Memory for events that took place at a specific time and place.

**Equilibration** In Piagetian theory, an innate self-regulatory process that begins with the discovery of a discrepancy between the child's cognitive structures or schemes and results, through accommodation and assimilation, in more organized and powerful schemes for effectively thinking about and adapting to the environment.

**Ethnic identity** The sense of belonging to a particular cultural group.

**Ethology** Theoretical orientation and discipline concerned with the evolutionary origins of behavior and its adaptive and survival value in animals, including humans.

**Exosystem** In Bronfenbrenner's ecological systems theory, environmental settings that indirectly affect the child by influencing the various microsystems forming the child's immediate environment.

**Experimental design** Research method in which one or more independent variables are manipulated to determine the effect on other, dependent, variables.

**Expiatory punishment** Young child's belief that punishment need not be related to a transgression as long as the punishment is severe enough.

**Expressive aphasia** Loss of the ability to speak fluently.

**Expressive characteristics**    Characteristics associated with emotions or relationships with people; usually considered feminine.

**Expressive style**    Type of early language production in which children use many social words.

**External locus of control**    Individual's sense that outside factors such as luck, fate, and other people primarily influence success and failure and the events that happen to him or her. Contrast with *internal locus of control*.

**Externality effect**    Tendency for infants younger than two months of age to focus on the external features of a complex stimulus and to explore the internal features less systematically.

**Failure to thrive**    Label applied to any child whose growth in height or weight is below the third percentile for children of the same age; may arise from inadequate social-emotional relationships with caregivers.

**Fast-mapping**    Deriving meanings of words from the context in which they are spoken.

**Fetal alcohol syndrome (FAS)**    Cluster of fetal abnormalities stemming from mother's consumption of alcohol; includes growth retardation, defects in facial features, and intellectual retardation.

**Fetal monitoring device**    Medical device used to monitor fetal heartbeat during delivery.

**Fetal period**    Period of prenatal development marked by relatively rapid growth of organs and preparation of body systems for functioning in postnatal environment. Begins about the eighth week after conception and ends at birth.

**Field experiment**    Experiment conducted in a "natural" real-world setting such as the child's home or school.

**Fluid intelligence**    Biologically based mental abilities that are relatively uninfluenced by cultural experiences.

**Focus on states**    Preoperational child's tendency to treat two or more connected events as unrelated.

**Formal operational stage**    In Piagetian theory, the last stage of development—approximately from eleven to fifteen years of age—in which thought is abstract and hypothetical.

**Fragile X syndrome**    Disorder associated with a pinched region of the X chromosome; a leading genetic cause of mental retardation in males.

**Fraternal twins**    Siblings sharing the same womb at the same time but who originate from two different eggs fertilized by two different sperm cells. Also called *dizygotic twins*.

**Gametes**    Sperm cells in males, egg cells in females, normally containing only twenty-three chromosomes.

**Gender constancy**    Knowledge, usually gained around age six or seven years, that one's gender does not change as a result of alterations in appearance, behaviors, or desires.

**Gender identity**    Knowledge, usually gained by age three years, that one is male or female.

**Gender schema**    Cognitive organizing structure for information relevant to sex typing.

**Gender stability**    Knowledge, usually gained by age four years, that one's gender does not change over time.

**Gender stereotypes**    Expectations or beliefs that individuals within a given culture hold about the behaviors characteristic of males and females.

**Gender-role development**    The process by which individuals acquire the characteristics and behaviors prescribed by their culture for their sex. Also called *sex-typing*.

**Gene**    Large segment of nucleotides within a chromosome that codes for the production of proteins and enzymes. These proteins and enzymes underlie traits and characteristics inherited from one generation to the next.

**Genetic counseling**    Medical and counseling specialty concerned with determining and communicating the likelihood that prospective parents will give birth to a baby with a genetic disorder.

**Genetic screening**    Systematic search for certain genotypes using a variety of tests to detect individuals at risk for developing genetic anomalies, bearing offspring with potential chromosome or gene defects, or having genetic susceptibility to environmental agents.

**Genital stage**    In Freudian theory, the final psychosexual stage, beginning with adolescence, in which sexual energy is directed to peers of the opposite sex.

**Genotype**    Total genetic endowment inherited by an individual.

**Germinal period**    Period lasting about ten to fourteen days following conception before the fertilized egg becomes implanted into the uterine wall. Also called *period of the zygote*.

**Gestational age**    Age of fetus derived from onset of mother's last menstrual period.

**Glial cells**    Brain cells that provide the material from which myelin is created, nourish neurons, and provide a scaffolding for neuron migration.

**Habituation**    Gradual decline in intensity, frequency, or duration of a response over repeated or lengthy occurrence of the same stimulus.

**Hedonistic reasoning**    Form of prosocial reasoning in which children say they will help in order to obtain material rewards.

**Heritability**    Proportion of variability in the phenotype that is estimated to be accounted for by genetic influences.

**Heterozygous**    Genotype in which two alleles of a gene are different. The effects on a trait will depend on how the two alleles interact.

**Heuristic strategies**  Methods of problem solving that involve higher-order analyses, such as subdividing the problem into smaller parts or comparing it with previously solved problems.

**Homozygous**  Genotype in which two alleles of a gene are identical, thus having the same effects on a trait.

**Human genome**  Entire inventory of nucleotide base pairs comprising the genes and chromosomes of humans.

**Huntington's disease**  Dominant genetic disorder characterized by involuntary movements of the limbs, mental deterioration, and premature death. Symptoms appear between thirty and fifty years of age and death within twenty years of onset of these symptoms.

**Hypothetical reasoning**  Ability to systematically generate and evaluate potential solutions to a problem.

**Identical twins**  Two individuals who originate from a single zygote (one egg fertilized by one sperm), which early in cell division separates to form two separate cell masses. Such twins have an identical genetic makeup. Also called *monozygotic twins.*

**Identity (personal)**  Broad, coherent, internalized view of who a person is, what a person wants to be, believes, and values that emerges during adolescence.

**Identity crisis**  Period, usually during adolescence, characterized by considerable uncertainty about the self and the role the individual is to fulfill in society.

**Identity**  In Eriksonian psychosocial theory, the acceptance of both self and society, a concept that must be achieved at every stage but is especially important during adolescence.

**Imaginary audience**  An individual's belief that others are examining and evaluating him.

**Immanent justice**  Young child's belief that punishment will inevitably follow a transgression.

**Imprinting**  Form of learning, difficult to reverse, during a sensitive period in development in which an organism tends to stay near a particular stimulus.

**Independent variable**  Variable manipulated by the experimenter; the suspected cause.

**Individual differences**  Unique characteristics that distinguish a person from other members of a larger group.

**Induction**  Parental control technique that relies on the extensive use of reasoning and explanation as well as the arousal of empathic feelings.

**Inflection**  Alteration to a word, such as tense or plural form, that indicates its syntactical function.

**Information processing**  Theoretical approach that views humans, much like computers, as having a limited ability to process information.

**Informed consent**  Subject's formal acknowledgment that he or she understands the purposes, procedures, and risks of a study and agrees to participate in it.

**Inner speech**  Interiorized form of private speech

**Instrumental characteristics**  Characteristics associated with acting upon the world; usually considered masculine.

**Instrumental competence**  Child's display of independence, self-control, achievement orientation, and cooperation.

**Intelligence quotient (IQ)**  Numerical score received on an intelligence test.

**Interactive synchrony**  Reciprocal, mutually engaging cycles of caregiver-child behaviors.

**Interagent consistency**  Consistency in application of disciplinary strategies among different caregivers.

**Intermodal perception**  The coordination of sensory information to perceive or make inferences about the characteristics of an object.

**Intermodal perception**  The coordination of sensory information to perceive or make inferences about the characteristics of an object.

**Internal locus of control**  Individual's sense that his or her own efforts and activities influence success and failure and the events that happen to him or her. Contrast with *external locus of control.*

**Internalized reasoning**  Form of prosocial reasoning in which internalized beliefs and principles are followed to fulfill societal obligations and maintain self-respect.

**Intra-agent consistency**  Consistency in a single caregiver's application of discipline from one situation to the next.

**Karyotype**  Pictorial representation of an individual's chromosomes.

**Kinetic cue**  Perceptual information provided by movement of eyes, head, body, or of objects in the environment; important source of information for depth perception, even for infants.

**Lagging-down growth**  Condition in which, after periods of rapid acceleration because of congenital or hormonal disorders, growth is slowed so that subsequent increases in height conform to those normally expected for the individual.

**Landmark**  Distinctive location or cue that the child uses to negotiate or represent a spatial environment.

**Latency**  In Freudian theory, a period from about six to eleven years of age, when libidinal energy is suppressed and energies are focused on intellectual, athletic, and social achievements appropriate to the adult years.

**Lateralization**  Process by which one hemisphere of the brain dominates the other. In most individuals the left hemisphere is more involved in language processing, whereas the right is more involved in processing spatial and emotional information.

**Learned helplessness**  Belief that one has little control over situations, perhaps because of lack of ability or inconsistent outcomes.

**Learning** Relatively permanent change in behavior as a result of such experiences as exploration, observation, and practice.

**Limited-resource model** Information-processing model that emphasizes the allocation of finite energy within the cognitive system.

**Long-term memory** Memory that holds information for extended periods of time.

**Longitudinal study** Research in which the same subjects are repeatedly tested over a period of time, usually years.

**Macrosystem** In Bronfenbrenner's ecological systems theory, major historical events and the broad values, practices, and customs promoted by a culture.

**Mastery orientation** Belief that achievements are based on one's own efforts rather than luck or other factors beyond one's control.

**Means-ends behavior** Deliberate behavior employed to attain a goal.

**Mediator** Cognitive process that bridges the gap between an environmental event and the individual's eventual response to it.

**Meiosis** Process of cell division that takes place to form the gametes; normally results in twenty-three chromosomes in each human egg and sperm cell rather than the full complement of forty-six chromosomes.

**Memory span** Number of stimulus items that can be recalled after a brief interval of time.

**Memory strategy** Mental activity, such as rehearsal, that enhances memory performance.

**Menarche** First occurrence of menstruation.

**Mesosystem** In Bronfenbrenner's ecological systems theory, the environment provided by the interrelationships among the various settings of the microsystem.

**Meta-analysis** Statistical examination of a body of research studies to assess the effect of the common central variable.

**Metacognition** Awareness and knowledge of cognitive processes.

**Metalinguistic awareness** Ability to reflect on language as a communication tool and on the self as a user of language.

**Metamemory** Understanding of memory as a cognitive process.

**Metaphor** Figurative language in which a term is transferred from the object it customarily designates to describe a comparable object or event.

**Microsystem** In Bronfenbrenner's ecological systems theory, the immediate environment provided in such settings as the home, school, workplace, and neighborhood.

**Mitosis** Process of cell division taking place in most cells of the human body that results in a full complement of forty-six chromosomes in each cell; reproduces identical genetic material in succeeding generations of cells.

**Moral realism** In Piaget's theory of moral development, the first stage of moral reasoning, in which moral judgments are made on the basis of the consequences of an act. Also called *heteronomy*.

**Moral relativism** In Piaget's theory of moral development, the second stage of moral reasoning, in which moral judgments are made on the basis of the actor's intentions. Also called *autonomy*.

**Morality of care and responsibility** Tendency to make moral judgments on the basis of concern for others.

**Morality of justice** Tendency to make moral judgments on the basis of reason and abstract principles of equity.

**Motherese** Simple, repetitive, high-pitched speech of caregivers to young children; includes many questions.

**Multistore model** Information-processing model that describes a sequence of mental structures through which information flows.

**Mutation** Sudden change in molecular structure of a gene; may occur spontaneously or be caused by an environmental event such as radiation. Some mutations are lethal, but others are not and may be passed on from one generation to the next in the form of alleles of a gene.

**Mutual exclusivity bias** Tendency for children to assume that unfamiliar words label new objects.

**Myelin** Sheath of fatty cells that insulates and speeds neural impulses by about tenfold.

**Natural domains** Concepts or categories that children acquire especially rapidly and effortlessly.

**Naturalistic observation** Study in which observations of naturally occurring behavior are made in real-life settings.

**Nature-nurture debate** Ongoing theoretical controversy over whether development is the result of the child's genetic endowment or the kinds of experiences he or she has had.

**Needs-oriented reasoning** Form of prosocial reasoning in which children express a concern for the physical or psychological needs of others.

**Negative correlation** Relationship in which changes in one variable are accompanied by systematic changes in another variable in the opposite direction.

**Negative punishment** The withdrawal or loss of a desired stimulus or reward that, upon its removal, weakens or decreases the frequency of a behavior.

**Negative reinforcement** Withdrawal of an aversive stimulus that, upon its removal, serves to strengthen a preceding response.

**Network** Model of semantic memory that consists of associations among closely related items.

**Neuron** Nerve cell within central nervous system electrochemically designed to transmit messages between cells.

**Niche picking** Tendency to actively select an environment compatible with a genotype.

**Nominals**  Words that label objects, people, or events; the first type of words most children produce.

**Norms**  Measure of average values and variations in some aspect of development such as physical size and motor skill development in relation to age.

**Nucleotide**  Repeating basic building block of DNA consisting of nitrogen-based molecules of adenine, thymine, cytosine, and guanine.

**Object concept**  Realization that objects exist even when they are not within view. Also called object permanence.

**Observational learning**  Learning that takes place by simply observing another person's behavior.

**Observer bias**  Tendency of researchers to interpret ongoing events as consistent with their research hypotheses.

**One-to-one correspondence**  Understanding that two sets are equivalent in number if each element in one set can be mapped onto a unique element in the second set with none left over.

**Open classroom**  Nontraditional educational approach that emphasizes peer interaction, free-flowing movement of students around different activity centers in the classroom, and structured opportunities for students to "discover" knowledge.

**Operant conditioning**  Type of learning in which patterns of behavior that are learned and the frequency with which they are performed depend on whether the behaviors produce rewarding or desired outcomes. Also called *instrumental conditioning.*

**Operation**  In Piagetian theory, mental action such as reversibility.

**Operational definition**  Specification of variables in terms of measurable properties.

**Oral stage**  In Freudian theory, the first psychosexual stage, between birth and about one year of age, during which libidinal energy is focused on the mouth.

**Ordinality**  Principle that a number refers to an item's order within a set, as in the third finisher in a race.

**Organization**  In Piagetian theory, the inborn tendency for structures and processes to become more systematic and coherent. Memory strategy in which subjects reorder items to be remembered on the basis of category or some other higher-order relationships.

**Overextension**  Tendency to apply a label to a broader category than the term actually signifies.

**Overregularization**  Inappropriate application of syntactic rules to words and grammatical forms that show exceptions.

**Parallel play**  Side-by-side independent play that is not interactive.

**Peer collaboration**  Peer-centered learning experience in which pairs of students work together on academic problems, usually without competing against other students.

**Peer**  Companion of approximately the same age and developmental level.

**Perception**  Process of organizing and interpreting sensory information.

**Perceptual differentiation**  Process postulated by Eleanor and James Gibson in which experience contributes to the ability to make increasingly finer perceptual discriminations and to distinguish stimulation arising from each sensory modality.

**Perinatal period**  Period beginning about the seventh month of pregnancy and continuing until about four weeks after birth.

**Period of the zygote**  *See* germinal period

**Permissive parent**  Parent who sets few limits on the child's behavior.

**Personal fable**  The belief that one is unique and perhaps even invulnerable.

**Perspective taking**  Ability to take the role of another person and understand what that person is thinking, feeling, or knows, often with the purpose of solving some problem in communicating or interacting with that individual.

**Phallic stage**  In Freudian theory, the third psychosexual stage, between about three and five years of age, when libidinal energy is focused on the genitals and resolution of unconscious conflict with the parent of the same sex leads to establishment of the superego.

**Phenotype**  Observable and measurable characteristics and traits of an individual; a product of the interaction of the genotype with the environment.

**Phoneme**  Smallest unit of sound that changes the meanings of words.

**Phonology**  Fundamental sound units and combinations of units in a given language.

**Pivot grammar**  Early two-word grammar in which one word is repeated and a series of other words fills the second slot.

**Placenta**  Support organ formed by cells from both blastocyst and uterine lining; serves as exchange site for oxygen, nutrients, and waste products.

**Plasticity**  Capacity of immature systems, including regions of the brain and the individual neurons within those regions, to take on different functions as a result of experience.

**Polygenic**  Phenotypic characteristic influenced by two or more genes.

**Positive correlation**  Relationship in which changes in one variable are accompanied by systematic changes in another variable in the same direction.

**Positive reinforcement**  Occurrence of a stimulus that strengthens a response when it follows that response. Also known as a reward.

**Postconventional level**  In Kohlberg's theory, the third level of moral reasoning, in which laws are seen as the result of a social contract and individual principles of conscience may emerge.

**Postnatal development**   Period in development following birth.

**Power assertion**   Parental control technique that relies on the use of forceful commands, physical punishment, and removal of material objects or privileges.

**Pragmatics**   Rules for using language effectively within a social context.

**Preconventional level**   In Kohlberg's theory, the first level of moral reasoning, in which morality is motivated by the avoidance of punishments and attainment of rewards.

**Prenatal development**   Period in development from conception to the onset of labor.

**Preoperational stage**   In Piagetian theory, the second stage of development—approximately from two to seven years of age—in which thought is now symbolic in form.

**Primacy effect**   Tendency for subjects to display good recall for early items in a list.

**Private speech**   Child's vocalized speech to himself that directs behavior

**Production deficiency**   Failure of children under age seven years to spontaneously generate memory strategies.

**Productive language**   Meaningful language spoken or otherwise produced by the individual.

**Prosocial behavior**   Positive social action performed to benefit others.

**Prosody**   Patterns of intonation, stress, and rhythm that communicate meaning in speech.

**Protodeclarative communication**   Use of a gesture to call attention to an object or event.

**Protoimperative communication**   Use of a gesture to issue a command or request.

**Proximodistal development**   Pattern that organs and systems of the body near the middle tend to develop earlier than those near the periphery.

**Psychometric model**   Theoretical perspective that quantifies individual differences in test scores to establish a rank order of abilities.

**Psychometrician**   Psychologist who specializes in the construction and interpretation of standardized tests.

**Psychosexual theory of development**   Freud's theory that many aspects of an individual's personality originate in an early and broad form of childhood sexuality. The focus of gratification of this sexuality, however, changes from one region of the body to another throughout various stages of development.

**Psychosocial theory of development**   Erikson's theory that personality development proceeds through eight stages during which adaptive modes of functioning are established to meet the variety of demands framed by society.

**Puberty**   Developmental period during which a sequence of physical changes takes place that transforms the individual from immaturity to one capable of reproduction.

**Punishment by reciprocity**   Belief that punishment should be related to the transgression.

**Punishment**   Aversive stimulus, or the removal of a pleasant stimulus, that decreases the frequency of a response when it is the outcome of that response.

**Quasi-experiment**   Study in which the assignment of subjects to experimental groups is determined by their natural experiences.

**Questionnaire**   Set of standardized questions administered to subjects in written form.

**Random assignment**   Use of principles of chance to assign subjects to treatment and control groups; avoids systematic bias.

**Range of reaction**   Range of phenotypic differences possible as a result of different environments interacting with a specific genotype. Also called *norm of reaction*.

**Realism**   The inability to distinguish between mental and physical entities.

**Recall memory**   Ability to reproduce stimuli that have previously been encountered.

**Recast**   Repetition of a child's utterance along with some new elements.

**Recency effect**   Tendency for subjects to show good recall for the last few items in a list.

**Receptive aphasia**   Loss of the ability to comprehend speech.

**Receptive language**   Ability to comprehend spoken speech.

**Recessive allele**   Allele whose characteristics do not tend to be expressed when part of a heterozygous genotype. Its genetic characteristics tend to be masked by other alleles.

**Recognition memory**   Ability to identify whether a stimulus has been previously encountered.

**Recovery from habituation**   Reinstatement of the intensity, frequency, or duration of a response to a stimulus that has changed. Also called *dishabituation*.

**Reduplicated babbling**   Repetition of simple consonant-vowel combinations in the early stages of language development.

**Referential communication**   Communication in situations that require the speaker to describe an object to a listener or to evaluate the effectiveness of a message.

**Referential style**   Type of early language production in which the child uses mostly nominals.

**Reflex**   Involuntary movement in response to touch, light, sound, and other forms of stimulation; controlled by subcortical neural mechanisms.

**Regulator gene**   Gene that switches other genes on and off.

**Rehearsal**  Memory strategy that involves repetition of items to be remembered.

**Reliability**  Degree to which a measure will yield the same results if administered repeatedly.

**Retrieval cue**  Aid or cue to extract information that has already been stored in memory.

**Reversibility**  In Piagetian theory, the ability to mentally reverse or negate an action or transformation.

**Rhythmical stereotypies**  Repeated sequences of movements such as leg kicking and hand waving or banging that seem to have no apparent goal.

**Rough-and-tumble play**  Active, physical play that carries no intent of imposing harm on another child.

**Route mapping**  Child's use of sequential directional changes to negotiate or represent a spatial environment.

**Saccade**  Rapid eye movement to inspect an object or to view a stimulus in the periphery of the visual field.

**Scaffolding**  Temporary aid provided by one person to encourage, support, and assist a lesser-skilled person in carrying out a task or completing a problem. The model provides knowledge and skills that are learned and gradually transferred to the learner.

**Scheme**  In Piagetian theory, the mental structure underlying a coordinated and systematic pattern of behaviors or thinking applied across similar objects or situations.

**Scientific method**  Use of objective, measurable, and repeatable techniques to gather information.

**Script**  Organized scheme or framework for commonly experienced events.

**Secondary reinforcer**  Object or person that attains rewarding value because of its association with a primary reinforcer.

**Secular trend**  Consistent pattern of change over generations.

**Self-concept**  Perceptions, conceptions, and values one holds about oneself.

**Self-control**  Ability to comply with sociocultural prescriptions concerning ethical or moral behavior.

**Self-esteem**  One's feelings of worth; extent to which one senses one's attributes and actions are good, desired, and valued.

**Self-regulation**  Process by which children are expected to control their own behaviors in accordance with the standards and desires of their caregivers and community, especially in the absence of other adults.

**Self**  Realization of being an independent, unique, stable, and self-reflective entity; the beliefs, knowledge, feelings, and characteristics that the individual ascribes to his or her own personhood.

**Semantic bootstrapping hypothesis**  The idea that children derive information about syntax from the meanings of words.

**Semantic memory**  Memory for general concepts or facts.

**Semantics**  Meanings of words or combinations of words.

**Semiotic function**  Ability to symbolize objects.

**Sensation**  Basic information in the external world processed by the sensory receptors.

**Sensitive period**  Brief period during which specific kinds of experiences have significant positive or negative consequences for development and behavior. Also called *critical period*.

**Sensorimotor stage**  In Piagetian theory, the first stage of cognitive development—from birth to approximately two years of age—in which thought is based primarily on action.

**Sensory store**  Memory store that holds information for very brief periods of time in a form that closely resembles the initial input.

**Separation protest**  Distress shown by the infant when the caregiver leaves the immediate environment.

**Sequential study**  Study that examines groups of children of different ages over a period of time; usually shorter than a longitudinal study.

**Sex segregation**  Clustering of individuals into same-sex groups.

**Sex typicality**  The extent to which a behavior is usually associated with one sex as opposed to the other.

**Sickle cell anemia**  Genetic blood disorder common in regions of Africa and other areas of the world where malaria is found and among descendants of these regions. Abnormal blood cells are unable to carry adequate amounts of oxygen.

**Sickle cell trait**  Symptoms shown by those possessing a heterozygous genotype for sickle cell anemia.

**Signaling behavior**  In ethological theory, a behavior such as crying or smiling that brings the caregiver physically close to the infant.

**Single-case design**  Study that follows only one or a few children over a period of time.

**Skeletal maturity**  Extent to which cartilage has ossified to form bone; provides the most accurate estimate of how much additional growth will take place in the individual.

**Smooth visual pursuit**  Consistent, unbroken tracking by the eyes that serves to maintain focus on a moving visual target.

**Social comparison**  Process in which individuals define themselves in relation to the skills, attributes, and qualities of others; believed to become especially important in contributing to self-concept during the middle childhood years.

**Social conventions**  Behavioral rules that regulate social interactions, such as dress codes and degrees of formality in speech.

**Social learning theory**  Theoretical approach emphasizing the importance of learning through observation and imitation of behaviors modeled by others.

**Social learning theory**  Theoretical approach emphasizing the importance of learning through observation and imitation of behaviors modeled by others.

**Social pretend play**  Play that makes use of imaginary and symbolic objects and social roles, often enacted among several children. Also called *sociodramatic play*.

**Social referencing**  Looking to another individual for emotional cues in interpreting a strange or ambiguous event.

**Socialization**  Process by which children acquire the social knowledge, skills, and attitudes valued by the larger society.

**Sociohistorical theory**  Vygotsky's theory of development emphasizing the historical (cultural) and social processes that are part of the context of development for every child.

**Sociometric nomination**  Peer assessment measure in which children are asked to name a specified number of peers who fit a certain criterion, such as "peers you would like to walk home with."

**Sociometric rating scale**  Peer assessment measure in which children rate peers on a number of social dimensions.

**Solitary play**  Individual play, performed without regard for what others are doing.

**Sound localization**  Ability to determine a sound's point of origin.

**Stage**  Developmental period during which the organization of thought and behavior is qualitatively different from that of an earlier or later period.

**Stereopsis**  Ability to perceive a single image of an object even though perceptual input is binocular and differs slightly for each eye; significant source of cues for depth perception.

**Strange Situation**  Standardized test that assesses the quality of infant-caregiver attachment.

**Stranger anxiety**  Fear or distress shown by an infant at the approach of an unfamiliar person.

**Structural gene**  Gene responsible for the production of enzymes and other protein molecules. Humans are estimated to have about 100,000 structural genes, some of which have been located on particular chromosomes.

**Structured interview**  Standardized set of questions administered orally to subjects.

**Structured observation**  Study in which behaviors are recorded as they occur within a situation constructed by the experimenter, usually in the laboratory.

**Subject reactivity**  Tendency of subjects who know they are under observation to alter natural behavior.

**Sudden infant death syndrome (SIDS)**  Sudden, unexplained death of infant or toddler as a result of failure to continue breathing during sleep.

**Superego**  In Freudian theory, a mental structure that monitors socially acceptable and unacceptable behavior.

**Syntax**  Grammatical rules that dictate how words can be combined.

**Systems theory**  Model for understanding the family that emphasizes the reciprocal interactions among various members.

**Telegraphic speech**  Early two-word speech that contains few modifiers, prepositions, or other connective words.

**Temperament**  Stable, early appearing constellation of individual personality attributes believed to have a hereditary basis; includes sociability, emotionality, and activity level.

**Teratogen**  Any environmental agent that can cause deviations in prenatal development. Consequences may range from death to behavioral problems.

**Test bias**  Idea that the content of traditional standardized tests does not adequately measure the competencies of children from diverse cultural backgrounds.

**Theory**  Set of ideas or propositions that helps organize or explain observable phenomena.

**Time-out**  Disciplinary strategy in which a child is removed from all possible sources of reinforcement, both positive and negative, after committing a transgression.

**Transactional theory**  Theoretical perspective in psychology that highlights the reciprocal relationship between child and environment, emphasizing that development is a seamless alloy formed by the child's being affected by and, in turn, actively influencing the environment.

**Triarchic theory**  Theory developed by Robert Sternberg that intelligence consists of three major components: (1) the ability to adapt to the environment; (2) the ability to employ fundamental information-processing skills; and (3) the ability to deal with novelty and automatize processing.

**Trisomy**  Condition in which an extra chromosome is present.

**Turn taking**  Alternating vocalization by parent and child.

**Turnabout**  Element of conversation that requests a response from the child.

**Ultrasonography**  Method of using sound wave reflections to provide a representation of the developing fetus. Used to estimate gestational age and to detect fetal physical abnormalities.

**Umbilical cord**  Conduit of blood vessels through which oxygen, nutrients, and waste products are transported between placenta and embryo.

**Unconditioned response (UCR)**  The response that is automatically elicited by the unconditioned stimulus (UCS).

**Unconditioned stimulus (UCS)**  A stimulus that, without prior training, elicits a reflexlike response (unconditioned response).

**Underextension**  Application of a label to a narrower class of objects than the term signifies.

**Uninvolved parent**  Parent who is emotionally detached from the child and focuses on his or her own needs as opposed to the child's.

**Validity**   Degree to which an assessment procedure actually measures the variable under consideration.

**Variable**   Factor having no fixed or constant value in a given situation.

**Vergence**   Ability of the eyes to rotate in opposite directions to fixate objects at different distances; improves rapidly during first few months after birth.

**Viability**   Ability of the baby to survive outside the mother's womb.

**Visual accommodation**   Visuomotor process by which small involuntary muscles change the shape of the lens of the eye so that images of objects seen at different distances are brought into focus on the retina.

**Visual acuity**   Ability to make fine discriminations among elements in a visual array by detecting contours, transitions in light patterns that signal borders and edges.

**Visual cliff**   Experimental apparatus used to test depth perception in which the surface on one side of a glass-covered table is made to appear far below the surface on the other side.

**Vocabulary spurt**   Period of rapid word acquisition that typically occurs early in language development.

**Wernicke's area**   Portion of the cerebral cortex that controls language comprehension.

**Working memory**   Short-term memory store in which mental operations such as rehearsal and categorization take place.

**X chromosome**   Larger of the two sex chromosomes associated with genetic determination of sex. Normally females have two X chromosomes; males, only one.

**Y chromosome**   Smaller of the two sex chromosomes associated with genetic determination of sex. Normally males have one Y chromosome; females, none.

**Zygote**   Fertilized egg cell.

**Zone of proximal development**   Range of various kinds of support and assistance provided by an expert (usually an adult) who helps children to carry out activities they currently cannot complete but will later be able to accomplish independently.

# References

Abel, E. L. (1980). Smoking during pregnancy: A review of effects on growth and development of offspring. *Human Biology, 52,* 593–625.

Abel, E. L. (1981). Behavioral teratology of alcohol. *Psychological Bulletin, 90,* 564–581.

Abel, E. L. (1982). Consumption of alcohol during pregnancy: A review of effects on growth and development of offspring. *Human Biology, 54,* 421–453.

Abel, E. L. (1989). *Behavioral teratogenesis and behavioral mutagenesis: A primer in abnormal development.* New York: Plenum Press.

Abel, E. L., & Sokol, R. J. (1987). Incidence of fetal alcohol syndrome and economic impact of FAS-related anomalies. *Drug and Alcohol Dependency, 19,* 51–70.

Abel, E. L., Rockwood, G. A., & Riley, E. P. (1986). The effects of early marijuana exposure. In E. P. Riley & C. V. Vorhees (Eds.), *Handbook of behavioral teratology.* New York: Plenum Press.

Aber, J. L., & Allen, J. P. (1987). Effects of maltreatment on young children's socioemotional development: An attachment theory perspective. *Developmental Psychology, 23,* 406–414.

Aboud, F. E., & Skerry, S. (1983). Self and ethnic concepts in relation to ethnic constancy. *Canadian Journal of Behavioral Science, 15,* 14–26.

Abramovitch, R., & Grusec, J. E. (1978). Peer imitation in a natural setting. *Child Development, 49,* 60–65.

Abramovitch, R., Corter, C., Pepler, D. J., & Stanhope, L. (1986). Sibling and peer interaction: A final follow-up and a comparison. *Child Development, 57,* 217–229.

Abramovitch, R., Pepler, D., & Corter, C. (1982). Patterns of sibling interaction among preschool-age children. In M. E. Lamb & B. Sutton-Smith (Eds.), *Sibling relationships: Their nature and significance across the lifespan.* Hillsdale, NJ: Erlbaum.

Abramson, L. (1991). Facial expressivity in failure to thrive and normal infants: Implications for their capacity to engage in the world. *Merrill-Palmer Quarterly, 37,* 159–182.

Abravanel, E. (1968). The development of intersensory patterning with regard to selected spatial dimensions. *Monographs of the Society for Research in Child Development, 33*(2, Serial No. 118).

Achenbach, T. M., Phares, V., Howell, C. T., Rauh, V. A., & Nurcombe, B. (1990). Seven-year outcome of the Vermont intervention program for low-birthweight infants. *Child Development, 61,* 1672–1681.

Acredolo, L. P., & Goodwyn, S. W. (1988). Symbolic gesturing in normal infants. *Child Development, 59,* 450–466.

Acredolo, L. P., & Goodwyn, S. W. (1990a). Sign language among hearing infants: The spontaneous development of symbolic gestures. In V. Volterra & C. J. Erting (Eds.), *From gesture to language in hearing and deaf children.* New York: Springer-Verlag.

Acredolo, L. P., & Goodwyn, S. W. (1990b). Sign language in babies: The significance of symbolic gesturing for understanding language development. In R. Vasta (Ed.), *Annals of child development* (Vol. 7). Greenwich, CT: JAI Press.

Acredolo, L. P., Pick, H. L., & Olsen, M. G. (1975). Environmental differentiation and familiarity as determinants of children's memory for spatial location. *Developmental Psychology, 11,* 495–501.

Adams, R. J. (1989). Newborns' discrimination among mid- and long-wavelength stimuli. *Journal of Experimental Child Psychology, 47,* 130–141.

Adams, R. J., Maurer, D., & Cashin, H. A. (1990). The influence of stimulus size on newborns' discrimination of chromatic from achromatic stimuli. *Vision Research, 30,* 2023–2030.

Adams, R. J., Maurer, D., & Davis, M. (1986). Newborns' discrimination of chromatic from achromatic stimuli. *Journal of Experimental Child Psychology, 41,* 267–281.

Adams, R. S., & Biddle, B. J. (1970). *Realities of teaching.* New York: Holt, Rinehart & Winston.

Adamson, L. B., & Bakeman, R. (1985). Affect and attention: Infants observed with mothers and peers. *Child Development, 56,* 582–593.

Adelson, E., & Fraiberg, S. (1974). Gross motor development in infants blind from birth. *Child Development, 45,* 114–126.

Ainsworth, M. D. S., Bell, S. M., & Stayton, D. J. (1974). Infant-mother attachment and social development: "Socialization" as a product of reciprocal responsiveness to signals. In M. R. Richards (Ed.), *The integration of the child into a social world.* London: Cambridge University Press.

Ainsworth, M. D. S., Blehar, M. C., Waters, E., & Wall, S. (1978). *Patterns of attachment: A psychological study of the strange situation.* Hillsdale, NJ: Erlbaum.

Alberts, B., Bray, D., Lewis, J., Raff, M., Roberts, K., & Watson, J. D. (1983). *Molecular biology of the cell.* New York: Garland.

Alessandri, S. M., & Lewis, M. (1993). Parental evaluation and its relation to shame and pride in young children. *Sex Roles, 29,* 335–343.

Alexander, I. E., & Babad, E. Y. (1981). Returning the smile of a stranger: Within-culture and cross-cultural comparisons of Israeli and American children. *Genetic Psychology Monographs, 103,* 31–77.

Alexander, K. L., & Entwistle, D. R. (1988). Achievement in the first 2 years of school: Patterns and processes. *Monographs of the Society for Research in Child Development, 53*(2, Serial No. 218).

Allen, J. P., Weissberg, R. P., & Hawkins, J. A. (1989). The relation between values and social competence in early adolescence. *Developmental Psychology, 25,* 458–464.

Alsaker, F. D. (1992). Pubertal timing, overweight, and psychological adjustment. *Journal of Early Adolescence, 12,* 396–419.

Alwitt, L. F., Anderson, D. R., Lorch, E. P., & Levin, S. R. (1980). Preschool children's visual attention to attributes of television. *Human Communication Research, 7,* 52–67.

Ambros, V., & Horvitz, H. R. (1984). Heterochronic mutants of the nematode *Caenorhabditis elegans. Science, 226,* 409–416.

American Academy of Pediatrics. Committee on Substance Abuse and Committee on Children with Disabilities. (1993). Fetal alcohol syndrome and fetal alcohol effects. *Pediatrics, 91,* 1004–1006.

American Academy of Pediatrics. Task Force on Infant Positioning and SIDS. (1992). Positioning and SIDS. *Pediatrics, 89,* 1120–1126.

American Association of University Women. (1991). *Short change in girls, short change in America* [Summary]. Washington, DC: American Association of University Women.

American Association of University Women. (1992). *How schools shortchange girls.* Washington, DC: AAUW Educational Foundation.

American Fertility Society. (1988). Ethical considerations of the new reproductive technologies. *Fertility and Sterility, 46* (Suppl. 2), 1S–7S.

American Medical Association. (1985). AMA diagnostic and treatment guidelines concerning child abuse and neglect. *Journal of the American Medical Association, 254,* 796–800.

American Psychiatric Association. (1987). *Diagnostic and statistical manual of mental disorders* (3rd ed., rev.). Washington, DC.

American Psychological Association. (1985). *Violence on television.* Washington, DC: APA Board of Ethical and Social Responsibility for Psychology.

Amsterdam, B. K. (1972). Mirror self-image reactions before age two. *Developmental Psychobiology, 5,* 297–305.

Anderson, D. R., & Levin, S. R. (1976). Young children's attention to "Sesame Street." *Child Development, 47,* 806–811.

Anderson, D. R., Choi, H. P., & Lorch, E. P. (1987). Attentional inertia reduces distractibility during young children's TV viewing. *Child Development, 58,* 798–806.

Anderson, D. R., Lorch, E. P., Field, D. E., & Sanders, J. (1981). The effects of TV program comprehensibility on preschool children's television viewing behavior. *Child Development, 52,* 151–157.

Anderson, D. R., Lorch, E. P., Field, D. E., Collins, P. A., & Nathan, J. G. (1986). Television viewing at home: Age trends in visual attention and time with TV. *Child Development, 57,* 1024–1033.

Anderson, K. E., Lytton, H., & Romney, D. M. (1986). Mothers' interactions with normal and conduct-disordered boys: Who affects whom? *Developmental Psychology, 22,* 604–609.

Andersson, B. (1992). Effects of day-care on cognitive and socioemotional competence of thirteen-year-old Swedish schoolchildren. *Child Development, 63,* 20–36.

Andiman, W. A., & Horstmann, D. M. (1984). Congenital and perinatal viral infections. In M. B. Bracken (Ed.), *Perinatal epidemiology.* New York: Oxford University Press.

Angoff, W. H. (1988). The nature-nurture debate, aptitudes, and group differences. *American Psychologist, 43,* 713–720.

Anisfeld, M. (1991). Neonatal imitation. *Developmental Review, 11,* 60–97.

Annett, M. (1973). Laterality of childhood hemiplegia and the growth of speech and intelligence. *Cortex, 9,* 4–33.

Anooshian, L. J., & Young, D. (1981). Developmental changes in cognitive maps of a familiar neighborhood. *Child Development, 52,* 341–348.

Antonov, A. N. (1947). Children born during the siege of Leningrad in 1942. *Journal of Pediatrics, 30,* 250–259.

Apgar, V. (1953). A proposal for a new method of evaluation of the newborn infant. *Anesthesia and Analgesia: Current Researches, 32,* 260–267.

Applebee, A. N., Langer, J. A., Mullis, I. V. S., & Jenkins, L. B. (1990). *The writing report card, 1984–1988.* Princeton, NJ: Educational Testing Service.

Appleton, T., Clifton, R., & Goldberg, S. (1975). The development of behavioral competence in infancy. In F. D. Horowitz (Ed.), *Review of child development research* (Vol. 4). Chicago: University of Chicago Press.

Arend, R., Gove, F. L., & Sroufe, L. A. (1979). Continuity of individual adaptation from infancy to kindergarten: A predictive study of ego-resiliency and curiosity in preschoolers. *Child Development, 50,* 950–959.

Ariès, P. (1962). *Centuries of childhood: A social history of family life* (R. Baldick, Trans.). New York: Vintage.

Aronfreed, J. (1969). The concept of internalization. In D. A. Goslin (Ed.), *Handbook of socialization theory and research.* Chicago: Rand McNally.

Aronfreed, J. (1976). Moral development from the standpoint of a general psychological theory. In T. Lickona (Ed.), *Moral development and moral behavior.* New York: Holt, Rinehart & Winston.

Arsenio, W. F., & Ford, M. E. (1985). The role of affective information in social-cognitive development: Children's differentiation of moral and conventional events. *Merrill-Palmer Quarterly, 31,* 1–17.

Artman, L., & Cahan, S. (1993). Schooling and the development of transitive inference. *Developmental Psychology, 29,* 753–759.

Asendorpf, J. B., & Baudonniére, P-M. (1993). Self-awareness and other-awareness: Mirror self-recognition and synchronic imitation among unfamiliar peers. *Developmental Psychology, 29,* 88–95.

Asher, S. R. (1983). Social competence and peer status: Recent advances and future directions. *Child Development, 54,* 1427–1434.

Asher, S. R. (1985). An evolving paradigm in social skill training research with children. In B. H. Schneider, K. H. Rubin, & J. E. Ledingham (Eds.), *Children's peer relations: Issues in assessment and intervention.* New York: Springer-Verlag.

Asher, S. R., & Dodge, K. A. (1986). The identification of socially rejected children. *Developmental Psychology, 22,* 444–449.

Asher, S. R., & Renshaw, P. D. (1981). Children without friends: Social knowledge and social skill training. In S. R. Asher & J. M. Gottman (Eds.), *The development of children's friendships.* Cambridge: Cambridge University Press.

Asher, S. R., & Wheeler, V. A. (1985). Children's loneliness: A comparison of rejected and neglected peer status. *Journal of Consulting and Clinical Psychology, 53,* 500–505.

Ashmead, D., McCarty, M. E., Lucas, L. S., & Belvedere, M. C. (1993). Visual guidance in infants' reaching toward suddenly displaced targets. *Child Development, 64,* 1111–1127.

Ashmead, D. H., Clifton, R. K., & Perris, E. E. (1987). Precision of auditory localization in human infants. *Developmental Psychology, 23,* 641–647.

Ashmead, D. H., Hill, E. W., & Talor, C. R. (1989). Obstacle perception by congenitally blind children. *Perception & Psychophysics, 46,* 425–433.

Aslin, R. N. (1987a). Motor aspects of visual development in infancy. In P. Salapatek & L. Cohen (Eds.), *Handbook of infant perception: From sensation to perception* (Vol. 1). Orlando, FL: Academic Press.

Aslin, R. N. (1987b). Visual and auditory development in infancy. In J. D. Osofsky (Ed.), *Handbook of infant development* (2nd ed.). New York: Wiley.

Aslin, R. N., & Dumais, S. T. (1980). Binocular vision in infants: A review and a theoretical framework. In H. W. Reese & L. P. Lipsitt (Eds.), *Advances in child development and behavior* (Vol. 15). New York: Academic Press.

Aslin, R. N., & Smith, L. B. (1988). Perceptual development. *Annual Review of Psychology, 39,* 435–473.

Aslin, R. N., Pisoni, D. B., & Jusczyk, P. W. (1983). Auditory development and speech perception in infancy. In M. M. Haith & J. J. Campos (Eds.), *Handbook of child psychology: Vol. II. Infancy and developmental psychobiology.* New York: Wiley.

Astington, J. W., Harris, P. L., & Olson, D. R. (1988). *Developing theories of mind.* New York: Cambridge University Press.

Atkins, W. T. (1988). Cocaine: The drug of choice. In I. J. Chasnoff (Ed.), *Drugs, alcohol, pregnancy and parenting.* Boston: Kluwer Academic Publishers.

Atkinson, R. C., & Shiffrin, R. M. (1968). Human memory: A proposed system and its control processes. In K. W. Spence & J. T. Spence (Eds.), *The psychology of learning and motivation: Advances in research and theory* (Vol. 2). New York: Academic Press.

Au, T. K., & Laframboise, D. E. (1990). Acquiring color names via linguistic contrast: The influence of contrasting terms. *Child Development, 61,* 1808–1823.

Autti-Rämö, I., Korkman, M., Hilakivi-Clarke, L., Lehtonen, M., Halmesmäki, E., & Granström, M. (1992). Mental development of 2-year-old children exposed to alcohol in utero. *Journal of Pediatrics, 120,* 740–746.

Avery, A. W. (1982). Escaping loneliness in adolescence: The case for androgyny. *Journal of Youth and Adolescence, 11,* 451–459.

Avis, J., & Harris, P. L. (1991). Belief-desire reasoning among Baka children: Evidence for a universal conception of mind. *Child Development, 62,* 460–467.

Aylward, E. H., Butz, A. M., Hutton, N., Joyner, M. L., & Vogelhut, J. W. (1992). Cognitive and motor development in infants at risk for human immunodeficiency virus. *American Journal of Diseases in Children, 146,* 218–222.

Aylward, G. P., Pfeiffer, S. I., Wright, A., & Verhulst, S. J. (1989). Outcome studies of low birth weight infants published in the last decade: A metaanalysis. *Journal of Pediatrics, 115,* 515–520.

Azen, C. G., Koch, R., Friedman, E. G., Berlow, S., Coldwell, J., Krause, W., Matalon, R., McCabe, E., O'Flynn, M., Peterson, R., Rouse, B., Scott, C.R., Sigman, B., Valle, D., & Warner, R. (1991). Intellectual development in 12-year-old children treated for phenylketonuria. *American Journal of Diseases of Children, 145,* 35-39.

Azmitia, M., & Perlmutter, M. (1989). Social influences on children's cognition: State of the art and future directions. In H. W. Reese (Ed.), *Advances in child development and behavior* (Vol. 22). New York: Academic Press.

Bachman, J. G. (1970). *The impact of family background and intelligence on tenth grade boys: Vol. 2. Youth in transition.* Ann Arbor: Survey Research Center, Institute for Social Research.

Backscheider, A. G., Shatz, M., & Gelman, S. A. (1993). Preschoolers' ability to distinguish living kinds as a function of regrowth. *Child Development, 64,* 1242–1257.

Bahrick, L. E. (1992). Infants' perceptual differentiation of amodal and modality-specific audio-visual relations. *Journal of Experimental Child Psychology, 53,* 180–199.

Bahrick, L. E. (1983). Infants' perception of substance and temporal synchrony in multimodal events. *Infant Behavior and Development, 6,* 429–451.

Baillargeon, R. (1987a). Object permanence in 3 1/2- and 4 1/2-month-old infants. *Developmental Psychology, 23,* 655–664.

Baillargeon, R. (1987b). Young children's reasoning about the physical and spatial characteristics of a hidden object. *Cognitive Development, 2,* 179–200.

Baillargeon, R., & DeVos, J. (1991). Object permanence in young infants: Further evidence. *Child Development, 62,* 1227–1246.

Baird, P. A., Anderson, T. W., Newcombe, H. B., & Lowry, R. B. (1988). Genetic disorders in children and young adults: A population study. *American Journal of Human Genetics, 42,* 677-693.

Baker-Sennett, J., Matusov, E., & Rogoff, B. (1993). Planning as a developmental process. In H. W. Reese (Ed.), *Advances in child development and behavior.* Vol. 24. San Diego, CA: Academic Press.

Baker-Ward, L., Ornstein, P. A., & Holden, D. J. (1984). The expression of memorization in early childhood. *Journal of Experimental Child Psychology, 37,* 555–575.

Baldwin, J. M. (1895). *Mental development in the child and the race.* New York: Macmillan.

Baldwin, J. M. (1930). [Autobiography]. In C. Murchison (Ed.), *A history of psychology in autobiography* (Vol. 1). Worcester, MA: Clark University Press.

Ball, S., & Bogatz, G. (1970). *The first years of Sesame Street: An evaluation.* Princeton, NJ: Educational Testing Service.

Ball, W., & Tronick, E. (1971). Infant responses to impending collision: Optical and real. *Science, 171,* 818–820.

Ballard, B. D., Gipson, M. T., Guttenberg, W., & Ramsey, K. (1980). Palatability of food as a factor influencing obese and normal-weight children's eating habits. *Behavior Research and Therapy, 18,* 598–600.

Balogh, R. D., & Porter, R. H. (1986). Olfactory preferences resulting from mere exposure in human neonates. *Infant Behavior and Development, 9,* 395–402.

Bandura, A. (1965). Vicarious processes: A case of no-trial learning. In L. Berkowitz (Ed.), *Advances in experimental social psychology* (Vol. 2). New York: Academic Press.

Bandura, A. (1969). *Principles of behavior modification.* New York: Holt, Rinehart & Winston.

Bandura, A. (1977a). Self-efficacy: Toward a unifying theory of behavioral change. *Psychological Review, 84,* 191–215.

Bandura, A. (1977b). *Social learning theory.* Englewood Cliffs, NJ: Prentice-Hall.

Bandura, A. (1986). *Social foundations of thought and action: A social cognitive theory.* Englewood Cliffs, NJ: Prentice-Hall.

Bandura, A. (1989). Social cognitive theory. In R. Vasta (Ed.), *Annals of child development: Vol. 6. Six theories of child development: Revised formulations and current issues.* Greenwich, CT: JAI Press.

Bandura, A., & Walters, R. H. (1959). *Adolescent aggression.* New York: Ronald Press.

Bandura, A., & Walters, R. H. (1963). *Social learning and personality development.* New York: Holt, Rinehart & Winston.

Bandura, A., Ross, D., & Ross, S. A. (1963a). Imitation of film-mediated aggressive models. *Journal of Abnormal and Social Psychology, 66,* 3–11.

Bandura, A., Ross, D., & Ross, S. A. (1963b). Vicarious reinforcement and imitative learning. *Journal of Abnormal and Social Psychology, 67,* 601–607.

Banks, M. S. (1980). The development of visual accommodation during early infancy. *Child Development, 51,* 646–666.

Banks, M. S., & Dannemiller, J. L. (1987). Infant visual psychophysics. In P. Salapatek & L. Cohen (Eds.), *Handbook of infant perception: From sensation to perception* (Vol. 1). Orlando, FL: Academic Press.

Banks, M. S., Aslin, R. N., & Letson, R. D. (1975). Sensitive period for the development of human binocular vision. *Science, 190,* 675–677.

Barahal, R. M., Waterman, J., & Martin, H. P. (1981). The social cognitive development of abused children. *Journal of Consulting and Clinical Psychology, 49,* 508–516.

Baran, A., & Pannor, R. (1989). *Lethal secrets.* New York: Warner Books.

Barden, R. C., Zelko, F., Duncan, S. W., & Masters, J. C. (1980). Children's consensual knowledge about the experiential components of emotion. *Journal of Personality and Social Psychology, 39,* 968–976.

Barenboim, C. (1981). The development of person perception in childhood and adolescence: From behavioral comparisons to psychological constructs to psychological comparisons. *Child Development, 52,* 129–144.

Barinaga, M. (1989). Manic depression gene put in limbo. *Science, 246,* 886–887.

Barker, R., & Gump, P. (1964). *Big school, small school: High school size and student behavior.* Stanford, CA: Standard University Press.

Barnard, K. E. (1987). Paradigms for intervention: Infant state modulation. In N. Gunzenhauser (Ed.), *Infant stimulation: For whom, what kind, when, and how much?* (Johnson & Johnson Baby Products Company Pediatric Round Table Series No. 13). Skilman, NJ: Johnson & Johnson.

Barnard, K. E., & Bee, H. L. (1983). The impact of temporally patterned stimulation on the development of preterm infants. *Child Development, 54,* 1156–1167.

Barnes, K. (1971). Preschool play norms: A replication. *Developmental Psychology, 5,* 99–103.

Baron-Cohen, S., Tager-Flusberg, H., & Cohen, D. J. (1993). *Understanding other minds: Perspectives from autism.* New York: Oxford University Press.

Barrera, M. E., & Maurer, D. (1981a). The perception of facial expressions by the three-month-old. *Child Development, 52,* 203–206.

Barrera, M. E., & Maurer, D. (1981b). Recognition of mother's photographed face by the three-month-old infant. *Child Development, 52,* 714–716.

Barrett, M. D. (1985). Issues in the study of children's single-word speech. In M. D. Barrett (Ed.), *Children's single-word speech.* Chichester, England: Wiley.

Barrett, M. D. (1986). Early semantic representations and early word usage. In S. A. Kuczaj & M. D. Barrett (Eds.), *The development of word meaning.* New York: Springer-Verlag.

Barrett, M. D. (1989). Early language development. In A. Slater & G. Bremner (Eds.), *Infant development.* London: Erl-baum.

Barth, J. M. (1989, April). *Parent-child relationships and children's transition to school.* Paper presented at the biennial meeting of the Society for Research in Child Development, Kansas City, MO.

Bartsch, K., & Wellman, H. (1989). Young children's attribution of action to beliefs and desires. *Child Development, 60,* 946–964.

Baruch, G. K., & Barnett, R. C. (1981). Fathers' participation in the care of their preschool children. *Sex Roles, 7,* 1043–1055.

Basser, L. S. (1962). Hemiplegia of early onset and the faculty of speech with special reference to the effects of hemispherectomy. *Brain, 85,* 427–460.

Bates, E. (1979). *The emergence of symbols: Cognition and communication in infancy.* New York: Academic Press.

Bates, E., Benigni, L., Bretherton, I., Camaioni, L., & Volterra, V. (1979). *The emergence of symbols: Cognition and communication in infancy.* New York: Academic Press.

Bates, E., Bretherton, I., & Snyder, L. (1988). *From first words to grammar.* Cambridge: Cambridge University Press.

Bates, E., Camaioni, L., & Volterra, V. (1975). The acquisition of performatives prior to speech. *Merrill-Palmer Quarterly, 21,* 205–224.

Bates, E., Thal, D., & Marchman, V. (1991). Symbols and syntax: A Darwinian approach to language development. In N. A. Krasnegor, D. M. Rumbaugh, R. L. Schiefelbusch, & M. Studdert-Kennedy (Eds.), *Biological and behavioral determinants of language*. Hillsdale, NJ: Erlbaum.

Bates, J. E., Maslin, C. A., & Frankel, K. A. (1985). Attachment security, mother-child interaction, and temperament as predictors of behavior-problem ratings at age three years. In I. Bretherton & E. Waters (Eds.), *Growing points of attachment theory and research. Monographs of the Society for Research in Child Development, 50*(1–2, Serial No. 209).

Bateson, P. P. G. (1979). How do sensitive periods arise and what are they for? *Animal Behaviour, 27,* 470–486.

Batson, C. D. (1990). How social an animal? The human capacity for caring. *American Psychologist, 45,* 336–346.

Batson, C. D., & Oleson, K. C. (1991). Current status of the empathy-altruism hypothesis. In M. S. Clark (Ed.), *Review of personality and social psychology: Prosocial behavior* (Vol. 12). Newbury Park, CA: Sage.

Bauer, P. J. (1993). Memory for gender-consistent and gender-inconsistent event sequences by twenty-five-month-old children. *Child Development, 64,* 285–297.

Bauer, P. J., & Mandler, J. M. (1992). Putting the horse before the cart: The use of temporal order in recall of events by one-year-old children. *Developmental Psychology, 28,* 441–452.

Baum, C. G., & Foreham, R. (1984). Social factors associated with adolescent obesity. *Journal of Pediatric Psychology, 9,* 293–302.

Baumrind, D. (1971). Current patterns of parental authority. *Developmental Psychology Monographs, 4*(1, Pt. 2).

Baumrind, D. (1972). From each according to her ability. *School Review, 80,* 161–197.

Baumrind, D. (1973). The development of instrumental competence through socialization. In A. D. Pick (Ed.), *The Minnesota symposia on child psychology* (Vol. 7). Minneapolis: University of Minnesota Press.

Baumrind, D. (1991). The influence of parenting style on adolescent competence and substance abuse. *Journal of Early Adolescence, 11,* 56–94.

Baumrind, D. (1993). The average expectable environment is not good enough: A response to Scarr. *Child Development, 64,* 1299-1317.

Baydar, N., & Brooks-Gunn, J. (1991). Effects of maternal employment and child-care arrangements on preschoolers' cognitive and behavioral outcomes: Evidence from the Children of the National Longitudinal Survey of Youth. *Developmental Psychology, 27,* 932–945.

Bayley, N. (1935). The development of motor abilities during the first three years. *Monographs of the Society for Research in Child Development, 1* (1, Serial No. 1), 1–26.

Bayley, N. (1936). *The California Infant Scale of Motor Development.* Berkeley and Los Angeles: University of California Press.

Bayley, N. (1949). Consistency and variability in the growth of intelligence from birth to eighteen years. *Journal of Genetic Psychology, 75,* 165–196.

Bayley, N. (1969). *Bayley Scales of Infant Development.* New York: The Psychological Corporation.

Bayley, N. (1993). *Bayley Scales of Infant Development* (2nd ed.). San Antonio: The Psychological Corporation.

Beal, C. R. (1987). Repairing the message: Children's monitoring and repair skills. *Child Development, 58,* 401–408.

Bear, G. G. (1989). Sociomoral reasoning and antisocial behaviors among normal sixth graders. *Merrill-Palmer Quarterly, 35,* 181–196.

Beauchamp, G. K., & Cowart, B. J. (1990). Preference for high salt concentrations among children. *Developmental Psychology, 26,* 539–545.

Beauchamp, G. K., & Moran, M. (1982). Dietary experience and sweet taste preferences in human infants. *Appetite, 3,* 139–152.

Beaudet, A. L., Scriver, C. R., Sly, W.S., Valle, D., Cooper, D. N., McKusick, V. A., & Schmidke, J. (1989). Genetics and biochemistry of variant human phenotypes. In C.R. Scriver, A. L. Beaudet, W. S. Sly, and D. Valle (Eds.), *The metabolic basis of inherited disease* (6th ed., Vol. I). New York: McGraw-Hill.

Beck, R. W., & Beck, S. H. (1989). The incidence of extended households among middle-aged black and white women. *Journal of Family Issues, 10,* 147–168.

Becker, H. J., & Sterling, C. W. (1987). Equity in school computer use: National data and neglected considerations. *Journal of Educational Computing Research, 3,* 289–311.

Becker, J. (1989). Preschoolers' use of number words to denote one-to-one correspondence. *Child Development, 60,* 1147–1157.

Becker, J. (1993). Young children's numerical use of number words: Counting in many-to-one situations. *Developmental Psychology, 29,* 458–465.

Beckman, D. A., & Brent, R. L. (1987). Etiology of human malformations. In N. Kretchmer, E. J. Quilligan, & J. D. Johnson (Eds.), *Prenatal and perinatal biology and medicine: Vol. 2. Disorder, diagnosis and therapy.* New York: Harwood Academic Publishers.

Beilin, H. (1989). Piagetian theory. In R. Vasta (Ed.), *Annals of child development: Vol. 6. Six theories of child development: Revised formulations and current issues.* Greenwich, CT: JAI Press.

Beilin, H. (1992). Piaget's enduring contribution to developmental psychology. *Developmental Psychology, 28,* 191-204.

Bell, M. A., & Fox, N. A. (1992). The relations between frontal brain electrical activity and cognitive development during infancy. *Child Development, 63,* 1142–1163.

Bell, R. Q. (1971). Stimulus control of parent or caretaker behavior by offspring. *Developmental Psychology, 4,* 63–72.

Bell, R. Q.(1968). A reinterpretation of the direction of effects in studies of socialization. *Psychological Review, 75,* 81–95.

Bell, R. Q., & Harper, L. V. (1977). *Child effects on adults.* Hillsdale, NJ: Erlbaum.

Bell, S. M., & Ainsworth, M. D. S. (1972). Infant crying and maternal responsiveness. *Child Development, 43,* 1171–1190.

Bellugi, U. (1967). *The acquisition of negation.* Unpublished doctoral dissertation, Harvard University.

Belmont, J. M. (1989). Cognitive strategies and strategic learning: The socio-instructional approach. *American Psychologist, 44,* 142–148.

Belmont, L., & Marolla, F. A. (1973). Birth order, family size, and intelligence. *Science, 182,* 1096–1101.

Belsky, J. (1980). Child maltreatment: An ecological integration. *American Psychologist, 35,* 320–335.

Belsky, J. (1981). Early human experience: A family perspective. *Developmental Psychology, 17,* 3–23.

Belsky, J. (1993). Etiology of child maltreatment: A developmental-ecological analysis. *Psychological Bulletin, 114,* 413–434.

Belsky, J., & Braungart, J. M. (1991). Are insecure-avoidant infants with extensive day-care experience less stressed by and more independent in the Strange Situation? *Child Development, 62,* 567–571.

Belsky, J., & Rovine, M. J. (1988). Nonmaternal care in the first year of life and the security of infant-parent attachment. *Child Development, 59,* 157–167.

Bem, S. L. (1974). The measurement of psychological androgyny. *Journal of Consulting and Clinical Psychology, 42,* 155–162.

Bem, S. L. (1975). Sex role adaptability: One consequence of psychological androgyny. *Journal of Personality and Social Psychology, 31,* 634–643.

Bem, S. L. (1981). Gender schema theory: A cognitive account of sex-typing. *Psychological Review, 88,* 354–364.

Bem, S. L. (1983). Gender schema theory and its implications for child development: Raising gender aschematic children in a gender schematic society. *Signs, 8,* 598–616.

Ben-Zeev, S. (1977). The influence of bilingualism on cognitive strategy and cognitive development. *Child Development, 48,* 1009–1018.

BenTsvi-Mayer, S., Hertz-Lazarowitz, R., & Safir, M. P. (1989). Teachers' selections of boys and girls as prominent pupils. *Sex Roles, 21,* 231–245.

Benbow, C. P., & Stanley, J. C. (1980). Sex differences in mathematical ability: Fact or artifact? *Science, 210,* 1262–1264.

Benbow, C. P., & Stanley, J. C. (1983). Sex differences in mathematical reasoning ability: More facts. *Science, 222,* 1029–1031.

Bender, B. G., Linden, M. G., & Robinson, A. (1987). Environment and developmental risk in children with sex chromosome abnormalities. *Journal of the Academy of Child and Adolescent Psychiatry, 26,* 499–503.

Benedict, H. (1979). Early lexical development: Comprehension and production. *Journal of Child Language, 6,* 183–200.

Benson, J. B. (1988). The significance and development of crawling in human infancy. In J. E. Clark & J. H. Humphrey (Eds.), *Advances in motor development* (Vol. 3). New York: AMS Press.

Bentur, Y., & Koren, G. (1991). The three most common occupation exposures reported by pregnant women: An update. *American Journal of Obstetrics and Gynecology, 165,* 429–437.

Berbaum, M. L., & Moreland, R. L. (1985). Intellectual development within transracial adoptive families: Retesting the confluence model. *Child Development, 56,* 207–216.

Berg, C. A., & Sternberg, R. J. (1985). Response to novelty: Continuity versus discontinuity in the developmental course of intelligence. In H. W. Reese (Ed.), *Advances in child development and behavior* (Vol. 19). New York: Academic Press.

Bergin, D. A., Ford, M. E., & Hess, R. D. (1993). Patterns of motivation and social behavior associated with microcomputer use of young children. *Journal of Educational Psychology, 85,* 437–445.

Berk, L. E. (1984). Development of private speech among low-income Appalachian children. *Developmental Psychology, 20,* 271–286.

Berk, L. E. (1986). Relationship of elementary school children's private speech to behavioral accompaniment to task, attention, and task performance. *Developmental Psychology, 22,* 671–680.

Berk, L. E. (1992). Children's private speech: An overview of theory and the status of research. In R. M. Diaz & L. E. Berk (Eds.), *Private speech: From social interaction to self-regulations.* Hillsdale, NJ: Erlbaum.

Berko, J. (1958). The child's learning of English morphology. *Word, 14,* 150–177.

Berman, A. L. (1987, Spring). The problem of adolescent suicide. *Division of Child, Youth, and Family Services Newsletter, 10*(2), American Psychological Association Division 37. pp. 1, 14.

Berndt, T. J. (1979). Developmental changes in conformity to peers and parents. *Developmental Psychology, 15,* 608–616.

Berndt, T. J. (1981). Relations between social cognition, nonsocial cognition, and social behavior: The case of friendship. In J. H. Flavell & L. D. Ross (Eds.), *Social cognitive development: Frontiers and possible futures.* Cambridge: Cambridge University Press.

Berry, J. W. (1966). Temne and Eskimo perceptual skills. *International Journal of Psychology, 1,* 207–229.

Berry, M. (1982). The development of the human nervous system. In J. W. T. Dickerson & H. McGurk (Eds.), *Brain and behavioural development.* London: Surrey University Press.

Bertenthal, B. I., & Fischer, K. W. (1978). Development of self-recognition in the infant. *Developmental Psychology, 14,* 44–50.

Bertoud-Papandropoulou, I. (1978). An experimental study of children's ideas about language. In A. Sinclair, R. J. Jarvella, & W. J. M. Levelt (Eds.), *The child's conception of language.* Heidelberg: Springer-Verlag.

Berwick, D. M. (1980). Nonorganic failure to thrive. *Pediatrics in Review, 1,* 265–270.

Best, C. T., Hoffman, H., & Glanville, B. B. (1982). Development of infant ear asymmetries for speech and music. *Perception & Psychophysics, 31,* 75–85.

Best, D. L. (1993). Inducing children to generate mnemonic organizational strategies: An examination of long-term retention and materials. *Developmental Psychology, 29,* 324–336.

Bialystok, E. (1986). Factors in the growth of linguistic awareness. *Child Development, 57,* 498–510.

Bialystok, E. (1991). Metalinguistic dimensions of bilingual language proficiency. In E. Bialystok (Ed.), *Language processing in bilingual children.* Cambridge, UK: Cambridge University Press.

Bierman, K. L. (1986). Process of change during social skills training with preadolescents and its relation to treatment outcome. *Child Development, 57,* 230–240.

Bigelow, B. J., & LaGaipa, J. J. (1975). Children's written descriptions of friendship: A multidimensional analysis. *Developmental Psychology, 11,* 857–858.

Bigelow, B. J., Tesson, G., & Lewko, J. H. (1992). The social rules that children use: close friends, other friends, and "other kids" compared to parents, teachers, and siblings. *International Journal of Behavioral Development, 15,* 315–335.

Bijou, S. W. (1989). Behavior analysis. In R. Vasta (Ed.), *Annals of child development: Vol 6. Six theories of child development: Revised formulations and current issues.* Greenwich, CT: JAI Press.

Biller, H. B. (1974). *Paternal deprivation: Family, school, sexuality and society.* Lexington, MA: Heath.

Binet, A., & Simon, T. (1905). Méthodes nouvelles pour le diagnostic du niveau intellectuel des anormaux. *L'Anée Psychologique, 11,* 191–244.

Bishop, S. M., & Ingersoll, G. M. (1989). Effects of marital conflict and family structure on the self-concepts of pre- and early adolescents. *Journal of Youth and Adolescence, 18,* 25–38.

Bivens, J. A., & Berk, L. E. (1990). A longitudinal study of the development of elementary school children's private speech. *Merrill-Palmer Quarterly, 36,* 443–463.

Bjorkland, D. F. (1987). How age changes in knowledge base contribute to the development of children's memory: An interpretive review. *Developmental Review, 7,* 93–130.

Bjorkland, D. F., & Harnishfeger, K. K. (1990). The resources construct in cognitive development: Diverse sources of evidence and a theory of inefficient inhibition. *Developmental Review, 10,* 48–71.

Bjorkland, D. F., Ornstein, P. A., & Haig, J. R. (1977). Development of organization and recall: Training in the use of organizational techniques. *Developmental Psychology, 13,* 175–183.

Black, B., & Hazen, N. L. (1990). Social status and patterns of communication in acquainted and unacquainted preschool children. *Developmental Psychology, 26,* 379–387.

Black, M. M., & Rollins, H. A., Jr. (1982). The effects of instructional variables on young children's organization and recall. *Journal of Experimental Child Psychology, 33,* 1–19.

Blackman, J. A. (1991). Neonatal intensive care: Is it worth it? *Pediatric Clinics of North America, 38,* 1497–1511.

Blake, J. (1989). Number of siblings and educational attainment. *Science, 245,* 32–36.

Blakemore, C., & Mitchell, D. E. (1973). Environmental modification of the visual cortex and the neural basis of learning and memory. *Nature* (London), *241,* 467–468.

Blasi, A. (1980). Bridging moral cognition and moral action: A critical review of the literature. *Psychological Bulletin, 88,* 1–45.

Blass, E. M., Ganchrow, J. R., & Steiner, J. E. (1984). Classical conditioning in newborn humans 2–48 hours of age. *Infant Behavior and Development, 7,* 223–235.

Blass, E. M., & Smith, B. A. (1992). Differential effects of sucrose, fructose, glucose, and lactose on crying in 1- to 3-day-old human infants: Qualitative and quantitative considerations. *Developmental Psychology, 28,* 804-810.

Blatt, M. M., & Kohlberg, L. (1975). The effects of classroom moral discussion upon children's level of moral judgment. *Journal of Moral Education, 4,* 129–161.

Blinder, B. J., & Goodman, S. L. (1986). Atypical eating disorders. *New Directions for Mental Health Services, 31,* 29–37.

Blinkov, S. M., & Glezer, I. I. (1968). *The human brain in figures and tables: A quantitative handbook.* New York: Basic Books.

Block, J. (1971). *Lives through time.* Berkeley, CA: Bancroft Books.

Block, J. H. (1973). Conceptions of sex role: Some cross-cultural and longitudinal perspectives. *American Psychologist, 28,* 512–526.

Block, J. H. (1983). Differential premises arising from differential socialization of the sexes: Some conjectures. *Child Development, 54,* 1335–1354.

Block, J. H., & Block, J. (1980). The role of ego-control and ego-resiliency in the organization of behavior. In W. A. Collins (Ed.), *The Minnesota symposia on child psychology: Vol. 13. Development of cognition, affect, and social relations.* Hillsdale, NJ: Erlbaum.

Block, J., & Robins, R. W. (1993). A longitudinal study of consistency and change in self-esteem from early adolescence to early adulthood. *Child Development, 64,* 909–923.

Bloom, B. S. (1982). The role of gifts and markers in the development of talent. *Exceptional Children, 48,* 510–522.

Bloom, L. (1973). *One word at a time.* The Hague: Mouton.

Bloom, L. (1991). *Language development from two to three.* Cambridge, UK: Cambridge University Press.

Bloom, L., Lightbown, P., & Hood, L. (1975). Structure and variation in child language and the acquisition of grammatical morphemes. *Monographs of the Society for Research in Child Development, 40*(2, Serial No. 160).

Bloom, P. (1990). Syntactic distinctions in child language. *Journal of Child Language, 17,* 343–355.

Bock, J. K., & Hornsby, M. E. (1981). The development of directives: How children ask and tell. *Journal of Child Language, 8,* 151–163.

Boehm, A. (1985). Educational applications of intelligence testing. In B. B. Wolman (Ed.), *Handbook of intelligence.* New York: Wiley.

Boehnke, K., Silbereisen, R. K., Eisenberg, N., Reykowski, J., & Palmonari, A. (1989). Developmental pattern of prosocial motivation: A cross-national study. *Journal of Cross-Cultural Psychology, 20,* 219–243.

Bogatz, G., & Ball, S. (1972). *The second year of Sesame Street: A continuing evaluation.* Princeton, NJ: Educational Testing Service.

Bohannon, J. N., & Stanowicz, L. (1988). The issue of negative evidence: Adult responses to children's language errors. *Developmental Psychology, 24,* 684–689.

Boismer, J. D. (1977). Visual stimulation and wake-sleep behavior in human neonates. *Developmental Psychobiology, 10,* 219–227.

Boldizar, J. P., Perry, D. G., & Perry, L. C. (1989). Outcome values and aggression. *Child Development, 60,* 571–579.

Bond, E. A. (1940). Tenth grade abilities and achievements. *Teachers College contributions to education.* No. 813.

Bonds, R. (1969). Growth, maturation, and performance of Philadelphia Negro and White elementary school children.

Unpublished doctoral dissertation, University of Pennsylvania, Philadelphia.

Bonitatibus, G. J., & Flavell, J. H. (1985). Effect of presenting a message in written form on young children's ability to evaluate its communication adequacy. *Developmental Psychology, 21,* 207–216.

Borke, H. (1973). The development of empathy in Chinese and American children between three and six years of age: A cross-culture study. *Developmental Psychology, 9,* 102–108.

Borke, H. (1975). Piaget's mountains revisited: Changes in the egocentric landscape. *Developmental Psychology, 11,* 240–243.

Bornstein, M. H., & Benasich, A. A. (1986). Infant habituation: Assessments of individual differences and short-term reliability at five months. *Child Development, 57,* 87–99.

Bornstein, M. H., & Krinsky, S. J. (1985). Perception of symmetry in infancy: The salience of vertical symmetry and the perception of pattern wholes. *Journal of Experimental Child Psychology, 39,* 1–19.

Bornstein, M. H., & Sigman, M. D. (1986). Continuity in mental development from infancy. *Child Development, 57,* 251–274.

Bornstein, M. H., Tal, J., Rahn, C., Galperín, G. Z., Pêcheux, M., Lamour, M., Toda, S., Azuma, H., Ogino, M., & Tamis-LeMonda, C. S. (1992). Functional analysis of the contents of maternal speech to infants of 5 and 13 months in four cultures: Argentina, France, Japan, and the United States. *Developmental Psychology, 28,* 593–603.

Borstelmann, L. J. (1983). Children before psychology: Ideas about children from antiquity to the late 1800s. In W. Kessen (Ed.), *Handbook of child psychology: Vol. I. History, theory, and methods.* New York: Wiley.

Boué, A., Boué, J., & Gropp, A. (1985). Cytogenetics of pregnancy wastage. In H. Harris & K. Hirschhorn (Eds.), *Advances in human genetics* (Vol. 14). New York: Plenum Press.

Bouchard, T. J., Jr. (1984). Twins reared together and apart: What they tell us about human diversity. In S. W. Fox (Ed.), *Individuality and determinism: Chemical and biological bases.* New York: Plenum Press.

Bouchard, T. J., Jr., & McGue, M. (1981). Familial studies of intelligence: A review. *Science, 212,* 1055–1059.

Bouchard, T. J., Jr., Lykken, D. T., McGue, M., Segal, N. L., & Tellegen, A. (1990). Sources of human psychological differences: The Minnesota Study of Twins Reared Apart. *Science, 250,* 223–228.

Bouchard, T. J., Jr., Lykken, D. T., McGue, M., Segal, N. L., & Tellegan, A. (1990). sources of human psychological differences: The Minnesota Study of Twins Reared Apart. *Science, 250,* 223-228.

Boucher, J. (1981). Immediate free recall in early childhood autism: Another point of behavioral similarity with the amnesic syndrome. *British Journal of Psychology, 72,* 211–215.

Bousha, D. M., & Twentyman, C. Y. (1984). Mother-child interactional style and abuse, neglect, and control groups: Naturalistic observations in the home. *Journal of Abnormal Psychology, 93,* 106–114.

Bowerman, M. (1978). The acquisition of word meaning: An investigation of some current conflicts. In N. Waterson & C. Snow (Eds.), *The development of communication.* New York: Wiley.

Bowlby, J. (1958). The nature of the child's tie to his mother. *International Journal of Psychoanalysis, 39,* 350–373.

Bowlby, J. (1969). *Attachment and loss: Vol. 1. Attachment.* New York: Basic Books.

Bowlby, J. (1973). *Attachment and loss. Vol. 2. Separation: Anxiety and anger.* New York: Basic Books.

Boyes, M. C., & Allen, S. G. (1993). Styles of parent-child interaction and moral reasoning in adolescence. *Merrill-Palmer Quarterly, 39,* 551–570.

Boykin, A. W. (1986). The triple quandry and the schooling of Afro-American children. In U. Neisser (Ed.), *The school achievement of minority children: New perspectives.* Hillsdale, NJ: Erlbaum.

Boysson-Bardies, B. de, Halle, P., Sagart, L., & Durand, C. (1989). A crosslinguistic investigation of vowel formants in babbling. *Journal of Child Language, 16,* 1–17.

Boysson-Bardies, B. de, Sagart, L., & Durand, C. (1984). Discernible differences in the babbling of infants according to target language. *Journal of Child Language, 11,* 1–15.

Brabeck, M. (1983). Moral judgment: Theory and research on differences between males and females. *Developmental Review, 3,* 274–291.

Brackbill, Y. (1975). Continuous stimulation and arousal level in infancy: Effects of stimulus intensity and stress. *Child Development, 46,* 364–369.

Brackbill, Y. (1979). Obstetrical medication and infant behavior. In J. D. Osofsky (Ed.), *Handbook of infant development.* New York: Wiley.

Brackbill, Y., & Nichols, P. L. (1982). A test of the confluence model of intellectual development. *Developmental Psychology, 18,* 192–198.

Brackbill, Y., McManus, K., & Woodward, L. (1985). *Medication in maternity: Infant exposure and maternal information.* Ann Arbor: University of Michigan Press.

Bradbard, M. R., Martin, C. L., Endsley, R. C., & Halverson, C. F. (1986). Influence of sex stereotypes on children's exploration and memory: A competence versus performance distinction. *Developmental Psychology, 22,* 481–486

Bradley, R. H. (1989). The use of the HOME inventory in longitudinal studies of child development. In M. H. Bornstein & N. A. Krasnegor (Eds.), *Stability and continuity in mental development: Behavioral and biological perspectives.* Hillsdale, NJ: Erlbaum.

Bradley, R. H., & Caldwell, B. M. (1976). The relation of infants' home environments to mental test performance at fifty-four months: A follow-up study. *Child Development, 47,* 1172–1174.

Bradley, R. H., & Caldwell, B. M. (1984). The relation of infants' home environments to achievement test performance in first grade: A follow-up study. *Child Development, 55,* 803–809.

Braine, M. D. S. (1976). Children's first word combinations. *Monographs of the Society for Research in Child Development, 41*(1, Serial No. 164).

Brainerd, C. J. (1978). *Piaget's theory of intelligence.* Englewood Cliffs, NJ: Prentice-Hall.

Brainerd, C. J. (1978b). The stage question in cognitive-developmental theory. *Brain and Behavioral Science, 2,* 173–213.

Brainerd, C. J., & Reyna, V. F. (1990). Gist is the grist: Fuzzy-trace theory and the new intuitionism. *Developmental Review, 10,* 3–47.

Brainerd, C. J., & Reyna, V. F. (1992). Explaining "memory free" reasoning. *Psychological Science, 3,* 332–339.

Brainerd, C. J., & Reyna, V. F. (1993). Memory independence and memory interference in cognitive development. *Psychological Review, 100,* 42–67.

Brand, E., Clingempeel, W. E., & Bowen-Woodward, K. (1988). Family relationships and children's psychological adjustment in stepmother and stepfather families: Findings and conclusions from the Philadelphia Stepfamily Research Project. In E. M. Hetherington & J. D. Arasteh (Eds.), *Impact of divorce, single-parenting, and stepparenting on children.* Hillsdale, NJ: Erlbaum.

Bray, J. H. (1988). Children's development during early remarriage. In E. M. Hetherington & J. D. Arasteh (Eds.), *Impact of divorce, single parenting, and stepparenting on children.* Hillsdale, NJ: Erlbaum.

Brazelton, T. B. (1973). *Neonatal Behavioral Assessment Scale.* Philadelphia: J. B. Lippincott.

Brazelton, T. B., Nugent, K. J., & Lester, B. M. (1987). Neonatal Behavioral Assessment Scale. In J. D. Osofsky (Ed.), *Handbook of infant development* (2nd ed.). New York: Wiley.

Bremner, J. G. (1978). Egocentric versus allocentric spatial coding in nine-month-old infants: Factors influencing the choice of code. *Developmental Psychology, 14,* 346–355.

Bremner, J. G., & Bryant, P. E. (1977). Place versus response as the basis for spatial errors made by young infants. *Journal of Experimental Child Psychology, 23,* 162–171.

Bretherton, I., & Beeghly, M. (1982). Talking about internal states: The acquisition of an explicit theory of mind. *Developmental Psychology, 18,* 906–921.

Bretherton, I., Fritz, J., Zahn-Waxler, C., & Ridgeway, D. (1986). Learning to talk about emotions: A functionalist perspective. *Child Development, 57,* 529–548.

Bril, B., & Breniére, Y. (1992). Postural requirements and progression velocity in young walkers. *Journal of Motor Behavior, 24,* 105–116.

Brody, E. B., & Brody, N. (1976). *Intelligence: Nature, determinants, and consequences.* New York: Academic Press.

Brody, G. H., & Forehand, R. (1986). Maternal perceptions of child maladjustment as a function of the combined influence of child behavior and maternal depression. *Journal of Consulting and Clinical Psychology, 54,* 237–240.

Brody, G. H., & Shaffer, D. (1982). Contributions of parents and peers to children's moral socialization. *Developmental Review, 2,* 31–75.

Brody, G. H., & Stoneman, Z. (1981). Selective imitation of same-age, older, and younger peer models. *Child Development, 52,* 717–720.

Brody, G. H., Stoneman, Z., & Burke, M. (1987). Family system and individual child correlates of sibling behavior. *American Journal of Orthopsychiatry, 57,* 561–569.

Brody, G. H., Stoneman, Z., & MacKinnon, C. E. (1986). Contributions of maternal child-rearing practices and play contexts to sibling interactions. *Journal of Applied Developmental Psychology, 7,* 225–236.

Brody, G. H., Stoneman, Z., & McCoy, J. K. (1992). Associations of maternal and paternal direct and differential behavior with sibling relationships: Contemporaneous and longitudinal analyses. *Child Development, 63,* 82–92.

Brody, G. H., Stoneman, Z., McCoy, J. K., & Forehand, R. (1992). Contemporaneous and longitudinal associations of sibling conflict with family relationship assessments and family discussion about sibling problems. *Child Development, 63,* 391–400.

Brodzinsky, D. M., Schecter, D. E., Braff, A. M., & Singer, L. M. (1984). Psychological and academic adjustment in adopted children. *Journal of Consulting and Clinical Psychology, 52,* 582–590.

Bronfenbrenner, U. (1964). Upbringing in collective settings in Switzerland and the U.S.S.R. *Proceedings of the XVIII International Congress of Psychology, Washington, DC.* Amsterdam: North-Holland.

Bronfenbrenner, U. (1970). *Two worlds of childhood: U.S. and U.S.S.R.* New York: Simon & Schuster.

Bronfenbrenner, U. (1977). Toward an experimental ecology of human development. *American Psychologist, 32,* 513–531.

Bronfenbrenner, U. (1979). *The ecology of human development.* Cambridge: Harvard University Press.

Bronfenbrenner, U. (1986). Ecology of the family as a context for human development: Research perspectives. *Developmental Psychology, 22,* 723–742.

Bronfenbrenner, U. (1989). Ecological systems theory. In R. Vasta (Ed.), *Annals of child development: Vol 6. Six theories of child development: Revised formulations and current issues.* Greenwich, CT: JAI Press.

Bronson, G. W. (1974). The postnatal growth of visual capacity. *Child Development, 45,* 873–890.

Bronson, G. W. (1990). Changes in infants' visual scanning across the 2- to 14-week age period. *Journal of Experimental Child Psychology, 49,* 101–125.

Bronson, W. (1981). Toddlers' behavior with age-mates: Issues of interaction, cognition, and affect. In L. Lipsitt (Ed.), *Monographs on infancy* (Vol. 1). Norwood, NJ: Ablex.

Brook, C. G. D. (1986). Turner syndrome. *Archives of Disease in Childhood, 61,* 305–309.

Brooks, R. B. (1992). Self-esteem during the school years: Its normal development and hazardous decline. *Pediatric Clinics of North America, 39,* 537–550.

Brooks-Gunn, J. (1984). The psychological significance of different pubertal events to young girls. *Journal of Early Adolescence, 4,* 315–327.

Brooks-Gunn, J. (1989). Pubertal processes and the early adolescent transition. In W. Damon (Ed.), *Child development today and tomorrow.* San Francisco: Jossey-Bass.

Brooks-Gunn, J., & Reiter, E. O. (1990). The role of pubertal processes. In S. S. Feldman & G. R. Elliott (Eds.), *At the threshold.* Cambridge, MA: Harvard University Press.

Brooks-Gunn, J., & Ruble, D. (1980). Menarche: The interaction of physiology, cultural, and social factors. In A. J. Dan, E. A. Graham, & C. P. Beecher (Eds.), *The menstrual cycle: A synthesis of interdisciplinary research.* New York: Springer-Verlag.

Brooks-Gunn, J., Klebanov, P. K., Liaw, F., & Spiker, D. (1993). Enhancing the development of low-birthweight, premature infants: Changes in cognition and behavior over the first three years. *Child Development, 64,* 736–754.

Brooks-Gunn, J., Warren, M. P., Samelson, M., & Fox, R. (1986). Physical similarity of and disclosure of menarcheal status to friends: Effects of grade and pubertal status. *Journal of Early Adolescence, 6,* 3–14.

Brophy, J. (1986). Teacher influences on student achievement. *American Psychologist, 41,* 1069–1077.

Brown, A. L. (1990). Domain-specific principles affect learning and transfer in children. *Cognitive Science, 14,* 107–133.

Brown, A. L., & Barclay, C. R. (1976). The effects of training specific mnemonics on the metamnemonic efficiency of retarded children. *Child Development, 47,* 71–80.

Brown, A. L., & Reeve, R. A. (1987). Bandwidths of competence: The role of supportive contexts in learning and development. In L. S. Liben (Ed.), *Development and learning: Conflict or congruence?* Hillsdale, NJ: Erlbaum.

Brown, A. L., & Scott, M. S. (1971). Recognition memory for pictures in preschool children. *Journal of Experimental Child Psychology, 11,* 401–412.

Brown, A. L., Campione, J. C., & Barclay, C. R. (1979). Training self-checking routines for estimating test readiness: Generalization from list learning to prose recall. *Child Development, 50,* 501–512.

Brown, A. L., Campione, J. C., Ferrara, R. A., Reeve, R. A., & Palincsar, A. S. (1991). Interactive learing and individual understanding: The case of reading and mathematics. In L. T. Landsmann (Ed.), *Culture, Schooling, and psychological development.* Norwood, NJ: Ablex.

Brown, A. L., Kane, M. J., & Echols, C. H. (1986). Young children's mental models determine analogical transfer across problems with a common goal structure. *Cognitive Development, 1,* 103–121.

Brown, B. B. (1989). The role of peer groups in adolescents' adjustment to secondary school. In T. J. Berndt & G. W. Ladd (Eds.), *Peer relationships in child development.* New York: Wiley.

Brown, B. B., Clasen, D. R., & Eicher, S. A. (1986). Perceptions of peer pressure, peer conformity dispositions, and self-reported behavior among adolescents. *Developmental Psychology, 22,* 521–530.

Brown, B. B., Mounts, N., Lamborn, S. D., & Steinberg, L. (1993). Parenting practices and peer group affiliation in adolescence. *Child Development, 64,* 467–482.

Brown, L. M., & Gilligan, C. (1992). *Meeting at the crossroads: Women's psychology and girls' development.* Cambridge, MA: Harvard University Press.

Brown, P. J., & Konner, M. (1987). An anthropological perspective on obesity. *Annals of the New York Academy of Sciences, 499,* 29–46.

Brown, R. (1973). *A first language: The early stages.* Cambridge: Harvard University Press.

Brown, R., & Hanlon, C. (1970). Derivational complexity and order of acquisition in child speech. In J. R. Hayes (Ed.), *Cognition and the development of language.* New York: Wiley.

Brown, R. M., & Fishman, R. H. B. (1984). An overview and summary of the behavioral and neural consequences of perinatal exposure to psychotropic drugs. In J. Yanai (Ed.), *Neurobehavioral teratology.* New York: Elsevier.

Brownlee, S. (1987, April). Lords of the flies. *Discover,* pp. 26–40.

Bruck, K. (1962). Temperature regulation in the newborn infant. *Biological Neonatorum, 3,* 65–119.

Bruner, J. S. (1981). Intention in the structure of action and interaction. In L. P. Lipsitt (Ed.), *Advances in infancy research* (Vol. 1). Norwood, NJ: Ablex.

Bruner, J. S. (1983). *Child's talk: Learning to use language.* New York: W. W. Norton.

Bryant, P. E., & Trabasso, T. (1971). Transitive inferences and memory in young children. *Nature, 232,* 456–458.

Buhrmester, D. (1990). Intimacy of friendship, interpersonal competence, and adjustment during preadolescence and adolescence. *Child Development, 61,* 1101–1111.

Buhrmester, D., & Furman, W. (1986). The changing functions of children's friendships: A neo-Sullivanian perspective. In V. Derlega & B. Winstead (Eds.), *Friendships and social interaction.* New York: Springer-Verlag.

Buhrmester, D., & Furman, W. (1987). The development of companionship and intimacy. *Child Development, 58,* 1101–1113.

Buhrmester, D., & Furman, W. (1990). Perceptions of sibling relationships during middle childhood and adolescence. *Child Development, 61,* 1387–1398.

Buitendijk, S., & Bracken, M. B. (1991). Medication in early pregnancy: Prevalence of use and relationship to maternal characteristics. *American Journal of Obstetrics and Gynecology, 165,* 33–40.

Bukowski, W. M., & Kramer, T. L. (1986). Judgments of the features of friendship among early adolescent boys and girls. *Journal of Early Adolescence, 6,* 331–338.

Bukowski, W. M., Gauze, C., Hoza, B., & Newcomb, A. F. (1993). Differences and consistency between same-sex and other-sex peer relationships during early adolescence. *Developmental Psychology, 29,* 255–263.

Bullinger, A. (1987, April). Action as tutor for the infant's tools of exploration. In M. Haith (Chair), *Perception and action: The acquisition of skill.* Symposium conducted at the biennial meeting of the Society for Research in Child Development, Baltimore.

Bumpass, L. L. (1990). What's happening to the American family? Interactions between demographic and institutional change. *Demography, 27,* 483–498.

Burgess, R. L., & Conger, R. D. (1978). Family interaction in abusive, neglectful, and normal families. *Child Development, 49,* 1163–1173.

Burkhauser, R. V., Duncan, G. J., Hauser, R., & Bernsten, R. (1991). Wife or frau, women do worse: A comparison of men and women in the United States and Germany after marital dissolution. *Demography, 28,* 353–360.

Burnett, C. A., Jones, J. A., Rooks, J., Chen, C. H., Tyler, C. W., & Miller, C. A. (1980). Home delivery and neonatal mortality in North Carolina. *Journal of the American Medical Association, 244,* 2741–2745

Burns, A. L., Mitchell, G., & Obradovich, S. (1989). Of sex role and strollers: Female and male attention to toddlers at the zoo. *Sex Roles, 20,* 309–315.

Burns, B., & Lipsitt, L. P. (1991). Behavioral factors in crib death: Toward an understanding of the sudden infant death syndrome. *Journal of Applied Developmental Psychology, 12,* 159–184.

Burns, K. A., Deddish, R. B., Burns, W. J., & Hatcher, R. P. (1983). Use of oscillating waterbeds and rhythmic sounds for premature infant stimulation. *Developmental Psychology, 19,* 746–751.

Burton, B. K., Schulz, C. J., & Burd, L. I. (1992). Limb anomalies associated with chorionic villus sampling. *Obstetrics and Gynecology, 79,* 726–730.

Bushnell, E. W. (1981). The ontogeny of intermodal relations: Vision and touch in infancy. In R. D. Walk & H. L. Pick, Jr. (Eds.), *Intersensory perception and sensory integration.* New York: Plenum Press.

Bushnell, E. W. (1985). The decline of visually guided reaching during infancy. *Infant Behavior and Development, 8,* 139–155.

Bushnell, E. W., & Boudreau, J. P. (1993). Motor development and the mind: The potential role of motor abilities as a determinant of aspects of perceptual development. *Child Development, 64,* 1005–1021.

Bushnell, I. W. R., Gerry, G., & Burt, K. (1983). The externality effect in neonates. *Infant Behavior and Development, 6,* 151–156.

Bushnell, I. W. R., Sai, F., & Mullin, J. T. (1989). Neonatal recognition of the mother's face. *British Journal of Developmental Psychology, 7,* 3–15.

Buss, A. H., & Plomin, R. (1975). *A temperament theory of personality development.* New York: Wiley-Interscience.

Buss, A. H., & Plomin, R. (1984). *Temperament: Early developing personality traits.* Hillsdale, NJ: Erlbaum.

Bussey, K., & Bandura, A. (1984). Influence of gender constancy and social power on sex-linked modeling. *Journal of Personality and Social Psychology, 47,* 1292–1302.

Bussey, K., & Bandura, A. (1992). Self-regulatory mechanisms governing gender development. *Child Development, 63,* 1236–1250.

Bussey, K., & Perry, D. G. (1982). Same-sex imitation: The avoidance of cross-sex models or the acceptance of same-sex models. *Sex Roles, 8,* 773–784.

Butler, N. R., & Goldstein, H. (1973). Smoking in pregnancy and subsequent child development. *British Medical Journal, 4,* 573–575.

Butler, R. (1989). Mastery versus ability appraisal: A developmental study of children's observations of peers' work. *Child Development, 60,* 1350–1361.

Butler, R. (1990). The effects of mastery and competitive conditions on self-assessment at different ages. *Child Development, 61,* 201–210.

Byers, T. (1992). The epidemic of obesity in American Indians. *American Journal of Diseases of Children, 146,* 285–286.

Byrne, B. M. (1984). The general/academic self-concept nomological network: A review of construct validation research. *Review of Educational Research, 54,* 427–456.

Byrnes, J. P., & Overton, W. F. (1988). Reasoning about logical connections: A developmental analysis. *Journal of Experimental Child Psychology, 46,* 194–218.

Caccia, N., Johnson, J. M., Robinson, G. E., & Barna, T. (1991). Impact of prenatal testing on maternal-fetal bonding: Chorionic villus sampling versus amniocentesis. *American Journal of Obstetrics and Gynecology, 165,* 1122–1125.

Cadoret, R. J., Cain, C. A., & Grove, W. M. (1980). Development of alcoholism in adoptees raised apart from alcoholic biologic relatives. *Archives of General Psychiatry, 37,* 561–563.

Cairns, R. B. (1983). The emergence of developmental psychology. In W. Kessen (Ed.), *Handbook of child psychology: Vol. I. History, theory, and methods.* New York: Wiley.

Cairns, R. B., & Ornstein, P. A. (1979). Developmental psychology. In E. Hearst (Ed.), *The first century of experimental psychology.* Hillsdale, NJ: Erlbaum.

Caldwell, B. M., & Bradley, R. H. (1978). *Home Observation for Measurement of the Environment.* Little Rock: University of Arkansas.

Calkins, S. D., & Fox, N. A. (1992). The relations among infant temperament, security of attachment, and behavioral inhibition at twenty-four months. *Child Development, 63,* 1456–1472.

Calvert, S. L., Huston, A. C., Watkins, B. A., & Wright, J. C. (1982). The relationship between selective attention to televised forms and children's comprehension of content. *Child Development, 53,* 601–610.

Camara, K. A., & Resnick, G. (1988). Interparental conflict and cooperation: Factors moderating children's post-divorce adjustment. In E. M. Hetherington & J. Arasteh (Eds.), *Impact of divorce, single-parenting, and stepparenting on children.* Hillsdale, NJ: Erlbaum.

Campione, J. C., & Brown, A. L. (1978). Toward a theory of intelligence: Contributions from research with retarded children. *Intelligence, 2,* 279–304.

Campione, J. C., Brown, A. L., & Ferrara, R. A. (1982). Mental retardation and intelligence. In R. J. Sternberg (Ed.), *Handbook of human intelligence.* Cambridge: Cambridge University Press.

Campos, J. J., Barrett, K. C., Lamb, M. E., Goldsmith, H. H., & Stenberg, C. (1983). Socioemotional development. In M. M. Haith & J. J. Campos (Eds.), *Handbook of child psychology: Vol. II. Infancy and developmental psychobiology.* New York: Wiley

Campos, J. J., Langer, A., & Krowitz, A. (1970). Cardiac responses on the visual cliff in prelocomotor human infants. *Science, 170,* 196–197.

Carey, S. (1978). The child as word learner. In M. Halle, J. Bresnan, & G. A. Miller (Eds.), *Linguistic theory and psychological reality.* Cambridge: MIT Press.

Carey, S. (1985). Are children fundamentally different thinkers and learners than adults? In S.F. Chipman, J.W. Segal, & R. Glaser (Eds.), *Thinking and learning skills* (Vol. 2). Hillsdale, NJ: Erlbaum.

Carey, S. (1985). *Conceptual changes in childhood.* Cambridge, MA: MIT Press.

Carlson, V., Cicchetti, D., Barnett, D., & Braunwald, K. (1989). Contributions of the study of maltreated infants to the development of the disorganized ("D") type of attachment relationship. In D. Cicchetti & V. Carlson (Eds.), *Child maltreat-ment: Theory and research on the causes and consequences of child abuse and neglect.* Cambridge: Cambridge University Press.

Carroll, J. J., & Gibson, E. J. (1981, April). *Infants' differentiation of an aperture and an obstacle.* Paper presented at the biennial meeting of the Society for Research in Child Development, Boston.

Carter, D. B. (1987). The roles of peers in sex role socialization. In D. B. Carter (Ed.), *Current conceptions of sex roles and sex-typing: Theory and research.* New York: Praeger.

Carter, D. B., & Levy, G. D. (1988). Cognitive aspects of early sex-role development: The influence of gender schemas on preschoolers' memories and preferences for sex-typed toys and activities. *Child Development, 59,* 782–792.

Carter, D. B., & McCloskey, L. A. (1984). Peers and the maintenance of sex-typed behavior: The development of children's understanding of cross-gender behavior in their peers. *Social Cognition, 2,* 294–314.

Carter, D. B., & Patterson, C. J. (1982). Sex roles as social conventions: The development of children's conceptions of sex role stereotypes. *Developmental Psychology, 18,* 812–824.

Casaer, P. (1993). Old and new facts about perinatal brain development. *Journal of Child Psychology and Psychiatry, 34,* 101–109.

Case, R. (1985). *Intellectual development: A systematic reinterpretation.* New York: Academic Press.

Case, R. (1992). *The mind's staircase: Exploring the conceptual underpinnings of children's thought and knowledge.* Hillsdale, NJ: Erlbaum.

Case, R., Kurland, D. M., & Goldberg, J. (1982). Operational efficiency and the growth of short term memory span. *Journal of Experimental Child Psychology, 33,* 386–404.

Casey, R. J. (1993). Children's emotional experience: Relations among expression, self-report, and understanding. *Developmental Psychology, 29,* 119–129.

Cassidy, J., & Asher, S. R. (1992). Loneliness and peer relations in young children. *Child Development, 63,* 350–365.

Cattell, J. M. (1890). Mental tests and measurements. *Mind, 15,* 373–381.

Cattell, R. B. (1971). *Abilities: Their structure, growth, and action.* Boston: Houghton Mifflin.

Cavior, N., & Dokecki, P. R. (1973). Physical attractiveness, perceived attitude similarity, and academic achievement as contributors to interpersonal attraction among adolescents. *Developmental Psychology, 9,* 44–54.

Ceci, S. J. (1991). How much does schooling influence general intelligence and its cognitive components? A reassessment of the evidence. *Developmental Psychology, 27,* 703–722.

Ceci, S. J., & Bruck, M. (1993). Suggestability of the child witness: A historical review and synthesis. *Psychological Bulletin, 113,* 403–439.

Ceci, S. J., Ross, D. F., & Toglia, M. P. (1987). Suggestibility of children's memory: Psychological implications. *Journal of Experimental Psychology: General, 116,* 38–49.

Centers for Disease Control. (1991). Body-weight perceptions and selected weight-management goals and practices of high school students—United States, 1990. *Morbidity and Mortality Weekly Report, 40,* 741–750.

Centers for Disease Control. (1992). Pregnancy risks determined from birth certificate data—United States, 1989. *Morbidity and Mortality Weekly Report, 41,* 556–564.

Centers for Disease Control. Rates of Cesarean delivery—United States 1991. (1993). *Morbidity and Mortality Weekly Report, 42,* 285–289.

Cernoch, J. M., & Porter, R. H. (1985). Recognition of maternal axillary odors by infants. *Child Development, 56,* 1593–1598.

Chapman, M., & Zahn-Waxler, C. (1981). *Young children's compliance and noncompliance to parental discipline in a natural setting.* Unpublished manuscript.

Chapman, M., Skinner, E. A., & Baltes, P. B. (1990). Interpreting correlations between children's perceived control and cognitive performance: Control, agency, or means-ends beliefs? *Developmental Psychology, 26,* 246–253.

Chasnoff, I. J. (1986). Perinatal addiction: Consequences of intrauterine exposure to opiate and nonopiate drugs. In I. J. Chasnoff (Ed.), *Drug use in pregnancy: Mother and child.* Lancaster, England: MTP Press.

Chasnoff, I. J. (1988). Cocaine: Effects on pregnancy and the neonate. In I. J. Chasnoff (Ed.), *Drugs, alcohol, pregnancy and parenting.* Boston: Kluwer Academic Publishers.

Chasnoff, I. J. (1992). Cocaine, pregnancy, and the growing child. *Current Problems in Pediatrics, 22,* 302–321.

Chasnoff, I. J., Hatcher, R., & Burns, W. J. (1980). Early growth patterns of methadone-addicted infants. *American Journal of Diseases of Children, 134,* 1049–1051.

Chen, M. (1985). A macro-focus on microcomputers: Eight utilization and effects issues. In M. Chen & W. Paisley (Eds.), *Children and microcomputers: Research on the newest medium.* Beverly Hills: Sage.

Chen, Z., & Daehler, M. W. (1989). Positive and negative transfer in analogical problem-solving by 6-year-olds. *Cognitive Development, 4,* 327–344.

Chess, S., & Thomas, A. (1982). Infant bonding: Mystique and reality. *American Journal of Orthopsychiatry, 52,* 213–222.

Chess, S., & Thomas, A. (1986). Developmental issues. In S. Chess & A. Thomas (Eds.), *Annual progress in child psychiatry and child development.* New York: Brunner/Mazel.

Chess, S., & Thomas, A. (1990). Continuities and discontinuities in temperament. In L. N. Robins & M. Rutter (Eds.). *Straight and devious pathways from childhood to adolescence.* Cambridge, UK: Cambridge University Press.

Chess, S., & Thomas, A. (1991). Temperament and the concept of goodness of fit. In J. Strelau & A. Angleitner (Eds.), *Explorations in temperament: International perspectives on theory and measurement.* New York: Plenum.

Cheyne, J. A. (1976). Development of forms and functions of smiling in preschoolers. *Child Development, 47,* 820–823.

Chi, M. T. H. (1978). Knowledge structure and memory development. In R. Siegler (Ed.), *Children's thinking: What develops?* Hillsdale, NJ: Erlbaum.

Chibucos, T., & Kail, P. R. (1981). Longitudinal examination of father-infant interaction and infant-father interaction. *Merrill-Palmer Quarterly, 27,* 81–96.

Children's Defense Fund. (1994). *The state of America's children yearbook.* Washington, DC: Children's Defense Fund.

Children's Defense Fund. (1988, April). Piecing together the teen pregnancy puzzle. *CDF Reports, 9,* pp. 1, 5–6.

Chiu, L. H. (1992–93). Self-esteem in American and Chinese (Taiwanese) children. *Current Psychology: Research & Reviews, 11,* 309–313.

Chomsky, N. (1957). *Syntactic structures.* The Hague: Mouton.

Chomsky, N. (1980). *Rules and representations.* New York: Columbia University Press.

Chomsky, N. (1986). *Knowledge of language: Its nature, origin, and use.* New York: Praeger.

Christenson, P. G. (1982). Children's perceptions of TV commercials and products: The effects of PSAs. *Communication Research, 9,* 491–524.

Chu, S. Y., Buehler, J. W., Oxtoby, M. J., & Kilbourne, B. W. (1991). Impact of the human immunodeficiency virus epidemic on mortality in children, United States. *Pediatrics, 87,* 806–810.

Chukovsky, K. (1963). *From two to five.* Berkeley and Los Angeles: University of California Press.

Cianfrani, T. (1960). *A short history of obstetrics and gynecology.* Springfield, IL: C. C. Thomas.

Cicchetti, D. (1987). Developmental psychopathology in infancy: Illustration from the study of maltreated youngsters. *Journal of Consulting and Clinical Psychology, 55,* 837–845.

Clark, E. V. (1973). What's in a word? On the child's acquisition of semantics in his first language. In T. E. Moore (Ed.), *Cognitive development and the acquisition of language.* New York: Academic Press.

Clark, E. V. (1987). The principle of contrast: A constraint on language acquisition. In B. MacWhinney (Ed.), *Mechanisms of language acquisition.* Hillsdale, NJ: Erlbaum.

Clark, E. V. (1988). On the logic of contrast. *Journal of Child Language, 15,* 317–336.

Clark, E. V. (1992). Conventionality and contrast: Pragmatic principles with lexical consequences. In A. Lehrer & E. F. Kittay (Eds.), *Frames, fields, and contrasts: New essays in semantic and lexical organization.* Hillsdale, NJ: Erlbaum.

Clark, J. E. (1988). Development of voluntary motor skill. In E. Meisami & P. S. Timiras (Eds.), *Handbook of human growth and developmental biology* (Vol. 1, part B). Boca Raton, FL: CRC Press.

Clarke, N., in consultation with Bennets, A. B. (1982). Vital statistics and nonhospital births: A mortality study of infants born out of hospitals in Oregon [Appendix]. In *Research Issues in the Assessment of Birth Settings.* Washington, DC: Institute of Medicine and National Research Council, National Academy Press.

Clarke-Stewart, A. (1982). *Daycare.* Cambridge: Harvard University Press.

Clarke-Stewart, K. A. (1989). Infant day care: Maligned or malignant? *American Psychologist, 44,* 266–273.

Clarke-Stewart, K. A., & Fein, G. G. (1983). Early childhood programs. In M. M. Haith & J. J. Campos (Eds.), *Handbook of child psychology: Vol. II. Infancy and developmental psychobiology.* New York: Wiley.

Clarren, S. K., Alvord, E. C., Suni, S. M., & Streissguth, A. P. (1978). Brain malformations related to prenatal exposure to ethanol. *Journal of Pediatrics, 92,* 64–67.

Clasen, D. R., & Brown, B. B. (1985). The multidimensionality of peer pressure in adolescence. *Journal of Youth and Adolescence, 14,* 451–468.

Clausen, J. (1991). Adolescent competence and the shaping of the life course. *American Journal of Sociology, 96,* 805–842.

Clements, D. H. (1986). Effects of Logo and CAI environments on cognition and creativity. *Journal of Educational Psychology, 78,* 309–318.

Clements, D. H., & Gullo, D. F. (1984). Effects of computer programming on young children's cognition. *Journal of Educational Psychology, 76,* 1051–1058.

Clifton, R., Perris, E., & Bullinger, A. (1991). Infants' perception of auditory space. *Developmental Psychology, 27,* 187–197.

Clifton, R. K., Muir, D. W., Ashmead, D. H., & Clarkson, M. G. (1993). Is visually guided reaching in early infancy a myth? *Child Development, 64,* 1099–1110.

Cobb, H. V. (1954). Role wishes and general wishes of children and adolescents. *Child Development, 25,* 161–171.

Cohen, L., & Campos, J. (1974). Father, mother and stranger as elicitors of attachment behaviors in infancy. *Developmental Psychology, 10,* 146–154.

Cohen, L. B., & Oakes, L. M. (1993). How infants perceive a simple causal event. *Developmental Psychology, 29,* 421–433.

Cohen, R. L. (1966). Experimental and clinical chemateratogenesis. *Advances in Pharmacology, 4,* 263–349.

Cohn, J. F., & Tronick, E. Z. (1983). Three-month-old infants' reaction to simulated maternal depression. *Child Development, 54,* 185–193.

Cohn, J. F., & Tronick, E. Z. (1987). Mother-infant face-to-face interaction: The sequence of dyadic states at 3, 6, and 9 months. *Developmental Psychology, 23,* 68–77.

Cohn, J. F., Matias, R., Tronick, E. Z., Connell, D., & Lyons-Ruth, D. (1986). Face-to-face interactions of depressed mothers and their infants. In E. Z. Tronick & T. M. Field (Eds.), *New directions for child development: No. 34. Maternal depression and infant disturbance.* San Francisco: Jossey-Bass.

Coie, J. D., & Dodge, K. A. (1983). Continuities and changes in children's social status: A five-year longitudinal study. *Merrill-Palmer Quarterly, 29,* 261–282.

Coie, J. D., & Dodge, K. A. (1988). Multiple sources of data on social behavior and social status in the school: A cross-age comparison. *Child Development, 59,* 815–829.

Coie, J. D., Dodge, K. A., & Coppotelli, H. (1982). Dimensions and types of social status: A cross-age perspective. *Developmental Psychology, 18,* 557–570.

Colby, A., Kohlberg, L., Gibbs, J., & Lieberman, M. (1983). A longitudinal study of moral judgment. *Monographs of the Society for Research in Child Development, 48*(1–2, Serial No. 200).

Cole, D. A. (1991). Change in self-perceived competence as a function of peer and teacher evaluation. *Developmental Psychology, 27,* 682–688.

Cole, M., Gay, J., Glick, J., & Sharp, D. W. (1971). *The cultural context of learning and thinking.* New York: Basic Books.

Cole, W., Emery, M., Horowitz, J. M., Towle, L. H., & Hequet, M. (1993, May 24). How should we teach our children about sex? *Time,* pp. 60–66.

Coleman, J. S., Campbell, E., & Mood, A. (1966). *Equality of educational opportunity.* Washington, DC: U.S. Office of Education.

Collins, F.S. (1992). Cystic fibrosis: Molecular biology and therapeutic implications. *Science, 256,* 774-779.

Collins, W. A. (1983). Social antecedents, cognitive processing, and comprehension of social portrayals on television. In E. T. Higgins, D. N. Ruble, & W. W. Hartup (Eds.), *Social cognition and social development.* Cambridge: Cambridge University Press.

Collins, W. A., Wellman, H., Keniston, A. H., & Westby, S. D. (1978). Age-related aspects of comprehension and inference from a televised dramatic narrative. *Child Development, 49,* 389–399.

Colombo, J., Mitchell, D. W., Coldren, J. T., & Freeseman, L. J. (1991). Individual differences in infant visual attention: Are short lookers faster processors or feature processors? *Child Development, 62,* 1247–1257.

Colombo, J., Mitchell, D. W., O'Brien, M., & Horowitz, F. D. (1987). The stability of visual habituation during the first year of life. *Child Development, 58,* 474–487.

Condry, J. C., & Condry, S. M. (1976). Sex differences: A study of the eye of the beholder. *Child Development, 47,* 812–819.

Condry, S. M., Condry, J. C., & Pogatshynik, L. W. (1978, August). *Sex differences: A study of the ear of the beholder.* Paper presented at the annual meeting of the American Psychological Association, Toronto.

Conger, R. D., Conger, K. J., Elder, G. H., Jr., Lorenz, F. O., Simons, R. L., & Whitbeck, L. B. (1992). A family process model of economic hardship and adjustment of early adolescent boys. *Child Development, 63,* 526–541.

Congregation for the Doctrine of the Faith. (1987, March 11). Instruction on respect for human life [Vatican document]. *The New York Times,* pp. A14–A17.

Connolly, K., & Elliott, J. (1972). The evolution and ontogeny of hand function. In N. B. Jones (Ed.), *The growth of competence.* Cambridge: Cambridge University Press.

Connor, J. M., Schackman, M. E., & Serbin, L. A. (1978). Sex-related differences in response to practice on a visual-spatial test and generalization to a related test. *Child Development, 49,* 24–29.

Consensus Development Conference. (1981). *Cesarean childbirth.* Bethesda, MD: National Institutes of Health.

Cook, T. D., Appleton, H., Conner, R. F., Shaffer, A., Tamkin, G., & Weber, S. J. (1975). *"Sesame Street" revisited.* New York: Russell Sage.

Cooley, C. H. (1902). *Human nature and the social order.* New York: Scribner's.

Cooper, J., Hall, J., & Huff, C. (1990). Situational stress as a consequence of sex-stereotyped software. *Personality and Social Psychology Bulletin, 16,* 419–429.

Coplan, J. (1993). New developments: Child development. *Current Problems in Pediatrics, 23,* 44-49.

Copper, R. L., Goldenberg, R. L., Cliver, S. P., DuBard, M. B., Hoffman, H. J., & Davis, R. O. (1993). Anthropometric assessment of body size differences of full-term male and female infants. *Obstetrics and Gynecology, 81,* 161–164.

Cordua, G. D., McGraw, K. O., & Drabman, R. S. (1979). Doctor or nurse: Children's perceptions of sex-typed occupations. *Child Development, 50,* 590–593.

Cornell, E. H., Heth, C. D., & Rowat, W. L. (1992). Wayfinding by children and adults: Response to instructions to use look-back and retrace strategies. *Developmental Psychology, 28,* 328–336.

Corrigan, R. (1979). Cognitive correlates of language: Differential criteria yield differential results. *Child Development, 50,* 617–631.

Costanzo, P. R., & Woody, E. Z. (1979). Externality as a function of obesity in children: Pervasive style or eating-specific attribute? *Journal of Personality and Social Psychology, 37,* 2286–2296.

Cournoyer, M., & Trudel, M. (1991). Behavioral correlates of self-control at 33 months. *Infant Behavior and Development, 14,* 497–503.

Coustan, D. R., & Felig, P. (1988). Diabetes mellitus. In G. N. Burrow & T. F. Ferris (Eds.), *Medical complications during pregnancy* (3rd ed.). Philadelphia: W. B. Saunders.

Cowan, W. M. (1979, September). The development of the brain. *Scientific American, 241,* pp. 113–133.

Cox, M. J., Owen, M. T., Lewis, J. M., & Henderson, V. K. (1989). Marriage, adult adjustment, and early parenting. *Child Development, 60,* 1015–1024.

Cox, M. J., Owen, T. J., Henderson, V. K., & Margand, N. A. (1992). Prediction of infant-father and infant-mother interaction. *Developmental Psychology, 28,* 474–483.

Crain, W. C. (1985). *Theories of development: Concepts and applications* (2nd ed.). Englewood Cliffs, NJ: Prentice-Hall.

Crain, W. C. (1992). *Theories of development: Concepts and applications* (3rd ed.). Englewood Cliffs, NJ: Prentice-Hall.

Crain-Thoreson, C., & Dale, P. S. (1992). Do early talkers become early readers? Linguistic precocity, preschool language, and emergent literacy. *Developmental Psychology, 28,* 421–429.

Crandall, R. (1973). The measurement of self-esteem and related concepts. In J. P. Robinson & P. R. Shaver (Eds.), *Measures of social psychological attitudes* (rev. ed.). Ann Arbor: Institute for Social Research.

Crandall, V. C. (1969). Sex differences in expectancy of intellectual and academic reinforcement. In C. P. Smith (Ed.), *Achievement-related motives in children.* New York: Russell Sage.

Cratty, B. J. (1986). *Perceptual and motor development in infants and children* (3rd ed.). Englewood Cliffs, NJ: Prentice-Hall.

Crick, N. R., & Ladd, G. W. (1993). Children's perceptions of their peer experiences: Attributions, loneliness, social anxiety, and social avoidance. *Developmental Psychology, 29,* 244–254.

Crnic, L. S., & Pennington, B. F. (1987). Developmental psychology and the neurosciences: An introduction. *Child Development, 58,* 533–538.

Crockenberg, S., & Litman, C. (1990). Autonomy as competence in 2-year-olds: Maternal correlates of child defiance, compliance, and self-assertion. *Developmental Psychology, 26,* 961–971.

Crockenberg, S., & Litman, C. (1991). Effects of maternal employment on maternal and two-year-old child behavior. *Child Development, 62,* 930–953.

Crockett, L., Losoff, M., & Petersen, A. C., (1984). Perceptions of the peer group and friendship in early adolescence. *Journal of Early Adolescence, 4,* 155–181.

Crook, C. (1987). Taste and olfaction. In P. Salapatek & L. Cohen (Eds.), *Handbook of infant perception: From sensation to perception* (Vol. 1). Orlando, FL: Academic Press.

Csikszentmihalyi, M., & Larson, R. (1984). *Being adolescent.* New York: Basic Books.

Cummings, E. M., Ianotti, R. J., & Zahn-Waxler, C. (1985). Influence of conflict between adults on the emotions and aggression of young children. *Developmental Psychology, 21,* 495–507.

Cummings, E. M., Zahn-Waxler, C., & Radke-Yarrow, C. (1981). Young children's responses to expressions of anger and affection by others in the family. *Child Development, 52,* 1274–1282.

Cummings, W. K. (1988). Policy options for values education. In W. K. Cummings, S. Gopinathan, & Y. Tomodu (Eds.), *The revival of values education in Asia and the West.* New York: Pergamon.

Curie-Cohen, M., Luttrell, L., & Shapiro, S. (1979). Current practice of artificial insemination by donor in the United States. *New England Journal of Medicine, 300,* 585–590.

Curtis, L. E., Siegel, A. W., & Furlong, N. E. (1981). Developmental differences in cognitive mapping: Configurational knowledge of familiar large-scale environments. *Journal of Experimental Child Psychology, 31,* 456–469.

Curtiss, S. (1977). *Genie: A psycholinguistic study of a modern-day 'wild child.'* New York: Academic Press.

Daehler, M. W., & Bukatko, D. (1977). Recognition memory for pictures in very young children: Evidence from attentional preferences using a continuous presentation procedure. *Child Development, 48,* 693–696.

Daehler, M. W., & Bukatko, D. (1985). *Cognitive development.* New York: Knopf.

Dalterio, S., & Bartke, A. (1979). Perinatal exposure to cannabinoids alters male reproductive function in mice. *Science, 205,* 1420–1422.

Damon, W. (1983). *Social and personality development: Infancy through adolescence.* New York: W. W. Norton.

Damon, W., & Hart, D. (1988). *Self-understanding in childhood and adolescence.* New York: Cambridge University Press.

Daniels, K. (1989). Waterbirth: The newest form of safe, gentle and joyous birth. *Journal of Nurse-Midwifery, 34,* 198–205.

Dark, V. J., & Benbow, C. P. (1993). Cognitive differences among the gifted: A review and new data. In D. K. Detterman (Ed.), *Current topics in human intelligence. Vol. 3. Individual differences and cognition.* Norwood, NJ: Ablex.

Darwin, C. (1877). A biographical sketch of an infant. *Mind, 2,* 285–294.

Darwin, C. (1965). *The expression of emotions in man and animals.* Chicago: University of Chicago Press. (Original work published 1872)

Dasen, P. R. (1972). Cross-cultural Piagetian research: A summary. *Journal of Cross-Cultural Psychology, 3,* 23–39.

De Maeyer, E. M. (1976). Protein-energy malnutrition. In G. Beaton & J. Bengoa (Eds.), *Nutrition in preventative medicine* (WHO Monograph Series No. 62). Geneva: World Health Organization.

DeBaryshe, B. D., Patterson, G. R., & Capaldi, D. M. (1993). A performance model for academic achievement in early adolescent boys. *Developmental Psychology, 29,* 795–804.

DeCasper, A. J., & Fifer, W. P. (1980). Of human bonding: Newborns prefer their mothers' voices. *Science, 208,* 1174–1176.

DeCasper, A. J., & Spence, M. J. (1986). Prenatal maternal speech influences newborns' perception of speech sounds. *Infant Behavior and Development, 9,* 133–150.

DeFries, J. C., Gervais, M. C., & Thomas, E. A. (1978). Response to 30 generations of selection for open-field activity in laboratory mice. *Behavior Genetics, 8,* 3–13.

DeLisi, C. (1988). The human genome project. *American Scientist, 76,* 488–493.

DeLisi, R., & Gallagher, A. M. (1991). Understanding of gender stability and constancy in Argentinian children. *Merrill-Palmer Quarterly, 37,* 483–502.

DeLoache, J. (1987). Rapid change in the symbolic functioning of young children. *Science, 238,* 1556–1557.

DeRegt, R. H., Minkoff, H. L., Feldman, J., & Schwartz, R. H. (1986). Relation of private or clinic care to the cesarean birth rate. *New England Journal of Medicine, 315,* 619–624.

de Villiers, P. A., & de Villiers, J. G. (1979). Form and function in the development of sentence negation. *Papers and Reports in Child Language, 17,* 57–64.

Deaux, K. (1993). Commentary: Sorry, wrong number—a reply to Gentile's call. *Psychological Science, 4,* 125–126.

Dekovic, M., & Janssens, J. (1992). Parents' child-rearing style and child's sociometric status. *Developmental Psychology, 28,* 925–932.

Demany, L., McKenzie, B., & Vurpillot, E. (1977). Rhythm perception in early infancy. *Nature, 266,* 718–719.

Demetras, M., Post, K., & Snow, C. (1986). Feedback to first language learners: The role of repetitions and clarification questions. *Journal of Child Language, 13,* 275–292.

*Demographic Yearbook, 1981.* (1983). New York: United Nations.

*Demographic Yearbook, 1988.* (1990). New York: United Nations.

*Demographic Yearbook, 1991.* (1993). New York: United Nations.

Dempster, F. N. (1981). Memory span: Sources of individual and developmental differences. *Psychological Bulletin, 89,* 63–100.

Denham, S. A., McKinley, M., Couchoud, E. A., & Holt, R. (1990). Emotional and behavioral predictors of preschool ratings. *Child Development, 61,* 1145–1152.

Dennis, W. (1960). Causes of retardation among institutional children: Iran. *Journal of Genetic Psychology, 96,* 47–59.

Dennis, W., & Dennis, M. G. (1940). The effect of cradling practices upon the onset of walking in Hopi children. *Journal of Genetic Psychology, 56,* 77–86.

Desmond, M. M., Franklin, R. R., Vallbona, C., Hill, R. M., Plumb, R., Arnold, H., & Watts, J. (1963). The clinical behavior of the newly born. *Journal of Pediatrics, 62,* 307–325.

Desmond, M. M., Rudolph, A. J., & Phitaksphraiwan, P. (1963). The clinical behavior of the newly born. *Journal of Pediatrics, 63,* 307–325.

Deur, J. L., & Parke, R. D. (1970). Effects of inconsistent punishment on aggression in children. *Developmental Psychology, 2,* 403–411.

Deutsch, M., Katz, I., & Jensen, A. R. (1968). *Social class, race, and psychological development.* New York: Holt, Rinehart & Winston.

Devitt, N. (1977). The transition from home to hospital birth in the United States, 1930–1960. *Birth and the Family Journal, 4,* 47–58.

Devoe, L. D., Murray, C., Youssif, A., & Arnaud, M. (1993). Maternal caffeine consumption and fetal behavior in normal third-trimester pregnancy. *American Journal of Obstetrics and Gynecology, 168,* 1105–1112.

Dewey, J. (1963). *The school and society.* New York: Macmillan. (Original work published 1938)

DiLalla, L. F. , & Gottesman, I. I. (1991). Biological and genetic contributors to violence—Widom's untold tale. *Psychological Bulletin, 109,* 125-129.

DiVitto, B., & Goldberg, S. (1979). The effect of newborn medical status on early parent-infant interactions. In T. M. Field, A. M. Sostek, S. Goldberg, & H. H. Shuman (Eds.), *Infants born at risk.* New York: S. P. Medical & ScientificBooks.

Diamond, A. (1985). The development of the ability to use recall to guide action as indicated by infants' performance on AB. *Child Development, 56,* 868–883.

Diamond, A. (1991). Neuropsychological insights into the meaing of object concept development. In S. Carey & R. Gelman (Eds.), *The epigenesis of mind: Essays on biology and cognition.* Hillsdale, NJ: Erlbaum.

Diamond, A. (1993, March). *Nature and causes of cognitive deficits in phenylketonuria (PKU) even with dietary treatment: Longitudinal study and animal model.* Presented at the 60th semiannual meeting of the Society for Research in Child Development, New Orleans, LA.

Diamond, A., & Goldman-Rakic, P. S. (1989). Comparison of human infants and rhesus monkeys on Piaget's AB task: Evidence for dependence on dorsolateral prefrontal cortex. *Experimental Brain Research, 74,* 24–40.

Diaz, R. M., & Klingler, C. (1991). Towards an explanatory model of the interaction between bilingualism and cognitive development. In E. Bialystok (Ed.), *Language processing in bilingual children.* Cambridge, UK: Cambridge University Press.

Diaz, R. M., Neal, C. J., & Vachio, A. (1991). Maternal teaching in the zone of the proximal development: A comparison of low- and high-risk dyads. *Merrill-Palmer Quarterly, 37,* 83–108.

Dick-Read, G. (1959). *Childbirth without fear.* New York: Harper & Row.

Dien, D. S. (1982). A Chinese perspective on Kohlberg's theory of moral development. *Developmental Review, 2,* 331–341.

Dietz, W. A. (1983). Childhood obesity: Susceptibility, cause, and management. *Journal of Pediatrics, 103,* 676–686.

Dion, K. K., & Berscheid, E. (1974). Physical attractiveness and peer perception among children. *Sociometry, 37,* 1–12.

Dix, T. H., & Grusec, J. E. (1985). Parent attribution processes in the socialization of children. In I. E. Sigel (Ed.), *Parental belief systems: The psychological consequences for children.* Hillsdale, NJ: Erlbaum.

Dix, T. H., Ruble, D. N., Grusec, J. E., & Nixon, S. (1986). Social cognition in parents: Inferential and affective reactions tochildren of three age levels. *Child Development, 57,* 879–894. Dix, T., Ruble, D. N., & Zambarano, R. J. (1989). Mothers' implicit theories of discipline: Child effects, parent effects, and the attribution process. *Child Development, 60,* 1373–1391.

Dixon, S., Tronick, E., Keeler, C., & Brazelton, T. B. (1981). Mother-infant interaction among the Gusii of Kenya. In T. M. Field, A. M. Sosteck, P. Vietze, & P. H. Leiderman (Eds.), *Culture and early interactions.* Hillsdale, NJ: Erlbaum.

Dodge, K. A. (1980). Social cognition and children's aggressive behavior. *Child Development, 51,* 162–170.

Dodge, K. A. (1982). Social information processing variables in the development of aggression and altruism in young children. In C. Zahn-Waxler, M. Cummings, & M. Radke-Yarrow (Eds.), *The development of altruism and aggression: Social and sociological origins.* New York: Cambridge University Press.

Dodge, K. A. (1986). A social information processing model of social competence in children. In M. Perlmutter (Ed.), *The Minnesota symposia on child psychology: Vol. 18. Cognitive perspectives on children's social and behavioral development.* Hillsdale, NJ: Erlbaum.

Dodge, K. A., & Somberg, D. R. (1987). Hostile attributional biases among aggressive boys are exacerbated under conditions of threats to self. *Child Development, 58,* 213–224.

Dodge, K. A., Coie, J. D., Pettit, G. S., & Price, J. M. (1990). Peer status and aggression in boys' groups: Developmental and contextual analyses. *Child Development, 61,* 1289–1309.

Dodge, K. A., Murphy, R. R., & Buchsbaum, K. (1984). The assessment of intention-cue detection skills in children: Implications for developmental psychopathology. *Child Development, 55,* 163–173.

Dodge, K. A., Pettit, G. S., McClaskey, C. L., & Brown, M. M. (1986). Social competence in children. *Monographs of the Society for Research in Child Development, 51*(2, Serial No. 213).

Dodge, K. A., Schlundt, D. C., Schocken, I., & Delugach, J. D. (1983). Social competence and children's sociometric status: The role of peer group entry strategies. *Merrill-Palmer Quarterly, 29,* 309–336.

Dodwell, P. C., Humphrey, G. K., & Muir, D. W. (1987). Shape and pattern perception. In P. Salapatek & L. Cohen (Eds.), *Handbook of infant perception: From perception to cognition* (Vol. 2). Orlando, FL: Academic Press.

Doherty, W. J., & Needle, R. H. (1991). Psychological adjustment and substance use among adolescents before and after parental divorce. *Child Development, 62,* 328–337.

Dollard, J., Doob, L. W., Miller, N. E., Mowrer, O. H., & Sears, R. R. (1939). *Frustration and aggression.* New Haven: Yale University Press.

Doman, G. (1983). *How to teach your baby to read* (2nd ed.). Garden City, NY: Doubleday.

Dornbush, S. M., Ritter, P. L., Leiderman, P. H., Roberts, D. F., & Fraleigh, M. J. (1987). The relation of parenting style to adolescent school performance. *Child Development, 58,* 1244–1257.

Dorozynski, A. (1986). How the new genetic therapy could change peoples' lives. *Impact of Science on Society,* 36, 313–319.

Dorr, A. (1983). No shortcuts to judging reality. In J. Bryant & D. R. Anderson (Eds.), *Children's understanding of television: Research on attention and comprehension.* New York: Academic Press.

Dorr, A. (1986). *Television and children: A special medium for a special audience.* Beverly Hills: Sage.

Doty, R. L., Shaman, P., Applebaum, S. L., Giberson, R., Sikorski, L., & Rosenberg, L. (1984). Smell identification ability: Changes with age. *Science, 226,* 141–143.

Douglas, V. I. (1983). Attentional and cognitive problems. In M. Rutter (Ed.), *Developmental neuropsychiatry.* New York: Guilford.

Drotar, D., Eckerle, D., Satola, J., Pallotta, J., & Wyatt, B. (1990). Maternal interactional behavior with nonorganic failure-to-thrive infants: A case comparison study. *Child Abuse and Neglect, 14,* 41–51.

Dubow, E. F., Tisak, J., Causey, D., Hryshko, A., & Reid, G. (1991). A two-year longitudinal study of stressful life events, social support, and social problem-solving skills: Contributions to children's behavioral and academic adjustment. *Child Development, 62,* 583–599.

Dumaret, A. (1985). IQ, scholastic performance and behaviour of sibs raised in contrasting environments. *Journal of Child Psychology and Psychiatry, 26,* 553–580.

Dumas, J. E., & Wahler, R. G. (1983). Predictors of treatment outcome in parent training: Mother insularity and socioeconomic disadvantage. *Behavioral Assessment, 5,* 301–313.

Dunham, P. J., Dunham, F., & Curwin, A. (1993). Joint-attentional states and lexical acquisition at 18 months. *Developmental Psychology, 29,* 827–831.

Dunn, J. (1988). Connections between relationships: Implications of research on mothers and siblings. In R. A. Hinde & J. Stevenson-Hinde (Eds.), *Relationships within families: Mutual influences.* Oxford: Clarendon Press.

Dunn, J., & Kendrick, C. (1982). *Siblings: Love, envy, and understanding.* Cambridge: Harvard University Press.

Dunn, J., & Shatz, M. (1989). Becoming a conversationalist despite (or because of) having an older sibling. *Child Development, 60,* 399–410.

Dunn, J., Bretherton, I., & Munn, P. (1987). Conversations about feeling states between mothers and their young children. *Developmental Psychology, 23,* 132–139.

Durkin, D. (1966). *Children who read early: Two longitudinal studies.* New York: Teachers College Press.

Dusek, J. B. (1987). Sex roles and adjustment. In D. B. Carter (Ed.), *Current conceptions of sex roles and sex typing: Theory and research.* New York: Praeger.

Dweck, C. S. (1975). The role of expectations and attributions in the alleviation of learned helplessness. *Journal of Personality and Social Psychology, 31,* 674–685.

Dweck, C. S. (1986). Motivational processes affecting learning. *American Psychologist, 41,* 1040–1048.

Dweck, C. S. (1991). Self-theories and goals: Their role in motivation, personality, and development. In R. Diestbier (Ed.), *Nebraska Symposium on Motivation, 1990* (Vol. 36). Lincoln: University of Nebraska Press.

Dweck, C. S., & Elliott, E. S. (1983). Achievement motivation. In E. M. Hetherington (Ed.), *Handbook of child psychology: Vol. IV. Socialization, personality, and social development.* New York: Wiley.

Dweck, C. S., & Reppucci, N. D. (1973). Learned helplessness and reinforcement responsibility in children. *Journal of Personality and Social Psychology, 25,* 109–116.

Dweck, C. S., Davidson, W., Nelson, S., & Enna, B. (1978). Sex differences in learned helplessness: II. The contingencies of evaluative feedback in the classroom and III. An experimental analysis. *Developmental Psychology, 14,* 268–276

Dweck, C. S., Goetz, T. E., & Strauss, N. L. (1980). Sex differences in learned helplessness: IV. An experimental and naturalistic study of failure generalization and its mediators. *Journal of Personality and Social Psychology, 38,* 441–452.

Dye, N. S. (1986). The medicalization of birth. In P. S. Eakins (Ed.), *The American way of birth.* Philadelphia: Temple University Press.

Eagly, A. H., & Steffen, V. J. (1986). Gender and aggressive behavior: A meta-analytic review of the social psychological literature. *Psychological Bulletin, 100,* 309–330.

Eakins, P. S. (1984). The rise of the free standing birth center: Principles and practice. *Women and Health, 9,* 49–64.

Easterbrooks, M. A., & Goldberg, W. A. (1984). Toddler development in the family: Impact of father involvement and parenting characteristics. *Child Development, 55,* 740–752.

Easterbrooks, M. A., & Goldberg, W. A. (1985). Effects of early maternal employment on toddlers, mothers, and fathers. *Developmental Psychology, 4,* 774–783.

Eccles, J. E. (1983). Expectancies, values, and academic behaviors. In J. T. Spence (Ed.), *Achievement and achievement motives: Psychological and sociological approaches.* San Francisco: W. H. Freeman.

Eccles, J. E. (1987). Adolescence: Gateway to androgyny? In D. B. Carter (Ed.), *Current conceptions of sex roles and sex typing: Theory and research.* New York: Praeger.

Eccles, J. E., & Jacobs, J. E. (1986). Social forces shape math attitudes and performance. *Signs, 11,* 367–380.

Eccles, J. S., & Midgely, C. (1988). Stage/environment fit: Developmentally appropriate classrooms for early adolescents. In R. E. Ames & C. Ames (Eds.), *Research on motivation in education* (Vol. 3). New York: Academic Press.

Eccles, J., Midgley, C., Wigfield, A., Buchanan, C. M., Reuman, D., Flanagan, C., & Mac Iver, D. (1993). Development during adolescence: The impact of stage-environment fit on young adolescents' experiences in schools and families. *American Psychologist, 48,* 90–101.

Eccles, J., Wigfield, A., Harold, R. D., & Blumenfeld, P. (1993). Age and gender differences in children's self- and task perceptions during elementary school. *Child Development, 64,* 830–847.

Eccles-Parsons, J., Adler, T., & Kaczala, C. (1982). Socialization of achievement attitudes and beliefs: Parental influences. *Child Development, 53,* 310–321.

Eckenrode, J., Laird, M., & Doris, J. (1993). School peformance and disciplinary problems among abused and neglected children. *Developmental Psychology, 29,* 53–62.

Eckerman, C. O., & Stein, M. R. (1990). How imitation begets imitation and toddlers' generation of games. *Developmental Psychology, 26,* 370–378

Eckerman, C. O., Whatley, J. L., & Kutz, S. L. (1975). Growth of social play with peers during the second year of life. *Developmental Psychology, 11,* 42–49.

Edelman, A. M., Kraemer, H. C., & Korner, A. F. (1982). Effects of compensatory movement stimulation on the sleep-wake behaviors of preterm infants. *Journal of the American Academy of Child Psychiatry, 21,* 555–559.

Eder, D., & Hallinan, M. T. (1978). Sex differences in children's friendships. *American Sociological Review, 43,* 237–250.

Eder, R. A. (1989). The emergent personologist: The structure and content of 3 1/2-, 5 1/2-, and 7 1/2-year-olds' concepts of themselves and other persons. *Child Development, 60,* 1218–1228.

Eder, R. A. (1990). Uncovering young children's psychological selves: Individual and developmental differences. *Child Development, 61,* 849–863.

Egeland, B., & Sroufe, L. A. (1981a). Attachment and early maltreatment. *Child Development, 52,* 44–52.

Egeland, B., & Sroufe, L. A. (1981b). Developmental sequelae of maltreatment in infancy. In R. Rizley & D. Cicchetti (Eds.), *New directions for child development: No. 11. Developmental perspectives on child maltreatment.* San Francisco: Jossey-Bass.

Egeland, B., Jacobvitz, D., & Papatola, K. (1987). Intergenerational continuity of abuse. In R. J. Gelles & J. B. Lancaster (Eds.), *Child abuse and neglect: Biosocial dimensions.* Hawthorne, NY: Aldine de Gruyter.

Egeland, B., Jacobvitz, D., & Sroufe, L. A. (1988). Breaking the cycle of abuse. *Child Development, 59,* 1080–1088.

Ehrenhaft, P. M., Wagner, J. L., & Herdman, R. C. (1989). Changing prognosis for very low birth weight infants. *Obstetrics and Gynecology, 74,* 528–535.

Ehrhardt, A. A., & Meyer-Bahlburg, H. F. L. (1981). Effects of prenatal sex hormones on gender-related behavior. *Science, 211,* 1312–1318.

Ehrhardt, A. A., Meyer-Bahlburg, H. F. L., Feldman, J. F., & Ince, S. E. (1984). Sex-dimorphic behavior in childhood subsequent to prenatal exposure to exogenous progestogens and estrogens. *Archives of Sexual Behavior, 13,* 457–477.

Eimas, P. D., Siqueland, E. R., Jusczyk, P., & Vigorito, J. (1971). Speech perception in infants. *Science, 171,* 303–306.

Eisenberg, N. (1982). Introduction. In N. Eisenberg (Ed.), *The development of prosocial behavior.* New York: Academic Press.

Eisenberg, N. (1986). *Altruistic emotion, cognition, and behavior.* Hillsdale, NJ: Erlbaum.

Eisenberg, N., & Lennon, R. (1983). Sex differences in empathy and related capacities. *Psychological Bulletin, 94,* 100–131.

Eisenberg, N., & Miller, P. A. (1987). The relation of empathy to prosocial and related behaviors. *Psychological Bulletin, 101,* 91–119.

Eisenberg, N., & Mussen, P. H. (1989). *The roots of prosocial behavior in children.* Cambridge: Cambridge University Press.

Eisenberg, N., & Shell, R. (1986). Prosocial moral judgment and behavior in children: The mediating role of cost. *Personality and Social Psychology Bulletin, 12,* 426–433.

Eisenberg, N., Boehnke, K., Schuhler, P., & Silbereisen, R. K. (1985). The development of prosocial behavior and cognition in German children. *Journal of Cross-Cultural Psychology, 16,* 69–82.

Eisenberg, N., Fabes, R. A., Bernzweig, J., Karbon, M., Poulin, R., & Hanish, L. (1993). The relations of emotionality and regulation to preschoolers' social skills and sociometric status. *Child Development, 64,* 1418–1438.

Eisenberg, N., Hertz-Lazarowitz, R., & Fuchs, I. (1990). Prosocial moral judgment in Israeli kibbutz and city children: A longitudinal study. *Merrill-Palmer Quarterly, 36,* 273–285.

Eisenberg, N., Miller, P. A., Shell, R., McNalley, S., & Shea, C. (1991). Prosocial development in adolescence: A longitudinal study. *Developmental Psychology, 27,* 849–857.

Eisenberg, N., Roth, K., Bryniarski, K. A., & Murray, E. (1984). Sex differences in the relationship of height to children's actual and attributed social and cognitive competencies. *Sex Roles, 11,* 719–734.

Eisenberg-Berg, N., & Hand, M. (1979). The relationship of preschoolers' reasoning about prosocial moral conflicts to prosocial behavior. *Child Development, 50,* 356–363.

Eisenberg-Berg, N., & Neal, C. (1979). Children's moral reasoning about their own spontaneous prosocial behavior. *Developmental Psychology, 15,* 228–229.

Ekman, P. (1972). Universals and cultural differences in facial expressions of emotion. In J. K. Cole (Ed.), *Nebraska symposium on motivation, 1971.* Lincoln: University of Nebraska Press.

Ekman, P. (1973). Cross-cultural studies of facial expression. In P. Ekman (Ed.), *Darwin and facial expression.* New York: Academic Press.

Elardo, R., & Bradley, R. H. (1981). The Home Observation for Measurement of the Environment (HOME) scale: A review of research. *Developmental Review, 1,* 113–145.

Elardo, R., Bradley, R. H., & Caldwell, B. M. (1975). The relation of infants' home environments to mental test performance from six to thirty-six months: A longitudinal analysis. *Child Development, 46,* 71–76.

Elias, S., & Annas, G. J. (1987). *Reproductive genetics and the law.* Chicago: Year Book Medical Publishers.

Elkind, D. (1976). *Child development and education.* New York: Oxford.

Elkind, D. (1978). *The child's reality: Three developmental themes.* Hillsdale, NJ: Erlbaum.

Elkind, D. (1981a). *Children and adolescents: Interpretive essays on Jean Piaget* (3rd ed.). New York: Oxford University Press.

Elkind, D. (1981b). *The hurried child.* Reading, MA: Addison-Wesley.

Elkind, D. (1984). *All grown up and no place to go: Teenagers in crisis.* Reading, MA: Addison-Wesley.

Elkind, D., Koegler, R. R., & Go, E. (1964). Studies in perceptual development: 2. Part-whole perception. *Child Development, 35,* 81–90.

Elliott, R., & Vasta, R. (1970). The modeling of sharing: Effects associated with vicarious reinforcement, symbolization, age, and generalization. *Journal of Experimental Child Psychology, 10,* 8–15.

Emde, R. N. (1980). Levels of meaning for infant emotions: A biosocial view. In W. A. Collins (Ed.), *The Minnesota symposia on child psychology: Vol. 13. Development of cognition, affect, and social relations.* Hillsdale, NJ: Erlbaum.

Emde, R. N., & Koenig, K. L. (1969). Neonatal smiling, frowning and rapid eye movement states. *Journal of the American Academy of Child Psychiatry, 8,* 57–67.

Emde, R. N., Biringen, Z., Clyman, R. B., & Oppenheim, D. (1991). The moral self of infancy: Affective core and procedural knowledge. *Developmental Review, 11,* 251–270.

Emde, R. N., Johnson, W. F., & Easterbrooks, M. A. (1987). The do's and don'ts of early moral development: Psychoanalytic tradition and current research. In J. Kagan & S. Lamb (Eds.), *The emergence of morality in young children.* Chicago: University of Chicago Press.

Emde, R. N., Plomin, R., Robinson, J., Corley, R., DeFries, J., Walker, D. W., Reznick, J. S., Campos, J., Kagan, J., & Zahn-Waxler, C. (1992). Temperament, emotion, and cognition at fourteen months: The MacArthur longitudinal twin study. *Child Development, 63,* 1427–1455.

Emery, R. E. (1989). Family violence. *American Psychologist, 44,* 321–328.

Emler, N. P., & Rushton, J. P. (1974). Cognitive-developmental factors in children's generosity. *British Journal of Social and Clinical Psychology, 13,* 277–281.

Engen, T., Lipsitt, L. P., & Kaye, H. (1963). Olfactory responses and adaptation in the human neonate. *Journal of Comparative and Physiological Psychology, 56,* 73–77.

English, P. C. (1978). Failure to thrive without organic reason. *Pediatric Annals, 7,* 774–781.

Enright, M. K., Rovee-Collier, C. K., Fagen, J. W., & Caniglia, K. (1983). The effects of distributed training on retention of operant conditioning in human infants. *Journal of Experimental Child Psychology, 36,* 512–524.

Epstein, C. J. (1989). Down syndrome (Trisomy 21). In C. R. Scriver, A. L. Beaudet, W. S. Sly, & D. Valle (Eds.), *The metabolic basis of inherited disease* (6th ed. Vol. I). New York: McGraw-Hill.

Epstein, J., & McPartland, J. (1976). The concept and measurement of the quality of school life. *American Educational Research Journal, 50,* 13–30.

Epstein, L. H., & Wing, R. R. (1987). Behavioral treatment of childhood obesity. *Psychological Bulletin, 101,* 331–342.

Epstein, L. H., Wing, R. R., & Valoski, A. (1985). Childhood obesity. In P. B. Penchanz (Ed.), *Pediatric clinics of North America, 32,* 363–380.

Erickson, M. F., Sroufe, L. A., & Egeland, B. (1985). The relationship between quality of attachment and behavior problems in preschool in a high-risk sample. In I. Bretherton & E. Waters (Eds.), *Growing points of attachment theory and research. Monographs of the Society for Research in Child Development, 50*(1–2, Serial No. 209).

Erikson, E. H. (1950). *Childhood and society.* New York: W. W. Norton.

Erikson, E. H. (1963). *Childhood and society* (2nd ed.). New York: W. W. Norton.

Eron, L. D. (1980). Prescription for reduction of aggression. *American Psychologist, 35,* 244–252.

Eron, L. D. (1987). The development of aggressive behavior from the perspective of a developing organism. *American Psychologist, 42,* 435–442.

Eron, L. D., & Huesmann, L. R. (1984). The relation of prosocial behavior to the development of aggression and psychopathology. *Aggressive Behavior, 10,* 243–253.

Eron, L. D., Laulicht, J. H., Walder, L. O., Farber, I. E., & Spiegel, J. P. (1961). Application of role and learning theories to the study of the development of aggression in children. *Psychological Reports, 9,* 291–334.

Erwin, P. (1985). Similarity of attitudes and constructs in children's friendships. *Journal of Experimental Child Psychology, 40,* 470–485.

Eskenazi, B. (1984). Neurobehavioral teratology. In M. B. Bracken (Ed.), *Perinatal epidemiology.* New York: Oxford University Press.

Estes, D., Wellman, H. M., & Woolley, J. D. (1989). Children's understanding of mental phenomena. In H. W. Reese (Ed.), *Advances in child development and behavior* (Vol. 22). New York: Academic Press.

Etaugh, C., Grinnell, K., & Etaugh, A. (1989). Development of gender labeling: Effect of age of pictured child. *Sex Roles, 21,* 769–773.

Evans, M. I., Drugan, A., Koppitch, F. C., III, Zador, I. E., Sacks, A. J., & Sokol, R. J. (1989). Genetic diagnosis in the first trimester: The norm for the 1990s. *American Journal of Obstetrics and Gynecology, 160,* 1332–1339.

Eyer, D. (1993). *Mother-infant bonding: A scientific fiction.* New Haven: Yale University Press.

Fabes, R. A., Eisenberg, N., McCormick, S. E., & Wilson, M. S. (1988). Preschoolers' attributions of the situational determinants of others' naturally occurring emotions. *Developmental Psychology, 24,* 376–385.

Fagan, J. F. (1984). The intelligent infant: Theoretical implications. *Intelligence, 8,* 1–9.

Fagan, J. F., & Montie, J. E. (1988). The behavioral assessment of cognitive well-being in the infant. In J. Kavanagh (Ed.), *Understanding mental retardation: Research accomplishments and new frontiers.* Baltimore: Paul H. Brookes.

Fagan, J. F., & Singer, L. T. (1983). Infant recognition memory as a measure of intelligence. In L. P. Lipsitt (Ed.), *Advances in infancy research* (Vol. 2). Norwood, NJ: Ablex.

Fagan, J. F., III. (1974). Infant recognition memory: The effects of length of familiarization and type of discrimination task. *Child Development, 45,* 351–356.

Fagan, J. F., Shepherd, P. A., & Montie, J. E. (1987). A screening test for infants at risk for mental retardation. *Journal of Developmental and Behavioral Pediatrics, 5,* 121–130.

Fagot, B. I. (1977). Consequences of moderate cross-gender behavior in preschool children. *Child Development, 48,* 902–907.

Fagot, B. I. (1978a). The influence of sex of child on parental reactions to toddler children. *Child Development, 49,* 459–465.

Fagot, B. I. (1978b). Reinforcing contingencies for sex-role behaviors: Effect of experience with children. *Child Development, 49,* 30–36.

Fagot, B. I. (1985). Changes in thinking about early sex role development. *Developmental Review, 5,* 83–98.

Fagot, B. I., & Leinbach, M. D. (1987). Socialization of sex roles within the family. In D. B. Carter (Ed.), *Current conceptions of sex roles and sex typing: Theory and research.* New York: Praeger.

Fagot, B. I., & Leinbach, M. D. (1989). The young child's gender schema: Environmental input, internal organization. *Child Development, 60,* 663–672.

Fagot, B. I., Leinbach, M. D., & O'Boyle, C. (1992). Gender labeling, gender stereotyping, and parenting behaviors. *Developmental Psychology, 28,* 225–230.

Falbo, T., & Cooper, C. R., (1980). Young children's time and intellectual ability. *Journal of Genetic Psychology, 173,* 299–300.

Falbo, T., & Polit, D. F. (1986). Quantitative review of the only child literature: Research evidence and theory development. *Psychological Bulletin, 100,* 176–189.

Fantz, R. L. (1961, May). The origin of form perception. *Scientific American, 204,* pp. 66–72.

Fantz, R. L., & Yeh, J. (1979). Configurational selectivities: Critical for development of visual perception and attention. *Canadian Journal of Psychology, 33,* 277–287.

Farrar, M. J. (1992). Negative evidence and grammatical morpheme acquisition. *Developmental Psychology, 28,* 90–98.

Faust, M. S. (1983). Alternative constructions of adolescent growth. In J. Brooks-Gunn & A. C. Petersen (Eds.), *Girls at puberty: Biological and psychosocial perspectives.* New York: Plenum Press.

Feingold, A. (1988). Cognitive gender differences are disappearing. *American Psychologist, 43,* 95–103.

Feldman, D. (1979). The mysterious case of extreme giftedness. In H. Passow (Ed.), *The gifted and talented.* Chicago: University of Chicago Press.

Feldman, H. A. (1982). Epidemiology of toxoplasma infections. *Epidemiological Review, 4,* 204–213.

Feldman, H., Goldin-Meadow, S., & Gleitman, L. (1978). Beyond Herodotus: The creation of language by linguistically deprived deaf children. In A. Locke (Ed.), *Action, symbol, and gesture: The emergence of language.* New York: Academic Press.

Feldman, W., Feldman, E., & Goodman, J. T. (1988). Culture versus biology: Children's attitudes toward thinness and fatness. *Pediatrics, 81,* 190–194.

Felner, R. D., & Adan, A. M. (1988). The School Transitional Environment Project: An ecological intervention and evaluation. In R. H. Price, E. L. Cowan, R. P. Lorion, I. Serrano-Garcia, & J. Ramos-McKay (Eds.), *14 ounces of prevention: A casebook for practitioners.* Washington, DC: American Psychological Association.

Felner, R. D., Ginter, M., & Primavera, J. (1982). Primary prevention during school transitions: Social support and environmental structure. *American Journal of Community Psychology, 10,* 277–290.

Fenson, L., Vella, D., & Kennedy, M. (1989). Children's knowledge of thematic and taxonomic relations at two years of age. *Child Development, 60,* 911–919.

Fernald, A. (1985). Four-month-olds prefer to listen to motherese. *Infant Behavior and Development, 8,* 181–195.

Fernald, A. (1991). Prosody in speech to children: Prelinguistic and linguistic features. In R. Vasta (Ed.), *Annals of child development: Vol. 8.* London: Jessica Kingsley.

Fernald, A., & Kuhl, P. (1987). Acoustic determinants of infant preference for motherese speech. *Infant Behavior and Development, 10,* 279–293.

Fernald, A., & Mazzie, C. (1983, April). *Pitch-marking of new and old information in mothers' speech to infants.* Paper presented at the biennial meeting of the Society for Research in Child Development, Detroit.

Fernald, A., & Mazzie, C. (1991). Prosody and focus in speech to infants and adults. *Developmental Psychology, 27,* 209–221.

Fernald, A., & Morikawa, H. (1993). Common themes and cultural variations in Japanese and American mothers' speech to infants. *Child Development, 64,* 637–656.

Feshbach, S., & Singer, R. (1971). *Television and aggression.* San Francisco: Jossey-Bass.

Feuerstein, R., Rand, Y., & Rynders, J. (1988). *Don't accept me as I am: Helping "retarded" people to excel.* New York: Plenum.

Fichtner, R. R., Sullivan, K. M., Zyrkowski, C. L., & Trowbridge, F. L. (1990). Racial ethnic differences in smoking, other risk factors, and low birthweight among low-income pregnant women, 1978–1988. *Morbidity and Mortality Weekly Report, 39,* 13–21.

Field, J., Muir, D., Pilon, R., Sinclair, M., & Dodwell, P. (1980). Infants' orientation to lateral sounds from birth to three months. *Child Development, 51,* 295–298.

Field, T. (1979). Differential behavior and cardiac responses of 3-month-olds to a mirror and a peer. *Infant Behavior and Development, 2,* 179–184.

Field, T. (1991). Quality infant day-care and grade school behavior and peformance. *Child Development, 6,* 863–870.

Field, T. M. (1977). Effects of early separation, interactive deficits, and experimental manipulations on infant-mother face-to-face interactions. *Child Development, 48,* 763–771.

Field, T. M. (1982). Affective displays of high-risk infants during early interactions. In T. Field & A. Fogel (Eds.), *Emotion and early interaction.* Hillsdale, NJ: Erlbaum.

Field, T. M. (1986). Interventions for premature infants. *Journal of Pediatrics, 109,* 183–191.

Field, T. M. (1987). Affective and interactive disturbances in infants. In J. D. Osofsky (Ed.), *Handbook of infant development* (2nd ed.). New York: Wiley.

Field, T. M., & Walden, T. A. (1982). Production and perception of facial expressions in infancy and early childhood. In H. W. Reese & L. P. Lipsitt (Eds.), *Advances in child development and behavior* (Vol. 16). New York: Academic Press.

Field, T. M., Cohen, D., Garcia, R., & Greenberg, R. (1984). Mother-stranger face discrimination by the newborn. *Infant Behavior and Development, 7,* 19–25.

Field, T. M., Healy, B., Goldstein, S., Perry, S., Bendell, D., Schanberg, S., Zimmerman, E. A., & Kuhn, C. (1988). Infants of depressed mothers show "depressed" behavior even with nondepressed adults. *Child Development, 59,* 1569–1579.

Field, T. M., Ignatoff, E., Stringer, S., Brennan, J., Greenberg, R., Widmayer, S., & Anderson, G. C. (1982). Nonnutritive sucking during tube feedings: Effects on preterm neonates in an intensive care unit. *Pediatrics, 70,* 381–384.

Field, T. M., Woodson, R., Cohen, D., Greenberg, R., Garcia, R., & Collins, K. (1983). Discrimination and imitation of facial expressions by term and preterm neonates. *Infant Behavior and Development, 6,* 485–489.

Field, T. M., Woodson, R., Greenberg, R., & Cohen, D. (1982). Discrimination and imitation of facial expressions by neonates. *Science, 218,* 179–181.

Field, T., Greenwald, P., Morrow, C., Healy, B., Foster, T., Guthertz, M., & Frost, P. (1992). Behavior state matching during interactions of preadolescent friends versus acquaintances. *Developmental Psychology, 28,* 242–250.

Finch, E. (1978). *Clinical assessment of short stature.* Unpublished medical school thesis, Yale University.

Findley, M. J., & Cooper, H. M. (1983). Locus of control and academic achievement. A literature review. *Journal of Personality and Social Psychology, 44,* 419–427.

Fine, M. (1988). Sexuality, schooling, and adolescent females: The missing discourse of desire. *Harvard Educational Review, 58,* 29–53.

Finn, J. D., & Achilles, C. M. (1990). Answers and questions about class size: A statewide experiment. *American Educational Research Journal, 27,* 557–577.

Finnie, V., & Russell, A. (1988). Preschool children's social status and their mothers' behavior and knowledge in the supervisory role. *Developmental Psychology, 24,* 789–801.

Fischbein, S. (1981). Heredity-environment influences on growth and development during adolescence. In L. Gedda, P. Parisi, & W. E. Nance (Eds.), *Twin research 3: Pt. B. Program in clinical and biological research.* New York: Liss.

Fischer, K. (1980). A theory of cognitive development: The control and construction of hierarchies of skills. *Psychological Review, 87,* 477–531.

Fischer, K. W., & Bidell, T. (1991). Constraining nativist inferences about cognitive capacities. In S. Carey & R. Gelman (Eds.), *The epigenesis of mind: Essays on biology and cognition.* Hillsdale, NJ: Erlbaum.

Fischer, K. W., & Farrar, M. J. (1988). Generalizations about generalization: How a theory of skill development explains both generality and specificity. In A. Demetriou (Ed.), *The neo-Piagetian theories of cognitive development: Toward an integration.* North-Holland: Elsevier.

Fischer, K., & Pipp, S. L. (1984). Processes of cognitive development: Optimal level and skill acquisition. In R. J. Sternberg (Ed.), *Mechanisms of cognitive development.* New York: W. H. Freeman.

Fish, M. C., Gross, A. L., & Sanders, J. S. (1986). The effect of equity strategies on girls' computer usage in school. *Computers in Human Behavior, 2,* 127–134.

Fishkin, J., Keniston, K., & MacKinnon, C. (1973). Moral reasoning and political ideology. *Journal of Personality and Social Psychology, 27,* 109–119.

Fishler, K., Azen, C. G., Henderson, R., Friedman, E. G., & Koch, R. (1987). Psychoeducational findings among children treated for phenylketonuria. *American Journal of Mental Deficiency, 92,* 65–73.

Fivush, R. (1984). Learning about school: The development of kindergartners' school scripts. *Child Development, 55,* 1697–1709.

Fivush, R., Kuebli, J., & Clubb, P. A. (1992). The structure of events and event representations: A developmental analysis. *Child Development, 63,* 188–201.

Flanagan, C. A. (1990). Change in family work status: Effects on parent-adolescent decision making. *Child Development, 61,* 163–177.

Flavell, J. H. (1963). *The developmental psychology of Jean Piaget.* New York: Van Nostrand Reinhold.

Flavell, J. H. (1970). Developmental studies of mediated memory. In H. W. Reese & L. P. Lipsitt (Eds.), *Advances in child development and behavior* (Vol. 5). New York: Academic Press.

Flavell, J. H. (1978). The development of knowledge about visual perception. In C. B. Keasey (Ed.), *Nebraska symposium on motivation* (Vol. 25). Lincoln: University of Nebraska Press.

Flavell, J. H. (1985). *Cognitive development* (2nd ed.). Englewood Cliffs, NJ: Prentice-Hall.

Flavell, J. H. (1988). The development of children's knowledge about the mind: From cognitive connections to mental representations. In J. W. Astington, P. L. Harris, & D. R. Olson (Eds.), *Developing theories of mind.* New York: Cambridge University Press.

Flavell, J. H. (1992). Cognitive development: Past, present, and future. *Developmental Psychology, 28,* 998–1005.

Flavell, J. H. (1993). Young children's understanding of thinking and consciousness. *Current Directions in Psychological Science, 2,* 40–43.

Flavell, J. H., & Wellman, H. M. (1977). Metamemory. In R. V. Kail & J. W. Hagen (Eds.), *Perspectives on the development of memory and cognition.* Hillsdale, NJ: Erlbaum.

Flavell, J. H., Beach, D. H., & Chinsky, J. M. (1966). Spontaneous verbal rehearsal in a memory task as a function of age. *Child Development, 37,* 283–299.

Flavell, J. H., Botkin, P. T., Fry, C. L., Jr., Wright, J. W., & Jarvis, P. E. (1968). *The development of roletaking and communication skills in children.* New York: Wiley.

Flavell, J. H., Friedrichs, A. G., & Hoyt, J. D. (1970). Developmental changes in memorization processes. *Cognitive Psychology, 1,* 324–340.

Flavell, J. H., Miller, P. H., & Miller, S. A. (1993). *Cognitive development* (3rd ed.). Englewood Cliffs, NJ: Prentice-Hall.

Flavell, J. H., Shipstead, S. G., & Croft, K. (1978). Young children's knowledge about visual perception: Hiding objects from others. *Child Development, 49,* 1208–1211.

Flavell, J. H., Zhang, X-D, Zou, H., Dong, Q., & Qi, S. (1983). A comparison of the appearance-reality distinction in the People's Republic of China and the United States. *Cognitive Psychology, 15,* 459–466.

Flavell, J. H., P. H., & Miller, S. A. (1993). *Cognitive Development* (3rd Ed.). Englewood Cliffs, NJ: Prentice Hall.

Flink, C., Boggiano, A. K., & Barrett, M. (1990). Controlling teaching strategies: Undermining children's self-determination and performance. *Journal of Personality and Social Psychology, 59,* 916–924.

Fodor, J. A. (1983). *The modularity of mind.* Cambridge: MIT Press.

Fogel, A. (1979). Peer- vs. mother-directed behavior in 1- to 3-month-old infants. *Infant Behavior and Development, 2,* 215–226.

Fogel, A. (1982). Early adult-infant face-to-face interaction: Expectable sequences of behavior. *Journal of Pediatric Psychology, 7,* 1–22.

Ford, C. S. (1964). *A comparative study of human reproduction* (Yale University Publications in Anthropology No. 32). New Haven: Yale University Press.

Fox, N. A. (1977). Attachment of kibbutz infants to mother and metapelet. *Child Development, 48,* 1228–1239.

Fox, N. A., & Davidson, R. J. (1986). Psychophysiological measures of emotion: New directions in developmental research. In C. E. Izard & P. B. Read (Eds.), *Measuring emotions in infants and children* (Vol. 2). Cambridge: Cambridge University Press.

Fox, R., Aslin, R. N., Shea, S. L., & Dumais, S. T. (1980). Stereopsis in human infants. *Science, 207,* 323–324.

Fraiberg, S. (1977). *Insights from the blind.* New York: Basic Books.

Francis, P. L., & McCroy, G. (1983, April). *Bimodal recognition of human stimulus configurations.* Paper presented at the biennial meeting of the Society for Research in Child Development, Detroit.

Frankenburg, W. K., & Dodds, J. B. (1967). The Denver Developmental Screening Test. *Journal of Pediatrics, 71,* 181–191.

Frankenburg, W. K., Dodds, J., Archer, P., Shapiro, H., & Bresnick, B. (1992). The Denver II: A major revision and restandardization of the Denver Developmental Screening Test. *Pediatrics, 89,* 91–97.

Franz, C. E., McClelland, D. C., & Weinberger, J. (1991). Childhood antecedents of conventional social accomplishment in midlife adults: A 36-year prospective study. *Journal of Personality and Social Psychology, 60,* 586–595.

Frauenglass, M. H., & Diaz, R. M. (1985). Self-regulatory functions of children's private speech: A critical analysis of recent challenges to Vygotsky's theory. *Developmental Psychology, 21,* 357–364.

Freedman, D. (1979). Ethnic differences in babies. *Human Nature, 2,* 26–43.

Freedman, J. L. (1984). Effect of television violence on aggressiveness. *Psychological Bulletin, 96,* 227–246.

Freedman, J. L. (1986). Television violence and aggression: A rejoinder. *Psychological Bulletin, 100,* 372–378.

Freud, A. (1958). Adolescence. In *Psychoanalytic study of the child* (Vol. 13). New York: International Universities Press.

Freud, S. (1922). *Beyond the pleasure principle.* London: Hogarth Press.

Freud, S. (1961). Some psychical consequences of the anatomical distinction between the sexes. In J. Strachey (Ed. and Trans.), *Standard edition of the complete psychological works of Sigmund Freud* (Vol. 19). London: Hogarth Press. (Original work published 1925)

Freud, S. (1965). *New introductory lectures on psychoanalysis* (J. Strachey, Trans.). New York: W. W. Norton. (Original work published 1933)

Frey, K. S., & Ruble, D. N. (1987). What children say about classroom performance: Sex and grade differences in perceived competence. *Child Development, 58,* 1066–1078.

Fried, P. A. (1986). Marijuana and human pregnancy. In I. J. Chasnoff (Ed.), *Drug use in pregnancy: Mother and child.* Lancaster, England: MTP Press.

Fried, P. A., & Watkinson, B. (1990). 36- and 48-month-neurobehavioral follow-up of children prenatally exposed to marijuana, cigarettes and alcohol. *Journal of Developmental and Behavioral Pediatrics, 11,* 49–58.

Friedman, E. (1978). *Labor: Clinical evaluation and management.* New York: Appleton-Century-Crofts.

Friedrich, L. K., & Stein, A. H. (1973). Aggressive and prosocial television programs and the natural behavior of preschool children. *Monographs of the Society for Research in Child Development, 38*(4, Serial No. 151).

Frisch, R. E. (1983). Fatness, puberty and fertility. In J. Brooks-Gunn & A. C. Petersen (Eds.), *Girls at puberty: Biological and psychosocial perspectives.* New York: Plenum Press.

Frith, U. (1985). Beneath the surface of developmental dyslexia. In K. E. Patterson, J. C. Marshall, & M. Coltheart (Eds.), *Surface dyslexia: Neuropsychologic and cognitive studies of phonological reading.* Hillsdale, NJ: Erlbaum.

Frith, U. (1993). Autism. *Scientific American, 268,* 108–114.

Frodi, A. M., & Lamb, M. E. (1980). Child abusers' responses to infant smiles and cries. *Child Development, 51,* 238–241.

Frodi, A. M., & Thompson, R. (1985). Infants' affective responses in the strange situation: Effects of prematurity and of quality of attachment. *Child Development, 56,* 1280–1290.

Frodi, A. M., Lamb, M. E., Leavitt, L. A., & Donovan, W. L. (1978). Fathers' and mothers' responses to infant smiles and cries. *Infant Behavior and Development, 1,* 187–198.

Frueh, T., & McGhee, P. (1975). Traditional sex-role development and amount of time spent watching television. *Developmental Psychology, 11,* 109.

Fry, D. B. (1966). The development of the phonological system in the normal and the deaf child. In F. Smith & G. A. Miller (Eds.), *The genesis of language.* Cambridge: MIT Press.

Fuchs, I., Eisenberg, N., Hertz-Lazarowitz, R., & Sharabany, R. (1986). Kibbutz, Israeli city, and American children's moral reasoning about prosocial moral conflicts. *Merrill-Palmer Quarterly, 32,* 37–50.

Fuligni, A. J., & Eccles, J. S. (1993). Perceived parent-child relationships and early adolescents' orientation toward peers. *Developmental Psychology, 29,* 622–632.

Fulker, O. W., & Eysenck, H. J. (1979). Nature, nurture and socio-economic status. In H. J. Eysenck (Ed.), *The structure and measurement of intelligence.* Berlin: Springer-Verlag.

Furman, W., & Bierman, K. L. (1984). Children's conceptions of friendship: A multimethod study of developmental changes. *Developmental Psychology, 20,* 925–931.

Furman, W., & Buhrmester, D. (1992). Age and sex differences in perceptions of networks of personal relationships. *Child Development, 63,* 103–115.

Furman, W., & Robbins, P. (1985). What's the point? Issues in the selection of treatment objectives. In B. H. Schneider, K. H. Rubin, & J. E. Ledingham (Eds.), *Children's peer relations: Issues in assessment and intervention.* New York: Springer-Verlag.

Furstenberg, F. F., Jr. (1987). The new extended family: The experience of parents and children after remarriage. In K. Paley & M. Ihinger-Tallman (Eds.), *Remarriage and stepparenting.* New York: Guilford Press.

Furstenberg, F. F., Jr., Brooks-Gunn, J., & Chase-Lansdale, L. (1989). Teenaged pregnancy and childbearing. *American Psychologist, 44,* 313–320.

Fuson, K. C. (1979). The development of self-regulating aspects of speech: A review. In G. Zivin (Ed.), *The development of self-regulation through private speech.* New York: Wiley.

Gaddis, A., & Brooks-Gunn, J. (1985). The male experience of pubertal change. *Journal of Youth and Adolescence, 14,* 61–69.

Gagné, R. M. (1968). *The conditions of learning.* New York: Holt, Rinehart & Winston.

Gagné, R. M., Briggs, L. J., & Wager, W. W. (1988). *Principles of instructional design* (3rd ed.). New York: Holt, Rinehart & Winston.

Gagnon, M., & Ladouceur, R. (1992). Behavioral treatment of child stutterers: Replication and extension. *Behavior Therapy, 23,* 113-129.

Gallahue, D. L. (1989). *Understanding motor development: Infants, children, adolescents.* Indianapolis, IN: Benchmark Press.

Galler, J. R., Ramsey, F. C., Morley, D. S., Archer, E., & Salt, P. (1990). The long-term effects of early Kwashiorkor compared with marasmus. IV. Performance on the National High School Entrance Exam. *Pediatric Research, 28,* 235–239.

Gallistel, C. R., Brown, A. L., Carey, S., Gelman, R., & Keil, F. C. (1991). Lessons from animal learning for the study of cognitive development. In S. Carey & R. Gelman (Eds.), *The epigenesis of mind: Essays on biology and cognition.* Hillsdale, NJ: Erlbaum.

Galotti, K. M. (1989). Approaches to studying formal and everyday reasoning. *Psychological Bulletin, 105,* 331–351.

Galton, F. (1883). *Inquiries into human faculty and its development.* London: Macmillan.

Gamoran, A. (1989). Measuring curriculum differentiation. *American Journal of Education, 97,* 129–143.

Ganiban, J., Wagner, S., & Cicchetti, D. (1990). Temperament and Down syndrome. In D. Cicchetti & M. Beeghly (Eds.), *Children with Down syndrome.* New York: Cambridge University Press.

Ganon, E. C., & Swartz, K. B. (1980). Perception of internal elements of compound figures by one-month-olds. *Journal of Experimental Child Psychology, 30,* 159–170.

Garabino, J. (1982). Sociocultural risk: Dangers to competence. In C. Kopp & J. Krakow (Eds.), *Child development in a social context.* Reading, MA: Addison-Wesley.

Garber, H. L. (1988). *The Milwaukee Project: Preventing mental retardation in children at risk.* Washington, DC: American Association on Mental Retardation.

Gardner, B. T., & Gardner, R. A. (1971). Two-way communication with an infant chimpanzee. In A. M. Schrier & F. Stollnitz (Eds.), *Behavior of nonhuman primates.* New York: Academic Press.

Gardner, D., Harris, P. L., Ohmoto, M., & Hamasaki, T. (1988). Japanese children's understanding of the distinction between real and apparent emotion. *International Journal of Behavioral Development, 11,* 203–218.

Gardner, H. (1983). *Frames of mind: The theory of multiple intelligences.* New York: Basic Books.

Gardner, H. (1986). The waning of intelligence tests. In R. J. Sternberg & D. K. Detterman (Eds.), *What is intelligence?* Norwood, NJ: Ablex.

Gardner, W., & Rogoff, B. (1990). Children's deliberateness of planning according to task circumstances. *Developmental Psychology, 26,* 480–487.

Garmezy, N. (1985). Stress-resistant children: The search for protective factors. In J. E. Stevenson (Ed.), *Recent research in developmental psychology.* (Journal of Child Psychology and Psychiatry Book Suppl. 4). Oxford: Pergamon Press.

Gavin, L. A., & Furman, W. (1989). Age differences in adolescent's perceptions of their peer groups. *Developmental Psychology, 25,* 827–834.

Gelman, R. (1969). Conservation acquisition: A problem of learning to attend to relevant attributes. *Journal of Experimental Child Psychology, 7,* 167–187.

Gelman, R. (1972). Logical capacity of very young children: Number invariance rules. *Child Development, 43,* 75–90.

Gelman, R., & Baillargeon, R. (1983). A review of some Piagetian concepts. In J. H. Flavell & E. M. Markman (Eds.), *Handbook of child psychology. Vol. III. Cognitive development.* New York: Wiley.

Gelman, R., & Gallistel, C. R. (1978). *The child's understanding of number.* Cambridge: Harvard University Press.

Gelman, R., & Meck, E. (1983). Preschoolers' counting: Principles before skill. *Cognition, 13,* 343–359.

Gelman, R., Spelke, E. S., & Meck, E. (1983). What preschoolers know about animate and inanimate objects. In D. Rogers & J. A. Sloboda (Eds.), *The acquisition of symbolic skills.* New York: Plenum.

Gelman, S. A., & Kremer, K. E. (1991). Understanding natural cause: Children's explanations of how objects and their properties originate. *Child Development, 62,* 396–414.

George, C., & Main, M. (1979). Social interactions of young abused children: Approach, avoidance, and aggression. *Child Development, 50,* 306–318.

Gerbner, G., Gross, L., Morgan, M., & Signorielli, N. (1986). Living with television: The dynamics of the cultivation process. In J. Bryant & D. Zillman (Eds.), *Perspectives on media effects.* Hillsdale, NJ: Erlbaum.

Geschwind. M., & Galaburda, A. M. (1987). *Cerebral lateralization.* Cambridge, MA: MIT Press.

Gesell, A. (1929). *Infancy and human growth.* New York: Macmillan.

Gesell, A., & Thompson, H. (1934). *Infant behavior: Its genesis and growth.* New York: McGraw-Hill.

Gesell, A., & Thompson, H. (1938). *The psychology of early growth.* New York: Macmillan.

Gewirtz, J. L., & Peláez-Nogureas, M. (1992). B. F. Skinner's legacy to human infant behavior and development. *American Psychologist, 47,* 1411-1422.

Ghim, H-R. (1990). Evidence for perceptual organization in infants: Perception of subjective contours by young infants. *Infant Behavior and Development, 13,* 221–248.

Ghim, H-R., & Eimas, P. D. (1988). Global and local processing by 3- and 4-month-old infants. *Perception & Psychophysics, 43,* 165–171.

Ghiselli, E. E. (1966). *The validity of occupational aptitude tests.* New York: Wiley.

Gibby, R. G., Sr., & Gibby, R. G., Jr. (1967). The effects of stress resulting from academic failure. *Journal of Clinical Psychology, 23,* 35–37.

Gibson, E. J. (1969). *Principles of perceptual learning and development.* New York: Appleton.

Gibson, E. J. (1982). The concept of affordances in development: The renascence of functionalism. In W. A. Collins (Ed.), *The Minnesota symposia on child psychology: Vol. 15. The concept of development.* Hillsdale, NJ: Erlbaum.

Gibson, E. J. (1988). Exploratory behavior in the development of perceiving, acting, and the acquiring of knowledge. *Annual Review of Psychology, 39,* 1–41.

Gibson, E. J., & Spelke, E. S. (1983). The development of perception. In J. H. Flavell & E. M. Markman (Eds.), *Handbook of child psychology: Vol. III. Cognitive development.* New York: Wiley.

Gibson, E. J., & Walker, A. (1984). Development of knowledge of visual-tactual affordances of substance. *Child Development, 55,* 453–460.

Gibson, E. J., Gibson, J. J., Pick, A. D., & Osser, H. (1962). A developmental study of the discrimination of letter-like forms. *Journal of Comparative and Physiological Psychology, 55,* 897–906.

Gibson, J. J. (1966). *The senses considered as perceptual systems.* Boston: Houghton Mifflin.

Gibson, J. J. (1979). *The ecological approach to visual perception.* Boston: Houghton Mifflin.

Gilligan, C. (1977). In a different voice: Women's conceptions of self and morality. *Harvard Educational Review, 47,* 481–517.

Gilligan, C. (1982). *In a different voice: Psychological theory and women's development.* Cambridge: Harvard University Press.

Gilligan, C. (1988). Remapping the moral domain: New images of self in relationship. In C. Gilligan, J. V. Ward, J. M. Taylor, & B. Bardige (Eds.), *Mapping the moral domain.* Cambridge, MA: Harvard University Press.

Gilligan, C., & Attanucci, J. (1988). Two moral orientations: Gender differences and similarities. *Merrill-Palmer Quarterly, 34,* 223–237.

Gilligan, C., & Wiggins, G. (1987). The origins of morality in early childhood relationships. In J. Kagan & S. Lamb (Eds.), *The emergence of morality in young children.* Chicago: University of Chicago Press.

Gilligan, C., Lyons, N. P., & Hanmer, T. J. (1990). *Making connections.* Cambridge, MA: Harvard University Press.

Gilligan, C., Lyons, N. P., & Hanmer, T. J. (Eds.). (1989). *Making connections: The relational worlds of adolescent girls at Emma Willard School.* Cambridge, MA: Harvard University Press.

Gillis, J. S. (1982). *Too tall, too small.* Champaign, IL: Institute for Personality and Ability Testing.

Ginsberg, H. (1972). *The myth of the deprived child: Poor children's intellect and education.* Englewood Cliffs, NJ: Prentice-Hall.

Ginsburg, H. P., & Opper, S. (1988). *Piaget's theory of intellectual development* (3rd ed.). Englewood Cliffs, NJ: Prentice-Hall.

Glass, D. C., Neulinger, J., & Brim, O. G. (1974). Birth order, verbal intelligence, and educational aspiration. *Child Development, 45,* 807–811.

Glazer, S. (1993). Preventing teen pregnancy: Is better sex education the answer? *CO Researcher, 3,* 409–418.

Gleason, J. B., & Perlmann, R. Y. (1985). Acquiring social variation in speech. In H. Giles & R. N. St. Clair (Eds.), *Recent advances in language, communication, and social psychology.* London: Erlbaum.

Gleason, J. B., & Weintraub, S. (1978). Input language and the acquisition of communicative competence. In K. Nelson (Ed.), *Children's language* (Vol. 1). New York: Gardner Press.

Gleitman, L. R., Gleitman, H., & Shipley, E. F. (1972). The emergence of the child as grammarian. *Cognition, 1,* 137–164.

Gleitman, L. R., Newport, E. L., & Gleitman, H. (1984). The current status of the motherese hypothesis. *Journal of Child Language, 11,* 43–79.

Gleuck, S., & Gleuck, E. (1950). *Unraveling juvenile delinquency.* Cambridge: Harvard University Press.

Glick, P. C. (1984). Marriage, divorce, and living arrangements: Prospective changes. *Journal of Family Issues, 5,* 7–26.

Glick, P. C. (1989). Remarried families, stepfamilies, and stepchildren: A brief demographic analysis. *Family Relations, 38,* 24–27.

Glick, P. C., & Lin, S. (1986). Recent changes in divorce and remarriage. *Journal of Marriage and the Family, 48,* 737–747.

Gnepp, J. & Chilamkurti, C. (1988). Children's use of personality attributions to predict other people's emotional and behavioral reactions. *Child Development, 59,* 743–754.

Goldberg, R. J. (1977, April). *Maternal time use and preschool performance.* Paper presented at the biennial meeting of the Society for Research in Child Development, New Orleans.

Goldberg, S. (1979). Premature birth: Consequences for the parent-infant relationship. *American Scientist, 67,* 582–590.

Goldberg, S. (1983). Parent-infant bonding: Another look. *Child Development, 54,* 1355–1382.

Goldenberg, R. L., Clivar, S. P., Cutter, G. R., Hoffman, H. J., Cassady, G., Davis, R. O., & Nelson, K. G. (1991). Black-white differences in newborn anthropometric measurements. *Obstetrics and Gynecology, 78,* 782–788.

Goldfield, B. A., & Reznick, J. S. (1990). Early lexical acquisition: Rate, content, and the vocabulary spurt. *Journal of Child Language, 17,* 171–183.

Goldschmid, M. L. (1967). Different types of conservation and non-conservation and their relation to age, sex, IQ, MA, and vocabulary. *Child Development, 38,* 1229–1246.

Goldschmid, M. L., & Bentler, P. M. (1968). *Concept assessment kit: Conservation.* San Diego: Educational and Industrial Testing Service.

Goldsmith, H. H., & Alansky, J. A. (1987). Maternal and infant temperamental predictors of attachment: A meta-analytic review. *Journal of Consulting and Clinical Psychology, 55,* 805–816.

Goldsmith, H. H., & Campos, J. J. (1982). Toward a theory of infant temperament. In R. N. Emde & R. J. Harmon (Eds.), *The development of attachment and affiliative systems.* New York: Plenum.

Goldsmith, H. H., & Campos, J. J. (1990). The structure of temperamental fear and pleasure in infants: A psychometric perspective. *Child Development, 61,* 1944–1964.

Goldsmith, H. H., & Gottesman, I. I. (1981). Origins of variation in behavioral style: A longitudinal study of temperament in young twins. *Child Development, 52,* 91–103.

Goldstein, H., Kaczmarek, L., Pennington, R., & Shafer, K. (1992). Peer-mediated intervention: Attending to, commenting on, and acknowledging the behavior of preschoolers with autism. *Journal of Applied Behavior Analysis, 25,* 289–305.

Golinkoff, R. M., Harding, C. G., Carlson, V., & Sexton, M. E. (1984). The infant's perception of causal events: The distinction between animate and inanimate objects. In L. L. Lipsitt & C. Rovee-Collier (Eds.), *Advances in infancy research. Vol. 3.* Norwood, NJ: Ablex.

Golub, M. S., Sassenrath, E. N., & Chapman, C. F. (1981). Regulation of visual attention in offspring of female monkeys treated with delta-9-tetrahydrocannabinol. *Developmental Psychobiology, 14,* 507–512.

Gomby, D. S., & Shiono, P. H. (1991). Estimating the number of substance-exposed infants. *The Future of Children: Drug Exposed Infants, 1,* 17–25.

Goodenough, F. L. (1931). *Anger in young children.* Minneapolis: University of Minnesota Press.

Goodman, G. S., & Reed, R. S. (1986). Age differences in eyewitness testimony. *Law and Human Behavior, 10,* 317–332.

Goodman, G. S., Levine, M., Melton, G. B., & Ogden, D. W. (1991). Child witnesses and the confrontation clause. *Law and Human Behavior, 15,* 13–29.

Goodman, G. S., Taub, E. P., Jones, D. P. H., England, P., Port, L. K., Rudy, L., & Prado, L. (1992). Testifying in criminal court. *Monographs of the Society for Research in Child Development, 57* (5, Serial No. 229).

Goodwin, D. W., Schulsinger, F., Hermansen, L., Guze, S. B., & Winokur, G. (1973). Alcohol problems in adoptees raised apart from alcoholic biological parents. *Archives of General Psychiatry, 28,* 238–243.

Goodwin, S. W., & Acredolo, L. P. (1993). Symbolic gesture versus word: Is there a modality advantage for onset of symbol use? *Child Development, 64,* 688–701.

Gopnik, A., & Meltzoff, A. N. (1986). Relations between semantic and cognitive development in the one-word stage: The specificity hypothesis. *Child Development, 57,* 1040–1053.

Gopnik, A., & Meltzoff, A. N. (1987). The development of categorization in the second year and its relation to other cognitive and linguistic attainments. *Child Development, 58,* 1523–1531.

Gopnik, A., & Meltzoff, A. N. (1992). Categorization and naming: Basic-level sorting in eighteen-month-olds and its relation to language. *Child Development, 63,* 1091–1103.

Gopnik, A., & Slaughter, V. (1991). Young children's understanding of changes in their mental states. *Child Development, 62,* 98–110.

Gorlin, R. J. (1977). Classical chromosome disorders. In J. J. Yunis (Ed.), *New chromosomal syndromes.* New York: Academic Press.

Gorman, H., & Bourne, L. E. (1983). Learning to think by learning Logo: Rule learning in third grade computer programmers. *Bulletin of the Psychonomic Society, 21,* 165–167.

Gorski, R. A. (1980). Sexual differentiation of the brain. In D. T. Krieger & J. C. Hughes (Eds.), *Neuroendocrinology.* New York: Rockefeller University Press.

Gorsky, P. A. (1991). Developmental intervention during neonatal hospitalization: Critiquing the state of the science. *Pediatric Clinics of North America, 38,* 1469–1479.

Gortmaker, S. L., Dietz, W. H., Jr., Sobol, A. M., & Wehler, C. A. (1987). Increasing pediatric obesity in the United States. *American Journal of Diseases of Children, 141,* 535–540.

Goswami, U. (1991). Analogical reasoning: What develops? A review of theory and research. *Child Development, 62,* 1–22.

Goswami, U. (1992). *Analogical reasoning in children.* Hillsdale, NJ: Erlbaum.

Goswami, U., & Brown, A. L. (1989). Melting chocolate and melting snowmen: Analogical reasoning and causal relations. *Cognition, 35,* 69–95.

Gottesman, I. I. (1963). Heritability of personality: A demonstration. *Psychological Monographs, 77* (Whole No. 572).

Gottesman, I. I., & Shields, J. (1982). *Schizophrenia: The epigenetic puzzle.* Cambridge: Cambridge University Press.

Gottfried, A. E., Gottfried, A. W., & Bathurst, K. (1988). Maternal employment when children are toddlers and kindergartners. In A. E. Gottfried & A. W. Gottfried (Eds.), *Maternal employment and children's development: Longitudinal research.* New York: Plenum Press.

Gottlieb, G. (1991). Experimental canalization of behavioral development: Theory. *Developmental Psychology, 27,* 4-13.

Gottman, J. M. (1983). How children become friends. *Monographs of the Society for Research in Child Development, 48*(2, Serial No. 201).

Gottman, J. M., & Parkhurst, J. T. (1980). A developmental theory of friendship and acquaintanceship processes. In W. A. Collins (Ed.), *The Minnesota symposia on child development: Vol. 13. Development of cognition, affect, and social relations.* Hillsdale, NJ: Erlbaum.

Gottman, J. M., Gonso, J., & Rasmussen, B. (1975). Social interaction, social competence, and friendship in children. *Child Development, 46,* 709–718.

Gouin-Decarie, T. (1969). A study of the mental and emotional development of the thalidomide child. In B. M. Foss (Ed.), *Determinants of infant behavior IV.* London: Methuen.

Gould, S. J. (1985, November). Geoffrey and the homeobox. *Natural History,* pp. 12–23.

Goy, R. (1970). Early hormonal influences on the development of sexual and sex-related behavior. In F. Schmitt, G. Quarton, T. Melnechuck, & G. Adelman (Eds.), *The neurosciences: Second study program.* New York: Rockefeller University Press.

Goyco, P. G., & Beckerman, R. C. (1990). Sudden infant death syndrome. *Current Problems in Pediatrics, 20,* 299–346.

Grady, D. (1987, June). The ticking of a time bomb in the genes. *Discover,* pp. 26–39.

Graham, S., Hudley, C., & Williams, E. (1992). Attributional and emotional determinants of aggression among African-American and Latino young adolescents. *Developmental Psychology, 28,* 731–740.

Gralinski, J. H., & Kopp, C. B. (1993). Everyday rules for behavior: Mothers' requests to young children. *Developmental Psychology, 29,* 573–584.

Granrud, C. E., Yonas, A., Smith, I. M. E., Arterberry, M. W., Glicksman, M. L., & Sorknes, A. C. (1984). Infants' sensitivity to accretion and deletion of texture as information for depth at an edge. *Child Development, 55,* 1630–1636.

Graves, N. B., & Graves, T. D. (1983). The cultural context of prosocial development: An ecological model. In D. L. Bridgeman (Ed.), *The nature of prosocial development: Interdisciplinary theories and strategies.* New York: Academic Press.

Green, J. E., Dorfmann, A., Jones, S. L., Bender, S., Patton, L., & Schulman, J. D. (1988). Chorionic villus sampling: Experience with an initial 940 cases. *Obstetrics and Gynecology, 71,* 208–212.

Greenberg, B. S. (1986). Minorities and the mass media. In J. Bryant & D. Zillman (Eds.), *Perspectives on mass media effects.* Hillsdale, NJ: Erlbaum.

Greenfield, P. M. (1976). Cross-cultural research and Piagetian theory: Paradox and progress. In K. Riegel & J. Meacham (Eds.), *The developing individual in a changing world* (Vol. 1). The Hague: Mouton.

Greenfield, P. M. (1984). A theory of the teacher in the learning activities of everyday life. In B. Rogoff & J. Lave (Eds.), *Everyday cognition: Its development in social context.* Cambridge: Harvard University Press.

Greenough, W. T., Black, J. E., & Wallace, C. S. (1987). Experience and brain development. *Child Development, 58,* 539–559.

Greif, E. B., & Gleason, J. B. (1980). Hi, thanks, and goodbye: More routine information. *Language in Society, 9,* 159–166.

Greif, E. B., & Ulman, K. J. (1982). The psychological impact of menarche on early adolescent females: A review of the literature. *Child Development, 53,* 1413–1430.

Greist, D., Wells, K. C., & Forehand, R. (1979). An examination of predictors of maternal perceptions of maladjustment in clinic-referred children. *Journal of Abnormal Psychology, 88,* 277–281.

Grimes, D., & Gross, G. (1981). Pregnancy outcomes in black women aged 35 and older. *Obstetrics and Gynecology, 58,* 614–620.

Grolnick, W. S., Ryan, R. M., & Deci, E. L. (1991). Inner resources for school achievement: Motivational mediators of children's perceptions of their parents. *Journal of Educational Psychology, 83,* 508–517.

Grossman, F. K., Pollack, W. S., & Golding, E. (1988). Fathers and children: Predicting the quality and quantity of fathering. *Developmental Psychology, 24,* 82–91.

Grossman, H. J. (1983). *Classification in mental retardation* (rev. ed.). Washington, DC: American Association on Mental Deficiency.

Grossman, K., Grossman, K. E., Spangler, G., Suess, G., & Unzner, L. (1985). Maternal sensitivity and newborns' orientation responses as related to quality of attachment in northern Germany. In I. Bretherton & E. Waters (Eds.), *Growing points of attachment theory and research. Monographs of the Society for Research in Child Development, 50*(1–2, Serial No. 209).

Grotevant, H. D., & Cooper, C. R. (1986). Individuation in family relationships. *Human Development, 29,* 82–100.

Gruen, G., Ottinger, D., & Zigler, E. (1970). Level of aspiration and the probability learning of middle- and lower-class children. *Developmental Psychology, 3,* 133–142.

Grusec, J. E. (1982). The socialization of altruism. In N. Eisenberg (Ed.), *The development of prosocial behavior.* New York: Academic Press.

Grusec, J. E. (1991). Socializing concern for others in the home. *Developmental Psychology, 27,* 338–342.

Grusec, J. E., & Redler, E. (1980). Attribution, reinforcement, and altruism: A developmental analysis. *Developmental Psychology, 16,* 525–534.

Grusec, J. E., & Skubiski, L. (1970). Model nurturance, demand characteristics of the modeling experiment, and altruism. *Journal of Personality and Social Psychology, 14,* 352–359.

Grusec, J. E. (1992). Social learning theory and developmental psychology: The legacies of Robert Sears and Albert Bandura. *Developmental Psychology, 28,* 776-786.

Guidubaldi, J., Perry, J. D., & Cleminshaw, H. K. (1984). The legacy of parental divorce: A nationwide study of family status and selected mediating variables on children's academic and social competencies. In B. B. Lahey & A. E. Kazdin (Eds.), *Advances in clinical child psychology* (Vol. 7). New York: Plenum Press.

Guilford, J. P. (1967). *The nature of human intelligence.* New York: McGraw-Hill.

Guilford, J. P. (1985). The structure-of-intellect model. In B. B. Wolman (Ed.), *Handbook of intelligence.* New York: Wiley.

Gump, P. V. (1978). School environments. In I. Altman & J. F. Wohlwill (Eds.), *Children and the environment.* New York: Plenum Press.

Gundy, J. H. (1987). The pediatric physical examination. In R. A. Hoekelman, S. Blatman, S. B. Friedman, N. M. Nelson, & H. M. Seidel (Eds.), *Primary pediatric care.* Washington, DC: C. V. Mosby.

Gunnar, M. R., Malone, S., Vance, G., & Fisch, R. O. (1985). Coping with aversive stimulation in the neonatal period: Quiet sleep and plasma cortisol levels during recovery from circumcision. *Child Development, 56,* 824–834.

Gunston, G. D., Burkimsher, D., Malan, H, & Sive, A. A. (1992). Reversible cerebral shrinkage in kwashiorkor: An MRI study. *Archives of Disease in Childhood, 67,* 1030–1032.

Gunzenhauser, N. (Ed.). (1987). *Infant stimulation: For whom, what kind, when, and how much?* (Johnson & Johnson Baby Products Company Pediatric Round Table Series No. 13). Skilman, NJ: Johnson & Johnson.

Gurucharri, C., & Selman, R. L. (1982). The development of interpersonal understanding during childhood, preadolescence, and adolescence: A longitudinal follow-up study. *Child Development, 53,* 924–927.

Gusella, J. L., Muir, D., & Tronick, E. Z. (1988). The effect of manipulating maternal behavior during an interaction on three- and six-month-olds' affect and attention. *Child Development, 59,* 1111–1124.

Guttentag, R. E. (1987). Memory and aging: Implications for theories of memory development during childhood. *Developmental Review, 5,* 56–82.

Hagerman, R. J. (1987). Fragile X syndrome. *Current Problems in Pediatrics, 17,* 625–674.

Hagerman, R. J. (1992). Fragile x syndrome: Advances and controversy. *Journal of Child Psychology and Psychiatry, 33,* 1127-1140.

Hainline, L., Turkel, J., Abramov, I., Lemerise, E., & Harris, C. M. (1984). Characteristics of saccades in human infants. *Vision Research, 24,* 1771–1780.

Haith, M. M. (1980). *Rules that babies look by: The organization of newborn visual activity.* Hillsdale, NJ: Erlbaum.

Haith, M. M. (1990). Progress in the understanding of sensory and perceptual processes in early infancy. *Merrill-Palmer Quarterly, 36,* 1–26.

Hakuta, K., & Diaz, R. M. (1985). The relationship between degree of bilingualism and cognitive ability: A critical discussion and some new longitudinal data. In K. E. Nelson (Ed.), *Children's language* (Vol. 5). Hillsdale, NJ: Erlbaum.

Halford, G. S. (1990). Is chilren's reasoning logical or analogical? Further comments on Piagetian cognitive developmental psychology. *Human Development, 33,* 356–361.

Hall, G. S. (1893). The contents of children's minds on entering school. *Pedagogical Seminary, 1,* 139–173.

Hall, J. A. (1978). Gender effects in decoding nonverbal cues. *Psychological Bulletin, 85,* 845–857.

Hall, J. A. (1984). *Nonverbal sex differences: Communication accuracy and expressive style.* Baltimore: Johns Hopkins University Press.

Hall, J. A., & Halberstadt, A. G. (1986). Smiling and gazing. In J. S. Hyde & M. C. Linn (Eds.), *The psychology of gender: Advances through meta-analysis.* Baltimore: Johns Hopkins University Press.

Hallinan, M. T. (1976). Friendship patterns in open and traditional classrooms. *Sociology of Education, 49,* 254–265.

Hallinan, M. T. (1990). The effects of ability grouping in secondary schools: A response to Slavin's best-evidence synthesis. *Review of Educational Research, 60,* 501–504.

Halmi, K. A. (1985). The diagnosis and treatment of anorexia nervosa. In D. Shaffer, A. A. Ehrhardt, & L. Greenhill (Eds.), *The clinical guide to child psychiatry.* New York: Free Press.

Halpern, D. F. (1986). *Sex differences in cognitive abilities.* Hillsdale, NJ: Erlbaum.

Halsey, C. L., Collin, M. F., & Anderson, C. G. (1993). Extremely low birth weight children and their peers: A comparison of preschool performance. *Pediatrics, 91,* 807–811.

Halverson, H. M. (1931). An experimental study of prehension in infants by means of systematic cinema records. *Genetic Psychology Monographs, 10,* 107–286.

Hamilton, V. J., & Gordon, D. A. (1978). Teacher-child interactions in preschool and task persistence. *American Educational Research Journal, 15,* 459–466.

Hanna, E., & Meltzoff, A. N. (1993). Peer imitation by toddlers in laboratory, home, and day-care contexts: Implications for social learning and memory. *Developmental Psychology, 29,* 701–710.

Hans, S. L. (1989). Developmental consequences of prenatal exposure to methadone. *Annals of the New York Academy of Science, 562,* 195–207.

Hans, S. L., Marcus, J., Jeremy, R. J., & Auerbach, J. G. (1984). Neurobehavioral development of children exposed in utero to opioid drugs. In J. Yanai (Ed.), *Neurobehavioral teratology.* New York: Elsevier.

Hansen, J. D. L. (1990). Malnutrition review. *Pediatric Reviews and Communication, 4,* 201–212.

Hanson, F. W., Tennant, F., Hume, S., & Brookhyser, K. (1992). Early amniocentesis: Outcome risks and technical problems at 12.8 weeks. *American Journal of Obstetrics and Gynecology, 166,* 1707–1711.

Harbison, R. D., & Mantilla-Plata, B. (1972). Prenatal toxicity, maternal distribution and placental transfer of tetrahydrocannabinol. *Journal of Pharmacology and Experimental Therapeutics, 180,* 446–453.

Hareven, T. (1985). Historical changes in the family and the life course: Implications for child development. In A. B. Smuts & J. W. Hagen (Eds.), *History and research in child development. Monographs of the Society for Research in Child Development, 50*(4–5, Serial No. 211).

Harkness, S., & Super, C. M. (1985). Child-environment interactions in the socialization of affect. In M. Lewis & C. Saarni (Eds.), *The socialization of emotions.* New York: Plenum Press.

Harlow, H. F., & Zimmerman, R. R. (1959). Affectional responses in the infant monkey. *Science, 130,* 421–432.

Harpin, V., Chellappah, G., & Rutter, N. (1983). Responses of the newborn infant to overheating. *Biology of the Neonate, 44,* 65–75.

Harriman, A. E., & Lukosius, P. A. (1982). On why Wayne Dennis found Hopi children retarded in age at onset of walking. *Perceptual and Motor Skills, 55,* 79–86.

Harris, G., & Booth, D. (1985). Sodium preference in food and previous dietary experience in 6-month-old infants. *IRCS Medical Science, 13,* 1177–1178.

Harris, P. L. (1983). Children's understanding of the link between situation and emotion. *Journal of Experimental Child Psychology, 36,* 490–509.

Harris, P. L., & Kavanaugh, R. D. (1993). Young children's understanding of pretense. *Monographs of the Society for Research in Child Development, 58* (1, Serial No. 231).

Harris, P. L., Brown, E., Marriott, C., Whittall, S., & Harmer, S. (1991). Monsters, ghosts and witches: Testing the limits of the fantasy-reality distinction. *British Journal of Developmental Psychology, 9,* 105–123.

Harris, P. L., Donnelly, K., Guz, G. R., & Pitt-Watson, R. (1986). Children's understanding of the distinction between real and apparent emotion. *Child Development, 57,* 895–909.

Harris, P. L., Guz, G. R., Lipian, M. S., & Man-Shu, Z. (1985). Insight into the time-course of emotion among Western and Chinese children. *Child Development, 56,* 972–988.

Harris, P. L., Olthof, T., & Meerum Terwogt, M. (1981). Children's knowledge of emotion. *Journal of Child Psychology and Psychiatry, 22,* 247–261.

Harris, R. T. (1991, March). Anorexia nervosa and bulimia nervosa in female adolescents. *Nutrition Today* pp. 30–34.

Harris, S., Mussen, P. H., & Rutherford, E. (1976). Some cognitive, behavioral, and personality correlates of maturity of moral judgment. *Journal of Genetic Psychology, 128,* 123–135.

Harrison, A. O., Wilson, M. N., Pine, C. J., Chan, S. Q., & Buriel, R. (1990). Family ecologies of ethnic minority children. *Child Development, 61,* 347–362.

Hart, C. H., De Wolf, D. M., Wozniak, P., & Burts, D. C. (1992). Maternal and paternal disciplinary styles: Relations with preschoolers' playground behavioral orientations and peer status. *Child Development, 63,* 879–892.

Hart, S. N., & Brassard, M. R. (1987). A major threat to children's mental health. *American Psychologist, 42,* 160–165.

Harter, S. (1980). A model of intrinsic mastery motivation in children: Individual differences and developmental change. In W. A. Collins (Ed.), *The Minnesota symposia on child psychology: Vol. 13. Development of cognition, affect, and social relations.* Hillsdale, NJ: Erlbaum.

Harter, S. (1982). A cognitive-developmental approach to children's use of affect and trait labels. In F. Serafice (Ed.), *Sociocognitive development in context.* New York: Guilford Press.

Harter, S. (1983). Developmental perspectives on the self-system. In E. M. Hetherington (Ed.), *Handbook of child psychology: Vol. IV. Socialization, personality, and social development.* New York: Wiley.

Harter, S. (1985). Processes underlying the construct, maintenance and enhancement of the self-concept in children. In J. Suls & A. Greenwald (Eds.), *Psychological perspectives on the self* (Vol. 3). Hillsdale, NJ: Erlbaum.

Harter, S. (1986). Cognitive-developmental processes in the integration of concepts about emotions and the self. *Social Cognition, 4,* 119–151.

Harter, S. (1987). The determinants and mediational role of global self-worth in children. In N. Eisenberg (Ed.), *Contemporary topics in developmental psychology.* New York: Wiley.

Harter, S. (1988). Developmental processes in the construction of the self. In T. D. Yawkey & J. E. Johnson (Eds.), *Integrative processes and socialization: Early to middle childhood.* Hillsdale, NJ: Erlbaum.

Harter, S., & Buddin, B. J. (1987). Children's understanding of the simultaneity of two emotions: A five-stage developmental acquisition sequence. *Developmental Psychology, 23,* 388–399.

Harter, S., & Monsour, A. (1992). Developmental analysis of conflict caused by opposing attributes in the adolescent self-portrait. *Developmental Psychology, 28,* 251–260.

Hartl, D. (1977). *Our uncertain heritage: Genetics and diversity.* Philadelphia: J. B. Lippincott.

Hartup, W. W. (1974). Aggression in childhood: Developmental perspectives. *American Psychologist, 29,* 336–341.

Hartup, W. W. (1977, Fall). Peers, play, and pathology: A new look at the social behavior of children. *Newsletter of the Society for Research in Child Development,* pp. 1–3.

Hartup, W. W. (1983). Peer relations. In E. M. Hetherington (Ed.), *Handbook of child psychology: Vol. IV. Socialization, personality, and social development.* New York: Wiley.

Hartup, W. W. (1989). Social relationships and their developmental significance. *American Psychologist, 44,* 120–126.

Hartup, W. W., & Coates, B. (1967). Imitation of a peer as a function of reinforcement from the peer group and rewardingness of the model. *Child Development, 38,* 1003–1016.

Hartup, W. W., & Sancilio, M. F. (1986). Children's friendships. In E. Shopler & G. B. Mesibov (Eds.), *Social behavior in autism.* New York: Plenum Press.

Hartup, W. W., French, D. C., Laursen, B., Johnston, M. K., & Ogawa, J. R. (1993). Conflict and friendship relations in middle childhood: Behavior in a closed field situation. *Child Development, 64,* 445–454.

Hartup, W. W., Laursen, B., Stewart, M. I., & Eastenson, A. (1988). Conflict and the friendship relations of young children. *Child Development, 59,* 1590–1600.

Hatfield, J. S., Ferguson, L. R., & Alpert, R. (1967). Mother-child interaction and the socialization process. *Child Development, 38,* 365–414.

Haubenstricker, J., & Seefeldt, V. (1986). Acquisition of motor skills during childhood. In V. Seefeldt (Ed.). *Physical activity and well-being.* Reston, VA: American Alliance for Health, Education, Recreation, and Dance.

Hauser, S. T., Powers, S. I., Noam, G. G., & Bowlds, M. K. (1987). Family interiors of adolescent ego development trajectories. *Family Perspectives, 21,* 263–282.

Hawkins, J., Sheingold, K., Gearhart, M., & Berger, C. (1982). Microcomputers in classrooms: Impact on the social life of elementary classrooms. *Journal of Applied Developmental Psychology, 3,* 361–373.

Hawn, P. R., & Harris, L. J. (1983). Hand differences in grasp duration and reaching in two- and five-month old infants. In G. Young, S. Segalowitz, C. M. Carter, & S. E. Trehub (Eds.), *Manual specialization and the developing brain.* New York: Academic Press.

Hay, D. F. (1985). Learning to form relationships in infancy: Parallel attainments with parents and peers. *Developmental Review, 5,* 122–161.

Hay, D. F., & Ross, H. S. (1982). The social nature of early conflict. *Child Development, 53,* 105–113.

Hay, D. F., Nash, A., & Pedersen, J. (1983). Interaction between 6-month-old peers. *Child Development, 54,* 557–562.

Headings, V. E. (1988). Screening the newborn population for congenital and genetic disorders. *Pediatric Reviews and Communications, 2,* 317–332.

Hearold, S. (1986). A synthesis of 1043 effects of television on social behavior. In G. A. Comstock (Ed.), *Public communications and behavior* (Vol. 1). New York: Academic Press.

Heath, S. B. (1983). *Ways with words.* Cambridge: Cambridge University Press.

Heath, S. B. (1989). Oral and literate traditions among black Americans living in poverty. *American Psychologist, 44,* 367–373.

Hebb, D. O. (1980). *Essay on mind.* Hillsdale, NJ: Erlbaum.

Held, R., Birch, E., & Gwiazda, J. (1980). Stereoacuity in human infants. *Proceedings of the National Academy of Sciences of the U.S.A., 77,* 5572–5574.

Hendrickse, R. G. (1991). Kwashiorkor: The hypothesis that incriminates aflatoxins. *Pediatrics, 88,* 376–379.

Henig, R. M. (1988, May 22). Should baby read? *The New York Times Magazine,* pp. 37–38.

Hertz-Lazarowitz, R., & Sharan, S. (1984). Enhancing prosocial behavior through cooperative learning in the classroom. In E. Staub, D. Bar-Tel, J. Karylowski, & J. Reykowski (Eds.), *Development and maintenance of prosocial behavior.* New York: Plenum Press.

Hess, R. D., & Miura, I. T. (1985). Gender differences in enrollment in computer camps and classes. *Sex Roles, 13,* 193–203.

Hetherington, E. M. (1989). Coping with family transitions: Winners, losers, and survivors. *Child Development, 60,* 1–14.

Hetherington, E. M., & Clingempeel, W. G. (1992). Coping with marital transitions: A family systems perspective. *Monographs of the Society for Research in Child Development* (2-3, Serial No. 227).

Hetherington, E. M., Cox, M., & Cox, R. (1982). Effects of divorce on parents and children. In M. Lamb (Ed.), *Nontraditional families.* Hillsdale, NJ: Erlbaum.

Heyman, G. D., Dweck, C. S., & Cain, K. M. (1992). Young children's vulnerability to self-blame and helplessness: Relationship to beliefs about goodness. *Child Development, 63,* 401–415.

Heyns, B. (1982). The influence of parents' work on children's school achievement. In S. B. Kamerman & C. D. Hayes (Eds.), *Families that work: Children in a changing world.* Washington, DC: National Academy Press.

Hicks, D. J. (1965). Imitation and retention of film-mediated aggressive peer and adult models. *Journal of Personality and Social Psychology, 2,* 97–100.

Higgins, E. T., & Parsons, J. E. (1983). Stages as subcultures: Social-cognitive development and the social life of the child. In E. T. Higgins, W. W. Hartup, & D. N. Ruble (Eds.), *Social cognition and social development: A sociocultural perspective.* New York: Cambridge University Press.

Hilgard, J. R. (1932). Learning and maturation in preschool children. *Journal of Genetic Psychology, 41,* 36–56.

Hill, C. R., & Stafford, F. P. (1980). Parental care of children: Time diary estimates of quantity, predictability, and variety. *Journal of Human Resources, 15,* 219–289.

Hill, J. P. (1987). Research on adolescents and their families: Past and prospect. In C. E. Irwin (Ed.), *Adolescent social behavior and health.* San Francisco: Jossey-Bass.

Hill, S. T., & Shronk, L. K. (1979). The effect of early parent-infant contact on newborn body temperature. *Journal of Obstetric and Gynecological Nursing, 8,* 287–290.

Hinde, R. A. (1965). Interaction of internal and external factors in integration of canary reproduction. In F. Beach (Ed.), *Sex and behavior.* New York: Wiley.

Hinde, R. A. (1989). Ethological and relationships approaches. In R. Vasta (Ed.), *Annals of child development: Vol 6. Six theories of child development: Revised formulations and current issues.* Greenwich, CT: JAI Press.

Hinde, R. A., Titmus, G., Easton, D., & Tamplin, A. (1985). Incidence of "friendship" and behavior to strong associates versus non-associates in preschoolers. *Child Development, 56,* 234–245.

Hirsch, B. J., & Rapkin, B. D. (1987). The transition to junior high school: A longitudinal study of self-esteem, psychological symptomatology, school life, and social support. *Child Development, 58,* 1235–1243.

Hirsch, J. (1975). Cell number and size as a determinant of subsequent obesity. In M. Winick (Ed.), *Childhood obesity.* New York: Wiley.

Hirsch-Pasek, K., Gleitman, L. R., & Gleitman, H. (1978). What does the brain say to the mind? A study of the detection and report of ambiguity by young children. In A. Sinclair, R. J. Jarvella, & W. J. M. Levelt (Eds.), *The child's conception of language.* Berlin: Springer-Verlag.

Hock, E., & DeMeis, D. K. (1990). Depression in mothers of infants: The role of maternal employment. *Developmental Psychology, 26,* 285–291.

Hodapp, R. M., & Zigler, E. (1990). Applying the developmental perspective to individuals with Down syndrome. In D. Cicchetti & M. Beeghly (Eds.), *Children with Down syndrome.* New York: Cambridge University Press.

Hoff-Ginsberg, E. (1986). Function and structure in maternal speech: Their relation to the child's development of syntax. *Developmental Psychology, 22,* 155–163.

Hoff-Ginsberg, E. (1990). Maternal speech and the child's development of syntax: A further look. *Journal of Child Language, 17,* 85–99.

Hoff-Ginsberg, E. (1991). Mother-child conversation in different social classes and communicative settings. *Child Development, 62,* 782–796.

Hoffman, L. W. (1979). Maternal employment: 1979. *American Psychologist, 34,* 859–865.

Hoffman, L. W. (1980). The effects of maternal employment on the academic attitudes and performance of school-age children. *School Psychology Review, 9,* 319–336.

Hoffman, L. W. (1984). Maternal employment and the young child. In M. Perlmutter (Ed.), *The Minnesota symposia on child psychology: Vol. 17. Parent-child interaction and parent-child relations in child development.* Hillsdale, NJ: Erlbaum.

Hoffman, L. W. (1989). Effects of maternal employment in the two-parent family. *American Psychologist, 44,* 283–292.

Hoffman, M. L. (1970). Moral development. In P. H. Mussen (Ed.), *Carmichael's manual of child psychology* (Vol. 2). New York: Wiley.

Hoffman, M. L. (1971). Identification and conscience development. *Child Development, 42,* 1071–1082.

Hoffman, M. L. (1975). Altruistic behavior and the parent-child relationship. *Journal of Personality and Social Psychology, 31,* 937–943.

Hoffman, M. L. (1976). Empathy, role-taking, guilt, and the development of altruistic motives. In T. Lickona (Ed.), *Moral development and moral behavior: Theory, research, and social issues.* New York: Holt, Rinehart & Winston.

Hoffman, M. L. (1981a). Is altruism part of human nature? *Journal of Personality and Social Psychology, 40,* 121–137.

Hoffman, M. L. (1981b). Perspectives on the difference between understanding people and understanding things. The role of affect. In J. H. Flavell & L. Ross (Eds.), *Social cognitive development: Frontiers and possible futures.* New York: Cambridge University Press.

Hoffman, M. L. (1982). Development of prosocial motivation: Empathy and guilt. In N. Eisenberg (Ed.), *The development of prosocial behavior.* New York: Academic Press.

Hoffman-Plotkin, D., & Twentyman, C. (1984). A multimodal assessment of behavioral and cognitive deficits in abused and neglected preschoolers. *Child Development, 52,* 13–30.

Hofsten, C. von. (1984). Developmental changes in the organization of prereaching movements. *Developmental Psychology, 20,* 378–388.

Hofsten, C. von, & Rönnqvist, L. (1993). The structuring of neonatal arm movement. *Child Development, 64,* 1046–1057.

Hoge, D. R., Smit, E. K., & Hanson, S. L. (1990). School experiences predicting changes in self-esteem of sixth- and seventh-graders. *Journal of Educational Psychology, 82,* 117–127.

Holbrook, S. M. (1990). Adoption, infertility, and the new reproductive technologies: Problems and prospects for social work and welfare policy. *Social Work, 35,* 333–337.

Holden, G. W. (1983). Avoiding conflict: Mothers as tacticians in the supermarket. *Child Development, 54,* 233–240.

Holden, G. W., & West, M. J. (1989). Proximate regulation by mothers: A demonstration of how differing styles affect young children's behavior. *Child Development, 60,* 64–69.

Hollenbeck, A. R., & Slaby, R. G. (1979). Infant visual and vocal responses to television. *Child Development, 50,* 41–45.

Hollenbeck, A. R., Gewirtz, J. L., & Sebris, S. L. (1984). Labor and delivery medication influences parent-infant interaction in the first post-partum month. *Infant Behavior and Development, 7,* 201–209.

Holmbeck, G. N., & Hill, J. P. (1991). Conflictive engagement, positive affect, and menarche in families with seventh-grade girls. *Child Development, 62,* 1030–1048.

Honzik, M. P., Macfarlane, J. W., & Allen, L. (1948). The stability of mental test performance between two and eighteen years. *Journal of Experimental Education, 17,* 309–329.

Hood, K. E., Draper, P., Crockett, L. J., & Petersen, A. C. (1987). The ontogeny and phylogeny of sex differences in development: A biopsychosocial synthesis. In D. B. Carter (Ed.), *Current conceptions of sex roles and sex typing: Theory and research.* New York: Praeger.

Hopkins, B., & Westra, T. (1990). Motor development, maternal expectations, and the role of handling. *Infant Behavior and Development, 13,* 117–122.

Hops, H., & Finch, M. (1985). Social competence and skill: A reassessment. In B. H. Schneider, K. H. Rubin, & J. E. Ledingham (Eds.), *Children's peer relations: Issues in assessment and intervention.* New York: Springer-Verlag.

Horn, J. L. (1968). Organization of abilities and the development of intelligence. *Psychological Review, 75,* 242–259.

Horn, J. L., & Cattell, R. B. (1967). Refinement and test of the theory of fluid and crystallized ability intelligences. *Journal of Educational Psychology, 57,* 253–270.

Horn, J. M. (1983). The Texas Adoption Project: Adopted children and their intellectual resemblance to biological and adoptive parents. *Child Development, 54,* 268–275.

Horn, J. M., Loehlin, J. C., & Willerman, L. (1979). Intellectual resemblance among adoptive and biological relatives: The Texas Adoption Project. *Behavior Genetics, 9,* 177–201.

Horowitz, F. D. (1987a). *Exploring developmental theories: Toward a structural/behavioral model of development.* Hillsdale, NJ: Erlbaum.

Horowitz, F. D. (1987b). Targeting infant stimulation efforts: Theoretical challenges for research and intervention. In N. Gunzenhauser (Ed.), *Infant stimulation: For whom, what kind, when, and how much?* (Johnson & Johnson Baby Products Company Pediatric Round Table Series No. 13). Skilman, NJ: Johnson & Johnson.

Horwitz, R. A. (1979). Psychological effects of the "open classroom." *Review of Educational Research, 49,* 71–86.

Howard, M., & McCabe, J. B. (1990). Helping teenagers postpone sexual involvement. *Family Planning Perspectives, 22,* 21–26.

Howe, M. J. A. (1990). *Sense and nonsense about hothouse children: A practical guide for parents and teachers.* Leicester, UK: British Psychological Society.

Howe, P. E., & Schiller, M. (1952). Growth responses of the school child to changes in diet and environmental factors. *Journal of Applied Physiology, 5,* 51–61.

Howes, C. (1983). Patterns of friendship. *Child Development, 54,* 1041–1053.

Howes, C. (1987a). Peer interaction of young children. *Monographs of the Society for Research in Child Development, 53*(1, Serial No. 217).

Howes, C. (1987b). Social competence with peers in young children. *Developmental Review, 7,* 252–272.

Howes, C. (1990). Can age of entry and the quality of childcare predict adjustment in kindergarten? *Developmental Psychology, 26,* 292–303.

Howes, C., Phillips, D. A., & Whitebook, M. (1992). Thresholds of quality: Implications for the social development of children in center-based child care. *Child Development, 63,* 449–460.

Howes, C., Unger, O., & Seidner, L. B. (1989). Social pretend play in toddlers: Parallels with social play and with solitary pretend. *Child Development, 60,* 77–84.

Hoy, E. A., Sykes, D. H., Bill, J. M., Halliday, H. L., McClure, B. G., & Reid, M. McC. (1992). The social competence of very-low-birthweight children: Teacher, peer, and self-perception. *Journal of Abnormal Child Psychology, 20,* 123–150.

Hubel, D. H., & Wiesel, T. N. (1979, September). Brain mechanisms of vision. *Scientific American, 241,* pp. 150–162.

Huebner, A., & Garrod, A. (1991). Moral reasoning in a karmic world. *Human Development, 34,* 341–352.

Huesmann, L. R., Eron, L. D., Klein, R., Brice, P., & Fischer, P. (1983). Mitigating the imitation of aggressive behaviors by changing children's attitudes about media violence. *Journal of Personality and Social Psychology, 44,* 899–910.

Huesmann, L. R., Lagerspetz, K., & Eron, L. D. (1984). Intervening variables and the TV violence-aggression relation: Evidence from two countries. *Developmental Psychology, 20,* 746–775.

Hughes, C., & Russell, J. (1993). Autistic children's difficulty with mental disengagement from an object: Its implications for theories of autism. *Developmental Psychology, 29,* 498–510.

Humphrey, T. (1964). Some correlations between the appearance of human fetal reflexes and the development of the nervous system. *Progress in Brain Research, 4,* 93–133.

Humphreys, A. P., & Smith, P. K. (1987). Rough and tumble, friendship, and dominance in schoolchildren: Evidence for continuity and change with age. *Child Development, 58,* 201–212.

Hunt, C. E., & Brouillette, R. T. (1987). Sudden infant death syndrome: 1987 perspective. *Journal of Pediatrics, 110,* 669–678.

Huntsinger, P. W. (1959). Differences in speed between American Negro and white children in the performance of the 35-yard-dash. *Research Quarterly, 30,* 366–368.

Huston, A. C. (1983). Sex typing. In E. M. Hetherington (Ed.), *Handbook of child psychology: Vol. IV. Socialization, personality, and social development.* New York: Wiley.

Huston, A. C. (1985). The development of sex typing: Themes from recent research. *Developmental Review, 5,* 1–17.

Huston, A. C., & Alvarez, M. M. (1990). The socialization context of gender role development in early adolescence. In R. Montemayor, G. R. Adams, & T. P. Gullota (Eds.), *From childhood to adolescence: A transitional period?* Newbury Park, CA: Sage.

Huston, A. C., Watkins, B. A., & Kunkel, D. (1989). Public policy and children's television. *American Psychologist, 44,* 424–433.

Huston, A. C., Wright, J. C., Rice, M. L., Kerkman, D., & St. Peters, M. (1990). Development of television viewing patterns in early childhood: A longitudinal investigation. *Developmental Psychology, 26,* 409–420.

Huttenlocher, J., Haight, W., Bryk, A., Seltzer, M., & Lyons, T. (1991). Early vocabulary growth: Relation to language input and gender. *Developmental Psychology, 27,* 236–248.

Huttenlocher, P. R. (1990). Morphometric study of human cerebral cortex development. *Neuropsychologia, 28,* 517–527.

Hwang, P. (1987). The changing role of Swedish fathers. In M. E. Lamb (Ed.), *The father's role: Cross-cultural perspectives.* Hillsdale, NJ: Erlbaum.

Hyde, J. S. (1984). How large are gender differences in aggression? A developmental meta-analysis. *Developmental Psychology, 20,* 722–736.

Hyde, J. S. (1986). Gender differences in aggression. In J. S. Hyde & M. C. Linn (Eds.), *The psychology of gender: Advances through meta-analysis.* Baltimore: Johns Hopkins University Press.

Hyde, J. S., & Linn, M. C. (1988). Gender differences in verbal ability: A meta-analysis. *Psychological Bulletin, 104,* 53–69.

Hyde, J. S., Fennema, E., & Lamon, S. J. (1990). Gender differences in mathematics performance: A meta-analysis. *Psychological Bulletin, 107,* 139–155.

Hymel, S., & Franke, S. (1985). Children's peer relations: Assessing self-perceptions. In B. H. Schneider, K. H. Rubin, & J. E. Ledingham (Eds.), *Children's peer relations: Issues in assessment and intervention.* New York: Springer-Verlag.

Hymel, S., & Rubin, K. H. (1985). Children with peer relationship and social skills problems: Conceptual, methodological, and developmental issues. In G. J. Whitehurst (Ed.), *Annals of child development* (Vol. 2). Greenwich, CT: JAI Press.

Hymel, S., Wagner, E., & Butler, L. J. (1990). Reputational bias: Views from the peer group. In S. R. Asher & J. D. Coie (Eds.), *Peer rejection in childhood.* Cambridge, UK: Cambridge University Press.

Indacochea, F. J., & Scott, G. B. (1992). HIV-1 infection and the acquired immunodeficiency syndrome in children. *Current Problems in Pediatrics, 22,* 166–204.

Inhelder, B., & Piaget, J. (1958). *The growth of logical thinking from childhood to adolescence.* New York: Basic Books.

Inhelder, B., & Piaget, J. (1964). *The early growth of logic in the child: Classification and seriation.* London: Routledge.

International Association for the Evaluation of Educational Achievement. (1988). *Science achievement in seventeen countries: A preliminary report.* Exeter, England: Pergamon Press.

Isabella, R. A. (1993). Origins of attachment: Maternal interactive behavior across the first year. *Child Development, 64,* 605–621.

Isabella, R. A., Belsky, J., & von Eye, A. (1989). Origins of infant-mother attachment: An examination of interactional synchrony during the infant's first year. *Developmental Psychology, 25,* 12–21.

Isensee, W. (1986, September 3). *The Chronicle of Higher Education, 33.*

Ishii-Kuntz, M., & Coltrane, S. (1992). Predicting the sharing of household labor: Are parenting and housework distinct? *Sociological Perspectives, 35,* 629–647.

Izard, C. E. (1978). On the ontogenesis of emotions and emotion-cognition relationships in infancy. In M. Lewis & L. A. Rosenblum (Eds.), *The development of affect.* New York: Plenum Press.

Izard, C. E., & Dougherty, L. M. (1982). Two complementary systems for measuring facial expressions in infants and children. In C. E. Izard (Ed.), *Measuring emotions in infants and children* (Vol. 1). Cambridge: Cambridge University Press.

Izard, C. E., & Malatesta, C. Z. (1987). Perspectives on emotional development: I. Differential emotions theory of early emotional development. In J. D. Osofsky (Ed.), *Handbook of infant development* (2nd ed.). New York: Wiley.

Izard, C. E., Haynes, O. M., Chisolm, G., & Baak, K. (1991). Emotional determinants of infant-mother attachment. *Child Development, 62,* 906–917.

Izard, C. E., Huebner, R. R., Risser, D., McGinnes, G., & Dougherty, L. (1980). The young infant's ability to produce discrete emotion expressions. *Developmental Psychology, 16*, 132–140.

Izard, C. E., Kagan, J., & Zajonc, R. B. (1984). Introduction. In C. E. Izard, J. Kagan, & R. B. Zajonc (Eds.), *Emotions, cognition, and behavior.* Cambridge: Cambridge University Press.

Jacklin, C. N. (1989). Female and male: Issues of gender. *American Psychologist, 44*, 127–133.

Jacklin, C. N., & Maccoby, E. E. (1978). Social behavior at thirty-three months in same-sex and mixed-sex dyads. *Child Development, 49*, 557–569.

Jacklin, C. N., DiPietro, J. A., & Maccoby, E. E. (1984). Sex-typing behavior and sex-typing pressure in child/parent interaction. *Archives of Sexual Behavior, 13*, 413–425.

Jacklin, C. N., Maccoby, E. E., & Doering, C. H. (1983). Neonatal sex-steroid hormones and timidity in 6–18 month-old boys and girls. *Developmental Psychobiology, 16*, 163–168.

Jacklin, C. N., Maccoby, E. E., Doering, C. H., & King, D. (1984). Neonatal sex-steroid hormones and muscular strength of boys and girls in the first three years. *Developmental Psychobiology, 17*, 301–310.

Jacklin, C. N., Wilcox, K. T., & Maccoby, E. E. (1988). Neonatal sex-steroid hormones and cognitive abilities at six years. *Developmental Psychobiology, 21*, 567–574.

Jackson, A. W., & Hornbeck, D. W. (1989). Educating young adolescents: Why we must restructure middle grade schools. *American Psychologist, 44*, 831–836.

Jackson, J. F. (1993). Human behavioral genetics, Scarr's theory, and her views on interventions: A critical review and commentary on their implications for African American children. *Child Development, 64*, 1318-1332.

Jackson, N. E. (1988). Precocious reading ability: What does it mean? *Gifted Child Quarterly, 32*, 200–204.

Jackson, S. (1987). Great Britain. In M. E. Lamb (Ed.), *The father's role: Cross-cultural perspectives.* Hillsdale, NJ: Erlbaum.

Jacobson, S. W. (1979). Matching behavior in the young infant. *Child Development, 50*, 425–430.

Jacobson, S. W., & Frye, K. F. (1991). Effect of maternal social support on attachment: Experimental evidence. *Child Development, 62*, 572–582.

Jacobvitz, R. S., Wood, M., & Albin, K. (1989, April). *Cognitive skills and young children's comprehension of television.* Paper presented at the biennial meeting of the Society for Research in Child Development, Kansas City, MO.

Jakibchuk, Z., & Smeriglio, V. L. (1976). The influence of symbolic modeling on the social behavior of preschool children with low levels of social responsiveness. *Child Development, 47*, 838–841.

James, S. (1978). Effect of listener age and situation on the politeness of children's directives. *Journal of Psycholinguistic Research, 7*, 307–317.

James, W. (1890). *The principles of psychology.* New York: Henry Holt.

James, W. (1892). *Psychology: The briefer course.* New York: Henry Holt.

Jellife, D. B., & Jelliffe, E. F. P. (1992). Causation of kwashiorkor: Toward a multifactorial consensus. *Pediatric, 90*, 110–113.

Jencks, C. (1972). *Inequality: A reassessment of the effect of family and schooling in America.* New York: Basic Books.

Jensen, A. R. (1969). How much can we boost IQ and scholastic achievement? *Harvard Educational Review, 39*, 1–123.

Jensen, A. R. (1980). *Bias in mental testing.* New York: Free Press.

Jensen, A. R. (1982). The chronometry of intelligence. In R. J. Sternberg (Ed.), *Advances in the psychology of human intelligence* (Vol. 1). Hillsdale, NJ: Erlbaum.

Jensen, A. R., & Munroe, E. (1979). Reaction time, movement time, and intelligence. *Intelligence, 3*, 121–126.

Johnson, C. N., & Wellman, H. (1982). Children's developing conceptions of the mind and brain. *Child Development, 53*, 222–234.

Johnson, J., & Newport, E. (1989). Critical period effects in second language learning: The influence of maturational state on the acquisition of English as a second language. *Cognitive Psychology, 21*, 60–99.

Johnson, M. H. (1992). Imprinting and the development of face recognition: From chick to man. *Current Directions in Psychological Science, 1*, 52–55.

Johnson, M. H., Dziurawiec, S., Ellis, H. D., & Morton, J. (1991). Newborns' preferential tracking of face-like stimuli and its subsequent decline. *Cognition, 40*, 1–21.

Johnston, J. R., & Campbell, L. E. G. (1987). Instability in family networks of divorced and disputing parents. In E. J. Lawler & B. Markovsky (Eds.), *Advanced in group processes* (Vol. 4). Greenwich, CT: JAI.

Johnston, J., Ettema, J., & Davidson, T. (1980). *An evaluaton of "Freestyle": A television series to reduce sex role stereotypes.* Ann Arbor: Institute for Social Research.

Jones, G. P., & Dembo, M. H. (1989). Age and sex role differences in intimate friendships during childhood and adolescence. *Merrill-Palmer Quarterly, 35*, 445–462.

Jones, H. E., & Bayley, N. (1941). The Berkeley Growth Study. *Child Development, 12*, 167–173.

Jones, K. L., & Smith, D. W. (1973). Recognition of the fetal alcohol syndrome in early infancy. *Lancet, 2*, 999–1001.

Jones, L. V. (1984). White-black achievement differences: The narrowing gap. *American Psychologist, 39*, 1207–1213.

Jones, M. C. (1957). The later careers of boys who were early- or late-maturing. *Child Development, 28*, 113–128.

Jones, M. C. (1965). Psychological correlates of somatic development. *Child Development, 36*, 899–911.

*Journal of Applied Behavior Analysis, 25*, 289-305.

Jusczyk, P. W., Friederici, A. D., Wessels, J. M. I., Svenkerud, V. Y., & Jusczyk, A. M (1993). Infants' sensitivity to the sound patterns of native language words. *Journal of Memory and Language, 32*, 402–420.

Jusczyk, P. W., Hirsh-Pasek, K., Kemler Nelson, D. G., Kennedy, L. J., Woodward, A. & Piwoz, J. (1992). Perception of acoustic correlates of major phrasal units by young infants. *Cognitive Psychology, 24*, 252–293.

Juster, F. T. (1987). A note on recent changes in time use. In F. T. Juster & F. Stafford (Eds.), *Studies in the measurement of time allocation.* Ann Arbor: Institute for Social Research.

Juvonen, J. (1992). Negative peer reactions from the perspective of the reactor. *Journal of Educational Psychology, 84,* 314–321.

Kagan, J. (1976). Emergent themes in human development. *American Scientist, 64,* 186–196.

Kagan, J. (1981). *The second year: The emergence of self-awareness.* Cambridge, MA: Harvard University Press.

Kagan, J., Kearsley, R. B., & Zelazo, P. R. (1978). *Infancy: Its place in human development.* Cambridge: Cambridge University Press.

Kagan, J., Reznick, J. S., & Snidman, N. (1988). Biological basis of childhood shyness. *Science, 240,* 167–171.

Kagan, J., Reznick, J. S., Clarke, C., Snidman, N., & Garcia-Coll, C. (1984). Behavioral inhibition to the unfamiliar. *Child Development, 55,* 2212–2225.

Kagan, J., Snidman, N., & Arcus, D. M. (1992). Initial reactions to unfamiliarity. *Current Directions in Psychological Science, 1,* 171-174.

Kahn, P. H., Jr., (1992). Children's obligatory and discretionary moral judgments. *Child Development, 63,* 416–430.

Kahneman, D. (1973). *Attention and effort.* Englewood Cliffs, NJ: Prentice-Hall.

Kail, R. (1986). Sources of age differences in speed of processing. *Child Development, 57,* 969–987.

Kail, R. (1990). *The development of memory in children* (3rd ed.). New York: W. H. Freeman.

Kail, R. (1991a). Development of processing speed in childhood and adolescence. In H. W. Reese (Ed.), *Advances in child development and behavior* (Vol. 23). San Diego, CA: Academic Press.

Kail, R. (1991b). Processing time declines exponentially during childhood and adolescence. *Developmental Psychology, 27,* 259–266.

Kail, R., & Pellegrino, J. W. (1985). *Human intelligence: Perspectives and prospects.* New York: W. H. Freeman.

Kaitz, M., Lapidot, P., Bronner, R., & Eidelman, A. I. (1992). Parturient women can recognize their infants by touch. *Developmental Psychology, 28,* 35–39.

Kaitz, M., Meschulach-Sarfaty, O., Auerbach, J., & Eidelman, A. (1988). A reexamination of newborns' ability to imitate facial expressions. *Developmental Psychology, 24,* 3–7.

Kajii, T., Kida, M., & Takahashi, K. (1973). The effect of thalidomide intake during 113 human pregnancies. *Teratology, 8,* 163–166.

Kalil, R. E. (1989, December). Synapse formation in the developing brain. *Scientific American, 261,* pp. 76–85.

Kanner, L. (1943). Autistic disturbances of affective contact. *Nervous Children, 2,* 217–250.

Kaplan, H., & Dove, H. (1987). Infant development among the Ache of Eastern Paraguay. *Developmental Psychology, 23,* 190–196.

Karmel, B. Z., & Maisel, E. B. (1975). A neuronal activity model for infant visual attention. In L. B. Cohen & P. Salapatek (Eds.), *Infant perception: From sensation to cognition* (Vol. 1). New York: Academic Press.

Karniol, R. (1989). The role of manual manipulative stages in the infant's acquisition of perceived control over objects. *Developmental Review, 9,* 205–233.

Katz, P. A. & Ksansnak, K. R. (1994). Developmental aspects of gender role flexibility and traditionality in middle childhood and adolescence. *Developmental Psychology, 30,* 272–282.

Katz, P. A. (1987). Variations in family constellation: Effects on gender schemata. In L. S. Liben & M. L. Signorella (Eds.), *New directions for child development: No. 38. Children's gender schemata.* San Francisco: Jossey-Bass.

Kaufman, A. S., & Kaufman, N. L. (1983). *K-ABC administration and scoring manual.* Circle Pines, MN: American Guidance Service.

Kaufman, A. S., Kamphaus, R. W., & Kaufman, N. L. (1985). New directions in intelligence testing: The Kaufman Assessment Battery for Children (K-ABC). In B. B. Wolman (Ed.), *Handbook of intelligence.* New York: Wiley.

Kaye, K., & Marcus, J. (1981). Infant imitation: The sensorimotor agenda. *Developmental Psychology, 17,* 258–265.

Kazmeier, K. J., Keenan, W. J., & Sutherland, J. M. (1977). Effects of elevated bilirubin and phototherapy on infant behavior. *Pediatric Research, 11,* 563.

Keane, S. P., & Parrish, A. E. (1992). The role of affective information in the determination of intent. *Developmental Psychology, 28,* 159–162.

Keasey, C. B. (1971). Social participation as a factor in the moral development of preadolescents. *Developmental Psychology, 5,* 216–220.

Keating, D. P., & Clark, L. V. (1980). Development of physical and social reasoning in adolescence. *Developmental Psychology, 16,* 23–30.

Keeney, T. J., Cannizzo, S. R., & Flavell, J. H. (1967). Spontaneous and induced rehearsal in a recall task. *Child Development, 38,* 953–966.

Keil, F. C. (1989). *Concepts, kinds, and cognitive development.* Cambridge, MA: MIT Press.

Kelley, M. L., Power, T. G., & Wimbush, D. D. (1992). Determinants of disciplinary practices in low-income black mothers. *Child Development, 63,* 573–582.

Kellman, P. J., & Spelke, E. S. (1983). Perception of partly occluded objects in infancy. *Cognitive Psychology, 15,* 483–524.

Kellman, P. J., Spelke, E. S., & Short, K. (1986). Infant perception of object unity from transitory motion in depth and vertical translation. *Child Development, 57,* 72–86.

Kelly, M. H. (1992). Using sound to solve syntactic problems: The role of phonology in grammatical category assignments. *Psychological Review, 99,* 349–364.

Kennell, J., Klaus, M., McGrath, S., Robertson, S. & Hinkley, C. (1991). Continuous emotional support during labor in a U.S. hospital. *Journal of the American Medical Associaton, 265,* 2197–2201.

Keogh, J., & Sugden, D. (1985). *Movement skill development.* New York: Macmillan.

Kerig, P. K., Cowan, P. A., & Cowan, C. P. (1993). Marital quality and gender differences in parent-child interaction. *Developmental Psychology, 29,* 931–939.

Kerlinger, F. N. (1964). *Foundations of behavioral research: Educational and psychological inquiry.* New York: Holt, Rinehart & Winston.

Kermani, E. J. (1992). Issues of child custody and our moral values in the era of new medical technology. *Journal of the American Academy of Child and Adolescent Psychiatry, 31,* 533-539.

Kerns, L. L., & Davis, G. P. (1986). Psychotropic drugs in pregnancy. In I. J. Chasnoff (Ed.), *Drug use in pregnancy: Mother and child.* Lancaster, England: MTP Press.

Kester, P. A. (1984). Effects of prenatally administered 17-alpha-hydroxyprogesterone caproate on adolescent males. *Archives of Sexual Behavior, 13,* 441–455.

Khayrallah, M., & Van Den Meiraker, M. (1987). LOGO programming and the acquisition of cognitive skills. *Journal of Computer-Based Instruction, 14,* 133–137.

Kindermann, T. A. (1993). Natural peer groups as contexts for individual development: The case of children's motivation in school. *Developmental Psychology, 29,* 970–977.

Kinsbourne, M., & Hiscock, M. (1983). The normal and deviant development of functional lateralization of the brain. In M. M. Haith & J. C. Campos (Eds.), *Infancy and developmental psychobiology: Vol. II. Handbook of child psychology.* New York: Wiley.

Kirkpatrick, S. W., & Sanders, D. M. (1978). Body image stereotypes: A developmental comparison. *Journal of Genetic Psychology, 132,* 87–95.

Kisilevsky, B. S., & Muir, D. W. (1991). Human fetal and subsequent newborn responses to sound and vibration. *Infant Behavior and Development, 14,* 1–26.

Kisilevsky, B. S., Muir, D. W., & Low, J. A. (1992). Maturation of human fetal responses to vibroacoustic stimulation. *Child Development, 63,* 1497–1508.

Kitchen, W. H., Ford, G. W., Rickards, A. L., Lissenden, J. V., & Ryan, M. M. (1987). Children of birth weight <1000 g: Changing outcome between ages 2 and 5 years. *Journal of Pediatrics, 110,* 283–288.

Klahr, D. (1978). Goal formation, planning, and learning by preschool problem solvers or: "My socks are in the dryer." In R. S. Siegler (Ed.), *Children's thinking: What develops?* Hillsdale, NJ: Erlbaum.

Klahr, D. (1989). Information-processing approaches. In R. Vasta (Ed.), *Annals of child development: Vol 6. Six theories of child development: Revised formulations and current issues.* Greenwich, CT: JAI Press.

Klahr, D., & Robinson, M. (1981). Formal assessment of problem solving and planning processes in preschool children. *Cognitive Psychology, 13,* 113–148.

Klaus, M., & Kennell, J. (1976). *Maternal infant bonding.* St. Louis: C. V. Mosby.

Klaus, M., & Kennell, J. (1982). *Parent-infant bonding.* St. Louis: C. V. Mosby.

Kleinman, J. C., Pierre, M. B., Madans, J. H., Land, G. H., & Schramm, W. F. (1988). The effects of maternal smoking on fetal and infant mortality. *American Journal of Epidemiology, 127,* 274–282.

Kleitman, N. (1963). *Sleep and wakefulness.* Chicago: University of Chicago Press.

Klima, E. S., & Bellugi, U. (1966). Syntactic regularities in the speech of children. In J. Lyons & R. J. Wales (Eds.), *Psycholinguistic papers: The proceedings of the 1966 Edinburgh conference.* Edinburgh: Edinburgh University Press.

Kline, J., Shrout, P., Stein, Z., Susser, M., & Warburton, D. (1980). Drinking during pregnancy and spontaneous abortion. *Lancet, 2,* 176–180.

Kline, M., Tschann, J. M., Johnston, J. R., & Wallerstein, J. S. (1989). Children's adjustment in joint and sole physical custody families. *Developmental Psychology, 25,* 430–438.

Knoppers, B. M., & LeBris, S. (1991). Recent advances in medically assisted conception: Legal, ethical, and social issues. *American Journal of Law and Medicine, 17,* 329-361.

Knowles, R. V. (1985). *Genetics, society and decisions.* Columbus, OH: Merrill.

Kobak, R. R., Cole, H. E., Ferenz-Gillies, R., & Fleming, W. S. (1993). Attachment and emotion regulation during mother-teen problem-solving: A control theory analysis. *Child Development, 64,* 231–245.

Kobasigawa, A. (1968). Inhibitory and disinhibitory effects of models on sex-inappropriate behavior in children. *Psychologia, 11,* 86–96.

Kobasigawa, A. (1974). Utilization of retrieval cues by children in recall. *Child Development, 45,* 127–134.

Kobayashi-Winata, H., & Power, T. G. (1989). Child rearing and compliance: Japanese and American families in Houston. *Journal of Cross-Cultural Psychology, 20,* 333–356.

Kochanska, G. (1993). Toward a synthesis of parental socialization and child temperament in early development of conscience. *Child Development, 64,* 325–347.

Koff, E., Rierdan, J., & Sheingold, K. (1982). Memories of menarche: Age, preparation, and prior knowledge as determinants of initial menstrual experience. *Journal of Youth and Adolescence, 11,* 1–9.

Kohlberg, L. (1958). *The development of modes of moral thinking and choice in the years 10 to 16.* Unpublished doctoral dissertation, University of Chicago.

Kohlberg, L. (1969). Stage and sequence: The cognitive-developmental approach to socialization. In D. A. Goslin (Ed.), *The handbook of socialization theory and research.* Chicago: Rand McNally.

Kohlberg, L. (1976). Moral stages and moralization: The cognitive developmental approach. In T. Lickona (Ed.), *Moral development and moral behavior: Theory, research, and social issues.* New York: Holt, Rinehart & Winston.

Kohlberg, L. (1984). *Essays on moral development: Vol. 2. The psychology of moral development.* San Francisco: Harper & Row.

Kohlberg, L. A. (1966). A cognitive-developmental analysis of children's sex-role concepts and attitudes. In E. E. Maccoby (Ed.), *The development of sex differences.* Stanford, CA: Stanford University Press.

Kohlberg, L., & Kramer, R. (1969). Continuities and discontinuities in childhood moral development. *Human Development, 12,* 93–120.

Kohlberg, L., Levine, C., & Hewer, A. (1983). *Moral stages: A current formulation and a response to critics.* Basel: Karger.

Kohlberg, L., Yaeger, J., & Hjertholm, E. (1968). Private speech: Four studies and a review of theories. *Child Development, 45,* 127–134.

Kolb, B. (1989). Brain development, plasticity, and behavior. *American Psychologist, 44,* 1203–1212.

Koneya, M. (1976). Location and interaction in row-and-column seating arrangements. *Environment and Behavior, 8,* 265–282.

Kopp, C. B. (1979). Perspectives on infant motor system development. In M. Bornstein & W. Kessen (Eds.), *Psychological development from infancy.* Hillsdale, NJ: Erlbaum.

Kopp, C. B. (1982). The antecedents of self-regulation: A developmental perspective. *Developmental Psychology, 18,* 199–214.

Kopp, C. B. (1987). The growth of self-regulation: Caregivers and children. In N. Eisenberg (Ed.), *Contemporary topics in developmental psychology.* New York: Wiley.

Kopp, C. B., & McCall, R. B. (1980). Stability and instability in mental performance among normal, at-risk, and handicapped infants and children. In P. B. Baltes & O. G. Grim, Jr. (Eds.), *Life-span development and behavior* (Vol. 4). New York: Academic Press.

Korner, A. F. (1972). State as a variable, as obstacle, and mediator of stimulation in infant research. *Merrill-Palmer Quarterly, 18,* 77–94.

Korner, A. F. (1987). Preventive intervention with high-risk newborns: Theoretical, conceptual, and methodological perspectives. In J. D. Osofsky (Ed.), *Handbook of infant development* (2nd ed.). New York: Wiley.

Korner, A. F., Schneider, P., & Forrest, T. (1983). Effects of vestibular-proprioceptive stimulation on the neurobehavioral development of preterm infants: A pilot study. *Neuropediatrics, 14,* 170–175.

Kotelchuk, M. (1975, August). *Father caretaking characteristics and their influence on infant-father interactions.* Paper presented at the meeting of the American Psychological Association, Chicago.

Kotelchuk, M. (1976). The infant's relationship to the father: Experimental evidence. In M. E. Lamb (Ed.), *The role of the father in child development.* New York: Wiley.

Kraemer, H. C., Korner, A., Anders, T., Jacklin, C. N., & Dimiceli, S. (1985). Obstetric drugs and infant behavior: A re-evaluation. *Journal of Pediatric Psychology, 10,* 345–353.

Krafchuk, E. E., Tronick, E. Z., & Clifton, R. K. (1983). Behavioral and cardiac responses to sound in preterm infants varying in risk status: A hypothesis of their paradoxical reactivity. In T. Field & A. Sostek (Eds.), *Infants born at risk: Physiological, perceptual, and cognitive processes.* New York: Grune & Stratton.

Krauss, R. H., & Glucksberg, S. (1969). The development of communication. *Child Development, 40,* 255–266.

Krebs, D., & Gilmore, J. (1982). The relationship among the first stages of cognitive development, role taking abilities, and moral development. *Child Development, 53,* 877–886.

Kremenitzer, J. P., Vaughan, H. G., Kurtzberg, D., & Dowling, K. (1979). Smooth-pursuit eye movements in the newborn infant. *Child Development, 50,* 442–448.

Kreutzer, M. A., Leonard, S. C., & Flavell, J. H. (1975). An interview study of children's knowledge about memory. *Monographs of the Society for Research in Child Development, 40*(1, Serial No. 159).

Krogman, W. M. (1972). *Child growth.* Ann Arbor, MI: University of Michigan Press.

Kroll, J. (1977). The concept of childhood in the Middle Ages. *Journal of the History of the Behavioral Sciences, 13,* 384–393.

Krumhansl, C. L., & Jusczyk, P. W. (1990). Infants' perception of phrase structure in music. *Psychological Science, 1,* 70–73.

Kuchuk, A., Vibbert, M., & Bornstein, M. H. (1986). The perception of smiling and its experiential correlates in three-month-old infants. *Child Development, 57,* 1054–1061.

Kuczaj, S. A., Borys, R. H., & Jones, M. (1989). On the interaction of language and thought: Some thoughts and developmental data. In A. Gellatly, D. Rogers, & J. A. Sloboda (Eds.), *Cognition and social worlds.* Oxford: Clarendon Press.

Kuczynski, L., Kochanska, G., Radke-Yarrow, M., & Girnius-Brown, O. (1987). A developmental interpretation of young children's noncompliance. *Developmental Psychology, 23,* 799–806.

Kuczynski, L., Zahn-Waxler, C., & Radke-Yarrow, M. (1987). Development and content of imitation in the second and third year of life: A socialization perspective. *Developmental Psychology, 23,* 276–282.

Kugelmass, S., & Breznitz, S. (1967). The development of intentionality in moral judgment in city and kibbutz adolescents. *Journal of Genetic Psychology, 111,* 103–111.

Kuhl, P. K. (1987). Perception of speech and sound in early infancy. In P. Salapatek & L. Cohen (Eds.), *Handbook of infant perception: From perception to cognition* (Vol. 2). Orlando, FL: Academic Press.

Kuhl, P. K., & Meltzoff, A. N. (1988). Speech as an intermodal object of perception. In A. Yonas (Ed.), *Minnesota symposia on child psychology: Vol. 20. The development of perception.* Hillsdale, NJ: Erlbaum.

Kuhl, P. K., & Miller, J. D. (1978). Speech perception by the chinchilla: Identification functions for synthetic VOT stimuli. *Journal of the Acoustical Society of America, 63,* 905–917.

Kuhl, P. K., & Padden, D. M. (1983). Enhanced discriminability at the phonetic boundary for the place feature in macaques. *Journal of the Acoustical Society of America, 73,* 1003–1010.

Kuhl, P. K., Williams, K. A., Lacerda, F., Stevens, K. N., & Lindblom, B. (1992). Linguistic experience alters phonetic perception in infants by 6 months of age. *Science, 255,* 606–608.

Kuhn, D., Nash, S. C., & Brucken, L. (1978). Sex role concepts of two- and three-year-olds. *Child Development, 49,* 445–451.

Kulik, J. A., Bangert, R. L., & Williams, G. W. (1983). Effects of computer-based teaching on secondary school students. *Journal of Educational Psychology, 75,* 19–26.

Kulik, J. A., Kulik, C. C., & Bangert-Drowns, R. L. (1985). Effectiveness of computer-based education in elementary schools. *Computers in Human Behavior, 1,* 59–74.

Kunkel, D., & Roberts, D. (1991). Young minds and marketplace values: Issues in children's television advertising. *Journal of Social Issues, 47,* 57–72.

Kupersmidt, J. B. (1983, April). Predicting delinquency and academic problems from childhood peer status. In J. D. Coie (Chair), *Strategies for identifying children at social risk: Longitudinal correlates and consequences.* Symposium conducted at the biennial meeting of the Society for Research in Child Development, Detroit.

Kurdek, L. A. (1978). Perspective-taking as the cognitive basis of children's moral development: A review of the literature. *Merrill-Palmer Quarterly, 24,* 3–28.

Kurdek, L. A. (1989). Siblings' reactions to parental divorce. *Journal of Divorce, 12,* 203–219.

Kurdek, L. A., & Berg, B. (1983). Correlates of children's adjustments to their parents' divorces. In L. A. Kurdek (Ed.), *New directions for child development: No. 19. Children and divorce.* San Francisco: Jossey-Bass.

Kurtines, W., & Greif, E. B. (1974). The development of moral thought: Review and evaluation of Kohlberg's approach. *Psychological Bulletin, 81,* 453–470.

La Greca, A. M., & Santogrossi, D. A. (1980). Social skills training with elementary school students: A behavioral group approach. *Journal of Consulting and Clinical Psychology, 48,* 220–227.

LaBarbera, J. D., Izard, C. E., Vietze, P., & Parisi, S. A. (1976). Four- and six-month-old infants' visual responses to joy, anger, and neutral expressions. *Child Development, 47,* 535–538.

LaFreniere, P., & Charlesworth, W. R. (1983). Dominance, attention, and affiliation in a preschool group: A nine-month longitudinal study. *Ethology and Sociobiology, 4,* 55–67.

Lackey, P. N. (1989). Adults' attitudes about assignments of household chores to male and female children. *Sex Roles, 20,* 271–281.

Ladd, G. W. (1983). Social networks of popular, average, and rejected children in school settings. *Merrill-Palmer Quartlerly, 29,* 283–307.

Ladd, G. W. (1989, April). *Children's friendships in the classroom: Precursors of early school adaptation.* Paper presented at the biennial meeting of the Society for Research in Child Development, Kansas City, MO.

Ladd, G. W. (1990). Having friends, keeping friends, making friends, and being liked by peers in the classroom: Predictors of children's early school adjustment? *Child Development, 61,* 1081–1100.

Ladd, G. W., & Asher, S. R. (1985). Social skill training and children's peer relations. In L. L'Abate & M. Milan (Eds.), *Handbook of social skills training.* New York: Wiley.

Ladd, G. W., & Golter, B. S. (1988). Parents' management of preschooler's peer relations: Is it related to children's social competencies? *Developmental Psychology, 24,* 109–117.

Ladd, G. W., & Hart, C. H. (1992). Creating informal play opportunities: Are parents' and preschoolers' initiations related to children's competence with peers? *Developmental Psychology, 28,* 1179–1187.

Ladd, G. W., & Price, J. M. (1987). Predicting children's social and school adjustment following the transition from preschool to kindergarten. *Child Development, 58,* 1168–1189.

Ladd, G. W., Price, J. M., & Hart, C. H. (1988). Predicting preschoolers' peer status from their playground behaviors. *Child Development, 59,* 986–992.

Lahey, B. B., Hammer, D., Crumrine, P. L., & Forehand, R. L. (1980). Birth order sex interactions in child behavior problems. *Developmental Psychology, 16,* 608–615.

Lamaze, F. (1970). *Painless childbirth: Psychoprophylactic method.* Chicago: Henry Regnery.

Lamb, M. E. (1976). *The role of the father in child development.* New York: Wiley.

Lamb, M. E. (1981). *The role of the father in child development* (rev. ed.). New York: Wiley.

Lamb, M. E. (1987). Introduction: The emergent American father. In M. E. Lamb (Ed.), *The father's role: Cross-cultural perspectives.* Hillsdale, NJ: Erlbaum.

Lamb, M. E., & Nash, A. (1989). Infant-mother attachment, sociability, and peer competence. In T. J. Berndt & G. W. Ladd (Eds.), *Peer relationships in child development.* New York: Wiley.

Lamb, M. E., & Roopnarine, J. L. (1979). Peer influences on sex-role development in preschoolers. *Child Development, 50,* 1219–1222.

Lamb, M. E., Easterbrooks, M. A., & Holden, G. (1980). Reinforcement and punishment among preschoolers: Characteristics and correlates. *Child Development, 51,* 1230–1236.

Lamb, M. E., Pleck, J. H., Charnov, E. L., & Levine, J. A. (1987). A biosocial perspective on paternal behavior and involvement. In J. B. Lancaster, J. Altmann, A. S. Rossi, & L. R. Sherrod (Eds.), *Parenting across the life span: Biosocial dimensions.* New York: Aldine de Gruyter.

Lamb, M. E., Thompson, R. A., Gardner, W., & Charnov, E. L. (1985). *Infant-mother attachment: The origins and developmental significance of individual differences in strange situation behavior.* Hillsdale, NJ: Erlbaum.

Lamb, S. (1991). First moral sense: Aspects of and contributors to a beginning morality in the second year of life. In W. M. Kurtines & J. L. Gewirtz (Eds.), *Handbook of moral behavior and development: Vol. 2. Research.* Hillsdale, NJ: Erlbaum.

Lamborn, S. D., Mounts, N. S., Steinberg, L., & Dornbusch, S. M. (1991). Patterns of competence and adjustment among adolescents from authoritative, authoritarian, indulgent, and neglectful families. *Child Development, 62,* 1049–1065.

Lampl, M., Veldhuis, J. D., & Johnson, M. L. (1992). Saltation and stasis: A model of human growth. *Science, 258,* 801–803.

Landau, S., Lorch, E. P., & Milich, R. (1992). Visual attention to and comprehension of television in attention-deficit hyperactivity disordered and normal boys. *Child Development, 63,* 928–937.

Landesman-Dwyer, S., Keller, L. S., & Streissguth, A. P. (1978). Naturalistic observations of newborns: Effects of maternal alcohol intake. *Alcoholism, 2,* 171–177.

Landesman-Dwyer, S., Ragozin, A. S., & Little, R. E. (1981). Behavioral correlates of prenatal alcohol exposure: A four-year follow-up study. *Neurobehavioral Toxicology and Teratology, 3,* 187–193.

Landry, S. H., Chapieski, M. L., Richardson, M. A., Palmer, J., & Hall, S. (1990). The social competence of children born prematurely: Effects of medical complications and parent behaviors. *Child Development, 61,* 1605–1616.

Lane, D. M., & Pearson, D. A. (1982). The development of selective attention. *Merrill-Palmer Quarterly, 28,* 317–345.

Langlois, J. H., & Downs, A. C. (1980). Mothers, fathers, and peers as socialization agents of sex-typed play behaviors in young children. *Child Development, 51,* 1237–1247.

Langlois, J. H., & Stephan, C. (1981). Beauty and the beast: The role of physical attractiveness in the development of peer relations and social behavior. In S. S. Brehm, S. H. Kassin, & F. X. Gibbons (Eds.), *Developmental social psychology.* New York: Oxford University Press.

Laosa, L. M. (1982). Families as facilitators of children's intellectual development at 3 years of age: A causal analysis. In L. M. Laosa & I. E. Sigel (Eds.), *Families as learning environments for children.* New York: Plenum Press.

Larkin, R. W. (1979). *Suburban youth in cultural crisis.* New York: Oxford University Press.

Larson, R., & Ham, M. (1993). Stress and "storm and stress" in early adolescence: The relationship of negative events with dysphoric affect. *Developmental Psychology, 29,* 130–140.

Larson, R., & Lampman-Petraitis, C. (1989). Daily emotional stress as reported by children and adolescents. *Child Development, 60,* 1250–1260.

Lask, B., & Bryant-Waugh, R. (1991). Early-onset anorexia nervosa and related eating disorders. *Journal of Child Psychology and Psychiatry, 33,* 281–300.

Laupa, M. (1991). Children's reasoning about three authority attributes: Adult status, knowledge, and social position. *Developmental Psychology, 27,* 321–329.

Lauritzen, P. (1990). What price parenthood? *The Hastings Center Report, 20,* 38–46.

Law, C. M. (1987). The disability of short stature. *Archives of Disease in Childhood, 62,* 855–859.

Lawrence, R. A. (1983). Early mothering by adolescents. In E. R. McAnarney (Ed.), *Premature adolescent pregnancy and parenthood,* New York: Grune & Stratton.

Lawson, M. (1980). Development of body build stereotypes, peer ratings, and self-esteem in Australian children. *Journal of Psychology, 104,* 111–118.

Lazar, I., & Darlington, R. (1982). Lasting effects of early education: A report from the Consortium for Longitudinal Studies. *Monographs of the Society for Research in Child Development, 47*(2–3, Serial No. 195).

LeBoyer, F. (1975). *Birth without violoence.* New York: Knopf.

Lee, L. C. (1971). The concommitant development of cognitive and moral modes of thought: A test of selected deductions from Piaget's theory. *Genetic Psychology Monographs, 83,* 93–146.

Lee, R. V. (1988). Sexually transmitted infections. In G. N. Burrow & T. F. Ferris (Eds.), *Medical complications during pregnancy.* Philadelphia: W. B. Saunders.

Lee, V. E., Brooks-Gunn, J., & Schnur, E. (1988). Does Head Start work? A 1-year follow-up comparison of disadvantaged children attending Head Start, no preschool, and other preschool programs. *Developmental Psychology, 24,* 210–222.

Lee, V. E., Brooks-Gunn, J., Schnur, E., & Liaw, F. (1990). Are Head Start effects sustained? A longitudinal follow-up comparison of disadvantaged children attending Head Start, no preschool, and other preschool programs. *Child Development, 61,* 495–507.

Lefkowitz, M. M. (1981). Smoking during pregnancy: Long-term effects on offspring. *Developmental Psychology, 17,* 192–194.

Leinbach, M. D., & Fagot, B. I. (1986). Acquisition of gender labels: A test for toddlers. *Sex Roles, 15,* 655–666.

Lemish, D., & Rice, M. (1986). Television as a talking picture book: A prop for language acquisition. *Journal of Child Language, 13,* 251–274.

Lempers, J. D., Flavell, E. R., & Flavell, J. H. (1977). The development in very young children of tacit knowledge concerning visual perception. *Genetic Psychology Monographs, 95,* 3–53.

Lempert, H. (1989). Animacy constraints on preschool children's acquisition of syntax. *Child Development, 60,* 237–245.

Lenke, R. R., & Levy, H. L. (1982). Maternal phenylketonuria—results of dietary therapy. *Journal of Obstetrics and Gynecology, 142,* 548–553.

Lenneberg, E. (1967). *Biological foundations of language.* New York: Wiley.

Lennon, R. T. (1985). Group tests of intelligence. In B. B. Wolman (Ed.), *Handbook of intelligence.* New York: Wiley.

Lennon, R., & Eisenberg, N. (1987). Emotional displays associated with preschoolers' prosocial behavior. *Child Development, 58,* 992–1000.

Lepper, M. R., & Gurtner, J. (1989). Children and computers: Approaching the twenty-first century. *American Psychologist, 44,* 170–178.

Lerner, R. M., & Lerner, J. V. (1977). Effects of age, sex, and physical attractiveness on child-peer relations, academic performance, and elementary school adjustment. *Developmental Psychology, 13,* 585–590.

Lerner, R. M., & Lerner, J. V. (1983). Temperament-intelligence reciprocities in early childhood: A contextual model. In M. Lewis (Ed.), *Origins of intelligence.* New York: Plenum Press.

Leslie, A. M. (1984). Spatiotemporal continuity and the perception of causality in infants. *Perception, 13,* 287–305.

Leslie, A. M., & Keeble, S. (1987). Do six-month-olds perceive causality? *Cognition, 25,* 265–288.

Leslie, A. M. (1982). The perception of causality in infants. *Perception, 11,* 15–30.

Lesser, G. S., Fifer, F., & Clark, D. H. (1965). Mental abilities of children of different social-class and cultural groups. *Monographs of the Society for Research in Child Development, 30*(4, Serial No. 102).

Lester, B. M., & Brazelton, T. B. (1982). Cross-cultural assessment of neonatal behavior. In D. Wagner & H. W. Stevenson (Eds.), *Cultural perspectives on child development.* San Francisco: W. H. Freeman.

Lester, B. M., & Dreher, M. (1989). Effects of marijuana use during pregnancy on newborn cry. *Child Development, 60,* 765–771.

Lester, B. M., Kotelchuk, M., Spelke, E., Sellers, M. J., & Klein, R. E. (1974). Separation protest in Guatemalan infants: Cross-cultural and cognitive findings. *Developmental Psychology, 10,* 79–85.

Levenson, R. L., Jr., Mellins, C. A., Zawadzki, R., Kairam, R., & Stein, Z. (1992). Cognitive assessment of human immunodeficiency virus-exposed children. *American Journal of Diseases in Children, 146,* 1479–1483.

Levine, R., & White, M. (1986). *Human conditions: The cultural basis for educational development.* New York: Routledge & Kegan Paul.

Levine, S. C., Jordan, N. C., & Huttenlocher, J. (1992). Development of calculation abilities in young children. *Journal of Experimental Child Psychology, 53,* 72–103.

Levitt, M. J., Guacci-Franco, N., & Levitt, J. L. (1993). Convoys of social support in childhood and early adolescence: Structure and function. *Developmental Psychology, 29,* 811-818.

Lewis, M. (1969). Infants' responses to facial stimuli during the first year of life. *Developmental Psychology, 1,* 75–86.

Lewis, M. (1983). On the nature of intelligence. In M. Lewis (Ed.), *Origins of intelligence.* New York: Plenum Press.

Lewis, M. (1989, April). *Self and self-conscious emotions.* Paper presented at the biennial meeting of the Society for Research in Child Development, Kansas City, MO.

Lewis, M. (1990). Social knowledge and social development. *Merrill-Palmer Quarterly, 36,* 93–116.

Lewis, M. L. (1993). Early socioemotional predictors of cognitive competency at 4 years. *Developmental Psychology, 29,* 1036–1045.

Lewis, M., & Brooks-Gunn, J. (1979). *Social cognition and the acquisition of self.* New York: Plenum Press.

Lewis, M., & Brooks-Gunn, J. (1981). Visual attention at three months as a predictor of cognitive functioning at two years of age. *Intelligence, 5,* 131–140.

Lewis, M., & Feiring, C. (1982). Some American families at dinner. In L. M. Laosa & I. E. Sigel (Eds.), *Families as learning environments for children.* New York: Plenum Press.

Lewis, M., & Freedle, R. O. (1973). Mother-infant dyad: The cradle of meaning. In P. Pilner, L. Krames, & T. Alloway (Eds.), *Communication and affect: Language and thought.* New York: Academic Press.

Lewis, M., & Michalson, L. (1983). *Children's emotions and moods: Developmental theory and measurement.* New York: Plenum Press.

Lewis, M., & Saarni, C. (1985). Culture and emotions. In M. Lewis & C. Saarni (Eds.), *The socialization of emotions.* New York: Plenum Press.

Lewis, M., & Weinraub, M. (1974). Sex of parent versus sex of child: Socio-emotional development. In R. C. Friedman, R. M. Riehart, & R. Vande Wiele (Eds.), *Sex differences in behavior.* New York: Wiley.

Lewis, M., Sullivan, M. W., Stanger, C., & Weiss, M. (1989). Self development and self-conscious emotions. *Child Development, 60,* 146–156.

Lewis, P. (1983). Drug usage in pregnancy. In P. Lewis (Ed.), *Clinical pharmacology in obstetrics.* Boston: Wright-PSG.

Lewis, T. L., Maurer, D., & Kay, D. (1978). Newborns' central vision: Whole or hole? *Journal of Experimental Child Psychology, 26,* 193–203.

Lewkowicz, D. J. (1988a). Sensory dominance in infants: 1. Six-month-old infants' response to auditory-visual compounds. *Developmental Psychology, 24,* 155–171.

Lewkowicz, D. J. (1988b). Sensory dominance in infants: 2. Ten-month-old infants' response to auditory-visual compounds. *Developmental Psychology, 24,* 172–182.

Liben, L. S., & Downs, R. M. (1993). Understanding person-space-map relations: Cartographic and developmental perspectives. *Developmental Psychology, 29,* 739–752.

Lickona, T. (1976). Research on Piaget's theory of moral development. In T. Lickona (Ed.), *Moral development and behavior: Theory, research, and social issues.* New York: Holt, Rinehart & Winston.

Lieberman, D. (1985). Research on children and microcomputers: A review of utilization and effect studies. In M. Chen & W. Paisley (Eds.), *Children and microcomputers: Research on the newest medium.* Beverly Hills: Sage.

Liebert, R. M., & Sprafkin, J. (1988). *The early window: Effects of television on children and youth* (3rd ed.). New York: Pergamon Press.

Liggon, C., Weston, J., Ambady, N., Colloton, M., Rosenthal, R., & Reite, M. (1992). Content-free voice analysis of mothers talking about their failure-to-thrive children. *Infant Behavior and Development, 15,* 507–511.

Lightfoot, D. (1982). *The language lottery: Toward a biology of grammars.* Cambridge, MA: MIT Press.

Lillard, A. S., & Flavell, J. H. (1990). Young children's preference for mental state versus behavioral descriptions of human action. *Child Development, 61,* 731–741.

Lillard, A. S., & Flavell, J. H. (1992). Young children's understanding of different mental states. *Developmental Psychology, 28,* 626–634.

Lin, C. C., & Fu, V. R. (1990). A comparison of child-rearing practices among Chinese, immigrant Chinese, and Caucasian-American parents. *Child Development, 61,* 429–433.

Linden, M. G., Bender, B. G., Harmon, R. J., Mrazek, D. A., & Robinson, A. (1988). 47,XXX: What is the prognosis? *Pediatrics, 82,* 619–630.

Linn, M. C. (1985). Fostering equitable consequences from computer learning environments. *Sex Roles, 13,* 229–240.

Linn, M. C., & Petersen, A. C. (1985). Emergence and characterization of sex differences in spatial ability: A meta-analysis. *Child Development, 56,* 1479–1498.

Linn, M. C., & Petersen, A. C. (1986). A meta-analysis of differences in spatial ability: Implications for mathematics and science achievement. In J. S. Hyde & M. C. Linn (Eds.), *The psychology of gender: Advances through meta-analysis.* Baltimore: Johns Hopkins University Press.

Linney, J. A., & Seidman, E. N. (1989). The future of schooling. *American Psychologist, 44,* 336–340.

Lipsitt, L. P. (1982). Infant learning. In T. M. Field, A. Huston, H. C. Quay, L. Troll, & G. E. Finley (Eds.), *Review of Human Development.* New York: Wiley.

Lipsitt, L. P., Engen, T., & Kaye, H. (1963). Developmental changes in the olfactory threshold of the neonate. *Child Development, 34,* 371–376.

Little, B. B., Snell, L. M., & Gilstrap, L. C., III. (1988). Methamphetamine abuse during pregnancy: Outcome and fetal effects. *Obstetrics and Gynecology, 72,* 541–544.

Livesley, W. J., & Bromley, D. B. (1973). *Person perception in childhood and adolescence.* London: Wiley.

Lobel, T. E., Bempechat, J., Gewirtz, J. C., Shoken-Tpaz, T., & Bashe, E. (1993). The role of gender-related information and self-endorsement of traits in preadolescents' inferences and judgments. *Child Development, 64,* 1285–1294.

Locke, J. (1961). *An essay concerning human understanding.* London: J. M. Dent and Sons. (Original work published 1690)

Locke, J. (1964). *Some thoughts concerning education.* In P. Gay (Ed.), *John Locke on education.* New York: Bureau of Publications, Teacher's College. (Original work published 1693)

Lockheed, M. E. (1985). Women, girls, and computers: A first look at the evidence. *Sex Roles, 13,* 115–122.

Lockman, J. J., & Thelen, E. (1993). Developmental biodynamics: Brain, body, behavior connections. *Child Development, 64,* 953–959.

Loeb, R. C., Horst, L., & Horton, P. J. (1980). Family interaction patterns associated with self-esteem in preadolescent girls and boys. *Merrill-Palmer Quarterly, 26,* 203–217.

Loehlin, J. C., Horn, J. M., & Willerman, L. (1990). Heredity, environment, and personality change: Evidence from the Texas Adoption Project. *Journal of Personality, 58,* 221-243.

Loehlin, J. C., Lindzey, G., & Spuhler, J. N. (1975). *Racial differences in intelligence.* San Francisco: W. H. Freeman.

Loehlin, J. C., Willerman, L., & Horn, J. M. (1988). Human behavior genetics. *Annual Review of Psychology, 39,* 101–133.

Long, N., & Forehand, R. (1987). The effects of parental divorce and marital conflict on children: An overview. *Journal of Developmental and Behavioral Pediatrics, 8,* 292–296.

Lorch, E. P., Bellack, D. R., & Augsbach, L. H. (1987). Young children's memory for televised stories: Effects of importance. *Child Development, 58,* 453–463.

Lorenz, K. Z. (1966). *On aggression* (M. K. Wilson, Trans.). New York: Harcourt, Brace, & World. (Original work published 1963)

Lovdal, L. T. (1989). Sex role messages in television commercials: An update. *Sex Roles, 21,* 715–724.

Lovegrove, W. L. (1991). The visual deficit hypothesis. In N. Singh & I. Beale (Eds.), *Progress in learning disabilities.* New York: Springer-Verlag.

Lowitzer, A. C. (1987). Maternal phenylketonuria: Cause for concern among women with PKU. *Research in Developmental Disabilities, 8,* 1–14.

Lozoff, B. (1983). Birth and "bonding" in non-industrialized societies. *Developmental Medicine and Child Neurology, 25,* 595–600.

Lucariello, J., Kyratzis, A., & Nelson, K. (1992). Taxonomic knowledge: What kind and when? *Child Development, 63,* 978–998.

Lummis, M., & Stevenson, H. W. (1990). Gender differences in beliefs and achievement: A cross-cultural study. *Developmental Psychology, 26,* 254–263.

Luria, A. R. (1961). *The role of speech in the regulation of normal and abnormal behavior.* New York: Liveright.

Luria, A. R. (1969). Speech and formation of mental processes. In M. Cole & I. Maltzman (Eds.), *A handbook of contemporary Soviet psychology.* New York: Basic Books.

Lutkenhaus, P., Bullock, M., & Geppert, U. (1987). Toddlers' actions: Knowledge, control, and the self. In F. Halisch & J. Kuhl (Eds.), *Motivation, intention, and volition.* Berlin: Springer.

Lykken, D. T. , McGue, M. Tellegen, A., & Bouchard, T. J., Jr. (1992). Emergenesis: Genetic traits that may not run in families. *American Psychologist, 47,* 1565–1577.

Lyon, T. D., & Flavell, J. H. (1993). Young children's understanding of forgetting over time. *Child Development, 64,* 789–800.

Lyons-Ruth, K., Alpern, L., & Repacholi, B. (1993). Disorganized infant attachment classification and maternal psychosocial problems as predictors of hostile-aggressive behavior in preschool children. *Child Development, 64,* 572–585.

Lytton, H., & Romney, D. M. (1991). Parents' differential socialization of boys and girls: A meta-analysis. *Psychological Bulletin, 109,* 267–296.

MacFarlane, J. A. (1975). Olfaction in the development of social preferences in the human neonate. In M. A. Hofer (Ed.), *Parent-infant interaction.* Amsterdam: Elsevier.

MacKinnon, C. E. (1988). Influences on sibling relations in families with married and divorced parents. *Journal of Social Issues, 9,* 469–477.

MacKinnon, C. E. (1989a). An observational investigation of sibling interactions in married and divorced families. *Developmental Psychology, 25,* 36–44.

MacKinnon, C. E. (1989b). Sibling interactions in married and divorced families: Influence of ordinal position, socioeconomic status, and play context. *Journal of Divorce, 12,* 221–251.

MacLeod, C. L., & Lee, R. V. (1988). Parasitic infections. In G. N. Burrow & T. F. Ferris (Eds.), *Medical complications during pregnancy.* Philadelphia: W. B. Saunders.

MacLusky, N. J., & Naftolin, F. (1981). Sexual differentiation of the nervous system. *Science, 211,* 1294–1303.

Maccoby, E. E. (1984a). Middle childhood in the context of the family. In W. A. Collins (Ed.), *Development during middle childhood: The years from six to twelve.* Washington, DC: National Academy Press.

Maccoby, E. E. (1984b). Socialization and developmental change. *Child Development, 55,* 317–328.

Maccoby, E. E. (1988). Gender as a social category. *Developmental Psychology, 24,* 755–765.

Maccoby, E. E. (1990). Gender and relationships: A developmental account. *American Psychologist, 45,* 513–520.

Maccoby, E. E., & Jacklin, C. N. (1974). *The psychology of sex differences.* Stanford, CA: Stanford University Press.

Maccoby, E. E., & Jacklin, C. N. (1980). Sex differences in aggression: A rejoinder and reprise. *Child Development, 51,* 964–980.

Maccoby, E. E., & Jacklin, C. N. (1987). Gender segregation in childhood. In H. W. Reese (Ed.), *Advances in child development and behavior* (Vol. 20). Orlando, FL: Academic Press.

Maccoby, E. E., & Martin, J. A. (1983). Socialization in the context of the family: Parent-child interaction. In E. M. Hetherington (Ed.), *Handbook of child psychology: Vol. IV. Socialization, personality, and social development.* New York: Wiley.

Macklin, R., & Delaney, S. R. (1991). Artificial means of reproduction and our understanding of the family. *The Hastings Center Report, 21,* 5-12.

Magnusson, D., Stattin, H., & Allen, V. (1986). Differential maturation among girls and its relations to social adjustment: A longitudinal perspective. In P. B. Baltes, D. L. Featherman, & R. M. Lerner (Eds.), *Life-span development and behavior* (Vol. 7). Hillsdale, NJ: Erlbaum.

Main, M., & Cassidy, J. (1988). Categories of response to reunion with the parent at age 6: Predictable from attachment classifications and stable over a 1-month period. *Developmental Psychology, 24,* 415–426.

Main, M., & Solomon, J. (1986). Discovery of a disorganized/disoriented attachment pattern. In T. B. Brazelton & M. W. Yogman (Eds.), *Affective development in infancy.* Norwood, NJ: Ablex.

Main, M., Kaplan, N., & Cassidy, J. (1985). Security in in-fancy, childhood, and adulthood: A move to the level of representation. In I. Bretherton & E. Waters (Eds.), *Growing points of attachment theory and research. Monographs of the Society for Research in Child Development, 50*(1–2, Serial No. 209).

Makin, J. W., & Porter, R. H. (1989). Attractiveness of lactating females' breast odors to neonates. *Child Development, 60,* 803–810.

Malatesta, C. Z., & Haviland, J. M. (1982). Learning display rules: The socialization of emotion expression in infancy. *Child Development, 53,* 991–1003.

Malatesta, C. Z., Culver, C., Tesman, J. R., & Shepard, B. (1989). The development of emotion expression during the first two years of life. *Monographs of the Society for Research in Child Development, 54*(1–2, Serial No. 219).

Malik, S. L., & Hauspic, R. C. (1986). Age at menarche among high altitude Bods of Ladakh (India). *Human Biology, 58,* 541–548.

Malina, R. M. (1975). *Growth and development: The first twenty years in man.* Minneapolis: Burgess.

Malina, R. M. (1980). Biosocial correlates of motor development during infancy and early childhood. In L. S. Greene & F. E. Johnstone (Eds.), *Social and biological predictors of nutritional status, physical growth, and neurological development.* New York: Academic Press.

Malinowski, B. (1927). *Sex and repression in savage society.* London: Routledge & Kegan Paul.

Mandler, J. (1992). How to build a baby: II. Conceptual primitives. *Psychological Review, 99,* 587-604.

Mandler, J. M. (1988). How to build a baby: On the development of an accessible representational system. *Cognitive Development, 3,* 113–136.

Mandler, J. M., Fivush, R., & Reznick, J. S. (1987). The development of contextual categories. *Cognitive Development, 2,* 339–354.

Mange, A. P., & Mange, E. J. (1990). *Genetics: Human aspects* (2nd ed.). Sunderland, MA: Sinauer.

Manis, F. R., Savage, P. L., Morrison, F. J., Horn, C. C., Howel, M. J., Szeszulski, P. A., & Holt, L. J. (1987). Paired associate learning in reading-disabled children: Evidence for a rule-learning deficiency. *Journal of Experimental Child Psychology, 43,* 25–43.

Mannarino, A. P. (1978). Friendship patterns and self-concept development in preadolescent males. *Journal of Genetic Psychology, 133,* 105–110.

Maratsos, M. P. (1983). Some current issues in the study of the acquisition of grammar. In J. H. Flavell & E. M. Markman (Eds.), *Handbook of child psychology: Vol. III. Cognitive development.* New York: Wiley.

Maratsos, M. P. (1989). Innateness and plasticity in language acquisition. In M. L. Rice & R. L. Schiefelbusch (Eds.), *The teachability of language.* Baltimore: Paul H. Brookes.

Maratsos, M. P., Kuczaj, S. A., II, Fox, D. E. C., & Chalkley, M. A. (1979). Some empirical studies in the acquisition of transformational relations. In W. A. Collins (Ed.), *Minnesota symposia on child psychology* (Vol. 12). Hillsdale, NJ: Erlbaum.

Marcia, J. (1980). Identity in adolescence. In J. Adelson (Ed.), *Handbook of adolescent psychology.* New York: Wiley.

Marcus, D. E., & Overton, W. F. (1978). The development of cognitive gender constancy and sex role preferences. *Child Development, 49,* 434–444.

Marcus, G. F., Pinker, S., Ullman, M., Hollander, M., Rosen, T. J., & Xu, F. (1992). Overregularization in language acquisition. *Monographs of the Society for Research in Child Development, 57,* N. 4 (Serial No. 228).

Marean, G. C., Werner, L. A., & Kuhl, P. K. (1992). Vowel categorization by very young infants. *Developmental Psychology, 28,* 395–405.

Marin, B. V., Holmes, D. L., Guth, M., & Kovac, P. (1979). The potential of children as eyewitnesses. *Law and Human Behavior, 3,* 295–305.

Marjoribanks, K. (1972). Ethnic and environmental influences on mental abilities. *American Journal of Sociology, 78,* 323–337.

Markman, E. M. (1987). How children constrain the possible meanings of words. In U. Neisser (Ed.), *Concepts and conceptual development: Ecological and intellectual factors in categorization.* Cambridge: Cambridge University Press.

Markman, E. M. (1989). *Categorization and naming in children: Problems of induction.* Cambridge, MA: MIT Press.

Markman, E. M. (1990). Constraints children place on word meanings. *Cognitive Science, 14,* 57–77.

Markman, E. M., & Siebert, J. (1976). Classes and collections: Internal organization and resulting holistic properties. *Cognitive Psychology, 8,* 561–577.

Markman, E. M., & Wachtel G. F. (1988). Children's use of mutual exclusivity to constrain the meanings of words. *Cognitive Psychology, 20,* 121–157.

Marland, S. (1972). *Education of the gifted and talented.* Report to the Congress of the United States by the U.S. Commission on Education. Washington, DC: U.S. Government Printing Office.

Marlow, N., Roberts, L., & Cooke, R. (1993). Outcome of 8 years for children with birth weights of 1250 g or less. *Archives of Disease in Childhood, 68,* 286–290.

Marr, D. B., & Sternberg, R. J. (1987). The role of mental speed in intelligence: A triarchic perspective. In P. A. Vernon (Ed.), *Speed of information-processing and intelligence.* Norwood, NJ: Ablex.

Marshall, R. E., Porter, F. L., Rogers, A. G., Moore, J., Anderson, B., & Boxerman, S. B. (1982). Circumcision: 2. Effects on mother-infant interaction. *Early Human Development, 7,* 367–374.

Marshall, W. A., & Tanner, J. M. (1970). Variations in the pattern of pubertal changes in boys. *Archives of Disease in Childhood, 45,* 13–23.

Martin, B. (1975). Parent-child relations. In F. D. Horowitz (Ed.), *Review of child development research* (Vol. 4). Chicago: University of Chicago Press.

Martin, C. L. (1991). The role of cognition in understanding gender effects. In H. W. Reese (Ed.), *Advances in child development and behavior* (Vol. 23). San Diego, CA: Academic Press.

Martin, C. L., & Halverson, C. F. (1981). A schematic processing model of sex typing and stereotyping in children. *Child Development, 52,* 1119–1134.

Martin, C. L., & Halverson, C. F. (1987). The roles of cognition in sex role acquisition. In D. B. Carter (Ed.), *Current conceptions of sex roles and sex typing: Theory and research.* New York: Praeger.

Martin, C. L., & Little, J. K. (1990). The relation of gender understanding to children's sex-typed preferences and gender stereotypes. *Child Development, 61,* 1427–1439.

Martin, H. P., & Beezley, P. (1976). Personality of abused children. In H. P. Martin (Ed.), *The abused child.* Cambridge: Ballinger.

Martin, J. B. (1987). Molecular genetics: Applications to the clinical neurosciences. *Science, 238,* 765–772.

Martin, J., Martin, D. C., Lund, C. A., & Streissguth, A. P. (1977). Maternal alcohol ingestion and cigarette smoking and their effects on newborn conditioning. *Alcoholism: Clinical and Experimental Research, 1,* 243–247.

Marvin, R. S. (1977). An ethological-cognitive model for the attenuation of mother-child attachment behavior. In T. M. Alloway, L. Krames, & P. Pliner (Eds.), *Advances in the study of communication and affect: Vol. 3. The development of social attachments.* New York: Plenum Press.

Masangkay, Z. S., McCluskey, K. A., McIntyre, C. W., Sims-Knight, J., Vaughn, B. E., & Flavell, J. H. (1974). The early development of inferences about the visual percepts of others. *Child Development, 45,* 357–366.

Massad, C. M. (1981). Sex role identity and adjustment during adolescence. *Child Development, 52,* 1290–1298.

Massaro, D. W., & Cowan, N. (1993). Information processing models: Microscopes of mind. In L. W. Porter & M. R. Rosenzweig (Eds.), *Annual Review of Psychology, 34,* 383–425.

Masters, J. C., Barden, R. C., & Ford, M. E. (1979). Affective states, expressive behavior, and learning in children. *Journal of Personality and Social Psychology, 37,* 380–390.

Masters, J. C., Ford, M. E., Arend, R., Grotevant, H. D., & Clark, L. V. (1979). Modeling and labeling as integrated determinants of children's sex-typed imitative behavior. *Child Development, 50,* 364–371.

Masur, E. F. (1982). Mothers' responses to infants' object-related gestures: Influences on lexical development. *Journal of Child Language, 9,* 23–30.

Matas, L., Arend, R. A., & Sroufe, L. A. (1978). Continuity of adaptation in the second year: The relationship between quality of attachment and later competence. *Child Development, 49,* 547–556.

Matheny, A. P., Jr. (1989). Children's behavioral inhibition over age and across situations. *Journal of Personality, 57,* 215–235.

Mathews, J. J., & Zadak, K. (1991). The alternative birth movement in the United States: History and current status. *Women & Health, 17,* 39–56.

Matias, R., & Cohn, J. F. (1993). Are max-specified infant facial expressions during face-to-face interaction consistent with differential emotions theory? *Developmental Psychology, 29,* 524–531.

Matsumoto, D., Haan, N., Yabrove, G., Theodorou, P., & Carney, C. C. (1986). Preschoolers' moral actions and emotions in prisoner's dilemma. *Developmental Psychology, 22,* 663–670.

Maudry, M., & Nekula, M. (1939). Social relations between children of the same age during the first two years of life. *Journal of Genetic Psychology, 54,* 193–215.

Maurer, D. (1983). The scanning of compound figures by young infants. *Journal of Experimental Child Psychology, 35,* 437–448.

Maurer, D. (1985). Infants' perception of facedness. In T. M. Field & N. A. Fox (Eds.), *Social perception in infants.* Norwood, NJ: Ablex.

Maurer, D., & Lewis, T, L. (1979). A physiological explanation of infants' early visual development. *Canadian Journal of Psychology, 33,* 232–252.

Mayer, R. E., & Fay, A. L. (1987). A chain of cognitive changes with learning to program in Logo. *Journal of Educational Psychology, 79,* 269–279.

McAnarney, E. R. (1987). Young maternal age and adverse neonatal outcome. *American Journal of Diseases of Children, 141,* 1053–1059.

McAnarney, E. R., & Stevens-Simon, C. (1990). Maternal psychological stress/depression and low birth weight. *American Journal of Diseases of Children, 144,* 789–792.

McBride, W. G. (1961). Thalidomide and congenital abnormalities. *Lancet, 2,* 1358.

McCabe, A., & Lipscomb, T. J. (1988). Sex differences in children's verbal aggression. *Merrill-Palmer Quarterly, 34,* 389–401.

McCall, R. B. (1979). *Infants.* Cambridge: Harvard University Press.

McCall, R. B. (1981). Nature-nurture and the two realms of development: A proposed integration with respect to mental development. *Child Development, 52,* 1–12.

McCall, R. B. (1984). Developmental changes in mental performance: The effect of birth of a sibling. *Child Development, 55,* 1317–1321.

McCall, R. B., & Carriger, M. S. (1993). A meta-analysis of infant habituation and recognition memory performance as predictors of later IQ. *Child Development, 64,* 57–79.

McCall, R. B., Appelbaum, M. I., & Hogarty, P. S. (1973). Developmental changes in mental performance. *Monographs of the Society for Research in Child Development, 38*(3, Serial No. 150).

McCall, R. B., Hogarty, P. S., & Hurlburt, N. (1972). Transitions in sensorimotor development and the prediction of childhood IQ. *American Psychologist, 27,* 728–748.

McCall, R. B., Parke, R. D., & Kavanaugh, R. D. (1977). Imitation of live and televised models in children one to three years of age. *Monographs of the Society for Research in Child Development, 42*(3, Serial No. 171).

McCartney, K., & Nelson, K. (1981). Children's use of scripts in story recall. *Discourse Processes, 4,* 59–70.

McCartney, K., Harris, M. J., & Bernieri, F. (1990). Growing up and growing apart: A developmental meta-analysis of twin studies. *Psychological Bulletin, 107,* 226–237.

McCartney, K., Scarr, S., Phillips, D., & Grajek, S. (1985). Day care as intervention: Comparisons of varying quality programs. *Journal of Applied Developmental Psychology, 6,* 247–260.

McClelland, D. C. (1973). Testing for competence rather than for "intelligence." *American Psychologist, 28,* 1–14.

McCormick, M. C., Gortmaker, S. L., & Sobol, A. M. (1990). Very low birth weight children: Behavior problems and school difficulty in a national sample. *Journal of Pediatrics, 117,* 687–693.

McCormick, M. C., Shapiro, S., & Starfield, B. H. (1982). Factors associated with maternal opinion of infant development: Clues to the vulnerable child? *Pediatrics, 69,* 537–543.

McCormick, M. C., Wessel, K. W., Krischer, J. P., Welcher, D. W., & Handy, J. B. (1981). Preliminary analysis of developmental observations in a survey of morbidity in infants. *Early Human Development, 5,* 377–393.

McDavid, J. W., & Harari, H. (1966). Stereotyping of names and popularity in grade-school children. *Child Development, 37,* 453–459.

McDonald, L., & Pien, D. (1982). Mother conversational behavior as a function of interactional intent. *Journal of Child Language, 9,* 337–358.

McGhee, P. E. (1979). *Humor: Its origin and development.* San Francisco: W. H. Freeman.

McGhee, P. E., & Frueh, T. (1980). Television viewing and the learning of sex role stereotypes. *Sex Roles, 6,* 179–188.

McGraw, M. B. (1935). *Growth: A study of Johnny and Jimmy.* New York: Appleton-Century.

McGraw, M. B. (1941). Neural maturation as exemplified in the changing reactions of the infant to pin prick. *Child Development, 12,* 31–42.

McGraw, M. B. (1943). *The neuromuscular maturation of the human infant.* New York: Columbia University Press.

McGregor, J. A., & French, J. I. (1991). *Chlamydia trachomatis* infection during pregnancy. *American Journal of Obstetrics and Gynecology, 165,* 1782–1789.

McGuire, J. (1988). Gender stereotypes of parents with two-year-olds and beliefs about gender differences in behavior. *Sex Roles, 19,* 233–240.

McGuire, K. D., & Weisz, J. R. (1982). Social cognition and behavior correlates of preadolescent chumship. *Child Development, 53,* 1478–1484.

McGurk, H., & MacDonald, J. (1976). Hearing lips and seeing voices. *Nature* (London), *264,* 746–748.

McKenna, J. J., Mosko, S., Dungy, C., & McAninch, J. (1990). Sleep and arousal patterns of co-sleeping human mother/infant pairs: A preliminary physiological study with implications for the study of sudden infant death syndrome (SIDS). *American Journal of Physical Anthropology, 83,* 331–347.

McKey, R. H., Condelli, L., Granson, H., Barrett, B., McConkey, C., & Plantz, M. (1985). *The impact of Head Start on children, families and communities* (Final report of the Head Start Evaluation, Synthesis and Utilization Project). Washington, DC: U.S. Government Printing Office.

McLaughlin, B. (1984). *Second-language acquisition in childhood: Vol. 2. School-age children.* Hillsdale, NJ: Erlbaum.

McLoyd, V. C. (1990). The impact of economic hardship on black families and children: Psychological distress, parenting, and socioemotional development. *Child Development, 61,* 311–346.

McLoyd, V. C., & Wilson, L. (1989). Maternal behavior, social support, and economic conditions as predictors of psychological distress in children. In V. C. McLoyd & C. Flanagan (Eds.), *New directions for child development: No. 46. Responses of children and adolescents to economic crisis.* San Francisco: Jossey-Bass.

McMahon, R. J., & Forehand, R. (1978). Nonprescription behavior therapy: Effectiveness of a brochure in teaching mothers to correct their children's inappropriate mealtime behaviors. *Behavior Therapy, 9,* 814–820.

McManus, I. C., & Bryden, M. P. (1991). Geschwind's theory of cerebral lateralization: Developing a formal, causal model. *Psychological Bulletin, 110,* 237–253.

McNally, S., Eisenberg, N., & Harris, J. D. (1991). Consistency and change in maternal child-rearing practices and values: A longitudinal study. *Child Development, 62,* 190–198.

McNeal, J. (1990, September). Children as customers. *American Demographics,* pp. 36–39.

Mead, G. H. (1934). *Mind, self, and society.* Chicago: University of Chicago Press.

Mead, M. (1967). *Male and female: A study of the sexes in a changing world.* New York: Morrow Quill. (Original work published 1949)

Medin, D. L. (1989). Concepts and conceptual structure. *American Psychologist, 44,* 1469–1481.

Mednick, S. A., Moffitt, T. E., & Stack, S. (1987). *The causes of crime: New biological approaches.* New York: Cambridge University Press.

Mehler, J., Jusczyk, P., Lambertz, G., Halsted, N., Bertoncini, J., & Amiel-Tison, C. (1988). A precursor of language acquisition in young infants. *Cognition, 29,* 143–178.

Meichenbaum, D. (1977). *Cognitive-behavior modification: An integrative approach.* New York: Plenum Press.

Meichenbaum, D., & Goodman, J. (1971). Training impulsive children to talk to themselves: A means of developing self-control. *Journal of Abnormal Psychology, 77,* 115–126.

Meltzoff, A. N. (1988a). Imitation, objects, tools, and the rudiments of language in human ontogeny. *Human Evolution, 3,* 45–64.

Meltzoff, A. N. (1988b). Infant imitation and memory: Nine-month-olds in immediate and deferred tests. *Child Development, 59,* 217–225.

Meltzoff, A. N., & Moore, M. K. (1983). Newborn infants imitate adult facial gestures. *Child Development, 54,* 702–709.

Meltzoff, A. N., & Moore, M. K. (1989). Imitation in newborn infants: Exploring the range of gestures imitated and the underlying mechanisms. *Developmental Psychology, 25,* 954–962.

Meltzoff, A. N., & Moore, M. K. (1992). Early imitation within a functional framework: The importance of person identity, movement, and development. *Infant Behavior and Development, 15,* 479–505.

Meltzoff, A., & Borton, R. (1979). Intermodal matching by human neonates. *Nature* (London), *282,* 403–404.

Mendelson, M. J., & Haith, M. M. (1976). The relation between audition and vision in the human newborn. *Monographs of the Society for Research in Child Development, 41*(4, Serial No. 167).

Meredith, H. V. (1978). *Human body growth in the first ten years of life.* Columbia, SC: The State Printing Co.

Merimee, T. J., Zapf, J., & Froesch, E. R. (1981). Dwarfism in the Pygmy: An isolated deficiency of insulin-like Growth Factor I. *New England Journal of Medicine, 305,* 965–968.

Merriman, W. E., & Bowman, L. L. (1989). The mutual exclusivity bias in children's word learning. *Monographs of the Society for Research in Child Development, 54*(3–4, Serial No. 220).

Merritt, T. A. (1981). Smoking mothers affect little lives. *American Journal of Diseases of Children, 135,* 501–502.

Mervis, C. (1984). Early lexical development: The contributions of mother and child. In C. Sophian (Ed.), *Origins of cognitive skills.* Hillsdale, NJ: Erlbaum.

Mervis, C., & Crisafi, M. (1982). Order of acquisition of subordinate-, basic-, and superordinate-level categories. *Child Development, 53,* 267–273.

Messer, D. J. (1981). The identification of names in maternal speech to infants. *Journal of Psycholinguistic Research, 10,* 69–77.

Meyer, M. B., & Tonascia, J. A. (1977). Maternal smoking, pregnancy complications, and perinatal mortality. *American Journal of Obstetrics and Gynecology, 128,* 494–502.

Michel, G. F. (1988). A neuropsychological perspective on infant sensorimotor development. In C. Rovee-Collier & L. P. Lipsitt (Eds.), *Advances in infancy research* (Vol. 5). Norwood, NJ: Ablex.

Michel, G. F., & Harkins, D. A. (1986). Postural and lateral asymmetries in the ontogeny of handedness during infancy. *Developmental Psychobiology, 19,* 247–258.

Michelson, L., Sugai, D. P., Wood, R. P., & Kazdin, A. E. (1983). *Social skills assessment and training with children.* New York: Plenum Press.

Michelsson, K., Sirvio, P., & Wasz-Hockert, D. (1977). Pain cry in fullterm asphyxiated newborn infants correlated with late findings. *Acta Paediatrica Scandinavica, 66,* 611–616.

Michotte, A. (1963). *The perception of causality.* New York: Basic Books.

Milich, R. (1984). Cross-sectional and longitudinal observations of activity level and sustained attention in a normative sample. *Journal of Abnormal Child Psychology, 12,* 261–275.

Miller, B., McCoy, J., Olson, T., & Wallace, C. (1986). Parental discipline and control attempts in relation to adolescent sexual attitudes and behavior. *Journal of Marriage and the Family, 48,* 503–512.

Miller, B. C., Card, J. J., Paikoff, R. L., & Peterson, J. L. (1992). *Preventing adolescent pregnancy.* Newbury Park, CA: Sage.

Miller, J. B. (1976). *Toward a new psychology of women.* Boston: Beacon Press.

Miller, J. B. (1991). The development of women's sense of self. In J. V. Jordan, A. G. Kaplan, J. B. Miller, I. P. Stiver, & J. L. Surrey (Eds.), *Women's growth in connection.* New York: Guilford.

Miller, N. B., Cowan, P. A., Cowan, C. P., Hetherington, E. M., & Clingempeel, W. G. (1993). Externalizing in preschoolers and early adolescents: A cross-study replication of a family model. *Developmental Psychology, 29,* 3–18.

Miller, N., & Maruyama, G. (1976). Ordinal position and peer popularity. *Journal of Personality and Social Psychology, 33,* 123–131.

Miller, P. H. (1985). Children's reasoning about the causes of human behavior. *Journal of Experimental Child Psychology, 39,* 343–362.

Miller, P. H., & Aloise, P. A. (1989). Young children's understanding of the psychological causes of behavior: A review. *Child Development, 60,* 257–285.

Miller, P. H., & Harris, Y. R. (1988). Preschoolers' strategies of attention on a same-different task. *Developmental Psychology, 24,* 628–633.

Miller, P. H., Kessel, F. S., & Flavell, J. H. (1970). Thinking about people thinking about people thinking about . . . A study of social cognitive development. *Child Development, 41,* 613–623.

Miller, P. H., Woody-Ramsey, J., & Aloise, P. A. (1991). The role of strategy effortfulness in strategy effectiveness. *Developmental Psychology, 27,* 738–745.

Miller-Jones, D. (1989). Culture and testing. *American Psychologist, 44,* 360–366.

Mills, J. L., Graubard, B. I., Harley, E. E., Rhoads, G. G., Berends, H. W. (1984). Maternal consumption and birth weight: How much drinking in pregnancy is safe? *Journal of the American Medical Association, 252,* 1875–1879.

Mills, R. S. L., & Grusec, J. E. (1989). Cognitive, affective, and behavioral consequences of praising altruism. *Merrill-Palmer Quarterly, 35,* 299–326.

Minkoff, H., Deepak, N., Menez, R., & Fikrig, S. (1987). Pregnancies resulting in infants with acquired immunodeficiency syndrome or AIDS-related complex: Follow-up of mothers, children, and subsequently born siblings. *Obstetrics and Gynecology, 69,* 288–291.

Minuchin, P. P. (1988). Relationships within the family: A systems perspective on development. In R. A. Hinde & J. Stevenson-Hinde (Eds.), *Relationships within families: Mutual influences.* Oxford: Clarendon Press.

Minuchin, P. P., & Shapiro, E. K. (1983). The school as a context for social development. In E. M. Hetherington (Ed.), *Handbook of child psychology: Vol. IV. Socialization, personality, and social development.* New York: Wiley.

Mischel, H. N., & Mischel, W. (1983). The development of children's knowledge of self-control strategies. *Child Development, 54,* 603–619.

Mischel, W. (1966). A social learning view of sex differences in behavior. In E. E. Maccoby (Ed.), *The development of sex differences.* Stanford, CA: Stanford University Press.

Mischel, W., & Mischel, H. N. (1977). Self-control and the self. In T. Mischel (Ed.), *The self: Psychological and philosophical issues.* Totowa, NJ: Rowan & Littlefield.

Mischel, W., Ebbesen, E. B., & Zeiss, A. R. (1972). Cognitive and attentional mechanisms in delay of gratification. *Journal of Personality and Social Psychology, 21,* 204–218.

Mischel, W., Shoda, Y., & Rodriguez, M. L. (1989). Delay of gratification in children. *Science, 244,* 933–938.

Mittendorf, R., Williams, M. A., Berkey, C. S., & Cotter, P. F. (1990). The length of uncomplicated human gestation. *Obstetrics and Gynecology, 75,* 929–932.

Miyake, K., Chen, S., & Campos, J. J. (1985). Infant temperament, mother's mode of interaction, and attachment in Japan: An interim report. In I. Bretherton & E. Waters (Eds.), *Growing points of attachment theory and research. Monographs of the Society for Research in Child Development, 50*(1–2, Serial No. 209).

Moely, B. E., Hart, S. S., Leal, L., Santulli, K. A., Rao, N., Johnson, T., & Hamilton, L. B. (1992). The teacher's role in facilitating memory and study strategy development in the elementary school classroom. *Child Development, 63,* 653–672.

Moely, B. E., Hart, S. S., Santulli, K. A., Leal, L., Kogut, D. J., McLain, E., Zhou, Z., & Johnson, T. D. (1989, April). *Teachers' cognitions about the memory processes of elementary school children: A developmental perspective.* Paper presented at the biennial meeting of the Society for Research in Child Development, Kansas City, MO.

Moely, B. E., Olson, F. A., Halwes, T. G., & Flavell, J. H. (1969). Production deficiency in young children's clustered recall. *Developmental Psychology, 1,* 26–34.

Moffat, R., & Hackel, A. (1985). Thermal aspects of neonatal care. In A. Gottfried & J. Gaiter (Eds.), *Infant stress under intensive care.* Baltimore: University Park Press.

Moffitt, T. E., Caspi, A., Belsky, J., & Silva, P. A. (1992). Childhood experience and the onset of menarche: A test of a sociobiological model. *Child Development, 63,* 47–58.

Molfese, D. L., & Molfese, V. J. (1979). Hemisphere and stimulus differences as reflected in the cortical responses of newborn infants to speech stimuli. *Developmental Psychology, 15,* 505–511.

Molfese, D. L., & Molfese, V. J. (1980). Cortical responses of preterm infants to phonetic and nonphonetic speech stimuli. *Developmental Psychology, 16,* 574–581.

Molfese, D. L., & Molfese, V. J. (1985). Electrophysiological indices of auditory discrimination in newborn infants: The bases for predicting later language development? *Infant Behavior and Development, 8,* 197–211.

Money, J., & Ehrhardt, A. A. (1972). *Man and woman, boy and girl: Differentiation and dimorphism of gender identity from conception to maturity.* Baltimore: Johns Hopkins University Press.

Monfries, M. M., & Kafer, N. F. (1987). Neglected and rejected children: A social-skills model. *Journal of Psychology, 121,* 401–407.

Moore, C. L. (1985). Another psychobiological view of sexual differentiation. *Developmental Review, 5,* 18–55.

Moore, K. L. (1988). *The developing human: Clinically oriented embryology* (4th ed.). Philadelphia: W. B. Saunders.

Moore, K. L. (1989). *Before we are born* (3rd ed.). Philadelphia: W. B. Saunders.

Moore, R. S., & Moore, D. N. (1975). *Better late than early.* New York: Reader's Digest Press.

Morgan, M. (1982). Television and adolescents' sex-role stereotypes: A longitudinal study. *Journal of Personality and Social Psychology, 43,* 947–955.

Morgan, M. (1987). Television, sex-role attitudes, and sex-role behavior. *Journal of Early Adolescence, 7,* 269–282.

Morison, P., & Maste, A. S. (1991). Peer reputation in middle childhood as a predictor of adaptation in adolescence: A seven-year follow-up. *Child Development, 62,* 991–1007.

Morrelli, G., Rogoff, B., Oppenheim, D., & Goldsmith, D. (1992). Cultural variation in infants' sleeping arrangements: Questions of independence. *Developmental Psychology, 28,* 604–613.

Morris, R., & Kratchowill, T. (1983). *Treating children's fears and phobias.* New York: Pergamon Press.

Morrongiello, B. A. (1984). Auditory temporal pattern perception in 6- and 12-month-old infants. *Developmental Psychology, 20,* 441–448.

Morrongiello, B. A. (1988). The development of auditory pattern perception skills. In C. Rovee-Collier & L. P. Lipsitt (Eds.), *Advances in infancy research* (Vol. 5). Norwood, NJ: Ablex.

Morrongiello, B. A., Fenwick, K. D., & Chance, G. (1990). Sound localization acuity in very young infants: An observer-based testing procedure. *Developmental Psychology, 26,* 75–84.

Moshman, D. (1990). The development of metalogical understanding. In W. F. Overton (Ed.), *Reasoning, necessity and logic: Developmental perspectives.* Hillsdale, NJ: Erlbaum.

Moshman, D., & Franks, B. A. (1986). Development of the concept of inferential validity. *Child Development, 57,* 153–165.

Moss, H. A. (1974). Early sex differences and mother-infant interaction. In R. C. Friedman, R. M. Richart, & R. L. Vande Wiele (Eds.), *Sex differences in behavior.* New York: Wiley.

Mossler, D. G., Marvin, R. S., & Greenberg, M. T. (1976). Conceptual perspective-taking in 2- to 6-year-old children. *Developmental Psychology, 12,* 85–86.

Movshon, J. A., & Van Sluyters, R. C. (1981). Visual neuronal development. *Annual Review of Psychology, 32,* 477–522.

Mulhern, R. K., Jr., & Passman, R. H. (1981). Parental discipline as affected by the sex of the parent, the sex of the child, and the child's apparent responsiveness to discipline. *Developmental Psychology, 17,* 604–613.

Muller, A. A., & Perlmutter, M. (1985). Preschool children's problem-solving interactions at computers and jigsaw puzzles. *Journal of Applied Developmental Psychology, 6,* 173–186.

Muller, H. J. (1927). Artificial transmutation of the gene. *Science, 66,* 84–87.

Mullis, I. V. S., & Jenkins, L. B. (1990). *The reading report card, 1971–1988.* Princeton, NJ: Educational Testing Service.

Munroe, R. H., Shimmin, H. S., & Munroe, R. L. (1984). Gender understanding and sex role preference in four cultures. *Developmental Psychology, 20,* 673–682.

Murphy, L. B. (1937). *Social behavior and child personality.* New York: Columbia University Press.

Mussen, P. H., & Jones, M. C. (1957). Self-conceptions, motivations, and interpersonal attitudes of late and early maturing boys. *Child Development, 28,* 243–256.

Mussen, P. H., & Jones, M. C. (1958). The behavior inferred motivations of late and early maturing boys. *Child Development, 29,* 61–67.

Mussen, P., Rutherford, E., Harris, S., & Keasey, C. (1970). Honesty and altruism among preadolescents. *Developmental Psychology, 3,* 169–194.

Náñez, J. E., Sr. (1988). Perception of impending collision in 3- to 6-week-old human infants. *Infant Behavior and Development, 11,* 447–463.

Nahmias, A. J., Keyserling, H. L., & Kernick, G. M. (1983). Herpes simplex. In J. S. Remington & J. O. Klein (Eds.), *Infectious diseases of the fetus and newborn infant.* Philadelphia: W. B. Saunders.

Narod, S. A., de Sanjosé, S., & Victora, C. (1991). Coffee during pregnancy: A reproductive hazard? *American Journal of Obstetrics and Gynecology, 164,* 1109–1114.

Nastasi, B. K., Clements, D. H., & Battista, M. T. (1990). Social-cognitive interactions, motivation, and cognitive growth in Logo programming and CAI problem-solving environments. *Journal of Educational Psychology, 82,* 150–158.

National Association for Perinatal Addiction Research and Education. (1988, October). Innocent addicts: High rate of prenatal drug abuse found. *ADAMHA News.*

National Center for Health Statistics. (1976). *Monthly Vital Statistics Report, 25*(3, Suppl).

National Center for Health Statistics. (1988). *Vital statistics of the United States 1986: Vol. 1. Natality.* (DHHS Publication No. PHS 88-1123). Washington, DC: U.S. Government Printing Office.

National Commission on Excellence in Education. (1983). *A nation at risk: The imperative for educational reform.* Washington, DC: U.S. Government Printing Office.

National Genetics Foundation. (1987). *Clinical genetics handbook.* Oradell, NJ: Medical Economics Books.

National Institutes of Mental Health. (1982). *Television and behavior: Ten years of scientific progress and implications for the eighties.* Rockville, MD: Author.

National Research Council, Committee on Mapping and Sequencing the Human Genome. (1988). *Mapping and sequencing the human genome.* Washington, DC: National Academy Press.

Neill, S. (1976). Aggressive and non-aggressive fighting in twelve- to thirteen-year-old pre-adolescent boys. *Journal of Child Psychology and Psychiatry, 17,* 213–220.

Neimark, E. D. (1979). Current status of formal operations research. *Human Development, 22,* 60–67.

Nelson, C. A., & Horowitz, F. D. (1987). Visual motion perception in infancy: A review and synthesis. In P. Salapatek & L. Cohen (Eds.), *Handbook of infant perception: From perception to cognition* (Vol. 2). Orlando, FL: Academic Press.

Nelson, D. G. K., Hirsh-Pasek, K., Jusczyk, P. W., & Cassidy, K. W. (1989). How the prosodic cues in motherese might assist language learning. *Journal of Child Language, 16,* 55–68.

Nelson, K. (1973). Structure and strategy in learning to talk. *Monographs of the Society for Research in Child Development, 38*(1–2, Serial No. 149).

Nelson, K. (1988). Constraints on word learning? *Cognitive Development, 3,* 221–246.

Nelson, K. (1991). Concepts and meaning in language development. In N. A. Krasnegor, D. M. Rumbaugh, R. L. Schiefelbusch, & M. Studdert-Kennedy (Eds.), *Biological and behavioral determinants of language development.* Hillsdale, NJ: Erlbaum.

Nelson, K. E. (1989). Strategies for first language teaching. In M. L. Rice & R. L. Schiefelbusch (Eds.), *The teachability of language.* Baltimore: Paul H. Brookes.

Nelson, K., & Gruendel, J. (1981). Generalized event representations: Basic building blocks of cognitive development. In M. E. Lamb & A. L. Brown (Eds.), *Advances in developmental psychology* (Vol. 1). Hillsdale, NJ: Erlbaum.

Nelson-LeGall, S. (1985). Motive-outcome matching and outcome foreseeability: Effects on attribution of intentionality and moral judgments. *Developmental Psychology, 21,* 332–337.

New, R. S., & Benigni, L. (1987). Italian fathers and infants: Cultural constraints on paternal behavior. In M. E. Lamb (Ed.), *The father's role: Cross-cultural perspectives.* Hillsdale, NJ: Erlbaum.

Newborg, J., Stock, J. R., & Wnek, L. (1984). *Battelle Developmental Inventory.* Allen, TX: LINC Associates.

Newcombe, N., & Huttenlocher, J. (1992). Children's early ability to solve perspective-taking problems. *Developmental Psychology, 28,* 635–643.

Newcomer, S., & Baldwin, W. (1992). Demographics of adolescent sexual behavior, contraception, pregnancy, and STDs. *Journal of School Health, 62,* 265–270.

Newport, E. L. (1977). Motherese: The speech of mothers to young children. In N. J. Castellan, D. B. Pisoni, & G. Potts (Eds.), *Cognitive theory* (Vol. 2). Hillsdale, NJ: Erlbaum.

Newport, E. L. (1990). Maturational constraints on language learning. *Cognitive Science, 14,* 11–28.

Newton, N. (1955). *Maternal emotions.* New York: P. B. Hoeber.

Nickel, H., & Kocher, E. M. T. (1987). West Germany and the German-speaking countries. In M. E. Lamb (Ed.), *The father's role: Cross-cultural perspectives.* Hillsdale, NJ: Erlbaum.

Nielsen, J. M. (1990). *Sex and gender in society: Perspectives on stratification* (2nd ed.). Prospect Heights, IL: Waverly.

Nielson Co. (1988). *1988 Nielson report on television.* Northbrook, IL: Author.

Niemiec, R., & Walberg, H. J. (1987). Comparative effects of computer-assisted instruction: A synthesis of reviews. *Journal of Educational Computing Research, 3,* 19–37.

Nilsson, L. (1977). *A child is born.* New York: Dell.

Nilsson, L. (1990). *A child is born.* New York: Dell.

Ninio, A., & Bruner, J. S. (1978). The achievement and antecedents of labelling. *Journal of Child Language, 5,* 1–15.

Noddings, N. (1992). *The challenge to care in schools: An alternative approach to education.* New York: Teachers College Press.

Norbeck, J. S., & Tilden, V. P. (1983). Life stress, social support, and emotional disequilibrium in complications of pregnancy:

A prospective, multivariate study. *Journal of Health and Social Behavior, 24,* 30–46.

Notzon, F. C., Placek, P. J., & Taffel, S. M. (1987). Comparisons of national cesarean-section rates. *New England Journal of Medicine, 316,* 386–389.

Novello, A. C., Wise, P. H., Willoughby, A., & Pizzo, P. A. (1989). Final report of the United States Department of Health and Human Services Secretary's Work Group on Pediatric Human Immunodeficiency Virus Infection and Disease: Content and implications. *Pediatrics, 84,* 547–555.

Nowakowski, R. S. (1987). Basic concepts of CNS development. *Child Development, 58,* 568–595.

Nowicki, S., & Strickland, B. (1973). A locus of control scale for children. *Journal of Consulting and Clinical Psychology, 40,* 148–154.

Nucci, L. P., & Turiel, E. (1978). Social interactions and the development of social concepts in preschool children. *Child Development, 49,* 400–407.

Nucci, L., & Turiel, E. (1993). God's word, religious rules, and their relaton to Christian and Jewish children's concepts of morality. *Child Development, 64,* 1475–1491.

Nuckolls, K. B., Cassel, J., & Kaplan, B. H. (1972). Psychosocial assets, life crisis, and the prognosis of pregnancy. *American Journal of Epidemiology, 95,* 431–441.

Nussbaum, R. L., & Ledbetter, D. H. (1986). Fragile X syndrome: A unique mutation in man. *Annual Review of Genetics, 20,* 109–145.

Oakes, J. (1985). *Keeping track: How schools structure inequality.* New Haven, CT: Yale University Press.

Oakes, L. M., & Cohen, L. B. (1990). Infant perception of a causal event. *Cognitive Development, 5,* 193–207.

Oakland, T. D. (1982). Nonbiased assessment in counseling: Issues and guidelines. *Measurement and Evaluation in Guidance, 15,* 107–116.

Oates, R. K. (1984). Similarities and differences between nonorganic failure to thrive and deprivation dwarfism. *Child Abuse and Neglect, 8,* 439–445.

Oates, R. K., Peacock, A., & Forrest, D. (1985). Long-term effects of nonorganic failure to thrive. *Pediatrics, 75,* 36–40.

Ochs, E. (1990). Indexicality and socialization. In J. W. Stigler, R. A. Shweder, & G. Herdt (Eds.), *Cultural psychology.* Cambridge: Cambridge University Press.

Offer, D. (1987). In defense of adolescents. *Journal of the American Medical Association, 257,* 3407–3408.

Ogbu, J. U. (1974). *The next generation: An ethnography of education in an urban neighborhood.* New York: Academic Press.

Ogbu, J. U. (1986). The consequences of the American caste system. In U. Neisser (Ed.), *The school achievement of minority children: New perspectives.* Hillsdale, NJ: Erlbaum.

Oldershaw, L., Walters, G. C., & Hall, D. K. (1986). Control strategies and noncompliance in abusive mother-child dyads: An observational study. *Child Development, 57,* 722–732.

Oller, D. K., & Eilers, R. E. (1982). Similarity of babbling in Spanish and English-learning babies. *Journal of Child Language, 9,* 565–577.

Oller, D. K., & Eilers, R. E. (1988). The role of audition in infant babbling. *Child Development, 59,* 441–449.

Olney, R., & Scholnick, E. (1976). Adult judgments of age and linguistic differences in infant vocalizations. *Journal of Child Language, 3,* 145–156.

Olsen, J. A., Weed, S. E., Ritz, G. M., & Jensen, L. C. (1991). The effects of three abstinence sex education programs on student attitudes toward sexual activity. *Adolescence, 26,* 631–641.

Olsho, L. W. (1984). Infant frequency discrimination. *Infant Behavior and Development, 7,* 27–35.

Olson, S. L., Bayles, K., & Bates, J. E. (1986). Mother-child interaction and children's speech progress: A longitudinal study of the first two years. *Merrill-Palmer Quarterly, 32,* 1–20.

Olson, S. L., Bates, J. E., & Kaskie, B. (1992). Caregiver-infant interaction antecedents of children's school-age cognitive ability. *Merrill-Palmer Quarterly, 38,* 309–330.

Olweus, D. (1980). Familial and temperamental determinants of aggressive behavior in adolescent boys: A causal analysis. *Developmental Psychology, 16,* 644–660.

Olweus, D., Mattsson, A., Schalling, D., & Low, H. (1980). Testosterone, aggression, physical, and personality dimensions in normal adolescent males. *Psychosomatic Medicine, 42,* 253–269.

Omark, D. R., & Edelman, M. S. (1975). Formation of dominance hierarchies in young children: Attention and perception. In T. Williams (Ed.), *Physical anthropology.* The Hague: Mouton.

Orenstein, S. R. (1992). Throwing out the baby with the bedding. *Clinical Pediatrics, 31,* 546–548.

Orenstein, W. A., Bart, K. J., Hinman, A. R., Preblud, S. R., Greaves, W. L., Doster, S. W., Stetler, W. C., & Sirotkin, B. (1984). The opportunity and obligation to eliminate rubella from the United States. *Journal of the American Medical Association, 251,* 1988–1994.

Ornstein, P. A., & Naus, M. J. (1978). Rehearsal processes in children's memory. In P. A. Ornstein (Ed.), *Memory development in children.* Hillsdale, NJ: Erlbaum.

Ornstein, P. A., Baker-Ward, L., & Naus, M. J. (1988). The development of mnemonic skill. In F. E. Weinert & M. Perlmutter (Eds.), *Memory development: Universal changes and individual differences.* Hillsdale, NJ: Erlbaum.

Ornstein, P. A., Naus, M. J., & Liberty, C. (1975). Rehearsal and organizational processes in children's memory. *Child Development, 46,* 818–830.

Orton, G. L. (1982). A comparative study of children's worries. *Journal of Psychology, 110,* 153–162.

Osherson, D. N., & Markman, E. M. (1975). Language and the ability to evaluate contradictions and tautologies. *Cognition, 2,* 213–226.

Ostrea, E. M., Brady, M., Gause, S., Raymundo, A. L., & Stevens, M. (1992). Drug screening of newborns by meconium analysis: A large-scale, prospective epidemiological study. *Pediatrics, 89,* 107–113.

Ostrer, H., & Hejtmancik, J. F. (1988). Prenatal diagnosis and carrier detection of genetic diseases by analysis of deoxyribonucleic acid. *Journal of Pediatrics, 112,* 679–687.

Ounsted, C., Oppenheimer, R., & Lindsay, J. (1974). Aspects of bonding failure: The psychopathology and psychotherapeutic treatment of families of battered children. *Developmental Medicine and Child Neurology, 16,* 447–452.

Over, R. (1987). Can human neonates imitate facial gestures? In B. E. McKenzie & R. H. Day (Eds.), *Perceptual development in early infancy: Problems and issues.* Hillsdale, NJ: Erlbaum.

Overview: Growing up—Del and Rey, Johnny and Jimmy, and nature versus nurture. (1987, July). *Scientific American,* pp. 30–32.

Owen, M. T., & Cox, M. J. (1988). Maternal employment and the transition to parenthood. In A. E. Gottfried & A. W. Gottfried (Eds.), *Maternal employment and children's development: Longitudinal research.* New York: Plenum Press.

O'Brien, M., Huston, A. C., & Risley, T. (1983). Sex-typed play of toddlers in a day care center. *Journal of Applied Developmental Psychology, 4,* 1–9.

O'Connor, N., & Hermelin, B. (1965). Sensory dominance. *Archives of General Psychiatry, 12,* 99–103.

O'Connor, R. D. (1972). Relative efficacy of modeling, shaping, and the procedures for modification of social withdrawal. *Journal of Abnormal Psychology, 79,* 327–334.

Paikoff, R. L., & Brooks-Gunn, J. (1991). Do parent-child relationships change during puberty? *Psychological Bulletin, 110,* 47–66.

Palincsar, A. S., & Brown, A. L. (1986). Interactive teaching to promote independent learning from text. *The Reading Teacher, 39,* 771–777.

Palinscar, A. S., & Brown, A. L. (1984). Reciprocal teaching of comprehension-fostering and comprehension-monitoring activities. *Cognition and Instruction, 1,* 117–175.

Palisin, H. (1986). Preschool temperament and performance on achievement tests. *Developmental Psychology, 22,* 766–770.

Palkovitz, R. (1985). Fathers' birth attendance, early contact, and extended contact with their newborns: A critical review. *Child Development, 56,* 392–406.

Palmer, S. E., & Kimchi, R. (1986). The information processing approach to cognition. In T. J. Knapp & L. C. Robertson (Eds.), *Approaches to cognition: Contrasts and controversies.* Hillsdale, NJ: Erlbaum.

Papert, S. (1980). *Mindstorms: Children, computers, and powerful ideas.* New York: Basic Books.

Papoušek, M. (1992). Early ontogeny of vocal communication in parent-infant interactions. In H. Papoušek, U. Jürgens, & M. Papoušek (Eds.), *Nonverbal vocal communication: Comparative and developmental approaches.* Cambridge, UK: Cambridge University Press.

Papoušek, H. (1967). Experimental studies of appetitional behavior in human newborns and infants. In H. W. Stevenson, E. H. Hess, & H. L. Rheingold (Eds.), *Early behavior.* New York: Wiley.

Papoušek, H., Papoušek, M., & Koester, L. S. (1986). Sharing emotionality and sharing knowledge: A microanalytic approach to parent-infant communication. In C. E. Izard & P. B. Read (Eds.), *Measuring emotions in infants and children* (Vol. 2). Cambridge: Cambridge University Press.

Paris, S. G., & Cross, D. R. (1983). Ordinary learning: Pragmatic connections among children's beliefs, motives, and actions. In J. Bisanz, G. L. Bisanz, & R. Kail (Eds.), *Learning in children: Progress in cognitive research.* New York: Springer-Verlag.

Parke, R. D. (1969). Effectiveness of punishment as an interaction of intensity, timing, agent nurturance, and cognitive structuring. *Child Development, 40,* 213–235.

Parke, R. D., & Collmer, C. W. (1975). Child abuse: An interdisciplinary analysis. In E. M. Hetherington (Ed.), *Review of child development research* (Vol. 5). Chicago: University of Chicago Press.

Parke, R. D., & O'Leary, S. (1976). Father-mother-infant interaction in the newborn period: Some findings, some observations, and some unresolved issues. In K. F. Riegel & J. Meacham (Eds.), *The developing individual in a changing world: Vol. 2. Social and environmental issues.* The Hague: Mouton.

Parke, R. D., & Slaby, R. G. (1983). The development of aggression. In E. M. Hetherington (Ed.), *Handbook of child psychology: Vol. IV. Socialization, personality, and social development.* New York: Wiley.

Parke, R. D., & Walters, R. H. (1967). Some factors influencing the efficacy of punishment training for inducing response inhibition. *Monographs of the Society for Research in Child Development, 32*(1, Serial No. 109).

Parke, R. D., MacDonald, K. B., Beitel, A., & Bhavnagri, N. (1988). The role of the family in the development of peer relationships. In R. D. Peters & R. J. McMahon (Eds.), *Social learning and systems approaches to marriage and the family.* New York: Brunner/Mazel.

Parker, J. G., & Asher, S. R. (1987). Peer relations and later personal adjustment: Are low-accepted children at risk? *Psychological Bulletin, 102,* 357–389.

Parker, J. G., & Asher, S. R. (1993). Friendship and friendship quality in middle childhood: Links with peer group acceptance and feelings of loneliness and social dissatisfaction. *Developmental Psychology, 29,* 611–621.

Parker, J. G., & Gottman, J. M. (1989). Social and emotional development in a relational context: Friendship interaction from early childhood to adolescence. In T. M. Berndt & G. W. Ladd (Eds.), *Peer relations in childhood.* New York: Wiley.

Parker, S. J., Zahr, L. K., Cole, J. G., & Brecht, M. (1992). Outcome after developmental intervention in the neonatal intensive care unit for mothers of preterm infants with low socioeconomic status. *Journal of Pediatrics, 120,* 780–785.

Parkhurst, J. T., & Asher, S. R. (1992). Peer rejection in middle school: subgroup differences in behavior, loneliness, and interpersonal concerns. *Developmental Psychology, 28,* 231–241.

Parmelee, A. H., & Sigman, M. (1983). Perinatal brain development and behavior. In M. Haith & J. Campos (Eds.), *Biology and infancy.* New York: Wiley.

Parsons, J. E. (1980). Psychosexual neutrality: Is anatomy destiny? In J. E. Parsons (Ed.), *The psychobiology of sex differences and sex roles.* New York: Hemisphere.

Parten, M. B. (1932). Social participation among pre-school children. *Journal of Abnormal and Social Psychology, 32,* 243–269.

Pass, R. F. (1987). Congenital and perinatal infections due to viruses and toxoplasma. In N. Kretchmer, E. J. Quilligan, & J. D. Johnson (Eds.), *Prenatal and perinatal biology and medicine: Vol. 2. Disorder, diagnosis, and therapy.* New York: Harwood Academic Publishers.

Pass, R. F., Stagno, S., Myers, G. J., & Alford, C. A. (1980). Outcome of symptomatic congenital cytomegalovirus infection: Results of long-term longitudinal follow-up. *Pediatrics, 66,* 758–762.

Patterson, D. (1987, August). The causes of Down syndrome. *Scientific American, 257,* pp. 52–61.

Patterson, G. R. (1976). The aggressive child: Victim and architect of a coercive system. In E. J. Mash, L. A. Hamerlynck, & L. C. Handy (Eds.), *Behavior modification and families.* New York: Brunner/Mazel.

Patterson, G. R. (1982). *A social learning approach: Vol. 3. Coercive family process.* Eugene, OR: Castalia.

Patterson, G. R. (1986). Performance models for antisocial boys. *American Psychologist, 41,* 432–444.

Patterson, G. R., & Fleischman, M. J. (1979). Maintenance of treatment effects: Some considerations concerning family systems and follow-up data. *Behavior Therapy, 10,* 168–185.

Patterson, G. R., & Reid, J. B. (1973). Intervention for families of aggressive boys: A replication study. *Behavior Research and Therapy, 11,* 383–394.

Patterson, G. R., Littman, R. A., & Bricker, W. (1967). Assertive behavior in children: A step toward a theory of aggression. *Monographs of the Society for Research in Child Development, 32*(5, Serial No. 113).

Patterson, G. R., Reid, J. B., Jones, R. R., & Conger, R. E. (1975). *A social learning approach: Vol. 1. Families with aggressive children.* Eugene, OR: Castalia.

Paxton, S. J., Wertheim, E. H., Gibbons, K., Szmukler, G. I., Hillier, L., & Petrovich, J. L. (1991). Body image satisfaction, dieting beliefs, and weight loss behaviors in adolescent girls and boys. *Journal of Youth and Adolescence, 20,* 362–379.

Pea, R. D., Kurland, D. M., & Hawkins, J. (1985). LOGO and the development of thinking skills. In M. Chen & W. Paisley (Eds.), *Children and microcomputers: Research on the newest medium.* Beverly Hills: Sage.

Pearson, D. A., & Lane, D. M. (1990). Reorientation in hyperactive and nonhyperactive children. Evidence for developmentally immature attention? In J. T. Enns (Ed.), *The development of attention: Research and theory.* Amsterdam: North-Holland.

Peckham, C. S., & Logan, S. (1993). Screening for toxoplasmosis during pregnancy. *Archives of Disease in Childhood, 68,* 3–5.

Pederson, F. A., Cain, R., Zaslow, M., & Anderson, B. (1982). Variation in infant experience associated with alternative family organization. In L. Laosa & I. Sigel (Eds.), *Families as learning environments for children.* New York: Plenum Press.

Pedlow, R., Sanson, A., Prior, M., & Oberklaid, F. (1993). Stability of maternally reported temperament from infancy to 8 years. *Developmental Psychology, 29,* 998–1007.

Peevers, B. H., & Secord, P. F. (1973). Developmental changes in attribution of descriptive concepts to persons. *Journal of Personality and Social Psychology, 27,* 120–128.

Pellegrini, A. D. (1988). Elementary-school children's rough-and-tumble play and social competence. *Developmental Psychology, 24,* 802–806.

Penner, S. G. (1987). Parental responses to grammatical and ungrammatical child utterances. *Child Development, 58,* 376–384.

Perlmutter, M., & Myers, N. A. (1979). Development of recall in 2- to 4-year-old children. *Developmental Psychology, 15,* 73–83.

Perris, E. E., Myers, N. A., & Clifton, R. K. (1990). Long-term memory for a single infancy experience. *Child Development, 61,* 1796–1807.

Perry, D. G., & Bussey, K. (1979). The social learning theory of sex differences: Imitation is alive and well. *Journal of Personality and Social Psychology, 37,* 1699–1712.

Perry, D. G., Perry, L. C., & Rasmussen, P. (1986). Cognitive social learning mediators of aggression. *Child Development, 52,* 700–711.

Perry, D. G., Williard, J. C., & Perry, L. C. (1990). Peers' perceptions of the consequences that victimized children provide aggressors. *Child Development, 61,* 1310–1325.

Persell, C. H. (1977). *Education and inequality: A theoretical and empirical synthesis.* New York: Free Press.

Petersen, A. C. (1980). Biopsychosocial processes in the development of sex-related differences. In J. Parsons (Ed.), *The psychobiology of sex differences and sex roles.* New York: Hemisphere.

Petersen, A. C., & Hamburg, B. (1986). Adolescence: A developmental approach to problems and psychopathology. *Behavior Therapy, 13,* 480–499.

Petersen, A. C., Compas, B. E., Brooks-Gunn, J., Stemmler, M., Ey, S., & Grant, K. E. (1993). Depression in adolescence. *American Psychologist, 48,* 155–168.

Peterson, A. C. (1987, September). Those gangly years. *Psychology Today,* pp. 28–34.

Peterson, A. C. (1988). Adolescent development. *Annual Review of Psychology, 39,* 583–607.

Peterson, D. R. (1984). Sudden infant death syndrome. In M. B. Bracken (Ed.), *Behavioral teratology.* New York: Oxford University Press.

Peterson, G. W., & Rollins, B. C. (1987). Parent-child socialization. In M. B. Sussman & S. K. Steinmetz (Eds.), *Handbook of marriage and the family.* New York: Plenum Press.

Peterson, L. (1983). Influence of age, task competence, and responsibility focus on children's altruism. *Developmental Psychology, 19,* 141–148.

Petitto, L. A., & Marentette, P. F. (1991). Babbling in the manual code: Evidence for the ontogeny of language. *Science, 251,* 1493–1496.

Pettersen, L., Yonas, A., & Fisch, R. O. (1980). The development of blinking in response to impending collision in preterm, full-term, and postterm infants. *Infant Behavior and Development, 3,* 155–165.

Pettit, G. S., Dodge, K. A., Bakshi, A., & Coie, J. D. (1990). The emergence of social dominance in young boys' play groups: Developmental differences and behavioral correlates. *Developmental Psychology, 26,* 1017–1025.

Phelps, E., & Damon, W. (1989). Problem solving with equals: Peer collaboration as a context for learning mathematics and spatial concepts. *Journal of Educational Psychology, 81,* 639–646.

Phelps, L., & Bajorek, E. (1991). Eating disorders of the adolescent: Current issues in etiology, assessment, and treatment. *School Psychology Review, 1991,* 9–22.

Phillips, D. (1984). The illusion of incompetence among academically competent children. *Child Development, 55,* 2000–2016.

Phillips, J. L. (1975). *The origins of intellect: Piaget's theory.* San Francisco: W. H. Freeman.

Phinney, J. S. (1989). Stages of ethnic identity in minority group adolescents. *Journal of Early Adolescence, 9,* 34–49.

Phinney, J. S. (1990). Ethnic identity in adolescents and adults: Review of research. *Psychological Bulletin, 108,* 499–514.

Phinney, J. S., & Rosenthal, D. A. (1992). Ethnic identity in adolescence: Process, context and outcome. In G. R. Adams, T. P. Gullotta, & R. Montemayor (Eds.), *Adolescent identity formation.* Newbury Park, CA: Sage.

Piaget, J. (1926). *The language and thought of the child.* New York: Harcourt Brace.

Piaget, J. (1929). *The child's conception of the world.* London: Routledge & Kegan Paul.

Piaget, J. (1929). *The child's conception of the world.* London: Routledge & Kegan Paul.

Piaget, J. (1930). *The child's conception of physical causality.* London: Routledge & Kegan Paul.

Piaget, J. (1952a). *The child's conception of number.* New York: W. W. Norton.

Piaget, J. (1952b). *The origins of intelligence in children.* New York: W. W. Norton.

Piaget, J. (1954). *The construction of reality in the child.* New York: Basic Books.

Piaget, J. (1962). *Play, dreams, and imitation in childhood.* New York: W. W. Norton.

Piaget, J. (1965). *The moral judgment of the child.* New York: Free Press. (Original work published 1932)

Piaget, J. (1970). *Psychology and epistemology.* New York: Norton.

Piaget, J. (1971). *Biology and knowledge: An essay on the relationship between organic regulations and cognitive processes.* Chicago: University of Chicago Press.

Piaget, J. (1974). *Understanding causality.* New York: Norton.

Piaget, J., & Inhelder, B. (1956). *The child's conception of space.* London: Routledge & Kegan Paul.

Pick, A. D. (1965). Improvement of visual and tactual discrimination. *Journal of Experimental Psychology, 69,* 331–339.

Pick, H. L., Jr. (1987). Information and the effects of early perceptual experience. In N. Eisenberg (Ed.), *Contemporary topics in developmental psychology.* New York: Wiley.

Pick, H. L., Jr. (1992). Eleanor J. Gibson: Learing to perceive and perceiving to learn. *Developmental Psychology, 28,* 787–794.

Pickens, J., & Field, T. (1993). Facial expressivity in infants of depressed mothers. *Developmental Psychology, 29,* 986–988.

Pillow, B. H. (1988). Young children's understanding of attentional limits. *Child Development, 59,* 38–46.

Pineau, A., & Streri, A. (1990). Intermodal transfer of spatial arrangement of the component parts of an object in infants aged 4–5 months. *Perception, 19,* 795–804.

Pinker, S. (1984). *Language learnability and language development.* Cambridge, MA: Harvard University Press.

Pinker, S. (1987). The bootstrapping problem in language acquisition. In B. MacWhinney (Ed.), *Mechanisms of language acquisition.* Hillsdale, NJ: Erlbaum.

Pinneau, S. R. (1961). *Changes in intelligence quotient: Infancy to maturity.* Boston: Houghton Mifflin.

Pinon, M. F., Huston, A. C., & Wright, J. C. (1989). Family ecology and child characteristics that predict young children's educational television viewing. *Child Development, 60,* 846–856.

Pinyerd, B. J. (1992). Assessment of infant growth. *Journal of Pediatric Health Care, 6,* 302–308.

Platt, L. D., Koch, R., Azen, C., Hanley, W. B., Levy, H. L., Matalon, R., Rouse, B., de la Cruz, F., & Walla, C. A. (1992). Maternal phenylketonuria collaborative study, obstetric aspects and outcome: The first 6 years. *American Journal of Obstetrics and Gynecology, 166,* 1150-1162.

Platt, S. A., & Sanislow, C. A. III. (1988). Norm-of-reaction: Definition and misinterpretation of animal research. *Journal of Comparative Psychology, 102,* 254-261.

Pleck, J. H. (1982). *Husbands' and wives' paid work, family work, and adjustment.* Working papers. Wellesley, MA: Wellesley College Center for Research on Women.

Pleck, J. H. (1983). Husbands' paid work and family roles: Current research issues. In H. Z. Lopata & J. H. Pleck (Eds.), *Research in the interweave of social roles: Families and jobs.* Greenwich, CT: JAI Press.

Plomin, R. (1986). *Development, genetics, and psychology.* Hillsdale, NJ: Erlbaum.

Plomin, R. (1987). Developmental behavioral genetics and infancy. In J. D. Osofsky (Ed.), *Handbook of infant development* (2nd ed.). New York: Wiley.

Plomin, R. (1989). Environment and genes: Determinants of behavior. *American Psychologist, 44,* 105–111.

Plomin, R. (1990). The role of inheritance in behavior. *Science, 248,* 183–188.

Plomin, R., & Daniels, D. (1987). Why are children in the same family so different from one another? *Behavioral and Brain Science, 10,* 1–16.

Plomin, R., & DeFries, J. C. (1980). Genetics and intelligence: Recent data. *Intelligence, 4,* 15–24.

Plomin, R., & DeFries, J. C. (1985). *Origins of individual differences in infancy: The Colorado Adoption Project.* Orlando, FL: Academic Press.

Plomin, R., & Rende, R. (1991). Human behavioral genetics. *Annual Reviews of Psychology, 42,* 161-190.

Plomin, R., Corley, R., DeFreis, J. C., & Fulker, D. W. (1990). Individual differences in television viewing in early childhood: Nature as well as nurture. *Psychological Science, 1,* 371-377.

Plomin, R., DeFries, J. C., & Loehlin, J. C. (1977). Genotype-environment interaction and correlation in the analysis of human behavior. *Psychological Bulletin, 84,* 309–322.

Plomin, R., DeFries, J. C., & McClearn, G. E. (1990). *Behavioral genetics: A primer* (2nd ed.). New York: W. H. Freeman.

Poche, C., McCubbrey, H., & Munn, T. (1982). The development of correct toothbrushing techniques in pre-school children. *Journal of Applied Behavior Analysis, 15,* 315–320.

Pogrebin, L. C. (1980). *Growing up free: Raising your kids in the 80's.* New York: McGraw-Hill.

Pollio, M. R., & Pickens, J. P. (1980). The developmental structure of figurative competence. In R. P. Honeck & R. R. Hoffman (Eds.), *Cognition and figurative language*. Hillsdale, NJ: Erlbaum.

Pollitt, E., Gorman, K. S., Engle, P. L., Martorell, R., & Rivera, J. (1993). Early supplementary feeding and cognition. *Monographs of the Society for Research in Child Development, 58* (7, Serial No. 235).

Pollock, L. A. (1983). *Forgotten children: Parent-child relations from 1500–1900*. Cambridge: Cambridge University Press.

Pomerleau, A., Bolduc, D., Malcuit, G., & Cossette, L. (1990). Pink or blue: Environmental gender stereotypes in the first two years of life. *Sex Roles, 22,* 359–367.

Poole, D. A., & White, L. T. (1991). Effects of question repetition on the eyewitness testimony of children and adults. *Developmental Psychology, 27,* 975–986.

Poole, D. A., & White, L. T. (1993). Two years later: Effects of question repetition and retention interval on the eyewitness testimony of children and adults. *Developmental Psychology, 29,* 844–853.

Porter, R. H., Balogh, R. D., & Makin, J. W. (1988). Olfactory influences on mother-infant interaction. In C. Rovee-Collier & L. P. Lipsitt (Eds.), *Advances in infancy research* (Vol. 5). Norwood, NJ: Ablex.

Porter, R. H., Makin, J. W., Davis, L. B., & Christensen, K. M. (1992). Breast-fed infants respond to olfactory cues from their own mother and unfamiliar lactating females. *Infant Behavior and Development, 15,* 85–93.

Postman, N. (1982). *The disappearance of childhood*. New York: Delacorte.

Powers, S. I., Hauser, S. T., & Kilner, L. A. (1989). Adolescent mental health. *American Psychologist, 44,* 200–208.

Prader, A. (1978). Catch-up growth. *Postgraduate Medical Journal, 54,* 133–146.

Prather, P. A., & Bacon, J. (1986). Developmental differences in part/whole identification. *Child Development, 57,* 549–558.

Pratt, M. W., Green, D., MacVicar, J., & Bountrogianni, M. (1992). The mathematical parent: Parental scaffolding, parenting style, and learning outcomes in long-division mathematics homework. *Journal of Applied Developmental Psychology, 13,* 17–34.

Premack, D. (1971). On the assessment of language competence in the chimpanzee. In A. M. Schrier & F. Stollnitz (Eds.), *Behavior of nonhuman primates: Vol. 4*. New York: Academic Press.

Pressley, M., & Levin, J. R. (1977). Task parameters affecting the efficacy of a visual imagery learning strategy in younger and older children. *Journal of Experimental Child Psychology, 24,* 53–59.

Preyer, W. (1888–1889). *The mind of the child* (H. W. Brown, Trans.). New York: Appleton. (Original work published 1882)

Price-Williams, D., Gordon, W., & Ramirez, M. (1969). Skill and conservation: A study of pottery-making children. *Developmental Psychology, 1,* 769.

Proffitt, D. R., & Bertenthal, B. I. (1990). Converging operations revisited: Assessing what infants perceive using discrimination measures. *Perception & Psychophysics, 47,* 1–11.

Pulkkinen, L. (1982). Self-control and continuity from childhood to adolescence. In P. B. Baltes & O. G. Brim (Eds.), *Life-span development and behavior* (Vol. 4). New York: Academic Press.

Purcell, P., & Stewart, L. (1990). Dick and Jane in 1989. *Sex Roles, 22,* 177–185.

Putallaz, M. (1987). Maternal behavior and children's sociometric status. *Child Development, 58,* 324–340.

Radin, N. (1981). The role of the father in cognitive, academic, and intellectual development. In M. E. Lamb (Ed.), *The role of the father in child development*. New York: Wiley.

Radin, N. (1982). Primary caregiving and role-sharing fathers. In M. E. Lamb (Ed.), *Nontraditional families: Parenting and child development*. Hillsdale, NJ: Erlbaum.

Radin, N., & Sagi, A. (1982). Childrearing fathers in intact families in Israel and the U.S.A. *Merrill-Palmer Quarterly, 28,* 111–136.

Radke-Yarrow, M., & Zahn-Waxler, C. (1984). Roots, motives, and patterns of children's prosocial behavior. In E. Staub, D. Bar-Tel, J. Karylowski, & J. Reykowski (Eds.), *Development and maintenance of prosocial behavior*. New York: Plenum Press.

Radke-Yarrow, M., Zahn-Waxler, C., & Chapman, M. (1983). Children's prosocial dispositions and behavior. In E. M. Hetherington (Ed.), *Handbook of child psychology: Vol. IV. Socialization, personality, and social development*. New York: Wiley.

Radziszewska, B., & Rogoff, B. (1988). Influence of adult and peer collaborators on children's planning skills. *Developmental Psychology, 24,* 840–848.

Radziszewska, B., & Rogoff, R. (1991). Children's guided participation in planning imaginary errands with skilled adult or peer partners. *Developmental Psychology, 27,* 381–389.

Raffaelli, M. (1989, April). *Conflict with siblings and friends in late childhood and early adolescence*. Paper presented at the biennial meeting of the Society for Research in Child Development, Kansas City, MO.

Rakic, P. (1981). Developmental events leading to laminar and areal organization of the neocortex. In F. O. Schmitt, F. G. Worden, G. Adelman, & S. G. Dennis (Eds.), *The organization of the cerebral cortex: Proceedings of a neurosciences research program colloquium*. Cambridge, MA: MIT Press.

Rallison, M. L. (1986). *Growth disorders in infants, children, and adolescents*. New York: Wiley.

Ramey, C. T., & Campbell, F. A. (1981). Educational intervention for children at risk for mild retardation: A longitudinal analysis. In P. Mittler (Ed.), *Frontiers of knowledge in mental retardation: Vol. 1. Social, educational, and behavioral aspects*. Baltimore: University Park Press.

Ramey, C. T., & Ramey, S. L. (1990). Intensive educational intervention for children of poverty. *Intelligence, 14,* 1–9.

Ramey, C. T., Bryant, D. M., & Suarez, T. M. (1987). Early intervention: Why, for whom, how, at what cost? In N. Gunzenhauser (Ed.), *Infant stimulation: For whom, what kind, when, and how much?* (Johnson & Johnson Baby Products Company Pediatric Round Table Series No. 13). Skilman, NJ: Johnson & Johnson.

Ramey, C. T., Bryant, D. M., Wasik, B. H., Sparling, J. J., Fendt, K. H., & LaVange, L. M. (1992). Infant Health and Development Program for low birth weight, premature infants: Program elements,. family participation, and child intelligence. *Pediatrics, 89,* 454–465.

Ramey, C. T., Lee, M. W., & Burchinal, M. R. (1989). Developmental plasticity and predictability: Consequences of ecological change. In M. H. Bornstein & N. A. Krasnegor (Eds.), *Stability and continuity in mental development: Behavioral and biological perspectives.* Hillsdale, NJ: Erlbaum.

Ratner, H. H. (1984). Memory demands and the development of young children's memory. *Child Development, 55,* 2173–2191.

Raven, J. C. (1962). *Coloured progressive matrices.* London: H. K. Lewis and Co.

Raven, J. C., Court, J. H., & Raven, J. (1985). *A manual for Raven's Progressive Matrices and vocabulary scales.* London: H. K. Lewis.

Redd, W. H., Morris, E. K., & Martin, J. A. (1975). Effects of positive and negative adult-child interaction on children's social preferences. *Journal of Experimental Child Psychology, 19,* 153–164.

Reisman, J. E. (1987). Touch, motion, and proprioception. In P. Salapatek & L. Cohen (Eds.), *Handbook of infant perception: From sensation to perception* (Vol. 1). Orlando, FL: Academic Press.

Reissland, N. (1988). Neonatal imitation in the first hour of life: Observations in rural Nepal. *Developmental Psychology, 24,* 464–469.

Renshaw, P. D. & Brown, P. J. (1993). Loneliness in middle childhood: Concurrent and longitudinal predictors. *Child Development, 64,* 1271–1284.

Reppucci, N. D. (1984). The wisdom of Solomon: Issues in child custody determination. In N. D. Reppucci, L. A. Weithorn, E. P. Mulvey, & J. Monahan (Eds.), *Children, mental health, and the law.* Beverly Hills, CA: Sage.

Resnick, L. B. (1986). The development of mathematical intuition. In M. Perlmutter (Ed.), *Perspectives on intellectual development: The Minnesota symposia on child psychology* (Vol. 19). Hillsdale, NJ: Erlbaum.

Resnick, M. B., Stralka, K., Carter, R. L., Ariet, M., Bucciarelli, R. L., Furlough, R. R., Evans, J. H., Curran, J. S., & Ausbon, W. W. (1990). Effects of birth weight and sociodemographic variables on mental development of neonatal intensive care unit survivors. *American Journal of Obstetrics and Gynecology, 162,* 374–378.

Rest, J. R. (1983). Morality. In J. H. Flavell & E. Markman (Eds.), *Handbook of child psychology: Vol. III. Cognitive development.* New York: Wiley.

Reznick, J. S., & Goldfield, B. A. (1992). Rapid change in lexical development in comprehension and production. *Developmental Psychology, 28,* 406–413.

Rheingold, H. L., & Cook, K. V. (1975). The contents of boys' and girls' rooms as an index of parents' behavior. *Child Development, 46,* 459–463.

Rhodes, W. A. & Brown (Eds. ). (1991). *Why some children succeed despite the odds.* New York: Praeger.

Rholes, W. S., & Ruble, D. N. (1984). Children's understanding of dispositional characteristics of others. *Child Development, 33,* 550–560.

Ribble, M. (1943). *The rights of infants.* New York: Columbia University Press.

Ricciuti, H. N. (1993). Nutrition and mental development. *Current Directions in Psychological Science, 2,* 43–46.

Rice, K. G. (1990). Attachment in adolescence: A narrative and meta-analytic review. *Journal of Youth and Adolescence, 19,* 511–538.

Rice, M. (1983). The role of television in language acquisition. *Developmental Review, 3,* 211–224.

Rice, M. L. (1989). Children's language acquisition. *American Psychologist, 44,* 149–156.

Rice, M. L., & Woodsmall, L. (1988). Lessons from television: Children's word learning when viewing. *Child Development, 59,* 420–429.

Rice, M. L., Huston, A. C., Truglio, R., & Wright, J. (1990). Words from "Sesame Street": Learning vocabulary while viewing. *Developmental Psychology, 26,* 421–428.

Richards, D. S., Frentzen, B., Gerhardt, K. J., McCann, M. E., & Abrams, R. M. (1992). Sound levels in the human uterus. *Obstetrics and Gynecology, 80,* 186–190.

Richards, H. G., Bear, G. G., Stewart, A. L., & Norman, A. D. (1992). Moral reasoning and classroom conduct: Evidence for a curvilinear relationship. *Merrill-Palmer Quarterly, 38,* 176–190.

Richards, M. H., & Ducket, E. (1994). The relationship of maternal employment to early adolescent daily experience with and without parents. *Child Development, 65,* 225–236.

Ricks, M. H. (1985). The social transmission of parental behavior: Attachment across generations. In I. Bretherton & E. Waters (Eds.), *Growing points of attachment theory and research. Monographs of the Society for Research in Child Development, 50*(1–2, Serial No. 209).

Rieber, L. P. (1990). Using computer animated graphics in science instruction with children. *Journal of Educational Psychology, 82,* 135–140.

Riesen, A. H. (1965). Effects of visual deprivation on perceptual function and the neural substrate. In J. de Ajuriaguerra (Ed.), *Dessafferentation expérimental et clinique.* Geneva: Georg.

Rieser, J., Yonas, A., & Wikner, K. (1976). Radial localization of odors by human newborns. *Child Development, 47,* 856–859.

Rieser, P. A. (1992). Educational, psychologic, and social aspects of short stature. *Journal of Pediatric Health Care, 6,* 325–332.

Robbins, W. J., Brody, S., Hogan, A. G., Jackson, C. M., & Green, C. W. (Eds.). (1928). *Growth.* New Haven: Yale University Press.

Roberts, L. (1991). Does the egg beckon sperm when the time is right? *Science, 252,* 214.

Robertson, M. A. (1984). Changing motor patterns during childhood. In J. R. Thomas (Ed.), *Motor development during childhood and adolescence.* Minneapolis, MN: Burgess.

Robins, L. N. (1978). Aetiological implications in studies of childhood histories relating to antisocial personality. In R. D. Hare & D. Schalling (Eds.), *Psychopathic behavior.* New York: Wiley.

Robinson, J. L., Kagan, J., Reznick, J. S., & Corley, R. (1992). The heritability of inhibited and uninhibited behavior: A twin study. *Developmental Psychology, 28,* 1030–1037.

Robinson, J. L., Kagan, J., Reznick, J. S., & Corley, R. (1992). The heritability of inhibited and uningibited behavior: A twin study. *Developmental Psychology, 28,* 1030-1037.

Rochat, P. (1992). Self-sitting and reaching in 5- to 8-month-old infants: The impact of posture and its development on early eye-hand coordination. *Journal of Motor Behavior, 24,* 210–220.

Rodgers, B. D., & Lee, R. V. (1988). Drug abuse. In G. N. Burrow & T. F. Ferris (Eds.), *Medical complications during pregnancy.* Philadelphia: W. B. Saunders.

Rodgers, R. R., Bronfenbrenner, U., & Devereux, E. C., Jr. (1968). Standards of social behavior among children in four cultures. *International Journal of Psychology, 3,* 31–41.

Roe, K. V., Drivas, A., Karagellis, A., & Roe, A. (1985). Sex differences in vocal interaction with mother and stranger in Greek infants: Some cognitive implications. *Developmental Psychology, 21,* 372–377.

Roffwarg, H. P., Muzio, J. N., & Dement, W. C. (1966). Ontogenetic development of the human sleep-dream cycle. *Science, 152,* 604–619.

Roggman, L. A., Langlois, J. H., & Hubbs-Tait, L. (1987). Mothers, infants, and toys: Social play correlates of attachment. *Infant Behavior and Development, 10,* 233–237.

Rogoff, B. (1981). Schooling and the development of cognitive skills. In H. C. Triandis & A. Heron (Eds.), *Handbook of cross-cultural psychology: Developmental psychology* (Vol. 4). Boston: Allyn & Bacon.

Rogoff, B. (1989). The joint socialization of development by young children and adults. In A. Gellatly, D. Rogers, & J. A. Sloboda (Eds.), *Cognition and social worlds.* Oxford: Clarendon Press.

Rogoff, B., & Morelli, G. (1989). Perspectives on children's development from cultural psychology. *American Psychologist, 44,* 343–348.

Rogoff, B., & Waddell, K. J. (1982). Memory for information organized in a scene by children from two cultures. *Child Development, 53,* 1224–1228.

Rogoff, B., Mistry, J., Göncü, A., & Mosier, C. (1993). Guided participation in cultural activity by toddlers and caregivers. *Monographs of the Society for Research in Child Development, 58*(8, Serial No. 236).

Rollins, B. C., & Thomas, D. L. (1979). Parental support, power, and control techniques in the socialization of children. In W. R. Burr, R. Hill, F. I. Nye, & I. L. Reiss (Eds.), *Contemporary theories about the family: Research-based theories* (Vol. 1). New York: Free Press.

Rosch, E., Mervis, C. B., Gray, W. D., Johnson, D. M., & Boyes-Braem, P. (1976). Basic objects in natural categories. *Cognitive Psychology, 8,* 382–439.

Rose, S. A., Feldman, J. F., & Wallace, I. F. (1992). Infant information processing in relation to six-year cognitive outcomes. *Child Development, 63,* 1126–1141.

Rose, S. A., Feldman, J. F., Wallace, I. F., & McCarton, C. (1989). Infant visual attention: Relation to birth status and developmental outcome during the first 5 years. *Developmental Psychology, 25,* 560–576.

Rose, S. A., Gottfried, A. W., & Bridger, W. H. (1981). Cross-modal transfer in 6-month-old infants. *Developmental Psychology, 17,* 661–669.

Rosekrans, M. A. (1967). Imitation in children as a function of perceived similarity to a social model and vicarious reinforcement. *Journal of Personality and Social Psychology, 7,* 307–315.

Rosen, K. S., & Rothbaum, F. (1993). Quality of parental caregiving and security of attachment. *Developmental Psychology, 29,* 358–367.

Rosenbaum, J. E. (1980). Social implications of educational grouping. *Review of Educational Research, 8,* 361–401.

Rosenberg, K. R. (1992). The evolution of modern human childbirth. *Yearbook of Physical Anthropology, 35,* 89–124.

Rosenblith, J. F., & Sims-Knight, J. E. (1985). *In the beginning: Development in the first two years of life.* Monterey, CA: Brooks/Cole.

Rosenfield, P., Lambert, N. M., & Black, A. (1985). Desk arrangement effects on pupil classroom behavior. *Journal of Educational Psychology, 77,* 101–108.

Rosengren, K. S., Gelman, S. A., Kalish, C. W., & McCormick, M. (1991). As time goes by: Children's early understanding of growth in animals. *Child Development, 62,* 1302–1320.

Rosenholtz, S. J., & Simpson, C. (1984). The formation of ability conceptions: Developmental trend or social construction? *Review of Educational Research, 54,* 31–63.

Rosenkoetter, L. I. (1973). Resistance to temptation: Inhibitory and disinhibitory effects of models. *Developmental Psychology, 8,* 80–84.

Rosenthal, D. (1970). *Genetic theory and abnormal behavior.* New York: McGraw-Hill.

Rosenthal, D. A., & Feldman, S. S. (1992). The nature and stability of ethnic identity in Chinese youth. *Journal of Cross-Cultural Psychology, 23,* 214–227.

Rosenthal, R., & Jacobson, L. (1968). *Pygmalion in the classroom: Teacher expectation and pupils' intellectual development.* New York: Holt, Rinehart & Winston.

Rosett, H. L., & Weiner, L. (1984). *Alcohol and the fetus, a clinical perspective.* New York: Oxford University Press.

Ross, D. M., & Ross, S. A. (1982). *Hyperactivity: Current issues, research, and theory* (2nd ed.). New York: Wiley.

Ross, G., Lipper, E. G., & Auld, P. A. M. (1991). Educational status and school-related abilities of very low birth weight premature children. *Pediatrics, 88,* 1125–1134.

Rosser, R. A. (1983). The emergence of spatial perspective taking: An information-processing alternative to egocentrism. *Child Development, 54,* 660–668.

Rossi, A. S. (1987). Parenthood in transition: From lineage to child to self-orientation. In J. B. Lancaster, J. Altmann, A. S. Rossi, & L. R. Sherrod (Eds.), *Parenting across the life span: Biosocial dimensions.* New York: Aldine de Gruyter.

Rothbart, M. K. (1986). Longitudinal home observations of infant temperament. *Developmental Psychology, 22,* 356–365.

Rothbart, M. K., & Derryberry, D. (1981). Development of individual differences in temperament. In M. E. Lamb & A. L. Brown (Eds.), *Advances in developmental psychology* (Vol. 1). Hillsdale, NJ: Erlbaum.

Rothberg, A. D., & Lits, B. (1991). Psychosocial support for maternal stress during pregnancy: Effect on birth weight. *American Journal of Obstetrics and Gynecology, 165,* 403–407.

Rothenberg, B. B. (1970). Children's social sensitivity and the relationship to interpersonal competence, intrapersonal comfort, and intellectual level. *Developmental Psychology, 2,* 335–350.

Rotnem, D. L. (1986). Size versus age: Ambiguities in parenting short-statured children. In B. Stabler & L. E. Underwood (Eds.), *Slow grows the child: Psychological aspects of growth delay.* Hillsdale, NJ: Erlbaum.

Rotter, J. B. (1966). Generalized expectancies for internal versus external locus of control of reinforcement. *Psychological Monographs: General and Applied, 80,* 1–28.

Rousseau, J. J. (1895). *Émile or treatise on education* (W. H. Payne, Trans.). New York: Appleton. (Original work published 1762)

Rovee-Collier, C. K. (1987). Learning and memory in infancy. In J. D. Osofsky (Ed.), *Handbook of infant development* (2nd ed.). New York: Wiley.

Rovee-Collier, C. K., & Lipsitt, L. P. (1987). Learning, adaptation, and memory in the newborn. In P. Stratton (Ed.), *Psychobiology of the human newborn.* New York: Wiley.

Rovee-Collier, C., & Hayne, H. (1987). Reactivation of infant memory: Implications for cognitive development. In H. W. Reese (Ed.), *Advances in child development and behavior* (Vol. 28). San Diego, CA: Academic Press.

Rovee-Collier, C., & Shyi, G. (1992). A functional and cognitive analysis of infant long-term retention. In M. L. Howe, C. J. Brainerd, & V. F. Reyna (Eds.), *Development of long-term retention.* New York: Springer-Verlag.

Rovee-Collier, C., Schechter, A., Shyi, G. C. W., & Shields, P. (1992). Perceptual identification of contextual attributes and infant memory retrieval. *Developmental Psychology, 28,* 307–318.

Rozin, P. (1990). Development in the food domain. *Developmental Psychology, 26,* 555–562.

Rubenstein, J., & Howes, C. (1976). The effects of peers on toddler interaction with mother and toys. *Child Development, 47,* 597–605.

Rubenstein, J., & Howes, C. (1979). Caregiving and infant behavior in day care and in homes. *Developmental Psychology, 15,* 1–24.

Rubin, K. H., & Everett, B. (1982). Social perspective-taking in young children. In S. G. Moore & C. R. Cooper (Eds.), *The young child: Reviews of research* (Vol. 3). Washington, DC: National Association for the Education of Young Children.

Rubin, K. H., & Krasnor, L. R. (1986). Social-cognitive and social behavioral perspectives on problem-solving. In M. Perlmutter (Ed.), *The Minnesota symposia on child psychology: Vol. 18. Cognitive perspectives on children's social and behavioral development.* Hillsdale, NJ: Erlbaum.

Rubin, K. H., & Schneider, F. W. (1973). The relationship between moral judgment, egocentrism, and moral behavior. *Child Development, 44,* 661–665.

Rubin, K. H., Fein, G. G., & Vandenberg, B. (1983). Play. In E. M. Hetherington (Ed.), *Handbook of child psychology: Vol. IV. Socialization, personality, and social development.* New York: Wiley.

Rubin, K. H., Maioni, T. L., & Hornung, M. (1976). Free play behaviors in middle- and lower-class preschoolers: Parten and Piaget revisited. *Child Development, 47,* 414–419.

Ruble, D. N. (1983). The development of social-comparison processes and their role in achievement-related self-socialization. In E. T. Higgins, D. Ruble, & W. W. Hartup (Eds.), *Social cognition and social development: A sociocultural perspective.* Cambridge: Cambridge University Press.

Ruble, D. N. (1987). The acquisition of self-knowledge: A self-socialization perspective. In N. Eisenberg (Ed.), *Contemporary topics in developmental psychology.* New York: Wiley.

Ruble, D. N., & Brooks-Gunn, J. (1982). The experience of menarche. *Child Development, 53,* 1557–1566.

Ruble, D. N., & Flett, G. L. (1988). Conflicting goals in self-evaluative information seeking: Developmental and ability level analyses. *Child Development, 59,* 97–106.

Ruble, D. N., Boggiano, A. K., Feldman, N. S., & Loebl, J. H. (1980). Developmental analysis of the role of social comparison in self-evaluation. *Developmental Psychology, 16,* 105–115.

Ruble, T. L. (1983). Sex stereotypes: Issues of change in the 1970s. *Sex Roles, 9,* 397–402.

Ruff, H. A., & Kohler, C. J. (1978). Tactual visual transfer in 6-month-old infants. *Infant Behavior and Development, 1,* 259–264.

Ruff, H. A., & Lawson, K. R. (1990). Development of sustained, focused attention in young children during free play. *Developmental Psychology, 26,* 85–93.

Rule, B. G., Nesdale, A. R., & McAra, M. J. (1974). Children's reactions to information about the intentions underlying an aggressive act. *Child Development, 45,* 794–798.

Rumbaugh, D. M., Gill, T. V., & von Glasersfeld, E. C. (1973). Reading and sentence completion by a chimpanzee (*Pan*). *Science, 182,* 731–733.

Rumberger, R. W. (1987). High school dropouts: A review of issues and evidence. *Review of Educational Research, 57,* 101–121.

Rushton, J. P. (1975). Generosity in children: Immediate and long-term effects of modeling, preaching, and moral judgment. *Journal of Personality and Social Psychology, 31,* 459–466.

Rushton, J. P. (1982). Social learning theory and the development of prosocial behavior. In N. Eisenberg (Ed.), *The development of prosocial behavior.* New York: Academic Press.

Russell, G. (1987). Fatherhood in Australia. In M. E. Lamb (Ed.), *The father's role: Cross-cultural perspectives.* Hillsdale, NJ: Erlbaum.

Russell, G., & Russell, A. (1987). Mother-child and father-child relationships in middle childhood. *Child Development, 58,* 1573–1585.

Rutter, M. (1979). Maternal deprivation 1972–1978: New findings, new concepts, new approaches. *Child Development, 50,* 283–305.

Rutter, M. (1983). Cognitive deficits in the pathogenesis of autism. *Journal of Child Psychology and Psychiatry, 24,* 513–532.

Rutter, M. (1983). School effects on pupil progress: Research findings and policy implications. *Child Development, 54,* 1–29.

Rutter, M. (1986). Meyerian psychobiology, personality development, and the role of life experiences. *American Journal of Psychiatry, 143,* 1077–1087.

Rutter, M. (1987). Psychosocial resilience and protective mechanisms. *American Journal of Orthopsychiatry, 57,* 316-331.

Rutter, M. (1991). Age changes in depressive disorders: Some developmental considerations. In J. Garber & K. A. Dodge (Eds.), *The development of emotion regulation and dysregulation.* Cambridge, UK: Cambridge University Press.

Rutter, M., & Garmezy, N. (1983). Developmental psychopathology. In E. M. Hetherington (Ed.), *Handbook of child psychology: Vol. IV. Socialization, personality, and social development.* New York: Wiley.

Rutter, M., & Madge, N. (1976). *Cycles of disadvantage.* London: Heinemann.

Rutter, M., Maughan, B., Mortimore, P., Ouston, J., & Smith, A. (1979). *Fifteen thousand hours: Secondary schools and their effects on children.* Cambridge: Harvard University Press.

Ryan, R. M., & Grolnick, W. S. (1986). Origins and pawns in the classroom: Self-report and projective assessments of individual differences in children's perceptions. *Journal of Personality and Social Psychology, 50,* 550–558.

Sadker, M. & Sadker, D. (1994). *Failing at fairness: How America's schools cheat girls.* New York: Charles Scribner's Sons.

Sagi, A., Lamb, M. E., Lewkowicz, K. S., Shoham, R., Dvir, R., & Estes, D. (1985). Security of infant-mother, -father, and -metapelet attachments among kibbutz-reared Israeli children. In I. Bretherton & E. Waters (Eds.), *Growing points of attachment theory and research. Monographs of the Society for Research in Child Development, 50*(1–2, Serial No. 209).

Salapatek, P. (1975). Pattern perception in early infancy. In L. B. Cohen & P. Salapatek (Eds.), *Infant perception: From sensation to cognition* (Vol. 1). New York: Academic Press.

Salomon, G., & Gardner, H. (1986). The computer as educator: Lessons from television research. *Educational Researcher, 15,* 13–19.

Salomon, G., Globerson, T., & Guterman, E. (1989). The computer as a zone of proximal development: Internalizing reading-related metacognitions from a reading partner. *Journal of Educational Psychology, 89,* 620–627.

Saltz, E., Campbell, S., & Skotko, D. (1983). Verbal control of behavior: The effects of shouting. *Developmental Psychology, 19,* 461–464.

Saltzman, R. L., & Jordan, M. C. (1988). Viral infections. In G. N. Burrow & T. F. Ferris (Eds.), *Medical complications during pregnancy.* Philadelphia: W. B. Saunders.

Salzinger, S., Feldman, R. S., Hammer, M., & Rosario, M. (1993). The effects of physical abuse on children's social relationships. *Child Development, 64,* 169–187.

Sameroff, A. J. (1968). The components of sucking in the human newborn. *Journal of Experimental Child Psychology, 6,* 607–623.

Sameroff, A. J. (1972). Learning and adaptation in infancy: A comparison of models. In H. W. Reese (Ed.), *Advances in child development and behavior* (Vol. 7). New York: Academic Press.

Sameroff, A. J. (1987). The social context of development. In N. Eisenberg (Ed.), *Contemporary topics in developmental psychology.* New York: Wiley.

Sameroff, A. J., & Cavanagh, P. J. (1979). Learning in infancy: A developmental perspective. In J. D. Osofsky (Ed.), *Handbook of infant development.* New York: Wiley.

Sameroff, A. J., & Chandler, P. J. (1975). Reproductive risk and the continuum of caretaking casualty. In F. D. Horowitz (Ed.), *Review of child development research* (Vol. 4). Chicago: University of Chicago Press.

Sameroff, A. J., Seifer, R., Baldwin, A., & Baldwin, C. (1993). Stability of intelligence from preschool to adolescence: The influence of social and family risk factors. *Child Development, 64,* 80–97.

Samuels, M., & Bennett, H. Z. (1983). *Well body, well earth: The Sierra Club environmental health sourcebook.* San Francisco: Sierra Club Books.

Samuels, M., & Samuels, N. (1986). *The well pregnancy book.* New York: Summit Books.

Santelli, J. S., & Beilenson, P. (1992). Risk factors for adolescent sexual behavior, fertility, and sexually transmitted diseases. *Journal of School Health, 62,* 271–279.

Santrock, J. W. (1975). Moral structure: The interrelations of moral behavior, moral judgment, and moral affect. *Journal of Genetic Psychology, 127,* 201–213.

Santrock, J. W., & Sitterle, K. A. (1987). Parent-child relationships in stepmother families. In K. Pasley & M. Ihinger-Tallman (Eds.), *Remarriage and stepparenting: Current research and theory.* New York: Guilford Press.

Savage-Rumbaugh, E. S., Murphy, J., Sevcik, R. A., Brakke, K. E., Williams, S. L., & Rumbaugh, D. M. (1993). Language comprehension in ape and child. *Monographs of the Society for Research in Child Development, 58,* (3–4, Serial No. 233).

Savin-Williams, R. C. (1979). Dominance hierarchies in groups of early adolescents. *Child Development, 50,* 923–935.

Savin-Williams, R. C. (1980). Dominance hierarchies in groups of middle to late adolescent males. *Journal of Youth and Adolescence, 9,* 75–85.

Sawin, D. B., & Parke, R. D. (1979). The effects of interagent inconsistent discipline on children's aggressive behavior. *Journal of Experimental Child Psychology, 28,* 525–538.

Saxby, L., & Bryden, M. P. (1985). Left visual field advantage in children for processing visual emotional stimuli. *Developmental Psychology, 20,* 253–261.

Saxe, G. B., Guberman, S. R., & Gearhart, M. (1987). Social processes in early number development. *Monographs of the Society for Research in Child Development, 52*(2, Serial No. 216).

Scafidi, F. A., Field, T. M., Schanberg, S. M., Bauer, C. R., Tucci, K., Roberts, J., Morrow, C., & Kuhn, C. M. (1990). Message stimulates growth in preterm infants: A replication. *Infant Behavior and Development, 13,* 167–188.

Scammon, R. E. (1930). The measurement of the body in childhood. In J. A. Harris, C. M. Jackson, D. G. Paterson, & R. E. Scammon (Eds.), *The measurement of man.* Minneapolis: University of Minnesota Press.

Scarr, S. (1981). Genetics and the development of intelligence. In S. Scarr (Ed.), *Race, social class, and individual differences in IQ.* Hillsdale, NJ: Erlbaum.

Scarr, S. (1987). Three cheers for behavior genetics: Winning the war and losing our identity. *Behavior Genetics, 17,* 219–228.

Scarr, S. (1992). Developmental theories for the 1990s: Development and individual differences. *Child Development, 63,* 1-19.

Scarr, S. (1993). Biological and cultural diversity: The legacy of Darwin for development. *Child Development, 64,* 1333-1353.

Scarr, S., & Carter-Saltzman, L. (1983). Genetics and intelligence. In J. L. Fuller & E. C. Simmel (Eds.), *Behavior genetics: Principles and applications.* Hillsdale, NJ: Erlbaum.

Scarr, S., & McCartney, K. (1983). How people make their own environments: A theory of genotype → environment effects. *Child Development, 54,* 424–435.

Scarr, S., & Weinberg, R. A. (1976). IQ test performance of black children adopted by white families. *American Psychologist, 31,* 726–739.

Scarr, S., & Weinberg, R. A. (1977). Intellectual similarities within families of both adopted and biological children. *Intelligence, 1,* 170–191.

Scarr, S., & Weinberg, R. A. (1978). The influence of "family background" on intellectual attainment. *American Sociological Review, 43,* 674–692.

Scarr, S., & Weinberg, R. A. (1983). The Minnesota adoption studies: Genetic differences and malleability. *Child Development, 54,* 260–267.

Scarr, S., Webber, P. L., Weinberg, R. A., & Wittig, M. A. (1981). Personality resemblance among adolescents and their parents in biologically related and adoptive families. *Journal of Personality and Social Psychology, 40,* 885–898.

Scarr-Salapatek, S., & Williams, M. L. (1973). The effects of early stimulation on low birth-weight infants. *Child Development, 44,* 94–101.

Schachter, F. F. (1982). Sibling deidentification and split-parent identification: A family tetrad. In M. E. Lamb & B. Sutton-Smith (Eds.), *Sibling relationships: Their nature and significance across the life-span.* Hillsdale, NJ: Erlbaum.

Schachter, F. F., Shore, E., Feldman-Rotman, S., Marquis, R. E., & Campbell, S. (1976). Sibling deidentification. *Developmental Psychology, 12,* 418–427.

Schafer, W. E., & Olexa, C. (1971). *Tracking and opportunity.* Scranton, PA: Chandler.

Schaffer, H. R., & Emerson, P. E. (1964). The development of social attachments in infancy. *Monographs of the Society for Research in Child Development, 29*(3, Serial No. 94).

Schaie, K. W. (1974). Translations in gerontology—from lab to life: Intellectual functioning. *American Psychologist, 29,* 802–807.

Schaie, K. W. (1983). The Seattle longitudinal study: A twenty-one year investigation of psychometric intelligence. In K. W. Schaie (Ed.), *Longitudinal studies of adult psychological development.* New York: Guilford Press.

Schaie, K. W., & Hertzog, C. (1986). Toward a comprehensive model of adult intellectual development: Contributions of the Seattle longitudinal study. In R. J. Sternberg (Ed.), *Advances in the psychology of human intelligence* (Vol. 3). Hillsdale, NJ: Erlbaum.

Schieffelin, B. B., & Ochs, E. (1983). A cultural perspective on the transition from prelinguistic to linguistic communication. In R. M. Golinkoff (Ed.), *The transition from prelinguistic to linguistic communication.* Hillsdale, NJ: Erlbaum.

Schlegel, A., & Barry, H. III. (1991). *Adolescence: An anthropological inquiry.* New York: Free Press.

Schlinger, H.D., Jr. (1992). Theory in behavior analysis: An application to child development. *American Psychologist, 47,* 1396-1410.

Schneider, B. H., & Byrne, B. M. (1985). Children's social skills training: A meta-analysis. In B. H. Schneider, K. H. Rubin, & J. E. Ledingham (Eds.), *Children's peer relations: Issues in assessment and intervention.* New York: Springer-Verlag.

Schneider, B., Trehub, S. E., Morrongiello, B. A., & Thorpe, L. A. (1986). Auditory sensitivity in preschool children. *Journal of the Acoustical Society of America, 79,* 447–452.

Schneider-Rosen, K., Braunwald, K., Carlson, V., & Cicchetti, D. (1985). Current perspectives on attachment theory: Illustrations from the study of maltreated infants. In I. Bretherton & E. Waters, (Eds.), *Growing points of attachment theory and research. Monographs of the Society for Research in Child Development, 50*(1–2, Serial No. 209).

Schnoll, S. H. (1986). Pharmacologic basis of perinatal addiction. In I. J. Chasnoff (Ed.), *Drug use in pregnancy: Mother and child.* Lancaster, England: MTP Press.

Schubert, J. B., Bradley-Johnson, S., & Nuttal, J. (1980). Mother-infant communication and maternal employment. *Child Development, 51,* 246–249.

Schulenberg, J., Asp, C. E., & Petersen, A. (1984). School from the young adolescent's perspective: A descriptive report. *Journal of Early Adolescence, 4,* 107–130.

Schuz, A. (1978). Some facts and hypotheses concerning dendritic spines and learning. In M. A. B. Brazier & H. Petsche (Eds.), *Architectonics of the cerebral cortex.* New York: Raven.

Schwartz, M., & Day, R. H. (1979). Visual shape perception in early infancy. *Monographs of the Society for Research in Child Development, 44*(7, Serial No. 182).

Scoville, R. (1983). Development of the intention to communicate: The eye of the beholder. In L. Feagans, C. Garvey, & R. Golinkoff (Eds.), *The origins and growth of communication.* Norwood, NJ: Ablex.

Scribner, S., & Cole, M. (1981). *The psychology of literacy.* Cambridge: Harvard University Press.

Scriver, C. R., & Clow, C. L. (1988). Avoiding phenylketonuria: Why parents seek prenatal diagnosis. *Journal of Pediatrics, 113,* 495–496.

Seavey, C. A., Katz, P. A., & Zalk, S. R. (1975). Baby X: The effects of gender labels on adult responses to infants. *Sex Roles, 1,* 103–109.

Secord, P., & Peevers, B. H. (1974). The development and attribution of person concepts. In T. Mischel (Ed.), *Understanding other persons.* Oxford: Blackwell.

Segall, M. H., Campbell, D. T., & Herskovits, M. J. (1966). *The influence of culture on perception.* New York: Bobbs-Merrill.

Self, P. A., Horowitz, F. D., & Paden, L. Y. (1972). Olfaction in newborn infants. *Developmental Psychology, 7,* 349–363.

Selman, R. L. (1976). Social-cognitive understanding: A guide to educational and clinical practice. In T. Lickona (Ed.), *Moral development and behavior: Theory, research, and social issues.* New York: Holt, Rinehart & Winston.

Selman, R. L. (1980). *The growth of interpersonal understanding: Developmental and clinical analysis.* New York: Academic Press.

Selman, R. L. (1981). The child as a friendship philosopher. In S. R. Asher & J. M. Gottman (Eds.), *The development of children's friendships.* Cambridge: Cambridge University Press.

Selman, R. L., & Byrne, D. F. (1974). A structural-developmental analysis of levels of role taking in middle childhood. *Child Development, 45,* 803–806.

Serbin, L. A., Connor, J. M., & Iler, I. (1979). Sex-stereotyped and nonstereotyped introductions of new toys in the preschool classroom: An observational study of teacher behavior and its effects. *Psychology of Women Quarterly, 4,* 261–265.

Serbin, L. A., Connor, J. M., Burchardt, C. J., & Citron, C. C. (1979). Effects of peer presence on sex-typing of children's play behavior. *Journal of Experimental Child Psychology, 27,* 303–309.

Serbin, L. A., O'Leary, K. D., Kent, R. N., & Tonick, I. J. (1973). A comparison of teacher response to the preacademic and problem behavior of boys and girls. *Child Development, 44,* 796–804.

Serbin, L. A., Powlishta, K. K., & Gulko, J. (1993). The development of sex typing in middle childhood. *Monographs of the Society for Research in Child Development, 58* (No. 2, Serial No. 232).

Serbin, L. A., Tonick, I. J., & Sternglanz, S. H. (1977). Shaping cooperative cross-sex play. *Child Development, 48,* 924–929.

Sergeant, J. (1988). From DSM-III attention deficit disorder to functional defects. In L. M. Bloomingdale & J. Sergeant (Eds.), *Attention deficit disorder: Criteria, cognition, intervention.* New York: Pergamon.

Shahar, S. (1990). *Childhood in the Middle Ages.* London: Routledge.

Shamai, S., & Coambs, R. B. (1992). The relative autonomy of schools and educational interventions for substance abuse, prevention, sex education and gender stereotyping. *Adolescence, 27,* 757–770.

Shankweiler, D., & Liberman, I. Y. (1990). *Phonology and reading disability: Solving the reading puzzle.* Ann Arbor: University of Michigan Press.

Shantz, C. (1983). Social cognition. In J. H. Flavell & E. M. Markman (Eds.), *Handbook of child psychology: Vol. III. Cognitive development.* New York: Wiley.

Shapira, A., & Madsen, M. C. (1969). Cooperative and competitive behavior of kibbutz and urban children in Israel. *Child Development, 4,* 609–617.

Shapiro, S., McCormick, M. C., Starfield, B. H., Krischer, J. P., & Bross, D. (1980). Relevance of correlates of infant deaths for significant morbidity at 1 year of age. *American Journal of Obstetrics and Gynecology, 136,* 363–373.

Sharp, D., Cole, M., & Lave, C. (1979). Education and cognitive development: The evidence from experimental research. *Monographs of the Society for Research in Child Development, 44*(1–2, Serial No. 178).

Shatz, C. J. (1992, September). The developing brain. *Scientific American,* pp. 60–67.

Shatz, M., & Gelman, R. (1973). The development of communication skills: Modification in the speech of young children as a function of listener. *Monographs of the Society for Research in Child Development, 38*(5, Serial No. 152).

Shaw, E., & Darling, J. (1985). *Strategies of being female.* Brighton, England: Harvester Press.

Sherif, M., Harvey, O. J., White, B. J., Hood, W. R., & Sherif, C. W. (1961). *Inter-group conflict and cooperation: The Robber's Cave experiment.* Norman: University of Oklahoma Press.

Shirley, M. M. (1931). *The first two years: A study of twenty-five babies: Vol. 1. Postural and locomotor development.* Minneapolis: University of Minnesota Press.

Shoda, Y., Mischel, W., & Peake, P. K. (1990). Predicting adolescent cognitive and self-regulatory competencies from preschool delay of gratification: Identifying diagnostic conditions. *Developmental Psychology, 26,* 978–986.

Shoop, J. G. (1992, October). "Fetal abuse" conviction overturned in Florida. *Trial.* pp. 70–76.

Shore, C. (1992). Virgin births and sterile debates. *Current Anthropology, 33,* 295-315.

Shostak, M. (1981). *Nisa: The life and words of a !Kung woman.* Cambridge: Harvard University Press.

Shrum, W., & Cheek, N. H. (1987). Social structure during the school years: Onset of the degrouping process. *American Sociological Review, 52,* 218–223.

Shultz, T. R. (1982). Causal reasoning in the social and nonsocial realms. *Canadian Journal of Behavior, 14,* 307–322.

Shultz, T. R., & Wells, D. (1985). Judging the intentionality of action-outcomes. *Developmental Psychology, 21,* 83–89.

Shultz, T. R., Wells, D., & Sarda, M. (1980). Development of the ability to distinguish intended actions from mistakes, reflexes, and passive movements. *British Journal of Social and Clinical Psychology, 19,* 301–310.

Shupert, C., & Fuchs, A. F. (1988). Development of conjugate human eye movements. *Vision Research, 28,* 585–596.

Shweder, R. A., Mahapatra, M., & Miller, J. G. (1987). Culture and moral development. In J. Kagan & S. Lamb (Eds.), *The emergence of morality in young children.* Chicago: University of Chicago Press.

Shy, K. K., Luthy, A. A., Bennett, F. C., Whitfield, M., Larson, E. G., Van Belle, G., Hughes, J. P., Wilson, J. A., & Stenchever, M. A. (1990). Effects of electronic fetal-heart-rate monitoring, as compared with periodic auscultation, on the neurological development of premature infants. *New England Journal of Medicine, 322,* 588–593.

Siegal, M. (1988). Children's knowledge of contagion and contamination as causes of illness. *Child Development, 59,* 1353–1359.

Siegel, A. W., Kirasic, K. C., & Kail, R. V., Jr. (1978). Stalking the elusive cognitive map: The development of children's representations of geographical space. In I. Altman & J. F. Wohlwill (Eds.), *Children and the environment.* New York: Plenum Press.

Siegel, L. S. (1993a). The development of reading. In H. W. Reese (Ed.), *Advances in child development and behavior: Vol. 24.* San Diego: Academic Press.

Siegel, L. S. (1993b). Phonological processing deficits as the basis of a reading disability. *Developmental Review, 13,* 246–257.

Siegler, R. S. (1989). Mechanisms of cognitive development. In M. R. Rosenzweig & L. W. Porter (Eds.), *Annual Review of Psychology, 40,* 353–379.

Siegler, R. S., & Crowley, K. (1991). The microgenetic method: A direct means for studying cognitive development. *American Psychologist, 46,* 606–620.

Siegler, R. S., & Jenkins, E. (1989). *How children discover new strategies.* Hillsdale, NJ: Erlbaum.

Siegler, R. S., & Richards, D. D. (1982). The development of intelligence. In R. J. Sternberg (Ed.), *Handbook of human intelligence.* Cambridge: Cambridge University Press.

Siegler, R. S., & Robinson, M. (1982). The development of numerical understandings. In H. W. Reese & L. P. Lipsitt (Eds.), *Advances in child development and behavior* (Vol. 16). New York: Academic Press.

Siegler, R. S., & Shrager, J. (1984). Strategy choices in addition and subtraction: How do children know what to do? In C. Sophian (Ed.), *Origins of cognitive skills.* Hillsdale, NJ: Erlbaum.

Sigelman, C. K., Carr, M. B., & Begley, N. L. (1986). Developmental changes in the influence of sex-role stereotypes on person perception. *Child Study Journal, 16,* 191–205.

Signorella, M. L. (1987). Gender schemata: Individual differences and context effects. In L. S. Liben & M. L. Signorella (Eds.), *New directions for child development: No. 38. Children's gender schemata.* San Francisco: Jossey-Bass.

Signorella, M. L., Bigler, R., & Liben, L. S. (1993). Developmental differences in children's gender schemata about others: A meta-analytic review. *Developmental Review, 13,* 147–183.

Signorielli, N. (1989). Television and conceptions about sex roles: Maintaining conventionality and the status quo. *Sex Roles, 21,* 341–360.

Silberstein, L., Gardner, H., Phelps, E., & Winner, E. (1982). Autumn leaves and old photographs: The development of metaphor preferences. *Journal of Experimental Child Psychology, 34,* 135–150.

Simmons, R. G., & Blyth, D. A. (1987). *Moving into adolescence: The impact of pubertal change and school context.* Hawthorne, NY: Aldine de Gruyter.

Simmons, R. G., Blyth, D. A., & McKinney, K. L. (1983). The social and psychological effects of puberty on white females. In J. Brooks-Gunn & A. C. Petersen (Eds.), *Girls at puberty.* New York: Plenum Press.

Simmons, R. G., Blyth, D. A., Van Cleave, E. F., & Bush, D. M. (1979). Entry into early adolescence: The impact of school structure, puberty, and early dating on self-esteem. *American Sociological Review, 44,* 948–967.

Simmons, R. G., Burgeson, R., Carlton-Ford, S., & Blyth, D. A. (1987). The impact of cumulative change in early adolescence. *Child Development, 58,* 1220–1234.

Simmons, R. G., Rosenberg, M., & Rosenberg, F. (1973). Disturbance in the self-image at adolescence. *American Sociological Review, 39,* 553–568.

Simner, M. L. (1971). Newborn's response to the cry of another infant. *Developmental Psychology, 5,* 136–150.

Sinclair, D. (1985). *Human growth after birth* (4th ed.). New York: Oxford University Press.

Singer, J. L., & Singer, D. G. (1983). Implications of childhood television viewing for cognition, imagination, and emotion. In J. Bryant & D. R. Anderson (Eds.), *Children's understanding of television: Research on attention and comprehension.* New York: Academic Press.

Singer, L. M., Brodzinsky, D. M., Ramsay, D., Steir, M., & Waters, E. (1985). Mother-infant attachment in adoptive families. *Child Development, 56,* 1543–1551.

Siqueland, E. R., & Lipsitt, L. P. (1966). Conditioned head turning in human newborns. *Journal of Experimental Child Psychology, 4,* 356–376.

Skinner, B. F. (1948). *Walden two.* New York: Macmillan.

Skinner, B. F. (1953). *Science and human behavior.* New York: Macmillan.

Skinner, B. F. (1957). *Verbal behavior.* New York: Appleton-Century-Crofts.

Skinner, B. F. (1971). *Beyond freedom and dignity.* New York: Knopf.

Skinner, B. F. (1974). *About behaviorism.* New York: Knopf.

Skinner, E. A., & Belmont, M. J. (1993). Motivation in the classroom: Reciprocal effects of teacher behavior and student engagement across the school year. *Journal of Educational Psychology, 85,* 571–581.

Skodak, M., & Skeels, H. M. (1949). A final follow-up study of one hundred adopted children. *Pedagogical Seminary and Journal of Genetic Psychology, 75,* 85–125.

Skuse, D. (1985). Nonorganic failure to thrive: A reappraisal. *Archives of Disease in Childhood, 60,* 173–178.

Slaby, R. G., & Crowley, C. G. (1977). Modification of cooperation and aggression through teacher attention to children's speech. *Journal of Experimental Child Psychology, 23,* 442–458.

Slaby, R. G., & Frey, K. S. (1975). Development of gender constancy and selective attention to same-sex models. *Child Development, 46,* 849–856.

Slaby, R. G., & Guerra, N. G. (1988). Cognitive mediators of aggression in adolescent offenders: 1. Assessment. *Developmental Psychology, 24,* 580–588.

Slater, A., Mattock, A., Brown, E., & Bremner, J. G. (1991). Form perception at birth: Cohen and Younger (1984) revisited. *Journal of Experimental Child Psychology, 51,* 395–406.

Slater, A., Morison, V., Somers, M., Mattock, A., Brown, E., & Taylor, D. (1990). Newborn and older infants' perception of partly occluded objects. *Infant Behavior and Development, 13,* 33–49.

Slater, A., Rose, D., & Morison, V. (1984). New-born infants' perception of similarities and differences between two- and three-dimensional stimuli. *British Journal of Developmental Psychology, 3,* 211–220.

Slaughter-Defoe, D. T., Nakagawa, K., Takanishi, R., & Johnson, D. J. (1990). Toward cultural/ecological perspectives on schooling and achievement in African- and Asian-American children. *Child Development, 61,* 363–383.

Slavin, R. E. (1987a). Ability grouping and student achievement in elementary schools: A best-evidence synthesis. *Review of Educational Research, 57,* 293–336.

Slavin, R. E. (1987b). Developmental and motivational perspectives on cooperative learning: A reconciliation. *Child Development, 58,* 1161–1167.

Slavin, R. E. (1990a). Achievement effects of ability grouping in secondary schools: A best-evidence synthesis. *Review of Educational Research, 60,* 471–499.

Slavin, R. E. (1990b). *Cooperative learning: Theory, research, and practice.* Englewood Cliffs, NJ: Prentice-Hall.

Smetana, J. G. (1988). Concepts of self and social conventions: Adolescents' and parents' reasoning about hypothetical and actual family conflicts. In M. R. Gunnar & W. A. Collins (Eds.), *The Minnesota symposia on child psychology: Vol. 21. Development during the transition to adolescence.* Hillsdale, NJ: Erlbaum.

Smetana, J. G., & Braeges, J. L. (1990). The development of toddlers' moral and conventional judgments. *Merrill-Palmer Quarterly, 36,* 329–346.

Smetana, J. G., Killen, M., & Turiel, E. (1991). Children's reasoning about interpersonal and moral conflicts. *Child Development, 62,* 629–644.

Smetana, J. G., Schlagman, N., & Adams, P. W. (1993). Preschool judgments about hypothetical and actual transgressions. *Child Development, 64,* 202–214.

Smilansky, S. (1968). *The effects of sociodramatic play on disadvantaged preschool children.* New York: Wiley.

Smilkstein, G., Helsper-Lucas, A., Ashworth, C., Montano, D., & Pagel, M. (1984). Prediction of pregnancy complications: An application of the biopsychosocial model. *Social Sciences & Medicine, 18,* 315–321.

Smith, B. L. (1988). The emergent lexicon from a phonetic perspective. In M. D. Smith & J. L. Locke (Eds.), *The emergent lexicon.* New York: Academic Press.

Smith, C. L., Gelfand, D. M., Hartmann, D. P., & Partlow, M. P. (1979). Children's causal attributions regarding help giving. *Child Development, 50,* 203–210.

Smith, I., Beasley, M. G., Wolff, O. H., & Ades, A. E. (1988). Behavior disturbance in 8-year-old children with early treated phenylketonuria. *Journal of Pediatrics, 112,* 403–408.

Smith, J. D., & Kemler-Nelson, D. G. (1984). Overall similarity in adults' classification: The child in all of us. *Journal of Experimental Psychology: General, 113,* 137–159.

Smith, L. B. (1989). From global similarities to kinds of similarities: The construction of dimensions in development. In S. Vosniadou & A. Ortony (Eds.), *Similarity and analogical reasoning.* New York: Cambridge University Press.

Smith, L. B., & Evans, P. M. (1989). Similarity, identity, and dimensions: Perceptual classification in children and adults. In B. E. Shepp & S. Ballesteros (Eds.), *Object perception: Structure and process.* Hillsdale, NJ: Erlbaum.

Smith, M. C. (1978). Cognizing the behavior stream: The recognition of intentional action. *Child Development, 49,* 736–743.

Smith, P. K., & Green, M. (1974). Aggressive behavior in English nurseries and playgroups: Sex differences and response of adults. *Child Development, 45,* 211–214.

Smith, T. E. (1988). Parental control techniques: Relative frequencies and relationships with situational factors. *Journal of Family Issues, 9,* 155–176.

Snarey, J. R. (1985). Cross-cultural universality of social-moral development: A critical review of Kohlbergian research. *Psychological Bulletin, 97,* 202–232.

Snow, C. E. (1977). The development of conversation between babies and mothers. *Journal of Child Language, 4,* 1–22.

Snow, C. E. (1984). Parent-child interaction and the development of communicative ability. In R. L. Schiefelbusch & J. Pickar (Eds.), *The acquisition of communicative competence.* Baltimore: University Park Press.

Snow, C. E. (1987a). Comment: Language and the beginnings of moral understanding. In J. Kagan & S. Lamb (Eds.), *The emergence of morality in young children.* Chicago: University of Chicago Press.

Snow, C. E. (1987b). Relevance of the notion of a critical period to language acquisition. In M. H. Bornstein (Ed.), *Sensitive periods in development.* Hillsdale, NJ: Erlbaum.

Sobal, J., & Stunkard, A. J. (1989). Socioeconomic status and obesity: A review of the literature. *Psychological Bulletin, 105,* 260–275.

Society for Research in Child Development. (1990, Winter). Ethical standards for research with children. *SRCD Newsletter.*

Solkoff, N., Yaffe, S., Weintraub, D., & Blase, B. (1969). Effects of handling on the subsequent development of premature infants. *Developmental Psychology, 1,* 765–768.

Sontag, L. W., Baker, C. T., & Nelson, V. L. (1958). Mental growth and personality development: A longitudinal study. *Monographs of the Society for Research in Child Development, 23*(2, Serial No. 68).

Sorce, J. F., Emde, R. N., Campos, J., & Klinnert, M. D. (1985). Maternal emotional signaling: Its effect on the visual cliff behavior of 1-year-olds. *Developmental Psychology, 21,* 195–200.

Spearman, C. (1904). "General intelligence," objectively determined and measured. *American Journal of Psychology, 15,* 72–101.

Spearman, C. (1923). *The nature of "intelligence" and the principles of cognition.* London: Macmillan.

Spearman, C. (1927). *The abilities of man.* London: Macmillan.

Spears, W., & Hohle, R. (1967). Sensory and perceptual processes in infants. In Y. Brackbill (Ed.), *Infancy and early childhood.* New York: Free Press.

Spelke, E. (1991). Physical knowledge in infancy: Reflections on Piaget's theory. In S. Carey & R. Gelman (Eds.), *The epigenesis of mind: Essays on biology and cognition.* Hillsdale, NJ: Erlbaum.

Spelke, E. S. (1976). Infants' intermodal perception of events. *Cognitive Psychology, 8,* 553–560.

Spelke, E. S. (1985). Perception of unity, persistence and identity: Thoughts on infants' conceptions of objects. In J. Mehler & R. Fox (Eds.), *Neonate cognition: Beyond the blooming, buzzing confusion.* Hillsdale, NJ: Erlbaum.

Spelke, E. S. (1987). The development of intermodal perception. In P. Salapatek & L. Cohen (Eds.), *Handbook of infant perception: From perception to cognition* (Vol. 2). Orlando, FL: Academic Press.

Spelke, E. S., & Owsley, C. J. (1979). Intermodal exploration and knowledge in infancy. *Infant Behavior and Development, 2,* 13–27.

Spelke, E., Hofsten, C. von, & Kestenbaum, R. (1989). Object perception in infancy: Interaction of spatial and kinetic information for object boundaries. *Developmental Psychology, 25,* 185–196.

Spence, S. H. (1986). Behavioural treatments of childhood obesity. *Journal of Child Psychology and Psychiatry, 27,* 447–453.

Spencer, M. B., & Markstrom-Adams, C. (1990). Identity processes among racial and ethnic minority children in America. *Child Development, 61,* 290–310.

Spitz, H. H. (1986). *The raising of intelligence.* Hillsdale, NJ: Erlbaum.

Spitz, R. (1946a). Anaclitic depression. *Psychoanalytic Study of the Child, 2,* 313–342.

Spitz, R. (1946b). Hospitalism: A follow-up report. *Psychoanalytic Study of the Child, 2,* 113–117.

Spivack, G., & Shure, M. B. (1974). *Social adjustment of young children.* San Francisco: Jossey-Bass.

Sprafkin, J. N., Liebert, R. M., & Poulos, R. W. (1975). Effects of a prosocial televised example on children's helping. *Journal of Experimental Child Psychology, 20,* 119–126.

Spreen, O., Tupper, D., Risser, A., Tuokko, H., & Edgell, D. (1984). *Human developmental neuropsychology.* New York: Oxford University Press.

Springer, K., & Keil, F. C. (1991). Early differentiation of causal mechanisms appropriate to biological and nonbiological kinds. *Child Development, 62,* 767–781.

Sroufe, L. A. (1983). Infant-caregiver attachment and patterns of adaptation in preschool: The roots of maladaptation and competence. In M. Perlmutter (Ed.), *The Minnesota symposia on child psychology: Vol. 16. Development and policy concerning children with special needs.* Hillsdale, NJ: Erlbaum.

Sroufe, L. A. (1985). Attachment classification from the perspective of infant-caregiver relationships and infant temperament. *Child Development, 56,* 1–14.

Sroufe, L. A., & Waters, E. (1976). The ontogenesis of smiling and laughter: A perspective on the organization of development in infancy. *Psychological Review, 83,* 173–189.

Sroufe, L. A., & Wunsch, J. P. (1972). The development of laughter in the first year of life. *Child Development, 43,* 1326–1344.

Sroufe, L. A., Bennett, C., Englund, M., & Urban, J. (1993). The significance of gender boundaries in preadolescence: Contemporary correlates and antecedents of boundary violation and maintenance. *Child Development, 64,* 455–466.

St. Peters, M. Fitch, M. Huston, A. C., Wright, J. C., & Eakins, D. J. (1991). Television and families: What do young children watch with their families? *Child Development, 62,* 1409–1423.

Staff. Stand and deliver. (1990). [Editorial]. *The Lancet, 335,* 761–762.

Staffieri, J. R. (1967). A study of social stereotypes of body image in children. *Journal of Personality and Social Psychology, 7,* 101–104.

Stahl, P. M. (1984). A review of joint and shared parenting literature. In J. Folberg (Ed.), *Joint custody and shared parenting.* Washington, DC: Bureau of National Affairs.

Stanbury, J. B., Wyngaarden, J. B., Frederickson, D. S., Goldstein, J. L., & Brown, M. S. (1988). Introduction. In C. R.

Scriver, A. L. Beaudet, W. S. Sly, & D. Valle (Eds.), *The metabolic basis of inherited disease* (6th ed Vol. I). New York: McGraw-Hill.

Stanovich, K. E. (1988). The right and wrong places to look for the cognitive locus of reading disability. *Annals of Dyslexia, 38,* 154–177.

Stanovich, K. E. (1992). Speculations on the causes and consequences of individual differences in early reading acquisition. In P. B. Gough, L. C. Ehri, & R. Treiman (Eds.), *Reading acquisition.* Hillsdale, NJ: Erlbaum.

Starfield, B., Shapiro, S., McCormick, M. C., & Bross, D. (1982). Mortality and morbidity in infants with intrauterine growth retardation. *Journal of Pediatrics, 101,* 978–983.

Stark, R. E. (1986). Prespeech segmental feature detection. In P. Fletcher & M. Garman (Eds.), *Language acquisition: Studies in first language development.* Cambridge: Cambridge University Press.

Stedman, L. C., & Kaestle, C. E. (1987). Literacy and reading performance in the United States from 1880 to the present. *Reading Research Quarterly, 22,* 8–46.

Stein, A. (1983). Pregnancy in gravidas over age 35 years. *Journal of Nurse-Midwifery, 28,* 17–20.

Steinberg, C. (1985). *TV facts.* New York: Facts on File Publications.

Steinberg, L. (1981). Transformations in family relations at puberty. *Developmental Psychology, 17,* 833–840.

Steinberg, L. (1988). Reciprocal relation between parent-child distance and pubertal maturation. *Developmental Psychology, 24,* 122–128.

Steinberg, L., Dornbusch, S. M., & Brown, B. B. (1992). Ethnic differences in adolescent achievement: An ecological perspective. *American Psychologist, 47,* 723–729.

Steinberg, L., Elmen, J. D., & Mounts, N. S. (1989). Authoritative parenting, psychosocial maturity, and academic success among adolescents. *Child Development, 60,* 1424–1436.

Steinberg, L., Fegley, S., & Dornbusch, S. M. (1993). Negative impact of part-time work on adolescent adjustment: Evidence from a longitudinal study. *Developmental Psychology, 29,* 171–180.

Steinberg, L., Greenberger, E., Garduque, L., & McAuliffe, S. (1982). High school students in the labor force: Some costs and benefits to schooling and learning. *Educational Evaluation and Policy Analysis, 4,* 363–372.

Steinberg, L., Lamborn, S. D., Dornbusch, S. M., & Darling, N. (1992). Impact of parenting practices on adolescent achievement: Authoritative parenting, school involvement, and encouragement to succeed. *Child Development, 63,* 1266–1281.

Steiner, J. E. (1979). Human facial expressions in response to taste and smell stimulation. In H. W. Reese & L. P. Lipsitt (Eds.), *Advances in child development and behavior* (Vol. 13). New York: Academic Press.

Stern, D. N. (1974). The goal and structure of mother-infant play. *Journal of the American Academy of Child Psychiatry, 13,* 402–421.

Sternberg, K. J., Lamb, M. E., Greenbaum, C., Cicchetti, D., Dawud, S., Cortes, R. M., Krispin, O., & Lorey, F. (1993). Effects of domestic violence on children's behavior problems and depression. *Developmental Psychology, 29,* 44–52.

Sternberg, R. J. (1981). A componential theory of intellectual giftedness. *Gifted Child Quarterly, 25,* 86–93.

Sternberg, R. J. (1985). *Beyond IQ: A triarchic theory of human intelligence.* Cambridge: Cambridge University Press.

Sternberg, R. J. (1986). Triarchic theory of intellectual giftedness. In R. J. Sternberg & J. E. Davidson (Eds.), *Conceptions of giftedness.* Cambridge, UK: Cambridge University Press.

Sternberg, R. J., & Nigro, G. (1980). Developmental patterns in the solution of verbal analogies. *Child Development, 51,* 27–38.

Sternberg, R. J., & Rifkin, B. (1979). The development of analogical reasoning processes. *Journal of Experimental Child Psychology, 27,* 195–232.

Sternberg, R. J., Conway, B. E., Ketron, J. L., & Bernstein, M. (1981). People's conceptions of intelligence. *Journal of Personality and Social Psychology, 41,* 37–55.

Stevenson, H. W., Chen, C., & Lee, S. (1993). Mathematics achievement of Chinese, Japanese, and American children: Ten years later. *Science, 259,* 53–58.

Stevenson, H. W., Lee, S., & Stigler, J. W. (1986). Mathematics achievement of Chinese, Japanese, and American children. *Science, 231,* 693–699.

Stevenson, H. W., Stigler, J. W., Lee, S., Lucker, G. W., Kitamura, S., & Hsu, C. (1985). Cognitive performance and academic achievement of Japanese, Chinese, and American children. *Child Development, 56,* 718–734.

Stevenson, H. W., Stigler, J. W., Lucker, G. W., & Lee, S. Y. (1986). Classroom behavior and achievement of Japanese, Chinese, and American children. In R. Glaser (Ed.), *Advances in instructional psychology.* Hillsdale, NJ: Erlbaum.

Stewart, G. D., Hassold, T. J., & Kunit, D. M. (1988). Trisomy 21: Molecular and cytogenetic studies of nondisjunction. In H. Harris & K. Hirschhorn (Eds.), *Advances in human genetics* (Vol. 17). New York: Plenum Press.

Stewart, L., & Pascual-Leone, J. (1992). Mental capacity constraints and the development of moral reasoning. *Journal of Experimental Child Psychology, 54,* 251–287.

Stigler, J. W., Lee, S., & Stevenson, H. W. (1987). Mathematics classrooms in Japan, Taiwan, and the United States. *Child Development, 58,* 1272–1285.

Stigler, J. W., Smith, S., & Mao, L.-W. (1985). The self-perception of competence by Chinese children. *Child Development, 56,* 1259–1270.

Stiles, J., Delis, D. C., & Tada, W. L. (1991). Global-local processing in preschool children. *Child Development, 62,* 1258–1275.

Stipek, D. J., & Hoffman, J. M. (1980). Children's achievement related expectancies as a function of academic performance histories and sex. *Journal of Educational Psychology, 72,* 861–865.

Stipek, D., Recchia, S., & McClintic, S. (1992). Self-evaluation in young chilren. *Monographs of the Society for Research in Child Development, 57,* (1, Serial No. 226).

Stipp, H., & Milavsky, J. R. (1988). U.S. television programming's effects on aggressive behavior of children and adolescents. *Current Psychology: Research & Reviews, 7,* 76–92.

Stolberg, A. L., & Anker, J. M. (1984). Cognitive and behavioral changes in children resulting from parental divorce and consequent environmental changes. *Journal of Divorce, 8,* 184–197.

Stout, J. W., & Rivara, F. P. (1989). School and sex education: Does it work? *Pediatrics, 83,* 375–379.

Straus, M. A., & Gelles, R. J. (1986). Societal change and change in family violence from 1975 to 1985 as revealed in two national surveys. *Journal of Marriage and the Family, 48,* 465–479.

Straus, M. A., Gelles, R. J., & Steinmetz, S. K. (1980). *Behind closed doors: Violence in the American family.* Garden City, NY: Doubleday.

Strayer, F. F., & Strayer, J. (1976). An ethological analysis of social agonism and dominance relations among preschool children. *Child Development, 47,* 980–989.

Streissguth, A. P., Barr, H. M., & Martin, D. C. (1983). Maternal alcohol use and neonatal habituation assessed with the Brazelton Scale. *Child Development, 54,* 1109–1118.

Streissguth, A. P., Barr, H. M., Sampson, P. D., Darby, B. L., & Martin, D. C. (1989). IQ at age 4 in relation to maternal alcohol use and smoking during pregnancy. *Developmental Psychology, 25,* 3–11.

Streissguth, A. P., Grant, T. M., Barr, H. M., Brown, Z. A., Martin, J. C., Mayock, D. E., Ramey, S. L., & Moore, L. (1991). Cocaine and the use of alcohol and other drugs during pregnancy. *American Journal of Obstetrics and Gynecology, 164,* 1239–1243.

Streissguth, A. P., Treder, R., Barr, H. M., Shepard, T., Bleyer, A., & Martin, D. (1984). Prenatal aspirin and offspring IQ in a large group. *Teratology, 29,* 59A–60A.

Strutt, G. F., Anderson, D. R., & Well, A. D. (1975). A developmental study of the effects of irrelevant information on speeded classification. *Journal of Experimental Child Psychology, 20,* 127–135.

Stunkard, A. J., Harris, J. R., Pedersen, N. L., & McClearn, G. E. (1990). The body-mass index of twins who have been reared apart. *New England Journal of Medicine, 322,* 1483–1487.

Stunkard, A. J., Sørensen, T. I., Hanis, C., Teasdale, T. W., Chakraborty, R., Schull, W. J., & Schulsinger, F. (1986). An adoption study of human obesity. *New England Journal of Medicine, 314,* 193–198.

Sturtevant, A. H. (1965). *A history of genetics.* New York: Harper & Row.

Sugarman, S. (1982). Developmental change in early representational intelligence: Evidence from spatial classification strategies and related verbal expressions. *Cognitive Psychology, 14,* 410–449.

Sugarman, S. (1983). *Children's early thought: Developments in classification.* New York: Cambridge University Press.

Sullivan, H. S. (1953). *The interpersonal theory of psychiatry.* New York: W. W. Norton.

Sullivan, S. A., & Birch, L. L. (1990). Pass the sugar, pass the salt: Experience dictates preference. *Developmental Psychology, 26,* 546–551.

Sulzer-Azaroff, B., & Mayer, G. R. (1977). *Applying behavior-analysis procedures with children and youth.* New York: Holt, Rinehart & Winston.

Summey, P. S. (1986). Cesarean birth. In P. S. Eakins (Ed.), *The American way of birth*. Philadelphia: Temple University Press.

Suomi, S. (1982). Biological foundations and developmental psychobiology. In C. B. Kopp & J. B. Krakow (Eds.), *The child: Development in a social context*. Reading, MA: Addison-Wesley.

Super, C. M. (1976). Environmental effects on motor development: The case of "African infant precocity." *Developmental Medicine and Child Neurology, 18,* 561–567.

Super, C. M., & Harkness, S. (1982). The infant's niche in rural Kenya and metropolitan America. In L. Adler (Ed.), *Issues in cross-cultural research*. New York: Academic Press.

Super, C. M., Herrera, M. G., & Mora, J. O. (1990). Long-term effects of food supplementation and psychosocial intervention on the physical growth of Colombian infants at risk of malnutrition. *Child Development, 61,* 29–49.

Surgeon General's Scientific Advisory Committee on Television and Social Behavior. (1972). *Television and growing up: The impact of televised violence* (DHEW Publication No. HSM 72–90). Washington, DC: U.S. Government Printing Office.

Surrey, J. L. (1991). The "self-in-relation": A theory of women's development. In J. V. Jordan, A. G. Kaplan, J. B. Miller, I. P. Stiver, & J. L. Surrey (Eds.), *Women's growth in connection*. New York: Guilford.

Susman, E. J., Inoff-Germain, G., Nottelmann, E. D., Loriaux, D. L., Cutler, G. B., Jr., & Chrousos, G. P. (1987). Hormones, emotional dispositions, and aggressive attributes in young adolescents. *Child Development, 58,* 1114–1134.

Sutton-Smith, B., & Rosenberg, B. G. (1970). *The sibling*. New York: Holt, Rinehart & Winston.

Svejda, M. J., Campos, J. J., & Emde, R. N. (1980). Mother-infant "bonding": Failure to generalize. *Child Development, 51,* 775–779.

Swain, I. U., Zelazo, P. R., & Clifton, R. K. (1993). Newborn infants' memory for speech sounds retained over 24 hours. *Developmental Psychology, 29,* 312–323.

Szajnberg, N., Ward, M. J., Krauss, A., & Kessler, D. B. (1987). Low birth-weight prematures: Preventive intervention and maternal attitude. *Child Psychiatry and Human Development, 17,* 152–165.

Tager-Flusberg, H. (1985). Putting words together: Morphology and syntax in the preschool years. In J. B. Gleason (Ed.), *The development of language*. Columbus, OH: Charles E. Merrill.

Talayesva, D. (1942). *Sun chief: The autobiography of a Hopi Indian*. New Haven: Yale University Press.

Tanner, J. M. (1962). *Growth at adolescence* (2nd ed.). Oxford: Blackwell.

Tanner, J. M. (1978). *Fetus into man: Physical growth from conception to maturity*. Cambridge: Harvard University Press.

Tanner, J. M., & Taylor, G. P. (1965). *Growth*. Alexandria, VA: Time/Life Books.

Tanner, J. M., Whitehouse, R. H., & Takaishi, M. (1966). Standards from birth to maturity for height, weight, height velocity, and weight velocity for British children 1965, Parts I and II. *Archives of Disease in Childhood, 41,* 613.

Taras, H. L., Sallis, J. F., Patterson, T. L., Nader, P. R., & Nelson, J. A. (1989). Television's influence on children's diet and physical activity. *Journal of Developmental and Behavioral Pediatrics, 10,* 176–180.

Taub, D. E., & Blinde, E. M. (1992). Eating disorders among adolescent female athletes: Influence of athletic participation and sport team membership. *Adolescence, 27,* 833–848.

Taylor, M. (1988). Conceptual perspective taking: Children's ability to distinguish what they know from what they see. *Child Development, 59,* 703–718.

Taylor, R. (1989). Cracking cocaine's legacy in babies of drug abusers. *The Journal of NIH Research, 1,* 29–31.

Teasdale, T. & Owen, K. (1985). Heredity and familial environment in intelligence and educational level—a sibling study. *Nature, 309,* 620–622.

Teller, D. Y., & Bornstein, M. H. (1987). Infant color vision and color perception. In P. Salapatek & L. Cohen (Eds.), *Handbook of infant perception: From sensation to perception* (Vol. 1). Orlando, FL: Academic Press.

Terman, L. M. (1916). *The measurement of intelligence*. Boston: Houghton Mifflin.

Terman, L. M. (1925). *Genetic studies of genius: Vol. 1. Mental and physical traits of a thousand gifted children*. Stanford, CA: Stanford University Press.

Terman, L. M. (1954). The discovery and encouragement of exceptional talent. *American Psychologist, 9,* 221–238.

Terman, L. M., & Merrill, M. A. (1937). *Measuring intelligence*. Boston: Houghton Mifflin.

Terman, L. M., & Merrill, M. A. (1973). *Stanford-Binet Intelligence Scale: Manual for the third revision*. Boston: Houghton Mifflin.

Terman, L. M., & Oden, M. H. (1959). *Genetic studies of genius: Vol. 4. The gifted group at midlife*. Stanford, CA: Stanford University Press.

Terrace, H. S., Pettito, L. A., Sanders, R. J., & Bever, T. G. (1979). Can an ape create a sentence? *Science, 206,* 891–900.

Tharp, R. G. (1989). Psychocultural variables and constants: Effects on teaching and learning in schools. *American Psychologist, 44,* 349–359.

Tharp, R. G., Jordan, C., Speidel, G. E., Au, K. H., Klein, T. W., Calkins, R. P., Sloat, K. C. M., & Gallimore, R. (1984). Product and process in applied developmental research: Education and the children of a minority. In M. E. Lamb, A. L. Brown, & B. Rogoff (Eds.), *Advances in developmental psychology* (Vol. 3). Hillsdale, NJ: Erlbaum.

Thase, M. W. (1988). The relationship between Down syndrome and Alzheimer's disease. In L. Nadel (Ed.), *The psychobiology of Down syndrome*. Cambridge, MA: MIT Press.

The crack children. (1990, February 12). *Newsweek*, pp. 62–63.

Thelen, E. (1979). Rhythmical stereotypies in normal human infants. *Animal Behavior, 27,* 699–715.

Thelen, E. (1983). Learning to walk is still an "old" problem: A reply to Zelazo. *Journal of Motor Behavior, 15,* 139–161.

Thelen, E., & Ulrich, B. D. (1991). Hidden skills: A dynamic systems analysis of treadmill stepping during the first year. *Monographs of the Society for Research in Child Development, 56*(1, Serial No. 223).

Thelen, E., Corbetta, D., Kamm, K., Spencer, J. P., Schneider, K., & Zernicke, R. F. (1993). The transition to reaching: Mapping

**711**

intention and intrinsic dynamics. *Child Development, 64,* 1058–1098.

Thelen, E., Kelso, J. A. S., & Fogel, A. (1987). Self-organizing systems and infant motor development. *Developmental Review, 7,* 39–65.

Thelen, E., Skala, K. D., & Kelso, J. A. S. (1987). The dynamic nature of early coordination: Evidence from bilateral leg movements in young infants. *Developmental Psychology, 23,* 179–186.

Thoman, A. (1993). Obligation and option in the premature nursery. *Developmental Review, 13,* 1–30.

Thoman, E. B., & Ingersoll, E. W. (1993). Learning in premature infants. *Developmental Psychology, 29,* 692–700.

Thomas, A., & Chess, S. (1977). *Temperament and development.* New York: Brunner/Mazel.

Thompson, C. (1982). Cortical activity in behavioural development. In J. W. T. Dickerson & H. McGurk (Eds.), *Brain and behavioural development.* London: Surrey University Press.

Thompson, L. A., Fagan, J. F., & Fulker, D. W. (1991). Longitudinal prediction of specific cognitive abilities from infant novelty preference. *Child Development, 62,* 530–538.

Thompson, R. A. (1990). Vulnerability in research: A developmental perspective on risk research. *Child Development, 61,* 1–16.

Thompson, R. A., Lamb, M. E., & Estes, D. (1982). Stability of infant-mother attachment and its relationship to changing life circumstances in an unselected middle-class sample. *Child Development, 53,* 144–148.

Thompson, S. K. (1975). Gender labels and early sex role development. *Child Development, 46,* 339–347.

Thompson, V. D. (1974). Family size: Implicit policies and assumed psychological outcomes. *Journal of Social Issues, 30,* 93–124.

Thorndike, R. L., Hagen, E. P., & Sattler, J. M. (1986). *The Stanford-Binet Intelligence Scale: Guide for administering and scoring* (4th ed.). Chicago: Riverside.

Thurstone, L. L. (1938). *Primary mental abilities.* Chicago: University of Chicago Press.

Thurstone, L. L. (1947). *Multiple factor analysis.* Chicago: University of Chicago Press.

Tieger, T. (1980). On the biological basis of sex differences in aggression. *Child Development, 51,* 943–963.

Tietjen, A. M. (1986). Prosocial moral reasoning among children and adults in a Papua New Guinea society. *Developmental Psychology, 22,* 861–868.

Tinbergen, N. (1951). *The study of instinct.* London: Oxford University Press.

Toda, S., & Fogel, A. (1993). Infant response to the still-face situation at 3 and 6 months. *Developmental Psychology, 29,* 532–538.

Toda, S., Fogel, A., & Kawai, M. (1990). Maternal speech to three-month-old infants in the United States and Japan. *Journal of Child Language, 17,* 279–294.

Tomasello, M. (1988). The role of joint attentional processes in early language development. *Language Sciences, 10,* 69–88.

Tomasello, M. (1992). The social bases of language acquisition. *Social Development, 1,* 68–87.

Tomasello, M., & Todd, J. (1983). Joint attention and lexical acquisition style. *First Language, 4,* 197–212.

Tomasello, M., Conti-Ramsden, G., & Ewert, B. (1990). Young children's conversations with their mothers and fathers: Differences in breakdown and repair. *Journal of Child Language, 17,* 115–130.

Tookey, P. A., Ades, A. E., & Peckham, C. S. (1992). Cytomegalovirus prevalence in pregnant women: The influence of parity. *Archives of Disease in Childhood, 67,* 779–783.

Touwen, B. C. L. (1974). The neurological development of the infant. In J. A. Davis & J. Dobbing (Eds.), *Scientific foundations of paediatrics.* Philadelphia: W. B. Saunders.

Trehub, S. E. (1987). Infants' perception of musical patterns. *Perception & Psychophysics, 41,* 635–641.

Trehub, S. E., Bull, D., & Thorpe, L. A. (1984). Infants' perception of melodies: The role of melodic contour. *Child Development, 55,* 821–830.

Trehub, S. E., Schneider, B. A., Morrongiello, B. A., & Thorpe, L. A. (1988). Auditory sensitivity in school-age children. *Journal of Experimental Child Psychology, 46,* 273–285.

Trehub, S. E., Thorpe, L. A., & Morrongiello, B. A. (1985). Infants' perception of melodies: Changes in a single tone. *Infant Behavior and Development, 8,* 213–223.

Treiber, F., & Wilcox, S. (1980). Perception of a "subjective" contour by infants. *Child Development, 51,* 915–917.

Trevarthen, W. (1987). *Human birth: An evolutionary perspective.* New York: Aldine de Gruyter.

Trevathen, W. R. (1987). *Human birth: An evolutionary perspective.* New York: Aldine de Gruyter.

Trevathen, W. R. (1988). Fetal emergence patterns in evolutionary perspective. *American Anthropologist, 90,* 674–681.

Trickett, P. K., & Susman, E. J. (1988). Parental perceptions of child-rearing practices in physically abusive and nonabusive families. *Developmental Psychology, 24,* 270–276.

Tronick, E. Z. (1987). The Neonatal Behavioral Assessment Scale as a biomarker of the effects of environmental agents on the newborn. *Environmental Health Perspectives, 74,* 185–189.

Tronick, E. Z. (1989). Emotions and emotional communication in infants. *American Psychologist, 44,* 112–119.

Tronick, E. Z., & Cohn, J. F. (1989). Infant-mother face-to-face interaction: Age and gender differences in coordination and the occurrence of miscoordination. *Child Development, 60,* 85–92.

Tronick, E. Z., Als, H., Adamson, L., Wise, S., & Brazelton, T. E. (1978). The infant's response to entrapment between contradictory messages in face-to-face interaction. *Journal of the American Academy of Child Psychiatry, 17,* 1–13.

Tronick, E. Z., Ricks, M., & Cohn, J. F., (1982). Maternal and infant affective exchange: Patterns of adaptation. In T. Field & A. Fogel (Eds.), *Emotion and early interaction.* Hillsdale, NJ: Erlbaum.

Tryon, R. C. (1940). Genetic differences in maze learning in rats. *Yearbook of the National Society for Studies in Education, 39,* 111–119.

Turiel, E. (1978). Social regulations and domains of social concepts. In W. Damon (Ed.), *New directions for child development: Vol. 1. Social cognition.* San Francisco: Jossey-Bass.

Turiel, E. (1983). *The development of social knowledge: Morality and convention.* Cambridge: Cambridge University Press.

Turiel, E., Hildebrandt, C., & Wainryb, C. (1991). Judging social issues. *Monographs of the Society for Research in Child Development, 56* (2, Serial No. 224).

Turkheimer, E. (1991). Individual and group differences in adoption studies of IQ. *Psychological Bulletin, 110,* 392–405.

Turkheimer, E., & Gottesman, I. I. (1991). Individual differences and the canalization of human behavior. *Developmental Psychology, 27,* 18–22.

Turner, S. M., & Mo, L. (1984). Chinese adolescents' self-concept as measured by the Offer Self-Image Questionnaire. *Journal of Youth and Adolescence, 13,* 131–142.

U.S. Bureau of the Census. (1978). *Statistical abstract of the United States* (98th ed.). Washington, DC: U.S. Government Printing Office.

U.S. Bureau of the Census. (1990a). *Statistical abstract of the United States* (110th ed.). Washington, DC: U.S. Government Printing Office.

U.S. Bureau of the Census. (1990b). Who's minding the kids? *Current population reports* (Series P-70, No. 20). Washington, DC: U.S. Government Printing Office.

U.S. Department of Health, Education, and Welfare. (1978). *Alcohol and health.* Rockville, MD: National Institute of Alcohol Abuse and Alcoholism.

U.S. Public Health Service. (1979). *Smoking and health* (A Report of the Surgeon General, U.S. Department of Health, Education, and Welfare Publication No. (PHS) 79–50066). Washington, DC: U.S. Public Health Service, Office on Smoking and Health.

Underwood, B., & Moore, B. (1982). Perspective-taking and altruism. *Psychological Bulletin, 91,* 143–173.

Underwood, L. E. (1991, March/April). Normal adolescent growth and development. *Nutrition Today,* pp. 11–16.

Uzgiris, I. (1968). Situational generality of conservation. In I. E. Sigel & F. H. Hooper (Eds.), *Logical thinking in children.* New York: Holt, Rinehart & Winston.

Valdez-Menchaca, M. C., & Whitehurst, G. J. (1992). Accelerating language development through picture book reading: A systematic extension to Mexican day care. *Developmental Psychology, 28,* 1106–1114.

Valian, V. (1986). Syntactic categories in the speech of young children. *Developmental Psychology, 22,* 562–579.

Valleroy, L. A., Harris, J. R., & Way, P. O. (1990). The impact of HIV infection on child survival in the developing world. *AIDS, 4,* 667–672.

Van Dyke, R. B. (1993). Pediatric human immunodeficiency virus infection and the acquired immunodeficiency syndrome. *American Journal of Diseases of Children, 147,* 524–525.

Vandell, D. L., & Mueller, E. C. (1980). Peer play and friendships during the first two years. In H. C. Foot, A. J. Chapman, & J. R. Smith (Eds.), *Friendship and social relations in children.* New York: Wiley.

Vandell, D. L., & Ramanan, J. (1992). Effects of early and recent maternal employment on children from low-income families. *Child Development, 63,* 938–949.

Vandell, D. L., & Wilson, K. S. (1982). Social interaction in the first year of life: Infants' social skills with peers versus mother. In K. H. Rubin & H. S. Ross (Eds.), *Peer relationships and social skills in childhood.* New York: Springer-Verlag.

Vandell, D. L., Henderson, V. K., & Wilson, K. S. (1988). A longitudinal study of children with day-care experiences of varying quality. *Child Development, 59,* 1286–1292.

Vandell, D. L., Wilson, K. S., & Buchanan, N. R. (1980). Peer interaction in the first year of life: An examination of its structure, content, and sensitivity to toys. *Child Development, 51,* 481–488.

Vandenberg, S. G., & Vogler, G. P. (1985). Genetic determinants of intelligence. In B. B. Wolman (Ed.), *Handbook of intelligence.* New York: Wiley.

Vandenberg, S. G., Singer, S. M., & Pauls, D. L. (1986). *The heredity of behavior disorders in adults and children.* New York: Plenum Press.

Varni, J. W., (1983). *Clinical behavioral pediatrics: An interdisciplinary biobehavioral approach.* New York: Pergamon Press.

Vaughn, B. E., Egeland, B., Sroufe, L. A., & Waters, E. (1979). Individual differences in infant-mother attachment at twelve and eighteen months: Stability and change in families under stress. *Child Development, 50,* 971–975.

Vaughn, B. E., Kopp, C. B., & Krakow, J. B. (1984). The emergence and consolidation of self-control from eighteen to thirty months of age: Normative trends and individual differences. *Child Development, 55,* 990–1004.

Vaughn, B. E., Taraldson, B., Crichton, L., & Egeland, B. (1980). Relationships between neonatal behavioral organization and infant behavior during the first year of life. *Infant Behavior and Development, 3,* 78–89.

Venezky, R. L. (1976). *Theoretical and experimental base for teaching reading.* The Hague: Mouton.

Vernon, P. A. (1983). Speed of information processing and general intelligence. *Intelligence, 7,* 53–70.

Vernon, P. E. (1966). Educational and intellectual development among Canadian Indians and Eskimos. *Educational Review, 18,* 79–91.

Veroff, J. (1969). Social comparison and the development of achievement motivation. In C. P. Smith (Ed.), *Achievement-related motives in children.* New York: Russell Sage.

Vinter, A. (1986). The role of movement in eliciting early imitations. *Child Development, 57,* 66–71.

Volling, B. R., & Belsky, J. (1992). The contribution of mother-child and father-child relationships to the quality of sibling interaction: A longitudinal study. *Child Development, 63,* 1209–1222.

Vorhees, C. V. (1986). Principles of behavioral teratology. In E. P. Riley & C. V. Vorhees (Eds.), *Handbook of behavioral teratology.* New York: Plenum Press.

Vosk, B., Forehand, R., Parker, J., & Rickard, K. (1982). A multimethod comparison of popular and unpopular children. *Developmental Psychology, 18,* 571–575.

Vuchinich, S., Hetherington, E. M., Vuchinich, R. A., & Clingempeel, W. G. (1991). Parent-child interaction and gender differences in early adolescents' adaptation to stepfamilies. *Developmental Psychology, 27,* 618–626.

Vurpillot, E. (1968). The development of scanning strategies and their relation to visual differentiation. *Journal of Experimental Child Psychology, 6,* 632–650.

Vurpillot, E., & Ball, W. A. (1979). The concept of identity and children's selective attention. In G. A. Hale & M. Lewis (Eds.), *Attention and cognitive development.* New York: Plenum Press.

Vuyk, R. (1981). *Overview and critique of Piaget's genetic epistemology 1965–1980* (Vols. 1 & 2). New York: Academic Press.

Vygotsky, L. S. (1962). *Thought and language* (E. Hanfmann & G. Vakar, Trans.). Cambridge: MIT Press.

Vygotsky, L. S. (1978). *Mind in society: The development of higher psychological processes.* Cambridge: Harvard University Press.

Waber, D. P. (1976). Sex differences in cognition: A function of maturation rate? *Science, 192,* 572–574.

Wachs, T. D. (1983). The use and abuse of environment in behavior-genetic research. *Child Development, 54,* 396–407.

Wachs, T. D., Bishry, Z., Sobhy, A., McCabe, G., Galal, O., & Shaheen, F. (1993). Relation of rearing environment to adaptive behavior of Egyptian toddlers. *Child Development, 64,* 586-604.

Waddington, C. H. (1971). Concepts of deveopment. In E. Tobach, L. R. Aronson, & E. Shaw (Eds.), *The biopsychology of development.* San Diego, CA: Academic Press.

Wadstroem, J. A. (1769). Metamorphosis humana, 1767. In C. von Linné, *Amoenitates academicae* (Vol. III, pp. 326–344).

Wagner, B. M., & Phillips, D. A. (1992). Beyond beliefs: Parent and child behaviors and children's perceived academic competence. *Child Development, 63,* 1380–1391.

Wagner, D. A. (1978). Memories of Morocco: The influence of age, schooling, and environment on memory. *Cognitive Psychology, 10,* 1–28.

Wagner, M. E., Schubert, H. J. P., & Schubert, D. S. P. (1985). Family size effects: A review. *Journal of Genetic Psychology, 146,* 65–78.

Wahler, R. G., & Dumas, J. E. (1984). Changing the observational coding styles of insular and noninsular mothers: A step toward maintenance of parent training effects. In R. F. Dangel & R. A. Polster (Eds.), *Parent training: Foundations of research and practice.* New York: Guilford Press.

Wahler, R. G., & Dumas, J. E. (1989). Attentional problems in dysfunctional mother-child interactions: An interbehavioral model. *Psychological Bulletin, 105,* 116–130.

Waldrop, M. F., & Halverson, C. F. (1975). Intensive and extensive peer behavior: Longitudinal and cross-sectional analyses. *Child Development, 46,* 19–26.

Walk, R. D. (1968). Monocular compared to binocular depth perception in human infants. *Science, 162,* 473–475.

Walk, R. D. (1981). *Perceptual development.* Monterey, CA: Brooks/Cole.

Walker, L. J. (1984). Sex differences in the development of moral reasoning: A critical review. *Child Development, 55,* 677–691.

Walker, L. J. (1989). A longitudinal study of moral reasoning. *Child Development, 60,* 157–166.

Walker, L. J., deVries, B., & Trevethan, S. D. (1987). Moral stages and moral orientations in real-life and hypothetical dilemmas. *Child Development, 58,* 842–858.

Walker, S. J. (1992). Supernatural beliefs, natural kinds, and conceptual structure. *Memory & Cognition, 20,* 655–662.

Walker-Andrews, A. S. (1986). Intermodal expression of expressive behaviors: Relation of eye and voice? *Developmental Psychology, 22,* 373–377.

Walker-Andrews, A. S., & Lennon, E. M. (1985). Auditory-visual perception of changing distance by human infants. *Child Development, 56,* 544–548.

Wallerstein, J. S., & Kelly, J. B. (1980). *Surviving the breakup: How children and parents cope with divorce.* New York: Basic Books.

Wallerstein, J. S., Corbin, S. B., & Lewis, J. M. (1988). Children of divorce: A ten-year study. In E. M. Hetherington & J. Arasteh (Eds.), *Impact of divorce, single-parenting, and step-parenting on children.* Hillsdale, NJ: Erlbaum.

Ward, S., Reale, G., & Levinson, D. (1972). Children's perceptions, explanations, and judgments of television advertising. In E. A. Rubenstein, G. A. Comstock, & J. P. Murray (Eds.), *Television and social behavior: Vol. 4. Television in day-to-day life: Patterns of use.* Washington, DC: U.S. Government Printing Office.

Warkany, J. (1983). Teratology: Spectrum of a science. In H. Kalter (Ed.), *Issues and reviews in teratology* (Vol. 1). New York: Plenum Press.

Warkany, J., & Schraffenberger, E. (1947). Congenital malformations induced in rats by roentgen rays. *American Journal of Roentgenology and Radium Therapy, 57,* 455–463.

Warshak, R. A., & Santrock, J. W. (1983). The impact of divorce on father-custody and mother-custody homes: The child's perspective. In L. Kurdek (Ed.), *New directions for child development: No. 19. Children and divorce.* San Francisco: Jossey-Bass.

Waters, E. (1978). The reliability and stability of individual differences in infant-mother attachment. *Child Development, 49,* 483–494.

Waters, E., & Deane, K. E. (1985). Defining and assessing individual differences in attachment relationships: Q-methodology and the organization of behavior in infancy and early childhood. In I. Bretherton & E. Waters (Eds.), Growing points of attachment theory and research. *Monographs of the Society for Research in Child Development, 50* (1–2, Serial No. 209).

Waters, E., Wippman, J., & Sroufe, L. A. (1979). Attachment, positive affect, and competence in the peer group: Two studies in construct validation. *Child Development, 50,* 821–829.

Watson, J. B. (1930). *Behaviorism.* New York: W. W. Norton.

Watson, J. S. (1971). Cognitive-perceptual development in infancy: Settings for the seventies. *Merrill-Palmer Quarterly, 17,* 139–152.

Watson, J. S., & Ramey, C. T. (1972). Reactions to response-contingent stimulation in early infancy. *Merrill-Palmer Quarterly, 18,* 219–227.

Wattenberg, W. W., & Clifford, C. (1964). Relation of self-concept to beginning achievement in reading. *Child Development, 35,* 461–467.

Wechsler, D. (1974). *Wechsler Intelligence Scale for Children—Revised.* New York: The Psychological Corporation.

Weinberg, R. (1989). Intelligence and IQ: Landmark issues and great debates. *American Psychologist, 44,* 98–104.

Weinberger, S. E., & Weiss, S. T. (1988). Pulmonary diseases. In G. N. Burrow & T. F. Ferris (Eds.), *Medical complications of pregnancy* (3rd ed.). Philadelphia: W. B. Saunders.

Weiner, B., & Handel, S. J. (1985). A cognition-emotion-action sequence: Anticipated emotional consequences of causal attributions and reported communication strategy. *Developmental Psychology, 21,* 102–107.

Weiner, L., & Morse, B. A. (1988). FAS: Clinical perspectives and prevention. In I. J. Chasnoff (Ed.), *Drugs, alcohol, pregnancy and parenting.* Boston: Kluwer Academic Publishers.

Weiss, B., Dodge, K. A., Bates, J. E., & Pettit, G. S. (1992). Some consequences of early harsh discipline: Child aggression and a maladaptive social information processing style. *Child Development, 63,* 1321–1335.

Weitsman, L. J. (1985). *The divorce revolution: The unexpected social and economic consequences for women and children in America.* New York: Free Press.

Weitzman, M., Gortmaker, S., & Sobol, A. (1992). Maternal smoking and behavior problems of children. *Pediatrics, 90,* 342–349.

Wellman, H. M. (1977). The early development of intentional memory. *Human Development, 20,* 86–101.

Wellman, H. M. (1990). *The child's theory of mind.* Cambridge, MA: MIT Press.

Wellman, H. M., & Estes, D. (1986). Early understanding of mental entities: A reexamination of childhood realism. *Child Development, 57,* 910–923.

Wellman, H. M., & Lempers, J. D. (1977). The naturalistic communicative abilities of two-year-olds. *Child Development, 48,* 1052–1057.

Welsh, M. C., Pennington, B. F., Ozonoff, S., Rouse, B., & McCabe, E. R. B. (1990). Neuropsychology of early-treated phenylketonuria: Specific executive function deficits. *Child Development, 61,* 1697–1713.

Wentworth, B. B., & Alexander, E. R. (1971). Seroepidemiology of infections due to members of the herpesvirus group. *American Journal of Epidemiology, 94,* 496–507.

Wentzel, K. R., & Erdley, C. A. (1993). Strategies for making friends: Relations to social behavior and peer acceptance in early adolescence. *Developmental Psychology, 29,* 819–826.

Werker, J. F. (1989). Becoming a native listener. *American Scientist, 77,* 54–59.

Werker, J. F., & Lalonde, C. E. (1988). Cross-language speech perception: Initial capabilities and developmental change. *Developmental Psychology, 24,* 672–683.

Werner, E. E. (1972). Infants around the world: Cross-cultural studies of psychomotor development from birth to two years. *Journal of Cross-Cultural Psychology, 3,* 111–134.

Werner, E., & Smith, R. (1982). *Vulnerable but invincible: A study of resilient children.* New York: McGraw-Hill.

Wertsch, J. V. (1985). *Vygotsky and the social formation of mind.* Cambridge: Harvard University Press.

Wertsch, J. V. (1989). A sociocultural approach to mind. In W. Damon (Ed.), *Child development today and tomorrow.* San Francisco: Jossey-Bass.

Wertsch, J. V., Minick, N., & Arns, F. J. (1984). The creation of context in joint problem solving. In B. Rogoff & J. Lave (Eds.), *Everyday cognition: Its development in social context.* Cambridge: Harvard University Press.

Wertsch, J. V., & Tulviste, P. (1992). L. S. Vygotsky and contemporary developmental psychology. *Developmental Psychology, 28,* 548–557.

Wertz, R. W., & Wertz, D. C. (1977). *Lying-in: A history of childbirth in America.* New York: Free Press.

Westinghouse Learning Corporation/Ohio University. (1969). *The impact of Head Start: An evaluation of the effects of Head Start on children's cognitive and affective development.* Washington, DC: Department of Commerce.

Wetzel, J. (1987). *American youth: A statistical snapshot.* Washington, DC: William T. Grant Foundation.

Wexler, K. (1982). A principle theory for language acquisition. In E. Wanner & L. Gleitman (Eds.), *Language acquisition.* Cambridge: Cambridge University Press.

Whalen, R. E. (1984). Multiple actions of steroids and their antagonists. *Archives of Sexual Behavior, 13,* 497–502.

White, B. L. (1971). *Human infants: Experience and psychological development.* Englewood Cliffs, NJ: Prentice-Hall.

White, J., & Labarba, R. (1976). The effects of tactile and kinesthetic stimulation on neonatal development in the premature infant. *Developmental Psychobiology, 9,* 569–577.

White, R. W. (1959). Motivation reconsidered: The concept of competence. *Psychological Review, 66,* 297–333.

White, S. D., & DeBlassie, R. R. (1992). Adolescent sexual behavior. *Adolescence, 27,* 183–191.

Whiting, B. B., & Edwards, C. P. (1988). *Children of different worlds.* Cambridge: Harvard University Press.

Whiting, B. B., & Whiting, J. W. M. (1975). *Children of six cultures: A psychocultural analysis.* Cambridge: Harvard University Press.

Widmayer, S. M., & Field, T. M. (1981). Effects of Brazelton demonstrations for mothers on the development of preterm infants. *Pediatrics, 67,* 711–714.

Widom, C. S. (1989). The cycle of violence. *Science, 244,* 160–166.

Wigfield, A., Eccles, J. S., Mac Iver, D., Reuman, D. A., & Midgley, C. (1991). Transitions during early adolescence: Changes in children's domain-specific self-perceptions and general self-esteem across the transition to junior high school. *Developmental Psychology, 27,* 552–565.

Wilder, G., Mackie, D., & Cooper, J. (1985). Gender and computers: Two surveys of computer-related attitudes. *Sex Roles, 13,* 215–228.

Willatts, P., & Rosie, K. (1989, April). *Planning by 12-month-old infants.* Paper presented at the biennial meeting of the Society for Research in Child Development, Kansas City, MO.

Williams, J. E., & Best, D. L. (1982). *Measuring sex stereotypes: A thirty nation study.* Beverly Hills, CA: Sage.

Wills, K. E., (1993). Neuropsychological functioning in children with spina bifida and/or hydrocephalus. *Journal of Clinical Child Psychology, 22,* 247–265.

Wilson, D. M., & Rosenfeld, R. G. (1987). Treatment of short stature and delayed adolescence. In C. P. Mahoney (Ed.), *Pediatric clinics of North America, 34,* 865–879.

Wilson, J. G. (1977). Current status of teratology: General principles and mechanisms derived from animal studies. In J. G. Wilson & F. C. Fraser (Eds.), *Handbook of teratology: Vol. 1. General principles and etiology.* New York: Plenum Press.

Wilson, M. N. (1986). The black extended family: An analytical consideration. *Developmental Psychology, 22,* 246–258.

Wilson, R. S. (1978). Synchronies in mental development: An epigenetic perspective. *Science, 202,* 939–948.

Wilson, R. S. (1983). The Louisville Twin Study: Developmental synchronies in behavior. *Child Development, 54,* 298–316.

Wilson, R. S. (1986). Continuity and change in cognitive ability profile. *Behavior Genetics, 16,* 45–60.

Wimmer, H., & Perner, J. (1983). Beliefs about beliefs: Representation and constraining function of wrong beliefs in young children's understanding of deception. *Cognition, 13,* 103–128.

Winer, G. A., Craig, R. K., & Weinbaum, E. (1992). Adults' failure on misleading weight-conservation tests: A developmental analysis. *Developmental Psychology, 28,* 109–120.

Winn, M. (1983). *Children without childhood.* New York: Pantheon Books.

Winner, E. (1979). New names for old things: The emergence of metaphoric language. *Journal of Child Language, 6,* 469–491.

Winner, E. (1986, August). Where pelicans kiss seals. *Psychology Today,* pp. 25–35.

Winstead, B. A. (1986). Sex differences in same-sex friendships. In V. J. Derlega & B. A. Winstead (Eds.), *Friendship and social interaction.* New York: Springer-Verlag.

Wissler, C. (1901). The correlation of mental and physical traits. *Psychological Monographs, 3,* 1–62.

Witelson, S. F. (1985). On hemisphere specialization and cerebral plasticity from birth: Mark II. In C. T. Best (Ed.), *Hemisphere function and collaboration in the child.* New York: Academic Press.

Witelson, S. F. (1987). Neurobiological aspects of language in children. *Child Development, 58,* 653–688.

Witkin, H. A., Mednick, S. A., Schulsinger, F., Bakkestrom, E., Christiansen, K. O., Goodenough, D. R., Hirschhorn, K., Lundsteen, C., Owen, D. R., Philip, J., Rubin, D. B., & Stocking, M. (1976). Criminality in XYY and XXY men. *Science, 193,* 547–555.

Wolf, T. M. (1973). Effects of live modeled sex-inappropriate play behavior in a naturalistic setting. *Developmental Psychology, 9,* 120–123.

Wolfe, D. A. (1985). Child-abusive parents: An empirical review and analysis. *Psychological Bulletin, 97,* 462–482.

Wolfe, D. A., Fairbank, J., Kelly, J. A., & Bradlyn, A. S. (1983). Child abusive parents' physiological responses to stressful and non-stressful behavior in children. *Behavioral Assessment, 5,* 363–371.

Wolff, P. H. (1969). The natural history of crying and other vocalizations in early infancy. In B. Foss (Ed.), *Determinants of infant behavior* (Vol. 4). London: Methuen.

Wolff, P. H. (1987). *The development of behavioral states and the expression of emotions in early infancy.* Chicago: University of Chicago Press.

Wood, D. J., Bruner, J. S., & Ross, G. (1976). The role of tutoring in problem solving. *Journal of Child Psychology and Psychiatry, 17,* 89–100.

Woods, N. S., Eyler, F. D., Behnke, M., & Conlon, M. (1993). Cocaine use during pregnancy: Maternal depressive symptoms and infant neurobehavior over the first month. *Infant Behavior and Development, 16,* 83–98.

Woolston, J. L. (1987). Obesity in infancy and early childhood. *Journal of the American Academy of Child and Adolescent Psychiatry, 26,* 123–126.

Worobey, J. (1985). A review of Brazelton-based interventions to enhance parent-infant interaction. *Journal of Reproductive and Infant Psychology, 3,* 64–73.

Worobey, J., & Belsky, J. (1982). Employing the Brazelton scale to influence mothering: An experimental comparison of three strategies. *Developmental Psychology, 18,* 736–743.

Wynn, K. (1992). Children's acquisition of the number words and the counting system. *Cognitive Psychology, 24,* 220–251.

Yakovlev, P. I., & Lecours, A. R. (1967). The myelogenetic cycles of regional maturation of the brain. In A. Minkowski (Ed.), *Regional development of the brain in early life.* Oxford: Blackwell.

Yarrow, L. J., Goodwin, M. S., Manheimer, H., & Milowe, I. D. (1973). Infancy experiences and cognitive and personality development at 10 years. In L. J. Stone, H. T. Smith, & L. B. Murphy (Eds.), *The competent infant: Research and commentary.* New York: Basic Books.

Yazigi, R. A., Odem, R. R., & Polakoski, K. L. (1991). Demonstration of specific binding of cocaine to human spermatozoa. *Journal of the American Medical Association, 266,* 1956–1959.

Yee, D. K., & Eccles, J. S. (1988). Parent perceptions and attributions for children's math achievement. *Sex Roles, 19,* 317–333.

Yen, I. H., Khoury, M. J., Erickson, J. D., James, L. M., Waters, G. D., & Berry, R. J. (1992). The changing epidemiology of neural tube defects, United States 1968–1989. *American Journal of Diseases of Children, 146,* 857–861.

Yendovitskaya, T. V. (1971). Development of attention. In A. V. Zaporozhets & D. B. Elkonin (Eds.), *The psychology of preschool children.* Cambridge: MIT Press.

Yogman, M. W. (1982). Observations on the father-infant relationship. In S. H. Cath, A. R. Gurwitt, & J. M. Ross (Eds.), *Father and child: Developmental and clinical perspectives.* Boston: Little, Brown.

Yogman, M. W., Dixon, S., Tronick, E., Als, H., Adamson, L., Lester, B. M., & Brazelton, T. B. (1977, April). *The goals and structure of face-to-face interaction between infants and their fathers.* Paper presented at the biennial meeting of the Society for Research in Child Development, New Orleans.

Yonas, A., & Owsley, C. (1987). Development of visual space perception. In P. Salapatek & L. Cohen (Eds.), *Handbook of infant perception: From perception to cognition* (Vol. 2). Orlando, FL: Academic Press.

Yoneshige, Y., & Elliott, L. L. (1981). Pure-tone sensitivity and ear canal pressure at threshold in children and adults. *Journal of the Acoustical Society of America, 70,* 1272–1276.

Young-Browne, G., Rosenfeld, H. M., & Horowitz, F. D. (1977). Infant discrimination of facial expression. *Child Development, 48,* 555–562.

Youngblade, L. M., & Belsky, J. (1992). Parent-child antecedents of 5-year-olds' close friendships: A longitudinal analysis. *Developmental Psychology, 28,* 700–713.

Youniss, J. (1980). *Parents and peers in social development: A Sullivan-Piaget perspective.* Chicago: University of Chicago Press.

Youniss, J., & Smollar, J. (1985). *Adolescent relations with mothers, fathers, and friends.* Chicago: University of Chicago Press.

Zagon, I. S., & McLaughlin, P. J. (1984). An overview of the neurobehavioral sequelae of perinatal opiod exposure. In J. Yanai (Ed.), *Neurobehavioral teratology.* New York: Elsevier.

Zahavi, S., & Asher, S. R. (1978). The effect of verbal instructions on preschool children's aggressive behavior. *Journal of School Psychology, 16,* 146–153.

Zahn-Waxler, C., & Radke-Yarrow, M. (1982). The development of altruism: Alternative research strategies. In N. Eisenberg-Berg (Ed.), *The development of prosocial behavior.* New York: Academic Press.

Zahn-Waxler, C., Friedman, S. L., & Cummings, E. M. (1983). Children's emotions and behaviors in response to infants' cries. *Child Development, 54,* 1522–1528.

Zahn-Waxler, C., Radke-Yarrow, M., & King, R. A. (1979). Child rearing and children's prosocial initiations toward victims of distress. *Child Development, 50,* 319–330.

Zahn-Waxler, C., Robinson, J. A., & Emde, R. N. (1991). The development of empathy in twins. *Developmental Psychology, 28,* 1038–1047.

Zajonc, R. B., & Markus, G. B. (1975). Birth order and intellectual development. *Psychological Review, 82,* 74–88.

Zajonc, R. B., Markus, H., & Markus, G. B. (1979). The birth order puzzle. *Journal of Personality and Social Psychology, 37,* 1325–1341.

Zaporozhets, A. V. (1965). The development of perception in the preschool child. *Monographs of the Society for Research in Child Development, 30*(2, Serial No. 100).

Zarbatany, L., Hartmann, D. P., & Rankin, D. B. (1990). The psychological functions of preadolescent peer activities. *Child Development, 61,* 1067–1080.

Zausmer, E., & Shea, A. M. (1984). Motor development. In S. M. Pueschel (Ed.), *The young child with Down syndrome.* New York: Human Sciences Press.

Zebrowitz, L. A., Kendall-Tackett, K., & Fafel, J. (1991). The influence of children's facial maturity on parental expectations and punishments. *Journal of Experimental Child Psychology, 52,* 221–238.

Zelazo, P. R. (1983). The development of walking: New find-ings and old assumptions. *Journal of Motor Behavior, 15,* 99–137.

Zelazo, P. R., Zelazo, N. A., & Kolb, S. (1972). "Walking" in the newborn. *Science, 176,* 314–315.

Zeskind, P. S. (1981). Behavioral dimensions and cry sounds of infants of differential fetal growth. *Infant Behavior and Development, 4,* 297–306.

Zeskind, P. S., & Lester, B. M. (1981). Analysis of cry features in newborns with differential fetal growth. *Child Development, 52,* 207–212.

Zeskind, P. S., & Ramey, C. T. (1981). Preventing intellectual and interactional sequelae of fetal malnutrition: A longitudinal, transactional and synergistic approach to development. *Child Development, 52,* 213–218.

Ziegler, C. B., Dusek, J. B., & Carter, D. B. (1984). Self-concept and sex-role orientation: An investigation of multidimensional aspects of personality development on adolescence. *Journal of Early Adolescence, 4,* 25–39.

Zigler, E. (1967). Familial mental retardation: A continuing dilemma. *Science, 155,* 292–298.

Zigler, E., & Berman, W. (1983). Discerning the future of early childhood intervention. *American Psychologist, 38,* 894–906.

Zigler, E., & Butterfield, E. C. (1968). Motivational aspects of changes in IQ test performance of culturally deprived nursery school children. *Child Development, 39,* 1–14.

Zigler, E., & Hodapp, R. M. (1986). *Understanding mental retardation.* Cambridge, UK: Cambridge University Press.

Zigler, E., & Muenchow, S. (1992). *Head Start: The inside story of America's most successful educational experiment.* New York: Basic Books.

Zigler, E., & Trickett, P. K. (1978). IQ, social competence, and evaluation of early childhood intervention programs. *American Psychologist, 33,* 789–798.

Zill, N. (1988). Behavior, achievement, and health problems among children in stepfamilies: Findings from a national survey of child health. In E. M. Hetherington & J. D. Arasteh (Eds.), *Impact of divorce, single-parenting, and stepparenting on children.* Hillsdale, NJ: Erlbaum.

Zimiles, H., & Lee, V. E. (1991). Adolescent family structure and educational progress. *Developmental Psychology, 27,* 314–320.

Zuckerman, B. (1988). Marijuana and cigarette smoking during pregnancy: Neonatal effects. In I. J. Chasnoff (Ed.), *Drugs, alcohol, pregnancy and parenting.* Boston: Kluwer Academic Publishers.

Zuckerman, B., & Bresnahan, K. (1991). Developmental and behavioral consequences of prenatal drug and alcohol exposure. *Pediatric Clinics of North America, 38,* 1387–1406.

Zuckerman, B., & Frank, D. A. (1992). "Crack kids": Not broken. *Pediatrics, 89,* 337–339.

# Credits

## Chapter 1

*Figure 1.2* Figure from Blass, E. M., & Smith, B. A., "Differential effects of sucrose, fructose, glucose, and lactose on crying in 1- to 3-day-old infants," *Developmental Psychology, 28,* pp. 804–810. Copyright © 1992 by the American Psychological Association. Reprinted by permission from the publisher and the author. *Figure 1.3* Gagnon, Mireille, and Robert Ladouceur, "Behavioral Treatment of Child Stutterers: Replication and Extension," *Behavior Therapy, Volume 23.* Copyright 1992 by the Association for Advancement of Behavior Therapy. Reprinted by permission of the publisher and the author. *Figure 1.4* Ornstein, P. A., Nans, M. J. and Liberty, C. (1975). Rehearsal and organization processes in children's memory. *Child Development, 46,* 818–830. © The Society for Research in Child Development, Inc. *Figure 1.5* Pinon, M. F., Hurston, A. C., and Wright, J. C. (1989). Family ecology and child characteristics that predict young children's educational television viewing. *Child Development, 60,* 846–856. © The Society for Research in Child Development, Inc.

## Chapter 2

*Figure 2.2* Goldstein, H., et al., (1992). "Peer-mediated intervention: Attending to, commenting on, and acknowledging the behavior of preschoolers with autism. *Journal of Applied Behavior Analysis, 25.* Used with permission of the publisher and the author. *Figure 2.4* Claire B. Kopp and Joanne B. Krakow (eds.), *The Child,* p. 648. Copyright ©1982 by Addison-Wesley Publishing Company, Inc. Reprinted by permission of the publisher and the author.

## Chapter 3

*Figure 3.1* Adapted from Isensee, W. (September 3, 1986). *The Chronicle of Higher Education.* Used with permission. *Figure 3.2* Alberts, B., Bray, D., Lewis, J., Raff, M. et al. (1983). *Molecular Biology of the Cell.* New York: Garland Publishing, Inc. Reprinted by permission. *Figure 3.6* From *Genetics, society & decisions* by Richard V. Kowles. Copyright ©1985 by Scott, Foresman and Company. Reprinted by permission of HarperCollins Publishers. *Figure 3.8* Scriver, C. et al., *The Metabolic Basis of Inherited Disease,* Sixth Edition. Copyright ©1989. Reproduced by permission of McGraw-Hill, Inc. *Table 3.4* Reprinted with the permission of the publishers from Developmental Theories for the 1990's: Development and Individual Differences by S. Scarr. *Child Development, 63,* p. 11. Copyright ©1992 The Society for Research in Child Development, Inc. *Table 3.5 Our uncertain heritage: Genetics and human diversity* by Daniel L. Hartl. Copyright ©1977 by Daniel L. Hartl. Reprinted by permission of HarperCollins Publisher.

## Chapter 4

*Figure 4.4* Reprinted with permission of the publishers from Maternal caffeine consumption and fetal behavior in normal third-trimester pregnancy by DeVoe, L. D. et. al. *American Journal of Obstetrics and Gynecology, 168,* p. 1109. Copyright ©1992 American Journal of Obstetrics & Gynecology. *Figure 4.3* Moore, K. L., *Before we are born,* 1989, 3rd Edition, W.B. Saunders Company. Reprinted by permission. *Figure 4.1* K. L. Moore, *The developing human,* 1988, 4th Edition, W.B. Saunders Company. Reprinted by permission. *Figure 4.5* Shapiro, S., McCormick, M. C., Starfield, B. H., et. al. Relevance of correlates of infant deaths for significant morbidity at one year of age. *American Journal of Obstetrics and Gynecology, 136:* 363–373, 1980. *Figure 4.7* Reprinted from *Science,* Vol. 152, p. 604–619. "Ontogenetic Development of the Human Sleep-Dream Cycle" by H. P. Roffwarg, J. N. Muzio, and W. C. Dement. Copyright ©1966 by the American Association for the Advancement of Science. *Table 4.4* Apgar, V. (1953). A proposal for a new method of evaluation of the new-born infant. *Anesthesia and Analgesia: Current Researches, 32,* 260–267. Reprinted by permission of International Anesthesia Research Society. *Table 4.3 Well body, well earth,* by Mike Samuels, M. D., and Hal Zina Bennett. Copyright ©1983 by Mike Samuels, M. D. and Hal Zina Bennett. Reprinted with permission of Sierra Club Books.

## Chapter 5

*Figure 5.1* Tanner, J. M., et. al. (1966). Standards from birth to maturity for height, weight, height velocity, and weight velocity for British children 1965, parts I and II. *Archives of Disease in Childhood, 41,* 613. Reprinted by permission. *Figure 5.5* From "The Development of the Brain," by William M. Cowan. Copyright ©1979 by Scientific American Inc. All rights reserved. *Figure 5.6* Connolly, K., and Elliot, J. (1972). The evolution and ontogeny of hand function. In N. B. Jones (Ed.) *The growth of competence.* Cambridge, England: Cambridge University Press. Reprinted by permission. *Figure 5.7* "Running and Throwing." Reprinted with permission from the American Alliance for Health, Physical Education, Recreation and Dance. *Figure 5.8* Marshall, W. A., and Tanner, Cambridge, MA: Harvard University Press. Copyright ©1978 by J. M. Tanner. *Figure 5.10* From Magnusson, D., et al. "Differential Maturation Among Girls and Its Relations to Social Adjustment: A Longitudinal Perspective." *Lifespan Development & Behavior,* Vol. 7. Copyright ©1986 Lawrence Erlbaum. Reprinted by permission of Lawrence Erlbaum Associates, Inc., Publishers and the author. *Figure 5.11* Newcomer, S. & Baldwin, W., "Demographics of adolescent sexual behavior, contraception, pregnancy, and STDs" from *Journal of School Health,* 62. Copyright © 1992 by the American School Health Association. Used with permission.

## Chapter 6

*Figure 6.10* Reprinted with the permission of the publishers from Maturation of human fetal responses to vibroacoustic stimulation, by Kisilevsky et. al. *Child Development, 63,* pp. 1497-1508. Copyright ©1992 The Society for Research in Child Development, Inc. *Figure 6.11* Pick, A. D. (1965). Improvement of visual and tactual discrimination. *Journal of Experimental Psychology, 69,* 331-339. Copyright 1969 by the American Psychological Association. Adapted by permission. *Figure 6.12* Elkind, D., Koeglar, R. R., and Go, E. (1964). Studies in perceptual development II: Part-whole perception. *Child Development, 35,* 81-90. © The Society for Research in Child Development, Inc. *Figure 6.3* From "The Origins of Form Perception," by Robert L. Fantz. Copyright © 1961 by Scientific American Inc. All rights reserved. *Figure 6.4* Salapatek, P. (1975). "Pattern Perception in Early Infancy." In L. B. Cohen & P. Salapatek (Eds.), *Infant Perception: From sensation to cognition (Vol. 1).* New York: Academic Press. Reprinted by permission of the publisher and the author. *Figure 6.6* Treiber, F., and Wilcox, S. (1980). "Perception of a 'subjective' contour by infants." Child Development, Inc. *Figure 6.7* Spelke, E. S. (1985). Perception of unity, persistence and identity: Thoughts on infants' conceptions of objects. From J. Mehler and R. Fox (Eds.), *Neonate Cognition: Beyond the Blooming, Buzzing Confusion.* Copyright © 1985 Lawrence Erlbaum. Reprinted by permission of Lawrence Erlbaum Associates, Inc., Publishers and the author.

## Chapter 7

*Figure 7.1* Fernald, A. (1985). Four-month-olds prefer to listen to motherese. Infant Behavior and Development, 8, 181-195. Reprinted with permission of Albex Publishing Corporation. *Figure 7.2* Nelson, K. (1973). Structure and strategy in learning to talk. Monographs of the Society For Research in Child Development, 38, (1-2, serial no. 149) © The Society for Research in Child Development, Inc. *Figure 7.3* Goldfield, B. A., and Reznick, J. S. (1990). Early lexical acquisition: Rate, content and the vocabulary spurt. *Journal of Child Language,* 17, 171-183, Reprinted by permission of Cambridge University Press. *Figure 7.4* Kraus, R. H., and Glucksberg, S. (1969). The development of communication. *Child Development, 40,* 255-266. © The Society for Research in Child Development, Inc. *Figure 7.6* Figure from Johnson, J. and Newport E. (1989), "Critical period effects in second language learning: The influence of maturational state on the acquisition of English as a second language," in *Cognitive Psychology, 21* 60-99. *Figure 7.7* Figure A1 From the Raven Standard Progressive Matrices is reproduced by permission of J. C. Raven Ltd. *Table 7.1* Braine, M. D. S. (1976). Children's first word combinations. Monographs of the Society for Research in Child Development, 41 (1, serial No. 164) © The Society for Research in Child Development, Inc. *Table 7.2* Modified and reprinted by permission of the publishers from *A first language* by

R. Brown, Cambridge, Mass: Harvard University Press, Copyright © 1973 by the President and Fellows of Harvard College. Reprinted by permission of Harvard University Press and International Thomson.

## Chapter 8

*Figure 8.2* Baillargeon, R. (1987). Object permanence in 3 1/2–4 1/2-month-old infants. *Developmental Psychology, 23,* 655-664. Copyright 1987 by the American Psychological Association. Reprinted by permission. *Figure 8.4* Reprinted from Cognition, Vol. 25, "Do six-month-olds perceive causality?" by A. M. Leslie and S. Keeble. Copyright © 1987 Elsevier Science Publishers. Used with permission from the publisher and the author. *Figure 8.6* From The origins of intellect: Piaget's theory by John L. Phillips, Jr. Copyright © 1969, and 1975 by W. H. Freeman and Company. Reprinted by permission. *Figure 8.7* Miller, P. H., Kessell, F. S., and Flavell, J. H. (1970). Thinking about people thinking about... A study of cognitive development. Child Development, Inc. *Figure 8.8* Gurucharri, C., and Selman, R. L. (1982). The development of interpersonal understanding during childhood. *Child Development,* 53, p. 926. © The Society for Research in Child Development, Inc. *Table 8.2* Selman, R. L. (1976). Social-cognitive understanding: A guide to educational and clinical practice. In T. Lickona (Ed.) *Moral Development and Behavior: Theory, Research, and Social Issues.* Holt, Rinehart and Winston. Reprinted by permission.

## Chapter 9

*Figure 9.1* From Vurpillot, E. (1968), "The development of scanning strategies and their relation to visual differentiation," *Journal of Experimental Child Psychology, 6,* 632-650. Reprinted by permission of Academic Press and the author. *Figure 9.2* Adapted from "Visual Attention and Comprehension of Television in Attention-Deficit Hyperactivity Disordered and Normal Boys" by S. Landau, E. P. Lorch, & R. Milich from *Child Development,* Vol. 63, p. 928-937. Copyright © 1992 The Society for Research in Child Development, Inc. Used with permission. *Figure 9.3* Fagan, J. F. (1979). Infant recognition memory: The effects of length of familiarization and type of discrimination task. *Child Development, 45,* 351-356. © The Society for Research in Child Development, Inc. *Figure 9.5* Dempster, F. N. (1981). "Memory Span: Sources of Individual and Developmental Differences," *Psychological Bulletin, 89,* 63-100. Copyright 1981 by the American Psychological Association. Reprinted by permission from the publisher and the author. *Figure 9.6* Ornstein, P. A., Naus , M. J., and Liberty, C. (1975). Rehearsal and organization processes in children's memory. *Child Development, 46,* 818-830. © The Society for Research in Child Development, Inc. *Figure 9.7* Kobasigwa, A. (1974). Utilization of retrieval cues by children in recall. *Child Development, 45,* 127-134. © The Society for Research in Child Development, Inc. *Figure 9.9* "Tower of Hanoi". Figure adapted from "Goal formation, planning, and learning by preschool problem solvers or 'My socks are in the dryer," by David Klahr. Copyright © 1978 by David Klahr. Used with permission. *Table 9.1* Ornstein, P.A., Naus, M. J., and Liberty, C. (1975). Rehearsal and organization processes in children's memory. *Child Development, 46,* 818-830. © The Society for Research in Child Development, Inc. *Table 9.2* Excerpt from "Interactive teaching to promote independent learning from text" by Annemarie Palinscar and Ann L. Brown, *The Reading Teacher,* April 1986. Reprinted with permission of Annemarie Palincsar and the International Reading Association.

## Chapter 10

*Figure 10.1* Guilford, J. P. (1985). The structure of intellect model. In B. B. Wolman (Ed.), *Handbook of Human Intelligence,* p. 230. Copyright © 1985 by John Wiley and Sons, Inc. Reprinted by permission of John Wiley and Sons, Inc. *Figure 10.3* Vandenberg, S. G. (1971). What do we need to know about the inheritance of intelligence and how do we know it? In R. Cancro (Ed.), *Intelligence: Genetic and Environmental Influences.* Figure 2, p. 184. Reprinted by permission of Grune and Stratton, Inc. *Figure 10.4* Simulated items similar to those in the Wechsler Intelligence Scale for Children-Revised. Copyright © by The Psychological Corporation. Reproduced by permission. All rights reserved. *Figure 10.5* Kaufman, A. S., and Kaufman, A. S. (1983). *Kaufman Assessment Battery for Children* (K-ABC). Circle Pines, MN: American Guidance Service, Inc. *Figure 10.6* Journal of Genetic Psychology, Vol. 75, p. 165-196. Reprinted with permission of Helen Dwight Reid Educational Foundation. Published by Heldref Publications. 1319 Eighteenth St., N.W., Washington, D.C. 20036-1802. Copyright © 1949. *Table 10.1* Siegler, R. S., and Richards, D. D. (1982). The development of intelligence. In R. J. Sternberg (Ed.), *Handbook of Human Intelligence,* Cambridge University Press, p. 889. Reprinted by permission. *Table 10.2* From the Bayley Scales of Infant Development. Copyright © 1969 by The Psychological Corporation. Reproduced by permission. All rights reserved. *Table 10.3* Adapted from Grossman, H. J. (1983). *Classification in mental retardation* (rev. ed.). Washington, DC: American Association on Mental Deficiency. *Table 10.4* Elardo, R., & Bradley, R. H. (1981), "The Home Observation for Measurement of the Environment (HOME) Scale: A Review of Research. *Developmental Review,* 1, 113-145. Reprinted by permission of Academic Press and the author.

## Chapter 11

*Figure 11.2* Larson, R. & Ham, M. (1993), "Stress and 'Storm and Stress' in early Adolescence: The relationship of negative events with dysphoric affect," *Developmental Psychology, 29,* 136. Copyright © 1993 by the American Psychological Association. *Figure 11.3* From Harlow, H. F., and Zimmerman, R. R. (1959). "Affectional Responses in the Infant Monkey," *Science,* 130, 421-432. Copyright 1959 by the American Association for the Advancement of Science. Reprinted by permission of the publisher and the author. *Figure 11.4* Shaffer, H. R., and Emerson, P. E.(1964). The development of social attachments in infancy. Monographs of the Society for Research in Child Development, 29, (3, serial No. 94) © The Society for Research in Child Development, Inc. *Figure 11.5* From T. Field and A. Fogel (Eds.), Emotion and Early Interaction, p. 109. Copyright © 1982 Lawrence Earlbaum. Reprinted by permission of Lawrence Earlbaum Associates, Inc., Publishers and the author. *Table 11.1* Bretherton, I., & Beeghly, M. (1982).

"Talking About Internal States: The Acquisition of an Explicit Theory of Mind," *Developmental Psychology, 18,* 906-921. Copyright 1982 by the American Psychological Association. Adapted by permission from the publisher and the author. *Table 11.2* M. M. Haith and J. J. Campos (Eds.), *Handbook of child psychology.* Vol II: Infancy and developmental psychobiology, p. 861. Copyright © 1983 by John Wiley and Sons, Inc. Reprinted by permission of John Wiley.

## Chapter 12

*Figure 12.1* Harter, S., & Monsour, A. (1992), "Developmental analysis of conflict caused by opposing attributes in the adolescent self-portrait," *Developmental Psychology, 28,* 251-260. Copyright © 1992 by the American Psychological Society. *Figure 12.3* Harter, S. (1987). The determinants and mediational role of global self-worth in children. In N. Eisenberg (Ed.), *Contemporary Topics in Developmental Psychology,* p. 227. Copyright © 1987 by John Wiley and Sons, Inc. Reprinted by permission of John Wiley and Sons, Inc. *Figure 12.4* From Mischel, W., Ebbesen, E. B., and Ziess, A. R. (1972), "Cognitive and Attentional Mechanisms in Delay of Gratification," *Journal of Personality and Social Psychology, 21,* 204-218. Copyright 1972 by the American Psychological Association. Reprinted by permission of the publisher and author. *Figure 12.5* Colby, A., Kohlberg, L., Gibbs, J., and Lieberman, M. (1983). A longitudinal study of moral judgement. *Monographs of the Society for Research in Child Development,* 48 (No. 1-2, Serial No. 200). © The Society for Research in Child Development, Inc. *Figure 12.6* Rushton, J. P. (1982). "Social Learning Theory and the Development of Prosocial Behavior." In N. Eisenber (Ed.), *The Development of Prosocial Behavior,* p. 89. Reprinted by permission of Academic Press and the author. *Table 12.1* Excerpts from *Essays on Moral Development Vol II: The Psychology of Moral Development* by Lawrence Kohlberg. Copyright © 1984 by Lawrence Kohlberg. Reprinted by permission of HarperCollins Publishers. *Table 12.3* From Eisenberg, N. (1986). *Altruistic Emotion, Cognition, and Behavior,* Hillsdale, NJ: Earlbaum, p. 144. Copyright © Lawrence Earlbaum. Reprinted by permission of Lawrence Earlbaum Associates, Inc, and the author.

## Chapter 13

*Figure 13.2* Hyde, J. S., Fennema, E., and Lamon, S. J. (1990). "Gender Differences is Mathematics Performance: a Meta-Analysis," *Psychological Bulletin,* 107, 139-155. Copyright 1990 by the American Psychological Association. Adapted by permission from the publisher and the author. *Figure 13.3* Linn, M. C., and Peterson, A. C. (1988). Emergence and characterization of sex differences in spatial ability: A meta-analysis. *Child Development,* 56, 1479-1498. © The Society for Research in Child Development, Inc. *Figure 13.4* Adapted from Self-regulatory mechanisms governing gender development by K. Bussy and A. Bandura from *Child Development,* Vol. 63, p. 1243. Copyright © 1992 The Society for Research in Child Development, Inc. Used with permission. *Figure 13.5* "The development of sex typing in middle childhood" from *Monographs of the Society for Research in Child Development,* 58 (No. 2, Serial No. 232), p. 35. Copyright © 1993 The Society for Research in

Child Development. Used with permission. *Figure 13.7* Frey, K. S., and Ruble, D. N. (1987). What children say about classroom performance: Sex and grade differences in perceived competence. *Child Development,* 58, 1066-1078. © The Society for Research in Child Development, Inc.

**Chapter 14**

*Figure 14.2* Peterson, G. W., and Rollins, B. C. (1987). Parent-child socialization. In M. B. Sussman and S. K. Steinmetz (Eds.) *Handbook of Marriage and the Family.* Reprinted by permission of Plenum Publishing Corporation. *Figure 14.3* Parke, R. D. (1969). Effectiveness as punishment as an interaction of intensity, timing, agent nurturance, and cognitive structuring. *Child Development* by Lawrence Kohlberg. Copyright © 1984 by Lawrence Kohlberg. Reprinted by permission of HarperCollins Publishers. *Figure 14.4* Robert J. McMahon and Rex Forehand, "Nonprescription Behavior Therapy: Effectiveness of a Brochure in Teaching Mothers to Correct Their Children's Inappropriate Mealtime Behavior," *Behavioral Therapy,* Volume 9, pages 814-820. Copyright 1978 by the Association for the Advancement of Behavior Therapy. Reprinted by permission of the publisher and the author. *Figure 14.5* From I. E. Sigel (Ed.), *Parental belief systems: The psychological consequences for children.* Copyright © 1985 by Lawrence Earlbaum. Reprinted by permission of Lawrence Earlbaum Associates, Inc. and the author. *Figure 14.7* Maccoby, E. E., and Martin, J. A. (1983). Socialization in the context of the Family: Parent-child interaction. In E. M. Hetherington (Ed.), *Handbook of child psychology.* Vol. 4. Socialization, personality, and social development. Copyright © 1983 by John Wiley and Sons, Inc. Reprinted by permission of John Wiley and Sons, Inc.

**Chapter 15**

*Figure 15.1* From Maccoby, E. E. and Jacklin, C. N. (1987). "Gender Segregation in Childhood." In H. W. Reese (Ed.), *Advances in Child Development and Behavior,* Vol. 20. Reprinted by permission of Academic Press and the author. *Figure 15.2* Berndt, T. J. (1979). "Developmental Changes in Conformity to Peers and Parents," *Developmental Psychology,* 15, 608-616. Copyright 1979 by the American Psychological Association. Reprinted by permission of the publisher and the author. *Figure 15.3* Asher, S. R. (1985). An evolving paradigm in social skill training research with children. In B. H. Schneider, K. H. Rubin, and J. E. Ledingham (Eds.), *Children's Peer Relations: Issues in Assessment and Intervention.* New York: Springer-Verlag. Reprinted with permission. *Figure 15.4* Dodge, K. A. (1986). A social information processing model of social competence in children. From M. Perlmutter (Ed.), The Minnesota Symposia on Child Psychology: Cognitive Perspectives on Children's Social and Behavioral Development, Vol. 18. Reprinted by permission of Lawrence Earlbaum Associates, Inc., Publishers. From M. Perlmutter (Ed.), The Minnesota symposia on child psychology: cognitive perspectives on children's social and behavioral development. Vol. 18. Copyright © 1986 Lawrence Earlbaum. Reprinted by permission of Lawrence Earlbaum Associates, Inc., Publishers and the author. *Figure 15.5* Jakibchuck, Z., and Smeriglio, V. L. (1976).

The influence of symbolic modeling on the social behavior of preschool children with low levels of social responsiveness. *Child Development,* 47, 838-841. © The Society for Research in Child Development, Inc. *Figure 15.6* Buhrmester, D., and Furham, W. (1986). The changing functions of friends in childhood: A neo-Sullivanism perspective. In V. J. Derlega and B. A. Winstead (Eds.), *Friendship and Social Interaction.* New York: Springer-Verlag. Reprinted with permission.

**Chapter 16**

*Figure 16.1* From the *Journal of Educational Psychology,* 83, p. 515, "Inner resources for school achievement: motivational mediators of children's perceptions of their parents" by W.S. Grolnick, R. M. Ryan, & E. L. Deci, Copyright © 1991 APA. Reprinted by permission of the publisher and the author. *Figure 16.3* From Stevenson, H. W., Lee, S., and Stigle, J. W. (1986). "Mathematics Achievement of Chinese, Japanese, and American Children." *Science,* 231, 693-699. Copyright 1986 by the American Association for the Advancement of Science. Reprinted by permission. *Figure 16.4* Becker, H. J., and Sterling, C. W. (1987). Equity in school computer use: National data and neglected considerations. *Journal of Educational Computing Research,* 3, 289-311. Copyright © 1987, Baywood Publishing Company, Inc. *Figure 16.5* Reprinted with permission from Liebert, R.M., and Sprafkin, J. (1988). *The early window: Effects of television on children and youth,* 3/e, 1988, Pergamon Press PLC. *Figure 16.6* Reprint with permission from Liebert, R. M., and Sprafkin J. (1988). *The early window: Effects of television on children and youth,* 3/e, 1988, Pergamon Press PLC. *Figure 16.7* Figure from *Social learning and personality development* by Albert Bandura and Richard H. Walters, reprinted by permission of Holt, Rinehart and Winston, Inc. *Table 16.1* Reprinted with permission from *Science achievement in seventeen countries: a preliminary report,* copyright 1988, Pergamon Press PLC. *Table 16.2* Horowitz, R. A. (1979). Psychological effects of the 'open classroom.' *Review of Educational Research,* 49, 71-86. Copyright 1979 by the American Educational Research Association. Reprinted by permission of the publisher.

1987 Rosenan. **p. 93:** Tony Mendoza/The Picture Cube. **p. 97:** (Figure 3.9) Billie Carstens/Denver Children's Hospital. **p. 99:** Hank Morgan/Photo Researchers. **p. 101:** Rob Nelson/Black Star. **p. 105:** Blair Seitz/Photo Researchers.

**Chapter 4 p. 115:** Algaze/The Image Works. **p. 117:** D. W. Fawcett/Photo Researchers. **pp. 122-123:** Lennart Nilsson, A CHILD IS BORN, Dell Publishing Company. **p. 130:** Dr. James Hanson. **p. 142:** Will & Deni McIntyre/Photo Researchers. **p. 144:** Nancy Durrell McKenna/Photo Researchers. **p. 146:** Jorgan Schytte/UNICEF. **p. 152:** © John Ficara/Woodfin Camp & Assoc.

**Chapter 5 p. 160:** © Catherine Karnow 1989/Woodfin Camp & Assoc. **p. 163:** Elizabeth Crews. **p. 170:** Nancy D. McKenna/Photo Researchers. **p. 178:** Leo de Wys, Inc./Sipa/Weddle. **p. 182:** © Laura Dwight. **p. 183:** © Susan Lapides. **p. 189:** Herbert Lanks/Superstock. **p. 191:** Ulrike Welsch. **p. 197:** Arlene Collins/Monkmeyer.

**Chapter 6 p. 204:** Matthew Neal McVay/Tony Stone Images. **p. 209:** Nadja Reissland. **p. 211:** Elizabeth Crews. **p. 218:** DEK/TexaStock. **p. 224:** (Figure 6.8) Enrico Ferorelli. **p. 231:** (Figure 6.9) Jacob E. Steiner. **p. 234:** Paul Damien/Tony Stone Images. **p. 236:** Frank Siteman/Stock Boston. **p. 239:** UN photo by J. Isaac.

**Chapter 7 p. 244:** Bob Daemmrich/Stock Boston. p. 252: Judith Kramer/The Image Works. **p. 257:** Cathlyn Melloan/Tony Stone Images. **p. 262:** Elizabeth Crews. **p. 268:** Bob Daemmrich/The Image Works. **p. 270:** Merrim/Monkmeyer. **p. 274:** Diana Rasche/Tony Stone Images. **p. 281:** Elizabeth Crews.

**Chapter 8 p. 286:** Lois Moulton/Tony Stone Images. **p. 291:** Goodman/Monkmeyer. **p. 295:** Sidney/Monkmeyer. **p. 301:** (Figure 8.3) Adele Diamond. **p. 307:** © Andy Caulfield/The Image Bank. **p. 318:** Arlene Collins/Monkmeyer.

**Chapter 9 p. 324** Antonio Bignami/The Image Bank. **p. 333:** (Figure 9.4) Courtesy of Carolyn Rovee-Collier. **p. 340:** Lawrence Migdale/Stock Boston. **p. 342:** Peter Southwick/Stock Boston. **p. 345:** (Figure 9.8) Dr. Peter Willatts. **p. 347:** Sobel/Klonsky/The Image Bank. **p. 355:** Cameramann International. **p. 357:** Bob Daemmrich/The Image Works.

**Chapter 10 p. 362:** © John Eastcott & Yva Momatiuk/The Image Works. **p. 368:** Francoia Darelet/The Image Bank.

**p. 371:** Alan Carey/The Image Works. **p. 372:** G. Carde/Photo Researchers. **p. 381:** Bob Daemmrich Photography. **p. 392:** © Leonard Lee Russ III/Photo Researchers. **p. 394:** Paul Conklin.

**Chapter 11 p. 399:** Kevin Horan/Stock Boston. **p. 403** left: David Frazier Photolibrary. **p. 403** right: David Frazier Photolibrary. **p. 408:** Dr. Tiffany Field. **p. 409:** (Figure 11.1) Kuchuk, A., Vibbert, M., & Bornstein, M. H. (1986). **p. 410:** David Young Wolff/Tony Stone Images. **p. 419:** Harlow Primate Laboratory, University of Wisconsin. **p. 426:** Lynne J. Weinstein/Woodfin Camp & Assoc. **p. 432:** Superstock.

**Chapter 12 p. 438:** Cathy Copeland. **p. 444:** L. Kolvoord/The Image Works. **p. 445:** Superstock. **p. 446:** (Figure 12.2) John S. Watson. **p. 450:** Peter M. Miller. **p. 455:** © Susan Lapides. **p. 461:** Richard Pan/The Image Bank. **p. 469:** David Austen/Stock Boston. **p. 476:** David Austen/Stock Boston. **p. 478:** D. Ogust/The Image Works. **p. 480:** © Phil Huber/Black Star.

**Chapter 13 p. 484:** © Judith D. Sedwick/The Picture Cube. **p. 491:** Rieder/Monkmeyer. **p. 492** left: © Kolvoord/The Image Works. **p. 492** right: Carol Palmer/The Picture Cube. **p. 493:** Andy Sacks/Tony Stone Images. **p. 496:** Elizabeth Crews. **p. 503:** Hazel Hankin/Stock Boston. **p. 507:** © Renee Lynn/Photo Researchers. **p. 510:** Bob Daemmrich/The Image Works. p 513: Elizabeth Crews.

**Chapter 14 p. 522:** © The Photo Works/Photo Researchers. **p. 528:** Jeffrey W. Myers/Stock Boston. **p. 530:** Elizabeth Crews. **p. 544:** Blair Seitz/Photo Researchers. **p. 551:** © Sarah Hood/Woodfin Camp & Assoc. **p. 555:** Bob Daemmrich.

**Chapter 15 p. 562** Bill Bachman/Photo Researchers. **p. 565:** Goodwin/Woodfin Camp & Assoc. **p. 570:** Bob Daemmrich/Stock Boston. **p. 576:** Joseph Schuyler/Stock Boston. **p. 580:** Bob Daemmrich/Stock Boston. **p. 583:** Elizabeth Crews/The Image Works. **p. 591:** Steven Burr Williams/The Image Bank.

**Chapter 16 p. 598:** Benn Mitchell/The Image Bank. **p. 605:** Bob Daemmrich/The Image Works. **p. 606:** George S. Zimbel/Monkmeyer. **p. 608:** Paul Conklin. **p. 614:** Wiley/Monkmeyer. **p. 624:** © Rob Nelson/Black Star. **p. 627:** Tom Pollack/Monkmeyer. **p. 631:** Albert Bandura

# Name Index

Kirasic, K. C., 309
Kirkpatrick, S. W., 173
Kisilevsky, B. S., 226, 233
Klahr, D., 56, 348
Klaus, M., 68, 147
Klebanov, P. K., 153
Kleinman, J. C., 131
Klima, E. S., 259
Kline, M., 558
Klingler, C., 280
Knoppers, B. M., 99
Knowles, R. V., 83, 87, 89, 96, 110, 125
Kobak, R. R., 428
Kobasigawa, A., 338, 339, 574
Kobayashi-Winata, H., 542
Kochanska, G., 460
Kocher, E. M. T., 546
Koegler, R. R., 238
Koenig, K. L., 406
Koester, L. S., 400
Koff, E., 194
Kohlberg, L., 455, 465, 466, 467, 469, 479, 486, 498, 516
Kohler, C. J., 235
Kolb, B., 176
Koneya, M., 604
Konner, M., 172
Kopp, C. B., 188, 381, 455, 456, 457
Koren, G., 141
Korner, A. F., 153, 154, 155, 407
Kotelchuk, M., 426
Kraemer, H. C., 146
Krafchuk, E. E., 210
Krakow, J. B., 455
Kramer, R., 469
Kramer, T. L., 590
Krasnor, L. R., 585, 586
Kratchowill, T., 412
Krauss, R. H., 261
Krebs, D., 316
Kremenitzer, J. P., 219
Kremer, K. E., 302
Kreutzer, M. A., 341
Krogman, W. M., 163
Kroll, J., 6
Krowitz, A., 224
Kruger, 464
Krumhansl, C. L., 227
Ksansnak, K. R., 511
Kuchuk, 409
Kuczaj, S. A., 279
Kuczynski, L., 210, 531
Kuebli, J., 342
Kugelmass, S., 464
Kuhl, P., 248
Kuhl, P. K., 228, 229, 234, 247
Kuhn, D., 503

Kulik, C. C., 621
Kulik, J. A., 621
Kunit, D. M., 93
Kunkel, D., 625, 632, 635
Kurdek, L. A., 467, 557
Kurland, D. M., 321, 326, 336, 622
Kurtines, W., 471
Kutz, S. L., 565
Kyratzis, A., 304

LaBarbera, J. D., 409
Lackey, P. N., 507
Ladd, G. W., 563, 580, 581, 583, 588, 611
Ladouceur, R., 25, 26
Laframboise, D. E., 255
LaFreniere, P., 572
LaGaipa, J. J., 591
Lagerspetz, K., 633
La Greca, A. M., 588
Lahey, B. B., 549
Laird, M., 540
Lalonde, C. E., 229
Lamaze, F., 147
Lamb, M. E., 431, 432, 509, 540, 545, 575
Lamb, S., 460
Lambert, N. M., 605
Lamborn, S. D., 529
Lamon, S. J., 20, 488, 489
Lampl, M., 163
Lampman-Petraitis, C., 415
Landau, S., 330, 331
Landesman-Dwyer, 131
Landry, S. H., 151
Lane, D. M., 329, 331
Langer, A., 224
Langlois, J. H., 425, 578
Laosa, L. M., 391
Larkin, R. W., 569
Larson, R., 415, 592
Lask, B., 197
Laupa, M., 465
Lave, C., 306, 355, 393
Lawrence, R. A., 199
Lawson, K. R., 328
Lawson, M., 173
Lazar, I., 395
LeBoyer, F., 147
LeBris, S., 99
Lecours, A. R., 321
Ledbetter, D. H., 96
Lee, L. C., 464
Lee, M. W., 394
Lee, R. V., 133, 135, 137, 138, 140
Lee, S., 618, 619
Lee, V. E., 558
Lefkowitz, M. M., 131
Leinbach, M. D., 501, 505, 506

Lemish, D., 630
Lempers, J. D., 261, 311
Lenneberg, E., 176, 177, 251, 266, 267
Lennon, E. M., 234
Lennon, R., 474, 490, 491
Lennon, R. T., 379
Leonard, S. C., 341
Lepper, M. R., 621
Lerner, J. M., 579
Lerner, R. M., 579
Leslie, A. M., 301, 302
Lesser, G. S., 387
Lester, B. M., 134, 146, 155, 190, 407, 421
Letson, R. D., 219
Levenson, R. L., 140
Levin, J. R., 338
Levin, S. R., 626
Levine, C., 466
Levine, R., 442
Levine, S. C., 308
Levinson, D., 635
Levitt, J. L., 18
Levitt, M. J., 18
Levy, G. D., 500, 501, 502
Lewis, J. M., 556
Lewis, M., 32, 369, 383, 404, 412, 418, 426, 441, 445, 506, 548
Lewis, T. L., 219
Lewko, J. H., 589
Lewkowicz, D. J., 234
Liaw, F., 153
Liben, L. S., 347, 504
Liberman, I. Y., 278
Liberty, C., 29, 336, 337, 338
Lickona, T., 464
Lieberman, D., 621, 623
Liebert, R. M., 626, 629, 634
Liggon, C., 170
Lightbown, P., 258
Lightfoot, D., 272
Lillard, A. S., 317
Lin, C. C., 542
Lin, S., 555
Linden, M. G., 95, 96
Lindsay, J., 540
Lindzey, G., 387
Linn, M. C., 489, 490, 624
Linney, J. A., 614
Lipper, E. G., 151
Lipsitt, L. P., 177, 181, 208, 230
Litman, C., 531, 553
Lits, B., 144
Littman, R. A., 575
Livesley, W. J., 441
Lobel, T. E., 511
Locke, J., 6
Lockheed, M. E., 624, 625

Siegel, A. W., 309, 310
Siegel, L. S., 278
Siegler, R. S., 308, 349, 350, 363, 364
Sigelman, C. K., 511
Sigman, M., 175
Sigman, M. D., 382
Signorella, M. L., 502, 504
Signorielli, N., 634
Silberstein, L., 265
Simmons, R. G., 195, 196, 452, 612
Simner, M. L., 472
Simon, T., 10, 365
Simpson, C., 614
Sims-Knight, J. E., 180, 189
Sinclair, D., 163, 166, 168
Singer, D. G., 630
Singer, J. L., 630
Singer, L. M., 430
Singer, L. T., 381
Singer, S. M., 111
Siqueland, E. R., 177
Sirvio, P., 407
Sitterle, K. A., 558
Skala, K. D., 183
Skeels, H. M., 108, 420
Skerry, S., 449
Skinner, B. F., 44, 48, 269
Skinner, E. A., 447, 614
Skodak, M., 108, 420
Skotko, D., 281
Skubiski, L., 477
Skuse, D., 170
Slaby, R. G., 499, 534, 585, 625
Slater, A., 216, 217, 222, 225
Slaughter, V., 318
Slaughter-Defoe, D. T., 617
Slavin, R. E., 607, 608, 609, 610
Smeriglio, V. L., 586, 587
Smetana, J. G., 453, 470, 471
Smilansky, S., 566
Smilkstein, G., 143
Smit, E. K., 603
Smith, B. A., 23
Smith, B. L., 254, 531
Smith, C. L., 476
Smith, I., 92
Smith, J. D., 238
Smith, L. B., 215, 235, 238, 239
Smith, P. K., 566
Smith, R., 102
Smith, S., 452
Smollar, J., 564
Snarey, J. R., 467, 469
Snidman, N., 109, 418
Snow, C., 270
Snow, C. E., 269, 274, 275
Snyder, L., 254

Sobal, J., 172
Sobol, A., 131
Society for Research in Child
      Development, 34
Sokol, R. J., 130
Solomon, J., 430
Somberg, D. R., 585
Sontag, L. W., 380
Sorce, J. F., 410
Spearman, C., 365, 366
Spears, W., 226
Spelke, E., 222
Spelke, E. S., 52, 222, 224, 233, 234, 235,
      247, 305
Spence, M. J., 226
Spence, S. H., 173
Spencer, M. B., 454
Spiker, D., 153
Spitz, H. H., 394
Spitz, R., 170, 420
Spivack, G., 588
Sprafkin, J., 626, 629
Sprafkin, J. N., 634
Spreen, O., 174, 175, 176
Springer, K., 305
Spuhler, J. N., 387
Sroufe, L. A., 406, 427, 428, 511, 539, 540,
      541, 582
Staffieri, J. R., 579
Stafford, F. P., 552
Stahl, P. M., 558
Stanbury, J. B., 89
Stanovich, K. E., 278
Stanowicz, L., 270
Starfield, B., 149
Stark, R. E., 250
Stattin, H., 195, 196
Stayton, D. J., 425
Stedman, L. C., 277
Steffen, V. J., 490
Stein, A., 142
Stein, A. H., 24, 633, 634
Stein, M. R., 210
Steinberg, L., 195, 527, 530, 602, 603
Steiner, J. E., 206, 230, 406
Steinmetz, S. K., 533
Stephan, C., 578
Sterling, C. W., 619
Stern, D. N., 410
Sternberg, R. J., 350, 363, 369, 370, 384,
      540
Sternglanz, S. H., 514
Stevenson, H. W., 443, 514, 618, 619
Stevens-Simon, C., 143
Stewart, G. W., 93, 94
Stewart, L., 471, 513
Stigler, J. W., 452, 618, 619

Stiles, J., 238
Stipek, D., 446
Stipek, D. J., 447
Stock, J. R., 186
Stolberg, A. L., 556
Stoneman, Z., 550, 551, 574
Stout, J. W., 199
Straus, M. A., 533
Strauss, N. L., 447
Strayer, F. F., 571, 572
Strayer, J., 571, 572
Streissguth, 131
Streissguth, A. P., 130, 131
Streri, A., 234
Strickland, B., 447
Strutt, G. F., 329
Stunkard, A. J., 172, 173
Suarez, T. M., 153
Sugarman, S., 303
Sugden, D., 182, 187
Sullivan, H. S., 595
Sullivan, S. A., 231
Sulzer-Azaroff, B., 535
Super, C. M., 156, 169, 171, 190, 417
Surrey, J. L., 518
Susman, E. J., 494, 541
Sutton-Smith, B., 549
Svejda, M. J., 68
Swain, I. U., 334
Swartz, K. B., 221
Szajnberg, N., 154

Tada, W. L., 238
Tager-Flusberg, H., 258, 319
Takahashi, K., 127
Takaishi, M., 164
Talor, C. R., 239
Tanner, J. M., 164, 166, 168, 171, 175
Taras, H. L., 635
Taub, D. E., 197
Taylor, M., 312
Teasdale, 107
Teller, D. Y., 220
Terman, L. M., 27, 375, 383, 384
Terrace, H. S., 272
Tesson, G., 589
Thal, D., 273
Tharp, R. G., 616, 617
Thase, M. W., 94
Thelen, E., 181, 182, 183, 184, 189, 190
Thoman, A., 153
Thoman, E. B., 153–154, 208
Thomas, A., 68, 109, 417
Thomas, E. A., 100
Thomas D. L., 533
Thompson, C., 156
Thompson, H., 11, 189

# Subject Index

cognitive-developmental theories on, 498–500

and nonsexist child rearing, 512

relational approach to, 517–518

social learning theory on, 496–498, 498 (fig.)

socialization in, 505–516, 509 (fig.), 516 (fig.)

and themes in development, 518–519

Gene disorders, 87–92

Gene expression, 81–84

Gene therapy, 84

Generalization, in learning, 349

Generalized other, 450–451

Genes, **77**, 79 (fig.)

    regulator, 85

    structural, 85

Genetic counseling, **97**, 97–98

Genetic counselors, 90

Genetic factors. *See also* Biological perspective

    in emotional development, 404

    in growth, 166, 168

    in intelligence or mental impairment, 385, 386, 387–388

    in obesity, 173

    and themes in development, 111–112

Genetic preadaptation, 188

Genetic screening, 97 (fig.)

Geneticists, behavioral, 100–102

Genital stage, **57**, 58 (table)

Genotype, **76**, 79 (fig.)

and environment, 102–106

German measles (rubella), 126, 137

Germinal period, **116**, 117–119, 118 (fig.)

Gesell, Arnold, 11

Gestational age, **121**

Gesture, as communication tool, 251

Gifted students, 383–385

    and sex differences in mathematics skills, 489

Glial cells, **175**

Gonadotropic hormones, 193

Gonads (testes), 78

Gonorrhea, and prenatal development, 138 (table), 140

Grammar. *See also* Syntax

    early, 257–258

    universal, 271

Grasping techniques, changes in, 184

Group identity experiment, 570–571

Grouping by ability (school), 609–610

Growth, vs. development, 162

Growth, physical, *see* Physical growth

Guided participation, 213

Guilford, J. P., 366, 367 (fig.)

Habituation, **210**, 216–217, 217 (fig.), 332

Habituation paradigm, 409

Hall, G. Stanley, 9–10

Head Start, 393–395

Health, and growth, 169

Hearing, by infants and newborns, 226–227

Hedonistic reasoning, **474**

Height

    growth in, 163

    social-emotional consequences of, 172

Hemophilia, 89 (table)

Hepatitis B, and prenatal development, 138 (table), 140

Hereditary transmission, 76–87

Heredity, 76. *See also* Nature-nurture debate

    and behavior, 106–111

    and themes in development, 111–112

Heritability, **108**

Heroin, as teratogen, 134–135

Herpes simplex, and prenatal development, 138 (table), 140

Heteronomy (Piaget), 463

Heterozygous genotype, **83**

Heuristic strategies, **622**

High-amplitude sucking, 217

Higher-order thinking, 344, 480. *See also* Formal reasoning; Problem–solving

Historical perspective, and childhood, 4–11. *See also* Socio-historical theory of Vygotsky

Home environment. *See also* Family; Fathers; Mothers; Parents

    measurement of, 390 (fig.), 390–391

    and sense of mastery, 446–447

Home Observation for Measurement of the Environment (HOME) inventory, 389, 390 (table), 391, 552

Homeostasis, of families, 525

Homozygous genotype, 83

Horizontal décalage, 292

Hormones

    and growth, 168–169

    and physical maturing, 193

    and sex differences, 493–494

Human development, *see* Development

Human genome, **77**, 77–78

Human growth hormone (HGH), 168, 172

Human immunodeficiency virus type 1 (HIV), 140

Humor, 263–264

Huntington's disease, **87**, 88 (table), 90

Hydantoins, 132 (table)

Hypertension, and prenatal development, 138 (table), 139 (table)

Hypothalamus, 168, 168 (fig.)

Hypotheses, 13

Hypothetical reasoning, **292**

Hypothyroidism, congenital, 88 (table)

I, *see* Identity; Self

Identical twins, **101**

Identification, with father, 460, 545

Identity (personal), **59**, 59 (table), 59–60, **452**, 452–454

    gender identity, 498, 500–501

Identity crisis, **453**

    and androgynous adolescents, 517

Illusion, Müller-Lyer (line-length), 240

Imaginary audience, **294**, 449

Imitation

    and cognitive skills, 356

    deferred, 209, 290

    and gender roles, 497

    in infancy, 208–209

    in language acqusition, 269, 270

Immanent justice, 463

Imprinting, 67, **67**, 420

In vitro fertilization, 99

Independent variables, 22

Individual differences, **10**, 42

    in cognitive development, 322, 359

    contextual approach to, 69, 71 (table)

    in development of self or values, 482

    in emotional development, 436

    and family environments, 109–110

    in gender development, 519

    and heredity vs. environment, 112

    information-processing approaches to, 56, 71 (table)

    in intelligence, 396

    in language development, 253–255, 283

    in learning and perceptual development, 241–242

    learning-theory approaches to, 48, 71 (table)

    in mental capabilities, 363

    in peer relations, 596

    in physical growth and motor skill development, 166, 201

    Piagetian approach to, 53, 71 (table)

    in prenatal development and birth, 123, 158

    psychosocial approach to, 60, 71 (table)

    in self-regulation, 457–458

PKU (phenylketonuria), 85, 89 (table), 91–92, 102
Placenta, **125**, 125–126
Planning, 347–348
Plasticity, **176**
    in brain development, 176–177, 267
Play
    cooperative, **565**
    and early peer relations, 564–566
    and gender role, 508–509, 509 (fig.)
    parallel, **565**
    rough–and–tumble, 493, **566**, 566–567, 580
    social pretend, **566**
    solitary, **565**
Politeness, in language, 260–261
Polygenic traits, **84**
Popularity among peers, 511, 577–582
Positive correlation, **21**
Positive reinforcement, **206**, **207**
Postconventional level, **465**, 467 (table)
Postnatal development, **116**
Postural control, 182
Postural reflexes, 179, 180 (table)
Poverty, and family relations, 543
Power, development of, 184, 185–186
Power assertion, **477**, 531
Pragmatics, **247**, 260–262
Preconventional level, **465**, 466 (table)
Preferential behaviors, 215
Preferential looking, 215 (fig.), 216, 216 (fig.)
Pregnancy, 115–116
Prelinguistic skills, 247–251
Prematurity, 429 (fig.), 429–430
    and child abuse, 540
Prenatal development, **116**
    changes in body proportions in, 165 (fig.)
    chronology of, 122–123
    and environment, 144–145
    and hearing in womb, 226
    stages of, 116–124
    and support within womb, 125–126
    and teratogens, 126–141
    and themes in development, 157–158
    and women's conditions, 141–144
Prenatal diagnosis, 124
Prenatal screening, 98
Preoperational stage (Piaget), 51 (table), **291**, 291–292
Prereaching, 183
Preschool children
    and attention, 327, 328, 329, 329 (fig.)
    and causality, 302
    emotional development in, 412
    friendships of, 589

    and moral development, 463, 470
    motor skills in, 184–187
    peer relations of, 566, 572
    and perception, 236, 237–238
    perspective taking by, 311 (fig.)
    and prosocial behavior, 473, 474
    self-regulation by, 280 (table), 280–281, 455–456, 457
    and sense of individuality, 449
    sex differences in aggression among, 490
    sex-typing of, 506
    and social comparison, 443
Pressure, infants' and newborns' perception of, 231–232
Preterm babies, 149
Preyer, Wilhelm, 8
Primacy effect, **336**
Primary reinforcers, 419
Primitive reflexes, 179, 179 (table)
Private speech, **280**, 456
Privileged information, research on, 312
Problem-solving, 344–346
    components of, 346–350
Production deficiency, **339**
Production processes, 48
Productive language, **253**
Progesterone, 494
Progestins, 133 (table)
Project Head Start, 393–395
Properties of objects, and concept development, 300–302, 301 (fig.)
Prosocial behaviors, **472**. *See also* Moral development; Values
    chronology of, 479
    and cooperative learning project, 480
    development of, 472–478, 475 (table), 479
    and play, 566, 567
    among siblings, 550–551
    and television, 633, 634
Prosody, **248**
Protodeclarative communication, **251**
Protoimperative communication, **251**
Proximodistal development, **165**
Psychoanalysis, and childhood, 10
Psychological states, understanding of, 310–317
Psychology, developmental, *see* Developmental psychology
Psychometric models, **365**
Psychometricians, **374**
Psychometrics, 365
    and fluid vs. crystallized intelligence, 367–368
    Guilford's structure-of-intellect approach, 366, 367 (fig.)

    Spearman's two–factor theory, 365–366
    Thurstone's primary abilities, 366
Psychosexual theory of development (Freud), **56**, 56–58, 58 (table), 458, 459–460
Psychosocial theory of development, 56, **58**
    of Erikson, 56, 57–60, 59 (table), 70–71 (table)
    and themes in development, 60–61, 70–71 (table)
Puberty, **192**, 192–193
    young people's views of, 194–196
Punishment, **207**, 532–534, 533 (fig.)
    expiatory, 463
    and moral development, 461
    physical, 37, 533
Punishment by reciprocity, **464**
Pupillary reflex, 218
Pygmalion effect, 613

Q-sort, 424–425
Quasi-experiments, **24**, 24–25, 27 (table)
Questionnaire, 15, **18**, 18–19, 21 (table)
Questionnaire method, and Hall, 9
Quickening, 121

Racism, and education, 617
Random assignment, **22**
    as impossible in some instances, 24
Range of reaction, **103**, 103 (fig.)
Rationalizing, 447
Raven Progressive Matrices, 279, 279 (fig.), 388
Reading difficulties, 277–278
Realism, **316**
Reasoning, formal, 350–352
Reasoning, moral, 458–459. *See also* Moral development
Reasoning, prosocial, 474–476
Recall, free, 29, 336, 336 (fig.)
Recall memory, **332**, 333 (fig.), 334–335
    developmental changes in, 335–343
Recasts, **270**, 274
Recency effect, **336**
Receptive aphasia, **266**, 266 (fig.)
Receptive language, **253**
Recessive allele, **83**
Reciprocal teaching, 356–357, 358 (table)
Reciprocity, in friendship, 592–593
Recognition memory, **332**, 333 (fig.), 334–335
Recovery from habituation, **210**, 216–217
Recursive thought, 312, 313 (fig.)
Reduplicated babbling, **249**